Lecture Notes in Artificial Intelligence 9693

Subseries of Lecture Notes in Computer Science

LNAI Series Editors

Randy Goebel
  University of Alberta, Edmonton, Canada
Yuzuru Tanaka
  Hokkaido University, Sapporo, Japan
Wolfgang Wahlster
  DFKI and Saarland University, Saarbrücken, Germany

LNAI Founding Series Editor

Joerg Siekmann
  DFKI and Saarland University, Saarbrücken, Germany

Leszek Rutkowski · Marcin Korytkowski
Rafał Scherer · Ryszard Tadeusiewicz
Lotfi A. Zadeh · Jacek M. Zurada (Eds.)

Artificial Intelligence and Soft Computing

15th International Conference, ICAISC 2016
Zakopane, Poland, June 12–16, 2016
Proceedings, Part II

 Springer

Editors

Leszek Rutkowski
Częstochowa University of Technology
Częstochowa
Poland

Marcin Korytkowski
Częstochowa University of Technology
Częstochowa
Poland

Rafał Scherer
Częstochowa University of Technology
Częstochowa
Poland

Ryszard Tadeusiewicz
AGH University of Science and Technology
Kraków
Poland

Lotfi A. Zadeh
University of California
Berkeley, CA
USA

Jacek M. Zurada
University of Louisville
Louisville, KY
USA

ISSN 0302-9743   ISSN 1611-3349 (electronic)
Lecture Notes in Artificial Intelligence
ISBN 978-3-319-39383-4   ISBN 978-3-319-39384-1 (eBook)
DOI 10.1007/978-3-319-39384-1

Library of Congress Control Number: 2016939934

LNCS Sublibrary: SL7 – Artificial Intelligence

Printed on acid-free paper

This Springer imprint is published by Springer Nature
The registered company is Springer International Publishing AG Switzerland

Preface

This volume constitutes the proceedings of the 15th International Conference on Artificial Intelligence and Soft Computing, ICAISC 2016, held in Zakopane, Poland, during June 12–16, 2016. The conference was organized by the Polish Neural Network Society in cooperation with the University of Social Sciences in Łódź and the Institute of Computational Intelligence at the Częstochowa University of Technology. Previous conferences took place in Kule (1994), Szczyrk (1996), Kule (1997) and Zakopane (1999, 2000, 2002, 2004, 2006, 2008, 2010, 2012, 2013, 2014, and 2015) and attracted a large number of papers and internationally recognized speakers: Lotfi A. Zadeh, Hojjat Adeli, Rafal Angryk, Igor Aizenberg, Shun-ichi Amari, Daniel Amit, Piero P. Bonissone, Jim Bezdek, Zdzisław Bubnicki, Andrzej Cichocki, Ewa Dudek-Dyduch, Włodzisław Duch, Pablo A. Estévez, Jerzy Grzymala-Busse, Martin Hagan, Yoichi Hayashi, Akira Hirose, Kaoru Hirota, Adrian Horzyk, Eyke Hüllermeier, Hisao Ishibuchi, Er Meng Joo, Janusz Kacprzyk, Jim Keller, Laszlo T. Koczy, Tomasz Kopacz, Adam Krzyzak, James Tin-Yau Kwok, Soo-Young Lee, Derong Liu, Robert Marks, Evangelia Micheli-Tzanakou, Kaisa Miettinen, Krystian Mikołajczyk, Henning Müller, Ngoc Thanh Nguyen, Andrzej Obuchowicz, Erkki Oja, Witold Pedrycz, Marios M. Polycarpou, José C. Príncipe, Jagath C. Rajapakse, Šarunas Raudys, Enrique Ruspini, Jörg Siekmann, Roman Słowiński, Igor Spiridonov, Boris Stilman, Ponnuthurai Nagaratnam Suganthan, Ryszard Tadeusiewicz, Ah-Hwee Tan, Shiro Usui, Fei-Yue Wang, Jun Wang, Bogdan M. Wilamowski, Ronald Y. Yager, Syozo Yasui, Gary Yen, and Jacek Zurada. The aim of this conference is to build a bridge between traditional artificial intelligence techniques and so-called soft computing techniques. It was pointed out by Lotfi A. Zadeh that "soft computing (SC) is a coalition of methodologies which are oriented toward the conception and design of information/intelligent systems. The principal members of the coalition are: fuzzy logic (FL), neurocomputing (NC), evolutionary computing (EC), probabilistic computing (PC), chaotic computing (CC), and machine learning (ML). The constituent methodologies of SC are, for the most part, complementary and synergistic rather than competitive." These proceedings present both traditional artificial intelligence methods and soft computing techniques. Our goal is to bring together scientists representing both areas of research. This volume is divided into five parts:

- Bioinformatics, Biometrics and Medical Applications
- Data Mining
- Artificial Intelligence in Modeling and Simulation
- Workshop: Visual Information Coding Meets Machine Learning
- Various Problems of Artificial Intelligence

The conference attracted 343 submissions from 35 countries and after the review process, 133 papers were accepted for publication. The ICAISC 2016 hosted the workshop "Visual Information Coding Meets Machine Learning: Large-Scale Challenges" (VICML 2016) organized by:

– Marcin Korytkowski, Częstochowa University of Technology, Poland
– Krystian Mikolajczyk, Imperial College, UK
– Rafał Scherer, Częstochowa University of Technology, Poland
– Sviatoslav Voloshynovskiy, University of Geneva, Switzerland

The workshop was supported by the project "Innovative Methods of Retrieval and Indexing Multimedia Data Using Computational Intelligence Techniques" funded by the National Science Centre. I would like to thank our participants, invited speakers, and reviewers of the papers for their scientific and personal contribution to the conference. I would also like to thank all the additional reviewers for their helpful reviews.

Finally, I thank my co-workers Łukasz Bartczuk, Piotr Dziwiński, Marcin Gabryel, and Marcin Korytkowski and the conference secretary, Rafał Scherer, for their enormous efforts that helped make the conference a very successful event. Moreover, I would like to appreciate the work of Marcin Korytkowski, who designed the Internet submission system.

June 2016   Leszek Rutkowski

Organization

ICAISC 2016 was organized by the Polish Neural Network Society in cooperation with the University of Social Sciences in Łódź and the Institute of Computational Intelligence at Częstochowa University of Technology.

ICAISC Chair

Honorary Chairs

Lotfi Zadeh	University of California, USA
Hojjat Adeli	The Ohio State University, USA
Jacek Żurada	University of Louisville, USA

General Chair

Leszek Rutkowski	Częstochowa University of Technology, Poland

Co-chairs

Włodzisław Duch	Nicolaus Copernicus University, Poland
Janusz Kacprzyk	Polish Academy of Sciences, Poland
Józef Korbicz	University of Zielona Góra, Poland
Ryszard Tadeusiewicz	AGH University of Science and Technology, Poland

ICAISC Program Committee

Rafał Adamczak, Poland
Cesare Alippi, Italy
Shun-ichi Amari, Japan
Rafal A. Angryk, USA
Jarosław Arabas, Poland
Robert Babuska, The Netherlands
Ildar Z. Batyrshin, Russia
James C. Bezdek, Australia
Marco Block-Berlitz, Germany
Leon Bobrowski, Poland
Piero P. Bonissone, USA
Bernadette Bouchon-Meunier, France
Tadeusz Burczynski, Poland
Andrzej Cader, Poland
Juan Luis Castro, Spain
Yen-Wei Chen, Japan
Wojciech Cholewa, Poland
Fahmida N. Chowdhury, USA

Andrzej Cichocki, Japan
Paweł Cichosz, Poland
Krzysztof Cios, USA
Ian Cloete, Germany
Oscar Cordón, Spain
Bernard De Baets, Belgium
Nabil Derbel, Tunisia
Ewa Dudek-Dyduch, Poland
Ludmiła Dymowa, Poland
Andrzej Dzieliński, Poland
David Elizondo, UK
Meng Joo Er, Singapore
Pablo Estevez, Chile
János Fodor, Hungary
David B. Fogel, USA
Roman Galar, Poland
Alexander I. Galushkin, Russia
Adam Gaweda, USA

Sarunas Raudys, Lithuania
Olga Rebrova, Russia
Vladimir Red'ko, Russia
Raúl Rojas, Germany
Imre J. Rudas, Hungary
Enrique H. Ruspini, USA
Khalid Saeed, Poland
Dominik Sankowski, Poland
Norihide Sano, Japan
Robert Schaefer, Poland
Rudy Setiono, Singapore
Paweł Sewastianow, Poland
Jennie Si, USA
Peter Sincak, Slovakia
Andrzej Skowron, Poland
Ewa Skubalska-Rafajłowicz, Poland
Roman Słowiński, Poland
Tomasz G. Smolinski, USA
Czesław Smutnicki, Poland
Pilar Sobrevilla, Spain
Janusz Starzyk, USA
Jerzy Stefanowski, Poland
Vitomir Štruc, Slovenia
Pawel Strumillo, Poland
Ron Sun, USA
Johan Suykens, Belgium
Piotr Szczepaniak, Poland
Eulalia J. Szmidt, Poland
Przemysław Śliwiński, Poland

Adam Słowik, Poland
Jerzy Świątek, Poland
Hideyuki Takagi, Japan
Yury Tiumentsev, Russia
Vicenç Torra, Spain
Burhan Turksen, Canada
Shiro Usui, Japan
Michael Wagenknecht, Germany
Tomasz Walkowiak, Poland
Deliang Wang, USA
Jun Wang, Hong Kong, SAR China
Lipo Wang, Singapore
Zenon Waszczyszyn, Poland
Paul Werbos, USA
Slawo Wesolkowski, Canada
Sławomir Wiak, Poland
Bernard Widrow, USA
Kay C. Wiese, Canada
Bogdan M. Wilamowski, USA
Donald C. Wunsch, USA
Maciej Wygralak, Poland
Roman Wyrzykowski, Poland
Ronald R. Yager, USA
Xin-She Yang, UK
Gary Yen, USA
John Yen, USA
Sławomir Zadrożny, Poland
Ali M.S. Zalzala, UAE

ICAISC Organizing Committee

Rafał Scherer, Secretary
Łukasz Bartczuk, Organizing Committee Member
Piotr Dziwiński, Organizing Committee Member
Marcin Gabryel, Finance Chair
Marcin Korytkowski, Databases and Internet Submissions

Additional Reviewers

R. Adamczak
M. Al-Dhelaan
E. Avila-Melgar
T. Babczyński
M. Białko
M. Blachnik
L. Bobrowski
P. Boguś
G. Boracchi
L. Borzemski
J. Botzheim
W. Bozejko
T. Burczyński
R. Burduk
C. Castro
K. Cetnarowicz
W. Cholewa
P. Cichosz
R. Czabański
I. Czarnowski
J. de la Rosa
J. Dembski
L. Diosan
L. Dutkiewicz
L. Dymowa
S. Ehteram
A. Fanea
I. Fister
M. Gabryel
P. Głomb
Z. Gomółka
M. Gorzałczany
D. Grabowski
E. Grabska
K. Grąbczewski
J. Grzymala-Busse
Y. Hayashi
P. Held
Z. Hendzel
F. Hermann
H. Hikawa
Z. Hippe
K. Hirota

A. Horzyk
E. Hrynkiewicz
R. Hyde
D. Jakóbczak
A. Janczak
T. Jiralerspong
J. Kacprzyk
W. Kamiński
V. Kecman
E. Kerre
P. Klęsk
L. Koczy
A. Kołakowska
J. Konopacki
J. Korbicz
M. Kordos
P. Korohoda
J. Koronacki
J. Kościelny
L. Kotulski
Z. Kowalczuk
M. Kraft
M. Kretowska
R. Kruse
B. Kryzhanovsky
A. Krzyzak
A. Kubiak
E. Kucharska
J. Kulikowski
O. Kurasova
V. Kurkova
M. Kurzyński
J. Kusiak
J. Kwiecień
A. Ligęza
A. Lisowska
M. Ławryńczuk
J. Łęski
B. Macukow
W. Malina
K. Malinowski
J. Mańdziuk
U. Markowska-Kaczmar

A. Martin
A. Materka
J. Mazurkiewicz
J. Mendel
J. Michalkiewicz
Z. Mikrut
S. Misina
W. Mitkowski
W. Moczulski
W. Mokrzycki
O. Mosalov
T. Munakata
G. Nalepa
M. Nashed
F. Neri
M. Nieniewski
S. Osowski
E. Ozcan
W. Palacz
G. Papa
A. Paszyńska
K. Patan
A. Pieczyński
A. Piegat
Z. Pietrzykowski
V. Piuri
P. Prokopowicz
A. Przybył
R. Ptak
A. Radzikowska
E. Rafajłowicz
E. Rakus-Andersson
A. Rataj
Ł. Rauch
L. Rolka
S. Rovetta
I. Rudas
F. Rudziński
S. Sakurai
N. Sano
A. Sashima
R. Scherer
P. Sevastjanov

A. Sędziwy
A. Skowron
K. Skrzypczyk
E. Skubalska-Rafajłowicz
K. Slot
D. Słota
A. Słowik
C. Smutnicki
A. Sokołowski
T. Sołtysiński
J. Stefanowski
E. Straszecka
V. Struc
B. Strug

P. Strumiłło
M. Studniarski
M. Sultana
J. Swacha
P. Szczepaniak
E. Szmidt
G. Ślusarczyk
J. Świątek
R. Tadeusiewicz
Y. Tiumentsev
S. Tomforde
V. Torra
J. Tvrdik
M. Urbański

T. Villmann
E. Volna
T. Walkowiak
Y. Wang
M. Wojciechowski
M. Wozniak
M. Wygralak
Q. Xiao
J. Yeomans
J. Zabrodzki
D. Zaharie
A. Zamuda
R. Zdunek

Contents – Part II

Bioinformatics, Biometrics and Medical Applications

Artificial Intelligence in Modeling and Simulation

Various Problems of Artificial Intelligence

Workshop: Visual Information Coding Meets Machine Learning

Contents – Part I

Fuzzy Systems and Their Applications

Pattern Classification

Agent Systems, Robotics and Control

Data Mining

Improving Automatic Classifiers Through Interaction

Silvia Acid$^{(\boxtimes)}$ and Luis M. de Campos

Department of Computer Science and Artificial Intelligence, Advanced Technical
School for Information Technology and Telecomunication, CITIC-UGR,
University of Granada, 18071 Granada, Spain
{acid,lci}@decsai.ugr.es

Abstract. We consider a scenario where an automatic classifier has
been built, but it sometimes decides to ask the correct label of an instance
to an oracle, instead of accepting its own prediction. This interactive classifier only knows with certainty the labels provided by the oracle. Our
proposal is to use this information to dynamically improve the behavior of the classifier, either increasing its accuracy when it is being used
autonomously or reducing the number of queries to the oracle. We have
tested our proposal by using twenty data sets and two adaptive classifiers from the Massive Online Analysis (MOA) open source framework
for data stream mining.

Keywords: Stream mining · Online classification · Interactivity · Reject
option

1 Introduction

In this paper we are concerned with the following situation: we have built a
classifier for a given classification problem, that is being used to classify new
instances. But the classifier can sometimes request the intervention of a human
(the oracle), who gives it the correct label of the instance being considered.
This may happen because the classifier is not enough sure about the label that
it is proposing for this instance. If the classifier does not ask the human the
correct label, there is some risk of permanently accepting a wrong classification
(the decisions made by the classifier will not be further revised). For example,
this may be the case of a model built to classify text documents into a set of
categories, or to classify emails.

In a previous paper [1] we studied two important questions related with this
interactive use of a classifier, namely how the performance of the interactive
classifier should be evaluated[1] and the way in which the system decides whether
or not to request a label to the oracle. In this paper we want to add a dynamic
component to the interactive classifier: as we assume that the oracle always gives

---

[1] The evaluation should not be based only on its predictive accuracy but should also
take into account the cost of the human intervention.

© Springer International Publishing Switzerland 2016
L. Rutkowski et al. (Eds.): ICAISC 2016, Part II, LNAI 9693, pp. 3–13, 2016.
DOI: 10.1007/978-3-319-39384-1_1

the correct answer when she is asked for the label of an instance, we could try to use this information to improve the behavior of the classifier, either increasing its accuracy when it is being used autonomously or reducing the number of queries to the oracle, or both.

It can be noticed that the proposed scenario shares many similarities with the learning with a reject option and the online learning approaches to classification.

In the scenario considered by the learning with a reject option approach [4,7], they try to build a model with the capacity to decide not to classify a given instance, because the model is not enough confident about its own prediction. In this case the instance must be manually classified by a human. However, they do not consider the possibility of updating the model as a consequence of the new information provided by the oracle for this instance (its label), together with the instance itself.

On the other hand, in the scenario proposed by the online learning [3,13] or learning from data streams [8,9] approaches, the goal is to update the learned model as soon as a new instance arrives and after we know its true class; it is assumed in this approach that soon after the prediction of the model for an instance is made, its true label will be revealed. This is only true in any problem that consists in predicting the (near) future.

The situation that we consider in this paper combines the two previous scenarios: we want to update the learned model, but we have not access to all the labels of the new instances arriving to the system but only to the labels of the examples classified by the oracle. We call this scenario interactive online classification.

The rest of the paper is organized in the following way: in Sect. 2 we give some necessary background about interactive classifiers. Section 3 describes our proposal to convert an interactive classifier into an interactive online classifier. In Sect. 4 we test our proposal by using twenty data sets and two adaptive classifiers from the Massive Online Analysis (MOA) [5] open source framework for data stream mining. Section 5 ends the paper with the conclusions and some proposals for future work.

2 Preliminaries

In order to evaluate the performance of an interactive classifier, we must take into account both its accuracy when it is used autonomously and the degree of interaction with the oracle. So, let n_c and n_w be the number of times that the classifier is used and it selects the correct and the wrong class for an instance, respectively. Also, let n_i be the number of times that the classifier asks the oracle (we assume that we have N instances to classify, so that $n_c + n_w + n_i = N$). In [1], the properties that a reasonable EMIC (Evaluation Measure for Interactive Classification) must possess were studied and two different EMIC were proposed. In this paper we will use the so called F_β measure [14]:

$$F_\beta = \frac{(1 + \beta^2)n_c}{(1 + \beta^2)N - n_i} \tag{1}$$

β is a parameter that controls the balance between precision and recall. In the experiments of this paper we will use $\beta = 0.5$ (which gives more importance to precision than to recall[2]).

Concerning the strategy that the interactive classifier can use to decide to ask the true class of an instance instead of classifying it, in [1] several alternatives based on the uncertainty sampling method [6,11] used in the active learning literature [12] were considered. We assume that given an instance $\mathbf{x}$, the classifier is able to obtain a posterior probability distribution of the class variable given the instance, $p(C|\mathbf{x})$, and then it predicts the most probable class, $c_{\mathbf{x}}^* = \arg\max_{c_i} p(c_i|\mathbf{x})$. Uncertainty sampling selects an instance for querying based on the level of uncertainty about its correct class. Let $\phi(p)$ be a measure of the confidence degree in the prediction obtained from the posterior probability $p(C|\mathbf{x})$. By fixing a threshold, α, on the degree of confidence, a decision rule according to which the system will decide whether or not to query the oracle can be established:

$$\begin{array}{c} \text{if } \phi(p) < \alpha \text{ then ask the oracle} \\ \text{else classify the instance} \end{array} \qquad (2)$$

In [1] several confidence measures were studied. In this paper we will use the measure of Maximum probability $\phi_m(p)$:

$$\phi_m(p) = \max_{c_i} p(c_i|\mathbf{x}) = p(c_{\mathbf{x}}^*|\mathbf{x}) \qquad (3)$$

$\phi_m(p)$ varies in the range $[\frac{1}{m}, 1]$, where m is the number of possible classes. $\phi_m(p) = \frac{1}{m}$ represents absolute lack of confidence (because in this case $p(c_i|\mathbf{x}) = \frac{1}{m}$ for all c_i), whereas $\phi_m(p) = 1$ means total confidence.

It is obvious that the threshold α used in combination with the confidence measure is a key parameter for the interactive classifier's decision strategy: the greater α the more interactive the classifier. If α is set to its maximum value (1 in the case of the confidence measure being considered) then the classifier is useless, it always queries; on the other extreme, if α is set to its minimum value, we obtain a non-interactive classifiers that never queries. Moreover, the same α may behave very differently depending on the specific algorithm used to build the base classifier and even the classification problem being considered. For these reasons it is very convenient to try to estimate a reasonable value for α taking into account both the problem to be solved and the base classifier to be used.

We will use the following strategy, proposed in [1]: we rank the training instances used to train the base classifier in decreasing order of their confidence measure and then look for the threshold which optimizes the selected performance measure (F_β in our case). We do it by tentatively making the threshold equal to the confidence measure of each training instance and computing the corresponding performance measure (for all the instances in the training set). We then select the threshold producing the best result. An example of this computation can be seen in Table 1.

---

[2] In [1], it was shown that with values of β lesser than or equal to 0.5, the interactive classifiers systematically outperform their non-interactive counterparts.

Table 1. Example of the strategy used to select the threshold α. Column ϕ represents the value of the confidence measure for each of the seven training instances; column c/w means whether the label predicted by the classifier coincides with the true label (c) or not (w); columns n_c, n_w and n_i count the number of correct and wrong classifications, and interactions, respectively, if we fix the value α to the corresponding ϕ value; column $F_{0.5}$ gives the values of the performance measure. In this case, in bold is marked the highest value for $F_{0.5}$, as well as its corresponding value for ϕ; thus, the threshold that optimizes the EMIC, is $\alpha = 0.74$.

ϕ	c/w	n_c	n_w	n_i	$F_{0.5}$
1.00	c	1	0	6	0.455
0.95	c	2	0	5	0.667
0.90	w	2	1	4	0.526
0.75	c	3	1	3	0.652
0.74	c	4	1	2	**0.741**
0.60	w	4	2	1	0.645
0.57	c	5	2	0	0.714

3   Interactive Online Classifiers

As mentioned in the introduction, our goal is to transform our interactive but static classifier into an online (dynamic) classifier that can improve its behavior from the information provided by the oracle when the classifier decides to query her instead of classifying an instance.

Obviously, any non-interactive classifier can be transformed into an interactive classifier, provided that it is able to give a numerical output for each possible category of the instance to be classified (which can be transformed into a posterior probability distribution where we apply the confidence measure and the decision rule in Eq. (2)). We will assume that the classifier being considered can work online, that is to say it can modify itself when a new instance together with its correct label are provided.

However, in the case of an online (non-interactive) classifier, it has access to all the new instances and their correct labels. Therefore, the new instances used to update the classifier are extracted from the same underlying distribution than the ones used to initially train it[3]. But it is not necessarily the case of the interactive online classifier, because the only instances that can be used to update it are those where the classifier is unsure, and this may introduce a bias in the classifier, perhaps decreasing its performance.

Therefore, what we want to evaluate is whether this is or not the case, i.e. whether the interactive online classifier can improve the performance of the initially trained (static) interactive classifier.

---

[3] In this paper we assume that the process is stationary and no concept drift occurs. The case of non-stationary problems, where a concept drift can modify the probability distribution, will be considered in future research.

Table 2. In the example in Table 1, we add a new instance with ϕ value 0.53, which is correctly classified. In bold are the new highest value for $F_{0.5}$ and the new best threshold, that decreases to $\alpha = 0.53$. If the new instance were classified incorrectly, then the value of $F_{0.5}$ for the confidence measure of the new instance would be 0.625 instead of 0.750 and the best threshold would still be $\alpha = 0.74$ as it was before, in italic.

ϕ	c/w	n_c	n_w	n_i	$F_{0.5}$
1.00	c	1	0	7	0.417
0.95	c	2	0	6	0.625
0.90	w	2	1	5	0.500
0.75	c	3	1	4	0.625
0.74	c	4	1	3	*0.714*
0.60	w	4	2	2	0.625
0.57	c	5	2	1	0.694
0.53	c	6	2	0	**0.750**

Another important point concerns the threshold α used by the decision rule in Eq. (2). As this threshold is computed from the initial training set, perhaps we should dynamically adapt it as new instances are used to update the classifier. Our proposal is to recompute this threshold each time a new instance (labeled by the oracle) is available, following the method explained in Sect. 2. It can be proven[4] that if we update the threshold in this way, it can only either remain equal or decrease. This is in agreement with our intuition that if we use more information to train a classifier, it will gain more confidence in its own predictions (thus decreasing α). An example of the re-computation of the threshold can be seen in Table 2.

4   Experimental Framework

In this section we are going to experimentally study the behavior of the interactive online classifiers. For all the experiments carried out we have used the MOA software [5], an open-source workbench for online learning from data streams, closely related to WEKA. We have selected two online base classifiers (to transform them into interactive and interactive online classifiers) and 20 different data streams, all easily available in MOA.

4.1   From Non-interactive to Online Interactive Classifiers

The first interactive classifier that we are going to test, proposed in [1], called *Theshold+NoLearn* (2TNL for short), comes from using any non-interactive base classifier to predict the class for a new arriving instance and, when this prediction

---

[4] By lack of space, we omit the proof of this result.

has low confidence, it will query the oracle for the true label. The degree of confidence will be measured using Eq. (3) and the uncertainty will be considered by using the decision rule in Eq. (2). The online base classifier is learned from the training data stream, and the threshold, α, is then estimated in the way described in Sect. 2 (see an example in Table 1). The threshold and the classifier, even though interactive, will remain unchanged for any further instances after the training. Although it does not learn any more, it will restrict itself to classify instances having a relatively high degree of confidence (trying to increase the EMIC measure in Eq. (1)).

As it has already been emphasized, the classifier only knows for sure the instances labeled by the oracle. Those labeled instances queried to the oracle have the same informative quality as the training set[5], and it could be a waste to miss some kind of learning. Thus, we propose a new interactive online classifier *Theshold+Learn* (3TLe for short), that adds any new acquired knowledge to the model by means of the own online classifier used in the training. Therefore, the new labeled instances are used to update the classifier. The threshold, the confidence indicator, remains as it was estimated from the training data stream, as in the previous interactive classifier.

Nevertheless, those instances labeled by the oracle could also be used to readjust the initial threshold estimated from the original training set. Thus, we propose another interactive online classifier called *Dynamic Threshold* (4Dyn). At any time this classifier will evaluate the confidence degree of the current instance, comparing it to the threshold (as in the previous cases), but once a query is submitted to the oracle the threshold can be updated (as explained in Sect. 3, see an example in Table 2). The new value of the threshold will be used by the interactive online classifier with the next instances, until a new query to the oracle occurs, in this case the threshold may be updated again.

As the baseline for our experiments, we will consider the non-interactive base classifier that never queries, denoted as 1NQ.

4.2   The Data Streams and the Base Classifiers

The two base online classifiers used are *NaiveBayes* and the *HoeffdingTreeNB* [10]. The second one is an incremental decision tree for streaming data with NaiveBayes classification at leaves.

For the experiment we have used 20 data streams created by means of four different streams generators available in MOA.

The *Agrawal* generator [2], simulates the granting of credit by means of 10 different functions or rules, that take into account 9 different attributes, e.g. academic degree, salary, value of the loan, etc. 3 of them are categorical and 6 numerical. *Hyperplane* generates data for a problem of predicting the class of a rotating hyperplane. We produce 3 different problems. For example, *hyperpl01* contains 10 continuous attributes, and the class attribute has two categories. The *sea* generator simulates 4 different concepts by means of rules based on 3

---

[5] The new instances are supposed to come from the same data distribution.

continuous attributes. Finally, we used the *Random tree* generator, that produces concepts that theoretically should favor decision tree learners. It constructs decision tree randomly according to several parameter settings, as number of classes, number of categorical and numerical attributes. The tree is used to determine the class label for new examples generated by assigning an uniformly distributed random value to the attributes. The attribute values as well as the class label determined via the tree become part of the data stream. We used 3 different concepts by using 2 simple and a complex random tree. More details of the data sets can be seen in Table 3.

Table 3. A summary of the 20 data streams used for the training and the evaluation of the classifiers. The total length of each data set is set to 101,000. The first thousand are used for the initial training process.

Name	Categorical	Numeric	Class	Name	Categorical	Numeric	Class
agrawal01	3	6	2	*hyperpl01*	0	10	2
agrawal02	3	6	2	*hyperpl02*	0	10	3
agrawal03	3	6	2	*hyperpl03*	0	50	5
agrawal04	3	6	2	*sea01*	0	3	2
agrawal05	3	6	2	*sea02*	0	3	2
agrawal06	3	6	2	*sea03*	0	3	2
agrawal07	3	6	2	*sea04*	0	3	2
agrawal08	3	6	2	*tree01*	5	5	2
agrawal09	3	6	2	*tree02*	5	5	3
agrawal10	3	6	2	*tree03*	10	40	5

By using any of the described generators we can obtain streams of any length, ready as input for the online classifiers. We used 1,000 instances for each of the described problems, as training data stream. Additionally we used 100,000 instances for testing and evaluating every classifier. Given the stochastic nature of the generators, the data were generated once and then saved. Thus, in order to perform a fair comparison, all the classifiers work on exactly the same data sets, so they begin from an identical starting point.

When evaluating online classifiers on a stream, every instance is used first for testing and after for updating the model. But, as the interactive classifiers have not access to the true label unless it is requested, the updating will be considered, only for the interactive online classifiers 3TLe and 4Dyn, when they ask the oracle. The main metric we compute during the evaluation process is the EMIC value in Eq. (1). Additionally we also compute two other metrics, Accuracy and Interactivity. Accuracy is the success rate over the instances actually classified autonomously, $\frac{n_c}{n_c+n_w}$[6]. Interactivity is the number of labels requested by the classifier, expressed in percentage, $100 * \frac{n_i}{N}$. This shows the degree of autonomy of the classifier.

---

[6] Without taking into account those instances labeled by the oracle, n_i.

Table 4. Average of the metrics used for the evaluation of the interactive classifiers based on *NaiveBayes*, using 100,000 instances. The average is computed over the 20 data streams.

	EMIC	Interactivity	Accuracy
1NQ	0.824	0.00	0.824
2TNL	0.835	18.74	0.876
3TLe	0.824	36.12	0.945
4Dyn	0.882	1.37	0.884

Table 5. Average of the metrics used for the evaluation of the interactive classifiers based on *HoeffdingTreeNB*, using 100,000 instances. The average is computed over the 20 data streams.

	EMIC	Interactivity	Accuracy
1NQ	0.820	0.00	0.820
2TNL	0.829	16.16	0.864
3TLe	0.711	2.51	0.714
4Dyn	0.837	1.13	0.839

A summary of the results of the comparative study of the interactive classifiers is displayed in Tables 4 and 5. We have made a separate study for each of the base classifiers *NaiveBayes* and *HoeffdingTreeNB* respectively. The values displayed are an average over the 20 data streams.

Regarding Table 4, the non-interactive classifier *NaiveBayes* 1NQ reaches an average Accuracy of 0.824. Due to its lack of interactivity, the EMIC value coincides with the Accuracy. 2TNL requests to the oracle the true label of 18.7 % of the 100,000 instances. This increases slightly Accuracy and EMIC, thus it avoids to commit some classification errors. 3TLe increases remarkably the Accuracy, reaching 0.945, at the expense of a high percentage of interactivity, 36.12 %. This means that, when the classifier is sure enough, its classification is mainly correct, but it asks for too much labeled instances, as many of them would be correctly classified otherwise. That penalty is reflected in the EMIC value, which is equal to the 1NQ's EMIC. This may be due to a threshold too high. On the other hand, the classifier 4Dyn performs very well. Its Accuracy is better than that of 1NQ and 2TNL, i.e., when it classifies it makes less errors. Moreover it pays a low price for this improvement, with an Interactivity of only 1.4 %. As a consequence, the EMIC value is much greater than the one of its competitors. As we will illustrate next, the queries to the oracle are posed more frequently at the beginning of the process, and after a while the classifier will continue almost autonomously.

The results in Table 5 are similar in many aspects to those in Table 4. 4Dyn is still the best classifier, although the differences with respect to the other classifiers are smaller, except with 3TLe, which performs quite poorly (with low

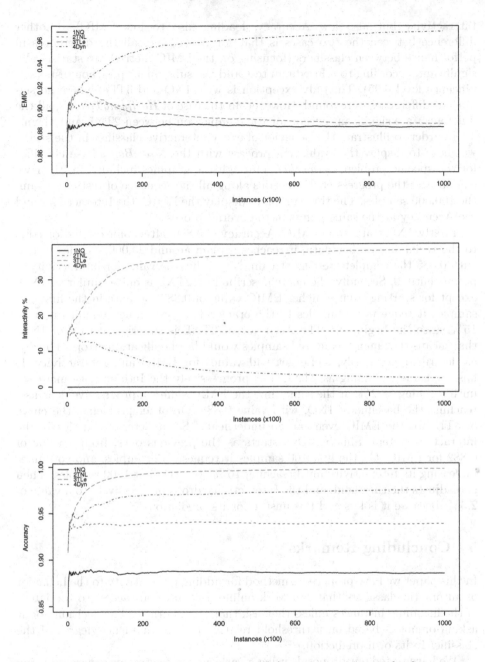

Fig. 1. Progress of the EMIC, Interactivity and Accuracy metrics on the data stream *agrawal07*, for each of the interactive classifier considered built over the base classifier *NaiveBayes* at the same points (steps of 100 samples) of the overall process. We can appreciate changes in the degree of the interactivity for *4Dyn* due to updating of α to lower values, that have impact on the EMIC curve, as this measure is a compound of the others.

Interactivity but also low Accuracy, leading also to low EMIC). Another difference between the two cases is that for *NaiveBayes* all the differences in performance between classifiers (focusing on the EMIC metric) are statistically significant, according to a Friedman test and the subsequent post hoc tests (significance level 0.05). The only exception is with 1NQ and 3TLe, where no significant differences were found. However, in the case of *HoeffdingTreeNB*, all the differences are significant except for the comparison between 2TNL and 4Dyn.

In order to illustrate the behavior of every interactive classifier in the study, we chose to display the evaluating process with the *NaiveBayes* base classifier for the specific problem *agrawal07*. Through the graphics included in Fig. 1 we can observe the progress of the metrics along all the sequence of testing stream, the 100.000 samples. The three graphics display the EMIC, the Interactivity and the Accuracy at the same points of the overall process.

Firstly, 1NQ starts from EMIC/Accuracy of 0.850, after some oscillations due to the variability on few data, it reaches a plain around 20,000 samples to end with 0.885 the complete testing stream. Naturally, the value for interactivity is permanently 0. Secondly, the curve described by 2TNL is quite similar to 1NQ, except for starting from a higher EMIC value of 0.882, because in the first 100 samples it requests 13 samples to the oracle. This percentage remains around 15 % since the beginning. The Accuracy of 2TNL is superior to that of 1NQ, that means that many requested samples would be classification errors. Thirdly, as described previously, 3TLe get bad values for EMIC and Interactivity. It has the same beginning as 2TNL, but progressively the Interactivity increases until reaching 38.2 %, at the same time the EMIC suffers a progressive decrease, reaching the baseline of 1NQ, with value 0.888. On other problems, the curve of 3TLe for the EMIC even can go underneath. So, it deteriorates clearly the interactive system. Finally, 4Dyn starts as the previous ones, from a value of 0.882 for EMIC. On the first 100 samples it requests 13 samples, and continues increasing its Interactivity until reaching 16 % after the first 1800 samples. Then it readjusts the threshold, and the Interactivity drops progressively to a value of 2.3 %, because it is less and less unsure for its predictions.

5   Concluding Remarks

In this paper we have proposed a method for adding interactivity to the behavior of automatic classifiers that can work online, but have not access to the labels of the incoming instances unless they ask them to an oracle. The decision about asking or not is based on a threshold relative to the confidence degree of the classifier in its own prediction.

We have tested our proposals using a variety of data streams generated using the MOA framework and two online base classifiers. The performance of the interactive online classifier that does not update its initial threshold is rather poor (probably due to the bias induced by the new instances used to update the classifier, which are always near the decision frontier). However, the interactive online classifier that recomputes its threshold performs excellently, both increasing the accuracy of the classifier when it is used autonomously and decreasing the number of queries to the oracle.

For future work, we plan to test our methods with other incremental/online classifiers beyond *NaiveBayes* and *HoeffdingTreeNB*. We also want to design alternative rules to decide whether the classifier should ask the oracle, for example allowing (in an random way) to occasionally ask when the classifier is quite sure of its prediction, in order to prevent the possible bias. Finally, we plan to study the problem of incorporating interactivity in the presence of concept drift.

Acknowledgements. This work has been funded by the Spanish Ministry of Economy and Competitiveness under the project TIN2013-42741-P and the European Regional Development Fund (ERDF-FEDER).

References

1. Acid, S., de Campos, L.M., Fernández, M.: Evaluation methods and strategies for the interactive use of classifiers. Int. J. Hum.-Comput. Stud. **70**(5), 321–331 (2012)
2. Agrawal, R., Imielinski, T., Swami, A.: Database mining: a performance perspective. IEEE Trans. Knowl. Data Eng. **5**(6), 914–925 (1993)
3. Auer, P., Cesa-Bianchi, N., Gentile, C.: Adaptive and self-confident on-line learning algorithms. J. Comput. Syst. Sci. **64**, 48–75 (2002)
4. Barlet, P.L., Wegkamp, M.H.: Classification with a reject option using a hinge loss. J. Mach. Learn. Res. **9**, 1823–1840 (2008)
5. Bifet, A., Holmes, G., Kirkby, R., Pfahringer, B.: MOA: massive online analysis. J. Mach. Learn. Res. **11**, 1601–1604 (2010)
6. Fu, Y., Zhu, X., Li, B.: A survey on instance selection for active lerning. Knowl. Inf. Syst. **35**, 249–283 (2013)
7. Fumera, G., Roli, F., Giacinto, G.: Reject option with multiple thresholds. Pattern Recogn. **33**(12), 2099–2101 (2000)
8. Gama, J.: Knowledge Discovery from Data Streams. Chapman and Hall/CRC, Boca Raton (2010)
9. Gama, J.: A survey on learning from data streams: current and future trends. Prog. Artif. Intell. **1**, 45–55 (2012)
10. Hulten, G., Spencer, L., Domingos, P.: Mining time-changing data streams. In: KDD-01, pp. 97–106. ACM Press (2001)
11. Lewis, D., Gale, W.: A sequential algorithm for training text classifiers. In: Proceedings of the ACM SIGIR Conference, pp. 3–12 (1994)
12. Settles, B.: Active learning literature survey. Computer Sciences Technical Report 1648, University of Wisconsin-Madison (2009)
13. Shalev-Shwartz, S.: Online learning and online convex optimization. Found. Trends Mach. Learn. **4**(2), 107–194 (2012)
14. van Rijsbergen, C.J.: Foundation of evaluation. J. Documentation **30**(4), 365–373 (1974)

Frequent Closed Patterns Based Multiple Consensus Clustering

Atheer Al-Najdi$^{(\boxtimes)}$, Nicolas Pasquier, and Frédéric Precioso

Univ. Nice Sophia Antipolis, CNRS, I3S, UMR 7271, 06900 Sophia Antipolis, France
{alnajdi,pasquier,precioso}@i3s.unice.fr

Abstract. Clustering is one of the major tasks in data mining. However, selecting an algorithm to cluster a dataset is a difficult task, especially if there is no prior knowledge on the structure of the data. Consensus clustering methods can be used to combine multiple base clusterings into a new solution that provides better partitioning. In this work, we present a new consensus clustering method based on detecting clustering patterns by mining frequent closed itemset. Instead of generating one consensus, this method both generates multiple consensuses based on varying the number of base clusterings, and links these solutions in a hierarchical representation that eases the selection of the best clustering. This hierarchical view also provides an analysis tool, for example to discover strong clusters or outlier instances.

Keywords: Unsupervised learning · Clustering · Consensus clustering · Ensemble clustering · Frequent closed patterns

1 Introduction

Clustering is the process of partitioning a dataset into groups, so that the instances in the same group are more similar to each other than to instances in any other group. This partitioning may lead to discover meaningful patterns in the dataset. Many clustering algorithms were developed in the last 50 years, and, most often, each algorithm produces different partitioning when applied to the same dataset, because they are designed to target a specific model (compact clusters, non-convex clusters...). Thus the question is: How to choose a clustering for a dataset from these many possibilities?

The most common solution is to use validation measure(s) to compare the results and select the one that gets the higher score [4, 7]. There are two general categories of validation measures: *Internal validation* that compares the clustering against a specific clustering model, and *external validation* that compares the clustering against true labels (class labels given on an evaluation set using domain knowledge). In both categories, many validation measures exist, and no one impartially evaluates the results of all clustering algorithms [20]. In real life, the user can have similar scores for different validation measures and/or for different clustering results, while the results are different in many aspects, like in the number of clusters or in the instance grouping into clusters.

© Springer International Publishing Switzerland 2016
L. Rutkowski et al. (Eds.): ICAISC 2016, Part II, LNAI 9693, pp. 14–26, 2016.
DOI: 10.1007/978-3-319-39384-1_2

Rather than depending on validation measures, another approach is to combine the multiple clustering solutions generated by several clustering algorithms and/or settings, in order to produce a final clustering which is better than each individual algorithm can produce. This technique is called *consensus clustering*, *aggregation of clusterings* or *ensemble clustering*, and the clustering algorithms to be combined are called *base clustering algorithms*. Many consensus clustering methods have been proposed, and some of them will be discussed in the next section. In this paper, we propose a new consensus clustering method named MultiCons. Instead of providing the user with a single solution, we generate multiple consensuses by varying the selection of base clusterings, then linking these multiple solutions in a hierarchical view. The user can then not only select the best solution, but also discover strong clusters in the dataset that do not change when varying the base clusterings. Hence, our proposed method is a combination of ensemble of consensus solutions with a visual data analysis tool.

The paper is organized as follows: Sect. 2 discusses some of the previous work in consensus clustering. Section 3 explains the proposed approach. Some experimental results are shown in Sect. 4, and we provide conclusions in Sect. 5.

2 Related Work

Consensus clustering refers to the problem of finding a single consensus clustering from a number of different inputs or base clusterings that have been obtained for a given dataset [11,24]. The advantage of this technique is to have a new clustering result that is at least as good as the best clustering achieved by the base methods.

Many consensus clustering methods were developed over the past years. In Asur *et al.* [1], six predefined clustering algorithms suitable for protein-protein datasets clustering were considered as base clusterings. A cluster membership matrix[1] is then built, and a consensus clustering method is applied over this matrix (agglomerative hierarchical clustering or recursive bisection) to obtain the final consensus. All the 6 base clusterings have K clusters, and if K is high the resulting binary membership matrix is sparse and the consensus clustering of this matrix is ineffective. Thus, PCA (Principle Components Analysis) is applied before the consensus clustering to reduce the dimensionality of the membership matrix into less, but more expressive, dimensions. These different consensus techniques were compared, and the authors conclude that the PCA based technique produced very efficient clustering and identified multiple functionalities of proteins.

Three consensus clustering methods were proposed by Strehl & Ghosh [18]. The first step for all their proposed consensus functions is to transform the given clusterings into a suitable hypergraph representation, where each cluster (column in the membership matrix) from any base clustering is considered as a hyperedge that connects several vertices (all the instances in this cluster) in a hypergraph. Based on this mapping, Strehl & Ghosh propose: (i) *Cluster-based Similarity*

---

[1] See Sect. 3.1 for a definition of cluster membership matrix.

Partitioning Algorithm (CSPA) which is based on an overall similarity matrix S built from the membership matrix H by using $S = \frac{1}{r}HH^\dagger$, where r is the number of base clusterings. The aforementioned hypergraph is built from this similarity matrix so that each hyperdge represents the sum of similarities between a given pair of vertices (i.e. each time the two considered vertices are clustered together by any base clustering, their similarity is increment by 1), then a graph-based clustering method (METIS) provides the consensus clustering; (ii) *HyperGraph-Partitioning Algorithm* (HGPA) all hyperedges as well as all vertices are equally weighted, then a hypergraph partitioning algorithm (HMETIS) defines the consensus by cutting a minimal number of edges; (iii) *Meta-CLustering Algorithm* (MCLA) follow the same ideas, but hyperedges weights are proportional to the similarity between vertices (instances) which is calculated using binary Jaccard measure. The resulting hypergraph is then clustered using METIS to generate K clusters. For each of these K meta-clusters, its hyperedges are collapsed into a single meta-hyperedge. Each meta-hyperedge has an association vector which contains an entry for each object describing its level of association with the corresponding meta-cluster.

With their algorithm *WClustering*, Li & Ding [11] proposed weighting the base clusterings to ensure removing redundant (similar) partitions, since this process produces better results compared to other methods that generate the consensus from brute-force averaging of the base clusterings. Weights are automatically determined by an optimization process. Experimental results showed that more accurate clustering was achieved by the k-means algorithm when applied to the weighted consensus similarity matrix, compared to the results of CSPA and HGPA. In Zhang & Li [24], the base clusterings are compared using pairwise similarity, and then divided into groups using K-means. On each group, one of the previously discussed consensus methods is used: PCA-based consensus algorithm [1], CSPA and HGPA from [18], and WClustering [11]. Thus, the final result is K consensuses for the user to select from.

The idea in Caruana *et al.* [2] is to generate many base clusterings, then build a similarity matrix for these different partitions using Rand index. This similarity matrix is passed to agglomerative hierarchical clustering to build a meta clustering. The dendrogram shows how the partitions are similar to each other, thus there is no final consensus. Instead, the user can analyze the resulting dendrogram to choose which clustering is the most relevant. To have a diversity in the base clusterings, feature weighting using Zipf distribution and PCA were used to produce different base clustering views.

For more information about consensus clustering methods, see Ghaemi *et al.* [5], Sarumathi *et al.* [17], and Vega-Pons & Ruiz-Shulcloper [20].

3   The Proposed Approach

Unlike consensus clustering methods that search for a *median partition* [20] to enhance the results of an ensemble of base clustering results, our objective is to identify hidden cluster structure in the dataset from the ensemble. Using the

Frequent Closed Itemsets (FCIs) [15] technique from pattern mining domain, we discover clustering patterns common to different sets of base clusterings. FCIs define both clustering patterns (fragments) common to all base clusterings, known as *data fragments* in [21], plus other "larger fragments" built from fewer base clusterings. Regrouping these fragments based on the number of base clusterings used to define them, patterns in each group can then be combined according to their common instances to build a consensus. Generated consensus clusters are then linked in a tree-shaped diagram to easily understand their building process and identify stable clusters. Algorithm 1 describes the successive steps of the proposed approach, as explained in the following subsections.

3.1   Cluster Membership Matrix

From the multiple clusterings of the dataset generated using a set of base clustering methods, a *cluster membership matrix* $\mathcal{M}$ is built. $\mathcal{M}$ is a binary matrix of $N \times M$ cells, where N is the number of dataset instances, and M is the number of cluster vectors (total number of clusters generated by all base clustering algorithms), as given in Definition 1.

Definition 1. *A cluster membership matrix $\mathcal{M}$ is a triplet $(\mathcal{I}, \mathcal{C}, \mathcal{R})$ where $\mathcal{I}$ is a finite set of instances represented as rows, $\mathcal{C}$ is a finite set of variables, each designating a cluster, represented as columns, and $\mathcal{R}$ is a binary relation defining relationships between rows and columns: $\mathcal{R} \subseteq \mathcal{I} \times \mathcal{C}$. Every couple $(i, c) \in \mathcal{R}$, where $i \in \mathcal{I}$ and $c \in \mathcal{C}$, means that the instance i belongs to the cluster c.*

Consider for example a dataset of nine instances $\mathcal{D} = \{1, 2, 3, 4, 5, 6, 7, 8, 9\}$ partitioned using five base clusterings into the five following partitions: $P1 = \{\{1, 2, 3\}, \{4, 5, 6, 7, 8, 9\}\}$, $P2 = \{\{1, 2, 3\}, \{4, 5, 6, 7, 8, 9\}\}$, $P3 = \{\{1, 2, 3, 4, 5\}, \{6, 7\}, \{8, 9\}\}$, $P4 = \{\{4, 5, 6, 7\}, \{1, 2, 3\}, \{8, 9\}\}$, and $P5 = \{\{4, 5, 6, 7\}, \{1, 2, 3\}, \{8, 9\}\}$. Table 1 shows the resulting cluster membership matrix consisting of 9 rows (instances) and 14 columns (total number of clusters in base clusterings). Each column P_j^i represents cluster j in partition i as a binary vector where values '1' identify the instances that belong to the cluster. In pattern mining domain, each column in $\mathcal{M}$ represents an item, as defined hereafter.

Definition 2. *An item of a cluster membership matrix $\mathcal{M} = (\mathcal{I}, \mathcal{C}, \mathcal{R})$ is a cluster identifier $c \in \mathcal{C}$ and an itemset is a non-empty finite set of items $C = \{c_1, ..., c_n\} \subseteq \mathcal{C}$ in $\mathcal{M}$. An itemset $C \subseteq \mathcal{C}$ is frequent in $\mathcal{M}$ iff its frequency, called support, in $\mathcal{M}$ defined as $support(C) = |\{I \in \mathcal{I} \mid \forall i \in I, \forall c \in C, \text{ we have } (i, c) \in \mathcal{R}\}|$ is greater than or equal to the user-defined minsupport threshold.*

3.2   Generating Clustering Patterns

The next step consists of generating the *Frequent Closed Patterns* (FCPs) from the cluster membership matrix $\mathcal{M}$. Each FCP associates a FCI (a closed set of cluster identifiers) and its corresponding set of instance identifiers, i.e., the

Table 1. Example cluster membership matrix.

Instance ID	P_1^1	P_2^1	P_1^2	P_2^2	P_1^3	P_2^3	P_3^3	P_1^4	P_2^4	P_3^4	P_1^5	P_2^5	P_3^5
1	1	0	1	0	1	0	0	0	1	0	0	1	0
2	1	0	1	0	1	0	0	0	1	0	0	1	0
3	1	0	1	0	1	0	0	0	1	0	0	1	0
4	0	1	0	1	1	0	0	1	0	0	1	0	0
5	0	1	0	1	1	0	0	1	0	0	1	0	0
6	0	1	0	1	0	1	0	1	0	0	1	0	0
7	0	1	0	1	0	1	0	1	0	0	1	0	0
8	0	1	0	1	0	0	1	0	0	1	0	0	1
9	0	1	0	1	0	0	1	0	0	1	0	0	1

identifiers of dataset instances that are common to all clusters in the FCI set. FCPs represent maximal sets, regarding inclusion, of base clusterings that agree on grouping a set of instances. Subsets of such sets of base clusterings that agree on grouping the same set of instances will not be considered.[2] Stated another way, FCPs are maximal rectangles in the membership matrix. See [23] for complexity considerations about FCIs and frequent pattern mining.

Definition 3. *A frequent closed pattern $P = (C, I)$ in the cluster membership matrix $M = (I, C, R)$ is a pair of sets $C \subset C$ and $I \subset I$ such that:*

(i) $\forall i \in I$ and $\forall c \in C$, we have $(i, c) \in R$.
(ii) $|I| \geq minsupport$, i.e., C is a frequent itemset.
(iii) $\nexists i' \in I$ such that $\forall c \in C$, we have $(i', c) \in R$.
(iv) $\nexists c' \in C$ such that $\forall i \in I$, we have $(i, c') \in R$.

Table 2 shows the set of the seven FCPs extracted from Table 1. Each row, identified by its FCP ID, represents an FCP. The support of each FCP corresponding to the size of its instance set, the *minsupport* parameter is set to 0 in order to consider clustering patterns, i.e., clusters of base clusterings, of all sizes.

3.3 Generating Multiple Consensuses

Building clustering consensuses from the FCPs is an iterative process that considers during each iteration all FCPs corresponding to a specific number, called *Decision Threshold* (DT), of base clusterings. The DT value represents the minimum number of base clusterings to consider for building a consensus. For the first consensus, we have DT = *MaxDT*, where *MaxDT* is the number of base clusterings used. The DT value is then sequentially decremented until DT = 1 to integrate in the new consensus another clustering view generated by a smaller

---

[2] Generating only clustering patterns of maximum agreement between base clusterings reduces processing time.

Table 2. Frequent closed patterns extracted from Table 1.

FCP IDs	Itemsets (FCIs)	Instance IDs
1	$\{P_2^1, P_2^2, P_1^3, P_1^4, P_1^5\}$	$\{4, 5\}$
2	$\{P_2^1, P_2^2, P_2^3, P_1^4, P_1^5\}$	$\{6, 7\}$
3	$\{P_2^1, P_2^2, P_3^3, P_3^4, P_3^5\}$	$\{8, 9\}$
4	$\{P_1^1, P_1^2, P_1^3, P_2^4, P_2^5\}$	$\{1, 2, 3\}$
5	$\{P_2^1, P_2^2, P_1^4, P_1^5\}$	$\{4, 5, 6, 7\}$
6	$\{P_1^3\}$	$\{1, 2, 3, 4, 5\}$
7	$\{P_2^1, P_2^2\}$	$\{4, 5, 6, 7, 8, 9\}$

number of base clusterings. During an iteration DT $= n$, all FCPs with an FCI of size n are combined with clusters of the previous iteration (for DT $= n+1$) making each consensus a complete clustering vector, i.e., covering all dataset instances:

Definition 4. *Having the first consensus,* $\mathbb{P}^{MaxDT} = \{P_1, P_2, ..., P_m\}$ *and the definition* $\mathbb{B}^{DT} = \mathbb{I}^{DT} \cup \mathbb{P}^{DT+1}$ *where* $\mathbb{I}^{DT}$ *is the instance sets of the FCPs built from DT base clusterings, and* $\mathbb{P}^{DT+1}$ *is the instance sets (clusters) of the previous consensus. A new consensus* $\mathbb{P}^{DT}$ *is the result of applying a consensus function* $\mathcal{Y}$ *on* $\mathbb{B}^{DT}$*, that is,* $\mathbb{P}^{DT} = \mathcal{Y}(\mathbb{B}^{DT}) = \{P_1, P_2, ..., P_k\}$ *such that* $P_i \cap P_j = \emptyset$*,* $\forall(i, j) \in \{1, ..., k\}$*,* $i \neq j$*, and* $\bigcup_{i=1}^{i=k} P_i = \mathcal{I}$*.*

The first consensus consists of instance sets of FCPs that define clustering patterns common to all base clusterings (lines 5–7 in Algorithm 1), or data fragments [21]. Consensuses are then iteratively built using results of the previous consensus (lines 9–32 in Algorithm 1) according to the following properties of instance sets. At each DT, an instance set $I \subseteq \mathcal{I}$ has one of the following three properties:

(i) Uniqueness: It does not intersect with any other set $I' \subseteq \mathcal{I}$, that is, $I \cap I' = \emptyset$.
(ii) Inclusion: It is a subset of another set $I' \subseteq \mathcal{I}$, that is, $I \subseteq I'$.
(iii) Intersection: It intersects with another set $I' \subseteq \mathcal{I}$, that is, $I \cap I' \neq \emptyset$, $I \setminus I' \neq \emptyset$ and $I' \setminus I \neq \emptyset$.

To build a new consensus, intersecting sets, that represent sets of instances that are close (very similar) in the data space,[3] of FCPs and clusters are merged (lines 23–27 in Algorithm 1). Instance sets having *inclusion* property are removed to consider the new clustering view (lines 17–22 in Algorithm 1). The merging process repeats until all instance sets have *uniqueness* property. Since only a small number of FCPs is used for generating each consensus, the process of generating consensuses is efficient, even when the total number of FCPs is large.

---

[3] This is the objective of clustering algorithms, yet they differ in how they define the similarity between instances.

Input   : Dataset to cluster.
Output: ConsTree tree of consensuses.

1 Generate multiple base clusterings of the dataset;
2 Build the cluster membership matrix $\mathcal{M}$;
3 Generate FCPs from $\mathcal{M}$ for *minsupport* = 0;
4 Sort the FCPs in ascending order of the size of their instance list;
5 $MaxDT \leftarrow$ Number of base clusterings;
6 $BiClust \leftarrow$ {instance sets of FCPs built from $MaxDT$ base clusters};
7 Assign a label to each set in $BiClust$ to build the first consensus vector and store it in a list of vectors $ConsVctrs$;
8 /* **Build the remaining consensuses** */;
9 **for** $DT = (MaxDT$ - $1)$ **to** 1 **do**
10 | $BiClust \leftarrow BiClust \cup$ {instance sets of FCPs built from DT base clusters};
11 | $N \leftarrow |BiClust|$ // **Nbr of sets in** $BiClust$;
12 | **repeat**
13 | | **for** $i = 1$ **to** N **do**
14 | | | $B_i \leftarrow i^{\text{th}}$ set in $BiClust$;
15 | | | **for** $j = 1$ **to** N, $j \neq i$ **do**
16 | | | | $B_j \leftarrow j^{\text{th}}$ set in $BiClust$;
17 | | | | **if** $B_i \subseteq B_j$ **then**
18 | | | | | Remove B_i from $BiClust$;
19 | | | | | Next i;
20 | | | | **else if** $B_j \subset B_i$ **then**
21 | | | | | Remove B_j from $BiClust$;
22 | | | | | Next j;
23 | | | | **else if** $B_i \cap B_j \neq \emptyset$ **then**
24 | | | | | $B_j \leftarrow B_i \cup B_j$;
25 | | | | | Remove B_i from $BiClust$;
26 | | | | | Next i;
27 | | | **end**
28 | | **end**
29 | **end**
30 | **until** *All sets in BiClust are unique*;
31 | Assign a label to each set in $BiClust$ to build a consensus vector and add it to $ConsVctrs$;
32 **end**
33 /* **Remove similar consensuses** */;
34 $ST \leftarrow$ Vector of '1's of length $MaxDT$;
35 **for** $i = MaxDT$ **to** 2 **do**
36 | $V_i \leftarrow i^{\text{th}}$ consensus in $ConsVctrs$;
37 | **for** $j = (i$ - $1)$ **to** 1 **do**
38 | | $V_j \leftarrow j^{\text{th}}$ consensus in $ConsVctrs$;
39 | | **if** $Jaccard(V_i, V_j) = 1$ **then**
40 | | | $ST[i] \leftarrow ST[i] + 1$;
41 | | | Remove $ST[j]$;
42 | | | Remove V_j from $ConsVctrs$;
43 | | **end**
44 | **end**
45 **end**
46 Build the tree of consensuses in $ConsVctrs$

Algorithm 1. The MultiCons approach.

Similar consensuses are then removed, and a *stability counter* (ST) is associated to each to count how many times it was generated, i.e., for how many different values of DT (lines 34–45 in Algorithm 1). For example, a consensus with ST = 3 means that this consensus is generated from 3 consecutive values of DT.

Considering the example in Table 1, the first consensus, with DT = 5, consists of instance sets of FCPs number 1 to 4 in Table 2, which FCI size is equal to the number of base clusterings. To build the next consensus, DT is decremented and FCP 5, that defines a pattern common to the 4 base clusterings 1, 2, 4 and 5, is integrated. FCPs 1 and 2 are removed as they are included in FCP 5, and the consensus for DT = 4 thus contains clusters {1,2,3}, {4,5,6,7} and {8,9}. This consensus represents the clustering agreement between at least 4 base clusterings. Since no FCP has an FCI of size 3, the consensus for DT = 3 is identical to the consensus for DT = 4. For DT = 2, FCP 7 is integrated, and replaces FCPs 3 and 5 that are included in FCP 7, resulting in the consensus: {{1,2,3}, {4,5,6,7,8,9}}. For DT = 1, FCP 6 is integrated, and FCP 4 that is included in FCP 6 is deleted. FCPs 6 and 7 are then merged as they intersect, and the consensus for DT = 1 thus results in grouping all instances in 1 cluster, which will become the root of the tree representation described hereafter. In the resulting consensus vector, consensuses for DT = 4 and DT = 3 are merged since they are identical resulting in consensus for DT = 4 having ST = 2. This consensus, that is the most stable generated, represents the best agreement between the 5 base partitions. It tells that at least 4 base clusterings agree on generating its clusters. Actually, the instances of clusters {1,2,3} and {8,9} are grouped together in the 5 base partitions, instances of the first never being grouped with other instances, and the instances of cluster {4,5,6,7} are grouped together in 4 partitions.

But, how can we recognize the best solution in operational situations? As stated before, our objective is to find as many clustering patterns of the hidden cluster structure (or close to it) as possible. This is why, instead of forcibly generate a median partition, we search for clustering patterns from different combinations of base clusterings, and then merge connected ones to build a structure of well separated patterns. However, we can also recommend the best solution as the one that is the most similar to the ensemble using the Jaccard index [10] similarity measure. The consensus with highest average Jaccard similarity with each partition in the ensemble is then recommended as the best solution. In the case of preceding example, this is consensus for DT = 4.

3.4   ConsTree: A Tree of Consensuses

After generating all consensuses, a tree graphical representation is built to visualize the different clustering results: The *ConsTree* tree of consensuses. Each level in the tree depicts a consensus, with nodes representing its clusters and edges representing inclusion relationships between instance sets of clusters of successive levels. The bottom level of the tree is the first consensus.

Definition 5. *A tree of consensuses is an ordered set $(\mathcal{L}, \preceq)$ of consensuses $\mathcal{L} = \bigcup_{DT=MaxDT}^{DT=MinDT} L^{DT}$ ordered in descending order of DT values. Let's denote $L^\alpha = \{P_1^\alpha, ..., P_m^\alpha\}$ and $L^\beta = \{P_1^\beta, ..., P_n^\beta\}$ the consensuses generated for α and β DT values respectively. Let's denote P_q^α the qth cluster in L^α and P_r^β the rth cluster in L^β, with $1 \le q \le m$ and $1 \le r \le n$. For $\alpha > \beta$ we have $L^\alpha \preceq L^\beta$, that is $\forall P_q^\alpha \in L^\alpha$, $\exists P_r^\beta \in L^\beta$ such that $P_q^\alpha \subseteq P_r^\beta$. L^α is a predecessor of L^β in the tree of consensuses.*

Figure 1 gives the Hasse diagram of the ConsTree for the example in Table 1. It shows at each level how clusters of the preceding lower level are merged to form new clusters, and the advised level, that is the consensus for DT = 4. We can also note the left branch showing the stable cluster {1,2,3} that is never merged except for root node.

Figure 2 shows another example ConsTree, resulting of the application of MultiCons to a dataset of 399 instances clustered using 10 base clusterings selected randomly, with random settings and K varied from 2 to 11. This tree consists of 7 levels, instead of 10 without merging of identical levels, as duplicated levels for DT = 2 and 3, for DT = 4, 5 and 6 are merged. Visualizing the tree enables the user to understand how the consensuses were built based on different combinations of base clusterings, and to discover strong partitions in the dataset: The cluster(s) that do not merge with others on a sequence of consensuses, which reflect strong intra-cluster similarity between their instances (as the ones circled in blue and red in Fig. 2). It may also highlight groups of instances that are far from being similar to other instances, such as the column of stable cluster circled in red and the similar column beside. Furthermore, the fact that these two columns merge into one cluster, circled in green, rather than merging with any of the previous stable clusters (circled in blue) provides more insight on the peculiar information they hold. The ST value can also point to the result that is more stable than others (the consensus for DT = 6), but as the clustering task is more related to the relevance of the found patterns to user preferences, the user may prefer to select the consensus at DT = 7

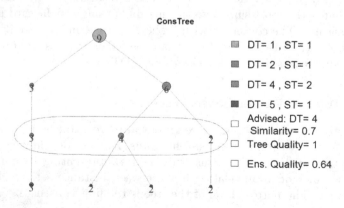

Fig. 1. ConsTree of example membership matrix Table 1.

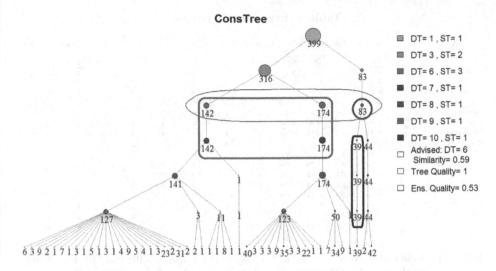

Fig. 2. Example of analysis from ConsTree visualization.

for example, because he/she prefers to separate the cluster of 83 instances at DT = 6 into 2 stable clusters as in DT = 7, as these 2 may reflect better patterns for him/her. Compared to classical ensemble approaches, that only provide one solution representing the clustering that is most similar to the ensemble, the tree of consensuses not only provides more information for the user to understand the strong relations in the data, but it also assists him/her to choose a final clustering based on his/her prior knowledge and preferences.

4 Experiments

We implemented the MultiCons algorithm using R language [16] on a DELL PRECISION M4800 with Intel® Core™ i7-4710MQ @ 2.50 GHz, 32 GB of RAM, and Microsoft Windows 10 Professional (64-bit) operating system. To generate the frequent closed patterns, we have used the FIST algorithm [13] implemented in Java from the website of the authors.[4] The output of MultiCons is represented as a graph with a vertex for each cluster of a consensus, and an edge between each pair of vertices in two consecutive consensuses representing two clusters related by inclusion. The *plot* function of the *igraph* R package [3] can plot the tree from a data frame defining these edges.

For each test, the base clusterings were generated by random selection of a set of clustering algorithms and/or parameter settings. Among the clustering algorithms used: K-means, PAM, DBSCAN, agglomerative hierarchical clustering, AGNES, DIANA, MCLUST, C-Means, FANNY, Bagged Clustering, and SOM. We compared the results of MultiCons against voting-based consensus

---

[4] Another possibility is to use the *arules* R package [6].

Table 3. Experimental results.

Dataset	E.Coli	Wine	Zoo	Breast cancer	Smiley	Shapes	Hyper cube	Chain link	Atom	Golf ball	Hepta	Terta
Size	336	178	101	699	500	2000	800	1000	800	4002	212	400
# attributes	7	13	16	9	2	2	3	3	3	3	3	3
# classes	8	3	7	2	4	4	8	2	2	1	7	4
# base clusterings	9	8	18	11	6	8	8	6	8	5	7	7
K range for ensemble	[2, 18]	[2, 10]	[4, 8]	[2, 6]	[2, 7]	[2, 9]	[4, 11]	[2, 7]	[2, 9]	[2, 6]	[4, 10]	[2, 8]
Ensemble min	0.19	0.28	0.29	0.35	0.40	0.46	0.41	0.24	0.46	0.17	0.36	0.50
Ensemble max	0.63	0.87	**0.86**	**0.90**	0.74	1	1	1	1	0.50	1	1
MultiCons	**0.72**	**0.92**	0.78	0.89	1	1	1	1	1	1	1	1
# clusters in MultiCons	15	4	5	3	4	4	8	2	2	1	7	4
SE	0.43	0.80	0.82	0.89	0.59	0.83	0.89	0.83	0.98	1	1	1
GV1	0.43	0.87	0.79	0.89	0.92	0.66	1	0.59	1	1	1	1
DWH	0.44	0.70	0.82	0.89	0.56	0.98	0.91	0.53	0.99	1	0.78	1
HE	0.49	0.89	0.82	0.89	0.78	0.84	1	0.64	0.98	1	0.78	1
SM	0.41	0.85	0.82	0.89	0.75	1	0.80	0.65	1	1	0.98	0.66
GV3	0.49	0.87	0.82	0.89	0.76	1	1	0.92	1	1	1	1
Soft/symdiff	0.36	0.80	0.83	0.89	0.57	1	1	0.92	1	1	1	1
Medoids	0.37	0.87	0.83	**0.90**	0.74	0.87	1	0.35	1	0.20	1	1

clustering algorithms available in R package CLUE [8], including the following consensus methods: SE, GV1, DWH, HE, SM, GV3, soft/symdiff, and consensus medoid. To validate the results of our consensus method and the CLUE methods, we compared the clustering results against the true class labels of the tested dataset using several external validation measures like NMI (Normalized Mutual Information) [18], Jaccard, cRand (Corrected Rand), and FM (Fowlkes and Mallows) [4,7] also in R package CLUE [9].

Table 3 presents results of experiments on benchmark datasets, with a summary description of the dataset, the base clusterings, and the quality of the achieved consensus results compared to the true class using Jaccard measure. The Jaccard measure was used because it gives a moderate trade-off between the similarity to the true class and the number of generated clusters [22]. Note that for voting methods in CLUE, all base clusterings in the ensemble must use the same K value. However, we did not impose this constraint in our tests, just set parameter K to the actual K, corresponding to the dataset true classes, for these methods. MultiCons, that does not require parameter K, generates multiple results with different numbers of clusters. The shown result of MultiCons is the one that is the most similar to the ensemble (the recommended consensus).

E.Coli and Wine datasets are available on the UCI Machine Learning Repository [12]. The Zoo, Breast Cancer, Smiley, Shapes and Hyper Cube datasets are available in the *mlbench* R package [14]. The other datasets are from Ultsch [19]. We can see that the MultiCons approach achieved very good results.

5 Conclusions

We presented a new multiple consensus clustering method that does not require parameter setting; yet it can build the appropriate number of clusters based on finding clustering patterns common to the set of base clusterings. This is a major distinction with other consensus methods that require at least parameter K, like CLUE methods, to generate K clusters in the consensus, as without prior domain knowledge, it is difficult to predict K.

To the best of our knowledge, the proposed method is the first to use frequent closed patterns to detect similarities among base clusterings and to build multiple consensuses from these. One of the benefits of using FCIs technique is efficiency: Execution time is not directly related to the size of the dataset, but depends instead on the number of base clusterings used and whether there are many similarities, or many conflicts, between base partitions. Thus, even for large datasets, few FCPs are generated if some clustering patterns are common to most base clusterings, while other methods based on distance matrices are constrained by the size of the dataset. Even when the number of FCPs is large, the greedy processing in MultiCons is fast, since at each consensus, it requires only few FCPs to work with. Tests showed that CLUE methods GV3 and soft/symdiff require a lot of both computation and memory compared to MultiCons for example.

In addition to providing a consensus clustering result, the ConsTree generated by MultiCons serves as a nice data analysis tool. It shows which clusters are stable, which reflect a strong intra-cluster similarity, leading to discovering meaningful patterns in the dataset. On the other hand, stable consensuses (if exist) suggest the existence of strong cluster structure in the dataset, which consists of well-separated clusters. The ConsTree not only provides one solution to the user, but it also allows he/she to choose another solution based on his/her preferences and prior knowledge for separating or merging certain clusters, for instance, the consensus below or above the suggested one.

References

1. Asur, S., Ucar, D., Parthasarathy, S.: An ensemble framework for clustering protein-protein interaction networks. Bioinformatics **23**(13), i29–i40 (2007)
2. Caruana, R., Elhawary, M., Nguyen, N., Smith, C.: Meta clustering. In: Proceedings of the IEEE ICDM Conference, pp. 107–118 (2006)
3. Csardi, G., Nepusz, T.: The igraph software package for complex network research. InterJournal Complex Systems, 1695 (2006). http://igraph.org
4. Dalton, L., Ballarin, V., Brun, M.: Clustering algorithms: on learning, validation, performance, and applications to genomics. Curr. Genomics **10**(6), 430 (2009)
5. Ghaemi, R., Sulaiman, M.N., Ibrahim, H., Mustapha, N.: A survey: clustering ensembles techniques. WASET **50**, 636–645 (2009)
6. Hahsler, M., Gruen, B., Hornik, K.: arules - a computational environment for mining association rules and frequent item sets. J. Stat. Softw. **14**(15), 1–25 (2005)
7. Halkidi, M., Batistakis, Y., Vazirgiannis, M.: On clustering validation techniques. J. Intell. Inf. Syst. **17**(2), 107–145 (2001)
8. Hornik, K.: A CLUE for CLUster Ensembles. J. Stat. Softw. **14**(12), 1–25 (2005)
9. Hornik, K.: CLUE: Cluster ensembles (2015). r package version 0.3-50 http://CRAN.R-project.org/package=clue
10. Jaccard, P.: The distribution of the flora in the alpine zone.1. New Phytol. **11**(2), 37–50 (1912). doi:10.1111/j.1469-8137.1912.tb05611.x
11. Li, T., Ding, C.: Weighted consensus clustering. In: Proceedings of the SIAM Conference on Data Mining, pp. 798–809 (2008)
12. Lichman, M.: UCI machine learning repository (2013). http://archive.ics.uci.edu/ml

13. Mondal, K.C., Pasquier, N., Mukhopadhyay, A., Maulik, U., Bandhopadyay, S.: A new approach for association rule mining and bi-clustering using formal concept analysis. In: Perner, P. (ed.) MLDM 2012. LNCS, vol. 7376, pp. 86–101. Springer, Heidelberg (2012)
14. Newman, D., Hettich, S., Blake, C., Merz, C.: UCI repository of machine learning databases (1998). http://www.ics.uci.edu/~mlearn/MLRepository.html
15. Pasquier, N., Bastide, Y., Taouil, R., Lakhal, L.: Efficient mining of association rules using closed itemset lattices. Inf. Syst. **24**(1), 25–46 (1999)
16. R Core Team: R: A Language and Environment for Statistical Computing. R Foundation for Statistical Computing, Vienna, Austria (2015). https://www.R-project.org/
17. Sarumathi, S., Shanthi, N., Sharmila, M.: A comparative analysis of different categorical data clustering ensemble methods in data mining. IJCA **81**(4), 46–55 (2013)
18. Strehl, A., Ghosh, J.: Cluster ensembles - a knowledge reuse framework for combining multiple partitions. JMLR **3**, 583–617 (2003)
19. Ultsch, A.: Clustering with SOM: U*C. In: Proceedings of the WSOM Workshop, pp. 75–82 (2005)
20. Vega-Pons, S., Ruiz-Shulcloper, J.: A survey of clustering ensemble algorithms. IJPRAI **25**(03), 337–372 (2011)
21. Wu, O., Hu, W., Maybank, S.J., Zhu, M., Li, B.: Efficient clustering aggregation based on data fragments. IEEE Trans. Syst. Man Cybern B Cybern. **42**(3), 913–926 (2012)
22. Xu, D., Tian, Y.: A comprehensive survey of clustering algorithms. Ann. Data Sci. **2**(2), 165–193 (2015)
23. Yang, G.: The complexity of mining maximal frequent itemsets and maximal frequent patterns. In: ACM SIGKDD, pp. 344–353 (2004)
24. Zhang, Y., Li, T.: Consensus clustering + meta clustering = multiple consensus clustering. In: Proceedings of the FLAIRS Conference (2011)

Complexity of Rule Sets Induced from Data Sets with Many Lost and Attribute-Concept Values

Patrick G. Clark[1], Cheng Gao[1], and Jerzy W. Grzymala-Busse[1,2(✉)]

[1] Department of Electrical Engineering and Computer Science,
University of Kansas, Lawrence, KS 66045, USA
patrick.g.clark@gmail.com, {cheng.gao,jerzy}@ku.edu
[2] Department of Expert Systems and Artificial Intelligence,
University of Information Technology and Management, 35-225 Rzeszow, Poland

Abstract. In this paper we present experimental results on rule sets induced from 12 data sets with many missing attribute values. We use two interpretations of missing attribute values: lost values and attribute-concept values. Our main objective is to check which interpretation of missing attribute values is better from the view point of complexity of rule sets induced from the data sets with many missing attribute values. The better interpretation is the attribute-value. Our secondary objective is to test which of the three probabilistic approximations used for the experiments provide the simplest rule sets: singleton, subset or concept. The subset probabilistic approximation is the best, with 5 % significance level.

Keywords: Incomplete data · Lost values · Attribute-concept values · Probabilistic approximations · MLEM2 rule induction algorithm

1 Introduction

The basic ideas of rough set theory are standard lower and upper approximations. A probabilistic approximation with a probability α is an extension of the standard approximation. For $\alpha = 1$, the probabilistic approximation is reduced to the lower approximation; for very small α, it is reduced to the upper approximation. Research on theoretical properties of probabilistic approximations was initiated in [1] and then was continued in, e.g., [2–5].

Incomplete data sets are analyzed using special approximations such as singleton, subset and concept [6,7]. Probabilistic approximations, for incomplete data sets and based on an arbitrary binary relation, were introduced in [8]. The first experimental results using probabilistic approximations were published in [9]. In experiments reported in this paper, we used three kinds of probabilistic approximations: singleton, subset and concept.

In this paper, we consider two interpretations of missing attribute values, lost values and attribute-concept values. Lost values indicate that the original values were erased, and as a result we should use only existing, specified attribute values for data mining. Attribute-concept values may be replaced by any specified attribute value for a given concept.

© Springer International Publishing Switzerland 2016
L. Rutkowski et al. (Eds.): ICAISC 2016, Part II, LNAI 9693, pp. 27–36, 2016.
DOI: 10.1007/978-3-319-39384-1_3

Experimental research on comparing different approaches to mining incomplete data was initiated in [10], where results of experiments on data sets with 35 % missing attribute values, using two interpretations of missing attribute values: lost values and "do not care" conditions, were presented.

Research on mining incomplete data with lost values and attribute-concept values, using different experimental setups, was presented in [11–14]. Results of initial research [10,12] show that the quality of rule sets, evaluated by an error rate computed by ten-fold cross validated, does not differ significantly with different combinations of missing attribute and probabilistic approximation type. On the other hand, for data sets with many lost values and attribute-concept values, experiments described in [13] show that the error rate was smaller for lost values.

In [11,14], complexity of rule sets induced from data with lost values and attribute-concept values was investigated. The results were not quite decisive, though the number of rules was always smaller for data sets with attribute-concept values, the results for the total number of rule conditions were not so conclusive.

Therefore the main objective of this paper is research on complexity of rule sets, in terms of the number of rules and total number of rule conditions, induced from data sets with many lost values and attribute-concept values using the Modified Learning from Examples Module version 2 (MLEM2) system for rule induction. The results of this paper show that the number of rules and the total number of conditions are always smaller for attribute-concept values than for lost values.

In our previous research [11,14], results on the best choice of probabilistic approximations (singleton, subset or concept) were not conclusive. So our secondary objective is to check which probabilistic approximation (singleton, subset or concept) is the best from the point of view of rule complexity. As results of our paper show, the best choice is the subset probabilistic approximation.

This paper starts with a discussion on incomplete data in Sect. 2 where we define approximations, attribute-value blocks and characteristic sets. In Sect. 3, we present singleton, subset and concept probabilistic approximations for incomplete data. Section 4 contains the details of our experiments. Finally, conclusions are presented in Sect. 5.

2   Incomplete Data

We assume that the input data sets are presented in the form of a decision table. An example of a decision table is shown in Table 1. Rows of the decision table represent cases, while columns are labeled by variables. The set of all cases will be denoted by U. In Table 1, $U = \{1, 2, 3, 4, 5, 6, 7\}$. Independent variables are called attributes and a dependent variable is called a decision and is denoted by d. The set of all attributes will be denoted by A. In Table 1, $A = \{Wind, Temperature, Humidity\}$. The value for a case x and an attribute a will be denoted by $a(x)$.

In this paper, we distinguish between two interpretations of missing attribute values: lost values, denoted by "?" and attribute-concept values, denoted by "−" [15,16]. Table 1 presents an incomplete data set affected by both lost values and attribute-concept values.

Table 1. A decision table

Case	Attributes			Decision
	Wind	Temperature	Humidity	Trip
1	low	?	low	yes
2	?	high	−	yes
3	high	−	low	yes
4	−	high	?	yes
5	high	low	−	no
6	low	high	?	no
7	?	?	high	no

One of the most important ideas of rough set theory [17] is an indiscernibility relation, defined for complete data sets. Let B be a nonempty subset of A. The indiscernibility relation $R(B)$ is a relation on U defined for $x, y \in U$ as defined by

$$(x, y) \in R(B) \text{ if and only if } \forall a \in B \ (a(x) = a(y))$$

The indiscernibility relation $R(B)$ is an equivalence relation. Equivalence classes of $R(B)$ are called *elementary sets* of B and are denoted by $[x]_B$. A subset of U is called B-*definable* if it is a union of elementary sets of B.

The set X of all cases defined by the same value of the decision d is called a *concept*. For example, a concept associated with the value *yes* of the decision *Trip* is the set $\{1, 2, 3, 4\}$. The largest B-definable set contained in X is called the B-*lower approximation* of X, denoted by $\underline{appr}_B(X)$, and defined as follows

$$\cup\{[x]_B \mid [x]_B \subseteq X\}.$$

The smallest B-definable set containing X, denoted by $\overline{appr}_B(X)$ is called the B-*upper approximation* of X, and is defined by

$$\cup\{[x]_B \mid [x]_B \cap X \neq \emptyset\}.$$

For a variable a and its value v, (a, v) is called a variable-value pair. A *block* of (a, v), denoted by $[(a, v)]$, is the set $\{x \in U \mid a(x) = v\}$ [18]. For incomplete decision tables the definition of a block of an attribute-value pair is modified in the following way.

− If for an attribute a there exists a case x such that $a(x) = ?$, i.e., the corresponding value is lost, then the case x should not be included in any blocks $[(a, v)]$ for all values v of attribute a,

- If for an attribute a there exists a case x such that the corresponding value is an attribute-concept value, i.e., $a(x) = -$, then the corresponding case x should be included in blocks $[(a, v)]$ for all specified values $v \in V(x, a)$ of attribute a, where $V(x, a)$ is defined by

$$\{a(y) \mid a(y) \text{ is specified}, y \in U, d(y) = d(x)\}$$

For the data set from Table 1, we have $V(2, Humidity) = \{low\}$, $V(3, Temperature) = \{high\}$, $V(4, Wind) = \{low, high\}$ and $V(5, Humidity) = \{high\}$. For the data set from Table 1 the blocks of attribute-value pairs are:

[(Wind, low)] = {1, 4, 6},
[(Wind, high)] = {3, 4, 5},
[(Temperature, low)] = {5}, and
[(Temperature, high)] = {2, 3, 4, 6},
[(Humidity, low)] = {1, 2, 3},
[(Humidity, high)] = {5, 7}.

For a case $x \in U$ and $B \subseteq A$, the *characteristic set* $K_B(x)$ is defined as the intersection of the sets $K(x, a)$, for all $a \in B$, where the set $K(x, a)$ is defined in the following way:

- If $a(x)$ is specified, then $K(x, a)$ is the block $[(a, a(x))]$ of attribute a and its value $a(x)$,
- If $a(x) = ?$ then the set $K(x, a) = U$, where U is the set of all cases,
- If $a(x) = -$, then the corresponding set $K(x, a)$ is equal to the union of all blocks of attribute-value pairs (a, v), where $v \in V(x, a)$ if $V(x, a)$ is nonempty. If $V(x, a)$ is empty, $K(x, a) = U$.

For Table 1 and $B = A$,

$K_A(1) = \{1\}$,
$K_A(2) = \{2, 3\}$,
$K_A(3) = \{3\}$,
$K_A(4) = \{3, 4, 6\}$,
$K_A(5) = \{5\}$,
$K_A(6) = \{4, 6\}$, and
$K_A(7) = \{5, 7\}$.

First we will quote some definitions from [19]. Let X be a subset of U. The B-*singleton lower approximation* of X, denoted by $\underline{appr}_B^{singleton}(X)$, is defined by

$$\{x \mid x \in U, K_B(x) \subseteq X\}.$$

The B-*singleton upper approximation* of X, denoted by $\overline{appr}_B^{singleton}(X)$, is defined by

$$\{x \mid x \in U, K_B(x) \cap X \neq \emptyset\}.$$

The B-*subset lower approximation* of X, denoted by $\underline{appr}_B^{subset}(X)$, is defined by

$$\cup \{K_B(x) \mid x \in U, K_B(x) \subseteq X\}.$$

The B-*subset upper approximation* of X, denoted by $\overline{appr}_B^{subset}(X)$, is defined by

$$\cup \{K_B(x) \mid x \in U, K_B(x) \cap X \neq \emptyset\}.$$

The B-*concept lower approximation* of X, denoted by $\underline{appr}_B^{concept}(X)$, is defined by

$$\cup \{K_B(x) \mid x \in X, K_B(x) \subseteq X\}.$$

The B-*concept upper approximation* of X, denoted by $\overline{appr}_B^{concept}(X)$, is defined by

$$\cup \{K_B(x) \mid x \in X, K_B(x) \cap X \neq \emptyset\} = \cup \{K_B(x) \mid x \in X\}.$$

For Table 1 and $X = \{5, 6, 7\}$, all A-singleton, A-subset and A-concept lower and upper approximations are:

$\underline{appr}_A^{singleton}(X) = \{5, 7\},$
$\overline{appr}_A^{singleton}(X) = \{4, 5, 6, 7\},$
$\underline{appr}_A^{subset}(X) = \{5, 7\},$
$\overline{appr}_A^{subset}(X) = \{3, 4, 5, 6, 7\},$
$\underline{appr}_A^{concept}(X) = \{5, 7\},$
$\overline{appr}_A^{concept}(X) = \{4, 5, 6, 7\}.$

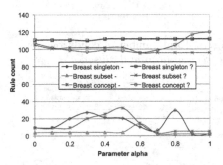

Fig. 1. Number of rules for the *breast cancer* data set

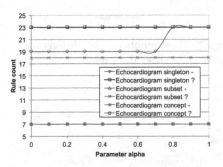

Fig. 2. Number of rules for the *echocardiogram* data set

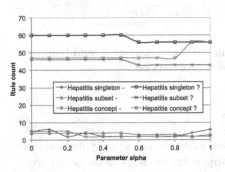

Fig. 3. Number of rules for the *hepatitis* data set

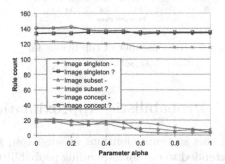

Fig. 4. Number of rules for the *image segmentation* data set

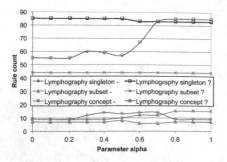

Fig. 5. Number of rules for the *lymphography* data set

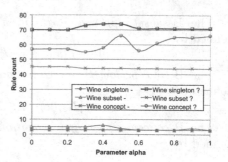

Fig. 6. Number of rules for the *wine recognition* data set

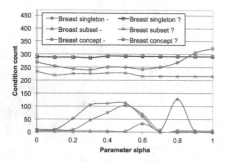

Fig. 7. Total number of conditions for the *breast cancer* data set

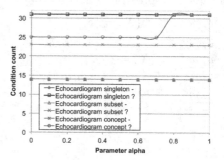

Fig. 8. Total number of conditions for the *echocardiogram* data set

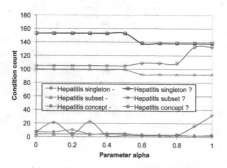

Fig. 9. Total number of conditions for the *hepatitis* data set

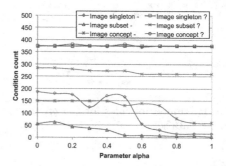

Fig. 10. Total number of conditions for the *image* data set

3 Probabilistic Approximations

In this section definitions of singleton, subset and concept approximations are extended to the corresponding probabilistic approximations. A B-singleton probabilistic approximation of X with the threshold α, $0 < \alpha \leq 1$, denoted by $appr_{\alpha,B}^{singleton}(X)$, is defined by

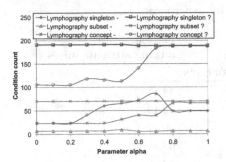

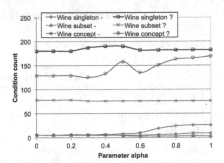

Fig. 11. Total number of conditions for the *lymphography* data set

Fig. 12. Total number of conditions for the *wine recognition* data set

$$\{x \mid x \in U, \ Pr(X \mid K_B(x)) \geq \alpha\},$$

where $Pr(X \mid K_B(x)) = \frac{|X \cap K_B(x)|}{|K_B(x)|}$ is the conditional probability of X given $K_B(x)$ and $|Y|$ denotes the cardinality of set Y. A B-subset probabilistic approximation of the set X with the threshold α, $0 < \alpha \leq 1$, denoted by $appr_{\alpha,B}^{subset}(X)$, is defined by

$$\cup\{K_B(x) \mid x \in U, \ Pr(X \mid K_B(x)) \geq \alpha\}.$$

A B-concept probabilistic approximation of the set X with the threshold α, $0 < \alpha \leq 1$, denoted by $appr_{\alpha,B}^{concept}(X)$, is defined by

$$\cup\{K_B(x) \mid x \in X, \ Pr(X \mid K_B(x)) \geq \alpha\}.$$

Note that if $\alpha = 1$, the probabilistic approximation is the standard lower approximation and if α is small, close to 0, in our experiments it is 0.001, the same definition describes the standard upper approximation.

For Table 1 and the concept $X = [(Trip, no)] = \{4, 5, 6\}$, there exist the following distinct probabilistic approximations:

$appr_{1.0,A}^{singleton}(X) = \{5, 7\}$,

$appr_{0.5,A}^{singleton}(X) = \{5, 6, 7\}$,

$appr_{0.333,A}^{singleton}(X) = \{4, 5, 6, 7\}$,

$appr_{1.0,A}^{subset}(X) = \{5, 7\}$,

$appr_{0.5,A}^{subset}(X) = \{4, 5, 6, 7\}$,

$appr_{0.333,A}^{subset}(X) = \{3, 4, 5, 6, 7\}$,

$appr_{1.0,A}^{concept}(X) = \{5, 7\}$,

$appr_{0.5,A}^{concept}(X) = \{4, 5, 6, 7\}$.

4   Experiments

Our experiments are based on six data sets that are available on the University of California at Irvine *Machine Learning Repository*. Basic information about these data sets is presented in Table 2.

Table 2. Data sets used for experiments

Data set	Number of			Percentage of missing attribute values
	Cases	Attributes	Concepts	
Breast cancer	277	9	2	44.81
Echocardiogram	74	7	2	40.15
Hepatitis	155	19	2	60.27
Image segmentation	210	19	7	69.85
Lymphography	148	18	4	69.89
Wine recognition	178	13	3	64.65

For every data set a set of templates was created. Templates were formed by replacing incrementally (with 5 % increment) existing specified attribute values by *lost* values. Thus, we started each series of experiments with no *lost* values, then we added 5 % of *lost* values, then we added additional 5 % of *lost* values, etc., until at least one entire row of the data sets was full of *lost* values. Then three attempts were made to change configuration of new *lost* values and either a new data set with extra 5 % of *lost* values were created or the process was terminated. Additionally, the same templates were edited for further experiments by replacing question marks, representing *lost* values by "−"s, representing *attribute-concept* values.

For any data set there was some maximum for the percentage of missing attribute values. For example, for the *Breast cancer* data set, it was 44.81 %. In our experiments we used only such incomplete data sets, with as many missing attribute values as possible. Note that for some data sets the maximum of the number of missing attribute values was less than 40 %, we have not used such data for our experiments.

For rule induction we used the Modified Learning from Examples Module version 2 (MLEM2) rule induction algorithm, a component of the Learning from Examples based on Rough Sets (LERS) data mining system [18]. Results of our experiments are presented in Figs. 1, 2, 3, 4, 5, 6, 7, 8, 9, 10, 11 and 12.

Our main objective was to select the better interpretation of missing attribute values: lost values or attribute-concept values in terms of complexity measured by the number of rules and the total number of conditions in rule sets. For any data set we compared the size of the rule set and the total number of conditions in the rule set for two interpretations of missing attribute values with the same type of probabilistic approximation. Our results show that the number of rules was always smaller for attribute-concept values than for lost values. Similarly, the total number of conditions was always smaller for attribute-concept values than for lost values.

Our secondary objective was to find the best kind of probabilistic approximations (singleton, subset or concept). Here the answer is more complicated.

For any data set we compared all three kinds of probabilistic approximations assuming the same type of missing attribute values using multiple comparisons based on Friedman's nonparametric test. As a result, the smallest number of rules is accomplished by subset approximations for eight out of 12 data sets (5 % significance level). For four data sets (*echocardiogram, hepatitis, image segmentation* and *wine recognition*, all with attribute-concept values), the difference is not statistically significant. The total number of conditions is also the smallest for subset approximations except two data sets (*echocardiogram* and *hepatitis*, both with attribute-concept values).

5 Conclusions

As follows from our experiments, the number of rules and the total number of conditions is always smaller for attribute-concept values than for lost values. Additionally, the best probabilistic approximation that should be used for rule induction from data with many missing attribute values is subset probabilistic approximation.

References

1. Pawlak, Z., Wong, S.K.M., Ziarko, W.: Rough sets: probabilistic versus deterministic approach. Int. J. Man Mach. Stud. **29**, 81–95 (1988)
2. Pawlak, Z., Skowron, A.: Rough sets: Some extensions. Inf. Sci. **177**, 28–40 (2007)
3. Yao, Y.Y.: Probabilistic rough set approximations. Int. J. Approximate Reasoning **49**, 255–271 (2008)
4. Yao, Y.Y., Wong, S.K.M.: A decision theoretic framework for approximate concepts. Int. J. Man Mach. Stud. **37**, 793–809 (1992)
5. Ziarko, W.: Probabilistic approach to rough sets. Int. J. Approximate Reasoning **49**, 272–284 (2008)
6. Grzymala-Busse, J.W.: Rough set strategies to data with missing attribute values. In: Notes of the Workshop on Foundations and New Directions of Data Mining, in conjunction with the Third International Conference on Data Mining, pp. 56–63 (2003)
7. Grzymala-Busse, J.W.: Data with missing attribute values: generalization of indiscernibility relation and rule induction. Trans. Rough Sets **1**, 78–95 (2004)
8. Grzymała-Busse, J.W.: Generalized parameterized approximations. In: Yao, J.T., Ramanna, S., Wang, G., Suraj, Z. (eds.) RSKT 2011. LNCS, vol. 6954, pp. 136–145. Springer, Heidelberg (2011)
9. Clark, P.G., Grzymala-Busse, J.W.: Experiments on probabilistic approximations. In: Proceedings of the 2011 IEEE International Conference on Granular Computing, pp. 144–149 (2011)
10. Clark, P.G., Grzymala-Busse, J.W., Rzasa, W.: Mining incomplete data with singleton, subset and concept approximations. Inf. Sci. **280**, 368–384 (2014)
11. Clark, P.G., Grzymala-Busse, J.W.: Complexity of rule sets induced from incomplete data with lost values and attribute-concept values. In: Proceedings of the Third International Conference on Intelligent Systems and Applications, pp. 91–96 (2014)

12. Clark, P.G., Grzymala-Busse, J.W.: Mining incomplete data with lost values and attribute-concept values. In: Proceedings of the IEEE International Conference on Granular Computing, pp. 49–54 (2014)
13. Clark, P.G., Grzymala-Busse, J.W.: Mining incomplete data with many lost and attribute-concept values. In: Ciucci, D., Wang, G., Mitra, S., Wu, W.-Z. (eds.) RSKT 2015. LNCS, vol. 9436, pp. 100–109. Springer, Heidelberg (2015)
14. Clark, P.G., Grzymala-Busse, J.W.: On the number of rules and conditions in mining incomplete data with lost values and attribute-concept values. In: Proceedings of the DBKDA 7-th International Conference on Advances in Databases, Knowledge, and Data Applications, pp. 121–126 (2015)
15. Grzymala-Busse, J.W., Wang, A.Y.: Modified algorithms LEM1 and LEM2 for rule induction from data with missing attribute values. In: Proceedings of the 5-th International Workshop on Rough Sets and Soft Computing in Conjunction with the Third Joint Conference on Information Sciences, pp. 69–72 (1997)
16. Stefanowski, J., Tsoukias, A.: Incomplete information tables and rough classification. Comput. Intell. **17**(3), 545–566 (2001)
17. Pawlak, Z.: Rough sets. Int. J. Comput. Inform. Sci. **11**, 341–356 (1982)
18. Grzymala-Busse, J.W.: A new version of the rule induction system LERS. Fundamenta Informaticae **31**, 27–39 (1997)
19. Grzymala-Busse, J.W., Rzasa, W.: Definability and other properties of approximations for generalized indiscernibility relations. Trans. Rough Sets **11**, 14–39 (2010)

On the Cesàro-Means-Based Orthogonal Series Approach to Learning Time-Varying Regression Functions

Piotr Duda[1(✉)], Lena Pietruczuk[1], Maciej Jaworski[1], and Adam Krzyzak[2]

[1] The Institute of Computational Intelligence,
Czestochowa University of Technology,
Armii Krajowej 36, 42-200 Czestochowa, Poland
{piotr.duda,lena.pietruczuk,maciej.jaworski}@iisi.pcz.pl
[2] Department of Computer Science and Software Engineering, Concordia University,
Montreal, QC H3G 1M8, Canada

Abstract. In this paper an incremental procedure for nonparametric learning of time-varying regression function is presented. The procedure is based on the Cesàro-means of orthogonal series. Its tracking properties are investigated and convergence in probability is shown. Numerical simulations are performed using the Fejer's kernels of the Fourier orthogonal series.

Keywords: Time-varying environment · Orthogonal series · Cesàro means · Convergence in probability

1 Introduction

Let $X_1, X_2 \ldots$ be a sequence of independent and identically distributed random variables in R^p with a common density function f. In this paper we will consider the following model

$$Y_n = \phi_n(X_n) + Z_n, \qquad n = 1, 2, \ldots, \tag{1}$$

where $\phi_n(\cdot)$, for $n = 1, 2, \ldots$, are unknown functions and Z_n are independent random variables with time-varying distributions such that

$$E(Z_n) = 0, \qquad EZ_n^2 = d_n, \qquad n = 1, 2, \ldots. \tag{2}$$

Our problem is to design a nonparametric procedure tracking changes of unknown functions $\phi_n(x)$, for $n = 1, 2, \ldots$, based on the observations $(X_1, Y_1), (X_2, Y_2), \ldots$, additionally assuming non-stationary noise. To solve this problem we propose to use a nonparametric technique based on the Cesàro means of orthogonal series.

It should be noted that the problem studied in this paper can be treated as a development of the kernel regression method for mining data stream (see e.g. [13,

© Springer International Publishing Switzerland 2016
L. Rutkowski et al. (Eds.): ICAISC 2016, Part II, LNAI 9693, pp. 37–48, 2016.
DOI: 10.1007/978-3-319-39384-1_4

19, 21, 35, 37, 51–55, 57]). Such problems have recently emerged as a very active branch of research activity and the main issue is to cope with distributions of data that may vary over time (see e.g. [7, 12, 14, 18, 41–48, 61, 62]). Our approach is derived from the techniques known in the literature as nonparametric density and regression estimation (see e.g. [39, 40]). Other approaches can be adopted from various techniques of soft computing, e.g. evolutionary and swarm optimizations [2, 3, 60], neural networks [4–6, 15–17, 20, 22, 23, 27–30, 36], fuzzy systems [1, 9–11, 26, 34, 38, 50, 58], support vectors machines [8], and rough sets [31–33].

The rest of the paper is organized as follows. In Sect. 2 the proposed algorithm is introduced along with the appropriate theorem showing its tracking properties. Section 3 contains experimental evaluation of the proposed method and the conclusions are drawn in Sect. 4.

2   Learning Algorithm and Its Convergence

To estimate the regression function $\phi_n(x)$ in model (1) we propose the orthogonal series based kernels in the form:

$$K_n(X_n, x) = \sum_{j=0}^{N(n)} (1 - \frac{j}{N(n)+1}) g_j(X_n) g_j(x), \tag{3}$$

and

$$K'_n(X_n, x) = \sum_{j=0}^{M(n)} (1 - \frac{j}{M(n)+1}) g_j(X_n) g_j(x) \tag{4}$$

where $\{g_j(\cdot)\}, j = 0, 1, 2, \ldots$ is a complete orthonormal system defined on $A \subset R^p$ such that

$$\max_x |g_j(x)| < G_j, \tag{5}$$

and where $M(n) \xrightarrow{n} \infty$, and $N(n) \xrightarrow{n} \infty$. More details about orthogonal series can be found in [24, 25, 56].

We propose to estimate the regression function $\phi_n(x)$ by the regression function estimate

$$\hat{\phi}_n(x) = \frac{\hat{R}_n(x)}{\hat{f}_n(x)}, \tag{6}$$

where $\hat{f}_n(x)$ is the estimator of the density function $f(x)$ and $\hat{R}_n(x)$ is the estimator of the function

$$R_n(x) = f(x)\phi_n(x), \tag{7}$$

for $n = 1, 2, \ldots$.

Estimators $\hat{f}_n(x)$ and $\hat{R}_n(x)$ are defined recursively as follows

$$\hat{f}_n(x) = \hat{f}_{n-1}(x) + \frac{1}{n}[K_n(X_n, x) - \hat{f}_{n-1}(x)], \tag{8}$$

$$\hat{R}_n(x) = \hat{R}_{n-1}(x) + c_n[Y_n K'_n(X_n, x) - \hat{R}_{n-1}(x)], \tag{9}$$

where $\hat{f}_0(x) = 0, \hat{R}_0(x) = 0$, and c_n is a decreasing sequence satisfying the following conditions:

$$\frac{c_n}{c_{n+1}} < const, \qquad c_n \xrightarrow{n} 0, \qquad \sum_{n=1}^{\infty} c_n = \infty. \tag{10}$$

An example of a sequence satisfying (10) is $c_n = 1/n^{\gamma}, 0 < \gamma \leq 1$.
Then the estimator $\hat{\phi}_n(x)$ takes the form

$$\hat{\phi}_n(x) = \frac{\hat{R}_{n-1}(x) + c_n[Y_n K'_n(x, X_n) - \hat{R}_{n-1}(x)]}{\hat{f}_{n-1}(x) + n^{-1}[K_n(x, X_n) - \hat{f}_{n-1}(x)]} \tag{11}$$

The block-diagram of procedure (6) is depicted in Fig. 1.

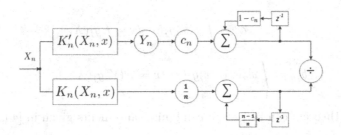

Fig. 1. The block-diagram of the procedure (6)

Let us denote:

$$s_n = d_n + \int_A \phi_n^2(u) f(u) du \tag{12}$$

and assume that

$$\int_A \phi_n^2(u) f(u) du < \infty \tag{13}$$

for $n = 1, 2, \ldots$.

Theorem 1. *Let us assume that conditions (5) and (13) are satisfied. If the following conditions hold*

$$c_n\left(\sum_{j=0}^{M(n)} G_j^2\right)^2 s_n \xrightarrow{n} 0, \qquad M(n) \xrightarrow{n} \infty \tag{14}$$

$$n^{-2}(\phi_n^2(x) + 1)\sum_{i=0}^{n}\left(\sum_{j=0}^{N(i)} G_j^2\right)^2 \xrightarrow{n} 0, \qquad N(n) \xrightarrow{n} \infty \tag{15}$$

$$c_n^{-1}|\phi_{n+1}(x) - \phi_n(x)| \to 0 \tag{16}$$

then

$$|\hat{\phi}_n(x) - \phi_n(x)| \xrightarrow{n} 0 \tag{17}$$

at every point $x \in A$ at which $f(x) \neq 0$ and

$$|\phi_n(x)|n^{-1}(\sum_{i=1}^{n}(\sum_{j=0}^{N(i)}(1 - \frac{j}{N(i)+1})a_j g_j(x) - f(x))) \xrightarrow{n} 0, \tag{18}$$

$$c_n^{-1}\left|\sum_{j=0}^{M(n)}(1 - \frac{j}{M(n)+1})b_{jn}g_j(x) - R_n(x)\right| \xrightarrow{n} 0 \tag{19}$$

where

$$a_j = \int_A f(x)g_j(x)dx = Eg_j(X_n), \tag{20}$$

$$b_{jn} = \int_A \phi_n(x)f(x)g_j(x)dx = E(Y_n g_j(X_n)). \tag{21}$$

Proof. The theorem can be proven combining arguments given in [40, 49].

Example. Let assume that

$$\phi_n(x) = n^\beta \phi(x), \tag{22}$$

with $\beta > 0$ and

$$c_n = n^{-\gamma} \tag{23}$$
$$M(n) = [k_M n^{q_M}] \tag{24}$$
$$N(n) = [k_N n^{q_N}] \tag{25}$$
$$d_n = k_d n^\alpha \tag{26}$$
$$G_j = k_G j^d, \tag{27}$$

where α, γ, q_M, q_N, k_M, k_N, k_d and k_G are positive numbers.

It is easily seen that if the following conditions are satisfied

$$4dq_M + 2q_M + 2\beta - \gamma < 0, \tag{28}$$
$$4dq_M + 2q_M + \alpha - \gamma < 0, \tag{29}$$
$$4dq_N + 2q_N + 2\beta < 1, \tag{30}$$
$$\beta + \gamma < 1, \tag{31}$$

then convergence (17) holds. One can check that if $\beta < \frac{1}{3}$ and $0 < \alpha < 1$, we can choose the values of parameters q_M, q_N and γ such that conditions (28)–(31) are satisfied and procedure (11) is able to track changes of time-varying regresion functions $\phi_n(\cdot)$ in model (1).

3   Experimental Results

We will investigate the performance of algorithm (6) using kernels (3) and (4) based on the Fourier orthogonal systems. Fourier orthonormal system has the form

$$\frac{1}{\sqrt{b-a}}, \sqrt{\frac{2}{b-a}}\cos 2\pi j\frac{x-a}{b-a}, \sqrt{\frac{2}{b-a}}\sin 2\pi j\frac{x-a}{b-a} \tag{32}$$

for $j = 1, 2, \dots$ and $[a, b] \subset R$. One can easily see that

$$\max_x |g_j(x)| \leq \text{const.} \tag{33}$$

The application of the Cesàro means for the Fourier orthogonal series leads to the so called Fejer's kernel. Let us define

$$F_q(X_n, x) = \frac{1}{2(q+1)}\left(\frac{\sin\frac{1}{2}(q+1)(X_n - x)}{\sin\frac{1}{2}(X_n - x)}\right)^2. \tag{34}$$

Now the kernels (3) and (4) can be expressed in the following way

$$K_n(X_n, x) = \pi^{-1}F_{N(n)}(X_n, x), \tag{35}$$

$$K'_n(X_n, x) = \pi^{-1}F_{M(n)}(X_n, x). \tag{36}$$

We will model a non-stationary system given by

$$Y_n = n^\beta \phi(X_n) + Z_n, \qquad n = 1, 2, \dots \tag{37}$$

where noise Z_n has a normal distribution with zero mean and $EZ_n^2 = d_n = n^\alpha$ for various values of parameters α and β. The sequence c_n is assumed to be $n^{-\gamma}$, $0 < \gamma < 1$.

3.1   The First Experiment

Assuming that $\phi(x) = \sin(\exp(x))$ in model (37) we set the values of parameters as follows (see Example in Sect. 2): $\alpha = 0.1$, $\beta = 0.1$, $\gamma = 0.695$, $q_N = 0.02$, $k_N = 50$, $q_M = 0.01$ and $k_M = 50$.

The first experiment has been conducted to carry out comparison between the value of estimator $\hat{\phi}_n(x)$ and the actual value of function $\phi_n(x)$ (see Fig. 2(a)), and also between the value of estimator $\hat{\phi}_n(x)$ and input-output data (see Fig. 2(b)). It can be observed that the shape of function is closely approximated by the estimator. Also the training data are well approximated by the values of $\hat{\phi}_n(x)$.

The next experiment shows the dependence of the value of n on the performance of algorithm (6) determined in one point. The obtained results for $x_0 = 0$ are shown in Fig. 3(a). In Fig. 3(b) the MSE is depicted with respect to number of data elements n. The MSE is computed as average of square differences between estimated and real values over 101 points, equally distributed in the

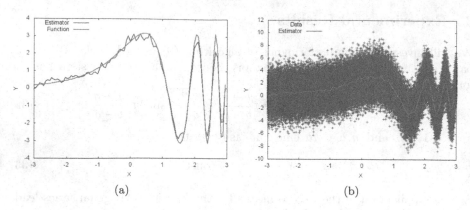

(a)   (b)

Fig. 2. The comparison of $\hat{\phi}_n(x)$ with: (a) actual value of $\phi_n(x)$ (b) input-output data for $n = 100000$

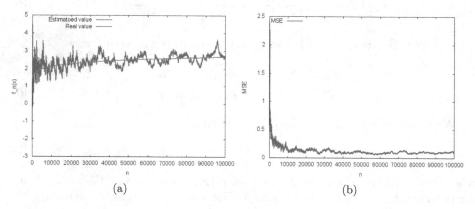

(a)   (b)

Fig. 3. (a) The comparison of $\hat{\phi}_n(x)$ and $\phi_n(x)$ at point $x = 0$; (b) The values of the MSE.

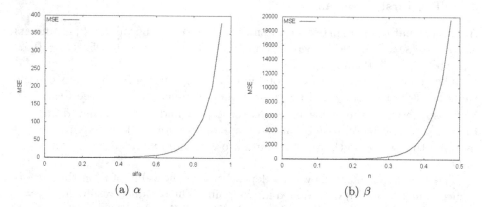

(a) α (b) β

Fig. 4. The dependence between the value of parameters α and β and the value of the *MSE*

considered interval. Those results confirmed that the growth of the number of training data n improves the accuracy.

The last two experiment show the dependence between the value of parameters α and β, and the accuracy of the algorithm. The obtained MSE is a mean of MSEs calculated for 50 different experiments. As previously $n = 100000$, $\gamma = 0.695$, $q_N = 0.02$, $k_N = 50$, $q_M = 0.01$, $k_M = 50$. In Fig. 4(a) the value of parameter α is considered in the interval $(0, 1)$, in Fig. 4(b) parameter β is changed from 0 to 0.5.

3.2 The Second Experiment

Assuming that $\phi(x) = 20(x^3 - x)$, $x \in [-3, 3]$, in model (37) we set the value of parameters as follows (see Example in Sect. 2): $\alpha = 0.15$, $\beta = 0.15$, $\gamma = 0.695$, $q_M = 0.1$, $k_M = 8$, $q_N = 0.1$, $k_N = 8$.

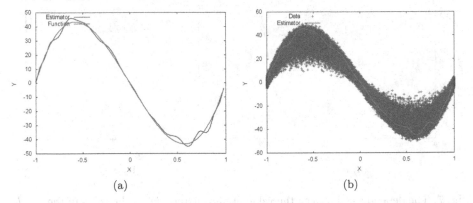

(a)   (b)

Fig. 5. The comparison of $\hat{\phi}_n(x)$ with: (a) actual value of $\phi_n(x)$ (b) input-output data for $n = 100000$

The first experiment has been conducted to compare the values of estimator $\hat{\phi}_n(x)$ and the actual value of function $\phi_n(x)$ (see Fig. 5(a)), and also the value of estimator $\hat{\phi}_n(x)$ and input-output data (see Fig. 5(b)). It can be observed that the shape of the function is mimicked by the shape of the estimator. Also the training data are well approximated by the values of $\hat{\phi}_n(x)$.

The next experiment shows the dependence of the value of n on the performance of algorithm (6) determined in one point. The obtained results for $x_0 = 0$ are shown in Fig. 6(a). In Fig. 6(b) the MSE is depicted with respect to number of data elements n. Those results confirmed that the growth of the number of training data n improves the accuracy.

The last two experiment show the dependence between the value of parameters α and β, and the accuracy of the algorithm. The obtained MSE is a mean of MSEs calculated for 50 different experiments. As previously $n = 100000$,

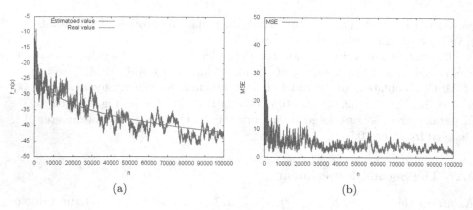

(a)   (b)

Fig. 6. (a) The comparison of $\hat{\phi}_n(x)$ and $\phi_n(x)$ at point $x = 0$; (b) The values of the MSE.

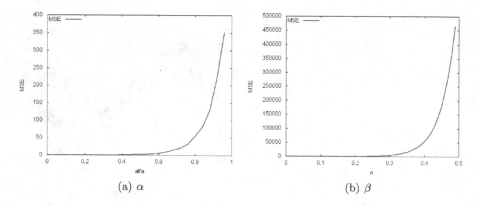

(a) α (b) β

Fig. 7. The dependence between the value of parameters β and the value of the MSE.

$\gamma = 0.695$, $q_M = 0.1$, $k_M = 8$, $q_N = 0.1$, $k_N = 8$. In Fig. 7(a) the value of parameter α is consider in the interval $(0, 1)$, in Fig. 7(b) parameter β is changed from 0 to 0.5.

4   Conclusions

In this paper we proposed a new method for estimation of time-varying regression functions ϕ_n. The method is based on the Cesàro means of the orthogonal series. It was shown that procedure (11) is able to track changes of time-varying regression functions $\phi_n(\cdot)$.

Acknowledgement. This work was supported by the Polish National Science Center under Grant No. 2014/15/B/ST7/05264.

References

1. Abbas, J.: The bipolar choquet integrals based on ternary-element sets. J. Artif. Intell. Soft Comput. Res. **6**(1), 13–21 (2016)
2. Aghdam, M.H., Heidari, S.: Feature selection using particle swarm optimization in text categorization. J. Artif. Intell. Soft Comput. Res. **4**(4), 231–238 (2015)
3. Bas, E.: The training of multiplicative neuron model based artificial neural networks with differential evolution algorithm for forecasting. J. Artif. Intell. Soft Comput. Res. **6**(1), 5–11 (2016)
4. Bilski, J., Smolag, J.: Parallel architectures for learning the RTRN and Elman dynamic neural networks. IEEE Trans. Parallel Distrib. Syst. **26**(9), 2561–2570 (2015)
5. Bilski, J., Smoląg, J., Żurada, J.M.: Parallel approach to the Levenberg-Marquardt learning algorithm for feedforward neural networks. In: Rutkowski, L., Korytkowski, M., Scherer, R., Tadeusiewicz, R., Zadeh, L.A., Zurada, J.M. (eds.) Artificial Intelligence and Soft Computing. LNCS, vol. 9119, pp. 3–14. Springer, Heidelberg (2015)
6. Bilski, J., Smoląg, J., Galushkin, A.I.: The parallel approach to the conjugate gradient learning algorithm for the feedforward neural networks. In: Rutkowski, L., Korytkowski, M., Scherer, R., Tadeusiewicz, R., Zadeh, L.A., Zurada, J.M. (eds.) ICAISC 2014, Part I. LNCS, vol. 8467, pp. 12–21. Springer, Heidelberg (2014)
7. Bose, R., van der Aalst, W., Zliobaite, I., Pechenizkiy, M.: Dealing with concept drifts in process mining. IEEE Trans. Neural Netw. Learn. Syst. **25**(1), 154–171 (2014)
8. Chu, J.L., Krzyżak, A.: The recognition of partially occluded objects with support vector machines, convolutional neural networks and deep belief networks. J. Artif. Intell. Soft Comput. Res. **4**(1), 5–19 (2014)
9. Cpalka, K., Rebrova, O., Nowicki, R., et al.: On design of flexible neuro-fuzzy systems for nonlinear modelling. Int. J. Gen. Syst. **42**(6), 706–720 (2013). Special Issue: SI
10. Cpalka, K., Zalasinski, M., Rutkowski, L.: New method for the on-line signature verification based on horizontal partitioning. Pattern Recogn. **47**(8), 2652–2661 (2014)
11. Cpalka, K., Rutkowski, L.: Flexible Takagi-Sugeno fuzzy systems. In: Proceedings of the IEEE International Joint Conference on Neural Networks (IJCNN), vol. 1–5, pp. 1764–1769 (2005)
12. Ditzler, G., et al.: Learning in nonstationary environments: a survey. Comput. Intell. Mag. IEEE **10**(4), 12–25 (2015)
13. Duda, P., Jaworski, M., Pietruczuk, L.: On pre-processing algorithms for data stream. In: Rutkowski, L., Korytkowski, M., Scherer, R., Tadeusiewicz, R., Zadeh, L.A., Zurada, J.M. (eds.) ICAISC 2012, Part II. LNCS, vol. 7268, pp. 56–63. Springer, Heidelberg (2012)
14. Elwell, R., Polikar, R.: Incremental learning of concept drift in nonstationary environments. IEEE Trans. Neural Netw. **22**(10), 1517–1531 (2011)
15. Galkowski, T., Rutkowski, L.: Nonparametric recovery of multivariate functions with applications to system identification. Proc. IEEE **73**, 942–943 (1985). New York
16. Galkowski, T., Rutkowski, L.: Nonparametric fitting of multivariable functions. IEEE Trans. Autom. Control **AC–31**, 785–787 (1986)

17. Galkowski, T.: Nonparametric estimation of boundary values of functions. Arch. Control Sci. **3**(1–2), 85–93 (1994)
18. Gama, J., Fernandes, R., Rocha, R.: Decision trees for mining data streams. Intell. Data Anal. **10**(1), 23–45 (2006)
19. Jaworski, M., Duda, P., Pietruczuk, L.: On fuzzy clustering of data streams with concept drift. In: Rutkowski, L., Korytkowski, M., Scherer, R., Tadeusiewicz, R., Zadeh, L.A., Zurada, J.M. (eds.) ICAISC 2012, Part II. LNCS, vol. 7268, pp. 82–91. Springer, Heidelberg (2012)
20. Jaworski, M., Er, M.J., Pietruczuk, L.: On the application of the parzen-type kernel regression neural network and order statistics for learning in a non-stationary environment. In: Rutkowski, L., Korytkowski, M., Scherer, R., Tadeusiewicz, R., Zadeh, L.A., Zurada, J.M. (eds.) ICAISC 2012, Part I. LNCS, vol. 7267, pp. 90–98. Springer, Heidelberg (2012)
21. Jaworski, M., Pietruczuk, L., Duda, P.: On resources optimization in fuzzy clustering of data streams. In: Rutkowski, L., Korytkowski, M., Scherer, R., Tadeusiewicz, R., Zadeh, L.A., Zurada, J.M. (eds.) ICAISC 2012, Part II. LNCS, vol. 7268, pp. 92–99. Springer, Heidelberg (2012)
22. Kitajima, R., Kamimura, R.: Accumulative information enhancement in the self-organizing maps and its application to the analysis of mission statements. J. Artif. Intell. Soft Comput. Res. **5**(3), 161–176 (2015)
23. Knop, M., Cierniak, R., Shah, N.: Video compression algorithm based on neural network structures. In: Rutkowski, L., Korytkowski, M., Scherer, R., Tadeusiewicz, R., Zadeh, L.A., Zurada, J.M. (eds.) ICAISC 2014, Part I. LNCS, vol. 8467, pp. 715–724. Springer, Heidelberg (2014)
24. Krzyzak, A., Pawlak, M.: Distribution-free consistency of a nonparametric kernel regression estimate and classification. IEEE Trans. Inf. Theor. **30**(1), 78–81 (1984)
25. Krzyzak, A.: The rates of convergence of kernel regression estimates and classification rules. IEEE Trans. Inf. Theor. **32**(5), 668–679 (1986)
26. Korytkowski, M., Rutkowski, L., Scherer, R.: Fast image classification by boosting fuzzy classifiers. Inf. Sci. **327**, 175–182 (2016)
27. Laskowski, Ł.: A novel hybrid-maximum neural network in stereo-matching process. Neural Comput. Appl. **23**(7–8), 2435–2450 (2013)
28. Laskowski, Ł., Jelonkiewicz, J., Hayashi, Y.: Extensions of hopfield neural networks for solving of stereo-matching problem. In: Rutkowski, L., Korytkowski, M., Scherer, R., Tadeusiewicz, R., Zadeh, L.A., Zurada, J.M. (eds.) Artificial Intelligence and Soft Computing. LNCS, vol. 9119, pp. 59–71. Springer, Heidelberg (2015)
29. Laskowski, Ł., Laskowska, M., Jelonkiewicz, J., Boullanger, A.: Molecular approach to hopfield neural network. In: Rutkowski, L., Korytkowski, M., Scherer, R., Tadeusiewicz, R., Zadeh, L.A., Zurada, J.M. (eds.) Artificial Intelligence and Soft Computing. LNCS, vol. 9119, pp. 72–78. Springer, Heidelberg (2015)
30. Miyajima, H., Shigei, N.: Performance comparison of hybrid electromagnetism-like mechanism algorithms with descent method. J. Artif. Intell. Soft Comput. Res. **5**(4), 271–282 (2015)
31. Mleczko, W., Kapuscinski, T., Nowicki, R.: Rough deep belief network - Application to incomplete handwritten digits pattern classification. In: Dregvaite, G., Damasevicius, R. (eds.) ICIST 2015. Communications in Computer and Information Science, pp. 400–411. Springer, Switzerland (2015)

32. Nowak, B.A., Nowicki, R.K., Starczewski, J.T., Marvuglia, A.: The learning of neuro-fuzzy classifier with fuzzy rough sets for imprecise datasets. In: Rutkowski, L., Korytkowski, M., Scherer, R., Tadeusiewicz, R., Zadeh, L.A., Zurada, J.M. (eds.) ICAISC 2014, Part I. LNCS, vol. 8467, pp. 256–266. Springer, Heidelberg (2014)

33. Nowicki, R.: Rough sets in the neuro-fuzzy architectures based on non-monotonic fuzzy implications. In: Rutkowski, L., Siekmann, J.H., Tadeusiewicz, R., Zadeh, L.A. (eds.) ICAISC 2004. LNCS (LNAI), vol. 3070, pp. 518–525. Springer, Heidelberg (2004)

34. Nowicki, R., Rutkowski, L.: Soft techniques for bayesian classification. In: Rutkowski, L., Kacprzyk, J. (eds.) Neural Networks and Soft Computing. Advances in Soft Computing, pp. 537–544. Springer, Heidelberg (2003)

35. Pietruczuk, L., Duda, P., Jaworski, M.: A new fuzzy classifier for data streams. In: Rutkowski, L., Korytkowski, M., Scherer, R., Tadeusiewicz, R., Zadeh, L.A., Zurada, J.M. (eds.) ICAISC 2012, Part I. LNCS, vol. 7267, pp. 318–324. Springer, Heidelberg (2012)

36. Pietruczuk, L., Zurada, J.M.: Weak convergence of the recursive parzen-type probabilistic neural network in a non-stationary environment. In: Wyrzykowski, R., Dongarra, J., Karczewski, K., Waśniewski, J. (eds.) PPAM 2011, Part I. LNCS, vol. 7203, pp. 521–529. Springer, Heidelberg (2012)

37. Pietruczuk, L., Duda, P., Jaworski, M.: Adaptation of decision trees for handling concept drift. In: Rutkowski, L., Korytkowski, M., Scherer, R., Tadeusiewicz, R., Zadeh, L.A., Zurada, J.M. (eds.) ICAISC 2013, Part I. LNCS, vol. 7894, pp. 459–473. Springer, Heidelberg (2013)

38. Rutkowska, D., Nowicki, R., Rutkowski, L.: Neuro-fuzzy architectures with various implication operators. In: Sinčák, P., Vaščák, J., Kvasnička, V., Mesiar, R. (eds.) State of the Art in Computational Intelligence. Advances in soft Computing, pp. 214–219. Springer, Heidelberg (2000)

39. Rutkowski, L.: Sequential estimates of probability densities by orthogonal series and their application in pattern classification. IEEE Trans. Syst. Man Cybern. **SMC–10**(12), 918–920 (1980)

40. Rutkowski, L.: Sequential estimates of a regression function by orthogonal series with applications in discrimination. In: Révész, P., Schmetterer, L., Zolotarev, V.M. (eds.) The First Pannonian Symposium on Mathematical Statistics. LNCS, pp. 236–244. Springer, New York (1981)

41. Rutkowski, L.: On Bayes risk consistent pattern recognition procedures in a quasistationary environment. IEEE Trans. Pattern Anal. Mach. Intell. **PAMI–4**(1), 84–87 (1982)

42. Rutkowski, L.: On-line identification of time-varying systems by nonparametric techniques. IEEE Trans. Automatic Control **AC–27**, 228–230 (1982)

43. Rutkowski, L.: On nonparametric identification with prediction of time-varying systems. IEEE Trans. Autom. Control **AC–29**, 58–60 (1984)

44. Rutkowski, L.: Nonparametric identification of quasi-stationary systems. Syst. Control Lett. **6**, 33–35 (1985). Amsterdam

45. Rutkowski, L.: The real-time identification of time-varying systems by nonparametric algorithms based on the Parzen kernels Int. J. Syst. Sci. **16**, 1123–1130 (1985). London

46. Rutkowski, L.: An application of multiple Fourier series to identification of multivariable nonstationary systems. Int. J. Syst. Sci. **20**(10), 1993–2002 (1989)

47. Rutkowski, L.: Nonparametric learning algorithms in the time-varying environments. Sig. Process. **18**, 129–137 (1989)

48. Rutkowski, L.: Adaptive probabilistic neural-networks for pattern classification in time-varying environment. IEEE Trans. Neural Netw. **15**, 811–827 (2004)

49. Rutkowski, L.: Generalized regression neural networks in time-varying environment. IEEE Trans. Neural Netw. **15**, 576–596 (2004)

50. Rutkowski, L., Cpalka, K.: Compromise approach to neuro-fuzzy systems. In: Intelligent Technologies - Theory and Applications: New Trends in Intelligent Technologies. Frontiers in Artificial Intelligence and Applications, vol. 76 pp. 85–90 (2002)

51. Rutkowski, L., Pietruczuk, L., Duda, P., Jaworski, M.: Decision trees for mining data streams based on the McDiarmid's bound. IEEE Trans. Knowl. Data Eng. **25**(6), 1272–1279 (2013)

52. Rutkowski, L., Jaworski, M., Duda, P., Pietruczuk, L.: Decision trees for mining data streams based on the gaussian approximation. IEEE Trans. Knowl. Data Eng. **26**(1), 108–119 (2014)

53. Rutkowski, L., Jaworski, M., Pietruczuk, L., Duda, P.: The CART decision trees for mining data streams. Inf. Sci. **266**, 1–15 (2014)

54. Rutkowski, L., Jaworski, M., Pietruczuk, L., Duda, P.: A new method for data stream mining based on the misclassification error. IEEE Trans. Neural Netw. Learn. Syst. **26**(5), 1048–1059 (2015)

55. Sakurai, S., Nishizawa, M.: A new approach for discovering top-K sequential patterns based on the variety of items. J. Artif. Intell. Soft Comput. Res. **5**(2), 141–153 (2015)

56. Sansone, G.: Orthogonal Functions, Pure and Applied Mathematics. Interscience Publishers, Inc., New York (1959)

57. Serdah, A., Ashour, W.: Clustering large-scale data based on modified affinity propagation algorithm. J. Artif. Intell. Soft Comput. Res. **6**(1), 23–33 (2016)

58. Starczewski, J.: Centroid of triangular and Gaussian type-2 fuzzy sets. Inf. Sci. **280**, 289–306 (2014)

59. Szegö, G.: Orthogonal Polynomials, vol. 23. American Mathematical Society Coll. Publ., Providence (1959)

60. Woźniak, M., Kempa, W.M., Gabryel, M., Nowicki, R.K., Shao, Z.: On applying evolutionary computation methods to optimization of vacation cycle costs in finite-buffer queue. In: Rutkowski, L., Korytkowski, M., Scherer, R., Tadeusiewicz, R., Zadeh, L.A., Zurada, J.M. (eds.) ICAISC 2014, Part I. LNCS, vol. 8467, pp. 480–491. Springer, Heidelberg (2014)

61. Ye, Y., Squartini, S., Piazza, F.: Online sequential extreme learning machine in nonstationary environments. Neurocomputing **116**, 94–101 (2013)

62. Zliobaite, I., Bifet, A., Pfahringer, B., Holmes, G.: Active learning with drifting streaming data. IEEE Trans. Neural Netw. Learn. Syst. **25**(1), 27–39 (2014)

Nonparametric Estimation of Edge Values
of Regression Functions

Tomasz Galkowski[1]([⊠]) and Miroslaw Pawlak[2,3]

[1] Institute of Computational Intelligence, Czestochowa University of Technology,
Czestochowa, Poland
tomasz.galkowski@iisi.pcz.pl
[2] Information Technology Institute, University of Social Sciences, Lodz, Poland
[3] Department of Electrical and Computer Engineering, University of Manitoba,
Winnipeg, Canada
pawlak@ee.umanitoba.ca

Abstract. In this article we investigate the problem of regression functions estimation in the edges points of their domain. We refer to the model $y_i = R(x_i) + \epsilon_i$, $i = 1, 2, \ldots n$, where x_i is assumed to be the set of deterministic inputs, $x_i \in D$, y_i is the set of probabilistic outputs, and ϵ_i is a measurement noise with zero mean and bounded variance. $R(.)$ is a completely unknown function. The possible solution of finding unknown function is to apply the algorithms based on the Parzen kernel [13,31]. The commonly known drawback of these algorithms is that the error of estimation dramatically increases if the point of estimation x is drifting to the left or right bound of interval D. This fact makes it impossible to estimate functions exactly in edge values of domain.

The main goal of this paper is an application of NMS algorithm (introduced in [11]), basing on integral version of the Parzen method of function estimation by combining the linear approximation idea. The results of numerical experiments are presented.

Keywords: Nonparametric estimation · Parzen kernel · Boundary problem · Regression

1 Introduction

The nonparametric algorithms have been proposed in literature for modelling and classification in stationary [4,8,14,33,34,36,42,43,46–48,56,57], quasi-stationary [37,40], and time-varying [15,38,39,41,44,45,49,50], environments. Another approaches of classification and modelling are derived from wide area of artificial intelligence methods like neural networks, fuzzy sets, genetic algorithms, see e.g. [1–3,5–7,19–23,26,27,29,30,35,51–54,58,59].

There is the substantial problem of regression functions estimation in the points situated near any edge of the domain and particularly exactly in it.

M. Pawlak carried out this research at ASS during his sabbatical leave from University of Manitoba.

L. Rutkowski et al. (Eds.): ICAISC 2016, Part II, LNAI 9693, pp. 49–59, 2016.
DOI: 10.1007/978-3-319-39384-1_5

We investigate the model of type $y_i = R(x_i) + \epsilon_i$, $i = 1, 2, \ldots n$, where x_i is assumed to be the set of deterministic inputs, $x_i \in D$, y_i is the set of probabilistic outputs, and ϵ_i is a measurement noise with zero mean and bounded variance. $R(.)$ is an unknown function. We have completely no assumption neither on its shape (like e.g. in the spline methods) nor on any mathematical formula with certain set of parameters to be found (so-called parametric approach). In this paper we use an approach known in the literature as a non-parametric estimation. The possible solutions of finding unknown function are based on Parzen kernel [9,13,31] or methods derived from orthogonal series [48]. Note that the Parzen kernel methods are much more often applied and analysed for estimation of probability density functions and/or regressions with probabilistic input than in a deterministic case.

Applications based on above methods bring satisfying results when the estimate is taken in the interior of the function $R(.)$ domain, whereas the error of estimation dramatically increases if the point of estimation x is coming up to the left or right bound of interval D in which measurements of R were taken, depending on some smoothing (bandwidth) parameter a_n. Figure 1 shows an example of classic Parzen estimation of a regression, particularly one may observe the boundary phenomenon in circled areas. The example regression function $R(x)$ (thin dashed line) is estimated in interval $D = [0, 1]$ (the points marked with small circles) basing on measurement data set - marked with +. Let us explain why estimators in the edges don't work satisfactory. Understanding the formula defining algorithm (1) the intuitive answer is that the estimator in the boundaries uses less number of measurements (input data) than in the interior of D. For the left boundary for instance, the kernel is applying only points belonging to the interval $(0, a_n]$, however the interval $[-a_n, 0)$ shows complete absence of them - because it is situated just outside domain. Also in the right boundary we have the same problem. Estimates in both situations tend to zero.

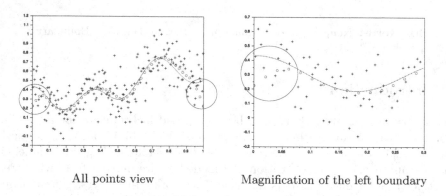

All points view   Magnification of the left boundary

Fig. 1. Regression function $R(x)$ and its classic Parzen estimates

This fact has its consequence in known theorems on bias and mean-square error convergence of the estimates. They are valid only in the interior of D.

Therefore the estimation method taken exactly in the edge points are still in the area of interest for many authors. There are a lot of works on the above problem occuring in the boundary regions. The first are taken by Gasser et al. [13], followed by Müller [28], Schuster [55] and Galkowski [10]. In the last years several authors still try to improve the previous results or/and propose new approaches to this problem, e.g. Karunamuni et al. [17,18], Kyung-Joon et al. [24], Poměnková-Dluhá [32], Chen [4], Hazelton et al. [16], Marshall et al. [25], Zhang et al. [60]. The main result of this paper is an algorithm based on the integral version of Parzen methods for an estimation of edge values of a function R. The linear approximation technique is combined in the proposed procedure. The numerical simulations results have been presented.

2   Kernel Estimation of Edge Values of Function

We consider a nonparametric estimator of unknown function $R(.)$ in the form

$$\hat{R}_n(x) = \frac{1}{a_n} \sum_{i=1}^{n} y_i \int_{D_i} K\left(\frac{x-u}{a_n}\right) du \tag{1}$$

where $K(.)$ is the kernel function described by (2), a_n is a smoothing parameter depending on the number of observations n. Interval D is partitioned into n disjunctive segments D_i such that $\cup D_i = [0,1]$, $D_i \cap D_j = \emptyset$ for $i \neq j$. The measurement points x_i are chosen from D_i, i.e.: $x_i \in D_i$. Kernel function is defined by Eq. (2):

$$\left. \begin{array}{ll} \text{(i)} & K(t) = 0, \text{ for } t \notin (-\tau, \tau), \tau > 0, \\ \text{(ii)} & \int_{-\tau}^{\tau} K(t)\, dt = 1 \\ \text{(iii)} & |K(t)| < \infty \end{array} \right\} \tag{2}$$

In the initial phase of the experiment we choose the points x_i and carry on measurements of R - in the presence of noise. We try to ensure sufficient representation of function R in domain D. The standard assumption in theorems on convergence is that the $max\, |D_i|$ tends to zero if n tends to infinity (see e.g. [8,9,13]). We may suppose that in the set of pairs (x_i, y_i) it is present the information on properties of function R, like its smoothness, for instance. Such supposition is underlying in such approaches like Markov chains - in the previous sequence of data it is encoded (somehow) the regularity allowing to forecast the future data.

In some papers authors describe methods using artificially expanded function e.g. by multinomial extension of function [60,61], or by mirrored reflection of held data [28,55], also by specially modified kernel functions used in the boundary region [13,62]. Ordinary mirroring of data implies assumption that the estimated function has local extreme (minimum or maximum) in the edge points ($x = 0$ or $x = 1$). This means that the first derivative of the function $R(.)$ is equal to zero. Of course, this is the strong limitation of class of unknown function.

The idea presented in this article is the variant of author's conception published at first in [11]. It is basing on auxiliary set of points outside domain D obtained by the original method of reflection of available data relatively to edge points, named the NMS algorithm. This reflection is "negative" and additionally "shifted" with a properly selected shift parameter. Figure 2 presents the main idea of the NMS algorithm.

The negative-mirror-shifted (NMS) algorithm combining the linear approximation is detailed in subsequent section. Without loss of generality we assume construction of the expansion of function $R(.)$ in the left boundary; the algorithm can be used analogously in the opposite (right) end of the interval D. The alternative method of finding the shift parameter is proposed in this article.

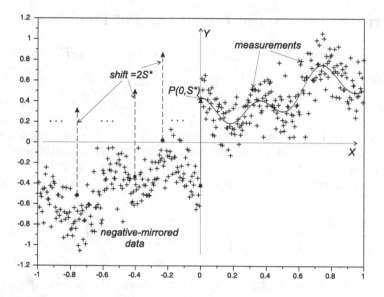

Fig. 2. The idea of the NMS algorithm with expanded set of input data

3   Description of the NMS Algorithm Combining the Linear Approximation

Note, that the proposed ideas are detailed for the left boundary of the domain D, but for the right boundary it is easy to make analogous reasoning. The function $R(.)$ is being extended beyond the left edge $x = 0$ and is redefined in the expanded interval $[-1,1]$ as follows:

$$\tilde{R}(x) = \begin{cases} R(x) & \text{for } x \in (0,1] \\ -R(-x) + 2S^* & \text{for } x \in [-1,0] \end{cases} \tag{3}$$

Let us mention that this method is similar to the odd expansion of function in a finite interval in order to apply the Fourier series theorem. Of course we shall not use this extension outside interval D, we do it only to improve the estimates inside the boundary region.

The crucial problem is to determine the shift parameter S^*. The method based on minimizing the special loss function presented in [11] gives the satisfactory results. Figures 3 shows some results of applying the NMS estimator introduced in [11]. An important problem is choosing the subset of measurements to be sufficient and productive in calculation of constant S^*. One may observe that it is enough to take measurements points belonging to the interval $(0, a_n]$, i.e. from the boundary region only. This makes shorter the time of calculations and improves significantly its efficiency.

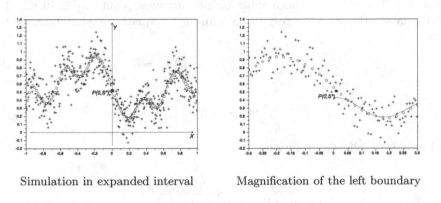

Simulation in expanded interval   Magnification of the left boundary

Fig. 3. Simulation of estimation of $R(x)$ applying NMS algorithm introduced in [11]

In this article we propose another way leading to finding of unknown constant S^*. We apply the method of linear approximation of functions. We assume the model of the following type

$$p(x) = ax + b \qquad (4)$$

is sufficiently good approximate of the unknown regression function $R(.)$ in the boundary region $(0, a_n]$. The problem of finding constant b^* is equivalent to finding S^* (because of $p(0) = b$), i.e.

$$b^* = S^* \qquad (5)$$

We take into account only points belonging to the interval $(0, a_n]$ as sufficiently preserving the smooth properties of function $R(.)$ close to the left edge of D. Our optimal linear model is in the form

$$\hat{p}(x) = a^* x + b^* \qquad (6)$$

We need to find constants a^* and b^*. Let us introduce the loss function in the form

$$\Gamma(a,b) = \int_0^{\partial a_n} (\hat{p}(x) - R(x))^2 dx \tag{7}$$

where integration is carried on in subinterval $(0, \partial a_n]$ corresponding almost to the interval $(0, a_n]$. Because we do not know $R(x)$ the integration is replaced by summing and values of $R(x)$ are substituted by measurements y_i and we obtain loss function estimator as follows

$$\hat{\Gamma}(a,b) = \sum_{j=1}^{n'} (\hat{p}(x_j) - y_j)^2 = \sum_{j=1}^{n'} (ax_j + b - y_j)^2 \tag{8}$$

where $j = 1, ..., n'$, n' is the number of measurement points $x_j \in (0, a_n]$. By differentiating Eq. (8), with respect to a and b by equating results to zeros we obtain

$$\hat{\Gamma}'_a = \sum_{j=1}^{n'} 2\left(ax_j + b - y_j\right) x_j = 0 \tag{9}$$

$$\hat{\Gamma}'_b = \sum_{j=1}^{n'} 2\left(ax_j + b - y_j\right) = 0. \tag{10}$$

It yields to following solutions

$$a^* = \frac{\sum_{j=1}^{n'} x_j y_j - \frac{1}{n'} \sum_{j=1}^{n'} y_j \sum_{j=1}^{n'} x_j}{\sum_{j=1}^{n'} x_j^2 - \frac{1}{n'} \left(\sum_{j=1}^{n'} x_j\right)^2} \tag{11}$$

$$b^* = \frac{\sum_{j=1}^{n'} y_j - a^* \sum_{j=1}^{n'} x_j}{n'}. \tag{12}$$

In view of condition (5) the shift constant S^* is found from Eq. (12).

Now we can adopt the estimated value S^* in the negatively mirrored extended set of measurements

$$\begin{aligned}
&[(x_{-n}, (y_{-n} + 2S^*)), (x_{-(n-1)}, (y_{-(n-1)} + 2S^*)), ... \\
&..., (x_{-1}, (y_{-1} + 2S^*)), (0, S^*), (x_1, y_1), ... \\
&..., (x_{n-1}, y_{n-1}), (x_n, y_n)]
\end{aligned} \tag{13}$$

New algorithm of estimation of the regression function, working with the expanded data set described by (13), is defined as follows

$$\hat{R}_n(x) = \frac{1}{a_n} \sum_{i=-n}^{+n} y_i \int_{D_i} K\left(\frac{x-u}{a_n}\right) du \tag{14}$$

It works in the points arbitrarily close to the left edge of interval D.

4 Simulation Study

The results of the simulation experiment are shown in Fig. 4.

Solid straight line shown on each picture is the approximating line in the short interval near left edge basing on observations $y_j : x_j \in (0, a_n]$. The standard assumption of theorems on convergence of the kernel regression estimators is that $a_n \to 0$ when $n \to \infty$ (see for instance [8,9,28,46]). Then the line tends to be tangent to the regression function at the edge point. This observation lets to gain less error of estimation of shift parameter S^*. Figure 4 presents results of four tests, i.e. four sets of randomly generated noisy measurements. Each simulation result depends on particular set of measurements. From presented plots one can see that the graph Test 2 shows the most precise approximation. Note that the directional factor's estimate a^* plays a smaller role in placement of point $P(0, S^*)$ than the estimate of $b^* = S^*$ - the shift constant in the NMS algorithm.

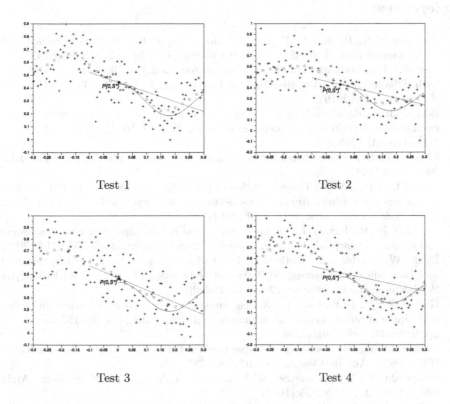

Test 1   Test 2

Test 3   Test 4

Fig. 4. Tests results for four random sets of measurements

5 Remarks and Extensions

The new approach of using the NMS method, based on the Parzen kernel algorithm, for estimation of regression function in boundary regions in deterministic case has been proposed. The adoption of linear approximation taken in boundary region $(0, a_n]$ can achieve acceptable precision by effective calculation of the shift parameter S^*. Using our procedure it is possible to determine the estimate of value of unknown function exactly in the edge point of domain. This way is simpler than one proposed in [11] and not worse as seen in simulations. One can see from the graphical results of simulation that the boundary effect is now strongly reduced or eliminated. Similar problems of reduction of boundary phenomenon probably could find the other solutions for instance basing on orthogonal nonparametric approach (see [15] or [48]). The multivariate case for resolving this problem shall be studied in future works.

References

1. Aghdam, M.H., Heidari, S.: Feature selection using particle swarm optimization in text categorization. J. Artif. Intell. Soft Comput. Res. **5**(4), 231–238 (2015)
2. Bas, E.: The Training of multiplicative neuron model artificial neural networks with differential evolution algorithm for forecasting. J. Artif. Intell. Soft Comput. Res. **6**(1), 5–11 (2016)
3. Bertini Jr., J.R., Carmo, N.M.: Enhancing constructive neural network performance using functionally expanded input data. J. Artif. Intell. Soft Comput. Res. **6**(2), 119–131 (2016)
4. Chen, S.X.: Beta kernel estimators for density functions. J. Stat. Plann. Infer. **139**, 2269–2283 (2009)
5. Chu, J.L., Krzyzak, A.: The recognition of partially occluded objects with support vector machines, convolutional neural networks and deep belief networks. J. Artif. Intell. Soft Comput. Res. **4**(1), 5–19 (2014)
6. Cierniak, R., Rutkowski, L.: On image compression by competitive neural networks and optimal linear predictors. Sig. Process.-Image Commun. **15**(6), 559–565 (2000)
7. Duch, W., Korbicz, J., Rutkowski, L., Tadeusiewicz, R. (eds.): Biocybernetics and Biomedical Engineering 2000. Neural Networks, vol. 6. Akademicka Oficyna Wydawnicza, EXIT, Warsaw (2000) (in Polish)
8. Galkowski, T., Rutkowski, L.: Nonparametric recovery of multivariate functions with applications to system identification. In: Proceedings of the IEEE, vol. 73, pp. 942–943, New York (1985)
9. Galkowski, T., Rutkowski, L.: Nonparametric fitting of multivariable functions. IEEE Trans. Autom. Control **AC–31**, 785–787 (1986)
10. Galkowski, T.: Nonparametric estimation of boundary values of functions. Arch. Control Sci. **3**(1–2), 85–93 (1994)
11. Gałkowski, T.: Kernel estimation of regression functions in the boundary regions. In: Rutkowski, L., Korytkowski, M., Scherer, R., Tadeusiewicz, R., Zadeh, L.A., Zurada, J.M. (eds.) ICAISC 2013, Part II. LNCS, vol. 7895, pp. 158–166. Springer, Heidelberg (2013)

12. Galkowski, T., Pawlak, M.: Nonparametric extension of regression functions outside domain. In: Rutkowski, L., Korytkowski, M., Scherer, R., Tadeusiewicz, R., Zadeh, L.A., Zurada, J.M. (eds.) ICAISC 2014, Part I. LNCS, vol. 8467, pp. 518–530. Springer, Heidelberg (2014)
13. Gasser, T., Muller, H.G.: Kernel estimation of regression functions. Lecture Notes in Mathematics, vol. 757. Springer, Heidelberg (1979)
14. Greblicki, W., Rutkowski, L.: Density-free bayes risk consistency of nonparametric pattern recognition procedures. Proc. IEEE **69**(4), 482–483 (1981)
15. Greblicki, W., Rutkowska, D., Rutkowski, L.: An orthogonal series estimate of time-varying regression. Ann. Inst. Stat. Math. **35**(1), 215–228 (1983)
16. Hazelton, M.L., Marshall, J.C.: Linear boundary kernels for bivariate density estimation. Stat. Prob. Lett. **79**, 999–1003 (2009)
17. Karunamuni, R.J., Alberts, T.: On boundary correction in kernel density estimation. Stat. Methodol. **2**, 191–212 (2005)
18. Karunamuni, R.J., Alberts, T.: A locally adaptive transformation method of boundary correction in kernel density estimation. J. Stat. Plann. Infer. **136**, 2936–2960 (2006)
19. Kitajima, R., Kamimura, R.: Accumulative information enhancement in the self-organizing maps and its application to the analysis of mission statements. J. Artif. Intell. Soft Comput. Res. **5**(3), 161–176 (2015)
20. Knop, M., Kapuscinski, T., Mleczko, W.K.: Video key frame detection based on the restricted Boltzmann machine. J. Appl. Math. Comput. Mech. **14**(3), 49–58 (2015)
21. Korytkowski, M., Nowicki, R., Scherer, R.: Neuro-fuzzy rough classifier ensemble. In: Alippi, C., Polycarpou, M., Panayiotou, C., Ellinas, G. (eds.) ICANN 2009, Part I. LNCS, vol. 5768, pp. 817–823. Springer, Heidelberg (2009)
22. Korytkowski, M., Rutkowski, L., Scherer, R.: Fast image classification by boosting fuzzy classifiers. Inf. Sci. **327**, 175–182 (2016)
23. Koshiyama, A.S., Vellasco, M., Tanscheit, R.: GPFIS-control: a genetic fuzzy system for control tasks. J. Artif. Intell. Soft Comput. Res. **4**(3), 167–179 (2014)
24. Kyung-Joon, C., Schucany, W.R.: Nonparametric kernel regression estimation near endpoints. J. Stat. Plann. Inf. **66**, 289–304 (1998)
25. Marshall, J.C., Hazelton, M.L.: Boundary kernels for adaptive density estimators on regions with irregular boundaries. J. Multivar. Anal. **101**, 949–963 (2010)
26. Laskowski, L.: A novel hybrid-maximum neural network in stereo-matching process. Neural Comput. Appl. **23**(7–8), 2435–2450 (2013)
27. Laskowski, L., Jelonkiewicz, J.: Self-correcting neural network for stereo-matching problem solving. Fundamenta Informaticae **138**, 1–26 (2015)
28. Müller, H.G.: Smooth optimum kernel estimators near endpoints. Biometrika **78**, 521–530 (1991)
29. Nikulin, V.: Prediction of the shoppers loyalty with aggregated data streams. J. Artif. Intell. Soft Comput. Res. **6**(2), 69–79 (2016)
30. Nowak, B.A., Nowicki, R.K., Starczewski, J.T., Marvuglia, A.: The learning of neuro-fuzzy classifier with fuzzy rough sets for imprecise datasets. In: Rutkowski, L., Korytkowski, M., Scherer, R., Tadeusiewicz, R., Zadeh, L.A., Zurada, J.M. (eds.) ICAISC 2014, Part I. LNCS, vol. 8467, pp. 256–266. Springer, Heidelberg (2014)
31. Parzen, E.: On estimation of a probability density function and mode. Anal. Math. Stat. **33**(3), 1065–1076 (1962)
32. Poměnková-Dluhá, J.: Edge Effects of Gasser-Müller Estimator, Mathematica 15, Brno, Masaryk University, pp. 307–314 (2004)

33. Rafajlowicz, E.: Nonparametric least squares estimation of a regression function statistics. J. Theor. Appl. Stat. **19**(3), 349–358 (1988)
34. Rafajlowicz, E., Schwabe, R.: Halton and hammersley sequences in multivariate nonparametric regression. Stat. Prob. Lett. **76**(8), 803–812. Elsevier (2006)
35. Rutkowska, A.: Influence of membership function's shape on portfolio optimization results. J. Artif. Intell. Soft Comput. Res. **6**(1), 45–54 (2016)
36. Rutkowski, L.: Sequential estimates of probability densities by orthogonal series and their application in pattern classification. IEEE Trans. Syst. Man Cybern. **SMC–10**(12), 918–920 (1980)
37. Rutkowski, L.: On bayes risk consistent pattern recognition procedures in a quasi-stationary environment. IEEE Trans. Pattern Anal. Mach. Intell. **PAMI–4**(1), 84–87 (1982)
38. Rutkowski, L.: Online identification of time-varying systems by nonparametric techniques. IEEE Trans. Autom. Control **27**(1), 228–230 (1982)
39. Rutkowski, L.: On nonparametric identification with prediction of time-varying systems. IEEE Trans. Autom. Control **AC–29**, 58–60 (1984)
40. Rutkowski, L.: Nonparametric identification of quasi-stationary systems. Syst. Control Lett. **6**, 33–35. Amsterdam (1985)
41. Rutkowski, L.: Real-time identification of time-varying systems by non-parametric algorithms based on parzen kernels. Int. J. Syst. Sci. **16**, 1123–1130 (1985)
42. Rutkowski, L.: A general approach for nonparametric fitting of functions and their derivatives with applications to linear circuits identification. IEEE Trans. Circuits Syst. **33**, 812–818 (1986)
43. Rutkowski, L.: Sequential pattern recognition procedures derived from multiple Fourier series. Pattern Recogn. Lett. **8**, 213–216 (1988)
44. Rutkowski, L.: Application of multiple fourier series to identification of multivariable nonstationary systems. Int. J. Syst. Sci. **20**(10), 1993–2002 (1989)
45. Rutkowski, L.: Non-parametric learning algorithms in the time-varying environments. Sig. Process. **18**(2), 129–137 (1989)
46. Rutkowski, L., Rafajłowicz, E.: On global rate of convergence of some nonparametric identification procedures. IEEE Trans. Autom. Control **AC–34**(10), 1089–1091 (1989)
47. Rutkowski, L.: Identification of MISO nonlinear regressions in the presence of a wide class of disturbances. IEEE Trans. Inf. Theory **IT–37**, 214–216 (1991)
48. Rutkowski, L.: Multiple fourier series procedures for extraction of nonlinear regressions from noisy data. IEEE Trans. Sig. Process. **41**(10), 3062–3065 (1993)
49. Rutkowski, L.: Generalized regression neural networks in time-varying environment. IEEE Trans. Neural Netw. **15**(3), 576–596 (2004)
50. Rutkowski, L.: Adaptive probabilistic neural networks for pattern classification in time-varying environment. IEEE Trans. Neural Netw. **15**(4), 811–827 (2004)
51. Rutkowski, L., Pietruczuk, L., Duda, P., Jaworski, M.: Decision trees for mining data streams based on the mcdiarmid's bound. IEEE Trans. Knowl. Data Eng. **25**(6), 1272–1279 (2013)
52. Rutkowski, L., Jaworski, M., Duda, P., Pietruczuk, L.: Decision trees for mining data streams based on the gaussian approximation. IEEE Trans. Knowl. Data Eng. **26**(1), 108–119 (2014)
53. Rutkowski, L., Jaworski, M., Pietruczuk, L., Duda, P.: The CART decision trees mining data streams. Inf. Sci. **266**, 1–15 (2014)
54. Rutkowski, L., Jaworski, M., Pietruczuk, L., Duda, P.: A new method for data stream mining based on the misclassification error. IEEE Trans. Neural Netw. Learn. Syst. **26**(5), 1048–1059 (2015)

55. Schuster, E.F.: Incorporating support constraints into nonparametric estimators of densities. Commun. Stat. Part A - Theory Methods **14**, 1123–1136 (1985)
56. Skubalska-Rafajlowicz, E.: Pattern recognition algorithms based on space-filling curves and orthogonal expansions. IEEE Trans. Inf. Theory **47**(5), 1915–1927 (2001)
57. Skubalska-Rafajlowicz, E.: Random projection RBF nets for multidimensional density estimation. Int. J. Appl. Math. Comput. Sci. **18**(4), 455–464 (2008)
58. Szarek, A., Korytkowski, M., Rutkowski, L., Scherer, R., Szyprowski, J.: Application of neural networks in assessing changes around implant after total hip arthroplasty. In: Rutkowski, L., Korytkowski, M., Scherer, R., Tadeusiewicz, R., Zadeh, L.A., Zurada, J.M. (eds.) ICAISC 2012, Part II. LNCS, vol. 7268, pp. 335–340. Springer, Heidelberg (2012)
59. Wang, Z., Zhang-Westmant, L.: New ranking method for fuzzy numbers by their expansion center. J. Artif. Intell. Soft Comput. Res. **4**(3), 181–187 (2014)
60. Zhang, S., Karunamuni, R.J.: On kernel density estimation near endpoints. J. Stat. Plann. Inf. **70**, 301–316 (1998)
61. Zhang, S., Karunamuni, R.J.: Deconvolution boundary kernel method in nonparametric density estimation. J. Stat. Plann. Inf. **139**, 2269–2283 (2009)
62. Zhang, S., Karunamuni, R.J.: Boundary performance of the beta kernel estimators. Nonparametric Stat. **22**, 81–104 (2010)

Hybrid Splitting Criterion in Decision Trees for Data Stream Mining

Maciej Jaworski[1(✉)], Leszek Rutkowski[1,2], and Miroslaw Pawlak[2,3]

[1] Institute of Computational Intelligence, Czestochowa University of Technology,
Armii Krajowej 36, 42-200 Czestochowa, Poland
{maciej.jaworski,leszek.rutkowski}@iisi.pcz.pl
[2] Information Technology Institute, University of Social Sciences,
90-113 Łódź, Poland
[3] Department of Electrical and Computer Engineering,
University of Manitoba, Winnipeg, Canada
pawlak@ee.umanitoba.ca

Abstract. In this paper the issue of splitting criteria used in decision tree induction algorithm designed for data streams is analyzed. A hybrid splitting criterion is proposed which combines two criteria established for two different split measure functions: the Gini gain and the split measure based on the misclassification error. The hybrid splitting criterion reveals advantages of its both component. The online decision tree with hybrid criterion demonstrates higher classification accuracy than the online decision trees with both considered single criteria.

Keywords: Data streams · Decision trees · Split measures · Hybrid splitting criterion

1 Introduction

The most promising methods used for data stream classification are algorithms based on decision trees. The most critical point in any decision tree induction algorithm is the choice of an attribute to split the considered node. In many commonly known algorithms, like CART [8], ID3 [37] or C4.5 [38], the choice is made using a data sample S assigned to the considered node. An attribute which maximizes some split measure function is chosen as a splitting one. In this paper only binary trees are taken into account, i.e. each node is split only into two children nodes: the 'left' one (with index L) and the 'right' one (with index R). Each data element is characterized by D attributes and belong to one of the K classes. Let us now introduce the following notation:

- $n_{q,i}(S)$ - number of elements in considered node that would be passed to the q-th child node if the split was made with respect to the i-th attribute ($q \in \{L, R\}$);

M. Pawlak carried out this research at USS during his sabbatical leave from University of Manitoba.

© Springer International Publishing Switzerland 2016
L. Rutkowski et al. (Eds.): ICAISC 2016, Part II, LNAI 9693, pp. 60–72, 2016.
DOI: 10.1007/978-3-319-39384-1_6

– $n_{q,i}^k(S)$ - number of elements from the k-th class in considered node that would be passed to the q-th child node if the split was made with respect to the i-th attribute ($q \in \{L, R\}$).

Then the most popular split measure functions for the i-th attribute can be expressed as follows:

(i) Information gain

$$\Delta g_i^I(S) = g^I(S) + \sum_{q \in \{L,R\}} \frac{n_{q,i}(S)}{n(S)} \sum_{k=1}^{K} \frac{n_{q,i}^k(S)}{n_{q,i}(S)} \log_2 \left(\frac{n_{q,i}^k(S)}{n_{q,i}(S)} \right) ; \quad (1)$$

(ii) Gini gain

$$\Delta g_i^G(S) = g^G(S) - \sum_{q \in \{L,R\}} \frac{n_{q,i}(S)}{n(S)} \left(1 - \sum_{k}^{K} \left(\frac{n_{q,i}^k(S)}{n_{q,i}(S)} \right)^2 \right) ; \quad (2)$$

(iii) Split measure based on misclassification error

$$\Delta g_i^M(S) = g^M(S) - \sum_{q \in \{L,R\}} \frac{n_{q,i}(S)}{n(S)} \left(1 - \max_{k \in \{1,...,K\}} \frac{n_{q,i}^k(S)}{n_{q,i}(S)} \right) , \quad (3)$$

where $g^I(S)$, $g^G(S)$ and $g^M(S)$ denote impurity measures: information entropy, Gini index and misclassification error, respectively.

The decision tree induction algorithms used for static data cannot be directly applied to data stream scenario. The reason is that data streams are potentially infinite sequences of data elements [1, 14, 15, 18, 43] and often arrive to the system with very high rates. Various methods and algorithms in this context, including learning in time-varying environment, have been developed in our previous papers [11–13, 20–22, 34–36] we are also working on adopting other techniques for this purpose [2, 3, 6, 7, 9, 25–27, 30–33, 44]. One of the most popular algorithms for data stream classification is the Very Fast Decision Tree algorithm (VFDT) [10], which applies the Hoeffding's inequality [16] to establish the desired splitting criterion. The VFDT algorithm and its core, i.e. the Hoeffding tree, stands as a basis for many decision tree induction algorithms designed for data streams [4, 5, 17, 24]. However, it was recently pointed out that the Hoeffding's inequality is irrelevant for establishing the splitting criteria for nonlinear split measures [28, 41, 42]. To solve this problem new statistical tools were proposed, i.e. the McDiarmid's inequality [19, 42] and the Gaussian approximation [39–41]. Additionally, in [41] an idea of hybrid splitting criterion was proposed. Such a criterion combines criteria for two different split measures, revealing advantages of both components. In this paper a hybrid splitting criterion combining criteria obtained for the Gini gain and for the misclassification-based split measure is proposed and analyzed.

The rest of the paper is organized as follows. In Sect. 2 a splitting criterion for the Gini gain is presented, whereas in Sect. 3 the splitting criterion for misclassification-based split measure is recalled. Both criteria are based on appropriate mathematical theorems. Section 4 contains a description of the hybrid splitting criterion, which is the main result of this paper. In Sect. 5 the experimental results are presented. Section 6 concludes the paper.

2   Splitting Criterion for Gini Gain

The idea of applying the McDiarmid's inequality [29], which is a generalization of the Hoeffding's one, as a statistical tool for deriving the splitting criteria in decision trees was proposed in [42]. The McDiarmid's theorem is presented below.

Theorem 1 (McDiarmid's Theorem). *Let $X_1, \ldots, X_n$ be a set of independent random variables and let $f(x_1, \ldots, x_n)$ be a function satisfying the following inequalities*

$$\sup_{x_1, \ldots, x_i, \ldots, x_n, \hat{x}_i} |f(x_1, \ldots, x_i, \ldots, x_n) - f(x_1, \ldots, \hat{x}_i, \ldots, x_n)| \leq c_i, \ \forall_{i=1,\ldots,n}. \quad (4)$$

Then for any $\epsilon > 0$ the following inequality is true

$$Pr\left(f(X_1, \ldots, X_n) - E\left[f(X_1, \ldots, X_n)\right] \geq \epsilon\right) \leq \exp\left(-\frac{2\epsilon^2}{\sum_{i=1}^{n} c_i^2}\right) = \delta. \quad (5)$$

The McDiarmid's theorem is applicable for any function, in particular for nonlinear split measures like information gain or Gini gain. Hence it can be applied to formulate theorems establishing new splitting criteria for various split measures. Splitting criterion for the Gini gain guarantees quite low number of data elements n to split the considered node, thus it has a practical meaning. For this reason the splitting criterion for the Gini gain will be presented below. First, a theorem concerning the comparison of Gini gain for any two attributes will be introduced.

Theorem 2 (McDiarmid's Inequality for Gini Gain). *Let $S = s_1, \ldots, s_n$ be a set of data elements (independent random variables) and let $\Delta g_i^G(S)$ and $\Delta g_j^G(S)$ be the Gini gain values, defined by (2), for the i-th and the j-th attribute, respectively. If the following condition is satisfied*

$$\Delta g_i^G(S) - \Delta g_j^G(S) > \sqrt{\frac{8 \ln (1/\delta)}{n(S)}}, \quad (6)$$

then with probability at least $1 - \delta$ the following inequality holds

$$E\left[\Delta g_i^G(S)\right] > E\left[\Delta g_j^G(S)\right]. \quad (7)$$

Proof. For the proof see [19,23].

Now the splitting criterion for Gini gain based on the McDiarmid's inequality can be formulated.

Corollary 1 (Splitting Criterion for Gini Gain Based on the McDiarmid's Inequality). *Let $S = s_1, \ldots, s_n$ be a set of data elements (independent random variables) and let $\Delta g^G_{i_{best}}(S)$ and $\Delta g^G_{i_{2nd\_best}}(S)$ be the Gini gain values, defined by (2), for attributes providing the highest and the second highest values of Gini gain, respectively. If the following condition is satisfied*

$$\Delta g^G_{i_{best}}(S) - \Delta g^G_{i_{2nd\_best}}(S) > \sqrt{\frac{8\ln(1/\delta)}{n(S)}}, \tag{8}$$

then, according to Theorem 2, with probability $(1-\delta)^{D-1}$ the following statement is true

$$i_{best} = \arg \max_{i=1,\ldots,D} \{E\left[\Delta g^G_i(S)\right]\} \tag{9}$$

and the i_{best}-th attribute is chosen to split the considered node.

3 Splitting Criterion for Misclassification-Based Split Measure

The Hoeffding's and the McDiarmid's inequalities are not the only possible statistical tools which can be used to establish splitting criteria for split measures. It turns out that a proper estimations for misclassification-based split measure can be derived using the Gaussian approximation. An appropriate theorem with the proof was presented in [41]. The theorem is recalled below.

Theorem 3 (Gaussian Approximation for Misclassification-Based Split Measure). *Let $S = s_1, \ldots, s_n$ be a set of data elements (independent random variables) and let $\Delta g^M_i(S)$ and $\Delta g^M_j(S)$ be the misclassification-based split measure values given by (3) for the i-th and the j-th attribute, respectively. If the following condition is satisfied*

$$\Delta g^M_i(S) - \Delta g^M_j(S) > z_{(1-\delta)}\sqrt{\frac{1}{2n(S)}}, \tag{10}$$

where $z_{(1-\delta)}$ is the $(1-\delta)$-th quantile of the standard normal distribution, then with probability $1-\delta$ for sufficiently high number $n(S)$ the following inequality holds

$$E\left[\Delta g^M_i(S)\right] > E\left[\Delta g^M_j(S)\right]. \tag{11}$$

Proof. For the proof see [41].

Now the splitting criterion for misclassification-based split measure based on the Gaussian approximation can be formulated.

Corollary 2 (Splitting Criterion for Misclassification-Based Split Measure Based on the Gaussian Approximation). *Let $S = s_1, \ldots, s_n$ be a set of data elements (independent random variables) and let $\Delta g_{i_{best}}^M (S)$ and $\Delta g_{i_{2nd\_best}}^M (S)$ be the misclassification-based split measures values for attributes providing the highest and the second highest values of misclassification-based split measure, respectively. If the following condition is satisfied*

$$\Delta g_{i_{best}}^M (S) - \Delta g_{i_{2nd\_best}}^M (S) > z_{(1-\delta)} \sqrt{\frac{1}{2n(S)}}, \qquad (12)$$

then, according to Theorem 3, with probability $(1-\delta)^{D-1}$ the following statement is true

$$i_{best} = \arg \max_{i=1,\ldots,D} \{ E \left[\Delta g_i^M (S) \right] \} \qquad (13)$$

and the i_{best}-th attribute is chosen to split the considered node.

4 Hybrid Splitting Criterion

Each aforementioned splitting criterion has its own advantages and drawbacks. The misclassification-based split measure induces trees which obtain quite satisfactory accuracies for the beginning stages of the tree development, i.e. after processing a relatively small number of data stream elements. Unfortunately, in further stages the value of accuracy stacks in a stable level. The reason is that the tree either does not grow anymore or the occasional splits of tree nodes do not introduce any sensible partitions of attribute values space. It is unlike in the case of Gini gain split measure. In this case much more data elements are required to make a decision about splitting the tree node. Therefore, at the beginning the induced trees demonstrates relatively low accuracies. The accuracy value grows slow as the data stream is processed. However, in the longer perspective, induced trees can provide very satisfactory classification results. Therefore, it is worth considering a hybrid splitting criterion, which would reveal advantages of both split measure functions in one decision tree simultaneously. The simplest way of merging two splitting criteria is to make a disjunction of them. The resulting splitting criterion determines that the split should be made if either the first or the second component criterion is met. Based on Theorems 2 and 3 the hybrid splitting criterion for misclassification-based split measure and Gini gain can be formulated [19].

Corollary 3 (Hybrid Splitting Criterion for Misclassification-Based Split Measure Based and Gini Gain). *Let $S = s_1, \ldots, s_n$ be a set of data elements (independent random variables), $\Delta g_{i_{G,best}}^G (S)$ and $\Delta g_{i_{G,2nd\_best}}^G (S)$ be the*

Gini gain values for attributes providing the highest and the second highest values of misclassification-based split measure, respectively and let $\Delta g_{i_{M,best}}^{M}(S)$ and $\Delta g_{i_{M,2nd\_best}}^{M}(S)$ be the misclassification-based split measures values for attributes providing the highest and the second highest values of misclassification-based split measure, respectively. If the following condition is satisfied

$$\Delta g_{i_{G,best}}^{G}(S) - \Delta g_{i_{G,2nd\_best}}^{G}(S) > \sqrt{\frac{8\ln{(1/\delta)}}{n(S)}}, \tag{14}$$

then, according to Theorem 2, with probability $(1-\delta)^{D-1}$ the following statement is true

$$i_{G,best} = \arg\max_{i=1,\dots,D}\{E\left[\Delta g_{i}^{G}(S)\right]\} \tag{15}$$

and the $i_{G,best}$-th attribute is chosen to split the considered node. Else, if the following condition holds

$$\Delta g_{i_{M,best}}^{M}(S) - \Delta g_{i_{M,2nd\_best}}^{M}(S) > z_{(1-\delta)}\sqrt{\frac{1}{2n(S)}}, \tag{16}$$

then, according to Theorem 3, with probability $(1-\delta)^{D-1}$ the following statement is true

$$i_{M,best} = \arg\max_{i=1,\dots,D}\{E\left[\Delta g_{i}^{M}(S)\right]\} \tag{17}$$

and the $i_{M,best}$-th attribute is chosen to split the considered node.

5 Experimental Section

In this section a comparison between online decision trees with various splitting criteria is investigated:

- online decision tree with Gini gain and splitting criterion presented in Corollary 1,
- online decision tree with misclassification-based split measure and splitting criterion presented in Corollary 2,
- online decision tree with hybrid splitting criterion presented in Corollary 3.

The experiments were carried out with probability $1 - \delta$ was set to 0.95. The Naive Bayes classifier was used as a classification procedure in tree leaves.

5.1 Datasets

The simulations were conducted using synthetic datasets. This datasets were generated using the Random Trees generator which was used to provide data for testing the VFDT algorithm and is described in [10]. The idea of the Random

Tree generator is as follows. First a random, synthetic decision tree is created. At each level of the tree, after the first d_{min} levels, each node has a chance ω to become a leaf. The higher value of parameter ω implies lower complexity of the tree. To the rest of nodes a splitting attribute is randomly assigned. It has to be an attribute which has not already occurred in the path from the root to the considered node. The maximum depth of the synthetic tree is d_{max} (at this level all nodes are replaced by leaves). After the whole tree is constructed, to each leave a class is randomly assigned. Then the training dataset is generated. For each data element the values of attributes are chosen in a random way. For each attribute the choice of each possible value is equally probable. Then the data element is sorted using the synthetic tree into a leaf, according to the splitting attributes assigned to the internal nodes. A class which was assigned to the achieved leaf is assigned to the considered data element.

Each synthetic tree represents a different data concept. For the purpose of the following simulations five datasets based on five different synthetic trees were generated. For all of them the following values of parameters were used: $d_{min} = 3$, $d_{max} = 18$ and $\omega = 0.15$. Datasets are characterized by different numbers of classes K, attributes D and possible values of attributes V (each attribute is nominal and has the same number of possible values). The values of parameters for applied datasets are summarized in Table 1.

Table 1. Datasets used in experiments.

Dataset	Number of attributes (D)	Number of values per attribute (V)	Number of classes (K)
S_1	10	2	2
S_2	10	2	3
S_3	10	3	3
S_4	20	2	2
S_5	20	2	3

To imitate the data stream as best as possible, every dataset contains very large number of data elements, i.e. $n(S_i) = 10^8$, $i = 1, \ldots, 5$. For each training dataset S_i a corresponding testing dataset $\hat{S}_i$, $i = 1, \ldots, 5$, of the size $n(\hat{S}_i) = 10^5$ was generated using the same synthetic tree as in the case of S_i.

5.2   Simulation Results

The results concerning the classification accuracies for datasets S_1-S_5 are presented in Figs. 1, 2, 3, 4 and 5, respectively.

As can be seen, at the beginning of data stream processing the accuracy of the tree with hybrid splitting criterion overlaps with the one obtained for misclassification-based split measure. It is the same for all five data elements

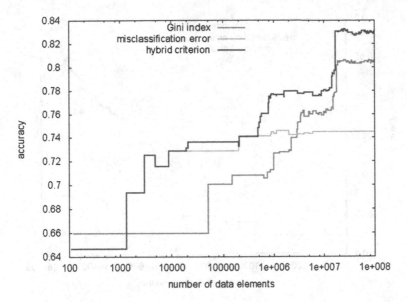

Fig. 1. A comparison of accuracies for online decision trees with splitting criterion based on Gini index, splitting criterion based on the misclassification error and hybrid splitting criterion for dataset S_1. Probability $1 - \delta = 0.95$.

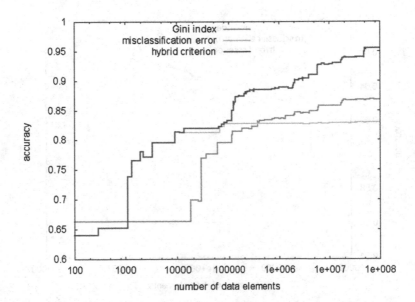

Fig. 2. A comparison of accuracies for online decision trees with splitting criterion based on Gini index, splitting criterion based on the misclassification error and hybrid splitting criterion for dataset S_2. Probability $1 - \delta = 0.95$.

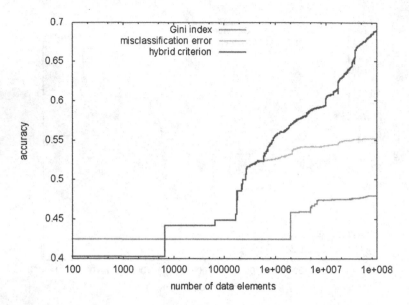

Fig. 3. A comparison of accuracies for online decision trees with splitting criterion based on Gini index, splitting criterion based on the misclassification error and hybrid splitting criterion for dataset S_3. Probability $1 - \delta = 0.95$.

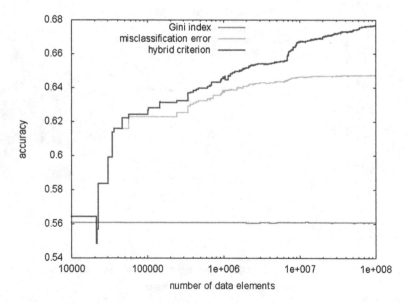

Fig. 4. A comparison of accuracies for online decision trees with splitting criterion based on Gini index, splitting criterion based on the misclassification error and hybrid splitting criterion for dataset S_4. Probability $1 - \delta = 0.95$.

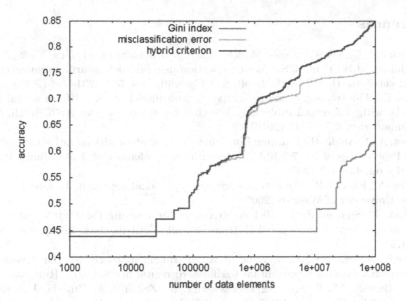

Fig. 5. A comparison of accuracies for online decision trees with splitting criterion based on Gini index, splitting criterion based on the misclassification error and hybrid splitting criterion for dataset S_5. Probability $1 - \delta = 0.95$.

used in the experiment. The difference occurs at the moment at which the first split using the Gini gain instead of misclassification-based split measure takes place. This event slightly increases the accuracy of the tree. Till the end of data stream processing the accuracy of decision tree with hybrid splitting criterion is higher than accuracy of the remaining two trees.

6   Conclusions

In this paper the problem of data stream classification using decision trees was investigated. One of the crucial points in decision tree induction algorithm designed for streaming data is a splitting criterion. The criterion is used to determine whether the number of data elements currently collected in the considered tree node is enough to make a decision about the split or not. In this paper a hybrid splitting criterion was proposed, combining criteria established for two different split measures: the Gini gain and the misclassification-based split measure. The hybrid splitting criterion reveals advantages of both components. The online decision tree with hybrid criterion outperforms the classification accuracy of online decision trees with single splitting criteria, what was demonstrated in numerical experiments.

Acknowledgments. This work was supported by the Polish National Science Center under Grant No. 2014/13/N/ST6/01848.

References

1. Aggarwal, C.: Data Streams: Models and Algorithms. Springer, New York (2007)
2. Aghdam, M.H., Heidari, S.: Feature selection using particle swarm optimization in text categorization. J. Artif. Intell. Soft Comput. Res. **5**(4), 231–238 (2015)
3. Bas, E.: The training of multiplicative neuron model based artificial neural networks with differential evolution algorithm for forecasting. J. Artif. Intell. Soft Comput. Res. **6**(1), 5–11 (2016)
4. Bifet, A., Gavaldà, R.: Learning from time-changing data with adaptive windowing. In: Proceedings of the 7th SIAM International Conference on Data Mining (SDM 2007), pp. 443–449 (2007)
5. Bifet, A., Kirkby, R.: Data stream mining: a practical approach. Technical report, The University of Waikato (2009)
6. Bilski, J., Smolag, J.: Parallel architectures for learning the RTRN and elman dynamic neural networks. IEEE Trans. Parallel Distrib. Syst. **26**(9), 2561–2570 (2015)
7. Bilski, J., Smolag, J., Zurada, J.M.: Parallel approach to the levenberg-marquardt learning algorithm for feedforward neural networks. In: Rutkowski, L., Korytkowski, M., Scherer, R., Tadeusiewicz, R., Zadeh, L.A., Zurada, J.M. (eds.) Artificial Intelligence and Soft Computing. LNCS, vol. 9119, pp. 3–14. Springer, Heidelberg (2015)
8. Breiman, L., Friedman, J., Olshen, R., Stone, C.: Classification and Regression Trees. Wadsworth and Brooks, Monterey (1984)
9. Cpałka, K., Rebrova, O., Nowicki, R., Rutkowski, L.: On design of flexible neuro-fuzzy systems for nonlinear modelling. Int. J. Gen. Syst. **42**(6), 706–720 (2013)
10. Domingos, P., Hulten, G.: Mining high-speed data streams. In: Proceedings of the 6th ACM SIGKDD International Conference on Knowledge Discovery and Data Mining, pp. 71–80 (2000)
11. Duda, P., Hayashi, Y., Jaworski, M.: On the strong convergence of the orthogonal series-type Kernel regression neural networks in a non-stationary environment. In: Rutkowski, L., Korytkowski, M., Scherer, R., Tadeusiewicz, R., Zadeh, L.A., Zurada, J.M. (eds.) ICAISC 2012, Part I. LNCS, vol. 7267, pp. 47–54. Springer, Heidelberg (2012)
12. Duda, P., Jaworski, M., Pietruczuk, L.: On pre-processing algorithms for data stream. In: Rutkowski, L., Korytkowski, M., Scherer, R., Tadeusiewicz, R., Zadeh, L.A., Zurada, J.M. (eds.) ICAISC 2012, Part II. LNCS, vol. 7268, pp. 56–63. Springer, Heidelberg (2012)
13. Er, M.J., Duda, P.: On the weak convergence of the orthogonal series-type Kernel regresion neural networks in a non-stationary environment. In: Wyrzykowski, R., Dongarra, J., Karczewski, K., Waśniewski, J. (eds.) PPAM 2011, Part I. LNCS, vol. 7203, pp. 443–450. Springer, Heidelberg (2012)
14. Gama, J.: Knowledge Discovery from Data Streams, 1st edn. Chapman & Hall/CRC, Boca Raton (2010)
15. Gama, J., Žliobaitė, I., Bifet, A., Pechenizkiy, M., Bouchachia, A.: A survey on concept drift adaptation. ACM Comput. Surv. **46**(4), 44:1–44:37 (2014)
16. Hoeffding, W.: Probability inequalities for sums of bounded random variables. J. Am. Stat. Assoc. **58**, 13–30 (1963)
17. Hulten, G., Spencer, L., Domingos, P.: Mining time-changing data streams. In: Proceedings of the 7th ACM SIGKDD International Conference on Knowledge Discovery and Data Mining, pp. 97–106 (2001)

18. Ikonomovska, E., Loskovska, S., Gjorgjevik, D.: A survey of stream data mining. In: Proceedings of the 8th National Conference with International Participation, ETAI, pp. 19–21 (2007)
19. Jaworski, M.: Data stream mining algorithms based on hybrid techniques. Ph.D. thesis, Institute of Computational Intelligence, Czestochowa University of Technology, Poland (2015)
20. Jaworski, M., Duda, P., Pietruczuk, L.: On fuzzy clustering of data streams with concept drift. In: Rutkowski, L., Korytkowski, M., Scherer, R., Tadeusiewicz, R., Zadeh, L.A., Zurada, J.M. (eds.) ICAISC 2012, Part II. LNCS, vol. 7268, pp. 82–91. Springer, Heidelberg (2012)
21. Jaworski, M., Er, M.J., Pietruczuk, L.: On the application of the Parzen-Type Kernel regression neural network and order statistics for learning in a nonstationary environment. In: Rutkowski, L., Korytkowski, M., Scherer, R., Tadeusiewicz, R., Zadeh, L.A., Zurada, J.M. (eds.) ICAISC 2012, Part I. LNCS, vol. 7267, pp. 90–98. Springer, Heidelberg (2012)
22. Jaworski, M., Pietruczuk, L., Duda, P.: On resources optimization in fuzzy clustering of data streams. In: Rutkowski, L., Korytkowski, M., Scherer, R., Tadeusiewicz, R., Zadeh, L.A., Zurada, J.M. (eds.) ICAISC 2012, Part II. LNCS, vol. 7268, pp. 92–99. Springer, Heidelberg (2012)
23. Jaworski, M., Rutkowski, L., Pietruczuk, L., Duda, P.: New frameworks and splitting criteria for decision trees in stream data mining. IEEE Trans. Neural Netw. Learn. Syst. (2016). (submitted for publication)
24. Kirkby, R.: Improving Hoeffding Trees. Ph.D. thesis, University of Waikato (2007)
25. Kitajima, R., Kamimura, R.: Accumulative information enhancement in the self-organizing maps and its application to the analysis of mission statements. J. Artif. Intell. Soft Comput. Res. 5(3), 161–176 (2015)
26. Korytkowski, M., Nowicki, R., Scherer, R.: Neuro-fuzzy rough classifier ensemble. In: Alippi, C., Polycarpou, M., Panayiotou, C., Ellinas, G. (eds.) ICANN 2009, Part I. LNCS, vol. 5768, pp. 817–823. Springer, Heidelberg (2009)
27. Korytkowski, M., Rutkowski, L., Scherer, R.: Fast image classification by boosting fuzzy classifiers. Inf. Sci. 327, 175–182 (2016)
28. Matuszyk, P., Krempl, G., Spiliopoulou, M.: Correcting the usage of the hoeffding inequality in stream mining. In: Tucker, A., Höppner, F., Siebes, A., Swift, S. (eds.) IDA 2013. LNCS, vol. 8207, pp. 298–309. Springer, Heidelberg (2013)
29. McDiarmid, C.: On the method of bounded differencies. In: Surveys in Combinatorics, pp. 148–188 (1989)
30. Miyajima, H., Shigei, N., Miyajima, H.: Performance comparison of hybrid electromagnetism-like mechanism algorithms with descent method. J. Artif. Intell. Soft Comput. Res. 5(4), 271–282 (2015)
31. Nowicki, R.: Rough sets in the neuro-fuzzy architectures based on monotonic fuzzy implications. In: Rutkowski, L., Siekmann, J.H., Tadeusiewicz, R., Zadeh, L.A. (eds.) ICAISC 2004. LNCS (LNAI), vol. 3070, pp. 510–517. Springer, Heidelberg (2004)
32. Nowicki, R., Nowicki, R.: Rough sets in the neuro-fuzzy architectures based on non-monotonic fuzzy implications. In: Rutkowski, L., Siekmann, J.H., Tadeusiewicz, R., Zadeh, L.A. (eds.) ICAISC 2004. LNCS (LNAI), vol. 3070, pp. 518–525. Springer, Heidelberg (2004)
33. Nowicki, R., Rutkowski, L.: Soft techniques for bayesian classification. In: Rutkowski, L., Kacprzyk, J. (eds.) Neural Networks and Soft Computing. Advances in Soft Computing, pp. 537–544. Physica-Verlag, A Springer–Verlag Company, Heidelberg (2003)

34. Pietruczuk, L., Duda, P., Jaworski, M.: A new fuzzy classifier for data streams. In: Rutkowski, L., Korytkowski, M., Scherer, R., Tadeusiewicz, R., Zadeh, L.A., Zurada, J.M. (eds.) ICAISC 2012, Part I. LNCS, vol. 7267, pp. 318–324. Springer, Heidelberg (2012)
35. Pietruczuk, L., Duda, P., Jaworski, M.: Adaptation of decision trees for handling concept drift. In: Rutkowski, L., Korytkowski, M., Scherer, R., Tadeusiewicz, R., Zadeh, L.A., Zurada, J.M. (eds.) ICAISC 2013, Part I. LNCS, vol. 7894, pp. 459–473. Springer, Heidelberg (2013)
36. Pietruczuk, L., Zurada, J.M.: Weak convergence of the recursive Parzen-Type probabilistic neural network in a non-stationary environment. In: Wyrzykowski, R., Dongarra, J., Karczewski, K., Waśniewski, J. (eds.) PPAM 2011, Part I. LNCS, vol. 7203, pp. 521–529. Springer, Heidelberg (2012)
37. Quinlan, J.R.: Induction of decision trees. Mach. Learn. 1(1), 81–106 (1986)
38. Quinlan, J.R.: C4.5: Programs for Machine Learning. Morgan Kaufmann Publishers Inc., San Francisco (1993)
39. Rutkowski, L., Jaworski, M., Pietruczuk, L., Duda, P.: The CART decision tree for mining data streams. Inf. Sci. 266, 1–15 (2014)
40. Rutkowski, L., Jaworski, M., Pietruczuk, L., Duda, P.: Decision trees for mining data streams based on the Gaussian approximation. IEEE Trans. Knowl. Data Eng. 26(1), 108–119 (2014)
41. Rutkowski, L., Jaworski, M., Pietruczuk, L., Duda, P.: A new method for data stream mining based on the misclassification error. IEEE Trans. Knowl. Data Eng. 26(5), 1048–1059 (2015)
42. Rutkowski, L., Pietruczuk, L., Duda, P., Jaworski, M.: Decision trees for mining data streams based on the McDiarmid's bound. IEEE Trans. Knowl. Data Eng. 25(6), 1272–1279 (2013)
43. Sakurai, S., Nishizawa, M.: A new approach for discovering top-k sequential patterns based on the variety of items. J. Artif. Intell. Soft Comput. Res. 5(2), 141–153 (2015)
44. Woźniak, M., Kempa, W.M., Gabryel, M., Nowicki, R.K., Shao, Z.: On applying evolutionary computation methods to optimization of vacation cycle costs in finite-buffer queue. In: Rutkowski, L., Korytkowski, M., Scherer, R., Tadeusiewicz, R., Zadeh, L.A., Zurada, J.M. (eds.) ICAISC 2014, Part I. LNCS, vol. 8467, pp. 480–491. Springer, Heidelberg (2014)

Data Intensive vs Sliding Window Outlier Detection in the Stream Data — An Experimental Approach

Mateusz Kalisch[1], Marcin Michalak[2(✉)], Marek Sikora[2,3], Łukasz Wróbel[3], and Piotr Przystałka[1]

[1] Institute of Fundamentals of Machinery Design, Silesian University of Technology, ul. Konarskiego 18a, 44-100 Gliwice, Poland
{Mateusz.Kalisch,Piotr.Przystalka}@polsl.pl
[2] Institute of Informatics, Silesian University of Technology, ul. Akademicka 16, 44-100 Gliwice, Poland
{Marcin.Michalak,Marek.Sikora}@polsl.pl
[3] Institute of Innovative Technologies EMAG, ul. Leopolda 31, 40-186 Katowice, Poland
Lukasz.Wrobel@ibemag.pl

Abstract. In the paper a problem of outlier detection in the stream data is raised. The authors propose a new approach, using well known outlier detection algorithms, of outlier detection in the stream data. The method is based on the definition of a sliding window, which means a sequence of stream data observations from the past that are closest to the newly coming object. As it may be expected the outlier detection accuracy level of this model becomes worse than the accuracy of the model that uses all historical data, but from the statistical point of view the difference is not significant. In the paper several well known methods of outlier detection are used as the basis of the model.

Keywords: Outlier detection · Data analysis · Classification · Time series

1 Introduction

Decision support systems can be considered as a higher level of abstraction of monitoring and diagnostic systems. In the past, a typical role of a diagnostic system was to measure, visualize and interpret the current values of monitored variables in the context of expert-derived knowledge (or some machine learning algorithms). The knowledge, represented in the model (diagnostic, prognostic), was constant in time. Nowadays it becomes more popular to analyze the stream data and refer them to the model that changes (is updated) as new data are coming. This kind of on-line analysis requires also an on-line application of data preparation techniques (replacing missing values, detection of outliers, preprocessing). Our point of interest is a decision support system dedicated to the

© Springer International Publishing Switzerland 2016
L. Rutkowski et al. (Eds.): ICAISC 2016, Part II, LNAI 9693, pp. 73–87, 2016.
DOI: 10.1007/978-3-319-39384-1_7

underground coal mining industry. The input data for this system are multivariate time series. Partially due to the nature of these data and due to the specific environment conditions, these data contain outliers and missing values. Previous works [30] showed that imputation of outliers at the level of 3 % of observations leads to the statistically significant worsening of the prediction accuracy.

The first objective of this paper is to check the effectiveness of methods of outliers identification available in the RapidMiner platform. RapidMiner is the core of the DISESOR decision support system [34]. The system processes stream data and, based on the on-line coming data, makes decisions regarding the predicted natural hazard state (e.g. seismic hazard) and the diagnostic states of machines (e.g. shearer).

Three approaches are presented in the paper. In the first approach the effectiveness of the methods for static datasets was tested. In this approach, all data (except the analyzed example) are available during the analysis. In the second approach, the analysis is based on the increasing — with the inflow of new measurements — dataset. This approach corresponds to the identification of outliers conducted online in a multidimensional time series. Finally, the third method includes the online identification of outliers too but is based on the analysis of the last recorded measurements (i.e. examples in a sliding time window of constant width). The research contributes to find the most efficient outlier identification methods for the data processed by the DISESOR system. In addition, thanks to the undertaken research it was possible to check whether the moving time window method allows to achieve satisfactory accuracy of outliers identification. The paper is organised as follows: next section gives the reader a context of the outlier detection problem, then a short description of works related to the streaming data analysis is presented. Afterwards, a presentation of a real data based time series, used in our experiments, is done, followed by the experiments explanation. The paper ends with some conclusions and perspectives of the further works.

2   Background

We can distinguish three main types of outliers: point outlier, context outlier and collective outlier. A point outlier is a single observation which differs from the data in its neighborhood and is the most intuitive interpretation of definitions presented above. A context outlier deals with the situation when the value of the point seems correct (does not exceed the typical range of values) but its occurrence in time is not typical. It can be observed especially in the time series analysis. Collective outliers are also typical for time series as they represent the situation when a subset of following observations does not behave typically.

A problem of outliers in data is very common in many fields of application of data analysis [24, 36, 40]. Three main approaches of outlier analysis can be found in the literature [26]:

– with no prior knowledge about the data, which is similar to unsupervised clustering,

– modelling the known normality and known abnormality,
– modelling the known normality with very few cases of abnormality.

Generally, two groups of outliers detection algorithms can be mentioned: statistical methods and methods based on spatial proximity.

For one-dimensional data, that have a normal distribution, a simple 3σ criterion can be applied: a value that differs from the mean value by more than three standard deviations is considered an outlying one. For this type of data the appearance of an outlier can be also checked with the Grubb's test [23].

Spatial proximity based methods of outlier detection generally take into consideration one of two distant measures: Euclidean or Mahalanobis. The Euclidean distance is intuitively the distance between k–dimensional objects x and y while the Mahalanobis distance is the distance between the object x and a set of objects, described with a centroid μ.

In the paper [43] a k–NN based approach for outliers is presented: "A point in a dataset is an outlier with respect to parameters k and d if no more than k points in the dataset are at a distance of d or less from p."

A similar idea is presented in [32]: if p of the k nearest neighbors of a data point ($p < k$) are closer than a specified threshold D, then the point is considered a normal one (not an outlier). A simplified version is based only on comparing the distance of the m–th closest neighbor with the threshold D (elimination of the k parameter) presented in [15].

A well known clustering algorithm DBSCAN [19] can also be used for the proximity based detection of outliers. On the basis of the ε–reachability and ε–connectivity it is possible to define a cluster as a subset of points, satisfying the density criterion. The points that do not belong to any cluster are considered a noise or — from the outliers detection point of view — outliers. The problem of data with regions of different points density was solved also in [12,13].

Another approach for finding outliers is called Minimum Volume Ellipsoid Estimation (MVE) [44]. It deals with finding the smallest possible permissible ellipsoid volume containing an assumed (usually 50 %) fraction of data points. The points not covered by the ellipsoid volume are considered outliers.

3   Related Works

The vast majority of current data-intensive applications such as decision support systems, high performance monitoring systems, telecommunications, manufacturing, sensor networks, and many others require appropriate data management and query processing engines. Traditional database management systems are not designed for real-time (hard or soft), rapid as well as continuous loading of individual data items. Moreover, these systems do not have a direct support for the continuous queries, that are needed in data stream applications. In response to these issues, data stream management systems are proposed to support a large class of continuous queries over continuous streams and traditional datasets. Currently, there are several research studies addressing models, methods and techniques in the context of data stream systems. The examples of the most advanced projects in this matter are STREAM [6], Borealis [1], TelegraphCQ [16]. The development of these systems entails the need to elaborate formal abstract semantics for simple continuous queries over streams using declarative, object-oriented or procedural languages. A detailed and comprehensive comparison of data stream management systems and stream query languages can be found in [8] or [55].

Knowledge discovery from data streams is another important field, which has recently attracted much attention. The main challenges taken into consideration by researchers and engineers can be classified into the following categories [2,20]: time series data streams, data stream clustering and classification, frequent pattern mining, change detection in data streams, stream cube analysis of multidimensional streams, sliding window computations and synopsis construction in data streams, dimensionality reduction and forecasting in data streams, distributed mining of data streams. Taking into account only the state of the art in the context of the subject of this paper it can be seen that a problem related to outlier detection in data streams represents a vibrant area of research.

Adaptive Outlier Detection for Data Streams (A-ODDS) is suggested in [46]. A-ODDS identifies outliers with respect to all received or/and temporally close data points. In this paper the authors used a real-life dataset collected from meteorological applications in order to present an efficient and online implementation of the technique. The performance study showed the superiority of A-ODDS over existing techniques in terms of accuracy and execution time.

In the paper [41] an incremental Local Outlier Factor algorithm (LOF) is given. This algorithm provides equivalent detection performance as the iterated static LOF algorithm while requiring significantly less computational time. The authors show experimental results on several synthetic and real-life datasets and indicate that the LOF algorithm can provide additional functionalities such as including detection of new behaviour or identification of masquerading outliers.

The authors of [17] introduced a new cluster-based approach which divides the stream in chunks and clusters, each chunk using k-median into variable number of clusters. Instead of storing a complete data stream chunk in memory the authors proposed to replace it with the weighted medians and to pass that information along with the newly arrived data chunk to the next phase.

Another clustering based framework for outlier detection in evolving data streams is proposed in [52]. This algorithm assigns weights to attributes depending upon their respective relevance. Experiment results show that the method gives a higher outlier detection rate and lower false alarm rate than other existing approaches such as Cluster based OutlieR Miner [18] and Local Outlier Factor [12].

The AnyOut algorithm capable of solving anytime outlier detection problem is introduced in [7]. The algorithm uses a cluster based approach to represent data in a hierarchical fashion. The authors compared their approach with established baseline algorithms finding comparable performance despite the largely reduced runtime.

The main objective of the paper [21] was to present an extensible framework that can be applied to perform a comparison of the state of the art algorithms for continuous outlier detection over data streams using the sliding window approach. In particular, four algorithms have been implemented and compared by the authors: STORM [5], Abstract-C [51], COD, and MCOD [33]. In the paper [42] a review of outlier detection methods over streaming data with data mining perspective is given. The authors discussed the merits and limitations of different outlier detection approaches such as statistical-based, depth-based, distance-based, density-based, cluster-based, sliding window-based and auto regression-based outlier detection methods.

4 Data Description (Underground Atmosphere Monitoring Time Series)

For the experiments of outliers detection a real time series with introduced outliers was used. The time series contains five variables which are real observations, coming from an underground atmosphere monitoring system installed at one of Polish coal mines. These five variables are as follows:

- AN: air flow (in [m/s]),
- MM: methane concentration (in [% CH$_4$]),
- $TP1, TP2$: air temperature (in [°C]),
- BA: air pressure (in [hPa]).

The data come from over 100 h of observations. All data were aggregated into 60 s intervals (originally, raw data were gathered every 2–3 s). Depending on the measuring device a different method of aggregation was applied: minimum (anemometer), maximum (methanometer) or average (thermometers and barometer). Aggregated data were also smoothed with the window of 24 previous observations. The Time series is presented in Fig. 1 and a brief statistical description of its variables is presented in Table 1.

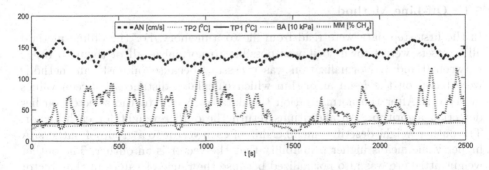

Fig. 1. Five independent time series.

Table 1. A brief statistical description of the considered independent time series.

	AN	MM	$TP1$	$TP2$	BA
min	0.100	0.1000	27.21	23.90	1090
Q_1	1.300	0.3000	28.33	24.68	1101
Q_2	1.400	0.4000	28.80	25.31	1105
$mean$	1.374	0.5048	28.91	25.47	1106
Q_3	1.500	0.6000	29.39	26.06	1109
max	1.800	3.0000	31.10	27.80	1131

5   Research

As it was mentioned before, the experiments were performed in the RapidMiner environment. Four methods of outlier detection were used, which are presented below. The experiments were performed on a set of 100 replications of a real time series. Each replication was made by a noising of original data and contained 5 % of observations modified as a one- or multi-dimensional outlier. Three models of outlier detection were compared:

- all-offline: all data are used for building a model for outlier detection and the model is applied on the same data;
- all-online: an incremental model; assuming a sequence of n observations as initial, starting from the $(n + 1)^{th}$ observation, a classification as an outlier is based on all previous observations (300th observation is checked as an outlier on the basis of 299 previous observations, 400th on the basis of 399 previous ones and so on);
- window-online: assuming a sequence of n observations as initial, starting from the $(n + 1)^{th}$ observation each newcoming observation is checked as an outlier due to the information about exactly n previous observations.

5.1   Off-Line Method

In the first step data were read from file to a memory. For the offline method all datasets were known so it was possible to normalize all of them to range between 0 and 1. Normalization was necessary because (almost) all methods were based on the k–nn algorithm which calculates distances between values in vectors. After the normalization the data were sent to the selected outlier detection algorithm. All algorithms return the outlier weight for each vector. The outlier weight describes membership of each vector to a group of outliers. A higher value means higher probability that the vector is an outlier. The outlier weight attribute was also normalized because the range of values in that vector depends on the values in the regular attributes. All vectors connected with outlier weights higher than the threshold value were considered outliers, the rest of them were assigned into group of regular vectors (Fig. 2).

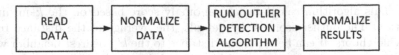

Fig. 2. Outlier detection process created for the all-offline mode

5.2 On-Line Methods

The main difference between online and offline methods was that in online methods vectors were added into the dataset continuously. As a consequence, for each new data vector a new model of outlier detection should be built. The repetition of building the model is called here iteration (Fig. 3).

It was not possible to normalize the whole dataset just before the main part of the process. The considered range of the dataset (connected to the window in single iteration) had to be normalized at the beginning of each iteration of the process. In the online method the authors also used two basic processes which worked similarly to processes described for the offline method. In the first process the window started with an initial number of vectors (e.g. 100) then in each iteration one vector was added into the considered dataset. The analyzed dataset for each iteration was normalized separately and sent to the outlier detection algorithm. The outlier weight calculated for the last vector was copied into the final dataset. In the second method the number of vectors sent to the outlier detection algorithm was always equal to the initial size of window. In each iteration one vector was added and one (the oldest one) was removed.

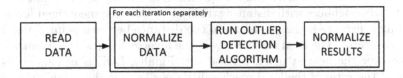

Fig. 3. Outlier detection process created for the all-online/window-online mode

5.3 Algorithms

The following four algorithms — implemented in the RapidMiner environment — were used in our experiments.

CDODE. The Detect Outlier (Densities) is an outlier detection algorithm that calculates the $DB(p, D)$–outliers (which is a short name for Distance-Based outlier detection using parameters p and D) for the given dataset [32]. This algorithm identifies outliers in the given dataset based on the data density. A $DB(p, D)$–outlier is an object which is at least D distance away from at least p proportion of all objects (p is a fraction of number of all objects).

GAS. This algorithm calculates the anomaly score based on the k–nn implementation. The outlier score is, by default, the average of the distance to the nearest neighbors. It can be set to the distance to the kth nearest neighbor which is similar to the algorithm proposed in [43] and does not require user to specify the distance parameter. The outlier score is calculated according to the used measure type. The higher the outlier, the more anomalous the instance.

INFLO. INFLO was introduced in 2006 [27]. This algorithm considers the circumstances when outliers are in the location where neighborhood density distributions are significantly different. For example, in the case of objects close to a denser cluster from a sparse cluster, this may give a wrong result. The algorithm is also based on the nearest neighbors set and considers the symmetric neighborhood relationship. In this approach a notion of the influence space is taken into consideration as a criterion for the object to be the outlier. The influence space considers both neighbors and reverse neighbors of an object. Assign each object in a database a influenced outlierness degree. A higher INFLO means that the object is an outlier. A normal instance has an outlier value of approximately 1, while outliers have values greater than 1.

LOF. LOF is one of the earliest local density based approaches proposed [12]. There are several steps in the calculation of LOF. The initial step involves getting the nearest neighbors set. The definition of the k–distance employed is the one proposed in the original paper in order to handle duplicates. The definition states that the k–distance(p) has at least k neighbors with distinct spatial coordinates that have a distance shorter than a specific limit or equal to it and at most $k - 1$ of such neighbors with distance strictly less than the mentioned level. The reachability distance is the maximum of the distance between point p and o and the k–distance(o). The local reachability is the inverse of the average reachability distance over the nearest neighborhood set. Finally, LOF is calculated as the average of the ratio of the local reachability density over the neighborhood set. The values of LOF oscillate with the change in the size of the neighborhood. Thus a range is defined for the size of the neighborhood. The maximum LOF over that range is taken as the final LOF score. A normal instance has an outlier value of approximately 1, while outliers have values greater than 1.

5.4   Results and Discussion

As it was mentioned earlier, experiments were performed on 100 datasets, derived from the real time series containing measurements from a real environment in an underground coal mining. One-dimensional and multidimensional outliers were introduced into the data with the level of 5 % of modified vectors, whose location was also known.

The experiments were performed in the RapidMiner environment and four mentioned methods of outlier detection were used. All methods return a rank for the object to be an outlier (in the context of the analyzed data). Because the real locations of outliers were known and due to the fact that the real outlier class represented only 5 % of the data (strongly unbalanced data) on AUC value was chosen as a measure for a specific outlier prediction quality. The experiments in the window-online mode were performed with the window length equal to 250 previous observations.

The main goal of the experiments was to check the efficiency of well known outlier detection algorithms, applied in different modes (offline and online). In Table 2 averaged results of 100 experiments for each outlier detection method are presented.

Table 2. Comparison of average AUC values for 100 repetition of data.

Method	An average AUC		
	All-offline	All-online	Window-online
CDODE	0.719	0.734	0.716
GAS	0.848	0.831	0.824
INFLO	0.781	0.803	0.795
LOF	0.855	0.839	0.832

Averaging of one hundred values is not enough to compare specific two algorithms. For the comparison of all-offline and all-online approaches two statistical tests were used: sign test and Wilcoxon's test. A minimal critical number of wins (or losses) for the set of 100 comparisons in the sign test is 60. Results are presented in Table 3.

As it can be observed, a change of the model implies a statistically significant change of the AUC — p-value for Wilcoxon's test takes values close to 0. The number of wins should be interpreted how many times (in 100 experiments) the all-offline method was better (in the terms of AUC) than the all-online. The number of losses points how many times the all-online mode gave better results than the all-offline one. The improvement of outliers detection can be seen in the case of two methods: CDODE and INFLO. The other two methods behave worse when applied in the on-line mode.

A similar detailed comparison was made to check whether the window-online approach is better than the all-online one — results are presented in the Table 4.

Table 3. Comparison of all-offline versus all-online methods of outlier detection.

Method	All-offline vs. All-online	
	Wins/Losses	Wilcoxon p-value
CDODE	38/62	0.011726
GAS	74/26	0.000178
INFLO	37/63	0.000121
LOF	69/31	0.001102

Table 4. Comparison of all-online versus window-online methods of outlier detection.

Method	All-online vs. Window-online	
	Wins/Losses	Wilcoxon p-value
CDODE	67/33	0.001904
GAS	57/43	0.058614
INFLO	58/42	0.063355
LOF	58/42	0.090058

Taking into consideration a sign test only for the CDODE algorithm, it can be clearly stated that the window-online mode gave statistically worse results. But looking at Wilcoxon's test p–values we observe small values for all four methods.

The efficiency of outlier detection methods in stream data could be also connected with the time of calculation. An average time of computation for all modes and four methods is presented in Table 5.

Table 5. Comparison of time of calculations for 100 time series.

Method	Time of calculations [s]		
	All-offline	All-online	Window-online
CDODE	<1	60–100	4–5
GAS	<1	90–100	4–5
INFLO	<1	90–100	4–5
LOF	<1	120–240	13

A very short time of calculations for the all-offline method does not surprise: only one iteration of building a model and its application takes place. Additionally, a difference between all-online and window-online time of calculation is easy to explain: in both approaches the same number of outlier detection models must be built (after any new data comes another iteration of model update must be done), but in the case of the window-online approach a time for building a model is much shorter due to the smaller amount of a data that are used in this process. It is also worth mentioning that the time of model building for the window-online approach will also become stable. In the case of the all-online approach, as the number of collected data increases, the time for building a model increases too.

Because four methods were applied in three modes of outlier detection in incoming data (all-offline, all-online and window-online) it was interesting to compare whether the differences of the methods results are statistically significant. The results of Friedman's test for all three methods point that there are statistically significant differences between different algorithms of outliers detection. Due to this fact the Nemeneyi test was applied. Critical distance diagrams are presented in Fig. 4.

The general conclusion is that the average ranking of all algorithms does not depend on the mode of outlier detection and only between two best algorithms — LOF and GAS — the difference becomes statistically insignificant.

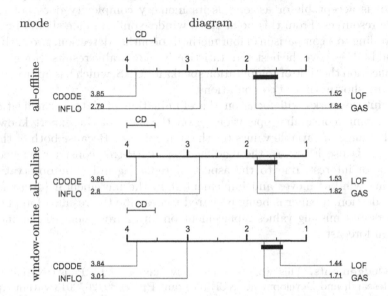

Fig. 4. CD diagrams comparing four outlier detection methods applied in three modes (from up to down): all-offline, all-online and window-online (average AUC criterion rankings on 100 time series)

6   Conclusion and Further Works

In this paper a problem of detecting outliers in the stream data was raised. As the reference point a model — called all-offline, taking into consideration all gathered data and apllied on this data — was examined. For the real application two online approaches were compared: the first one — called all-online — which takes all previously observed objects and the second one — called window-online — which takes into consideration only the constant number of the last observations. For the comparison a set of four algorithms of outlier detection was examined.

Generally, it can be claimed that the methods which take into consideration the all available data give more accurate models of outlier detection than the window-online method. This solution should not be recommended for stream data. As online diagnostic systems require a response in a finite and limited time the increasing time of computation of all-online methods (implied by an increase amount of data that the model is built of) suggest that sliding window models should be taken into consideration. The main advantage applying the window-online mode is a constant time of calculation.

Our recommendation is to merge the all-online and window-online approaches as follows: let us start from the all-online mode of outlier detection and continue as long as the time of building the model for the new data (including the time of outlier replacement and the building of the diagnostic state or a prediction response) is acceptable or as long as its memory complexity does not exceed available resources. From this point the a window-online mode should be used.

According to a comparison of four methods of outlier detection, two of them — GAS and LOF — gave the best and statistically comparable results. However, in a real application the time of computation speaks for GAS, which has approximately three times shorter time of computations.

Our future works will focus on the ellimination of data normalization — what is a time consuming operation — on the basis of the expert knowledge about the range of variable values (or the nameplates). Because both of the two best methods use FP-trees, the modification of FP-tree construction becomes our point of interest, due to the aspect of replacing only one observation as the sliding window moves and implement it in the incremental (decremental) way. In addition, a paper is being prepared to describe the results of application of outliers and missing values replacement on an improvement of classification algorithm forecasts.

Acknowledgements. This work was partially supported by Polish National Centre for Research and Development (NCBiR) grant PBS2/B9/20/2013 within Applied Research Programmes. The infrastructure was supported by "PL-LAB2020" project, contract POIG.02.03.01-00-104/13-00.

References

1. Abadi, D., Carney, D., Çetintemel, U., et al.: Aurora: a new model and architecture for data stream management. VLDB J. **12**(2), 120–139 (2003)
2. Aggarwal, C.: An Introduction to Data Streams. Springer, USA (2007)
3. Aggarwal, C.: Outlier Analysis. Springer, New York (2013)
4. Aggarwal, C., Yu, P.: Outlier detection for high dimensional data. In: Proceedings of ACM SIGMOD International Conference on Management of Data, pp. 37–46 (2001)
5. Angiulli, F., Fassetti, F.: Distance-based outlier queries in data streams: the novel task and algorithms. Data Min. Knowl. Discov. **20**(2), 290–324 (2010)
6. Arvind, A., Brian, B., Shivnath, B., John, C., Keith, I., Rajeev, M., Utkarsh, S., Jennifer, W.: Stream: the stanford data stream management system (2004)
7. Assent, I., Kranen, P., Baldauf, C., Seidl, T.: AnyOut: anytime outlier detection on streaming data. In: Lee, S., Peng, Z., Zhou, X., Moon, Y.-S., Unland, R., Yoo, J. (eds.) DASFAA 2012, Part I. LNCS, vol. 7238, pp. 228–242. Springer, Heidelberg (2012)
8. Babcock, B., Babu, S., Datar, M., Motwani, R., Widom, J.: Models and issues in data stream systems. In: Proceedings of the 21st ACM SIGMOD-SIGACT-SIGART Symposium on Principles of Database Systems, pp. 1–16 (2002)

9. Barkow, S., Bleuler, S., Prelić, A., Zimmermann, P., Zitzler, E.: BicAT: a biclustering analysis toolbox. Bioinformatics **22**(10), 1282–1283 (2006)
10. Barnett, V., Lewis, T.: Outliers in Statistical Data. Wiley, New York (1994)
11. Basu, S., Meckesheimer, M.: Automatic outlier detection for time series: an appli-
    cation to sensor data. Knowl. Inf. Syst. **11**(2), 137–154 (2007)
12. Breunig, M., Kriegel, H.-P., Ng, R., Sander, J.: LOF: identifying density-based local
    outliers. In: Proceedings of ACM SIGMOD International Conference on Manage-
    ment of Data, pp. 93–104 (2000)
13. Breunig, M.M., Kriegel, H.-P., Ng, R.T., Sander, J.: OPTICS-OF: identifying local
    outliers. In: Żytkow, J.M., Rauch, J. (eds.) PKDD 1999. LNCS (LNAI), vol. 1704,
    pp. 262–270. Springer, Heidelberg (1999)
14. Bu, Y., Leung, T.-W., Fu, A., et al.: WAT: finding top-K discords in time series
    database. In: Proceedings of the 2007 SIAM International Conference on Data
    Mining (2007)
15. Byers, S., Raftery, A.: Nearest-neighbor clutter removal for estimating features in
    spatial point processes. J. Am. Stat. Assoc. **93**(442), 577–584 (1988)
16. Chandrasekaran, S., Cooper, O., Deshpande, A., et al.: TelegraphCQ: continuous
    dataflow processing. In: Proceedings of the 2003 ACM SIGMOD International
    Conference on Management of Data, pp. 668–668 (2003)
17. Dhaliwal, P., Bhatia, M., Bansal, P.: A cluster-based approach for outlier detection
    in dynamic data streams (KORM: k-median OutlieR miner). J. Comput. **2**(2), 74–
    80 (2010)
18. Elahi, M., Li, K., Nisar, W., et al.: Efficient clustering-based outlier detection
    algorithm for dynamic data stream. In: 5th International Conference on Fuzzy
    Systems and Knowledge, Discovery, pp. 298–304 (2008)
19. Ester, M., Kriegel, H.-P., Sander, J., Xu, X.: A density-based algorithm for discov-
    ering clusters in large spatial databases with noise. In: Proceedings of the Second
    International Conference on Knowledge Discovery and Data Mining, pp. 226–231
    (1996)
20. Gama, J.: Knowledge Discovery from Data Streams. Chapman and Hall/CRC,
    Boca Raton (2010)
21. Georgiadis, D., Kontaki, M., Gounaris, A., et al.: Continuous outlier detection in
    data streams: an extensible framework and state-of-the-art algorithms. In: Pro-
    ceedings of ACM SIGMOD International Conference on Management of Data, pp.
    1061–1064 (2013)
22. Grubbs, F.: Procedures for detecting outlying observations in samples. Technomet-
    rics **11**(1), 1–21 (1969)
23. Grubbs, F.: Sample criteria for testing outlying observations. Ann. Math. Stat.
    21(1), 27–58 (1950)
24. Gupta, M., Gao, J., Aggarwal, C., Han, J.: Outlier detection for temporal data: a
    survey. IEEE Trans. Knowl. Data Eng. **26**(9), 2250–2267 (2014)
25. Hawkins, D.: Identification of Outliers. Springer, Netherlands (1980)
26. Hodge, V., Austin, J.: A survey of outlier detection methodologies. Artif. Intell.
    Rev. **22**(2), 85–126 (2004)
27. Jin, W., Tung, A.K.H., Han, J., Wang, W.: Ranking outliers using symmetric
    neighborhood relationship. In: Ng, W.-K., Kitsuregawa, M., Li, J., Chang, K. (eds.)
    PAKDD 2006. LNCS (LNAI), vol. 3918, pp. 577–593. Springer, Heidelberg (2006)
28. John, G.: Robust decision trees: removing outliers from databases. In: Knowledge
    Discovery and Data Mining, pp. 174–179. AAAI Press (1995)

29. Johnson, T., Kwok, I., Ng, R.: Fast computation of 2-dimensional depth contours. In: International Conference on Knowledge Discovery and Data Mining, pp. 224–228 (1998)
30. Kalisch, M., Michalak, M., Sikora, M., Wróbel, Ł., Przystałka, P.: Influence of outliers introduction on predictive models quality. Comm. Comp. Inf. Sci. (2016, to appear)
31. Keogh, E., Lin, J., Fu, A.: HOT SAX: efficiently finding the most unusual time series subsequence. In: Fifth IEEE International Conference on Data Mining (2005)
32. Knorr, E., Ng, R.: Algorithms for mining distance-based outliers in large datasets. In: Proceedings of the 24rd International Conference on Very Large Data Bases, pp. 392–403 (1998)
33. Kontaki, M., Gounaris, A., Papadopoulos, A., et al.: Continuous monitoring of distance-based outliers over data streams. In: IEEE International Conference on Data Engineering, pp. 135–146 (2011)
34. Kozielski, M., Sikora, M., Wróbel, Ł.: DISESOR - decision support system for mining industry. Ann. Comput. Sci. Inf. Syst. **5**, 67–74 (2015)
35. Kriegel, H.P., Schubert, M., Zimek, A.: Angle-based outlier detection in high-dimensional data. In: Proceedings of the 14th ACM SIGKDD International Conference on Knowledge Discovery and Data Mining, pp. 444–452 (2008)
36. Kuna, H., Garcia-Martinez, R., Villatoro, F.: Outlier detection in audit logs for application systems. Inf. Syst. **44**, 22–33 (2014)
37. Le, N., Martin, R., Raftery, A.: Modeling flat stretches, time series using mixture transition distribution models. J. Am. Stat. Assoc. **91**(436), 1504–1515 (1996)
38. Ma, J., Perkins, S.: Online novelty detection on temporal sequences. In: Proceedings of 9th SIGKDD International Conference on Knowledge Discovery and Data Mining, pp. 613–618 (2003)
39. Nag, A., Mitra, A., Mitra, S.: Multiple outlier detection in multivariate data using self-organizing maps title. Comput. Stat. **20**(2), 245–264 (2005)
40. Orzechowski, P., Boryczko, K.: Parallel approach for visual clustering of protein databases. Comput. Inf. **29**(6), 1221–1231 (2010)
41. Pokrajac, D., Lazarevic, A., Latecki, L.J.: Incremental local outlier detection for data streams. In: IEEE Symposium on Computational Intelligence and Data Mining, pp. 504–515 (2007)
42. Prakash, C., Prashant, C.: Outlier detection techniques over streaming data in data mining: a research perspective. Int. J. Recent Technol. Eng. **1**(2), 157–162 (2013)
43. Ramaswamy, S., Rastogi, R., Shim, K.: Efficient algorithms for mining outliers from large data sets. In: Proceedings of ACM SIGMOD International Conference on Management of Data, pp. 427–438 (2000)
44. Rousseeuw, P.: Multivariate estimation with high breakdown point. In: Mathematical Statistics and Applications (Vol. B). Reidel, Dordrecht (1985)
45. Ruts, I., Rousseeuw, P.: Computing depth contours of bivariate point clouds. Comput. Stat. Data Anal. **23**(1), 153–168 (1996)
46. Sadik, S., Gruenwald, L.: Online outlier detection for data streams. In: Proceedings of the 15th Symposium on International Database Engineering and Applications, pp. 88–96 (2011)
47. Schölkopf, B., Williamson, R., Smola, A., et al.: Support vector method for novelty detection. Adv. Neural Inf. Process. Syst. **12**, 582–588 (2000)

48. Shekhar, S., Lu, C.-T., Zhang, P.: Detecting graph-based spatial outliers: algorithms and applications (a summary of results). In: Proceedings of the Seventh ACM SIGKDD International Conference on Knowledge Discovery and Data Mining, pp. 371–376 (2001)
49. Torr, P., Murray, D.: Outlier detection and motion segmentation. In: Proceedings of SPIE, vol. 2059, pp. 432–443 (1993)
50. Tukey, J.: Exploratory Data Analysis. Addison-Wesley Publishing Company, Reading (1977)
51. Yang, D., Rundensteiner, E., Ward, M.: Neighbor-based pattern detection for windows over streaming data. In: Proceedings of the 12th International Conference on Extending Database Technology: Advances in Database Technology, pp. 529–540 (2009)
52. Yogita, T., Toshniwal, D.: A framework for outlier detection in evolving data streams by weighting attributes in clustering. Procedia Technol. **6**, 214–222 (2012)
53. Wei, L., Keogh, E., Xi, X.: SAXually explicit images: finding unusual shapes. In: Sixth International Conference on Data Mining, pp. 711–720 (2006)
54. Weisberg, S.: Applied Linear Regression. Wiley, Hoboken (2005)
55. Widera, M., Kozielski, S.: Strumieniowe systemy zarządzania danymi - przegląd rozwiązań (in Polish), in: Bazy danych. Modele, technologie, narzędzia. [Vol. 1]: Architektura, metody formalne, bezpieczeństwo, 257–266, WKŁ (2005)

Towards Feature Selection for Appearance Models in Solar Event Tracking

Dustin J. Kempton$^{(\boxtimes)}$, Michael A. Schuh, and Rafal A. Angryk

Department of Computer Science, Georgia State University,
P.O. Box 5060, Atlanta, GA 30302-5060, USA
{dkempton1,mschuh,angryk}@cs.gsu.edu

Abstract. Classification of solar event detections into two classes, of either the same object at a later time or an entirely different object, plays a significant role in multiple hypothesis solar event tracking. Many features for this task are produced when images from multiple wavelengths are used and compounded when multiple image parameters are extracted from each of these observations coming from NASA's Solar Dynamics Observatory. Furthermore, each different event type may require different sets of features to accurately accomplish this task. A feature selection algorithm is required to identify important features extracted from the available images and that can do so without a high computational cost. This work investigates the use of a simple feature subset selection method based on the ANOVA F-Statistic measure as a means of ranking the extracted image parameters in various wavelengths. We show that the feature subsets that are obtained through selecting the top K features ranked in this manner produce classification results as good or better than more complicated methods based on searching the feature subset space for maximum-relevance and minimum-redundancy. We intend for the results of this work to lay the foundations of future work towards a robust model of appearance to be used in the tracking of solar phenomena.

1 Introduction

In February 2010, NASA launched the Solar Dynamics Observatory (SDO), the first mission of NASA's Living with a Star program, which is a long term project dedicated to the study of the Sun and its impacts on human life. The SDO mission is an invaluable instrument for space weather monitoring, which can have great impacts on space and air travel, power grids, GPS, and communications satellites. Prior to the launch of the SDO mission, a multi-institutional team called the Feature Finding Team (FFT) began work on software modules to process SDO's Atmospheric Imaging Assembly (AIA) images, and generate object data with spatiotemporal characteristics. These module-reported objects are of solar phenomena (events) that are of great interest to the solar physics research community. As such, the object data is directly reported to the Heliophysics Event Knowledge base (HEK) [6], and is available to the general public

© Springer International Publishing Switzerland 2016
L. Rutkowski et al. (Eds.): ICAISC 2016, Part II, LNAI 9693, pp. 88–101, 2016.
DOI: 10.1007/978-3-319-39384-1_8

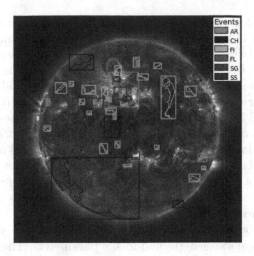

Fig. 1. An image from the SDO mission, with labeled solar phenomena coming from HEK overlaid. Labels include: (AR) Active Region, (CH) Coronal Hole, (FI) Filament, (FL) Flare, (SG) Sigmoid, and (SS) Sunspot. Image reproduced with permission of [13].

through the online iSolSearch graphical interface[1]. An example of both the image data and the object data can be seen in Fig. 1. Some of the reported events can be seen in the wavelength being displayed, like Active Regions, while others are only visible in other wavelengths, like Sun Spots.

There are approximately 70,000 high resolution (4,096 by 4,096 pixel) AIA images reported daily, with one image obtained every ten seconds [9]. This high rate of data reporting makes having human examination of every image in detail for new and interesting solar phenomena untenable. To aid the search for new and interesting solar phenomena, research of a system for content-based image retrieval is currently under development. In some of the prior work done in this area by [2,3], sets of image parameters were extracted, and Table 1 lists these parameters. These parameters were chosen because of their ability to be quickly calculated and their demonstrated usefulness on images of similar composition, such as medical x-rays.

For similar reason as the development of CBIR, a tracking algorithm was developed in [7,8] to facilitate the spatiotemporal analysis of the data reported to the HEK by the FFT modules. In the tracking algorithm, individually reported object detections are linked into sets of object detection reports called tracks. Their research utilized the image parameters extracted as part of the CBIR system, and one of the crucial components of such tracking algorithms is an appearance model that is able to discriminate among different targets.

The process of tracking multiple objects in video data, commonly referred to as multiple hypothesis tracking, is a difficult and only partially solved problem in computer vision. The problem can be broken into two independent steps that

---

[1] https://www.lmsal.com/isolsearch.

address separate issues of the overall problem [4]. The first of these steps is the detection of targets in each frame of the video data, and is independent of any knowledge of time, which is what the FFT software modules accomplish and report to the HEK. In the second step of multiple hypothesis tracking, targets are linked into the most likely trajectories based on some model of likelihood.

In the search for the most likely target trajectories, the likelihood of detections being linked is based on a cost function that incorporates several different aspects of similarity of potential detections. In the previous work done by [8], this likelihood function incorporated similarity of trajectory movement and appearance, among other factors. Our work is complementary to the work done in [8], in that we describe a method of selecting a subset of the image wavelengths and extracted image parameters for comparing object detections and selecting the most likely trajectories.

The main contribution of this work is to find a method of feature subset selection for a set of image wavelengths and image parameters. The selected features should show promising results when attempting to differentiate between detections that are the same tracked object at a later period in time and a completely different tracked object. The feature subset selection method should also be a relatively inexpensive operation that does not require an exhaustive search of all combinations of image parameters across several wavelengths, because detection differentiation accuracy may benefit from selecting features periodically as the sun goes through its solar cycle. By utilizing the information discovered here, we are determined to build an object appearance model to improve the results of the tracking work done by [7,8].

The remainder of this paper is organized as follows, Sect. 2 describes the different feature selection algorithms tested. In Sect. 3 we will provide an overview of the data we utilize from NASA's Solar Dynamic Observatory (SDO) mission, describe how we assess the features found by each algorithm, and then discuss the results. Finally, in Sect. 4, we conclude our discussion with our vision of future research.

2   Feature Selection

In the task of differentiating between detections of the same object at a later time and detections of differing objects, identifying the most characterizing features of the observed data, i.e., feature selection, is a critical step that is used to select a subset of the input for use in classification. There are numerous advantages to utilizing feature selection, some of which include: (1) the reduction of the number of dimensions in the problem and hence reduction of the computational cost of classification; (2) reducing noise in the input data and subsequently increasing classification accuracy. Given the input data D as a set of N samples and M features $X = \{x_i, i = 1, \ldots, M\}$, and the target classification variable c, the problem of feature selection is that of finding from the $M - dimensional$ observation space, $\Re^M$, a subspace of m features, $\Re^m$, which "optimally" characterize c, and with $m \ll M$ [11].

In general, there are two approaches to feature selection: filters and wrappers [5]. In the filter type of feature selection, features are selected based upon some intrinsic characteristic of the feature that determines its power to discriminate between the targeted classes. One such method is to use a simple statistical test such as the ANOVA F-test. This type of selection has an advantage of being relatively easy to compute and that the characteristics are uncorrelated to the learning methods that will be applied to the data, which leads to better generalization. In the wrapper type of feature selection, the selection of features is "wrapped" around some learning method and the features usefulness is directly evaluated by the estimated accuracy of the learning method. However, this method generally entails significant computational cost in the search for an optimal set of features.

In the following subsections we describe three different feature selection methods that we evaluate in this paper. The first is a simple filter type that selects the Top-K features based upon some ranking criteria. The second method is a hybrid filter and wrapper method that first utilizes the ranking of features and then utilizes a learning method to evaluate the addition of each ranked result. Finally, the third method is a more complex filter type that again utilizes the same ranking of features that the first two do, but then also uses a measure of redundancy of the features to exclude some of the ranked results.

2.1 Top-K Rank

In this filter method of feature selection, we select the K top-ranked features, where the ranking method looks to order the features by their relevance to the target class c. Here we have chosen the F-Statistic between the features and the classification variable as the scoring method used for the ordering of features. In this, the F-Statistic of feature x_i in P classes denoted by c is as follows:

$$F(x_i, c) = \frac{\sum_j^P n_j(\bar{x}_{ij} - \bar{x}_i)^2/(P-1)}{\sigma^2} \tag{1}$$

where $\bar{x}_i$ is the mean value of feature x_i across all classes, $\bar{x}_{ij}$ is the mean value of x_i within the jth class, n_j is number of samples of x_i within in the jth class, P is the number of classes, and

$$\sigma = [\sum_j^P (n_j - 1)\sigma_j^2]/(n - P) \tag{2}$$

is the pooled variance across all classes (where σ_j is the variance of x_i within the jth class) [5]. Using the value returned by the F-Statistic as the relevance of the tested feature, we order the features by descending value and choose the Top-K.

2.2   Top-K Forward Selection

This method combines both the filter and wrapper methods of feature selection. The steps of this method are as follows:

1. Rank features by F-Stat as was done in $Top - K$ method
2. Evaluate classification accuracy of top ranked feature
3. Add next highest ranked feature to the subset and evaluate accuracy
4. If accuracy increases, keep the feature in the subset and remove it otherwise
5. If we reach the number of features we want, then stop, otherwise repeat starting from step 3.

This selective addition method evaluates the classification accuracy of the feature subset by using a Naïve Bayes' classifier as a simple learning method wrapper.

2.3   Top-K Redundancy Limiting Forward Selection

This method is similar to the previous method in that feature subset $\bar{X}_i$ is obtained by adding the next highest ranked feature not already attempted, from the ranked list of all features, to the feature subset $\bar{X}_{i-1}$, and the resultant feature set $\bar{X}_i$ is evaluated using some selection criteria. However, instead of utilizing a learning method and evaluating if the addition increases classification accuracy as the selection criteria, this method utilizes a redundancy limiting condition. The redundancy value is calculated using the Pearson's correlation coefficient $cor(x_i, x_j)$ as follows:

$$R_i = \frac{1}{(|\bar{X}_i| * (|\bar{X}_i| + 1))/2} \sum_{i,j} |cor(x_i, x_j)| \tag{3}$$

where $|cor(i,j)|$ is the absolute value of the Pearson's correlation coefficient between the ith and j^{th} feature. The feature added to subset $\bar{X}_i$, at each step, is kept if it does not increase the redundancy (R_i) of the feature subset by some threshold amount, say 5 % over the redundancy R_{i-1} of the previous set $\bar{X}_{i-1}$.

3   Experiments

3.1   Data

The data used in this work was created by combining multiple parts, the first of which is a set of image parameters calculated on raster image data, which is described in the next subsection. The second part of our dataset is the detected objects that are instances of Active Regions and Coronal Holes produced by the SPoCA-suite [15]. This suite operates in the framework of the Feature Finding Team project [9], to extract these detections from AIA images in the 193Å Extreme UltraViolet (EUV) wavelength, and uploads the found detections every four hours to the HEK [6].

The two event types, Active Region and Coronal Hole, were used because of the tracking information generated by the SPoCA detection module that we use as ground truth to determine which detections are of the same object at a later time and detections of another object all together. We obtained tracked detections of both Active Regions and Coronal Holes from January 2012 to December 2013 and separated them into their subsequent one month date ranges. The tracked detections that were obtained were from work done in [8] and contain tracking information from the original SPoCA detection module.

Raster Data-Image Parameters. The images used in this work are the extracted image parameters from the original full resolution 4096 by 4096 pixel images returned from the SDO AIA instrument. As was mentioned in Sect. 1, the parameters were originally evaluated for use in solar content-based image retrieval of full-disk images in [3,10], and were later shown to be useful in identifying similar regions of SDO AIA images in [2]. These pre-calculated parameters were later made available in [13], which was then extended to encompass a larger date range in [12] and made available online[2]. The labels used in this text, names, and equations can be seen in Table 1.

The image parameters are calculated by dividing each 4096 by 4096 pixel image into 64 by 64 pixel cells, and applying each of the formulas in Table 1 to the resultant area. The calculated value for each of the cells are used to construct histograms from the cells intersecting an object detection. The image parameter extraction process effectively reduces the full-resolution images to 10 sets of 64 by 64 cell raster images, for each wavelength image coming from the SDO AIA instrument. There are 9 wavelengths that we can utilize; 94Å, 131Å, 171Å, 193Å, 211Å, 304Å, 335Å, 1600Å, and 1700Å. In total, this gives 90 different possible choices of image parameter and wavelength to use in feature value calculation.

Vector Data: Event Reports. The vector data that we received contains the following pieces of information:

- *Identifier:* a unique identifier for this detection report.
- *Time Stamp:* the reported starting time of the detection report.
- *Center Point:* the reported center of the detection report.
- *Minimum Bounding Rectangle:* a set of five points that produces the minimum sized rectangle that encompasses the detected object.
- *Boundary Polygon:* a set of points that constitute the polygon representation of the boundary of the detected object.
- *Next Detection Identifier:* the unique identifier of the next detection in the same set of object detections that make up the tracked object set, if such an detection report exists. Otherwise this field is empty.

These objects are in Helioprojective Cartesian (HPC) coordinate system, which was converted to a pixel-based coordinate system, so that the detections coordinates corresponded with the proper location on the raster data.

---

[2] http://dmlab.cs.montana.edu/solar/.

Table 1. Image parameters, where L stands for the number of pixels in the cell, z_i is the intensity value of the i-th pixel, m is the mean, and $p(z_i)$ is the histogram value of intensity value z_i. The fractal dimension is calculated on the box-counting method where $N(\varepsilon)$ is the number of boxes of side length ε required to cover the image cell.

Label	Name	Equation
P1	Entropy	$E = -\sum\limits_{i=0}^{L-1} p(z_i)log_2 p(z_i)$
P2	Mean	$m = \frac{1}{L}\sum\limits_{i=0}^{L-1} z_i$
P3	Std. Deviation	$\sigma = \sqrt{\frac{1}{L}\sum\limits_{i=0}^{L-1}(z_i - m)^2}$
P4	Fractal Dim.	$D_0 = -\lim\limits_{\varepsilon\to 0}\left(\frac{logN(\varepsilon)}{log(\varepsilon)}\right)$
P5	Skewness	$\mu_3 = \sum\limits_{i=0}^{L-1}(z_i - m)^3 p(z_i)$
P6	Kurtosis	$\mu_4 = \sum\limits_{i=0}^{L-1}(z_i - m)^4 p(z_i)$
P7	Uniformity	$U = \sum\limits_{i=0}^{L-1} p^2(z_i)$
P8	Rel. Smoothness	$R = 1 - \frac{1}{1+\sigma_2(z)}$
P9	T. Contrast	see [14]
P10	T. Directionality	see [14]

3.2   Feature Extraction and Feature Ranking

Each instance of an event report contains several cells of an image parameter inside its boundary. In order to compare two event reports and get a feature value, we extract a 20 bin histogram of the cells that fall within the bounding box of an event report and repeat this for both reports. We then compare these histograms using a common histogram comparison method and use the resultant value of the comparisons as our feature value. In the case of feature ranking we use the histogram intersection as the feature value, where we define intersection as the sum of the minimum bin count between the two histograms being compared or:

$$d(H_1, H_2) = \sum_{I}^{N} min(H_1(I), H_2(I)) \tag{4}$$

Where $H_k(I)$ is the value of the histogram bin at index I of N bins in histogram k. This was chosen as an approximation of the amount of mutual information between the two histograms and was found to generalize the best for ranking through trying several different comparison methods. This histogram construction and comparison is done for each of the image parameters that were described in Sect. 3.1 which are selected using the feature selection methods described in Sect. 2.

In the feature ranking process, we utilized each of the tracked objects from one month that have more than one detection in their trajectory and used each temporally sequential pair in these trajectories as a comparison point belonging to the same object class. We also took the first detection of each of these pairs and compared them to another detection from the data set that was known to be from another trajectory. These comparisons were then labeled as being in the different object class. This process results in a balanced 50/50 split between the two classes. It is these sets that were used in the three feature ranking processes described in Sect. 2.

To ensure that feature ranking was not biased by the month that we selected as the ranking data, we repeated the ranking of the features in several different months. In repeating the ranking, we saw that the top 10 ranked features stayed within the top 20 ranking and generally moved by only a few positions. We also saw that the top ranked feature for each event type generally stayed in the top 3 positions across all the tested months.

3.3 Experimental Framework

We asses classification performance using the "Leave-One-Out Cross Validation" (LOOCV) method. In order to perform the cross validation, we took the 24 months of data that we had available and set one month aside for testing, while training on the remaining 23. In the training process, we used a similar feature extraction method of comparing histograms from the same trajectory and different trajectories as was used in the ranking process. However, we use 23 months of training data in our evaluations instead of the one month that was used in ranking. In the task of classification, we consider an object to be classified properly if the classifier gives the detection from the same tracked object a higher probability of being in the class it belongs than its partner selected from the other class. This choice is based on the fact that, in the tracking algorithm of [8], the path a tracked object takes is affected more by this difference than by whether the object from the same path is more strongly associated with the incorrect class than it is with the correct one.

In our experimental evaluation, histogram distances were evaluated by the Bhattacharyya coefficient instead of the histogram intersection that was used in ranking. The Bhattacharyya coefficient is an approximate measure of the amount of overlap between two statistical samples which approximates the chi-square measure statistic for small distances. However, the Bhattacharyya coefficient does not have the drawback of infinite values arising when comparing empty histograms as can happen with the chi-squared statistic [1]. The use of this coefficient in experimental evaluation was included to show that the wavelength and parameter pair features obtained from the selection methods are effective features regardless of feature comparison method.

In the experiments, we compare the Top-K ranking selection method against the wrapper method of Top-K Forward Selection and the redundancy limiting selection method of Top-K Redundancy Limiting Forward Selection. The selected features are fed to a Naïve Bayes' classifier and tested against the testing month. We average the classification accuracy in each of the 24 months in the dataset. The distribution of the classification accuracy for each of the 24 months is displayed in the boxplots of Fig. 6.

3.4   Results

We include Fig. 2 to show how the F-Stat values for each of the features compares to the rest of the features in our dataset. As can be seen from the charts, the top 10 to 20 features indicate a significant separation of features values between the two classes, while the latter features are not as cleanly separated. We also include the top 10 ranked features for each event type in Table 2. In this table, it can be seen that the features of most importance, as determined by F-Stat ranking, are from wavelengths that are not used in the detection of these solar phenomena. For instance, the wavelength that is used in the detection of these phenomena (193Å) does not show up in the ranking until the 8th or 9th position in the list. This may indicate some heretofore unrecognized information about these event types contained in wavelengths other than those used for detection of these particular event types.

In Figs. 3, 4 and 5 we display the progression of our three feature selection methods when we do not limit the number of features they return. The feature numbers range from 1 to 90 and are ordered in their ranked order of descending F-Stat value, though not all features are selected in all methods. Whenever a feature is not selected by a method the score from the previously selected feature is copied to the location in the chart representing the non-selected feature.

Figure 3 displays the sum of the average redundancy in each class as calculate by Eq. 3, in this case we have two classes. As can be seen from the charts, the Top-K selection method ramps up to a maximum around 20 features, which indicates there is a not insignificant amount of redundancy between the first 20 features. This redundancy average then begins to decline indicating that the

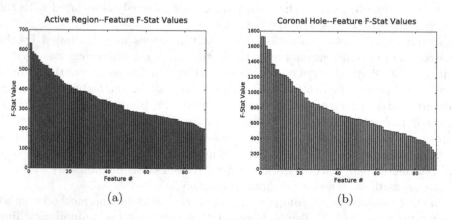

Fig. 2. (a) Active Regions, (b) Coronal Holes: F-Stat values of all 90 features ordered by their F-Stat value.

Table 2. Top 10 ranked wavelength/parameter pairs for Active Regions and Coronal Holes using F-Stat values.

Parameter #	Active Regions		Coronal Holes	
	Wave	Param	Wave	Param
1	1600Å	P2	1600Å	P2
2	1700Å	P3	1700Å	P2
3	1600Å	P3	1600Å	P3
4	211Å	P2	1700Å	P3
5	1700Å	P2	304Å	P2
6	335Å	P5	335Å	P2
7	335Å	P8	211Å	P2
8	1700Å	P1	193Å	P2
9	193Å	P2	131Å	P2
10	335Å	P1	171Å	P2

latter features do not include significant redundancy with the previously added features. It can also be seen that the Accuracy Search method does not add all of the first 20 features and hence limits the total amount of redundancy in the selected feature set. Similarly, the Redundancy Limit method does as is intended and limits the redundancy in the selected feature set by only adding features that do not significantly increase the total redundancy among the selected features.

In Fig. 4, we display the average relevancy of the selected features in the feature set returned by the various selection methods. The average is the average of the F-Stat as calculated by Eq. 1 for each selected feature. As can be seen from the charts, the Accuracy Search method tends to keep the overall relevancy higher than the other two methods. This is not unexpected as it would be sensible

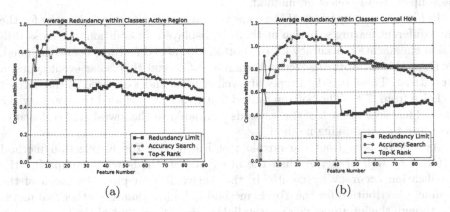

(a)   (b)

Fig. 3. (a) for Active Regions, (b) for Coronal Holes: Average Redundancy per feature selected within classes as measured by Eq. 3

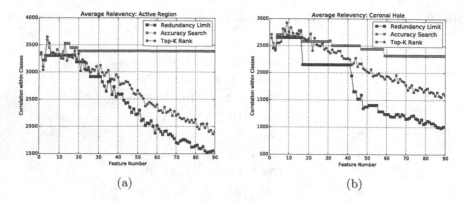

Fig. 4. (a) for Active Regions, (b) for Coronal Holes: Average Relevancy per feature selected where relevancy is the F-Stat value of Eq. 1.

to expect that the most relevant features would also be those that produce the best classification results. Similarly, in the Redundancy Limit method, the overall relevancy is lower than the other two methods due to the exclusion of the more relevant but more redundant features of higher rank.

In Fig. 5, with both Active Regions and Coronal Holes, we see the classification accuracy rise quickly in the first 10 features and then plateaus after about 20 features. This is true for all three selection methods even though the Redundancy Limit and Accuracy Search methods don't add every feature in the first 20. For instance, the Redundancy Limit method only adds less than 10 of the first 40 features of Coronal holes as it is trying to keep the added redundancy low. By doing so it also limits the most relevant features and hence leads to a lower classification accuracy. Similarly, the Accuracy Search method only adds 10 of the first 20 features and then no other features are added from the rest of the dataset as they don't increase the accuracy of classification within the ranking month. This too leads to lower accuracy of classification when compared to the simpler Top-K selection method.

In Fig. 6 the comparison of the cross validation classification accuracy for the three different feature selection methods is displayed. In addition, the cross validation classification accuracy for the bottom 20 ranked features is also included. We show this for both the Active Region and Coronal Hole solar event types in our dataset. These two data types are well studied and were used as the dataset of choice from [7,8]. The bottom ranked features were included to show how the selected features by each of the methods compared to the lowest ranked features according to our ranking method.

As can be seen from the boxplots of Fig. 6, the Top-K selection method performs as well or better than the other two methods when comparing the classification accuracy by month. In the Active Region plot, the mean of the accuracy distribution for the Top-K method is higher than the other two methods, though the interquartile range is slightly more than that of the Redundancy Limit method. Similarly for the Coronal Hole plot, the mean is higher on the Top-K method though the interquartile range is slightly larger than that of the Accuracy Search method.

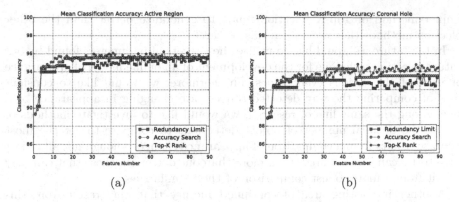

(a)   (b)

Fig. 5. (a) for **Active Regions**, (b) for **Coronal Holes**: Mean classification accuracy percentage for month after selection month.

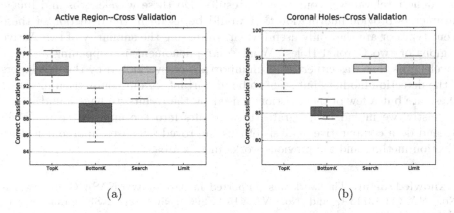

(a)   (b)

Fig. 6. (a) **Active Regions**, (b) **Coronal Holes**: Cross validation accuracy for all 24 months of data. **TopK** uses top 20 features selected with the Top-K method. **BottomK** uses the bottom 20 features selected with Top-K method just ranked in reverse order. **Search** uses the search method to select up to 20 features. **Limit** uses the limit method to select up to 20 features.

4   Conclusion and Future Work

The results of these experiments allowed us to show that a reasonable level of accuracy in classifying two detections as being either the same tracked object or a different tracked object can be achieved with a subset of the dimensionality reducing image parameters made available in previous research on content-based image retrieval. We also show that we can arrive at a suitable combination of image parameters from various wavelengths by using a simple feature subset selection method of ranking on the F-Statistic value. The observations that we found when evaluating the ranking position across several months, coupled with the results seen in the classification task, lead us to the conclusion that the simpler method of Top-K selection tends to generalize better than the other selection methods that we used in this research.

In the future we would like to utilize the subsets of parameters found by our feature selection technique for the development of an online model of appearance for each of the various event types. Furthermore, we would like to consider ways of comparing the way detected objects are changing in appearance over time. Along the same line of research, we would like to investigate methods of finding the optimal number of object detections to compare to get the most accurate results from a comparison of appearance change. Though not all object trajectories can be compared using more than one detection, those that can may benefit from a more robust comparison of their similarities.

Another interesting area of continued inquiry that may result from this research is to investigate the unexpected results of wavelengths previously thought to be unrelated to Active Region and Coronal Hole comparison showing the highest relevancy in our ranking results. Do these wavelengths and image parameters provide information that would be useful in the detection of these event types or are they only useful when comparing the similarity of two Active Regions or two Coronal Holes? What solar phenomena is happening at these wavelengths that was either ruled unimportant or overlooked by the developers of the detection modules but seem to be important for our comparison method? These are but a few of the questions raised by the results we have found.

Lastly, we intend to integrate these results into the appearance model in [8], and do a comparative analysis of this improved set based upon our feature selection method and the previous works in this area.

Acknowledgment. This work was supported in part by two NASA Grant Awards (No. $NNX11AM13A$, and No. $NNX15AF39G$), and one NSF Grant Award (No. AC1443061).

References

1. Aherne, F.J., Thacker, N.A., Rockett, P.I.: The Bhattacharyya metric as an absolute similarity measure for frequency coded data. Kybernetika **34**(4), 363–368 (1998). http://eudml.org/doc/33362
2. Banda, J., Liu, C., Angryk, R.: Region-based querying of solar data using descriptor signatures. In: 2013 IEEE 13th International Conference on Data Mining Workshops (ICDMW), pp. 1–7, December 2013. http://dx.doi.org/10.1109/ICDMW.2013.127
3. Banda, J., Angryk, R.: An experimental evaluation of popular image parameters for monochromatic solar image categorization. In: 2010 Twenty-Third FLAIRS Conference, pp. 380–385, May 2010
4. Berclaz, J., Fleuret, F., Fua, P.: Multiple object tracking using flow linear programming. In: 2009 Twelfth IEEE International Workshop on Performance Evaluation of Tracking and Surveillance (PETS-Winter), pp. 1–8, December 2009. http://dx.doi.org/10.1109/PETS-WINTER.2009.5399488

5. Ding, C., Peng, H.: Minimum redundancy feature selection from microarray gene expression data. In: Proceedings of the 2003 IEEE Bioinformatics Conference, CSB 2003, pp. 523–528, August 2003. http://dx.doi.org/10.1109/CSB.2003.1227396

6. Hurlburt, N., Cheung, M., Schrijver, C., Chang, L., Freeland, S., Green, S., Heck, C., Jaffey, A., Kobashi, A., Schiff, D., Serafin, J., Seguin, R., Slater, G., Somani, A., Timmons, R.: Heliophysics event knowledge base for the solar dynamics observatory (sdo) and beyond. In: Chamberlin, P., Thompson, B. (eds.) The Solar Dynamics Observatory, pp. 67–78. Springer, US (2012). http://dx.doi.org/10.1007/978-1-4614-3673-7_5

7. Kempton, D., Pillai, K., Angryk, R.: Iterative refinement of multiple targets tracking of solar events. In: 2014 IEEE International Conference on Big Data (Big Data), pp. 36–44, October 2014. http://dx.doi.org/10.1109/BigData.2014.7004402

8. Kempton, D., Angryk, R.: Tracking solar events through iterative refinement. Astron. Comput. **13**, 124–135 (2015). http://dx.doi.org/10.1016/j.ascom.2015.10.005

9. Martens, P., Attrill, G., Davey, A., Engell, A., Farid, S., Grigis, P., Kasper, J., Korreck, K., Saar, S., Savcheva, A., Su, Y., Testa, P., Wills-Davey, M., Bernasconi, P., Raouafi, N.E., Delouille, V., Hochedez, J., Cirtain, J., DeForest, C., Angryk, R., De Moortel, I., Wiegelmann, T., Georgoulis, M., McAteer, R., Timmons, R.: Computer vision for the solar dynamics observatory (sdo). Sol. Phys. **275**(1–2), 79–113 (2012). http://dx.doi.org/10.1007/s11207-010-9697-y

10. McInerney, P., Banda, J., Angryk, R.: On using sift descriptors for image parameter evaluation. In: 2013 IEEE 13th International Conference on Data Mining Workshops (ICDMW), pp. 32–39, December 2013. http://dx.doi.org/10.1109/ICDMW.2013.123

11. Peng, H., Long, F., Ding, C.: Feature selection based on mutual information criteria of max-dependency, max-relevance, and min-redundancy. IEEE Trans. Pattern Anal. Mach. Intell. **27**(8), 1226–1238 (2005). http://dx.doi.org/10.1109/TPAMI.2005.159

12. Schuh, M., Angryk, R.: Massive labeled solar image data benchmarks for automated feature recognition. In: 2014 IEEE International Conference on Big Data (Big Data), pp. 53–60, October 2014. http://dx.doi.org/10.1109/BigData.2014.7004404

13. Schuh, M., Angryk, R., Pillai, K., Banda, J., Martens, P.: A large-scale solar image dataset with labeled event regions. In: 2013 20th IEEE International Conference on Image Processing (ICIP), pp. 4349–4353, September 2013. http://dx.doi.org/10.1109/ICIP.2013.6738896

14. Tamura, H., Mori, S., Yamawaki, T.: Textural features corresponding to visual perception. IEEE Trans. Syst. Man Cybern. B Cybern. **8**(6), 460–473 (1978). http://dx.doi.org/10.1109/TSMC.1978.4309999

15. Verbeeck, C., Delouille, V., Mampaey, B., De Visscher, R.: The spoca-suite: software for extraction, characterization, and tracking of active regions andcoronal holes on euv images. Astron. Astrophys. **561**, A29 (2014). http://dx.doi.org/10.1051/0004-6361/201321243

Text Mining with Hybrid Biclustering Algorithms

Patryk Orzechowski[1]([⊠]) and Krzysztof Boryczko[2]

[1] Department of Automatics and Bioengineering,
AGH University of Science and Technology,
Mickiewicza Av. 30, 30-059 Cracow, Poland
patrick@agh.edu.pl
[2] Department of Computer Science,
AGH University of Science and Technology,
Mickiewicza Av. 30, 30-059 Cracow, Poland
boryczko@agh.edu.pl

Abstract. Text data mining is the process of extracting valuable information from a dataset consisting of text documents. Popular clustering algorithms do not allow detection of the same words appearing in multiple documents. Instead, they discover general similarity of such documents. This article presents the application of a hybrid biclustering algorithm for text mining documents collected from Twitter and symbolic analysis of knowledge spreadsheets. The proposed method automatically reveals words appearing together in multiple texts. The proposed approach is compared to some of the most recognized clustering algorithms and shows the advantage of biclustering over clustering in text mining. Finally, the method is confronted with other biclustering methods in the task of classification.

1 Introduction

Finding similarity between documents enables grouping documents in collections, possibly contributing to significant reduction of database query time [32]. Common clustering techniques such as hierarchical clustering, k-means, shared nearest neighbours or deep learning networks are capable of detecting similarities within texts based on the comparison of the words used [12,18,19,27,30]. Nonetheless, the majority of the studies aim at classification, wherein the documents are assigned into fully separated clusters. Whilst the usefulness of such an approach is unquestionable, the content of many documents may cover multiple subjects, thus the issues raised within each document should not be restricted to merely a single cluster. This justifies the formation of other types of algorithms for text mining, with analogical representation in the field of clustering: soft or fuzzy clustering [9,29].

Extracting keywords from particular documents and comparing them with similar ones provides means for aggregation of knowledge regarding the content. One of the popular data mining techniques intended to detect local similarities

© Springer International Publishing Switzerland 2016
L. Rutkowski et al. (Eds.): ICAISC 2016, Part II, LNAI 9693, pp. 102–113, 2016.
DOI: 10.1007/978-3-319-39384-1_9

within the dataset is biclustering (also called co-clustering). Biclustering algorithms, as opposed to classic clustering approaches, take into account rows and columns of the input matrix simultaneously. Some biclustering methods have been successfully applied for text classification [4,10,17,23]. Various biclustering methods have also gained recognition in multiple domains, such as biology and biomedicine, genetics, marketing and text mining [3,13,20,22].

In this article we propose the application of a newly developed hybrid biclustering technique for mining text datasets. We present the Propagation-Based Biclustering Algorithm (PBBA) and the scope of its application towards different types of text datasets. By analysing the content of documents collected from a popular social network, Twitter (i.e. tweets), we compare the proposed approach with the most popular clustering methods popularly used for this task. We also present the application of the algorithm to knowledge spreadsheets in symbolic datasets. Finally, using the example of a popular 20 newsgroup dataset, the algorithm is compared to other state-of-the-art text mining methods in a scenario that lies beyond its design, namely a classification task. The low effectiveness of the proposed approach with regard to this task is discussed.

2   Methodology

Hybrid methods emerged from combining selected aspects of some other existing methods, which allow them to be applied for different types of data. Those methods make use of the techniques, structures or metrics used by other algorithms. The final result provided by a hybrid solution is determined as a combination or aggregation of its components obtained during the process of its execution. Another distinct feature of hybrid algorithms is their broader scope of application. For example, the approach presented herein has been already successfully applied not only to text data, but also to gene expression datasets [28], symbolic datasets, analysis of production data and many other uses.

2.1   Algorithm

The hybrid biclustering algorithm presented here, named the Propagation-Based Biclustering Algorithm (PBBA), has already been successfully applied to various biological datasets [26,28]. The PBBA mechanism inspired by neural networks and associative artificial intelligence [14,15] originates from two biclustering methods: Bimax [31] and xMotifs [24].

Bimax. The Bimax algorithm [31] is a fast divide-and-conquer approach developed for binary data biclustering (in other cases the data needs to be binarized with a given threshold). The algorithm locates all inclusion-maximal biclusters within a given input matrix by dividing rows and columns of the matrix into three smaller submatrices, one of which contains only zeros and may be disregarded in further iterations. Afterwards, the algorithm is applied recursively to the two remaining, possibly overlapping submatrices.

xMotifs. The motivation of the xMotifs algorithm [24] was to provide a representation for gene expression data. An xMotif is an acronym for a conserved gene expression motif. Taking text mining into consideration, this could be a distinct analogy to determining a set of words to characterize each document. Biclusters (or xMotifs) generated with this algorithm need to fulfil a minimum size (here: number of documents), conservation (analogous to the same number of occurrences of any given term) and maximality criteria (analogy of maximum number of terms common with a given xMotif that remains outside the bicluster).

Artificial Associative Intelligence. Artificial associative systems are designed to contextually recall and combine separate pieces of information to form knowledge in a process which resembles recalling information by a human [15]. The neural graphs on which the systems are based, consist of elements which react separately depending on the repeatability and frequency of their input signals triggered by sequences of objects (facts, rules, algorithms etc.).

Propagation-Based Biclustering Algorithm (PBBA). The PBBA algorithm iterates the consecutive rows and seeds non-zero values in each row [26, 28]. The pattern created hereby serves to discover similar rows sharing at least one common value in column with the pattern. Subsets with seed row are detected by finding the nearest row with the exact value appearing in the particular column. A special mechanism is carried out to prevent the creation of non-maximum subsets. A general concept of the algorithm is presented in Fig. 1.

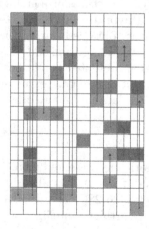

Fig. 1. The mechanism of PBBA - for each row, the algorithm seeks for the nearest row with the same value in a particular column.

Detailed information about the algorithm is presented hereafter. Similarly to Bimax, a minimum size of biclusters needs to be specified, otherwise PBBA (similarly to Bimax) may generate millions of overlapping biclusters. The modifications of the original version of PBBA involved ranking of the input matrix. The cardinality of the terms appearing in each document served as a basis for determining the ranks within the input matrix for the algorithm.

Algorithm 1. Propagation-based biclustering algorithm (PBBA)

---

procedure PBBA(matrix A)
  $M_{all} \leftarrow \emptyset$ ▷ set with all biclusters
  $R_{all} \leftarrow \emptyset$ ▷ set with restricted motifs
  for $i \leftarrow n \ldots 1$ **do**   ▷ set each row as seed
    $M_i \leftarrow \emptyset$ ▷ store all biclusters common with i-th pattern
    $M_i \leftarrow$ insert($M_i, R_i, B(i, A_{i*})$)   ▷ add seed to retrieved biclusters
    $mask \leftarrow A_{i*}$ ▷ propagate the motif to further rows
    $\{lev, pat\} \leftarrow$ next_level($mask$)
    while $pat \neq \emptyset$ **do**   ▷ proceed through all rows similar to $seed$
      $M_i \leftarrow$ insert($M_i, R_i, B(lev \cup i, pat)$)   ▷ intersect lev with M_i
      $R_{lev} \leftarrow R_{lev} \cup \{pat\}$ ▷ forbid addition of any subset of pat
      $mask(\{j : mask(j) = lev\}) \leftarrow v(mask(j))$ ▷ proceed to next row
      $\{lev, pat\} \leftarrow$ next_level($mask$)
    end while
    $M_{all} \leftarrow M_{all} \cup M_i$;
  end for
  print(M_{all})
end procedure

---

3   Results

This section presents the results of algorithm application to various datasets. The PBBA algorithm has been implemented in C++. Three different scenarios have been carried out. First, the algorithm has been applied to the data obtained from Twitter[1] to measure its performance in discovering commonly appearing phrases within tweets. Two clustering methods have been used as references: k-means and hierarchical clustering. Secondly, the algorithm has been applied to a knowledge spreadsheet of US consumer complaints and finally to a 20 newsgroups dataset, which is popularly used for the task of classification.

3.1   Scenario 1: Application to Social Network Data

Tweets are short, up to 140 characters, text messages that are sent by the users of one of the most popular social networks, Twitter. Twitter was queried for 50000 entries containing the "#data" tag published since 2000-01-01. All the data was collected on 2015-04-21. As a result, a total of 44394 documents has been collected. The most common terms (appearing in at least 600 tweets) with *wordcloud* package [8], as presented in Fig. 2.

The data was obtained with *twitteR* package [11], an R-based Twitter client, and processed with text mining (*tm*) package [6,7]. The preprocessing involved removing links, usernames, "RT" (used as an abbreviation of "retweet") and symbols ("&" etc.). All sentences were transformed to lower case. All English stop words were removed ("he's", "we'd" etc.), punctuation and white spaces

---

[1] twitter.com.

Fig. 2. The wordcloud of the most common terms appearing in Tweets together with the #data tag.

were ignored. Limits on the size of a tweet may cause tweets to be cut at the end of the message. Therefore, the additional removal considered the case of beginning of an unfinished link ("htt") at the end of the tweet. Finally, all the words of at least 3 letters were used to form a document-term matrix. *SnowballC* package [1] was used for stemming words. The statistics for words that appeared at least 1000 times in the database are presented in Fig. 3.

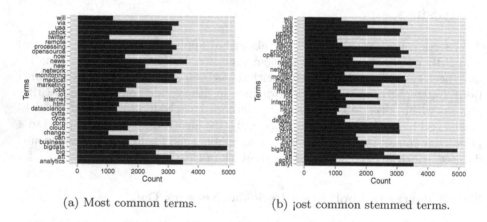

(a) Most common terms.   (b) ¡ost common stemmed terms.

Fig. 3. Most common terms appearing in tweets with the #data tag.

As the majority of words appeared only in a few tweets, sparse terms were removed from the matrix. Notice that the term-document matrix has not been sparsified as in [35] as that produced incorrect results. Terms were accepted with at least 0.1 % non-zero values across all documents. As a result, the original matrix shrank to 1290 terms and contained 301659 out of 406716 values. The stemmed matrix featured 1238 terms and 323410 non-zero values.

The PBBA was set to detect terms that appeared in at least 10 different tweets. At least two terms needed to appear in the same tweet. The input matrix for the PBBA contained words and their occurrences in the text, forming a document-term matrix with zeroes indicating lack of term in a document. The effect of stemming the words has been also presented.

Task 1: All Tweets. The PBBA algorithm detected 11036 biclusters in total for the non-stemmed dataset and 14576 biclusters for the stemmed dataset. The statistics of most common terms appearing in the same tweet with the #data tag for the stemmed and not stemmed datasets are presented in Table 1.

Table 1. Text biclusters detected by PBBA for the Twitter dataset - the most common terms used in the same tweet for (a) not stemmed and (b) stemmed dataset. Difference in occurrences of terms is the result of merging words with the same root.

Tweets	Terms in the same tweet	Tweets	Terms in the same tweet
4828	bigdata data	4828	bigdata data
3575	data news	3575	data news
3345	data network	3460	data network
3260	data processing	3352	data process
3257	data medical	3261	data medic

(a) Not stemmed dataset   (b) Stemmed dataset

For both datasets, twenty of the most popular terms used in the tweets had the same roots. This indicates that the most popular terms appear in the vast majority of the tweets in their exact form. A slight difference may be noticed within the "processing-process" term, which is considered the same phrase in the stemmed database.

Task 2: Unique Tweets. The second scenario involved biclustering on unique tweets only. We filtered documents that have not been retweeted and those which had the same content. Thus, the size of the dataset was reduced to 17083 for non-stemmed and 17594 for stemmed terms. The procedure applied guaranteed that each tweet or retweet with the same content was counted once only.

All word associations presented in Table 2 are commonly used together. This makes PBBA an interesting choice for the analysis of the common data within different documents. On the other hand, the sensitivity of PBBA for variants of similar words could also be considered as the curse of the algorithm, as all tweets that differ by one word only would result in generation of other bicluster(s).

Comparison with K-means. To determining the optimum number of clusters, we adapted a technique described by Hothorn [16] explained hereafter. After normalizing the data, we tested different numbers of clusters (from 2 to 200) and plotted the within-group sum of squares for each partition. As k-means require setting a random seed, the results obtained in multiple runs of the algorithm

Table 2. Text biclusters detected by PBBA for unique tweets - the most common terms used in the same tweet for (a) not stemmed and (b) stemmed dataset. Notice that different terms occurred the most often in each of cases.

Tweets	Terms in the same tweet
1495	data via
1490	bigdata data
1382	analytics data
1097	data jobs
940	big data

(a) Not stemmed dataset

Tweets	Terms in the same tweet
1519	data via
1501	bigdata data
1423	analyt data
1337	data job
996	data market

(b) Stemmed dataset

were different. Nonetheless, in all scenarios taken into account the WCSS measure reached very high values. We concluded that no consensus on the optimum setting of the number of clusters for k-means may be reached. Thus, we decided to take into consideration 42 clusters for stemmed and non-stemmed data. The results of clustering with k-means are presented in Table 3. We selected a couple of the most repetitive terms, sorted in decreasing order, similarly to Zhao [35], to serve as representative for the tweets.

Table 3. Example clusters for Twitter obtained with k-means, for (a) non-stemmed and (b) stemmed dataset.

Tweets	Terms in the same tweet
28279	data via analytics new
4444	bigdata data analytics datascience
3070	cyca opensource remote uptick
1052	html gamedev appdev internet
739	apply now jobs looking

(a) Non-stemmed dataset

Tweets	Terms in the same tweet
24980	data via analyt new
4077	bigdata analyt data datasci
3070	cyca opensourc remot uptick
1625	use data via bigdata
1387	job now appli hire

(b) Stemmed dataset

Clustering in multiple cases revealed one large cluster (with over half of the tweets from the dataset), a couple of smaller clusters (with a couple of hundreds of tweets) and multiple small clusters. Clustering performed fine if the whole content of the tweet was exact. This was the issue with one of commonly retweeted contents. PBBA easily managed to detect commonly used phrases and built biclusters of different sizes around them.

Comparison with Hierarchical Clustering. We compared the results from PBBA and k-means with those obtained from clustering using Hierarchical Clustering. After removing terms that had over 98 % and 99 % of sparsity, the remaining 96 terms (117 in case of the stemmed dataset) were normalized and divided into 20 different clusters with original Ward's minimum variance criterion used to form spherical clusters [25]. Hierarchical clustering managed to find some connotations of the words between different tweets. It detected a couple of meaningful clusters, such as "jobs apply now" and "change enter", or "html internet", but also a meaningless "news network medical processing monitoring att opensource usa remote cytta cyca uptick". The majority of terms fell into multiple one-term-size clusters or into a single big cluster with non-related values. Different levels of threshold didn't change that. In all cases, "data" formed its own cluster.

3.2   Scenario 2: Symbolic Datasets

One of the very popular types of datasets operating on symbolic representations of structures instead of using numeric data only is called knowledge spreadsheet for symbolic computing [33]. In this particular domain, the semantics determine the symbolic relations between the structures.

An example of a symbolic dataset is the consumer complaint database[2] collected on 2015-07-22. It contains 409400 consumer complaints regarding financial products and the current status of the cases. It covers the product name, sub-product, company name, US state, information if the answer has been delivered on time and whether the customer was satisfied with it.

In this scenario, as each symbolic expression may be substituted by a number, PBBA allows us to discover inner logic behind the dataset. An exemplary advanced analysis difficult to perform on a pivot table is presented in Table 4. The analysis concerns the most popular response to a complaint and its punctuality for different companies. Thus, biclusters with at least 3 columns containing the product name, company name and the response timeliness have been considered.

Table 4. The most popular responses to complaints and their punctuality for individual companies

Bicluster size	Product	Company	Timely response
23493×3	Mortgage	Bank of America	No
14614×3	Mortgage	Wells fargo	No
11879×3	Mortgage	Ocwen	No
9769×3	Mortgage	JPMorgan chase	No
7738×3	Mortgage	Bank of America	Yes
6863×3	Mortgage	Nationstar mortgage	No

Analysis of the PBBA results offers an easy way to get a valuable insight into different structures within the data. For example, the majority of untimely responses that ended up with explanations concerned mortgages (84131 cases),

---

[2] catalog.data.gov/dataset/consumer-complaint-database.

debt collection (35881 cases) and credit reporting (26174 cases). Comparing the responses that were given on time, the majority of them concerned mortgages (28289 cases), debt collection (10137 cases) and bank accounts or services (6823 cases). The most popular state for complaints on mortgages that ended with explanations was California (CA), covering 20926 cases, out of which in 14773 cases the answer was outside and 5179 within time limitations (some of the cases are still under consideration). The next states were Florida (FL) with 10075 cases and New York (NY) with 4959 cases. Depending on the desired query, a different logic behind the dataset may be discovered.

3.3   Scenario 3: Classification of a 20 Newsgroups Dataset

The third scenario involves the application of the algorithm to the task of classification. A very popular 20 newsgroups dataset[3] has been used as a reference. This database contains set of almost 20000 articles collected from 20 different groups, some of which are very closely related to each other. For comparison, a database from Hussain et al. [17] has been taken, provided by Grimal[4]. The dataset is divided into 6 separate subsets: M2 (500 documents and 2 clusters), M5 (500 documents, 5 clusters), M10 (500 documents and 10 clusters), NG1 (400 documents and 2 clusters), NG2 (1000 documents and 5 clusters) and NG3 (1600 documents and 8 clusters). Each subset contains 10 folds with documents selected randomly using the k-medoids algorithm [17].

In concordance with other studies, micro-average precision was used for assessing the PBBA effectiveness [5]. The PBBA algorithm has been run on each fold of the dataset. In each case, PBBA has generated multiple overlapping biclusters. Including the smallest sizes of the biclusters caused PBBA to perform excessively long computations and generate as many as millions of small biclusters. On the other hand, disregarding the smallest biclusters meant that multiple documents have not been included in any of the biclusters. In this cas, we have decided to match them with an artificial empty class and treat as false positives. As the number of biclusters in PBBA is unknown beforehand, the bicluster matching a specific class the most has been considered as the right one.

For each dataset taken into considerations, the results obtained with PBBA have been unsatisfactory. Even for the theoretically easiest task (M2), the micro-average precision of PBBA was around 0.1, far below the results presented in literature. Modifying the PBBA parameters for the minimum bicluster size did not increase the score, as the level of misclassified documents went up.

We conclude that the PBBA algorithm is unsuitable for performing hard classification of text datasets Chi-sim [17] or other co-clustering methods are far more suitable for this task.

---

[3] http://www.qwone.com/~jason/20Newsgroups/.
[4] membres-lig.imag.fr/grimal/code/XSim.tar.gz.

4   Conclusions

Providing personalized content to users, such as recommendations, increases user involvement with a service. These days, personalized recommendation systems [21] or contextual advertising systems [2,34] match users with the service content. With a high dose of probability, this functionality is already implemented in Twitter, as users are recommended to follow certain people. We assume that recommendations utilizes context similarity.

This paper presents the concept of hybrid biclustering algorithms. Those are methods combining selected techniques from existing solutions. The major advantage of hybrid biclustering algorithms is the broader area of their application. Using the example of PBBA, we proved that the said algorithms may provide an insight into textual data. Analysis of common terms with biclustering detected much more realistic word connotations compared with clustering. This was particularly visible when considering unique tweets. Thus, the technique may be applied to dividing documents into multiple overlapping groups based on their content.

We noticed that term stemming may further increase the accuracy of the results obtained. For the stemmed dataset, PBBA managed to detect biclusters of larger size. This proves that the stemming provides better compression of data as terms originating from the same word are merged together. It should be noted, however, that multiple tweets in our dataset were not written in English. Therefore, stemming analysis becomes much more susceptible to errors.

Analysis of symbolic datasets in knowledge spreadsheets proved that a hybrid biclustering algorithm may successfully retrieve statistical information from a given dataset. This includes the information regarding the most commonly co-appearing values in a dataset. This application of the algorithm resembles aspect filtering or pivot tables.

A classification task revealed the algorithm weakness, involving generating multiple overlapping biclusters. PBBA failed to provide a correct division in each of the subsets of a 20 newsgroups dataset. Nonetheless, the criterion was very rigorous. Perhaps developing a mechanism of merging biclusters could increase the algorithm performance. Nonetheless, it is doubtful whether such a technique may outperform state of the art methods.

Acknowledgments. This research was funded by the Polish National Science Center (NCN), grant No. 2013/11/N/ST6/03204. This research was supported in part by PL-Grid Infrastructure.

References

1. Bouchet-Valat, M.: SnowballC: Snowball stemmers based on the C libstemmer UTF-8 library (2014). http://CRAN.R-project.org/package=SnowballC. r package version 0.5.1

2. Broder, A., Fontoura, M., Josifovski, V., Riedel, L.: A semantic approach to contextual advertising. In: Proceedings of the 30th Annual International ACM SIGIR Conference on Research and Development in Information Retrieval, pp. 559–566. ACM (2007)

3. Busygin, S., Prokopyev, O., Pardalos, P.M.: Biclustering in data mining. Comput. Oper. Res. **35**(9), 2964–2987 (2008)

4. de Castro, P.A.D., de França, F.O., Ferreira, H.M., Von Zuben, F.J.: Applying biclustering to text mining: an immune-inspired approach. In: de Castro, L.N., Von Zuben, F.J., Knidel, H. (eds.) ICARIS 2007. LNCS, vol. 4628, pp. 83–94. Springer, Heidelberg (2007). http://dl.acm.org/citation.cfm?id=1776274.1776284

5. Dhillon, I.S., Mallela, S., Modha, D.S.: Information-theoretic co-clustering. In: Proceedings of the Ninth ACM SIGKDD International Conference on Knowledge Discovery and Data Mining, pp. 89–98. ACM (2003)

6. Feinerer, I., Hornik, K.: tm: Text Mining Package (2014). http://CRAN.R-project.org/package=tm. r package version 0.6

7. Feinerer, I., Hornik, K., Meyer, D.: Text mining infrastructure in r. J. Stat. Softw. **25**(5), 1–54 (2008). http://www.jstatsoft.org/v25/i05/

8. Fellows, I.: wordcloud: Word Clouds (2014). http://CRAN.R-project.org/package=wordcloud. r package version 2.5

9. Filippone, M., Masulli, F., Rovetta, S., Mitra, S., Banka, H.: Possibilistic approach to biclustering: an application to oligonucleotide microarray data analysis. In: Priami, C. (ed.) CMSB 2006. LNCS (LNBI), vol. 4210, pp. 312–322. Springer, Heidelberg (2006)

10. Franca, F.O.D.: Scalable Overlapping Co-clustering of Word-Document Data, pp. 464–467. IEEE (2012). http://ieeexplore.ieee.org/lpdocs/epic03/wrapper.htm?arnumber=6406666

11. Gentry, J.: twitteR: R Based Twitter Client (2015). http://CRAN.R-project.org/package=twitteR. r package version 1.1.8

12. Hartigan, J.A., Wong, M.A.: Algorithm as 136: a k-means clustering algorithm. Appl. Stat. **28**, 100–108 (1979)

13. Henriques, R., Madeira, S.: Biclustering with flexible plaid models to unravel interactions between biological processes. IEEE/ACM Trans. Comput. Biol. Bioinf. **PP**(99), 1–1 (2015)

14. Horzyk, A.: Information freedom and associative artificial intelligence. In: Rutkowski, L., Korytkowski, M., Scherer, R., Tadeusiewicz, R., Zadeh, L.A., Zurada, J.M. (eds.) ICAISC 2012, Part I. LNCS, vol. 7267, pp. 81–89. Springer, Heidelberg (2012). http://dx.doi.org/10.1007/978-3-642-29347-4_10

15. Horzyk, A.: How does human-like knowledge come into being in artificial associative systems?. In: Proceedings of the 8-th International Conference on Knowledge, Information and Creativity Support Systems, Krakow, Poland (2013)

16. Hothorn, T., Everitt, B.S.: A Handbook of Statistical Analyses using R, 3rd edn. Chapman and Hall/CRC, Boca Raton (2014)

17. Hussain, S.F., Bisson, G., Grimal, C.: An improved co-similarity measure for document clustering. In: Proceedings of the 2010 Ninth International Conference on Machine Learning and Applications, ICMLA 2010, pp. 190–197 (2010). http://dx.doi.org/10.1109/ICMLA.2010.35

18. Jain, A.K.: Data clustering: 50 years beyond k-means. Pattern Recogn. Lett. **31**(8), 651–666 (2010)

19. Jiang, Z., Li, L., Huang, D., Jin, L.: Training word embeddings for deep learning in biomedical text mining tasks. In: 2015 IEEE International Conference on Bioinformatics and Biomedicine (BIBM), pp. 625–628. IEEE (2015)

20. Kaiser, S.: Biclustering: Methods, Software and Application. Ph.D. thesis, Ludwig-Maximilians-Universitt Mnchen (2011)
21. Liang, T.P., Lai, H.J., Ku, Y.C.: Personalized content recommendation and user satisfaction: theoretical synthesis and empirical findings. J. Manag. Inf. Syst. **23**(3), 45–70 (2006)
22. Madeira, S.C., Oliveira, A.L.: Biclustering algorithms for biological data analysis: a survey. IEEE/ACM Trans. Comput. Biol. Bioinf. **1**(1), 24–45 (2004)
23. Mimaroglu, S., Uehara, K.: Bit sequences and biclustering of text documents. In: icdmw, pp. 51–56. IEEE (2007)
24. Murali, T., Kasif, S.: Extracting conserved gene expression motifs from gene expression data. Proc. Pacific Symp. Biocomputing **3**, 77–88 (2003)
25. Murtagh, F., Legendre, P.: Wards hierarchical agglomerative clusteringmethod: which algorithms implement wards criterion? J. Classif. **31**(3), 274–295 (2014)
26. Orzechowski, P., Boryczko, K.: Propagation-based biclustering algorithm for extracting inclusion-maximal motifs. Computing and Informatics (2016), in print
27. Orzechowski, P., Boryczko, K.: Parallel approach for visual clustering of protein databases. Comput. Inform. **29**(6+), 1221–1231 (2010). http://www.cai.sk/ojs/index.php/cai/article/view/140
28. Orzechowski, P., Boryczko, K.: Hybrid biclustering algorithms for data mining. In: Squillero, G., Burelli, P. (eds.) EvoApplications 2016. LNCS, vol. 9597, pp. 156–168. Springer, Heidelberg (2016). doi:10.1007/978-3-319-31204-0_11
29. Peters, G., Crespo, F., Lingras, P., Weber, R.: Soft clustering fuzzy and rough approaches and their extensions and derivatives. Int. J. Approximate Reasoning **54**(2), 307–322 (2013). http://www.sciencedirect.com/science/article/pii/S0888613X12001739
30. Poikolainen, I., Neri, F., Caraffini, F.: Cluster-based population initialization for differential evolution frameworks. Inf. Sci. **297**, 216–235 (2015)
31. Prelić, A., Bleuler, S., Zimmermann, P., Wille, A., Bühlmann, P., Gruissem, W., Hennig, L., Thiele, L., Zitzler, E.: A systematic comparison and evaluation of biclustering methods for gene expression data. Bioinformatics **22**(9), 1122–1129 (2006)
32. Steinbach, M., Karypis, G., Kumar, V., et al.: A comparison of document clustering techniques. In: KDD Workshop on Text Mining, vol. 400, Boston, MA, pp. 525–526 (2000)
33. Travers, M., Paley, S.M., Shrager, J., Holland, T.A., Karp, P.D.: Groups: knowledge spreadsheets for symbolic biocomputing. Database 2013, bat061 (2013)
34. Zhang, K., Katona, Z.: Contextual advertising. Mark. Sci. **31**(6), 980–994 (2012)
35. Zhao, Y.: R and Data mining: examples and case studies. Elsevier Science (2012). http://books.google.com.au/books?id=FEOh08LBD9UC

A Modification of the Silhouette Index for the Improvement of Cluster Validity Assessment

Artur Starczewski[1(✉)] and Adam Krzyżak[2,3]

[1] Institute of Computational Intelligence, Częstochowa University of Technology,
Al. Armii Krajowej 36, 42-200 Częstochowa, Poland
artur.starczewski@iisi.pcz.pl
[2] Department of Computer Science and Software Engineering,
Concordia University, Montreal, Canada
krzyzak@cs.concordia.ca
[3] Department of Electrical Engineering,
Westpomeranian University of Technology, 70-313 Szczecin, Poland

Abstract. In this paper a modification of the well-known *Silhouette* validity index is proposed. This index, which can be considered a measure of the data set partitioning accuracy, enjoys significant popularity and is often used by researchers. The proposed modification involves using an additional component in the original index. This approach improves performance of the index and provides better results during a clustering process, especially when changes of cluster separability are big. The new version of the index is called the *SILA* index and its maximum value identifies the best clustering scheme. The performance of the new index is demonstrated for several data sets, where the popular algorithm has been applied as underlying clustering techniques, namely the *Complete-linkage* algorithm. The results prove superiority of the new approach as compared to the original *Silhouette* validity index.

Keywords: Clustering · Cluster validity · Silhouette index

1 Introduction

Clustering allows partitioning of data into homogeneous subsets (called clusters), inside which elements are similar to each other while being different from items in other groups. It is also called unsupervised learning or unsupervised classification. Nowadays, a large number of clustering algorithms exist that have found use in various fields such as data mining, bioinformatics, exploration data, etc. Clustering methods can be applied to designing neural networks and neuro-fuzzy systems [2–10,16–18,30–32,37,44]. However, the results of clustering algorithms are

A. Krzyżak carried out this research at WUT during his sabbatical leave from Concordia University.

© Springer International Publishing Switzerland 2016
L. Rutkowski et al. (Eds.): ICAISC 2016, Part II, LNAI 9693, pp. 114–124, 2016.
DOI: 10.1007/978-3-319-39384-1_10

strongly dependent on the right choice of input parameters. Hence, for the same data but for different input parameters a clustering algorithm can produce different results. It should be noted that the number of clusters is significant input parameter of many clustering algorithms, which is often selected in advance. Thus, the key issue is how to properly evaluate results of data clustering. In the literature on the subject, three main techniques are used to evaluate partitioning of data sets, and they include external, internal or relative approaches [13,38]. The relative methods are very popular and widely used by researchers. In this approach a clustering algorithm provides data partitioning for different values of input parameters and next partitioning schemes are compared to find the best results. For this purpose cluster validity indices are used. A great number of such indices have been introduced so far, e.g., [1,11,12,14,22,39,40,45–47].

In this paper, a cluster validity index called the *SILA* index being a modification of the *Silhouette* index is proposed. This modification allows us to improve the index performance. Notice that the *Silhouette* index is often used by many researchers to evaluate clustering results. Unfortunately, in some cases it fails to detect correct partitioning of data sets. A detailed explanation of this problem is presented in Sect. 2. The proposed *SILA* index contains a component which corrects the index value when changes of cluster separability are considerable during a partitioning process (see Eq. (10)). In order to present the effectiveness of the new validity index several experiments were performed for various data sets. This paper is organized as follows: Sect. 2 presents the *Silhouette* index and detailed description of its properties. Section 3 describes a new validity index, which is a modification of the Silhouette index. Section 4 illustrates experimental results on artificial and real-life data sets. Finally, Sect. 5 presents conclusions.

2   Description of the Silhouette Index

Let us denote K-partition scheme of a data set X by $C = \{C_1, C, ..., C_K\}$, where C_k indicates k_{th} cluster, $k = 1, .., K$. Moreover, a mean of within-cluster distances, named $a(\mathbf{x})$, is defined as the average distance between a pattern $\mathbf{x}$ which belongs to C_k and the rest of patterns $\mathbf{x}_k$ also belonging to this cluster, such that

$$a(\mathbf{x}) = \frac{1}{n_k - 1} \sum_{\mathbf{x}_k \in C_k} d(\mathbf{x}, \mathbf{x}_k) \tag{1}$$

where n_k is the number of patterns in C_k and $d(\mathbf{x}, \mathbf{x}_k)$ is a function of the distance between $\mathbf{x}$ and $\mathbf{x}_k$. Furthermore, the mean of distances of $\mathbf{x}$ to the other patterns $\mathbf{x}_l$ belonging to the cluster C_l, where $l = 1, ..., K$ and $l \neq k$, can be written as:

$$\delta(\mathbf{x}, \mathbf{x}_l) = \frac{1}{n_l} \sum_{\mathbf{x}_l \in C_l} d(\mathbf{x}, \mathbf{x}_l) \tag{2}$$

where n_l is the number of patterns in C_l. Thus, the smallest distance $\delta(\mathbf{x}, \mathbf{x}_l)$ can be defined as:

$$b(\mathbf{x}) = \min_{\substack{l,k=1 \\ l \neq k}}^{K} \delta(\mathbf{x}, \mathbf{x}_l) \tag{3}$$

The so-called *silhouette width* of the pattern $\mathbf{x}$ can be expressed as follows:

$$S(\mathbf{x}) = \frac{b(\mathbf{x}) - a(\mathbf{x})}{max\,(a(\mathbf{x}), b(\mathbf{x}))} \tag{4}$$

Finally, the *Silhouette* index is defined as:

$$SIL = \frac{1}{n} \sum_{\mathbf{x} \in X} S(\mathbf{x}) \tag{5}$$

where n is the number of patterns in the data set X. Thus, this index can be also represented by:

$$SIL = \frac{1}{n} \sum_{\mathbf{x} \in X} \frac{b(\mathbf{x}) - a(\mathbf{x})}{\max(a(\mathbf{x}), b(\mathbf{x}))}. \tag{6}$$

The *Silhouette* index is also called the *SIL* index. Unlike most of the validity indices, the *SIL* index can be used for clusters of arbitrary shapes. It should be noted that the index is based on two components, i.e., $b(\mathbf{x})$ and $a(\mathbf{x})$. As given above, the first component is the smallest of the mean distances of $\mathbf{x}$ to the patterns belonging to other clusters. Then, $a(\mathbf{x})$ is defined as the average distance between $\mathbf{x}$ and the rest of the patterns belonging to the same cluster. Notice that $a(\mathbf{x})$ can be also considered a measure of cluster compactness, whereas the numerator of $S(\mathbf{x})$, which is the difference between $b(\mathbf{x})$ and $a(\mathbf{x})$, can be considered a measure of cluster separability (see Eq. (4)). It should be noted that the value of the *silhouette width* is from the interval $[-1, 1]$ and the element $\mathbf{x}$ is assigned to the right cluster when $S(\mathbf{x})$ is close to 1, but when it is nearly -1, $\mathbf{x}$ is located in a wrong cluster. Hence, a maximum value of the *Silhouette* index indicates the right partition scheme. Moreover, it should be observed that the measure of cluster separability (numerator of Eq. (6)) essentially influences results of this index and in some cases it can fail to detect correct data partitioning. For example, this can happen when differences of distances between clusters are large. Figure 1 presents an example of 2–dimensional data set, which contains three clusters labelled by numbers 1, 2 and 3. Notice that the distances between the clusters are very different. Moreover, it can be seen that these clusters have several elements per class and large differences of distances between them. Thus, the distance between clusters 1 and 2 is about $d1$; then, between clusters 2 and 3 it is $d2$, and between 3 and 1 it is $d3$. It can be noted that the distance $d1$ (or $d3$) is much larger than $d2$. Let us denote by c^* the correct number of clusters in the data set, so it is $c^* = 3$. When the number of clusters K is more than c^*, the natural existing compact clusters are subdivided into small ones by a clustering algorithm. In this case, the minimum distance between clusters is small, which also makes this index value small (see Eq. (4)). However, when $K = c^*$, the value of $b(\mathbf{x})$ is equal to about $d1$ for $\mathbf{x}$ belonging to cluster 1. Whereas $b(\mathbf{x})$ is about $d2$ for $\mathbf{x}$ belonging to the cluster 2 (or 3). Consequently, a large distance between clusters 1 and 2 (or 1 and 3) makes that the value of the factor $b(\mathbf{x})$ calculated for cluster 1 is also much higher than $a(\mathbf{x})$ and the *Silhouette* index is high (see Eq. (6)). But when $K < c^*$, the value of the index can be even higher than for $K = c^*$. This is because clusters 2 and 3

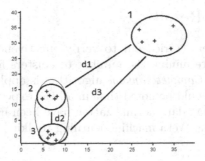

Fig. 1. An example of a data set consisting of three clusters

are merged and now two new clusters are also far from each other. This means that $b(\mathbf{x})$ for both clusters is large in comparison to $a(\mathbf{x})$, which does not actually increase so much. Consequently, the sum of values of *silhouette widths* can be higher for $K < c^*$ than for $K = c^*$. Thus, due to large differences between cluster distances, the index can indicate an incorrect number of clusters. In the next section, a modification of the index is proposed so as to overcome this drawback.

3   Modification of the Silhouette Index

The modification involves an additional component which corrects values of the index. Thus, the new index, called the $SILA$ index, is defined as follows:

$$SILA = \frac{1}{n} \left(\sum_{\mathbf{x} \in X} (S(\mathbf{x}) \cdot A(\mathbf{x})) \right) \tag{7}$$

where the $S(x)$ is the *silhouette width* (Eq. (4)). Whereas, the additional component $A(\mathbf{x})$ is expressed as:

$$A(\mathbf{x}) = \frac{1}{(1 + a(\mathbf{x}))} \tag{8}$$

Thus, the new index can be represented in the following way:

$$SILA = \frac{1}{n} \left(\sum_{\mathbf{x} \in X} \left(\frac{b(\mathbf{x}) - a(\mathbf{x})}{\max(a(\mathbf{x}), b(\mathbf{x}))} \cdot A(\mathbf{x}) \right) \right) \tag{9}$$

or

$$SILA = \frac{1}{n} \left(\sum_{\mathbf{x} \in X} \left(\frac{b(\mathbf{x}) - a(\mathbf{x})}{\max(a(\mathbf{x}), b(\mathbf{x}))} \cdot \frac{1}{(1 + a(x))} \right) \right) \tag{10}$$

In the next section the results of the experimental studies are presented to confirm the effectiveness of this approach.

4   Experimental Results

Several experiments were carried out to verify effectiveness of the new index. They are related to determining the number of clusters for artificial and real-life data sets when the *Complete-linkage* algorithm is applied as the underlying clustering method. It should be noted that in all the experiments the Euclidean distance and the min-max data normalization have been used. This approach is often applied, e.g., in the Weka machine learning toolkit [43].

4.1   Data Sets

Figures 2 and 3 show the randomly generated artificial data sets which were used in the experiments. Moreover, Table 1 presents their detailed description. These data consist of various numbers of clusters and elements per class. For instance, the first three of them called *Data* 1, *Data* 2 and *Data* 3 are 2- dimensional with 3, 5 and 8 clusters, respectively. The next three sets called *Data* 4, *Data* 5 and *Data* 6 are 3-dimensional with 4, 7 and 9 clusters, respectively. As it can be observed in Figs. 2 and 3 clusters are mostly circular and located in various distances from each other with some of them being quite close. For example, in Fig. 2 cluster sizes and distances between clusters are very different and they are located in two cluster groups in general. On the other hand, Fig. 3 presents various large clusters of 3-dimensional data sets. Here, distances between clusters are also very different and clusters create some groups. Whereas the real-life data were drawn from the UCI repository [20], and their detailed description is presented in Table 2. In experiments with the data sets, the *Complete-linkage* method as the underlying clustering algorithm was used for partitioning of the data. The number of clusters K was varied from $K_{max} = \sqrt{n}$ to $K_{min} = 1$. This value is an accepted rule in the clustering literature [23]. Moreover, in Figs. 4, 5 and 6 a comparison of the variations of the *Silhouette* and the *SILA* indices with respect to the number of clusters is presented. It can be seen that the *SILA* index provides the correct number of clusters for the all data sets. On the contrary, the *Silhouette* index incorrectly selects the partitioning schemes and thus the index mainly provides high distinct peaks when the number of clusters $K = 2$. This means that when the clustering algorithm merges clusters into larger ones and distances between them are large, influence of the separability measure is significant and consequently, this index provides incorrect results. On the other hand, despite the fact that the differences of distances between clusters are large, the *SILA*-index generates clear peaks which are related to the correct partitioning of these data. It can be observed that for real-life data sets both indices found the right number of clusters for the *Iris* data. However, for the *Ecoli* and the *Glass* data the *Silhouette* index indicates the number of clusters $K = 2$. On the other hand, the *SILA* index provides better results for the *Glass*, i.e., $K = 5$. Thus, for these sets, the number of clusters is determined more precisely by the *SILA*-index. Notice that when the number of clusters $K > c^*$ the component $A(\mathbf{x})$ poorly reduces values of this index because the clusters sizes are not so large.

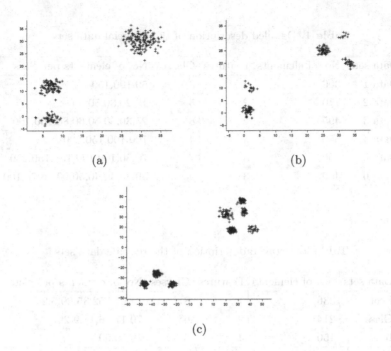

Fig. 2. 2-dimensional artificial data sets: (a) *Data* 1, (b) *Data* 2 and (c) *Data* 3

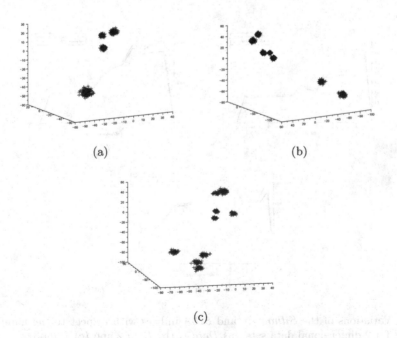

Fig. 3. 3-dimensional artificial data sets: (a) *Data* 4, (b) *Data* 5 and (c) *Data* 6

Table 1. Detailed description of the artificial data sets

Data sets	No. of elements	Features	Classes	No. of elements per class
Data 1	300	2	3	50,100,150
Data 2	170	2	5	10,20,30,50,60
Data 3	495	2	8	25,30,50,50,60,80,100,100
Data 4	550	3	4	100,100,150,200
Data 5	800	3	7	70,80,100,100,100,150,200
Data 6	460	3	9	30,30,40,40,50,50,50,70,100

Table 2. Detailed description of the real-life data sets

Data sets	No. of elements	Features	Classes	No. of elements per class
Ecoli	336	7	8	143,77,52,35,20,5,2,2
Glass	214	9	6	70,17,76,13,9,29
Iris	150	4	3	50,50,50

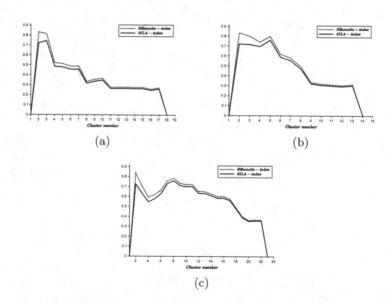

Fig. 4. Variations of the *Silhouette* and *SILA* indices with respect to the number of clusters for 2-dimensional data sets: (a) *Data* 1, (b) *Data* 2 and (c) *Data* 3

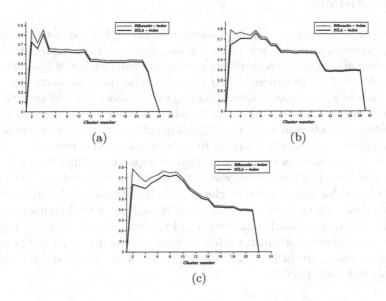

Fig. 5. Variations of the *Silhouette* and *SILA* indices with respect to the number of clusters for 3-dimensional data sets: (a) *Data* 4, (b) *Data* 5 and (c) *Data* 6

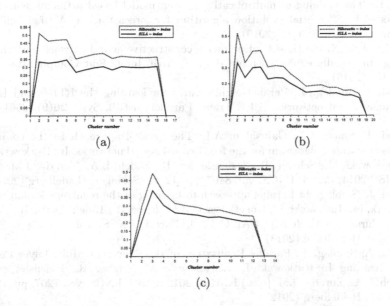

Fig. 6. Variations of the *Silhouette* and *SILA* indices with respect to the number of clusters for real-life data sets: (a) *Glass*, (b) *Ecoli* and (c) *Iris*

5   Conclusions

In this paper, a new cluster validity index called the $SILA$ index was proposed. It should be noted that this new index is a modification of the $Silhouette$ index, which is very often used by researchers to evaluate partitioning of data. Furthermore, unlike most other indices the $SILA$ index (also the $Silhouette$ index) can be used for arbitrary shaped clusters. As mentioned above, the $Silhouette$ index can indicate incorrect partitioning scheme when there are large differences of distances between clusters in a data set. Consequently, the new index contains an additional component which improves its performance and overcomes the drawback. This component uses a measure of cluster compactness which increases when a cluster size increases considerably and it reduces the high values of the index caused by large differences between clusters. To investigate the behaviour of the proposed validity index the $Complete-linkage$ is used as the underlying clustering algorithm. All the presented results confirm high efficiency of the $SILA$ index. It should also be noticed that cluster validity indices can be used during a process of designing various neuro-fuzzy structures [15,19,21,24–29,41,42] and stream data mining algorithms [33–36].

References

1. Baskir, M.B., Türksen, I.B.: Enhanced fuzzy clustering algorithm and cluster validity index for human perception. Expert Syst. Appl. **40**, 929–937 (2013)
2. Bas, E.: The training of multiplicative neuron model based artificial neural networks with differential evolution algorithm for forecasting. J. Artif. Intell. Soft Comput. Res. **6**(1), 5–11 (2016)
3. Bertini, J.R., Nicoletti, M.C.: Enhancing constructive neural network performance using functionally expanded input data. J. Artif. Intell. Soft Comput. Res. **6**(2), 119–131 (2016)
4. Bilski, J., Smolag, J.: Parallel architectures for learning the RTRN and Elman dynamic neural networks. IEEE Trans. Parallel Distrib. Syst. **26**(9), 2561–2570 (2015)
5. Bilski, J., Smolag, J., Galushkin, A.I.: The parallel approach to the conjugate gradient learning algorithm for the feedforward neural networks. In: Rutkowski, L., Korytkowski, M., Scherer, R., Tadeusiewicz, R., Zadeh, L.A., Zurada, J.M. (eds.) ICAISC 2014, Part I. LNCS, vol. 8467, pp. 12–21. Springer, Heidelberg (2014)
6. Bilski, J., Smolag, J.: Parallel approach to learning of the recurrent jordan neural network. In: Rutkowski, L., Korytkowski, M., Scherer, R., Tadeusiewicz, R., Zadeh, L.A., Zurada, J.M. (eds.) ICAISC 2013, Part I. LNCS, vol. 7894, pp. 32–40. Springer, Heidelberg (2013)
7. Bilski, J., Smolag, J.: Parallel Realisation of the Recurrent Multi Layer Perceptron Learning. In: Rutkowski, L., Korytkowski, M., Scherer, R., Tadeusiewicz, R., Zadeh, L.A., Zurada, J.M. (eds.) ICAISC 2012, Part I. LNCS, vol. 7267, pp. 12–20. Springer, Heidelberg (2012)
8. Cpalka, K., Rutkowski, L.: Flexible Takagi-Sugeno fuzzy systems. In: Proceedings of the International Joint Conference on Neural Networks (IJCNN), vols 1-5 Book Series: IEEE International Joint Conference on Neural Networks, pp. 1764–1769 (2005)

9. Cpaka, K., Rebrova, O., Nowicki, R., Rutkowski, L.: On design of flexible neuro-fuzzy systems for nonlinear modelling. Int. J. Gen Syst **42**(6), 706–720 (2013)
10. Duch, W., Korbicz, J., Rutkowski, L., Tadeusiewicz, R. (eds.): Biocybernetics and biomedical engineering 2000. Neural Networks, vol. 6, Akademicka Oficyna Wydawnicza, EXIT, (2000)
11. Fränti, P., Rezaei, M., Zhao, Q.: Centroid index: cluster level similarity measure. Pattern Recognit. **47**(9), 3034–3045 (2014)
12. Fred, L.N., Leitao, M.N.: A new cluster isolation criterion based on dissimilarity increments. IEEE Trans. Pattern Anal. Mach. Intell. **25**(8), 944–958 (2003)
13. Jain, A., Dubes, R.: Algorithms for Clustering Data. Prentice-Hall, Englewood Cliffs (1988)
14. Kim, M., Ramakrishna, R.S.: New indices for cluster validity assessment. Pattern Recogn. Lett. **26**(15), 2353–2363 (2005)
15. Korytkowski, M., Rutkowski, L., Scherer, R.: Fast image classification by boosting fuzzy classifiers. Inf. Sci. **327**, 175–182 (2016)
16. Korytkowski, M., Rutkowski, L., Scherer, R.: From ensemble of fuzzy classifiers to single fuzzy rule base classifier. In: Rutkowski, L., Tadeusiewicz, R., Zadeh, L.A., Zurada, J.M. (eds.) ICAISC 2008. LNCS (LNAI), vol. 5097, pp. 265–272. Springer, Heidelberg (2008)
17. Koshiyama, A.S., Vellasco, M., Tanscheit, R.: GPFIS-Control: a genetic fuzzy system for control tasks. J. Artif. Intell. Soft Comput. Res. **4**(3), 167–179 (2014)
18. Laskowski, Ł., Jelonkiewicz, J.: Self-correcting neural network for stereo-matching problem solving. Fundamenta Informaticae **138**(4), 457–482 (2015)
19. Li, X., Er, M.J., Lim, B.S., et al.: Fuzzy regression modeling for tool performance prediction and degradation detection. Int. J. Neural Syst. **20**(5), 405–419 (2010)
20. Lichman, M.: UCI Machine Learning Repository. University of California, School of Information and Computer Science, Irvine (2013). http://archive.ics.uci.edu/ml
21. Miyajima, H., Shigei, N., Miyajima, H.: Performance comparison of hybrid electromagnetism-like mechanism algorithms with descent method. J. Artif. Intell. Soft Comput. Res. **5**(4), 271–282 (2015)
22. Ozkan, I., Türksen, I.B.: MiniMax ε-stable cluster validity index for Type-2 fuzziness. Inf. Sci. **184**(1), 64–74 (2012)
23. Pal, N.R., Bezdek, J.C.: On cluster validity for the fuzzy c-means model. IEEE Trans. Fuzzy Syst. **3**(3), 370–379 (1995)
24. Patgiri, C., Sarma, M., Sarma, K.K.: A class of neuro-computational methods for assamese fricative classification. J. Artif. Intell. Soft Comput. Res. **5**(1), 59–70 (2015)
25. Rigatos, G., Siano, P.: Flatness-based adaptive fuzzy control of spark-ignited engines. J. Artif. Intell. Soft Comput. Res. **4**(4), 231–242 (2014)
26. Rutkowski, L., Cpalka, K.: Flexible neuro-fuzzy systems. IEEE Trans. Neural Networks **14**(3), 554–574 (2003)
27. Rutkowski, L., Przybyl, A., Cpalka, K.: Novel online speed profile generation for industrial machine tool based on flexible neuro-fuzzy approximation. IEEE Trans. Industr. Electron. **59**(2), 1238–1247 (2012)
28. Rutkowski, L., Cpalka, K.: Designing and learning of adjustable quasi-triangular norms with applications to neuro-fuzzy systems. IEEE Trans. Fuzzy Syst. **13**(1), 140–151 (2005)
29. Rutkowski, L., Cpalka, K.: A general approach to neuro-fuzzy systems. In: 10th IEEE International Conference on Fuzzy Systems, vols. 1–3: Meeting the Grand Challenge: Machines that Serve People, pp. 1428–1431 (2001)

30. Rutkowski, L., Cpalka, K.: A neuro-fuzzy controller with a compromise fuzzy reasoning. Control Cybern. **31**(2), 297–308 (2002)
31. Rutkowski, L., Przybył, A., Cpałka, K., Er, M.J.: Online Speed Profile Generation for Industrial Machine Tool Based on Neuro-fuzzy Approach. In: Rutkowski, L., Scherer, R., Tadeusiewicz, R., Zadeh, L.A., Zurada, J.M. (eds.) ICAISC 2010, Part II. LNCS, vol. 6114, pp. 645–650. Springer, Heidelberg (2010)
32. Rutkowski, L., Cpalka, K.: Compromise approach to neuro-fuzzy systems. Technol. Book Ser. Frontiers Artif. Intell. Appl. **76**, 85–90 (2002)
33. Rutkowski, L., Pietruczuk, L., Duda, P., Jaworski, M.: Decision trees for mining data streams based on the McDiarmids bound. IEEE Trans. Knowl. Data Eng. **25**(6), 1272–1279 (2013)
34. Rutkowski, L., Jaworski, M., Pietruczuk, L., Duda, P.: Decision trees for mining data streams based on the Gaussian approximation. IEEE Trans. Knowl. Data Eng. **26**(1), 108–119 (2014)
35. Rutkowski, L., Jaworski, M., Pietruczuk, L., Duda, P.: A new method for data stream mining based on the misclassification error. IEEE Trans. Neural Networks Learn. Syst. **26**(5), 1048–1059 (2015)
36. Rutkowski, L., Jaworski, M., Pietruczuk, L., Duda, P.: The CART decision tree for mining data streams. Inf. Sci. **266**, 1–15 (2014)
37. Saitoh, D., Hara, K.: Mutual learning using nonlinear perceptron. J. Artif. Intell. Soft Comput. Res. **5**(1), 71–77 (2015)
38. Sameh, A.S., Asoke, K.N.: Development of assessment criteria for clustering algorithms. Pattern Anal. Appl. **12**(1), 79–98 (2009)
39. Shieh, H.-L.: Robust validity index for a modified subtractive clustering algorithm. Appl. Soft Comput. **22**, 47–59 (2014)
40. Starczewski, A.: A new validity index for crisp clusters. Pattern Anal. Appl. (2015). doi:10.1007/s10044-015-0525-8
41. Starczewski, J., Rutkowski, L.: Interval type 2 neuro-fuzzy systems based on interval consequents. In: Rutkowski, L., Kacprzyk, J. (eds.) Neural Networks and Soft Computing. Advances in Soft Computing, pp. 570–577. Springer-Verlag, Physica-Verlag HD, Heidelberg (2003)
42. Starczewski, J.T., Rutkowski, L.: Connectionist structures of type 2 fuzzy inference systems. In: Wyrzykowski, R., Dongarra, J., Paprzycki, M., Waśniewski, J. (eds.) PPAM 2001. LNCS, vol. 2328, p. 634. Springer, Heidelberg (2002)
43. Weka 3: Data mining software in Java. University of Waikato, New Zealand. http://www.cs.waikato.ac.nz/ml/weka
44. Wozniak, M., Polap, D., Nowicki, R., Napoli, C., Pappalardo, G., Tramontana, E.: Novel approach toward medical signals classifier. In: 2015 International Joint Conference on Neural Networks (IJCNN), Killarney, Irlandia (2015). doi:10.1109/IJCNN.2015.7280556
45. Wu, K.L., Yang, M.S., Hsieh, J.N.: Robust cluster validity indexes. Pattern Recogn. **42**, 2541–2550 (2009)
46. Zalik, K.R.: Cluster validity index for estimation of fuzzy clusters of different sizes and densities. Pattern Recogn. **43**, 3374–3390 (2010)
47. Zhang, D., Ji, M., Yang, J., Zhang, Y., Xie, F.: A novel cluster validity index for fuzzy clustering based on bipartite modularity. Fuzzy Sets Syst. **253**, 122–137 (2014)

Similarities, Dissimilarities and Types of Inner Products for Data Analysis in the Context of Machine Learning

A Mathematical Characterization

Thomas Villmann[1]([✉]), Marika Kaden[1], David Nebel[1], and Andrea Bohnsack[2]

[1] Computational Intelligence Group,
University of Applied Sciences Mittweida, Mittweida, Germany
`thomas.villmann@hs-mittweida.de`
[2] Staatliche Berufliche Oberschule Kaufbeuren, Kaufbeuren, Germany

Abstract. Data dissimilarities and similarities are the key ingredients of machine learning. We give a mathematical characterization and classification of those measures based on structural properties also involving psychological-cognitive aspects of similarity determination, and investigate admissible conversions. Finally, we discuss some consequences of the obtained taxonomy and their implications for machine learning algorithms.

1 Introduction

Data in machine learning are usually compared in terms of dissimilarities or similarities. These values maybe obtained either by mathematical calculations or by other judgements like human rater values. Examples are the Euclidean and other distance measures, correlations or divergences but also questionnaire scales, joint probabilities etc. Often, the specific origin of the dissimilarity/similarity values is not known or at least not easy to explore for the data analyst. Thus, respective tasks have to deal just with the given dissimilarity/similarity matrix. Otherwise, algorithms and computational approaches in machine learning frequently require data assumptions to be fulfilled. For example, support vector machines, designed for classification learning, suppose a symmetric positive definite kernel matrix frequently interpreted as similarity relations [1–3], whereas online learning vector quantization models assume differentiable dissimilarities [4,5].

The prevailing methodology in machine learning applications is to convert dissimilarities in similarities and vice versa under mild conditions supposing an almost *similar behavior*. The respective assumption usually is based on an intuitive understanding of the concept of proximity. This intuitive thinking, however, can be misleading and, hence, result in false interpretation of the approaches regarding their abilities for data analysis. For example, kernel methods like support vector machines are frequently identified as a similarity based approach although, as we will explore later in detail, this is not valid for all kernels. Thus we plead for a more faithful purpose of these aspects.

© Springer International Publishing Switzerland 2016
L. Rutkowski et al. (Eds.): ICAISC 2016, Part II, LNAI 9693, pp. 125–133, 2016.
DOI: 10.1007/978-3-319-39384-1_11

However, a precise categorization of proximity measures is only available from the geometric interpretation of dissimilarity so far, mainly influenced by the mathematical definition of metrics. A finer grained differentiation is provided by Pekalska and Duin in [6] but still starting from the mathematical distance definition. Otherwise, the similarity paradigm is intensively studied in psychology and cognitive science [7–9]. It is pointed out that several aspects of mathematical distances like symmetry or triangle inequality are apparently not valid in many situations.

Starting with the pioneering work from Tversky [8,10] a more conceptual way was suggested based on a feature-theoretical contrast model considering the difference between common and distinguishing features of objects [11]. This approach leads to a better understanding of similarities based on weaker assumptions, which are made according to plausibility arguments and can be related to paradigms in information processing [8,12]. Yet, it turns out that most attempts of those more sophisticated and cognitive approaches return to the geometrical distance interpretation during the detailed considerations [11,13–15]. To our best knowledge only two authors remained in the conceptual line for formal description of similarities based on properties figured out to be important object discrimination in perception and tried to characterize it mathematically [12,16]. Both approaches as well as the early Tversky-approach have in common that they do not differentiate several kinds of similarity.

The aim of the present paper is to characterize similarities based on properties in relation to dissimilarity measures. For this purpose, we start with the cognitive understanding of similarity and the respective mathematical description as already done in the mentioned approaches. Thereafter, we fine tune the similarity categorization scheme according to the thoroughly defined kinds of dissimilarities. Further, we shortly discuss aspects of equivalent measures and show implications for machine learning applications.

2   Mathematical Description of Similarity Types and Its Relation to Dissimilarities

In this section we develop a scheme to relate kinds of similarities to adequate dissimilarity types based on mathematical properties. For this purpose, we start with the basic (mathematical) assumptions made in cognitive science for similarities, turn over to dissimilarities and extend both lines in the sequel to obtain a mirror-inverted description scheme. Thereby we match our differentiation to categories for dissimilarities suggested by Pekalska and Duin in [6].

As pointed out by Santini and Jain in [16], the mathematical distance axioms seem to be too rigid for a system of similarities. The common sense in cognitive science according to the contrast model is to endow a similarity measure (map)

$$s : X \times X \to \mathbb{R}$$

for the object space X with at least the following properties [8]:

1. Maximum or dominance principle: $s\left(x,x\right) \geq s\left(x,y\right)$ and $s\left(x,x\right) \geq s\left(y,x\right)$
2. Non-negativity: $s\left(x,y\right) \geq 0$

whereby $s\left(x,y\right)$ increases with x and y sharing more properties and decreases with the number and the degree of discriminative features, i.e. the similarity is a function of object commonalities and differences. We denote a similarity s, fulfilling the maximum principle, as a basic similarity. If additionally for the similarity s the non-negativity is given, it is said to be a primitive similarity. As an example for basic similarity could serve a negative distance measure $-d$, as it is used for the affinity propagation clustering [17], or negative divergences [5,18].

Accordingly to basic similarities, we suppose

1. Minimum principle: $d\left(x,x\right) \leq d\left(x,y\right)$ and $d\left(x,x\right) \leq d\left(y,x\right)$
2. Non-negativity: $d\left(x,y\right) \geq 0$

for a basic/primitive dissimilarity

$$d : X \times X \to \mathbb{R}.$$

The maximum principle and the non-negativity as basic properties of similarities are usually accompanied by a consistency requirement often chosen as $s\left(x,x\right) = c_s$ with $c_s = 1\ \forall x$. Here, we propose a more gradual definition with either an arbitrary constant c_s or data dependent $c_s\left(x\right)$ to take a local view. For dissimilarities, the minimum principle and the non-negativity usually come along with the consistency property $d\left(x,x\right) = c_d\left(x\right)$ yielding a weakly-consistent dissimilarity. The consistency is often tightened to be c_d independent from x or required as $d\left(x,x\right) = 0$ (reflexivity). A reflexive dissimilarity obeying these properties is denoted as hollow metric [6]. Definiteness as well as inequality constraints lead to further dissimilarity variants. We collect the complementary mathematical properties of similarities and dissimilarities in Table 1.

Adequately, we can assign these properties to respective types of dissimilarity and similarity measures. To be in agreement with earlier taxonomies we follow the classification scheme by [6] but with finer granularity and explicitly related to the above identified properties. We depict the respectively obtained dissimilarity types in Table 2.

Accordingly, we now introduce respective types for similarities following the already harmonized properties given in Table 1. Table 3 depicts this mathematical similarity categorization. We remark and emphasize at this point that this mathematical categorization is still in agreement with the cognitive-psychological approach of similarity from Tversky [8,10]. Further, it is also consistent with information processing paradigms [8,12].

With these definitions we are able to classify dis-/similarity measures precisely regarding their mathematical properties. In the next session we will relate similarities to (semi-) inner products.

Table 1. Complementary mathematical properties for dissimilarity and similarity measures. The properties are motivated by cognitive-psychological deliberations as well as geometrical thoughts.

	$d(\mathbf{x}, \mathbf{y})$	$s(\mathbf{x}, \mathbf{y})$	
MIN	minimum principle $d(x,x) \leq d(x,y) \wedge d(y,y) \leq d(x,y)$	maximum principle $s(x,x) \geq s(x,y) \wedge s(y,y) \geq s(x,y)$	MAX
NN	non-negativity $d(x,y) \geq 0$	$s(x,y) \geq 0$	NN
wC	weak consistency $d(x,x) = c_d(x)$ $(c_d(x), c_s(x) : X \to \mathbb{R})$	$s(x,x) = c_s(x)$	wC
sC	strong consistency $d(x,x) = c_d$ $c_d, c_s \in \mathbb{R}$	$s(x,x) = c_s$	sC
R	reflexivity $d(x,x) = 0$	normalized sC $d(x,x) = 1$	nC
S	symmetry $d(x,y) = d(y,x)$	$s(x,y) = s(y,x)$	S
D	definiteness (non-degeneration) $d(x,y) = d(x,x) \vee d(x,y) = d(y,y) \Rightarrow x = y$	$s(x,y) = s(x,x) \vee s(x,y) = s(y,y) \Rightarrow x = y$	D
T	triangle inequality $d(x,y) + d(y,z) \geq d(x,z)$	reverse triangle inequality $s(x,y) + s(y,z) \leq s(x,z)$	rT
UM	ultra-metric inequality $\max\{d(x,y), d(y,z)\} \geq d(x,z)$	reverse ultra-sim. inequality $\min\{s(x,y), s(y,z)\} \geq s(x,z)$	rUS

Table 2. Types of dissimilarities regarding the properties identified in Table 1.

Dissimilarities/properties	MIN	NN	Consistency			S	D	Inequalities	
			wC	sC	R			T	UM
Basic dis	x								
Primitive dis	x	x							
Weakly-consistent dis	x	x	x						
Strongly-consistent dis	x	x		x					
General dis. (hollow metric)	x	x			x				
Pre dis. (pre-metric)	x	x			x	x			
Usual dis. (quasi-metric)	x	x			x	x	x		
Semi-metric	x	x			x	x		x	
Distance (metric)	x	x			x	x	x	x	
Ultra metric	x	x			x	x	x		x

Table 3. Kinds of similarity measures based on the complementary properties of similarities compared with dissimilarities according to Table 1.

Similarities/properties	MAX	NN	Consistency			S	D	Inequalities	
			wC	sC	nC			rT	rUS
Basic sim	x								
Primitive sim	x	x							
Weakly-consistent sim	x	x	x						
Weak sim	x		x						
Strongly-consistent sim	x	x		x					
General sim. (hollow sim.)	x	x			x				
Pre-sim	x	x			x	x			
Usual sim. (quasi-sim.)	x	x			x	x	x		
Semi-sim	x	x			x	x		x	
(Minkowsky-like) sim	x	x			x	x	x	x	
Ultra sim	x	x			x	x	x		x

3   Similarities and (semi-) Inner Products

Inner products of Hilbert spaces are the basic ingredients for several machine learning approaches. Specifically, for support vector machines (SVM, [1,2]), kernels are computational convenient realizations of inner products of maybe infinite dimensional Hilbert spaces, which are uniquely related to the kernel feature mapping of the data into this space [3]. Yet, in the SVM context, a kernel is frequently interpreted as a kind of data similarity. Unfortunately, this interpretation is not correct in general. To see this, we remember the basic properties of (semi-) inner products:

Definition 1 (Inner Product). *Let X be a vector space over $\mathbb{C}$ with zero vector x_0. An **inner product** $\langle \cdot, \cdot \rangle_X : X \times X \to \mathbb{C}$ is a map such that the conditions*

(a) Hermitian symmetry: $\langle x, y \rangle_X = \overline{\langle y, x \rangle_X}$
(b) Positive definiteness: $\langle x, x \rangle_X > 0$ for $x \neq x_0$
(c) Non-degeneration: $\langle x, x \rangle_X = 0 \implies x = x_0$
(d) Linearity in the first argument: $\langle \lambda x + z, y \rangle_X = \lambda \langle x, y \rangle_X + \langle z, y \rangle_X$
(e) Sesqui-linearity in the second argument: $\langle x, \lambda y \rangle_X = \bar{\lambda} \langle x, y \rangle_X$

are valid.

Note, if X is a real space then $\langle \cdot, \cdot \rangle_X : X \times X \to \mathbb{R}$ is valid and the Hermitian symmetry degenerates to the usual symmetry. An inner product fulfills the Cauchy-Schwarz-inequality

$$|\langle x, y \rangle_X|^2 \leq \langle x, x \rangle_X \langle y, y \rangle_X \tag{1}$$

and generates by $\|x\|_X = \sqrt{\langle x, x \rangle_X}$ a norm. Obviously, $\|x - y\|_X$ determines a distance in X.

We immediately observe that an inner product may take negative value. Hence, the most basic requirements of similarities, the maximum principle and the non-negativity can not be ensured for general inner products and, hence, kernels cannot automatically serve as similarity measures. Yet, for special kernels these requirements may be fulfilled: The Gaussian kernel

$$\kappa\left(x, y\right) = \exp\left(\frac{-\|x - y\|^2}{2\sigma^2}\right) \tag{2}$$

is always positive. If we further assume normalized data with respect to the kernel-norm generated by this kernel, the consistency property delivers the maximum principle for the kernel by the Cauchy-Schwarz-inequality. More precisely, the Gaussian kernel constitutes a Minkowski-like similarity for normalized data according to the taxonomy given in Table 3.

Consider now a weaker concept than inner products, the so-called **semi-inner products** $[\cdot, \cdot]_X$ (SIP). A SIP violates the Hermitian symmetry such that the sesqui-linearity of inner products in the second argument is lost. However, the fulfillment of the Cauchy-Schwarz-inequality (1) is explicitly required also for SIPs such that SIP-spaces remain normed spaces [19]. Famous examples for SIP-spaces are the l_p-spaces for $p \neq 2$ [20].

As for kernels, SIPs are not similarity measures due to the same arguments, although SIPs can be used in under certain condition also for SVM-like algorithms [21].

In contrast to SIPs, an **indefinite inner product** $\langle \cdot | \cdot \rangle_X$ (IIP) may violate the positive definiteness condition of the inner product definition and may degenerate. In consequence the Cauchy-Schwarz-inequality (1) is not longer hold for IIPs. However, for real vector spaces an IIP remains to be a real bilinear form. IIPs, are used for relational methods in machine learning [22]. Since the Cauchy-Schwarz-inequality does not hold for IIPs, the maximum principle of similarities is violated according to the above arguments. Hence, the interpretability of relational methods is weakened.

4   Relations Between Dissimilarities and Similarities in the Context of Machine Learning Approaches

As mentioned in the introduction, in context of machine learning, frequently similarities and dissimilarities are converted into each other or are synonymously used. Otherwise, kernel methods often rely on the implicit non-linear mapping to expect better results. As we have seen before, kernel could be taken as similarity under certain circumstances. Now we take a closer look to similarities regarding their topological properties in comparison to dissimilarities and shortly discuss consequences for machine learning approaches.

Definition 2 (Rank Equivalence for Similarities and Dissimilarities).
Two dissimilarities d and $\widehat{d}$ are said to be rank-equivalent if $\forall x, y, v, w \in X$ the following relations hold for d and $\widehat{d}$

1. $d(x,y) < d(v,w)$ iff $\widehat{d}(x,y) < \widehat{d}(v,w)$
2. $d(x,y) = d(v,w)$ iff $\widehat{d}(x,y) = \widehat{d}(v,w)$.

Two similarities s and $\widehat{s}$ are said to be rank-equivalent if $\forall x, y, v, w \in X$ the following relations hold for s and $\widehat{s}$

3. $s(x,y) < s(v,w)$ iff $\widehat{s}(x,y) < \widehat{s}(v,w)$
4. $s(x,y) = s(v,w)$ iff $\widehat{s}(x,y) = \widehat{s}(v,w)$.

A dissimilarity d and a similarity s are said to be rank-equivalent if $\forall x, y, v, w \in X$ the following relations hold for s and d

5. $s(x,y) < s(v,w)$ iff $d(x,y) > d(v,w)$
6. $s(x,y) = s(v,w)$ iff $d(x,y) = d(v,w)$.

This definition leads to the following important observation:

Remark 1. If two dissimilarities d and $\widehat{d}$ are given and $d(x,y) = f\left(\widehat{d}(x,y)\right)$ with f being a monotonously increasing function, both dissimilarities d and $\widehat{d}$ are rank-equivalent.

According to his remark we can replace in the famous k-nearest-neighbor classifier (kNN, [23]) respective rank-equivalent distances without a change in the classification behavior of the kNN. For example, if a Gaussian kernel distances is considered, this distance is rank-equivalent to the Euclidean distance. Hence, the respective classification ability of kNN remains unchanged if we replace them by each other. Otherwise, vector quantizers may benefit during learning: The prototype vectors are distributed following the magnification law according to the data density [24], which depends on the underlying dissimilarity measure [25]. After training of those vector quantization models, we can return to a rank-equivalent dissimilarity with lower computational costs in case of time restricted applications. For example, a Gaussian kernel distance generated by the kernel (2), as used for learning in vector quantization based on kernels [4, 26], could be replaced by the simpler Euclidean distance after training, because the Gaussian kernel distance is rank-equivalent to the Euclidean distance. Moreover, according to the above definitions of rank-equivalence, the Gaussian kernel itself taken as similarity measure is rank equivalent to the Euclidean distance.

Similar thoughts may apply also for support vector machines.

Obviously, it is easy to generate a dissimilarity from a similarity measure. A convenient way is just to take

$$(d(x,y))^2 = s(x,x) + s(y,y) - s(x,y) - s(y,x) \tag{3}$$

whereas the reverse way is more complicate. However, the topological equivalence is not guaranteed. For example, if s is the Euclidean inner product, then d is the squared Euclidean distance. However, unit circles with respect to d do not have an analogue for s, in general. To see this, we consider $X = \mathbb{R}^2$ and a constant Euclidean inner product

$$s(x, y) = x_1 y_1 + x_2 y_2 = c$$

for a fixed $x \in \mathbb{R}^2$. Depending on x, the set S of solutions for y of this equation can take different values: for $x = \mathbf{0}$ we obtain $S = \emptyset$, whereas for $x = (a, 0)$ with $a \neq 0$ we get $S = \left\{ \left(\frac{1}{a}, y_2 \right) : y_2 \in \mathbb{R} \right\}$ determining a straight line. Thus, comparison of unit (constant) circles around x according to d and s show substantial topological differences. Similarly, topological changes occur if flipping or clipping is applied for relational methods in case of Pseudo-Euclidean data [22].

5   Conclusion

In this contribution we consider and define types of similarities and dissimilarities from a mathematical point of view. These types are based on structural properties and are in agreement with earlier approaches as well as involve psychological-cognitive aspects of similarity theory. One immediate consequence of these investigation is that one has to distinguish carefully between similarities and kernels/inner products although both can be seen as counterparts to dissimilarities.

Further, in the sense of this paper, we remark that Robust Soft LVQ (RSLVQ, [27]), originally introduced as a probabilistic variant of LVQ, can be seen as a similarity-based algorithm. The reason for this is that the probabilities are estimated by Gaussians, which are, in fact, kernels. Hence, they are similarities in the view of this paper.

In this sense, a canonical generalization of RSLVQ would be to apply other similarities than Gaussian kernels but keeping the optimization strategy. However, if other similarities replace the Gaussians in RSLVQ we obtain a ratio of summarized similarities, which can still serve as probabilistic assignments of data to classes. In consequence, we model the probabilities not longer by Gaussians but by a mixture of similarities in that case. Respective studies are planned for the future.

In summary, a general reassessment of kernels, inner products and dis-/similarities in machine learning is demanded for an adequate application use.

References

1. Schölkopf, B., Smola, A.: Learning with Kernels. MIT Press, Cambridge (2002)
2. Steinwart, I.: On the influence of the kernel on the consistency of support vector machines. J. Mach. Learn. Res. **2**, 67–93 (2001)
3. Steinwart, I., Christmann, A.: Support Vector Machines. Information Science and Statistics. Springer, Heidelberg (2008)
4. Villmann, T., Haase, S., Kaden, M.: Kernelized vector quantization in gradient-descent learning. Neurocomputing **147**, 83–95 (2015)

5. Villmann, T., Haase, S.: Divergence based vector quantization. Neural Comput. **23**(5), 1343–1392 (2011)
6. Pekalska, E., Duin, R.P.W.: The Dissimilarity Representation for Pattern Recognition: Foundations and Applications. World Scientific, Singapore (2006)
7. Shepard, R.N.: Toward a universal law of generalization for psychological science. Science **237**(11), 1317–1323 (1987)
8. Tversky, A.: Features of similarity. Psychol. Rev. **84**(4), 324–352 (1977)
9. Osherson, D.N.: New axioms for the contrast model of similarity. J. Math. Psychol. **31**, 93–103 (1987)
10. Tversky, A., Gati, I.: Studies of similarity. In: Rosch, E., Lloyd, B.B. (eds.) Cognition and Categorization, pp. 79–98. Erlbaum, Hillsdale (1978)
11. Tversky, A., Gati, I.: Similarity, separability, and the triangle inequality. Psychol. Rev. **89**(2), 123–154 (1982)
12. Lin, D.: An information-theoretic definition of similarity. In: Proceedings of the 15th International Conference on Machine Learning, pp. 296–304. Morgan Kaufmann (1998)
13. Jäkel, F., Schölkopf, B., Wichmann, F.A.: Does cognitive science need kernels? Trends Cogn. Sci. **13**(9), 381–388 (2009)
14. Jäkel, F., Schölkopf, B., Wichmann, F.A.: Similarity, kernels, and the triangle inequality. J. Math. Psychol. **52**, 297–303 (2008)
15. Tversky, A., Krantz, D.H.: The dimensional representation and the metric structure of similarity data. J. Math. Psychol. **7**, 572–590 (1970)
16. Santini, S., Jain, R.: Similarity measures. IEEE Trans. Pattern Anal. Mach. Intell. **21**(9), 871–883 (1999)
17. Frey, B.J., Dueck, D.: Clustering by message passing between data points. Science **315**, 972–976 (2007)
18. Cichocki, A., Amari, S.-I.: Families of alpha- beta- and gamma- divergences: flexible and robust measures of similarities. Entropy **12**, 1532–1568 (2010)
19. Lumer, G.: Semi-inner-product spaces. Trans. Am. Math. Soc. **100**, 29–43 (1961)
20. Giles, J.R.: Classes of semi-inner-product spaces. Trans. Am. Math. Soc. **129**, 436–446 (1967)
21. Zhang, H., Xu, Y., Zhang, J.: Reproducing kernel banach spaces for machine learning. J. Mach. Learn. Res. **10**, 2741–2775 (2009)
22. Hammer, B., Hofmann, D., Schleif, F.-M., Zhu, X.: Learning vector quantization for (dis-)similarities. Neurocomputing **131**, 43–51 (2014)
23. Duda, R.O., Hart, P.E.: Pattern Classification and Scene Analysis. Wiley, New York (1973)
24. Zador, P.L.: Asymptotic quantization error of continuous signals and the quantization dimension. IEEE Trans. Inf. Theor. **IT–28**, 149–159 (1982)
25. Villmann, T., Claussen, J.-C.: Magnification control in self-organizing maps and neural gas. Neural Comput. **18**(2), 446–469 (2006)
26. Schleif, F.-M., Villmann, T., Hammer, B., Schneider, P., Biehl, M.: Generalized derivative based kernelized learning vector quantization. In: Fyfe, C., Tino, P., Charles, D., Garcia-Osorio, C., Yin, H. (eds.) IDEAL 2010. LNCS, vol. 6283, pp. 21–28. Springer, Heidelberg (2010)
27. Seo, S., Obermayer, K.: Soft learning vector quantization. Neural Comput. **15**, 1589–1604 (2003)

Bioinformatics, Biometrics and Medical Applications

Detection of Behavioral Data Based on Recordings from Energy Usage Sensor

Piotr Augustyniak[✉]

AGH University of Science and Technology,
30 Mickiewicza Ave., 30-059 Kraków, Poland
august@agh.edu.pl

Abstract. Monitoring of human behavior in the natural living habitat requires a hidden yet accurate measurement. Several previous attempts showed, that this can be achieved by recording and analysing interactions of the supervised human with sensorized equipment of his or her household. We propose an imperceptible single-sensor measurement, already applied for energy usage profiling, to detect the usage of electrically powered domestic appliances and deduct important facts about the operator's functional health. This paper proposes a general scheme of the system, discusses the personalization and adaptation issues and reveals benefits and limitations of the proposed approach. It also presents experimental results showing reliability of device detection based on their load signatures and areas of applicability of the load sensor to analyses of device usage and human performance.

1 Introduction

One of the hottest challenges of current data sensing, transmitting and automatic understanding technologies are context-aware ecosystems for human wellbeing. This topic integrates experiences from telemedicine, behavioral sciences, modern telecommunication and data processing towards a better surveillance of people with various limitations (e.g. elderly or disabled), deeper understanding their needs and risk factors and intuitive interfacing them to the technology-fitted habitat. Continuous recording in human in natural living conditions was first recognized in cardiology, and is currently widespread in various forms of telecare services. The home, being human's natural habitat plays particular role as personal reference (i.e. where the privacy is expected), place of growing, learning, aging and formation of habits. Unfortunately, according to statistics, the household is also a place of grand majority of accidents and life-threatening events. Interpreting the behavioral data in context of security measures is recently focussed as a primary way to rise the life quality and comfort. The other aspect is that people behavior is closely related to energy consumption. Several fuel-related and environmental factors may be explained by exploring common human habits in daily routine. Finally, human performance, including physiological and psychological factors has systematically been studied for affective computing [5].

© Springer International Publishing Switzerland 2016
L. Rutkowski et al. (Eds.): ICAISC 2016, Part II, LNAI 9693, pp. 137–146, 2016.
DOI: 10.1007/978-3-319-39384-1_12

This paradigm assumes interfacing of human-specific feelings (as fear, sadness, joy or satisfaction) to the smart environment able to adapt accordingly.

In this paper we study the possibility of application of imperceptible load sensor for accurate tracking of the inhabitant's behavior, learning individual habits profile and detecting aberrations. Pursuing of people at home raises questions on potential privacy infringement, however, used ethically, may be a source of invaluable data on daily risk factors or provide markers of potential health setback.

A particular attention was paid to the imperceptible design of the sensor. At a price of limitation of its metrological excellence, which can be partly compensated by the software, the sensor remains invisible and does not interfer with the human behavior.

2   Related Work

The usage of home appliances as behavioral sensors was previously studied by the author [2], however our previous attempt was relying on individual device-embedded usage sensors. These provide unambiguous information on device-specific parameters captured by microprocessor-based and Wi-Fi enabled sensor board. Multiple sensorized devices have been integrated in a wireless network to record equipment usage in the whole household, analyse a typical behavioral model and abnormalities and next infer about possible psychophysical status setback of the inhabitant. Similar approach was also presented by Lai et al. [8] and assumes the usage of a household appliance-based sensor network for complementary reporting on human behavior, understanding the habits and evaluating performance in an intelligent environment.

Several recent papers of human behavior are focused on activity recognition with vision analysis systems [6,9,10]. Besides privacy issues, particularly prominent in video surveillance, they offer best reliability-to-price ratio in smart home setups. Vision-based systems are employed to track human mobility in two principal sorts of applications: assessment of the functional health and therapy efficiency [13] or recognition of danger [11]. Many other studies employing various stationary and wearable sensors were performed either to detect a particular event (e.g. a fall [3]), or to supervise the human in partticular activity (e.g. bathing [7]), or to balance between the sensors complexity and recognition accuracy [1].

A separate study revealed, that if detection of psychophysiological setback is a goal, no accurate activity description is necessary. Several systems with adaptive learning have been proposed for continuous screening of human behavior and report irregularities without indicating them in the behavior description domain. The paper by Vu et al. [16] proposed a predictive model exploiting the regularity of human motion found in the real traces, places visited and contacts made in daily activities. In 2013, Ros et al. proposed a new approach for the behavior recognition problem based on learning automata and fuzzy temporal windows [14]. Their system learns the normal behaviors, and uses that knowledge to recognize normal and abnormal human activities in real time. In addition, it is able to adapt online to environmental variations, changes in human habits, and temporal information, defined as an interval of time when the behavior should be performed. The learning approach presented in these papers was adopted to our newly proposed system for behavioral data collection.

Although the results presented are consistent, the usage of stationary video sensors or wearable sensors leads to alteration in human habitat and habits. Therefore we put forward the imperceptibility of the sensor at the price of recognition accuracy. One of such hidden sensors of potentially high performance is smart energy usage recorder. Such devices are not widespread in our homes, yet already identified by researchers as prospective information sources for profiling energy consumption in various types of households [15]. Various techniques were proposed as far for accurate detection of particular devices in the household, and even products from specific manufacturers [12,17]. These sensors usually exploit three electrical characteristics of the load: the active and reactive power, the current raising curve, and oscillatory properties of the load. Based on device-dependent load signatures Belley et. al. [4] proposed a human activity recognition system to control assistive services for Alzheimer-suffering inhabitant. This is as far the only known attempt to using energy usage sensors in secret assessment of human performance.

3   Materials and Methods

3.1   General Assumption and System Design

A primary assumption of our approach is the maximum secrecy and autonomy of the sensor. Besides the initial agreement to installation, the user is in no way involved in maintenance of the sensor, battery replacement etc. We also assumme that the sensor is mounted at the appartment's power clamps (together with the meter and fuses) and that the apartment is occupied by a single person under surveillance. Finally, we assumme that each kind of domestic equipment is represented by a unique device in specified location. All these assumptions fit well to a real-life scenario of independently living elder with configured environment and established habits.

Figure 1 presents a diagram flow of our system applying energy usage sensor to extract operator's behavioral data. Technically writting the sensor is a small integrated system-on-a-chip microprocessor-based device with multichannel analog front-end, dedicated processing software, data memory and transmission gateway. It features excellent MIPs/mW ratio sufficient for on-board calculation of complex signal transformation, detection of load transients and classification of patterns to recognize individual device signatures. For each considered device the usage profile is stored in a dedicated timeline record being a departure point to calculations of versatile usage statistics. All records considered together are a source of information for individual energy usage and pricing profiles and for predicting adequate supply at any time. A contextual analysis of

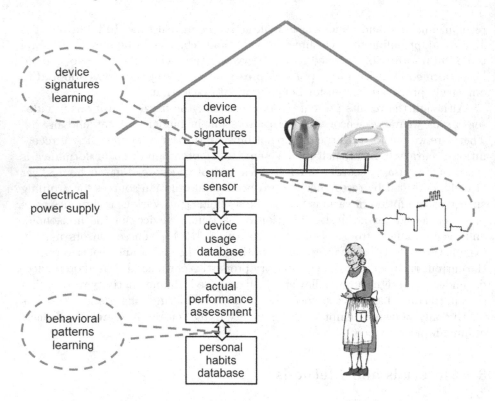

Fig. 1. Diagram flow of a elderly surveillance system using energy usage sensor to extract behavioral data.

the records leads to detecting of selected human actions and to calculate statistics of their regular performance. Each irregularity revealed may be interpreted as a sign of possible psychophysical status setback. In the experimental setup a wireless link, complying with WiFi ad-hoc connection protocol, was used to transmit the data on device-related events to the analysing computer.

3.2 Classification of Device Roles in Surveillance

Particular domestic appliances play different roles in operator's activity recognition. Several categories can be distinguished based on their operating modes. These are presented below:

1. Operator-independent, immobile - this category includes appliances which operation indirectly depends on the human's action; an example is a refrigerator turning on and off automatically.
2. Operator-dependent, mobile - this category includes devices directly operated by a human, however their mobility does not allow to determine the operator's and device location; examples are a hair dryer and an iron that can be plugged into any wall socket in the apartment.

3. Operator-dependent, immobile - this category includes devices directly operated by the human, which allow to determine their usage and operator's
position; example of such appliances is an electric mixer.

The categories were listed above in the order of increasing utility in operator's
behavior tracking. Devices from the third category are most useful, since they
allow to determine the usage statistics and location of the human. Nevertheless, the necessity of continuous presence of the operator, commonly perceived
as a drawback of the appliance design, determines the operator's location for
their whole operation time. Unfortunately, devices that require human action
to put them on but switch off automatically are much wider represented in the
household (e.g. electric kettle, microwave). Location of these devices indicates
the operator's position at the switch-on event, however during the remaining
operation time untill switch-off, the operator's position is undetermined.

3.3   Device Usage Description

Detection of the device usage was implemented following [4], but due to a
surveillance-specific purpose, the event's database was designed alternately. We
define *the event* as a record of switch-on or switch-off operation attributed with
device category-dependent relevance mark, temporal and context information.
Each event was recognized by the sensor on-board software and the behavioral
data available via wireless link has a form of information structure containing:

– device and event type (on/off) identifier, and
– time stamp (with resolution of 1 s).

Each structure representing the current event also repeats data for five prece-
dent events of different devices in ascending time order. As the overall information stream is very tiny, the data redundancy does not increase it very much, but
gives the advantageous context for interpretation of the current event without
the necessity of screening all possible appliance-related records.

3.4   System Learning and Surveillance Stages

Besides the usage statistics and energy saving information, two kinds of data are
particularly interesting from a behavior analysis viewpoint: operator's mobility,
defined as the minimal interval of time between activation of two distant immobile appliances (category 3) and repeatability of daily sequences of activating
operator-dependent appliances (categories 2 and 3). In our system both these
factors are subject to learning, modelling and recognition of possible abnormalities of performance. To this point, all devices representing categories 2 and 3
have their specific database entries collecting two usage aspects:

– contextual usage of other appliances, and
– length of the appliance activation.

Similarly, detection of activation of any appliance of category 3 launches the time recording procedure terminated by detection of activation of any other appliance of category 3, measuring the operator's transfer time (and corresponding motion speed) and attributing it to the later device.

These two records descriptive for human's behavior are subjects to machine learning in order to calculate their statistical model based on average (i.e. most expected) values and typical (i.e. allowable) deviations. During the surveillance stage, new events are detected, categorized and provide their quantitative description to the database. Next they are compared to a device-specific threshold distinguishing the current event as:

- variant of regular performance contributing to re-learning and adapting of the normal class kernel, or
- irregular performance, not contributing to re-learning, but triggering an adequate alert.

4   Tests and Results

4.1   Implementation Constraints

The implementation used a single piece of hardware built accordingly to [4]. The device continuously measures the line load and stores samples ($f_s = 1$ kHz) in a loopback buffer (10 s). A load transient defined as $\Delta I > 20$ mA triggers the measurement of the buffered data yielding maximum values of active and reactive power, transient time and spectral features of three dominant harmonic frequencies. These values, called *load signature*, were stored in the database as the event description. The database is first initialized with load signature patterns, recorded in the sensor learning phase, where any electrical equipment in the household is manually turned on and off. In a next off-line step, these values subject to recognition of device and event type, where the load signature patterns are used as classification kernels (k-nearest neighbors method). Since the classification is only about 96–99% accurate and the usage of a new device, unknown at sensor learning stage, is not excluded, we added new item called '*unknown load event*' to the outcome event list.

The load sensor trained with given device set was then used to measure human performance in an example experimental household. The energy saving results and device-oriented usage data were put aside, giving priority to calculations of two behavior-specific sequences: mobility of the subject between two switch-on episodes (category 3) and regularity of devices' usage (categories 2 and 3). The respective behavioral databases were created accordingly for each recognizable device: hair dryer and iron (both used in bathroom only), electric kettle, microwave, toaster, coffee maker, oven and electric mixer. Other devices (e.g. refrigerator or stereo) were excluded as either automatically or remotely switched and thus not representative for operator's behavior. Each database consists of a statictically processed typical behavioral pattern and up to five most recently recorded patterns ordered by their time stamp.

4.2   Experiment Setup

Three volunteers played predefined scenarios arranged as excerpts from daily living activities. In the system learning stage, they were roughly instructed to perform usual morning activities (MA), evening activities (EA) and housekeeping actions (HA) up to their habitual routine within a time limit of 60 min. The only requisite was the usage of both bathroom and kitchen devices, and we prefer the usage of as many various devices as possible. We collected behavioral patterns from five repetitions of all subjects and all tested scenarios. Each appliance was used at least three times by each volunteer. Calculations of statistical behavioral models including most typical devices' usage sequence and duration and the shortest bathroom to kitchen transfer time with their respective deviation data concluded the learning stage.

In the system testing stage the volunteers first repeated their action as in the previous stage, what allowed to confirm the correctness of action detection. Next, they were asked to perform predefined irregular operations of household devices consisting in:

- significant changing of usage durations,
- changing the events sequence order, or
- limitation of operator's mobility.

The newly detected behavior was compared with the patterns in the database and classified as regular or irregular. Regular behavior cases were used for kernel adjustment, while irregular cases triggered an adequate alert. The applied testing protocol allowed us to assess the correctness of irregular operation detection and surveillance system adaptivity.

4.3   Results

Test results for device recognition accuracy are presented in Table 1 for all volunteers and all scenarios. Table 2 summarizes results of device usage frequency and length typical for three considered scenarios and Table 3 presents results of irregular behavior detection in all cases.

5   Discussion

As Table 1 shows, particular domestic devices are reliably identified by the sensor, under the condition of their uniqueness in the household. The operation events detected by specific load signatures determine the location of the operator for most devices (automatically switching devices, like a refrigerator, were recognized by the sensor, but excluded from the behavioral studies). Shortest time between termination of the usage of bathroom appliance (hair dryer, iron) and beginning of the usage of kitchen appliance (kettle, microwave) represents the operator's transfer speed and his or her mobility, under the condition of a single operating person. The transfer time was not calculated as the average, since the activity of the operator between these events is undetermined.

Table 1. Device recognition accuracy

Device name	Recognition accuracy %
Hair dryer	96.3
Iron	98.5
Electric kettle	99.1
Microwave	97.2
Toaster	95.4
Coffee maker	96.7
Oven	98.9
Electric mixer	97.0
Average	97.4

Table 2. Device usage frequency ([%]) and average duration ([s])

Device name	Morning Activity (MA)	Evening Activity (EA)	Housekeeping Action (HA)
Hair dryer	15/180	25/240	10/240
Iron	10/300	70/2700	20/600
Electric kettle	100/100	30/100	100/180
Microwave	20/120	0/n.a	35/600
Toaster	50/300	0/n.a	30/400
Coffee maker	75/180	15/180	30/180
Oven	0/n.a	15/3600	70/1800
Electric mixer	10/120	20/600	20/600

Table 2 gives a more detailed insight to the probability and the most expected duration of devices' usage. In the form as presented in Table 2, the data may be used to predict the energy supply necessary in mornings and evenings of each working day or in the late morning on Saturdays when housekeeping actions are usually performed. These data may also be interesting to build a personalized profile of energy consumption, device usage and thus individual habits of each inhabitant. Moreover, such complex activities may easily be classified by device type and usage characteristics. Although safety improvement falls besides the scope of this paper, it is worth to mention that erroneous operation of devices may also be detected based on comparison of actual and habitual usage profiles.

Analysis of differences in behavior allows for drawing more general characteristics of the operating individuals. The data in Table 3 show that the volunteer Vol1 is quicker than Vol2, but performs more chaotically. On the other hand, Vol3 is slower than both others, but his performance is the most regular. Other conclusions are drawn from the comparison of morning and evening activities which

Table 3. Results of irregular behavior detection and operator's mobility

Volunteer and scenario identifier	Changing of events duration [%]	Changing the events sequence order [%]	Average bathroom to kitchen transfer time [s]
Vol1.MA	93.3	96.7	5.5
Vol1.EA	89.7	92.1	5.2
Vol1.HA	81.4	67.4	6.1
Vol2.MA	96.4	98.1	6.1
Vol2.EA	94.3	96.0	5.8
Vol2.HA	88.2	84.4	6.8
Vol3.MA	91.1	94.3	5.4
Vol3.EA	89.7	92.1	5.2
Vol3.HA	77.2	57.4	5.6

are usually more regular and housekeeping actions, where operator's behavior randomly depends on the actual tasks.

Despite a total invisibility of the load sensor and satisfactory results presented here, we have to point out numerous limitations of usage of the load signature-based approach to deduce about inhabitant's behavior. First is the single-chip collective sensing made for the whole household, which allows to use regular of-the-shelf domestic appliances, at the price of ambiguous identification of devices, their status, operator and location. Second is the limited number of electrically powered devices in the technical ecosystem of the monitored person. Few other devices of everyday use like tap, broom, chair on even garmet used in routine activities are out of range of the load signature detection. Finally, the psychophysical status of the supervised human is only partly represented in interactions with his or her environment. This is usually compensated by wearable sensors, which are hard to be imperceptible to the wearer unless implanted.

Acknowledgement. This scientific work is supported by the AGH University of Science and Technology in years 2015–2016 as a research project No. 11.11.120.612.

References

1. Augustyniak, P., Smolen, M., Mikrut, Z., Katoch, E.: Seamless tracing of human behavior using complementary wearable and house-embedded sensors. Sensors **14**(5), 7831–7856 (2014)
2. Augustyniak, P., Kantoch, E.: Turning domestic appliances into a sensor network for monitoring of activities of daily living. J. Med. Imaging Health Inf. **5**, 1662–1667 (2015)
3. Bagala, F., et al.: Evaluation of accelerometer-based fall detection algorithms on real-world falls. PLoS ONE **7**, e37062 (2012)

4. Belley, C., Gaboury, S., Bouchard, B., Bouzouane, A.: Activity recognition in smart homes based on electrical devices identification. In: Proceedings of the 6th International Conference on Pervasive Technologies Related to Assistive Environments, Rhodes, Greece, pp. 1–8 (2013). doi:10.1145/2504335.2504342
5. Bobek, S., Porzycki, K., Nalepa, G.J.: Learning sensors usage patterns in mobile context-aware systems. In: Ganzha, M., Maciaszek, L.A., Paprzycki, M. (eds.) Proceedings of the Federated Conference on Computer Science and Information Systems FedCSIS 2013, Krakow, Poland, 8–11 September 2013, pp. 993–998. IEEE (2013)
6. Brdiczka, O., Crowley, J.L., Reignier, P.: Learning situation models in a smart home. IEEE Trans. Syst. Man Cybern. Part B Cybern. **39**(1), 56–63 (2009)
7. Bujnowski, A., Skalski, L., Wtorek, J.: Monitoring of a bathing person. J. Med. Imaging Health Inform. **2**, 27–34 (2012)
8. Lai, Y.-X., Lai, C.-B., Huang, Y.-M., Chao, H.-C.: Multi-appliance recognition system with hybrid SVM/GMM classifier in ubiquitous smart home. Inf. Sci. **230**, 39–55 (2013)
9. Lapalu, J., Bouchard, K., Bouzouane, A., Bouchard, B., Giroux, S.: Unsupervised mining of activities for smart home prediction. In: Proceedings of the 4th International Conference on Ambient Systems, Networks and Technologies, Procedia Computer Science, vol. 19, pp. 503–510 (2013)
10. Li, C., Hua, T.: Human action recognition based on template matching. Procedia Eng. **15**, 2824–2830 (2011)
11. Luhr, S., West, G., Venkatesh, S.: Recognition of emergent human behaviour in a smart home: a data mining approach. Pervasive Mob. Comput. **3**, 95–116 (2007)
12. Maitre, J., Glon, G., Gaboury, S., Bouchard, B., Bouzouane, A.: Efficient appliances recognition in smart homes based on active and reactive power, fast fourier transform and decision trees. Papers from the 2015 Association for the Advancement of Artificial Intelligence Workshop, pp. 24–29 (2015)
13. Robben, S., Krse, B.: Longitudinal residential ambient monitoring: correlating sensor data to functional health status. In: Proceedings of the 7th International Conference on Pervasive Computing Technologies for Healthcare (PervasiveHealth), pp. 244–247 (2013)
14. Ros, M., Cullar, M.P., Delgado, M., Vila, A.: Online recognition of human activities and adaptation to habit changes by means of learning automata and fuzzy temporal windows. Inf. Sci. **220**, 86–101 (2013)
15. Ruzzelli, A.G., Nicolas, C., Schoofs, A., OHare, G.M.P.: Real-time recognition and profiling of appliances through a single electricity sensor. In: Proceedings of the 7th Annual IEEE Communications Society Conference on Sensor, Mesh and Ad Hoc Communications and Networks, Boston, MA, USA, 21–25 June 2010, pp. 1–9 (2010)
16. Vu, L., Do, Q., Nahrstedt, K.: Jyotish: constructive approach for context predictions of people movement from joint Wifi/Bluetooth trace. Pervasive Mob. Comput. **7**, 690–704 (2011)
17. Zoha, A., Gluhak, A., Imran, M.A., Rajasegarar, S.: Non-intrusive load monitoring approaches for disaggregated energy sensing: a survey. Sensors **12**(12), 16838–16866 (2012). doi:10.3390/s121216838

Regularization Methods for the Analytical Statistical Reconstruction Problem in Medical Computed Tomography

Robert Cierniak[1]([✉]), Anna Lorent[1], Piotr Pluta[1], and Nimit Shah[2]

[1] Institute of Computational Intelligence, Czestochowa University of Technology,
Armii Krajowej 36, 42-200 Czestochowa, Poland
robert.cierniak@iisi.pcz.pl

[2] Department of Electrical Engineering, M.S. University of Baroda, Vadodara, India

Abstract. The main purpose of this paper is to present the properties of our novel statistical model-based iterative approach to the image reconstruction from projections problem regarding its condition number. The reconstruction algorithm based on this concept uses a maximum likelihood estimation with an objective adjusted to the probability distribution of measured signals obtained using x-ray computed tomography. We compare this with some selected methods of regularizing the problem. The concept presented here is fundamental for 3D statistical tailored reconstruction methods designed for x-ray computed tomography.

Keywords: Image reconstruction from projections · X-ray computed tomography · Statistical reconstruction algorithm · Overfitting · Regularization

1 Introduction

This paper is concerned with the problem of formulating image reconstruction from projections algorithms, which are most important for the development of a basic medical imaging technique which is called Computed Tomography (CT). The main challenge in x-ray computed tomography is to improve the resolution of reconstructed images and/or decrease the x-ray intensity, while maintaining the quality of the CT images obtained. It is argued that x-ray radiation is harmful to the health of patients being examined because it can lead to many serious illnesses, and this therefore creates a barrier to the development of this x-ray medical imaging technique. It is for that reason that statistical reconstruction methods are being so intensively developed. Because the signals are adapted to the specific statistics of a given technique, the algorithms can yield a reduction in the radiation dose experienced during human body examination. Unfortunately, limiting the intensity of x-ray radiation during an examination, and thereby limiting the x-ray dose absorption, means a deterioration of the images obtained,

© Springer International Publishing Switzerland 2016
L. Rutkowski et al. (Eds.): ICAISC 2016, Part II, LNAI 9693, pp. 147–158, 2016.
DOI: 10.1007/978-3-319-39384-1_13

i.e. a decrease of the low contrast resolution parameter (one of the most important parameters used to describe the quality of a scanner). This is governed by the following relationship:

$$SNR \propto \sqrt{D} \tag{1}$$

where: D is the dose of x-ray radiation absorbed by a patient.

Relation (1) shows a strong connection between the dose absorbed by a patient and the quality of the reconstructed image. This presents a barrier to limiting the intensity directly, because the x-ray dose absorbed by a patient is proportional to the intensity of the x-ray used during the examination. That is why a new idea has emerged to decrease the dose, without degradation of the reconstructed image, by using an appropriately formulated reconstruction algorithm. This idea is exemplified by statistical image reconstruction algorithms, which take into account the probabilistic conditions present in the measurement systems of CT scanners, so as to limit the influence of this noise on the images obtained from the measurements. There are several statistical iterative reconstruction algorithms and iterative image based denoising algorithms that have been commercially developed and introduced, for example Adaptive Statistical Iterative Reconstruction (ASIR), Iterative Reconstruction in Image Space (ARIS), Adaptive Iterative Dose Reduction (AIDR) or iDose algorithms, which perform reconstruction processing iteratively in order to decrease the noise in the images. The most interesting, from a scientific point of view, is the model-based iterative reconstruction (MBIR) approach (see e.g. [1,2]). In this approach, in the likelihood term of the objective, the physical measurements are compared with calculated sinogram values. Matrix **A**, an operator transforming the reconstructed image into a sinogram space, is established in a manner similar to the methodology used in series-expansion reconstruction methods such as, for example, in algebraic reconstruction techniques. The matrix form of the reconstruction problem formulation in these approaches enables us, in our opinion, to classify them as "algebraic" methods. The commercial system Veo is based on this idea. As opposed to this solution, we propose an analytical statistical problem formulation. This idea has been presented in the literature in original work published by the author of this paper for parallel scanner geometry e.g. in [3–5,8], for fan-beam geometry in [6,7,10], and for spiral cone-beam geometry as presented in [9,11]. However, the approach is still under intensive research. At the moment, the most important direction of these studies is to show the advantages of our approach over algebraic forms of the statistical reconstruction problem. In particular, these considerations are addressed by an assessment of the condition number of our analytical approach. It is important to evaluate how a problem is conditioned in the context of the overfitting effect (typical for learning processes in soft computing techniques, see e.g. [12,13]), and consequently the need to regularize this problem, especially in such kind inverse problems which are mostly ill-conditioned.

2 Condition Number of the Analytical Statistical Reconstruction Problem

We have previously formulated our novel 2D analytical approximate reconstruction problem for scanners with parallel geometry (see e.g. [7]). There the formulation of the reconstruction problem is reduced to the weighted least squares (WLS) estimation problem, and can be written as follows:

$$
\mu_{min} = \arg\min_{\mu} \left(\frac{n_0}{2} \sum_{i=1}^{I} \sum_{j=1}^{J} \frac{1}{\sigma_{ij}^2} \cdot \left(\sum_{\bar{i}} \sum_{\bar{j}} \mu^* \left(x_{\bar{i}}, y_{\bar{j}} \right) \cdot h_{\Delta i, \Delta j} - \tilde{\mu} \left(x_i, y_j \right) \right)^2 \right),
$$

(2)

where coefficients $h_{\Delta i, \Delta j}$ are

$$
h_{\Delta i, \Delta j} = \Delta_\alpha \sum_{\psi=0}^{\Psi-1} int \left(\Delta i \cos \psi \Delta_\alpha + \Delta j \sin \psi \Delta_\alpha \right),
$$

(3)

and $\tilde{\mu}(i,j)$ is an image obtained by way of a back-projection operation; $int(\Delta s)$ is an interpolation function used in the back-projection operation; σ_{ij}^2 is a variance determined for every pixel in the image obtained after the back-projection operation; every projection is carried out after a rotation by Δ_α.

It is fundamental for our approach to consider the properties of the problem formulated by relation (2). It is convenient for this purpose to write this formula in the following form:

$$
\mu_{min} = \arg\min_{\mu} \left(\frac{n_0}{2} \| \mathbf{W} \left(\mathbf{H}\mu - \tilde{\mu} \right) \|_2^2 \right),
$$

(4)

where: $\mathbf{W} = [w_k] = [\frac{1}{\sigma_k^2}]$; $\mu^* = [\mu_l^*]$, and $\mu_l^* = \mu^* (x_{l\ div\ I+1}, y_{l\ mod\ I})$; $\tilde{\mu} = [\tilde{\mu}_k]$, and $\tilde{\mu}_k = \tilde{\mu} (x_{k\ div\ I+1}, y_{k\ mod\ I})$; $\mathbf{H} = [H_{kl}]$, and $H_{kl} = h_{\Delta i, \Delta j} = h_{(l-1)\ mod\ I-(k-1)\ mod\ I,(l-1)\ div\ I-(k-1)\ div\ I}$. The WLS expressed in this way is not over-determined and has a unique solution. This means that it can be reduced to a least squares (LS) problem.

For this kind of inverse problem, it is crucial to evaluate its sensitivity to perturbation, caused both by the limited accuracy of the model and by errors in the measurements. Sensitivity analysis is usually performed using an evaluation of the condition number of a given problem. In this case, we are actually dealing with linear least squares, and we can estimate the relative error of the solution obtained (see [14]), as follows:

$$
\frac{\| \delta\mu \|_2}{\| \mu_0 \|_2} \le \kappa_2 \left(1 + \kappa_2 \frac{\| e_0 \|_2}{\| \mu_0 \| \sigma_{max}} \right) \frac{\| \delta\mathbf{H} \|_2}{\| \mathbf{H} \|_2} + \kappa_2 \frac{\| \delta\tilde{\mu} \|_2}{\| \mu_0 \|_2 \sigma_{min}}
$$

(5)

where: $\kappa_2 = \sigma_{max}/\sigma_{min}$ is the spectral matrix condition number; σ_{max} and σ_{min} are the largest and the smallest singular values of the matrix $\mathbf{H}$; μ_0 is the solution of problem (4); $e_0 = \mathbf{H}\mu^* - \tilde{\mu}$ is the least squares residual. The matrix $\mathbf{H}$ is a normal matrix so $\sigma_{\max} = \lambda_{\max}$ and $\sigma\min = \lambda\min$, where $\lambda_{\max}$ and $\lambda\min$ are the largest and the smallest eigenvalues of the matrix $\mathbf{H}$ (all eigenvalues of $\mathbf{H}$ are positive).

Taking into account only the first term on the left side of the inequality (4) it is easy to overestimate the spectral norm relative condition number by at most a factor of $\sqrt{2}$ [14], assessing the influence of the model inaccuracy on the results obtained, as

$$\chi_2^{LS,rel}(\mathbf{H}) = \frac{\frac{\|\delta\mu\|_2}{\|\mu_0\|_2}}{\frac{\|\delta\mathbf{H}\|_2}{\|\mathbf{H}\|_2}} \leq \left(\frac{\|\mathbf{e}_0\|_2}{\|\mu_0\|_2\,\lambda_{\min}} + 1\right)\kappa_2 \tag{6}$$

As was mentioned earlier, problem (3) has a single unique solution, and $\|\mathbf{e}_0\| = 0$, leading to

$$\chi_2^{LS,rel}(\mathbf{H}) \leq \kappa_2. \tag{7}$$

The above relation allows us to estimate the condition number of the least squares problem based on the condition number of the matrix $\mathbf{H}$. It only remains to determine this condition number. This is not an easy matter because of the huge dimensions of the matrix: $2I^2 \times 2I^2$. Fortunately, matrix $\mathbf{H}$ is a symmetrical Toeplitz-Block-Toeplitz (TBT) matrix, and it is possible to evaluate a condition number for this matrix using the TBT modified to a circulant matrix $\mathbf{H}^c$ [15]. The reason for this manipulation is that it is easy to determine the condition number for a circulant matrix using the 2D FFT of the appropriately formed first column of this matrix. Condition number κ_2^c is equal in this case to the ratio of the maximum and minimum magnitudes of the spectrum of this column. It is shown in [15] that $\kappa_2 \leq \kappa_2^c$. For instance, for an image of resolution of 1024×1024 and $\kappa_2^c = 6604$, then

$$\chi_2^{LS,rel}(\mathbf{H}) \leq \kappa_2(\mathbf{H}^c) \approx 2245. \tag{8}$$

Analogously, we can estimate the influence of measurement errors (in this case noise) on the accuracy of the reconstructed image, considering only the second term on the left side of the inequality (4), as follows:

$$\chi_2^{LS,rel}(\tilde{\mu}) = \frac{\frac{\|\delta\mu\|_2}{\|\mu_0\|_2}}{\frac{\|\delta\tilde{\mu}\|_2}{\|\tilde{\mu}\|_2}} \leq \kappa_2 \frac{\|\tilde{\mu}\|_2}{\sigma_{\min}\|\mu_0\|_2}. \tag{9}$$

We can also evaluate this condition number using experiments with mathematical phantoms. In this case the ratio $\frac{\|\tilde{\mu}\|_2}{\|\mu_0\|_2}$ has a value of 2544. The lowest eigenvalue of the matrix $\mathbf{H}^c$ which was determined to calculate $\kappa_2(\mathbf{H}^c)$ is $\lambda_{\min}^c = 2.84$, and taking into account the fact that $\lambda_{\min} > \lambda_{\min}^c$ [15], we obtain an upper bound for the condition number established to assess the error in the reconstructed image from perturbations in the data obtained from x-ray measurements, where these perturbations may be due to measurement noise:

$$\chi_2^{LS,rel}(\tilde{\mu}) \leq \frac{\kappa_2^c(\mathbf{H}^c)}{\lambda_{\min}^c}\frac{\|\tilde{\mu}\|_2}{\|\mu_0\|_2} \approx 4.9 \cdot 10^6. \tag{10}$$

The results presented in Eqs. (8) and (10) show that the reconstruction problem (2) is middle-conditioned for inaccuracy in the model and strongly ill-conditioned for errors in measured data (noise). Therefore, problem (2) needs to be regularized in some way, often by the introduction of an additional term. This term usually has a form which limits large values of $\|\mu\|$ in the reconstructed image, and can be interpreted as a prior knowledge that $\|\mu\|$ for this image will be relatively small. It relates to the maximum a posteriori (MAP) estimate framework. In our case, this Bayesian framework can be expressed as follows:

$$\mu_{\min}^* = \arg\min_{\mu^*} \left(\frac{n_0}{2} \sum_{i=1}^{I} \sum_{j=1}^{J} \frac{1}{\sigma_{ij}^2} \cdot \left(\sum_{\bar{i}} \sum_{\bar{j}} \mu^* (x_{\bar{i}}, y_{\bar{j}}) \cdot h_{\Delta i, \Delta j} - \tilde{\mu} (x_i, y_j) \right)^2 + f(\mu) \right),$$
(11)

where $f(\mu)$ is some scalar regularization term. This regularization term may take different forms, however, functions which are based on the generalized Gaussian Markov random fields (q-GGMRFs) approach are often preferred and are able, in a controlled way, to preserve the edges in the reconstructed image, which has the following form [1]:

$$f_{qGGMRF}(\mu) = \frac{1}{pr^p} \sum_{\{k,\bar{k}\} \in C} d_{k,\bar{k}} \frac{|\mu_k - \mu_{\bar{k}}|^p}{1 + \left| \frac{\mu_k - \mu_{\bar{k}}}{u} \right|^{p-q}},$$
(12)

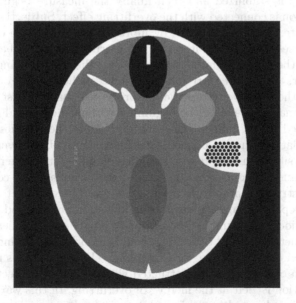

Fig. 1. View of the original images of the phantoms used in the experiments: FORBILD phantom (window center $C = 1.05 \cdot 10^{-3}$, window width $W = 0.1 \cdot 10^{-3}$).

where: C is the set of all pairs of neighboring pixels; $d_{k,\bar{k}}$ are directional weighting coefficients, which are chosen as the inverse of the distance between the center pixel and the elements in C; the constants p, q and u determine properties of function (12) (for details see [1]).

Another interesting approach to this method is total variation (TV) regularization. In this case, the following form of the prior term can be used (for details see e.g. [16]):

$$f_{TV}(\mu) = \sum_{i,j} \left((\mu(x_{i+1}, y_j) - \mu(x_i, y_j))^2 + (\mu(x_i, y_{j+1}) - \mu(x_i, y_j))^2 + \beta \right)^{\frac{1}{2}},$$

$$(13)$$

where β is a small constant used for keeping the term differentiable with respect to image intensity.

Unfortunately, supplying the regularization term causes several serious problems. Firstly, there is a trade off in the reconstruction process between a measure of consistency with experimental data and the smoothness of the image obtained. Moreover, the additional term complicates the calculations performed during the reconstruction process, especially as the form of this term usually has a complicated derivation. The regularization method proposed by us is based on the concept of early stopping (see e.g. [17]), and eliminates these drawbacks or it at least reduces their influence. This method of regularization is based on the observation that an iterative reconstruction process firstly decreases the error measure until it is stabilized and then finally the measure begins to increase. This phenomenon is connected with the overfitting effect. Subjectively, this effect is manifested, iteration by iteration, by more visible noise. The early stopping approach proposes stopping the iterative reconstruction process before the "egoistic" fitting of the pixels begins to dominate over the global fitting of the whole image. However, the error $e(i, j)$ is large in places where edges occur. One can observe during the iterative reconstruction procedure that the first relatively flat regions of the image appear, in the beginning without noise, and only later are the bones formed in the image. Unfortunately, before these bones are correctly shaped, those flat regions are blurred by noise because of the overfitting effect. To prevent this situation, we propose a slightly modified iterative reconstruction procedure. Because the optimized objective from formula (2) is convex, we can start our reconstruction procedure from any stage. Therefore, let us begin from an especially prepared image obtained using any standard method (e.g. applying some FBP method). We could use, according to a particular medical case, a window with parameters W_s and C_s, and we could smooth the starting image inside this window to a constant value, for example C_s. Because of this manipulation, the given region of interest is reconstructed with a denoising effect and the rest of the cross-section is "left at the mercy" of overfitting. In this way the prepared starting image is subjected to the iterative reconstruction process, some results of which are depicted in Tables 1, 2 and 3.

Table 1. View of the images (window centre $C = 1.05 \cdot 10^{-3}$, window width $W = 0.1 \cdot 10^{-3}$) using the following form of regularization term: q $-$ GGRMF ($c_2 = 10^{-13}$, $p = 2$, $q = 1.2$, $u = 10$)

It.	Reconstructed images	MSE
	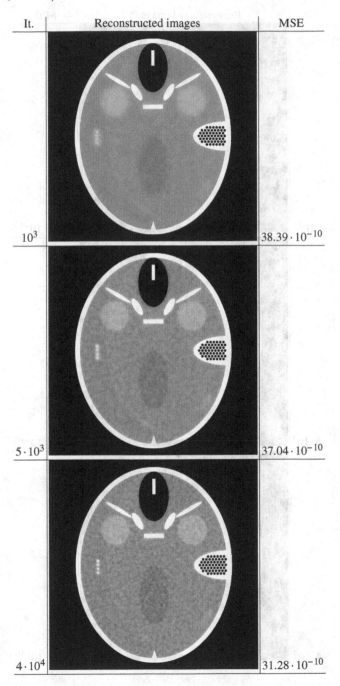	
10^3		$38.39 \cdot 10^{-10}$
$5 \cdot 10^3$		$37.04 \cdot 10^{-10}$
$4 \cdot 10^4$		$31.28 \cdot 10^{-10}$

Table 2. View of the images (window centre $C = 1.05 \cdot 10^{-3}$, window width $W = 0.1 \cdot 10^{-3}$) using the following form of regularization term: TV ($c_2 = 10^{-4}$, $\beta = 10^{-10}$)

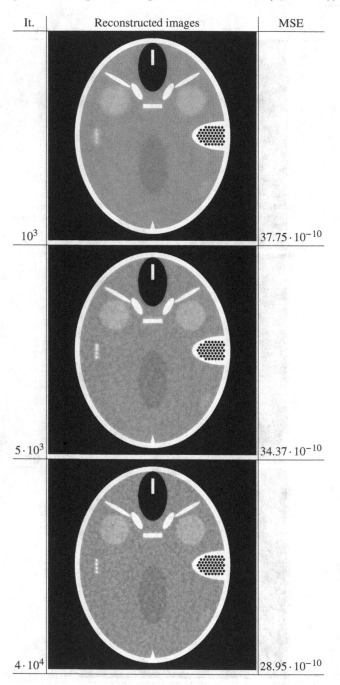

It.	Reconstructed images	MSE
10^3		$37.75 \cdot 10^{-10}$
$5 \cdot 10^3$		$34.37 \cdot 10^{-10}$
$4 \cdot 10^4$		$28.95 \cdot 10^{-10}$

Table 3. View of the images (window centre $C = 1.05 \cdot 10^{-3}$, window width $W = 0.1 \cdot 10^{-3}$) without regularization term

It.	Reconstructed images	MSE
	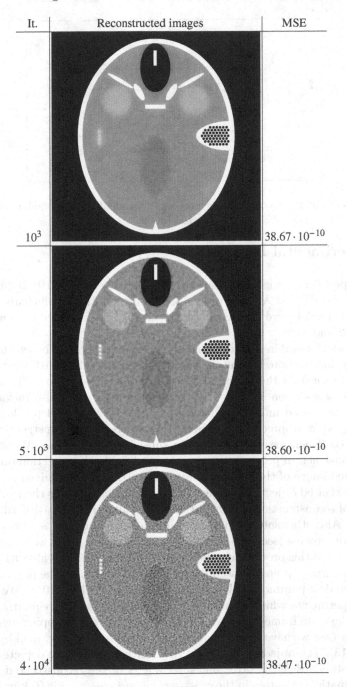	
10^3		$38.67 \cdot 10^{-10}$
$5 \cdot 10^3$		$38.60 \cdot 10^{-10}$
$4 \cdot 10^4$		$38.47 \cdot 10^{-10}$

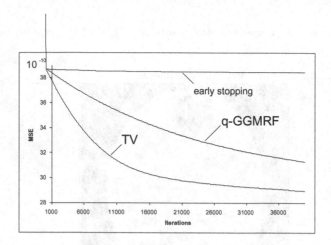

Fig. 2. Results of the reconstruction process, dependent on the number of iterations during the calculation of the reconstructed image.

3   Experimental Results

In our experiments, we have adapted the well-known FORBILD phantom of the head (see Fig. 1). All the values of the attenuation coefficients placed in the original model were divided by a factor 10^{-3} to facilitate the calculations (Tables 1, 2 and 3).

The model formed in this way was used to generate projections with a Poisson probability distribution. During the simulations, we fixed $L = 1024$ measurement points (detectors) on the screen at virtual parallel projections. The number of projections was chosen as $\Psi = 1610$ rotation angles per half-rotation and the size of the processed image was fixed at $I \times I = 1024 \times 1024$ pixels. The coefficients $h_{\Delta i, \Delta j}$ were precomputed before we started the reconstruction process and these coefficients were fixed for the subsequent processing. We started the actual reconstruction procedure and performed the back-projection operation to get a blurred image of the x-ray attenuation distribution in a given cross-section of the investigated object. The image obtained in this way was then subjected to a process of reconstruction (optimization) using an iterative statistically-tailored procedure. Also other soft computing techniques can find their application in this optimization process (see e.g. [18–23]). It is worth noting that we can choose the starting point of this procedure to be a result of using the FBP algorithm, and we used such an image prepared according to the description in the previous section with the window parameters $W_s = 2.1 \cdot 10^{-3}$ and $C_s = 1.05 \cdot 10^{-3}$. We have performed experiments which examined two approaches to the regularization: one using the Bayesian framework and the other with the early stopping methodology (in the first case we have used two forms of the prior term described by formulas (12) and (13). The objective results of these investigations are depicted in Fig. 2 using the standard MSE error measure. Views of the reconstructed images of the mathematical phantom in the cross-section are presented in Tables 1, 2 and 3.

4   Conclusion

The use of an analytical scheme of signal processing allows us to avoid very serious difficulties associated with the algebraic formulation of the reconstruction problem, which are particularly noticeable in reconstruction algorithms for spiral scanners. Simulations have been performed, which have shown that the proposed statistical approach allows us to design an iterative reconstruction procedure based both on a Bayesian framework, i.e. with the introduction of a prior term into the objective, and on a framework without any regularization term. The processing of our original reconstruction procedure is stable even if we do not use any additional regularization term. This simplification reduces the computation time in comparison with the Bayesian framework (by approximately a factor 1.5) without significant decreasing the quality of the reconstructed image (in particular in the subjective assessment). In contrast with the algebraic approach (ICD algorithm) used in the 3D MBIR technique, our analytical problem is much better conditioned (in the algebraic case the condition number of the WLS problem is approximately $\chi_2^{LS,rel}(\mathbf{A}) \approx 1.7 \cdot 10^4$ and $\chi_2^{LS,rel}(\mathbf{p}) \approx 1.5 \cdot 10^9$). Additionally, the computational complexity of every iteration of the reconstruction procedure is approximately proportional to $I^4 \times (num\_rec\_slices)^2 \times num\_measur$, and our method is much more attractive for a 3D implementation (approximately $2I^2 \log_2 I$ for one iteration of the reconstruction procedure).

References

1. Thibault, J.-B., Sauer, K.D., Bouman, C.A., Hsieh, J.: A three-dimensional statistical approach to improved image quality for multislice helical CT. Med. Phys. **34**(11), 4526–4544 (2007)
2. Zhou, Y., Thibault, J.-B., Bouman, C.A., Sauer, K.D., Hsieh, J.: Fast model-based x-ray CT reconstruction using spatially non-homogeneous ICD optimization. IEEE Trans. Image Process. **20**(1), 161–175 (2011)
3. Cierniak, R.: A novel approach to image reconstruction from discrete projections using hopfield-type neural network. In: Rutkowski, L., Tadeusiewicz, R., Zadeh, L.A., Żurada, J.M. (eds.) ICAISC 2006. LNCS (LNAI), vol. 4029, pp. 890–898. Springer, Heidelberg (2006)
4. Cierniak, R.: A new approach to tomographic image reconstruction using a Hopfield-type neural network. Int. J. Artif. Intell. Med. **43**(2), 113–125 (2008)
5. Cierniak, R.: A new approach to image reconstruction from projections problem using a recurrent neural network. Int. J. Appl. Math. Comput. Sci. **183**(2), 147–157 (2008)
6. Cierniak, R.: A novel approach to image reconstruction problem from fan-beam projections using recurrent neural network. In: Rutkowski, L., Tadeusiewicz, R., Zadeh, L.A., Zurada, J.M. (eds.) ICAISC 2008. LNCS (LNAI), vol. 5097, pp. 752–761. Springer, Heidelberg (2008)
7. Cierniak, R.: New neural network algorithm for image reconstruction from fan-beam projections. Neurocomputing **72**, 3238–3244 (2009)
8. Cierniak, R.: An analytical iterative statistical algorithm for image reconstruction from projections. Appl. Math. Comput. Sci. **24**(1), 7–17 (2014)

9. Cierniak, R.: A three-dimentional neural network based approach to the image reconstruction from projections problem. In: Rutkowski, L., Scherer, R., Tadeusiewicz, R., Zadeh, L.A., Zurada, J.M. (eds.) ICAISC 2010, Part I. LNCS, vol. 6113, pp. 505–514. Springer, Heidelberg (2010)

10. Cierniak, R.: Neural network algorithm for image reconstruction using the grid-friendly projections. Australas. Phys. Eng. Sci. Med. **34**, 375–389 (2011)

11. Cierniak, R., Knas, M.: An analytical statistical approach to the 3D reconstruction problem. In: Proceedings of the 12th International Meeting on Fully Three-Dimensional Image Reconstruction in Radiology and Nuclear Medicine, pp. 521–524 (2013)

12. Chu, J.L., Krzyźak, A.: The recognition of partially occluded objects with support vector machines, convolutional neural networks and deep belief networks. J. Artif. Intell. Soft. Comput. Res. **4**(1), 5–19 (2014)

13. Bas, E.: The training of multiplicative neuron model artificial neural networks with differential evolution algorithm for forecasting. J. Artif. Intell. Soft. Comput. Res. **6**(1), 5–11 (2016)

14. Grcar, J.F.: Optimal sensivity analysis of linear least squares. Technical report LBNL-52434, lawrance Berkeley National Laboratory (2003)

15. Golub, G.H., Van Loan, C.F.: Matrix Computations, 3rd edn. Johns Hopkins University Press, Baltimore (1996)

16. Aujol, J.-F.: Some first-order algorithms for total variation based image restoration. J. Math. Imaging Vision **34**(3), 307–327 (2009)

17. Raskutti, G., Wainwright, M.J., Yu, B.: Early stopping and non-parametric regression: an optimal data-dependent stopping rule. J. Mach. Learn. Res. **15**, 335–366 (2014)

18. Chen, M., Ludwig, S.A.: Particle swarm optimization based fuzzy clustering approach to identify optimal number of clusters. J. Artif. Intell. Soft. Comput. Res. **4**(1), 43–56 (2014)

19. Aghdam, M.H., Heidari, S.: Feature selection using particle swarm optimization in text categorization. J. Artif. Intell. Soft. Comput. Res. **5**(4), 231–238 (2015)

20. El-Samak, A.F., Ashour, W.: Optimization of traveling salesman problem using affinity propagation clustering and genetic algorithm. J. Artif. Intell. Soft. Comput. Res. **5**(4), 239–245 (2015)

21. Leon, M., Xiong, N.: Adapting differential evolution algorithms for continuous optimization via greedy adjustment of control parameters. J. Artif. Intell. Soft. Comput. Res. **6**(2), 103–118 (2016)

22. Miyajima, H., Shigei, N., Miyajima, H.: Performance comparison of hybrid electromagnetism-like mechanism algorithms with descent method. J. Artif. Intell. Soft. Comput. Res. **5**(4), 271–282 (2015)

23. Rutkowska, A.: Influence of membership function's shape on portfolio optimization results. J. Artif. Intell. Soft. Comput. Res. **6**(1), 45–54 (2016)

A Case-Based Approach
to Nosocomial Infection Detection

Ricardo Faria[1], Henrique Vicente[2], António Abelha[3], Manuel Santos[4],
José Machado[3], and José Neves[3(✉)]

[1] Departamento de Informática, Universidade do Minho, Braga, Portugal
ricardo.mof@hotmail.com
[2] Departamento de Quimica, Escola de Ciências e Tecnologia,
Universidade de Évora, Évora, Portugal
hvicente@uevora.pt
[3] Centro ALGORITMI, Universidade do Minho, Braga, Portugal
{abelha,jmac,jneves}@di.uminho.pt
[4] Centro ALGORITMI, Universidade do Minho, Guimarães, Portugal
mfs@dsi.uminho.pt
http://algoritmi.uminho.pt

Abstract. The nosocomial infections are a growing concern because
they affect a large number of people and they increase the admission time
in healthcare facilities. Additionally, its diagnosis is very tricky, requiring
multiple medical exams. So, this work is focused on the development of a
clinical decision support system to prevent these events from happening.
The proposed solution is unique once it caters for the explicit treatment
of incomplete, unknown, or even contradictory information under a logic
programming basis, that to our knowledge is something that happens for
the first time.

Keywords: Nosocomial infection · Healthcare · Knowledge representation and reasoning · Logic programming · Case-based reasoning ·
Similarity analysis

1 Introduction

This paper addresses the Nosocomial Infections (NI) theme and describes an
attempt to predict such occurrences, using Case Based Reasoning (CBR). In
developed countries 7 % of the hospitalized patients contract a nosocomial infection, while for underdeveloped ones this rate is about 10 % [1]. Moreover, each
year more than 4 million patients are affected by nosocomial taints in Europe
and 1.7 million in the USA. There are several factors that affect the probability
of contracting a NI. For instance, in the Intensive Care Units there is a high
rate of occurrence of NI. Many patients probably acquire respiratory infections
while seeking care for other diseases and waiting in ambulatory care facilities,
especially in overcrowded settings in developing countries, or during epidemic

L. Rutkowski et al. (Eds.): ICAISC 2016, Part II, LNAI 9693, pp. 159–168, 2016.
DOI: 10.1007/978-3-319-39384-1_14

periods [2–4]. Furthermore, the immune state of the patient and performed clinical procedures may also contribute to the occurrence of the problem. The prediction of the NI requires a proactive strategy able to take into account all these factors. Thus, this work is focused on the development of a predictive model to estimate the NI according to a historical dataset, under a CBR approach to problem solving [5,6]. Indeed, CBR is used especially when similar cases have similar terms and solutions, even when they have different backgrounds [6]. It must be also highlighted that up to the present, CBR systems have been unable to deal with incomplete, contradictory, or even unknown information. As a matter of fact the approach to CBR presented in this work will be a generic one and will have a focus on such a setting. It brings to evidence that the first step to be tackled is related with the construction of the Case-Base, able to handle with those different types of data, information or knowledge. This has been achieved by analyzing the objects and their attributes in terms of its data quality and the confidence that one may have that they really stands for the events whim whom are related.

2   Knowledge Representation and Reasoning

Many approaches to knowledge representation and reasoning have been proposed using the Logic Programming (LP) epitome, namely in the area of Model Theory [11,12], and Proof Theory [13–15]. In the present work the proof theoretical approach in terms of an extension to the LP language is followed. An Extended Logic Program is a finite set of clauses, given in the form:

$$\{p \leftarrow p_1, \ldots, p_n, \text{not } q_1, \ldots, \text{not } q_m$$
$$?p_1 \wedge \ldots \wedge p_n \wedge \text{not } q_1 \wedge \ldots \wedge \text{not } q_m, (n, m \geq 0)$$
$$exception_{p1} \ldots exception_{pj} (j \leq m, n)\} :: scoring_{value}$$

where ? is a domain atom denoting falsity, the p_i, q_j, and p are classical ground literals, i.e., either positive atoms or atoms preceded by the classical negation sign [14], where stands for a strong statement that speaks for itself, and not denotes negation-by- failure, or in other words, a flop in proving a given statement, once it was not declared explicitly. Under this formalism, every program is associated with a set of abducibles [11,12], given here in the form of exceptions to the extensions of the predicates that make the program, i.e., they denote declarations whose truth cannot be ruled out. The term scoring value stands for the relative weight of the extension of a specific predicate with respect to the extensions of the peers ones that make the inclusive or global program. In order to evaluate the knowledge that stems from a logic program, an assessment of the Quality-of-Information (QoI), given by a truth-value in the interval $0 \ldots 1$, that stems from the extensions of the predicates that make a program, inclusive in dynamic environments, aiming at decision-making purposes, was set [16–18]. Thus, $QoI_i = 1$ when the information is known (positive) or false (negative) and $QoI_i = 0$ if the information is unknown. Finally for situations where the extension of $predicate_i$ is unknown but can be taken from a set of terms, the

$QoI_i \in]0 \ldots 1[$ [17]. The objective is to build a quantification process of QoI and measure one's confidence, here represented as DoC, that stands for Degree of Confidence that the argument values of a given predicate with relation to their domains fit into a given interval [19]. Therefore, the universe of discourse is engendered according to the information presented in the extensions of a given set of predicates, according to productions of the type:

$$predicate_i - \bigcup_{j=1}^{m} clause_j(x_i, \ldots, x_n) :: QoI_i :: DoC_i \qquad (1)$$

3   A Case Study

Aiming to develop a predictive model to estimate the occurrence of Nosocomial Infection (NI) a database was set. The data was taken from the health records of patients at a major health care institution in the north of Portugal. This section demonstrates briefly the process of extraction, transformation and loading. Moreover, shows how all the information comes together and how it is processed.

3.1   Extract, Transform and Load

To feed the CBR process it was necessary to gather data from several sources and carry out an Extract, Transform and Load (ETL) process to organize the information. The information was organized in a star schema, which consists of a collection of tables that are logically related to each other [20]. To obtain a star schema it was essential to follow a few steps. In the former one it was necessary to understand the problem in study and gather the parameters that have influence in the final outcome. There are several variables that have influence in the NI occurrence and can be grouped in two categories. The ones that are directly related with the patient and the ones that have to do with hospital environment during inpatient care. The variables chosen are presented in Fig. 1 (Sect. 3.2). The following stage was related with the dimensions that would be needed to define these parameters on the facts table. Finally, information from several sources was collected, transformed according the fact and dimension table and loaded to fact table.

3.2   Data Processing

After having obtained the star schema it is possible to build up a knowledge database given in terms of the extensions of the relations depicted in Fig. 1, which stand for a situation where one has to manage information in order to predict the occurrence of NI. Under this scenario some incomplete and/or unknown data is also available. For instance, in case 1, the Bed Occupancy Rate (BOR) is unknown, which is represented by the symbol $\perp$, while the Intrinsic Risk

Factors range in the interval $[4, 5]$. The Treatment Related Factors and Intrinsic/Extrinsic Risk Factors tables are filled with 0 (zero) and 1 (one) denoting, respectively, absence/no or presence/yes. The values presented in the Treatment Related Factors and Intrinsic/Extrinsic Risk Factors columns of Nosocomial Infection table are the sum of the correspondent tables, ranging between $0 \ldots 5, 0 \ldots 9$ and $0 \ldots 8$, respectively. The Time of Inpatient Care was computed based on Admission and Discharge Date, while in the Gender column of Nosocomial Infection table 0 (zero) and 1 (one) stand, respectively, for Female (F) and Male (M). The values shown in the Service column denote the service where the patient was admitted, ranging between $1 \ldots 60$, while BOR column is populated with 0 (zero), one (1) or two (2) according to the bed occupancy rate. Thus, 0 (zero) denotes $BOR < 70\%$; 1 (one) stands for a BOR ranging in interval $70 \ldots 85$; and 2 (two) denotes a $BOR > 85\%$. The Descriptions column stands for free text fields that allow for the registration of relevant patient features. Applying the algorithm presented in [19] to all the fields that make the knowledge base for nosocomial infection detection (Fig. 1) excluding of such a process the Description ones, and looking to the DoCs values obtained as described in [19], it is possible to set the arguments of the predicate nosocomial infections detection ($ni_{detection}$) referred to below, that also denotes the objective function with respect to the problem under analyze.

$$ni_{detection} : Age, Gen_{der}, TimeOfInpatientcare, Serv_{ice}, BOR,$$
$$Treatment Related$$
$$Factors, Intrinsic Risk Factors, Extrinsic Risk Factors \rightarrow \{0, 1\}$$

where 0 (zero) and 1 (one) denote, respectively, the truth values false and true. Exemplifying the application of the reduction algorithm presented in [20], to a term (patient) that presents feature vector ($Age = 53, Gen = 1, ToI = 19, Serv = 26, BOR = 2, TRF = [3, 4], IRF = \bot, ERF = 4$), and applying the procedure referred to above, one may get:

Begin,
```
The predicate's extension that map the Universe-of-Discourse
for the term under observation is set
```

$$\{$$
$$\neg ni_{detection}(Age, Gen, ToI, Serv, BOR, TRF, IRF, ERF)$$
$$\leftarrow ni_{detection}(Age, Gen, ToI, Serv, BOR, TRF, IRF, ERF)$$

$$ni_{detection} \frac{(53, 1, 19, 26, 2, [3, 4], \bot, 4))}{\underbrace{attribute's \quad values}} :: 1 :: DoC$$
$$\underbrace{[22.98][0, 1][2, 124][1, 61][0, 2][0, 5][0, 9][0, 8]}_{attribute's \quad domains}$$

$$\} :: 1$$

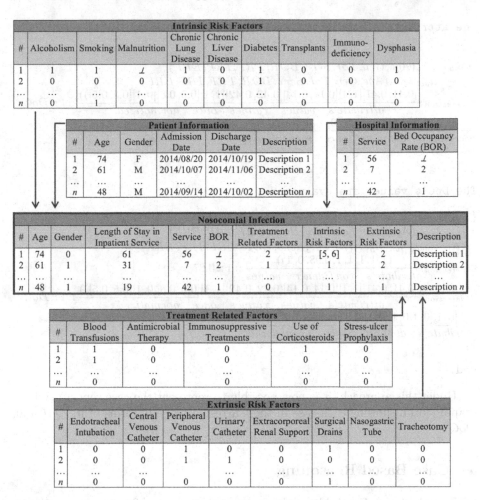

Fig. 1. A fragment of the knowledge base to predict the occurrence of nosocomial infections.

The attribute's values ranges are rewritten

$$
\{
$$
$$
\neg ni_{detection}(Age, Gen, ToI, Serv, BOR, TRF, IRF, ERF)
$$
$$
\leftarrow ni_{detection}(Age, Gen, ToI, Serv, BOR, TRF, IRF, ERF)
$$
$$
ni_{detection} \frac{([53,53][1,1][19,19][26,26][2,2][3,4][0,9][4,4]))}{attribute's \ \ values} :: 1 :: DoC
$$
$$
\frac{[22.98][0,1][2,124][1,61][0,2][0,5][0,9][0,8]}{attribute's \ \ domains}
$$
$$
\} :: 1
$$

The attribute's boundaries are set to the interval [0,1]

$\{$
$\neg ni_{detection}(Age, Gen, ToI, Serv, BOR, TRF, IRF, ERF)$
$\quad \leftarrow ni_{detection}(Age, Gen, ToI, Serv, BOR, TRF, IRF, ERF)$
$ni_{detection} \dfrac{([0.41, 0.41][1, 1][0.14, 0.14][0.42, 0.42][1, 1][0.6, 0.8][0, 1][0.5, 0.5]))}{attribute's \quad values \quad ranges \quad once \quad normalized} :: 1 :: DoC$
$\dfrac{[0, 1][0, 1]0, 1][0, 1][0, 1][0, 1][0, 1][0, 1]}{attribute's \quad domains \quad once \quad normalized}$
$\} :: 1$

The DoC's values are evaluated

$\{$
$\neg ni_{detection}(Age, Gen, ToI, Serv, BOR, TRF, IRF, ERF)$
$\quad \leftarrow ni_{detection}(Age, Gen, ToI, Serv, BOR, TRF, IRF, ERF)$
$ni_{detection} \dfrac{(1, 1, 1, 1, 1, 0.98, 0, 1))}{attribute's \quad confidence \quad values} :: 1 :: 0.87$
$ni_{detection} \dfrac{([0.41, 0.41][1, 1][0.14, 0.14][0.42, 0.42][1, 1][0.6, 0.8][0, 1][0.5, 0.5]))}{attribute's \quad values \quad ranges \quad once \quad normalized} :: 1 :: DoC$
$\dfrac{[0, 1][0, 1]0, 1][0, 1][0, 1][0, 1][0, 1][0, 1]}{attribute's \quad domains \quad once \quad normalized}$
$\} :: 1$

End.

Under this approach, it is now possible to represent the case repository in a graphic form, showing each case in the Cartesian plane in terms of its QoI and DoC.

4   Case Based Reasoning

CBR methodology for problem solving stands for an act of finding and justifying the solution to a given problem based on the consideration of similar past ones, by reprocessing or adapting their data or knowledge [5–10,15,21]. In CBR - the cases - are stored in a Case Base, and those cases that are similar or close to a new one are used in the problem solving process. Indeed, and unlike other problem solving methodologies, namely those that use Decision Trees or Artificial Neural Networks, relatively little work is done offline. Undeniably, in almost all the situations, the work is performed at query time (Fig. 2). Really, the main difference between this new approach and the typical CBR one relies on the fact that it allows for the handling of incomplete, unknown, or even contradictory data, information or knowledge [21], i.e., in [5] the working data is merely nominal and nuncupative, does not allowing for the handling of incomplete, unknown and even contradictory data, information or knowledge. On the other hand, each attribute of a given relation or predicate is to be understood not only in terms of its data quality, but also subject to an assessment if its boundaries with respect to its domains are the more appropriate ones, considering the problem under

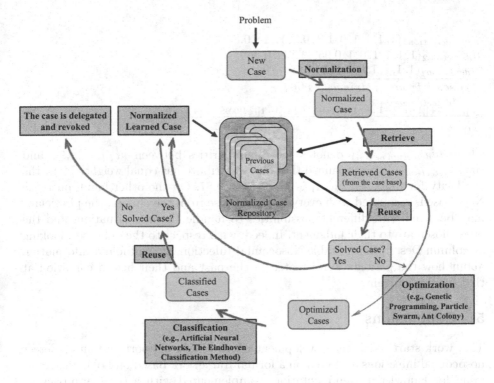

Fig. 2. A new approach to the CBR cycle.

equation, i.e., one has to have a confidence measure that a particular attribute, taken values in a given interval, fits into a given domain.

When faced to a new case, the system is able to retrieve all cases that meet such a structure and optimize such a population, i.e., it considers the attributes DoC value of each case or of their optimized counterparts when analyzing similarities among them. Thus, under the occurrence of a new case, the goal is to find similar cases in the knowledge base. Having this in mind, the reduction algorithm given in [19] is applied to the new case that presents feature vector ($Age = 67, Gen = 0, ToI = 37, Serv = 18, BOR = 1, TRF = 3, IRF = [2,4], ERF = 2, Description = Description\ new$), with the results:

$$\underline{ni_{detection\,new}(1,1,1,1,1,1,0.98,1) :: 1 :: 0.997}$$
$$new\quad case$$

Then, the New Case may be set into the Cartesian plane, and by using data mining techniques, like clustering, one may identify the clusters close to the New One. The New Case is compared with every retrieved case from the cluster using a similarity function sim, given in terms of the average of the modulus of the arithmetic difference between the arguments of each case of the selected cluster and those of the New Case (Description will not be object of attention in this work). Thus, one may get:

$$\frac{\begin{array}{l} ni_{detection1}(1,1,1,1,0,1,1,0.97) :: 1 :: 0.871 \\ ni_{detection2}(1,1,1,1,0,1,0.95,1) :: 1 :: 0.869 \\ ni_{detectionj}(1,1,1,1,0,1,0,1) :: 1 :: 0.750 \end{array}}{cases \quad from \quad retrieved \quad cluster}$$

$$ni_{detection\,new \to 1} = \frac{||1-1||+||1-1||1-1||+||1-1||+||1-0||+||1-1||+||0.98-1||+||1-0.97||}{8}$$
$$= 0.13$$

where $ni_{detection\,new \to 1}$ denotes the dissimilarities between $ni_{detection\,new}$ and the $ni_{detection1}$. It was assumed that every attribute has equal weight. Thus, the similarity for $ni_{detection\,new \to 1}$ is $1 - 0.13 = 0.87$. On the other hand, once the New Case is compared with every retrieved case from the cluster, the physicians may be faced with different possibilities to handle the new situation, and the ones chosen are to their judgment. Indeed, with respect to the old cases, looking at column Description in table Nosocomial Infection, we will found information about how the patients were treated in the past and their health condition at that precise moment.

5 Conclusions

This work starts with the development of a decision support system to detect nosocomial infections, centered on a formal framework based on Logic Programming for Knowledge Representation, complemented with a CBR approach to problem solving that caters for the handling of incomplete, unknown, or even contradictory information. With this approach the retrieval stage was optimized and the computational time was shortened in 32.7 % when compared with classic CBR implementations. Moreover, this approach allows the user to define the weights of the cases attributes on the fly, letting the user to choose the strategy he/she prefers. This feature gives the user the possibility to narrow the search for similar cases at runtime. It is also mandatory to specify and to implement an independent CBR system to automatically choose which strategy is the most reliable to a specific problem.

Acknowledgements. This work has been supported by COMPETE: POCI-01-0145-FEDER-007043 and FCT (Fundação para a Ciência e Tecnologia) within the Project Scope: UID/CEC/00319/2013.

References

1. World Health Organization: Report on the burden of endemic health care associated infection worldwide: A systematic review of the literature. WHO Press, Geneva (2011)
2. Rigor, H., Machado, J., Abelha, A., Neves, J., Alberto, C.: A web-based system to reduce the nosocomial infection impact in healtcare units. In: WEBIST 2008 - 4th International Conference on Web Information Systems and Technologies, pp. 264–268 (2008)

3. Silva, E., Cardoso, L., Portela, F., Abelha, A., Santos, M.F., Machado, J.: Predicting nosocomial infection by using data mining technologies. In: Rocha, A., Correia, A.M., Costanzo, S., Reis, L.P. (eds.) New Contributions in Information Systems and Technologies. AISC, vol. 354, pp. 189–198. Springer, Heidelberg (2015)
4. Damani, N.N.: Manual of Infection Control Procedures, 2nd edn. Greenwich Medical Media, New York (2003)
5. Aamodt, A., Plaza, E.: Case-based reasoning: foundational issues, methodological variations, and system approaches. AI Commun. **7**, 39–59 (1994)
6. Balke, T., Novais, P., Andrade, F., Eymann, T.: From real-world regulations to concrete norms for software agents - a case-based reasoning approach. In: Poblet, M., Schild, U., Zeleznikow, J. (eds.) Proceedings of the Workshop on Legal and Negotiation Decision Support Systems (LDSS 2009), pp. 13–28. Huygens Editorial, Barcelona (2009)
7. Carneiro, D., Novais, P., Andrade, F., Zeleznikow, J., Neves, J.: Using case-based reasoning to support alternative dispute resolution. In: de Leon F. de Carvalho, A.P., Rodríguez-González, S., De Paz Santana, J.F., Rodríguez, J.M.C. (eds.) Distributed Computing and Artificial Intelligence. AISC, vol. 79, pp. 123–130. Springer, Heidelberg (2010)
8. Carneiro, D., Novais, P., Andrade, F., Zeleznikow, J., Neves, J.: Using case-based reasoning and principled negotiation to provide decision support for dispute resolution. Knowl. Inf. Syst. **36**, 789–826 (2013)
9. Guessoum, S., Laskri, M.T., Lieber, J.: Respidiag: a case-based reasoning system for the diagnosis of chronic obstructive pulmonary disease. Expert Syst. Appl. **41**, 267–273 (2014)
10. Ping, X.-O., Tseng, Y.-J., Lin, Y.-P., Chiu, H.-J., Feipei Lai, F., Liang, J.-D., Huang, G.-T., Yang, P.-M.: A multiple measurements case-based reasoning method for predicting recurrent status of liver cancer patients. Comput. Ind. **69**, 12–21 (2015)
11. Kakas, A., Kowalski, R., Toni, F.: The role of abduction in logic programming. In: Gabbay, D., Hogger, C., Robinson, I. (eds.) Handbook of Logic in Artificial Intelligence and Logic Programming, vol. 5, pp. 235–324. Oxford University Press, Oxford (1998)
12. Pereira, L.M., Anh, H.T.: Evolution prospection. In: Nakamatsu, K., Phillips-Wren, G., Jain, L.C., Howlett, R.J. (eds.) New Advances in Intelligent Decision Technologies. SCI, vol. 199, pp. 51–63. Springer, Heidelberg (2009)
13. Neves, J.: A logic interpreter to handle time and negation in logic databases. In: Muller, R., Pottmyer, J. (eds.) Proceedings of the 1984 Annual Conference of the ACM on the 5th Generation Challenge, pp. 50–54. Association For Computing Machinery, New York (1984)
14. Neves, J., Machado, J., Analide, C., Abelha, A., Brito, L.: The halt condition in genetic programming. In: Neves, J., Santos, M.F., Machado, J.M. (eds.) EPIA 2007. LNCS (LNAI), vol. 4874, pp. 160–169. Springer, Heidelberg (2007)
15. Analide, C., Abelha, A., Machado, J., Neves, J.: An agent based approach to the selection dilemma in CBR. In: Badica, C., Mangioni, G., Carchiolo, V., Burdescu, D.D. (eds.) Intelligent Distributed Computing, Systems and Applications. SCI, vol. 162, pp. 35–44. Springer, Heidelberg (2008)
16. Lucas, P.: Quality checking of medical guidelines through logical abduction. In: Coenen, F., Preece, A., Mackintosh, A. (eds.) Proceedings of AI-2003 (Research and Developments in Intelligent Systems XX), pp. 309–321. Springer, London (2003)

17. Machado, J., Abelha, A., Novais, P., Neves, J., Neves, J.: Quality of service in healthcare units. In: Bertelle, C., Ayesh, A. (eds.) Proceedings of the ESM 2008, pp. 291–298. Eurosis - ETI Publication, Ghent (2008)
18. Peixoto, H., Santos, M., Abelha, A., Machado, J.: Intelligence in interoperability with AIDA. In: Chen, L., Felfernig, A., Liu, J., Raś, Z.W. (eds.) ISMIS 2012. LNCS, vol. 7661, pp. 264–273. Springer, Heidelberg (2012)
19. Fernandes, F., Vicente, H., Abelha, A., Machado, J., Novais, P., Neves, J.: Artificial neural networks in diabetes control. In: Proceedings of the 2015 Science and Information Conference (SAI 2015), pp. 362–370. IEEE Edition (2015)
20. O'Neil, P., O'Neil, B., Chen, X.: Star Schema Benchmark. Revision 3, 5 June 2009. http://www.cs.umb.edu/poneil/StarSchemaB.pdf
21. Neves, J., Analide, C., Fernandes, B., Freitas, M., Vicente, H.: A Logic Programming approach to Case-Based Reasoning (in preparation)

Computational Classification of Melanocytic Skin Lesions

Katarzyna Grzesiak-Kopeć[(✉)], Maciej Ogorzałek, and Leszek Nowak

Department of Information Technologies,
Jagiellonian University in Krakow, Krakow, Poland
{katarzyna.grzesiak-kopec,maciej.ogorzalek,leszek.nowak}@uj.edu.pl

Abstract. The increasing incidence of melanoma skin cancer is alarming. The lack of objective diagnostic procedures encourages development of computer aided approaches. Presented research uses three different machine learning methods, namely the Naive Bayes classifier, the Random Forest and the K* instance-based classifier together with two meta-learning algorithms: the Bootstrap Aggregating (Bagging) and the Vote Ensemble Classifier. Diagnostic accuracy of the selected methods, such as sensitivity and specificity and the area under the ROC curve, are discussed. The obtained results confirm that clinical history context and dermoscopic structures present in the images are important and can give accurate diagnostic classification of the lesions.

Keywords: Computer aided diagnostic · Machine learning · Melanoma

1 Introduction

Melanoma has become the fifth most common cancer for men and the seventh for women. The incidence of melanoma is increasing at a rate faster than for any other solid tumour [19]. Early detection is crucial for efficient treatment of this disease giving the overall 5-year survival rate for patients is about 98 %. When the cancerous changes reach the lymph nodes the survival rate is reduced to 62 %. Once the disease reaches metastasis to distant organs the survival rate becomes as low as 16 % [3]. Despite that these alarming indicators have increased public and physician awareness, still the visual inspection of skin lesions yields diagnostic accuracy of about 60 %. Experienced and well-trained dermatologists with the use of dermoscopy and different clinical procedural assessments such as the ABCD rule, the Menzies scoring method or 7-point checklist [16] achieve about 75–85 % diagnostic efficiency for the early melanoma cases [4]. Among them, simultaneous assessment of the diagnostic value of all dermoscopy features shown by the lesion, proved to be the most reliable procedure [7].

Dermoscopic diagnosis is very complex and often subjective. Because of this it often suffers from poor reproducibility and low accuracy especially for inexperienced dermatologists. On the other hand the most skilled specialists in the clinical diagnosis of melanoma seem to unconsciously rely on cognitive and

© Springer International Publishing Switzerland 2016
L. Rutkowski et al. (Eds.): ICAISC 2016, Part II, LNAI 9693, pp. 169–178, 2016.
DOI: 10.1007/978-3-319-39384-1_15

comparative processes rather than any algorithm of morphologic criteria [11]. Hence, in recent years, there has been rising interest in the development of quantitative computer-aided diagnosis systems. Computers can provide an objective second opinion based on analysis of images of pigmented skin lesions. There are many approaches to extract handcoded visual features from dermoscopy images and apply different machine learning methods [1]. Some of them take into account geometry, color and texture [18] of the lesion, while the others use image processing methods [30]. There are also packages that combine both the dermoscopic images and the clinical history context, namely the information like age, gender, location etc. [2].

One of the most popular method that allows for calculation of TDS coefficient (Total Dermoscopy Score) is the ABCD rule [16]. The A, B, C and D values correspond to different features of the lesion: (A) asymetry, (B) border, (C) color, and (D) dermoscopic structures. The TDS coefficient is calculated using the following formula:

$$TDS = A \cdot 1.3 + B \cdot 0.1 + C \cdot 0.5 + D \cdot 0.5$$

Last decade gave us many specific approaches for calculating A, B, C values which have been successfully integrated in software packages [26,27]. Nevertheless, computer aided calculation of D parameter is very difficult since the dermoscopic structures are hard to define, detect and assess.

Still little work can be found on classification of cutaneous lesions from standard images like convolutional neural network [9]. However, taking into account the significant progress that has been made in computer vision classification techniques, one of the challenges in visual screening is the visual similarity among skin disorders.

The aim of the research is the development of computer-aided diagnosis system to provide the physician with an objective second opinion. Because pattern analysis shows the best diagnostic performance among the clinical evaluation algorithms [7] we have decided to verify the influence of the features provided in The Interactive Atlas of Dermoscopy [5] on the pigmented skin lesions diagnosis. The preliminary results achieved with use of the Naive Bayes classifier [32], the Random Forest [6], the K* instance-based classifier [8] and the AQ21 multitask learning [21] were presented in [12]. In this paper further evaluation of the adopted approach is given. The meta learning algorithms are applied, namely the Bootstrap Aggregating (Bagging) and the Vote Ensemble Classifiers. Diagnostic accuracy of these methods, such as sensitivity and specificity and the area under the receiver operating characteristic curve, are discussed.

The achieved results confirm that dermoscopic structures can enhance accurate melanoma recognition. It would be of great assistance if some global characteristics for such a lesions were automatically recognized. The image processing and feature extraction procedures could be applied to identify visual patterns perceived by experienced clinicians. The visual similarity among skin disorders has to be investigated.

2   Related Works

The subject of melanoma detection using dermoscopic imaging has been widely studied for many years. Review articles of automated melanoma detection [1] and evaluating the diagnostic accuracy of the different clinical algorithms [28] have been published. Different machine learning methods have been applied, mainly neural networks, support vector machines (SVM), k-Nearest Neighbors (kNN) classification algorithms etc. In some cases, it was accompanied by a segmentation using wavelets or other image processing techniques. Besides the melanoma recognition, there have also been studied skin lesion patterns that are indicative of melanoma, like *blue whitish veil* [17] or *globules* [23]. In recent years, deep learning methods for computer vision applied to skin cancer images have been gaining in popularity.

Nevertheless, all the research suffers from the lack of annotated data. It is also very difficult to reliably compare different approaches using different set of samples. That is why, the International Society for Digital Imaging of the Skin is developing digital imaging standards and creating a public archive of clinical and dermoscopic images of skin lesions [14].

3   Measures of Diagnostic Accuracy

Diagnostic accuracy helps to measure the ability of a test to discriminate between the healthy cases (negative cases) and the disease cases (positive cases). It may be quantified by different measures such as sensitivity and specificity, predictive values, the area under the ROC curve and others. However, all these measures are extremely sensitive to the design of the study and may not be regarded fixed as indicators of a test performance [31].

There are no perfect diagnostic procedures and they can only make an approximate (in the statistical sense) distinction between the negative and the positive cases. Examined values above the certain cut-off do not always indicate a disease. Therefore, for any test four groups of cases are considered:

– true positive (TP) - the actually positive cases classified as *positive*,
– false positive (FP) - the actually positive cases classified as *negative*,
– true negative (TN) - the actually negative cases classified as *negative*,
– false negative (FN) - the actually negative cases classified as *positive*.

Sensitivity and *specificity* constitute the basic measures of performance of diagnostic tests. Sensitivity measures the proportion of positives that are correctly identified ($\frac{TP}{TP+FN}$). Hence, it relates to the potential of a test to recognize sick people who are correctly identified as having the condition. Specificity measures the proportion of negatives that are correctly identified as such ($\frac{TN}{TN+FP}$). Therefore, it relates to the test ability to recognize people who are correctly identified as not having the condition. Considering melanoma diagnosis, on one hand, non-invasive diagnostic methods with high sensitivity are necessary to curb the mortality rate of patients. On the other hand, the poor specificity of current diagnostic strategies is driving biopsy rates to alarming levels [25].

Another widely used and effective method for evaluating the quality or performance of diagnostic tests is the receiver operating characteristic (ROC) curve. The ROC curve is defined as a plot of test sensitivity as the y coordinate versus its 1-specificity or false positive rate (FPR) as the x coordinate. The area under the receiver operating characteristic curve (AUC) is a measure of the overall performance of a diagnostic test and is interpreted as the average value of sensitivity for all possible values of specificity [24]. The closer AUC is to 1, the better the overall diagnostic performance of the test. However, in some clinical cases not only the AUCs is important but also the actual shape of the curve. In the case of melanoma diagnosis, the cutoff range for a positive test should be chosen to provide good sensitivity, because false negative test results may have serious consequences. Nevertheless, the inaccurately adjusted cutoff range for a positive test may cause incorrect classification of many false positive decisions that may lead to unnecessary medical costs and patients anxiety.

4   Computer-Aided Diagnosis

Credible computer-assisted screening of possible patients before actual diagnosis performed by skilled medical personnel, could limit both the mortality rate and the negative biopsy rate.

4.1   Data Set Description

In this work, the samples description provided in The Interactive Atlas of Dermoscopy [5] is used for evaluation. There are 1010 clinical cases of melanoma (275) and benign lesions (735). All the selected attributes (features) are derived from [5] and no image processing to extract new features was performed.

The skin lesions samples are characterized by 14 properties: age, sex, location, diameter, elevation, global feature, pigment network, streaks, pigmentation, regression structures, globules, blue whitish veil, hypo-pigmentation and vascular structures. All of them are considered to be diagnostic significant and used in the clinical evaluation. Most of them stand for the visual patterns that proved to be better diagnostic indicators than other clinical procedural assessment algorithms. In [12] the data description and numerical data that confirm differential structures criteria discriminant power were presented. Since the best results for each classifier were achieved after removing the *sex* attribute from the samples, the same approach in this research is adopted.

All the available attributes, except of the age and location ones, are categorical variables of a fixed number of possible values. The patients were divided into 6 age groups: *baby* from 0 to 10, *teenager* from 11 to 19, *young* from 20 to 30, *adult* from 31 to 50, *old* from 51 to 70 and *very_old* from 71 to 90. The diameter value ranges from 2 to 40 mm and at the first attempt was divided into 3 subsets (intervals), but during the ongoing experiments, the five section division of the possible values gave better performance results: {2 mm, ..., 3.5 mm}, {4 mm,..., 9 mm}, {10 mm,..., 18 mm}, {19 mm,..., 30 mm}, {32 mm,..., 40 mm}.

4.2 Classification Algorithms

The first questions to ask when choosing a machine learning classifier are: the size and the type of available input data and the expected output. The number of 1010 samples is not a huge one, that is why high bias/low variance classifiers (e.g., Naive Bayes) should have an advantage over low bias/high variance classifiers (e.g., kNN) that would tend to overfit. Having mostly categorical input data, classifiers that can accept this kind of input data without any additional preprocessing and coding (e.g., Decision Trees) would be better choice than the others (e.g., Neural Networks).

Taking all this factors into account three different approaches from the statistical learning techniques have been chosen: the Naive Bayes classifier, the Random Forest and the K* instance-based classifier. The Naive Bayes classifier is a very simple model that performs pretty well in practice. It converges very fast if the conditional independence assumption actually holds, but is unable to learn any relationships among input features. However, the feature dependencies are easily learnt by Decision Trees that need no tuning of parameters, like e.g. SVMs. Even though classical Decision Trees tends to overfit easily, the ensemble methods like Random Forests (boosted tree) have overcome this problem. Recent work shows that Random Forests often outperform SVMs in classification tasks [15,29]. Since the "no free lunch theorem" is proving that when comparing machine learning algorithms over infinitely many datasets there will be no absolute best one, we have decided to apply also an instance-based classifier K*. It evaluates instances using an entropy-based distance function and performs well across a wide range of schemes, and in almost all cases is better than the other instance-based learning machines [8].

Since the experiments conducted in [12] show that all the selected statistical learning techniques have comparable levels of performance measured by the area under the ROC curve and the rate of correctly classified samples, a more thorough analysis of the ROC curve is needed. Also two different meta learning algorithms are applied, namely the Bootstrap Aggregating (Bagging) and the Vote Ensemble Classifier. The bagging is an ensemble meta-algorithm that reduces variance and helps to avoid overfitting. It is usually, but not necessarily, applied to decision trees and improves the stability and accuracy of the selected approach. The vote meta classifier allows to use many different classifiers and use different combinations of their outputs to give the final classification decision (e.g. majority voting).

In all cases, the WEKA [13] tool implementation was applied.

4.3 Results

The input feature vector was the same for the all experiments. It contained 13 categorical variables: age, location, diameter, elevation, global feature, pigment

Table 1. Results for the Naive Bayes classifier, the Random Forest and the K* instance-based classifier.

	Naive Bayes		Random Forest		K*	
classified as	YES	NO	YES	NO	YES	NO
real YES	**211**	64	193	82	200	75
real NO	80	655	50	**685**	56	679
Sensitivity	0.725		**0.794**		0.792	
Specificity	**0.911**		0.893		0.904	
	AUC = **0.921**		AUC = 0.913		AUC = 0.914	

Table 2. Results for the bagging applied to: the Naive Bayes classifier, the Random Forest and the K* instance-based classifier.

BAGGING	Naive Bayes		Random Forest		K*	
classified as	YES	NO	YES	NO	YES	NO
real YES	**212**	63	194	81	199	76
real NO	78	657	31	**701**	54	681
Sensitivity	0.731		**0.851**		0.787	
Specificity	**0.913**		0.896		0.9	
	AUC = 0.922		AUC = **0.937**		AUC = 0.923	

Table 3. Results for the vote applied to: the Naive Bayes classifier, the Random Forest and the K* instance-based classifier.

VOTE	Average of Probabilities		Maximum Probability	
classified as	YES	NO	YES	NO
real YES	210	65	**211**	64
real NO	52	**683**	60	675
Sensitivity	**0.802**		0.779	
Specificity	0.913		0.913	
	AUC = **0.932**		AUC = 0.93	

network, streaks, pigmentation, regression structures, globules, blue whitish veil, hypo-pigmentation and vascular structures. The age attribute had 6 different values and the diameter had 5 values. For each selected learning method the $10 - fold$ cross validation test was applied to gain a justifiable estimation of its accuracy. The $n - fold$ cross validation procedure randomly divides the whole data set into n subsets of samples. After that, n different models are trained using data from $n - 1$ sets and validated using the remaining one (the holdout fold). The process is repeated for each of the n folds.

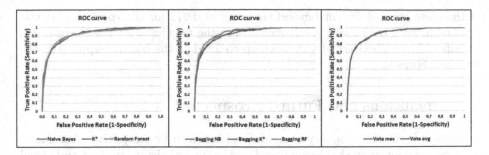

Fig. 1. The ROC curves: (1) the Naive Bayes classifier (NB $AUC = 0.921$), the Random Forest (RF $AUC = 0.913$) and the K* instance-based classifier (K* $AUC = 0.914$); (2) BAGGING NB ($AUC = 0.922$), BAGGING RF ($AUC = \mathbf{0.937}$) and BAGGING K* ($AUC = 0.923$); (3) VOTE the average of probabilities ($AUC = 0.932$), VOTE the maximum probability ($AUC = 0.93$).

The numerical results of the experiments with the Naive Bayes classifier, the Random Forest and the K* instance-based classifier are presented in Table 1. As we can see, the Naive Bayes classifier has the highest number of true positive classifications (211/275), while the Random Forest has the highest number of true negative ones (685/735). All the classifiers show much better specificity than sensitivity which is apparently caused by the small number of positive cases in the training set. The highest sensitivity and the highest AUC is reached by the Naive Bayes classifier. The ROC curves for the three classifiers are only slightly different and are presented in Fig. 1. The next stage of the experiment was to test the ability of selected meta heuristics to improve the results achieved so far. The first approach to check was the bagging, which trains each model in the ensemble using a randomly drawn subset of the training set. By sampling with replacement it reduces variance and improves the stability of the original algorithm. The outcome of the bagging applied to the Naive Bayes classifier, the Random Forest and the K* instance-based classifier is given in Table 2. This procedure usually comes with decision trees and such a combination gave the best results in our case too. Applying the bagging approach to the Random Forest classifier, the sensitivity of the method has increased from 0.794 to 0.851 and the AUC reached 0.937 (Fig. 1). The second selected meta approach was the vote. The vote approach combines different classifiers and gives different combinations of probability estimates for the final classification. The vote ensemble was built with the use of the Naive Bayes classifier, the Random Forest and the K* instance-based classifier. From miscellaneous probabilities combination rules, the most reliable output was produced by the average of probabilities and the maximum of probabilities (see Table 3), they reached $AUC = 0.932$ and $AUC = 0.93$ respectively. Even though, both combinations gave much better classification than each of the single classifier in the ensemble separately (Table 1), they did not improve the result achieved by the bagging ($AUC = 0.937$). For this ensemble, both the ROC curves are almost identical (Fig. 1). It is worth mentioning that, none of the meta-heuristics went beyond the limit of 0.913 for the specificity. It was reached in both tested voting schemes and in the bagging with the Naive Bayes classifier. The highest sensitivity went up to 0.851 in the bagging applied to the Random Forest.

5   Conclusions and Future Prospects

Dermoscopic diagnosis is very complex and tends to be subjective. Automatic diagnosis of pigmented skin lesion based on the clinical history context and visual structures can give some quantitative measure of images, be more accurate and objective. Our paper sums up the results obtained with a use of the Naive Bayes classifier, the Random Forest, the K* instance-based classifier, and two meta learning algorithms, namely the bagging and the vote ensemble classifiers. The experiments confirmed the correct selection of classifiers which was based on the input data characteristics. Taking into account insufficient number of the positive cases (with melanoma), applying the bagging to the Random Forest raised up its sensitivity to 0.851 and gave $AUC = 0.937$.

The achieved results confirm that dermoscopic structures can enhance accurate melanoma recognition. It would be of great assistance if some global characteristics for such a lesions were automatically recognized. The image processing and feature extraction procedures could be applied to identify visual patterns perceived by experienced clinicians. The visual similarity among skin disorders has to be investigated.

Acknowledgment. This research has been supported by The National Centre for Research and Development (NCBR) grant TANGO1/266877/NCBR/2015.

References

1. Abder-Rahman, A.A., Deserno, T.M.: A systematic review of automated melanoma detection in dermatoscopic images and its ground truth data. In: Proceedings of the SPIE 8318, Medical Imaging: Image Perception, Observer Performance, and Technology Assessment, 83181 (2012)
2. Alcn, J.F., Ciuhu, C., Kate, W., et al.: Automatic imaging system with decision support for inspection of pigmented skin lesions and melanoma diagnosis. IEEE J. Sel. Top. Sign. Proces. **3**(1), 14–25 (2009)
3. American Cancer Society, Cancer Facts & Figures (2014). http://www.cancer.org/acs/groups/content/@research/documents/webcontent/acspc-042151.pdf. Accessed 16 Nov 2014
4. Argenziano, G., Soyer, H.P., Chimenti, S., et al.: Dermoscopy of pigmented skin lesions: results of a consensus meeting via the Internet. J. Am. Acad. Dermatol. **48**, 679–693 (2003)
5. Argenziano, G., Soyer, H.P., De Giorgio, V., et al.: Interactive Atlas of Dermoscopy. Edra Medical Publishing & New Media, Milan (2000)
6. Breiman, L.: Random forests. Mach. Learn. **45**(1), 5–32 (2001)

7. Carli, P., Quercioli, E., Sestini, S., et al.: Pattern analysis, not simplified algorithms, is the most reliable method for teaching dermoscopy for melanoma diagnosis to residents in dermatology. Br. J. Dermatol. **148**(5), 981–984 (2003)
8. Cleary, J.G., Trigg, L.E.: K*: An instance-based learner using an entropic distance measure. In: 12th International Conference on Machine Learning, pp. 108–114 (1995)
9. Codella, N., Cai, J., Abedini, M., et al.: Deep learning, sparse coding, and SVM for melanoma recognition in dermoscopy images. In: Zhou, L., Wang, L., Wang, Q., Shi, Y. (eds.) MLMI 2015. LNCS, pp. 118–126. Springer, Switzerland (2015)
10. van Erkel, A.R., Pattynama, P.M.: Th: Receiver operating characteristic (ROC) analysis: Basic principles and applications in radiology. Eur. J. Radiol. **27**(2), 88–94 (1997)
11. Gachon, J., Beaulieu, P., Sei, J.F., Gouvernet, J., et al.: First prospective study of the recognition process of melanoma in dermatological practice. Arch. Dermatol. **141**(4), 434–438 (2005)
12. Grzesiak-Kopeć, K., Nowak, L., Ogorzałek, M.: Automatic diagnosis of melanoid skin lesions using machine learning methods. In: Rutkowski, L., Korytkowski, M., Scherer, R., Tadeusiewicz, R., Zadeh, L.A., Zurada, J.M. (eds.) ICAISC 2015, pp. 577–585. Springer, Switzerland (2015)
13. Hall, M., Frank, E., Holmes, G., et al.: The WEKA data mining software: an update. SIGKDD Explor. **11**(1), 10–18 (2009)
14. International Society for Digital Imaging of the Skin. http://www.ifcc.org/ifccfiles/docs/190404200805.pdf. Accessed 20 Dec 2015
15. Jia, S., Hu, X., Sun, L.: The comparison between random forest and support vector machine algorithm for predicting-hairpin motifs in proteins. Engineering **5**, 391–395 (2013)
16. Johr, R.H.: Dermoscopy: alternative melanocytic algorithms - the ABCD rule of dermatoscopy, menzies scoring method, and 7-point checklist. Clin. Dermatol. **20**, 240–247 (2002)
17. Madooei, A., Drew, M.S., Sadeghi, M., Atkins, M.S.: Automatic detection of blue-white veil by discrete colour matching in dermoscopy images. In: Mori, K., Sakuma, I., Sato, Y., Barillot, C., Navab, N. (eds.) MICCAI 2013, Part III. LNCS, vol. 8151, pp. 453–460. Springer, Heidelberg (2013)
18. Manousaki, A.G., Manios, A.G., Tsompanaki, E.I., et al.: A simple digital image processing system to aid in melanoma diagnosis in an everyday melanocytic skin lesion unit: a preliminary report. Int. J. Dermatol. **45**(4), 402–410 (2006)
19. Melanoma research gathers momentum: The Lancet, 385(9985): 2323 (2015)
20. Menzies, S.W., Bischof, L., Talbot, H., et al.: The performance of solarscan: an automated dermoscopy image analysis instrument for the diagnosis of primary melanoma. Arch. Dermatol. **141**, 1388–1396 (2005)
21. Michalski, R.S., Kaufman, K., Pietrzykowski, J., et al.: Natural Induction and Conceptual Clustering: A Review of Applications, Reports of the Machine Learning and Inference Laboratory, MLI 06–3, George Mason University, Fairfax, VA, (Updated: 23 August 2006) June 2006
22. Nowak, L.A., Pawłowski, M.P., Grzesiak-Kopeć, G.-K., Ogorzałek, M.J.: Color calibration model of skin lesion images for computer-aided diagnostic. In: Proceedings of the Operations Research and its Applications in Engineering, Technology and Management 2013 (ISORA 2013), pp. 1–5 (2013)
23. Nowak, L., Grzesiak-Kopeć, K., Ogorzałek, M.: Melanocytic globules detection in skin lesion images. In: Proceedings of the ISORA 2015, Luoyang, China, 21–24 August, pp. 215–219 (2015)

24. Obuchowski, N.A.: Receiver operating characteristic curves and their use in radiology. Radiology **229**, 3–8 (2003)
25. Oliveria, S.A., Selvam, N., Mehregan, D., et al.: Biopsies of nevi in children and adolescents in the United States, 2009 through 2013. JAMA Dermatol. **151**(4), 447–448 (2015)
26. Ogorzałek, M., Surówka, G., Nowak, L., Merkwirth, C.: Computational intelligence and image processing methods for applications in skin cancer diagnosis. In: Fred, A., Filipe, J., Gamboa, H. (eds.) BIOSTEC 2009. CCIS, vol. 52, pp. 3–20. Springer, Heidelberg (2010)
27. Ogorzałek, M.J., Nowak, L., Surówka, G., Alekseenko, A.: Modern Techniques for Computer-Aided Melanoma Diagnosis, Melanoma in the Clinic - Diagnosis, Management and Complications of Malignancy, Prof. Mandi Murph (Ed.). InTech (2011). ISBN: 978-953-307-571-6
28. Rajpara, S.M., Botello, A.P., Townend, J., Ormerod, A.D.: Systematic review of dermoscopy and digital dermoscopy/artificial intelligence for the diagnosis of melanoma. Br. J. Dermatol. **161**(3), 591–604 (2009)
29. Statnikov, A., Aliferis, C.F.: Are random forests better than support vector machines for microarray-based cancer classification? In: Proceedings of the AMIA Annual Symposium 2007, pp. 686–690 (2007)
30. Surówka, G., Grzesiak-Kopeć, K.: Different learning paradigms for the classification of melanoid skin lesions using wavelets. In: Conference Proceedings of the IEEE Engineering in Medicine and Biology Society, pp. 3136–3139 (2007)
31. Imundić, A.M.: Measures of diagnostic accuracy: basic definitions. http://www.ifcc.org/ifccfiles/docs/190404200805.pdf. Accessed 20 Dec (2015)
32. Zhang, H.: The optimality of naive bayes. In: FLAIRS Conference (2004)

Finding Free Schedules for RNA Secondary Structure Prediction

Marek Palkowski[(✉)]

Faculty of Computer Science and Information Systems,
West Pomeranian University of Technology in Szczecin,
Zolnierska 49, 71210 Szczecin, Poland
mpalkowski@wi.zut.edu.pl
http://www.wi.zut.edu.pl

Abstract. An approach permitting to build free schedules for the RNA folding algorithm is proposed. The statements can be executed in parallel as soon as all their operands are available. This technique requires exact dependence analysis for automatic parallelization of the Nussinov algorithm. To describe and implement the algorithm the dependence analysis by Pugh and Wonnacott was chosen where dependencies are found in the form of tuple relations. The approach has been implemented and verified by means of the islpy and CLooG tools as a part of the TRACO compiler. The experimental study presents speed-up, scalability and costs of parallelism of the output code. Related work and future tasks are described.

Keywords: Computational biology · Free schedules · The Nussinov algorithm · Automatic loop parallelization · RNA folding

1 Introduction

Bioinformatics algorithms are being developed to simulate sub-fields like RNA and protein folding or sequence alignment. Expensive and time consuming experimental methods are required to obtain the results for these sub-fields. Parallelization of molecular biology programs is still a challenging task for developers and researchers. Fortunately, many of these algorithms involve mathematical operations over affine control loops which iteration space can be represented by polyhedral model.

RNA Secondary Structure Prediction is an important current problem in bioinformatics. RNA is a single-stranded nucleic acid with four nucleotide base subunits. It serves as an intermediate in protein synthesis from DNA and can catalyze various biological reactions. The RNA prediction is a computational heavy problem with available parallelism. However, the automatic parallelization of RNA is a challenging task.

In this paper finding free schedules for RNA is presented. RNA folding is realized by means of the Nussinov algorithm. Automatic parallelization for this

© Springer International Publishing Switzerland 2016
L. Rutkowski et al. (Eds.): ICAISC 2016, Part II, LNAI 9693, pp. 179–188, 2016.
DOI: 10.1007/978-3-319-39384-1_16

method is not trivial because of dependencies existence. To solve this problem, the technique from paper [2] is used to calculate time partitioning with parallel fragments of code. Experiments are carried out to analyze speed-up and quality of the optimized and multi-threaded code. Related techniques and future approach development are considered.

2   Background

Dependence analysis produces execution-order constraints between statements/instructions and is required for correct loop parallelization. Two statement instances I and J are *dependent* if both access the same memory location and if at least one access is a write. The presented approach requires an exact representation of loop-carried dependences and consequently an exact dependence analysis which detects a dependence if and only if it actually exists. The dependence analysis proposed by Pugh and Wonnacott [17] was chosen, where dependencies are represented with dependence relations.

A dependence relation is a tuple relation of the form $[input\ list] \rightarrow [output\ list]$: *formula*, where *input list* and *output list* are the lists of variables and/or expressions used to describe input and output tuples and *formula* describes the constraints imposed upon *input list* and *output list* and it is a Presburger formula built of constraints represented with algebraic expressions and using logical and existential operators [17].

Standard operations on relations and sets are used, such as intersection ($\cap$), union ($\cup$), difference ($-$), domain (dom R), range (ran R), relation application ($S' = R(S)$: $e' \in S'$ iff exists e s.t. $e \rightarrow e' \in R, e \in S$). The detailed description of these operations is presented in [7,17].

The Presburger arithmetic operations are realized by means of islpy [8], a library for manipulating sets and relations of integer points bounded by linear constraints.

Definition 1. A fair source is a source that is not the destination of another dependence. Given a dependence relation R, describing all the dependencies in a loop, set, *FS*, including all fair sources can be calculated as domain(R) − range(R).

Definition 2 [5]. The *free schedule* is the function that assigns discrete time of execution to each loop statement instance as soon as its operands are available, that is, it is mapping $\sigma : LD \rightarrow \mathbb{Z}$ such that

$$\sigma(p) = \begin{cases} 0 \ if\ there\ is\ no\ p_1 \in LD\ s.t.\ p_1 \rightarrow p \\ 1 + max(\sigma(p_1), \sigma(p_2), ..., \sigma(p_n)); p, p_1, p_2, ..., p_n \in LD; \\ p_1 \rightarrow p, p_2 \rightarrow p, ..., p_n \rightarrow p, \end{cases} \tag{1}$$

where $p, p_1, p_2, ..., p_n$ are loop statement instances, LD is the loop domain, $p_1 \rightarrow p, p_2 \rightarrow p, ..., p_n \rightarrow p$ mean that the pairs p_1 and p, p_2 and p, ...,p_n and p are dependent, p represents the destination and $p_1, p_2, ..., p_n$ represent the sources of

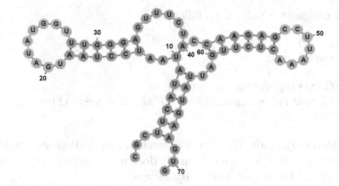

Fig. 1. RNA secondary structure visualization using the *forna* tool [16].

dependences, n is the number of operands of statement instance p (the number of dependences whose destination is statement instance p).

3   The Nussinov Algorithm

In this section, we outline the Nussinov algorithm and the program loop nests with dependencies. The algorithm of Nussinov is an approach to predict possible RNA secondary structure (folding), discovering parts that have complementary sequences. Let s be a sequence of length n. The algorithm solves the problem of RNA non-crossing secondary structure prediction by means of base pair maximization with input s. Let N be a $n \times n$ Nussinov matrix and $\sigma(i, j)$ be a function which returns 1 if $s[i]$ is complementary to $s[j]$, 0 otherwise. Initialization of the algorithm is defined as follows:

$$N[i, i] = 0, 0 \le i < n, N[i, i - 1] = 0, 0 < i < n. \qquad (2)$$

Next, the following recursion is computed [12]:

$$N[i, j] = max \left\{ \begin{matrix} N[i, j - 1] \\ max_{i \le k < j-1}(N[i, k - 1] + 1 + N[k + 1, j - 1]) * \sigma i, j) \end{matrix} \right\},$$
$$0 \le i < n, 0 < j < n, i < j. \qquad (3)$$

A visualization of the algorithm is presented in Fig. 1.

The following C/C++ code represents the RNA folding computations [11]:

```
for (i = N-1; i >= 0; i--) {
  for (j = i+1; j < N; j++) {
    for (k = 0; k < j-i; k++) {
      S[i][j] = MAX(S[i][k+i] + S[k+i+1][j], S[i][j]); // s0
    }
    S[i][j] = MAX(S[i][j], S[i+1][j-1] + can_pair(RNA, i, j)); // s1
  }
}
```

The function *can_pair* is defined as follows:

```
for(i=0; i<n; i++)
   RNA[i] = rand() % 4;
...
int can_pair(int *input, int a, int b){
   return ((((input[a] + input[b]) == 3) && (a < b - 1))) ? 1 : 0;
}
```

This function only reads *RNA* array items and loop indices values. Hence, the *can_pair* function is memory safe because it does not generate any dependencies. It is omitted in the further dependence analysis.

The studied loop contains the following number of statements:

$$\sum_{i=0}^{n-1}(i*(i+1)+i) \tag{4}$$

For example, RNA folding includes $4.179*10^7$ statements for parameter N = 500.

Dependence relations were calculated by means of the Petit analyser [17]. The Nussinov loop does not include the independent operations. It means that all statements are connected by dependence relations.

R00 is a relation whose sources and destinations are the instances of statement *s0*.

```
R00 :={[i,j,k] -> [i,j',j-i] : j < j' < N && 0 <= k && i+k < j && 0 <= i}
union {[i,j,k] -> [i',j,i-i'-1] : 0 <=i'< i && j < N && 0 <= k && i+k < j}
union {[i,j,k] -> [i,j,k'] : 0 <= k < k' && j < N && 0 <= i && i+k' < j}
```

R01 is a relation whose sources and destinations are the instances of statements *s0* and *s1*, respectively.

```
R01 : ={[i,j,k] -> [i-1,j+1] : j <= N-2 && 0 <= k && i+k < j && 1 <= i}
union   {[i,j,k] -> [i,j] : j < N && 0 <= k && i+k < j && 0 <= i}
```

R10 is a relation whose sources and destinations are the instances of statements *s1* and *s0*, respectively.

```
R10 : ={[i,j] -> [i,j',j-i] : 0 <= i < j < j' < N} union
{[i,j] -> [i',j,i-i'-1] : 0 <= i' < i < j < N}
```

R11 is a relation whose sources and destinations are the instances of statements *s1*.

```
R11 : = {[i,j] -> [i-1,j+1] : 1 <= i < j <= N-2}
```

4   Finding a Free Schedule for the RNA Folding Loop

In this section, the technique to compute free schedules for the Nussinov algorithm is presented. The approach can be applied automatically if the loop bounds are known and non-parametric. Otherwise, free schedules can be applied only in runtime.

The idea of the algorithm presented in paper [2] is as follows. All operations originated by each statement are divided into two sets, which contain the independent and dependent operations (sources and destinations), respectively. For the second set, the algorithm firstly collects operations for which all operands are available. They form the operations of *layer0*. Next, these operations are eliminated from *layer0*. The algorithm finds again those operations for which all operands are available and repeats this procedure until the second set of operations becomes empty [2].

Algorithm 1. Finding free schedules for RNA folding

```
 1:  S10 = R00 ∪ R10                        16:        L0 = S10(Lay1)
 2:  S20 = R00 ∪ R01                        17:        L1 = S11(Lay0)
 3:  S11 = R11 ∪ R01                        18:        J0 = J0 − Lay0
 4:  S21 = R11 ∪ R10                        19:        J1 = J1 − Lay1
 5:  I0 = domain(S20)                       20:     end if
 6:  I1 = domain(S21)                       21:     D0 = S10(J1)
 7:  for i = 0; ; i + + do   ▷ Infinity loop 22:     D1 = S11(J0)
 8:     if i = 0 then                        23:     Lay0 = L0 − D0
 9:        J0 = range(S10)                   24:     Lay1 = L1 − D1
10:        J1 = range(S11)                   25:     if Lay0 = ∅ ∩ Lay1 = ∅ then
11:        FS0 = I0 − J0  ▷ Fair sources     26:        Break       ▷ End of algorithm
                           for s0           27:     end if
12:        FS1 = I1 − J1  ▷ Fair sources     28:     Lay = Lay0 ∪ Lay1
                           for s1           29:     codegen(Lay)    ▷ Generate  loop
13:        L0 = S10(FS1)                                            for i-th Lay
14:        L1 = S11(FS0)
15:     else                                30: end for
```

The Nussinov algorithm is based on the imperfectly nested loop which contains two statements. Hence, the brief of the algorithm is reduced to two statements and four dependence relations. In paper [2], finding a free schedule for an imperfectly nested loop with any number of statements is explained in details.

Two sets of the dependencies are computed for each statement $s0$ and $s1$. The first one, $S1j$ includes the dependence relations whose destinations are the instances of statement j, $j = 0,1$. The second set, $S2j$ includes the dependence relations whose sources are originated with statement j, $j = 0,1$. Hence, we have four sets: $S10$, $S20$ for $s0$ and $S11$, $S21$ for $s1$.

Next, for each statement the sources of the dependencies are calculated as the domains of the relations, belonging to set $S2j$, and unite them into one set Ij. The algorithm produces $I0$ and $I1$.

For $s0$ and $s1$ the destinations of the dependencies are calculated as the ranges of the relations, belonging to set $S1j$, and unite them into one set Jj. The algorithm produces $J0$ and $J1$.

Next, all fair sources FSj are computed as the difference between Ij and Jj. Sets FSj form layer 0 of the operations that must be executed firstly.

The dependence destinations, that are linked up with the FSj by a chain of synchronization of length one or more, are computed as follows $Lj = S1j(FSk)$, where $k \neq j$, $S1j(FSk)$ are the sets of the fair dependence sources that are the sources of the dependencies represented with relations $S1j$.

The dependence destinations, that are linked up with the fair dependence sources by a chain of synchronization of length two or more, are computed as follows $Dj = S1j(Jk)$, where $j=0,1$, $k \neq j$, Jj are the sets of the dependence destinations that are the dependence sources represented with relations $S1j$.

The set $Layj$, $Layj := Lj - Dj$, includes the operations belonging to the first layer. These sets are united into one set Lay, which is a base to generate code by means of the code generator for the polyhedral models, CLooG [1].

Next layers are computed as follows. The dependence destinations Lj are computed that are linked up with the fair dependence sources by a chain of synchronization of length i or more. $Lj = S1j(Layk)$ are the sets representing the operations of layer i and originated by the sources of the dependencies represented with $S1j$. New values of sets Lj are computed.

Next, the dependence destinations are computed that are linked up with the fair dependence sources by a chain of synchronization of length $i+1$ or more, $Dj = S1j(Jk)$. The algorithm produces new values of the sets $D0$ and $D1$.

Next, the dependence destinations are computed that are linked up with the fair dependence sources by a chain of synchronization of length i. The algorithm calculates $Layj = Lj - Dj$ again, unites these sets into one set of the next layer and generates code. The procedure is repeated until there are no operations in each $Layj$ set.

The presented approach produces $2*N - 3$ layers separated by barrier constructs. For example, we have 997 layers for $N = 500$. Averaging, we have about one barrier for $4.192*10^4$ statements. However, the granularity of a parallel code grows together with the parameter N and faster than the amount of synchronization points. In other words, for bigger values of N we have a larger number of statements per one synchronization point.

5   Experiments

This section presents experimental study on speed-up and scalability of the scheduled code. According to the free schedule rule, loops in layers include only independent statements. Hence, the loop nests in a kernels construct are converted by the compiler into parallel kernels that run efficiently on a multi-core CPU. Below, an example of the output code is presented for $N = 500$. The result includes the OpenMP directives [13] that supports a shared memory multiprocessing. Arrays S and RNA are shared by all threads.

```
#pragma omp parallel shared(S,RNA)
{
// layer 0
#pragma omp for
 for (c0 = 0; c0 <= 1498; c0 += 1)
  S[c0][c0+1] = MAX(S[c0][c0+1], S[c0+1][c0+1-1] + can_pair(RNA,c0,c0+1));
// layer 1
#pragma omp for
 for (c0 = 0; c0 <= 1497; c0 += 1)
   for (c1 = c0 + 2; c1 <= min(c0 + 3, 1499); c1 += 1) {
    if (c1 == c0 + 2)
     S[c0][c0+2] = MAX(S[c0][0+c0] + S[0+c0+1][c0+2], S[c0][c0+2]);
     S[c0][c1] = MAX(S[c0][1+c0] + S[1+c0+1][c1], S[c0][c1]);
    }
// layer 2
#pragma omp for
 for (c0 = 0; c0 <= 1497; c0 += 1)
  S[c0][c0+2] = MAX(S[c0][c0+2], S[c0+1][c0+2-1] + can_pair(RNA,c0,c0+2));
// layer 3
#pragma omp for
 for (c0 = 0; c0 <= 1496; c0 += 1)
   for (c1 = c0 + 3; c1 <= min(c0 + 5, 1499); c1 += 1) {
    if (c0 + 4 >= c1)
     S[c0][c1] = MAX(S[c0][-c0+c1-3+c0] + S[-c0+c1-3+c0+1][c1],S[c0][c1]);
     S[c0][c1] = MAX(S[c0][2+c0] + S[2+c0+1][c1], S[c0][c1]);
    }
...
... <<next layers>> ...
} // pragma omp parallel
```

To reduce costs of multi-threading, the cardinality of the set *Lay* is calculated. For layers with more than one thousand statements, loops are parallelized with the OpenMP directive, *pragma omp for*. Otherwise, statements are executed on a single thread and surrounded by the *pragma omp single* directive.

To carry out experiments, we have used a computer with two processors Intel Xeon E5-2695 v2 (2.4 GHz, 24 cores, 30 MB Cache) and 128 GB RAM. Source and target codes of the examined programs are available as a part of the TRACO compiler [3], traco.sourceforge.net.

All programs were compiled with the -O3 flag of optimization. The performance of the generated code without (*traco-gcc*) and with OpenMP directives (*traco-gcc-openmp*) is studied to compare it with the original code compiled by means of the GNU Compiler Collections (*gcc* 4.8.2) and the Intel C++ Compiler (*icc* 15.0.2 with the *-parallel* flag). The experiments are carried out for four sizes of problem: N = 1000, 1500, 2000 and 2500.

Execution of the optimized code without the OpenMP directives is always shorter than the computation time of the original code, whereas the generated parallel code is more efficient for four or more processors. The output code is also scalable due to which the best performance is achieved using all available processors. The results are presented on Fig. 2.

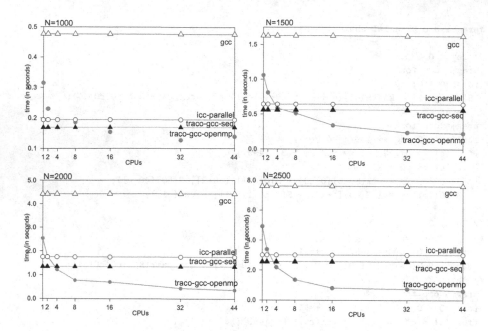

Fig. 2. Times of ICC, GCC and TRACO (with and without the OpenMP directives) for various sizes of the Nussinov algorithm.

6 Related Work

To the best knowledge of the author of this article, there is not any automatic polyhedral tool that can parallelize or optimize the general form of this RNA folding algorithm. Commonly known and very efficient source-to-source compilers like Pluto [4] or POCC [14] are useless to transform the Nussinov algorithm loop directly because there is no affine transformation allowing to tile or parallelize the loop being not permutable. Furthermore, the free scheduling of TRACO cannot be applied [3] as well because a composition of the dependence relations, R^k is computable only as the approximate form. Automatic parallelization of Intel C++ Compiler [6] is unlikely to optimize the studied code because of the dependencies existence. Nevertheless, the general form of the Nussinov code is parallelizable with the help of runtime, semi-automatic or manual techniques.

Mullapudi and Bondhugula presented dynamic tiling for Zukers optimal RNA secondary structure prediction [11]. The $O(n_3)$ loop in Zukers algorithm has the same dependence patterns as the Nussinov algorithm. 3D iterative tiling for dynamic scheduling is only calculated in runtime. Hence, runtime overheads for task and data management is significant.

Many algorithms exist for the RNA secondary structure prediction problem along with the sequential and parallel implementations. GTfold [10] implements the minimum free energy algorithm on shared memory architectures using OpenMP [13] parallelization. The GTfold implementation does not perform tiling to improve temporal locality.

Lavenier et al. [18] provide an excellent overview of the Zukers algorithm and its mapping to a GPU architecture. They implemented the algorithms in UNAFold [9] on Graphic Processing Units (GPUs) exploiting parallelism at multiple levels using CUDA.

Tanveer Pathan presented RNA Secondary Structure Prediction using AphaZ [15] as a case-study for polyhedral equational programming. The approach deduces the fast-i-loops algorithm for evaluation of internal loops in the RNA secondary structure prediction algorithm. However, the optimization is not fully automated. The tools require the input C program to comply with specific formats. They are still under development, so the problem of extracting equations from a generic C program is generally unsolved [15].

7   Conclusion

In this paper we presented finding a free schedule for RNA secondary structure prediction. For a non-parametrized loop, the transformation can be done in compilation-time. In the case of parametrized loop, the output code can be generated only at run-time. The speed-up of the approach for known loop bounds has been analyzed by means of a multi-core machine. The synchronization significance has been studied for various problem sizes.

In future we are going to study the following problems: (i) loop tiling and interchange for temporal locality improvement; (ii) finding the number and the form of layers for parametrized loops in a general case; (iii) the usage of GPU computing for synchronization costs reduction.

Regularity of the layers pattern is so promising that fully automatic transformation may be possible for parametrized codes of Nussinov and Zuker during compilation-time. This challenge deserves more attention from the research community, who parallelize algorithms in bioinformatics.

Acknowledgments. Thanks to the Miclab Team (miclab.pl) from the Technical University of Czestochowa (Poland) who provided access to high performance multi-core machines for the experimental study presented in this paper.

References

1. Bastoul, C.: Code generation in the polyhedral model is easier than you think. In: PACT 2013 IEEE International Conference on Parallel Architecture and Compilation Techniques, Juan-les-Pins, pp. 7–16, September 2004
2. Beletskyy, V., Siedlecki, K.: Finding free schedules for non-uniform loops. In: Kosch, H., Böszörményi, L., Hellwagner, H. (eds.) Euro-Par 2003. LNCS, vol. 2790, pp. 297–302. Springer, Heidelberg (2003). http://dx.doi.org/10.1007/978-3-540-45209-6_44
3. Bielecki, W., Palkowski, M.: A parallelizing and optimizing compiler - TRACO (2013). http://traco.sourceforge.net

4. Bondhugula, U., Hartono, A., Ramanujam, J., Sadayappan, P.: A practical automatic polyhedral parallelizer and locality optimizer. SIGPLAN Not. **43**(6), 101–113 (2008)
5. Darte, A., Robert, Y., Vivien, F.: Scheduling and Automatic Parallelization. Birkhauser, Boston (2000)
6. Intel: Intel C++ and Fortran Compilers (2015). https://software.intel.com/en-us/intel-compilers
7. Kelly, W., Maslov, V., Pugh, W., Rosser, E., Shpeisman, T., Wonnacott, D.: The omega library interface guide. Technical report, College Park, MD, USA (1995)
8. Kloeckner, A.: islpy documentation (2015). http://documen.tician.de/islpy/
9. Markham, N., Zuker, M.: Unafold. In: Keith, J. (ed.) Bioinformatics. Methods in Molecular Biology, vol. 453, pp. 3–31. Humana Press, Totowa (2008)
10. Mathuriya, A., Bader, D.A., Heitsch, C.E., Harvey, S.C.: Gtfold: a scalable multicore code for rna secondary structure prediction. In: Proceedings of the 2009 ACM Symposium on Applied Computing, SAC 2009, pp. 981–988. ACM, New York (2009)
11. Mullapudi, R.T., Bondhugula, U.: Tiling for dynamic scheduling. In: Rajopadhye, S., Verdoolaege, S. (eds.) Proceedings of the 4th International Workshop on Polyhedral Compilation Techniques, Vienna, Austria, January 2014
12. Nussinov, R., Pieczenik, G., Griggs, J.R., Kleitman, D.J.: Algorithms for loop matchings. SIAM J. Appl. Math. **35**(1), 68–82 (1978)
13. OpenMP Architecture Review Board: OpenMP application program interfaceversion 4.0 (2013). http://www.openmp.org/mp-documents/OpenMP4.0.0.pdf
14. Park, E., Pouchet, L.N., Cavazos, J., Cohen, A., Sadayappan, P.: Predictive modeling in a polyhedral optimization space. In: 9th IEEE/ACM International Symposium on Code Generation and Optimization (CGO 2011), pp. 119–129. IEEE Computer Society press, Chamonix, April 2011
15. Pathan, T.: RNA secondary structure prediction using AlphaZ. Ph.D. thesis, Colorado State University (2010)
16. Peter Kerpedjiev, S.H., Hofacker, I.L.: Forna (force-directed RNA): simple and effective online RNA secondary structure diagrams. Bioinformatics **31**, 3377–3379 (2015). http://bioinformatics.oxfordjournals.org/content/early/2015/07/15/bioinformatics.btv372.full.pdf
17. Pugh, W., Wonnacott, D.: An exact method for analysis of value-based array data dependences. In: Banerjee, U., Gelernter, D., Nicolau, A., Padua, D.A. (eds.) LCPC 1993. LNCS, vol. 768, pp. 546–566. Springer, Heidelberg (1994)
18. Rizk, G., Lavenier, D.: GPU accelerated RNA folding algorithm. In: Allen, G., Nabrzyski, J., Seidel, E., van Albada, G.D., Dongarra, J., Sloot, P.M.A. (eds.) ICCS 2009, Part I. LNCS, vol. 5544, pp. 1004–1013. Springer, Heidelberg (2009)

A Kinect-Based Support System for Children with Autism Spectrum Disorder

Aleksandra Postawka$^{(\boxtimes)}$ and Przemysław Śliwiński

Faculty of Electronics, Wroclaw University of Science and Technology,
Wroclaw, Poland
{aleksandra.postawka,przemyslaw.sliwinski}@pwr.edu.pl

Abstract. Since the number of autistic children births increases each year, Autism Spectrum Disorder has become a serious community problem. In this paper we present the development of an integrated system for children with autism (surveillance, rehabilitation and daily life assistance). The hierarchical classifier for human position recognition has been developed and the scalable symbols codebook for Hidden Markov Models has been created. For data acquisition Microsoft Kinect 2.0 depth sensor is used. A few experiments for basic action models have been conducted and the preliminary results are satisfactory. The obtained classifiers will be used in further work.

Keywords: Position recognition · Action recognition · Autism Spectrum Disorder · Hidden Markov Models · Kinect

1 Introduction

Autism Spectrum Disorder (ASD) has become a serious community problem. According to the newest report published in National Health Statistic Reports (13.11.2015) the estimated prevalence of ASD based on 2014 is 2.24 % (about 1 in 45) and in comparison to the numbers obtained in earlier years this rate is still rising. Each autism vary in the type and intensity of present symptoms, so that autistic children behave in a very individual way. For every person a different approach is needed [1].

Since last two decades several applications concerning autism have been created. A significant part of them is based on observation that cartoon characters and toy-like creatures have a positive contribution to autism therapy. Numerous research concern robots involvement in therapy so as to improve social skills usually lacking in this kind of mental impairment (e.g. [2,3]). Another group of applications undertakes the problem of communication disorders. For instance, the authors in [4] describe a software teaching autistic children to communicate their needs by pointing at proper pictures and in [5] animations with recorded sentences are used in order to reduce impairments in speech (echolalia, irrelevant speech).

© Springer International Publishing Switzerland 2016
L. Rutkowski et al. (Eds.): ICAISC 2016, Part II, LNAI 9693, pp. 189–199, 2016.
DOI: 10.1007/978-3-319-39384-1_17

In recent years more and more frequent is the use of Kinect sensor in autistic people therapy and observation. For example, in [6] author propose using short games for Kinect as an auxiliary tool in autistic children education. Teaching children with ASD the proper greeting behaviors in [7] combine the use of cartoon creatures and self-modeling (obtained by replacing the character's face with child's face) - as children with ASD prefer their own images than others. The evaluation of the task execution is based on calculation of the distances between skeleton joints received from Kinect. In [8] Kinect is used for children tantrum behavior extraction. The four types of behavior are recognized: beating others, ignoring others, requesting, and crying or being depressed.

There are also few applications supporting the therapy indirectly. In [1] the data mining techniques are used to evaluate the effects of current therapy and therefore to more appropriately match the children to therapy. Authors in [9] propose an integrated system as an ABA therapy support with a broad therapy database, data analysis engine and an expert system. Another work [10] deals with interpretation and understanding of the mechanisms in problematic behaviors based on heart rate patterns. A few rules for predicting inappropriate behavior have been developed.

In our previous work [11] we proposed a multi-purpose system for i.a. autistic children surveillance, rehabilitation and assistance (hints for daily life activities). All these modules are based on position recognition in order to obtain position numbers sequences representing subsequent movements. However, because of the intended use of this system the classifier has to be different from gesture recognition in [12] or [13]. The system has to be scalable in order to provide the capability of attaching new actions. In behavior modeling (e.g. for the purpose of potential danger prevention) essential is the information about *main position* which is standing, sitting, lying etc. On the other hand, surveillance or rehabilitation modules need quite accurate information about the *hands position* within a given main position. Therefore a hierarchical position classifier has been developed. Firstly the main position is calculated and then - for chosen main positions - the hands positions are estimated.

Action modeling and recognition is realized with the help of Hidden Markov Models (HMMs). The choice of this method has been motivated in [11].

The joints coordinates are obtained from the Microsoft Kinect 2.0 device by the skeleton structure. Because of the use of depth sensor only, both the observed person and the activities details cannot be recognized from such recording. Therefore the privacy is not violated.

In Sect. 2 the system outline has been presented. Sections 3 and 4 describe the main position and hands position classifiers, respectively. Section 5 is devoted to used in application formal modeling tools. In Sect. 6 the conducted experiments and their results have been presented. Section 7 contains overall conclusions and future work.

2 System Overview

The system overview has been presented in Fig. 1. The majority of planned system modules uses position classification. Therefore the *Position classifier* (composed of two subclassifiers) is the basic module and a lot of attention have been paid to its precision and proper work.

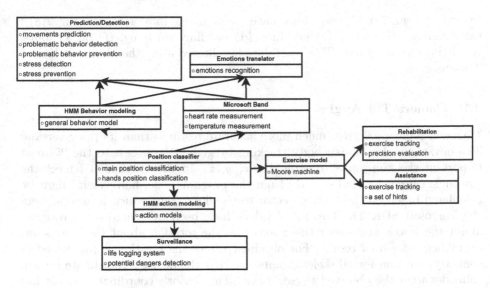

Fig. 1. System overview

Rehabilitation and *Assistance* modules use this classifier directly, since the exercise tracking needs to recognize the actual position. The precision of movements in Rehabilitation module is evaluated based on the *Exercise model* proposed as a Moore machine. Such model is also used in the Assistance module where the next expected movement is displayed as a hint.

The *Surveillance* module uses the position classifier directly by modeling the actions with HMMs. The recognized activities (as well as recognized positions) may be written into the life logging system or may be used as dangers detection in the case of actions labeled as dangerous.

Emotions translator and *Prediction/Detection* modules are based on behavior modeling. Behavior HMM models are created based on long time child's observation. Using such model the next child's movement may be predicted and their emotional state may be estimated. The Microsoft Band can be applied as the additional data source since the information about observed person's heart rate may be very valuable. It is already known that a problematic behavior prediction is possible based on heart rate monitoring [10]. The heart rate changes may also be modeled with the use of HMMs and provide some information about the current emotional state.

In this paper first of all the common part of all system modules - Position classifier - is being investigated. Also the results of preliminary experiments with HMM action modeling have been included. The remaining components of the system will be developed in our further work.

3   Main Position Classifier

In our system 7 main positions have been taken into account (Fig. 2(a)): (a) standing, (b) sitting, (c) kneeling, (d) bending, (e) lying, (f) on all fours, (g) sitting on the ground. The input data is collected using the Microsoft Kinect 2.0 sensor.

3.1   Camera Tilt Angles

Microsoft Kinect 2.0 gives much more accurate readings than its prior version. The device enables human body tracking by giving the access to the 25 most important skeleton joints (coordinates x, y, z). In this version of Kinect the tilt angle cannot be read directly from the program code, however it might be calculated based on the normal vector to the floor plane which is accessible in the Microsoft SDK 2.0. Two angle values have been calculated - the rotation about the x axis and about the z axis - as the rotation about the y axis has no influence for final results. For obtained values the rotation is performed in contrary direction for all skeleton joints as that the device's coordinate system coincides with the observed person's one. The sensor's coordinate system has been shown in Fig. 2(b).

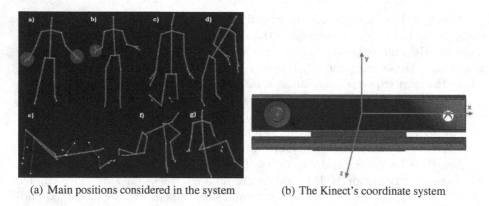

(a) Main positions considered in the system   (b) The Kinect's coordinate system

Fig. 2. (a) Main positions considered in the system (b) Kinect sensor coordinate system

3.2   Test Set and Data Set Preparation

Firstly, the raw data set for all considered positions in diverse variants (Fig. 3(a)) has been collected based on the recording of a single person performing a list of activities twice. Such a file is comprised of records which describe subsequent body frames. Each row contains coordinates values and tracking state for all skeleton joints. Secondly, the records have been manually assigned to classes (main positions numbers). A few body frames have been also rejected, when data received from Kinect were very inaccurate or it was hard to determine the class belonging (the transitions between positions). The class number assignment has been realized with the use of computer program illustrating the skeleton projected to the 2D plane (Fig. 3(b)). Finally, such data set has been divided into training set and test set in the way that one of the activities list performances is a training set and the other one is a test set (5592 and 3682 rows, respectively).

3.3   Decision Tree

The final features for decision tree based classification have been chosen after a long development process. The first ideas and preliminary experiments have been described in [11], then the recognition accuracy for these feature selection scheme has been presented in [14]. The real time classification problems resulted in new ideas for features modification.

Initially the four features $f_1, \ldots, f_4$ have been chosen. Each one of them is the cosine of an angle between the vector $[0, 1, 0]$ and the corresponding vector. The feature f_1 is based on the vector connecting the Spine Base and Spine Shoulder joints and it is used to determine if the person is leaning or straight. It makes it possible to unambiguously distinguish standing position from bending, lying

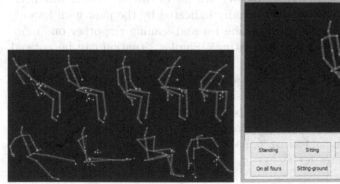

(a) Variants of the same position   (b) Program used for data set preparation

Fig. 3. (a) Examples of different possible variants of the same position for sitting on the chair (top) and sitting on the ground (bottom) (b) Program used for data set preparation

Fig. 4. Example of positions combined by two different poses with leading position indicated by lower y value

and on all fours positions. The vector used for f_2 calculation connects the knees center k_c and the Spine Base joint. This feature distinguishes the positions with different direction of thigh bones. Similarly, f_3 is calculated for vector which connects the ankles center a_c and knees center and it separates positions with horizontal or vertical direction of crossbones. The feature f_4 is based on the vector connecting Spine Base and ankles center so it indicates positions with ankles and hip on the same height such as lying and sitting on the ground. The centers k_c and a_c are the points calculated based on the coordinates for left P_{left} and right P_{right} knee or ankle due to the following rule.

$P_c[x] = (P_{left}[x] + P_{right}[x])/2.0;$
$P_c[z] = (P_{left}[z] + P_{right}[z])/2.0;$
if $(P_{left}[y] < P_{right}[y])$ **then**
$\quad|\quad P_c[y] = P_{left}[y];$
else
$\quad|\quad P_c[y] = P_{right}[y];$
end

The y coordinate is not calculated as arithmetic average as it has been observed that the leading position is usually indicated by the joint with lower y value. For example, while standing on one leg and leaning the other one more important is standing position (than sitting). Similar situation can be noticed for leading kneeling position (Fig. 4).

The tests have revealed that skeleton joints in kneeling position are very inaccurate. If the observed person is turned sideways at least a little (as in Fig. 2(a) in case (c)) the precision enables proper position recognition. Nevertheless, if the person kneels opposite, the angle calculated by feature f_3 is not even close to $90°$. Therefore an additional feature f_5 has been chosen as an Euclidean distance between the y coordinates for k_c and a_c. This feature is used only if kneeling position is not recognized.

The feature selection and comparison order is based on logic and observations. As particularly described in [11] the parameters are calculated using Matlab script. For each feature and corresponding data set the histograms for data division are created and their densities are estimated. The intersection of density functions is calculated and such obtained value is later used in the decision tree.

The developed classifier provides the capability of main position recognition independently of body orientation in the OXZ plane, body proportions or its distance from Kinect camera so that the classifier can be applied to arbitrary new persons. The sequences of position numbers obtained by the classifier are forwarded as *observation symbols* to HMMs described in Sect. 5. The experiments results have been presented in Sect. 6.

4   Hands Position Classifier

Hands position classifier may be used for diverse types of tasks and depending on its intended use different variant of classifier is needed. For general action recognition one symbol for both hands superposition is used and then treated as an observation symbol in HMMs. In the case of rehabilitation each hand may be considered separately, depending on the task. It can be also interesting to obtain the information about each hand's position separately with comparison possibility, e.g. for motion parallelism analysis. In presented method symbols are assigned to each hand separately and such obtained numbers are merged into one symbol which enables to return to previous form in a simple way.

The input joints are independent of Kinect tilt angle as described in Sect. 3 as we use the same skeleton instance. The symbols should be independent of body orientation in the OXZ plane and body location, thus firstly some translations and rotations are performed. All skeleton joints are translated by a vector connecting the Spine Shoulder joint and the origin of the coordinate system, so that the Spine Shoulder is moved to the origin of the coordinate system. Then an angle between the vector connecting Left Shoulder and Right Shoulder joints and the x axis is calculated. Upper body joints are rotated by the additive inverse of the angle value. Such prepared skeleton is used for feature extraction.

The feature vector is comprised of three features $h_1, \ldots, h_3$. For each hand the radius vector v for its position in relation to corresponding shoulder as origin is calculated. In the case of right hand the vector v is reflected by the z axis as that it can be considered similarly like left hand's one. The feature h_1 is calculated as an angle between projection of the vector v to the OXZ plane and x axis. The feature h_2 is an angle between the vector v and y axis. The third feature h_3 is calculated as a relative length of the vector v (the quotient of $|v|$ and the length of the whole arm). The range of possible values for features $h_1 - h_3$ has been measured experimentally.

The range of possible values for each feature h_i has been divided into m_i equal intervals (although the intervals do not have to be equal). For each frame (skeleton) feature h_i assumes a value z_i corresponding to the interval it belongs, $z_i \in \{0; m_i - 1\}$. The algorithm can be generalized for N features. An ancillary variable M is calculated by (1). The symbol s_N for one hand is calculated by the recursive formula (2):

$$M = \prod_{i=1}^{N} m_i \tag{1}$$

$$\begin{cases} s_0 = 0 \\ s_i = s_{i-1} + z_i \dfrac{M}{\prod_{k=1}^{i} m_k} \end{cases} \tag{2}$$

Applying this procedure results in two symbols s_{left} and s_{right} for left and right hand, respectively. In order to get an unique set of symbols $S = \{s_t\}$, $s_t \in \{0, \ldots, M^2\}$ the formula (3) can be applied. From such combined symbol s_t we can retrieve the earlier right and left hand symbols with formulas (4) and (5).

$$s_t = s_{left} \cdot M + s_{right} \tag{3}$$
$$s_{right} = s_t \bmod M \tag{4}$$
$$s_{left} = \left\lfloor \tfrac{s_t}{M} \right\rfloor. \tag{5}$$

5   Action Modeling and Recognition

For action modeling and recognition the Hidden Markov Models have been used. There are three computational problems in HMMs [11]: *learning, decoding* and *evaluation*. During the learning process the models are created based on the sequence of observation symbols (here - the position numbers sequence describing the given action). The evaluation algorithm is used both in learning phase and during the action recognition - we obtain the probability that the given observation symbol sequence has been generated by given model. This probability value is being used for evaluation (comparison) of obtained models and for determination if a new sequence of observations could be generated by chosen model. During the decoding process the knowledge about the most probable state sequence for the given model and given observation sequence is gained.

In our work the learning process has been realized with the use of *Baum-Welch algorithm*. For decoding the hidden state sequence the *Viterbi algorithm* has been implemented. The evaluation problem has been solved with the *forward-backward procedure*.

The training sequences for chosen activities have been recorded using main position classifier described in Sect. 3. The models have been created for a few simple actions basing on main position changes (symbols description is presented in the table below): 0-1, 1-0, 0-2, 2-0, 0-6, 6-0, 2-6, 6-2, 6-4, 4-6, 2-5, 5-2. Because of different complexity of actions the *left-to-right* model structure [13] has been used.

In the case of main positions it was quite easy to find proper symbol sequence describing a given action. For more detailed activities some additional software is needed which would enable displaying subsequent frames in understandable for human way and selecting interesting sequence. In next stages of this project the cooperation with psychologists and autistic children's parents is planned, so it should be easy for them to choose interesting sequence of movements. This software is under development right now.

Symbol	Main position
0	Standing
1	Sitting on the chair
2	Kneeling
3	Bending
4	Lying
5	On all fours
6	Sitting on the ground

6   Experiments and Results

The data set with assigned class numbers for main position classifier has been divided into training set and test set, each containing many variants of all positions. In practice two complete recordings have been created separately. The efficiency of developed classifier is 99.67 % and 99.34 % for the training and test set, respectively. The results are satisfactory as well as the realtime recognition. To the high rate of recognition contributes the rejection of transitional positions and inaccurate data during the preparation of training and test sets. The most frequently confused positions are sitting on the chair and sitting on the ground. This problem results from inaccurate Kinect's skeleton joints estimation. Unfortunately Kinect is designed for players being usually in a standing position.

Action	P_{O_1}	P_{O_2}	P_{O_3}	P_{O_a}	P_{O_p}
0 - 1	−19.13	−21.27	−28.37	−22.92	−21.98
1 - 0	−5.93	−5.64	−6.23	−5.94	−5.34
0 - 2	−19.44	−19.44	−6.97	−15.28	−7.95
2 - 0	−21.80	−16.98	−18.25	−19.01	−25.69
0 - 6	−238.91	−107.14	−86.47	−144.18	−32.96
6 - 0	−36.32	−29.90	−35.15	−33.79	−32.96
2 - 6	−25.75	−18.09	−31.25	−25.03	−29.78
6 - 2	−19.58	−22.88	−20.01	−20.82	−38.99
6 - 4	−2.96	−2.65	−2.53	−2.71	−2.53
4 - 6	−3.11	−2.97	−2.68	−2.92	−2.80
2 - 5	−2.60	−3.52	−3.38	−3.17	−2.72
5 - 2	−2.81	−2.83	−3.60	−3.08	−3.95

There was a following class balance in the training/test set: 15 %/8 % (standing), 28 %/19 % (sitting on the chair), 11 %/13 % (kneeling), 7 %/7 % (bending), 9 %/11 % (lying), 14 %/11 % (on all fours), 16 %/31 % (sitting on the ground). In the chosen method, which is based on density functions estimation, the class balance seems not to be significant. However, it may be important in such algorithms as k-Nearest Neighbors.

For all created models (described in Sect. 5) a few tests have been performed. Different symbol sequences have been chosen for learning and for verification. As the forward variable value (evaluation) tends to 0 exponentially along with the increasing number of observations, some transformation has been performed according to [15], so that instead of posterior probability $P(O|\lambda)$ of observation sequence O given model λ the logarithmic value $P_O = log[P(O|\lambda)]$ has been calculated. In table below the preliminary results (for chosen actions) of conducted experiments with different observation sequences O_i for given action have been presented. The value P_{O_a} is the average of P_{O_i} values. The value P_{O_p} is calculated for pattern sequence (used for model learning). All of the chosen actions have been recognized correctly.

7   Conclusions and Future Work

The hierarchical classifier for human body positions has been developed. The classification of 7 main positions (standing, sitting etc.) is separated from hands positions classification. The method for symbol codebook creation for hands has been developed.

A few experiments for action modeling and recognition based on main positions with the use of Hidden Markov Models have been conducted. The preliminary results are satisfactory and have been presented in this paper. In the nearest future we plan to apply hands position classifier to more detailed activities recognition. The skeleton data for autistic children will be recorded and in cooperation with psychologists some basic activities models will be created.

With the use of hands position classifier also the assistance and rehabilitation modules will be developed. In accordance with the psychologist's guidelines the exercises for autistic children will be prepared. The experiments will be held mainly at a special school for children with autism.

Main position recognition will be also used for behavior modeling (HMMs) and the attempt of emotions recognition will be made. The emotional state will be estimated with the use of some additional information about the observed person's heart rate. For the heart rate acquisition the Microsoft Band will be used.

Acknowledgement. This work was supported by the statutory funds of the Faculty of Electronics B50311, Wroclaw University of Science and Technology, Wroclaw, Poland.

References

1. Leroy, F., Irmscher, A., Charlop, M.: Data mining techniques to study therapy success with autistic children. In: International Conference on Data Mining (2006)

2. Torres, N.A., Clark, N., Ranatunga, I.: Implementation of interactive arm playback behaviors of social robot zeno for autism spectrum disorder therapy. In: Proceedings of the 5th International Conference on PETRA, article no. 21 (2012)
3. Feil-Seifer, D., Mataric, M.: Robot-assisted therapy for children with autism spectrum disorders. In: Proceedings of the 7th International Conference on IDC, pp. 49–52 (2008)
4. Israel, M.L., Ruthel, L., Bates, M., Smith, N.: Software to teach nonverbal persons with severe autism and retardation to communicate by pointing to pictures. In: IEEE Proceedings of the Johns Hopkins National Search for Computing Applications to Assist Persons with Disabilities, pp. 80–83 (1992)
5. Hetzroni, O., Tannous, J.: Effects of a computer-based intervention program on the communicative functions of children with autism. J. Autism Dev. Disord. **34**, 95–113 (2004)
6. Boutsika, E.: Kinect in education: a proposal for children with autism. In: 5th International Conference on Software Development and Technologies for Enhancing Accessibility and Fighting Info-exclusion, vol. 27, pp. 123–129 (2014)
7. Uzuegbunam, N., Wong, W.H., Cheung, S.S., Ruble, L.: MEBook: kinect-based self-modeling intervention for children with autism. In: IEEE International Conference on Multimedia and Expo (ICME), pp. 1–6 (2015)
8. Yu, X., Wu, L., Liu, Q., Zhou, H.: Children tantrum behaviour analysis based on kinect sensor. In: Third Chinese Conference on IVS, pp. 49–52 (2011)
9. Adamus, E., Kołodziejczyk, J.: A system for behavioral therapy support for autistic children. Electr. Rev. **88**, 276–279 (2012)
10. Freeman, R., Grzymala-Busse, J., Harvey, M.: Functional behavioral assessment using the LERS data mining system–strategies for understanding complex physiological and behavioral patterns. J. Intell. Inf. Syst. **21**, 173–181 (2003)
11. Postawka, A., Śliwiński, P.: Recognition and modeling of atypical children behavior. In: Rutkowski, L., Korytkowski, M., Scherer, R., Tadeusiewicz, R., Zadeh, L.A., Zurada, J.M. (eds.) ICAISC 2015. LNAI, vol. 9119, pp. 757–767. Springer, Heidelberg (2015)
12. Liu, T., Song, Y., Gu, Y., Li, A.: Human action recognition based on depth images from microsoft kinect. In: Fourth Global Congress on Intelligent Systems, pp. 200–204 (2013)
13. Starner, T.: Visual Recognition of American Sign Language Using Hidden Markov Models. Massachusetts Institute of Technology (1995)
14. Postawka, A., Nikodem, M., Śliwiński, P.: Daily life assistant. In: Proceedings of the WECC2015 (2015)
15. Stamp, M.: A Revealing Introduction to Hidden Markov Models (2012)

From Biometry to Signature-As-A-Service: The Idea, Architecture and Realization

Leszek Siwik[1(✉)], Lukasz Mozgowoj[2], and Krzysztof Rzecki[3]

[1] AGH University of Science and Technology, Krakow, Poland
siwik@agh.edu.pl
[2] Biotrustis Biometric Trust Information Systems, Krakow, Poland
lukasz.mozgowoj@biotrustis.com
[3] Cracow University of Technology, Krakow, Poland
krz@iti.pk.edu.pl

Abstract. The purpose of this article is to discuss the motivation and benefits of developing and releasing a cloud service providing digital signature in software and infrastructure as-a-service model. Additionally, since users authorization and authentication is based on biometry (analyzing the blood vessels system) the end user doesnt have to be equipped with any additional smart-cards or devices for storing the private key and performing crypto-operations, and the only what he needs to digitally sign data, files or documents is a web browser and his finger. Podpiszpalcem.pl is the service realizing the above idea and is presented in this paper.

1 Introduction

In 1976, W. Diffie and M. Hellman proposed a new schema of cryptographic key exchange [6] that has given rise to asymmetric cryptography (cryptography with a public key). It was clear then that cryptography would start a new era when it was able to provide not only classic cryptographic services and algorithms for protecting data (just encrypting) but also some kinds of additional (extra) services such as digital signature, time-stamping, or "digital notary" [1,15,16].

New algorithms, along with the appropriate cryptographic protocols, became more important when the popularity of e-services exploded. In the e-world, such elements as digital signature, digital authorization and authentication, and time-stamping are even more important than classically understood cryptography used merely for encrypting and protecting the privacy of data transferred in public networks. In the case of some particular e-services (e.g., e-payments, e-banking, and e-offices), such "extra functionalities" of cryptography have been a sine qua non condition of providing real (not only informative) e-services. It takes place, for instance, in the case of fully-functional access to financial and banking products and services.

Unfortunately, although we have not only (theoretical) algorithms and protocols but many fully functional environments implementing the public key

© Springer International Publishing Switzerland 2016
L. Rutkowski et al. (Eds.): ICAISC 2016, Part II, LNAI 9693, pp. 200–209, 2016.
DOI: 10.1007/978-3-319-39384-1_18

infrastructure concepts [17] and, the more so, components for building and con-
figuring the PKI infrastructure available on any software and hardware platform [18] time passed, and the popularization of digital signature as well as
the number of (e)-services using this technology were far, far below what was
expected (until today, it has actually been rather marginal), and solutions such
as SMS tokens became definitely more popular.

The natural question thus arises if it is possible to propose a solution which
takes all advantages from the concepts, algorithms, and protocols of asymmetric
cryptography; i.e., giving not only encryption but also some "extra services" like
non-repudiation, time stamping, etc., but which:

– would be (extremely) easy to provide digital signature and cryptoservices, for
  instance, in SaaS or IaaS model [5, 11];
– would provide not only actual but also "psychologically" realized high-level
  security being simultaneously as simple in daily (and occasional) use as only
  possible.

The attempt to propose the concept and realize a prototype of the system addressing the postulates given above was undertaken in project UDA-
POIG.01.04.00-12-041/11-00; i.e.: "The server-side digital signature platform
with biometric authorization – bioPKI". The goal of this paper is to shine a
light on podpiszpalcem.pl a first web page for signing documents with biometric
authorization as the sample application of bioPKI platform and realization of
the Signature-as-a-Service idea.

2   The Concept of BioPKI System

The main goal of bioPKI project was: to propose the architecture of a server-side
digital-signature platform in such a way, that any additional dongles, cards, or
chips that the user must have in contemporary solutions could be eliminated
preserving at least the same security level as before. The important question is
the compatibility of the centralized digital signature system with the legal system
being in force. Well, it depends on the particular country and legal system. There
are countries, like Poland, where according to the Polish Digital Signature Act
proposed solution cannot be considered and certified as a "qualified" one so in
a legal sense, a digital signature made on the platform will not be considered
as valid as a traditional, hand-written signature. Nevertheless, research on the
platform like bioPKI is absolutely justified, since there are countries and legal
systems where centralized, server-side digital signature is qualified as being in
force. For instance:

– the idea of performing digital signature "remotely" (i.e., on the server-side)
  has been positively judged by the Forum of European Supervisory Authorities
  for Electronic Signatures – the association of official authorities responsible
  for defining any digital signature aspects in EU member countries;
– the server-side digital signature system (authorized with SMS-tokens) has
  been successfully launched in Austria [18];

– scientists from Graz University of Technology published a document with a positive assessment of the server-side digital signature system for mobile devices [14]. The document confirms that signatures made remotely can be considered as "qualified" ones.

The one of two main top-level assumptions of the bioPKI platform is that the end-user doesn't have to be equipped with any additional dongles, chips, tokens, cards, etc [12,13].

There is, of course, a fundamental question whether this is possible at all; i.e., if it is possible to store private keys remotely on the server and assure the highest-possible security level without additional cards, dongles, tokens, etc. without utilizing such nonsensical or trivial approaches like SMS-tokens, logins and passwords, PINs, etc.

According to the (pre)design analysis, the decision was made to use one of the biometric authentication technology. In such an approach my biological PIN controlling access to my private key is always with me, and I don't need any additional dongles, cards, or tokens. It also provides not only an actual, but also a psychologically-perceived high security level my finger, face, or eye are always with me and under my own control.

3   The Biometry and the Security

Mechanisms and algorithms based on biometry are relatively new and, simultaneously, a promising direction of research on identification, authentication, and authorization [3,4,10].

From the bioPKI platform perspective, the main advantage of using biometry is eliminating any additional dongles or cards, which was one of the main assumptions of this project.

There are several biometric identification and/or verification methods available on the market including: eye-iris, face recognition, fingerprint, hand-geometry, voice-recognition or finger-vein just to mention the most important [7,9]. In Table 1, a relative and qualitative comparison of the aforementioned methods is presented. The comparison is made for the sake of the most important features found in each biometric identification method: i.e., accuracy and precision, efficiency, and security.

Techniques based on recognition of the blood vessel system are considered particularly interesting, since this is (much) more secure than fingerprint or face recognition, and equally secure as eye-iris recognition (yet, faster and more precise). It also has the important feature of requiring a live body, since positive authorization is possible when the blood (hemoglobin, in fact) flows through the circulatory system of a live person's finger. So any additional subsystems and algorithms for vitality detecting are not required.

Equally important here is the accuracy of the given methods. When the given method has been selected so called Equal Error Rate (EER) value has been analyzed.

Table 1. Qualitative and relative comparison of selected biometric verification methods

Bio feature	Security level	Accuracy	Efficiency
Iris	High	High, $ERR = 0,01\%$	Average
Finger print	Average	Average, $ERR =\sim 2\%$	Average
Face	Low	Low, $ERR =\sim 20\%$	Average
Hand geometry	Average	Average, $ERR =\sim 1\%$	Average
Voice	Low	Low, $ERR =\sim 6\%$	Average
Finger vein	High	High, $ERR =\sim 0.8\%$	High

EER refers to such point on Detection Error Tradeoff (DET) curve where False Accept Rate (FAR) equals to False Reject Rate (FRR). Generally speaking verification or identification system makes a decision by comparing the match score s to a threshold η. So, taking a set of genuine and impostor match scores, FRR can be defined as the rate of genuine scores that are less than the threshold η where FAR can be defined as the rate of impostor scores that are greater than or equal to η.

So, formally FRR and FAR can be defined as [10]:

$$FAR(\eta) = p(s \geq \eta) \mid \omega_0) = \int_{\eta}^{\infty} p(s \mid \omega_0)\delta s \tag{1}$$

$$FRR(\eta) = p(s < \eta) \mid \omega_1) = \int_{-\infty}^{\eta} p(s \mid \omega_1)\delta s \tag{2}$$

where $p(s \mid \omega_0)$ and $p(s \mid \omega_1)$ are the probability density functions of the genuine and impostor scores respectively and ω_0 and ω_1 denotes impostor and genuine classes. Intuitively, the lower is the value of ERR the better is the method of verification.

3.1 The Biometry of Finger Blood Vessels

Finger-vein method consists in exposing the finger to a light near the infrared band. Part of the light is absorbed by (live) hemoglobin, and the rest passes through the finger without any changes. Consequently, it is possible to generate the image of the blood vessels in a (live) finger. Important factor here is that the system of blood vessels is not publicly available (for instance cannot be taken from the glass as fingerprints). It is also unique to each person and doesn't change during his lifetime. Also, it is impossible to use a finger that has been amputated or is no longer viable (i.e., alive). The ERR value oscillates in this case below 1 % (c.a. 0.8 %).

The Finger Vein solution assumes three methods of scanning and analyzing the system of blood vessels; i.e., using a light reflection, light transmission, and a side-exposure approach. In the approach based on light reflection, the source of light is located on the same side as the camera. Part of the light is absorbed by hemoglobin, and the rest reflected light is captured by the camera. Reflection from the skin surface results in the image of the blood vessel system with low contrast. The reader in such an approach can be small and open [8].

In the approach based on light transmission, the source of light and the camera are located on opposite sides of the finger. The light which penetrates the finger is partially absorbed by hemoglobin, and the rest is captured by the camera. In this method, a high-contrast image is obtained and the reader has to be bigger and closed.

The side-exposure method is the most-advanced technique, as it combines the advantages of the previous methods to some extent. In this method, a high-contrast image is obtained, but the reader can be small and open.

The most important features of the Finger Vein solution are as follows:

- it is "theft resistant" biometric data is located inside live finger(s),
- every single scanning of the finger results in slightly different image of the blood vessel system (different location of the finger in the reader, different humidity, temperature, etc.),
- high accuracy the False Rejection Rate (FRR) value is lower than 0,01 % and the False Acceptance Rate (FAR) value is lower than 0,0001 %,
- the system of blood vessels is unique to each person (even identical twins) and does not vary over a person's lifetime,
- the clarity of blood vessels allows for a fast analysis and efficient comparison and matching,
- it is impossible to reconstruct the image of the blood vessels system on the basis of the pattern stored in the biometric data store. In practice, the computational complexity is too high.

4   Podpiszpalcem.pl: A Signature as a Service Solution

In Fig. 1, the top-level architectural design of the proposed server-side digital signature system with biometric authorization is presented. Within the system boundaries there are distinguished: services, biometric authorization system, digital signature service and (d)e(n)cryption with biometric authorization and hardware security module [2].

BioPKI platform has been considered as a system which allows for automation of (pre-existing) (e)services offered by such institutions as governmental offices (wills, applications, etc.), banks (wills, applications, authorization and confirmation of transactions, etc.), clinics (patient files, prescriptions, insurance verification, etc.) or drugstores (prescription realization, insurance verification, etc.). External systems can be integrated with bioPKI platform directly or indirectly through podpiszpalcem.pl service for instance what has been schematically presented in Fig. 1.

More architectural and functional details of bioPKI platform as well as the flow(s) of basic operations have been presented and discussed in [19]. In the case of podpiszpalcem.pl service, from among four possible matching schemes

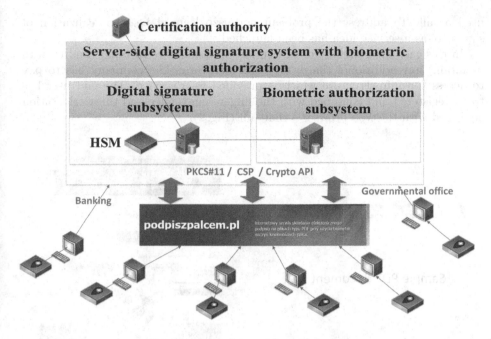

Fig. 1. Top level bioPKI architecture

i.e. matchonthecard, matchonthedevice, matchontheserver and matchonthehost
[19] match-on-the-server mode is assumed.

In this mode of operation, the authorization server is equipped with IDs of all
users registered in the system, along with their biometric data patterns. When
the cryptographic operation requiring access to the private key is performed,
the data taken by the reader and the one stored in the system is compared in
the authorization subsystem, and (according to the results) access to the private
key is allowed or rejected. The idea of server-side digital signature system (with
biometric authorization) is really interesting since the biometry (the finger vein
in particular) is one of the most convenient and one of the strongest possible
authorization factor and the user does not have to be equipped with additional
(smart)cards or dongles for storing his private key.

Hardware and software infrastructure, its configuration, orchestration, security and maintenance is the crucial part of every single (PKI-based) digital signature system. In proposed approach it is obviously the more so critical since
private keys are stored and the cryptographic operation are performed not inside
distributed and user-possessed (smart)cards but in one central place i.e. on the
server(s).

The question so arises how the solutions can be provided to the users. The
assumption that every single company is going to build its own server-side
infrastructure to make it possible to use biometric digital signature by their
employees and/or customers would kill the idea and the solution wouldn't be

used at all. To address the problem podpiszpalcem.pl i.e. the realization of signature-as-a-service idea has been launched.

In this case the company or institution does not have to build (and then to maintain) any additional (hardware) infrastructure. The company has to pay to access the infrastructure which is provided as a service. The end user has to be registered and equipped with the finger-vein reader and the work-station equipped with the web browser – thats all (Fig. 2).

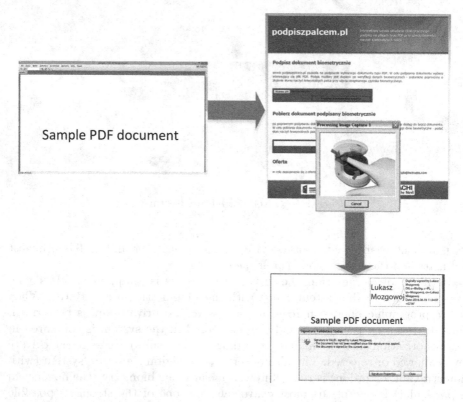

Fig. 2. Podpiszpalcem.pl digital signature with biometric authorization as a service

Podpiszpalcem.pl is the practical realization of the idea of the service providing digital signature in Software-as-a-Service/Infrastructure-as-a-Service model from one single place available for many companies, enterprises and institutions without building separate (hardware and software) infrastructure (which is crucial, complex and expensive in this case).

4.1   Deployment and Registration Procedure

In short, deployment of podpiszpalcem.pl in particular company or institution looks as follows (see Fig. 3):

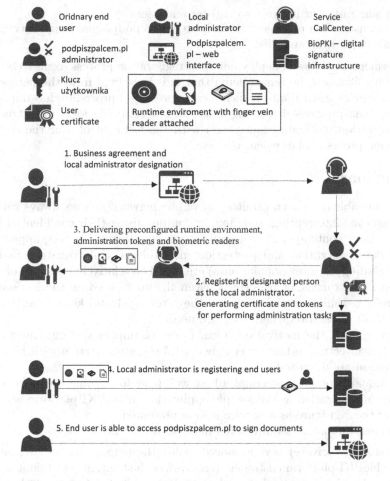

Fig. 3. Podpiszpalcem.pl deployment and registration process

- The business agreement including the number of users, price and payment terms and conditions, supported types of files and documents is signed
- Local administrator of the service i.e. the person or persons who will be responsible for registering end users in the corporate or institution is designated. Local administrator is registered in the system
- Runtime environment for administrator is prepared. In particular at this stage:
  - SSL certificate for accessing podpiszpalcem.pl (and registering end users) is generated
  - One-time administrative tokens for performing administration tasks are generated
  - Virtual machine is preconfigured
- All required elements i.e. biometric readers, administration tokens and administration run-time environment with preinstalled certificate are delivered to the customer

– Local administrator is ready to register end users
– The end-user when registered is ready to access podpiszpalcem.pl service and sign his documents and files.

Aforementioned flow of deployment and registration process seems to be complicated but it has to be remembered that it is presented from the perspective of the enterprise/institution. In such a case, presented procedure has important advantage i.e.: provides digital signature as a service (no local infrastructure, no configuration, no maintenance etc.) with the full control over the end-user registration process (who, when, why etc.).

5   Summary

When vulnerable data is transmitted in public network(s), one always runs the risk of someone intercepting, spoofing, or compromising their confidential information. Many contemporary communication applications are equipped with built-in data encryption and protection mechanisms. Unfortunately, many of them (including the most popular ones) are based on relatively insecure solutions based on PINs, tokens, or passwords. Even the ones based on the key security often prefer usability over security and they store (private) keys directly in the file system of the station where they are used.

In this paper, the motivation, idea, basic assumptions, requirements, and top-level architecture of the server-side digital signature system with biometric authorization are discussed.

Additionally, podpiszpalcem.pl a first web page for signing documents with biometric authorization as the sample application of bioPKI platform and realization of the Signature-as-a-Service idea is presented.

The most important requirements have been met: i.e.:

– since storing (private) keys is moved inside the (super) secure environment of the bioPKI platform customers (enterprises, institutions etc.) dont have to build and maintain critical, complex (and expensive) software and hardware infrastructure;
– since key access is authorized biometrically, any other devices, cards or dongles for authorization and authentication have been eliminated (as they are awkward in everyday use).

When the platform was designed, the integration layer consisting of cryptographic libraries implementing CSP and PKCS#11 standards was assumed and then implemented. Thus, any application, system, or middle-tier compatible with any of these two standards (in practice, almost any software requiring cryptographic operation and not being closed hermetic solutions) can be integrated with bioPKI easily and smoothly.

Acknowledgments. The research presented in this paper was partially supported by the AGH University of Science and Technology Statutory Fund no. 11.11.230.124 and by research project UDA-POIG.01.04.00-12-041/11-00; i.e.: "The server-side digital signature platform with biometric authorization - bioPKI".

References

1. Ballad, B., Ballad, T., Banks, E.: Access Control, Authentication, and Public Key Infrastructure, 1st edn. Jones & Bartlett, Boston (2010)
2. Bement, A.L.: Security requirements for cryptographic modules. Information Technology Laboratory, National Institute of Standards and Technology (2001)
3. Bhattacharyya, D., Ranjan, R., Alisherov, A., Choi, M.: Biometric authentication: a review. Int. J. u- e- Serv Sci. Technol. **2**(3), 13–28 (2009)
4. Boulgouris, N.V., Plataniotis, K.N., Micheli-Tzanakou, E.: Biometrics: Theory, Methods, and Applications. IEEE Press Series on Computational Intelligence, 1st edn. Wiley-IEEE Press, New York (2009)
5. Chapman, M.R.: SaaS Enterpreneur: The definite guide to success in your cloud application business, Softletter (2012)
6. Diffie, W., Hellman, M.E.: New directions in cryptography. IEEE Trans. Infor. Theor. **22**(6), 644–654 (1976)
7. Heseltine, T., Pears, N., Austin, J., Chen, Z., Recognition, F.: A Comparison of Appearance-Based approaches. In: Sun C., Talbot, H., Ourselin, S., Adriaansen, T. (eds.) Proceedings of VIIth Digital Image Computing: Techniques and Applications, Sydney, 10–12 December 2003 (2003)
8. Himaga, M., Kou, K.: Finger vein authentication technology and financial applications. In: Ratha, N.K., Govindaraju, V. (eds.) Advances in Biometrics. Springer, London (2008)
9. Huang B., Dai Y., Li R., Tang W., Li W., Finger-vein authentication based on wide line detector and pattern normalization. In: International Conference on Pattern Recognition (2010)
10. Jain, A.K., Ross, A.A., Nandakumar, K.: Introduction to Biometrics, 1st edn. Springer, USA (2011)
11. McGrath, M.P.: Understanding PaaS. OReilly Media, Sebastopol (2012)
12. Menezes A.J., van Oorschot P.C., Vanstone S.A.: Handbook of Applied Cryptography. Edycja V (2005)
13. Mitnick, K.D., Simon, W.L., Wozniak, S.: The Art of Deception Controlling the Human Element of Security. Wiley Publishing, Indianapolis (2002)
14. Orthacker, C., Centner, M., Kittl, C.: Qualified mobile server signature. In: Rannenberg, K., Varadharajan, V., Weber, C. (eds.) Security and Privacy Silver Linings in the Cloud. IFIP Advances in Information and Communication Technology. Springer, Heidelberg (2010)
15. Schneier, B.: Applied cryptography, 2nd edn. John Wiley and Sons, New York (1996)
16. Vacca, J.R., Infrastructure, P.K.: Public Key Infrastructure: Building Trusted Applications and Web Services, 1st edn. Auerbach Publications, Boca Raton (2004)
17. Rzecki, K., Siwik, L., Wojnarowicz, J.: Selected environments implementing the public key infrastructure. In: International Conference on Information Security in Computer Systems (2003)
18. Rzecki, K., Siwik, L.: Certification authority in linux system. In: 4th Conference: Computermethods and Systems in Scientific Research and Engineering Design (MSK) (2003)
19. Siwik, L., Mozgowoj, L.: Server-side encrypting and digital signature platform with biometric authorization. Int. J. Comput. Netw. Inf. Secur. **7**(4), 57–64 (2015)

Self Organizing Maps for 3D Face Understanding

Janusz T. Starczewski[1(✉)], Sebastian Pabiasz[2], Natalia Vladymyrska[1],
Antonino Marvuglia[3], Christian Napoli[4], and Marcin Woźniak[5]

[1] Institute of Computational Intelligence, Czestochowa University of Technology,
Czestochowa, Poland
janusz.starczewski@iisi.pcz.pl
[2] Radom Academy of Economics, Radom, Poland
sebastian.pabiasz@gmail.com
[3] Environmental Research and Innovation Department,
Luxembourg Institute of Science and Technology,
Esch-sur-Alzette, Luxembourg, Luxembourg
[4] Department of Mathematics and Informatics, University of Catania, Catania, Italy
[5] Institute of Mathematics, Silesian University of Technology, Gliwice, Poland

Abstract. Landmarks are unique points that can be located on every
face. Facial landmarks typically recognized by people are correlated with
anthropomorphic points. Our purpose is to employ in 3D face recognition such landmarks that are easy to interpret. Face understanding is
construed as identification of face characteristic points with automatic
labeling of them. In this paper, we apply methods based on Self Organizing Maps to understand 3D faces.

Keywords: Understanding of images · 3D face recognition · Self Organizing Maps

1 Introduction

Three-dimensional facial recognition appears as to be a powerful approach
for biometric person identification outperforming existing two-dimensional
approaches. Among numerous approaches to image recognition [5,6,8,9,11,13–
15,19] and to 3D face recognition [17,18,24], we have focused on solutions based
on the characteristic points (*landmarks*). Automatic understanding of the face
landmarks proposed in this paper should significantly speed up the recognition
process.

In our previous works, we have presented several approaches to determine
three-dimensional facial landmarks [22] and recognition results based on these
methods [20,21]. In this work, we move toward understanding of faces, which
relies on interpretability of three-dimensional characteristic points. The key idea
is to employ a Self Organizing Map (SOM) which preserves a surface topology
in the three-dimensional space. By preserving the network topology, we automatically maintain the relationship between face landmarks represented by the
network nodes. Such approach provides an immediate and simultaneous identification of characteristic points on faces to be recognized.

L. Rutkowski et al. (Eds.): ICAISC 2016, Part II, LNAI 9693, pp. 210–217, 2016.
DOI: 10.1007/978-3-319-39384-1_19

2   Three-Dimensional Facial Landmarks

In this section, we present a new three-dimensional face representation, which is based on our recognition methods. Initially, let the input set be organized in the form of a depth-map. Our task is to examine the possibility of extracting face landmarks (with no explicit relation to anthropometric points) on the basis of extremes. We assume that each row and each column is represented in function forms. Besides, each function can be classified as one of the four types of values:

local minimum of a function at a specified window size,
local maximum of a function at a specified window size,
global minimum of a function,
global maximum of a function.

Therefore, our method consists of two phases (Algorithm 1.1). The first phase extracts characteristic points from columns, and the second one performs the same operation from rows. In each step, only points of the selected range are analyzed.

```
for x = 1 → COLUMNS do
  for y = 1 → WINDOW_SIZE do
    find_Local_Minimum
    find_Local_Maximum
    if is_Global_Minimum_in_Range then
      save_Global_Minimum
    end if
    if is_Global_Maximum_in_Range then
      save_Global_Maximum
    end if
  end for
end for
for x = 1 → ROWS do
  for y = 1 → WINDOW_SIZE do
    find_Local_Minimum
    find_Local_Maximum
    if is_Global_Minimum_in_Range then
      save_Global_Minimum
    end if
    if is_Global_Maximum_in_Range then
      save_Global_Maximum
    end if
  end for
end for
```

Algorithm 1.1. The first state of landmark extraction

In our algorithm, the height of each point is the smallest distance from the straight line matching the function at the window borders (Fig. 1).

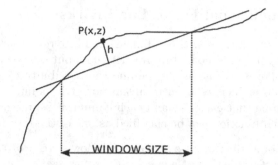

Fig. 1. Determination of the height of the point

Discussed characteristic points have been collected into the following groups:

all, all local and global landmarks from columns and rows,
col-l, local landmarks from columns,
col-g, global landmarks from columns,
glob, global landmarks from columns and rows,
row-l, local landmarks from rows,
row-g, global landmarks from rows.

3   Toward 3D Face Understanding Using SOM Analysis

In this section, we present a new research on 3D face understanding. This research gives the answer for the question whether a Self Organizing Map (SOM) carry information that can be interpreted somehow.

For this purpose, the characteristic points, defined in the previous section, were analyzed using a Kohonen SOM (see e.g. [10]). We made use of a standard rectangular two-dimensional grid of a fixed resolution that was stretched over clusters of points in the three-dimensional space. Figure 2(a) presents a face with marked characteristic points, obtained through the SOM analysis. Our task was to check whether, on the base of obtained points, it is possible to interpret the same part of the other faces.

Figure 2(b) presents a face with marked characteristics points obtained by the SOM. Intentionally we distinguished a group of face characteristic points located close to the nose.

We have compared all groups of points (*all, glob, row-l, ...*). The results we achieved in *glob* group. Figure 3 presents some of the results. In frames, there are marked points which are similar to the previously selected *nose-zone*. This experiment based on 10 3D scans taken from 10 different people. At each scan, we found a group of points that is similar to the selected (nose-zone).

Table 1 shows results of recognition of the nose area in all groups of points. A test set contains 8 faces taken from 6 people. Faces 1a and 1b belong to the same person, differing only in pose. The pattern recognition process is referred

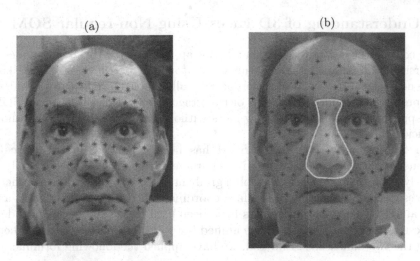

Fig. 2. Face with marked characteristic points: (a) obtained SOM, (b) region of points to be recognized in other faces (nose - middle zone)

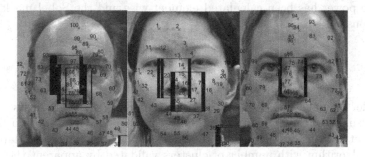

Fig. 3. Face with marked groups of points which are similar to *nose-zone*

Table 1. Search results of nose area in groups. First value determines — correct areas, second — all areas (correct+incorrect)

			Face no.				
	1a	1b	2	3	4	5	6
all	6/48	4/43	1/16	2/35	2/12	1/12	3/6
glob	3/4	3/5	2/3	3/5	4/7	2/3	1/1
row-l	9/41	11/36	2/5	1/6	2/5	1/13	4/6
row-g	0/12	0/9	1/5	1/48	1/12	0/28	0/14
col-l	11/43	8/37	1/4	6/15	2/6	3/9	2/6
col-g	6/12	5/8	1/3	2/6	3/8	1/6	1/6

to the face 1a. In our simulations, we make use of a set of biometric three-dimensional images *NDOff-2007* [7]. The advantage of this collection is that, for a single person, there are several variants of face orientation.

4   Understanding of 3D Faces Using Non-regular SOM

As a consequence of previous research, we apply SOMs with labeled nodes to understand face characteristic features. The topology of a proposed SOM have to be non-regular, as the localization of naturally labeled face features is indeed. The proposed here method consist of two stages: generation of an initial SOM, and application of the SOM to new faces without modification of neighborhood coefficients.

In the first stage, the initial SOM has been expanded on a generic 3D face model with prior identification of characteristic points by cluster analysis. Namely, we have made use of the Sobel gradient detector to find more significant changes in the Z-dimension of the face coordinates according to X- and Y-axes separately. Then the both gradients have been used to calculate a magnitude of the resultant vector, hence, we have unified both positive and negative gradients along the two dimensions. In detail, we have applied the following formula:

$$I = \sqrt{(conv\,(\mathbf{h}, \mathbf{I}))^2 + conv\,(\mathbf{h}', \mathbf{I})^2} \tag{1}$$

where the power has been calculated element-wise and the Sobel mask for the convolutions has been chosen as

$$\mathbf{h} = \begin{vmatrix} 1 & 0 & -1 \\ 2 & 0 & -2 \\ 1 & 0 & -1 \end{vmatrix}. \tag{2}$$

In order to make SOMs to be sensitive to magnitude of gradients, we have been choosing the training points randomly with the probability proportional to the gradient magnitudes. Such points have been clustered by the standard Fuzzy C-Means algorithm with number of clusters validated by apparent their utility as characteristic points (see e.g. [4]). During multiple runs of the algorithm, we have decided to limit the number of centers to 27 characteristic points. The averaged labeled points are illustrated in Fig. 4.

Then the real distances between the 3D characteristic points on the generic model surface have been used as lateral distances. For simplicity of calculations, we have omitted the distances of 3rd and higher level of neighborhood. Consequently, the Gaussian neighborhood grades could be stored in an array for calculations in the next stage. The resultant SOM, which is plotted in Fig. 5, has been set as the initial map for further identification of 3D face characteristic points.

In the second stage, we have trained the SOM on 6 subsequent 3D faces with an exponentially decreasing learning factor. The result can be observed in Fig. 6.

The trained SOMs in all cases positively localized noses and lips. Moreover, almost in all faces, eye corners have been labeled correctly. The localization of envelope characteristic features, as a *cranium*, *chin* or *zygoma*, depend strongly on the particular shape of the face. Apparently because of the observed thick neck in Fig. 6(d), the *chin* characteristic point has been moved downward. Although the results are very promising, there is still need of further work on training of the SOM. The model should be robust to each kind of uncertainties, especially that

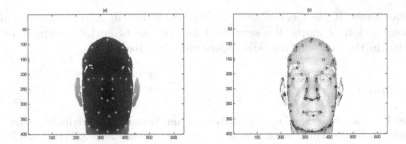

Fig. 4. Interpretable characteristic points (indicated by *stars*) obtained by FCM clustering: (a) shaded representation of the 3D generic model, (b) reference to single-run FCM clusters (indicated by *circles*) on the face model after the Sobel transformation.

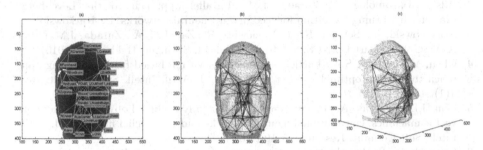

Fig. 5. Face features understanding: (a) initial SOM with labeled features, (b) and (c) expansion of the SOM on a 3D face to be understood (actual features indicated by *plus* sings).

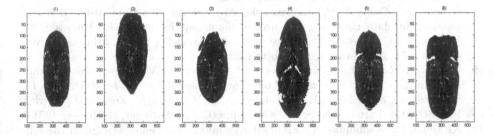

Fig. 6. Understanding of six 3D faces with the labeled version of SOM

localized in the envelope face features. We are positive to solve such problems by introducing uncertainty in the SOM model and processing it with the aid of fuzzy logic, the rough set theory and other kinds of neural networks [1–3,12,16,23].

5   Conclusions

We have demonstrated that SOMs and a new method derived from them are able to interpret obtained nodes as face characteristic points toward understanding of human faces. It has been observed that variability in poses adversely affect the construction of maps. We suppose that the use of surface normals or the Laplacian in the face analysis will reduce this drawback.

References

1. Bas, E.: The training of multiplicative neuron model based artificial neural networks with differential evolution algorithm for forecasting. J. Artif. Intell. Soft Comput. Res. **6**(1), 5–11 (2016)
2. Bilski, J., Smolag, J.: Parallel architectures for learning the RTRN and elman dynamic neural networks. IEEE Trans. Parallel Distrib. Syst. **26**(9), 2561–2570 (2015)
3. Bilski, J., Smoląg, J., Żurada, J.M.: Parallel approach to the Levenberg-Marquardt learning algorithm for feedforward neural networks. In: Rutkowski, L., Korytkowski, M., Scherer, R., Tadeusiewicz, R., Zadeh, L.A., Zurada, J.M. (eds.) ICAISC 2015, Part I. LNCS, vol. 9119, pp. 3–14. Springer, Heidelberg (2015)
4. Chen, M., Ludwig, S.A.: Particle swarm optimization based fuzzy clustering approach to identify optimal number of clusters. J. Artif. Intell. Soft Comput. Res. **4**(1), 43–56 (2014)
5. Chu, J.L., Krzyźak, A.: The recognition of partially occluded objects with support vector machines, convolutional neural networks and deep belief networks. J. Artif. Intell. Soft Comput. Res. **4**(1), 5–19 (2014)
6. Cierniak, R., Rutkowski, L.: On image compression by competitive neural networks and optimal linear predictors. Sig. Proc. Image Comm. **15**(6), 559–565 (2000)
7. Faltemier, T., Bowyer, K., Flynn, P.: Rotated profile signatures for robust 3d feature detection. In: 8th IEEE International Conference on Automatic Face Gesture Recognition, FG 2008, pp. 1–7, September 2008
8. Grycuk, R., Gabryel, M., Korytkowski, M., Scherer, R.: Content-based image indexing by data clustering and inverse document frequency. In: Kozielski, S., Mrozek, D., Kasprowski, P., Małysiak-Mrozek, B. (eds.) BDAS 2014. CCIS, vol. 424, pp. 374–383. Springer, Heidelberg (2014)
9. Grycuk, R., Gabryel, M., Korytkowski, M., Scherer, R., Voloshynovskiy, S.: From single image to list of objects based on edge and blob detection. In: Rutkowski, L., Korytkowski, M., Scherer, R., Tadeusiewicz, R., Zadeh, L.A., Zurada, J.M. (eds.) ICAISC 2014, Part II. LNCS, vol. 8468, pp. 605–615. Springer, Heidelberg (2014)
10. Kitajima, R., Kamimura, R.: Accumulative information enhancement in the self-organizing maps and its application to the analysis of mission statements. J. Artif. Intell. Soft Comput. Res. **5**(3), 161–176 (2015)
11. Knop, M., Kapuściński, T., Mleczko, W.K.: Video key frame detection based on the restricted boltzmann machine. J. Appl. Math. Comput. Mech. **14**(3), 49–58 (2015)
12. Korytkowski, M., Nowicki, R., Scherer, R.: Neuro-fuzzy rough classifier ensemble. In: Alippi, C., Polycarpou, M., Panayiotou, C., Ellinas, G. (eds.) ICANN 2009, Part I. LNCS, vol. 5768, pp. 817–823. Springer, Heidelberg (2009)
13. Korytkowski, M., Rutkowski, L., Scherer, R.: Fast image classification by boosting fuzzy classifiers. Inf. Sci. **327**, 175–182 (2016)
14. Laskowski, L.: A novel hybrid-maximum neural network in stereo-matching process. Neural Comput. Appl. **23**(7–8), 2435–2450 (2013)

15. Laskowski, Ł., Jelonkiewicz, J., Hayashi, Y.: Extensions of hopfield neural networks for solving of stereo-matching problem. In: Rutkowski, L., Korytkowski, M., Scherer, R., Tadeusiewicz, R., Zadeh, L.A., Zurada, J.M. (eds.) ICAISC 2015. LNCS, vol. 9119, pp. 59–71. Springer, Heidelberg (2015)
16. Laskowski, Ł., Laskowska, M., Jelonkiewicz, J., Boullanger, A.: Molecular approach to hopfield neural network. In: Rutkowski, L., Korytkowski, M., Scherer, R., Tadeusiewicz, R., Zadeh, L.A., Zurada, J.M. (eds.) ICAISC 2015. LNCS, vol. 9119, pp. 72–78. Springer, Heidelberg (2015)
17. Lei, Y., Bennamoun, M., Hayat, M., Guo, Y.: An efficient 3D face recognition approach using local geometrical signatures. Pattern Recogn. **47**(2), 509–524 (2014)
18. Li, H., Huang, D., Morvan, J.M., Wang, Y., Chen, L.: Towards 3d face recognition in the real: a registration-free approach using fine-grained matching of 3d keypoint descriptors. Int. J. Comput. Vis. **113**(2), 128–142 (2015)
19. Mleczko, W.K., Kapuscinski, T., Nowicki, R.K.: Rough deep belief network - application to incomplete handwritten digits pattern classification. In: Dregvaite, G., Damasevicius, R. (eds.) ICIST 2015. CCIS, vol. 538, pp. 400–411. Springer International Publishing, Switzerland (2015)
20. Pabiasz, S., Starczewski, J.T., Marvuglia, A.: SOM vs FCM vs PCA in 3D face recognition. In: Rutkowski, L., Korytkowski, M., Scherer, R., Tadeusiewicz, R., Zadeh, L.A., Zurada, J.M. (eds.) ICAISC 2015, Part II. LNCS, vol. 9120, pp. 120–129. Springer, Heidelberg (2015)
21. Pabiasz, S., Starczewski, J.T., Marvuglia, A.: A new three-dimensional facial landmarks in recognition. In: Rutkowski, L., Korytkowski, M., Scherer, R., Tadeusiewicz, R., Zadeh, L.A., Zurada, J.M. (eds.) ICAISC 2014, Part II. LNCS, vol. 8468, pp. 179–186. Springer, Heidelberg (2014)
22. Pabiasz, S., Starczewski, J.T.: A new approach to determine three-dimensional facial landmarks. In: Rutkowski, L., Korytkowski, M., Scherer, R., Tadeusiewicz, R., Zadeh, L.A., Zurada, J.M. (eds.) ICAISC 2013, Part II. LNCS, vol. 7895, pp. 286–296. Springer, Heidelberg (2013)
23. Starczewski, J.T.: Advanced Concepts in Fuzzy Logic and Systems with Membership Uncertainty. Studies in Fuzziness and Soft Computing, vol. 284. Springer, Heidelberg (2013)
24. Wechsler, H., Phillips, J.P., Bruce, V., Soulie, F.F., Huang, T.S.: Face Recognition: From Theory to Applications, vol. 163. Springer Science & Business Media, Heidelberg (2012)

A New Approach to the Dynamic Signature Verification Aimed at Minimizing the Number of Global Features

Marcin Zalasiński[1(✉)], Krzysztof Cpałka[1], and Yoichi Hayashi[2]

[1] Institute of Computational Intelligence, Częstochowa University of Technology, Częstochowa, Poland
{marcin.zalasinski,krzysztof.cpalka}@iisi.pcz.pl
[2] Department of Computer Science, Meiji University, Tokyo, Japan
hayashiy@cs.meiji.ac.jp

Abstract. Identity verification using the dynamic signature is an important biometric issue. Its big advantage is that it is commonly socially acceptable. Verification based on so-called global features is one of the most effective methods used for this purpose. In this paper we propose an approach which minimises a number of the features used during verification process due to check how the number of features affects the classification result. The paper contains the simulation results for the public MCYT-100 database of the dynamic signatures.

Keywords: Behavioural biometrics · Dynamic signature verification · Global features · Flexible neuro-fuzzy system · One-class classifier

1 Introduction

Signature is a commonly used form of authentication, so identity verification using this biometric attribute is not controversial as in the case of certain biometric characteristics such as fingerprint or face.

Dynamic signature is behavioural biometric attribute which contains information about dynamics of signing process. The dynamics of the signature is difficult to see and forge, so taking it into account in the systems used for identity verification increases efficiency of this process.

Approaches used to the dynamic signature verification can be divided into four main groups: **(a)** global feature-based methods (see e.g. [27,49, 56,90,96,97]), **(b)** function-based methods (see e.g. [25,36,39]), **(c)** regional-based methods (see e.g. [16–18,26,35,38,91–95]) and **(d)** hybrid methods (see e.g. [19,53,57]).

In this paper we consider the approach based on so-called global features (e.g. signing time, number of pen-ups, etc.). These features are extracted from the signature and they are used during training and verification phase. We use a set of global features well known in the literature and proposed in [27]. However, proposed algorithm does not depend on the used set of features.

© Springer International Publishing Switzerland 2016
L. Rutkowski et al. (Eds.): ICAISC 2016, Part II, LNAI 9693, pp. 218–231, 2016.
DOI: 10.1007/978-3-319-39384-1_20

In this paper we focus on minimizing the number of global features used during verification process due to check how the number of features affects the classification result. We start our simulation from the set of 80 global features and next we reduce them gradually to 10 features.

In verification process we use a neuro-fuzzy one-class classifier, proposed by us earlier (see e.g. [16,93]). It does not require supervised learning, has an uniform structure for all users and is distinguished by the interpretability of rules included in the base of rules. It is worth to note that many computational intelligence methods (see e.g. [1–7,20–24,31,32,34,37,42,48,59–64,72–74,76,79,82,88]) are successfully used in pattern recognition, modelling and optimization issues.

This paper is organised into 4 sections. Section 2 contains description of the new method for dynamic signature verification aimed at minimising the number of global features. Section 3 shows simulation results. Conclusions are drawn in Sect. 4.

2 Description of the New Method for Dynamic Signature Verification Aimed at Minimizing the Number of Global Features

Idea of the proposed method can be summarized as follows: (a) It uses a set of 80 global features which have been systematized in the paper [27]. However, this method does not depend on the base set of features, which can be modified. (b) It determines weight of importance for each feature, individually for each signer. Higher value of the weight means that the feature is more characteristic for the considered user and it will be more important during classification process. (c) It selects M the most characteristic global features for each user, which are used in the classification phase. (d) It uses authorial one-class classifier which is based on the capacities of the flexible fuzzy system (see e.g. [10,15,16,28,51,52,62,63,66–71,93]). The classifier takes into account the weights of importance of features.

The algorithm starts from the training phase in which weights of importance of features are computed, the most characteristic features are selected and parameters of the classifier are determined.

2.1 Training Phase

At the beginning of the training phase, user i ($i = 1, 2, \ldots, I$, I is a number of the users) has to create J reference signatures using a digital input device, e.g. graphic tablet. Next, all global features are determined for all J signatures. They are stored in the matrix $\mathbf{G}_i$ which has the following structure:

$$\mathbf{G}_i = \begin{bmatrix} g_{i,1,1} & g_{i,2,1} & \cdots & g_{i,N,1} \\ g_{i,1,2} & g_{i,2,2} & \cdots & g_{i,N,2} \\ & & \vdots & \\ g_{i,1,J} & g_{i,2,J} & \cdots & g_{i,N,J} \end{bmatrix} = \begin{bmatrix} \mathbf{g}_{i,1} \\ \mathbf{g}_{i,2} \\ \vdots \\ \mathbf{g}_{i,N} \end{bmatrix}^T, \tag{1}$$

where $\mathbf{g}_{i,n} = \begin{bmatrix} g_{i,n,1} & g_{i,n,2} & \cdots & g_{i,n,J} \end{bmatrix}$, $g_{i,n,j}$ is the value of the global feature n, $n = 1, 2, \ldots, N$, determined for the signature j, $j = 1, 2, \ldots, J$, created by the user i, N is the number of the global features. As already mentioned, the detailed method of determining each of the considered features is described in [27].

Matrix $\mathbf{G}_i$ is used to determine value of the vector $\bar{\mathbf{g}}_i$ which contains average values of each global feature of all reference signatures J of the user i. It is described as follows:

$$\bar{\mathbf{g}}_i = [\bar{g}_{i,1}, \bar{g}_{i,2}, \ldots, \bar{g}_{i,N}], \tag{2}$$

where $\bar{g}_{i,n}$ is the average value of global feature n of training signatures of the user i, computed using the following formula:

$$\bar{g}_{i,n} = \frac{1}{J} \sum_{j=1}^{J} g_{i,n,j}. \tag{3}$$

Next, weights of importance of features are determined. They are based on the dispersion measure of the distances between global features of the reference signatures and average values of them. Weight $w_{i,n}$ of the global feature n of the user i is determined as follows:

$$w_{i,n} = 1 - \frac{\frac{1}{J}\sqrt{\sum_{j=1}^{J} \left(|\bar{g}_{i,n} - g_{i,n,j}| - \frac{1}{J}\sum_{j=1}^{J} |\bar{g}_{i,n} - g_{i,n,j}| \right)^2}}{\left| \max_{j=1,\ldots,J} \{|\bar{g}_{i,n} - g_{i,n,j}|\} - \min_{j=1,\ldots,J} \{|\bar{g}_{i,n} - g_{i,n,j}|\} \right|}. \tag{4}$$

Having weights of importance, we select M global features which values of weights are the highest. We assume that they are the most characteristic for the user i and they will be used in the verification phase.

Next, we determine last parameters used by our classifier - the values of maximum distances $maxd_{i,m}$ of global feature m $(m = 1, 2, \ldots, M)$ of the user i between average value of global feature and the values of global features of the reference signatures. It is determined as follows:

$$maxd_{i,m} = \max_{j=1,\ldots,J} \{|\bar{g}_{i,m} - g_{i,m,j}|\}. \tag{5}$$

The distance $maxd_{i,m}$ determines instability of the signature of the user i in the context of the feature m. Value of the distance has an impact on the work of the signature classifier (see Fig. 1).

Average values of global features, indexes of selected the most characteristic global features and determined parameters of the classifier have to be stored in the database, because they will be used in the verification phase.

Next, a classifier is created. We use a flexible neuro-fuzzy system of the Mamdani type (see e.g. [10,11,13,14]). Neuro-fuzzy systems (see e.g. [12,29,33,40,50,77,78,81]) combine the natural language description of fuzzy systems (see e.g. [41,43,85,98]) and the learning properties of neural networks (see e.g. [8, 44–47, 80, 83, 84, 86, 87]). This system is based on the rules in the form if-then. The fuzzy rules contain fuzzy sets which represent the values, e.g. "low" and "high", of the input and output linguistic variables. In our method the input linguistic variables are dependent on the similarity between the global features of test signature and average values of global features computed on the basis of training signatures. The system uses M selected features. Output linguistic variables describe the reliability of the signature. In our method parameters of input fuzzy sets are individually selected for each user. Please note that if training signatures are more similar to each other, the tolerance of our classifier is lower ($maxd_{i,m}$ takes smaller values).

The flexibility of the classifier results from the possibility of using weights of importance, which have been previously determined individually for each user. Taking into account these weights is possible thanks to the use of aggregation operators named the weighted triangular norms proposed by us earlier (see e.g. [11, 69, 75]).

Our classifier works on the basis of two fuzzy rules presented as follows:

$$
\begin{cases}
R^{(1)}: & \begin{bmatrix} \text{IF } \left(dtst_{i,1} \text{ is } A_{i,1}^1\right) \middle| w_{i,1} \text{ AND } \left(dtst_{i,2} \text{ is } A_{i,2}^1\right) \middle| w_{i,2} \text{ AND} \\ \vdots \\ \text{AND } \left(dtst_{i,M} \text{ is } A_{i,M}^1\right) \middle| w_{i,M} \text{ THEN } y_i \text{ is } B^1 \end{bmatrix} \\
R^{(2)}: & \begin{bmatrix} \text{IF } \left(dtst_{i,1} \text{ is } A_{i,1}^2\right) \middle| w_{i,1} \text{ AND } \left(dtst_{i,2} \text{ is } A_{i,2}^2\right) \middle| w_{i,2} \text{ AND} \\ \vdots \\ \text{AND } \left(dtst_{i,M} \text{ is } A_{i,M}^2\right) \middle| w_{i,M} \text{ THEN } y_i \text{ is } B^2 \end{bmatrix}
\end{cases}, \quad (6)
$$

where:

- $dtst_{i,m}$, $i = 1, 2, \ldots, I$, $m = 1, 2, \ldots, M$, $j = 1, 2, \ldots, J$, are input linguistic variables in the system for the signature verification. Values of $dtst_{i,m}$ are determined as follows:

$$
dtst_{i,m} = \bar{g}_{i,m} - gtst_{i,m}, \quad (7)
$$

where $\bar{g}_{i,m}$ is the average value of global feature m of the user i and $gtst_{i,m}$ is the value of global feature m of the test signature of the user i.
- $A_{i,m}^1$, $A_{i,m}^2$, $i = 1, 2, \ldots, I$, $m = 1, 2, \ldots, M$, are input fuzzy sets related to the global feature number m of the user i. Fuzzy sets $A_{i,1}^1, A_{i,2}^1, \ldots, A_{i,M}^1$ represent values "high" assumed by input linguistic variables. Analogously, fuzzy sets $A_{i,1}^2, A_{i,2}^2, \ldots, A_{i,M}^2$ represent values "low" assumed by input linguistic variables. Thus, each rule contains M antecedents. In the fuzzy classifier of the signature used in the simulations we applied a Gaussian membership function (see Fig. 1) for all input fuzzy sets.
- y_i, $i = 1, 2, \ldots, I$, is output linguistic variable interpreted as reliability of signature considered to be created by the signer i.
- B^1, B^2 are output fuzzy sets shown in Fig. 1. Fuzzy set B^1 represents value "high" of output linguistic variable. Analogously, fuzzy set B^2 represents value

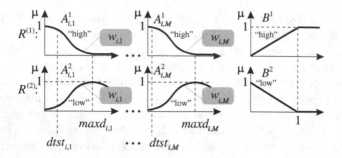

Fig. 1. Input and output fuzzy sets of the flexible neuro-fuzzy system of the Mamdani type for user i signature verification.

"low" of output linguistic variable. In the fuzzy classifier of the signature used in the simulations we applied the membership function of type γ (see e.g. [65]) in the rule 1 and the membership function of type L (see e.g. [65]) in the rule 2. Please note that the membership functions of fuzzy sets B^1 and B^2 are the same for all users (their parameters do not depend on the chosen global features of the dynamic signature and their values).

- $maxd_{i,m}$, $i = 1, 2, \ldots, I$, $m = 1, 2, \ldots, M$, can be equated with the border values of features of individual users (see formula (5)).
- $w_{i,m}$, $i = 1, 2, \ldots, I$, $m = 1, 2, \ldots, M$, are weights of importance related to the global feature number m of the user i (see formula (4)).

Please note that regardless of the set of features chosen individually for the user, the interpretation of the input and output fuzzy sets is uniform. Moreover, the way of the signature classification is interpretable (see [30]).

When training of the system for the user i ends, identity verification on the basis of his/her signature can be performed.

2.2   Identity Verification Phase

First the user whose identity will be verified creates one test signature and claims his/her identity as i. Next, information about average values of global features characteristic for the user i and parameters of the classifier of the user i created during training phase are downloaded from the database. Next, system determines global features of the test signature and values of parameters $dtst_{i,m}$ (see Eq. 7). Finally, verification is performed using our flexible neuro-fuzzy one-class classifier of Mamdani type. A signature is true if the following assumption is satisfied:

$$\bar{y}_i = \cfrac{T^* \left\{ \begin{array}{c} \mu_{A_{i,1}^1}(dtst_{i,1}), \ldots, \mu_{A_{i,M}^1}(dtst_{i,M}) ; \\ w_{i,1}, \ldots, w_{i,M} \end{array} \right\}}{\left(T^* \left\{ \begin{array}{c} \mu_{A_{i,1}^1}(dtst_{i,1}), \ldots, \mu_{A_{i,M}^1}(dtst_{i,M}) ; \\ w_{i,1}, \ldots, w_{i,M} \end{array} \right\} + \atop T^* \left\{ \begin{array}{c} \mu_{A_{i,1}^2}(dtst_{i,1}), \ldots, \mu_{A_{i,M}^2}(dtst_{i,M}) ; \\ w_{i,1}, \ldots, w_{i,M} \end{array} \right\} \right)} > cth_i, \qquad (8)$$

where $T^* \{\cdot\}$ is the algebraic weighted t-norm (see [9,11,69]), $\mu_A(\cdot)$ is a Gaussian membership function (see e.g. [65]), $\bar{y}_i$, $i = 1, 2, \ldots, I$, is the value of the output signal of applied neuro-fuzzy system described by rules (6), $cth_i \in [0, 1]$ is a coefficient determined experimentally for each user to eliminate disproportion between FAR and FRR error (see e.g. [89]).

Formula (8) was created by taking into account in the description of system simplification resulting from the spacing of fuzzy sets, shown in Fig. 1. The simplifications are as follows: $\mu_{B^1}(0) = 0$, $\mu_{B^1}(1) \approx 1$, $\mu_{B^2}(0) \approx 1$, $\mu_{B^2}(1) = 0$, where $\mu_{B^1}(\cdot)$ is a membership function of class L (see e.g. [65]) and $\mu_{B^2}(\cdot)$ is a membership function of class γ (see e.g. [65]).

3   Simulation Results

Simulations were performed using authorial test environment written in C# and public MCYT-100 dynamic signature database (see [58]). It contains a set of dynamic signatures of 100 users (25 genuine signatures and 25 forged ones for each signer).

For each user from the MCYT-100 database we repeated 5 times the training phase and the test phase. The results obtained for all users have been averaged. During training phase we used 5 randomly selected genuine signatures of considered user and during verification phase we used 15 genuine and 15 forged signatures of the user. We performed the simulations starting from 80 global features and next we reduce them gradually to 10 features.

Results of the simulations are presented in Table 1. It contains values of the errors FAR (False Acceptance Rate) and FRR (False Rejection Rate) achieved by our method for different number of selected global features. It can be noted that initially the value of average classification error falls for lower number of used global features and it is the lowest for 50 features. After that, error value grows for lower number of features. It is also worth to note that it rapidly rises for less than 30 global features. The variation of the average classification error depending on the number of used features is shown in Fig. 2.

Moreover, in Table 2 we present the best result obtained by our method in comparison to the global feature-based methods of other authors. In this comparison we take into account methods which use maximum 5 reference signatures during training phase and use so-called skilled forgeries during verification phase. Skilled forgeries are signatures created by forgers which saw how considered user creates his/her genuine signatures. It is worth to note that our method achieves a very good accuracy in comparison to the other ones.

Table 1. Results of the simulations performed by our system using the MCYT-100 database for different number of selected global features.

Number of global features	Average FAR	Average FAR	Average error
80	5.64 %	1.24 %	3.44 %
70	5.42 %	1.38 %	3.40 %
60	5.22 %	1.51 %	3.37 %
50	**3.85 %**	**1.99 %**	**2.92 %**
40	5.36 %	2.61 %	3.99 %
30	5.15 %	3.64 %	4.40 %
20	6.60 %	6.12 %	6.36 %
10	12.17 %	9.00 %	10.59 %

Table 2. Comparison of the results for the dynamic signature verification methods taking into account methods based on global features using maximum 5 reference signatures and tested using so-called skilled forgeries.

Method	Average FAR	Average FAR	Average error
Fierrez-Aguilar et al. [27]	–	–	5.61 %
Lumini, Nanni [49]	–	–	4.50 %
Nanni [54]	–	–	5.20 %
Nanni, Lumini (a) [55]	–	–	7.60 %
Nanni, Lumini (b) [56]	–	–	8.40 %
Our method	3.85 %	1.99 %	2.92 %

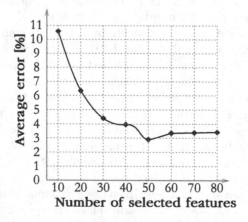

Fig. 2. Variation of the average classification error depending on the number of used features.

4 Conclusions

In this paper we propose a new approach to the dynamic signature verification aimed at minimizing the number of global features. Proposed method selects the most characteristic global features which are used during verification phase. Classification is performed using authorial flexible neuro-fuzzy one-class classifier. It is worth to note that during training of the classifier forged signatures are not necessary. Our simulations have shown that the method is the most effective for 50 global features. Moreover, the proposed algorithm worked with a very good accuracy in comparison to the methods of other authors.

Acknowledgment. The project was financed by the National Science Centre (Poland) on the basis of the decision number DEC-2012/05/B/ST7/02138.

References

1. Akimoto, T., Ogata, T.: Experimental development of a focalization mechanism in an integrated narrative generation system. J. Artif. Intell. Soft Comput. Res. 5(3), 177–188 (2015)
2. Bartczuk, Ł.: Gene expression programming in correction modelling of nonlinear dynamic objects. Adv. Intell. Syst. Comput. **429**, 125–134 (2016)
3. Bartczuk, Ł., Przybył, A., Koprinkova-Hristova, P.: New method for nonlinear fuzzy correction modelling of dynamic objects. In: Rutkowski, L., Korytkowski, M., Scherer, R., Tadeusiewicz, R., Zadeh, L.A., Zurada, J.M. (eds.) ICAISC 2014, Part I. LNCS, vol. 8467, pp. 169–180. Springer, Heidelberg (2014)
4. Bartczuk, Ł., Rutkowska, D.: Type-2 fuzzy decision trees. In: Rutkowski, L., Tadeusiewicz, R., Zadeh, L.A., Zurada, J.M. (eds.) ICAISC 2008. LNCS (LNAI), vol. 5097, pp. 197–206. Springer, Heidelberg (2008)
5. Bartczuk, Ł., Rutkowska, D.: Medical diagnosis with Type-2 fuzzy decision trees. In: Kącki, E., Rudnicki, M., Stempczyńska, J. (eds.) Computers in Medical Activity. AISC, vol. 65, pp. 11–21. Springer, Heidelberg (2009)
6. Bello, O., Holzmann, J., Yaqoob, T., Teodoriu, C.: Application of artificial intelligence methods in drilling system design and operations: a review of the state of the art. J. Artif. Intell. Soft Comput. Res. 5(2), 121–139 (2015)
7. Chu, J.L., Krzyżak, A.: The recognition of partially occluded objects with support vector machines, convolutional neural networks and deep belief networks. J. Artif. Intell. Soft Comput. Res. 4(1), 5–19 (2014)
8. Cierniak, R., Rutkowski, L.: On image compression by competitive neural networks and optimal linear predictors. Sig. Process.: Image Commun. **156**, 559–565 (2000)
9. Cpalka, K.: A method for designing flexible neuro-fuzzy systems. In: Rutkowski, L., Tadeusiewicz, R., Zadeh, L.A., Żurada, J.M. (eds.) ICAISC 2006. LNCS (LNAI), vol. 4029, pp. 212–219. Springer, Heidelberg (2006)
10. Cpałka, K.: A new method for design and reduction of neuro-fuzzy classification systems. IEEE Trans. Neural Netw. **20**, 701–714 (2009)
11. Cpałka, K.: On evolutionary designing and learning of flexible neuro-fuzzy structures for nonlinear classification. Nonlinear Anal. Ser. A: Theory Methods Appl. **71**, 1659–1672 (2009)

12. Cpałka, K., Łapa, K., Przybył, A.: A new approach to design of control systems using genetic programming. Inf. Technol. Control **44**(4), 433–442 (2015)
13. Cpałka, K., Łapa, K., Przybył, A., Zalasiński, M.: A new method for designing neuro-fuzzy systems for nonlinear modelling with interpretability aspects. Neurocomputing **135**, 203–217 (2014)
14. Cpałka, K., Rebrova, O., Nowicki, R., Rutkowski, L.: On design of flexible neuro-fuzzy systems for nonlinear modelling. Int. J. Gen. Syst. **42**, 706–720 (2013)
15. Cpałka, K., Rutkowski, L.: Flexible Takagi-Sugeno neuro-fuzzy structures for nonlinear approximation. WSEAS Trans. Syst. **4**(9), 1450–1458 (2005)
16. Cpałka, K., Zalasiński, M.: On-line signature verification using vertical signature partitioning. Expert Syst. Appl. **41**, 4170–4180 (2014)
17. Cpałka, K., Zalasiński, M., Rutkowski, L.: New method for the on-line signature verification based on horizontal partitioning. Pattern Recogn. **47**, 2652–2661 (2014)
18. Cpałka, K., Zalasiński, M., Rutkowski, L.: A new algorithm for identity verification based on the analysis of a handwritten dynamic signature. Appl. Soft Comput. (2016, in press). http://dx.doi.org/10.1016/j.asoc.2016.02.017
19. Doroz, R., Porwik, P., Orczyk, T.: Dynamic signature verification method based on association of features with similarity measures. Neurocomputing **171**, 921–931 (2016)
20. Duda, P., Hayashi, Y., Jaworski, M.: On the strong convergence of the orthogonal series-type kernel regression neural networks in a non-stationary environment. In: Rutkowski, L., Korytkowski, M., Scherer, R., Tadeusiewicz, R., Zadeh, L.A., Zurada, J.M. (eds.) ICAISC 2012, Part I. LNCS, vol. 7267, pp. 47–54. Springer, Heidelberg (2012)
21. Duda, P., Jaworski, M., Pietruczuk, L.: On pre-processing algorithms for data stream. In: Rutkowski, L., Korytkowski, M., Scherer, R., Tadeusiewicz, R., Zadeh, L.A., Zurada, J.M. (eds.) ICAISC 2012, Part II. LNCS, vol. 7268, pp. 56–63. Springer, Heidelberg (2012)
22. Dziwiński, P., Avedyan, E.D.: A new approach to nonlinear modeling based on significant operating points detection. In: Rutkowski, L., Korytkowski, M., Scherer, R., Tadeusiewicz, R., Zadeh, L.A., Zurada, J.M. (eds.) Artificial Intelligence and Soft Computing. LNCS, vol. 9120, pp. 364–378. Springer, Heidelberg (2015)
23. Dziwiński, P., Bartczuk, Ł., Przybył, A., Avedyan, E.D.: A new algorithm for identification of significant operating points using swarm intelligence. In: Rutkowski, L., Korytkowski, M., Scherer, R., Tadeusiewicz, R., Zadeh, L.A., Zurada, J.M. (eds.) ICAISC 2014, Part II. LNCS, vol. 8468, pp. 349–362. Springer, Heidelberg (2014)
24. Er, M.J., Duda, P.: On the weak convergence of the orthogonal series-type kernel regresion neural networks in a non-stationary environment. In: Wyrzykowski, R., Dongarra, J., Karczewski, K., Waśniewski, J. (eds.) PPAM 2011, Part I. LNCS, vol. 7203, pp. 443–450. Springer, Heidelberg (2012)
25. Faundez-Zanuy, M.: On-line signature recognition based on VQ-DTW. Pattern Recogn. **40**, 981–992 (2007)
26. Fierrez, J., Ortega-Garcia, J., Ramos, D., Gonzalez-Rodriguez, J.: HMM-based on-line signature verification: feature extraction and signature modeling. Pattern Recogn. Lett. **28**, 2325–2334 (2007)
27. Fiérrez-Aguilar, J., Nanni, L., Lopez-Peñalba, J., Ortega-Garcia, J., Maltoni, D.: An on-line signature verification system based on fusion of local and global information. In: Kanade, T., Jain, A., Ratha, N.K. (eds.) AVBPA 2005. LNCS, vol. 3546, pp. 523–532. Springer, Heidelberg (2005)

28. Gabryel, M., Cpałka, K., Rutkowski, L.: Evolutionary strategies for learning of neuro-fuzzy systems. In: Proceedings of the I Workshop on Genetic Fuzzy Systems, Granada, pp. 119–123 (2005)
29. Gabryel, M., Korytkowski, M., Scherer, R., Rutkowski, L.: Object detection by simple fuzzy classifiers generated by boosting. In: Rutkowski, L., Korytkowski, M., Scherer, R., Tadeusiewicz, R., Zadeh, L.A., Zurada, J.M. (eds.) ICAISC 2013, Part I. LNCS, vol. 7894, pp. 540–547. Springer, Heidelberg (2013)
30. Gacto, M.J., Alcala, R., Herrera, F.: Interpretability of linguistic fuzzy rule-based systems: an overview of interpretability measures. Inf. Sci. **181**, 4340–4360 (2011)
31. Gałkowski, T., Rutkowski, L.: Nonparametric recovery of multivariate functions with applications to system identification. Proc. IEEE **73**(5), 942–943 (1985)
32. Gałkowski, T., Rutkowski, L.: Nonparametric fitting of multivariate functions. IEEE Trans. Autom. Control **AC–31**(8), 785–787 (1986)
33. Grycuk, R., Gabryel, M., Korytkowski, M., Scherer, R., Voloshynovskiy, S.: From single image to list of objects based on edge and blob detection. In: Rutkowski, L., Korytkowski, M., Scherer, R., Tadeusiewicz, R., Zadeh, L.A., Zurada, J.M. (eds.) ICAISC 2014, Part II. LNCS, vol. 8468, pp. 605–615. Springer, Heidelberg (2014)
34. Held, P., Dockhorn, A., Kruse, R.: On merging and dividing social graphs. J. Artif. Intell. Soft Comput. Res. **5**(1), 23–49 (2015)
35. Huang, K., Hong, Y.: Stability and style-variation modeling for on-line signature verification. Pattern Recogn. **36**, 2253–2270 (2003)
36. Jeong, Y.S., Jeong, M.K., Omitaomu, O.A.: Weighted dynamic time warping for time series classification. Pattern Recogn. **44**, 2231–2240 (2011)
37. Jimenez, F., Kanoh, M., Yoshikawa, T., Furuhashi, T., Nakamura, T.: Effect of robot utterances using onomatopoeia on collaborative learning. J. Artif. Intell. Soft Comput. Res. **4**(2), 125–131 (2014)
38. Khan, M.A.U., Khan, M.K., Khan, M.A.: Velocity-image model for online signature verification. IEEE Trans. Image Process. **15**, 3540–3549 (2006)
39. Kholmatov, A., Yanikoglu, B.: Identity authentication using improved online signature verification method. Pattern Recogn. Lett. **26**, 2400–2408 (2005)
40. Korytkowski, M., Nowicki, R., Scherer, R.: Neuro-fuzzy rough classifier ensemble. In: Alippi, C., Polycarpou, M., Panayiotou, C., Ellinas, G. (eds.) ICANN 2009, Part I. LNCS, vol. 5768, pp. 817–823. Springer, Heidelberg (2009)
41. Korytkowski, M., Rutkowski, L., Scherer, R.: From ensemble of fuzzy classifiers to single fuzzy rule base classifier. In: Rutkowski, L., Tadeusiewicz, R., Zadeh, L.A., Zurada, J.M. (eds.) ICAISC 2008. LNCS (LNAI), vol. 5097, pp. 265–272. Springer, Heidelberg (2008)
42. Korytkowski, M., Rutkowski, L., Scherer, R.: Fast image classification by boosting fuzzy classifiers. Inf. Sci. **327**, 175–182 (2016)
43. Koshiyama, A.S., Vellasco, M.M., Tanscheit, R.: GPFIS-control: a genetic fuzzy system for control tasks. J. Artif. Intell. Soft Comput. Res. **4**(3), 167–179 (2014)
44. Laskowski, Ł., Laskowska, M.: Probing of synthesis route. J. Solid State Chem. **220**, 221–226 (2014)
45. Laskowski, Ł., Laskowska, M., Bałanda, M., Fitta, M., Kwiatkowska, J., Dziliński, K., Karczmarska, A.: Raman and magnetic analysis. Microporous Mesoporous Mater. **200**, 253–259 (2014)
46. Laskowska, M., Laskowski, Ł., Jelonkiewicz, J.: SBA-15 mesoporous silica activated by metal ions-verification of molecular structure on the basis of Raman spectroscopy supported by numerical simulations. J. Mol. Struct. **1100**, 21–26 (2015)

47. Laskowska, M., Laskowski, Ł., Jelonkiewicz, J., Boullanger, A.: Molecular approach to hopfield neural network. In: Rutkowski, L., Korytkowski, M., Scherer, R., Tadeusiewicz, R., Zadeh, L.A., Zurada, J.M. (eds.) Artificial Intelligence and Soft Computing. LNCS, vol. 9119, pp. 72–78. Springer, Heidelberg (2015)
48. Lee, P.M., Hsiao, T.C.: Applying LCS to affective image classification in spatial-frequency domain. J. Artif. Intell. Soft Comput. Res. 4(2), 99–123 (2014)
49. Lumini, A., Nanni, L.: Ensemble of on-line signature matchers based on overcomplete feature generation. Expert Syst. Appl. 36, 5291–5296 (2009)
50. Łapa, K., Cpałka, K., Wang, L.: New method for design of fuzzy systems for nonlinear modelling using different criteria of interpretability. In: Rutkowski, L., Korytkowski, M., Scherer, R., Tadeusiewicz, R., Zadeh, L.A., Zurada, J.M. (eds.) ICAISC 2014, Part I. LNCS, vol. 8467, pp. 217–232. Springer, Heidelberg (2014)
51. Łapa, K., Zalasiński, M., Cpałka, K.: A new method for designing and complexity reduction of neuro-fuzzy systems for nonlinear modelling. In: Rutkowski, L., Korytkowski, M., Scherer, R., Tadeusiewicz, R., Zadeh, L.A., Zurada, J.M. (eds.) ICAISC 2013, Part I. LNCS, vol. 7894, pp. 329–344. Springer, Heidelberg (2013)
52. Łapa, K., Przybył, A., Cpałka, K.: A new approach to designing interpretable models of dynamic systems. In: Rutkowski, L., Korytkowski, M., Scherer, R., Tadeusiewicz, R., Zadeh, L.A., Zurada, J.M. (eds.) ICAISC 2013, Part II. LNCS, vol. 7895, pp. 523–534. Springer, Heidelberg (2013)
53. Moon, J.H., Lee, S.G., Cho, S.Y., Kim, Y.S.: A hybrid online signature verification system supporting multi-confidential levels defined by data mining techniques. Int. J. Intell. Syst. Technol. Appl. 9, 262–273 (2010)
54. Nanni, L.: An advanced multi-matcher method for on-line signature verification featuring global features and tokenised random numbers. Neurocomputing 69, 2402–2406 (2006)
55. Nanni, L., Lumini, A.: Advanced methods for two-class problem formulation for on-line signature verification. Neurocomputing 69, 854–857 (2006)
56. Nanni, L., Lumini, A.: Ensemble of Parzen window classifiers for on-line signature verification. Neurocomputing 68, 217–224 (2005)
57. Nanni, L., Maiorana, E., Lumini, A., Campisi, P.: Combining local, regional and global matchers for a template protected on-line signature verification system. Expert Syst. Appl. 37, 3676–3684 (2010)
58. Ortega-Garcia, J., Fierrez-Aguilar, J., Simon, D., Gonzalez, J., Faundez-Zanuy, M., Espinosa, V., Satue, A., Hernaez, I., Igarza, J.-J., Vivaracho, C., Escudero, D., Moro, Q.-I.: MCYT baseline corpus: a bimodal biometric database. IEE Proc.-Vis. Image Sig. Process. 150, 395–401 (2003)
59. Rutkowski, L.: Identification of MISO nonlinear regressions in the presence of a wide class of disturbances. IEEE Trans. Inf. Theory 37(1), 214–216 (1991)
60. Rutkowski, L.: Sequential estimates of probability densities by orthogonal series and their application in pattern classification. IEEE Trans. Syst. Man Cybern. 10(12), 918–920 (1980)
61. Rutkowski, L.: On-line identification of time-varying systems by nonparametric techniques. IEEE Trans. Autom. Control 27(1), 228–230 (1982)
62. Rutkowski, L.: On nonparametric identification with prediction of time-varying systems. IEEE Trans. Autom. Control 29(1), 58–60 (1984)
63. Rutkowski, L.: A general approach for nonparametric fitting of functions and their derivatives with applications to linear circuits identification. IEEE Trans. Circuits Syst. 33(8), 812–818 (1986)
64. Rutkowski, L.: Adaptive probabilistic neural networks for pattern classification in time-varying environment. IEEE Trans. Neural Netw. 15(4), 811–827 (2004)

65. Rutkowski, L.: Computational Intelligence. Springer, Heidelberg (2008)
66. Rutkowski, L., Cpałka, K.: Flexible Structures of Neuro-Fuzzy Systems. Quo Vadis Computational Intelligence. Studies in Fuzziness and Soft Computing, vol. 54. Springer, Heidelberg (2000)
67. Rutkowski, L., Cpałka, K.: Compromise approach to neuro-fuzzy systems. In: Sincak, P., Vascak, J., Kvasnicka, V., Pospichal, J. (eds.) Intelligent Technologies - Theory and Applications, vol. 76, pp. 85–90. IOS Press (2002)
68. Rutkowski L., Cpałka K.: Flexible weighted neuro-fuzzy systems. In: Proceedings of the 9th International Conference on Neural Information Processing (ICONIP 2002), Orchid Country Club, Singapore, 18–22 November 2002
69. Rutkowski, L., Cpałka, K.: Flexible neuro-fuzzy systems. IEEE Trans. Neural Netw. **14**, 554–574 (2003)
70. Rutkowski, L., Cpałka, K.: Neuro-fuzzy systems derived from quasi-triangular norms. In: Proceedings of the IEEE International Conference on Fuzzy Systems, Budapest, 26–29 July 2004, vol. 2, pp. 1031–1036 (2004)
71. Rutkowski, L., Cpałka, K.: Designing and learning of adjustable quasi triangular norms with applications to neuro-fuzzy systems. IEEE Trans. Fuzzy Syst. **13**, 140–151 (2005)
72. Rutkowski, L., Jaworski, M., Pietruczuk, L., Duda, P.: Decision trees for mining data streams based on the gaussian approximation. IEEE Trans. Knowl. Data Eng. **26**(1), 108–119 (2014)
73. Rutkowski, L., Jaworski, M., Pietruczuk, L., Duda, P.: The CART decision tree for mining data streams. Inf. Sci. **266**, 1–15 (2014)
74. Rutkowski, L., Pietruczuk, L., Duda, P., Jaworski, M.: Decision trees for mining data streams based on the McDiarmid's bound. IEEE Trans. Knowl. Data Eng. **25**(6), 1272–1279 (2013)
75. Rutkowski, L., Przybył, A., Cpałka, K.: Novel online speed profile generation for industrial machine tool based on flexible neuro-fuzzy approximation. IEEE Trans. Ind. Electron. **59**, 1238–1247 (2012)
76. Rutkowski, L., Rafajłowicz, E.: On optimal global rate of convergence of some nonparametric identification procedures. IEEE Trans. Autom. Control **34**(10), 1089–1091 (1989)
77. Scherer, R.: Neuro-fuzzy systems with relation matrix. In: Rutkowski, L., Scherer, R., Tadeusiewicz, R., Zadeh, L.A., Zurada, J.M. (eds.) ICAISC 2010, Part I. LNCS, vol. 6113, pp. 210–215. Springer, Heidelberg (2010)
78. Scherer, R., Rutkowski, L.: Relational equations initializing neuro-fuzzy system. In: Proceedings of the 10th Zittau Fuzzy Colloquium, Zittau, Germany, pp. 18–22 (2002)
79. Starczewski, J.T., Bartczuk, L., Dziwiński, P., Marvuglia, A.: Learning methods for Type-2 FLS based on FCM. In: Rutkowski, L., Scherer, R., Tadeusiewicz, R., Zadeh, L.A., Zurada, J.M. (eds.) ICAISC 2010, Part I. LNCS, vol. 6113, pp. 224–231. Springer, Heidelberg (2010)
80. Szarek, A., Korytkowski, M., Rutkowski, L., Scherer, R., Szyprowski, J.: Application of neural networks in assessing changes around implant after total hip arthroplasty. In: Rutkowski, L., Korytkowski, M., Scherer, R., Tadeusiewicz, R., Zadeh, L.A., Zurada, J.M. (eds.) ICAISC 2012, Part II. LNCS, vol. 7268, pp. 335–340. Springer, Heidelberg (2012)
81. Szarek, A., Korytkowski, M., Rutkowski, L., Scherer, R., Szyprowski, J.: Forecasting wear of head and acetabulum in hip joint implant. In: Rutkowski, L., Korytkowski, M., Scherer, R., Tadeusiewicz, R., Zadeh, L.A., Zurada, J.M. (eds.) ICAISC 2012, Part II. LNCS, vol. 7268, pp. 341–346. Springer, Heidelberg (2012)

82. Szczypta, J., Przybył, A., Wang, L.: Evolutionary approach with multiple quality criteria for controller design. In: Rutkowski, L., Korytkowski, M., Scherer, R., Tadeusiewicz, R., Zadeh, L.A., Zurada, J.M. (eds.) ICAISC 2014, Part I. LNCS, vol. 8467, pp. 455–467. Springer, Heidelberg (2014)

83. Smyczyńska, J., Hilczer, M., Smyczyńska, U., Stawerska, R., Tadeusiewic, R., Lewiński, A.: Artificial neural models - a novel tool for predictying the efficacy of growth hormone (GH) therapy in children with short stature. Neuroendocrinol. Lett. (ISSN: 0172-780X, ISSN-L: 0172-780X) **36**(4), 348–353 (2015)

84. Smyczyńska, U., Smyczyńska, J., Hilczer, M., Stawerska, R., Lewiński, A., Tadeusiewicz, R.: Artificial neural networks - a novel tool in modelling the effectiveness of growth hormone (GH) therapy in children with GH deficiency. Pediatr. Endocrinol. **14**(2), 9–18 (2015)

85. Starczewski, J.T., Rutkowski, L.: Connectionist structures of Type 2 fuzzy inference systems. In: Wyrzykowski, R., Dongarra, J., Paprzycki, M., Waśniewski, J. (eds.) PPAM 2001. LNCS, vol. 2328, p. 634. Springer, Heidelberg (2002)

86. Tadeusiewicz, R.: Neural networks as a tool for modeling of biological systems. Bio-Algorithms Med-Syst. **11**(3), 135–144 (2015)

87. Tadeusiewicz, R.: Neural networks in mining sciences - general overview and some representative examples. Arch. Min. Sci. **60**(4), 971–984 (2015)

88. Wang, X., Liu, X., Japkowicz, N., Matwin, S.: Automated approach to classification of mine-like objects using multiple-aspect sonar images. J. Artif. Intell. Soft Comput. Res. **4**(2), 133–148 (2014)

89. Yeung, D.-Y., Chang, H., Xiong, Y., George, S., Kashi, R., Matsumoto, T., Rigoll, G.: SVC2004: first international signature verification competition. In: Zhang, D., Jain, A.K. (eds.) ICBA 2004. LNCS, vol. 3072, pp. 16–22. Springer, Heidelberg (2004)

90. Zalasiński, M., Łapa, K., Cpałka, K.: New algorithm for evolutionary selection of the dynamic signature global features. In: Rutkowski, L., Korytkowski, M., Scherer, R., Tadeusiewicz, R., Zadeh, L.A., Zurada, J.M. (eds.) ICAISC 2013, Part II. LNCS, vol. 7895, pp. 113–121. Springer, Heidelberg (2013)

91. Zalasiński, M., Cpałka, K.: A New Method of On-line Signature Verification Using a Flexible Fuzzy One-Class Classifier, pp. 38–53. Academic Publishing House EXIT (2011)

92. Zalasiński, M., Cpałka, K.: Novel algorithm for the on-line signature verification. In: Rutkowski, L., Korytkowski, M., Scherer, R., Tadeusiewicz, R., Zadeh, L.A., Zurada, J.M. (eds.) ICAISC 2012, Part II. LNCS, vol. 7268, pp. 362–367. Springer, Heidelberg (2012)

93. Zalasiński, M., Cpałka, K.: New approach for the on-line signature verification based on method of horizontal partitioning. In: Rutkowski, L., Korytkowski, M., Scherer, R., Tadeusiewicz, R., Zadeh, L.A., Zurada, J.M. (eds.) ICAISC 2013, Part II. LNCS, vol. 7895, pp. 342–350. Springer, Heidelberg (2013)

94. Zalasiński, M., Cpałka, K., Er, M.J.: New method for dynamic signature verification using hybrid partitioning. In: Rutkowski, L., Korytkowski, M., Scherer, R., Tadeusiewicz, R., Zadeh, L.A., Zurada, J.M. (eds.) ICAISC 2014, Part II. LNCS, vol. 8468, pp. 216–230. Springer, Heidelberg (2014)

95. Zalasiński, M., Cpałka, K., Er, M.J.: A new method for the dynamic signature verification based on the stable partitions of the signature. In: Rutkowski, L., Korytkowski, M., Scherer, R., Tadeusiewicz, R., Zadeh, L.A., Zurada, J.M. (eds.) Artificial Intelligence and Soft Computing. LNCS, vol. 9120, pp. 161–174. Springer, Heidelberg (2015)

96. Zalasiński, M., Cpałka, K., Hayashi, Y.: New method for dynamic signature verification based on global features. In: Rutkowski, L., Korytkowski, M., Scherer, R., Tadeusiewicz, R., Zadeh, L.A., Zurada, J.M. (eds.) ICAISC 2014, Part II. LNCS, vol. 8468, pp. 231–245. Springer, Heidelberg (2014)

97. Zalasiński, M., Cpałka, K., Hayashi, Y.: New fast algorithm for the dynamic signature verification using global features values. In: Rutkowski, L., Korytkowski, M., Scherer, R., Tadeusiewicz, R., Zadeh, L.A., Zurada, J.M. (eds.) Artificial Intelligence and Soft Computing. LNCS, vol. 9120, pp. 175–188. Springer, Heidelberg (2015)

98. Zhao, W., Lun, R., Espy, D.D., Ann, R.M.: Realtime motion assessment for rehabilitation exercises: integration of kinematic modeling with fuzzy inference. J. Artif. Intell. Soft Comput. Res. 4(4), 267–285 (2014)

An Idea of the Dynamic Signature Verification Based on a Hybrid Approach

Marcin Zalasiński[1]([✉]), Krzysztof Cpałka[1], and Elisabeth Rakus-Andersson[2]

[1] Institute of Computational Intelligence,
Częstochowa University of Technology, Częstochowa, Poland
{marcin.zalasinski,krzysztof.cpalka}@iisi.pcz.pl
[2] Department of Mathematics and Science,
Blekinge Institute of Technology, Karlskrona, Sweden
Elisabeth.Andersson@bth.se

Abstract. Dynamic signature verification is a very interesting biometric issue. It is difficult to realize because signatures of the user are characterized by relatively high intra-class and low inter-class variability. However, this method of an identity verification is commonly socially acceptable. It is a big advantage of the dynamic signature biometric attribute. In this paper we propose a new hybrid algorithm for the dynamic signature verification based on global and regional approach. We present the simulation results of the proposed method for BioSecure DS2 database, distributed by the BioSecure Association.

Keywords: Behavioural biometrics · Dynamic signature · Hybrid approach · Flexible neuro-fuzzy system · One-class classifier

1 Introduction

A dynamic signature is a behavioural biometric attribute, which contains information about dynamics of the signing process. It is acquired using a digital input device, e.g. graphic tablet. This is a very important attribute, because it is commonly socially acceptable. However, identity verification using the dynamic signature is a difficult process, because of relatively high intra-class and low inter-class variability. Moreover, during training phase a biometric system does not have reference signatures of forgers, so in this case the use of the one-class classifier is required.

In the literature one can find four main approaches to the dynamic signature analysis: **(a)** global feature based approach (see e.g. [25,51,57]), **(b)** function based approach (see e.g. [23,41,55]), **(c)** regional based approach (see e.g. [24, 26,38,89,90]) and **(d)** hybrid approach (see e.g. [17,56,58]). In this paper we present a new hybrid method for the dynamic signature verification.

The method proposed in this paper is a hybrid of two approaches used for the dynamic signature verification - the first one based on the regions (see e.g. [14,15,89]) and the second one based on the global features (see e.g. [91–93]).

© Springer International Publishing Switzerland 2016
L. Rutkowski et al. (Eds.): ICAISC 2016, Part II, LNAI 9693, pp. 232–246, 2016.
DOI: 10.1007/978-3-319-39384-1_21

These approaches differ in selection of the most characteristic features of the signature and creation of the signatures' templates. During training phase our method evaluates created templates of the signature and the most characteristic ones are the most important during test phase. Verification process is realized using our authorial neuro-fuzzy one-class classifier with weights of importance. It is worth to note that many computational intelligence methods (see e.g. [1–7, 18–22, 28, 30, 32, 34, 35, 39, 40, 42, 44, 50, 59–67, 73–75, 78, 81, 86]) are successfully used in pattern recognition, modelling and optimization issues.

Simulations of the proposed method have been performed using BioSecure (BMDB) dynamic signatures database distributed by the BioSecure Association [36].

This paper is organized into 4 sections. Section 2 contains description of the new method for the dynamic signature verification based on a hybrid approach. Section 3 shows simulation results. Conclusions are drawn in Sect. 4.

2 Description of the New Method for the Dynamic Signature Verification Based on a Hybrid Approach

In this section we propose a new algorithm for an identity verification based on the global features and partitions of the dynamic signatures. Exemplary global features are duration of signing process, number of pen-ups and time moment of maximum velocity of the signature. In turn, partitions are associated with signature regions in which pen velocity is low or high and pen pressure is low or high in the initial, middle, and final time moments of the signing process. Operation of the method bases on the creation of the templates of global features and trajectories in the partitions (Sect. 2.1). The templates are used to determine parameters of the system evaluating similarity of the signatures (Sect. 2.2). Classification of the signatures is described in Sect. 2.3.

2.1 Creation of the Templates

Templates of the signature are created on the basis of the reference signatures and they are used during verification process. In the proposed hybrid method, there are two types of the templates.

The templates of the first type (using regional approach) are extracted from the regions called partitions, which are a combination of horizontal and vertical sections of the signature.

At the beginning of this process, reference signatures of the user should be pre-processed by commonly used methods (see e.g. [26, 38]) in order to match length, rotation, scale and offset.

Each reference signature j ($j = 1, 2, \ldots, J$, where J is the number of reference signatures) of the user i ($i = 1, 2, \ldots, I$, where I is the number of users) is represented by the following signals: (a) horizontal trajectory $\mathbf{x}_{i,j} = [x_{i,j,k=1}, x_{i,j,k=2}, \ldots, x_{i,j,k=K_i}]$, where K_i is the number of signal samples and k is an index of the signal sample ($k = 1, 2, \ldots, K_i$),

(b) vertical trajectory $\mathbf{y}_{i,j} = [y_{i,j,k=1}, y_{i,j,k=2}, \ldots, y_{i,j,k=K_i}]$, (c) pen veloc-
ity $\mathbf{v}_{i,j} = [v_{i,j,k=1}, v_{i,j,k=2}, \ldots, v_{i,j,k=K_i}]$ and (d) pen pressure $\mathbf{z}_{i,j} = [z_{i,j,k=1}, z_{i,j,k=2}, \ldots, z_{i,j,k=K_i}]$. In order to simplify the description of the algorithm
we use the symbol $\mathbf{a}_{i,j} = [a_{i,j,k=1}, a_{i,j,k=2}, \ldots, a_{i,j,k=K_i}]$ to describe both shape sig-
nals ($a \in \{x, y\}$) and the symbol $\mathbf{s}_{i,j} = [s_{i,j,k=1}, s_{i,j,k=2}, \ldots, s_{i,j,k=K_i}]$ to describe
both dynamics signals ($s \in \{v, z\}$).

The purpose of the partitioning is to assign each point of the signature to
the single hybrid partition resulting from a combination of the vertical and
the horizontal section.

The vertical sections are indicated by the elements of the vector $\mathbf{pv}_i = \left[pv_{i,k=1}, pv_{i,k=2}, \ldots, pv_{i,k=K_i} \right]$ determined as follows:

$$
pv_{i,k} = \begin{cases} 1 \text{ for } & 0 < k \leq \frac{K_i}{P} \\ 2 \text{ for } & \frac{K_i}{P} < k \leq \frac{2K_i}{P} \\ \quad \vdots \\ P \text{ for } & \frac{(P-1)K_i}{P} < k \leq K_i \end{cases}, \tag{1}
$$

where P is the number of the vertical sections.

Next, horizontal sections are created. Each of them represents high and
low velocity and high and low pressure in individual moments of sign-
ing. Horizontal sections indicated by the elements of the vector $\mathbf{ph}_i^{\{s\}} = \left[ph_{i,k=1}^{\{s\}}, ph_{i,k=2}^{\{s\}}, \ldots, ph_{i,k=K_i}^{\{s\}} \right]$ are determined as follows:

$$
ph_{i,k}^{\{s\}} = \begin{cases} 1 \text{ for } s_{i,j=jBase,k} < avgv_{i,p=pv_{i,k}^{\{s\}}}^{\{s\}} \\ 2 \text{ for } s_{i,j=jBase,k} \geq avgv_{i,p=pv_{i,k}^{\{s\}}}^{\{s\}} \end{cases}, \tag{2}
$$

where $jBase$ is an index of the base signature selected during pre-processing
(see [14, 15]), $avgv_{i,p}^{\{s\}}$ is an average value of the signal s in the vertical section
indicated by the index p:

$$
avgv_{i,p}^{\{s\}} = \frac{1}{Kv_{i,p}} \sum_{k=\left(\frac{(p-1)\cdot K_i}{P^{\{s\}}}+1 \right)}^{k=\left(\frac{p\cdot K_i}{P^{\{s\}}} \right)} s_{i,j=jBase,k}, \tag{3}
$$

where $Kv_{i,p}$ is the number of samples in the vertical section p, $s_{i,j=jBase,k}$ is
the sample k of the signal $s \in \{v, z\}$ describing dynamics of the signature.

The intersection of the vertical and horizontal section is the partition.

The templates of the signatures are averaged fragments of the reference
signatures represented by the shape trajectories. The partition contains two
templates. Template $\mathbf{tc}_{i,p,r}^{\{s,a\}} = \left[tc_{i,p,r,k=1}^{\{s,a\}}, tc_{i,p,r,k=2}^{\{s,a\}}, \ldots, tc_{i,p,r,k=Kc_{i,p,r}^{\{s,a\}}}^{\{s,a\}} \right]$, where
$Kc_{i,p,r}^{\{s,a\}}$ is the number of samples in the partition (p, r), which describes frag-
ments of the reference signatures in the partition (p, r) of the user i, associated

with the signal a (x or y), created on the basis of the signal s (v or z), is determined as follows:

$$tc_{i,p,r,k}^{\{s,a\}} = \frac{1}{J} \sum_{j=1}^{J} a_{i,j,p,r,k}^{\{s\}},$$ (4)

where $\mathbf{a}_{i,j,p,r}^{\{s\}} = \left[a_{i,j,p,r,k=1}^{\{s\}}, a_{i,j,p,r,k=2}^{\{s\}}, \cdots, a_{i,j,p,r,k=Kc_{i,p,r}^{\{s,a\}}}^{\{s\}} \right]$ is a trajectory of the reference signature j of the user i created on the basis of the signal s, which belongs to the partition (p, r).

Next, creation of the templates of the second type (using global approach) is performed.

This approach bases on a set of global features describing the dynamics of the signature, which have been systematized in the paper [25]. Determination of the templates starts from the creation of global features matrix $\mathbf{G}_i$.

Matrix $\mathbf{G}_i$, which contains all considered global features of all J training signatures of the user i, has the following structure:

$$\mathbf{G}_i = \begin{bmatrix} g_{i,1,1} & g_{i,2,1} & \cdots & g_{i,N,1} \\ g_{i,1,2} & g_{i,2,2} & \cdots & g_{i,N,2} \\ & & \vdots & \\ g_{i,1,J} & g_{i,2,J} & \cdots & g_{i,N,J} \end{bmatrix} = \begin{bmatrix} \mathbf{g}_{i,1} \\ \mathbf{g}_{i,2} \\ \vdots \\ \mathbf{g}_{i,N} \end{bmatrix}^T,$$ (5)

where $\mathbf{g}_{i,n} = \left[g_{i,n,1} \, g_{i,n,2} \cdots g_{i,n,J} \right]$, $g_{i,n,j}$ is a value of the global feature n, $n = 1, 2, \ldots, N$, determined for the signature j created by the user i, N is the number of the global features.

Matrix $\mathbf{G}_i$ is used to determine value of the vector $\bar{\mathbf{g}}_i$ which contains templates of global features. This vector is described as follows:

$$\bar{\mathbf{g}}_i = [\bar{g}_{i,1}, \bar{g}_{i,2}, \ldots, \bar{g}_{i,N}],$$ (6)

where $\bar{g}_{i,n}$ is the template of n-th global feature of the user i, computed using the following formula:

$$\bar{g}_{i,n} = \frac{1}{J} \sum_{j=1}^{J} g_{i,n,j}.$$ (7)

Next, parameters of the classifier are determined.

2.2 Determination of the Classifier Parameters

In the verification phase our method uses a flexible neuro-fuzzy system (see e.g. [9–13, 27, 29, 33, 43, 52–54, 69–72, 76, 77, 80, 88]). Neuro-fuzzy systems combine the natural language description of fuzzy systems (see e.g. [45, 94]) and the learning properties of neural networks (see e.g. [8, 46–49, 79, 82–85]). However, our authorial system is a one-class classifier. Moreover, it uses weights of importance of the templates, which have individual character for the user i.

Values of the templates weights are based on a dispersion of the reference signatures signals or global features and also on an average distance between the template and the reference signatures signals or global features.

First, to compute weight of importance for the template created using regional approach, average distance $\bar{d}_{i,p,r}^{\{s,a\}}$ between signatures signals and the template has to be computed as follows:

$$\bar{d}_{i,p,r}^{\{s,a\}} = \frac{1}{J} \sum_{j=1}^{J} \sqrt{\sum_{k=1}^{Kc_{i,p,r}^{\{s,a\}}} \left(tc_{i,p,r,k}^{\{s,a\}} - a_{i,j,p,r,k} \right)^2}. \tag{8}$$

Next, dispersion of the reference signatures signals $\sigma_{i,p,r}^{\{s,a\}}$ has to be calculated:

$$\sigma_{i,p,r}^{\{s,a\}} = \sqrt{\frac{1}{J} \sum_{j=1}^{J} \left(\bar{d}_{i,p,r}^{\{s,a\}} - \sqrt{\sum_{k=1}^{Kc_{i,p,r}^{\{s,a\}}} \left(tc_{i,p,r,k}^{\{s,a\}} - a_{i,j,p,r,k} \right)^2} \right)^2}. \tag{9}$$

Weight $wr_{i,p,r}^{\{s,a\}}$ for the template created using regional approach is determined as follows:

$$wr_{i,p,r}^{\{s,a\}} = 1 - \frac{\bar{d}_{i,p,r}^{\{s,a\}} \cdot \sigma_{i,p,r}^{\{s,a\}}}{\max\limits_{p=1,\dots,P;r=1,2} \left\{ \bar{d}_{i,p,r}^{\{s,a\}} \cdot \sigma_{i,p,r}^{\{s,a\}} \right\}}. \tag{10}$$

After determination of the weights of importance of the templates created on the basis of the regional approach, we determine the weights $wg_{i,n}$ associated with the templates created using global approach. They are determined as follows:

$$wg_{i,n} = 1 - \frac{\frac{1}{J} \sum_{j=1}^{J} |\bar{g}_{i,n} - g_{i,n,j}|}{\frac{1}{J} \sum_{j=1}^{J} |\bar{g}_{i,n} - g_{i,n,j}| + \sqrt{\frac{1}{J} \sum_{j=1}^{J} (\bar{g}_{i,n} - g_{i,n,j})^2}}. \tag{11}$$

Having weights of importance, we also have to determine the parameters describing differences between the reference signatures and the templates, which are used in the construction of fuzzy rules used by the flexible-neuro fuzzy system in the classification process. For the templates created using regional approach they are determined as follows:

$$dmaxr_{i,j,p,r}^{\{s,a\}} = \max_{j=1,\dots,J} \left\{ \sqrt{\sum_{k=1}^{Kc_{i,p,r}^{\{s,a\}}} \left(tc_{i,p,r,k}^{\{s,a\}} - a_{i,j,p,r,k} \right)^2} \right\}. \tag{12}$$

Next, determination of the parameters $dmaxg_{i,n}$ used in the classification process for the templates created by global approach is performed:

$$dmaxg_{i,n} = \max_{j=1,\ldots,J} \left\{ |\bar{g}_{i,n} - g_{i,n,j}| \right\}. \tag{13}$$

After determination of parameters of neuro-fuzzy system used for the dynamic signature verification, classification of the test signature of the user claiming to be user i can be performed.

2.3 Classification

Sections 2.1 and 2.2 are related to the actions taken in the so-called training phase. In that phase each user of considered biometric system creates reference signatures used for determination of individual parameters of the classification system. In this section we consider the test phase for the signature of the user claiming to be signer i.

The user whose identity should be verified creates one test signature. Next, this signature should be pre-processed. Then, it is partitioned and global features of it are also determined.

Next step of the classification phase is determination of the similarities of the test signature to the template. Similarities to the templates created using regional approach $dtstr_{i,p,r}^{\{s,a\}}$ are determined as follows:

$$dtstr_{i,p,r}^{\{s,a\}} = \sqrt{ \sum_{k=1}^{Kc_{i,p,r}^{\{s,a\}}} \left(tc_{i,p,r,k}^{\{s,a\}} - atst_{i,p,r,k}^{\{s,a\}} \right)^2 }, \tag{14}$$

where $atst_{i,p,r,k}^{\{s,a\}}$ is the test signature trajectory fragment.

After determination of these similarities, we calculate similarities of the test signature to the templates created using global approach $dtstg_{i,n}$. They are determined as follows:

$$dtstg_{i,n} = |\bar{g}_{i,n} - gtst_{i,n}|, \tag{15}$$

where $gtst_{i,n}$ is a global feature of the test signature.

Next, the system evaluates similarity of the test signature to the templates. It is realized on the basis of the values of similarities $dtstr_{i,p,r}^{\{s,a\}}$ and $dtstg_{i,n}$. The classifier also takes into account the weights $wr_{i,p,r}^{\{s,a\}}$ and $wg_{i,n}$. The response of the flexible neuro-fuzzy one-class classifier is the basis for the evaluation of the signature reliability.

Due to simplify a notation of the fuzzy rules, we will use the following additional variables:

- $dtst_{i,q} \in \left\{ dtstr_{i,p,r}^{\{s,a\}}, dtstg_{i,n} \right\}$ - which is the similarity of the test signature determined using regional or global approach, where q ($q = 1, \ldots, Q$, where Q is a sum of the templates' number created using regional and global approaches) is an index of considered similarity,

- $w_{i,q} \in \left\{ wr_{i,p,r}^{\{s,a\}}, wg_{i,n} \right\}$ - which is the weight of importance determined using regional or global approach,
- $dmax_{i,q} \in \left\{ dmaxr_{i,p,r}^{\{s,a\}}, dmaxg_{i,n} \right\}$ - which is the parameter describing differences between the reference signatures and the templates determined using regional or global approach.

The proposed system used for classification works on the basis of two fuzzy rules presented as follows:

$$
\begin{cases}
R^{(1)} : \begin{bmatrix} \textbf{IF} \left(dtst_{i,1} \textbf{is} A_{i,1}^1 \right) |w_{i,1} \textbf{ AND} \ldots \textbf{AND} \left(dtst_{i,Q} \textbf{is} A_{i,Q}^1 \right) |w_{i,Q} \\ \textbf{THEN} y_i \textbf{is} B^1 \end{bmatrix} \\
R^{(2)} : \begin{bmatrix} \textbf{IF} \left(dtst_{i,1} \textbf{is} A_{i,1}^2 \right) |w_{i,1} \textbf{ AND} \ldots \textbf{AND} \left(dtst_{i,Q} \textbf{is} A_{i,Q}^2 \right) |w_{i,Q} \\ \textbf{THEN} y_i \textbf{is} B^2 \end{bmatrix}
\end{cases}, \quad (16)
$$

where

- $dtst_{i,q}$ are input linguistic variables. Values "high" and "low" taken by these variables are Gaussian fuzzy sets $A_{i,q}^1$ and $A_{i,q}^2$ (see Fig. 1).
- y_i $(i = 1, \ldots, I)$ is output linguistic variable meaning "similarity of the test signature to the reference signatures of the user i". Value "high" of this variable is the fuzzy set B^1 of γ type and value "low" is the fuzzy set B^2 of L type (see Fig. 1).
- $w_{i,q}$ are weights of the templates.

The test signature is recognized as genuine if the assumption $\bar{y}_i > cth_i$ is satisfied, where $\bar{y}_i$ is the value of the output signal of neuro-fuzzy system described by the (16):

$$
\bar{y}_i \approx \frac{T^* \left\{ \mu_{A_{i,1}^1} (dtst_{i,1}), \ldots, \mu_{A_{i,Q}^1} (dtst_{i,Q}); w_{i,1}, \ldots, w_{i,Q} \right\}}{\left(\begin{array}{l} T^* \left\{ \mu_{A_{i,1}^1} (dtst_{i,1}), \ldots, \mu_{A_{i,Q}^1} (dtst_{i,Q}); w_{i,1}, \ldots, w_{i,Q} \right\} \\ +T^* \left\{ \mu_{A_{i,1}^2} (dtst_{i,1}), \ldots, \mu_{A_{i,Q}^2} (dtst_{i,Q}); w_{i,1}, \ldots, w_{i,Q} \right\} \end{array} \right)}, \quad (17)
$$

where $T^* \{\cdot\}$ is the weighted t-norm (see e.g. [68]) and $cth_i \in [0, 1]$ is a coefficient determined experimentally for each user to eliminate disproportion between FAR and FRR error (see e.g. [87]). The values of this coefficient are usually close to 0.5. Formula (17) was established by taking into account the following simplification, resulting from the spacing of the fuzzy sets shown in Fig. 1: $\mu_{B^1}(0) = 0$, $\mu_{B^1}(1) \approx 1$, $\mu_{B^2}(0) \approx 1$ and $\mu_{B^2}(1) = 0$.

3 Simulation Results

During simulations we used dynamic signature BioSecure DS2 database distributed by the BioSecure Association. Tests were performed using an application implemented in C#. We repeated 5 times the simulation procedure, taking each

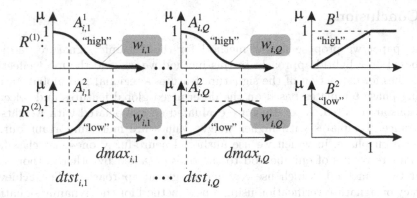

Fig. 1. Input and output fuzzy sets used in the rules (16) of the flexible neuro-fuzzy system for evaluation of similarity of the test signature to the reference signatures in the hybrid global-regional method for the dynamic signature verification.

time 5 training signatures and 20 test signatures (10 genuine signatures and 10 ones prepared by so-called skilled forgers). In the simulations we assumed that $P^{\{s\}} = 2$.

The results of the simulations are presented in Table 1, which contains values of the errors FAR (False Acceptance Rate) and FRR (False Rejection Rate) achieved by our method in comparison to the regional and global methods proposed by us earlier and the methods of other authors. Please note that the new method for the dynamic signature verification based on a hybrid approach has the best accuracy in comparison to the methods presented in Table 1.

Table 1. Comparison of the accuracy of different methods for the signature verification for the BioSecure database.

Method	Average FAR	Average FRR	Average error
Methods of other authors [37]	-	-	3.48 % – 30.13 %
Algorithm based on Horizontal Partitioning, AHP (Cpałka et al. (2014) [15])	2.94 %	4.45 %	3.70 %
Algorithm based on Vertical Partitioning, AVP (Cpałka, Zalasiński (2014) [14])	3.13 %	4.15 %	3.64 %
Algorithm based on Global Features, AGF (Zalasiński et al. (2015) [92])	3.29 %	3.82 %	3.56 %
Algorithm based on Hybrid Partitioning, AHP (Cpałka et al. (2016) [16])	3.36 %	3.30 %	3.33 %
Our method	**2.17 %**	**1.34 %**	**1.76 %**

4   Conclusions

In this paper we propose a new method for the dynamic signature verification based on a hybrid approach. In this method we use two the most effective approaches for extraction of the signature features - regional and global. In the training phase templates based on the determined global features and selected partitions are created. Next, they are evaluated and associated with weights of importance. Templates with higher weight values are more important during classification phase, in which we use authorial neuro-fuzzy one-class classifier. We compare results of our method to the ones obtained by other authors and to our three methods which use regional or global approaches. The achieved accuracy of signature verification using a new method for the dynamic signature verification confirms that combination of the approaches is a very good solution for the identity verification task using dynamic signature.

Acknowledgment. The project was financed by the National Science Centre (Poland) on the basis of the decision number DEC-2012/05/B/ST7/02138.

References

1. Akimoto, T., Ogata, T.: Experimental development of a focalization mechanism in an integrated narrative generation system. J. Artif. Intell. Soft Comput. Res. **5**(3), 177–188 (2015)
2. Bartczuk, Ł.: Gene expression programming in correction modelling of nonlinear dynamic objects. In: Borzemski, L., Grzech, A., Świątek, J., Wilimowska, Z. (eds.) ISAT 2015 - Part I. Advances in Intelligent Systems and Computing, vol. 429, pp. 125–134. Springer, Heidelberg (2016)
3. Bartczuk, Ł., Przybył, A., Koprinkova-Hristova, P.: New method for nonlinear fuzzy correction modelling of dynamic objects. In: Rutkowski, L., Korytkowski, M., Scherer, R., Tadeusiewicz, R., Zadeh, L.A., Zurada, J.M. (eds.) ICAISC 2014, Part I. LNCS, vol. 8467, pp. 169–180. Springer, Heidelberg (2014)
4. Bartczuk, Ł., Rutkowska, D.: Type-2 fuzzy decision trees. In: Rutkowski, L., Tadeusiewicz, R., Zadeh, L.A., Zurada, J.M. (eds.) ICAISC 2008. LNCS (LNAI), vol. 5097, pp. 197–206. Springer, Heidelberg (2008)
5. Bartczuk, Ł., Rutkowska, D.: Medical diagnosis with type-2 fuzzy decision trees. In: Kkacki, E., Rudnicki, M., Stempczyńska, J. (eds.) Computers in Medical Activity. Advances in Intelligent and Soft Computing, vol. 65, pp. 11–21. Springer, Heidelberg (2009)
6. Bello, O., Holzmann, J., Yaqoob, T., Teodoriu, C.: Application of artificial intelligence methods in drilling system design and operations: a review of the state of the art. J. Artif. Intell. Soft Comput. Res. **5**(2), 121–139 (2015)
7. Chu, J.L., Krzyżak, A.: The recognition of partially occluded objects with support vector machines, convolutional neural networks and deep belief networks. J. Artif. Intell. Soft Comput. Res. **4**(1), 5–19 (2014)
8. Cierniak, R., Rutkowski, L.: On image compression by competitive neural networks and optimal linear predictors. Sig. Process. Image Commun. **15**(6), 559–565 (2000)

9. Cpalka, K.: A method for designing flexible neuro-fuzzy systems. In: Rutkowski, L., Tadeusiewicz, R., Zadeh, L.A., Żurada, J.M. (eds.) ICAISC 2006. LNCS (LNAI), vol. 4029, pp. 212–219. Springer, Heidelberg (2006)

10. Cpałka, K., Łapa, K., Przybył, A.: A new approach to design of control systems using genetic programming. Inf. Technol. Control **44**(4), 433–442 (2015)

11. Cpałka, K., Łapa, K., Przybył, A., Zalasiński, M.: A new method for designing neuro-fuzzy systems for nonlinear modelling with interpretability aspects. Neurocomputing **135**, 203–217 (2014)

12. Cpałka, K., Rebrova, O., Nowicki, R., Rutkowski, L.: On design of flexible neuro-fuzzy systems for nonlinear modelling. Int. J. Gen. Syst. **42**(6), 706–720 (2013)

13. Cpałka, K., Rutkowski, L.: Flexible Takagi-Sugeno neuro-fuzzy structures for nonlinear approximation. WSEAS Trans. Syst. **4**(9), 1450–1458 (2005)

14. Cpałka, K., Zalasiński, M.: On-line signature verification using vertical signature partitioning. Expert Syst. Appl. **41**, 4170–4180 (2014)

15. Cpałka, K., Zalasiński, M., Rutkowski, L.: New method for the on-line signature verification based on horizontal partitioning. Pattern Recogn. **47**, 2652–2661 (2014)

16. Cpałka, K., Zalasiński, M., Rutkowski, L.: A new algorithm for identity verification based on the analysis of a handwritten dynamic signature. Appl. Soft Comput. (2016, in press). http://dx.doi.org/10.1016/j.asoc.2016.02.017

17. Doroz, R., Porwik, P., Orczyk, T.: Dynamic signature verification method based on association of features with similarity measures. Neurocomputing **171**, 921–931 (2016)

18. Duda, P., Hayashi, Y., Jaworski, M.: On the strong convergence of the orthogonal series-type kernel regression neural networks in a non-stationary environment. In: Rutkowski, L., Korytkowski, M., Scherer, R., Tadeusiewicz, R., Zadeh, L.A., Zurada, J.M. (eds.) ICAISC 2012, Part I. LNCS, vol. 7267, pp. 47–54. Springer, Heidelberg (2012)

19. Duda, P., Jaworski, M., Pietruczuk, L.: On pre-processing algorithms for data stream. In: Rutkowski, L., Korytkowski, M., Scherer, R., Tadeusiewicz, R., Zadeh, L.A., Zurada, J.M. (eds.) ICAISC 2012, Part II. LNCS, vol. 7268, pp. 56–63. Springer, Heidelberg (2012)

20. Dziwiński, P., Avedyan, E.D.: A new approach to nonlinear modeling based on significant operating points detection. In: Rutkowski, L., Korytkowski, M., Scherer, R., Tadeusiewicz, R., Zadeh, L.A., Zurada, J.M. (eds.) ICAISC 2015, Part II. LNCS, vol. 9120, pp. 364–378. Springer, Heidelberg (2015)

21. Dziwiński, P., Bartczuk, Ł., Przybył, A., Avedyan, E.D.: A new algorithm for identification of significant operating points using swarm intelligence. In: Rutkowski, L., Korytkowski, M., Scherer, R., Tadeusiewicz, R., Zadeh, L.A., Zurada, J.M. (eds.) ICAISC 2014, Part II. LNCS, vol. 8468, pp. 349–362. Springer, Heidelberg (2014)

22. Er, M.J., Duda, P.: On the weak convergence of the orthogonal series-type kernel regresion neural networks in a non-stationary environment. In: Wyrzykowski, R., Dongarra, J., Karczewski, K., Waśniewski, J. (eds.) PPAM 2011, Part I. LNCS, vol. 7203, pp. 443–450. Springer, Heidelberg (2012)

23. Faúndez-Zanuy, M.: On-line signature recognition based on VQ-DTW. Pattern Recogn. **40**, 981–992 (2007)

24. Faúndez-Zanuy, M., Pascual-Gaspar, J.M.: Efficient on-line signature recognition based on multi-section vector quantization. Formal Pattern Anal. Appl. **14**, 37–45 (2011)

25. Fierrez-Aguilar, J., Nanni, L., Lopez-Peñalba, J., Ortega-Garcia, J., Maltoni, D.: An on-line signature verification system based on fusion of local and global information. In: Kanade, T., Jain, A., Ratha, N.K. (eds.) AVBPA 2005. LNCS, vol. 3546, pp. 523–532. Springer, Heidelberg (2005)
26. Fierrez, J., Ortega-Garcia, J., Ramos, D., Gonzalez-Rodriguez, J.: HMM-based on-line signature verification: feature extraction and signature modeling. Pattern Recogn. Lett. **28**, 2325–2334 (2007)
27. Gabryel, M., Cpałka, K., Rutkowski, L.: Evolutionary strategies for learning of neuro-fuzzy systems. In: Proceedings of the I Workshop on Genetic Fuzzy Systems, Granada, pp. 119–123 (2005)
28. Gabryel, M., Grycuk, R., Korytkowski, M., Holotyak, T.: Image indexing and retrieval using GSOM algorithm. In: Rutkowski, L., Korytkowski, M., Scherer, R., Tadeusiewicz, R., Zadeh, L.A., Zurada, J.M. (eds.) ICAISC 2015, Part I. LNCS, vol. 9119, pp. 706–714. Springer, Heidelberg (2015)
29. Gabryel, M., Korytkowski, M., Scherer, R., Rutkowski, L.: Object detection by simple fuzzy classifiers generated by boosting. In: Rutkowski, L., Korytkowski, M., Scherer, R., Tadeusiewicz, R., Zadeh, L.A., Zurada, J.M. (eds.) ICAISC 2013, Part I. LNCS, vol. 7894, pp. 540–547. Springer, Heidelberg (2013)
30. Gabryel, M., Woźniak, M., Damaševičius, R.: An application of differential evolution to positioning queueing systems. In: Rutkowski, L., Korytkowski, M., Scherer, R., Tadeusiewicz, R., Zadeh, L.A., Zurada, J.M. (eds.) Artificial Intelligence and Soft Computing. LNCS, vol. 9120, pp. 379–390. Springer, Heidelberg (2015)
31. Galkowski, T., Pawlak, M.: Nonparametric extension of regression functions outside domain. In: Rutkowski, L., Korytkowski, M., Scherer, R., Tadeusiewicz, R., Zadeh, L.A., Zurada, J.M. (eds.) ICAISC 2014, Part I. LNAI, vol. 8467, pp. 518–530. Springer, Heidelberg (2014)
32. Gałkowski, T., Rutkowski, L.: Nonparametric recovery of multivariate functions with applications to system identification. Proc. IEEE **73**(5), 942–943 (1985)
33. Grycuk, R., Gabryel, M., Korytkowski, M., Scherer, R., Voloshynovskiy, S.: From single image to list of objects based on edge and blob detection. In: Rutkowski, L., Korytkowski, M., Scherer, R., Tadeusiewicz, R., Zadeh, L.A., Zurada, J.M. (eds.) ICAISC 2014, Part II. LNAI, vol. 8468, pp. 605–615. Springer, Heidelberg (2014)
34. Grycuk, R., Gabryel, M., Korytkowski, M., Scherer, R.: Content-based image indexing by data clustering and inverse document frequency. In: Kozielski, S., Mrozek, D., Kasprowski, P., Małysiak-Mrozek, B., Kostrzewa, D. (eds.) BDAS 2014. CCIS, vol. 424, pp. 374–383. Springer, Heidelberg (2014)
35. Held, P., Dockhorn, A., Kruse, R.: On merging and dividing social graphs. J. Artif. Intell. Soft Comput. Res. **5**(1), 23–49 (2015)
36. Homepage of Association BioSecure. http://biosecure.it-sudparis.eu. Accessed 29 Dec 2015
37. Houmani, N., Garcia-Salicetti, S., Mayoue, A., Dorizzi, B.: BioSecure Signature Evaluation Campaign 2009 (BSEC 2009): Results. http://biometrics.it-sudparis. eu/BSEC2009/downloads/BSEC2009_results.pdf. Accessed 29 Dec 2015
38. Ibrahim, M.T., Khan, M.A., Alimgeer, K.S., Khan, M.K., Taj, I.A., Guan, L.: Velocity and pressure-based partitions of horizontal and vertical trajectories for on-line signature verification. Pattern Recogn. **43**, 2817–2832 (2010)
39. Jaworski, M., Er, M.J., Pietruczuk, L.: On the application of the parzen-type kernel regression neural network and order statistics for learning in a non-stationary environment. In: Rutkowski, L., Korytkowski, M., Scherer, R., Tadeusiewicz, R., Zadeh, L.A., Zurada, J.M. (eds.) ICAISC 2012, Part I. LNCS, vol. 7267, pp. 90–98. Springer, Heidelberg (2012)

40. Jaworski, M., Pietruczuk, L., Duda, P.: On resources optimization in fuzzy clustering of data streams. In: Rutkowski, L., Korytkowski, M., Scherer, R., Tadeusiewicz, R., Zadeh, L.A., Zurada, J.M. (eds.) ICAISC 2012, Part II. LNCS, vol. 7268, pp. 92–99. Springer, Heidelberg (2012)
41. Jeong, Y.S., Jeong, M.K., Omitaomu, O.A.: Weighted dynamic time warping for time series classification. Pattern Recogn. **44**, 2231–2240 (2011)
42. Jimenez, F., Kanoh, M., Yoshikawa, T., Furuhashi, T., Nakamura, T.: Effect of robot utterances using onomatopoeia on collaborative learning. J. Artif. Intell. Soft Comput. Res. **4**(2), 125–131 (2014)
43. Korytkowski, M., Nowicki, R., Scherer, R.: Neuro-fuzzy rough classifier ensemble. In: Alippi, C., Polycarpou, M., Panayiotou, C., Ellinas, G. (eds.) ICANN 2009, Part I. LNCS, vol. 5768, pp. 817–823. Springer, Heidelberg (2009)
44. Korytkowski, M., Rutkowski, L., Scherer, R.: Fast image classification by boosting fuzzy classifiers. Inf. Sci. **327**, 175–182 (2016)
45. Koshiyama, A.S., Vellasco, M.M., Tanscheit, R.: Gpfis-control: a genetic fuzzy system for control tasks. J. Artif. Intell. Soft Comput. Res. **4**(3), 167–179 (2014)
46. Laskowski, Ł., Laskowska, M.: Functionalization of SBA-15 mesoporous silica by Cu-phosphonate units: probing of synthesis route. J. Solid State Chem. **220**, 221–226 (2014)
47. Laskowski, Ł., Laskowska, M., Bałanda, M., Fitta, M., Kwiatkowska, J., Dziliński, K., Karczmarska, A.: Mesoporous silica SBA-15 functionalized by nickel-phosphonic units: Raman and magnetic analysis. Microporous Mesoporous Mater. **200**, 253–259 (2014)
48. Laskowski, Ł., Laskowska, M., Jelonkiewicz, J., Boullanger, A.: Molecular approach to hopfield neural network. In: Rutkowski, L., Korytkowski, M., Scherer, R., Tadeusiewicz, R., Zadeh, L.A., Zurada, J.M. (eds.) ICAISC 2015, Part I. LNCS, vol. 9119, pp. 72–78. Springer, Heidelberg (2015)
49. Laskowski, Ł., Laskowska, M., Jelonkiewicz, J., Boullanger, A.: Spin-glass implementation of a hopfield neural structure. In: Rutkowski, L., Korytkowski, M., Scherer, R., Tadeusiewicz, R., Zadeh, L.A., Zurada, J.M. (eds.) ICAISC 2014, Part I. LNCS, vol. 8467, pp. 89–96. Springer, Heidelberg (2014)
50. Lee, P.M., Hsiao, T.C.: Applying LCS to affective image classification in spatial-frequency domain. J. Artif. Intell. Soft Comput. Res. **4**(2), 99–123 (2014)
51. Lumini, A., Nanni, L.: Ensemble of on-line signature matchers based on overcomplete feature generation. Expert Syst. Appl. **36**, 5291–5296 (2009)
52. Łapa, K., Cpałka, K., Wang, L.: New method for design of fuzzy systems for nonlinear modelling using different criteria of interpretability. In: Rutkowski, L., Korytkowski, M., Scherer, R., Tadeusiewicz, R., Zadeh, L.A., Zurada, J.M. (eds.) ICAISC 2014, Part I. LNCS, vol. 8467, pp. 217–232. Springer, Heidelberg (2014)
53. Łapa, K., Zalasiński, M., Cpałka, K.: A new method for designing and complexity reduction of neuro-fuzzy systems for nonlinear modelling. In: Rutkowski, L., Korytkowski, M., Scherer, R., Tadeusiewicz, R., Zadeh, L.A., Zurada, J.M. (eds.) ICAISC 2013, Part I. LNCS, vol. 7894, pp. 329–344. Springer, Heidelberg (2013)
54. Łapa, K., Przybył, A., Cpałka, K.: A new approach to designing interpretable models of dynamic systems. In: Rutkowski, L., Korytkowski, M., Scherer, R., Tadeusiewicz, R., Zadeh, L.A., Zurada, J.M. (eds.) ICAISC 2013, Part II. LNCS, vol. 7895, pp. 523–534. Springer, Heidelberg (2013)
55. Maiorana, E.: Biometric cryptosystem using function based on-line signature recognition. Expert Syst. Appl. **37**, 3454–3461 (2010)

56. Moon, J.H., Lee, S.G., Cho, S.Y., Kim, Y.S.: A hybrid online signature verification system supporting multi-confidential levels defined by data mining techniques. Int. J. Intell. Syst. Technol. Appl. **9**, 262–273 (2010)
57. Nanni, L., Lumini, A.: Advanced methods for two-class problem formulation for on-line signature verification. Neurocomputing **69**, 854–857 (2006)
58. Nanni, L., Maiorana, E., Lumini, A., Campisi, P.: Combining local, regional and global matchers for a template protected on-line signature verification system. Expert Syst. Appl. **37**, 3676–3684 (2010)
59. Pietruczuk, L., Duda, P., Jaworski, M.: A new fuzzy classifier for data streams. In: Rutkowski, L., Korytkowski, M., Scherer, R., Tadeusiewicz, R., Zadeh, L.A., Zurada, J.M. (eds.) ICAISC 2012, Part I. LNCS, vol. 7267, pp. 318–324. Springer, Heidelberg (2012)
60. Pietruczuk, L., Duda, P., Jaworski, M.: Adaptation of decision trees for handling concept drift. In: Rutkowski, L., Korytkowski, M., Scherer, R., Tadeusiewicz, R., Zadeh, L.A., Zurada, J.M. (eds.) ICAISC 2013, Part I. LNCS, vol. 7894, pp. 459–473. Springer, Heidelberg (2013)
61. Pietruczuk, L., Zurada, J.M.: Weak convergence of the recursive parzen-type probabilistic neural network in a non-stationary environment. In: Wyrzykowski, R., Dongarra, J., Karczewski, K., Waśniewski, J. (eds.) PPAM 2011, Part I. LNCS, vol. 7203, pp. 521–529. Springer, Heidelberg (2012)
62. Rutkowski, L.: On-line identification of time-varying systems by nonparametric techniques. IEEE Trans. Autom. Control **27**(1), 228–230 (1982)
63. Rutkowski, L.: A general approach for nonparametric fitting of functions and their derivatives with applications to linear circuits identification. IEEE Trans. Circ. Syst. **33**(8), 812–818 (1986)
64. Rutkowski, L.: Non-parametric learning algorithms in time-varying environments. Sig. Process. **182**, 129–137 (1989)
65. Rutkowski, L.: Identification of MISO nonlinear regressions in the presence of a wide class of disturbances. IEEE Trans. Inf. Theory **37**(1), 214–216 (1991)
66. Rutkowski, L.: Multiple Fourier series procedures for extraction of nonlinear regressions from noisy data. IEEE Trans. Sig. Process. **41**(10), 3062–3065 (1993)
67. Rutkowski, L.: Adaptive probabilistic neural networks for pattern classification in time-varying environment. IEEE Trans. Neural Netw. **15**(4), 811–827 (2004)
68. Rutkowski, L.: Computational Intelligence. Springer, Berlin (2008)
69. Rutkowski, L., Cpałka, K.: Flexible structures of neuro-fuzzy systems. In: Sincak, P., Vascak, J. (eds.) Quo Vadis Computational Intelligence. Studies in Fuzziness and Soft Computing, vol. 54, pp. 479–484. Springer, Heidelberg (2000)
70. Rutkowski, L., Cpałka, K.: Compromise approach to neuro-fuzzy systems. In: Sincak, P., Vascak, J., Kvasnicka, V., Pospichal, J. (eds.) Intelligent Technologies - Theory and Applications, vol. 76, pp. 85–90. IOS Press, Amsterdam (2002)
71. Rutkowski, L., Cpałka, K.: Flexible weighted neuro-fuzzy systems. In: Proceedings of the 9th International Conference on Neural Information Processing (ICONIP 2002), Orchid Country Club, Singapore, 18–22 November 2002, CD (2002)
72. Rutkowski, L., Cpałka, K.: Neuro-fuzzy systems derived from quasi-triangular norms. In: Proceedings of the IEEE International Conference on Fuzzy Systems, Budapest, 26–29 July, vol. 2, pp. 1031–1036 (2004)
73. Rutkowski, L., Jaworski, M., Pietruczuk, L., Duda, P.: Decision trees for mining data streams based on the gaussian approximation. IEEE Trans. Knowl. Data Eng. **26**(1), 108–119 (2014)
74. Rutkowski, L., Jaworski, M., Pietruczuk, L., Duda, P.: The CART decision tree for mining data streams. Inf. Sci. **266**, 1–15 (2014)

75. Rutkowski, L., Pietruczuk, L., Duda, P., Jaworski, M.: Decision trees for mining data streams based on the McDiarmid's bound. IEEE Trans. Knowl. Data Eng. **25**(6), 1272–1279 (2013)
76. Scherer, R.: Neuro-fuzzy systems with relation matrix. In: Rutkowski, L., Scherer, R., Tadeusiewicz, R., Zadeh, L.A., Zurada, J.M. (eds.) ICAISC 2010, Part I. LNCS, vol. 6113, pp. 210–215. Springer, Heidelberg (2010)
77. Scherer, R., Rutkowski, L.: Relational equations initializing neuro-fuzzy system. In: Proceedings of the 10th Zittau Fuzzy Colloquium, Zittau, Germany, pp. 18–22 (2002)
78. Starczewski, J.T., Bartczuk, Ł., Dziwiński, P., Marvuglia, A.: Learning methods for type-2 FLS based on FCM. In: Rutkowski, L., Scherer, R., Tadeusiewicz, R., Zadeh, L.A., Zurada, J.M. (eds.) ICAISC 2010, Part I. LNCS, vol. 6113, pp. 224–231. Springer, Heidelberg (2010)
79. Szarek, A., Korytkowski, M., Rutkowski, L., Scherer, R., Szyprowski, J.: Application of neural networks in assessing changes around implant after total hip arthroplasty. In: Rutkowski, L., Korytkowski, M., Scherer, R., Tadeusiewicz, R., Zadeh, L.A., Zurada, J.M. (eds.) ICAISC 2012, Part II. LNCS, vol. 7268, pp. 335–340. Springer, Heidelberg (2012)
80. Szarek, A., Korytkowski, M., Rutkowski, L., Scherer, R., Szyprowski, J.: Forecasting wear of head and acetabulum in hip joint implant. In: Rutkowski, L., Korytkowski, M., Scherer, R., Tadeusiewicz, R., Zadeh, L.A., Zurada, J.M. (eds.) ICAISC 2012, Part II. LNCS, vol. 7268, pp. 341–346. Springer, Heidelberg (2012)
81. Szczypta, J., Przybył, A., Wang, L.: Evolutionary approach with multiple quality criteria for controller design. In: Rutkowski, L., Korytkowski, M., Scherer, R., Tadeusiewicz, R., Zadeh, L.A., Zurada, J.M. (eds.) ICAISC 2014, Part I. LNCS, vol. 8467, pp. 455–467. Springer, Heidelberg (2014)
82. Smyczyńska, J., Hilczer, M., Smyczyńska, U., Stawerska, R., Tadeusiewicz, R., Lewiński, A.: Artificial neural models - a novel tool for predicting the efficacy of growth hormone (GH) therapy in children with short stature. Neuroendocrinol. Lett. **36**(4), 348–353 (2015). ISSN: 0172-780X, ISSN-L: 0172-780X
83. Smyczyńska, U., Smyczyńska, J., Hilczer, M., Stawerska, R., Lewiński, A., Tadeusiewicz, R.: Artificial neural networks - a novel tool in modelling the effectiveness of growth hormone (GH) therapy in children with GH deficiency. Pediatr. Endocrinol. **14**, no. 2(51), 9–18 (2015)
84. Tadeusiewicz, R.: Neural networks as a tool for modeling of biological systems. Bio-Algorithms Med-Syst. **11**(3), 135–144 (2015)
85. Tadeusiewicz, R.: Neural networks in mining sciences - general overview and some representative examples. Arch. Min. Sci. **60**(4), 971–984 (2015)
86. Wang, X., Liu, X., Japkowicz, N., Matwin, S.: Automated approach to classification of mine-like objects using multiple-aspect sonar images. J. Artif. Intell. Soft Comput. Res. **4**(2), 133–148 (2014)
87. Yeung, D.-Y., Chang, H., Xiong, Y., George, S.E., Kashi, R.S., Matsumoto, T., Rigoll, G.: SVC2004: first international signature verification competition. In: Zhang, D., Jain, A.K. (eds.) ICBA 2004. LNCS, vol. 3072, pp. 16–22. Springer, Heidelberg (2004)
88. Zalasiński, M., Cpałka, K.: A new method of on-line signature verification using a flexible fuzzy one-class classifier, In: pp. 38–53. Academic Publishing House EXIT (2011)

89. Zalasiński, M., Cpałka, K.: New approach for the on-line signature verification based on method of horizontal partitioning. In: Rutkowski, L., Korytkowski, M., Scherer, R., Tadeusiewicz, R., Zadeh, L.A., Zurada, J.M. (eds.) ICAISC 2013, Part II. LNCS, vol. 7895, pp. 342–350. Springer, Heidelberg (2013)
90. Zalasiński, M., Cpałka, K., Er, M.J.: New method for dynamic signature verification using hybrid partitioning. In: Rutkowski, L., Korytkowski, M., Scherer, R., Tadeusiewicz, R., Zadeh, L.A., Zurada, J.M. (eds.) ICAISC 2014, Part II. LNCS, vol. 8468, pp. 216–230. Springer, Heidelberg (2014)
91. Zalasiński, M., Cpałka, K., Hayashi, Y.: New method for dynamic signature verification based on global features. In: Rutkowski, L., Korytkowski, M., Scherer, R., Tadeusiewicz, R., Zadeh, L.A., Zurada, J.M. (eds.) ICAISC 2014, Part II. LNCS, vol. 8468, pp. 231–245. Springer, Heidelberg (2014)
92. Zalasiński, M., Cpałka, K., Hayashi, Y.: New fast algorithm for the dynamic signature verification using global features values. In: Rutkowski, L., Korytkowski, M., Scherer, R., Tadeusiewicz, R., Zadeh, L.A., Zurada, J.M. (eds.) Artificial Intelligence and Soft Computing. LNCS, vol. 9120, pp. 175–188. Springer, Heidelberg (2015)
93. Zalasiński, M., Łapa, K., Cpałka, K.: New algorithm for evolutionary selection of the dynamic signature global features. In: Rutkowski, L., Korytkowski, M., Scherer, R., Tadeusiewicz, R., Zadeh, L.A., Zurada, J.M. (eds.) ICAISC 2013, Part II. LNCS, vol. 7895, pp. 113–121. Springer, Heidelberg (2013)
94. Zhao, W., Lun, R., Espy, D.D., Ann Reinthal, M.: Realtime motion assessment for rehabilitation exercises: Integration of kinematic modeling with fuzzy inference. J. Artif. Intell. Soft Comput. Res. 4(4), 267–285 (2014)

Artificial Intelligence in Modeling and Simulation

A New Method for Generating Nonlinear Correction Models of Dynamic Objects Based on Semantic Genetic Programming

Łukasz Bartczuk[1](✉) and Alexander I. Galushkin[2]

[1] Institute of Computational Intelligence, Częstochowa University of Technology,
Częstochowa, Poland
lukasz.bartczuk@iisi.pcz.pl
[2] Moscow Institute of Physics and Technology, Moscow, Russia
neurocomputer@yandex.ru

Abstract. The purpose of nonlinear correction modelling of dynamic object is to use an approximated linear model of an object and determine corrections of this model in an appropriate way, taking into account the specificity of modelled nonlinearity. In this paper a new method for generating the coefficients of correction matrices is proposed. This method uses a mathematical formulas determined automatically by the Gene Expression Programming algorithm extended by semantic operator.

Keywords: Nonlinear modeling · Correction modeling · Genetic programming · Fuzzy system

1 Introduction

Genetic programming is a computational intelligence paradigm that allows automatic creation of computer programs by mimicking processes of biological evolution (see e.g. [25,37]). It has been successfully used to solve many challenging problems [38]. One of the branches of genetic programming that has been dynamically developed in recent years is the semantic genetic programming, which in the process of evolving programs takes into account not only syntax but also their semantics.

In this paper we try to combine some aspects of semantic genetic programming with Gene Expression Programming algorithm [23–25] and apply it to correction modelling of nonlinear dynamic objects. Modelling of such objects can be realized by many different methods including methods of computational intelligence like neural networks (see e.g. [9,31]), fuzzy systems (see e.g. [7,10–20,35,36,41–43,47,59–63,68–70,74,80–87]), population based algorithms (see e.g. [26,72,73,76]). It is worth to note that many computational intelligence methods (see e.g. [8,21,22,28–30,32,40,45,48–57,64–67,71,75,78,79]) are successfully used in pattern recognition, modelling and optimization issues.

In general the nonlinear system dynamics is described by the following equation:

© Springer International Publishing Switzerland 2016
L. Rutkowski et al. (Eds.): ICAISC 2016, Part II, LNAI 9693, pp. 249–261, 2016.
DOI: 10.1007/978-3-319-39384-1_22

$$\frac{d\mathbf{x}}{dt} = f(\mathbf{x}, \mathbf{u}), \tag{1}$$

where: $\mathbf{x}$ is the vector of state variables, $f(\mathbf{x}, \mathbf{u})$ is a nonlinear function that represents the changes of object state and $\mathbf{u}$ is the vector of input values. Because creating and analysing nonlinear models in form of Eq. (1) is not a trivial task, in practice they are often approximated by linear models:

$$\frac{d\mathbf{x}}{dt} = f(\mathbf{x}, \mathbf{u}) = \mathbf{A}\mathbf{x} + \mathbf{B}\mathbf{u} + \eta g(\mathbf{x}, \mathbf{u}), \tag{2}$$

where: A, B are system and input matrices respectively, $g(\mathbf{x}, \mathbf{u})$ is a separate nonlinear part of the system and η determines the impact of function $g(\cdot)$ on the entire object. The Eq. (2) can be used for modelling any nonlinear object, however, determination of function $g(\cdot)$ for whole range of the operation for the modelled object is difficult or not possible. For this reason the range of modelling of weakly nonlinear objects is usually limited only to the surroundings of some typical operating point $(\mathbf{x}_s, \mathbf{v}_s)$.

In papers [3,4] we have proposed the solution to increase accuracy of the method described above by the procedure based on equivalent linearization technique [6]. In such a case the state Eq. (2) can be shown as follows:

$$\frac{dx}{dt} = f(\mathbf{x}, \mathbf{u}) = \mathbf{A}_{eq}\mathbf{x} + \mathbf{B}\mathbf{u} + e(\mathbf{x}, \mathbf{u}), \tag{3}$$

where: $\mathbf{A}_{eq} = \mathbf{A} + \mathbf{P}_{\mathbf{A}}$ and $e(\mathbf{x}, \mathbf{u})$ is an error term. The purpose of correction matrix $\mathbf{P}_{\mathbf{A}}$ is nonlinear modelling of the relationship between the known approximated linear model and unknown nonlinear model that is constructed. The correction matrix values depend on the selected operating point, so they should be changed during moving away from this point. From this reason we assumed that values of the matrix $\mathbf{P}_{\mathbf{A}}$ are not constant but they are functions that take into account the current state $\mathbf{x}$ of the object being modelled, so $\mathbf{A}_{eq}(x) = \mathbf{A} + \mathbf{P}_{\mathbf{A}}(\mathbf{x})$. Due to this, these values may change with the change of the current operating point. In this paper in order to discover functional dependency that allows us to generate an adequate values of correction matrix $\mathbf{P}_{\mathbf{A}}(\mathbf{x})$ we use Gene Expression Programming algorithm extended by semantic operator.

2   Genetic Programming and Gene Expression Programming Algorithm

Genetic algorithms are computational intelligence methods inspired by biological evolution that are used to solve optimization problems (see e.g. [58]). They allow simultaneous analysis of multiple solutions represented by the individuals whose parameters are stored in the form of linear chromosomes. In each iteration of the algorithm, the individuals are transformed into new, hopefully better in the sense of chosen fitness function and only the best of them are passed to the next iteration.

Genetic programming is an adaptation of this concept for automatic creation of computer programs to solve the posed problem (see e.g. [25,37,38]). In classical genetic programming algorithms each individual represents one program which is encoded in the form of a chromosome tree composed of non-terminal symbols (functions) and terminal symbols (constants and inputs parameters).

Gene Expression Programming is a tool which - like genetic programming - allows computer programs to evolve (see e.g. [23–25]). However, unlike the genetic programming, it encodes a program as a linear chromosome which allows the use of classical genetic operators. An advantage of this representation is the possibility of using genetic operators known from classic genetic algorithms.

In original algorithm proposed by Ferreira (presented in Fig. 1) the population contains μ individuals and each of them encodes one function. A chromosome $\mathbf{C}_{ch}$, $ch = 1, \ldots, \mu$ of each individual is composed of three parts:

$$\mathbf{C}_{ch} = \{\mathbf{C}_{ch}^{\text{head}}, \mathbf{C}_{ch}^{\text{tail}}, \mathbf{C}_{ch}^{\text{constants}}\}, \tag{4}$$

where: $\mathbf{C}_{ch}^{\text{head}}$ can contain information about non-terminal and terminal symbols and its length $|\mathbf{C}_{ch}^{\text{head}}|$ is arbitrary, $\mathbf{C}_{ch}^{\text{tail}}$ can contain information about non-terminals only and its length can be computed with the following formula:

$$|\mathbf{C}_{ch}^{\text{tail}}| = |\mathbf{C}_{ch}^{\text{head}}| * (f_{\max} - 1) + 1, \tag{5}$$

where: $f_{\max}$ is a maximum arity of a non-terminal symbol. Part $\mathbf{C}_{ch}^{\text{constant}}$ contains numerical constants and its length is arbitrary too.

As already mentioned, in the GEP algorithm we can use classical genetic operators due to the organization of the chromosome. However, contrary to classical genetic programming where crossover and mutation operate locally modifying only part of the program, in the case of this algorithm these operators can significantly modify the solution due to the program encoding.

```
begin
    P←Initialization();
    Evaluation(P);
    while Stop condition is not fulfilled do
        O←∅;
    repeat
        parent₁←Selection(P);
        parent₂←Selection(P);
        offspring←Crossover(parent₁, parent₂);
        Mutation(offspring);
        O←O ∪ offspring;
    until count(O) < μ;
    end
    Evaluation(O);
    P←Reproduction(P,offspring);
end
```

Fig. 1. Gene Expression Programming algorithm

3   Semantics in Genetic Programming

One of the problems of genetic programming is the possibility that during the process of evolution new individuals that are created can have different structures (encoding programs having different syntax) but the same semantics (providing the same results). This leads to a population having a low diversity of individuals, which in turn slows down finding the best solution.

In recent years there have been many articles describing the various methods of genetic programming, taking into account not only the syntax of created program but also its semantics (see e.g. [4,5,27,39,44,46,77]). A semantics (in the article [27] also called functionality) in the genetic programming is usually defined as the difference of the row outputs of two programs. The research in this area have relied mostly on the use of semantics in the genetic operators like crossover and mutation (see e.g. [4,5,77]). In addition, in the paper [27] the semantic tournament selection operator has been proposed. This method is designed to ensure that offspring will be semantically different from their parents.

It should be noted that all those methods have been proposed for classical genetic programming which encodes programs in the form of chromosomes tree.

4   Semantics in Gene Expression Programming

In this paper we explore the possibility of using semantics in Gene Expression Programming.

As mentioned above, crossover and mutation operators in the Gene Expression Programming algorithm may cause simultaneously modification of multiple segments of programs. Therefore, the usage of operators described in papers [4,5,77] seems to be too computational expensive (due to the possible large number of fragments of programs needed to analyse). Moreover, the operator of semantic selection of parental individuals [27] does not guarantee that individuals produced as a result of genetic operators will be different form their parents. This is mainly due to the presence of non-coding regions in the chromosome. If the crossover or mutation point falls in this area, the offsprings would be the same as their parents in the terms of semantics.

For these reasons, it seems that the most effective approach that allows the use of semantic information in the Gene Expression Programming algorithm is the operation of adding newly created individual into offspring population. The new individual is added into the offspring population only if this population does not contain the solution that is semantically similar. However, if new offspring and the existing one have similar semantics, then the one with higher value of fitness function is preserved in the offspring population. The proposed, extended version of the Gene Expression Programming algorithm is presented in Fig. 2.

```
    begin
        P←Initialization();
        Evaluation(P);
        while Stop condition is not fulfilled do
            O←∅;
            repeat
                parent₁←Selection(P);
                parent₂←Selection(P);
                offspring←Crossover(parent₁, parent₂);
                Mutation(offspring);
                if ∀o ∈ O: semanticsₒ <> semanticsₒffspring then
                    Evaluate(offspring);
                    O←O ∪ offspring;
                else
                    o ←find(O, o' → semanticsₒ' = semanticsₒffspring);
                    if fitnessₒ < fitnessₒffspring then
                        Evaluate(offspring);
                        replace(O,o,offspring);
                    end
                end
            until count(O) < μ;
        end
        P←Reproduction(P,offspring);
    end
```

Fig. 2. Gene Expression Programming algorithm with semantic offsprings selection

5 Semantic Gene Expression Programming in Modelling of Nonlinear Dynamic Objects

In our implementation of semantic version of Gene Expression Programming algorithm we assume that:

- Chromosome is composed from m such 3-tuples, each of them encodes one of m equations required by the model:

$$\mathbf{C}_{ch} = \bigcup_{j=1}^{m}\{\mathbf{C}_{ch,j}^{head}, \mathbf{C}_{ch,j}^{tail}\} \cup \bigcup_{j=1}^{m}\{\mathbf{C}_{ch,j}^{constants}\}. \tag{6}$$

- Fitness function is a dependency determining the difference between output signals $\hat{x}_j$, $j = 1,\ldots,m$ generated by the created model at step $k+1$ and corresponding to reference x_j values:

$$fAcc(\mathbf{X}) = \frac{1}{m \cdot K}\sqrt{\sum_{j=1}^{m}\sum_{k=1}^{K}(x_j(k+1) - \hat{x}_j(k+1))^2}. \tag{7}$$

- We use simple one point crossover with replacement genes as a crossover operation. This operation is carried out separately for part of a chromosome describing the structure of the correction functions and for parts that contain numeric constants.
- We use multigene mutation as a mutation operation. Similarly to the crossover, this operation is performed separately for part of a chromosome describing the structure of the correction functions and for parts that contain numeric constants.
- We use elitist selection mechanism, so the best individual from parental population is carrying over to the next population unaltered.
- Similarity of two functions (f_1, f_2) finding by Gene Expression Programming is defined in similar way as in paper [77] e.g.

$$\text{Similarity}(f_1, f_2) = \frac{\sum_{i=1}^{N} |p_i - q_i|}{N} \tag{8}$$

where: p_i, q_i is a value computed for i-th sample point, respectively for function f_1 and f_2. In case of our simulations we split domain of each input variable into S equidistant points, so $N = S^D$, D is a number of input variable However, because in one chromosome we encode M different functions, we assume that the two chromosomes are semantically the same if values of Eq. (8) computed for each corresponding function are lower than a threshold α, so:

$$\text{AreTheSame}(I_1, I_2) = \bigvee_{j=1}^{m} \left(\text{Similarity}(f_{1,j}, f_{2,j}) < \alpha \right). \tag{9}$$

6   Simulation Results

To examine the effectiveness of applying Gene Expression Programming algorithm to nonlinear correction modelling of dynamic objects we considered two problems (1) harmonic oscillator and (2) the nonlinear electrical circuit with solar generator and DC drive system. The harmonic oscillator can be defined using the following formula:

$$\frac{d^2 x}{dt^2} + 2\zeta \frac{dx}{dt} + \omega^2 x = 0, \tag{10}$$

where ζ, ω are oscillator parameters and $x(t)$ is a reference value of the modelled process as function of time. We used the following state variables $x_1(t) = dx(t)/dt$ and $x_2(t) = x(t)$. In such a case the system matrix $\mathbf{A}$ and the matrix of corrections coefficients $\mathbf{P_A}$ is described as follows:

$$\mathbf{A} = \begin{bmatrix} 0 & \omega \\ -\omega & 0 \end{bmatrix} \qquad \mathbf{P_A} = \begin{bmatrix} 0 & p_{12}(\mathbf{x}) \\ p_{21}(\mathbf{x}) & 0 \end{bmatrix}.$$

In our experiments the parameter ω was modified in simulation according with a formula:

$$\omega(x) = 2\pi - \frac{\pi}{(1 + |2 \cdot x|^6)}. \tag{11}$$

In the second experiment the nonlinear electrical circuit with solar generator and DC drive system was modelled [1,33]. In this case the following state variables were used: $x_1(k) = -\frac{I_s}{C}e^{-au(k)} - \frac{1}{C}i(k) + \frac{I_s + I_0}{C}$, $x_2(k) = \frac{1}{L}i(k) - \frac{R_m}{L}u(k) - \frac{K_x}{L}\Omega(k)$, $x_3(k) = \frac{K_x}{L}u(k) - \frac{K_r}{J}\Omega(k)$, where: $u(k)$ is the generator voltage, $i(k)$ is the rotor current, $\Omega(k)$ is DC motor rotational speed. Parameters of the circuit were chosen as in [33] and they had the following values: $R_m = 12.045\Omega$, $L = 0.1H$, $C = 500\mu F$, $K_x = 0.5Vs$, $K_r = 0.1Vs^2$, $J = 10^{-3}Ws^3$, $I_0 = 2A$, $I_s = 1.28 \cdot 10^{-5}A$, $a = 0.54V^{-1}$. In this experiment we also assumed that the system matrix $\mathbf{A}$ and correction matrix $\mathbf{P_A}$ have values:

$$\mathbf{A} = \begin{bmatrix} -2163.86 & 2000.00 & 0.00 \\ 10.00 & -120.45 & -5.00 \\ 0.00 & 500.00 & -100.00 \end{bmatrix} \quad \mathbf{P_A} = \begin{bmatrix} p_{11}(\mathbf{x}) & 0 & 0 \\ 0 & 0 & 0 \\ 0 & 0 & 0 \end{bmatrix}.$$

The values of the matrix $\mathbf{A}$ were determined with Taylor's series expansion linearization method [34] in point $[22.15, 0, 0]$.

For both problems the simulations have been split into two groups. In the first group the simulations have been conducted with classic Gene Expression Programming without using semantic approach and in the second group the offspring individuals have been selected on the basis of the semantic information. The parameters of evolutionary process that we use in the simulations are shown in Table 1 and the obtained results are presented in Table 2.

Table 1. Parameters of Gene Expression Programming algorithm used in simulations

Functions set F	Harmonic oscillator	Nonlinear electric circuit
	$\{+, -, \cdot, /, \text{abs}, \text{pow}\}$	$\{+, -, \cdot, /, \text{pow}, \exp, \log\}$
Head size $|\mathbf{C}_{ch}^{head}|$	10	10
Number of constants $|\mathbf{C}_{ch}^{constants}|$	5	5
Constants range	$[-5, 5]$	$[-100, 100]$
Number of epochs	1000	1000
Population size μ	50	50
Probability of crossover p_c	0.7	0.7
Probability of mutation p_m	0.3	0.1
Similarity threshold α	1	1
Number of simulations	30	30

The obtained results can be summarized as follows:

- For both problems the semantic approach made it possible to obtain better results in terms of the RMSE error than the basic version of the Gene Expression Programming algorithm.

Table 2. Obtained results of simulations

Problem	Harmonic oscillator			Nonlinear electric circuit		
	GEP with semantic op.	GEP	Improvement	GEP with semantic op.	GEP	Improvement
Minimum RMSE	0.017	0.024	**29.16 %**	0.016	0.028	**42.85 %**
Average RMSE	0.046	0.064	**28.12 %**	0.051	0.147	**65.30 %**
Number of simulations in which the RMSE was below 0.05	18	8	**55.55 %**	17	8	**52.94 %**

– For both problems the semantic approach allows us to obtain a model that gives satisfactory results more often than the basic version of the Gene Expression Programming algorithm.

7   Conclusions

The proposed method of generating formulas enabling the determination of correction matrix coefficients in the modelling of nonlinear dynamic objects allows us to obtain good results. It should be noted that the Gene Expression Programming can create a model that achieves the same level of the RMSE error as the model created by the proposed semantic version of this algorithm. However, the extension of Gene Expression Algorithm by semantic operator allows us to reduce the number of epochs required to obtain satisfactory results.

Acknowledgment. The project was financed by the National Science Center on the basis of the decision number DEC-2012/05/B/ST7/02138.

References

1. Barland, M., et al.: Commende optimal d'un systeme generateur photovoltaique converisseur statique - receptur. Revue Phys. Appl. **19**, 905–915 (1984)
2. Bartczuk, Ł., Przybył, A., Dziwiński, P.: Hybrid state variables - fuzzy logic modelling of nonlinear objects. In: Rutkowski, L., Korytkowski, M., Scherer, R., Tadeusiewicz, R., Zadeh, L.A., Zurada, J.M. (eds.) ICAISC 2013, Part I. LNCS, vol. 7894, pp. 227–234. Springer, Heidelberg (2013)
3. Bartczuk, Ł., Przybył, A., Koprinkova-Hristova, P.: New method for nonlinear fuzzy correction modelling of dynamic objects. In: Rutkowski, L., Korytkowski, M., Scherer, R., Tadeusiewicz, R., Zadeh, L.A., Zurada, J.M. (eds.) ICAISC 2014, Part I. LNCS, vol. 8467, pp. 169–180. Springer, Heidelberg (2014)
4. Beadle, L., Johnson, C.: Semantically driven crossover in genetic programming. In: 2008 IEEE Congress on Evolutionary Computation (CEC), pp. 111–116 (2008)
5. Beadle, L., Johnson, C.: Semantically driven mutation in genetic programming. In: 2009 IEEE Congress on Evolutionary Computation (CEC), pp. 1336–1342 (2009)

6. Caughey, T.K.: Equivalent linearization techniques. J. Acoust. Soc. Am. **35**(11), 1706–1711 (1963)
7. Chaibakhsh, A., Chaibakhsh, N., Abbasi, M., Norouzi, A.: Orthonormal basis function fuzzy systems for biological wastewater treatment processes modeling. J. Artif. Intell. Soft Comput. Res. **2**(4), 343–356 (2012)
8. Chen, Q., Abercrombie, R.K., Sheldon, F.T.: Risk assessment for industrial control systems quantifying availability using Mean Failure Cost (MFC). J. Artif. Intell. Soft Comput. Res. **5**(3), 205–220 (2015)
9. Cierniak, R., Rutkowski, L.: On image compression by competitive neural networks and optimal linear predictors. Sig. Process.: Image Commun. **156**, 559–565 (2000)
10. Cpalka, K.: A method for designing flexible neuro-fuzzy systems. In: Rutkowski, L., Tadeusiewicz, R., Zadeh, L.A., Żurada, J.M. (eds.) ICAISC 2006. LNCS (LNAI), vol. 4029, pp. 212–219. Springer, Heidelberg (2006)
11. Cpałka, K.: On evolutionary designing and learning of flexible neuro-fuzzy structures for nonlinear classification. Nonlinear Anal. Ser. A: Theory Methods Appl. Elsevier **71**, 1659–1672 (2009)
12. Cpałka, K., Łapa, K., Przybył, A.: A new approach to design of control systems using genetic programming. Inf. Technol. Control **44**(4), 433–442 (2015)
13. Cpałka, K., Łapa, K., Przybył, A., Zalasiński, M.: A new method for designing neuro-fuzzy systems for nonlinear modelling with interpretability aspects. Neurocomputing **135**, 203–217 (2014)
14. Cpałka, K., Rebrova, O., Nowicki, R., Rutkowski, L.: On design of flexible neuro-fuzzy systems for nonlinear modelling. Int. J. Gener. Syst. **42**(6), 706–720 (2013)
15. Cpałka, K., Rutkowski, L.: A new method for designing and reduction of neuro-fuzzy systems. In: Proceedings of the 2006 IEEE International Conference on Fuzzy Systems (IEEE World Congress on Computational Intelligence, WCCI 2006), Vancouver, BC, Canada, pp. 8510–8516 (2006)
16. Cpałka, K., Rutkowski, L.: Flexible Takagi-Sugeno fuzzy systems. In: Proceedings of the International Joint Conference on Neural Networks 2005, Montreal, pp. 1764–1769 (2005)
17. Cpałka, K., Rutkowski, L.: 2005, Flexible Takagi-Sugeno neuro-fuzzy structures for nonlinear approximation. WSEAS Trans. Syst. **4**(9), 1450–1458 (2005)
18. Cpałka, K., Zalasiński, M.: On-line signature verification using vertical signature partitioning. Expert Syst. Appl. **41**(9), 4170–4180 (2014)
19. Cpałka, K., Zalasiński, M., Rutkowski, L.: New method for the on-line signature verification based on horizontal partitioning. Pattern Recogn. **47**, 2652–2661 (2014)
20. Cpałka, K., Zalasiński, M., Rutkowski, L.: A new algorithm for identity verification based on the analysis of a handwritten dynamic signature. Appl. Soft Comput. **43**, 47–56 (2016)
21. Dziwiński, P., Bartczuk, L., Przybył, A., Avedyan, E.D.: A new algorithm for identification of significant operating points using swarm intelligence. In: Rutkowski, L., Korytkowski, M., Scherer, R., Tadeusiewicz, R., Zadeh, L.A., Zurada, J.M. (eds.) ICAISC 2014, Part II. LNCS, vol. 8468, pp. 349–362. Springer, Heidelberg (2014)
22. Dziwiński, P., Avedyan, E.D.: A new approach to nonlinear modeling based on significant operating points detection. In: Rutkowski, L., Korytkowski, M., Scherer, R., Tadeusiewicz, R., Zadeh, L.A., Zurada, J.M. (eds.) Artificial Intelligence and Soft Computing. LNCS, vol. 9120, pp. 364–378. Springer, Heidelberg (2015)
23. Ferreira, C.: Gene Expression Programming in Problem Solving. Soft Computing and Industry. Springer, London (2002)

24. Ferreira, C.: Gene expression programming: a new algorithm for solving problems. Complex Syst. **13**(2), 87–129 (2001)
25. Ferreira, C.: Gene Expression Programming: Mathematical Modeling by an Artificial Intelligence, 2nd edn. Springer, Germany (2006)
26. Folly, K.: Parallel PBIL applied to power system controller design. J. Artif. Intell. Soft Comput. Res. **3**(3), 215–223 (2013)
27. Galvan-Lopez, E., Cody-Kenny, B., Trujillo, L., Kattan, A.: Using semantics in the selection mechanism in genetic programming: a simple method for promoting semantic diversity. In: 2013 IEEE Congress on Evolutionary Computation (CEC), pp. 2972–2979 (2013)
28. Gałkowski, T.: Kernel estimation of regression functions in the boundary regions. In: Rutkowski, L., Korytkowski, M., Scherer, R., Tadeusiewicz, R., Zadeh, L.A., Zurada, J.M. (eds.) ICAISC 2013, Part II. LNCS, vol. 7895, pp. 158–166. Springer, Heidelberg (2013)
29. Gałkowski, T., Rutkowski, L.: Nonparametric recovery of multivariate functions with applications to system identification. Proc. IEEE **73**(5), 942–943 (1985)
30. Gręblicki, W., Rutkowski, L.: Density-free Bayes risk consistency of nonparametric pattern recognition procedures. Proc. IEEE **69**(4), 482–483 (1981)
31. Ismail, S., Pashilkar, A.A., Ayyagari, R., Sundararajan, N.: Neural-sliding mode augmented robust controller for autolanding of fixed wing aircraft. J. Artif. Intell. Soft Comput. Res. **2**(4), 317–330 (2012)
32. Jimenez, F., Yoshikawa, T., Furuhashi, T., Kanoh, M.: An emotional expression model for educational-support robots. J. Artif. Intell. Soft Comput. Res. **5**(1), 51–57 (2015)
33. Jordan, A.J.: Linearization of non-linear state equation, Bulletin of the Polish academy of science. Tech. Sci. **54**(1), 63–73 (2006)
34. Kaczorek, T., Dzieliński, A., Dąbrowski L., Łopatka R.: The basis of control theory, WNT, Warsaw (2006) (in Polish)
35. Korytkowski, M., Rutkowski, L., Scherer, R.: From ensemble of fuzzy classifiers to single fuzzy rule base classifier. In: Rutkowski, L., Tadeusiewicz, R., Zadeh, L.A., Zurada, J.M. (eds.) ICAISC 2008. LNCS (LNAI), vol. 5097, pp. 265–272. Springer, Heidelberg (2008)
36. Korytkowski, M., Rutkowski, L., Scherer, R.: Fast image classification by boosting fuzzy classifiers. Inf. Sci. **327**, 175–182 (2016)
37. Koza, J.R.: Genetic Programming - On the Programming of Computers by Means of Natural Selection. The MIT Press, Cambridge (1992)
38. Koza, J.R.: Human-competitive results produced by genetic programming. Genet. Programm. Evolvable Mach. **11**(3–4), 251–284 (2010)
39. Krawiec, K.: Genetic programming: where meaning emerges from program code. Genet. Programm. Evolvable Mach., Springer **15**(1), 75–77 (2014)
40. Lin, C.H., Dong, F.Y., Hirota, K.: Common driving notification protocol based on classified driving behavior for cooperation intelligent autonomous vehicle using vehicular ad-hoc network technology. J. Artif. Intell. Soft Comput. Res. **5**(1), 5–21 (2015)
41. Łapa, K., Cpałka, K., Wang, L.: New method for design of fuzzy systems for nonlinear modelling using different criteria of interpretability. In: Rutkowski, L., Korytkowski, M., Scherer, R., Tadeusiewicz, R., Zadeh, L.A., Zurada, J.M. (eds.) ICAISC 2014, Part I. LNCS, vol. 8467, pp. 217–232. Springer, Heidelberg (2014)

42. Łapa, K., Przybył, A., Cpałka, K.: A new approach to designing interpretable models of dynamic systems. In: Rutkowski, L., Korytkowski, M., Scherer, R., Tadeusiewicz, R., Zadeh, L.A., Zurada, J.M. (eds.) ICAISC 2013, Part II. LNCS, vol. 7895, pp. 523–534. Springer, Heidelberg (2013)

43. Łapa, K., Zalasiński, M., Cpałka, K.: A new method for designing and complexity reduction of neuro-fuzzy systems for nonlinear modelling. In: Rutkowski, L., Korytkowski, M., Scherer, R., Tadeusiewicz, R., Zadeh, L.A., Zurada, J.M. (eds.) ICAISC 2013, Part I. LNCS, vol. 7894, pp. 329–344. Springer, Heidelberg (2013)

44. Machado, P., Correia, J.: Semantic aware methods for evolutionary art. In: Proceedings of the 2014 Annual Conference on Genetic and Evolutionary Computation (GECCO 2014), pp. 301–308 (2014)

45. Miyajima, H., Shigei, N., Miyajima, H.: Performance comparison of hybrid electromagnetism-like mechanism algorithms with descent method. J. Artif. Intell. Soft Comput. Res. 5(4), 271–282 (2015)

46. Pawlak, T.P., Wieloch, B., Krawiec, K.: Review and comparative analysis of geometric semantic crossovers. Genet. Programm. Evolvable Mach. Springer 16(3), 351–386 (2015)

47. Przybył, A., Cpałka, K.: A new method to construct of interpretable models of dynamic systems. In: Rutkowski, L., Korytkowski, M., Scherer, R., Tadeusiewicz, R., Zadeh, L.A., Zurada, J.M. (eds.) ICAISC 2012, Part II. LNCS, vol. 7268, pp. 697–705. Springer, Heidelberg (2012)

48. Rigatos, G.G., Siano, P.: Flatness-based adaptive fuzzy control of spark-ignited engines. J. Artif. Intell. Soft Comput. Res. 4(4), 231–242 (2014)

49. Rutkowski, L.: On nonparametric identification with prediction of time-varying systems. IEEE Trans. Autom. Control 29(1), 58–60 (1984)

50. Rutkowski, L.: Nonparametric identification of quasi-stationary systems. Syst. Control Lett. 6(1), 33–35 (1985)

51. Rutkowski, L.: Real-time identification of time-varying systems by non-parametric algorithms based on Parzen kernels. Int. J. Syst. Sci. 16(9), 1123–1130 (1985)

52. Rutkowski, L.: A general approach for nonparametric fitting of functions and their derivatives with applications to linear circuits identification. IEEE Trans. Circuits Syst. 33(8), 812–818 (1986)

53. Rutkowski, L.: Sequential pattern-recognition procedures derived from multiple Fourier-series. Pattern Recogn. Lett. 8(4), 213–216 (1988)

54. Rutkowski, L.: Application of multiple Fourier-series to identification of multivariable non-stationary systems. Int. J. Syst. Sci. 20(10), 1993–2002 (1989)

55. Rutkowski, L.: Non-parametric learning algorithms in time-varying environments. Sig. Process. 182, 129–137 (1989)

56. Rutkowski, L.: Multiple Fourier series procedures for extraction of nonlinear regressions from noisy data. IEEE Trans. Sig. Process. 41(10), 3062–3065 (1993)

57. Rutkowski, L.: Adaptive probabilistic neural networks for pattern classification in time-varying environment. IEEE Trans. Neural Netw. 15(4), 811–827 (2004)

58. Rutkowski, L.: Computational Intelligence: Methods and Techniques. Springer, Heidelberg (2008)

59. Rutkowski, L., Cpałka, K.: Flexible Structures of Neuro-Fuzzy Systems. Quo Vadis Computational Intelligence. Studies in Fuzziness and Soft Computing, pp. 479–484. Springer, Heidelberg (2000)

60. Rutkowski, L., Cpałka, K.: A general approach to neuro-fuzzy systems. In: The 10th IEEE International Conference on Fuzzy Systems, Melbourne, pp. 1428–1431 (2001)

61. Rutkowski, L., Cpałka, K.: Compromise approach to neuro-fuzzy systems. In: Sincak, P., Vascak, J., Kvasnicka, V., Pospichal, J. (eds.) Intelligent Technologies - Theory and Applications, vol. 76, pp. 85–90. IOS Press (2002)
62. Rutkowski, L., Cpałka, K.: A neuro-fuzzy controller with a compromise fuzzy reasoning. Control Cybern. **31**(2), 297–308 (2002)
63. Rutkowski, L., Cpałka, K.: Neuro-fuzzy systems derived from quasi-triangular norms. In: Proceedings of the IEEE International Conference on Fuzzy Systems, Budapest, 26–29 July 2004, vol. 2, pp. 1031–1036 (2004)
64. Rutkowski, L., Jaworski, M., Pietruczuk, L., Duda, P.: Decision trees for mining data streams based on the gaussian approximation. IEEE Trans. Knowl. Data Eng. **26**(1), 108–119 (2014)
65. Rutkowski, L., Jaworski, M., Pietruczuk, L., Duda, P.: The CART decision tree for mining data streams. Inf. Sci. **266**, 1–15 (2014)
66. Rutkowski, L., Pietruczuk, L., Duda, P., Jaworski, M.: Decision trees for mining data streams based on the McDiarmid's bound. IEEE Trans. Knowl. Data Eng. **25**(6), 1272–1279 (2013)
67. Rutkowski, L., Przybył, A., Cpałka, K., Er, M.J.: Online speed profile generation for industrial machine tool based on neuro-fuzzy approach. In: Rutkowski, L., Scherer, R., Tadeusiewicz, R., Zadeh, L.A., Zurada, J.M. (eds.) ICAISC 2010, Part II. LNCS, vol. 6114, pp. 645–650. Springer, Heidelberg (2010)
68. Rutkowski, L., Przybył, A., Cpałka, K.: Novel on-line speed profile generation for industrial machine tool based on flexible neuro-fuzzy approximation. IEEE Trans. Ind. Electr. **59**, 1238–1247 (2012)
69. Starczewski, J.T., Bartczuk, Ł., Dziwiński, P., Marvuglia, A.: Learning methods for Type-2 FLS based on FCM. In: Rutkowski, L., Scherer, R., Tadeusiewicz, R., Zadeh, L.A., Zurada, J.M. (eds.) ICAISC 2010, Part I. LNCS, vol. 6113, pp. 224–231. Springer, Heidelberg (2010)
70. Starczewski, J.T., Rutkowski, L.: Connectionist structures of Type 2 fuzzy inference systems. In: Wyrzykowski, R., Dongarra, J., Paprzycki, M., Waśniewski, J. (eds.) PPAM 2001. LNCS, vol. 2328, pp. 634–642. Springer, Heidelberg (2002)
71. Sugiyama, H.: Pulsed power network based on decentralized intelligence for reliable and lowloss electrical power distribution. J. Artif. Intell. Soft Comput. Res. **5**(2), 97–108 (2015)
72. Szczypta, J., Przybył, A., Cpałka, K.: Some aspects of evolutionary designing optimal controllers. In: Rutkowski, L., Korytkowski, M., Scherer, R., Tadeusiewicz, R., Zadeh, L.A., Zurada, J.M. (eds.) ICAISC 2013, Part II. LNCS, vol. 7895, pp. 91–100. Springer, Heidelberg (2013)
73. Szczypta, J., Przybył, A., Wang, L.: Evolutionary approach with multiple quality criteria for controller design. In: Rutkowski, L., Korytkowski, M., Scherer, R., Tadeusiewicz, R., Zadeh, L.A., Zurada, J.M. (eds.) ICAISC 2014, Part I. LNCS, vol. 8467, pp. 455–467. Springer, Heidelberg (2014)
74. Theodoridis, D.C., Boutalis, Y.S., Christodoulou, M.A.: Robustifying analysis of the direct adaptive control of unknown multivariable nonlinear systems based on a new neuro-fuzzy method. J. Artif. Intell. Soft Comput. Res. **1**(1), 59–79 (2011)
75. Thiagarajan, R., Rahman, M., Gossink, D., Calbert, G.: A data mining approach to improve military demand forecasting. J. Artif. Intell. Soft Comput. Res. **4**(3), 205–214 (2014)
76. Tran, V.N., Brdys, M.A.: Optimizing control by robustly feasible model predictive control and application to drinking water distribution systems. J. Artif. Intell. Soft Comput. Res. **1**(1), 43–57 (2011)

77. Uy, N.Q., Hoai, N.X., O'Neill, M., McKay, R.I., Galvan-Lopez, E.: Semantically-based crossover in genetic programming: application to real-valued symbolic regression. Genet. Programm. Evolvable Mach. **12**(2), 91–119 (2011)
78. Wang, G., Zhang, S.: ABM with behavioral bias and applications in simulating China stock market. J. Artif. Intell. Soft Comput. Res. **5**(4), 257–270 (2015)
79. Wang, Z., Zhang-Westmant, L.: New ranking method for fuzzy numbers by their expansion center. J. Artif. Intell. Soft Comput. Res. **4**(3), 181–187 (2014)
80. Zalasiński, M., Cpałka, K.: Novel algorithm for the on-line signature verification. In: Rutkowski, L., Korytkowski, M., Scherer, R., Tadeusiewicz, R., Zadeh, L.A., Zurada, J.M. (eds.) ICAISC 2012, Part II. LNCS, vol. 7268, pp. 362–367. Springer, Heidelberg (2012)
81. Zalasiński, M., Cpałka, K.: New approach for the on-line signature verification based on method of horizontal partitioning. In: Rutkowski, L., Korytkowski, M., Scherer, R., Tadeusiewicz, R., Zadeh, L.A., Zurada, J.M. (eds.) ICAISC 2013, Part II. LNCS, vol. 7895, pp. 342–350. Springer, Heidelberg (2013)
82. Zalasiński, M., Cpałka, K.: Novel algorithm for the on-line signature verification using selected discretization points groups. In: Rutkowski, L., Korytkowski, M., Scherer, R., Tadeusiewicz, R., Zadeh, L.A., Zurada, J.M. (eds.) ICAISC 2013, Part I. LNCS, vol. 7894, pp. 493–502. Springer, Heidelberg (2013)
83. Zalasiński, M., Cpałka, K., Er, M.J.: New method for dynamic signature verification using hybrid partitioning. In: Rutkowski, L., Korytkowski, M., Scherer, R., Tadeusiewicz, R., Zadeh, L.A., Zurada, J.M. (eds.) ICAISC 2014, Part II. LNCS, vol. 8468, pp. 216–230. Springer, Heidelberg (2014)
84. Zalasiński, M., Cpałka, K., Er, M.J.: A new method for the dynamic signature verification based on the stable partitions of the signature. In: Rutkowski, L., Korytkowski, M., Scherer, R., Tadeusiewicz, R., Zadeh, L.A., Zurada, J.M. (eds.) Artificial Intelligence and Soft Computing. LNCS, vol. 9120, pp. 161–174. Springer, Heidelberg (2015)
85. Zalasiński, M., Cpałka, K., Hayashi, Y.: New method for dynamic signature verification based on global features. In: Rutkowski, L., Korytkowski, M., Scherer, R., Tadeusiewicz, R., Zadeh, L.A., Zurada, J.M. (eds.) ICAISC 2014, Part II. LNCS, vol. 8468, pp. 231–245. Springer, Heidelberg (2014)
86. Zalasiński, M., Cpałka, K., Hayashi, Y.: New fast algorithm for the dynamic signature verification using global features values. In: Rutkowski, L., Korytkowski, M., Scherer, R., Tadeusiewicz, R., Zadeh, L.A., Zurada, J.M. (eds.) Artificial Intelligence and Soft Computing. LNCS, vol. 9120, pp. 175–188. Springer, Heidelberg (2015)
87. Zalasiński, M., Łapa, K., Cpałka, K.: New algorithm for evolutionary selection of the dynamic signature global features. In: Rutkowski, L., Korytkowski, M., Scherer, R., Tadeusiewicz, R., Zadeh, L.A., Zurada, J.M. (eds.) ICAISC 2013, Part II. LNCS, vol. 7895, pp. 113–121. Springer, Heidelberg (2013)

A New Method for Generating of Fuzzy Rules for the Nonlinear Modelling Based on Semantic Genetic Programming

Łukasz Bartczuk[1](✉), Krystian Łapa[1], and Petia Koprinkova-Hristova[2]

[1] Institute of Computational Intelligence, Częstochowa University of Technology,
Częstochowa, Poland
{lukasz.bartczuk,krystian.lapa}@iisi.pcz.pl
[2] Institute of Information and Communication Technologies,
Bulgarian Academy of Sciences, Sofia, Bulgaria
pkoprinkova@bas.bg

Abstract. In this paper we propose a new approach for nonlinear modelling. It uses capabilities of the Takagi-Sugeno neuro-fuzzy systems and population based algorithms. The aim of our method is to ensure that created model achieves appropriate accuracy and is as compact as possible. In order to obtain this aim we incorporate semantic information about created fuzzy rules into process of evolution. Our method was tested with the use of well-known benchmarks from the literature.

Keywords: Nonlinear modeling · Genetic programming · Fuzzy system

1 Introduction

Nonlinear modelling is an important and dynamically developed branch of science and engineering. Its main purpose is to create models of e.g. objects or physical phenomena, with characteristics developed on the basis of observation of their responses to the input values, which cannot be defined by linear formulas. Such models have a great practical importance because they allow to ensure predictability, which guarantees safety, decreases costs and ensures control. In literature we can find many different approaches to perform this task. Some of them are based on analytical methods (see e.g. [36]) and the others are based on computational methods like neural networks (see e.g. [3,33]), fuzzy systems (see e.g. [7,10–14,16–20,40,45,46,50,56–59,64,65,73,80,81,83–86,88]), population based algorithms (see e.g. [29,69,70,75]).

In this paper we propose a new approach to nonlinear modelling that is based on Takagi-Sugeno fuzzy system. Such a systems are commonly used to solve the regression and system identification tasks (see e.g. [17,35,37,71,72]). There are many different methods that can be used to create such systems. In this paper we propose a hybrid population based method that combines the possibilities of classical genetic algorithm (see e.g. [41,54]) and semantic genetic programming

© Springer International Publishing Switzerland 2016
L. Rutkowski et al. (Eds.): ICAISC 2016, Part II, LNAI 9693, pp. 262–278, 2016.
DOI: 10.1007/978-3-319-39384-1_23

(see e.g. [4,5,30,43]). Genetic algorithms are computational intelligence methods inspired by biological evolution that allow solving optimization problems (see e.g. [54]). They allow simultaneous analysis of multiple solutions represented by the individuals whose parameters are stored in the form of linear chromosomes. In each iteration of algorithm, the individuals are transformed into new, hopefully better in the sense of chosen fitness function and only the best of them are passed to the next iteration. Semantic genetic programming is an adaptation of this concept for automatic creation of computer programs that in the process of evolution takes into account not only the syntax of the program but also its meaning (see e.g. [4,5,30,43]). It is worth to note that many computational intelligence methods (see e.g. [9,15,26,27,31,34,44,49,52,53,60–63,66,68,74,77, 78]) are successfully used in pattern recognition, modelling and optimization issues.

In our approach the genetic algorithm is used to determine parameters of fuzzy sets and genetic programming is used to determine the structure of fuzzy rules. The main purpose of our method is to ensure that obtained system is as accurate and as compact as possible, thus the possibilities of interpretation of created model should be increased. In order to obtain this aim in the process of evolution we also used some semantic aspect of fuzzy rules. It should be noted that the proposed method can be also used to generate fuzzy systems that are used for modelling of nonlinear dynamic objects.

2   Intelligent System for Nonlinear Modelling

Neuro-fuzzy systems (see e.g. [39,54,79–82,87]) combine the learning properties of neural networks and the natural language description of fuzzy systems (see e.g. [22–25,47,48]). In this paper we consider simple multi-input, single-output (MISO) Takagi-Sugeno neuro-fuzzy system, but it should be noted that presented considerations can be easily generalized also for multiple-output systems.

The MISO Takagi Sugeno fuzzy system (see e.g. [17,35,37,71,72]) performs mapping $\mathbf{X} \rightarrow \mathbf{Y}$, where $\mathbf{X} \subset \mathbf{R}^n$ and $\mathbf{Y} \subset \mathbf{R}$. If we assume that a collection $\mathcal{A}_i = \{A_{i,1}, \ldots, A_{i,R}\}$ is defined on $\mathbf{X}_i$ for each system input $i = 1, \ldots n$, where R is a number of elements of collection $\mathcal{A}_i$ and n is a number of system inputs, then such system contains a collection of K fuzzy IF – THEN rules in the form:

$$\mathcal{R}^k : \text{IF } x_1 \text{ is } A_{k,1} \text{ AND} \ldots \text{AND } x_n \text{ is } A_{k,n} \text{ THEN } y_1 \text{ is } c_{k,0} + c_{k,1}x_1 + \cdots + c_n^k x_n, \quad (1)$$

where $\mathbf{x} = [x_1, \ldots, x_n] \in \mathbf{X}$ is a vector of input variables, $y_1 \in \mathbf{Y}$ is an output value, $c = [c_0, \ldots, c_n]$ is a vector of real parameters. $A_{k,1}, \ldots, A_{k,n}, k = 1, \ldots, K$ are fuzzy sets characterized by the membership functions $\mu_{A_{k,i}}(x_i), i = 1, \ldots, n$; $j = 1, \ldots, m$; $k = 1, \ldots, K$.

The output of Takagi-Sugeno system is obtained as a weighted sum of outputs provided by each rule and is defined as follows:

$$\overline{y} = \frac{\sum\limits_{k=1}^{K} \overline{y_1}^k \cdot \mu_{A^k}(\overline{\mathbf{x}})}{\sum\limits_{k=1}^{K} \mu_{A^k}(\overline{\mathbf{x}})}, \quad (2)$$

where: $\bar{\mathbf{x}} = [\bar{x}_1, \ldots, \bar{x}_n]$ is a vector of input signals of the system, $\mu_{A^k}(\bar{\mathbf{x}}) = T_{i=1}^n \left(\mu_{A_{k,i}}(\bar{x}_i) \right)$ is a degree of fulfillment of the k-th fuzzy rule, T is a t-norm operator, $\bar{y}_1^{\,k}$ is a value of functional dependency contained in the conclusion of k-th fuzzy rule computed for input values $\bar{\mathbf{x}}$.

It should be noted that this kind of fuzzy systems can not directly guarantee the obtaining of models which can be easily analyzed. Therefore, in the proposed method of determining structure and parameters of the fuzzy system we have taken into account some constraints to get a model whose knowledge can be easily analyzed. This method is described in the next section.

3   Evolutionary Construction of Fuzzy System

In order to create a Takagi-Sugeno neuro-fuzzy system presented in the previous section we used a hybrid approach with combines two population based algorithms: genetic programming (see e.g. [28,42]) and classical genetic algorithm (see e.g. [11,12,45,54]).

In our method the genetic programming has been used to identify the structure of the fuzzy rules and the genetic algorithm to determine the parameters of fuzzy sets. The proposed algorithm is presented in Fig. 1 and its details are described in the following sections.

```
 1 begin
 2      P←Initialization();
 3      Evaluation(P);
 4      while Stop condition is not fulfilled do
 5          O←∅;
 6          repeat
 7              parent₁←Selection(P);
 8              parent₂←Selection(P);
 9              offspring←Crossover(parent₁, parent₂);
10              O←O ∪ offspring;
11          until |O| < μ;
12          Mutation(O);
13          Prune(O);
14          Expending(O);
15          RuleBaseModification(O);
16          RemoveSimilarRules(O);
17          Evaluation(O);
18          P←Reproduction(P,O);
19      end
20 end
```

Fig. 1. Hybrid algorithm to create Takagi-Sugeno fuzzy system to nonlinear modelling combining classic genetic algorithm and semantic genetic programming.

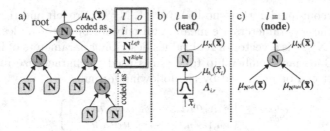

Fig. 2. Representation of premises of fuzzy rule: (a) tree, (b) leaf, (c) node.

3.1   Chromosome Encoding

The population $\mathbf{P}$ contains μ individuals and each of them encodes the complete fuzzy system. The chromosome $\mathbf{X}_{ch}$ of each individual, $ch = 1, \cdots, \mu$ is composed of two elements:

$$\mathbf{X}_{ch} = \{\mathbf{X}_{ch}^{\text{fsets}}, \mathbf{X}_{ch}^{\text{rls}}\} \tag{3}$$

where: $\mathbf{X}_{ch}^{\text{fsets}}$, $\mathbf{X}_{ch}^{\text{rls}}$ encodes information about fuzzy sets from $\mathcal{A}_i$ collections, and information about structures of fuzzy rules, respectively.

Each fuzzy rule which can be described by Eq. (1) can be represented in the tree form. In such a structure every internal node defines the fuzzy operator and leaves (possibly negated) linguistic terms. Because each fuzzy rule must contain an implication as root node, in our algorithm we assume that this node is present in the tree, thus the tree describes only the premises of the rule (Fig. 2). For these reasons in our method, each rule is represented as tuple: $\{\mathbf{N}_k^{\text{root}}, [c_{0,k}, c_{1,k}, ..., c_{n,k}]\}$ and the whole system as:

$$\mathbf{X}_{ch}^{\text{rls}} = \left\{ \begin{array}{l} \{\mathbf{N}_1^{\text{root}}, [c_{1,0}, c_{1,1}, ..., c_{1,n}]\}, \\ \{\mathbf{N}_2^{\text{root}}, [c_{2,0}, c_{2,1}, ..., c_{2,n}]\}, \\ \qquad\qquad ..., \\ \{\mathbf{N}_K^{\text{root}}, [c_{K,0}, c_{K,1}, ..., c_{K,n}]\} \end{array} \right\}, \tag{4}$$

where $\mathbf{N}_k^{\text{root}}$ is a root node of premises of k-th rule, $k = 1, ... K$, and the $[c_{k,0}, c_{k,1}, ..., c_{k,n}]$ is a vector of real values describes coefficients of the functional dependency contained in conclusion of the k-th rule.

In the implementation of our system, we assumed that each tree node $\mathbf{N}$ is also represented as a tuple of elements:

$$\mathbf{N} = \{l, o, i, r, \mathbf{N}^{Left}, \mathbf{N}^{Right}\}, \tag{5}$$

where $l \in \{0, 1\}$ is an indicator that node is a leaf ($l = 0$) or fuzzy operator node ($l = 1$), $o \in \{0, 1\}$ defines kind of fuzzy operator (when $l = 0$) or determines whether the input is negated or not (when $l = 1$), $i = 1, ..., n$ is the input of fuzzy system $r = 1, ..., R$ is the r-th fuzzy set contained in the collection $\mathcal{A}_i$ (these two parameters have meaning only for leaves nodes and allow determination of the fuzzy set contained in these nodes), $\mathbf{N}^{Left}$, $\mathbf{N}^{Right}$ are left and right subtrees of node $\mathbf{N}$ (these parameters are meaningful only for operator nodes).

The part $\mathbf{X}^{\text{fsets}}_{ch}$ is a vector of real values describing parameters of input fuzzy sets. If the Gaussian membership function is used to characterize inputs fuzzy sets, this part can be described by the following formula:

$$\mathbf{X}^{\text{fsets}}_{ch} = \left\{ \begin{array}{l} s_{1,1}, \sigma_{1,1}, \ldots, s_{1,R}, \sigma_{1,R}, \ldots, \\ s_{n,1}, \sigma_{n,1}, \ldots, s_{n,R}, \sigma_{n,R} \end{array} \right\}, \tag{6}$$

where: $s_{i,r}$, $\sigma_{i,r}$ are centers and widths of Gaussian membership functions ($i = 1, \ldots, n$, $r = 1, \ldots, R$).

3.2 Chromosome Initialization

In the initialization the number $K \in [K^{min}, K^{max}]$ of fuzzy rules and their structure are generated at random (line 2 in Fig. 1). During the initialization step the parameters of the vector $\mathbf{X}^{\text{fsets}}_{ch}$, as well as values describing coefficients of functional dependency contained conclusions of fuzzy rules $c_{k,i}$, $i = 0, \ldots, n$, $k = 1, \ldots, K$ are set to random numbers within the range of corresponding input or output. The initial form of the fuzzy rule is determined as a result of a recursive function:

$$\text{init}(lvl, l) = \left\{ \begin{array}{ll} \left\{ 1, o', i', r', \text{null}, \text{null} \right\} & \text{for } \{l = 1 \text{ or } lvl \geq lvl^{\max}\} \\ \left\{ \begin{array}{l} 0, o', i', r', \\ \text{init}(lvl + 1, l'), \\ \text{init}(lvl + 1, l') \end{array} \right\} & \text{for } \{l = 0 \text{ and } lvl < lvl^{\max}\} \end{array} \right. \tag{7}$$

where: lvl is a depth (level) of current node, $lvl^{\max}$ is the maximum acceptable depth of the tree, $l' = U_c(0, 1)$, $o' = U_c(0, 1)$, $i' = U_c(1, n)$, $r' = U_c(1, R)$ are random integer values generated with uniform distribution from defined range determined respectively for l, o, i, r parameters of the node $\mathbf{N}$. As a result this function returns a tuple describing the node $\mathbf{N}$ of the tree. It should be noted that the kind of the created node is determined randomly if its depth is lower than the maximum depth of the tree and is always a fuzzy set node on this level.

3.3 Evolution of Chromosomes

The modification of individuals contained in the population $\mathbf{P}$ is carried out mainly through the mechanisms of crossover and mutation. During the crossing operation (line 9 in Fig. 1) a new individual is created and its genes are determined in the following manner:

- first, genes $\mathbf{X}^{\text{fsets}}_{ch}$ are crossed by well-known genetic algorithm method (one-point crossover) (see e.g. [54]),
- then genes $\mathbf{X}^{\text{rls}}_{ch}$ are set by random selection of $K \in [K^{min}, K^{max}]$ fuzzy rules from selected parents.

The process of mutating individuals belonging to a population $\mathbf{P}$ is implemented by four operators:

- the mutation operator (line 12 in Fig. 1), which randomly changes the values of genes $\mathbf{X}_{ch}^{\text{fsets}}$, as well as the parameters i and r contained in the nodes of the tree. In this step, the coefficients $c_{j,k}$ are also updated, but the modification is carried out using the following formulas:

$$c_0 \leftarrow c_0 \cdot m_r \cdot U_r\left(-1,1\right) \cdot \left(y^{\text{max}} - y^{\text{min}}\right), \tag{8}$$

and

$$c_i \leftarrow c_i \cdot m_r \cdot U_r\left(-1,1\right) \cdot \left(\frac{y^{\text{max}}}{\max\left\{\left|x_i^{\text{min}}\right|, \left|x_i^{\text{max}}\right|\right\}} - \frac{y^{\text{min}}}{\max\left\{\left|x_i^{\text{min}}\right|, \left|x_i^{\text{max}}\right|\right\}} \right). \tag{9}$$

where: $U_r(-1,1)$ means the real random number from specified range and m_r is a parameter which defines the mutation range.
- The pruning operator (line 13 in Fig. 1) which replaces one randomly chosen operator node with newly created leaf node.
- The expanding operator (line 14 in Fig. 1) puts in the place of randomly chosen leaf the newly created operator node. It should be noted that this operation can be conducted only when the depth of selected leaf is lower then maximum permissible tree depth $lvl_N < lvl^{\text{max}}$.
- The rule base modification operator (line 15 in Fig. 1) randomly adds a new fuzzy rule to the system (when $K < K^{\text{max}}$) or removes a randomly selected one (when $K > K^{\text{min}}$).

3.4   Usage of Semantic Information in the Process of Evolution

Because crossover and mutation operators are proceeded in random fashion there is possibility that we obtain more than one rule that have different syntax but the same semantics. The semantics is a concept that is considered in many different field of science, so there is no one strict definition of it. In this paper we take the same assumption as other researcher (see e.g. [4,5,30]) that combine semantic information and genetic programming algorithm and define semantic as a raw output of function (or in this case fuzzy rule). With this assumption we can define the degree of similarity of two fuzzy rules as a following function:

$$simi\left(k,l\right) = 1 - \frac{1}{Z \cdot m} \sum_{z=1}^{Z} \frac{\left|\mu_{A^k}\left(\bar{\mathbf{x}}_z\right) \cdot \bar{y}_1^k\left(\bar{\mathbf{x}}_z\right) - \mu_{A^l}\left(\bar{\mathbf{x}}_z\right) \cdot \bar{y}_1^l\left(\bar{\mathbf{x}}_z\right)\right|}{y_1^{\text{max}} - y_1^{\text{min}}}, \tag{10}$$

where: $\bar{\mathbf{x}}_z$ is an vector of input values of z-th sample contained in training set, Z is the number of training samples, $\bar{y}_1^b(\bar{\mathbf{x}}_z)$, $b \in \{k,l\}$ is a value of functional dependency contained in rule k or l, y_1^{min}, y_1^{max} are minimum and maximum output values contained in training set. In the literature on genetic programming we can find different ways to incorporate the semantics information into the process of evolution (see e.g. [4,5,30]). In the conducting simulations (Sect. 4) we have considered three different approach to use this information:

- **Case 1.** With use of operator RemoveSimilarRules (line 16 in Fig. 1) of algorithm we randomly remove one of two fuzzy rules if their degree of similarity is greater than an arbitrary threshold c_{simi}.
- **Case 2.** With use of ff$_{simi}$ component of fitness function (see Sect. 3.5),
- **Case 3.** With use a combination of both above methods.

3.5   Evaluation of Individual

Each solution (individual) is evaluated according to the following fitness function:

$$\text{ff}\left(\mathbf{X}_{ch}\right) = RMSE \cdot \left(w_{cmpl} + \text{ff}_{cmpl}\left(\mathbf{X}_{ch}\right)\right) \cdot \left(w_{simi} + \text{ff}_{simi}\left(\mathbf{X}_{ch}\right)\right), \qquad (11)$$

where: $RMSE$ determines the accuracy of the neuro-fuzzy system encoded in $\mathbf{X}_{ch}$ chromosome defined as a root mean square error (see e.g. [54]), ff$_{cmpl}(\mathbf{X}_{ch})$ is a penalty function, which purpose is to reduce the complexity of the fuzzy system, and ff$_{simi}(\mathbf{X}_{ch})$ is a penalty function which aim is to reduce the fitness of an individual describing fuzzy system which contains similar rules. Parameters w_{cmpl} and w_{simi} determine the impact of a penalties on evaluation of the individual. The function ff$_{cmpl}(\mathbf{X}_{ch})$ is defined as:

$$\text{ff}_{cmpl}\left(\mathbf{X}_{ch}\right) = \frac{nodes + leaves}{N^{\max}\left(2^{lvl^{\max}} - 1\right)}, \qquad (12)$$

where: $nodes$, $leaves$ are the total numbers of nodes and leaves that are contained in all fuzzy rules describing by individual $\mathbf{X}_{ch}$. The component ff$_{simi}(\mathbf{X}_{ch})$ is defined as a following function:

$$\text{ff}_{simi}\left(\mathbf{X}_{ch}\right) = \frac{2!\left(K - 2\right)}{K!} \cdot \sum_{k=1}^{K-1} \sum_{l=k+1}^{K} simi\left(k, l\right). \qquad (13)$$

4   Simulations Results

In order to prove validity of our method we used five well-known benchmarks of nonlinear modelling (see Table 1). For the simulations the following values of

Table 1. Nonlinear modelling benchmarks used in the simulations.

Label	Benchmark problem	Number of inputs (n)	Number of outputs (m)	Number of data rows (Z)
AM	Auto MPG [51]	7	1	392
ASN	Airfoil Self-Noise [6]	5	1	1503
CS	Compresive Strenght [76]	8	1	1030
HF	HANG function [67]	2	1	50
MC	Machine CPU [38]	7	1	209

Table 2. Simulation results. $QUAL$ stands for quality of obtained solutions calculated as: $RMSE \cdot \text{ff}_{cmpl}(\mathbf{X}_{ch}) \cdot \text{ff}_{simi}(\mathbf{X}_{ch})$ (fitness function values cannot be compared due to different way of calculating it in different cases). Case 0 stands for standard solution.

Label	Case	ff	$RMSE$	ff_{cmpl}	ff_{simi}	K	$QUAL$
AM	0	3.342	2.980	0.122	0.856	3.500	0.310
	1	3.264	2.934	0.112	0.791	3.150	0.261
	2	0.894	3.041	0.116	0.527	3.250	0.185
	3	0.649	**2.917**	**0.101**	**0.404**	**3.000**	**0.119**
ASN	0	4.940	4.432	0.115	0.521	3.450	0.264
	1	4.858	4.421	0.099	0.524	**3.000**	0.229
	2	0.525	4.432	0.109	**0.214**	3.300	**0.103**
	3	0.589	**4.292**	**0.098**	0.250	3.050	0.106
CS	0	9.914	8.878	0.117	0.817	3.350	0.846
	1	9.239	**8.432**	**0.102**	0.789	**3.000**	0.680
	2	2.401	9.272	0.122	0.462	3.400	0.520
	3	1.603	8.799	0.104	**0.330**	3.050	**0.301**
HF	0	0.241	0.213	0.129	0.872	4.000	0.024
	1	0.274	0.249	0.100	0.858	3.100	0.021
	2	0.091	**0.195**	0.138	0.824	4.200	0.022
	3	0.087	0.202	**0.097**	**0.787**	**3.000**	**0.015**
MC	0	19.306	**16.835**	0.147	0.976	4.250	2.411
	1	19.832	17.633	**0.125**	0.929	3.600	**2.044**
	2	10.990	19.677	0.151	0.971	4.100	2.876
	3	10.218	19.596	0.131	**0.922**	**3.550**	2.361

Table 3. Obtained improvement of proposed method in comparison with standard method. Quality stands for $QUAL$ from Table 2. AVG stands for average improvement for all benchmarks.

Improvement in	Case	ASN	AM	CS	HF	MC	AVG
$RMSE$	1	0.26 %	1.54 %	5.03 %	-16.62 %	-4.74 %	-2.91 %
	2	0.00 %	-2.06 %	-4.44 %	8.82 %	-16.88 %	-2.91 %
	3	3.15 %	2.10 %	0.89 %	5.49 %	-16.40 %	**-0.95%**
ff_{cmpl} (complexity)	1	13.62 %	7.52 %	12.44 %	22.50 %	15.02 %	14.22 %
	2	5.16 %	4.87 %	-4.15 %	-6.67 %	-2.56 %	-0.67 %
	3	14.08 %	16.81 %	11.06 %	25.00 %	10.99 %	**15.59%**
ff_{simi} (similarity)	1	-0.53 %	7.62 %	3.41 %	1.59 %	4.77 %	3.37 %
	2	58.93 %	38.44 %	43.47 %	5.49 %	0.51 %	29.37 %
	3	52.02 %	52.83 %	59.60 %	9.70 %	5.48 %	**35.93%**
$QUAL$ (quality)	1	13.38 %	15.88 %	19.68 %	11.06 %	15.24 %	15.05 %
	2	61.05 %	40.23 %	38.51 %	8.07 %	-19.27 %	25.72 %
	3	60.08 %	61.58 %	64.39 %	35.99 %	2.07 %	**44.82%**

Table 4. Exemplary fuzzy rules obtained for benchmark: AM and ASN. Corresponding fuzzy sets are shown in Fig. 3.

Label	Fuzzy rules notation
AM	$R_1:$ IF (x_5 IS $A_{5,5}$ AND x_7 IS $A_{7,4}$ AND x_1 IS $A_{1,4}$) THEN $y_1 = $ ($21.00 + 6.29x_1 + +0.20x_2 + 0.14x_3 + +0.01x_4 + 4.05x_5 + +0.63x_6 + 25.36x_7$)
	$R_2:$ IF (x_3 IS $A_{3,2}$ AND x_2 IS $A_{2,1}$) THEN $y_1 = $ ($22.22 - 0.60x_1 + -0.03x_2 - 0.18x_3 + -0.01x_4 - 1.27x_5 + +0.81x_6 + 4.37x_7$)
	$R_3:$ IF (x_3 IS $A_{3,2}$ AND x_5 IS $A_{5,3}$) THEN $y_1 = $ ($23.09 - 0.32x_1 + +0.01x_2 - 0.06x_3 + +0.00x_4 + -0.16x_5 + +0.22x_6 - 3.77x_7$)
ASN	$R_1:$ IF (x_2 IS $A_{2,1}$ AND x_3 IS $A_{3,2}$ AND x_1 IS $A_{1,4}$) THEN $y_1 = $ ($141.37 + 0.00x_1 + -0.94x_2 - 124.40x_3 + +0.06x_4 - 847.70x_5$)
	$R_2:$ IF (x_1 IS $A_{1,1}$ AND x_3 IS $A_{3,3}$) THEN $y_1 = $ ($131.52 + 0.00x_1 + -0.15x_2 - 21.53x_3 + +0.09x_4 - 191.18x_5$)
	$R_3:$ IF (x_2 IS $A_{2,4}$ AND x_5 IS $A_{5,2}$ AND x_4 IS $A_{4,5}$) THEN $y_1 = $ ($134.17 + 0.00x_1 + -0.62x_2 - 54.27x_3 + +0.10x_4 - 95.59x_5$)

parameters were set: maximum deep level of tree $deep = 5$, minimum number of rules $N^{\min} = 3$, maximum number of rules $N^{\max} = 5$, probability of gene mutation $p_m = 0.3$, probability of tree pruning $p_p = 0.2$, probability of tree expanding $p_e = 0.15$, probability of rule inserting $p_r = 0.1$, impact of complexity component $w_{cmpl} = 1.0$, impact of similarity component $w_{simi} = 0.5$, arbitrary threshold $c_{simi} = 0.1$, $\mu = 100$, number of iterations $= 1000$. For each benchmark simulations were repeated 50 times.

Simulation results are presented in Table 2. The exemplary fuzzy sets are shown in Fig. 3 and fuzzy rules corresponding to them are presented in Tables 4 and 5.

Table 5. Exemplary fuzzy rules obtained for benchmark: CS, HF and MC. Corresponding fuzzy sets are shown in Fig. 3.

label	fuzzy rules notation

CS

R_1 : IF
$$\begin{pmatrix} x_6 \text{ IS } A_{6,4} \\ \text{AND} \\ x_1 \text{ IS } A_{1,3} \\ \text{AND} \\ x_8 \text{ IS } A_{8,4} \\ \text{AND} \\ x_3 \text{ IS } A_{3,1} \end{pmatrix}$$ THEN $y_1 = $
$$\begin{pmatrix} 23.23 + 0.09x_1 + \\ +0.05x_2 + 0.03x_3 + \\ -0.01x_4 + 0.93x_5 + \\ -0.02x_6 - 0.03x_7 + \\ +0.08x_8 \end{pmatrix}$$

R_2 : IF
$$\begin{pmatrix} x_2 \text{ IS } A_{2,1} \\ \text{AND} \\ x_3 \text{ IS } A_{3,2} \\ \text{AND} \\ x_5 \text{ IS } A_{5,1} \\ \text{AND} \\ x_6 \text{ IS } A_{6,1} \\ \text{AND} \\ x_7 \text{ IS } A_{7,5} \\ \text{AND} \\ x_1 \text{ IS } A_{1,5} \end{pmatrix}$$ THEN $y_1 = $
$$\begin{pmatrix} 28.55 + 0.12x_1 + \\ +0.20x_2 + 0.12x_3 + \\ +0.29x_4 + 0.23x_5 + \\ +0.00x_6 + 0.08x_7 + \\ +0.15x_8 \end{pmatrix}$$

R_3 : IF
$$\begin{pmatrix} x_8 \text{ IS } A_{8,1} \\ \text{AND} \\ x_7 \text{ IS } A_{7,3} \end{pmatrix}$$ THEN $y_1 = $
$$\begin{pmatrix} 61.91 - 0.08x_1 + \\ +0.08x_2 - 0.04x_3 + \\ -0.76x_4 - 1.26x_5 + \\ -0.05x_6 + 0.00x_7 + \\ +0.24x_8 \end{pmatrix}$$

HF

R_1 : IF
$$\begin{pmatrix} x_2 \text{ IS } A_{2,4} \\ \text{AND} \\ x_1 \text{ IS } A_{1,5} \end{pmatrix}$$ THEN $y_1 = $
$$\begin{pmatrix} 3.33 + \\ -0.24x_1 + \\ -0.22x_2 \end{pmatrix}$$

R_2 : IF
$$\begin{pmatrix} x_1 \text{ IS } A_{1,1} \\ \text{AND} \\ x_2 \text{ IS } A_{2,1} \end{pmatrix}$$ THEN $y_1 = $
$$\begin{pmatrix} 3.54 + \\ +0.34x_1 + \\ +0.81x_2 \end{pmatrix}$$

R_3 : IF
$$\begin{pmatrix} x_2 \text{ IS } A_{2,2} \\ \text{AND} \\ x_1 \text{ IS } A_{1,3} \end{pmatrix}$$ THEN $y_1 = $
$$\begin{pmatrix} 1.84 + \\ +0.18x_1 + \\ -0.34x_2 \end{pmatrix}$$

MC

R_1 : IF
$$\begin{pmatrix} x_5 \text{ IS } A_{5,4} \\ \text{AND} \\ x_4 \text{ IS } A_{4,3} \end{pmatrix}$$ THEN $y_1 = $
$$\begin{pmatrix} 22.05 + 0.69x_1 + \\ +0.03x_2 + 0.01x_3 + \\ +0.40x_4 - 11.51x_5 + \\ +1.44x_6 - 0.34x_7 \end{pmatrix}$$

R_2 : IF
$$\begin{pmatrix} x_3 \text{ IS } A_{3,4} \\ \text{AND} \\ x_4 \text{ IS } A_{4,2} \end{pmatrix}$$ THEN $y_1 = $
$$\begin{pmatrix} -20.66 - 0.01x_1 + \\ +0.00x_2 + 0.01x_3 + \\ -1.50x_4 + 10.55x_5 + \\ -0.06x_6 + 0.54x_7 \end{pmatrix}$$

R_3 : IF
$$\begin{pmatrix} x_7 \text{ IS } A_{7,5} \\ \text{AND} \\ x_5 \text{ IS } A_{5,2} \\ \text{AND} \\ x_4 \text{ IS } A_{4,5} \end{pmatrix}$$ THEN $y_1 = $
$$\begin{pmatrix} 783.09 + 0.66x_1 + \\ +0.00x_2 + 0.01x_3 + \\ +1.07x_4 + 10.49x_5 + \\ +4.93x_6 + 0.30x_7 \end{pmatrix}$$

R_4 : IF
$$\begin{pmatrix} x_7 \text{ IS } A_{7,2} \\ \text{AND} \\ x_6 \text{ IS } A_{6,3} \end{pmatrix}$$ THEN $y_1 = $
$$\begin{pmatrix} 15.77 - 0.01x_1 + \\ +0.01x_2 + 0.00x_3 + \\ +0.62x_4 - 0.37x_5 + \\ +0.05x_6 + 0.10x_7 \end{pmatrix}$$

272   Ł. Bartczuk et al.

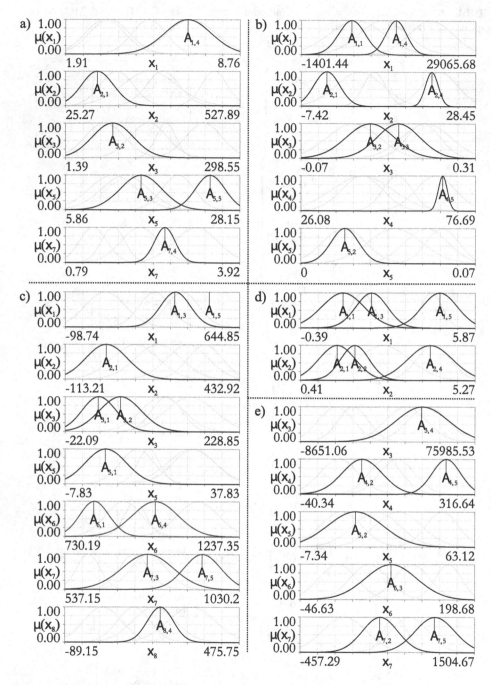

Fig. 3. Exemplary fuzzy sets obtained for benchmark: (a) AM, (b) ASF, (c) CS, (d) HF, (e) MC. Corresponding fuzzy rules are presented Tables 4 and 5. Grey fuzzy sets stands for not used (by any fuzzy rule) fuzzy sets.

The simulation results can be summed up as follows:

- Obtained rmse is very similar to rmse from standard method (better in 66 % of results - see Table 3),
- For cases with reducing similar rules (case 1 and 3) 14.22 % and 15.59 % of complexity improvement was achieved (with no negative effect on system rmse - see Table 3),
- For cases with similarity component considered in fitness function (case 2 and 3) 29.37 % and 35.93 % improvement in distinguishability of the rules was achieved (see Table 3). Improvement level depends highly from benchmark,
- Overall improvement for all cases was significantly positive (15.05 % for case 1, 25.72 % for case 2, 44.82 % for case 3 - see quality improvement in Table 3),
- Obtained fuzzy sets and fuzzy rules are clear and interpretable (see Fig. 3, Tables 4 and 5).

5   Conclusions

Proposed method for generating fuzzy rules for the nonlinear modeling based on semantic genetic programming allows us to obtain good results. The semantic improvement was obtained by three approaches: by removing similar rules, by considering similarity of rules in the fitness function and by using both approaches simultaneously. For all approaches a significant improvement in complexity reduction and distinguishability of the fuzzy rules was achieved with no negative effect on system rmse. The proposed method is effective and can be used in any other algorithms for nonlinear modelling.

Acknowledgment. The project was financed by the National Science Center on the basis of the decision number DEC-2012/05/B/ST7/02138.

References

1. Bartczuk, Ł., Przybył, A., Dziwiński, P.: Hybrid state variables - Fuzzy logic modelling of nonlinear objects. In: Rutkowski, L., Korytkowski, M., Scherer, R., Tadeusiewicz, R., Zadeh, L.A., Zurada, J.M. (eds.) ICAISC 2013, Part I. LNCS, vol. 7894, pp. 227–234. Springer, Heidelberg (2013)
2. Bartczuk, Ł., Przybył, A., Koprinkova-Hristova, P.: New method for nonlinear fuzzy correction modelling of dynamic objects. In: Rutkowski, L., Korytkowski, M., Scherer, R., Tadeusiewicz, R., Zadeh, L.A., Zurada, J.M. (eds.) ICAISC 2014, Part I. LNCS, vol. 8467, pp. 169–180. Springer, Heidelberg (2014)
3. Bas, E.: The training of multiplicative neuron model based artificial neural networks with differential evolution algorithm for forecasting. J. Artif. Intell. Soft Comput. Res. **6**(1), 5–11 (2016)
4. Beadle, L., Johnson, C.: Semantically driven crossover in genetic programming. In: 2008 IEEE Congress on Evolutionary Computation (CEC), pp. 111–116 (2008)
5. Beadle, L., Johnson, C.: Semantically driven mutation in genetic programming. In: 2009 IEEE Congress on Evolutionary Computation (CEC), pp. 1336–1342 (2009)

6. Brooks, T.F., Pope, D.S., Marcolini, A.M.: Airfoil self-noise and prediction, Technical report, NASA RP-1218 (1989)
7. Chaibakhsh, A., Chaibakhsh, N., Abbasi, M., Norouzi, A.: Orthonormal basis function fuzzy systems for biological wastewater treatment processes modeling. J. Artif. Intell. Soft Comput. Res. 2(4), 343–356 (2012)
8. Chang, W.-J., Chang, W., Liu, H.-H.: Model-based fuzzy modeling and control for autonomous underwater vehicles in the horizontal plane. J. Mar. Sci. Technol. 11(3), 155–163 (2003)
9. Chen, Q., Abercrombie, R.K., Sheldon, F.T.: Risk assessment for industrial control systems quantifying availability using mean failure cost (MFC). J. Artif. Intell. Soft Comput. Res. 5(3), 205–220 (2015)
10. Cpalka, K.: A method for designing flexible neuro-fuzzy systems. In: Rutkowski, L., Tadeusiewicz, R., Zadeh, L.A., Żurada, J.M. (eds.) ICAISC 2006. LNCS (LNAI), vol. 4029, pp. 212–219. Springer, Heidelberg (2006)
11. Cpałka, K.: On evolutionary designing and learning of flexible neuro-fuzzy structures for nonlinear classification. Nonlinear Anal. Ser. A Theor. Methods Appl. 71, 1659–1672 (2009). Elsevier
12. Cpałka, K., Łapa, K., Przybył, A., Zalasiński, M.: A new method for designing neuro-fuzzy systems for nonlinear modelling with interpretability aspects. Neurocomputing 135, 203–217 (2014)
13. Cpałka, K., Rebrova, O., Nowicki, R., Rutkowski, L.: On design of flexible neuro-fuzzy systems for nonlinear modelling. Int. J. Gen. Syst. 42(6), 706–720 (2013)
14. Cpałka, K., Rutkowski, L.: Flexible Takagi-Sugeno fuzzy systems. In: Proceedings of the 2005 IEEE International Joint Conference on Neural Networks, IJCNN 2005, vol. 3, pp. 1764–1769 (2005)
15. Cpałka, K., Rutkowski, L.: Flexible Takagi-Sugeno neuro-fuzzy structures for nonlinear approximation. WSEAS Trans. Syst. 4(9), 1450–1458 (2005)
16. Cpałka, K., Rutkowski, L.: A new method for designing and reduction of neuro-fuzzy systems, In: Proceedings of the 2006 IEEE International Conference on Fuzzy Systems (IEEE World Congress on Computational Intelligence, WCCI 2006), Vancouver, BC, Canada, pp. 8510–8516 (2006)
17. Cpałka, K., Rutkowski, L.: Flexible Takagi-Sugeno fuzzy systems. In: Proceedings of the International Joint Conference on Neural Networks 2005, Montreal, pp. 1764–1769 (2005)
18. Cpałka, K., Zalasiński, M.: On-line signature verification using vertical signature partitioning. Expert Syst. Appl. 41(9), 4170–4180 (2014)
19. Cpałka, K., Zalasiński, M., Rutkowski, L.: New method for the on-line signature verification based on horizontal partitioning. Pattern Recogn. 47, 2652–2661 (2014)
20. Cpałka, K., Zalasiński, M., Rutkowski, L.: A new algorithm for identity verification based on the analysis of a handwritten dynamic signature. Appl. Soft comput. 43, 47–56 (2016)
21. Delgado, M.R., Zuben, F.V., Gomide, F.: Coevolutionary genetic fuzzy systems: a hierarchical collaborative approach. Fuzzy Sets Syst. 141, 89–106 (2004). Elsevier
22. Dziwiński, P., Bartczuk, Ł., Starczewski, J.T.: Fully controllable ant colony system for text data clustering. In: Rutkowski, L., Korytkowski, M., Scherer, R., Tadeusiewicz, R., Zadeh, L.A., Zurada, J.M. (eds.) EC 2012 and SIDE 2012. LNCS, vol. 7269, pp. 199–205. Springer, Heidelberg (2012)
23. Dziwiński, P., Rutkowska, D.: Algorithm for generating fuzzy rules for WWW document classification. In: Rutkowski, L., Tadeusiewicz, R., Zadeh, L.A., Żurada, J.M. (eds.) ICAISC 2006. LNCS (LNAI), vol. 4029, pp. 1111–1119. Springer, Heidelberg (2006)

24. Dziwiński, P., Rutkowska, D.: Ant focused crawling algorithm. In: Rutkowski, L., Tadeusiewicz, R., Zadeh, L.A., Zurada, J.M. (eds.) ICAISC 2008. LNCS (LNAI), vol. 5097, pp. 1018–1028. Springer, Heidelberg (2008)
25. Dziwiński, P., Starczewski, J.T., Bartczuk, L.: New linguistic hedges in construction of interval type-2 FLS. In: Rutkowski, L., Scherer, R., Tadeusiewicz, R., Zadeh, L.A., Zurada, J.M. (eds.) ICAISC 2010, Part II. LNCS, vol. 6114, pp. 445–450. Springer, Heidelberg (2010)
26. Dziwiński, P., Bartczuk, L., Przybył, A., Avedyan, E.D.: A new algorithm for identification of significant operating points using swarm intelligence. In: Rutkowski, L., Korytkowski, M., Scherer, R., Tadeusiewicz, R., Zadeh, L.A., Zurada, J.M. (eds.) ICAISC 2014, Part II. LNCS, vol. 8468, pp. 349–362. Springer, Heidelberg (2014)
27. Dziwiński, P., Avedyan, E.D.: A new approach to nonlinear modeling based on significant operating points detection. In: Rutkowski, L., Korytkowski, M., Scherer, R., Tadeusiewicz, R., Zadeh, L.A., Zurada, J.M. (eds.) Artificial Intelligence and Soft Computing. LNCS, vol. 9120, pp. 364–378. Springer, Heidelberg (2015)
28. Ferreira, C.: Gene Expression Programming: Mathematical Modeling by an Artificial Intelligence, 2nd edn. Springer, Germany (2006)
29. Folly, K.: Parallel Pbil applied to power system controller design. J. Artif. Intell. Soft Comput. Res. 3(3), 215–223 (2013)
30. Galvan-Lopez, E., Cody-Kenny, B., Trujillo, L., Kattan, A.: Using semantics in the selection mechanism in genetic programming: a simple method for promoting semantic diversity. In: 2013 IEEE Congress on Evolutionary Computation (CEC), pp. 2972–2979 (2013)
31. Gałkowski, T., Rutkowski, L.: Nonparametric recovery of multivariate functions with applications to system identification. Proc. IEEE 73(5), 942–943 (1985)
32. Hoffman, F., Nelles, O.: Genetic programming for model selection of TSK-fuzzy systems. Inf. Sci. 136, 7–28 (2001). Elsevier
33. Ismail, S., Pashilkar, A.A., Ayyagari, R., Sundararajan, N.: Neural-sliding mode augmented robust controller for autolanding of fixed wing aircraft. J. Artif. Intell. Soft Comput. Res. 2(4), 317–330 (2012)
34. Jimenez, F., Yoshikawa, T., Furuhashi, T., Kanoh, M.: An emotional expression model for educational-support robots. J. Artif. Intell. Soft Comput. Res. 5(1), 51–57 (2015)
35. Johansen, T.A., Shorten, R., Murray-Smith, R.: On the interpretation and identification of dynamic Takagi-Sugeno fuzzy models. IEEE Trans. Fuzzy Syst. 8(3), 297–313 (2000)
36. Kaczorek, T., Dzieliński, A., Dąbrowski L., Łopatka R.: The Basis of Control Theory, WNT, Warsaw (2006) (in Polish)
37. Kamyar, M.: Takagi-Sugeno Fuzzy Modeling for Process Control Industrial Automation, Robotics and Artificial Intelligence (EEE8005), School of Electrical, Electronic and Computer Engineering, vol. 8 (2008)
38. Kibler, D., Aha, D.: Instance-based prediction of real-valued attributes. In: Proceedings of the CSCSI (Canadian AI) Conference (1988)
39. Koprinkova-Hristova, P.: Backpropagation through time training of a neuro-fuzzy controller. Int. J. Neural Syst. 20(5), 421–428 (2010)
40. Korytkowski, M., Rutkowski, L., Scherer, R.: Fast image classification by boosting fuzzy classifiers. Inf. Sci. 327, 175–182 (2016)
41. Koshiyama, A.S., Vellasco, M., Tanscheit, R.: Gpfis-control: a genetic fuzzy system for control tasks. J. Artif. Intell. Soft Comput. Res. 4(3), 167–179 (2014)

42. Koza, J.R.: Genetic programming - On the Programming of Computers by Means of Natural Selection. The MIT Press, Cambridge (1992)

43. Krawiec, K.: Genetic programming: where meaning emerges from program code. Genet. Program. Evolvable Mach. **15**(1), 75–77 (2014). Springer

44. Lin, C.H., Dong, F.Y., Hirota, K.: Common driving notification protocol based on classified driving behavior for cooperation intelligent autonomous vehicle using vehicular ad-hoc network technology. J. Artif. Intell. Soft Comput. Res. **5**(1), 5–21 (2015)

45. Łapa, K., Przybył, A., Cpałka, K.: A new approach to designing interpretable models of dynamic systems. In: Rutkowski, L., Korytkowski, M., Scherer, R., Tadeusiewicz, R., Zadeh, L.A., Zurada, J.M. (eds.) ICAISC 2013, Part II. LNCS, vol. 7895, pp. 523–534. Springer, Heidelberg (2013)

46. Łapa, K., Zalasiński, M., Cpałka, K.: A new method for designing and complexity reduction of neuro-fuzzy systems for nonlinear modelling. In: Rutkowski, L., Korytkowski, M., Scherer, R., Tadeusiewicz, R., Zadeh, L.A., Zurada, J.M. (eds.) ICAISC 2013, Part I. LNCS, vol. 7894, pp. 329–344. Springer, Heidelberg (2013)

47. Laskowski, Ł.: A novel hybrid-maximum neural network in stereo-matching process. Neural Comput. Appl. **23**(7–8), 2435–2450 (2013). Springer

48. Laskowski, Ł., Jelonkiewicz, J.: Self-correcting neural network for stereo-matching problem solving. Fundamenta Informaticae **138**(4), 457–482 (2015). IOS Press

49. Miyajima, H., Shigei, N., Miyajima, H.: Performance comparison of hybrid electromagnetism-like mechanism algorithms with descent method. J. Artif. Intell. Soft Comput. Res. **5**(4), 271–282 (2015)

50. Przybył, A., Cpałka, K.: A new method to construct of interpretable models of dynamic systems. In: Rutkowski, L., Korytkowski, M., Scherer, R., Tadeusiewicz, R., Zadeh, L.A., Zurada, J.M. (eds.) ICAISC 2012, Part II. LNCS, vol. 7268, pp. 697–705. Springer, Heidelberg (2012)

51. Quinlan, R.: Combining instance-based and model-based learning. In: Proceedings on the Tenth International Conference of Machine Learning, pp. 236–243 (1993)

52. Rigatos, G.G., Siano, P.: Flatness-based adaptive fuzzy control of spark-ignited engines. J. Artif. Intell. Soft Comput. Res. **4**(4), 231–242 (2014)

53. Rutkowski, L.: Adaptive probabilistic neural networks for pattern classification in time-varying environment. IEEE Trans. Neural Netw. **15**(4), 811–827 (2004)

54. Rutkowski, L.: Computational Intelligence: Methods and Techniques. Springer, Heidelberg (2008)

55. Rutkowski, L., Cpałka, K.: Flexible structures of neuro-fuzzy systems. Quo Vadis Computational Intelligence, Studies in Fuzziness and Soft Computing, Springer **54**, 479–484 (2000)

56. Rutkowski, L., Cpałka, K.: A general approach to neuro-fuzzy systems. In: The 10th IEEE International Conference on Fuzzy Systems, 2001, Melbourne, pp. 1428–1431 (2001)

57. Rutkowski, L., Cpałka, K.: Compromise approach to neuro-fuzzy systems. In: Sincak, P., Vascak, J., Kvasnicka, V., Pospichal, J. (eds.) Intelligent Technologies - Theory and Applications. IOS Press, vol. 76, pp. 85–90 (2002)

58. Rutkowski, L., Cpałka, K.: Compromise approach to neuro-fuzzy systems. In: Sincak, P., Vascak, J., Kvasnicka, V., Pospichal, J. (eds.) Intelligent Technologies - Theory and Applications, vol. 76, pp. 85–90. IOS Press, Amsterdam (2002)

59. Rutkowski, L., Cpałka, K.: Neuro-fuzzy systems derived from quasi-triangular norms. In: Proceedings of the IEEE International Conference on Fuzzy Systems, Budapest, 26–29 July 2014, vol. 2, pp. 1031–1036 (2004)

60. Rutkowski, L., Jaworski, M., Pietruczuk, L., Duda, P.: Decision trees for mining data streams based on the gaussian approximation. IEEE Trans. Knowl. Data Eng. **26**(1), 108–119 (2014)
61. Rutkowski, L., Jaworski, M., Pietruczuk, L., Duda, P.: The CART decision tree for mining data streams. Inf. Sci. **266**, 1–15 (2014)
62. Rutkowski, L., Pietruczuk, L., Duda, P., Jaworski, M.: Decision Trees for mining data streams based on the McDiarmid's bound. IEEE Trans. Knowl. Data Eng. **25**(6), 1272–1279 (2013)
63. Rutkowski, L., Przybył, A., Cpałka, K., Er, M.J.: Online speed profile generation for industrial machine tool based on neuro-fuzzy approach. In: Rutkowski, L., Scherer, R., Tadeusiewicz, R., Zadeh, L.A., Zurada, J.M. (eds.) ICAISC 2010, Part II. LNCS, vol. 6114, pp. 645–650. Springer, Heidelberg (2010)
64. Rutkowski, L., Przybył, A., Cpałka, K.: Novel on-line speed profile generation for industrial machine tool based on flexible neuro-fuzzy approximation. IEEE Trans. Industr. Electron. **59**, 1238–1247 (2012)
65. Rutkowski, L., Przybył, A., Cpałka, K., Er, M.J.: Online speed profile generation for industrial machine tool based on neuro-fuzzy approach. In: Rutkowski, L., Scherer, R., Tadeusiewicz, R., Zadeh, L.A., Zurada, J.M. (eds.) ICAISC 2010, Part II. LNCS, vol. 6114, pp. 645–650. Springer, Heidelberg (2010)
66. Starczewski, J.T., Bartczuk, Ł., Dziwiński, P., Marvuglia, A.: Learning methods for type-2 FLS based on FCM. In: Rutkowski, L., Scherer, R., Tadeusiewicz, R., Zadeh, L.A., Zurada, J.M. (eds.) ICAISC 2010, Part I. LNCS, vol. 6113, pp. 224–231. Springer, Heidelberg (2010)
67. Sugeno, M., Yasukawa, T.: A fuzzy logic based approach to qualitative modeling. IEEE Trans. Fuzzy Syst. **1**, 7–31 (1993)
68. Sugiyama, H.: Pulsed power network based on decentralized intelligence for reliable and lowloss electrical power distribution. J. Artif. Intell. Soft Comput. Res. **5**(2), 97–108 (2015)
69. Szczypta, J., Przybył, A., Cpałka, K.: Some aspects of evolutionary designing optimal controllers. In: Rutkowski, L., Korytkowski, M., Scherer, R., Tadeusiewicz, R., Zadeh, L.A., Zurada, J.M. (eds.) ICAISC 2013, Part II. LNCS, vol. 7895, pp. 91–100. Springer, Heidelberg (2013)
70. Szczypta, J., Przybył, A., Wang, L.: Evolutionary approach with multiple quality criteria for controller design. In: Rutkowski, L., Korytkowski, M., Scherer, R., Tadeusiewicz, R., Zadeh, L.A., Zurada, J.M. (eds.) ICAISC 2014, Part I. LNCS, vol. 8467, pp. 455–467. Springer, Heidelberg (2014)
71. Takagi, T., Sugeno, M.: Fuzzy identification of systems and its application to modeling and control. IEEE Trans. Syst. Man Cybern. **15**(1), 116–132 (1985)
72. Tsakonas, A.: Local and global optimization for Takagi-Sugeno fuzzy system by memetic genetic programming. Expert Syst. Appl. **40**(8), 3282–3298 (2013)
73. Theodoridis, D.C., Boutalis, Y.S., Christodoulou, M.A.: Robustifying analysis of the direct adaptive control of unknown multivariable nonlinear systems based on a new neuro-fuzzy method. J. Artif. Intell. Soft Comput. Res. **1**(1), 59–79 (2011)
74. Thiagarajan, R., Rahman, M., Gossink, D., Calbert, G.: A data mining approach to improve military demand forecasting. J. Artif. Intell. Soft Comput. Res. **4**(3), 205–214 (2014)
75. Tran, V.N., Brdys, M.A.: Optimizing control by robustly feasible model predictive control and application to drinking water distribution systems. J. Artif. Intell. Soft Comput. Res. **1**(1), 43–57 (2011)
76. Yeh, I.C.: Modeling of strength of high performance concrete using artificial neural networks. Cem. Concr. Res. **28**(12), 1797–1808 (1998)

77. Wang, G., Zhang, S.: ABM with behavioral bias and applications in simulating China stock market. J. Artif. Intell. Soft Comput. Res. 5(4), 257–270 (2015)
78. Wang, Z., Zhang-Westmant, L.: New ranking method for fuzzy numbers by their expansion center. J. Artif. Intell. Soft Comput. Res. 4(3), 181–187 (2014)
79. Zalasiński, M., Cpałka, K.: A New Method of On-Line Signature Verification Using a Flexible Fuzzy One-Class Classifier. Academic Publishing House EXIT, Warsaw (2011)
80. Zalasiński, M., Cpałka, K.: Novel algorithm for the on-line signature verification. In: Rutkowski, L., Korytkowski, M., Scherer, R., Tadeusiewicz, R., Zadeh, L.A., Zurada, J.M. (eds.) ICAISC 2012, Part II. LNCS, vol. 7268, pp. 362–367. Springer, Heidelberg (2012)
81. Zalasiński, M., Cpałka, K.: New approach for the on-line signature verification based on method of horizontal partitioning. In: Rutkowski, L., Korytkowski, M., Scherer, R., Tadeusiewicz, R., Zadeh, L.A., Zurada, J.M. (eds.) ICAISC 2013, Part II. LNCS, vol. 7895, pp. 342–350. Springer, Heidelberg (2013)
82. Zalasiński, M., Cpałka, K.: Novel algorithm for the on-line signature verification using selected discretization points groups. In: Rutkowski, L., Korytkowski, M., Scherer, R., Tadeusiewicz, R., Zadeh, L.A., Zurada, J.M. (eds.) ICAISC 2013, Part I. LNCS, vol. 7894, pp. 493–502. Springer, Heidelberg (2013)
83. Zalasiński, M., Cpałka, K., Er, M.J.: New method for dynamic signature verification using hybrid partitioning. In: Rutkowski, L., Korytkowski, M., Scherer, R., Tadeusiewicz, R., Zadeh, L.A., Zurada, J.M. (eds.) ICAISC 2014, Part II. LNCS, vol. 8468, pp. 216–230. Springer, Heidelberg (2014)
84. Zalasiński, M., Cpałka, K., Er, M.J.: A new method for the dynamic signature verification based on the stable partitions of the signature. In: Rutkowski, L., Korytkowski, M., Scherer, R., Tadeusiewicz, R., Zadeh, L.A., Zurada, J.M. (eds.) Artificial Intelligence and Soft Computing. LNCS, vol. 9120, pp. 161–174. Springer, Heidelberg (2015)
85. Zalasiński, M., Cpałka, K., Hayashi, Y.: New method for dynamic signature verification based on global features. In: Rutkowski, L., Korytkowski, M., Scherer, R., Tadeusiewicz, R., Zadeh, L.A., Zurada, J.M. (eds.) ICAISC 2014, Part II. LNCS, vol. 8468, pp. 231–245. Springer, Heidelberg (2014)
86. Zalasiński, M., Cpałka, K., Hayashi, Y.: New fast algorithm for the dynamic signature verification using global features values. In: Rutkowski, L., Korytkowski, M., Scherer, R., Tadeusiewicz, R., Zadeh, L.A., Zurada, J.M. (eds.) Artificial Intelligence and Soft Computing. LNCS, vol. 9120, pp. 175–188. Springer, Heidelberg (2015)
87. Zalasiński, M., Łapa, K., Cpałka, K.: New algorithm for evolutionary selection of the dynamic signature global features. In: Rutkowski, L., Korytkowski, M., Scherer, R., Tadeusiewicz, R., Zadeh, L.A., Zurada, J.M. (eds.) ICAISC 2013, Part II. LNCS, vol. 7895, pp. 113–121. Springer, Heidelberg (2013)
88. Zhao, W., Lun, R., Espy, D., Reinthal, A.M.: Realtime motion assessment for rehabilitation exercises: integration of kinematic modeling with fuzzy inference. J. Artif. Intell. Soft. Comput. Res. 4(4), 267–285 (2014)

A New Approach for Using the Fuzzy Decision Trees for the Detection of the Significant Operating Points in the Nonlinear Modeling

Piotr Dziwiński[1(✉)] and Eduard D. Avedyan[2]

[1] Institute of Computational Intelligence, Częstochowa University of Technology,
Częstochowa, Poland
piotr.dziwinski@iisi.pcz.pl
[2] Moscow Institute of Physics and Technology, Dolgoprudny, Russia
avedian@mail.ru

Abstract. The paper presents a new approach for using the fuzzy decision tress for the detection of the significant operating points from non-invasive measurements of the nonlinear dynamic object. The PSO-GA algorithm is used to identify the unknown values of the system matrix describing the nonlinear dynamic object. It is defined in the terminal nodes of the fuzzy decision tree. The new approach was tested on the nonlinear electrical circuit. The obtained results prove efficiency of the new approach for using fuzzy decision tree for the detection of the significant operating points in the nonlinear modeling.

Keywords: Nonlinear modeling · Non-invasive identification · Significant operating point · Particle swarm optimization · Genetic algorithm · Electrical circuit · Takagi-Sugeno system · Fuzzy decision trees

1 Introduction

Non-invasive identification of nonlinear dynamic objects relies on discovering of the mathematical model allowing the reproduction of the reference values with a sufficient precision. The reference values are obtained from the non-invasive measurements of the nonlinear dynamic object. The determination of the sufficiently precise mathematical model for object is generally very hard or even impossible. Practically created mathematical models of the nonlinear dynamic objects are the approximate models, they cannot describe all phenomena enough precisely.

A large number of mathematical models which can describe the nonlinear systems on universal way were proposed in the literature, among others, neural networks [6,20,36,38,49] treated as black box models, fuzzy systems [8,12,21, 25,30,31,50], type 2 fuzzy inference systems [47], flexible fuzzy systems [17, 32,37,53,56], neuro-fuzzy systems [9–11,16,18,33,39,51,52,54,55], interval type 2 neuro-fuzzy systems [46] flexible neuro-fuzzy systems [13,17,19,40], Takagi-Sugeno fuzzy system [14,15,29] and flexible Takagi-Sugeno fuzzy systems [44,45], type-2 fuzzy decision trees [3,4] and other systems [28].

© Springer International Publishing Switzerland 2016
L. Rutkowski et al. (Eds.): ICAISC 2016, Part II, LNAI 9693, pp. 279–292, 2016.
DOI: 10.1007/978-3-319-39384-1_24

The methods mentioned earlier enable modeling in an universal way but do not provide enough precision of the reproduction of the reference values. Much better results can be obtained by using a hybrid approach.

In the hybrid approach approximate linear or nonlinear model can be used. It allows reproduction of the reference values with a sufficient precision only in the certain equilibrium point. Whereas the universal model can determine the values of the parameters of the approximate model in different equilibrium points and between them. This approach ensures obtaining a sufficient precision of the identification in the entire area of the work of the nonlinear dynamic object. Bartczuk [5] has proposed new method for nonlinear fuzzy connection modelling of dynamic objects. He has used gene expression programming [2].

This article describes a new approach for using the fuzzy decision trees [35, 41–43, 48], for selection of the important inputs from measurements as criterion of the significant operating points detection. The splitting node is created in the decision fuzzy tree for each selected input. The terminal nodes of the tree contains the system matrix values for the detected operating points. Finally, the obtained fuzzy decision tree is converted to Takagi-Sugeno fuzzy system.

The remainder of this paper is organized as follows. Section 2 describes modeling of nonlinear dynamic object by the algebraic equations and on the basis of the state variable technique. It also describes modeling of the system matrix in the operating points. Section 3 deals with fuzzy modeling of the system matrix in the operating points using the fuzzy decision tree. The Sect. 4 presents the algorithm of the significant operating point detection using decision tree method. Finally, Sect. 6 shows simulation results which prove the effectiveness of the new approach for suing the fuzzy decision trees for the detection of the significant operating points in the nonlinear modeling.

2   Identification of the Nonlinear Dynamic Object

Let us consider the nonlinear dynamic object described by the algebraic equations and based on the state variable technique [37]

$$\frac{d\mathbf{x}(t)}{dt} = \mathbf{A}(t)\mathbf{x}(t) + \mathbf{B}(t)\mathbf{u}(t), \tag{1}$$

$$\mathbf{y}(t) = \mathbf{C}\mathbf{x}(\mathbf{t}), \tag{2}$$

where $\mathbf{A}(t)$, $\mathbf{B}(t)$ are the system state and input matrices respectively, $\mathbf{u}(t)$, $\mathbf{y}(t)$ are the input and output signals respectively, $\mathbf{x}(t)$ is the vector of the state variables. The algebraic equations based on the state variable technique, delivered by the experts, usually cannot describe dynamic nonlinear object enough precisely. There are phenomena that are not described in sufficient detail by experts. Overall accuracy of such a model may be too low for many practical applications. The developed nonlinear model can reproduce the behavior of the nonlinear dynamic object with a sufficient precision only in some equilibrium point called operating point. In this work we use a hybrid approach which increases effectiveness of the nonlinear dynamic object modeling. It is done by the identification of the system matrix values of the nonlinear model in the terminal nodes of the fuzzy decision tree.

In the hybrid approach the entire model can be described by algebraic equations and on the basis of the state variable technique, while the system matrix $\hat{\mathbf{A}}(t)$ has different values of the elements in different operating points. The global model is defined as follows:

$$f_g(\mathbf{x}(t), \mathbf{u}(t)) = \hat{\mathbf{A}}(t)\mathbf{x}(t) + \mathbf{B}(t)\mathbf{u}(t). \tag{3}$$

In the global model the values of the system matrix $\hat{\mathbf{A}}(t)$ may depend on input $\mathbf{u}(t)$ or internal state of the object $\mathbf{x}(t)$. Thus, the values of the system matrix $\hat{\mathbf{A}}(t)$ in the individual operating points can be described by specific function $\zeta^l_{ij}(\mathbf{u}(t), \mathbf{x}(t))$ in the following way

$$\hat{a}_{ij}(t) = \sum_{l=1}^{l=L} \zeta^l_{ij}(\mathbf{u}(t), \mathbf{x}(t))a^l_{ij}(t), \tag{4}$$

where: $\hat{a}_{ij}(t)$ is the resulting value of the system matrix element, $a^l_{ij}(t)$ is the value of the system matrix in operating point l, $\zeta^l_{ij}(\mathbf{u}(t), \mathbf{x}(t))$ is the function describing the activation level of the element of the system matrix at the operating point. So, the local linear or nonlinear model is described by using Eq. (5).

$$f_l(\mathbf{x}(t), \mathbf{u}(t)) = \hat{\mathbf{A}}^l(t)\mathbf{x}(t) + \mathbf{B}(t)\mathbf{u}(t). \tag{5}$$

In the proposed approach we select important inputs from the measured values $\mathbf{x}(t)$, $\mathbf{u}(t)$ using fuzzy decision tree method.

3   Fuzzy Decision Tree Modeling of the System Matrix in the Significant Operating Points

The change of the system matrix $\hat{\mathbf{A}}(t)$ values that takes place between operating points usually does not occur rapidly, but in a smooth manner which is difficult to describe by using the mathematical model. The values of the system matrix existing in the operating points pass fluently among themselves and overlap. So, for activation level description of the system matrix in the operating points we use a fuzzy decision tree. The tree contains two types of nodes: the inner nodes and terminal nodes. The inner nodes of the tree contain a split fuzzy function. The terminal nodes contain the function $f^{(l)}$, determining the system matrix values for the detected operating points. In the fuzzy tree, all terminal nodes can be active, so final value of the matrix is calculated as weighted average of the all terminal nodes. An example of the fuzzy decision tree for nonlinear system identification is presented in the Fig. 1.

The fuzzy decision tree is interpreted as the Takagi-Sugeno fuzzy system by reading all paths from the root of the tree to all terminal nodes (tree leaves).

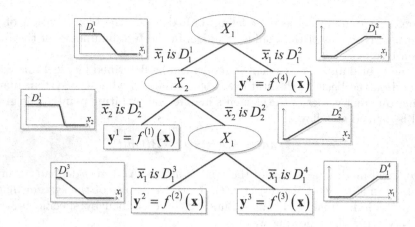

Fig. 1. The example of the fuzzy decision tree.

For the tree show in the Fig. 1 it can be obtained the set of the rules presented in the Eqs. (6–9).

$$R^{(1)} : \text{ IF } \bar{x}_1 \text{ is } D_1^1 \text{ and } \bar{x}_2 \text{ is } D_2^1 \text{ THEN } \mathbf{y}^1 = f^{(1)}(\mathbf{x}) \tag{6}$$

$$R^{(2)} : \text{ IF } \bar{x}_1 \text{ is } D_1^1 \text{ and } \bar{x}_2 \text{ is } D_2^2 \text{ and } \bar{x}_1 \text{ is } D_1^3 \text{ THEN } \mathbf{y}^2 = f^{(2)}(\mathbf{x}) \tag{7}$$

$$R^{(3)} : \text{ IF } \bar{x}_1 \text{ is } D_1^1 \text{ and } \bar{x}_2 \text{ is } D_2^2 \text{ and } \bar{x}_1 \text{ is } D_1^4 \text{ THEN } \mathbf{y}^3 = f^{(3)}(\mathbf{x}) \tag{8}$$

$$R^{(4)} : \text{ IF } \bar{x}_1 \text{ is } D_1^2 \text{ THEN } \mathbf{y}^4 = f^{(4)}(\mathbf{x}) \tag{9}$$

The first occurrence of the premise $\bar{x}_1$ in the rules $R^{(2)}$ and $R^{(3)}$ can be omitted, if we use the some type of the T-norms - for example minimum. The general form of the Takagi-Sugeno fuzzy system is presented in Eq. (10).

$$R^{(l)} : \text{ IF } \bar{\mathbf{x}} \text{ is } \mathbf{D}^l \text{ THEN } \mathbf{y}^l = f^{(l)}(\mathbf{x}), \tag{10}$$

where: $\bar{\mathbf{x}} = [\bar{x}_1, \bar{x}_2, \ldots, \bar{x}_N] \in \mathbf{X}$, $y^l \in \mathbf{Y}^l$, $\mathbf{D}^l = D_1^l \times D_2^l \times \ldots \times D_N^l$, $D_1^l, D_2^l, \ldots, D_N^l$, are the fuzzy sets described by the membership functions $\mu_{D_i^l}(\bar{x}_i)$, $i = 1, \ldots, N$, $l = 1, \ldots, n$, L is the number of the rules and N is the number of the inputs of the Takagi-Sugeno neuro-fuzzy system, $f^{(l)}$ is the function describing values of the system matrix activated by the $R^{(l)}$ fuzzy rule.

Assuming the aggregate method as weighted average, we obtain well known formula described by the Eq. (11).

$$\mathbf{y} = f(\bar{\mathbf{x}}) = \frac{\sum_{l=1}^{L} f^{(l)}(\mathbf{x}) \cdot \mu_{\mathbf{D}^l}(\bar{\mathbf{x}})}{\sum_{l=1}^{L} \mu_{\mathbf{D}^l}(\bar{\mathbf{x}})}. \tag{11}$$

The terminal nodes of the fuzzy decision tree correspond to the fuzzy rules of the Takagi-Sugeno fuzzy system and describe the identified significant operating points.

4   Fuzzy Decision Tree Method for the Detection of the Operating Points

The automatic detection of the operating points in nonlinear modeling is the very hard and time-consuming task. In the most researches the authors focus on solutions using grouping and classification algorithms to initially determine the potential areas that stand for the operating points. Unfortunately, the most part of them require complete data set or its random samples to determine initial areas.

Dziwiński [23,24] has proposed new method of the identification of the significant operating points. He has used single linear or nonlinear model described by the system matrix. The values of the matrix in the operating points were described by the Takagi-Sugeno fuzzy system. He uses the Particle Swarm Optimization supported by the Genetic Algorithm (PSO-GA) to determine the parameters of the system matrix and parameters of the fuzzy rules. The PSO is frequently used by the authors for solving the hard combinatorial problems [1,7,34] as well as genetic algorithms [27]. Real-word modeling problems usually involve a large number of the candidate inputs for the splitting features. In the case of the nonlinear dynamic objects identification, the selection of the important inputs is sometimes difficult due to nonlinearities. Thus, the input selection is a crucial step to obtain the simple model using only inputs, that are important for the detecting the operating points. The methods found in the literature [35,41–43,48] can generally be divided in two groups: model-free methods and model-based methods. Mendonca [35] has used two approaches: top-down and bottom-up. In the top-down approach, he selects the all of the input variables, and removes the one with the worst performance at each stage. In the bottom-up approach, he starts with only one input.

At each stage, he builds the fuzzy model for each of the n considered inputs. Next, he evaluates models using different performance criterion. Finally, he selects the best one. The mentioned approach has the drawback. It requires estimating the $2*N$ fuzzy models at each stage of splitting, so it is very computationally expensive.

In this paper we propose new approach for using the fuzzy decision tree model based method for the detection of the significant operating points. It is done by using the decision tree method at each stage of the operating points identification algorithm [24]. The new approach is presented in the Algorithm 1. We start with only one input and add successively the most relevant one on the each stage of the construction. In the new approach we expand measurement region until the Takagi-Sugeno fuzzy system can model the changes of the system matrix in the same way as in work [24]. It is done by calculating error at the end of the used time interval (12)

$$\epsilon(t_{max}^{(e)}) = (\mathbf{y}'(t_{max}^{(e)}) - \mathbf{y}(t_{max}^{(e)}))^2 \tag{12}$$

where: $\mathbf{y}'(t_{max}^{(e)})$ is the obtained output for the created model in the $t_{max}^{(e)}$ time of the simulation, $\mathbf{y}(t_{max}^{(e)})$ is the measured reference value.

Algorithm 1. Pseudocode of the identification algorithm of the operating points using fuzzy decision tree.

Algorithm Build_Fuzzy_Decision_Tree $(\mathbf{u}(t), \mathbf{x}(t), \mathbf{y}(t), S)$

> **Data:** $\mathbf{u}(t), \mathbf{x}(t), \mathbf{y}(t)$ - measurements, $t = 0, (T_s), T_{max}, T_s$ - time steep, T_{max} - total time of the measurements, S - the set of the available inputs (splitting attributes),
>
> **Result:** FDT - fuzzy decision tree, $\theta_l = \{\mathbf{D}^l, \hat{\mathbf{A}}^l\}$, $\theta_l \in \Theta$, Θ - set of the operating points corresponding to the terminal nodes of the FDT, $l = 1, \ldots, L$, L - number of the detected operating points,
>
> Set initially: $\Theta \in \emptyset$, $L = 0$, $e = 0$, e - the current epoch in the PSO-GA algorithm;
>
> Add the root node to the FDT, for the first operating point:
>
> $L \leftarrow L + 1, \Theta \leftarrow \Theta \cup \theta_L$
>
> Determine the start time for the $t_{max}^{(e)}$:
>
> **while** $\epsilon(t_{max}^{(e)}) < \epsilon_{max}$ **do**
>> $t_{max}^{(e)} \leftarrow t_{max}^{(e)} + T_s$;
>> Determine the $\epsilon(t_{max}^{(e)})$
>
> **repeat**
>> **repeat**
>>> Perform the single iteration of the PSO-GA algorithm for the current set of the operating points Θ encoded in the FDT, $e = e + 1$;
>>>
>>> For the best solution $\Theta \Leftarrow$ PSO-GA$(t_{max}^{(e)}, \mathbf{u}(t), \mathbf{x}(t), \mathbf{y}(t))$ determine the error at the end of the time interval $\epsilon(t_{max}^{(e)})$ (12)
>>>
>>> Extend the time interval according to the error criterion:
>>> **while** $\epsilon(t_{max}^{(e)}) < \epsilon_{min}$ **do**
>>>> $t_{max}^{(e)} \leftarrow t_{max}^{(e)} + T_s$;
>>>> Determine the $\epsilon(t_{max}^{(e)})$
>>>
>>> Determine the value of the $RMSE^{(e)}$ error
>> **until** $t_{max}^{(e)} > t_{max}^{(e-z)} \mid RMSE^{(e)} < RMSE^{(e-z)}$;
>>
>> Choose the best terminal node n_t corresponding to the fuzzy rule $R^{(l)}$ on the basis of the activity at the end of the measurements
>>
>> $\mu_{\mathbf{D}^l}(\bar{\mathbf{m}}(t_{max}^{(e)})) = \arg \max_{i=1,\ldots,L} (\mu_{\mathbf{D}^i}(\bar{\mathbf{m}}(t_{max}^{(e)})))$ (6-9), $\bar{\mathbf{m}}(t_{max}^{(e)})$ is the fuzzy values of the splitting attributes at the end of the measurements;
>>
>> **Select_Best_Candidate_Split**$(FDT, n_t, S, \mathbf{m}(t))$;
>>
>> Update the operating point for the replaced terminal node with split node;
>>
>> Add new operating point θ_L for the new terminal node $(n_t^1$ or $n_t^2)$:
>>
>> $L \leftarrow L + 1, \Theta \leftarrow \Theta \cup \theta_L$;
>
> **until** $t_{max}^{(e)} < T_{max}$ & $RMSE^{(e)} > RMSE_{min}$;

Algorithm 2. The pseudocode of the function for select of the best candidate split

---

Function Select_Best_Candidate_Split (FDT,n_t,**S**,**m**(t))

    Data: FDT - the actual fuzzy decision tree, n_t - the selected terminal node for the split, **S** - the set of the all candidate splits , **m**(t) - available measurements for the set of the splits **S**

    Result: $n_{s_{best}}$ the splitting node,n_t^1,n_t^2 - the new terminal node in the FDT

    Expand the $t_{max}^{(e)}$ on the basis of the ϵ_{max} value:

    $tt_{max} = t_{max}^{(e)}$, $t_{max}^{(e)}$ - time of the measurements used in the epoch e;

    while $\epsilon(tt_{max}) < \epsilon_{max}$ **do**

        $tt_{max} \leftarrow tt_{max} + T_s$;

        Determine the $\epsilon(tt_{max})$

    for *all candidate splits s in* **S** **do**

        Replace the terminal node n_t with the split node n_s and split s;

        Create two terminal nodes n_t^1 and n_t^2 and add to split node n_s;

        if $m_s(t_{max}^{(e)}) < m_s(tt_{max})$ **then**

            Copy the system matrix values from the split node n_s to the terminal nodes n_t^1;

            Estimate the system matrix values for the terminal nodes n_t^2 for the time tt_{max} solving the algebraic equation based on the state variable technique in the discrete form;

        else

            Copy the system matrix values from the split node n_s to the terminal nodes n_t^2;

            Estimate the system matrix values for the terminal nodes n_t^1 for the time tt_{max} solving the algebraic equation based on the state variable technique in the discrete form;

        Evaluate the obtained fuzzy decision tree using the $RMSE$ error measure

    Select and keep the candidate split s_{best}, the split node $n_{s_{best}}$ and the terminal nodes n_t^1,n_t^2 which produces the lowest $RMSE$ error and the best version of the modified fuzzy decision tree FDT

If measured error $RMSE^{(e)}$ does not decrease for the specific number of the epochs (z) or the maximal time of the used measurements t_{max}^e does not increase, then we select the best candidate split using **Select_Best_Candidate_Split** function presented in the Algorithm 2. The presented function replaces the selected best terminal node n_t with the best splitting node $n_{s_{best}}$ and adds two terminal nodes (one contains the copy of the best terminal node). The new terminal node (n_t^1 or n_t^2) corresponds to a new operating point encoded in fuzzy decision tree. The modified FDT is again identified by using PSO-GA algorithm. The algorithm ends when it has used all measurement data and error $RMSE$ reaches the $RMSE_{min}$ value.

5   Experimental Results

Experiments were done for the identification of the nonlinear electrical circuit
with the nonlinear Zener diode [24]. The Fig. 2 presents the reference values
collected for the experimental electrical circuit. The task of the algorithm is the
modeling of the reference values $U_c^{ref}(t)$ using replacement electrical circuit and
on the basis of the value of the error $\epsilon(t) = U_c(t) - U_c^{ref}(t)$. So, the unknown
element of the electrical circuit is only Zener diode which is modeled by using
replacement resistance R_{zd}. As a results of the experiments we obtained three
operating points described by the fuzzy decision tree presented in the Fig. 3. The
fuzzy decision tree contains membership functions shown in the Fig. 4.

$$R^{(1)} : \text{ IF } \bar{x}_1 \text{ is } D_1^1 \text{ and } \bar{x}_1 \text{ is } D_1^3 \text{ THEN } \quad a_{11} = -4.05 \tag{13}$$

$$R^{(2)} : \text{ IF } \bar{x}_1 \text{ is } D_1^1 \text{ and } \bar{x}_1 \text{ is } D_1^4 \text{ THEN } \quad a_{11} = -2.13 \tag{14}$$

$$R^{(3)} : \text{ IF } \bar{x}_1 \text{ is } D_1^2 \text{ THEN } \quad a_{11} = -9.13 \tag{15}$$

$$R^{(1)} : \text{ IF } \bar{x}_1 \text{ is } D_1^3 \text{ THEN } \quad a_{11} = -4.05 \tag{16}$$

The obtained fuzzy rules from the FDT presented in the Fig. 3 are shown in
Eqs. (13–15). The Eq. (13) can be shorten to the form presented in Eq. (16). We
obtain a very small error $\epsilon(t)$ presented in the Fig. 5.

The obtained very small error proves the rightness of the new approach for
using the fuzzy decision trees for detection of the significant operating points

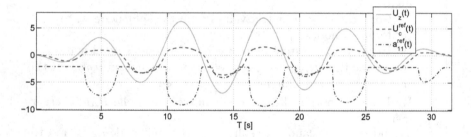

Fig. 2. The reference characteristics of the experimental circuit.

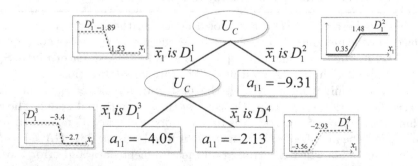

Fig. 3. The fuzzy decision tree obtained from the experiments.

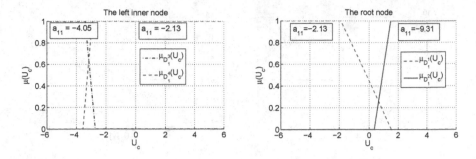

Fig. 4. The obtained membership functions for the identified operating points described by the nodes of the fuzzy decision tree.

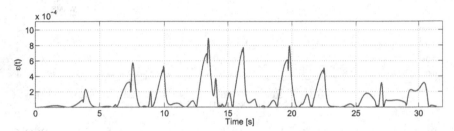

Fig. 5. The error $\epsilon(t)$ for the obtained voltage $U_c(t)$ and reference voltage $U_c^{ref}(t)$ in the function of the time simulation.

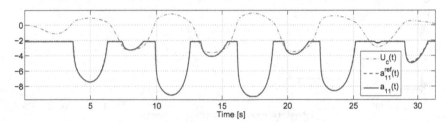

Fig. 6. The reference values $a_{11}^{ref}(t)$ and the obtained values $a_{11}(t)$ of the system matrix for the obtained voltage U_c.

in nonlinear modeling. Moreover, we obtain a very well approximation of the system matrix what is shown in the Fig. 6. Moreover, on the basis of the obtained value of the a_{11}, the characteristic of the Zener diode $i_d = f(U_d)$ is determined and presented in the Fig. 7. The evaluation of the obtained results is done by Weighted Root Mean Square Error measure (WRMSE) [22]. The progress of the new method in the function of the epochs number is illustrated in the Fig. 8. The observed local growth of the obtained errors is associated with extension of the measurement used for the identification of the operating points presented in the Fig. 9.

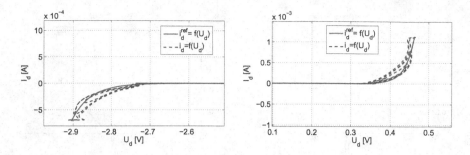

Fig. 7. The reference and the obtained characteristic for the Zener diode.

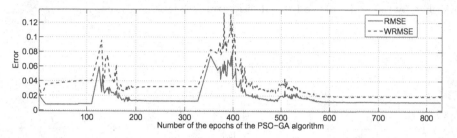

Fig. 8. The obtained errors in the function of the epochs number in the PSO-GA algorithm.

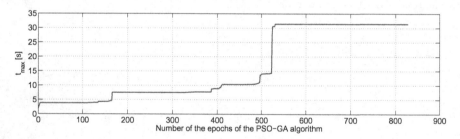

Fig. 9. The measurement time used for the identification of the operating points in the function of the epochs number.

6   Conclusions

The very good results have been obtained in the new approach for using fuzzy decision trees for the significant operating points detection. However additional experiments with more complicate nonlinear object are needed. The nonlinear object in the operating points should contain states which can be determined depending on the different inputs.

Acknowledgment. The project was financed by the National Science Centre (Poland) on the basis of the decision number DEC-2012/05/B/ST7/02138.

References

1. Aghdam, M.H., Heidari, S.: Feature selection using particle swarm optimization in text categorization. J. Artif. Intell. Soft Comput. Res. 5(4), 231–238 (2015)
2. Bartczuk, Ł.: Gene expression programming in correction modelling of nonlinear dynamic objects. In: Borzemski, L., Grzech, A., Świątek, J., Wilimowska, Z. (eds.) ISAT 2015 - Part I. Advances in Intelligent Systems and Computing, vol. 429, pp. 125–134. Springer, Heidelberg (2016)
3. Bartczuk, Ł., Rutkowska, D.: Medical diagnosis with Type-2 fuzzy decision trees. In: Kącki, E., Rudnicki, M., Stempczyńska, J. (eds.) Computers in Medical Activity. AISC, vol. 65, pp. 11–21. Springer, Heidelberg (2009)
4. Bartczuk, Ł., Rutkowska, D.: Type-2 fuzzy decision trees. In: Rutkowski, L., Tadeusiewicz, R., Zadeh, L.A., Zurada, J.M. (eds.) ICAISC 2008. LNCS (LNAI), vol. 5097, pp. 197–206. Springer, Heidelberg (2008)
5. Bartczuk, Ł., Przybył, A., Koprinkova-Hristova, P.: New method for nonlinear fuzzy correction modelling of dynamic objects. In: Rutkowski, L., Korytkowski, M., Scherer, R., Tadeusiewicz, R., Zadeh, L.A., Zurada, J.M. (eds.) ICAISC 2014, Part I. LNCS, vol. 8467, pp. 169–180. Springer, Heidelberg (2014)
6. Bas, E.: The training of multiplicative neuron model based artificial neural networks with differential evolution algorithm for forecasting. J. Artif. Intell. Soft Comput. Res. 6(1), 5–11 (2016)
7. Chen, M., Ludwig, S.A.: Particle swarm optimization based fuzzy clustering approach to identify optimal number of clusters. J. Artif. Intell. Soft Comput. Res. 4(1), 43–56 (2014)
8. Chiu, S.: Fuzzy model identification based on cluster estimation. J. Intell. Fuzzy Syst. 2(3), 267–278 (1994)
9. Cpalka, K.: A method for designing flexible neuro-fuzzy systems. In: Rutkowski, L., Tadeusiewicz, R., Zadeh, L.A., Żurada, J.M. (eds.) ICAISC 2006. LNCS (LNAI), vol. 4029, pp. 212–219. Springer, Heidelberg (2006)
10. Cpałka, K.: On evolutionary designing and learning of flexible neuro-fuzzy structures for nonlinear classification. Nonlinear Anal. Ser. A Theory Methods Appl. 71, 1659–1672 (2009). Elsevier
11. Cpałka, K., Łapa, K., Przybył, A., Zalasiński, M.: A new method for designing neuro-fuzzy systems for nonlinear modelling with interpretability aspects. Neurocomputing 135, 203–217 (2014). Elsevier
12. Cpałka, K., Łapa, K., Przybył, A.: A new approach to design of control systems using genetic programming. Inf. Technol. Control 44(4), 433–442 (2015)
13. Cpałka, K., Rebrova, O., Nowicki, R., Rutkowski, L.: On design of flexible neuro-fuzzy systems for nonlinear modelling. Int. J. Gen. Syst. 42(6), 706–720 (2013)
14. Cpałka, K., Rutkowski, L.: Flexible takagi-sugeno fuzzy systems. In: Proceedings of the International Joint Conference on Neural Networks, Montreal, pp. 1764–1769 (2005)
15. Cpałka, K., Rutkowski, L.: Flexible takagi sugeno neuro-fuzzy structures for nonlinear approximation. WSEAS Trans. Syst. 4(9), 1450–1458 (2005)
16. Cpałka, K., Rutkowski, L.: A new method for designing and reduction of neuro-fuzzy systems. In: Proceedings of the 2006 IEEE International Conference on Fuzzy Systems (IEEE World Congress on Computational Intelligence, WCCI 2006), Vancouver, pp. 8510–8516 (2006)
17. Cpałka, K., Zalasiński, M.: On-line signature verification using vertical signature partitioning. Expert Syst. Appl. 41(9), 4170–4180 (2014)

18. Cpałka, K., Zalasiński, M., Rutkowski, L.: A new algorithm for identity verification based on the analysis of a handwritten dynamic signature. Appl. Soft Comput. (2016, in press). http://dx.doi.org/10.1016/j.asoc.2016.02.017
19. Cpałka, K., Zalasiński, M., Rutkowski, L.: New method for the on-line signature verification based on horizontal partitioning. Pattern Recogn. **47**, 2652–2661 (2014)
20. Duch, W., Korbicz, J., Rutkowski, L., Tadeusiewicz, R. (eds.): Biocybernetics and Biomedical Engineering 2000. Neural Networks, vol. 6, Akademicka Oficyna Wydawnicza, EXIT, Warsaw 2000 (in Polish)
21. Dziwiński, P., Rutkowska, D.: Algorithm for generating fuzzy rules for WWW document classification. In: Rutkowski, L., Tadeusiewicz, R., Zadeh, L.A., Żurada, J.M. (eds.) ICAISC 2006. LNCS (LNAI), vol. 4029, pp. 1111–1119. Springer, Heidelberg (2006)
22. Dziwiński, P., Bartczuk, Ł., Przybył, A., Avedyan, E.D.: A new algorithm for identification of significant operating points using swarm intelligence. In: Rutkowski, L., Korytkowski, M., Scherer, R., Tadeusiewicz, R., Zadeh, L.A., Zurada, J.M. (eds.) ICAISC 2014, Part II. LNCS, vol. 8468, pp. 349–362. Springer, Heidelberg (2014)
23. Dziwiński, P., Avedyan, E.D.: A new approach to nonlinear modeling based on significant operating points detection. In: Rutkowski, L., Korytkowski, M., Scherer, R., Tadeusiewicz, R., Zadeh, L.A., Zurada, J.M. (eds.) ICAISC 2015, Part II. LNCS, vol. 9120, pp. 364–378. Springer, Heidelberg (2015)
24. Dziwiński, P.: A new method of the intelligent modeling of the nonlinear dynamic objects with fuzzy detection of the operating points. In: Rutkowski, L., Korytkowski, M., Scherer, R., Tadeusiewicz, R., Zadeh, L.A., Zurada, J.M. (eds.) ICAISC 2016, Part II. LNAI, vol. 9693, pp. 293–305. Springer, Heidelberg (2016)
25. Eftekhari, M., Zeinalkhani, M.: Extracting interpretable fuzzy models for nonlinear systems using gradient-based continuous ant colony optimization. Fuzzy Inf. Eng. **5**, 255–277 (2013). Springer
26. Eftekhari, M., Deai, B., Katebi, S.D.: Gradient-based ant colony optimization for continuous spaces. Esteghlal J. Eng. **25**, 33–45 (2006)
27. El-Samak, A.F., Ashour, W.: Optimization of traveling salesman problem using affinity propagation clustering and genetic algorithm. J. Artif. Intell. Soft Comput. Res. **5**(4), 239–245 (2015)
28. Gałkowski, T., Rutkowski, L.: Nonparametric recovery of multivariate functions with applications to system identification. Proc. IEEE **73**(5), 942–943 (1985)
29. Juang, C.-F.: A hybrid of genetic algorithm and particle swarm optimization for recurrent network design. IEEE Trans. Syst. Man Cybern. Part B Cybern. **34**(2), 997–1006 (2004)
30. Korytkowski, M., Rutkowski, L., Scherer, R.: From ensemble of fuzzy classifiers to single fuzzy rule base classifier. In: Rutkowski, L., Tadeusiewicz, R., Zadeh, L.A., Zurada, J.M. (eds.) ICAISC 2008. LNCS (LNAI), vol. 5097, pp. 265–272. Springer, Heidelberg (2008)
31. Łapa, K., Cpałka, K., Wang, L.: New method for design of fuzzy systems for nonlinear modelling using different criteria of interpretability. In: Rutkowski, L., Korytkowski, M., Scherer, R., Tadeusiewicz, R., Zadeh, L.A., Zurada, J.M. (eds.) ICAISC 2014, Part I. LNCS, vol. 8467, pp. 217–232. Springer, Heidelberg (2014)
32. Łapa, K., Przybył, A., Cpałka, K.: A new approach to designing interpretable models of dynamic systems. In: Rutkowski, L., Korytkowski, M., Scherer, R., Tadeusiewicz, R., Zadeh, L.A., Zurada, J.M. (eds.) ICAISC 2013, Part II. LNCS, vol. 7895, pp. 523–534. Springer, Heidelberg (2013)

33. Łapa, K., Zalasiński, M., Cpałka, K.: A new method for designing and complexity reduction of neuro-fuzzy systems for nonlinear modelling. In: Rutkowski, L., Korytkowski, M., Scherer, R., Tadeusiewicz, R., Zadeh, L.A., Zurada, J.M. (eds.) ICAISC 2013, Part I. LNAI, vol. 7894, pp. 329–344. Springer, Heidelberg (2013)
34. Ludwig, S.A.: Repulsive self-adaptive acceleration particle swarm optimization approach. J. Artif. Intell. Soft Comput. Res. **4**(3), 189–204 (2014)
35. Mendonca, L.F.: Decision tree search methods in fuzzy modeling and classification. Int. J. Approximate Reasoning **44**, 106–123 (2007)
36. Arain, M.A., Hultmann Ayala, H.V., Ansari, M.A.: Nonlinear system identification using neural network. In: Chowdhry, B.S., Shaikh, F.K., Hussain, D.M.A., Uqaili, M.A. (eds.) IMTIC 2012. CCIS, vol. 281, pp. 122–131. Springer, Heidelberg (2012)
37. Przybył, A., Cpałka, K.: A new method to construct of interpretable models of dynamic systems. In: Rutkowski, L., Korytkowski, M., Scherer, R., Tadeusiewicz, R., Zadeh, L.A., Zurada, J.M. (eds.) ICAISC 2012, Part II. LNAI, vol. 7268, pp. 697–705. Springer, Heidelberg (2012)
38. Rutkowski, L.: Adaptive probabilistic neural networks for pattern classification in time-varying environment. IEEE Trans. Neural Netw. **15**(4), 811–827 (2004)
39. Rutkowski, L., Cpałka, K.: Compromise approach to neuro-fuzzy systems. In: Sincak, P., Vascak, J., Kvasnicka, V., Pospichal, J. (eds.) Intelligent Technologies - Theory and Applications, vol. 76, pp. 85–90. IOS Press, Amsterdam (2002)
40. Rutkowski, L., Cpałka, K.: Flexible structures of neuro-fuzzy systems. In: Sincak, P., Vascak, J. (eds.) Quo Vadis Computational Intelligence. Studies in Fuzziness and Soft Computing, vol. 54, pp. 479–484. Springer, Heidelberg (2000)
41. Rutkowski, L., Jaworski, M., Pietruczuk, L., Duda, P.: Decision trees for mining data streams based on the gaussian approximation. IEEE Trans. Knowl. Data Eng. **26**(1), 108–119 (2014)
42. Rutkowski, L., Jaworski, M., Pietruczuk, L., Duda, P.: The CART decision tree for mining data streams. Inf. Sci. **266**, 1–15 (2014)
43. Rutkowski, L., Pietruczuk, L., Duda, P., Jaworski, M.: Decision trees for mining data streams based on the McDiarmid's bound. IEEE Trans. Knowl. Data Eng. **25**(6), 1272–1279 (2013)
44. Rutkowski, L., Przybył, A., Cpałka, K., Er, M.J.: Online speed profile generation for industrial machine tool based on neuro-fuzzy approach. In: Rutkowski, L., Scherer, R., Tadeusiewicz, R., Zadeh, L.A., Zurada, J.M. (eds.) ICAISC 2010, Part II. LNAI, vol. 6114, pp. 645–650. Springer, Heidelberg (2010)
45. Starczewski, J.T., Bartczuk, Ł., Dziwiński, P., Marvuglia, A.: Learning methods for type-2 FLS based on FCM. In: Rutkowski, L., Scherer, R., Tadeusiewicz, R., Zadeh, L.A., Zurada, J.M. (eds.) ICAISC 2010, Part I. LNAI, vol. 6113, pp. 224–231. Springer, Heidelberg (2010)
46. Starczewski, J., Rutkowski, L.: Interval type 2 neuro-fuzzy systems based on interval consequents. In: Rutkowski, L., Kacprzyk, J. (eds.) Neural Networks and Soft Computing, pp. 570–577. Physica-Verlag, A Springer-Verlag Company, Heidelberg (2003)
47. Starczewski, J.T., Rutkowski, L.: Connectionist structures of type 2 fuzzy inference systems. In: Wyrzykowski, R., Dongarra, J., Paprzycki, M., Waśniewski, J. (eds.) PPAM 2001. LNCS, vol. 2328, pp. 634–642. Springer, Heidelberg (2002)
48. Tambouratzis, T., Souliou, D., Chalikias, M., Gregoriades, A.: Maximising accuracy and efficiency of traffic accident prediction combining information mining with computational intelligence approaches and decision trees. J. Artif. Intell. Soft Comput. Res. **4**(1), 31–42 (2014)

49. Xinghua, L., Jiang, M., Jike, G.: A method research on nonlinear system identification based on neural network. In: Zhu, R., Ma, Y. (eds.) Information Engineering and Applications. Lecture Notes in Electrical Engineering, vol. 154(1), pp. 234–240. Springer, London (2012)
50. Zalasiński, M., Cpałka, K.: Novel algorithm for the on-line signature verification. In: Rutkowski, L., Korytkowski, M., Scherer, R., Tadeusiewicz, R., Zadeh, L.A., Zurada, J.M. (eds.) ICAISC 2012, Part II. LNCS, vol. 7268, pp. 362–367. Springer, Heidelberg (2012)
51. Zalasiński, M., Cpałka, K., Er, M.J.: A new method for the dynamic signature verification based on the stable partitions of the signature. In: Rutkowski, L., Korytkowski, M., Scherer, R., Tadeusiewicz, R., Zadeh, L.A., Zurada, J.M. (eds.) Artificial Intelligence and Soft Computing. LNCS, vol. 9120, pp. 161–174. Springer, Heidelberg (2015)
52. Zalasiński, M., Cpałka, K., Er, M.J.: New method for dynamic signature verification using hybrid partitioning. In: Rutkowski, L., Korytkowski, M., Scherer, R., Tadeusiewicz, R., Zadeh, L.A., Zurada, J.M. (eds.) ICAISC 2014, Part II. LNCS, vol. 8468, pp. 216–230. Springer, Heidelberg (2014)
53. Zalasiński, M., Cpałka, K.: Novel algorithm for the on-line signature verification using selected discretization points groups. In: Rutkowski, L., Korytkowski, M., Scherer, R., Tadeusiewicz, R., Zadeh, L.A., Zurada, J.M. (eds.) ICAISC 2013, Part I. LNAI, vol. 7894, pp. 493–502. Springer, Heidelberg (2013)
54. Zalasiński, M., Cpałka, K., Hayashi, Y.: New fast algorithm for the dynamic signature verification using global features values. In: Rutkowski, L., Korytkowski, M., Scherer, R., Tadeusiewicz, R., Zadeh, L.A., Zurada, J.M. (eds.) Artificial Intelligence and Soft Computing. LNCS, vol. 9120, pp. 175–188. Springer, Heidelberg (2015)
55. Zalasiński, M., Cpałka, K., Hayashi, Y.: New method for dynamic signature verification based on global features. In: Rutkowski, L., Korytkowski, M., Scherer, R., Tadeusiewicz, R., Zadeh, L.A., Zurada, J.M. (eds.) ICAISC 2014, Part II. LNCS, vol. 8468, pp. 231–245. Springer, Heidelberg (2014)
56. Zalasiński, M., Łapa, K., Cpałka, K.: New algorithm for evolutionary selection of the dynamic signature global features. In: Rutkowski, L., Korytkowski, M., Scherer, R., Tadeusiewicz, R., Zadeh, L.A., Zurada, J.M. (eds.) ICAISC 2013, Part II. LNCS, vol. 7895, pp. 113–121. Springer, Heidelberg (2013)

A New Method of the Intelligent Modeling of the Nonlinear Dynamic Objects with Fuzzy Detection of the Operating Points

Piotr Dziwiński[1(✉)] and Eduard D. Avedyan[2]

[1] Institute of Computational Intelligence,
Częstochowa University of Technology, Częstochowa, Poland
piotr.dziwinski@iisi.pcz.pl
[2] Moscow Institute of Physics and Technology, Dolgoprudny, Russia
avedian@mail.ru

Abstract. The paper presents a new method of the intelligent modeling of the nonlinear dynamic objects with online detection of significant operating points from non-invasive measurements of the nonlinear dynamic object. The PSO-GA algorithm is used to identify the unknown values of the system matrix describing the nonlinear dynamic object in the detected operating points. The Takagi-Sugeno fuzzy system determines the values of the system matrix in the detected operating points. The new method was tested on the nonlinear electrical circuit with the three operating points. The obtained results prove efficiency of the new method of the intelligent modeling of the nonlinear dynamic objects with fuzzy detection of the operating points.

Keywords: Nonlinear modeling · Non-invasive identification · Significant operating point · Particle swarm optimization · Genetic algorithm · Electrical circuit · Takagi-Sugeno fuzzy system

1 Introduction

Non-invasive identification of nonlinear dynamic objects relies on discovering of the mathematical model allowing the reproduction of the reference values with a sufficient precision. The reference values are obtained from the non-invasive measurements of the nonlinear dynamic object. The determination of the sufficiently precise mathematical model for object is generally very hard or even impossible. Practically created mathematical models of the nonlinear dynamic objects are the approximate models, they cannot describe all phenomena enough precisely.

A large number of mathematical models which can describe the nonlinear systems on universal way were proposed in the literature, among others, neural networks [6,21,37,39,54] treated as black box models, fuzzy systems [12,31,32, 55], flexible fuzzy systems [18,33,38,58,61], neuro-fuzzy systems [9–11,16,19, 34,49,56,57,59,60], flexible neuro-fuzzy systems [13,18,20,43], interval type 2

© Springer International Publishing Switzerland 2016
L. Rutkowski et al. (Eds.): ICAISC 2016, Part II, LNAI 9693, pp. 293–305, 2016.
DOI: 10.1007/978-3-319-39384-1_25

neuro-fuzzy systems [51,52] Takagi-Sugeno system [14,15,29], flexible Takagi-Sugeno systems [49] and other systems [28].

The methods mentioned earlier enable modeling in an universal way but do not provide enough precision of the reproduction of the reference values. Much better result, can be obtained by using a hybrid approach.

In the hybrid approach approximate linear or nonlinear model can be used. It allows reproduction of the reference values with a sufficient precision only in the certain equilibrium point. Whereas the universal model can determine the values of the parameters of the approximate model in different equilibrium points and between them. This approach ensures obtaining a sufficient precision of the identification in the entire area of the work of the nonlinear dynamic object.

Eftekhari [26] has used substractive clustering algorithm [8,22] to discover potential areas of applying local linear models which were identified subsequently. The structure obtained in this way was learned by using ant colony optimization for continuous space [27]. Starczewski [50] has created the Type-2 fuzzy rules based on FCM for describing clusters. Korytkowski has used boosting fuzzy classifiers [30]. Rutkowski has proposed new method for data stream mining [44]. Dziwiński [23,24] has proposed a new approach for identification of the operating points. He extends the measurement area as long as the identified local linear model can reproduce reference values with a sufficient precision. He uses the Particle Swarm Optimization supported by the Genetic Algorithm (PSO-GA) to determine the parameters of the system matrix and parameters of the fuzzy rules. The PSO is frequently used by the authors for solving the hard combinatorial problems [1,7,36] as well as genetic algorithms [25]. Bartczuk [5] proposed a new method for nonlinear fuzzy correction modeling of dynamic objects. He applied gene expression programming [2].

We describe a new method of the intelligent modeling which is a modification of the approach proposed by Dziwiński [24]. The new proposed method contains the improved way the global model description. It was done by using the Takagi-Sugeno fuzzy system for modeling of the system matrix.

The remainder of this paper is organized as follows. Section 2 describes modeling of nonlinear dynamic object by the algebraic equations and on the basis of the state variable technique. It also describes modeling of the system matrix in the operating points. Section 3 deals with fuzzy modeling of the values of the system matrix in the operating points using the Takagi-Sugeno fuzzy system. The Sect. 4 presents the algorithm of the significant operating point detection including the modification for modeling of the values of the system matrix. The Sect. 5 describes nonlinear electrical circuit and placeholder circuit with the three operating points. Finally, Sect. 6 shows simulation results which prove the effectiveness of the new method of the intelligent modeling.

2   Identification of the Nonlinear Dynamic Object

Let us consider the nonlinear dynamic object described by the algebraic equations and based on the state variable technique [38]

$$\frac{d\mathbf{x}(t)}{dt} = \mathbf{A}(t)\mathbf{x}(t) + \mathbf{B}(t)\mathbf{u}(t), \tag{1}$$

$$\mathbf{y}(t) = \mathbf{C}\mathbf{x(t)}, \tag{2}$$

where $\mathbf{A}(t)$, $\mathbf{B}(t)$ are the system and input matrices respectively, $\mathbf{u}(t)$, $\mathbf{y}(t)$ are the input and output signals respectively, $\mathbf{x}(t)$ is the vector of the state variables. The algebraic equations based on the state variable technique, delivered by the experts, usually cannot describe dynamic nonlinear object enough precisely. There are phenomena that are not described in sufficient detail by experts. Overall accuracy of such a model may be too low for many practical applications. The developed nonlinear model can reproduce the behavior of the nonlinear dynamic object with a sufficient precision only in some equilibrium point called operating point. In this work we propose hybrid approach which increases effectiveness of the modeling of the nonlinear dynamic object. It is done by the identification the system matrix values of the nonlinear model in determined operating points. In the hybrid approach the entire model can be described by algebraic equations and on the basis of the state variable technique, while the system matrix $\hat{\mathbf{A}}(t)$ has different values of the elements in different operating points. The global model is defined as follows:

$$f_g(\mathbf{x}(t), \mathbf{u}(t)) = \hat{\mathbf{A}}(t)\mathbf{x}(t) + \mathbf{B}(t)\mathbf{u}(t). \tag{3}$$

In the global model the values of the system matrix $\hat{\mathbf{A}}(t)$ may depend on input $\mathbf{u}(t)$ or internal state of the object $\mathbf{x}(t)$. Thus, the values of the system matrix $\hat{\mathbf{A}}(t)$ in the individual operating points can be described by specific function $\zeta_{ij}^l(\mathbf{u}(t), \mathbf{x}(t))$ in the following way

$$\hat{a}_{ij}(t) = \sum_{l=1}^{l=L} \zeta_{ij}^l(\mathbf{u}(t), \mathbf{x}(t)) a_{ij}^l(t), \tag{4}$$

where: $\hat{a}_{ij}(t)$ is the resulting value of the element of the system matrix, $a_{ij}^l(t)$ is the value of the system matrix in operating point l, $\zeta_{ij}^l(\mathbf{u}(t), \mathbf{x}(t))$ is the function describing the activation level of the element of the system matrix at the operating point. So, the local linear or nonlinear model is described by using Eq. (5).

$$f_l(\mathbf{x}(t), \mathbf{u}(t)) = \hat{\mathbf{A}}^l(t)\mathbf{x}(t) + \mathbf{B}(t)\mathbf{u}(t). \tag{5}$$

In the proposed approach we select important inputs from the measured values $\mathbf{x}(t)$, $\mathbf{u}(t)$ on the basis of the experts' knowledge. Selected inputs are used for the identification of the operating points and for the activating inputs of the Takagi-Sugeno fuzzy system described in the next chapter. The selection of the inputs can be performed by decision tree methods [3,4,45–47,53].

3   Fuzzy Modeling of the System Matrix in the Significant Operating Points

The change of the system matrix $\hat{\mathbf{A}}(t)$ values that takes place between operating points usually does not occur rapidly, but in a smooth manner which is difficult to describe by using the mathematical model. The values of the system matrix existing in the operating points pass fluently among themselves and overlap. However, for modeling the activity level of the system matrix described by the function $\zeta_{ij}^l(\mathbf{u}(t), \mathbf{x}(t))$, the Takagi-Sugeno neuro-fuzzy system is perfectly suitable.

The construction of the most neuro-fuzzy structures [14] is based on the Mamdani reasoning type described by using t-norm, for example product or minimum. They require defuzzification of the output values, thus they cannot be applied easily for modeling of the system matrix opposed to Takagi-Sugeno neuro-fuzzy system. This system includes dependences between a premise **IF** and a consequent **THEN** of the rule in the form

$$R^{(l)} : \text{ IF } \bar{\mathbf{x}} \text{ is } \mathbf{D}^l \text{ THEN } \mathbf{y}^l = f^{(l)}(\mathbf{x}), \tag{6}$$

where: $\bar{\mathbf{x}} = [\bar{x}_1, \bar{x}_2, \ldots, \bar{x}_N] \in \bar{\mathbf{X}}$, $\mathbf{y}^l \in \mathbf{Y}^l$, $\mathbf{D}^l = D_1^l \times D_2^l \times \ldots \times D_N^l$, $D_1^l, D_2^l, \ldots, D_N^l$, are the fuzzy sets described by the membership functions $\mu_{D_i^l}(\bar{x}_i)$, $i = 1, \ldots, N$, $l = 1, \ldots, n$, L is the number of the rules and N is the number of the inputs of the Takagi-Sugeno neuro-fuzzy system, $f^{(l)}$ is the function described system matrix for the (l) fuzzy rule.

Assuming the aggregate method as weighted average, we obtain well known formula described by the Eq. (7).

$$y = f(\bar{\mathbf{x}}) = \frac{\sum_{l=1}^{L} f^{(l)}(\mathbf{x}) \cdot \mu_{\mathbf{D}^l}(\bar{\mathbf{x}})}{\sum_{l=1}^{L} \mu_{\mathbf{D}^l}(\bar{\mathbf{x}})}. \tag{7}$$

Through replacing the function $f^{(l)}(\mathbf{x})$ by the elements of the system matrix a_{ij}^l we obtain MIMO system described by Eq. (8).

$$\hat{a}_{ij}(t) = \frac{\sum_{l=1}^{L} a_{ij}^l \cdot \mu_{\mathbf{D}_{ij}^l}(\bar{\mathbf{m}}(t-1))}{\sum_{l=1}^{L} \mu_{\mathbf{D}_{ij}^l}(\bar{\mathbf{m}}(t-1))}, \tag{8}$$

where: a_{ij}^l is the value of the system matrix in the l operating point, $\mathbf{m}(t-1) = \{u_i(t-1), x_j(t-1)\}$ are the values of the inputs obtained from non-invasive measurements in the time $(t-1)$, i,j are the indexes selected by the expert as important during the detection of the significant operating points, $\bar{\mathbf{m}}(t)$ are the fuzzy values of the $\mathbf{m}(t)$. So, the local linear or nonlinear model in the operating point l is defined through the set of the parameters $\theta_l = \{\mathbf{D}^l, \hat{\mathbf{A}}^l\}$.

4   Fuzzy Detection of the Operating Points

The automatic detection of the operating points in nonlinear modeling is the very hard and time-consuming task. In the most researches the authors focus on solutions using grouping and classification algorithms to initially determine the potential areas that stand for the operating points. Unfortunately, the most part of them require complete data set or its random samples to determine initial areas.

Algorithm 1. Pseudocode of the identification algorithm of the operating points.

Algorithm IdentifyOperatingPoints $(\mathbf{u}(t), \mathbf{x}(t), \mathbf{y}(t), \mathbf{m}(t))$

Data: $\mathbf{u}(t), \mathbf{x}(t), \mathbf{y}(t), t = 0, (T_s), t_{max}^{(e)}, T_s$ - time steep, T_{max} - total time of the measurements, $\mathbf{m}(t)$ - input measurements important for detecting operating points.

Result: $\theta_l = \{\mathbf{D}^l, \hat{\mathbf{A}}^l\}, \theta_l \in \Theta, l = 1, \ldots, L, L$ - number of the detected operating points.

Set initially: $\Theta \in \emptyset, L = 0, e = 0, e$ - the current epoch in the PSO-GA algorithm;

repeat

    Add new operating point: $L \leftarrow L + 1, \Theta \leftarrow \Theta \cup \theta_L$;

    Determine the initial time for the used time of the measurements $t_{max}^{(e)}$ on the basis of the expert knowledge and the changes in the value of the selected inputs $\mathbf{m}(t)$.

    repeat

        Perform the single epoch of the PSO-GA algorithm for the current set of the operating points Θ, $e = e + 1$;

        For the best solution $\Theta \Leftarrow$ PSO-GA$(t_{max}^{(e)}, \mathbf{u}(t), \mathbf{x}(t), \mathbf{y}(t))$ determine the error at the end of the time interval $\epsilon(t_{max}^{(e)})$ (9)

        Extend the time interval according to the error criterion:

        while $\epsilon(t_{max}^{(e)}) < \epsilon_{min}$ **do**

            $t_{max}^{(e)} \leftarrow t_{max}^{(e)} + T_s$;

            Determine the $\epsilon(t_{max}^{(e)})$

        if $t_{max}^{(e)} > t_{max}^{(e-1)}$ **then**

            Refresh the initial values of the parameters of the fuzzy sets $\mathbf{D}^l$ for the membership function:

$$\mu_{\mathbf{D}^l}(\bar{\mathbf{m}}(t_{max}^{(e)}) = \arg \max_{i=1,\ldots,L} (\mu_{\mathbf{D}^i}(\bar{\mathbf{m}}(t_{max}^{(e)})))$$

        Determine the value of the $RMSE^{(e)}$ error

    until $t_{max}^{(e)} > t_{max}^{(e-z)} \mid RMSE^{(e)} < RMSE^{(e-z)}$;

until $t_{max}^{(e)} < T_{max}$ & $RMSE^{(e)} > RMSE_{min}$;

M. Eftekhtari [26] has used substractive clustering algorithm to discover regions of the measurements which can be potential candidates for operating points. Dziwiński has [24] proposed algorithm for the identification of significant operating points. He expands measurement region until the identified local linear model was able to reproduce reference values. Otherwise he, adds the new operating point. For all operating points he repeats the identification process using

PSO-GA algorithm. He describes the global model using linear combination of the local linear models activated by the fuzzy rules of the Takagi-Sugeno fuzzy model. In the solution mentioned earlier the separate linear model is created for each operating point.

In this paper we propose a new improved method of the identification of the operating points, where we use a single linear or nonlinear model described by the system matrix. The values of the matrix elements are determined by the Takagi-Sugeno fuzzy system. The values of the matrix and the parameters of the membership functions are determined by the PSO-GA algorithm [23] for each operating point. The evaluation of the obtained results is done by Weighted Root Mean Square Error measure (WRMSE) [23]. The identification algorithm of the operating points is presented in the Algorithm (1). In the algorithm we expand the measurement region until the Takagi-Sugeno fuzzy system is able to describe changes of the system matrix. It was done by calculating error at the end of the used time interval (9).

$$\epsilon(t_{max}^{(e)}) = (\mathbf{y}'(t_{max}^{(e)}) - \mathbf{y}(t_{max}^{(e)}))^2 \tag{9}$$

where: $\mathbf{y}'(t_{max}^{(e)})$ is the obtained output for the created model in the time $t_{max}^{(e)}$ of the simulation, $\mathbf{y}(t_{max}^{(e)})$ is the measured reference value. If measured error $RMSE^{(e)}$ does not decrease for the specific number of the epochs (z) or the maximum time t_{max}^e of used measurements does not increase, then we add the new fuzzy rule describing the new operating point. For all operating points (fuzzy rules of the Takagi-Sugeno fuzzy system) we repeat identification process using PSO-GA algorithm.

5   The Nonlinear Model with the Zener Diode

The simulations were performed for the electrical circuit with the nonlinear Zener diode presented in Fig. 1a. Zener diode has three operating points: forward state, reverse state and Zener breakdown state for the breakdown voltage. The approximate linear model with the replacement resistance for the Zener diode

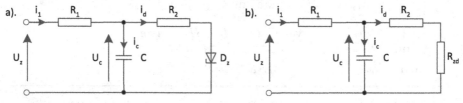

U_z - input voltage, U_c - capacitor voltage, R_1 - input resistance ($4,7\ k\Omega$), R_2 - resistance in branch with the diode (980Ω), C - capacitor ($100\mu F$), D_z - Zener diode with known characteristic, R_{zd} - unknown replacement resistance of the Zener diode.

Fig. 1. The experimental and replacement electrical circuit.

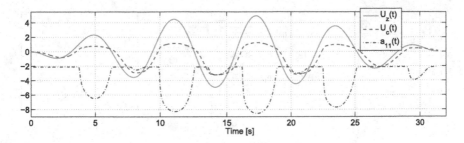

Fig. 2. The reference characteristics of the experimental circuit.

R_{zd} has been designed and is presented in Fig. 1b. In the electrical circuit, the internal state of the model is described by the value of the voltage U_c on the capacitor C. The derived algebraic equation based on the state variable technique in a discrete form is shown in the Eq. (10). The obtained algebraic equation includes the replacement resistance for the branch with the Zener diode R_{zd}.

$$\left[U_c^{k+1} \right] = \left[U_c^k \right] + \left[a_{11} \cdot T_s \right] \left[U_c^k \right] + \left[b_{11} \cdot T_s \right] \left[U_z^k \right], \tag{10}$$

$$a_{11} = \left(\frac{1}{C} \cdot \left(-\frac{1}{R_1} - \frac{1}{R_2 + R_{zd}} \right) \right) \tag{11}$$

$$b_{11} = \frac{1}{C \cdot R_1}, \tag{12}$$

where: U_c^k, U_c^{k+1} are voltages of the capacitor C in the integration steps (k) and $(k+1)$ respectively, U_z^k is the input voltage in the integration step k, T_s is the integration step (5 ms).

The Fig. 2 presents the reference values collected for the experimental electrical circuit. The values a_{11}^k of the system matrix are obtained from the Eq. (13)

$$a_{11}^k = \frac{U_c^k - U_c^{k-1} - b_{11} \cdot U_z^{k-1} \cdot T_s}{U_c^{k-1} \cdot T_s}. \tag{13}$$

The task of the algorithm is the modeling of the reference values $U_c^{ref}(t)$ using replacement electrical circuit and on the basis of the value of the error $\epsilon(t) = U_c(t) - U_c^{ref}(t)$. So, the unknown element of the electrical circuit is only Zener diode which is modeled using replacement resistance R_{zd}. However, Takagi-Sugeno neuro-fuzzy system determines the values of the element a_{11}^k of the system matrix in the identified operating points.

6   Experimental Results

Experiments were done for the identification of the nonlinear electrical circuit with the nonlinear Zener diode presented in Fig. 1a replaced by replacement resistance R_{zd} presented in Fig. 1b. As a result of the experiments we obtained

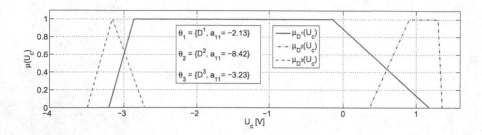

Fig. 3. The obtained membership functions for the identified operating points θ_1, θ_2 and θ_3.

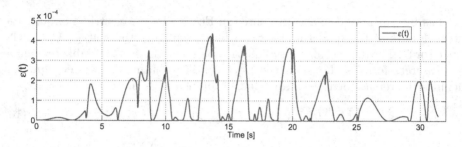

Fig. 4. The error $\epsilon(t)$ for the obtained voltage $U_c(t)$ and reference voltage $U_c^{ref}(t)$ in the function of the time simulation.

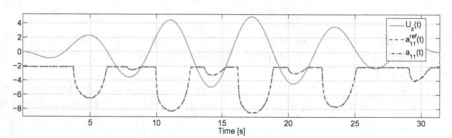

Fig. 5. The reference values $a_{11}^{ref}(t)$ and the obtained values $a_{11}(t)$ of the system matrix for the input voltage $U_z(t)$.

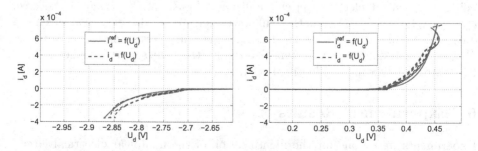

Fig. 6. The reference and the obtained characteristic for the Zener diode.

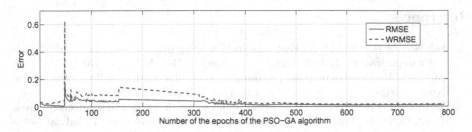

Fig. 7. The obtained errors in the function of the epochs number in the PSO-GA algorithm.

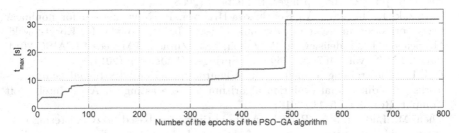

Fig. 8. The measurement time $t_{max}^{(e)}$ used for the identification of the operating points in the function of the epochs number.

three operating points shown in the Fig. 3 with the $\epsilon(t)$ error calculated for the reference data $U_c^{ref}(t)$ presented in the Fig. 4.

The obtained very small error proves the rightness of the new method for the intelligent modeling of the nonlinear dynamic objects with the fuzzy detection of the operating points. Moreover, we obtained very well approximation of the system matrix what is shown in the Fig. 5. On the basis of the obtained values of the a_{11}^k, the characteristic of the Zener diode $i_d = f(U_d)$ was determined and presented in the Fig. 6. The progress of the new method in the function of the epochs number is illustrated in the Fig. 7. The observed local growth of the obtained errors is associated with extension the time $t_{max}^{(e)}$ of the measurements used for the identification of the operating points presented in the Fig. 8.

7   Conclusions

The very good results have been obtained in the new method of the intelligent modeling. However, the important problem of the selection of the important inputs from the data measurements, used for detection of the operating points, remains to solve and can be done by using decision tree methods [3, 4, 45–47, 53].

Acknowledgments. The project was financed by the National Science Centre (Poland) on the basis of the decision number DEC-2012/05/B/ST7/02138.

References

1. Aghdam, M.H., Heidari, S.: Feature selection using particle swarm optimization in text categorization. J. Artif. Intell. Soft Comput. Res. **5**(4), 231–238 (2015)
2. Bartczuk, Ł.: Gene expression programming in correction modelling of nonlinear dynamic objects. Adv. Intell. Syst. Comput. **429**, 125–134 (2016)
3. Bartczuk, Ł., Rutkowska, D.: Medical diagnosis with Type-2 fuzzy decision trees. In: Kącki, E., Rudnicki, M., Stempczyńska, J. (eds.) Computers in Medical Activity. AISC, vol. 65, pp. 11–21. Springer, Heidelberg (2009)
4. Bartczuk, Ł., Rutkowska, D.: Type-2 fuzzy decision trees. In: Rutkowski, L., Tadeusiewicz, R., Zadeh, L.A., Zurada, J.M. (eds.) ICAISC 2008. LNCS (LNAI), vol. 5097, pp. 197–206. Springer, Heidelberg (2008)
5. Bartczuk, Ł., Przybył, A., Koprinkova-Hristova, P.: New method for nonlinear fuzzy correction modelling of dynamic objects. In: Rutkowski, L., Korytkowski, M., Scherer, R., Tadeusiewicz, R., Zadeh, L.A., Zurada, J.M. (eds.) ICAISC 2014, Part I. LNCS, vol. 8467, pp. 169–180. Springer, Heidelberg (2014)
6. Bas, E.: The training of multiplicative neuron model based artificial neural networks with differential evolution algorithm for forecasting. J. Artif. Intell. Soft Comput. Res. **6**(1), 5–11 (2016)
7. Chen, M., Ludwig, S.A.: Particle swarm optimization based fuzzy clustering approach to identify optimal number of clusters. J. Artif. Intell. Soft Comput. Res. **4**(1), 43–56 (2014)
8. Chiu, S.: Fuzzy model identification based on cluster estimation. J. Intell. Fuzzy Syst. **2**(3), 267–278 (1994)
9. Cpalka, K.: A method for designing flexible Neuro-fuzzy systems. In: Rutkowski, L., Tadeusiewicz, R., Zadeh, L.A., Żurada, J.M. (eds.) ICAISC 2006. LNCS (LNAI), vol. 4029, pp. 212–219. Springer, Heidelberg (2006)
10. Cpałka, K.: On evolutionary designing and learning of flexible neuro-fuzzy structures for nonlinear classification. Nonlinear Anal. Ser. A: Theor. Methods Appl. **71**, 1659–1672 (2009). Elsevier
11. Cpałka, K., Łapa, K., Przybył, A., Zalasiński, M.: A new method for designing neuro-fuzzy systems for nonlinear modelling with interpretability aspects. Neurocomputing **135**, 203–217 (2014). Elsevier
12. Cpałka, K., Łapa, K., Przybył, A.: A new approach to design of control systems using genetic programming. Inf. Technol. Control **44**(4), 433–442 (2015)
13. Cpałka, K., Rebrova, O., Nowicki, R., Rutkowski, L.: On design of flexible Neuro-Fuzzy systems for nonlinear modelling. Int. J. Gen. Syst. **42**(6), 706–720 (2013)
14. Cpałka, K., Rutkowski, L.: Flexible Takagi-Sugeno fuzzy systems, Neural Networks. In: Proceedings of the 2005 IEEE International Joint Conference on IJCNN 2005, vol. 3, pp. 1764–1769 (2005)
15. Cpałka, K., Rutkowski, L.: Flexible takagi sugeno neuro-fuzzy structures for nonlinear approximation. WSEAS Trans. Syst. **4**(9), 1450–1458 (2005)
16. Cpałka, K., Rutkowski, L.: A new method for designing and reduction of Neuro-fuzzy systems. In: Proceedings of the 2006 IEEE International Conference on Fuzzy Systems (IEEE World Congress on Computational Intelligence, WCCI 2006), Vancouver, pp. 8510–8516 (2006)
17. Cpałka, K., Łapa, K., Przybył, A., Zalasiński, M.: A new method for designing neuro-fuzzy systems for nonlinear modelling with interpretability aspects. Neurocomputing **135**, 203–217 (2014)

18. Cpałka, K., Zalasiń, S.M.: On-line signature verification using vertical signature partitioning. Expert Syst. Appl. **41**(9), 4170–4180 (2014)
19. Cpałka, K., Zalasiński, M., Rutkowski, L.: A new algorithm for identity verification based on the analysis of a handwritten dynamic signature. Appl. Soft. Comput. **43**, 47–56 (2016). http://dx.doi.org/10.1016/j.asoc.2016.02.017
20. Cpałka, K., Zalasiński, M., Rutkowski, L.: New method for the on-line signature verification based on horizontal partitioning. Pattern Recogn. **47**, 2652–2661 (2014)
21. Duch, W., Korbicz, J., Rutkowski, L., Tadeusiewicz, R. (eds.): Biocybernetics and Biomedical Engineering 2000. Neural Networks, vol. 6, Akademicka Oficyna Wydawnicza, EXIT, Warsaw, (in Polish) (2000)
22. Dziwiński, P., Rutkowska, D.: Algorithm for generating fuzzy rules for WWW document classification. In: Rutkowski, L., Tadeusiewicz, R., Zadeh, L.A., Żurada, J.M. (eds.) ICAISC 2006. LNCS (LNAI), vol. 4029, pp. 1111–1119. Springer, Heidelberg (2006)
23. Dziwiński, P., Bartczuk, Ł., Przybył, A., Avedyan, E.D.: A new algorithm for identification of significant operating points using swarm intelligence. In: Rutkowski, L., Korytkowski, M., Scherer, R., Tadeusiewicz, R., Zadeh, L.A., Zurada, J.M. (eds.) ICAISC 2014, Part II. LNCS, vol. 8468, pp. 349–362. Springer, Heidelberg (2014)
24. Dziwiński, P., Avedyan, E.D.: A new approach to nonlinear modeling based on significant operating points detection. In: Rutkowski, L., Korytkowski, M., Scherer, R., Tadeusiewicz, R., Zadeh, L.A., Zurada, J.M. (eds.) Artificial Intelligence and Soft Computing. LNCS, vol. 9120, pp. 364–378. Springer, Heidelberg (2015)
25. El-Samak, A.F., Ashour, W.: Optimization of traveling salesman problem using affinity propagation clustering and genetic algorithm. J. Artif. Intell. Soft Comput. Res. **5**(4), 239–245 (2015)
26. Eftekhari, M., Zeinalkhani, M.: Extracting interpretable fuzzy models for nonlinear systems using gradient-based continuous ant colony optimization. Fuzzy Inf. Eng. **5**, 255–277 (2013). Springer
27. Eftekhari, M., Deai, B., Katebi, S.D.: Gradient-based ant colony optimization for continuous spaces. Esteghlal J. Eng. **25**, 33–45 (2006)
28. Gałkowski, T., Rutkowski, L.: Nonparametric recovery of multivariate functions with applications to system identification. Proc. IEEE **73**(5), 942–943 (1985)
29. Juang, C.-F.: A hybrid of genetic algorithm and particle swarm optimization for recurrent network design. IEEE Trans. Syst. Man Cybern. Part B Cybern. **34**(2), 997–1006 (2004)
30. Korytkowski, M., Rutkowski, L., Scherer, R.: Fast image classification by boosting fuzzy classifiers. Inf. Sci. **327**, 175–182 (2016)
31. Korytkowski, M., Rutkowski, L., Scherer, R.: From ensemble of fuzzy classifiers to single fuzzy rule base classifier. In: Rutkowski, L., Tadeusiewicz, R., Zadeh, L.A., Zurada, J.M. (eds.) ICAISC 2008. LNCS (LNAI), vol. 5097, pp. 265–272. Springer, Heidelberg (2008)
32. Łapa, K., Cpałka, K., Wang, L.: New method for design of fuzzy systems for nonlinear modelling using different criteria of interpretability. In: Rutkowski, L., Korytkowski, M., Scherer, R., Tadeusiewicz, R., Zadeh, L.A., Zurada, J.M. (eds.) ICAISC 2014, Part I. LNCS, vol. 8467, pp. 217–232. Springer, Heidelberg (2014)
33. Łapa, K., Przybył, A., Cpałka, K.: A new approach to designing interpretable models of dynamic systems. In: Rutkowski, L., Korytkowski, M., Scherer, R., Tadeusiewicz, R., Zadeh, L.A., Zurada, J.M. (eds.) ICAISC 2013, Part II. LNCS, vol. 7895, pp. 523–534. Springer, Heidelberg (2013)

34. Łapa, K., Zalasiński, M., Cpałka, K.: A new method for designing and complexity reduction of Neuro-fuzzy systems for nonlinear modelling. In: Rutkowski, L., Korytkowski, M., Scherer, R., Tadeusiewicz, R., Zadeh, L.A., Zurada, J.M. (eds.) ICAISC 2013, Part I. LNCS, vol. 7894, pp. 329–344. Springer, Heidelberg (2013)
35. Li, X., Er, M.J., Lim, B.S.: Fuzzy regression modeling for tool performance prediction and degradation detection. Int. J. Neural Syst. **20**, 405–419 (2010)
36. Ludwig, S.A.: Repulsive self-adaptive acceleration particle swarm optimization approach. J. Artif. Intell. Soft Comput. Res. **4**(3), 189–204 (2014)
37. Arain, M.A., Hultmann Ayala, H.V., Ansari, M.A.: Nonlinear system identification using neural network. In: Chowdhry, B.S., Shaikh, F.K., Hussain, D.M.A., Uqaili, M.A. (eds.) IMTIC 2012. CCIS, vol. 281, pp. 122–131. Springer, Heidelberg (2012)
38. Przybył, A., Cpałka, K.: A new method to construct of interpretable models of dynamic systems. In: Rutkowski, L., Korytkowski, M., Scherer, R., Tadeusiewicz, R., Zadeh, L.A., Zurada, J.M. (eds.) ICAISC 2012, Part II. LNCS, vol. 7268, pp. 697–705. Springer, Heidelberg (2012)
39. Rutkowski, L.: Adaptive probabilistic neural networks for pattern classification in time-varying environment. IEEE Trans. Neural Networks **15**(4), 811–827 (2004)
40. Rutkowski, L.: A general approach for nonparametric fitting of functions and their derivatives with applications to linear circuits identification. IEEE Trans. Circ. Syst. **33**(8), 812–818 (1986)
41. Rutkowski, L.: Application of multiple Fourier-series to identification of multivariable non-stationary systems. Int. J. Syst. Sci. **20**(10), 1993–2002 (1989)
42. Rutkowski, L., Cpałka, K.: Compromise approach to neuro-fuzzy systems. In: Sincak, P., Vascak, J., Kvasnicka, V., Pospichal, J. (eds.) Intelligent Technologies - Theory and Applications, vol. 76, pp. 85–90. IOS Press, The Netherlands (2002)
43. Rutkowski, L., Cpałka, K.: Flexible structures of neuro-fuzzy systems. Quo Vadis Comput. Intell. Stud. Fuzziness Soft. Comput. **54**, 479–484 (2000). Springer
44. Rutkowski, L., Jaworski, M., Pietruczuk, L., Duda, P.: A new method for data stream mining based on the misclassification error. IEEE Trans. Neural Netw. Learn. Syst. **26**(5), 1048–1059 (2015)
45. Rutkowski, L., Jaworski, M., Pietruczuk, L., Duda, P.: Decision trees for mining data streams based on the gaussian approximation. IEEE Trans. Knowl. Data Eng. **26**(1), 108–119 (2014)
46. Rutkowski, L., Jaworski, M., Pietruczuk, L., Duda, P.: The CART decision tree for mining data streams. Inf. Sci. **266**, 1–15 (2014)
47. Rutkowski, L., Pietruczuk, L., Duda, P., Jaworski, M.: Decision trees for mining data streams based on the McDiarmid's bound. IEEE Trans. Knowl. Data Eng. **25**(6), 1272–1279 (2013)
48. Rutkowski, L., Przybył, A., Cpałka, K.: Novel online speed profile generation for industrial machine tool based on flexible neuro-fuzzy approximation. IEEE Trans. Ind. Electron. **59**(2), 1238–1247 (2012)
49. Rutkowski, L., Przybył, A., Cpałka, K., Er, M.J.: Online speed profile generation for industrial machine tool based on neuro-fuzzy approach. In: Rutkowski, L., Scherer, R., Tadeusiewicz, R., Zadeh, L.A., Zurada, J.M. (eds.) ICAISC 2010, Part II. LNCS, vol. 6114, pp. 645–650. Springer, Heidelberg (2010)
50. Starczewski, J.T., Bartczuk, Ł., Dziwiński, P., Marvuglia, A.: Learning methods for type-2 FLS based on FCM. In: Rutkowski, L., Scherer, R., Tadeusiewicz, R., Zadeh, L.A., Zurada, J.M. (eds.) ICAISC 2010, Part I. LNCS, vol. 6113, pp. 224–231. Springer, Heidelberg (2010)

51. Starczewski, J., Rutkowski, L.: Interval type 2 neuro-fuzzy systems based on interval consequents. In: Rutkowski, L., Kacprzyk, J. (eds.) Neural Networks and Soft Computing, pp. 570–577. Physica-Verlag, A Springer-Verlag Company, Heidelberg (2003)
52. Starczewski, J.T., Rutkowski, L.: Connectionist structures of type 2 fuzzy inference systems. In: Wyrzykowski, R., Dongarra, J., Paprzycki, M., Waśniewski, J. (eds.) PPAM 2001. LNCS, vol. 2328, pp. 634–642. Springer, Heidelberg (2002)
53. Tambouratzis, T., Souliou, D., Chalikias, M., Gregoriades, A.: Maximising accuracy and efficiency of traffic accident prediction combining information mining with computational intelligence approaches and decision trees. J. Artif. Intell. Soft Comput. Res. 4(1), 31–42 (2014)
54. Xinghua, L., Jiang, M., Jike, G.: A method research on nonlinear system identification based on neural network. Information Engineering and Applications. LNEE, vol. 154, pp. 234–240. Springer, London (2012)
55. Zalasiński, M., Cpałka, K.: Novel algorithm for the on-line signature verification. In: Rutkowski, L., Korytkowski, M., Scherer, R., Tadeusiewicz, R., Zadeh, L.A., Zurada, J.M. (eds.) ICAISC 2012, Part II. LNCS, vol. 7268, pp. 362–367. Springer, Heidelberg (2012)
56. Zalasiński, M., Cpałka, K., Er, M.J.: A new method for the dynamic signature verification based on the stable partitions of the signature. In: Rutkowski, L., Korytkowski, M., Scherer, R., Tadeusiewicz, R., Zadeh, L.A., Zurada, J.M. (eds.) Artificial Intelligence and Soft Computing. LNCS, vol. 9120, pp. 161–174. Springer, Heidelberg (2015)
57. Zalasiński, M., Cpałka, K., Er, M.J.: New method for dynamic signature verification using hybrid partitioning. In: Rutkowski, L., Korytkowski, M., Scherer, R., Tadeusiewicz, R., Zadeh, L.A., Zurada, J.M. (eds.) ICAISC 2014, Part II. LNCS, vol. 8468, pp. 216–230. Springer, Heidelberg (2014)
58. Zalasiński, M., Cpałka, K.: Novel algorithm for the on-line signature verification using selected discretization points groups. In: Rutkowski, L., Korytkowski, M., Scherer, R., Tadeusiewicz, R., Zadeh, L.A., Zurada, J.M. (eds.) ICAISC 2013, Part I. LNCS, vol. 7894, pp. 493–502. Springer, Heidelberg (2013)
59. Zalasiński, M., Cpałka, K., Hayashi, Y.: New fast algorithm for the dynamic signature verification using global features values. In: Rutkowski, L., Korytkowski, M., Scherer, R., Tadeusiewicz, R., Zadeh, L.A., Zurada, J.M. (eds.) Artificial Intelligence and Soft Computing. LNCS, vol. 9120, pp. 175–188. Springer, Heidelberg (2015)
60. Zalasiński, M., Cpałka, K., Hayashi, Y.: New method for dynamic signature verification based on global features. In: Rutkowski, L., Korytkowski, M., Scherer, R., Tadeusiewicz, R., Zadeh, L.A., Zurada, J.M. (eds.) ICAISC 2014, Part II. LNCS, vol. 8468, pp. 231–245. Springer, Heidelberg (2014)
61. Zalasiński, M., Łapa, K., Cpałka, K.: New algorithm for evolutionary selection of the dynamic signature global features. In: Rutkowski, L., Korytkowski, M., Scherer, R., Tadeusiewicz, R., Zadeh, L.A., Zurada, J.M. (eds.) ICAISC 2013, Part II. LNCS, vol. 7895, pp. 113–121. Springer, Heidelberg (2013)

Why Systems of Temporal Logic Are Sometimes (Un)useful?

Krystian Jobczyk[1]([⊠]) and Antoni Ligęza[2]

[1] University of Caen, Caen, France
krystian.jobczyk@unicaen.fr
[2] AGH University of Science and Technology, Kraków, Poland
ligeza@agh.edu.pl

Abstract. This paper is aimed at the evaluating of utility of 3 temporal logics: linear temporal logic (LTL) and Halpern-Shoham interval logic from the point of view of the engineering practice. We intend to defend the thesis that chosen systems are only partially capable of satisfying typical requirements of engineers.

Keywords: Linear temporal logic · Halpern-Shoham logic · Engineering evaluation

1 Introduction

Many of rich formal systems are often enigmatic. Their high expressive power is obtained at the cost of their undecidability, incompleteness or losing of other "nice" meta-logical property. The classical example of Peano's Arithmetic of natural number seems to have some analogons in a class of modal-temporal logics such as: *Linear Temporal Logic* (LTL) or its younger competitor – the so-called *Halpern-Shoham logic* (denoted later as HS) – capable of expressing the temporal Allen's interval relations from [1] in a modal way. Although a precise characterization of a capability of temporal systems (especially their expressive power) is a difficult task, it was shown by L. Maximova in [14] that LTL with operator 'next' does not respect the so-called Beth property, what means that not all implicit definitions of this system can be explicitly expressed in its language. It seems to justify that an expressive power of LTL is (at least partially) elusive. Similarly, most of subsystems of the Halpern-Shoham logic share such "nice" meta-logical properties as a decidability of satisfiability problem of PSPACE-completeness of the model-checking problem.

It seems that more practical aspects of dealing with these logic systems are much more elusive and completely non-problematic ones – especially in the light of their (experimentally confirmable) utility in engineering practice and, independently of their theoretical – or even philosophical provenance (see: [19]). Nevertheless, an unlimited belief in a non-restricted practical utility of these systems seems to contrast with many situation of engineering practice, when

© Springer International Publishing Switzerland 2016
L. Rutkowski et al. (Eds.): ICAISC 2016, Part II, LNAI 9693, pp. 306–316, 2016.
DOI: 10.1007/978-3-319-39384-1_26

seemingly simple formula requires a mixed formulas and some portion of fibred semantics, what exceeds possibilities of the considered temporal systems. Furthermore, a success of some practical tasks with respect to temporal logic – such as encoding some piece of information about the robot motion environment in Büchi automata depends on more theoretic results about these systems. For that reason, more practical capabilities of temporal systems must not be more transparent than their purely theoretical features. In particular, it is not clear, which properties of an robot activity and its work space in temporal logic motion planning can be effectively expressed in known temporal systems.

Objectives of the Paper. With respect to it, we intend to propose a kind of retrospective evaluation of these two well-known temporal systems from the point of view of their'engineering' utility. We venture to formulate and defend a thesis that neither LTL nor the Halpern-Shoham logic are capable of expressing (in a complete way) the common engineering requirements imposed on (even typical) robot's activities in problems of motion planning. For that reason, we distinguish a handful of such requirements concerning the system specification, actions of robot and a nature of time. This issue forms a main objective of this paper.

Paper's Motivation and State of Art. The main paper's motivation forms a lack of a broader comparative discussion on a real expressive power of well-known systems of temporal logic from the point of view of engineering requirements. The considerations of the paper stem from the earlier approaches to time representation in the framework of LTL – introduced in [18] by Amir Pnueli (in a point-wise way) – and of the Halpern-Shoham interval temporal logic introduced in [9]. This last type of logic has emerged as a workable alternative approach to more standard point-wise ones and it was broadly discussed in such works as: [7,8,15,16]. However, majority of them elucidates only a variety of meta-logical features of this system and its subsystems. Some practical aspects of temporal problem modeling in terms of some preferential extension of HS-system was discussed in [11].

An optimistic thesis about an utility of LTL in motion planning for mobile robots was expressed in [5,6] and in search control knowledge for planning in [3]. The role of LTL as a support of the discrete events based model was discussed by Antonniotti in [2]. The part of this paper referring to LTL was also presented in [10] and also – as a basis for further fuzzy LTL-extensions – in [12]. A comparative monograph of Emerson [4] gives a broad overlook at the nature of the mutual relationships between modal logic and temporal logic. We are also interested in such temporal systems, which have a natural modal connotation or representation. This fact determined a subject of our analysis: LTL and Halpern- Shoham logic – as (probably) the most representative systems of temporal logic, involved in two different semantics types: the point-wise (LTL) and the interval-based one (HS). For that reason, they could be seen as, somehow, mutually complementary logical systems. For these purposes, we omit well-known Temporal Logic of Action of L. Lamport as a non-modal system, although actions in temporal framework will be a subject of our interest. It also appears that the evaluation of the Lamport's system requires some analysis, which essentially exceeds the thematic scope of this paper. Although HS conceptually stems from the Allen's algebra of interval relations, we omit a description of the last one, since it does not form a logical system in a strict sense.

Paper's Organization. In Sect. 2 we formulate our initial problem in a form of some paradigmatic example pf temporal planning with a robot per- forming tasks in block's world. The main paper's body forms Sect. 3, where we present three systems of temporal logic: LTL and HS and we evaluate their capability of expressing the requirements imposed on the robot's task and its realization. In Sect. 4 we formulate concluding remarks and we give an outline of future research.

2   The Problem Formulation and Its Justification

It has been said that a main paper's objective is to evaluate the ability of cho- sen modal-temporal systems to express the several engineering requirements in examples of temporal planning. In order to realize this goal, we firstly extract a handful of such requirements from a paradigmatic example of the temporal plan- ning with a robot performing the task to relocate the blocks in a given workspace P. Secondly, we check which of the extracted engineering requirements (referring to the robot environments, robot tasks and their temporal requirements) can be captured by *Linear Temporal Logic* and its interval-based competitor, the *Halpern-Shoham logic*.

Problem: We formulate the problem-example that will be addressed in this paper as follows: Consider a robot R that is capable of moving in a square environment with k-rooms $P_1^*, P_2, \ldots, P_k$ and a corridor *Corr* for some natural $k > 3$ with blocks A, B, C located somewhere in rooms $P_1, P_2, \ldots, P_k$. Consider that R performs the task: carry all the blocks and put them together in a corridor in an alphabetic order (firstly A, secondly B, finally C). Consider that the robot's activity has the following temporal constraints:

- Take a block B not earlier than $t_0 > 0$ after putting the block A in a corridor;
- Do not take two blocks in the same time;
- The room searching cannot be automatically finished by the robot;
- Visit the rooms $P_1, P_2, \ldots, P_k$ in any order;
- Since a moment t_A visit the rooms in the order: P_1, P_2, P_3.

It easy to see that our problem seems to be a paradigmatic one for all class of similar problems and can be a convenient basis for further analysis and attempt of a new system construction. In fact, it contains typical commonly considered commands, tasks, actions concerning robot's activity and its admissible environ- ment. Secondly, such a particularity degree corresponds well with a particularity degree of typical engineering requirements imposed on similar systems.

3   Engineering Requirements of the Problem-Situation

The above example allows us to distinguish the following engineering requirements imposed on the environment of the robot activity, its temporal constraints for its activity and the system specification.

System Specification

1. *Sequencing:* Carry the blocks in alphabetical order: A, B, C.
2. *Coverage:* Go to rooms: $P_1, P_2, \ldots, P_k$.
3. *Conditions:* If you find a block A, B or C, take it; otherwise stay where you are.
4. *Conceptualization of the robot's activity:* Point-wise events (block A in P_k etc.) and actions on events as processes in time-intervals (the room searching by a robot R, the carrying of the blocks etc.)
5. *Nature of actions:* Some actions finish in the last action event, but some of them can last further automatically in a future (see: the room searching by a robot).

Temporal Requirements

1. *Temporal sequencing:* Take a block B not earlier than $t_0 > 0$ after putting the block A in a corridor;
   Since the moment t_A firstly visit the room P_1, after that P_2 and finally P_3.
2. *Temporal coverage:* Do not take two blocks in the same time;
3. *Action duration:* The duration time of some actions (like a room searching) can be longer than some time-interval I_1, but shorter than a time-interval I_2.
4. *Nature of time:* The states should be accessible from the'earlier states in a discrete linear time, but potentially – also in a continuous time.

3.1   Linear Temporal Logic (LTL) and Engineering Requirements

In order to evaluate whether LTL is capable of expressing all of the desired engineering requirements, above extracted from the above problem-situation of the robot's activity, we will describe the syntax and semantics of LTL and distinguish the special class of LTL-formulas that could be especially useful for expressing of the above problem-situation.

Syntax. Bi-modal language of LTL is obtained from standard propositional language (with the Boolean constant $\top$) by adding temporal-modal operators such as: *always in a past* (H), *always in a future* (G), *eventually in the past* (P), *eventually in the future* (F), *next and until* ($\mathcal{U}$) and *since* ($\mathcal{S}$) – co-definable with "until". The set FOR of LTL-formulas is given as follows:

$$\phi := \phi|\neg\phi|\phi \vee \psi|\phi\mathcal{U}\psi|\phi\mathcal{S}\psi|H\phi|P\phi|F\phi|Next(\phi) \tag{1}$$

Some of the above operators of temporal-modal types are together co-definable as follows: $F\phi = \top\mathcal{U}$, $P\phi = \top\mathcal{S}\phi$ and classically: $F\phi = \neg G\phi$ and $P\phi = \neg H\phi$.

Semantics. LTL is traditionally interpreted in models based on the point-wise time-flow frames $\mathcal{F} = \langle T, < \rangle$ and dependently on a set of states S. In result, we consider pairs (t, s) (for $t \in T$ representing a time point and $s \in S$) as states of LTL- models. Anyhow, we often consider a function $f : T \mapsto S$ that associates a time-point $t \in T$ with some state $s \in S$ and we deal with pairs (t, f) instead of (t, s). Hence the satisfaction relation $\models$ is defined as follows:

- $(t, f) \models G\phi \iff (\forall t' > t) t' \models \phi$, $(t, f) \models H\phi \iff (\forall t < t') t' \models \phi$.
- $(t, f) \models F\phi \iff (\exists t' > t) t' \models \phi$, $(t, f) \models P\phi \iff (\exists t < t') t' \models \phi$.
- $(t_1, f) \models \phi S\psi \iff$ there is $t_2 < t_1$ such that $t_2, f \models \psi$ and $t, f \models \phi$ for all $t \in (t_1, t_2)$
- $(t_1, f) \models \phi \mathcal{U}\psi \iff$ there is $t_2 > t_1$ such that $t_2, f \models \psi$ and $t, f \models \phi$ for all $t \in (t_1, t_2)$
- $(t_k, f) \models Next(\phi) \iff (t_{k+1}, f) \models \phi, k \in \mathbb{N}$.

Specific Set of Formulas of LTL. Due to the observation from [6], we distinguish a class of special formulas of $\mathcal{L}(LTL)$ of two sorts. The first class $X = \{object--names : \psi_1^c, \psi_2^c, \ldots, P_1, \ldots, P_k, Corr, A, B, C; events : A^{P_1}, B^{P_2}, etc.\}$ will describe the robot's environments and its evolution; the second one $-$ Y $= \{actions : see(), move(), \ldots, go(), take(), a_1, a_2, \ldots etc.\}$ $-$ the robot's 'behavior' and activity.

In accordance with our intentions, object-names will be denoted by concrete objects in a considered situations, the events-names by 'real' events such as that "block" A is located in a room P_1 etc. In a similar way we encode actions as propositions. It not difficult to observe that LTL, enriched as above, is (at least partially) capable of describing the situation of the robot's activity and partially express desired requirements as follows.

System Specification

1. *Sequencing:* Carry the blocks in alphabetical order: A, B, C.
   $F(Go(P_1)) \wedge F(Go(P_2)) \wedge \ldots F(Go(P_k))$.
2. *Coverage:* Go to rooms: $P_1, P_2, \ldots, P_k$.
   $Go(P_1) \wedge Go(P_2) \wedge \ldots Go(P_k)$
3. *Conditions:* If you find a block A, B or C, take it; otherwise stay where you are.
   $(See(A) \to take(A)) \wedge (See(B) \to take(B)) \wedge (See(C) \to take(C))$.

Robot's Environments

1. The blocks A, B, C initially located somewhere in rooms $P_1, \ldots P_k$ but not in a corridor Corr.
   $A^{P_i} \wedge B^{P_j} \wedge C^{P_l} \wedge \neg(A^{Corr} \wedge B^{Corr} \wedge C^{Corr})$
2. The corridor as a final place of the location of blocks A, B, C.

Temporal Requirements

1. Temporal coverage: Do not take two blocks in the same time:
   $\neg G(take(A) \wedge take(B) \wedge take(C))$
2. *Nature of time:* The states should be accessible from the 'earlier' states in a discrete linear time, but potentially– also in a continuous time.

Independently of such a (relative big) expressive power of LTL, we can observe a difficulty with the expressing of such temporal requirements as delays and move of actions in time (after t_o, longer than t_1, but not shorten than t_2 etc.).

3.2   The Plan Construction and LTL

At the end of the paragraph we shall briefly evaluate how the LTL formalism can support plan constructions. We will refer to planning operators classically understood as a sequence of the appropriate actions (expressed in terms of its preconditions and effects). we will focus our attention on the robot's actions that we distinguished in the above engineering requirements. In our case we can approximate a plan construction as follows.

$go(r, P_1, P_2, \ldots P_k)$:
   robot r goes to the room P_1 and-after that – to the adjacent rooms $P_2, \ldots P_k$
   preconditions: • adjacent(P_1, P_2) ... adjacent (P_{k-1}, P_k)
      • blocks are initially located somewhere in rooms $P_1, P_2 \ldots P_k$,
      but not in a corridor $Corr$:
      $A^{P_i} \wedge B^{P_j} \wedge C^{P_l} \wedge \neq (A^{Corr} \wedge B^{Corr} \wedge C^{Corr})$
   effects: $see(r, A^{P_i}) \wedge see(r, B^{P_j}) \wedge see(r, C^{P_l})$ for $i, j, l \in \{1, 2 \ldots k\}$

$take(r, A, Corr)$
   robot r takes a block A from P_i to the corridor $Corr$
   preconditions: • non-empty(P_i), empty(Corr): $A^{P_j}, \neg Corr^A \wedge \neg Corr^B \wedge$
$\neg Corr^C$
   effects: empty(A^{P_i}), non-empty(corridor):
   $\neg A^{P_i}, Corr^A$

$take(r, B, Corr)$
   robot r takes a block B from P_j to the corridor $Corr$
   preconditions: • non-empty(P_i), empty(Corr): $B^{P_j}, \neg Corr^A \wedge \neg Corr^B \wedge$
$\neg Corr^C$
   effects: empty(A^{P_i}), non-empty(corridor):
   $\neg B^{P_i}, Corr^B$

$take(r, C, Corr)$
   robot r takes a block C from P_j to the corridor $Corr$
   preconditions: • non-empty(P_i), empty(Corr): $C^{P_j}, \neg Corr^A \wedge \neg Corr^B \wedge$
$\neg Corr^C$
   effects: empty(A^{P_i}), non-empty(corridor):
   $\neg C^{P_i}, Corr^B$

4 Halpern-Shoham Logic and Its "Engineering" Expressive Power

The Halpern-Shoham logic (denoted later as HS) forms a modal representation of temporal relations between intervals, originally defined by [1]: "after" (or "meets"), ("later"), "begins" (or "start"), ("during"), "end" and "overlap" ; see also [9]. These relations correspond to the modal HS operators: $\langle A \rangle$ for "after", $\langle B \rangle$ for "begins", $\langle L \rangle$ for "later", etc. The syntax of HS entities ϕ is defined by:

$$\phi := p \,|\, \neg\phi \,|\, \phi \wedge \phi \,|\, \langle X \rangle \phi \,|\, \langle \bar{X} \rangle \phi, \tag{2}$$

where p is a propositional variable and $\langle \bar{X} \rangle$ denotes a modal operator for the inverse relation w. r. t. $X \in \{A, B, D, E, O, L\}$ being a set of Allen's relations (Fig. 1).

Generally, the semantics of HS is given in terms of interval models. Denoting by $\mathcal{P}(\mathbb{N})$ the set of all closed intervals $[i, j]$ for $i, j \in \mathbb{N} \le \omega$, the interval HS-model is defined as n-tuple $M = \langle \mathcal{P}(\mathbb{N}), X, V \rangle$, where $X \in \{A, B, D, E, O, L\}$ and $V : \mathcal{P}(N) \mapsto \mathcal{P}(Prop)$ is a valuation for propositional letters $Prop$ of $\mathcal{L}(HS)$.

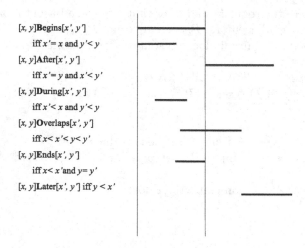

$[x, y]\mathbf{Begins}[x', y']$
  iff $x' = x$ and $y' < y$
$[x, y]\mathbf{After}[x', y']$
  iff $x' = y$ and $x' < y'$
$[x, y]\mathbf{During}[x', y']$
  iff $x' < x$ and $y' < y$
$[x, y]\mathbf{Overlaps}[x', y']$
  iff $x < x' < y < y'$
$[x, y]\mathbf{Ends}[x', y']$
  iff $x < x'$ and $y = y'$
$[x, y]\mathbf{Later}[x', y']$ iff $y < x'$

Fig. 1. The visual presentation of Allen's interval relations

Many different types of interval-based models for HS are known and used in theoretic contexts. We omit a detailed description of their taxonomy, we only mentioned that they are often conceived to be based on generalized Kripke frames, i.e. as a triple: $\langle W, X, Lab \rangle$, where W is a (non-empty) domain, Lab is a usual labeling and $X \in \{A, B, D, E, O, L\}$. If $\phi \in \mathcal{L}(HS)$, M is a (generalized) Kripke frame-based model, and $I \in W$, then the satisfaction for the HS-operators is given as follows:

$$M, I \models \langle X \rangle \phi \iff \exists I' \text{ that} I \, X \, I' \text{ and } M, I' \models \phi. \tag{3}$$

Let us observe that this generally depicted HS-syntax can be naturally specified in order to express that some object occurs somewhere or some events or actions hold somewhere, in a temporal period. It is enough to incorporate a handful of atomic propositions as names of environments objects (rooms-names, blocks-names etc.) and some new basis-propositions: HOLDS(P, i) (property P holds during interval i), OCCURS(E, i) (event E happens over interval i) and $take()$, $go()$, $move()$ to denote the simple robot's actions. In particular, an event that a block A is located in P_1 over interval i can be expressed by OCCURS(A^{P_1}). Such an extended system will be denote as HS*. In such a way, several of our desired engineering requirements can be easily formulated in HS*.

System Specification

1. *Sequencing:* Carry the blocks in alphabetical order: A, B, C.
   $HOLDS(take(A), i) \land HOLDS(take(B), j) \ldots \land HOLDS(take(C), k) \land$
   $starts(i, j) \land starts(j, k)$
2. *Coverage:* Go to rooms: $P_1, P_2, \ldots, P_k$.
   $HOLDS(go(P1)) \land HOLDS(go(P2)) \land HOLDS(go(P3))$
3. *Conditions:* If you find a block A, B or C, take it; otherwise stay where you are.
   $HOLDS(see(A, i)) \rightarrow HOLDS(take(A, j)) \land meets(i; j)$

Robot's Environments

1. The blocks A, B, C initially located somewhere in rooms $P_1, \ldots, P_k$, but not in a corridor Corr.
2. The corridor as a final place of the location of blocks A, B, C.

The lack of direct possibility to express such adjectives as "initially" of "finally" can be avoided by referring the initial activities and robot's actions to some interval i and final actions to some interval j such that i starts j or– equivalently – j finishes i. In this way we introduce, somehow, the chronology in the class of the considered events and actions. Then the conditions 2 and 3 (of robot's environment) can be formally represented as follows:

$$OCCURS(A^{P_1 \lor P_2 \ldots P_k}, i) \land OCCURS(B^{P_1 \lor P_2 \ldots P_k}, i) \land OCCURS(C^{P_1 \lor P_2 \ldots P_k}, i)$$

$$\land \neg OCCURS(A^{Corr}, j) \land OCCURS(B^{Corr}, j) \land OCCURS(C^{Corr}, j)$$

$$\land finishes(j, i).$$

Nevertheless, these examples does not illustrate any proper expressive power of HS-system as a possibility of their presentation in terms of HS-syntax forms a natural consequence of defining this syntax over a relatively "rich" piece of a descriptive logic language. It seems that the proper expressive power of HS could be easier elucidated with respect to such aspects of the robot's activity in its polygonal environment as orientation. Due to observation from [marcinkowski] – a HS-operator D (for "during"-relation) seems to especially promising tool. Unexpectedly, it is not difficult to overcome some insensitivity of this operator to a difference between past and future and lest and right by introducing some additional variables L (for "left"), R (for "right") and $\widehat{s_0}, \widehat{s_1}, \ldots, \widehat{s_k}$ for a representation of the robot's states $s_0 \ldots s_k$ (in its environment and as states of an automaton encoding its "behavior".)

$$[D](\widehat{s_0} \to L) \tag{4}$$

$$\langle D \rangle R \wedge \langle D \rangle L \tag{5}$$

$$[D](L \to \neg R) \tag{6}$$

$$[D](take(A) \to go(Corr)) \wedge \langle D \langle (take(B) \to go(P_1)) \tag{7}$$

A formula (4) asserts that a temporal interval I (associated to a robot's action, say A) that satisfies s_0, satisfies also L. It could have the following spatial interpretation: always a robot's state s_0 is located somewhere "on the left" (of the robot's environment). A formula (5) expresses some more general environment's feature: there is an interval labeled with R and an interval labeled with L, what means that there is a left and a right part of the robot's environment. The last formula (7) asserts – in the temporal interpretation–that there are always temporal intervals (connected with an initial one by a "during"-relation), where if a robot takes a block A, than should go to the corridor $Corr$ or there exists (at least one) such an interval, where it goes to a room P_1 provided that it takes a block B. It follows from semantics of D-operator. Let us investigate it for a first part of (7). In fact, a satisfaction of $[D](take(A) \to go(Corr))$ means for all intervals I' such that I during I' it holds: $I' \models (take(A) \to go(Corr))$. It easy to observe that –if we assume that our robot moves from left to right – the spatial properties of the robot's environment can be translated to a temporal interpretation of the robot's behavior.

It seems that the similar experiments with other HS-operators could be equally promising from the considered perspective. However, there are some crucial restrictions imposed on them. In fact, each logical representation of features of robot's environments and its "behavior" should be later, somehow, operationally exploited, for example in a sense of an encoding by automata. It is known that a D-operator gives such a chance – due to results from [13]. The similar promising results can be expected with operators $A\bar{A}B\bar{B}$ as they are associated to ω-regular languages recognized by Büchi automata –due to [17]. Capability of another operators are not clear and their engineering utility seems to be now slightly doubtful– at least for authors of this paper.

To make the matter worse, it seems that some difficulties with the expressing of temporal requirements such as a linear and discrete nature of time are shared by **HS*** and all its subsystems. It does not change, however, the fact that **HS*** is more 'sensitive' for a distinction between 'possible' and "necessary" as-essentially-a modal system. Furthermore, actions and events cannot be distinguished in this logic type. The explicit way to express them leads via defining a HS-syntax over some fragments of description logic. The above established properties of considered temporal systems LTL and **HS*** are presented in the table below.

Properties	$\mathcal{L}$(LTL)	HS* logic
• Time linearity	Yes	No
• Way of time representation	Point-wise	Intervals
• Nature of time	Discrete, continuous	No
• Distinction between events and actions	Partial	Partial
• Different actions types	No	No
• Possibility to express the processes	Partial	Partial
• Possibility to express the moves and delays in time	No	No
• Representation of events in time	Non-concrete	Non-concrete
• Capability to be operationally exploited (especially in automata)	High	Restricted to some subsystems with such operators as: $D, A, \bar{A}, B, \bar{B}$

5 Conclusions and Future Works

In this paper, we have evaluated two most representative types of temporal modal logic: Linear Temporal Logic and Halpern-Shoham logic. We formulated and defended a thesis that these formalisms only partially satisfy typical engineer's requirements imposed on robot's activity in a block's world. We find this attempt promising for further extensions. The natural direction of the current investigation can be an evaluation of the expressive power of well- known temporal logic of action of L. Lamport − not only from the practical, but also from a theoretical point of view. It seems to be also promising to compare LTL with other powerful systems such as Transparent Intensional Logic (TIL).

Nevertheless, it appears that the most important common shortcoming of all these systems is their non-sensibility for different types of actions, processes and events. For example, these systems are not capable of capturing a difference between actions to events. Moreover, there is sometimes a need of a sharp distinguishing between actions that can last in a future independently of their initiator and its intentions and actions, which do not have such a property. This issue seems to be a promising subject of future research.

References

1. Allen, J.: Maintaining knowledge about temporal intervals. Commun. ACM **26**(11), 832–843 (1983)
2. Antonniotti, M., Mishra, B.: Discrete event models+ temporal logic = supervisory controller: Automatic synthesis of locomotion controllers. In: Proceedings of IEEE International Conference on Robotics and Automation (1999)
3. Bacchus, F., Kabanza, F.: Using temporal logic to express search control knowledge for planning. Artif. Intell. **116**, 123–191 (2000)
4. Emerson, A.: Temporal and modal logic. In: Handbook of Theoretical Computer Science, vol. B, pp. 995–1072 (1990)
5. Fainekos, G., Kress-gazit, H., Pappas, G.: Hybrid controllers for path planning: a temporal logic approach. In: Proceeding of the IEEE International Conference on Decision and Control, Sevilla, pp. 4885–4890, December 2005
6. Fainekos, G., Kress-gazit, H., Pappas, G.: Temporal logic moton planning for mobile robots. In: Proceeding of the IEEE International Conference on Robotics and Automaton, pp. 2032–2037 (2005)
7. Gabbay, D., Kurucz, A., Wolter, F., Zakharyaschev, M.: Many-Dimentional Modal Logics: Theory and Application. Elsevier, Amsterdam (2003)
8. Goronko, V., Montanari, A., Sciavicco, G.: A road map of interval temporal logics and duration calculi. J. Appl. Non-Classical Logics **14**, 9–54 (2004)
9. Halpern, J., Shoham, Y.: A propositional modal logic of time intervals. J. ACM **38**, 935–962 (1991)
10. Jobczyk, K., Ligeza, A.: Systems of temporal logic for a use of engineering. Towards a more practical approach. In: Intelligent Systems for Computer Modelling. Proceedings of the 1st Europe-Middle Asian Conference on Computer Modelling EMACOM, pp. 147–157 (2015)
11. Jobczyk, K., Ligeza, A., Karczmarczuk, J.: Fuzzy temporal approach to the handling of temporal interval relations and preferences. In: Proceedings of INISTA (2015)
12. Jobczyk, K., Ligeza, A., Kluza, K.: Selected temporal logic systems: an attempt at engineering evaluation. In: Rutkowski, L., et al. (eds.) Proceedings of the 15th International Conference, ICAISC 2016, Zakopane, pp. 219–229. Springer, Heidelberg (2016)
13. Marcinkowski, J., Michaliszyn, J.: The last paper on the halpern-shoham interval temporal logic (2010)
14. Maximova, L.: Temporal logics with operator 'the next' do not have interpolation or beth property. Sibirskii Matematicheskii Zhurnal **32**(6), 109–113 (1991)
15. Montanari, A., Pratt-Hartmann, I., Sala, P.: Decidability of the logic of a reflexive sub-interval relations overfinite linear orders. In: Proceeding of TIME
16. Montanari, A., Puppies, G., Sala, P., Sciavicco, G.: Decidability of the interval temporal logic abb on natural numbers. In: Proceeding of 27th Symposium on Theoretical Aspects of Computer Science STACS, Monterey, CA, pp. 597–608 (2010)
17. Montanari, A., Sala, P.: Interval logics and ωB-regular languages. In: Dediu, A.-H., Martín-Vide, C., Truthe, B. (eds.) LATA 2013. LNCS, vol. 7810, pp. 431–443. Springer, Heidelberg (2013)
18. Pnueli, A.: The temporal logic of programs. In: Proceedings of the 18th Annual Symposium on Foundation of Computer Science, pp. 46–57 (1977)
19. van Benthem, J., Bezhanishvili, G.: Modal logic of space. In: Aiello, M., Pratt-Hartmann, I., Van Benthem, J. (eds.) Handbook of Spatial Logics, pp. 217–298. Springer, Netherlands (2007)

New Integral Approach to the Specification of STPU-Solutions

Krystian Jobczyk[1,2]([⊠]), Antoni Ligeza[2], and Krzysztof Kluza[2]

[1] University of Caen, Caen, France
krystian.jobczyk@unicaen.fr
[2] AGH University of Science and Technology, Kraków, Poland
{ligeza,kluza}@agh.edu.pl

Abstract. This paper is aimed at proposing some new formal system of a fuzzy logic – suitable for representation the "before" relation between temporal intervals. This system and an idea of the integral-based approach to the representation of the Allen's relations between temporal intervals is later used for a specification of a class of solutions of the so-called Simple Temporal Problem under Uncertainty and it extends the classical considerations of R. Dechter and L. Khatib in this area.

Keywords: Simple temporal problem under uncertainty · Fuzzy logic · Integral approach · Specification of solutions

1 Introduction

In [2] R. Dechter introduced the so-called *Simple Temporal Problem* as a restriction of the framework of Temporal Constraint Satisfaction Problems, tractable in polynomial time. In order to address the lack of expressiveness in standard STPs, Khatib in [10] proposed some extended version of STP – the so-called *Simple Temporal Problem with Preferences* (STPP). The lack of flexibility in execution of standard STPs was a motivation factor to introduce the so-called *Simple Temporal Problem under Uncertainty* (STPU) in [14]. In order to capture both the possible situations of acting with preferences and under uncertainty, the *Simple Temporal Problem with Preferences under Uncertainty* (STPPU) was described in [13]. Due to – [2] – *The Simple Temporal Problems*(STPs) is a kind of such a Constraints Satisfaction Problem, where a constraint between time-points X_i and X_j is represented in the constraint graph as an edge $X_i \rightarrow X_j$, labeled by a single interval $[a_{ij}, b_{ij}]$ that represents the constraint $a_{ij} \leq X_j - X_i \leq b_{ij}$. Solving an STP means finding an assignment of values to variables such that all temporal constraints are satisfied. Due to [14] – *The Simple Temporal Problem under Uncertainty* extends STP by distinguishing *contingent* events, whose occurrence is controlled by exogenous factors often referred to as "Nature".

Independently of this research path, H-J. Ohlbach proposed in [11] a new integral-based approach to the fuzzy representation of the well-known Allen relations between temporal intervals[1] – initially introduced by J. Allen in [1]. This paper

---

[1] Such as "before", "after", "during".

© Springer International Publishing Switzerland 2016
L. Rutkowski et al. (Eds.): ICAISC 2016, Part II, LNAI 9693, pp. 317–328, 2016.
DOI: 10.1007/978-3-319-39384-1_27

analysis combines both research paths. In fact, we intend to propose a new-integral-based fuzzy logic system – capable of expressing the chosen relation "before" in terms of Ohlbach's integrals – in this paper. The chosen "before" relation was chosen as some operationally "nice" and paradigmatic example among all Allen's relations, which can be modeled in a similar way. This system is conceived as some extension of the Fuzzy Integral Logic of Pavelka-Hajek from [4] – developed in [8] and –for Allen's relations in [9]. This *manouvre* is dictated by the second main paper purpose: to demonstrate how the integral-based approach to the modelling of Allen's relations allows us to differentiate a potential class of STPU-solutions. Although the specification of a class of the STPU-solutions was made by means of some analytic tools, the introduced formalism supports this analysis, it constitutes its foundation and ensures – thanks the completeness theorem – a coherence between a description of STPU-problems in terms of the proposed formalism and the proposed semantics. An algebraic approach to some unique temporal problems such as scheduling with defects was proposed in [3].

1.1   Paper's Motivation and Formulation of an Initial Problem

The main motivation factor of the current analysis is a lack of an approach to the STPU-solving – capable of elucidating of an "evolution" of solutions. In particular, there is no integral-based approach – in spite of integral-based representation of Allen relations between intervals. In addition, it seems that a theoretic, meta-logical establishing of the STPU[2] has not been discussed yet in a specialist literature. Some possibilities of modelling of preferences in fuzzy temporal contexts were, somehow, demonstrated by authors of this paper in [5–7], but without the explicit referring to STP and its extensions. From the more practical point of view this paper analysis are motivated by the following example of the STPU:

Example: *Consider a satellite which performs a task to observe a volcano Etna in some time-interval [0; 80]. The cloudiness can take place in time interval $j(x) = [20; 50]$, but it comes out gradually in this time-interval. When to begin the observation task (beginning from the initial time-point) in order to maximize a chance for finishing the satellite observation in a given time-interval [0; 80]?*

We associate this main problem to the following (sub)problems supporting its solution in terms of the features of "before"-relation.

Problem 1: *Does the Allen relation "before" take a one or many values in the integral-based depiction? If many, show which values from [0,1]-interval can be taken by this relation in their integral-based depiction for linear functions.*

Problem 2: *If the "before"-relation can be evaluated by values from [0,1], decide for which real parameters $C > 0$ this relation takes values no smaller than 0,7?*

---

[2] Establishing as completeness of system describing the STPU w.r.t its models.

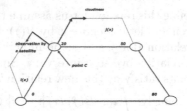

Fig. 1. STPU for observation task of the satellite

2   Terminological Background

The proper analysis will be prefaced by introducing a terminological background regarding concepts of the fuzzy intervals, operations on them and the Ohlbach's representation of Allen's interval relations.

Definition 1 *(Fuzzy Interval). Assume that $f : \mathcal{R} \mapsto [0.1]$ is a total integrable function (not necessary continuous). Than the fuzzy interval i_f (corresponding to a function f) is defined as follows: $i_f = \{(x, y), \subseteq \mathcal{R} \times [0.1] | y \le f(x)\}$.*

A fuzzy set (in a comparison with a crisp one) is illustrated on the picture (Fig. 2):

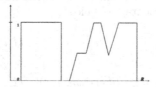

Fig. 2. A crisp and a fuzzy interval

Operations of an intersection and a union of two fuzzy intervals are defined with a use of the appropriate t-norms. Classically: $(i \cap j)(x) =^{def} min\{i(x), j(x)\}$ and $(i \cup j)(x) =^{def} max\{i(x), j(x)\}$.

Some Basic Transformations on Fuzzy Sets. We can associate some additional transformation with fuzzy intervals – presented in details in [11,12]. We restrict their list to the following, especially useful:

$$identity(i) =^{def} \quad i,$$

$$integrate^+(x) =^{def} \int_{-\infty}^{x} i(y)dy/|i|,$$

$$integrate^-(x) =^{def} \int_{x}^{+\infty} i(y)dy/|i|,$$

$$cut_{x_1,x_2}(x) = 0, \text{ if } x < x_1 \text{ or } x_2 \le x; i(x) - \text{ otherwise.}$$

1. Before. In order to define this relation let us assume that some point-interval relation:'p before j' is given and let us denote it by $B(j)$. In order to extend $B(j)$ to the interval-interval relation (for j and some interval i), we should average this point-interval *before*-relation over the interval i. Since fuzzy intervals form subsets of R^2, all these points satisfying this new relation $before(i,j)$ are given by the appropriate integral, namely: $\int i(x)B(j)dx/|i|$. ($|i|$ normalizes this integral to be smaller than 1.)

Infinite Intervals: This general methods should be somehow modified w.r.t the situation when either i or j or both intervals are infinite. If i is $[a,\infty)$-type, than nothing can be after i, thus $before(i,j)$ must yield 0. For a contrast, if j is $(-\infty, a]$-type, than nothing can be before j, what leads to the same value 0.

It remains the case, when i is $(-\infty, a]$-type, but j is finite or of $[a,\infty)$-type. In this case we should find some alternative, because $\int i(x)B(j)dx$ will be infinite. Therefore we take an intersection $i\cap_{min}j$ instead of the whole infinite i. Since j is not of a $(-\infty, a]$-type, the intersection $i\cap_{min}j$ must be finite and the $before(i,j)$ is given by:

$$before(i,j) =^{def} \int (i(x)\cap_{min} B(j))dx/|i(x)\cap_{min} j(x)|.$$

In results, for some point-interval relation $B(j)$ the new interval-interval relation $before(i,j)$ should be represented as below:

$$before(i,j) = \begin{cases} 0 & if\ i = \emptyset\ or\ i = [a,\infty)\ or\ j = \emptyset \\ 1 & if\ \ i = (\infty, a]\ and\ i \cap j = \emptyset \\ \int i(x) \cap_{min} B(j)/|i(x) \cap_{min} j(x)| & if\ i = (\infty, a] - type \\ \int i(x)B(j)/|i(x)| & otherwise \end{cases}$$

In order to solve this problem we will consider two fuzzy intervals $i(x)$ and $j(x)$. For simplicity (but without losing of generality) we can take into account a single Allen relation $before(i,j)(x)$ between them localized w.r.t the y-axis as given on the picture (Fig. 3):

Fig. 3. Fuzzy intervals $i(x)$ and $j(x)$

3   Some Extension of the Fuzzy Integral Logic of Hajek for the Fuzzy Allen Relation "before"

3.1   Requirements of the Construction

We will extend the *Fuzzy Integral Logic* of Hajek from [4] in order to express the interval-interval relation "before". In order to render it in a language of our system we need introduce a new relation symbol, say $B(i,j)$ for atomic terms i, j (denoted by fuzzy intervals). In accordance with the Ohlbach's definition of this relation, one also need introduce the following: a) a symbol, say $B(i)(x)$ to represent the atomic interval-point relation $before(i, x)$ (an interval i is'before' a point x) and b) a constant for normalization factor N. The point-interval relation $B(i)(x)$ etc. will be denoted by a symbol: $\hat{B}_x^i$. Because of the need of a clear distinction between the FLI -syntax and its semantics with Allen's relations – the fuzzy intervals $i(x), j(x)$ will be represented in the FLI -syntax by formulas ϕ_x^i and ϕ_x^j (resp.). In results, we will write: $\int \psi_t^i \hat{B}_t^j dt$ instead of the Ohlbach's formula: $\int i(x) B(j)(x) dx$ etc.

3.2   Syntax and Semantics

Language. For these purposes we introduce our *FLI* in an appropriate language L of Lukasiewicz Propositional Logic (LukPL) with the following connectives and constants: $\rightarrow, \neg, \Longleftrightarrow, \wedge$ (weak conjunction), $\otimes$ (strong conjunction), $\vee$ (weak disjunction), $\oplus$ (strong disjunction) and propositional constants 0 and 1. We extend by new constants: $\hat{r}_1, \hat{r}_2, \hat{r}_3 \ldots$, representing in the language $\mathcal{L}(FLI)$ the rational numbers: $\hat{r}_1, \hat{r}_2, \ldots, s_1, s_2 \ldots$ etc. We enrich this language by $\exists-$ and $\forall-$ quantifiers to the full language of Rational Pavelka Predicate Logic RPL$\forall$. The alphabet of $\mathcal{L}$(FLI) consists of[3]:

- propositional variables: $\phi, \chi, \psi, \ldots, a_i, b_i, \ldots x, y, t \ldots$
- functional symbols: $\phi_t, \phi_{x-t}, \chi_t, \chi_{x-t}, \ldots$
- predicates (of point-interval relations): $\hat{B}_t^i, \hat{D}_t^i, \hat{M}_t^i, \hat{S}_t^i, \hat{F}_t^i \ldots$
- rational constant names: $\hat{r}_1, \hat{r}_2, \ldots \hat{0}, \hat{1}$, scalar constants: $\hat{N}, \widehat{M} \ldots$ etc.
- quantifiers: $\forall, \exists | \int () dx, \int \int () dx dy, \int_0^\infty () dt, \int_{t_0}^{t_1} () dt \ldots$
- operations: $\rightarrow, \neg, \vee, \wedge, \bullet, \oplus, \otimes, = .$

Set of Formulas FOR: The class of well-formed formulas *FOR* of $\mathcal{L}$(FLI) form *propositional variables* and *rational constants* as *atomic* formulas. The next - formulas obtained from given $\phi, \chi \in FOR$ by operations $\neg, \vee, \wedge, \rightarrow, \oplus, \otimes, \forall, \exists, \int () dx$ and the formulas obtained from $\phi_i, \chi_i \in FOR$ by

---

[3] This system is a (slightly modified) system introduced in [8].

operations $\neg, \vee, \wedge, \rightarrow, \oplus, \otimes, \bullet, \forall, \exists, \int_0^\infty ()dt, \int_0^{t_0} ()dt, \int_{t_0}^{t_1} ()dt$. Finally, formulas obtained from $\phi_i \in FOR$ and rational numbers by operations $\neg, \vee, \wedge, \rightarrow, \oplus, \otimes, \bullet$ belong to FOR as well. These classes of formulas exhaust the list of FOR of $\mathcal{L}(\text{FLI})$.

Example: $\int_0^\infty \phi_t \bullet \chi_{x-t} dt \rightarrow \hat{r} \in FOR$, but $\int \phi dx \rightarrow \int_0^\infty \chi_t dt$ does not.

The mentioned system FLI arises in $\mathcal{L}(\text{FLI})$ by assuming the following

Axioms: – partially considered by Hajek in [4]:

$$\int (\neg \phi) dx = \neg \int \phi dx, \quad \int (\phi \rightarrow \chi) dx \rightarrow \left(\int \phi dx \rightarrow \int \chi dx \right)$$

$$\int (\phi \otimes \chi) dx = \left(\left(\int \phi dx \rightarrow \int (\phi \wedge \chi) dx \right) \rightarrow \int \chi dx \right)$$

$$\int \int \phi dx dy = \int \int \phi dy dx^4 \text{ (Fubini theorem)}:$$

and new axioms defining the algebraic properties of convolutions[5]:

$$\int_0^\infty \phi_t \bullet \chi_{x-t} dt = \int_0^\infty \phi_{x-t} \bullet \chi_t dt$$

$$\hat{r} \int_0^\infty \phi_t \bullet \chi_{x-t} dt = \int_0^\infty (\hat{r}\phi_t) \bullet \chi_{x-t} dt, (\text{r}-constant) \text{ (associativity)}[6]$$

$$\int_0^\infty \phi_t \bullet (\chi_{x-t} \oplus \psi_t) dt = \int_0^\infty \phi_t \bullet \chi_{x-t} dt \oplus \int_0^\infty \phi_t \bullet \psi_{x-t} dt \text{ (distributivity)}$$

As inference rules we assume *Modus Ponens*, generalization rule for $\int -symbol$

and two new specific rules: $\dfrac{\phi}{\int \phi dx}, \dfrac{\phi \rightarrow \chi}{\int \phi dx \rightarrow \int \chi dx}$ and the same rules for

indexed formulas and convolution integrals.

Semantics. Our intention is to semantically represent $\int$-formulas of $\mathcal{L}(\text{FLI})$ by 'semantic' integrals. Because all of the considered point-interval relations $D(p, j), M(p, j)$ etc. are functions for the fixed j, than such "semantic" integrals can be defined on a class of the appropriate functions.

More precisely, we will understand such integrals I as a mapping $I : f \in Alg \mapsto If(x) \in [0, 1]$ (where Alg is an algebra of functions from $M \neq \emptyset$ to $[0.1]$ containing each rational function $r \in [0.1]$ and closed on $\Rightarrow$ (see: [4], p. 240))

---

[4] If both sides are defined.

[5] We only present the axioms for convolution in the infinite domain. The axioms in other cases are introduced in the same way.

[6] That is wrt the scalar multiplication.

satisfying the conditions corresponding to the presented axioms of $\mathcal{L}(\text{FLI})$. For example, it holds:

$$I(1 - f)dx = 1 - Ifdx, \ I(f \Rightarrow g)dx \leq (Ifdx \Rightarrow Igdx) \tag{1}$$

$$I(Ifdx)dy = I(Ifdy)dx \tag{2}$$

$$I(f(t)g(x - t)dt = Ig(t)f(x - t)dt \tag{3}$$

$$rIf(t)g(x - t)dt = I(rf(t))g(x - t)dt \tag{4}$$

We omit the whole presentation of these corresponding conditions. They can be found in [8] and partially in [4].

Interpretation. Let assume that $Int = (\triangle, \|\phi\|)$ with $\triangle \neq \emptyset$ and a (classical fuzzy) truth-value interpretation–function: $\|\|$ of formulas of $\mathcal{L}(\text{FLI})$. The propositions of Łukasiewicz logic are interpreted in the sense of $\|\|$ as follows: $\|\neg(\psi)\| = 1 - x$, $\| \rightarrow (\phi, \psi)\| = min\{1, 1 - x + y\}$, $\| \wedge (\phi, \psi)\| = min\{x, y\}$, $\| \wedge (\phi, \psi)\| = max\{x, y\}$, $\| \otimes (\phi, \psi)\| = max\{0, x + y - 1\}$, and $\| \oplus (\phi, \psi)\| = min\{1, x + y\}$ for any $x, y \in$ MV-algebra A^7.

We inductively expand now this interpretation for new elements of the grammar $\mathcal{L}(\text{FLI})$ as below. **Definition of the Model:** We define a *model* M as a

syntax ($\phi \in \mathcal{L}(FLI)$)	fuzzy semantics ($\|\phi\|_{FLI}$)
a_i, b_i	objects A_i, B_i for $i \in \{1, \ldots, k\}$
ϕ_i	functions $f(i)$ for $i \in \{x, t, x - t, t - x\}$
$\int \phi dx, \left(\int_0^\infty \phi dx \right)$	$Ifdx, (I_0^\infty fdx)$
$\phi_i \bullet \chi_i$	$\|\phi_i\| \star \|\chi_i\|$ (i like above)
$\phi \otimes \chi$	$min\{1, \|\phi\| + \|\chi\|\}$
$(\|\phi_i \otimes \chi_i\|)$	$min\{1, \|\phi_i\| + \|\chi_i\|\}$
$\int_0^\infty \phi_t \bullet \chi_{x-t} dt$	$I_0^\infty g(t) \star f(x - t))dt$
$\widehat{r} \int_0^\infty dt$	$\|\widehat{r}\| \star \|I_0^\infty f\|dt = rI_0^\infty fdt$
$\dfrac{\int \phi_t^i \bullet \widehat{B}_{x-t}^j dt}{\widehat{N}}$	$I \dfrac{i(t)B(j)(x-t)\star f(x-t))dt}{N}$

n-tuple of the form: $M = \langle |M|, \{r_0, r_1, ..\}, f_i, If_i dx, I_0^\infty f_i g_j dt \rangle$ where $|M|$ is a countable (or finite) set $\{r_0, r_1, \ldots\}$, f_i are respectively: a set of rational numbers belonging to $|M|$, and atomic integrable functions. If_i are integrals on the algebra Alg of subsets of $|M|$ and $I_0^\infty f_i g_j dt$ are convolutions of f_i and g_j.

---

[7] We omit a detailed definition of MV-algebra as a structure that algebraically interprets a language of a fuzzy logic, it can be easily found in [4].

FLI turns out to be complete w.r.t such a model and undecidable. If a model M is given, we write $\|\phi\|_{M,v}$ for a denotation of the *truth value under evaluation* v for each formula of $\mathcal{L}(FLI)$ as a function: $\mathcal{L}(FLI) \to [0,1]$. If M is a model and v is a valuation, than: $\|\hat{r}\|_{M,v} = r, \|x\|_{M,v} = a \in [0,1]$ for a variable x and for a predicate $Pred(t_1, \ldots, t_k)$ it holds: $\|Pred(t_1, \ldots t_k)\|_{M,v} = Rel(\|t_1\|_{M,v}, \ldots \|t_k\|_{M,v})$ for Rel interpreting $Pred$ in a model M.

Example 1: Consider two intervals $i(x)$ and $j(x)$ such that $i, j \subseteq [a, b]$ and two actions A and B associated with $i(x)$ and $j(x)$ (resp.) Let denote this by $i(x)^A$ and $j(x)^B$ The fact that action A is parallel to B can be represented by an integral-based $during(i(x)^A, j(x)^B)$-relation and interpreted by a model

$$\mathcal{M} = \langle [a, b], i^A, j^B, \int_a^b i^A D(i(x)^A, j(x)^B) dx / |i^A| \rangle.$$

Completeness Theorem for FLI: *For each theory T over predicate $\mathcal{L}$ (FLI) and for each formula $\phi \in \mathcal{L}(FLI)$ it holds: $|\phi|_{FLI} = \|\phi\|_{FLI}$.*

Proof is very similar to the completeness proof for the Hajek's integral logic from [4], so it will be omitted here.

4   Solving of the Problem

In this section we intend to solve the main problem – defined and depicted on a picture in the introductory section with two problems associated to it. Anyhow, we preface this solution by considerations focused on analytic features of $before(i, j)$-relation in terms of integrals. In particular, we present a graph of the function representing this relation provided that the atomic point-interval relation is linear. We decide on this linearity assumption because of a simplicity of the further analysis.

4.1   A Formal Depiction of the Problem and Some Introductory Assumptions

We begin with the formal depiction of the presented problems. For that reason, let us note that the interval-interval definition of Allen's relation $before(i, j)(x)$ is of the type:

$$before(i, j)(x) = \frac{\int i(x)j(x)dx}{max_a \int i(x - a)j(x)dx} \tag{5}$$

According to the above requirement let us consider their unique form for $i(x)$ and $j(x)$ given by linear functions, i.e. $\begin{cases} i(x) = & Ax, A > 0, B < 0, \\ j(x) = & Bx, A < 0, B > 0 \end{cases}$ (see: Fig. 1)

Than:

$$(1) = \frac{AB\int x^2 dx}{AB\int(x-a)x dx} = \frac{\int x^2 dx}{\int(x^2-ax)dx} = \frac{x^3}{3[\frac{x^3}{3}-\frac{ax^2}{2}]} = \frac{x^3}{3[\frac{2x^3-3ax^2}{6}]} = \frac{2x^3}{2x^3-3ax^2}$$

$$(6)$$

for some done $a \in R$.

It remains now to investigate the function $f(x) = \frac{2x^3}{2x^3-3ax^2}$ in order to find its values in the fuzzy interval $[0,1]$.

4.2   Investigation of Properties of the Considered Allen's Before-Relation in the Integrals-Based Representation

In this subsection we check the analytic properties of the function $\frac{2x^3}{2x^3-3ax^2}$ representing the considered Allen's relation $before(i,j)(x)$ for fuzzy intervals $i(x)$ and $j(x)$ given by linear functions.

(a) **Domain of** $f(x)$.
$2x^3 - 3ax^2 \neq 0 \iff x \neq 0$ or $x \neq 3/2a$, so $x \in R/\{0, 3/2a\}$.

(b) **Limits:**
$\lim_{x\to-\infty} \frac{3x^3}{2x^3-3ax^2} = [\frac{-\infty}{-\infty}] = 1$, $\lim_{x\to\infty} \frac{3x^3}{2x^3-3ax^2} = [\frac{\infty}{\infty}] = 1$,
$\lim_{x\to(\frac{3}{2}a)-} \frac{2x^3}{2x^3-3ax^2} = [\frac{2(\frac{3a}{2})^3}{0-}] = -\infty$, $\lim_{x\to(\frac{3}{2}a)+} \frac{2x^3}{2x^3-3ax^2} = [\frac{2(\frac{3a}{2})^3}{0+}] = \infty$.
$\lim_{x\to(\frac{0}{0})-} \frac{2x^3}{2x^3-3ax^2} = [\frac{0}{0-}] = 0$, $\lim_{x\to(\frac{0}{0})+} \frac{2x^3}{2x^3-3ax^2} = [\frac{0}{0+}] = 0$.

It allows us to visualize the graph of the function as follows: Therefore, $0 \leq \frac{2x^3}{2x^3-3ax^2} \leq 1$ for $x \in (-\infty, 0)$ (Fig. 4).

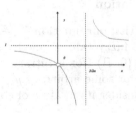

Fig. 4. An outline of the function $\frac{2x^3}{2x^3-3ax^2}$

4.3   Some Modification of the Initial Assumptions

Let us note that the above solution holds by assumption that intervals $i(x)$ and $j(x)$ meets in a point $x = 0$ as on the picture. One needs therefore a function $F(x-B) = \frac{2(x-B)^3}{2(x-B)^3-3a(x-B)^2}$. Its graph stems from the earlier graph of $\frac{2x^3}{2x^3-3ax^2}$ via translation by a vector $(0, B)$. It looks like this: We are now interested in the

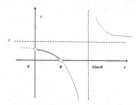

Fig. 5. A diagram of a function $f(x)$ in the required vector translation.

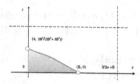

Fig. 6. The fragment of a graph of a function $F(x - B)$, which we are interested in – as a visual representation of our problem solution.

part of this graph between $x_0 = 0$ and $x_1 = $ B. Immediately from the graph one can see that for $x = B$ the function $F(x - B)$ is not defined, but $\lim_{B \to 0} F(x - B) = 0$. On can easily compute that $F(0 - B) = \frac{-2B^3}{-2B^3 - 3B^2a} = \frac{2B^3}{-B^3 + 3B^2a} < 1$. It can be visualized as follows: Therefore, the investigated function takes the values from the interval $I = (0; \frac{2B^3}{2B^3 + 3B^2a})$ (Figs. 5 and 6).

Example: For B $= 1$ we obtain an interval $I_1 = (0, \frac{2}{2+3a})$ for done $a \in R$.

4.4 Further Properties of This Integral-Based Representation of Allen's Before-Relation

At the end we intend to show that our function $\frac{2x^3}{2x^3 - 3ax^2}$ is uniformly continuous. It means that the change the fuzzy values (one for another) is "lazy" and non-radical in the whole interval $(0, B)$ (for arbitrary pairs of x_1 and x_2 from this interval if only $|x_1 - x_2| < \rho$ for some arbitrary $\rho > 0$.)

For this purpose let us consider its module of continuity:

$$|\frac{2x_1^3}{2x_1^3 - 3ax_1^2} - \frac{2x_2^3}{2x_2^3 - 3ax_2^2}| = |\frac{2x_1^3(2x_2^3 - 3ax_2^2) - 2x_2^3(2x_1^3 - 3ax_1^2)}{(2x_1^3 - 3ax_1^2)(2x_2^3 - 3ax_2^2)}| = \quad (7)$$

$$|\frac{-6ax_1^3x_2^2 + 6ax_2^3x_1^3}{(2x_1^3 - 3ax_1^2)(2x_2^3 - 3ax_2^2)}| = |\frac{6ax_1^2x_2^2(x_2 - x_1)}{(2x_1^3 - 3ax_1^2)(2x_2^3 - 3ax_2^2)}| \leq \frac{6a|x_1 - x_2|}{M} = \frac{6a\rho}{M}, \quad (8)$$

where M is the appropriate lower bound of the last denominator. Hence $\forall \epsilon > 0 : |\frac{2x_1^3}{2x_1^3 - 3ax_1^2} - \frac{2x_2^3}{2x_2^3 - 3ax_2^2}| < \epsilon$ if only assume $\rho \leq \frac{M\epsilon}{6a}$, what justifies a desired uniform continuity of our function.

4.5   Solving of the Main Problem

The arrangements, presented above, allow us to solve the main problem with
the observation task of a satellite and the problems associated to it in the introductory part. In order to make it let us recall that:

$$before(i,j) = \frac{\int i(x)Bef(j)(x)dx}{max_a \int i(x-a)Bef(j)(x)dx}, \tag{9}$$

for some point-interval relation $Bef(j)(x)$. Meanwhile, we have just shown that
for linear functions defining the fuzzy intervals this general definition can be
given by:

$$before(i,j) = \frac{2x^3}{2x^3 - 3ax^2} \tag{10}$$

and $0 \le before(i,j)(x) \le 1$ holds for $x \in (0; \frac{2C^3}{2C^3+3C^2a})$. Nevertheless, by our
assumption $C = 20$ (min) we obtain that: $x \in (0; \frac{2\bullet20^3}{2\bullet20^3+3\bullet20^2a}) = (0; \frac{2\bullet8000}{2\bullet8000+1200a})$.
Assuming for simplicity $a = 1$ we can get $x \in (0; \frac{16000}{17200}) = (0; 0,9302)$.
    Therefore, our function takes values from $(0; 0,9302)$.

Problem 2: *For which parameters $C > 0$ the $before(i,j)(x)$ -relation takes values no smaller than 0,7?*

Solution: $0,7 \le \frac{2C^3}{2C^3+3C^2}$. It is equivalent to $0 \le \frac{2C^3}{2C^3+3C^2} - \frac{0,7\bullet(2C^3+2C^2)}{2C^3+3C^2} = \frac{1,3(C^3-2,1C^2)}{2C^3+3C^2}$. Let's consider the equation $\frac{1,3(C^3-2,1C^2)}{2C^3+3C^2} = 0$ (for $C \ne 0$). It leads
to the equation $1,3(C^3 - 2,1C^2 = 0 \iff C^2(1,3C - 2,1) = 0 \iff 1,3C = 2,1 \iff C = \frac{2,1}{1,3}$. Therefore, our inequality holds for $C \in (-\infty; 0) \bigcup(\frac{21}{13}; \infty)$.
Because we are only interested in $C > 0$, so the only solution is given by an
interval $(\frac{21}{13}; \infty)$.

5   Concluding Remarks

It has emerged that the integral-based approach to the Allen temporal relations
allows us to specify the class of STPU-solutions. It also appears that the intuitively graspable point-solutions are preserved as the appropriate ones – as a
board case solution in considered situations. Finally, the construction of a fuzzy
logic system and its completeness ensures that models of STPU (in terms of
before-relation) really refer to the formal descriptions of STPU in the appropriate languages. It seems that the similar procedures can be repeated for other
Allen relations in the integral-based Ohlbach's depiction.
    Anyhow, the considered STPU-problem belongs to the class of relatively ele-
mentary problems. It seems that many similar problems, with a higher compli-
cation degree – such as STPPU-problems – could be investigated in the similar
way. In this perspective, the analysis of the current paper seems to be open.

Acknowledgement. Authors of this paper are grateful to Katarzyna Grobler for some useful remarks and comments.

References

1. Allen, J.: Maintaining knowledge about temporal intervals. Commun. ACM **26**(11), 832–843 (1983)
2. Dechter, R.: Temporal causal networks. Artif. Intell. **49**, 61–95 (1991)
3. Grobler-Debska, A., Kucharska, E., Dudek-Dyduch, E.: Idea of switching algebraic-logical models in flow-shop scheduling problem with defects. In: Methods and Models in Automaton and Robotics (MMAR), pp. 532–537 (2013)
4. Hajek, P.: Metamathematics of Fuzzy Logic. Kluwer Academic Publishers, Dordrecht (1998)
5. Jobczyk, K., Ligeza, A.: Temporal planning in terms of a fuzzy integral logic (fli) versus temporal planning in pddl. In: Proceedings of INISTA, pp. 1–8 (2015)
6. Jobczyk, K., Ligeza, A., Bouzid, M., Karczmarczuk, J.: Comparative approach to the multi-valued logic construction for preferences. In: Rutkowski, L., Korytkowski, M., Scherer, R., Tadeusiewicz, R., Zadeh, L.A., Zurada, J.M. (eds.) Artificial Intelligence and Soft Computing. LNCS, vol. 9119, pp. 172–183. Springer, Heidelberg (2015)
7. Jobczyk, K., Ligeza, A., Karczmarczuk, J.: Fuzzy temporal approach to the handling of temporal interval relations and preferences. In: Proceedings of INISTA (2015)
8. Jobczyk, K., Bouzid, M., Ligeza, A., Karczmarczuk, J.: Fuzzy integral logic expressible by convolutions. In: Proceeding of ECAI 2014, pp. 1042–1043 (2014)
9. Jobczyk, K., Bouzid, M., Ligeza, A., Karczmarczuk, J.: Fuzzy logic for representation of temporal verbs and adverbs 'often' and 'many times'. In: Proceeding of LENSL 2011 Tokyo (2014)
10. Khatib, L., Morris, P., Morris, R., Rossi, F.: Temporal reasoning about preferences. In: Proceedings of IJCAI-01, pp. 322–327 (2001)
11. Ohlbach, H.: Relations between time intervals. In: 11th Internal Symposium on Temporal Representation and Reasoning, vol. 7, pp. 47–50 (2004)
12. Ohlbach, H.-J.: Fuzzy time intervals and relations-the futire library. Research Report PMS-04/04, Inst. f. Informatik, LMU Munich (2004)
13. Rossi, F., Yorke-Smith, N., Venable, K.: Temporal reasoning with preferences and uncertainty. Proc. AAAI **8**, 1385–1386 (2003)
14. Vidal, T., Fargier, H.: Handling contingency in temporal constraints networks: from consistency to controllabilities. J. Exp. Tech. Artif. Intell. **11**(1), 23–45 (1999)

Towards Verification of Dialogue Protocols: A Mathematical Model

Magdalena Kacprzak[1]($\boxtimes$), Anna Sawicka[2], and Andrzej Zbrzezny[3]

[1] Bialystok University of Technology, Bialystok, Poland
m.kacprzak@pb.edu.pl
[2] Polish-Japanese Academy of Information Technology, Warsaw, Poland
asawicka@pja.edu.pl
[3] Jan Długosz University, Czestochowa, Poland
a.zbrzezny@ajd.czest.pl

Abstract. Formal dialogue systems are an important trend in current research on the process of communication. They can be used as the schema of the dialogue conducted between artificial entities or as a simplified form of human dialogue with a machine or a human being with a man. In this work we introduce a mathematical model of dialogue, which is inspired by dialogue games. This model will be used as a semantic structure in verification of properties of dialogue protocols. For this purpose, the semantics of the dialogue games has been translated into interpreted systems that are commonly used in the model checking approach. The newly created model will be applied to develop methods and techniques for automated analysis of dialogues.

Keywords: Formal dialogue system · Protocol · Verification

1 Introduction

Fast progress in modern technology has resulted in the need for dialogues carried out between two machines or a machine and a man. The development of a protocol to be followed during a conversation between the machine and the man is complex and challenging. It requires natural language processing and analysis. However, it appears that in some applications, the dialogue can be executed according to very strict rules. It is then a little trivial, but still retains these elements and features that are necessary for the analysis. As examples of such limited dialogues we can consider dialogue games [4,11,23,25,27]. In this approach, a dialogue is treated as some kind of a game played between two parties. Rules of this game define principles for the exchange of messages between parties in order to meet some assumptions. For example, in Hamblin system [8,14] these rules prevent making argumentative mistakes. In contrast, Lorenzen system [15,17] is intended to validate formulas of some logic [12,28]. Each game should have three basic categories of rules. The first one, called *locution rules*, defines a set of actions (speech acts) the player is allowed to use.

© Springer International Publishing Switzerland 2016
L. Rutkowski et al. (Eds.): ICAISC 2016, Part II, LNAI 9693, pp. 329–339, 2016.
DOI: 10.1007/978-3-319-39384-1_28

These actions express communication intentions of players. The second type of rules defines possible answers to legal moves. For example, if a player claims some sentence T, the opponent can agree with him by performing *concede T* or challenge T by performing *why T*. These rules are called *structural rules*. The third group of rules applies to effects of actions. In dialogue games all actions relate to verbal expression: confirming, rejecting, questioning or arguing them. Therefore, only public declarations (commitments) of players are changed. As a result, a set containing publicly uttered statements is assigned to each player. The result of an action is a change in this set. These rules are called *effect rules*.

The dialogues, which we intend to analyze, are simple argumentation dialogues that human can use to communicate with the software agents. The purpose of these dialogues is to train and support psychologists who work with people with reduced cognitive skills. One of the main tasks of our research is to design a protocol for such communication. This protocol specifies the restrictions and rules which determine what players can say and when. One of the basic assumptions of our approach is that dialogue participants speak the same language. On the one hand, the protocol must meet specific requirements. On the other hand, designed, specified protocol has its own character and we need to verify what properties have a dialogue in accordance with this protocol. For this purpose, we use the method of model checking applied in verification of multi-agent systems (MAS). Main approaches in this field are based on combining bounded model checking (BMC) with symbolic verification using translations to either ordered binary decision diagrams (BDDs) [10] or propositional logic (SAT) [21]. Properties of MAS are expressed in logics which are combinations of the epistemic logic with either branching [24] or linear time temporal logic [9]. These logics are interpreted over interleaved interpreted systems (IIS) [16] or interpreted systems themselves [7]. IIS are systems in which only one action at a time is performed in a global transition. It is the ideal semantics also to interpret the properties of dialogue games.

In this work we introduce a mathematical, general model for dialogue systems. This model refers to the tradition of model checking. Therefore, the first step of the research is to translate locution, structural and effect rules into the concept of interpreted systems. This is not a trivial task, because we need to find a bridge between two different structures. The difficulty of the translation lies in the fact that we should postpone dialogue system rules to notions such as a protocol function, a transition relation, and an evolution function. The initial, much poorer version of this model was described in [13]. In this article, we define among others legal answer function and we formalize all rules of the protocol by means of this new function. We also introduce a concept of numbered and double numbered actions. Subsequently, we will offer new modal language to express properties and adjust the appropriate model checking techniques to verify them. The property, which is within the range of our interests is primarily the reachability, i.e. whether after a concrete dialogue it is possible to achieve a state that satisfies a condition α. For example, if one of the participants can convince his opponent to a statement φ. Another interesting property to verify is whether there is a dialogue compatible with the protocol, after which some condition α is true. Such a condition is determined by the outcome rule and depends on the type of dialogue that is analyzed.

2   General Framework for Argumentation Dialogues

There are many different dialogue systems [4,12,18,20,26]. The general specification for argumentation dialogues, which we use in our research, is described in [22]. In accordance with this specification, dialogues are assumed to be for two parties arguing about a single dialogue *topic* T - the *proponent* P who defends T and the *opponent* O who challenges T. Both are equipped with a set of commitments that are understood as publicly incurred standpoints.

Definition 1. *A* dialogue system *for argumentation is a pair* $(\mathcal{L}, \mathcal{D})$, *where* $\mathcal{L}$ *is a logic for argumentation and* $\mathcal{D}$ *is a dialogue system proper.*

The elements of the above top-level definition are defined as follows.

Definition 2. *A logic for argumentation* $\mathcal{L}$ *is a tuple* $(L_t, R, Args, \rightarrow)$, *where* L_t *is a logical language called the topic language, R is a set of inference rules over L_t, Args is a set of arguments, and $\rightarrow$ is a binary relation of defeat defined on Args.*

Definition 3. *A dialogue system proper is a triple* $\mathcal{D} = (L_c, Pr, C)$ *where L_c is a communication language (the set of locution rules), Pr is a protocol (the set of structural rules) for L_c, and C is a set of effect rules of locutions in L_c.*

The protocol for L_c is defined in terms of the notion of a dialogue, which in turn is defined using the notion of a move. The set M of *moves* is defined as $\mathbb{N} \times \{P, O\} \times L_c \times \mathbb{N}$, where the four elements of a move m are denoted as follows: $id(m)$ - the *identifier* of the move, $pl(m)$ - the *player* of the move, $s(m)$ - the *speech act* (locution) performed in m, and $t(m)$ - the *target* of m. The set of dialogues, denoted by $M^{\leq \infty}$, is the set of all sequences $m_1, \ldots, m_i, \ldots$ from M such that 1) for every i, $id(m_i) = i$ (the identifier of move m_i is i); 2) $t(m_1) = 0$ (the target of move m_1 is assumed to be 0); and 3) for every $i > 1$ $t(m_i) = j$ for some $j < i$ (the target of move m_i is one of the preceding moves). The set of *finite dialogues*, denoted by $M^{< \infty}$, is the set of all finite sequences that satisfy these conditions. When d is a dialogue and m a move, then (d, m) will denote the continuation of d with m.

The key notion for the dialogue system is the protocol. A *protocol* on the set of moves M is a set $Pr \subseteq M^{< \infty}$ satisfying the condition that whenever d is in Pr, all initial sequences beginning with d are also in Pr. A partial function $\overline{Pr} : M^{< \infty} \rightarrow 2^M$ is derived from Pr as follows: $\overline{Pr}(d) =$ undefined whenever $d \notin Pr$; otherwise $\overline{Pr}(d) = \{m : (d, m) \in Pr\}$. The elements of the domain $dom(\overline{Pr})$ are called the *legal finite dialogues*. $\overline{Pr}(d)$ is the set of moves permitted after d. If d is a legal dialogue and $\overline{Pr}(d) = \emptyset$, then d is said to be a *terminated* dialogue.

Every utterance from L_c can influence participants' commitments. The results of utterances are determined by commitment rules, which are specified as a commitment function. A *commitment function* is a function: $C : M^{<\infty} \times \{P, O\} \to 2^{L_t}$, such that $C(\emptyset, i) = \emptyset$ for $i \in \{P, O\}$. $C(d, i)$, for a participant $i \in \{P, O\}$ and a dialogue $d \in M^{<\infty}$, denotes a player i's commitments following the execution of d.

3 Interpreted System for Dialogue Game

In this section we define a new model for argumentation dialogue games as presented in Sect. 2. This model uses the concept of interpreted systems and Kripke structures. In our further research we will interpret in this model formulas of a modal logic adequate to express properties describing the dynamics of dialogue systems and properties that allow prediction of players' behavior. The obtained Kripke structure will be used to perform model checking for dialogue protocols.

The set of players of a dialogue game consists of two players: W and B, $Pl = \{W, B\}$. To each player $p \in Pl$, we assign a set of actions Act_p and a set of possible local states L_p. By $\overline{p}$ we denote the opponent of p.

Every action from Act_p can influence participant's commitments. We assume that the set Act_p contains also the special empty (null) action ε. Players' commitments are elements of topic language and are represented by *commitment sets*. Every action (except null action) is synonymous with locution expressed by specific player. The results of locutions are determined by evolution function and are specified afterwards. As we describe player's local state as a set of commitments, L_p denotes possible commitment sets of player p. Next, Act denotes the Cartesian product of the players actions, i.e. $Act = Act_W \times Act_B$. The global action $a \in Act$ is a pair of actions $a = (a_W, a_B)$, where $a_W \in Act_W$, $a_B \in Act_B$ and at least one of these actions is the empty action. This means that players can not speak at the same time and player cannot reply to his own moves.

Also, we need to order performed global actions and indicate which actions correspond with which ones and therefore we define double-numbered global action set $Num_2Act = \mathbb{N} \times \mathbb{N} \times Act$. During the dialogue, we assign to each performed global action two numbers: the first one (ascending) indicates order (starting from the value 1). The second one points out to which earlier action this action is refering (0 at the begining of the dialogue means that we are not refering to any move). Therefore, we define numbered global action set $Num_1Act = \mathbb{N} \times Act$. The element of this set has additional information about action it refers to. If we want to find out whether we can use some global action one more time, we should check if the possible move containing the same global action refer to the different earlier move. We define function $Denum : Num_2Act \to Num_1Act$, which maps double-numbered global action to the numbered global action. We understand dialogue d as a sequence of moves and in particular we denote $d_{1..n} = d_1, ..., d_n$, where $d_i \in Num_2Act$, $d_i = (i, j, act)$, $j \in \mathbb{N}$, $j < i$, $act \in Act$.

A global state g is a triple consisting of dialogue and players' commitment sets corresponding to a snapshot of the system at a given time

$g = (d(g), C_W(g), C_B(g))$, $g \in G$ where G is the set of global states. Given a global state $g = (d(g), C_W(g), C_B(g))$, we denote by $d(g)$ a sequence of moves executed on a way to state g and by $C_p(g)$ - the commitment set of player p (by $C_{\overline{p}}(g)$ we denote the commitment set of the p's opponent).

An *interpreted system* for a dialogue game is a tuple

$$IS = (I, \{L_p, Act_p\}_{p \in Pl})$$

where $I \subseteq G$ is the set of initial global states. Let $\alpha, \beta, \varphi, \psi_1, \ldots, \psi_n, \gamma_1, \ldots, \gamma_n \in Form(PV)$, i.e., be formulas defined over the set PV which is a set of atomic propositions under which a content of speech acts is specified. Locutions used in players' actions are the same for both players: $Act_W = Act_B = \{\varepsilon, claim\varphi, concede\varphi, why\varphi, \varphi \ since \ \{\psi_1, \ldots, \psi_n\}, retract\varphi, question\varphi\}$.

We define *legal answers function* $F_{LA} : Num_2Act \to 2^{Num_1Act}$, which maps double-numbered action to the set of possible numbered actions. This function is symmetrical for both players.

- $F_{LA}(i, j, (\varepsilon, \varepsilon)) = \emptyset$.
- $F_{LA}(i, j, (claim \ \varphi, \varepsilon)) = \{(i, act) : act \in \{(\varepsilon, why \ \varphi), (\varepsilon, concede \ \varphi), (\varepsilon, claim \ \neg\varphi)\}$,
- $F_{LA}(i, j, (why \ \varphi, \varepsilon)) = \{(i, act) : act \in \{(\varepsilon, \varphi \ since \ \{\psi_1, \ldots, \psi_n\}), (\varepsilon, retract \ \varphi)\}$,
- $F_{LA}(i, j, (\varphi \ since \ \{\psi_1, \ldots, \psi_n\}, \varepsilon)) = \{(i, act) : act \in \{(\varepsilon, why \ \alpha), (\varepsilon, concede \ \beta), (\varepsilon, \neg\varphi \ since \ \{\gamma_1, \ldots, \gamma_n\})\}$, where $\alpha \in \{\psi_1, \ldots, \psi_n\}$ and $\beta \in \{\varphi, \psi_1, \ldots, \psi_n\}$,
- $F_{LA}(i, j, (concede \ \varphi, \varepsilon)) = \{(i, act) : act \in \{(\varepsilon, \varepsilon), (\varepsilon, claim \ \alpha), (\varepsilon, \alpha \ since \ \{\psi_1, \ldots, \psi_n\})\}$, for some $\alpha, \psi_1, \ldots, \psi_n \in Form(PV)$
- $F_{LA}(i, j, (retract \ \varphi, \varepsilon)) = \{(i, act) : act \in \{(\varepsilon, \varepsilon), (\varepsilon, claim \ \alpha), (\varepsilon, \alpha \ since \ \{\psi_1, \ldots, \psi_n\})\}$, for some $\alpha, \psi_1, \ldots, \psi_n \in Form(PV)$
- $F_{LA}(i, j, (question \ \varphi, \varepsilon)) = \{(i, act) : act \in \{(\varepsilon, retract \ \varphi), (\varepsilon, claim \ \varphi), (\varepsilon, claim \ \neg\varphi)\}$,

The actions executed by players are selected according to a *protocol function* $Pr : G \to 2^{Num_2Act}$, which maps a global state g to the set of possible double-numbered global actions. The function Pr satisfies the following rules.

(R1) For $\iota \in I$ $Pr(\iota) = \{(1, 0, (claim \ \varphi, \ \varepsilon)), (1, 0, (question \ \varphi, \varepsilon)), (1, 0, (\varphi \ since \ \{\psi_1, \ldots, \psi_n\}, \varepsilon))\}$
(R2) $Pr((d_{1..k-1}, (k, l, (\varepsilon, \varepsilon)), C_W(g), C_B(g))) = \{(k + 1, numact) : numact \in F_{LA}(k, l, (\varepsilon, \varepsilon))$
(R3) $Pr((d_{1..k-1}, (k, l, (claim \ \varphi, \varepsilon)), C_W(g), C_B(g))) = \{(k + 1, numact) : numact \in F_{LA}(k, l, (claim \ \varphi, \varepsilon))\}$
(R4) $Pr((d_{1..k-1}, (k, l, (why \ \varphi, \varepsilon)), C_W(g), C_B(g))) = \{(k + 1, numact) : numact \in F_{LA}(k, l, (why \ \varphi, \varepsilon))\}$
(R5) $Pr((d_{1..k-1}, (k, l, (\varphi \ since \ \{\psi_1, \ldots, \psi_n\}, \varepsilon)), C_W(g), C_B(g))) = \{(k + 1, numact) : numact \in F_{LA}(k, l, (\varphi \ since \ \{\psi_1, \ldots, \psi_n\}, \varepsilon))\}$

(R6) $Pr((d_{1..k-1}, (k, l, (concede\ \varphi, \varepsilon)), C_W(g), C_B(g))) = \{(k+1, numact) :$
$numact \in ((\bigcup_{i<=k} FLA(d_i) \cap \{(n, (\varepsilon, \alpha)) : n < k, \alpha \in Act_B\})$
$\backslash \{Denum(d_i) : i = 1, .., k\})\}$

After opponent's locution *concede* the player can use one from possible answers for all previous opponent's moves, excluding these ones which he has already used.

(R7) $Pr((d_{1..k-1}, (k, l, (retract\ \varphi, \varepsilon)), C_W(g), C_B(g))) = \{(k+1, numact) :$
$numact \in ((\bigcup_{i<=k} FLA(d_i) \cap \{(n, (\varepsilon, \alpha)) : n < k, \alpha \in Act_B\})$
$\backslash \{Denum(d_i) : i = 1, .., k\})\} \cup \{(k+1, x, (\varepsilon, why\ \beta)) : \exists_{x<k}\ d_x = (x, y, (\beta$
$since\ \varphi, \varepsilon))\}$ for some $\varphi, \beta \in Form(PV)$

Again, after opponent's locution *retract*φ the player can use one from possible answers for all previous opponent's moves, excluding these ones which he has already used but also he can ask for reason for β if φ was previously used to justify β.

These rules for player B are analogous.

Locution *claim* can start a dialogue or can be introduced during the dialogue, but only if it can lead to the conflict resolution and termination of discussion. Such a *claim* should refer to previous actions in the dialogue and do not start a completely new topic, which has no connection with previous ones. Therefore *claim* cannot be introduced after locutions, which demand immediate answer (locutions *why* and *since*). Also, after player's *claim* α, the opponent can utter (among others) the only possible subsequent *claim* – *claim* $\neg\alpha$ because the answer to the first locution should reveal opponent's attitude to player's statement.

To avoid infinite dialogues, at the beginning of the game we limit the number of possible introduced atomic sentences and the number of uttered locutions *claim*. In our system, we consider only finite dialogues, that is why we need the above rules preventing infinite ones. Similar rules are constructed e.g. for locution *since*, which can also start a new thread of the discussion.

Finally, we define *global (partial) evolution function* $t : G \times Num_2Act \rightarrow G$, which determines results of actions. This function is symmetrical for both players. Let $d(g) = d(g)_{1,...,m}$, then:

- $t(g, (m+1, j, (claim\ \varphi, \varepsilon))) = g'$ iff $\varphi \notin C_W(g) \wedge C_W(g') = C_W(g) \cup \{\varphi\}$ $\wedge\ d(g') = (d(g)_{1,...,m}, (m+1, j, (claim\ \varphi, \varepsilon)))$,
- $t(g, (m+1, j, (concede\ \varphi, \varepsilon))) = g'$ iff $\varphi \in C_B(g) \wedge C_W(g') = C_W(g) \cup \{\varphi\}$ $\wedge\ d(g') = (d(g)_{1,...,m}, (m+1, j, (concede\ \varphi, \varepsilon)))$,
- $t(g, (m+1, j, (why\ \varphi, \varepsilon))) = g'$ iff $C_W(g') = C_W(g) \wedge d(g') = (d(g)_{1,...,m}, (m+1, j, (why\ \varphi, \varepsilon)))$,
- $t(g, (m+1, j, (\varphi\ since\ \{\psi_1, \ldots, \psi_n\}, \varepsilon))) = g'$ iff $C_W(g') = C_W(g) \cup \{\varphi, \psi_1, .., \psi_n\} \wedge d(g') = (d(g)_{1,...,m}, (m+1, j, (\varphi\ since\ \{\psi_1, \ldots, \psi_n\}, \varepsilon)))$,
- $t(g, (m+1, j, (retract\ \varphi, \varepsilon))) = g'$ iff $C_W(g') = C_W(g) \backslash \{\varphi\} \wedge d(g') = (d(g)_{1,...,m}, (m+1, j, (retract\ \varphi, \varepsilon)))$,

– $t(g, (m + 1, j, (question \ \varphi, \varepsilon))) = g'$ iff $C_W(g') = C_W(g) \wedge d(g') = (d(g)_{1,...,m}, (m + 1, j, (question \ \varphi, \varepsilon)))$.

4   Example of Formal Dialogue

The following example shows the dialogue, which is compatible with the protocol as described in the previous section. This dialogue is between two persons Alice and Bob:

[1] A: Taxes should not be raised.
[2] B: I rather think that they should be raised.
[3] A: Why do you think they should be raised?
[4] B: I think so because state needs more money for health care and education and that is the only way to get them.
[5] A: Why do you think that is the only way to get them?
[6] B: Probably you are right, that is not the only way.
[7] A: So why do you think taxes should be raised?
[8] B: It seems that maybe they should not.
[9] A: I think they shouldn't be raised because tax increase would kill economic growth and higher taxes mean jobs loss.
[10] B: You convinced me, they should not be raised.

We introduce some abbreviations to construct the game based on the above dialogue: α – "taxes should be raised", β – "state needs more money for health care and education", θ – "raising taxes is the only way to get money", δ – "tax increase would kill economic growth", λ – "higher taxes mean jobs loss".

Corresponding dialogue looks then as follows:

A: $(1, 0, (claim \ \neg\alpha, \ \varepsilon))$
B: $(2, 1, (\varepsilon, claim \ \alpha))$
A: $(3, 2, (why \ \alpha, \ \varepsilon))$
B: $(4, 3, (\varepsilon, \alpha \ since \ \{\beta,\theta\}))$
A: $(5, 4, (why \ \theta, \ \varepsilon))$
B: $(6, 5, (\varepsilon, retract \ \theta))$
A: $(7, 4, (why \ \alpha \ , \ \varepsilon))$
B: $(8, 7, (\varepsilon, retract \ \alpha))$
A: $(9, 4, (\neg\alpha \ since \ \{\delta, \lambda\}, \ \varepsilon))$
B: $(10, 9, (\varepsilon, concede \ \neg\alpha \ ))$

Alice starts a dialogue by stating that taxes should not be raised (move 1) and Bob claims the opposite (that they should) in the next move. When asked for justification (move 3), he gives two premises (move 4). Alice asks for reasons for the second premise (move 5), but because Tom hasn't got anything to support his claim, he retracts from this premise in move 6. Because the justification for rising taxes presented in move 4 is not valid any more, Alice ask one more time for tax increase justification (move 7). It is noteworthy that this move does not refer to the immediately preceding move (like all previous moves), but contains reference to the move 4, where the first justification for tax increase took place. Move 7 can be executed according to the rule (**R7**). In this rule we are excluding from possible moves set these ones, which have been already executed. Even though the global action $(why \ \alpha, \ \varepsilon)$ used in move 7 was already used in move 3, these two are different numbered global actions, because they refer to the different earlier moves. Apparently, Bob has no more arguments for his standpoint that raising taxes is a good idea and he retracts from it in move 8. Then, according to rules (**R7**) and (**R5**), Alice in move 9 can reply also to one of previous moves of Bob, and she decides to reply directly to move 4 and justify the opposite thesis (that we should not raise taxes) by giving two premises. (We could also interpret this reply as a reference to move 8.) Bob accepts these arguments and concedes that taxes should not be raised (move 10), what was originally proposed by Alice.

5 Notes on Verification of Dialogue Protocols

Mathematical model for argumentative dialogue games presented in Sect. 3 provides a basis for applying the methods of model checking to verify the correctness of dialogue protocols relative to the properties that the protocols should satisfy. Model checking [1,5,6,19] is an automatic verifying technique for concurrent systems such as: digital systems, distributed systems, real time systems, multiagent systems, communication protocols, cryptographic protocols, concurrent programs, dialogue systems, and many others. To be able to check automatically whether the system satisfies a given property, one must first create a *model* of the system, and then describe in a formal language both the created model and the property.

Therefore, we associate with the given interpreted system a *Kripke structure*, that is the basis for the application of model checking. A Kripke structure is defined as a tuple

$$M = (G, Act, T, I, AP, V)$$

consisting of a set of global states G, a set of actions Act (in our approach Num_2Act), a set of initial states $I \subseteq G$, a transition relation $T \subseteq G \times Act \times G$ such that T is left-total, a set of atomic propositions AP, and a valuation function $V : G \to 2^{AP}$ that assigns to each state a set of atomic propositions that are assumed to be true at that state.

To formulate properties of dialogue protocols suitable propositional temporal logics are applied. The most commonly used are: linear temporal logic (LTL), computation temporal logic (CTL), a full branching time logic (CTL*), the universal and existential fragments of these logics, and other logics which are their modifications and extensions. One of the most important practical problems in the model checking is the exponential growth of number of states of the Kripke structure. That is why, in future work we intend to focus on symbolic model checking of dialogue protocols. Symbolic model checking avoids building a state graph; instead, sets and relations are represented by Boolean formulae. One of the possible methods of symbolic model checking is bounded model checking (BMC) [2,3]. It uses a reduction of the problem of truth of a temporal formula in a Kripke structure to the problem of satisfiability of formulae of the classical propositional calculus. The reduction is achieved by a translation of the transition relation and a translation of a given property to formulae of classical propositional calculus.

The standard BMC algorithm, starting with $k = 0$, creates for a given Kripke structure M and a given formula φ, a propositional formula $[M, \varphi]_k$. Then the formula $[M, \varphi]_k$ is converted to a satisfiability equivalent propositional formula in conjunctive normal form and forwarded to a SAT-solver. If the tested formula is unsatisfiable, then k is increased (usually by 1) and the process is repeated. The BMC algorithm terminates if either the formula $[M, \varphi]_k$ turns out to be satisfiable for some k, or k becomes greater than a certain, M-dependent, threshold (e.g. the number of states of M). Exceeding this threshold means that the formula φ is not true in the Kripke structure M. On the other hand, satisfiability of $[M, \varphi]_k$, for some k means that the formula φ is true in M.

6 Conclusions

Dialogue is the primary means of interpersonal communication. Structured dialogue represents a class of dialogue practices developed as a means of orienting the dialogic discourse toward problem understanding and consensual action. It can be used as a practice in e.g. education or business. In our research we analyze dialogues and communication processes. We decided to build on the tradition of formal dialogue systems to propose a concise model of a dialogue game. Natural dialogue may be simplified so as to keep only the essential elements. A simplified dialogue can be successfully used for scientific, educational and illustrative purposes. Its realization requires the elaboration of a protocol. A protocol is in simple terms a set of rules that guide the conversation and a powerful tool to help facilitate the structuring of conversation. Its form closely depends on what type of dialogue we want to carry out: persuasive, negotiating, argumentation, etc. For example, the aim of the dialogue may be to move towards consensus on difficult (disputed) issues. That is why there is a need to identify which protocol is best for a concrete application, what you can specify examining its properties. The aim of our research is dialogue protocol verification with the use of model checking. The first step was to establish a mathematical model, which will be a semantic structure for describing the properties of these protocols. Further work will focus on the development of adequate methods of verification.

Acknowledgments. Kacprzak's contribution was supported by the Bialystok University of Technology grant S/W/1/2014.

References

1. Baier, C., Katoen, J.-P.: Principles of Model Checking. MIT Press, Cambridge (2008)
2. Biere, A., Cimatti, A., Clarke, E., Fujita, M., Zhu., Y.: Symbolic model checking using SAT procedures instead of BDDs. In: Proceedings of the ACM/IEEE Design Automation Conference (DAC 1999), pp. 317–320 (1999)
3. Biere, A., Cimatti, A., Clarke, E.M., Strichman, O., Zhu, Y.: Bounded model checking. Adv. Comput. **58**, 117–148 (2003)
4. Budzynska, K., Kacprzak, M., Sawicka, A., Yaskorska, O.: Dialogue Dynamics: Formal Approach, IFS PAS (2015)
5. Clarke, E.M., Emerson, E.A., Sistla, A.P.: Automatic verification of finite state concurrent systems using temporal logic specifications: a practical approach. In: Conference Record of the Tenth Annual ACM Symposium on Principles of Programming Languages, Austin, pp. 117–126. ACM Press (1983)
6. Clarke, E.M., Grumberg, O., Peled, D.: Model Checking. MIT Press, Cambridge (2001)
7. Fagin, R., Halpern, J.Y., Moses, Y., Vardi, M.: Reasoning About Knowledge. MIT Press, Cambridge (1995)
8. Hamblin, C.: Fallacies. Methuen, London (1970)
9. van der Hoek, W., Wooldridge, M.J.: Model checking knowledge and time. In: Bošnački, D., Leue, S. (eds.) SPIN 2002. LNCS, vol. 2318, pp. 95–111. Springer, Heidelberg (2002)
10. Jones, A.V., Lomuscio, A.: Distributed BDD-based BMC for the verification of multi-agent systems. In: Proceedings of of AAMAS 2010, pp. 675–682 (2010)
11. Kacprzak, M., Dziubinski, M., Budzynska, K.: Strategies in dialogues: a game-Theoretic approach. In: Computational Models of Argument, Frontiers in Artificial Intelligence and Applications, vol. 266, pp. 333–344 (2014)
12. Kacprzak, M., Sawicka, A.: Identification of formal fallacies in a natural dialogue. Fundamenta Informaticae **135**(4), 403–417 (2014)
13. Kacprzak, M., Sawicka, A., Zbrzezny, A.: Dialogue systems: modeling and prediction of their dynamics. In: Proceedings of AECIA 2015. Advances in Intelligent Systems and Computing, pp. 421–431 (2016)
14. Kacprzak, M., Yaskorska, O.: Dialogue protocols for formal fallacies. Argumentation **28**(3), 349–369 (2014)
15. Keiff, L.: Dialogical logic. In: The Stanford Encyclopedia of Philosophy (2011)
16. Lomuscio, A., Penczek, W., Qu, H.: Partial order reduction for model checking interleaved multi-agent systems. In: Proceedings of AAMAS 2010, pp. 659–666 (2010)
17. Lorenz, K., Lorenzen, P.: Dialogische logik. WBG, Darmstadt (1978)
18. Mackenzie, J.D.: Question begging in non-cumulative systems. J. Philos. Logic **8**, 117–133 (1979)
19. Meski, A., Penczek, W., Szreter, M., Wozna-Szczesniak, B., Zbrzezny, A.: BDD-versus SAT-based bounded model checking for the existential fragment of linear temporal logic with knowledge: algorithms and their performance. Auton. Agent Multi-Agent Syst. **28**, 558–604 (2014)
20. Parsons, S., Wooldridge, M., Amgoud, L.: Properties and complexity of some formal inter-agent dialogues. J. Logic Comp. **13**, 347–376 (2003)
21. Penczek, W., Lomuscio, A.: Verifying epistemic properties of multi-agent systems via bounded model checking. Fundamenta Informaticae **55**(2), 167–185 (2003)

22. Prakken, H.: Coherence and flexibility in dialogue games for argumentation. J. Logic Comput. **15**, 1009–1040 (2005)
23. Rahman, S., Tulenheimo, T.: From games to dialogues and back: towards a general frame for validity. In: Majer, O., Pietarinen, A.-V., Tulenheimo, T. (eds.) Games: Unifying Logic, Language, and Philosophy, pp. 153–208. Springer, The Netherlands (2009)
24. Raimondi, F., Lomuscio, A.: Automatic verification of multi-agent systems by model checking via OBDDs. J. Appl. Logic **5**(2), 235–251 (2007)
25. Visser, J., Bex, F., Reed, C., Garssen, B.: Correspondence between the pragma-dialectical discussion model and the argument interchange format. Stud. Logic Grammar Rhetoric **23**(36), 189–224 (2011)
26. Walton, D.N., Krabbe, E.C.W.: Commitment in Dialogue: Basic Concepts of Inter-personal Reasoning. State University of N.Y. Press, Albany (1995)
27. Wells, S., Reed, C.: A domain specific language for describing diverse systems of dialogue. J. Appl. Logic **10**(4), 309–329 (2012)
28. Yaskorska, O., Budzynska, K., Kacprzak, M.: Proving propositional tautologies in a natural dialogue. Fundamenta Informaticae **128**(1–2), 239–253 (2013)

Transient Solution for Queueing Delay Distribution in the $GI/M/1/K$-type Mode with "Queued" Waking up and Balking

Wojciech M. Kempa[1], Marcin Woźniak[1]([⊠]), Robert K. Nowicki[2],
Marcin Gabryel[2], and Robertas Damaševičius[3]

[1] Institute of Mathematics, Silesian University of Technology, ul. Kaszubska 23,
44-100 Gliwice, Poland
{Wojciech.Kempa,Marcin.Wozniak}@polsl.pl
[2] Institute of Computational Intelligence, Czestochowa University of Technology,
Al. Armii Krajowej 36, 42-200 Czestochowa, Poland
{Robert.Nowicki,Marcin.Gabryel}@iisi.pcz.pl
[3] Software Engineering Department, Kaunas University of Technology, Studentu 50,
Kaunas, Lithuania
Robertas.Damasevicius@ktu.lt

Abstract. Time-dependent behavior of queueing delay distribution in the $GI/M/1/K$-type model with the "queued" server's waking up and balking is studied. After each idle period the server is being "queued" woken up, i.e. the processing is being started at the moment the number of packets accumulated in the buffer reaches the fixed level N. Moreover, each incoming packet can balk (resign from service) and leave the system irrevocably, with probability $1 - \beta$, and join the queue with probability β, where $0 < \beta \leq 1$.

Keywords: Balking · Finite-buffer queue · N-policy · Queueing delay · Transient state

1 Queueing Model

We deal with a finite-buffer $GI/M/1/K$-type queueing model in which interarrival times are independent and generally distributed random variables with a CDF (Cumulative Distribution Function) $F(\cdot)$, and the arriving packets are being processed singly according to an exponentially distributed service time with mean μ^{-1}, applying FIFO service discipline. The total number of packets present in the system is bounded by a non-random value K, i.e. there is a buffer of capacity $K - 1$ packets and one place "in service" [14,16–18]. We assume that the system begins the operation together with an arrival of the first packet, while the server initializes the processing at the moment at which the number of packets accumulated in the buffer queue and waiting for service reaches the fixed level N, where $1 \leq N \leq K$ (the so called "N-policy"), so, as one can say, the server is being woken up by an increasing queue length [1–5]. When the server

© Springer International Publishing Switzerland 2016
L. Rutkowski et al. (Eds.): ICAISC 2016, Part II, LNAI 9693, pp. 340–351, 2016.
DOI: 10.1007/978-3-319-39384-1_29

becomes idle it is being turned off and starts the processing again if it finds N packets accumulated in the buffer, and so on. Moreover, each of incoming packets can balk (resign from the processing) with probability $1 - \beta$, or join the queue with probability β, where $0 < \beta \le 1$. Obviously, each arriving packet that finds the buffer saturated, does not join the buffer queue and leaves the system without service (is lost). This type of modeling can be applied in various mass service systems, i.e. industrial control systems where risk management is important for production efficiency [6]; large-scale data base to increase quality of service for local and remote clients [7]; game management systems and dedicated strategies where better quality of service can enable better playability [8,9]; energy management systems [10–13] and other similar in type queueing systems [19–23].

It is clear that the evolution of the system can be considered on successive buffer loading periods $L_1, L_2, ...$, during which the level of buffer saturation is increasing from 1 to N, followed by busy cycles $C_1, C_2, ...$, consisting of busy periods, beginning at the moment of Nth arrival and during which the queue empties, and idle periods (times of waiting for the first arrival after the queue becomes empty). Since successive arrival epochs are Markov (renewal) moments in the $GI/M/1/K$-type queue (see e.g. [15]), then (L_k) and (C_k), $k = 1, , 2, ...$, are sequences of independent random variables with the same CDFs, treating each sequence separately. In the paper we will often equate buffer loading periods and busy cycles with their respective durations.

2   Analysis of a Buffer Loading Period

Let us analyze, firstly, the queueing delay distribution at arbitrary time epoch t during the first buffer loading period L_1, which begins at $t = 0$ together with the first arrival occurrence. Let $F^{j*}(\cdot)$ denote the j-fold Stieltjes convolution of the CDF $F(\cdot)$ with itself, namely

$$F^{0*}(t) = 1, \quad F^{j*}(t) = \int_0^t F^{(j-1)*}(t - y)dF(y), \quad j \ge 1, \tag{1}$$

and denote

$$f(s) \stackrel{def}{=} \int_0^\infty e^{-st}dF(t), \quad \text{Re}(s) > 0. \tag{2}$$

Let $G_{L,k}(\cdot)$ be a CDF of the kth buffer loading period duration L_k. Obviously, we have

$$G_L(t) = G_{L,k}(t)$$

$$= \mathbf{P}\{\text{the } (N - 1)\text{th packet physically join the buffer queue before } t\}$$

$$= \sum_{i=N-1}^\infty \left[F^{i*}(t) - F^{(i)*}(t) \right] \sum_{r=N-1}^i \binom{r-1}{N-2} \beta^{N-1}(1 - \beta)^{r-N+1}, \tag{3}$$

where $i \ge 1$.

Indeed, if exactly i packets $(i \geq N - 1)$ appear in the arrival stream up to time t, then the notation r stands for the number of packet being the last one for initialization the processing (the $(N-1)$th physically joining the buffer queue) [26, 27]. Hence, among $(r - 1)$ first arriving jobs $N - 2$ should be "accepting" (each with probability β) and $r - N + 1$ must be "dropped" (each with probability $(1 - \beta)$). Obviously, the rth packet should be "enqueued" (with probability β) in the buffer.

Denoting by $\widetilde{g}_L(\cdot)$ the LST (= Laplace Stieltjes transform) of CDF $G_L(\cdot)$, namely

$$\widetilde{g}_L(s) \overset{def}{=} \int_0^\infty e^{-st} dG_L(t), \quad \mathrm{Re}(s) > 0, \tag{4}$$

we get from (3)

$$\widetilde{g}_L(s) = s^{-1}[1 - f(s)] \sum_{r=N-1}^i f^r(s) \binom{r-1}{N-2} \beta^{N-1}(1-\beta)^{r-N+1}. \tag{5}$$

Observe that the following representation is justified:

$$\mathbf{P}\{(v(t) > x) \cap (t \in L_1)\} = \sum_{i=0}^\infty \int_{y=0}^t dF^{i*}(y) \sum_{k=0}^{\max(i, N-2)} \binom{i}{k} \beta^k(1-\beta)^{i-k}$$

$$\times \int_{u=t-y}^\infty dF(u) \Bigg[\beta \sum_{r=N-k-2}^\infty \binom{r-1}{N-k-3} \beta^{N-k-2}(1-\beta)^{r-N+k+2} \int_{z=0}^\infty dF^{r*}(z)$$

$$+ (1 - \beta) \sum_{r=N-k-1}^\infty \binom{r-1}{N-k-2} \beta^{N-k-1}(1-\beta)^{r-N+k+1} \int_{z=0}^\infty dF^{r*}(z) \Bigg]$$

$$\times e^{-\mu(x-y-u-z+t)} \sum_{j=0}^k \frac{[\mu(x+y-u-z+t)]^j}{j!}. \tag{6}$$

Indeed, on the right side of (5) i denotes the number of packets which physically join the buffer queue before time t entering before t, except for one occurring exactly at $t = 0$. After time period $y + u + v$ the buffer loading period completes and a busy period begins. A "virtual" packet entering the system exactly at epoch t waits more than time x if and only if the time needed for the buffer to become empty plus the time period duration from t to the buffer loading completion epoch exceeds x.

In further considerations we use the LT of $\mathbf{P}\{(v(t) > x) \cap (t \in L_1)\}$, so let us introduce the following notation:

$$\widetilde{v}^L(s, x) \overset{def}{=} \int_0^\infty e^{-st} \mathbf{P}\{(v(t) > x) \cap (t \in L_1)\} dt, \quad \mathrm{Re}(s) > 0. \tag{7}$$

3   Analysis of Queueing Delay in the Busy Cycle

In this section we derive the closed-form representation for the LT of the queueing delay distribution "inside" a single busy cycle of the system, by using the methodology based on the idea of embedded Markov chain, continuous version of total probability law and an auxiliary result from linear algebra. Let us suppose, for a time, that the system may start the processing not necessarily with N packets accumulated in the buffer queue but with arbitrary number of n packets, where $1 \leq n \leq K$. Moreover, let us assume that $t = 0$ is the start moment of the first busy cycle C_1. Introduce the following notation:

$$V_n^C(t, x) = \mathbf{P}\{(v(t) > x) \cap (t \in C_1) \,|\, X(0) = n\}, \ 1 \leq n \leq K, \ x > 0, \ t > 0, \quad (8)$$

where $X(t)$ stands for the number of packets present in the system exactly at time t. In fact, $V_n^C(\cdot, \cdot)$ denotes the tail distribution function of the queueing delay on the first busy cycle C_1, conditioned by the number of packets accumulated in the buffer at the initial moment of C_1.

Utilizing the fact that successive arrival epochs are Markov moments and applying the total probability law with respect to the first arrival epoch after $t = 0$, we get the following system of integral equations:

$$V_n^C(t, x) = \sum_{i=0}^{n-1} \int_0^t \frac{(\mu y)^i}{i!} e^{-\mu y} \Big[\beta V_{n-i+1}^C(t - y, x) + (1 - \beta) V_{n-i}^C(t - y, x) \Big] dF(y)$$

$$+ \overline{F}(t) e^{-\mu(t+x)} \sum_{i=0}^{n-1} \frac{(\mu t)^i}{i!} \sum_{j=0}^{n-i-1} \frac{(\mu x)^j}{j!}, \quad (9)$$

where $1 \leq n \leq K - 1$, and

$$V_K^C(t, x) = \int_0^t e^{-\mu y} V_K^C(t - y, x) dF(y)$$

$$+ \sum_{i=1}^{K-1} \int_0^t \frac{(\mu y)^i}{i!} e^{-\mu y} \Big[\beta V_{K-i+1}^C(t - y, x) + (1 - \beta) V_{K-i}^C(t - y, x) \Big] dF(y)$$

$$+ \overline{F}(t) e^{-\mu(t+x)} \sum_{i=1}^{K-1} \frac{(\mu t)^i}{i!} \sum_{j=0}^{K-i-1} \frac{(\mu x)^j}{j!}. \quad (10)$$

Let us comment (9)–(10) briefly. The integral on the right side of (9) presents the situation in which the first packet arrives at time $0 < y < t$. Then the number of packets at Markov moment y equals $n - i + 1$ if the packet joins the queue (with probability β) or $n - i$ if the arriving packet resigns from service (with probability $1 - \beta$), where $0 \leq i \leq n - 1$ denotes the number of completed services up to time y. The second summand on the right side of (9) relates to the situation in which the first arrival occurs after t. In such a case exacly $0 \leq i \leq n - 1$ items must be processed till t and at most $n - i - 1$ during time x. Let us observe that there are only two differences between (9) and (10). The first summand on the right side of (10) describes the case in which there are no departures before t : the "virtual" packet entering exactly at time t is then dropped due to the buffer overflow. The second difference is in the sum from $i = 1$ to $K - 1$ in the case of the first arrival occurring after t. Indeed, if any packet is completely served before t, the "virtual" one is dropped since the buffer is still saturated at time t.

Denote

$$\widetilde{v}_n^C(s, x) \stackrel{def}{=} \int_0^\infty e^{-st} V_n^C(t, x) dt, \quad n \geq 1, \tag{11}$$

$$a_n(s) \stackrel{def}{=} \int_0^\infty e^{-(s+\mu)t} \frac{(\mu t)^n}{n!} dF(t), \quad n \geq 0, \tag{12}$$

$$\varphi_n(s, x) \stackrel{def}{=} - \int_0^\infty e^{-(s+\mu)t - \mu x} \overline{F}(t)$$

$$\times \left[\sum_{i=0}^{n-1} \frac{(\mu t)^i}{i!} \sum_{j=0}^{n-i-1} \frac{(\mu x)^j}{j!} - \delta_{n,K} \sum_{j=0}^{K-1} \frac{(\mu x)^j}{j!} \right] dt, \tag{13}$$

where $\mathrm{Re}(s) > 0$. Introducing (11)–(13) into the system (9)–(10), we obtain

$$\widetilde{v}_n^C(s, x) = \sum_{i=0}^{n-1} a_i(s) \left[\beta \widetilde{v}_{n-i+1}^C(s, x) + (1 - \beta) \widetilde{v}_{n-i}^C(s, x) \right] - \varphi_n(s, x), \tag{14}$$

where $1 \leq n \leq K - 1$, and

$$[1 - a_0(s)] \widetilde{v}_K^C(s, x) = \sum_{i=1}^{K-1} a_i(s) \left[\beta \widetilde{v}_{K-i+1}^C(s, x) + (1 - \beta) \widetilde{v}_{K-i}^C(s, x) \right] - \varphi_K(s, x). \tag{15}$$

If we define now another functional sequence $(\alpha_i(s))$ in the following way:

$$\alpha_0(s) \stackrel{def}{=} \beta a_0(s), \quad \alpha_i(s) \stackrel{def}{=} (1 - \beta) a_{i-1}(s) + \beta a_i(s), \quad i \geq 1, \tag{16}$$

and, moreover, take

$$\psi_n(s, x) \stackrel{def}{=} \varphi_n(s, x) - (1 - \beta) a_{n+1}(s) \widetilde{v}_1^C(s, x), \quad n \geq 1, \tag{17}$$

we can obtain from (14)

$$\alpha_0(s) \widetilde{v}_2^C(s, x) - \widetilde{v}_1^C(s, x) = \psi_1(s, x), \tag{18}$$

that gives immediately

$$\widetilde{v}_1^C(s, x) = \frac{\varphi_1(s, x) - \alpha_0(s) \widetilde{v}_2^C(s, x)}{(1 - \beta) a_0(s) - 1}, \tag{19}$$

and

$$\sum_{k=-1}^{n-2} \alpha_{k+1}(s) \widetilde{v}_{n-k}^C(s, x) - \widetilde{v}_n^C(s, x) = \psi_n(s, x), \quad 2 \leq n \leq K. \tag{20}$$

Besides, the Eq. (15) can be transformed in the following way:

$$\tilde{v}_K^C(s,x) = \left[1 - a_0(s) - \hat{\alpha}_1(s)\right]^{-1}\left(\sum_{i=1}^{K-1}\hat{\alpha}_{i+1}(s)\tilde{v}_{K-i}^C(s,x) - \varphi_i(s,x)\right), \quad (21)$$

where

$$\hat{\alpha}_i(s,x) \stackrel{def}{=} \beta a_i(s)I\{1 \le i \le K-1\} + (1-\beta)a_{i-1}(s)I\{2 \le i \le K\}, \quad (22)$$

and $I\{A\}$ stands for the indicator of the random event A.

In [24] (see also [25]) the infinite-sized system of type (20) is considered, where $n \ge 2$ and is not bounded. From the theory stated in [24] follows that each solution of (20) with infinite number of equations can be written as

$$\tilde{v}_n^C(s,x) = A(s,x)R_{n-1}(s) + \sum_{k=2}^{n} R_{n-k}(s)\psi_k(s,x), \quad n \ge 2, \quad (23)$$

where $A(s,x)$ is independent on n, and successive terms of the sequence $(R_n(s))$ can be found recursively in the following way:

$$R_0(s) = 0, \quad R_1(s) = \alpha_0^{-1}(s),$$

$$R_{n+1}(s) = R_1(s)\left(R_n(s) - \sum_{i=0}^{n}\alpha_{i+1}(s)R_{n-i}(s)\right), \quad (24)$$

where $n \ge 1$.

Since in the system (20) the number of equations is finite, we can utilize the equality (21) as a boundary condition and find $A(s,x)$ explicitly. Indeed, using (21) and (23) in (21), and comparing with (23) written for $n = K$, we obtain

$$A(s,x)R_{K-1}(s) + \sum_{i=2}^{K} R_{K-i}(s)\psi_i(s,x) = \left[1 - a_0(s) - \hat{\alpha}_1^{-1}(s)\right]^{-1}$$

$$\left\{\sum_{i=1}^{K-2}\hat{\alpha}_{i+1}(s)\left[A(s,x)R_{K-i-1}(s) + \sum_{j=2}^{K-i} R_{K-i-j}(s)\psi_j(s,x)\right]\right.$$

$$\left. + \hat{\alpha}_k(s)\left[(1-\beta)a_0(s) - 1\right]^{-1}\left[\varphi_1(s,x) - A(s,x)\right] - \varphi_k(s,x)\right\}. \quad (25)$$

Taking into consideration (17) and the following substitutions:

$$\gamma(s) \stackrel{def}{=} \left[(1-\beta)a_0(s) - 1\right]^{-1}, \quad \eta(s) \stackrel{def}{=} \left[1 - a_0(s) - \hat{\alpha}_1(s)\right]^{-1}, \quad (26)$$

we get from (25)

$$
A(s,x)R_{K-1}(s) + \sum_{i=2}^{K} R_{K-i}(s)\Big[\varphi_i(s,x) - (1-\beta)\gamma(s)a_{i-1}(s)
$$

$$
\times \big(\varphi_1(s,x) - A(s,x)\big)\Big] = \eta(s)\Bigg\{\sum_{i=1}^{K-2}\widehat{\alpha}_{i+1}(s)\Big[A(s,x)R_{K-i-1}(s)
$$

$$
+ \sum_{j=2}^{K-i} R_{K-i-j}(s)\Big(\varphi_j(s,x) - (1-\beta)\gamma(s)a_{j-1}(s)\big(\varphi_1(s,x) - A(s,x)\big)\Big)\Big]
$$

$$
+ \widehat{\alpha}_k(s)\gamma(s)\big(\varphi_1(s,x) - A(s,x)\big) - \varphi_k(s,x)\Bigg\}. \tag{27}
$$

Now, from (27) we can eliminate $A(s,x)$ in the following way:

$$
A(s,x) = \Delta_1^{-1}(s)\Delta_2(s,x), \tag{28}
$$

where

$$
\Delta_1(s) \overset{def}{=} R_{K-1}(s) + (1-\beta)\gamma(s)\sum_{i=2}^{K} R_{K-i}(a)a_{i-1}(s)
$$

$$
- \eta(s)\Bigg[\sum_{i=1}^{K-2}\widehat{\alpha}_{i+1}(s)\Big(R_{K-i-1}(s) + (1-\beta)\gamma(s)\sum_{j=2}^{K-i} R_{K-i-j}(s)a_{j-1}(s)\Big)
$$

$$
- \widehat{\alpha}_k(s)\gamma(s)\Bigg] \tag{29}
$$

and

$$
\Delta_2(s,x) \overset{def}{=} \sum_{i=2}^{K} R_{K-i}(s)\Big((1-\beta)\gamma(s)\varphi_1(s,x)a_{i-1}(s) - \varphi_i(s,x)\Big)
$$

$$
+ \eta(s)\Bigg\{\sum_{i=2}^{K-2}\widehat{\alpha}_{i+1}(s)\Big[\sum_{j=2}^{K-i} R_{K-i-j}(s)\Big(\varphi_j(s,x) - (1-\beta)\gamma(s)\varphi_1(s,x)a_{j-1}(s)\Big)\Big]
$$

$$
+ \gamma(s)\varphi_1(s,x)\widehat{\alpha}_k(s) - \varphi_k(s,x)\Bigg\}. \tag{30}
$$

Now, from (19) and (23), taking into consideration (17) and (28), the following theorem follows:

Theorem 1. *The formulae for the LT $\widetilde{v}_n^C(s,x)$ of the conditional queueing delay tail distribution in the busy cycle of the $GI/M/1/K$-type model with probability $(1-\beta)$ of balking are following:*

$$
\widetilde{v}_1^C(s,x) = \gamma(s)\big[\varphi_1(s,x) - \Delta_1^{-1}(s)\Delta_2(s,x)\big] \tag{31}
$$

and

$$\tilde{v}_n^C(s, x) = \Delta_1^{-1}(s)\Delta_2(s, x)R_{n-1}(s)$$

$$+ \sum_{i=2}^{n} R_{n-i}(s)\Big[\varphi_i(s, x) - (1 - \beta)\gamma(s)a_{i+1}(s)\big(\varphi_1(s, x) - \Delta_1^{-1}(s)\Delta_2(s, x)\big)\Big], \quad (32)$$

where $\mathrm{Re}(s) > 0$, $2 \leq n \leq K$, *and the formulae for* $a_k(s)$, $\varphi_k(s, x)$, $R_k(s)$, $\gamma(s)$, $\Delta_1(s)$ *and* $\Delta_2(s, x)$, *can be found in* (12), (13), (24), (26), (29) *and* (30), *respectively.*

4   Busy Cycle Duration

In this section, by using the same methodology as in the previous one, we find a representation for the LT of the busy cycle C_k, $k \geq 1$, duration, conditioned by the initial level of buffer saturation (we assume temporarily, as previously, that the busy cycle may begin with any number $1 \leq n \leq K$ of packets present in the system). Introduce the following notation:

$$\tilde{h}_n^C(s) \overset{def}{=} \tilde{h}_n^{C_k}(s) = \int_0^\infty e^{-st}d\mathbf{P}\{C_k < t \mid X(0) = n\}dt, \quad (33)$$

where $\mathrm{Re}(s) > 0$ and $1 \leq n \leq K$.

Applying the total probability law we obtain

$$\tilde{h}_n^C(s) = \sum_{i=0}^{n-1} \int_0^\infty e^{-(s+\mu)x}\frac{(\mu x)^i}{i!}\Big[\beta\tilde{h}_{n-i+1}(s) + (1-\beta)\tilde{h}_{n-i}(s)\Big]dF(x)$$

$$+ \int_{x=0}^\infty \Big(\int_{y=0}^x e^{-(s+\mu)y}\frac{\mu^n}{(n-1)!}y^{n-1}dy\Big)dF(x) \quad (34)$$

and

$$\big[1 - a_0(s)\big]\tilde{h}_K^C(s) = \sum_{i=1}^{K-1} \int_0^\infty e^{-(s+\mu)x}\frac{(\mu x)^i}{i!}\Big[\beta\tilde{h}_{K-i+1}(s)$$

$$+ (1-\beta)\tilde{h}_{K-i}(s)\Big]dF(x) + \int_{x=0}^\infty \Big(\int_{y=0}^x e^{-(s+\mu)y}\frac{\mu^K}{(K-1)!}y^{K-1}dy\Big)dF(x). \quad (35)$$

Denoting

$$\phi_n(s) \overset{def}{=} -\int_{x=0}^\infty \Big(\int_{y=0}^x e^{-(s+\mu)y}\frac{\mu^n}{(n-1)!}y^{n-1}dy\Big)dF(x), \quad (36)$$

we can rewrite (34)–(35) in the following form (compare (14)–(15):

$$\tilde{h}_n^C(s) = \sum_{i=0}^{n-1} a_i(s)\Big[\beta\tilde{h}_{n-i+1}^C(s) + (1-\beta)\tilde{h}_{n-i}^C(s)\Big] - \phi_n(s), \quad (37)$$

where $1 \leq n \leq K - 1$, and

$$[1 - a_0(s)]\tilde{h}_K^C(s) = \sum_{i=1}^{K-1} a_i(s)\left[\beta\tilde{h}_{K-i+1}^C(s) + (1 - \beta)\tilde{v}_{K-i}^C(s)\right] - \phi_K(s). \quad (38)$$

Hence, immediately, we obtain the following result (compare Theorem 1)

Theorem 2. *The representations for the LT* $\tilde{h}_n^C(s, x)$ *of the conditional distribution of the busy cycle duration in the* $GI/M/1/K$-*type model with probability* $(1 - \beta)$ *of balking are following:*

$$\tilde{h}_1^C(s) = \gamma(s)\left[\phi_1(s) - \Delta_1^{-1}(s)\Delta_2^{\#}(s)\right] \quad (39)$$

and

$$\tilde{h}_n^C(s) = \Delta_1^{-1}(s)\Delta_2^{\#}(s)R_{n-1}(s)$$
$$+ \sum_{i=2}^{n} R_{n-i}(s)\left[\phi_i(s) - (1 - \beta)\gamma(s)a_{i+1}(s)(\phi_1(s) - \Delta_1^{-1}(s, x)\Delta_2^{\#}(s))\right], \quad (40)$$

where $\operatorname{Re}(s) > 0$, $2 \leq n \leq K$,

$$\Delta_2^{\#}(s) \stackrel{def}{=} \sum_{i=2}^{K} R_{K-i}(s)\left((1 - \beta)\gamma(s)\phi_1(s)a_{i-1}(s) - \phi_i(s)\right)$$
$$+ \eta(s)\left\{\sum_{i=2}^{K-2} \hat{\alpha}_{i+1}(s)\left[\sum_{j=2}^{K-i} R_{K-i-j}(s)\left(\phi_j(s) - (1 - \beta)\gamma(s)\phi_1(s)a_{j-1}(s)\right)\right]\right.$$
$$\left. + \gamma(s)\phi_1(s)\hat{\alpha}_k(s) - \phi_k(s)\right\}. \quad (41)$$

and the formulae for $a_k(s)$, $\phi_k(s)$, $R_k(s)$, $\gamma(s)$ *and* $\Delta_1(s)$ *can be found in (12), (36), (24), (26) and (29) and respectively.*

5   General Result

In this section, utilizing the renewal-theory approach and analytical results obtained in previous sections, we prove the following general theorem:

Theorem 3. *The formula for the transient queueing delay* $v(t)$ *conditional tail distribution in the* $GI/M/1/K$-*type model with* N-*policy and balking probability* $(1 - \beta)$ *is following:*

$$\int_0^\infty e^{-st}\mathbf{P}\{v(t) > x\}dt = \frac{\tilde{v}^L(s, x) + \tilde{g}^L(s)\tilde{v}_N^C(s, x)}{1 - \tilde{h}_N^C(s)\tilde{g}^L(s)}, \quad (42)$$

where the formulae for $\tilde{g}^L(s)$, $\tilde{v}^L(s, x)$, $\tilde{v}_N^C(s, x)$ *and* $\tilde{h}_N^C(s)$ *are defined in (4), (7), (32) and (40), respectively.*

Proof. Let us observe that

$$\mathbf{P}\{v(t) > x\} = \sum_{k=1}^{\infty}\Big(\mathbf{P}\{(v(t) > x) \cap (t \in L_k)\}$$

$$+ \mathbf{P}\{(v(t) > x) \cap (t \in C_k)\}\Big). \qquad (43)$$

Furthermore, since all terms of sequences (L_k) and (C_k), $k \geq 1$, are independent and identically distributed random variables ("inside" each sequence treated separately), we get

$$\mathbf{P}\{(v(t) > x) \cap (t \in L_k)\}$$

$$= \int_0^t \mathbf{P}\{(v(t-y) > x) \cap (t - y \in L_1)\}d(G_L * H_N^C)^{(k-1)*}(y) \qquad (44)$$

and, similarly,

$$\mathbf{P}\{(v(t) > x) \cap (t \in C_k)\}$$

$$= \int_0^t \mathbf{P}\{(v(t-y) > x) \cap (t - y \in C_1)\}d[(G_L)^{k*} * (H_N^C)^{(k-1)*}](y), \qquad (45)$$

where

$$H_N^C(t) \overset{def}{=} \mathbf{P}\{C_k < t \,|\, X(0) = N\}, \quad t > 0, k \geq 1, \qquad (46)$$

denotes conditional CDF of busy cycle duration in the original system with N-policy and packet balking.

Introducing Laplace transforms into Eqs. (44)–(45), by virtue of (43), we get the conclusion (42). □

6   Conclusions

In this article we present theoretical model for time-dependent behavior of queueing delay distribution in the $GI/M/1/K$-type system with the "queued" server's waking up and balking. Theorems presented in Sects. 2–5 give general result applicable in modeling of data base systems where information retrieval is based on efficient server in-built management i.e. where multimedia files are indexed for further classification [28–30]. However for mathematical modeling is also important to have applications in real systems, like for examples shown in Sect. 1. Model given in this article have many of them since theoretical assumptions can be easily adapted for various situations by calculating system parameters. Calculations give values of input and output parameters responsible for positioning. In these calculations it is possible to use evolutionary strategies [31] or genetic algorithms [32] since these types of programming enable easier numerical operations on complex mathematical systems like in queueing.

Further work will be focused on validation of the system in practical examples, where applied model will be used for positioning of mass service systems for better quality of service and more efficient energy usage.

References

1. Gabryel, M., Nowicki, R.K., Woźniak, M., Kempa, W.M.: Genetic cost optimization of the $GI/M/1/N$ finite-buffer queue with a single vacation policy. In: Rutkowski, L., Korytkowski, M., Scherer, R., Tadeusiewicz, R., Zadeh, L.A., Zurada, J.M. (eds.) ICAISC 2013, Part II. LNCS, vol. 7895, pp. 12–23. Springer, Heidelberg (2013)
2. Woźniak, M.: On applying cuckoo search algorithm to positioning GI/M/1/N finite-buffer queue with a single vacation policy. In: Proceedings of the 12th Mexican International Conference on Artificial Intelligence - MICAI 2013, Mexico City, Mexico, 24–30 November 2013, pp. 59–64. IEEE (2013)
3. Woźniak, M., Kempa, W.M., Gabryel, M., Nowicki, R.K.: A finite-buffer queue with single vacation policy - analytical study with evolutionary positioning. Int. J. Appl. Math. Comput. Sci. **24**(4), 887–900 (2014)
4. Woźniak, M., Kempa, W.M., Gabryel, M., Nowicki, R.K., Shao, Z.: On applying evolutionary computation methods to optimization of vacation cycle costs in finite-buffer queue. In: Rutkowski, L., Korytkowski, M., Scherer, R., Tadeusiewicz, R., Zadeh, L.A., Zurada, J.M. (eds.) ICAISC 2014, Part I. LNCS, vol. 8467, pp. 480–491. Springer, Heidelberg (2014)
5. Woźniak, M., Gabryel, M., Nowicki, R.K., Nowak, B.: An application of firefly algorithm to position traffic in NoSQL database systems. In: Kunifuji, S. (ed.) Advances in Intelligent Systems and Computing - KICSS 2014, vol. 416, pp. 259–272. Springer, Switzerland (2016)
6. Chen, Q., Abercrombie, R., Sheldon, F.: Risk assessment for industrial control systems quantifying availability using Mean Failure Cost (MFC). J. Artif. Intell. Soft Comput. Res. **5**(3), 205–220 (2015)
7. Serdah, A., Ashour, W.: Clustering large-scale data based on modified affinity propagation algorithm. J. Artif. Intell. Soft Comput. Res. **6**(1), 23–33 (2016)
8. Waledzik, K., Mandziuk, J.: An automatically generated evaluation function in general game playing. IEEE Trans. Comput. Intell. AI Games **6**(3), 258–270 (2014)
9. Swiechowski, M., Mandziuk, J.: Self-adaptation of playing strategies in general game playing. IEEE Trans. Comput. Intell. AI Games **6**(4), 367–381 (2014)
10. Birvinskas, D., Jusas, V., Martišius, I., Damaševičius, R.: Fast DCT algorithms for EEG data compression in embedded systems. COMSIS J. **12**(1), 49–62 (2015)
11. Birvinskas, D., Jusas, V., Martisius, I., Damaševičius, R.: Data compression of EEG signals for artificial neural network classification. Inf. Technol. Control **42**(3), 238–241 (2013)
12. Napoli, C., Bonanno, F., Capizzi, G.: Exploiting solar wind time series correlation with magnetospheric response by using an hybrid neuro-wavelet approach. Proc. Int. Astron. Union **6**(s274), 156–158 (2010)
13. Napoli, C., Bonanno, F., Capizzi, G.: Some remarks on the application of RNN and PRNN for the charge-discharge simulation of advanced lithiumions battery energy storage. In: Proceedings of Power Electronics, Electrical Drives, Automation and Motion (SPEEDAM), pp. 941–945. IEEE (2012)
14. Abate, J., Choudhury, G.L., Whitt, W.: An introduction to numerical transform inversion and its application to probability models. In: Probability, C., Grassmann, W. (eds.) Computational Probability, pp. 257–323. Kluwer, Boston (2000)
15. Cohen, J.W.: The Single Server Queue. North-Holland, Amsterdam-New York-Oxford (1982)

16. Jiang, F.-Ch., Huang, D.-C., Wang, K.-H.: Design approaches for optimizing power consumption of sensor node with N-policy $M/G/1$. In: Proceedings of QTNA 2009, Singapore, 29–31 July 2009

17. Jiang, F.-C., Huang, D.-C., Tang, C.-T., Wang, K.-H.: Mitigation techniques for the energy hole problem in sensor networks using N-policy $M/G/1$ queueing models. In: Proceedings of the IET International Conference: Frontier Computing Theory, Technologies and Applications 2010, Taichung, 4–6 August 2010

18. Jiang, F.-C., Huang, D.-C., Tang, C.-T., Leu, F.Y.: Lifetime elongation for wireless sensor network using queue-based approaches. J. Supercomputing **59**, 1312–1335 (2012)

19. Kempa, W.M.: The virtual waiting time for the batch arrival queueing systems. Stochast. Anal. Appl. **22**(5), 1235–1255 (2004)

20. Kempa, W.M.: The transient analysis of the queue-length distribution in the batch arrival system with N-policy, multiple vacations and setup times. AIP Conf. Proc. **1293**, 235–242 (2010)

21. Kempa, W.M.: Departure process in finite-buffer queue with batch arrivals. In: Al-Begain, K., Balsamo, S., Fiems, D., Marin, A. (eds.) ASMTA 2011. LNCS, vol. 6751, pp. 1–13. Springer, Heidelberg (2011)

22. Kempa, W.M.: On transient queue-size distribution in the batch arrival system with the N-policy and setup times. Math. Commun. **17**, 285–302 (2012)

23. Kempa, W.M.: The virtual waiting time in a finite-buffer queue with a single vacation policy. In: Al-Begain, K., Fiems, D., Vincent, J.-M. (eds.) ASMTA 2012. LNCS, vol. 7314, pp. 47–60. Springer, Heidelberg (2012)

24. Korolyuk, V.S.: Boundary-Value Problems for Compound Poisson Processes. Naukova Dumka, Kiev (1975) (in Russian)

25. Korolyuk, V.S., Bratiichuk, N.S., Pirdzhanov, B.: Boundary-Value Problems for Random Walks. Ylym, Ashkhabad (1987) (in Russian)

26. Lee, H.W., Lee, S.S., Park, J.O., Chae, K.-C.: Analysis of the $M^X/G/1$ queue with N-policy and multiple vacations. J. Appl. Probab. **31**(2), 476–496 (1994)

27. Mancuso, V., Alouf, S.: Analysis of power saving with continuous connectivity. Comput. Netw. **56**, 2481–2493 (2012)

28. Korytkowski, M., Scherer, R., Staszewski, P., Woldan, P.: Bag-of-features image indexing and classification in microsoft SQL server relational database. In: Proceedings of CYBCONF 2015, Gdynia, Poland, 24–26 June 2015, pp. 478–482. IEEE (2015)

29. Grycuk, R., Gabryel, M., Scherer, R., Voloshynovskiy, S.: Multi-layer architecture for storing visual data based on WCF and microsoft SQL server database. In: Rutkowski, L., Korytkowski, M., Scherer, R., Tadeusiewicz, R., Zadeh, L.A., Zurada, J.M. (eds.) Artificial Intelligence and Soft Computing. LNCS, vol. 9119, pp. 715–726. Springer, Heidelberg (2015)

30. Korytkowski, M., Rutkowski, L., Scherer, R.: Fast image classification by boosting fuzzy classifiers. Inf. Sci. **327**, 175–182 (2016)

31. Kasthurirathna, D., Piraveenan, M., Uddin, S.: Evolutionary stable strategies in networked games: the influence of topology. J. Artif. Intell. Soft Comput. Res. **5**(2), 83–95 (2015)

32. El-Samak, A., Ashour, W.: Optimization of traveling salesman problem using affinity propagation clustering and genetic algorithm. J. Artif. Intell. Soft Comput. Res. **5**(4), 239–245 (2015)

Some Novel Results of Collective Knowledge Increase Analysis Using Euclidean Space

Van Du Nguyen$^{(\boxtimes)}$ and Ngoc Thanh Nguyen

Faculty of Computer Science and Management, Wroclaw University of Technology,
Wyb. St. Wyspianskiego 27, 50-370 Wroclaw, Poland
{van.du.nguyen,ngoc-thanh.nguyen}@pwr.edu.pl

Abstract. The collective knowledge increase, in general, is understood as an additional amount of knowledge in a collective in comparison with the average of the knowledge states given by collective members on the same subject in the real world. These knowledge states reflect the real knowledge state of the subject, but only to some degree because of the incompleteness and uncertainty. In this work, we investigate the influence of the inconsistency degree on the collective knowledge increase in a collective by taking into account the number of collective members. In addition, by means of experiments we prove that the amount of knowledge increase in a collective with higher inconsistency degree is better than that in a collective with lower inconsistency degree.

1 Introduction

Collective knowledge is understood as a common knowledge state of a whole collective consisting of autonomous units such as experts or agents on a common subject in the real world [1]. The knowledge states of collective members reflect the real knowledge state concerning some issues of the subject, but only to some degree because of the incompleteness and uncertainty. In addition, we assume that the real knowledge state exists but it is not known by the autonomous units when they are being asked for giving their knowledge states about the subject. Thus, in processing collective knowledge, the following cases may take place:

- The real knowledge state exists dependently on the knowledge states in a collective.
- The real knowledge state exists independently of the knowledge states in a collective.

The main difference between these cases is due to the ways in which the knowledge states of the collective members are used. In both of them the knowledge states of the collective members are taken into account to determine the collective knowledge of the collective. However, in the first way the collective knowledge is interpreted as some assessments for a concrete subject such as a collective opinion on a movie. In this case the collective knowledge and the real knowledge state are identical. Both of them are dependent on the knowledge

© Springer International Publishing Switzerland 2016
L. Rutkowski et al. (Eds.): ICAISC 2016, Part II, LNAI 9693, pp. 352–363, 2016.
DOI: 10.1007/978-3-319-39384-1_30

states given by the collective members. Thus we name this case as *subjective case*. In the second way the collective knowledge reflects the real knowledge state regarding a concrete subject to some degree. For example, weather forecasts from the meteorological stations for the next day for a specific region. In this case the real knowledge state (the weather state of the region when the next day comes) exists, but it is independent of the collective knowledge which is determined on the basic of collective members' knowledge states (forecasts from the meteorological stations). Thus we name this case as *objective case*. In [2] the author has worked out many consensus-based algorithms to determine the collective knowledge of a collective for different knowledge representations such as logical, relational structures and ontology.

So far, according to Tziner [3] and Barrick [4], the performance of a group is an average of individual performances. This statement was confirmed by Neuman in a similar research [5]. Additionally, team knowledge is greater than the collection of members' knowledge and it is the result of interactions among members in a collective [6]. Through simulation, Hutchins has also concluded that team knowledge can be greater than external or internal knowledge of team members, and it is the consequence of interactions of factors in the sociotechnical system [7]. However, the limitation of these works is only based on some statistic involving members' performances. No mathematical model has been worked out for proving these statements. Besides, in [2,8] the authors have proved that the collective knowledge is better than the worst knowledge state in a collective. In case all knowledge states to the same degree reflect the real knowledge state, then the collective knowledge is the best one in comparison with all knowledge states in the collective. In [9] through experiments analysis, the number of collective members positively affects the collective knowledge, that is collectives with more members will give better collective knowledge than collectives with fewer members. The better collective knowledge means the closer one to the real knowledge state of the subject. However, how about the difference between the average of knowledge states in a collective and the collective knowledge? We named it as *collective knowledge increase*. It can be considered as an additional amount of knowledge in a collective in comparison with the average of knowledge states given by collective members. This concept is different from the concept of new knowledge elements generated in a collective [10] or a *"surplus"* element as in [11]. The measure of collective knowledge increase in a collective is based on the difference between the average of the distances from the real knowledge state to the knowledge states and the distance from the real knowledge state to the collective knowledge. Although collective knowledge determination is an important task, the influence of some factors such as the inconsistency degree and the number of collective members on the collective knowledge increase in a collective is also an important issue. The inconsistency degree, in general, presents the coherence and density levels of the knowledge states in the collective [2]. In some situations, it is helpful in giving a proper solution such as in [12,13]. However, in others, it can be undesired one as in decision making process because of in this case more consistent participants' opinions is better than that containing some conflicts [14–18]. In this work, we investigate the problem of the influence of the inconsistency degree on the collective knowledge increase in a collective by taking into account the number of collective members. For this aim, based on the Euclidean space, we will propose a formal model to determine how the inconsistency degree influences the collective knowledge increase in a collective for objective case. With some restrictions, the hypothesis *"the higher is the inconsistency degree, the better is the collective knowledge increase in a collective"* is true. This is the main contribution of the paper.

The rest of the paper is organized as follows. Section 2 recalls some basic notions related to collective of knowledge states, collective knowledge determination, function for measuring the increase of collective knowledge in a collective. In Sect. 3, the proposed method is presented. The experimental results and their evaluation will be provided in Sect. 4. Finally, conclusion and future work are pointed out in Sect. 5.

2   Basic Notions

2.1   Collective of Knowledge States

Let U be a set of objects representing the potential elements of knowledge referring to a subject in the real world. The structure of elements of the set U can be logic expressions, relational structures, ontology, etc. The elements of set U can be inconsistent with each other. By 2^U we denotes the set of all subsets of U and $\prod_k (U)$ is the set of all k-element subsets (with repetitions) of set U for $k \in N$ (N is the set of natural numbers), and let $\prod (U)$ be the set of all non-empty finite subsets with repetitions of set U as follows:

$$\prod (U) = \bigcup_{k=1}^{\infty} \prod_k (U) \qquad (1)$$

A set $X \in \prod (U)$ is called a collective and can represent the knowledge states given by autonomous units on the same subject. In this work, based on the Euclidean space, a collective of knowledge states (or collective for short) is described as follows:

$$X = \{x_i = (x_{i1}, x_{i2}, ..., x_{im}) : i = 1, 2, ..., n\} \qquad (2)$$

where $x_{ij} \in R, j = 1, 2, ..., m$; n is the number of collective members; R is the set of real numbers; m is the number of dimensions. Each element of the collective, given by an autonomous unit, is a multi-dimensional vector. In addition, each dimension represents the value of an issue of the subject which autonomous units are invited for giving their knowledge states (for example *max temperature* is an issue belonging to the subject of weather forecast).

Definition 1. *A collective $X \in \prod (U)$ is called:*

- *homogeneous, if all its knowledge states are identical, meaning $X = \{n * x\}$ where $x \in U$ and n is a natural number.*
- *heterogeneous, if it is not homogeneous.*

2.2 Knowledge of a Collective

As aforementioned, the collective knowledge of a collective is often determined from the basic of the knowledge states in that collective. According to [2] there exist many consensus-based algorithms which have been proposed to determine the collective knowledge of a collective for different knowledge representations such as: relational structures, ontology, etc. A consensus choice has usually been understood as a general agreement in situations where participants have not agreed on some matters [19]. A full degree of agreement (i.e. unanimity) is not required because it is difficult to achieve in practice [20]. Consensus models have been proved to be useful in solving conflict which arisen in the process of collective knowledge determination [19,21,22]. There exist two popular consensus-based criteria for determining the knowledge of a collective [2]. They are: 1-Optimality and 2-Optimality or O_1 and O_2 for short.

Let x^* be the collective knowledge of collective X consisting of n knowledge states referring to the same subject in the real world. Then the collective knowledge of a collective which determined by:

- Criterion O_1 if: $\sum_{i=1}^{n} d(x^*, x_i) = \min_{y \in U} \sum_{i=1}^{n} d(y, x_i)$
- Criterion O_2 if: $\sum_{i=1}^{n} d^2(x^*, x_i) = \min_{y \in U} \sum_{i=1}^{n} d^2(y, x_i)$

where $d(x_i, x_j)$ represents the distance from x_i to x_j, $\sum_{i=1}^{n} d(x^*, x_i)$ is the sum of distances from x^* to the knowledge states of collective X and $\sum_{i=1}^{n} d^2(x^*, x_i)$ is the sum of squared distances from x^* to the knowledge states of collective X. In case of using criterion O_2, the collective knowledge x^* has the following form:

$$x^* = \frac{1}{n} \left(\sum_{i=1}^{n} x_{i1}, \sum_{i=1}^{n} x_{i2}, ..., \sum_{i=1}^{n} x_{im} \right). \tag{3}$$

2.3 Increase of Collective Knowledge

Generally, the collective knowledge increase is understood as an additional amount of knowledge in a collective. It's different from the concept of new knowledge elements generated in a collective as mentioned in [10] or a *"surplus"* element as in [11]. Concretely, we consider the following definition.

Definition 2. *The collective knowledge increase in a collective is defined by a function Inc as follows:*

$$Inc : \prod (U) \rightarrow [-1, 1] \tag{4}$$

where $\prod (U)$ is set of non-empty subset with repetitions of universe U.

Definition 3. *Let x^*, y^* represent collective knowledge of collectives X and Y, respectively, let r be the real knowledge state. Function Inc should satisfy the following conditions:*

1. $\forall X \in \prod (U)$:
   (a) $\forall x_i \in X$: if $((r = x_i) \wedge (r = x^*))$, then $Inc(X) = 0$.

(b) $\forall x_i \in X$: *if* $((d(r, x_i) = 1) \wedge (r = x^*))$, *then* $Inc(X) = 1$.
(c) $\forall x_i \in X$: *if* $((r = x_i) \wedge (d(r, x^*) = 1))$, *then* $Inc(X) = -1$.

2. $\forall X, Y \in \prod(U)$: *if* $((r = x^* = y^*) \wedge (d(r, X) \geq d(r, Y)))$, *then* $Inc(X) \geq Inc(Y)$.

The first condition deals with some special cases of the collective knowledge increase. In case collective X is homogeneous and its knowledge states are identical to the real knowledge state, then there is no additional amount of knowledge in the collective. Inversely, in case all of the knowledge states have the maximal distance to the real knowledge state while the collective knowledge is identical to the real knowledge state, then the value of collective knowledge increase is maximal. Otherwise, this value is minimal in case all knowledge states are identical to the real knowledge sate, but the collective knowledge has maximal distance to the real knowledge state.

The second condition aims to reflect the large degree of collective knowledge increase in a collective in comparison with others. If the knowledge states of collective X are further from the real knowledge state than those of collective Y and the collective knowledge of these collectives are identical to the real knowledge state $(r = x^* = y^*)$, then the collective knowledge increase of collective X must be higher than that of collective Y.

Definition 4. *Function Inc satisfying above conditions has the following form:*

$$Inc(X) = \frac{d(r, X)}{n} - d(r, x^*) \tag{5}$$

According to Definition 4, function *Inc* takes into account the difference between the average of the distances from the real knowledge state to the knowledge states and the distance from the collective knowledge to the real knowledge state. However, in case the distance from the real knowledge state to the collective knowledge is greater than the average of the distances from the real knowledge state to the collective members, the value of collective knowledge increase is negative. However, similar to the problem of GDP (Gross Domestic Product) increase, sometimes it can be negative. In addition, this function also reflects the large degree of the collective knowledge increase in a collective in comparison with other collective. For example, there are two collectives $X = \{x_1, x_2\}$ and $Y = \{y_1, y_2\}$ as in Fig. 1. The collective knowledge of collectives X and Y $(x^*$ and y^* respectively) are identical to the real knowledge state. In this case, the collective knowledge increase in collective X is higher than that in collective Y.

3   The Influence of the Inconsistency Degree on the Collective Knowledge Increase

3.1   Inconsistency Degree Measure

Generally, inconsistency degree presents the coherence and density levels of the knowledge states of collective members [2]. Its measure is based on the distances

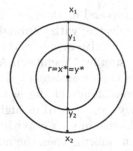

Fig. 1. Collective knowledge increase in collectives X and Y

between the knowledge states in a collective. According to [2], the author has defined five functions serve for measuring the inconsistency degree of a collective. However, in the paper, we concentrate on analyzing the influence of function c_3 on the collective knowledge increase in a collective. This function is considered as a representative of the inconsistency degree of collective members. The measure of inconsistency degree is taken into account the average of the distances between the knowledge states in a collective.

$$c_3(X) = \begin{cases} \frac{2}{n(n-1)} \sum_{i=1}^{n-1} \sum_{j=i+1}^{n} d(x_i, x_j) & n > 1 \\ 0 & \text{otherwise} \end{cases} \tag{6}$$

where $d(x_i, x_j)$ is the distance between knowledge states x_i and x_j in collective X.

3.2 The Proposed Method

In this section, we propose a method to determine the influence of the inconsistency degree on the collective knowledge increase as mentioned in Introduction section. For this aim, two cases involving adding members to or removing members from collectives which causes the inconsistency degree of the collectives to be down or up are investigated. This serves for proving the hypothesis *"the higher is the inconsistency degree, the better is the collective knowledge increase in a collective"*. The general idea of the proposed method is described in Fig. 2.

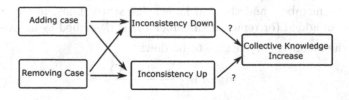

Fig. 2. Two cases of the proposed method

The detailed steps of the proposed method are described in the Fig. 3. With adding case, we start from a collective with minimal number of collective members *(n)*. Then the number of collective members is increased up to the maximal number of members *(m)* (each step by 1 member). An added member is a member in the set U which causes the inconsistency degree of the collective to be down or up. Meaning the inconsistency of the new collective in step *(k+1)* is smaller (in case of inconsistency to be down) or higher (in case of inconsistency to be up) than that of the collective in step k. With removing case, however, we start from a collective with m members. Then the number of collective members is decreased down to n members (each step by 1 member). Similar as adding case, the inconsistency of a new collective in step *(k+1)* (after removing 1 member) is smaller or higher than that of the collective at in step k.

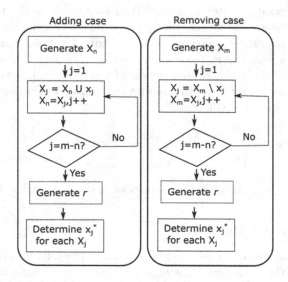

Fig. 3. The procedure of the proposed method

The most important tasks in the procedure are generating a new member (x_j) and the real knowledge state (r). Because of randomly generating reason, adding or removing a member can cause the value of collective knowledge increase to be higher or lower. This is dependent on the relationship between an added member (or a removed member) and the real knowledge state. Thus, in this work, the criterion for an added (or removed) member (y) is described as follows [23]:

– Causing the inconsistency degree to be down:

$$d(y, X) \leq \frac{\sum d(x_i, X)}{n - 1} \tag{7}$$

– Causing the inconsistency degree to be up:

$$d(y, X) \geq \frac{\sum d(x_i, X)}{n - 1} \tag{8}$$

As aforementioned, the criterion for simulating the real knowledge state is also an important task because it exists independently of the set of knowledge states in a collective and it's not known when the autonomous units are being invited for giving their knowledge states about a subject in the real world. In this work, the real knowledge state (r) is simulated when the collective has reached the maximal number of members (for adding case) or the minimal number of members (for removing case). The criterion is described as follows:

$$d(r, x^*) \leq \frac{\sum d(x^*, X)}{n} \qquad (9)$$

According to this criterion, the real knowledge state is not too far from the common knowledge state of a whole collective. The knowledge states in a collective are randomly generated. In this work, the set U is a set of points in the circle of radius 1.0, center $(0, 0)$. The knowledge states in a collective represent autonomous units' knowledge about the same subject in real world. A collective is a set with repetitions of n members belonging to the set U.

4   Simulation Experiments and Their Analysis

Since the problem of choosing the number of collective members should be enough for a given subject is a difficult and complicated task. Thus, in this paper, the minimal number of collective members begins with an odd number as mentioned in [2,24]. The choosing of the maximal number of collective members is based on the stability of the inconsistency degree in a collective after adding members. In simulation experiments we use 3 as the minimal number of collective members and 250 as the maximal number of collective members. The experimental results are described in the following figures:

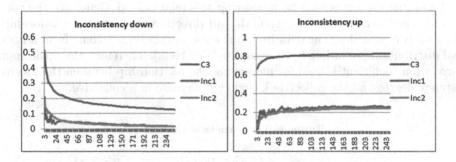

Fig. 4. Adding case with maximal 250 members

In the above figures c_3 is inconsistency degree of a collective; $Inc1$ and $Inc2$ are the collective knowledge increase satisfying criteria O_1 and O_2 respectively. Firstly, Fig. 4 contains the results for experiments in case of adding members such that causes the inconsistency degree of the collective to be down (the left

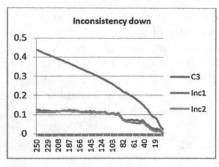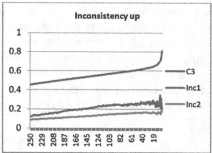

Fig. 5. Removing case with maximal 250 members

one) and to be up (the right one). Similarly, Fig. 5 presents the experimental results in case of removing members such that causes the inconsistency degree of the collective to be down (the left one) and to be up (the right one).

According to these figures, adding members to (or removing members from) a collective such that causes the inconsistency degree of the collective to be down does not positively affect the collective knowledge increase in a collective. Inversely, adding members to (or removing members from) a collective which causes the inconsistency degree of the collective to be up will cause the collective knowledge increase in a collective to be higher. From this fact we can conclude that the nature of collective knowledge increase is due to the inconsistency degree of a collective. In other words, with some restrictions, collectives with more inconsistency degree will give better collective knowledge increase than that of collectives with lower inconsistency degree.

However, whether the relationship between the inconsistency degree and the collective knowledge increase in a collective is statistically significant? For this aim, a statistical test is used for measuring this relationship. Generally, the correlation coefficient reflects the strength and direction of the linear relationship between two variables. The data from our experiments do not come from a normal distribution (according to the Shapiro-Wilk tests). Therefore, the Spearman correlation coefficient is used for measuring the relationship between the inconsistency degree and the collective knowledge increase in a collective.

Table 1. The statistical analysis

		Criterion O_1		Criterion O_2	
		Rho	$p\text{-}value$	Rho	$p\text{-}value$
Adding case	Inconsistency down	0.9749	$< 2.2e - 16$	0.9999	$< 2.2e - 16$
	Inconsistency up	0.8325	$< 2.2e - 16$	0.9864	$< 2.2e - 16$
Removing case	Inconsistency down	0.9504	$< 2.2e - 16$	0.9870	$< 2.2e - 16$
	Inconsistency up	0.9444	$< 2.2e - 16$	0.9209	$< 2.2e - 16$

According to Table 1, the relationship between the inconsistency degree and the collective knowledge increase in a collective is very strong for both adding and removing cases. In addition, the values of *p-value* in all situations are very small $(< 2.2e - 16)$. Therefore, the correlation coefficients in these situations are statistically significant. Thus, through experiments analysis we can conclude that the inconsistency degree positively affects the collective knowledge increase in a collective. For more detail we consider the following theorems:

Theorem 1. *For a given collective $X = \{x_1, x_2, ..., x_n\}$*
Let x^* be its collective knowledge. Let $Y = X \cup \{x^*\}$, y^* be the knowledge of collective Y.

1. *If $d(r, x_1) = d(r, x_2) = ... = d(r, x_n)$, then $Inc(X) \geq Inc(Y)$*
2. *If $d^2(x^*, X) = \min_{z \in U} d^2(z, X) \wedge d^2(y^*, Y) = \min_{z \in U} d^2(z, Y)$, then $Inc(X) \geq Inc(Y)$*

Proof. The proof for this theorem is not included because of page limit.   □

According to Theorem 1, with some restrictions, in case the collective knowledge of a collective is added to that collective, the collective knowledge increase in the added collective *(Y)* will not be higher than that in the original collective *(X)*. Concretely, in case all of the knowledge states of collective X to the same degree reflect the real knowledge state, the collective knowledge increase in collective X is higher than that in collective Y. In addition, in case of satisfying criterion O_2, the collective knowledge increase of collective X is also always higher than that of collective Y.

Theorem 2. *For a given collective $X = \{x_1, x_2, ..., x_n\}, Y = \{y_1, y_2, ..., y_n\}$*
Let x^*, y^* represent their collective knowledge (satisfying criterion O_2) respectively.
If $(d(r, X) = d(r, Y) \wedge c_3(X) \leq c_3(Y))$, then $Inc(X) \geq Inc(Y)$.

Proof. The proof for this theorem is not included because of page limit.   □

From Theorem 2, we can state that the smaller inconsistency degree is not always useful and it positively affects the collective knowledge increase in a collective. This is consistent with the results of the statistical analysis as in [12,13]. Inversely, the inconsistency degree plays an important role in giving a bettter collective knowledge increase in a collective. From this theorem we can conclude that, with some restrictions, the hypothesis *"the higher is the inconsistency degree, the better is the collective knowledge increase in a collective"* is true.

5   Conclusion and Future Work

In this paper, we have investigated the problem of collective knowledge increase for objective case by taking into account the number of collective members.

Through experiments analysis, adding or removing members which causes decreasing the inconsistency degree does not cause the value of collective knowledge increase in a collective to be higher. Inversely, the collective knowledge increase in a collective to be higher in case of adding or removing members which causes increasing the inconsistency degree. In addition, if the added members are the collective knowledge, then the value of collective knowledge increase is not higher than that in the original collective. From these results we can state that with some restrictions the inconsistency positively effects on the collective knowledge increase in a collective. Concretely, the hypothesis *"the higher is the inconsistency degree, the better is the collective knowledge increase in a collective"* is true.

The future work should determine the number of collective members for a given degree of collective knowledge increase; the upper limit of knowledge increase in a collective by taking into account the number of collective members; the influence of the inconsistency degree on the collective knowledge increase in case of updating knowledge states in a collective. With these problems paraconsistent logics could be useful [25].

Acknowledgement. This research is partially funded by Vietnam National University Ho Chi Minh City (VNU-HCM) under grant number C2014-26-05.

References

1. Nguyen, N.T.: Processing inconsistency of knowledge in determining knowledge of collective. Cybern. Syst. **40**(8), 670–688 (2009)
2. Nguyen, N.T.: Advanced Methods for Inconsistent Knowledge Management. Springer, London (2008)
3. Tziner, A., Eden, D.: Effects of crew composition on crew performance: does the whole equal the sum of its parts? J. Appl. Psychol. **70**(1), 85–93 (1985)
4. Barrick, M.R., Stewart, G.L., Neubert, M.J., Mount, M.K.: Relating member ability and personality to work-team processes and team effectiveness. J. Appl. Psychol. **83**(3), 377–391 (1998)
5. Neuman, G.A., Wagner, S.H., Christiansen, N.D.: The relationship between work-team personality composition and the job performance of teams. Group Organ. Manag. **24**(1), 28–45 (1999)
6. Klimoski, R., Mohammed, S.: Team mental model: construct or metaphor? J. Manag. **20**(2), 403–437 (1994)
7. Hutchins, E.: The social organization of distributed cognition. In: Resnick, L.B., Levine, J.M., Teasley, S.D. (eds.) Perspectives on Socially Shared Cognition, pp. 283–307. American Psychological Association, Washington, DC (1991)
8. Nguyen, N.T.: Inconsistency of knowledge and collective intelligence. Cybern. Syst. **39**(6), 542–562 (2008)
9. Nguyen, V.D., Nguyen, N.T.: A method for improving the quality of collective knowledge. In: Nguyen, N.T., Trawiński, B., Kosala, R. (eds.) ACIIDS 2015. LNCS, vol. 9011, pp. 75–84. Springer, Heidelberg (2015)
10. Maleszka, M., Nguyen, N.T.: Integration computing and collective intelligence. Expert Syst. Appl. **42**(1), 332–340 (2015)

11. Hecker, A.: Knowledge beyond the individual? Making sense of a notion of collective knowledge in organization theory. Organ. Stud. **33**(3), 423–445 (2012)
12. Shermer, M.: The Science of Good and Evil. Henry Holt, New York (2004)
13. Surowiecki, J.: The Wisdom of Crowds. Anchor, New York (2005)
14. Herrera-Viedma, E., Herrera, F., Chiclana, F., Luque, M.: Some issues on consistency of fuzzy preference relations. Eur. J. Oper. Res. **154**(1), 98–109 (2004)
15. Francisco, C., Mata, F., Martinez, L., Herrera-Viedma, E., Alonso, S.: Integration of a consistency control module within a consensus model. Int. J. Uncertainty Fuzziness Knowl. Based Syst. **16**(supp01), 35–53 (2008)
16. Xu, Z.: An automatic approach to reaching consensus in multiple attribute group decision making. Comput. Ind. Eng. **56**(4), 1369–1374 (2009)
17. Wu, Z., Xu, J.: A concise consensus support model for group decision making with reciprocal preference relations based on deviation measures. Fuzzy Sets Syst. **206**, 58–73 (2012)
18. Wu, Z., Xu, J.: A consistency and consensus based decision support model for group decision making with multiplicative preference relations. Decis. Support Syst. **52**(3), 757–767 (2012)
19. Day, W.H.E.: The Consensus Methods as Tools for Data Analysis. In: Bock, H.H. (ed.) IFC 1987: Classifications and Related Methods of Data Analysis. Springer, Heidelberg (1988)
20. Kline, J.A.: Orientation and group consensus. Cent. States Speech J. **23**(1), 44–47 (1972)
21. Barthelemy, J.P., Guenoche, A., Hudry, O.: Median linear orders: heuristics and a branch and bound algorithm. Eur. J. Oper. Res. **42**(3), 313–325 (1989)
22. Nguyen, N.T.: Using consensus methods for determining the representation of expert information in distributed systems. In: Cerri, S.A., Dochev, D. (eds.) AIMSA 2000. LNCS (LNAI), vol. 1904, pp. 11–20. Springer, Heidelberg (2000)
23. Nguyen, V.D., Nguyen, N.T.: An influence analysis of the inconsistency degree on the quality of collective knowledge for objective case. In: Nguyen, N.T., Trawiński, B., Fujita, H., Hong, T.-P. (eds.) ACIIDS 2016. LNCS, vol. 9621, pp. 23–32. Springer, Heidelberg (2016)
24. Nguyen, N.T.: Criteria for consensus susceptibility in conflicts resolving. In: Inuiguchi, M., Hirano, S., Tsumoto, S. (eds.) Rough Set Theory and Granular Computing, pp. 223–232. Springer, Heidelberg (2003)
25. Nakamatsu, K., Abe, J.: The paraconsistent process order control method. Vietnam J. Comput. Sci. **1**(1), 29–37 (2014)

Ontological Approach to Design Reasoning with the Use of Many-Sorted First-Order Logic

Wojciech Palacz[✉], Ewa Grabska, and Grażyna Ślusarczyk

The Faculty of Physics, Astronomy and Applied Computer Science,
Jagiellonian University, ul. Łojasiewicza 11, 30-348 Kraków, Poland
{wojciech.palacz,ewa.grabska,grazyna.slusarczyk}@uj.edu.pl

Abstract. This paper is a continuation and extension in developing the knowledge-based decision support design system (called HSSDR) which communicates with the designer via drawings. Graph-based modeling of conceptualization in the CAD process, which enables the system to automatically transform design drawings into appropriate graph-based data structures, is considered. Hierarchical graphs with bonds are proposed as a representation of designs. An ontological commitment between design conceptualization and internal representations of solutions, which enables us to capture intended design models, is described. Moreover, the first-order logic (FOL) of HSSDR is replaced by many-sorted FOL that makes it possible to define different sorts in specification of functions and predicates in semantics and design constraint verification.

1 Introduction

This paper is focused on maintaining ontological compatibility between drawings and their graph-based representations in a CAD process. Design drawings are created on the basis of the conceptualization characteristic for a given design domain. Conceptualization concerns objects, concepts, and other entities that are assumed to exist in the considered domain of discourse, and the relationships that hold among them.

The drawings by which a CAD system communicates with the designer are usually converted to some internal data structures. In many CAD programs those structures are graph-based, because graphs are well-suited to model sub-components of the designed object and relations between those subcomponents. An example of such a system is HSSDR (Hypergraph System Supporting Design and Reasoning) described in [3]. It was developed as a tool for designing floor layouts and validating their correctness in respect to an adjustable set of rules.

Every action undertaken by the designer modifies a displayed drawing and this modification is in turn reflected in the HSSDR's internal data structure in the form of a hierarchical graph. Every modification done by the designer triggers a constraint verification round. Design constraints are specified as logic formulas. Two constraint sets, which verify compliance with fire code regulations and check if all paths leading to certain important rooms are monitored by cameras, were considered in [3].

© Springer International Publishing Switzerland 2016
L. Rutkowski et al. (Eds.): ICAISC 2016, Part II, LNAI 9693, pp. 364–374, 2016.
DOI: 10.1007/978-3-319-39384-1_31

Experiences gained during implementation and testing of the original version of HSSDR have suggested two potential improvements. The first one is concerned with the way of modeling parts of the layout. Areas, rooms and walls were treated as elements of the domain of discourse, while other objects, like doors and cameras, as properties (attributes) of these elements. This approach caused the lack of ontological compatibility between conceptualization and the hypergraph representation of drawings. This paper proposes a new representation in the form of hierarchical graphs with bonds, which makes it possible to include all of the objects as elements of the domain of discourse.

Another proposed improvement concerns the language in which the design constraints are specified. The FOL is replaced by many-sorted FOL. It allows for enhanced syntactic checking of the constraints.

This paper is organized as follows: Sect. 2 gives some insights in human-computer interaction in the context of computer-aided design. Section 3 presents the current modeling system, while Sect. 4 then proposes its modifications. In Sect. 5 a new type of hierarchical graphs, so called the graphs with bonds, is defined. Sections 6 and 7 consider the reasoning mechanism of HSSDR based on many-sorted FOL language, while reasoning examples are given in Sect. 8. The paper ends with a conclusion.

2 Human-Computer Interaction in CAD

During the conceptual design the designer has to describe the domain of discourse being a subset of his/her cognitive domain. There exists the need to keep in mind objects, concepts, and other entities that are assumed to exist in the considered domain of discourse, and the relationships that hold among them. Conceptualization is one of the most challenging aspects of designing because it forces designers to considers many disparate factors. According to [2] a conceptualization can be defined as follows.

Definition 1. *A conceptualization is a pair* $C = (\Delta, \Theta)$, *where:* Δ *is a set called the universe of discourse, and* Θ *is a set of relations on* Δ.

During the computer aided design process externalization of designer's conceptualization takes the form of design drawings. They are generated by the designer with the use of a visual editor and constitute the first type of representation storing information about design solutions. Design drawings are composed of transformed basic shapes which are specified on the basis of the conceptualization. The design drawing can be formally defined as follows.

Definition 2. *Let* F *be a set of admissible transformations of the form* $f : R^n \to R^n$. *Let* S *be a finite set of basic shapes being bounded subsets of* R^n *such that for each two* $s, s' \in S$ *and* $f \in F$, $f(s) = s' \Rightarrow s = s'$. *Let* $Q \subset S \times F$ *be a space configuration.*

A design drawing with configuration Q *is specified as* $Z(Q) = \cup_{(s,f) \in Q} f(s)$.

In HSSDR the designer can generate an *observable world state* in the form of a design drawing (Fig. 1). In each step of the design process the designer can change his conceptualization, i.e., number of elements of the domain of discourse Δ and/or relations of Θ on Δ because both the requirements and the design become more refined as the project proceeds. The conceptualization for the designer's world can be represented by the sequence of observable world states and denoted by W. The conceptualization which includes all entities and relations defined for W is denoted by $\mathcal{C}_W$.

The designer communicates with the design system using a visual design language, i.e., a set of design drawings. Let us consider the specialized CAD editor for designing floor layout composed of polygons which are placed on an orthogonal grid. These polygons represent functional areas or rooms. According to designer's convention each line shared by polygons in the drawing is associated with one of two relations. Lines with a door symbol on them represent the accessibility relation among components, while continuous lines shared by polygons denote the adjacency relation between them. An example of a floor layout generated by the designer with the use of the editor is shown in Fig. 1.

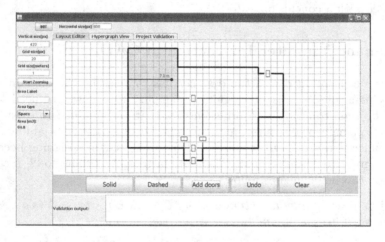

Fig. 1. The design drawing representing a floor-layout created by the designer in HSSDR

A majority of visual languages is characterized by a vocabulary being a finite set of basic shapes and a finite set of rules specifying possible configurations of these shapes. Basic shapes of visual languages and their spatial relationships correspond to concepts and relations defined by the conceptualization of the discourse domain. Each specialized design domain has its own visual language related to concepts of this domain [4, 5].

3   The Current Modeling System

The Hypergraph System Supporting Design and Reasoning described in [3] is a system for designing floor layouts using the top-down methodology. HSSDR communicates with its users by means of a simple visual language of diagrams. It also checks if the current state of the layout satisfies design constraints specified as a set of FOL formulas.

A user starts by drawing an outline of an apartment. This outline is then divided by drawing a polyline. The resulting areas are further divided into sub-areas. The user continues dividing them, stopping when she reaches the level of rooms. Doors and cameras can be added either during, or after this process.

HSSDR internally uses a hierarchical hypergraph as its main data structure (see Fig. 2). Every user action modifying the displayed diagram is reflected in this hypergraph.

The hypergraph consists of two types of hyperedges: those representing rooms and areas, and those representing adjacency and accessibility relations. Functional areas and groups of rooms are at higher hierarchy levels, while single rooms are at the bottom. Graph nodes correspond to walls. Attributes are used to store rooms positions, as well as wall lengths, number and positions of doors and cameras, room labels, etc.

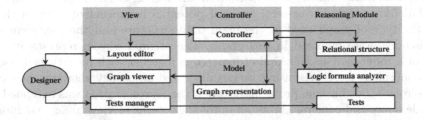

Fig. 2. The internal architecture of HSSDR

The design constraints are stored in external text files, thus they can be easily modified or replaced at any time, even in the middle of a design session. Constraints can refer to elements of the layout (rooms, walls, doors and cameras) and to a fixed set of relations and functions (adjacency between two rooms, room type, distance between two doors, etc.). Thanks to the use of widely known FOL formalisms they are readable by developers, experts and users.

The constraints are logic sentences, and as such can be evaluated as true or false in context of a specific relational structure [1]. HSSDR defines a structure which reflects the current state of the hypergraph. Results of evaluation are presented to the user; all false results are flagged as constraint violations.

An example of such results can be seen in Fig. 3. The text field near the bottom shows the name of the file and the message associated with the failed test. The layout element which failed this test is marked red on the diagram.

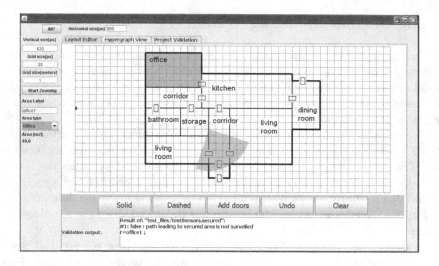

Fig. 3. A finished layout which does not fulfill one of design constraints

4   The New System

Experiences gained during implementation and testing of the original version of HSSDR have pointed to several areas of potential improvement. One of them was the type of graph used as the main data structure and the way elements of discourse were modeled in this graph. The original way of representing an area or a room by a special kind of hyperedge together with its attached nodes was convenient for representing accessibility and adjacency relations between areas/rooms, but became problematic when the representation was extended to include doors and cameras. From an ontological point of view areas and rooms are treated as elements of the domain of discourse, while other objects as doors and cameras as properties (attributes) of these elements. In other words, there does not exist ontological commitment between conceptualization and its representation in the form attributed hypergraph. Therefore, this paper proposes a new model which uses hierarchical graphs with bonds. This type of graphs makes it possible to include all of the object as elements of the domain of discourse. Bonds are distinguished graph nodes which can specify arguments of relations on different levels of detail.

Another proposed improvement concerns the language, in which the design constraints are specified. The original HSSDR used FOL; it can be replaced by many-sorted FOL. Introduction of sorts divides the domain of discourse into subsets: of rooms, of doors, of numbers, of room types, etc. Predicates and functions used in formulas are annotated with information about sorts of their arguments and results. This allows for enhanced syntactic checking of formulas.

The new system keeps the name HSSDR, but the first letter now stands for a hierarchical graph, not for a hypergraph. So, it can refer to any kind of a hierarchical graph, from graphs described in [7], through hypergraphs used by the previous version of HSSDR and B-graphs proposed for the new version, to other kinds which may be used in the future. For example, multi-hierarchical graphs seem promising as models for multi-storey buildings and other cases where single hierarchy based on spatial containment is insufficient.

5   Hierarchical B-Graphs

B-graphs are meant to represent objects and their fragments or elements (known as bonds) that can be used as arguments of relations. Relations are defined between bonds. We distinguish two kinds of bonds: engaged and free, which correspond to arguments of existing and potential relations, respectively. This distinction of bonds is essential for defining operations on graphs that reflect modifications of design drawings.

B-graphs used in this paper are hierarchical, because of the need to represent nested areas. Hierarchy also allows for sub-bonds (for example, a room has walls as its fragments and one of them has a door – this door is a fragment of the room, but also is subordinate to the wall). Instead of one set of nodes, B-graphs have two: a set of object nodes and a set of bond nodes. They also have a set of edges. Every edge connects bonds belonging to two different objects. HSSDR needs to store additional information about layout elements, therefore B-graphs allow for labels and attributes on nodes and edges.

Let Σ be a finite alphabet used to label object nodes, bond nodes and edges. Let A be a nonempty, finite set of attributes. For every attribute $a \in A$, let D_a be a fixed, nonempty set of its admissible values, known as the domain of a.

Definition 3. *A B-graph G is a tuple $G = (O, B, E, bd, s, t, ch, lab, atr)$, where:*

- *O, B, E are pairwise disjoint finite sets, whose elements are respectively called object nodes, bond nodes, and edges,*
- *$bd : O \to 2^B$ is a function assigning sets of bond nodes to object nodes in such a way that $\forall x \in B \; \exists ! y \in O : x \in bd(y)$, i.e., each bond belongs to exactly one object,*
- *$s, t : E \to B$ are functions assigning to edges source and target bond nodes, respectively, in such a way that $\forall e \in E \; \exists x, y \in O : s(e) \in bd(x) \land t(e) \in bd(y) \land x \neq y$,*
- *$ch : O \cup B \cup E \to 2^{O \cup B \cup E}$ is a child nesting function such that:*
  - *$\forall x, y, z \in O \cup B \cup E : x \in ch(y) \land x \in ch(z) \Rightarrow y = z$, i.e., a graph element cannot be nested in two different places,*
  - *$\forall x \in O \cup B \cup E : x \notin ch^+(x)$, i.e., a graph element cannot be its own descendant,*
  - *$\forall x \in B, \; \forall y \in O : x \in bd(y) \Rightarrow x \in ch(y) \lor (\exists z \in B : x \in ch(z) \land z \in bd(y))$, i.e., a bond must be nested either in its object, or in some other bond belonging to this object,*
- *$lab : O \cup B \cup E \to \Sigma$ is a labelling function,*
- *$atr : O \cup B \cup E \to 2^A$ is an attributing function.*

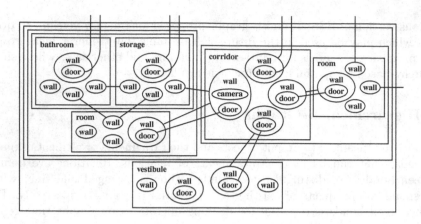

Fig. 4. A part of a graph model corresponding to the layout displayed in Fig. 3

A part of the B-graph being the internal representation of the layout shown in Fig. 3 is presented in Fig. 4. Bonds without the outgoing edges in Fig. 4 represent free bonds.

A graph instance is obtained by adding attribute values. Each design drawing is represented by a corresponding B-graph instance defined as follows.

Definition 4. *An instance I of a B-graph G is a pair $I = (G, val)$ where $G = (O, B, E, bd, s, t, ch, lab, atr)$ and $val : O \cup B \cup E \times A \to D$, with $D = \bigcup_{a \in A} D_a$, is a partial function assigning attribute values in such a way that $val(x, a)$ is defined if and only if $a \in atr(x)$ and $val(x, a) \in D_a$ if defined.*

The proposed B-graphs allow for maintaining ontological compatibility between drawings and their graph-based representations.

Definition 5. *Let W denote the designer's world and $C_W = (\Delta_W, \Theta_W)$ be a conceptualization for W. Let $G_W = (O, B, E, bd, s, t, ch, lab, atr)$ be a family of B-graphs representing world states of W.*

An ontological commitment between C_W and G_W is a mapping $\Im_W : \Delta_W \cup \Theta_W \to O \cup B \cup E$, such that for each C_w, where $w \in W$, there exists B-graph $g_w \in G_W$ such that concepts of Δ_W are mapped to object and bond nodes of g_w and relations of Θ_W to edges of g_w.

6 Many-Sorted First-Order Logic

The explicit specification of design constraints related to the reasoning mechanism based on representation of drawings in the form of B-graph instances must be formal, i.e., the expressions must be defined in a formal language. We use a many-sorted FOL language which introduces representing distinct kinds of objects to reason about [6]. The concept of sort allows one to specify for functions and relations what sorts of their domains and ranges are required.

The formal description of many-sorted FOL formulas starts with the following definition of a signature.

Definition 6. *A signature σ is a tuple $\sigma = (S, X, C, F, P)$, where:*

- *$S = \{s_1, s_2, \ldots, s_k\}$ is a set of sorts,*
- *X is a set of variables, which is partitioned into subsets $X_1 \ldots X_k$ with each X_i containing variables of sort s_i,*
- *C is a set of constant symbols, which is partitioned into subsets $C_1 \ldots C_k$ with each C_i containing constants of sort s_i,*
- *F is a set of n-ary function symbols the type $s_{i_1} \times \cdots \times s_{i_n} \to s_{i_{n+1}}$, where $n \geq 0$, and each $s_{i_j} \in S$,*
- *P is a set of n-ary predicate symbols of the type $s_{i_1} \times \cdots \times s_{i_n}$, where $n \geq 0$, and each $s_{i_j} \in S$.*

Definitions of σ-terms and σ-formulas are analogous to the definitions of these concepts for the classic FOL language. A formula where all variables are bound by quantifiers is known as a sentence. Sentences are either true or false, but only after all symbols used in formulas are assigned a specific semantics. This semantic information is provided by a relational structure defined as follows.

Definition 7. *For a signature σ, a σ-relational structure R is a map with the following properties:*

- *each sort s_i is mapped to a nonempty set A_i,*
- *each constant symbol $c \in C_i$ is mapped to an element of A_i,*
- *each function symbol $f : s_{i_1} \times \cdots \times s_{i_n} \to s_{i_{n+1}}$ is mapped to a function $f^R : A_{i_1} \times \cdots \times A_{i_n} \to A_{i_{n+1}}$,*
- *each predicate symbol $p : s_{i_1} \times \cdots \times s_{i_n}$ is mapped to a subset $p^R \subset A_{i_1} \times \cdots \times A_{i_n}$.*

7 Reasoning Module of HSSDR

The HSSDR's reasoning module interprets symbols of the logic language signature on the basis of B-graphs representing design drawings. This interpretation should be compatible with the ontological commitment between conceptualization and graph structures (Definition 5). On the basis of this assumption the vocabulary of the reasoning module is defined.

In HSSDR the following sorts are defined: *areas, walls, doors, sensors, labels* and *numbers*. There are constants representing labels ("hall", "bathroom", etc.) and numbers. There are functions: *type* : *areas* $\to$ *labels*, *width*, *length* : *areas* $\to$ *numbers*, *doorsDist* : *doors* $\times$ *doors* $\to$ *numbers* (returns a distance between two pairs of doors in a single room), and standard arithmetic operators, either *numbers* $\times$ *numbers* $\to$ *numbers* or *numbers* $\to$ *numbers*.

Two-argument predicates: *adjacent, accessible* : *areas* $\times$ *areas*, *doors InRoom* : *doors* $\times$ *areas* (returns true if the doors are embedded in a wall of the room), *sensorInRoom* : *sensors* $\times$ *areas*, *isPassageWatched* : *doors* $\times$ *doors* (returns true if every path between two pairs of doors in a single room is watched by one or more sensors), and standard arithmetic comparison operators: $numbers \times numbers$.

One-argument predicates (i.e., sort subsets): $Areas : areas$, $Rooms : areas$, $Walls : walls$, $Doors : doors$, $ExternalDoors : doors$, and $Sensors : sensors$.

Only Rooms and ExternalDoors define proper subsets of their sorts. Other predicates always return true, and thus define sets equal to their whole sorts. From the formal point of view these predicates are not necessary, and are provided only because constraint writers sometimes prefer to write constraints with explicitly specified quantifier ranges, e.g., $forall\ a\ in\ Rooms:\ type(a) = $ "bank vault" $=>\ exists\ s\ in\ Sensors:\ sensorInRoom(s,\ a)$.

For a given B-graph I representing a layout, the corresponding relational structure R is constructed as follows:

- $A_{areas} = O_I$, $A_{walls} = \{x \in B_I : lab_I(x) = $ "wall" $\}$, $A_{doors} = \{x \in B_I : lab_I(x) = $ "door"$\}$, $A_{sensors} = \{x \in B_I : lab_I(x) = $"sensor"$\}$, $A_{labels} = \Sigma$, $A_{numbers} = \mathbb{R}$,
- label and number constants are mapped to themselves,
- $type^R(x) = lab_I(x)$, $width^R(x) = val_I(x,$ "width"$)$, $length^R(x) = val_I(x,$ "length"$)$, $doorsDist^R(x, y)$ is implemented algorithmically,
- arithmetic operators are defined as themselves,
- $adjacent^R = \{(x, y) \subset O_I \times O_I$: exists $e \in E_I$ such that $s_I(e) \in bd_I(x), t_I(e) \in bd_I(y), lab_I(e) = $ "adjacent"$\}$,
- $acessible^R = \{(x, y) \subset O_I \times O_I$: exists $e \in E_I$ such that $s_I(e) \in bd_I(x), t_I(e) \in bd_I(y), lab_I(e) = $ "acessible"$\}$,
- $doorsInRoom^R = \{(x, y) \subset B_I \times O_I : lab_I(x) = $ "door", $x \in bd_I(y)\}$,
- $sensorInRoom^R = \{(x, y) \subset B_I \times O_I : lab_I(x) = $ "sensor", $x \in bd_I(y)\}$,
- $isPassageWatched^R \subset B_I \times B_I$ is calculated by Java code,
- arithmetic comparisons are defined as themselves,
- $Areas^R = A_{areas}$, $Rooms^R = \{x \in O_I : ch_I(x) \cap O_I = \emptyset\}$, $Walls^R = A_{walls}$, $Doors^R = A_{doors}$, $ExternalDoors^R = \{x \in A_{doors}$: there is no $e \in E_I$ such that $s_I(e) = x\}$, $Sensors^R = A_{sensors}$.

8   Reasoning Examples

This section provides several examples of tests, written in a form acceptable to HSSDR.

The following constraint requires at least one bedroom present in the layout: $exists\ x:\ type(x) = $"Bedroom". The HSSDR's reasoning module, when loading this formula, will recognize x as a variable of an unspecified sort and "Bedroom" as a constant of the labels sort. Since x is used as an argument of the $type$ function, it apparently must be of the areas sort. This function produces results of the labels sort, which means that both sides of the equality sign are of the same sort. The formula is syntactically correct. The reasoning module uses exhaustive search when evaluating formulas with quantifiers. In this case, since x is of the areas sort, it will loop over all areas (and rooms) currently present in the layout – that is, over elements of the $Areas^R$ set.

The constraint of the form *exists r: type(r) > 42* is syntactically invalid, because results of the *type* function belong to the labels sort, and cannot be compared with constants of the numbers sort.

The last example checks if all path leading to secured areas are watched by sensors. Originally presented in [8], here it was adapted to many-sorted logic. Results produced by this test can be seen on screenshots in Figs. 3 and 5. At first, the test fails because a thief can enter through the doors in the dining room and walk unobserved through kitchen to the office. Adding a second sensor in the kitchen secures this path. In the similar way the satisfaction of standard architectural norms can be checked.

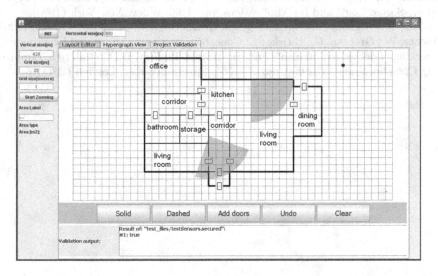

Fig. 5. Corrected version of the layout from Fig. 3.

9   Conclusions

This paper presents how graphs can be combined with logic-based knowledge representation techniques, where knowledge is represented explicitly by symbolic terms and reasoning is the manipulation of these terms. In the proposed approach the semantics of logical formulas build over many-sorted signature uses relational structures based on B-graph instances.

In our future research we shall focus attention on modelling multi-storey buildings with the use of multi-hierarchical graph representations with bonds.

References

1. Fagin, R., Halpern, J.Y., Moses, Y., Vardi, M.Y.: Reasoning About Knowledge. The MIT Press, Cambridge (2003)
2. Genesereth, M.R., Nilsson, N.J.: Logical Foundations of Artifical Intelligence. Morgan Kaufmann, Los Altos (1987)
3. Grabska, E., Borkowski, A., Palacz, W., Gajek, Sz.: Hypergraph system supporting design and reasoning. In: Huhnt, W. (ed.) Computing in Engineering EG-ICE Conference 2009, pp. 134–141. Shaker Verlag (2009)
4. Grabska, E., Łachwa, A., Ślusarczyk, G.: New visual languages supporting design of multi-storey buildings. Adv. Eng. Inform. **26**, 681–690 (2012)
5. Kraft, B., Nagl, M.: Visual knowledge specification for conceptual design: definition and tool support. Adv. Eng. Inform. **21**, 67–83 (2007)
6. Manzano, M.: Introduction to many-sorted logic. In: Meinke, K., Tucker, J.V. (eds.) Many-Sorted Logic and Its Applications, pp. 3–86. Wiley, New York (1993)
7. Palacz, W.: Algebraic hierarchical graph transformation. JCSS **68**, 497–520 (2004)
8. Palacz, W., Grabska, G., Gajek, Sz.: Conceptual designing supported by automated checking of design requirements and constraints. In: Frey, D.D., et al. (eds.) Improving Complex Systems Today, pp. 257–265. Springer-Verlag, London (2011)

Local Modeling with Local Dimensionality Reduction: Learning Method of Mini-Models

Andrzej Piegat[✉] and Marcin Pietrzykowski

Faculty of Computer Science and Information Technology,
West Pomeranian University of Technology, Żołnierska 49, 71-210 Szczecin, Poland
{apiegat,mpietrzykowski}@wi.zut.edu.pl

Abstract. The paper presents a new version on the mini-models method
(MM-method). Generally, the MM-method identifies not the full global
model of a system but only a local model of the neighborhood of the query
point of our special interest. It is an instance-based learning method
similarly as the k-nearest algorithm, GRNN network or RBF network
but its idea is different. In the MM-method the learning process is based
on a group of points that is constrained by a polytope. The first MM-
method was described in previous publications of authors. In this paper
a new version of the MM-method is presented. In comparison to the
previous version it was extended by local dimensionality reduction. As
experiments have shown this reduction not only simplifies local models
but also in most cases allows for increasing the local model precision.

Keywords: Mini-model · Local self-learning · Function approximation ·
Instance-based learning · Local dimensionality reduction

1 Introduction

The mini-models idea is new but the method itself already was described in
many publications. Mini-models based on polytopes in 2D- and 3D-space were
described in publications of authors [1–4]. The method could also work in multidimensional space what was described in following papers [5,6]. The unique
characteristic of MM-method is that the method uses sample points only from
the local neighborhood of the query. This is the consequences of the fact that
very often we are only interested in an answer to a specific query point. This
kind of an answer does not require identification of the full function over a great
inputs domain of the problem. Thus, learning process of MM-method is in fact
the identification process of a mathematical function which describes the dependence between input and output variables only in some part of the space. It
creates a local constrained model that can be simple e.g. the linear regression.
The set of points which is used in the learning process of a MM is contained in a
basic polytope. This area is called *mini-model area* or a *mini-model domain* and
is defined in the input space of the problem. In the general case for n-dimensional
space the mini-model area has character of a n-1-dimensional convex polytope.

© Springer International Publishing Switzerland 2016
L. Rutkowski et al. (Eds.): ICAISC 2016, Part II, LNAI 9693, pp. 375–383, 2016.
DOI: 10.1007/978-3-319-39384-1_32

I could be based on any type of polytope. Previous publications described mini-models based on simplex, n-cube and n-orthoplex. The MM-area can also have hyper-ellipsoidal shape [7].

The MM-method is an supervised instance-based learning algorithm (memory-based learning). Methods in this group instead of performing explicit generalization, compare new problem instances with instances from training, which are stored in the memory [8,9]. In this type of algorithm complexity can grow with the data. On the other side instance-based learning methods have great ability to adapt its model to previously unseen data. It simply could add a new instance to the memory. Examples of instance-based learning algorithm are the k-nearest neighbor algorithm [10], GRNN network [11] or RBF network [12]. The k-NN method can be considered as a special case of a mini-model method. More expanded comparison between this two methods could be found in previous authors' publications.

The concept of mini-models method was developed by A. Piegat [1,2]. However, the learning method applied and investigated in first mini-models was rather inappropriate for higher space dimensions. The latest versions of the method described in publications [5–7] are able to work in multidimensional space and are competitive. The main aim of this paper is to present the MM-method based on n-dimensional simplex using a local dimensionality reduction. There are several methods used for the dimensionality reduction such as: Principal Component Analysis (PCA) [13,14], Linear Discriminant Analysis (LDA) [14,15], manifold learning [16], Locally Linear Embedding (LLE) [17] and others. All that methods reduce dimensionality in the whole problem domain. The authors assumed that all input variables in particular part of the domain are not equally important. For example in one part of the domain a variable which is statistically important could be completely unimportant and add unnecessary noise in other distant part of the same domain. In the multidimensional space it is very difficult to partition the input space to a regular sectors, and to ensure suitable number of data items in every sector. This problem is strictly connected to the "curse of dimensionality". Thus, the MM-method tries to check significance of the variables for each query.

The method consists of two groups of algorithms: algorithms for defining the local neighborhood of the query point and algorithms for mathematical modeling on the mini-model area. The version of the method described in this article uses linear regression for mathematical modeling. In order to reduce space dimensionality the algorithm checks which variables are statistically significant using t-student test [18,19]. This approach can increase method efficiency and indicate which input variables are insignificant in some part of the domain. Moreover, answer for specified query point after discrimination of unimportant variables will be more accurate.

2   Mini-Model Method: Algorithms

The algorithms of the MM-method was described in few previous publications [5,6]. However the method is relatively new and the main steps of the algorithm should be recalled. The method consists of two groups of algorithms: algorithms for defining the local neighborhood of the query point (learning part of the algorithm) and algorithms for mathematical modeling on the mini-model area (learning and operating parts of the algorithm).

2.1   Defining Mini-Model Area

The first part of the algorithm is the data points' conversion from Cartesian coordinate system into spherical coordinate system [20,21]. The transformation occurs only in the input space. The output is used in the process of the mathematical model output-calculation. It means that in the general case, $n+1$-dimensional data point is converted into coordinate system based on n-sphere. The query point $Q = x_{Q1}, x_{Q2}, \ldots, x_{Qn}, y_Q$ is assumed to be the local coordinate system center. Values of input variables $x_{Q1}, x_{Q2}, \ldots, x_{Qn}$ are known, but the value of output variable y_Q is to be calculated. All data points p_i are transformed into spherical coordinate system where they are defined by radius $r \in [0, \infty)$ (distance from the center) and angles $\varphi_{i1}, \varphi_{i2}, \ldots, \varphi_{i(n-2)} \in [0; \pi), \varphi_{i(n-1)} \in [0; 2\pi)$. The set of points P can be denoted as:

$$P = \{p_1, p_2, \ldots, p_i, \ldots, p_I\}$$
$$p_i = (x_{i1}, \ldots, x_{in}, y_i) = (r_i, \varphi_{i1}, \ldots, \varphi_{i(n-1)}, y_i). \tag{1}$$

The mini-model area, in the general case is a polytope and contains J faces. A particular polyhedron face j is a part of a plane F_j. In further considerations the whole plane F_j will be called *face*. The face is defined by point G_j, which will be called *face generation point*. It was assumed that the plane is orthogonal to the vector $\overrightarrow{QG_j}$. Each face is defined as:

$$F_j = \left\{ G_j, p_i : \varphi_{ij} < \frac{\pi}{2} \wedge r_i = \frac{r_j}{\cos \varphi_{ij}} \right\} \tag{2}$$

where φ_{ij} is the angle value between vectors $\overrightarrow{QG_j}, \overrightarrow{Qp_i}$. The angle value can be computed using the dot product, which for Cartesian coordinates is given by (3).

$$\varphi_{ij} = \arccos \frac{x_{i1}x_{j1} + \cdots + x_{in}x_{jn}}{\sqrt{x_{i1}^2 + \cdots + x_{in}^2}\sqrt{x_{j1}^2 + \cdots + x_{jn}^2}} \tag{3}$$

After simplifications formula (4) for spherical coordinates was obtained.

$$\varphi_{ij} = \arccos(\cos \varphi_{i1} \cos \varphi_{j1} + \sin \varphi_{i1} \sin \varphi_{j1}($$
$$\cos \varphi_{i2} \cos \varphi_{j2} + \sin \varphi_{i2} \sin \varphi_{j2}($$
$$\cdots \tag{4}$$
$$\cos \varphi_{i(n-2)} \cos \varphi_{j(n-2)} + \sin \varphi_{i(n-2)} \sin \varphi_{j(n-2)}($$
$$\cos(\varphi_{i(n-1)} - \varphi_{j(n-1)})) \cdots))).$$

The face in fact divides all the space into two half-spaces. The first half-space consists of data points which may be included into the area of a mini-model. The set of points which may be included in face F_j is defined by (5).

$$I_j = \left\{ p_i : \varphi_{ij} \geq \frac{\pi}{2} \cup \left(\varphi_{ij} < \frac{\pi}{2} \wedge r_i \leq \frac{r_j}{\cos \varphi_{ij}} \right) \right\}. \tag{5}$$

The second half-space consists of data points which are certainly excluded from the figure area. This set of points E_j is defined by (6).

$$E_j = \left\{ p_i : \varphi_{ij} < \frac{\pi}{2} \wedge r_i > \frac{r_j}{\cos \varphi_{ij}} \right\}. \tag{6}$$

Every face divides the space in the way described above. Intersections of half-spaces (which include data points) of all faces contain points which are included into the polyhedron area. Set of points Z included in the polyhedron is given by (7).

$$Z = I_1 \cap I_2 \cap \cdots \cap I_J. \tag{7}$$

The way how a face divides 3D space into two half-spaces is presented in Fig. 1. Data points marked by triangles are certainly excluded from the mini-model area whilst points marked by squares are possibly included into the area. Whether the point will be included in the mini-model area or not depends also on its position in relation to other faces. Only points included by all faces will be included in the mini-model area.

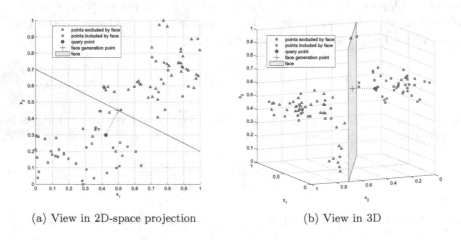

(a) View in 2D-space projection   (b) View in 3D

Fig. 1. Example of space partition by a face.

In the process of the mini-model learning the model-area rotation is of great importance. It can be realized by multiplying coordinates of faces "generation points" by appropriate rotation matrix. In the general case there are $\binom{n}{2}$ rotation matrices. Every rotation occurs as rotations parallel to a 2D plane, not as a rotation around an axis. This way of rotation understanding is consistent with 2D-space where only one plane exists, and with 3D-space where three planes exists.

2.2 Mathematical Modeling on the Mini-Model Area

On the defined mini-model area, any method of mathematical modeling can be uses e.g.: linear regression, polynomial approximation, mean value, fuzzy reasoning, neural network, etc. After defining the local neighborhood, a mini-model uses data points which are inside of the mini-model area. In this paper authors use linear regression as the method of mathematical modeling. Selected method is basic algorithm that can model only linear dependency. Linear regression is not complex enough for a mathematical modeling in entire domain of real world dataset. However, in the task of local modeling linear regression is suitable for finding local data dependency in a small constrained part of the domain. At the first step algorithm try to determine which variables are linearly dependent, then they are discarded. Next, t-statistics is used to determine which variables is statistically important. Process of removing insignificant variables usually results in smaller model error. Discarding unimportant variables of the model is in fact a local dimensionality reduction. This approach could indicate which input variables are insignificant in particular part of the domain. Insignificant variable in one part of the domain could be statistically important in other distant part of the domain. This is of great advantage over the global dimensionality reduction which analyses data points in whole system domain. The proposed method do it only locally around the query point. Local dimensionality reduction has a lot of benefits. First of all it makes the model simpler, with a smaller number of inputs. Secondly, it gives information which variables are unimportant and can be omitted in some parts of the domain. It is of great advantages in a situation in which we would like to collect additional data samples around the query point. Moreover answer for a specified query point after discrimination of unimportant variables will be more accurate. There are other statistical methods that can check regression fit e.g. F-test. Nevertheless, t-test allows us to check model parameters and remove variables which are statistically unimportant.

2.3 Mini-Model Learning

The learning process is heuristic and usually involves random way of changing the location of points G_j. During the learning process numerous mini-models' areas are found. Linear regression uses data points which are inside of the mini-model area. Firstly these points are checked if they contain linearly dependent variables. If some variables are linearly dependent, then they are discarded. Then algorithm identifies linear regression model [18,19]:

$$Y = \beta_0 + \beta_1 x_1 + \beta_2 x_2 + \cdots + \beta_n x_n + \epsilon \tag{8}$$

At the next step t-statistics is used to determine which variables are statistically important. T-statistics is computed for all coefficients. The coefficient with highest value of p is removed from the model as the most insignificant one. Then new linear regression model is computed with t-statistics for remaining coefficients. The whole procedure is repeated until all remaining coefficients are statistically important or the minimal number of coefficients in the model is achieved. The whole procedure is repeated iteratively because unimportant variable could interfere t-statistics for other variables in the model. Then the mini-model calculates numeric answer for the query point, and the error committed on learning data. In the next step the MM-algorithm tries to find another mini-model area, computes regression model, performs local dimensionality reduction, calculates new error, the mini-model answer etc. The model which makes the smallest error is chosen as the optimal one. Not every mini-model area is valid. The area has to satisfy following initial MM-properties:

- minimal number of points inside the mini-model area,
- maximal number of points inside the mini-model area,
- ratio between the minimal and the maximal lengths of vectors $\overrightarrow{QG_j}$,
- query point should not be extrapolated by learning points (it is not always possible and sometimes is not required or necessary).

There is no simple rule of how to choose initial values of the properties. The range of points inside the mini-model area depends on learning data. The lower boundary has to be greater than dimensionality of the problem space. Sometimes for certain query point, there exist no valid mini-model area which satisfies initial constraints. In such situation the mini-model is unable to return a reliable numeric answer.

In the experiments authors used many times the learning procedure which included the whole figure rotation and changing radiuses of faces generation points. All the moving-parameters were taken at random. The ratio between the minimal and the maximal radii values has to be greater than 0.5 in order to prevent the figure over-stretching.

3 Results of Experiments

The MM-method was compared with other instance-based learning methods: k-NN method, RBF network, GRNN network, local linear regression [22]. MM-method and k-NN method work on points from local neighborhood. They can be compared with use of leave-one-out cross validation method. General Regression Neural Network (GRNN), Radial Basis Function Network (RBF) were tested with use of the 10-fold cross validation. The experiments were conducted on six datasets from UCI Machine Learning [23]:

- Boston Housing - (x_3 - proportion of non-retail business acres per town, x_5 - nitric oxides concentration (parts per 10 million), x_6 - average number of rooms per dwelling, x_7 - proportion of owner-occupied units built prior to 1940, x_{10} - full-value property-tax rate per \$ 10,000, x_{11} - pupil-teacher ratio by town, x_{13} - % lower status of the population) (506 instances),
- Concrete Compressive Strength - (all available input attributes) (1029 instances),

- Auto MPG - (all available input attribute except: x_8 - origin, x_9 - car name) (391 instances),
- Concrete Slump Test - (all available input attribute, output attribute: 28-day Compressive Strength) (102 instances),
- Yacht Hydrodynamics - (all available input attribute) (307 instances),
- Servo - (all available input attributes) (166 instances)

Results of experiments are presented in Table 1. Experiments were performed with the optimal values of all parameters for all tested methods. Mini-models were based on n-simplexes, and used the linear regression to calculate the model answer. The dimension of the polytope was appropriate for the dimension of input space. The table also contains information about allowed range of points inside the mini-model area. The MM-method was tested in two variants with and without local dimensionality reduction. For a regression analysis significant level was set to 0.05, minimal number of coefficients in the model to 2. The method discarded the result for particular query point if it was unable to find a valid mini-model area. Results of experiments have shown that in this situation usually the mean absolute error was very high.

Table 1. Comparison of effectiveness of tested methods.

		Housing	Concrete	Auto	Slump	Yacht	Servo
MM-method	error	0.0551	0.0483	0.0529	0.0500	0.0167	0.0493
	samples	25 - 40	20 - 40	20 - 60	8 - 20	12 - 25	10 - 25
MM-method with dim. red	error	0.0532	0.0478	0.0525	0.0451	0.0189	0.0442
	samples	25 - 40	20 - 40	50 - 80	20 - 40	10 - 20	15 - 30
k-NN	error	0.0567	0.0722	0.0531	0.0600	0.0371	0.0437
	k	4	1	3	2	2	3
Local linear regression	error	0.0534	0.0705	0.0498	0.0554	0.0296	0.0378
	learn. error	0.08	0.06	0.09	0.14	0.03	0.06
GRNN	error	0.0545	0.0699	0.0502	0.0621	0.0385	0.0381
	spread	0.1	0.03	0.08	0.1	0.07	0.05
RBF	error	0.0517	0.0511	0.0512	0.0257	0.0220	0.0528
	spread	0.8	1.0	1.0	2.0	2.9	0.7
	learn. error	0.004	0.003	0.004	0.0008	0.003	0.002

4 Conclusion

Mini-models have competitive accuracy with other tested instance based-learning methods. Generally, the proposed approach with local dimensionality reduction improves the method accuracy. The investigated variant of the method achieved worse result in comparison to the basic version only for one tested dataset. The authors assumed that particular input variables in different part of the domain are not equally important. For example in one part of the domain particular variable which globally is statistically important could be less important or completely unimportant and could add unnecessary noise in other distant part of the domain. It gives an edge over global dimensionality reduction methods that analyses the variables in the whole system domain. The proposed approach increases the method efficiency and indicates which input variables are insignificant in some part of the domain. It has a great advantages in the situation in which we would like to collect additional data samples around query point. Moreover the model found in this way is simpler.

Very important parameter in the model learning process is the points' range. Too small range results in an over-fitted model, whereas too wide range causes the MM calculates the answer from too many distinct samples. Generally, MM-method with local dimensionality reduction requires a wider points' range to achieve optimal results in comparison to the basic MM version. Probably this is caused by the fact that mini-model requires more data samples for a proper identification of variables significance. Choosing too small points' range results with inappropriate identification of variable significance and the error committed by the MM is high. The presented variant of the method is rather simple. In multidimensional space, volume of the n-simplex is smaller than e.g. volume of n-cube and the model area is more constrained than in case of figures with higher number of faces. Mini-models can take into account the tendency existing in the neighborhood of the query point. This extrapolation properties allow for better modeling in places with information gaps. Great advantage of mini-models is the ability of detecting situations in which the mini-model cannot satisfy its initial criteria and thus it is unable to return a reliable numeric answer. Global models have not this property.

References

1. Piegat, A., Wasikowska, B., Korzeń, M.: Application of the self-learning, 3-point mini-model for modelling of unemployment rate in Poland. [in Polish] Studia Informatica, nr 27, University of Szczecin, pp. 59–69 (2010)
2. Piegat, A., Wasikowska, B., Korzeń, M.: Differences between the method of mini-models and the k-nearest neighbors an example of modeling unemployment rate in Poland. Information Systems in Management IX-Business Intelligence and Knowledge Management, pp. 34–43. WULS Press, Warsaw (2011)
3. Pietrzykowski, M.: The use of linear and nonlinear mini-models in process of data modeling in a 2D-space. Nowe trendy w Naukach Inzynieryjnych, pp. 100–108. CREATIVETIME, Krakow (2011)
4. Pietrzykowski, M.: Effectiveness of mini-models method when data modelling within a 2D-space in an information deficiency situation. J. Theor. Appl. Comput. Sci. 6(3), 21–27 (2012)
5. Pietrzykowski, M.: Comparison between mini-models based on multidimensional polytopes and k-nearest neighbor method: case study of 4D and 5D problems. In: Wiliński, A., El Fray, I., Pejaś, J. (eds.) Soft Computing in Computer and Information Science. Advances in Intelligent Systems and Computing, vol. 342, pp. 107–118. Springer, Switzerland (2015)

6. Pietrzykowski, M., Piegat, A.: Geometric approach in local modeling: learning of mini-models based on n-dimensional simplex. In: Rutkowski, L., Korytkowski, M., Scherer, R., Tadeusiewicz, R., Zadeh, L.A., Zurada, J.M. (eds.) Artificial Intelligence and Soft Computing. LNCS, vol. 9120, pp. 460–470. Springer, Heidelberg (2015)

7. Pluciński, M.: Application of mini-models to the interval information granules processing. In: Wiliński, A., El Fray, I., Pejaś, J. (eds.) Soft Computing in Computer and Information Science. Advances in Intelligent Systems and Computing, vol. 342, pp. 37–48. Springer, Switzerland (2015)

8. Russell, S., Norvig, P.: Artificial Intelligence: A Modern Approach, 2nd edn. Prentice Hall, Englewood Cliffs (2003). ISBN 0-13-080302-2

9. Kotsiantis, S.B., Zaharakis, I.D., Pintelas, P.E.: Machine learning: a review of classification and combining techniques. Artif. Intell. Rev. **26**(3), 159–190 (2006)

10. Destercke, S.: A K-nearest neighbours method based on imprecise probabilities. Soft. Comput. **16**(5), 833–844 (2012)

11. Celikoglu, H.B.: Application of radial basis function and generalized regression neural networks in non-linear utility function specification for travel mode choice modelling. Math. Comput. Model. **44**(7–8), 640–658 (2006)

12. Lin, C.L., Wang, J.F., Chen, C.Y., Chen, C.W., Yen, C.W.: Improving the generalization performance of RBF neural networks using a linear regression technique. Expert Syst. Appl. **36**(10), 12049–12053 (2009)

13. Zou, H., Hastie, T., Tibshirani, R.: Sparse principal component analysis. J. Comput. Graph. Stat. **15**(2), 265–286 (2006)

14. Martinez, A.M., Kak, A.C.: PCA versus LDA. IEEE Trans. Pattern Anal. Mach. Intell. **23**(2), 228–233 (2001)

15. Ji, S.W., Ye, J.P.: Generalized linear discriminant analysis: a unified framework and efficient model selection. IEEE Trans. Neural Netw. **19**(10), 1768–1782 (2008)

16. Law, M.H.C., Jain, A.K.: Incremental nonlinear dimensionality reduction by manifold learning. IEEE Trans. Pattern Anal. Mach. Intell. **28**(3), 377–391 (2006)

17. Donoho, D.L., Grimes, C.: Hessian eigenmaps: locally linear embedding techniques for high-dimensional data. Proc. Nat. Acad. Sci. U.S.A. **100**(10), 5591–5596 (2003)

18. Kutner, M.H., Nachtsheim, C.J., Neter, J., et al.: Applied Linear Statistical Models. McGraw-Hill/Irwin, Chicago (2005). ISBN 9780073108742

19. Rice, J.A.: Mathematical Statistics and Data Analysis. Duxbury Press, India (2006). ISBN 9780534399429

20. Bronshtein, I., Semendyayev, K., Musiol, G., Muhlig, H.: Handbook of Mathematics. Springer, Heidelberg (2007). ISBN 9783540721215

21. Moon, P., Spencer, D.: Field theory handbook: Including Coordinate Systems, Differential Equations, and Their Solutions. Springer, Heidelberg (1988). ISBN 9780387027326

22. Ruppert, D., Wand, M.P.: Multivariate locally weighted least-squares regression. Ann. Stat. **22**(3), 1346–1370 (1994)

23. UCI Machine Learning Repository. http://archive.ics.uci.edu/ml/

Evolutionary Multiobjective Optimization of Liquid Fossil Fuel Reserves Exploitation with Minimizing Natural Environment Contamination

Leszek Siwik[(⊠)], Marcin Los, Marek Kisiel-Dorohinicki, and Aleksander Byrski

AGH University of Science and Technology, Krakow, Poland
{siwik,los,doroh,olekb}@agh.edu.pl

Abstract. One of exploitation methods of liquid fossil fuel deposits depends on pumping chemicals to the geological formation and 'sucking out' the fuel that is pushed out by the solution. This method became particularly popular in the case of extraction of shale gases. A real problem here is however a natural environment contamination caused mainly by chemicals soaking through the geological formations to ground-waters.

The process of pumping the chemical fluid into the formation and extracting the oil/gas is modeled here as a non-stationary flow of the non-linear fluid in heterogeneous media.

The (poly)optimization problem of extracting oil in such a process is then defined as a multiobjetcive optimization problem with two contradictory objectives: maximizing the amount of the oil/gas extracted and minimizing the contamination of the ground-waters.

To solve the problem defined a hibridized solver of multiobjective optimization of liquid fossil fuel extraction (LFFEP) integrating population-based heuristic (i.e. NSGA-II algorithm for approaching the Pareto frontier) with isogeometric finite element method IGA-FEM method for modeling non-stationary flow of the non-linear fluid in heterogeneous media is presented along with some preliminary experimental results.

1 Introduction

One of exploitation methods of liquid fossil fuel deposits is 'fracking' consisting in pumping to the deposit of certain chemical solutions and 'sucking out' the fuel that is pushed out by the solution. This method became particularly popular in the case of extraction of shale gases. However a real problem becomes correct placing of the pumps injecting the chemical solutions to the deposit as well as the pumps sucking out the fuel in such a way to maximize the amount of the fuel extracted but minimizing the contamination of groundwater at the same time. The latter aspect is often neglected by the oil extracting companies.

Meanwhile, the environmental impact of the extraction of liquid fossil fuels (oil/gas) bearing formation by pumping water with some chemical components, in particular its influence on the contamination of the groundwater is a crucial aspect.

© Springer International Publishing Switzerland 2016
L. Rutkowski et al. (Eds.): ICAISC 2016, Part II, LNAI 9693, pp. 384–394, 2016.
DOI: 10.1007/978-3-319-39384-1_33

Thus, leveraging a population-based technique, we aim at developing dedicated metaheuristics, taking into consideration multiple criteria to produce Pareto-optimal results. In the case of exploiting of liquid fossil fuel reserves the amount of fossil fuel received and the amount of water lost in the ground waters (as well as the amount of chemicals pumped into the formation) have to be considered. Optimization of such process could help to a large extent in planning environmental-friendly oil drilling procedures, reducing the negative effects of the industry on our planet.

Unfortunately, it requires complicated expensive numerical models, involving non-linear high order models possible to solve by means of the modern isogeometric finite element method solvers (IGA-FEM). Simultaneously, the problem requires multi-objective inverse problem formulation (minimization of the environmental impact, while maximization of the amount of extracting oil).

The significance of developing comprehensive methods for solving multiobjective optimization problems is undisputed since in the real-life almost any single decision, designing or optimization task has to deal with many contradictory objectives (the price and the quality, the quality and the duration, the price and the functionality, the profit and the risk etc.). The goal of our research is to develop an appropriate model and effective solvers dedicated for efficient and accurate simulation of such process before the actual extraction starts. Considering multiple (contradictory) criteria, will allow for early preparation for the extraction in particular geological conditions, lowering the costs of the whole process, reducing the risks of failures and enhancing the environmental safety.

For the last 20 years a variety of evolutionary multi-criteria optimization techniques have been proposed [1]. In the Deb's typology of evolutionary multiobjective algorithms (EMOAs) firstly the elitist (which give the best individuals the opportunity to be directly carried over to the next generation) and non-elitist ones are distinguished [1]. Deb's typology includes also so-called *constrained EMOAs*—i.e. algorithms and techniques that enable handling constraints connected with problem that is being solved.

For preliminary experiments, as the stochastic algorithm for the inverse algorithm, population-based state-of-the-art algorithm i.e. NSGA-II algorithm has been used.

When we solve difficult inverse problem, we need a fast and accurate solver for the primal problem solution, as well as a sophisticated methodology for solving the inverse problem, calling the primal problem many times to get the fitness or gradient estimates. Therefore we propose to hybridize IGA-FEM solvers with population-based metaheuristics to obtain high-quality Pareto-optimal frontiers of multi-objective optimization of liquid fossil fuel reserve extraction with minimal environmental contamination and maximal oil yield.

Recently, the isogeometric finite element method (IGA-FEM) [7] became the state-of-the-art method for performing accurate simulations of difficult time dependent problems. This is because the IGA-FEM utilizes B-splines and Non-uniform rational B-splines (NURBS) [8] as basis functions and thus provide a global higher continuity of the numerical solution, especially when the simulated physical phenomena requires higher order partial differential equations (PDE). Additionally there are linear computational cost solvers allowing for fast accurate solution of the system of linear equations obtained from IGA-FEM simulations [9,10]. That is why during research the IGA-FEM solver has been used as the primal problem solver modeling the process of pumping the water into oil/gas bearing formations as the non-linear flow in heterogeneous media.

2   Problem Formulation

The problem of extracting of the oil/gas by pumping the chemical fluid into the formation can be modeled as non-stationary flow of the non-linear fluid in heterogeneous media, following [11]. The time dependent problem is given by:

$$
\begin{cases}
\dfrac{\partial u}{\partial t} - L(u) = f(\mathbf{x}, t) & \text{in } \Omega \times [0, T] \\
\nabla u \cdot \hat{\mathbf{n}} = 0 & \text{in } \partial \Omega \times [0, T] \\
u(\mathbf{x}, 0) = u_0(\mathbf{x}) & \text{in } \Omega
\end{cases}
\tag{1}
$$

where $L(u)$ is defined according to [11]. We transform the time dependent problem into weak form

$$
\left(v, \frac{\partial u}{\partial t}\right)_\Omega + b(v, u) = (v, f)_\Omega \quad \forall v \in V
\tag{2}
$$

where:

$$
b(v, u) = (v, L(u))_\Omega
\tag{3}
$$

and

$$
(f_1, f_2)_\Omega = \int_\Omega f_1 f_2 \, dx
\tag{4}
$$

We can utilize Forward Euler scheme:

$$
\frac{\partial u}{\partial t} \approx \frac{u_{t+1} - u_t}{\Delta t}
\tag{5}
$$

mixed with the isogeometric finite element method formulation

$$
\left(v, \frac{u_{t+1} - u_t}{\Delta t}\right)_\Omega + b(v, u) = (v, f)_\Omega \quad \forall v \in V
\tag{6}
$$

$$
(v, u_{t+1})_\Omega = (v, u_t)_\Omega + \Delta t \left[(v, f)_\Omega - b(v, u)\right] \forall v \in V
\tag{7}
$$

The problem 7 is equivalent to a sequence of isogeometric L2 projection problems. The particular case of the non-linear flow in heterogeneous media is given by:

$$
\frac{\partial u(x)}{\partial t} - \nabla \cdot (K(x) \nabla u) = h(x, t)
\tag{8}
$$

where u – pressure, K – permeability of the medium, h – forcing arising from pumps and sinks, domain $D = [0,1]^3$. Permeability is given by

$$K(x, u, \mu) = K_q(x)e^{\mu u} \tag{9}$$

and K_q is the prescribed formation map.

We can use the time step of order of magnitude $\Delta t = 10^{-6}$ (depending on mesh size) due to stability constraints arising from Courant Friedrichs Lewy (CFL) condition.

Pumps and sinks can be located arbitrarily inside the domain. Let us define an auxiliary function

$$\phi(t) = \begin{cases} \left(\frac{t}{r} - 1\right)^2 \left(\frac{t}{r} + 1\right)^2 & \text{for } t \leq r \\ 0 & \text{for } t > r \end{cases} \tag{10}$$

for some constant r (in our case, $r = 0.15$). Function ϕ assumes value 1 at $t = 0$ and falls smoothly to 0 at $t = r$. For each pump $p \in P$ and sink $s \in S$ let x_p and x_s denote its position, respectively. Forcing h is computed as

$$h(x, t) = \sum_{p \in P} \phi(\|x_p - x\|) - \sum_{s \in S} u(x, t)\phi(\|x_s - x\|) \tag{11}$$

that is, a pump or sink affects area around it in a radius r, and sink draining strength depends on pressure. The total amount D of drained liquid is calculated as a time integral of draining part in the above equation, i.e.

$$D = \sum_{s \in S} \int_0^T u(x, t)\phi(\|x_s - x\|)\, dt \tag{12}$$

Groundwater region Ω_G is defined as set of points with $z < 0.2$. Contamination is computed as an integral of u in that region at the end of the simulation, that is

$$C(T) = \int_{\Omega_G} u(x, T)\, dx \tag{13}$$

We solve the problem over the cube $\Omega = [0,1]^3$ domain.

On a very high level, the problem undertaken can be formulated as follows: where the pumps injecting the chemical solutions to the formation as well as where the pumps sucking the shale gas should be located in the formation to ensure maximum volume of extracted fuel (maximum gain) and minimum contamination of the ground waters (minimum lost).

We gain a classical multiobjective optimization problem with two contradictory objectives.

From the mathematical point of view, multi-objective (or multi-criteria) optimization problem (MOOP) is formulated as follows ([1,2]):

$$MOOP \equiv \begin{cases} Min/Max: & f_l(\bar{x}), \quad l = 1, 2 \dots, L \\ Taking\ into\ consideration: & \\ g_j(\bar{x}) \geq 0, & j = 1, 2 \dots, J \\ h_k(\bar{x}) = 0, & k = 1, 2 \dots, K \\ x_i^{(L)} \leq x_i \leq x_i^{(U)}, & i = 1, 2 \dots, N \end{cases}$$

The set of constraints, both: equalities $(h_k(\bar{x}))$, as well as inequalities $(g_j(\bar{x}))$, and constraints related to the decision variables, i.e. lower bounds $(x_i^{(L)})$ and upper bounds $(x_i^{(U)})$, define so called searching space—feasible alternatives $(\mathscr{D})$.

In our case, the multiobjective optimization of **L**iquid **F**ossil **F**uel **E**xtraction **P**roblem (**LFFEP**) respecting the environmental impact can be formulated as follows:

$$MOOP = LFFEP \equiv \begin{cases} Max: \ D = \sum_{s \in S} \int_0^T u(x,t)\phi\left(\|x_s - x\|\right) dt & (amount\ of\ drained\ liquid) \\ Min: \ C(T) = \int_{\Omega_G} u(x,T)\,dx & (contamination) \\ Taking\ into\ consideration: \\ \quad D \geq 0 \ and\ C(T) \geq 0 \\ \quad 0 \leq x_i \leq 1, \quad i = 1, 2, 3 \end{cases}$$

In the course of this paper multi-objective optimization in the Pareto sense is considered, so solving defined problem means determining of all feasible and non-dominated alternatives from the set $(\mathscr{D})$. Such defined set is called Pareto set $(\mathscr{P})$ and in objective space it forms so called Pareto frontier $(\mathscr{PF})$.

3   Computational Method

To solve defined problem of multiobjective optimization of liquid fossil fuels extraction we proposed hybridization of population-based multiobjective algorithm (i.e. NSGA-II) with dedicated solver for primal/inverse problems e.g. modern isogeometric finite element method solver IGA-FEM.

The multiobjective optimization algorithm is responsible for approaching the set of non-dominated solutions (i.e. Pareto set and Pareto frontiers respectively) with appropriate selection, crossing-over, mutation etc. whereas IGA-FEM solver is responsible for simulating distribution of chemicals in the geological formation and computing the amount of extracted fuel and contamination of groundwater depending on the localization of pumps and sinks.

NSGA-II [1] is the most commonly and widely used evolutionary algorithm for multiobjective optimization. It is based on non-dominated sorting procedure ensuring that the better the individual is (it is non-dominated, or dominated only once (by non-dominated individuals) etc.) it is the higher probability that the individual is directly carried over to the next generation. The algorithm is just a state-of-the-art in the multiobjective optimization field and is constantly improved (recently NSGA-III algorithm has been proposed which is non-dominated sorting based algorithm for solving many-objective optimization problems [19]).

In our research implementation of NSGA-II available in jMetal framework [16] has been used as the starting point. Individuals are represented as the matrix of coordinates of pumps and sinks location in the formation. To evaluate every single individual IGA-FEM solver is launched which is used here as a black box, with the input describing the location of the pumps (where the chemicals are pushed into the formation) and the sinks (where the oil is extracted). The IGA-FEM solver provides the amount of extracted oil and the contamination of groundwaters for given coordinates of pumps and sinks. Graphically, proposed approach can be presented as in Fig. 1.

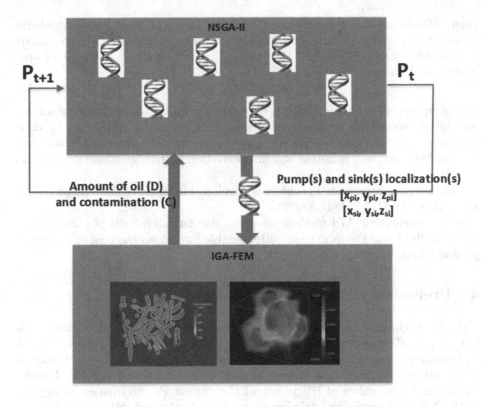

Fig. 1. Proposed solver of LFFEP: hybridization of NSGA-II and IGA-FEM

3.1 IGA-FEM Solver

In our IGA-FEM simulation each time step involves solving an L2 projection problem, as shown in Sect. 2, i.e. solving a system of linear equations where the matrix is the Gram matrix of chosen basis functions. For this purpose we use ADI method [9,10].

The ADI method has been originally introduced in papers [3–6] to solve parabolic, hyperbolic and elliptic partial differential equations. Recently, the method has been extended to isogeometric finite element methods simulations. Its sequential implementation delivers linear computational cost with respect to mesh size [9,10] and the parallel version scales well up to 1,000 processors [13]. The method has been applied as a fast solver to 2D non-stationary problem [9], as well as the preconditioner for ILUPCG iterative solvers in case of solution of non-stationary PDE over complex geometries [10].

The method exploits a special structure of Gram matrix of our basis functions, which are constructed as a tensor product of one-dimensional basic B-splines, i.e. basis functions are defined as

$$B_{ijk}(x,y,z) = B_i(x)B_j(y)B_k(z) \tag{14}$$

where B_α are one-dimensional basic B-splines. This is possible due to simplicity of domain geometry and boundary conditions. It can be shown that Gram matrix of such basis can be expressed as a tensor product of Gram matrices of one-dimensional bases:

$$M = M_x \otimes M_y \otimes M_z \qquad (15)$$

This property allows us to reduce problem of solving system $Mx = b$ to solving multiple systems with smaller matrices M_x, M_y and M_z, which can be done efficiently (in linear time with respect to the number of unknowns), since they are banded. Detailed exposition and full derivation of the algorithm can be found in [12].

The solver for the primal problem is developed in frame of the PRELUDIUM grant DEC-2014/15/N/ST6/04662.

The isogeometric ADI method allows to simulate the effects of pumping the chemical fluid into the formation with possible impact on the contamination of groundwaters.

4   Preliminary Experimental Results

We have performed initial tests using NSGA-II optimization algorithm available in jMetal framework. We were seeking positions of a single pump and sink to minimize groundwater contamination and maximize the amount of drained liquid oil concentrated in a sphere located in the center of a cubic domain. Figure 2a depicts values of HV metric of the current Pareto frontier during one of the NSGA-II executions. Obviously not actual values of HV metrics but the tendency is important here showing that the solver is approaching better and better approximation of the Pareto frontier. As the matter of fact Hyper volume ratio (HVR) metrics would be better here but since we don't know the true Pareto frontier we are not able to calculate the ratio between the Hypervolume of obtained approximation and the Hypervolume of the true Pareto frontier that is why we use hypervolume as the quality indicator here.

Figure 2b depicts a selection of Pareto-optimal solutions (sinks and pumps) found by the algorithm (selected non dominated solutions found by hibridized NSGAII–IGA-FEM solver).

Due to the large number of simulation executions required by the algorithm we used a relatively small number of iterations (10,000) to make the time required to carry out the computation reasonable. This number of iterations is still large enough to avoid the problem observed when the number of iterations was small. In such case the results hardly depend on position of pump and optimal placement of the sink is simply the center of the initial oil distribution, since during very small number of iterations the distribution does not change its shape significantly and so the optimal solution is to put the sink in the place where it can drain the most from the initial distribution (e.g. where the pressure is highest). In the Fig. 2b we can see that while in most cases optimal sink positions are still close to the center, there is some variety and there are even solutions with sinks significantly distant from the center.

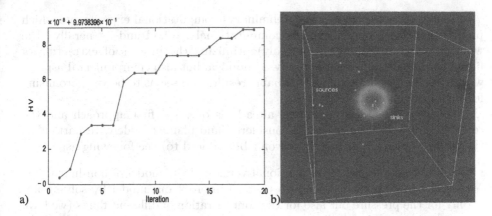

Fig. 2. HV metric during one of the tests (a) and Location of pumps and sinks in Pareto-optimal solutions found (initial oil pressure distribution displayed in the background) (b)

5   Conclusions and the Future Work

One of exploitation methods of liquid fossil fuel deposits depends on pumping chemicals to the geological formation and 'sucking out' the fuel that is pushed out by the solution. This method became particularly popular in the case of extraction of shale gases. However a real problem is natural environment contamination caused mainly by chemicals soaking through the geological formations to groundwaters.

Thus developing a models and solvers describing the process of extracting liquid fossil fuels respecting not only economical aspects but also the impact on natural environment is a crucial in this context.

In the paper we presented our first approach for describing, modeling and solving the problem.

First, we modeled the process of extracting of the oil/gas by pumping the chemical fluid into the formation as non-stationary flow of the non-linear fluid in heterogeneous media.

Next we defined the problem of extracting liquid fossil fuels as a multiobjetcive problem with two contradictory objectives: maximizig the amount of the oil/gas extracted and minimizing the contamination of the groundwaters.

Then we developed the IGA-FEM solver for solving an L2 projection of the problem defined in Sect. 2, i.e. solving a system of linear equations where the matrix is the Gram matrix of chosen basis functions. For this purpose we used ADI method [9,10].

Next we developed a hibridized solver of multiobjective optimization of fossil fuel extraction (LFFEP) integrating population-based heuristic (i.e. NSGA-II algorithm for approaching the Pareto frontier) with isogeometric finite element method IGA-FEM method for modeling a non-stationary flow of the non-linear fluid in heterogeneous media.

Finally, we performed some (preliminary) computational experiments which proved that the proposed models computational method and—generally—the whole process and approach of (poly)optimizing the process of extracting of liquid fossil fuels respecting not only economical but also environmental aspects works, allows for obtaining very valuable results and seems to be very promising for further research.

Of course, what has been done already is only the first approach and the research will be continued and is considered and planned widely. In particular, the future works will include (but won't be reduced to) the following aspects:

- We plan to develop three dimensional version of the model of non-linear flow in heterogeneous media. We also plan to improve our model by solving not only for the pressure but also for the concentration of different fluids (we have groundwaters, water with chemicals that is pumped to the formation, and the oil formations).
- We plan to investigate the relation between the IGA-FEM mesh size, and the accuracy of the primal and inverse problem solution. In particular, we would like to find the compromise between the computational cost (execution time, memory usage, number of processors used) of the IGA-FEM solver and the resulting accuracy of the inverse problem solution.
- Next step will be also developing the tool-set based on evolutionary multi-agent system dedicated for solving multi-criteria optimization problem describing the exploitation of liquid fossil fuel reserves. Several versions of Evolutionary Multi-Agent System for Multi-Objective optimization have already been developed [17,18]. The most appropriate version will be then selected and adjusted by implementing dedicated operators, representation etc. to solve efficiently inverse problems in general and the LFFEP in particular. Also some additional aspects will be taken into consideration while dedicated EMAS will be constructed i.e. the noisiness as well as the ability for handling many (not only multi) objectives. Such mechanisms as hierarchical [20] approaches and coevolutionary interactions are going to be examined in particular [21–23].
- We plan also to perform some research on hybridization of population-based (e.g. EMAS) heuristics and iterative solvers of LFFEP (working along with IGA-FEM solver) such as Incomplete LU Preconditioned Conjugated Gradients (ILUPCG) available from SLATEC library [14], Broyden-Fletcher-Goldfar-Shanno (BFGS) algorithm (The BFGS is a quasi-Newton method utilizing the approximation to the Hessian matrix) or other iterative solvers available through SLATEC or PETSc [15] libraries.
- Finally, we will use the available computing power of the ACC Cyfronet supercomputing facilities by utilizing Scalarm data farming platform (www.scalarm.com) to parallelize and distribute computations in supercomputing environment.

Acknowledgments. The research presented in this paper was partially supported by the AGH University of Science and Technology Statutory Fund no. 11.11.230.124.

References

1. Deb, K.: Multi-Objective Optimization using Evolutionary Algorithms. Wiley, New York (2008)
2. Abraham, A., Jain, L.C., Goldberg, R.: Evolutionary Multiobjective Optimization Theoretical Advances and Applications. Springer, London (2005)
3. Peaceman, D.W., Rachford, H.H.: The numerical solution of parabolic and elliptic differential equations. J. Soc. Ind. Appl. Math. **3**, 28–41 (1955)
4. Douglas, J., Rachford, H.: On the numerical solution of heat conduction problems in two and three space variables. Trans. Am. Math. Soc. **82**, 421439 (1956)
5. Wachspress, E.L., Habetler, G.: An alternating-direction-implicit iteration technique. J. Soc. Ind. Appl. Math. **8**, 403423 (1960)
6. Birkhoff, G., Varga, R.S., Young, D.: Alternating direction implicit methods. Adv. Comput. **3**, 189273 (1962)
7. Bazilevs, Y., Calo, V.M., Cottrell, J.A., Evans, J.A., Lipton, S., Scott, M.A., Sederberg, T.W.: Isogeometric analysis using T-splines. Comput. Methods Appl. Mech. Eng. **199**, 229–263 (2010)
8. Hughes, T.J.R., Cottrell, J.A., Bazilevs, Y.: Isogeometric analysis: CAD, finite elements NURBS, exact geometry and mesh refinement. Comput. Methods Appl. Mech. Eng. **194**(39), 4135–4195 (2005)
9. Gao, L., Calo, V.M.: Fast isogeometric solvers for explicit dynamics. Comput. Methods Appl. Mech. Eng. **274**(1), 19–41 (2014)
10. Gao, L., Calo, V.M.: Preconditioners based on the alternating-direction-implicit algorithm for the 2D steady-state diffusion equation with orthotropic heterogeneous coefficients. J. Comput. Appl. Math. **273**(1), 274–295 (2015)
11. Alotaibi, M., Calo, V.M., Efendiev, Y., Galvis, J., Ghommem, M.: Global-local nonlinear model reduction for flows in heterogeneous porous media. Comput. Methods Appl. Mech. Eng. **292**(1), 122–137 (2015)
12. Łoś, M., Woźniak, M., Paszyński, M., Dalcin, L., Calo, V.M.: Dynamics with matrices possesing Kronecker product structure. Procedia Comput. Sci. **51**, 286–295 (2015)
13. Woźniak, M., Los, M., Paszyński, M., Dalcin, L., Calo, V.M.: Parallel fast isogeometric solvers for explicit dynamic, accepted to Computing and Informatics (2015)
14. SLATEC Common Mathematical Library (1993). http://www.netlib.org/slatec/
15. Balay, S., Abhyankar, S., Adams, M.F., Brown, J., Brune, P., Buschelman, K., Eijkhout, V., Gropp, W.D., Kaushik, D., Knepley, M.G., Curfman McInnes, L., Rupp, K., Smith, B.F., Zhang, H.: PETSc (2014). http://www.mcs.anl.gov/petsc
16. Nebro, A.J., Durillo, J.J., Vergne, M.: Redesigning the jMetal Multi-Objective Optimization Framework. In: Proceedings of the Companion Publication of the 2015 Annual Conference on Genetic and Evolutionary Computation, GECCO Companion (2015)
17. Byrski, A., Drezewski, R., Siwik, L., Kisiel-Dorohinicki, M.: Evolutionary multi-agent systems, The Knowledge Engineering Review (2015)
18. Dreżewski, R., Siwik, L.: A review of agent-based Co-Evolutionary algorithms for multi-objective optimization. In: Tenne, Y., Goh, C.-K. (eds.) Computational Intelligence in Optimization. ALO, vol. 7, pp. 177–209. Springer, Heidelberg (2010)
19. Yuan, Y., Xu, H., Wang, B.: An improved NSGA-III procedure for evolutionary many-objective optimization. In: Proceedings of the 2014 Annual Conference on Genetic and Evolutionary Computation, GECCO 2014. ACM (2014)

20. Ciepiela, E., Kocot, J., Siwik, L., Drezewski, R.: Hierarchical approach to evolutionary. In: International Conference on Computational Science, Krakow (2008)
21. Drezewski, R., Siwik, L.: Co-evolutionary multi-agent system with sexual selection mechanism for multi-objective optimization. In: Proceedings of the IEEE World Congress on Computational Intelligence (WCCI 2006). IEEE (2006)
22. Drezewski, R., Siwik, L.: Multi-objective optimization using co-evolutionary multi-agent system with host-parasite mechanism. In: International Conference on Computational Science, Reading (2006)
23. Drezewski, R., Siwik, L.: Co-evolutionary multi-agent system with predator-prey mechanism for multi-objective optimization. In: International Conference on Adaptive and Natural Computing Algorithms, Warsaw (2007)

SOMA Swarm Algorithm in Computer Games

Ivan Zelinka[(⊠)] and Michal Bukacek

Department of Computer Science, Faculty of Electrical Engineering
and Computer Science, VSB-Technixal University of Ostrava,
17. listopadu 2172/15, 708 00 Ostrava-Poruba, Czech Republic
`ivan.zelinka@vsb.cz, michal@bukacek.cz`
`http://navy.cs.vsb.cz`

Abstract. This participation is focused on artificial intelligence techniques and their practical use in computer game. The aim is to show how game player (based on evolutionary algorithms) can replace a man in two computer games. The first one is strategy game StarCraft: Brood War, briefly reported here. Implementation used in our experiments use classic techniques of artificial intelligence environments, as well as unconventional techniques, such as evolutionary computation. The second game is Tic-Tac-Toe in which SOMA has also take a role of player against human player. This provides an opportunity for effective, coordinated movement in the game fitness landscape. Research reported here has shown potential benefit of evolutionary computation in the field of strategy games and players strategy mining based on their mutual interactions.

Keywords: StarCraft · Tic-Tac-Toe · SOMA · Evolutionary algorithms · Game · Intelligence · Player

1 Introduction

In last years artificial intelligence (AI) plays an important role in various technological applications and branches of science. One of interesting challenge come from game domain that, in fact, represent various mathematical problems with different level of complexity. As an example can serve Chess, Tic-Tac-Toe amongst the others. Various methods from AI has been used for that purpose. In this paper is discussed use of evolutionary algorithms (EAs), especially Self-Organizing Migrating Algorithm (SOMA) in computer game Star Craft[1]. In this game was SOMA used in realtime regime so that trajectories of an individuals were one-to-one trajectories of game bot warriors, as already reported in [30]. This application will be mentioned briefly here, for full info we recommend to read [30].

The second and till now unpublished use of evolutionary algorithms, in this case again SOMA, is well known game Tic-Tac-Toe, that is now available at Google Play[2], so anyone can test it. SOMA is evolutionary algorithm, more

---

[1] http://eu.blizzard.com/en-gb/games/hots/landing/.
[2] https://play.google.com/store/apps/details?id=cz.bukacek.soma_tictactoe.

© Springer International Publishing Switzerland 2016
L. Rutkowski et al. (Eds.): ICAISC 2016, Part II, LNAI 9693, pp. 395–406, 2016.
DOI: 10.1007/978-3-319-39384-1_34

close to the swarm class algorithms. Evolutionary algorithms are a powerful tool for solving many problems of engineering applications. They are usually used where the solution of a given problem analytically is unsuitable or unrealistic. If implemented in a suitable manner, there is no need for frequent user intervention into the actions of the equipment in which they are used.

The majority of the problems of engineering applications can be defined as optimization problems, for example, finding the optimum trajectory of a robot or the optimum thickness of the wall of a pressure tank or the optimum setting of the regulator's parameters. In other words, the problem solved can be transformed into a mathematical problem defined by a suitable prescription, whose optimization leads to finding the arguments of the objective function, which is its goal.

Countless examples illustrating this problem [1] can be found. The solution of such problems usually requires working with the arguments of optimized functions, where the definition ranges of these arguments may be of a heterogeneous character, such as, for example, the range of integers, real or complex numbers, etc. Moreover, it may happen (depending on the case) that for certain subintervals from the permitted interval of values, the corresponding argument of the optimized function may assume values of various types (integers, real, complex,..). Besides this, various penalizations and restrictions can play a role within optimization, not only for given arguments, but also for the functional value of the optimized function. In many cases, the analytical solution of such an optimization problem is possible, nevertheless, considerably complicated and tedious. Evolutionary algorithms solve problems in such an elegant manner that they became very popular and are used in many engineering fields.

From the point of view of the most general classification, the evolutionary algorithms belong to heuristic algorithms. Heuristic algorithms are either *deterministic* or *stochastic*. The algorithms of the second group differ in that their certain steps use random operations, which means that the results of the solutions obtained with their use may differ in the individual runs of the program. It is therefore meaningful to run the program several times and select the best solution obtained.

As a representative example of evolutionary algorithms can be mentioned for example Genetic algorithm (GA) [8,14], Evolutionary strategies (ES) [26] and Schwefel [15], Ant Colony Optimization (ACO) [16], Particle Swarm (PS) or SOMA (Self-Organizing Migrating Algorithm) [17], Memetic Algorithms (MA) [18–21]. Differential Evolution (DE) [22] or the latest Firefly [24] (FF), CoCoo algorithm [23] (CC) or Bat algorithm (BA) [25] amongst the others [2–13].

These algorithms can be divided according to the principles of their action, complexity of the algorithm, etc. Of course, this classification is not the only possibility, nevertheless, because it fits the current state rather well, it can be considered as one of the possible views on the classical and modern optimization methods.

The evolutionary algorithms can be essentially used for the solution of very heterogeneous problems. Of course, for the solution of the optimization problems, there are many more algorithms than were indicated here. Because their description would exceed the framework of this text, we can only refer to the corresponding literature, where the algorithms indicated above are described in more details.

2   Experiment Design

SOMA has been applied to two different kind of games. The first was StarCraft [30] and the second one Tic-Tac-Toe. In [29,30] is SOMA application focused on techniques of artificial intelligence (AI) applications and practical utilization. The goal of the [29,30] (and its results partially reported here) is to implement computer player replacing human in real time strategy StarCraft: Brood War. The implementation uses "conventional" techniques from artificial intelligence, as well as unconventional techniques, such as evolutionary computation. The computer player behavior is provided by implementation of decision-making tree together with evolutionary algorithm called SOMA, used to remote movement of combat units. Code was written in Java programming language in which was created system, that ensures behavior of computer player in an easy way in implementation of artificial intelligence. Particular implementation of SOMA algorithm provides an opportunity for efficient, coordinated movement of combat units over the map. The work [29] and its results reported in [30] has shown great benefit of evolutionary techniques in the field of real time strategy games.

The second game, reported here was Tic-Tac-Toe. Evolution has been applied in this game and application at Google Play[3], is fully accessible at the moment. In Tic-Tac-Toe has been used SOMA as well.

2.1   Selected Algorithm and Its Setting

SOMA (Fig. 1) is a stochastic optimization algorithm that is modeled based on the social behavior of competitive-cooperating individuals [17]. It was chosen because it has been proved that this algorithm has the ability to converge towards the global optimum [17]. SOMA works on a population of candidate solutions in loops, called migration loops. The population is initialized by uniform random distribution over the search space at the beginning of the search. In each loop, the population is evaluated and the solution with the lowest cost value becomes the Leader. Apart from the Leader, in one migration loop, all individuals will traverse the searched space in the direction of the leader. Mutation, the random perturbation of individuals, is an important operation for SOMA. It ensures diversity amongst all the individuals and it also provides a means to restore lost information in a population. Mutation is different in SOMA as compared with other EAs. SOMA uses a parameter called PRT to achieve perturbations. This parameter has same effect for SOMA as mutation for EAs. The PRT vector defines the final movement of an active individual in the search space. The randomly generated binary perturbation vector controls the allowed dimensions for an individual. If an element of the perturbation vector is set to zero, then the individual is not allowed to change its position in the corresponding dimension. An individual will travel over a certain distance (called the PathLength) towards the leader in finite steps of the defined length. If the PathLength is chosen to be greater than one, then the individual will overshoot the leader. This path is

---

[3] https://play.google.com/store/apps/details?id=cz.bukacek.soma_tictactoe.

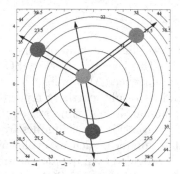

Fig. 1. SOMA principle.

perturbed randomly. The main principle of SOMA, i.e. traveling of an individual over space of possible solutions is depicted at Fig. 1.

The initial parameters set of SOMA for our experiments are in Table 1. They can be also set in the Android program, as demonstrated in Figs. 2, 3 and 4 .

Table 1. SOMA AllToOne parameter setting for Tic-Tac-Toe. For remaining strategies was used the same as in application on Google Play https://play.google.com/store/apps/details?id=cz.bukacek.soma_tictactoe

Parameter	Value
PathLength	3
Step	0.11
PRT	0.1
D	2
PopSize	20
Migration	10
MinDiv	-1 (i.e. not applied)

For more details about SOMA, see [17]. SOMA can be also regarded as a member of swarm intelligence class algorithms. In the same class is the algorithm particle swarm, which is also based on population of particles, which are mutually influenced amongst themselves. Some similarities as well as differences are between SOMA and particle swarm, for details see [27,28].

2.2   Cost Function Definition

The cost function, used to evaluate fitness of the strategy depend on game structure and number of players of course. Here we discuss briefly two cost functions: StarCraft: Brood War and Tic-Tac-Toe in order to show its difference and complexity.

Fig. 2. SOMA setting in Tic-Tac-Toe. General setting.

Fig. 3. SOMA setting in Tic-Tac-Toe. SOMA strategy setting.

Game in which an artificial intelligence was created is well-known real time strategy game StarCraft: Brood War. Similarly to other strategic games here it is also crucial to provide sufficient amount of materials for creating army in order to win. Materials are to be found on several places on the map as well as at the starting position. Game provides a choice of selecting from three races. Protoss are strong extraterrestrial beings. They have strong but expensive units. Zergs appear to be primitive and overgrown insects. Although, theirs units are of a cheap price, they are much weaker than units of Protoss. This race finds its victory in numbers. Last race are Terrans; race of humans being a compromise between already mentioned races have balanced prices and efficiency of theirs units. For a creation of the artificial intelligence a Zergs race has been chosen. For the creation of the artificial intelligence were used casual techniques such as decision making tree or unconventional techniques in the form of evolutionary algorithms, specifically SOMA algorithm. The algorithm should have arranged a movement of the combat units on the map. This at first appeared as an inappropriate as it would pointlessly search the whole map when an enemy is to be situated only at the places with a raw materials. Each member of the unit would be searching the map individually which is not advantageous as the army would become scattered. Game also further would not allow random placement of a population on the map. Staring positions of the units can be only near the structures meant for production of the units. With an incorrect objective function would be rising problems with the speed of finding the enemy. Only the contact with the enemy would stabilize the searching and the searching units would be attracted to this place. Few of the problems can be solved by the right setting of the parameters of SOMA algorithm and suitable implementation of

Fig. 4. SOMA setting in Tic-Tac-Toe. SOMA parameters setting.

the objective function. Other problems could not be solved this way. Parameter PathLength was set to a value 1 for the units to stay on the position of the leader. Parameter Step was not a bigger success at this situation as an interface of the game enabled to command the course of a unit. The unit was particularly searching by Step long as its own. Meaning Step = 0.5. Parameter PRT was selected near 1 so the units would not deviate from each other so much and at least some random searching came to pass. PRT was set to value 0.8. Parameter $D = 2$ because I was looking for the places on the map which were given by coordinates x and y. PopSize was a changeable parameter. Each produced combat unit was added to population and was its part until its death. All the finishing parameters (Migrations, MinDiv) were unwanted because algorithm SOMA was working through whole game if there were any units present. The positions of the enemy units were included in the fitness function as well as important positions on the map. SOMA algorithm thus optimized dynamic function in terms of mobility of the enemy units. This is how the function looked like:

$$Fitness = \sum_{i=0}^{m} hp_i w_i - \sum_{j=1}^{n} d_{bj} w_j - \sum_{k=1}^{p} d_{Mk} w_k - \sum_{l=0}^{q} d_{IPl} w_l \tag{1}$$

m is a number of units in radius 100 from the individual, hp_i is a number of hit points of the enemy unit in the radius 100 from the individual, n is a number of starting positions, d_{Bj} is a distance of starting positions from the individual, p is a number of positions with the materials, d_{Mk} is a distance of the individual from the position with the materials, q is a number of important positions on the map (e.g. last clash with an enemy, strategically important positions), d_{IPl} is a distance from the important point, w_x is an assigned weight of each item, can be

Fig. 5. Zerg units driven by SOMA in combat action in [30].

changeable with values $w_i = 10$, $w_j = 5$, $w_k = 0.1$, $w_l = 1$. The largest value was set to the enemy units. The more there were the enemies in the presence of the individual the bigger was a value of fitness. The closer was the individual to enemy starting position the bigger was its fitness. Starting position itself was set to 0. The biggest problem was a non-random placement of the population and inefficiency of the random search of the map. The position of the headquarters of the enemy is known. It is one of the starting positions. These problems were solved by the division of the population into two classes (as already reported): static and dynamic. Dynamic individual is not interesting at all. It is classical individual who yields to recombination and mutation. It is migrating individual in the terminology of SOMA algorithm. Static individuals on the other hand are not migrating. They are placed on the important positions at the map. Meaning positions with materials and starting positions. They can be also placed on the position of each built structure. Their role is important because of the static individual, at the starting position of the enemy, is calculated the biggest fitness. And they attract all of the units albeit from only one position. If they encounter the enemy on their route this kind of individual is chosen as a leader (in the terms of the highest value of the enemy hit points). If is enemy to attack any of our structures, this structure is chosen to be a leader (there is a static individual) from the same reason as stated. And the leader will attract attacking friendly units from unprotected enemy base. So these individuals create also alarm system. The strategy was quick attack (rush) at unprepared enemy. The screenshot from many battle situations is in Fig. 5, results of the fights are reported in [30].

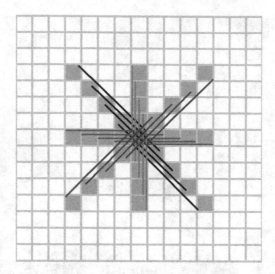

Fig. 6. TicTacToe cost function (see Eq. 2) principle.

On the contrary, in the Tic-Tac-Toe was cost function defined according to the Fig. 6 and is in principle captured in Eq. 2. The principle is that (Fig. 6). All experiments were done with one human player against 4 SOMA strategies (AllToOne, AllToOnenRand, AllToAll, AllToAllAdaptive) in 100 experiments in total (i.e. 25 experiments per strategy).

$$f(x) = Max(a, b)$$
$$a = \sum_i^4 \sum_j^5 10^{\left(\sum_{k=1}^5 x_{i,j,k}\right)-1} \text{ ... weight of defence strategy}$$
$$b = \sum_l^4 \sum_m^5 10^{\left(\sum_{n=1}^5 x_{l,m,n}\right)-1} \text{ ... weight of attack strategy} \tag{2}$$

x ... an individual position at Tic $-$ Tac $-$ Toe dashboard
i, l ... No. of possible paths
j, m ... No. of possible quintuples
k, n ... No. of occupied positions on $j_{th}(m_{th})$ quintuple

The cost function In fact algorithm, not a mathematical formula, in (2) is based on ideal case depicted in Fig. 6. Lets assume optimal case that individual from population is set into central position. Then it has to check all possible quintuples (related to its position, Fig. 6), i.e. 5 in each of 4 directions. In each direction is tested No. of occupied (or free, depend on strategy - attack, defence) positions. When summarized, then maximal fitness is selected and used to put SOMA's mark (green circle). It has to be said **that formula (2) is valid for optimal case, i.e. if position under fitness calculation would be on the edge, then number of tested positions would be restricted and limited and also case** when some quintuple has mixed marks (circle-cross), cannot be used too. Restrictions and edge situations are not mentioned in (2).

3   Results

While in StarCraft game has been done statistical set of experiments (thanks to automatic combat PC against SOMA) and reported in [30], in Tic-Tac-Toe we have made manual experiments and it can be stated that Tic-Tac-Toe driven by SOMA id exhibiting very good performance and many times win over the human player. A 100 manual experiments has been done here for each strategy and results are in the Table 2.

Table 2. Results - SOMA against human player.

Strategy	SOMA	Human
AllToOne	85	15
AllToOneRand	73	27
AllToAll	91	9
AllToAllAdaptive	95	5

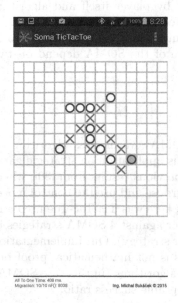

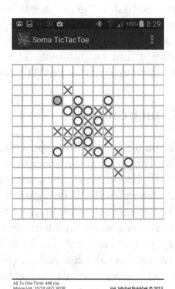

Fig. 7. Tic-Tac-Toe screenshot. Game in process - strategy AllToOne, green circle - SOMA, blue cross - human. (Color figure online)

Fig. 8. Tic-Tac-Toe screenshot. Game in process - strategy AllToOne, green circle - SOMA, blue cross - human. (Color figure online)

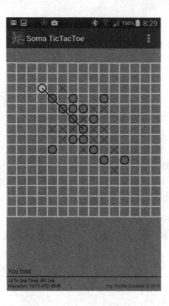

Fig. 9. Tic-Tac-Toe screenshot. End of game. SOMA won, green circle - SOMA, blue cross - human. (Color figure online)

True is that all experiments are influenced by player itself and algorithm setting. The screenshot from one game is depicted in Figs. 7, 8 and 9. If SOMA parameters would be set differently in non-optimal way, then of course the performance would be different. Thus performance of the SOMA depend on two factors: human skills and SOMA setting.

4   Conclusion

In this paper we have demonstrated use of SOMA swarm class algorithm on Tic-Tac-Toe game and also mention our previous application on strategic game StarCraft: Brood War [30]. Comparing to our previous results from [30], where SOMA dynamics has been modifies for game purpose and used to control movement of the combat units in order to win battle, here was Tic-Tac-Toe used and all experiments were done with one human player against 4 SOMA strategies in 100 experiments in total (i.e. 25 experiments per strategy). Our implementation and obtained results has shown (remember this is not mathematical proof but numerical demonstration) that EAs and swarm algorithms (in this case SOMA) are applicable for such class of games with acceptable success ratio.

Acknowledgment. The following grants are acknowledged for the financial support provided for this research: Grant Agency of the Czech Republic - GACR P103/15/06700S and SP2016/175.

References

1. Back, T., Fogel, B., Michalewicz, Z.: Handbook of Evolutionary Computation. Institute of Physics, London (1997)
2. Kirkpatrick, S., Gelatt Jr., C., Vecchi, M.: Optimization by simulated annealing. Science **220**(4598), 671–680 (1983)
3. Cerny, V.: Thermodynamical approach to the traveling salesman problem: an efficient simulation algorithm. J. Opt. Theor. Appl. **45**(1), 41–51 (1985)
4. Telfar, G.: Acceleration Techniques for Simulated Annealing. M.Sc. thesis. Victoria University of Wellington, New Zealand (1996)
5. Russell, S.J., Norvig, P.: Artificial Intelligence: A Modern Approach, 2nd edn. Prentice Hall, Upper Saddle River (2003). pp. 111–114, ISBN 0-13-790395-2
6. Rego, C., Alidaee, B.: Metaheuristic Optimization via Memory and Evolution: Tabu Search and Scatter Search. Springer, New York (2005). ISBN: 978-1402081347
7. Davis, L.: Handbook of Genetic Algorithms. Van Nostrand Reinhold, Berlin (1996)
8. Goldberg, D.: Genetic Algorithms in Search, Optimization, and Machine Learning. Addison-Wesley Publishing Company Inc., Boston (1989). ISBN 0201157675
9. Michalewicz, Z.: Genetic Algorithms + Data Structures = Evolution Programs. Springer, Berlin (1996)
10. Chu, P.: A Genetic Algorithm Approach for Combinatorial Optimisation Problems. Ph.D. thesis. The Management School Imperial College of Science, Technology and Medicine, London 181 (1997)
11. Glover, F., Laguna, M.: Tabu Search. Springer, New York (1997). ISBN 0-7923-8187-4
12. Michalewicz, Z., Fogel, D.B.: How to Solve It: Modern Heuristics. Springer, Berlin (2000)
13. Reeves, C.: Modern Heuristic Techniques for Combinatorial Problems. Blackwell Scientific Publications, Oxford (1993)
14. Holland, J.: Adaptation in Natural and Artificial Systems. University of Michigan Press, Ann Arbor (1975)
15. Schwefel, H.: Numerische Optimierung von Computer-Modellen (PhD thesis). Reprinted by Birkhuser (1974)
16. Dorigo, M., Sttzle, T.: Ant Colony Optimization. MIT Press, Cambridge (2004). ISBN: 978-0262042192
17. Zelinka, I.: SOMA - Self Organizing Migrating Algorithm. In: Onwubolu, B.B. (ed.) New Optimization Techniques in Engineering, pp. 167–218. Springer, New York (2004). ISBN 3-540-20167X
18. Goh, C., Ong, Y., Tan, K.: Multi-Objective Memetic Algorithms. Springer, Heidelberg (2009). ISBN 978-3-540-88050-9
19. Schonberger, J.: Operational Freight Carrier Planning, Basic Concepts, Optimization Models and Advanced Memetic Algorithms. Springer, Heidelberg (2005). ISBN 978-3-540-25318-1
20. Onwubolu, G., Babu, B.: New Optimization Techniques in Engineering. Springer, New York (2004). pp. 167–218, ISBN 3-540-20167X
21. Hart, W., Krasnogor, N., Smith, J.: Recent Advances in Memetic Algorithms. Springer, Heidelberg (2005). ISBN 978-3-540-22904-9
22. Price, K.: An introduction to differential evolution. In: Corne, D., Dorigo, M., Glover, F. (eds.) New Ideas in Optimisation, pp. 79–108. McGraw Hill International, UK (1999)

23. Yang, X.-S., Deb, S.: Cuckoo search via Lvy flights. In: World Congress on Nature and Biologically Inspired Computing (NaBIC 2009), pp. 210–214. IEEE Publications (2009)
24. Yang, X.-S.: Firefly algorithms for multimodal optimization. In: Watanabe, O., Zeugmann, T. (eds.) SAGA 2009. LNCS, vol. 5792, pp. 169–178. Springer, Heidelberg (2009)
25. Yang, X.-S.: A new metaheuristic bat-inspired algorithm. In: Gonzalez, J.R., et al. (eds.) Nature Inspired Cooperative Strategies for Optimization (NISCO 2010). Studies in Computational Intelligence, vol. 284, pp. 65–74. Springer, Berlin (2010)
26. Rechenberg, I.: Evolutionsstrategie - Optimierung technischer Systeme nach Prinzipien der biologischen Evolution (Ph.D. thesis), Printed in Fromman-Holzboog, 1973 (1971)
27. Eberhart, R.C., Kennedy, J.: A new optimizer using particle swarm theory. In: Proceedings of the Sixth International Symposium on Micromachine and Human Science, Nagoya, Japan, pp. 39–43 (1995)
28. Clerc, M.: Particle Swarm Optimization. ISTE Publishing Company, London (2006). ISBN 1-905209-04-5
29. Sikora, L.: StarCraft: Brood War - Strategy Powered by the SOMA Swarm Algoritmh, Diploma thesis, VSB-TU Ostrava
30. Zelinka, I., Sikora, L.: StarCraft: brood war - strategy powered by the SOMA swarm algorithm. In: IEEE Conference on Computational Intelligence and Games, Taiwan (2015, accepted, in print)

Various Problems of Artificial Intelligence

Tabu Search Algorithm with Neural Tabu Mechanism for the Cyclic Job Shop Problem

Wojciech Bożejko[1(✉)], Andrzej Gnatowski[1], Teodor Niżyński[1],
and Mieczysław Wodecki[2]

[1] Department of Automatics, Mechatronics and Control Systems,
Faculty of Electronics, Wrocław University of Technology,
Janiszewskiego 11-17, 50-372 Wrocław, Poland
{wojciech.bozejko,andrzej.gnatowski,teodor.nizynski}@pwr.edu.pl
[2] Institute of Computer Science, University of Wrocław,
Joliot-Curie 15, 50-383 Wrocław, Poland
mwd@ii.uni.wroc.pl

Abstract. In the work there is a NP-hard cyclic job shop problem of tasks scheduling considered. To its solution there was tabu search algorithm implemented using neural mechanism to prevent looping of the algorithm. There were computational experiments conducted that showed statistically significant efficacy of the proposed tabu method as compared to classical list of forbidden moves.

Keywords: Discrete optimization · Tabu search · Scheduling

1 Introduction

The modern market has a huge demand for cheap, differentiated products. Hence, the importance of cyclic mass production, where more copies of the product are manufactured in recurring fixed intervals (cycle time). To maximize the number of goods produced in unit time, the aim is to minimize the cycle time. In order to do this there is a model of this problem implemented, allowing the use of optimization algorithms. Depending on the specific production process and expected accuracy of mapping the reality, there is General Assembly Line Problems [1] or cyclic extensions of classical scheduling problems applied. The considered in this work cyclical job shop problem belongs to a class of strongly NP-hard problems. Strong NP-hardness results in the fact that the possibility to use the exact algorithms is limited to a small instances of the problem and enables the of use heuristics and metaheuristics for larger instances. Analysis of the state of knowledge about many varieties of cyclic job shop problem was presented in the work [17].

To solve the considered in the work problem there was tabu search (TS) algorithm used. It is one of the most widely used algorithms to solve combinatorial optimization problems, including cyclic multi-machine problems [6,7,14]. In the paper, in place of classic tabu list, there is a proposal to use the mechanism based

© Springer International Publishing Switzerland 2016
L. Rutkowski et al. (Eds.): ICAISC 2016, Part II, LNAI 9693, pp. 409–418, 2016.
DOI: 10.1007/978-3-319-39384-1_35

on the concept of an artificial neural network. On one hand, it prevents generation of already considered solutions, on the other hand, it provides much better
diversification of the process of the solution space search. In general, the idea
of using advanced mathematical modeling constitutes promising way in solving
hard optimization problems [8,9,11,13]. In particular, neural approach was used
not only in an algorithm solving the traveling salesman problem [16], but also
in other problems of tasks scheduling [10,12].

2   Problem Definition

In the paper, cyclic job shop scheduling problem is considered. The problem
can be formulated as follows. There are m work stations (hereinafter denomi-
nated as *the machines*), numbered in consecutive order, forming the set $\mathcal{M} =
\{1, 2, \ldots, m\}$. On the machines, n tasks (jobs) from the set $\mathcal{J} = \{1, 2, \ldots, n\}$
are being processed in a cyclical manner. Task $j \in \mathcal{J}$ requires n_j operations
numbered as follows:

$$(l_{j-1}+1, l_{j-1}+2, \ldots, l_{j-1}+n_j), \quad l_j = \begin{cases} \sum_{i=1}^{j} n_i & \text{for } j = 1, 2, \ldots, n, \\ 0 & \text{for } j = 0, \end{cases} \quad (1)$$

to be executed in predefined order.

The set $\mathcal{O} = \{1, 2, \ldots, o\}$ consists of all the operations that are required to
finish the tasks from the set $\mathcal{J}$. Each operation $i \in \mathcal{O}$ must be being executed
continuously on the machine v_i for $p_i > 0$ time, and each machine can execute
at most one operation at a time. Therefore, m disjoint sets of the operations can
be defined: $\mathcal{O}_k = \{j \in \mathcal{O} : v_j = k\}$, $k = 1, \ldots m$. The set $\mathcal{O}_k$ consists of all the
operations that are executed on the machine $k \in \mathcal{M}$ and has a size of $m_k = |\mathcal{O}_k|$.
A set of operations that must be processed in a single cycle ($\mathcal{O}$) is called MPS
(*Minimal Part Set*). MPSes are processed cyclically, e.g. each operation $i \in \mathcal{O}$
must be executed every T time units, where T is *a cycle time*. The sequence
of operation execution on the machine $k \in \mathcal{M}$ is denoted by the permutation
$\pi_k = (\pi_k(1), \ldots, \pi_k(m_k))$, where $\pi_k(i) \in \mathcal{O}_k$ is an operation on the position i
in π_k. The order of execution for all the machines is represented by the m-tuple
$\pi = (\pi_1, \pi_2, \ldots, \pi_m)$. Let $\Pi_k, k \in \mathcal{M}$ be a set of possible permutations of the
operations from the set $\mathcal{O}_k$. Then $\pi \in \Pi = \Pi_1 \times \Pi_2 \times \cdots \times \Pi_m$.

A solution of the problem is defined by the cycle time T and the schedule
$S^x = (S_1^x, S_2^x, \ldots, S_o^x)$, where S_i^x is the moment in time when, in x-th MPS, the
execution of the operation $i \in \mathcal{O}$ is being started. The schedule is subject to the
following constraints:

$$S_i^x + p_i \leq S_{i+1}^x, \qquad \text{for} \quad i \in \mathcal{O}_k, \ k \in \mathcal{M}, \qquad (2)$$

$$S_{\pi_k(i)}^x + p_{\pi_k(i)} \leq S_{\pi_k(i+1)}^x, \qquad \text{for} \quad i = 1, \ldots, m_k - 1, \ k \in \mathcal{M}, \qquad (3)$$

$$S_i^x \geq 0, \qquad \text{for} \quad i \in \mathcal{O}, \qquad (4)$$

$$S_{\pi_k(m_k)}^x + p_{\pi_k(m_k)} \leq S_{\pi_k(1)}^{x+1}, \qquad \text{for} \quad k \in \mathcal{M}, \qquad (5)$$

$$S_i^x + T = S_i^{x+1}, \qquad \text{for} \quad i \in \mathcal{O}, \qquad (6)$$

where $x = 1, 2, \ldots$ is the number of MPS.

Definition 1. *For a given order of execution π, the minimal cycle time $T(\pi)$ is the lowest value of a cycle time T, for which π is feasible, e.g. at least one schedule S^x that satisfies the constraints from Eqs. (2)–(6) exists.*

Therefore, the problem of the minimum cycle time is reduced to finding such $\pi^* \in \Pi$ that minimizes the minimal cycle time

$$T(\pi^*) = \min_{\pi \in \Pi}\{T(\pi)\}. \qquad (7)$$

Passage from π to the solution in the form of cycle time T and schedule S^x boils down not only to designation of $T(\pi)$ but also finding an acceptable schedule. Therefore, the important issue is determining the minimum cycle time for a given order of operations, i.e. permutation $\pi \in \Pi$.

3   The Minimum Cycle Time

In order to determine the minimum cycle time there was a method presented in the works [4,6] adopted. Let us consider shifted to the left schedule of operation execution which meets the constraints of (2) and (5). Then the values of the following completion times of the operations can be calculated with the use of the formula:

$$S_{\pi_k(i)}^x = \begin{cases} -\infty & \text{for} \quad x = 0, \\ S_{\pi_k(i-1)}^x + p_{\pi_k(i)} & \text{for} \quad \pi_k(i) = l_{j-1}+1, \, j \in \mathcal{J} \\ S_{\pi_k(m_k)}^{x-1} & \text{for} \quad i = 0, \\ \max\left\{S_{\pi_k(i-1)}^x; \, S_{\pi_k(i)-1}^x\right\} + p_{\pi_k(i)} & \text{otherwise,} \end{cases}$$
$$(8)$$

where: $k \in \mathcal{M}$, $i \in \{1, 2, \ldots, m_k\}$, $x = 1, 2, \ldots$. It is easy to notice that for any permissible order of operations on the machines $\pi \in \Pi$ (order for which it is possible to find at least one acceptable schedule), it is possible to perform the calculation from the Eq. 8. Let ^kS denote schedule anchored in the operation $\pi_k(1)$, e.g. $^kS_{\pi_k(i)}^1 = p_{\pi_k(i)}$. To fulfill the condition from the Eq. 6 there must occur:

$$T \geq {}^kS_{\pi_k(1)}^x - {}^kS_{\pi_k(1)}^{x-1}, \quad k = 1, 2, \ldots, m, \qquad (9)$$

where after transformations

$$T \geq {}^kS_{\pi_k(1)}^x - ({}^kS_{\pi_k(1)}^1 + T(x - 1 - 1)). \qquad (10)$$

Since $^kS_{\pi_k(1)}^1 = 0$, therefore

$$T \geq \frac{{}^kS_{\pi_k(1)}^x}{x - 1}, \qquad (11)$$

ultimately the condition that must be met by the minimum cycle time:

$$T(\pi) \geq \frac{{}^k S^x_{\pi_k(1)}}{x - 1}, \ k \in \mathcal{M}, \ x = 2, 3, \ldots . \tag{12}$$

Finally the minimum cycle time for a fixed solutions $\pi \in \Pi$ can be determined with the use of the equation:

$$T(\pi) = \max \left\{ \frac{{}^k S^x_{\pi_k(1)}}{x - 1} : \ x = \{2, 3, \ldots m\}, \ k \in \mathcal{M} \right\}. \tag{13}$$

As shown in [5], with the use of the discussed method, the cycle time can be designated in time $O(om^2)$.

4 Solution Method

To solve the considered in the work problem there was, proposed in the work [15], metaheuristic tabu search algorithm adopted. In order to avoid locking in local minima, a list of prohibited moves was used in it. In the literature one can find many modifications of the original algorithm used in tasks scheduling problems [3, 18, 20]. A scheme of the proposed method (denoted in short as NTS) is shown in Fig. 1. In its description, the numbers in parentheses indicate the number of the block in diagram.

The algorithm starts by designation of allowable initial solution π^0 (block (1)). *The starting procedure* is a simple heuristics determining such order of operations execution on machines, in which all operations from the tasks i are performed before operations from tasks j, if $i < j$. The best solution found so far was denoted with the use of π^*, whereas the current solution π, *iter* is the number of iterations of the algorithm from the last improvement of the order π^*. In block (2) there is *the neighborhood* generated, i.e. the set of $N(\pi)$ solutions (neighbors) of the solution π, created with the use of a specific operator. In this algorithm the neighborhood block N_1 was modeled on the example from the works of Nowicki and Smutnicki [18]. Its definition in terms of cyclical problems can be found in [14]. Elements of the neighborhood are generated by swapping the order of performing of the first operation from each block with the second operation of the block, and the last operation of each block with the one before last operation. If the designated neighborhood is empty (3) there is a *recurrence* (11) performed. The mechanism of a recurrence is a diversification scheme applied in order to leave unpromising search areas. For this purpose there is a list of good long-term solutions used. It is created with the solutions of the objective function value less than the best found so far (improving π^*). The solution is stored along with the neighborhood omitting the best neighbor (to avoid re-following of the same path). The recurrence is performed when one of the conditions is met:

1. neighborhood of the current solution is empty (3);
2. algorithm cyclically visits the same solutions (10);

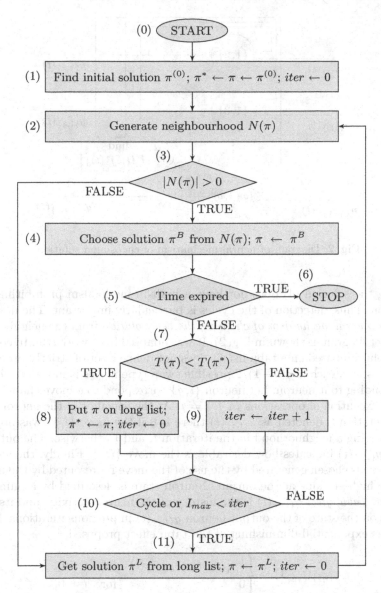

Fig. 1. Flowchart of tabu search algorithm

3. number of iterations, without improving the best solution found so far, exceeds the predetermined value I_{max} depending on the current iteration (10).

The algorithm proceeds to solve the oldest solution from the long-term list, at the same time deleting it from the list. As demonstrated by computational experiments, the algorithm deprived of condition 2, has a tendency to fall into cycles of small length. This results from the fact that neural mechanism for

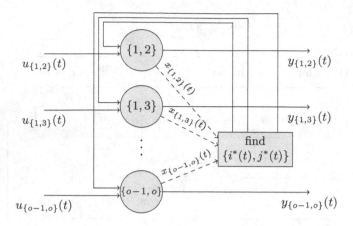

Fig. 2. Diagram of neural mechanism of choosing a solution

choosing the solution (4) does not have a built-in mechanism prohibiting their formation. Thus, detection of the cycles is particularly important. The next step (4) is the *neural mechanism of choosing the best solution* from the neighborhood (the exact diagram is shown in Fig. 2). It was adapted from work [19]. In contrast to the solution based on a tabu list, it does not define a set of strictly prohibited moves. Instead, each of $o(o-1)/2$ possible swap type moves is modeled with the corresponding to it neuron. Let neuron $\{i,j\}$ correspond to a move changing the order of execution of operations i i j, $i \neq j$. At the entrance of the neuron $\{i,j\}$ in the iteration t, denoted as $u_{\{i,j\}}(t)$ there is 0 if the move $\{i,j\}$ was not used when creating a neighborhood in the iteration t, and 1 otherwise. The output of neuron $y_{\{i,j\}}(t)$ indicates how desirable is the move $\{i,j\}$. Finally, the solution $\pi^B \in N(\pi)$ is chosen generated by the use of the move represented by the neuron with the highest value at the output. Neuron state is described by a number of variables. *Tabu effect* $\gamma_{\{i,j\}}(t)$ is the history of the neuron activity, and its value depends on the state of the output neuron $y_{\{i,j\}}(t)$ in previous iterations. In [19] there was exponential diminishing of the tabu effect proposed:

$$\gamma_{\{i,j\}}(t+1) = \begin{cases} k\gamma_{\{i,j\}}(t) + y_{\{i,j\}}(t) & \text{for } t > 0, \\ 0 & \text{for } t = 0, \end{cases} \tag{14}$$

where k is a coefficient that allows one to modify the pace of decline. *Gain effect* informs one about the quality of the move and is described by the equation

$$\eta_{\{i,j\}}(t+1) = \begin{cases} \alpha \frac{T(\pi(t)_{\{i,j\}})}{T(\pi^*(t))} & \text{for } u_{\{i,j\}}(t+1) = 1, \\ \infty & \text{for } u_{\{i,j\}}(t+1) = 0, \end{cases} \tag{15}$$

where $\pi(t)_{\{i,j\}}$ is the permutation defined by swapping of the order of execution of operations i and j in solution π from iteration t; α is the coefficient of scalability, $\pi^*(t)$ is best obtained order of execution π^* defined by the first t iteration of the algorithm. Finally, the output neuron is calculated by the formula:

$$y_{\{i,j\}}(t+1) = \frac{1}{2} |\{i,j\} \cap \{i^*(t), j^*(t)\}|, \tag{16}$$

where $i^*(t)$ i $j^*(t)$ are arbitrarily selected pair of operations satisfying the condition:

$$x_{\{i^*(t),j^*(t)\}}(t) = \min\left\{x_{\{k,l\}}(t) : k,l \in \mathcal{O} \wedge k \neq l\right\}, \tag{17}$$
$$x_{\{i,j\}}(t) = \eta_{\{i,j\}}(t) + \gamma_{\{i,j\}}(t). \tag{18}$$

Thus the value $y_{\{i,j\}}(t) \in \{0, 0.5, 1\}$ reflects the degree to which the move $\{i, j\}$ is similar to the best move $\{i^*(t), j^*(t)\}$. Blocks (5) and (7) are responsible for stopping the execution of the algorithm after a fixed period of time. In blocks (7–9) the value of the best so far determined order π^* is updated. Blocks (10–11) were discussed earlier. In order to evaluate the effect of the application of a neural network on the quality of the results, there was standard TS algorithm proposed differing from the NTS algorithm by the block principle activity (4). In the TS the prohibitions mechanism is implemented with the use of a tabu list which is the short-term history of searches. The attributes of the visited by the algorithm solutions are added to it. The solution π is described with an unordered pair of operations $\{i, j\}$, $v_i = v_j = s$, where changing the order of tasks execution on the machine s led to creation of π. When the length of the list reaches the maximum fixed value of L_{max}, before adding the next solution, the oldest one is deleted from the list. In case where, in a particular step, all elements of the neighborhood are on the tabu list, the successive solutions are deleted from it, beginning with the oldest, until at least one of the neighbors is not prohibited. In addition, there is an aspiration criterion introduced: every neighbor of objective function value less than the current best solution is not prohibited, even if it is on the tabu list. In the algorithm, there was a strategy of choosing a neighbor of the smallest value of the objective function adopted.

5 Computational Experiments

Both the NTS algorithm and the classic TS algorithm were implemented in C++ using Visual Studio 2015 Professional. The study was conducted on a PC equipped with an Intel i7-4930K CPU clocked at 4.31 GHz processor, 32 GB of RAM and the operating system Widows 8.1 64-bit. Due to the lack of benchmarks for the tested varieties of the problem there were test examples from the OR-Library used [2]: ft6, ft10, ft20 and la01 - la40 for the job shop problem, assuming that the operations are carried out periodically. In the preliminary studies there were the parameters of algorithms established. In the TS algorithm there was the length of the tabu list determined on $L_{max} = 7$, $I_{max} = 5000 + t/10$, where t denotes the number of iterations. In the NTS there were $\alpha = 12$, $k = 0.98$, $I_{max} = 5000 + t/10$ adopted. For each instance determined the relative deviation of the smallest of determining minimum cycle time

Table 1. Values Dev for TS and NTS algorithms.

Instance		Dev [%]		Instance		Dev [%]		Instance		Dev [%]	
Name	$n \times m$	TS	NTS	Name	$n \times m$	TS	NTS	Name	$n \times m$	TS	NTS
la01	10×5	2.79	0.51	la16	10×10	34.88	36.00	la31	30×10	9.13	8.38
la02	10×5	2.65	1.45	la17	10×10	8.54	8.16	la32	30×10	21.03	0.91
la03	10×5	2.62	2.45	la18	10×10	28.84	31.37	la33	30×10	15.76	0.41
la04	10×5	8.01	7.00	la19	10×10	16.96	20.98	la34	30×10	18.93	7.49
la05	10×5	29.02	11.47	la20	10×10	16.67	12.35	la35	30×10	7.80	0.98
la06	15×5	14.31	13.84	la21	15×20	17.23	17.76	la36	15×15	27.36	21.53
la07	15×5	11.07	11.00	la22	15×20	21.05	11.27	la37	15×15	47.37	42.11
la08	15×5	0.44	0.56	la23	15×20	1.21	1.17	la38	15×15	43.16	41.23
la09	15×5	3.74	0.42	la24	15×20	8.77	12.24	la39	15×15	19.76	23.48
la10	15×5	0.40	0.71	la25	15×20	12.19	10.16	la40	15×15	15.92	19.05
la11	20×5	12.39	11.97	la26	20×10	5.52	4.51	ft06	6×6	11.24	11.24
la12	20×5	1.96	0.27	la27	20×10	15.09	5.61	ft10	10×10	17.35	10.16
la13	20×5	4.23	3.61	la28	20×10	0.89	1.78	ft20	20×5	6.36	5.92
la14	20×5	0.02	0.00	la29	20×10	3.41	3.19				
la15	20×5	8.32	7.65	la30	20×10	17.21	17.01				

$T(\pi)$ from its estimate a lower T^{LB}, defined as:

$$Dev = \frac{T(\pi) - T^{LB}}{T^{LB}} \cdot 100\,\%, \tag{19}$$

where $T^{LB} = \max_{1 \leq i \leq m} \left\{ \sum_{j \in O_i} p_j \right\}$, was obtained by each of the algorithms in time of $100\,$s. The results of the experiment are given in Table 1 and presented in Fig. 3. NTS algorithm is much better for larger sizes of instances. Unfortunately, while the average result for the proposed method was lower by $13.34\,\%$ - $10.67\,\%$ $= 2.67\,\%$, in case of an instance: la08, la10, la16, la18, la19, la21, la24, la28, la39, la40 there was no improvement in the results observed.

The results of TS and NTS algorithms were compared with the use of the Wilcoxon-Mann-Whitney two-sample rank-sum test. It was assumed that the test examples are representative sample of the population. Let D_{TS} denote the population of the relative deviations of the smallest designated by TS algorithm minimum cycle time $T(\pi)$ from its lower estimate $T(\pi^{LB})$ for all instances of the problem. Population D_{NTS} was defined in a similar way. It is assumed that under the null hypothesis H_0, the probability of an observation from the population D_{TS} exceeding an observation from the second population D_{NTS} equals the probability of an observation from D_{NTS} exceeding an observation from D_{TS}: $P(D_{TS} > D_{NTS}) = P(D_{TS} < D_{NTS})$. The alternative hypothesis H_1 was: $P(D_{TS} > D_{NTS}) > P(D_{TS} < D_{NTS})$. The test does not conclude on $P(D_{TS} = D_{NTS})$. The test was performed using the software environment for statistical computing R obtaining $V = 736, p = 0.000763$. At the significance

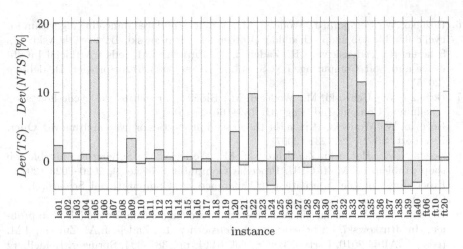

Fig. 3. Differences in the quality of the results of TS and MTS algorithms activity on test examples

level of $p = 0.05$ rejected the hypothesis H_0 was rejected to adopt H_1 hypothesis. Thus, the test enabled the recognition of the results obtained by using the NTS as better than the results of the TS algorithm.

6   Concluding Remarks

In the paper there was a modified tabu search algorithm with neural prohibitions mechanism proposed. The promoted model is the equivalent of the biological mechanism of forgetting - the move is not explicitly prohibited or allowed. The use of statistical Wilcoxon-Mann-Whitney test, on the solutions of problem instances from OR-Library, allows the recognition of the results obtained with the proposed algorithm as better than the results obtained with the use of the modified tabu search.

References

1. Battaïa, O., Dolgui, A.: A taxonomy of line balancing problems and their solution approaches. Int. J. Prod. Econ. **142**(2), 259–277 (2013)
2. Beasley, J.E.: OR-Library: distributing test problems by electronic mail. J. Oper. Res. Soc. **41**(11), 1069–1072 (1990)
3. Ben-Daya, M., Al-Fawzan, M.: A tabu search approach for the flow shop scheduling problem. Eur. J. Oper. Res. **109**(1), 88–95 (1998)
4. Bożejko, W., Gnatowski, A., Pempera, J., Wodecki, M.: Parallel tabu search meta-heuristics for the cyclic job shop scheduling problem. Computers and Industrial Engineering (2015, Submitted)
5. Bożejko, W., Gniewkowski, U., Pempera, J., Wodecki, M.: Cyclic hybrid flowshop scheduling problem with machine setups. Procedia Comput. Sci. **29**, 2127–2136 (2014)

6. Bożejko, W., Pempera, J., Wodecki, M.: Parallel simulated annealing algorithm for cyclic flexible job shop scheduling problem. In: Rutkowski, L., Korytkowski, M., Scherer, R., Tadeusiewicz, R., Zadeh, L.A., Zurada, J.M. (eds.) Artificial Intelligence and Soft Computing. LNCS, vol. 9120, pp. 603–612. Springer, Heidelberg (2015)

7. Bożejko, W., Uchroski, M., Wodecki, M.: Block approach to the cyclic flow shop scheduling. Comput. Ind. Eng. **81**, 158–166 (2015)

8. Bożejko, W., Wodecki, M.: On the theoretical properties of swap multimoves. Oper. Res. Lett. **35**(2), 227–231 (2007)

9. Bożejko, W., Hejducki, Z., Uchroński, M., Wodecki, M.: Solving the flexible job shop problem on Multi-GPU. Procedia Computer Science, 9, 2020–2023 (2012). Proceedings of the International Conference on Computational Science, ICCS (2012)

10. Bożejko, W., Uchroński, M.: A neuro-tabu search algorithm for the job shop problem. In: Rutkowski, L., Scherer, R., Tadeusiewicz, R., Zadeh, L.A., Zurada, J.M. (eds.) ICAISC 2010, Part II. LNCS, vol. 6114, pp. 387–394. Springer, Heidelberg (2010)

11. Bożejko, W., Uchroński, M., Wodecki, M.: The new golf neighborhood for the exible job shop problem. Procedia Comput. Sci. **1**(1), 289–296 (2010). ICCS

12. Bożejko, W., Uchroński, M., Wodecki, M.: Parallel neuro-tabu search algorithm for the job shop scheduling problem. In: Rutkowski, L., Korytkowski, M., Scherer, R., Tadeusiewicz, R., Zadeh, L.A., Zurada, J.M. (eds.) ICAISC 2013, Part II. LNCS, vol. 7895, pp. 489–499. Springer, Heidelberg (2013)

13. Bożejko, W., Uchroński, M., Wodecki, M.: Block approach to the cyclic flow shop scheduling. Comput. Ind. Eng. **81**, 158–166 (2015)

14. Brucker, P., Heitmann, S., Hurink, J.: Flow-shop problems with intermediate buffers. OR Spectrum **25**(4), 549–574 (2003)

15. Glover, F.: Future paths for integer programming and links to artificial intelligence. Comput. Oper. Res. **13**(5), 533–549 (1986)

16. Hasegawa, M., Ikeguchi, T., Aihara, K.: Combination of chaotic neurodynamics with the 2-opt algorithm to solve traveling salesman problems. Phys. Rev. Lett. **79**(12), 2344 (1997)

17. Levner, E., Kats, V., de Pablo, D.A.L., Cheng, T.E.: Complexity of cyclic scheduling problems: a state-of-the-art survey. Comput. Ind. Eng. **59**(2), 352–361 (2010)

18. Nowicki, E., Smutnicki, C.: A fast taboo search algorithm for the job shop problem. Manag. Sci. **42**(6), 797–813 (1996)

19. Solimanpur, M., Vrat, P., Shankar, R.: A neuro-tabu search heuristic for the flow shop scheduling problem. Comput. Oper. Res. **31**(13), 2151–2164 (2004)

20. Taillard, E.: Some efficient heuristic methods for the flow shop sequencing problem. Eur. J. Oper. Res. **47**(1), 65–74 (1990)

Parallel Tabu Search Algorithm with Uncertain Data for the Flexible Job Shop Problem

Wojciech Bożejko[1(✉)], Mariusz Uchroński[2], and Mieczysław Wodecki[3]

[1] Department of Control Science and Mechatronics, Faculty of Electronics,
Wrocław University of Technology, Janiszewskiego 11-17, 50-372 Wrocław, Poland
wojciech.bozejko@pwr.edu.pl
[2] Wrocław Centre of Networking and Supercomputing,
Wyb. Wyspiańskiego 27, 50-370 Wrocław, Poland
mariusz.uchronski@pwr.edu.pl
[3] Institute of Computer Science, University of Wrocław,
Joliot-Curie 15, 50-383 Wrocław, Poland
mwd@ii.uni.wroc.pl

Abstract. In many real production systems the parameters of individual operations are not deterministic. Typically, they can be modeled by fuzzy numbers or distributions of random variables. In this paper we consider the flexible job shop problem with machine setups and uncertain times of operation execution. Not only we present parallel algorithm on GPU with fuzzy parameters but also we investigate its resistance to random disturbance of the input data.

1 Introduction

In the process of solving classical tasks scheduling problems all tasks parameters (e.g. execution times) are known. In case of uncertain data, first – assuming a certain size (from many possible), then – finding the solution to obtained in this way deterministic scheduling problem – results in reaching not very stable solutions. Therefore, data uncertainty is modeled either with the use of stochastic methods or with the theory of fuzzy numbers. The first attempt [8] requires knowledge of certain statistic data from the past. The main disadvantage of this method is the difficulty in obtaining and verifying not only probability distribution of parameters but also their moments (e.g. mean). In case of research on new problems or the use of new technologies, knowledge concerning statistic data from the past usually does not exist. That is why the approach based on the use of the theory of fuzzy numbers is in this case fully justified. The first studies concerning solving scheduling problems with fuzzy data relate to PERT method [10], and also to classical single and multi-machine problems [1,11].

2 Problem Formulation

Flexible job shop problem can be defined as follows. There is a set of tasks $\mathcal{J} = \{1, 2, \ldots, n\}$ given, which should be executed on the machines from the set

© Springer International Publishing Switzerland 2016
L. Rutkowski et al. (Eds.): ICAISC 2016, Part II, LNAI 9693, pp. 419–428, 2016.
DOI: 10.1007/978-3-319-39384-1_36

$\mathcal{M} = \{1, 2, \ldots, m\}$. There is a breakup of a set of machines into types, i.e. machines of the same functional properties. The task is a sequence of some operations. Each operation should be performed on the suitable type of machine in a fixed period of time. Between sequentially executed operations there should be setup of machines performed. The solution to the problem relies in the allocation of operations to the appropriate type of machines and determination of the order of operations on each machine, to minimize the time of execution of all tasks.

Let $\mathcal{O} = \{1, 2, \ldots, o\}$ be the set of all operations. It can be divided into the subsequences of operations corresponding to the tasks, where the task $j \in \mathcal{J}$ is a sequence of o_j operations which will be successively performed on the respective machines (in the so-called technological order). These operations are indexed by numbers $(l_{j-1} + 1, \ldots, l_{j-1} + o_j)$, where $l_j = \sum_{i=1}^{j} o_i$ is the number of the first operation of the task j, $j = 1, 2, \ldots, n$, whereas $l_0 = 0$, and $o = \sum_{i=1}^{n} o_i$.

The set of machines $\mathcal{M} = \{1, 2, \ldots, m\}$ can be partitioned into q subsets of machines of the same type (*nests*), whereas i-th ($i = 1, 2, \ldots, q$) type $\mathcal{M}^i$ includes m_i machines, which are indexed by numbers $(t_{i-1} + 1, \ldots, t_{i-1} + m_i)$, where $t = \sum_{j=1}^{i} m_j$ is the number of machines in the first i types, $i = 1, 2, \ldots, q$, and $t_0 = 0$, and $m = \sum_{j=1}^{m} m_j$.

Operation $v \in \mathcal{O}$ should be performed in the nest $\mu(v)$, i.e. on one of machines from the set $\mathcal{M}^{\mu(v)}$ in time p_{vj}, where $j \in \mathcal{M}^{\mu(v)}$.

Let $\mathcal{O}^k = \{v \in \mathcal{O} : \mu(v) = k\}$ be a set of operations executed in k-th ($k = 1, 2, \ldots, q$) nest. A sequence of disjoint sets of operations will be executed in k-th ($k = 1, 2, \ldots, q$) nest. A sequence of disjoint sets of operations $\mathcal{Q} = [\mathcal{Q}_1, \mathcal{Q}_2, \ldots, \mathcal{Q}_m]$, such that for every $k = 1, 2, \ldots, q$, $\mathcal{O}^k = \bigcup_{i=t_{k-1}+1}^{t_{k-1}+m_k} \mathcal{Q}_i$, is called the *allocation of operations from the set* $\mathcal{O}$ *to machines from the set* $\mathcal{M}$. In turn, the sequence $[\mathcal{Q}_{t_{k-1}+1}, \mathcal{Q}_{t_{k-1}+2}, \ldots, \mathcal{Q}_{t_{k-1}+m_k}]$ is the allocation of operations to machines in the i-th nest.

Any feasible solution of the flexible job shop problem is a pair $(\mathcal{Q}, \pi(\mathcal{Q}))$, where $\mathcal{Q}$ is the allocation of operations to machines and $\pi(\mathcal{Q}) = (\pi_1, \pi_2, \ldots, \pi_m)$ is a m-tuple of permutations (or permutation in short) denoting the order of performing operations on individual machines. In the further part, for simplicity of notation, any feasible solution will be denoted by $\Theta = (\mathcal{Q}, \pi)$. By Φ there is a set of all feasible solutions for the flexible job shop problem denoted.

2.1 Graph Model

Any solution $\Theta = (\mathcal{Q}, \pi) \in \Phi$ can be represented by the directed graph with burdened vertices and arcs $G(\Theta) = (\mathcal{V}, \mathcal{R} \cup \mathcal{E}(\Theta))$, where $\mathcal{V}$ is a set of vertices, and $\mathcal{R} \cup \mathcal{E}(\Theta)$ is a set of arcs, whereby:

1. The set $\mathcal{V} = \mathcal{O} \cup \{s, c\}$, where s and c are additional operations representing respectively: 'start' and 'end'. The vertex $v \in \mathcal{V} \setminus \{s, c\}$ is characterized by two features:
   - $\lambda(v)$ – the number of a machine $v \in \mathcal{O}$ on which the operation is to be executed,
   - $p_{v,\lambda(v)}$ – the time of execution of the operation $v \in \mathcal{O}$ on machine $\lambda(v)$.

The weighs of additional vertices s and c equal zero.

2. The set $\mathcal{R}$ contains arcs connecting successive operations of the same task. Weight of an arc is equal to the time of machine setup. The set also includes arcs from the vertex s for the first operation of each task and arcs for the last operation of each task to the vertex of the c. The weight of the arcs is zero.

3. Arcs from the set $\mathcal{E}(\Theta)$ combine operations performed on the same machine. The weight of this arc is zero.

Remark 1. The pair $\Theta = (\mathcal{Q}, \pi)$ is a feasible solution for the flexible job shop problem if and only if the graph $G(\Theta)$ does not contain cycles.

2.2   Block Eliminating Properties

The sequence of vertices $(v_1, v_2, \ldots, v_k)$ of the graph $G(\Theta)$ such that $(v_i, v_{i+1}) \in \mathcal{R} \cup \mathcal{E}(\Theta)$ for $i = 1, 2, \ldots, k-1$ is called *a path* from the vertex v_1 to v_k. Let $C(\nu, v)$ denote the longest path (called *critical path*) in the graph $G(\Theta)$ from the vertex ν do v $(\nu, v \in \mathcal{V})$, and $L(\nu, v)$ the length (the sum of weighs of vertices) of the path.

It is easy to notice that the execution time of all operations $C_{max}(\Theta)$ consistent with the assignment of operations $\mathcal{Q}$ and the sequence π is equal to the length $L(s, c)$ of the critical path $C(s, c)$ in graph $G(\Theta)$. Solution of the flexible job shop problem is reduced to designation of $\Theta = (\mathcal{Q}, \pi)$ in the set Φ, for which the corresponding graph $G(\Theta)$ has the shortest critical path, i.e. minimizes $L(s, c)$.

Critical path $C(s, c) = (s, v_1, v_2, \ldots, v_w, c)$, where $v_i \in \mathcal{O}$ $(1 \leqslant i \leqslant w)$, in graph $G(\Theta)$ can be divided into the subsequences of vertices $\mathcal{B} = [B_1, B_2, \ldots, B_r]$ called *components* of the critical path $C(s, c)$, where:

(a) component contains further operations performed directly one after the other, on the same machine,

(b) intersection of any two components is empty,

(c) component is the maximum (due to the inclusion) subset of operations from the critical path fulfilling the constraints (a)–(b).

In the further part there will be considered only the components containing at least two elements. The component B_k $(k = 1, 2, \ldots, r)$ on machine M_i $(i = 1, 2, \ldots, m)$ from the nest t $(t = 1, 2, \ldots, q)$ will be denoted by $B_k = (\pi_i(a_k), \pi_i(a_{k+1}), \ldots, \pi_i(b_k))$, where $1 \leqslant a_k < b_k \leqslant |\mathcal{Q}^i|$. The operations $\pi(a_k)$ i $\pi(b_k)$ are called respectively *first* and *last*.

For any component $B_k = (\pi_i(a_k), \pi_i(a_k + 1), \ldots, \pi_i(b_k))$, by Φ^k we denote the set of all permutations from the set $\{\pi_i(a_k + 1), \pi_i(a_k + 2), \ldots, \pi_i(b_k - 1)\}$. Let $\beta^* \in \Phi^k$ be the permutation such that

$$\Psi(\beta^*) = min\{\Psi(\gamma) : \gamma \in \Phi^k\}, \tag{1}$$

where $\Psi(\gamma) = s_{\pi_i(a_k), \gamma(1)} + \sum_{i=a_k+1}^{b_k-1} s_{\gamma(i), \gamma(i+1)} + s_{\gamma(b_k-1), \pi_i(b_k)}$ is the length of the path $(\pi_i(a_k), \gamma(1), \gamma(2), \ldots, \gamma(b_k - 1), \pi_i(b_k))$.

Remark 2. Permutation β^* represents the shortest path between $\pi_i(a_k)$ and $\pi_i(b_k)$) in $G(\Theta)$ including vertices from the set $\{\pi_i(a_k+1), \pi_i(a_k+2), \ldots, \pi_i(b_k-1)\}$.

The sequence of operations executed on k-th machine $\widehat{B}^k = (\pi_i(a_k), \beta^*, \pi_i(b_k))$ is called k-th **block**, whereas permutation β^* – internal block. By designating blocks on critical path of the solution Θ we generate some new solution of value of not more than the value of solution Θ. This procedure can be seen as some form of local optimization (improvement of Θ).

Theorem 1. *If $\widehat{B}_k$ is a block from critical path, then any change of the order of operation from internal block does not generate a solution of lower value of the objective function.*

The proof is similar to that of Theorem 3 from the work by Bożejko et al. [5].

This property (i.e. *block elimination property*) will be used to generate the neighborhood in both sequential algorithm and parallel algorithm solving the flexible job shop problem with machine setups. The above theorem implies that any improvement of the value of the current solution can only be achieved by: (1) swapping some operations from some internal block before the first or the last operation of this block, or (2) moving the operation to another, from the same nest, machine.

3   Tabu Search Algorithm

To solve the problem considered in this work there will be tabu search algorithm with golf neighborhood used (Bożejko et al. [3]). It is generated by the combination of insert type (i-move) and transfer (t-move) moves (see [2]). The first – changes the order of operations on a machine, whereas the second – transfers operation to another machine (from the same nest). Ideas for generating the neighborhood solution Θ can be represented as follows:

1. generate graph $G(\Theta)$,
2. determine critical path in graph $G(\Theta)$, then perform partitioning of the set of operations from the path into components,
3. in accordance with block definition determine the sequence of operations for each component,
4. generate golf neighborhood using block elimination properties (Theorem 1).

If B is a component of the critical path in the graph $G(\Theta)$, then determination of the order of an operation that fulfills the constraints of the block definition requires the determination of the shortest path (permutation) between the first and the last operation in B.

It is easy to notice that in case of the considered problem the process comes down to solving the traveling salesman problem (TSP) in the graph, wherein vertices are the operations of B and the distance between vertices are setup times. This is an NP-hard problem, this is why to find a good approximate solution the 2-*opt* algorithm will be used, one of the most popular approximate algorithms for the TSP. The use of heuristic algorithm results in the fact that one of the conditions from the block definition cannot be fulfilled. As a consequence, 'good' elements can be eliminated from the neighborhood.

3.1   Parallel Algorithm on GPU

In the tabu search algorithm, for any solution $\Theta = (\mathcal{Q}, \pi)$, there should be created a graph $G(\Theta) = (\mathcal{V}, \mathcal{R} \cup \mathcal{E}(\Theta))$, then there should be a critical path, components and blocks designated. Next, using the block eliminating properties there should be generated the neighborhood from which the best element is chosen. As the graph contains o vertices, the parallel algorithm designating the longest path between all pairs of vertices needs time of $O(o)$ using o^2 processors.

Theorem 2. *The sequence of blocks $\mathcal{B} = (B_1, B_2, \ldots, B_r)$ on the critical path $C(s, c)$ for any solution $\Theta \in \Phi$ can be determined on CREW PRAM machine in time $O(1)$ with the use of $O(o)$ processors.*

Proof. Let each of the processors be assigned to the vertex v from critical path. It is sufficient if the processor checks whether the number of machines allocated to its vertex $\lambda(v)$ is the same as the number of the machine $\lambda(u)$ assigned to the next vertex u from the critical path. If the numbers of machines are different, the next block starts from the vertex u.

Theorem 3. *Neighborhood $\mathcal{N}(\Theta)$ of the solution Θ of the flexible job shop problem generated by t-moves can be searched in time $O(o)$ with the use of $O(om)$ processor CREW PRAM machine.*

Proof. The considered neighborhood consists of $O(om)$ elements. Let each of the processors be assigned to one element from the neighborhood. Designation of the objective function for any solution requires time $O(o)$. Therefore, the whole search process of the neighborhood requires time $O(o)$.

Proposal 1. *Speedup of the method based on Theorem 3 is $O(om)$, whereas the cost equals $O(o^2m)$. The presented method is cost-optimal. Its efficiency equals $O(1)$.*

Theorem 4. *The neighborhood of the solution generated by t-moves can be searched in the time $O(mo)$ with the use of $O(o)$ processor CREW PRAM machine.*

Proof. The considered neighborhood consists of $O(om)$ elements. Let each of the processors be assigned to one of the operations $i \in \mathcal{O}$, $i = 1, 2, \ldots, o$. For each operation it is possible to generate $O(m)$ solutions using t-moves. Determination of the value of the objective function of a single solution takes time $O(o)$. Therefore, the whole process takes time $O(mo)$.

Proposal 2. *Speedup of the method based on Theorem 4 is $O(o)$. The cost is $O(o^2m)$. The presented method is cost-optimal.*

4 Fuzzy Times of Tasks Execution

Let p_{vj} $(j \in \mathcal{M}^{\mu(v)})$ be the time of execution of operation $v \in \mathcal{O}$ in the nest $\mu(v)$, i.e. on one of the machines from the set $\mathcal{M}^{\mu(v)}$. We assume that the uncertain times of operations execution will be represented by the membership function γ represented by four numbers $\widehat{p}_{v,j} = (p_{v,j}^{min}, p_{v,j}^{med1}, p_{v,j}^{med2}, p_{v,j}^{max})$ such that:

- $(p_{v,j}^{min} \leqslant p_{v,j}^{med1} \leqslant p_{v,j}^{med2} \leqslant p_{v,j}^{max})$,
- $\gamma(x) = 0$ for $x \leqslant p_{v,j}^{min}$ or $x \geqslant p_{v,j}^{max}$,
- $\gamma(p_{v,j}^{med1}) = \gamma(p_{v,j}^{med2}) = 1$,
- γ is increasing in the interval $[p_{v,j}^{min}, p_{v,j}^{med1}]$ and decreasing in the interval $[p_{v,j}^{med2}, p_{v,j}^{max}]$,

which can be represented as:

$$\gamma(x) = \begin{cases} \frac{x - p_{v,j}^{min}}{p_{v,j}^{med1} - p_{v,j}^{min}} & \text{for } x \in [p_{v,j}^{min}, p_{v,j}^{med1}), \\ 1 & \text{for } x \in [p_{v,j}^{med1}, p_{v,j}^{med2}), \\ \frac{p_{v,j}^{max} - x}{p_{v,j}^{max} - p_{v,j}^{med2}} & \text{for } x \in [p_{v,j}^{med2}, p_{v,j}^{max}]. \end{cases} \qquad (2)$$

Graphical representation of the function $\gamma(x)$ has a trapezoidal shape, therefore, fuzzy numbers represented by it are called trapezoidal fuzzy numbers. A special case of trapezoidal fuzzy number is a triangular fuzzy number. By substituting $p_{v,j}^{med} = p_{v,j}^{med1} = p_{v,j}^{med2}$ to (2) we obtain a membership function for the triangular fuzzy number. Definitions of arithmetic activities and computing maximum/minimum of fuzzy numbers is defined in the work of Dubois [7]. Therefore, when the times of operations execution are fuzzy numbers, then the completion times of operations and completion date the of all tasks executions are also fuzzy numbers.

In the optimization algorithms certain values (for instance goal function values) are repeatedly compared with one another. Therefore, there is a need in mapping of the number of fuzzy into the real numbers (*defuzzification*). In literature the most often cited features of defuzzification are: last of maximum, mean of maxima values and center of area.

Last of Maximum Defuzzification Function. Let $(m_1, m_2, \ldots m_l)$ be a sequence of local maximum values of the fuzzy number $\widehat{a}$ of the membership function $\gamma(x)$, $x \in \mathbb{R}$. First of maximum defuzzification function is defined as $LOM(\widehat{a}) = m_i$, where $i = \max_{1 \leqslant j \leqslant l} \arg m_j$.

Mean of Maxima Defuzzification Function. Let $(m_1, m_2, \ldots m_l)$ be a sequence of local maximum values of the fuzzy number $\widehat{a}$ of the membership function $\gamma(x)$, $x \in \mathbb{R}$. First of maximum defuzzification function is defined as $MOM(\widehat{a}) = \left\lceil \frac{1}{l} \sum_{i=1}^{l} m_i \right\rceil$.

Center Area Defuzzification Function. Let $\widehat{a}$ be a fuzzy number of membership function $\gamma(x)$, $x \in \mathbb{R}$. Center area defuzzification function is defined as

$COA(\widehat{a}) = \left\lceil \frac{\int x\gamma(x)\,dx}{\int \gamma(x)\,dx} \right\rceil$. In order to determine the 'center area' defuzzification function for trapezoidal fuzzy number (2) let us adapt the following simplification:

$$\gamma(x) = \begin{cases} \frac{x-a}{b-a} & \text{for } x \in [a, b), \\ 1 & \text{for } x \in [b, c), \\ \frac{d-x}{d-c} & \text{for } x \in [c, d]. \end{cases} \tag{3}$$

For each of the intervals we calculate the corresponding integrals.

$$\int_a^b x \frac{x-a}{b-a}\,dx = \frac{1}{b-a}\int_a^b x^2 - ax\,dx = \frac{1}{b-a}\left[\frac{x^3}{3} - \frac{ax^2}{2}\right]_a^b = -\frac{1}{6}(a-b)(a+2b).$$

$$\int_c^d x \frac{d-x}{d-c}\,dx = \frac{1}{d-c}\int_c^d dx - x^2\,dx = \frac{1}{d-c}\left[\frac{dx^2}{2} - \frac{x^3}{3}\right]_c^d = -\frac{1}{6}(c-d)(2c+d).$$

$$\int_a^b \frac{x-a}{b-a}\,dx = \frac{1}{b-a}\int_a^b x - a\,dx = \frac{1}{b-a}\left[ax - \frac{x^2}{2}\right]_a^b = \frac{b-a}{2}.$$

$$\int_c^d \frac{d-x}{d-c}\,dx = \frac{1}{d-c}\int_c^d d - x\,dx = \frac{1}{d-c}\left[dx - \frac{x^2}{2}\right]_c^d = \frac{d-c}{2}.$$

$$\int_b^c x\,dx = \left[\frac{x^2}{2}\right]_b^c = \frac{1}{2}(c^2 - b^2), \quad \int_b^c 1\,dx = [x]_b^c = c - b.$$

Using the calculated integrals we ultimately obtain:

$$COA(\widehat{a}) = \left\lceil \frac{\int x\gamma(x)\,dx}{\int \gamma(x)\,dx} \right\rceil = \left\lceil \frac{a^2 + ab + b^2 - c^2 - cd - d^2}{3(a+b-c-d)} \right\rceil. \tag{4}$$

4.1 Block Properties for the Fuzzy Times of Operation Execution

Since the operations execution times and moments of their completion are fuzzy numbers, there can be a **fuzzy critical path** $\widehat{C}(s, c)$ determined with the use of defuzzification function and then its division into blocks

$$\widehat{B} = [\widehat{B}_1, \widehat{B}_2, \ldots, \widehat{B}_r]. \tag{5}$$

In deterministic version of the problem block properties enable the elimination of worse solutions from the search process. This can significantly reduce the size of the analyzed solution space. In case of modeling of uncertain times of operations execution with the use of fuzzy numbers there can be two models, using eliminating block properties, taken into consideration.

In the first model – determination of the starting moment of the operation execution – relies in computing of a maximum of two fuzzy numbers (termination moments of the technological $\widehat{C}_t$ and machine $\widehat{C}_m$) predecessor, resulting in obtaining the fuzzy number $\widehat{C}_x = \max\{\widehat{C}_t, \widehat{C}_m\}$. Since the number $\widehat{C}_x$ does not have to be any of the numbers $\widehat{C}_t$ and $\widehat{C}_m$, critical path determination is not possible. By introducing additional parameters describing the degree of similarity between the determined number of a maximum $\widehat{C}_x$ and the numbers $\widehat{C}_t$ and $\widehat{C}_m$ there can be *quasi critical path* determined.

In turn, in the second model, using the defuzzification function, there can be the termination moments of technological C_t and machine C_m predecessor determined. Then, it is possible to clearly determine the time of commencement of new operations as the fuzzy number C_x (defuzzification maximum):

$$C_x = \max\{defuz(\widehat{C}_t), defuz(\widehat{C}_m)\}. \tag{6}$$

In this case, it is possible to clearly determine the critical path.

4.2   Resistance of Algorithms to Data Disturbances

Resistance of an algorithm is the property that allows its users to determine the influence of data disturbances on changes in the value of the objective function. For the problem considered in the work, let $\delta = [p_{v,j}]_{o \times 1}$ be time vector of (deterministic) times of execution of separate operations. By $D(\delta)$ we denote the set of data generated from δ by the disturbance in times of operations execution. The disturbance relies in changing the elements of $p = [p_{v,j}]_{o \times 1}$ into randomly generated values.

Let $A = \{TS, TSF\}$, where TS and TSF are respectively deterministic and fuzzy algorithms (i.e. for the data represented by fuzzy numbers). By π_δ^A we denote a solution (permutation) determined by the algorithm A for data δ. Then $C_{max(\pi_\delta^A, \varphi)}$ is a termination point, when the tasks are executed in the order π (defined by algorithm A) and φ is a time vector of individual operations execution. The average relative error for the disturbed data from a set $D(\delta)$ is

$$\Delta(A, \delta, D(\delta)) = \frac{1}{|D(\delta)|} \sum_{\varphi \in D} \frac{C_{max(\pi_\delta^A, \varphi)} - C_{max(\pi_\delta^{TS}, \varphi)}}{C_{max(\pi_\delta^{TS}, \varphi)}}. \tag{7}$$

If Ω is a set of deterministic instances of the problem, then the resistance coefficient of an algorithm A on the set Ω is defined as follows:

$$S(A, \Omega) = \frac{1}{|\Omega|} \sum_{\delta \in \Omega} \Delta(A, \delta, D(\delta)). \tag{8}$$

The lower the value of the coefficient, the greater the resistance to random disturbances of solutions determined by the algorithm A.

5   Computational Experiments

Parallel algorithms: deterministic pTSGPU and fuzzy pFzTSGPU were implemented in C++ with the use of CUDA. The MPI library was used for communication between the GPU computing cards. Computational experiments were performed on HP server equipped with Intel i7 CPU (3.33 GHz) and Tesla GPU S2050 running at 64-bit operating system Linux Ubuntu 10.04.4 LTS. The calculations were made separately for the triangular and trapezoidal representation of fuzzy numbers. Their goal was to determine the resistance coefficient and to investigate the effect of defuzzification function on its value.

Representation of Triangular Fuzzy Numbers. As the basis there were examples from work [4] for flexible job shop problem taken. For each deterministic instance there was 100 *disturbed* instances determined. They were generated, in accordance with the uniform distribution, in the interval$[\max\{1, \lceil p_i - p_i/3 \rceil\}, \lceil p_i + p_i/6 \rceil]$.

Fuzzy times of operations execution were generated as follows. If p_i ($i = 1, 2, \ldots, o$) are deterministic times, then the fuzzy times are represented by three $(p_i^{min}, p_i^{med}, p_i^{max})$, where$p_i^{min} = \max\{1, \lceil p_i - p_i/3 \rceil\}$, $p_i^{med} = p_i$, $p_i^{max} = \lceil p_i + p_i/6 \rceil$. For each group of instances there were, in accordance with (7), the values of (minimum and maximum average) parameters Δ established, which are presented in Table 1. The resistance coefficient of pTSGPU algorithm is $S(pTSGPU, \Omega) = 3.41\%$, whereas pFzTSGPU algorithm – $S(pFzTSGPU, \Omega) = 3.45\%$. Resistances of both algorithms differ very little from each other. It results among others, from the fact that fuzzy values of tasks termination moments (after defuzzification) are little different from the tasks set termination moments for deterministic data.

Table 1. Resistance coefficients of algorithms to data perturbances.

Instance			pTSGPU			pFzTSGPU		
Name	$n \times m$	Flex	Δ_{min}	Δ_{aprd}	Δ_{max}	Δ_{min}	Δ_{aprd}	Δ_{max}
Mk01	10×6	2.09	0.315	0.618	0.861	0.268	0.528	0.775
Mk02	10×6	4.10	0.052	0.292	0.468	0.138	0.298	0.441
Mk03	15×8	3.01	0.086	0.271	0.598	0.165	0.396	0.554
Mk04	15×8	1.91	−0.039	0.350	0.625	0.210	0.396	0.584
Mk05	15×4	1.71	−0.037	0.006	0.069	−0.053	0.012	0.075
Mk06	10×15	3.27	0.725	0.860	1.052	0.506	0.942	1.164
Mk07	20×5	2.83	0.080	0.283	0.418	0.026	0.283	0.490
Mk08	20×10	1.43	0.103	0.161	0.232	0.120	0.230	0.350
Mk09	20×10	2.53	0.159	0.451	0.865	0.047	0.216	0.360
Mk10	20×15	2.98	−0.087	0.011	0.314	0.008	0.148	0.286

Representation of Trapezoidal Fuzzy Numbers. If p_i is the time of execution of i-th operation, then the fuzzy time of its execution $\widehat{p}_i = (p_i^{min}, p_i^{med1}, p_i^{med2}, p_i^{max})$, where $p_i^{min} = \max\{1, \lceil p_i - 3p_i/4 \rceil\}$, $p_i^{med1} = \lceil p_i - p_i/5 \rceil$, $p_i^{med2} = \lceil p_i + p_i/5 \rceil$ and $p_i^{max} = \lceil p_i + 3p_i/4 \rceil$ The disturbed data were generated in the same way as in the case of experiments concerning triangular fuzzy numbers. For each example of deterministic data (including the disturbed data) with the use of NEH [9] algorithm, there was a solution determined. The solution was used when calculating the resistance coefficient (8). One of the purposes of the carried out numerical experiments was to study the influence of defuzzification function on the resistance of the obtained solutions. Following calculations were done: $S(A_d)$ – resistance of the deterministic algorithm, $S_\Psi(A_f)$ – resistance of fuzzy algorithm with defuzzification function $\Psi \in \{LOM, MOM, COA\}$. In this case, solutions to all three versions of the fuzzy algorithm (average over all test instances: $S_{LOM}(A_f) = 7.64$, $S_{COA}(A_f) = S_{COA}(A_f) = 8.37$) are more resistant to data disturbances than solutions designated by deterministic algorithm $(S(A_d) = 9.07)$. The most resistant are the solutions, when as 'the last of maximum' defuzzification function is used.

6   Remarks and Conclusions

In the paper there was a job shop problem with uncertain times of operations execution represented by fuzzy numbers presented. To its solution there was parallel tabu search algorithm for the GPU (in deterministic versions and for fuzzy numbers) implemented. In the design of the algorithm there were blocks eliminating properties used. For each deterministic instance there was 100 random examples of disturbed data generated. On their basis there were resistance coefficients of algorithms to input disturbance generated. There was also the influence of defuzzification functions on the resistance of the algorithm examined.

References

1. Balin, S.: Parallel machine scheduling with fuzzy processing times using a robust genetic algorithm and simulation. Inf. Sci. **161**, 3551–3569 (2011)
2. Bożejko, W., Wodecki, M.: On the theoretical properties of swap multimoves. Oper. Res. Lett. **35**(2), 227–231 (2007)
3. Bożejko, W., Uchroski, M., Wodecki, M.: The new golf neighborhood for the flexible job shop problem. In: Proceedings of the ICCS 2010, Procedia Computer Science 1, pp. 289–296. Elsevier (2010)
4. Bożejko, W., Uchroski, M., Wodecki, M.: Solving the flexible job shop problem on Multi-GPU. In: Proceedings of the ICCS 2012, Procedia Computer Science 9, pp. 378–394. Elsevier (2012)
5. Bożejko, W., Uchroski, M., Wodecki, M.: Block approach to the cyclic flow shop scheduling. Comput. Ind. Eng. **81**, 158–166 (2015)
6. Brandimarte, P.: Routing and scheduling in a flexible job shop by tabu search. Ann. Oper. Res. **41**, 157–183 (1993)
7. Dubois, D., Prade, H.: Theorie des Possibilites. Applications a la representation des connaissances en informatique. Masson, Paris (1988)
8. Hodgson, T.J., King, R.E., Stanfield, P.M.: Ready-time scheduling with stochastic service time. Oper. Res. **45**(5), 779–783 (1997)
9. Nawaz, M., Enscore, E.E., Ham, I.: A heuristic algorithm for the m-machine, n-job flow-shop sequencing problem. OMEGA Int. J. Manag. Sci. **11**, 91–95 (1983)
10. Prade, H.: Uzing fuzzy set theory in a scheduling problem. Fuzzy Sets Syst. **2**, 153–165 (1979)
11. Sowiski, R., Hapke, M.: Scheduling under Fuzziness. Physica-Verlag, New York (2000)

A Method of Analysis and Visualization of Structured Datasets Based on Centrality Information

Wojciech Czech[✉] and Radosław Łazarz

Institute of Computer Science, AGH University of Science and Technology,
Kraków, Poland
czech@agh.edu.pl

Abstract. We present a new method of quantitative graph analysis and visualization based on vertex centrality measures and distance matrices. After generating distance k-graphs and collecting frequency information about their vertex descriptors, we obtain generic, multidimensional representation of a graph, invariant to graph isomorphism. The histograms of vertex centrality measures, organized in a form of B-matrices, allow to capture subtle changes in network structure during its evolution and provide robust tool for graph comparison and classification. We show that different types of B-matrices and their extensions are useful in graph analysis tasks performed on benchmark complex networks from Koblenz and IAM datasets. We compare the results obtained for proposed B-matrix extensions with performance of other state-of-art graph descriptors showing that our method is superior to others.

1 Introduction

The importance of complex network analysis and structural pattern recognition has grown rapidly in recent decade. Large sets of structured data emerge in various areas of science, such as information technology, computational science, sociology, medicine or economics. In consequence of this situation, there is an increasing need for versatile tools that could facilitate the process of working with such forms of knowledge.

Efficient graph mining relies on computationally feasible methods of analyzing structural properties of graphs, in particular the tools for graph comparison, which allow computing similarity/dissimilarity measures required by machine learning algorithms [9]. Contrary to vectors, graphs are structures, which do not allow straightforward computing of distances and inner products. In order to overcome gap between statistical and structural pattern recognition, numerous approaches for measuring inter-graph similarity have been developed [9]. Inexact graph matching can be implemented based on the concept of graph edit distance (GED), understood as a minimal cost associated with a set of elementary edit operations transforming one graph into another [4,18]. The methods based on graph edit distance were shown to have many successful applications,

© Springer International Publishing Switzerland 2016
L. Rutkowski et al. (Eds.): ICAISC 2016, Part II, LNAI 9693, pp. 429–441, 2016.
DOI: 10.1007/978-3-319-39384-1_37

nevertheless due to significant computational complexity, their feasibility is limited to medium-size graphs with hundreds of vertices. The next group of graph comparison tools, namely graph kernels provide framework for implicit embedding of graphs into vector space [5,6]. Graph kernels, being similarity measures, build the link between kernel methods from statistical learning theory and structural patterns. They are constructed using product graphs and different graph sub-structures including shortest paths [23], random walks [1], treelets [10], graphlets [19] and can be applied for attributed or unattributed graphs. Till now, multiple types of graph kernels were proposed and verified on real-world data such as molecules, protein-protein interaction networks or documents.

An alternative approach to kernel-based implicit graph embedding applies direct transformation of graph to vector using graph invariants. The set of methods following this scenario is classified as explicit graph embedding. The construction of vector representing graph is typically non-injective mapping, which results in partial lost of information about its structure. Nevertheless, the variety of available graph invariants enables sophisticated feature extraction and provides easy-to-use vector data for classical machine learning algorithms. The most recent studies in the field introduced feature vectors based on random walks and commute times [16] performing well in image clustering and motion tracking applications. In [25], the authors presented a model of graph structure which provides embedding of vertices into vector space and facilitates constructing multi-dimensional graph representations based on spectral properties of heat kernel matrix. Prototype-based graph embedding computes dissimilarity representation based on distances from pre-defined prototype graphs. Its recent results are presented in works [3,13], describing the problem of optimal prototype selection. The method designed for image recognition presented in [11] is based on graph of words substructure enumeration and constructs long, sparse vectors, later on reduced to lower dimension using kernel Principal Component Analysis (kPCA) or Independent Component Analysis (ICA). In [21], graph characterization using Schrödinger operator is presented. This work represents the group of embedding methods utilizing properties of diffusion process on a graph. In this case quantum effects are added resulting in robust graph structure descriptors.

Our goal in this work is to combine subpattern embedding based on distance k-graphs with scalar vertex centrality measures to obtain robust graph representation useful in graph learning and visualization. In the work [8] we presented a new method of graph embedding which uses selected invariants of distance k-graphs, specifically vertex degree B-matrices as a framework for graph embedding. Here, we extend our study presenting B-matrices constructed from vertex descriptors such as clustering coefficient, eccentricity, closeness and betweenness [2] and their application for analysis of vascular networks. The motivation behind this work is to retrieve more specific topological features of graphs and apply them in graph learning tasks.

The rest of this work is organized as follows. In Sect. 2 we describe the concept of graph embedding based on distance k-graphs. Specifically, we present B-matrices constructed from degree histograms of distance k-graphs. Next, in Sect. 3 we describe extensions of B-matrices relying on vertex centrality measures and other vertex descriptors from theory of complex networks. Section 4 presents selected results of analyzing complex networks from IAM and Koblenz databases. Section 5 concludes the paper offering final remarks and describing future work plans.

2   Graph Invariants Based on Distance Information

In [7,8] we presented how to use the ordered set of distance k-graphs to generate isomorphism invariants robust in graph comparison. In this section, we briefly describe most important notions and explain why the specific types of distance k-graph invariants, namely degree B-matrices are useful in graph embedding and visualization. The similar framework will be used in Sect. 3 for defining new variants of B-matrices capturing more specific topological features of graphs.

Definition 1 (Vertex Distance k-graph). *For an undirected graph $G = (V(G), E(G))$ we define vertex distance k-graph $G_k^{\mathcal{V}}$ as a graph with vertex set $V(G_k^{\mathcal{V}}) = V(G)$ and edge set $E(G_k^{\mathcal{V}})$ so that $\{u, v\} \in E(G_k^{\mathcal{V}})$ iff $d_G(u, v) = k$.*

$d_G(u, v)$ is dissimilarity measure between vertex u and v, in particular the length of the shortest path between u and v. It follows that $G_1^{\mathcal{V}} = G$ and for $k > diameter(G)$, $G_k^{\mathcal{V}}$ is an empty graph. For a given graph G the invariants of G-derived vertex k-distance graphs can be aggregated to form new descriptor of length $diameter(G)$. In particular, the histograms of vertex degrees for $G_k^{\mathcal{V}}$ graphs can be row-packed to 2D graph representation called vertex B-matrix.

Definition 2 (Vertex B-matrix). *For a given function $f : V \to X$ and an ordered set of disjoint categories $b_1, \ldots, b_n : \underset{i \in \{1,\ldots,n\}}{\forall} b_i \subseteq X \wedge \bigcup_{i=1}^{n} b_i = X$ (called bins), the vertex B-matrix is defined as:*

$$B_{k,l}^{\mathcal{V}} = |\{v : v \in V(G_k^{\mathcal{V}}) \wedge f(v) \in b_l\}| \tag{1}$$

The rows of vertex B-matrix are in fact histograms of particular vertex-domain function for the subsequent distance k-graphs. The sample degree-based vertex B-matrices computed by authors for web graphs from SNAP database [14] are presented in Figs. 1a and b. Even more powerful B-matrices can be constructed using edge k-distance graphs.

Definition 3 (Edge Distance). *Let $G = (V(G), E(G))$ be an undirected, unweighted, simple graph. The distance from a vertex $w \in V(G)$ to an edge $e_{uv} = \{u, v\} \in E(G)$, denoted as $d_G^{\mathcal{E}}(w, e_{uv})$, is the mean of distances $d_G(w, u)$ and $d_G(w, v)$.*

For unweighted graphs $d_G^{\mathcal{E}}$ has integer or half-integer values. For a selected vertex w, integer values of $k = d_G^{\mathcal{E}}(w, e_{uv})$ occur for edges e_{uv} whose endpoints are equidistant from w. This means that e_{uv} belongs to odd closed walk of length $2k + 1$ starting and ending at w.

Poland

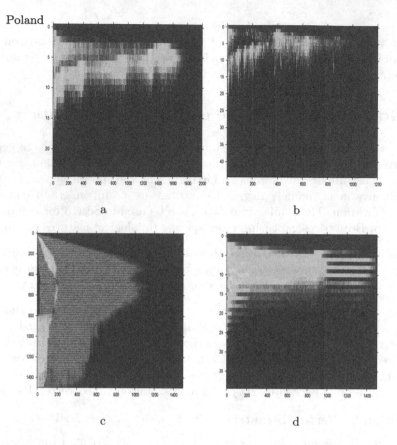

a

b

c

d

Fig. 1. Degree B-matrices generated for selected networks from Stanford Large Network Dataset Collection: a. Web Google network (875713 vertices, 4322051 edges, vertex B-matrix), b. Web Stanford network (281903 vertices, 1992636 edges, vertex B-matrix), c. Road network of Pennsylvania (1088092 vertices, 1541898 edges, edge B-matrix), d. Youtube online social network (1134890 vertices, 2987624 edges, edge B-matrix).

Definition 4 (Edge Distance k-graph). *We define edge distance k-graph as a bipartite graph $G_k^{\mathcal{E}} = (U(G_k^{\mathcal{E}}), V(G_k^{\mathcal{E}}), E(G_k^{\mathcal{E}})) = (V(G), E(G), E(G_k^{\mathcal{E}}))$ such that for each $w \in V(G)$ and $e_{uv} \in E(G)$, $\{w, e_{uv}\} \in E(G_k^{\mathcal{E}})$ iff $d_G^{\mathcal{E}}(w, e_{uv}) = k$.*

The maximal value of k for which $G_k^{\mathcal{E}}$ is non-empty is $2 \times diameter(G)$. The descriptors of graph G constructed based on edge distance k-graphs bring more discriminating information than ones obtained for vertex distance k-graphs.

Definition 5 (Edge B-matrix). *For a given function $f : U \to X$ and an ordered set of disjoint categories $b_1, \ldots, b_m : \underset{i \in \{1, \ldots, m\}}{\forall} b_i \subseteq X \wedge \bigcup_{i=1}^{m} b_i = X$ (called bins), the edge B-matrix is defined as:*

$$B_{k,l}^{\mathcal{E}} = |\{v : v \in U(G_{k/2}^{\mathcal{E}}) \wedge f(v) \in b_l\}| \tag{2}$$

Specifically, for $f(v) = degree(v)$, i-th row of $B^{\mathcal{E}}$ represents histogram of vertex degrees for members of set $U(G^{\mathcal{E}}_{0.5i})$, being a part of bipartite graph $G^{\mathcal{E}}_{0.5i}$. Two sample degree-based edge B-matrices computed by authors for graphs from SNAP database [14] are presented in Figs. 1c and d.

Both types of B-matrices provide useful tool for visual comparison of networks. Moreover, a set of diverse local and global features can be extracted from $B^{\mathcal{V}}$ and $B^{\mathcal{E}}$ by selecting rectangular fragments of B-matrices and packing them to long pattern vectors, used afterwards in machine learning. For lower-dimensional representation, the aggregated statistics of B-matrix rows (e.g. relative standard deviation) can be computed to obtain graph embeddings of size proportional to graph diameter. The space complexity of B-matrices generation is approximately $\mathcal{O}(n \times diameter(G))$, much less than $O(n^2)$ for distance matrices. This makes them feasible for studying real-world complex networks, as diameter of complex networks typically is proportional to $\log(n)$ or even $\log(\log(n))$. The time complexity of distance k-graphs generation depends on the density of a graph and varies from $\mathcal{O}(n^2)$ for sparse networks to $\mathcal{O}(n^3)$ for dense ones.

3   B-Matrix Extensions

In this section we introduce extended versions of B-matrices, based on different vertex-domain functions f (see Definitions 2 and 5). To this end, we recall two vertex centrality measures from theory of complex networks [2] that is *closeness* and *betweenness*. Any other vertex descriptor can be used as well. Our aim is to capture more relevant graph features than using vertex degree descriptor, being a local topological measure. Centrality measures identify vertices, which are crucial from the perspective of information flow in a graph. Their distribution gives insight about graph anatomy, e.g. answers a question if there is a small group of chief vertices or the majority of them are equivalent. Additionally, we consider *clustering coefficient* [2] as an local-type descriptor alternative to *degree*, and *eccentricity*, which measures maximum distance between given vertex and any other vertex.

Definition 6 (Closeness). *Closeness of vertex v is defined as a reciprocal of a sum of distances from v to all other vertices, normalised by the minimal value of such sum:*

$$CL(v) = \frac{n-1}{\sum_{u \in V(G)} d_G(u,v)}, \tag{3}$$

where $n = |V(G)|$.

In case of disconnected graphs an alternative definition can be used (known also as *harmonic centrality*).

$$CL(v) = \sum_{u \neq v} \frac{1}{d_G(u,v)} \tag{4}$$

Higher values of *closeness* are achieved for vertices located in the center of graph, that is their average distance to other vertices is relatively low. The shape of *closeness* distribution indicates how compact a graph is.

Definition 7 (Betweenness). *Shortest-path betweenness is defined as a fraction of the shortest paths between pairs of vertices in a graph that pass through given vertex:*

$$BC(v) = \sum_{\substack{s \neq v \neq t \in V(G) \\ s \neq t}} \frac{\sigma_{st}(v)}{\sigma_{st}}, \tag{5}$$

where $\sigma_{st}(v)$ is the number of the shortest paths from s to t which pass through v and σ_{st} denotes the total number of the shortest paths from s to t.

It measures to what extent a given vertex is needed by other vertices to transfer information through the shortest paths. The betweenness centrality for a graph G with n vertices is an average of betweenness centrality for each vertex:

$$BC(G) = \frac{1}{n} \sum_{v \in V(G)} BC(v). \tag{6}$$

Definition 8 (Clustering Coefficient). *The clustering coefficient of vertex v defined as:*

$$C(v) = \frac{2|\{u : e_{uv} \in E(G)\}|}{k_v(k_v - 1)}, \tag{7}$$

where $e_{uv} = \{u, v\}$ and $k_v = degree(v)$, is a ratio of a number of connections between neighbors of vertex v, denoted by $|\{u : e_{uv} \in E(G)\}|$, to a number of links that could possibly exist between them, i.e., $k_v(k_v - 1)/2$.

This vertex descriptor measures neighborhood connectivity and indicates small-worldliness of a network [24]. Clustering coefficient describes local topology of a graph, reflecting how close the neighborhood of a given vertex is to form a complete graph. The clustering coefficient for a graph G with n vertices is an average of clustering coefficients for each vertex:

$$C(G) = \frac{1}{n} \sum_{v \in V(G)} C(v). \tag{8}$$

Definition 9 (Eccentricity). *The eccentricity of vertex v defined as*

$$E(v) = \max_{u \neq v} d_G(v, u), \tag{9}$$

where $d_G(v, u)$ is the length of the shortest path between v and u, is the greatest distance between vertex v an any other vertex.

The computational cost of generating B-matrices based on *closeness*, *betweenness* and *eccentricity* is $\mathcal{O}(n^2 \times diameter(G))$ for sparse graphs and $\mathcal{O}(n^3 \times diameter(G))$ (for each distance k-graph allpair shortest paths problems has to be resolved). In the next section we compare discriminative properties of different B-matrices and present how different variants of B-matrices can be used for graph visualization and classification.

4   Experiments on Visualization and Classification

We perform experiments on two graph datasets. The first one contains real-world graphs from the Koblenz Network Collection [12], including social, cellular, transportation and technological networks. In the experiment on classification we used IAM Database [17], which forms a benchmark dataset for structural pattern recognition algorithms. The goal of the experiments is to verify discriminative capablilites of different B-matrices and prove that they help to understand underlying structured data.

4.1   Visualization

The aim of graph visalization is to reveal structural properties of underlying data in a form easily comprehensible by human eye. Apart from variety of graph drawing methods relying on construction of 2D layout for vertices and marking edges with lines or curves, several different approaches were developed. This includes general and domain-specific techniques such as area-based treemapping [20] or BioFabric [15]. Also B-matrices, forming 2D representations of graphs can be used for pictorial presentation of structural features. They are particularly interesting form of graph visualization because of their intrinsic invariance under node relabeling. In this section we demonstrate selected visual discriminating features of generic B-matrices. For each vertex descriptor we present two sample visualizations, computed using the same number of categories.

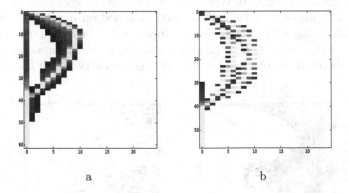

a   b

Fig. 2. Vertex B-matrices based on closeness: a. Euroroad network (1174 vertices, 1417 edges), b. US power grid network (4941 vertices, 6594 edges). Y axis represents k, X axis - category index.

Figure 2 depicts vertex B-matrices based on vertex closeness constructed for Euroroad and US power grid networks. These graphs are sparse and have median shortest path lengths 15 and 17 accordingly. As shown in Fig. 2, an average closeness of vertex distance k-graph grows until k reaches median path length and then starts to decrease. The vertex distance k-graph for k equal median shortest path length is most densely connected and centralized. Next, with growing k the vertex distance k-graphs become sparse and typically not connected. For Euroroad (Fig. 2a), we also observe that skewness of closeness distribution is changing from negative ($k < 20$) to zero and positive ($k > 30$). This reflects loosing centralized structure by subsequent vertex distance k-graphs (number of distant vertices grows, dense center disappears). This effect is not so clearly visible for US power grid (Fig. 2b), which gives more complex, bimodal closeness distributions reflecting disassortativity of underlying graph. The vertical stripe present on Fig. 2a (for all k's) is an effect caused by a number of small not-connected components (islands) and isolated vertices, which account for low values of closeness. This type of artifact depicts the k for which isolated vertices occur (see Fig. 2b, row 30).

In Fig. 3 we present vertex B-matrices based on betweenness centrality computed for the two mentioned networks. Close to median shortest path length ($k = 15$, $k = 17$) the visualizations follow the same pattern. Starting from broad distributions of betweenness centrality, they achieve narrow distributions close to median shortest path, next evolving towards broad distributions again, to end-up with all samples assigned to a single category. Euroroad network exhibits positive-skewed betweeness values for $k < 30$, what confirms that the network does not have too many bridges (vertices which play significant role in a transport through shortest paths). By contrast, US power grid network gives more complex distribution pattern with a number of negatively-skewed betweenness distributions indicating presence of vertices crucial in diffusion processes.

Figure 4 presents the next type of vertex B-matrix, constructed using vertex eccentricity measure, which ranks vertices based on maximum length of a shortest path to any other vertex. As a consequence, the distribution for $k = 1$ spans between the radius of a graph and graph diameter. Euroroad matrix is not connected, therefore we observe low values of eccentricity for all k's and several

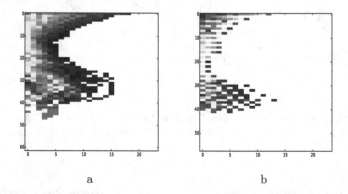

a   b

Fig. 3. Vertex B-matrices based on betweenness centrality: a. Euroroad network (1174 vertices, 1417 edges), b. US power grid network (4941 vertices, 6594 edges). Y axis represents k, X axis - category index.

head categories. This is in parallel to observation made for closeness B-matrix. Note that eccentricities are computed for each connected component separately, therefore value ∞ does not appear. With a growing k, the average eccentricity moves to zero and finally all vertices of distance k-graph (for $k = diameter(G) + 1$) become isolated.

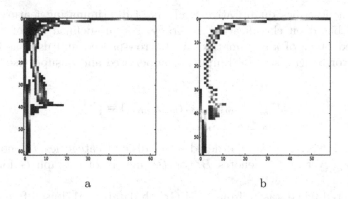

a   b

Fig. 4. Edge B-matrices based on eccentricity: a. Euroroad network (1174 vertices, 1417 edges), b. US power grid network (4941 vertices, 6594 edges). Y axis represents k, X axis - category index.

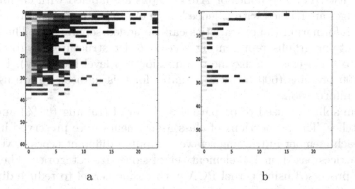

a   b

Fig. 5. Edge B-matrices based on clustering coefficient: a. Euroroad network (1174 vertices, 1417 edges), b. US power grid network (4941 vertices, 6594 edges). Y axis represents k, X axis - category index.

The vertex B-matrices based on clustering coefficient, presented in Fig. 5 reveal significant structural difference between Euroroad and US power grid networks. The latter exhibits small-world property, which is preserved by vertex distance k-graphs for $k < 7$ (Fig. 5b). For k close to median shortest path length, the vertex distance k-graphs becomes unclustered. B-matrix of Euroroad graph exhibits positively-skewed distributions for $k < 32$. This is partially caused by a number of small not-connected components but also intrinsic low local clustering of road network. The structural difference between two analyzed networks is reflected in local (lower k's) and global (higher k's) scale.

4.2   Classification

This section describes quantitative analysis of discriminating features of new B-matrices based on classification accuracy. For pre-defined set of categories and selected range of k's, B-matrix can be row-packed and used as fixed-size feature vector being a standard input for supervised and unsupervised learning algorithms.

$$D^\star_{long}(k_{min}, k_{max}, l_{min}, l_{max}) = [B^\star_{k,l}]$$
$$k_{min} \leq k \leq k_{max}, \ l_{min} \leq l \leq l_{max} \tag{10}$$

where $(b_1, \ldots, b_l, \ldots, b_n)$ is an ordered set of disjoint categories, l denotes index of i-th category and $B^\star$ denotes $B^\mathcal{V}$ or $B^\mathcal{E}$ matrix of a graph G for a given function f.

We selected two datasets from IAM Graph database [17] used frequently for benchmarking structural pattern recognition algorithms. The database contains 9 datasets of labeled graphs. Each one is divided into training, validation and testing sets. The **Aids** dataset is unbalanced and contains 2000 graphs representing molecular compounds divided into two classes: active (400) and inactive (1600) against HIV. The nodes of **Aids** graphs are labeled with chemical symbols and edges are labeled with valence but in our experiments we are using only structural information (label statistics can be added separately). The **Protein** dataset contains graphs representing second order structure of proteins. It is divided into 6 EC classes (enzyme commission top level hierarchy). Each class contains 100 proteins (600 in total). Again, for this dataset we are using only structural information.

Random split was used to prepare single pair of training (85 %) and testing (15 %) batches. The proportions of class assignments were preserved in created sets. For each member in training set we computed different types of vertex and edge B-matrices based on 100-element set of same-size categories. The training batch was processed using kernel PCA with cosine kernel to reduce dimensionality of input feature space to 15 % of original one. Additionally, we tested two other graph descriptors. First one - state-of-art multidimensional graph invariant based on quantum random walks and Schrödinger operator [22]. Second one - simple feature vector composed of aggregated statistics of vertex degrees and clustering coefficients (average value, standard devication, skewness, kurtosis).

The experiment on classification was performed using Support Vector Machines (SVM) with radial basis function kernel. The accuracy of classifier was evaluated by repeating random split 100 times and reporting average and standard deviation of each test run. The results are presented in Table 1.

The best results were obtained for edge B-matrix based on closeness, both for **Aids** and **Protein** datasets. The features generated based on B-matrices of all kinds outperform simple descriptor as well as descriptor based on quantum

Table 1. Classification accuracy achieved on **Aids** and **Protein** datasets using SVM and different input graph descriptors (B-m stand for B-matrix).

Descriptor	Aids		Protein	
	Accuracy	StdDev	Accuracy	StdDev
Edge degree B-m	97.24	1.37	28.72	4.51
Edge clustering coefficient B-m	96.33	2.04	22.61	3.77
Edge closeness B-m	**99.04**	**0.83**	**33.06**	6.01
Edge betweeness B-m	97.88	1.45	25.83	4.77
Edge eccentricity B-m	98.83	1.07	29.89	5.74
Vertex degree B-m	97.05	1.04	32.83	4.97
Vertex clustering coefficient B-m	97.38	1.78	29.22	5.52
Vertex closeness B-m	98.42	1.04	30.11	4.71
Vertex betweeness B-m	98.75	1.16	25.39	4.12
Vertex eccentricity B-m	98.88	1.22	27.89	7.28
Schrödinger operator	92.9	3.50	22.82	4.37
Simple	88.5	2.75	20.23	4.88
ZeroR	80.00	-	16.70	-

random walks. The new B-matrices (based on *closeness, betweenness, eccentricity*) perform better than B-matrices based on degree, nevertheless differences in accuracy achieved for top 3 descriptors is less than 1 %.

5 Discussion and Conclusions

We proposed a new method of graph embedding by generalization of previously reported approach based on vertex/edge distance k-graphs and their degree distributions. Our method uses ordered set of distance k-graphs as a basis for generating 2D permutation invariants useful in visual inspection of graph structure and in supervised or unsupervised learning of structural patterns. The described extension takes advantage of several common vertex invariants, namely centrality measures, to construct more robust variants of B-matrices.

In the experimental section we presented which structural features of graphs can be visualized using B-matrices of different types. Nevertheless, many visual features of B-matrices are still difficult to interpret and require further study. Furthermore, B-matrices can be successfully used as a method of embedding graphs into multidimensional vector spaces. The experiments on classification confirmed that the new approach is a solid framework for capturing relevant graph features.

Acknowledgments. This research is supported by the Polish National Center of Science (NCN) DEC-2013/09/B/ST6/01549.

References

1. Bai, L., Hancock, E.R.: Graph kernels from the jensen-shannon divergence. J. Math. Imaging Vis. **47**(1–2), 60–69 (2013)
2. Boccaletti, S., Latora, V., Moreno, Y., Chavez, M., Hwang, D.: Complex networks: structure and dynamics. Phys. Rep. **424**(4–5), 175–308 (2006)
3. Borzeshi, E.Z., Piccardi, M., Riesen, K., Bunke, H.: Discriminative prototype selection methods for graph embedding. Pattern Recogn. **46**(6), 1648–1657 (2013)
4. Bunke, H.: On a relation between graph edit distance and maximum common subgraph. Pattern Recogn. Lett. **18**(8), 689–694 (1997)
5. Bunke, H., Riesen, K.: Recent advances in graph-based pattern recognition with applications in document analysis. Pattern Recogn. **44**(5), 1057–1067 (2011)
6. Bunke, H., Riesen, K.: Towards the unification of structural and statistical pattern recognition. Pattern Recogn. Lett. **33**(7), 811–825 (2012)
7. Czech, W.: Graph descriptors from B-Matrix representation. In: Jiang, X., Ferrer, M., Torsello, A. (eds.) GbRPR 2011. LNCS, vol. 6658, pp. 12–21. Springer, Heidelberg (2011)
8. Czech, W.: Invariants of distance k-graphs for graph embedding. Pattern Recogn. Lett. **33**(15), 1968–1979 (2012)
9. Foggia, P., Percannella, G., Vento, M.: Graph matching and learning in pattern recognition in the last 10 years. Int. J. Pattern Recogn. Artif. Intell. **28**(01), 1554–1585 (2014)
10. Gaüzere, B., Brun, L., Villemin, D.: Two new graphs kernels in chemoinformatics. Pattern Recogn. Lett. **33**(15), 2038–2047 (2012)
11. Gibert, J., Valveny, E., Bunke, H.: Dimensionality reduction for graph of words embedding. In: Jiang, X., Ferrer, M., Torsello, A. (eds.) GbRPR 2011. LNCS, vol. 6658, pp. 22–31. Springer, Heidelberg (2011)
12. Kunegis, J.: Akonect: the koblenz network collection. In: Proceedings of the 22nd International Conference on World Wide Web Companion. International World Wide Web Conferences Steering Committee, pp. 1343–1350 (2013)
13. Lee, W.-J., Duin, R.P.W.: A labelled graph based multiple classifier system. In: Benediktsson, J.A., Kittler, J., Roli, F. (eds.) MCS 2009. LNCS, vol. 5519, pp. 201–210. Springer, Heidelberg (2009)
14. Leskovec, J., Sosič, R.: SNAP: a general purpose network analysis and graph mining library in C++, June 2014. http://snap.stanford.edu/snap
15. Longabaugh, W.J.: Combing the hairball with biofabric: a new approach for visualization of large networks. BMC Bioinform. **13**(1), 275 (2012)
16. Qiu, H., Hancock, E.: Clustering and embedding using commute times. IEEE Trans. Pattern Anal. Mach. Intell. **29**(11), 1873–1890 (2007)
17. Riesen, K., Bunke, H.: Iam graph database repository for graph based patternrecognition and machine learning. In: da Vitoria Lobo, N., Kasparis, T., Roli, F., Kwok, J.T., Georgiopoulos, M., Anagnostopoulos, G.C., Loog, M. (eds.) SSPR&SPR 2008. LNCS, pp. 287–297. Springer, Heidelberg (2008)
18. Riesen, K., Bunke, H.: Approximate graph edit distance computation by means of bipartite graph matching. Image Vis. Comput. **27**(7), 950–959 (2009)
19. Shervashidze, N., Petri, T., Mehlhorn, K., Borgwardt, K.M., Vishwanathan, S.: Efficient graphlet kernels for large graph comparison. In: International Conference on Artificial Intelligence and Statistics, pp. 488–495 (2009)
20. Shneiderman, B., Plaisant, C.: Treemaps for space-constrained visualization of hierarchies (1998)

21. Suau, P., Hancock, E.R., Escolano, F.: Analysis of the Schrödinger operator in the context of graph characterization. In: Hancock, E., Pelillo, M. (eds.) SIMBAD 2013. LNCS, vol. 7953, pp. 190–203. Springer, Heidelberg (2013)
22. Suau, P., Hancock, E.R., Escolano, F.: Graph characteristics from the Schrödinger operator. In: Kropatsch, W.G., Artner, N.M., Haxhimusa, Y., Jiang, X. (eds.) GbRPR 2013. LNCS, vol. 7877, pp. 172–181. Springer, Heidelberg (2013)
23. Vishwanathan, S.V.N., Schraudolph, N.N., Kondor, R., Borgwardt, K.: Graph kernels. J. Mach. Learn. Res. **11**, 1201–1242 (2010)
24. Watts, D., Strogatz, S.: Collective dynamics of small-world networks. Nature **393**(6684), 440–442 (1998)
25. Xiao, B., Hancock, E., Wilson, R.: A generative model for graph matching and embedding. Comput. Vis. Image Underst. **113**(7), 777–789 (2009)

Forward Chaining with State Monad

Konrad Grzanek[(⊠)]

IT Institute, University of Social Science (SAN), Sienkiewicza 9, 90-113 Lodz, Poland
kgrzanek@spoleczna.pl

Abstract. Production systems use forward chaining to perform the reasoning, in this case - matching rules with facts. The Rete algorithm is an effective forward chaining realization. With the growing popularity of functional programming style, questions arise, how well suitable the style is for implementing complex algorithms in the Artificial Intelligence, like Rete. We present selected implementation details of our custom realization of the algorithm in purely functional programming language Haskell. This paper also discusses usability and usefulness of some advanced means of expression, that are common in functional style, for performing the task.

Keywords: Production systems · Forward chaining · Rete · Functional Programming · State monad · Lenses

1 Introduction

An architecture of a typical expert system consists of a base of facts (*knowledge base*), the internal representation of *(inference) rules*, and the *inference engine* that does the actual task of applying rules to facts [4]. Usually, when a solution is found, the system undertakes some actions. These actions may be modifying the knowledge base, the rule-set, or simply informing the user about the success (solution found). An important issue here is also solving conflicts; the situations in which more than one solution is found. This is a description of a *rule-based* approach, one of the most transparent and robust ways of encoding expert knowledge [5]. Rules are in a way the central concept in this approach. We call them *productions* and the software systems based on this approach are called the *production systems*. Usually a production consists of a set of *conditions* (also called *predicates*) and a set of *actions*.

The inference process in the production systems consists of iteratively applying *modus ponens* ($P \rightarrow Q, P \vdash Q$) to the conditions of the rules and to the facts in the knowledge base, to find the facts matching the conditions. Matches cause a series of transitions from the current system state, through the actions (of productions) that modify the knowledge base and/or the rule-set, to the next state with an updated base of facts and rule-set, until the occurrence of inference conditions that actually stop the whole process. Then we get either a solution to some problem or a state that means the impossibility of continuing due to the lack of further matches. This process called *forward chaining* [1–3] is one of the

© Springer International Publishing Switzerland 2016
L. Rutkowski et al. (Eds.): ICAISC 2016, Part II, LNAI 9693, pp. 442–452, 2016.
DOI: 10.1007/978-3-319-39384-1_38

two major mechanisms found in the rule-based inference engines. The other one, known as *backward chaining* is the core of famous *Prolog* - the general purpose logic programming language.

In [19] we described an implementation of a production system in a purely functional programming language Haskell. The implementation was based on a *Software Transactional Memory* (see [18]) and was essentially a projection of mutable character of Rete onto the *STM monad*. This paper presents another approach - the *State monad* as a carrier of (simulated) explicit mutations [20]. We also discuss some functional means of expression and show their usefulness for implementing complex algorithms.

2   Motivations and Novelty

Production systems with forward chaining are, by nature, stateful. Unfortunately, with the advent of multi-core architectures and growing demands for concurrency support in software, the imperative programming style doesn't scale with respect to human effort while developing more and more complex concurrent systems. Forward chaining belongs to a class of highly complex algorithms, even when implemented without concurrency support. To make it robust, reliable, and concurrent at the same time, special approaches are necessary, like the ones described in this paper.

Choosing a functional programming style over traditional one (presumably imperative, object-oriented) for implementing Rete is a novelty on its own. But we go deeper with it to get us closer to achieving the following functional advantages over the traditional products:

Rollbacks. The ability to roll back the computational process when performing forward chaining opens a way to provide the users of the production system with the ability to execute roll-back actions in productions. This in turn opens the door for both defining new business rules ("break and return to the starting point", a *backtracking*-like behavior) and for performing "speculative" runs of the inference process, during which we add some new facts (possibly random ones) and observe the system behavior, making conclusions and rolling back in the end. This may be called reversible reasoning schemes.

Transactional Updates of Rete State. Production systems with forward chaining are naturally "predisposed" to be implemented with the use of transactions. Unfortunately, the accessible production systems of industrial quality do not admit to implement this feature[1]. The transactional approach was described extensively in [19]. *The solution given in this paper goes further by treating all state changes as transitions between the elements of persistent (immutable) collection of subsequent Rete states.* And the user of Rete implementation, either the programmer or an end-user of an expert system engine *has access to all these states.*

---

[1] In particular we mean *Drools* http://www.drools.org, *Microsoft Business Rules Engine* http://msdn.microsoft.com/en-us/library/aa561216.aspx and *CLIPS* http://clipsrules.sourceforge.net/.

Robust Concurrency. Contemporary production systems are intended to be used in concurrent, multi-core world. Transactions are the only known means to implement concurrent updates of data (facts and rule-set in this case) in a provably correct way.

Insight into Inference. A production system implemented from the ground up is completely transparent for us. In particular, it is possible (and expedient) to design its API in such way, that it would allow us to write routines to perform observations of how the facts are matched against the production conditions. As mentioned above, the programmer can access all states in the chain of state-transitions to make any kind of actions or analyses on them. The abilities of performing detailed analysis of the process may be highly valuable.

3   Rete Algorithm - An Overview

The basis of forward chaining is searching for facts that match the conditions of rules. In a naive approach the production system must re-evaluate conditions of all rules against all facts gathered in the knowledge base after any act of manipulating facts or the rule-set. This highly ineffective process makes this approach unusable in practical scenarios due to a poor scalability (despite that it is not an $NP-$hard problem). It is worth mentioning here that in large production systems a number of hundreds of thousands rules and millions of facts is not unusual (see [8]).

Rete algorithm developed by Forgy in early 1970s [7] is the established first-class algorithm that performs the matching in an effective way. Its outstanding characteristics led to its wide adoption in the expert systems domain. Commercial products like Drools, CLIPS, and Microsoft Business Rules Engine (part of BizTalk) are examples of its use in a production environment. It has been a subject of research and was used in research projects.

Our implementation relies on work of R. B. Doorenbos. He is a designer of an optimization called Rete/UL and an author of a clear and comprehensive description of the algorithm [8].

The basic Rete achieves a demanded high performance by using two techniques:

1. Storing all the match results, including the partial ones, in a specified graph (this is where the name of the algorithm comes from - "Rete" in Latin means "net" or "comb"). This in turn eliminates the need to re-evaluate matching of all facts against all conditions.
2. Sharing the network structure between productions. It is a source of massive optimization in the situations when we have a large number of productions having the same or similar sets of conditions.

Facts in Rete are represented by tuples $(object, attribute, value)$ called, for brevity, *Wmes* (*Working Memory Elements*). The main role of the network is to propagate Wmes starting from the working memory, through the graph nodes, down to so called *production nodes*, where the appropriate *actions* are fired. The following Fig. 1 presents a network for three productions $P1, P2, P3$ that share the structure of the graph. At the figure the production nodes are called like the productions: $P1, P2, P3$ (see the bottom of the network).

Between the working memory and the production nodes there is a non trivial network structure. Its first layer are the α *memory* nodes. Their role is to store the Wmes matching constant tests in productions. The α memories pass their Wmes to *join nodes* (symbol $\bowtie$) where the join operations are performed. The role of joins is to find wmes that match more than one condition within a production. Cross-condition variable value tests are performed here, regarding that conditions may use variables, e.g. like in ($\langle x \rangle$ *is red*), where $\langle x \rangle$ is a variable. Matching Wmes are grouped into *Tokens* and stored in β *memories* (symbolized by a white rectangle with β at the diagram). Tokens represent matches for the production's conditions "so far" accordingly to the network level of the join node that "produced" them. The production nodes receive complete (full) tokens from above and then fire their actions.

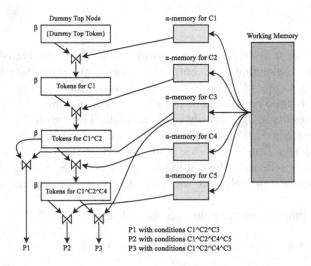

Fig. 1. Rete network for three productions with node sharing exposed. Source: [8] (re-edited in [19]).

Figure 2 shows a concrete situation for one production and a group of Wmes. Tokens are symbolized by curly braces, e.g. $\{w1, w2, w3\}$ is a token with three Wmes: $w1, w2,$ and $w3$.

By convention, the α memories are called the α *part* of the network, and the other nodes are the β *part*. When an α memory passes a Wme to a join node, it is called a *right activation* of the node. When a β memory passes a token into its child join node, we call it *left activation. beta* memories and production nodes may only be left-activated.

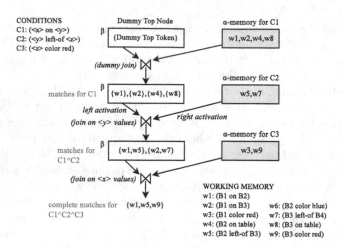

Fig. 2. Instantiated network for a single production. Source: [8] (re-edited in [19]).

4 Lenses

Functional purity at its core assumes immutability [9]. Any transformation of a value or values belonging to a compound object (algebraic data-type/record) requires making a copy of the object being operated on. In a presence of chains of referentially related compound objects the task of making all necessary copies is tedious and results in ugly, hardly readable code. The idea of *lenses* is a simple yet powerful remedy for these problems. Precisely speaking, the essential construct is called *van Laarhoven lens*, as described in [13,14]. Over the years it resulted in a comprehensive Haskell library by Kmett [15]. Our Rete implementation uses lenses extensively, but we use our own simple realization [17] based on [16].

A lens is a function of the following signature:

type $Lens\ s\ a = Functor\ f \Rightarrow (a \rightarrow f\ a) \rightarrow s \rightarrow f\ s$

It acts as a generalized composable accessor. In the above a is a type of accessed or modified property value in a compound object of type s.

To modify a compound object component using a transformation function $a \rightarrow a$ using $Lens\ s\ a$ (for property type a on object s) one can use the following *over* operator:

$over :: Lens\ s\ a \rightarrow (a \rightarrow a) \rightarrow s \rightarrow s$
$over\ ln\ f = runIdentity \circ ln\ (Identity \circ f)$

Accessing a property value is possible with *view*:

$view :: Lens\ s\ a \rightarrow s \rightarrow a$
$view\ ln = getConst \circ ln\ Const$

and finally to set a property value one can use *set*:

$$set :: Lens\ s\ a \rightarrow a \rightarrow s \rightarrow s$$
$$set\ ln = over\ ln \circ const$$

The reader may notice that both *over* and *set* return *s*, that is a newly created compound object with modified property. Examples of use of all the operators defined in this section will follow later on.

5   State Monad and Rete Monad

Our implementation simulates statefulness of the original Rete algorithm by using a specialized variant of *state monad* [10,12]. In essence, the state monad is a type of a function that takes a state *s* and returns it coupled with a value of type *a*:

newtype *State s a = State* { *runState :: s $\rightarrow$ (a, s)* }

To make things encapsulated, a specialized constructor *state* is used:

$$state :: (s \rightarrow (a, s)) \rightarrow State\ s\ a$$

From now on we may think treat objects *State s a* as state processors.

The monadic operator *return* [11] simply takes a value *x* and wraps it within the state processor, as follows:

$$return :: a \rightarrow State\ s\ a$$
$$return\ x = state\ (\lambda st \rightarrow (x, st))$$

And the *bind* operator uses a state processor *st* and a function *k* - a state-processor factory to create a new processor from the result of the first one:

$$(\ggeq) :: State\ s\ a \rightarrow (a \rightarrow State\ s\ b) \rightarrow State\ s\ b$$
$$pr \ggeq k = state\ \$\ \lambda st \rightarrow$$
$$\textbf{let}\ (x, st') = runState\ pr\ st$$
$$\textbf{in}\ runState\ (k\ x)\ st'$$

Storing a new state within the monad is implemented as a *put* operator:

$$put\ newState = state\ \$ \setminus \_ \rightarrow ((), newState)$$

and *get* makes the currently stored state a value in the monad (see the first component of the tuple returned by the state processor):

$$get = state\ \$\ \lambda st \rightarrow (st, st)$$

Mechanisms of exiting the monad come in two variants. The first one called *evalState* returns a value of type *a* using a state processor and an initial state of type *s*:

$$evalState :: State\ s\ a \rightarrow s \rightarrow a$$
$$evalState\ pr\ st = fst\ (runState\ pr\ st)$$

The other, *execState*, returns the resulting state instead:

$$execState :: State\ s\ a \rightarrow s \rightarrow s$$
$$execState\ pr\ st = snd\ (runState\ pr\ st)$$

To make the described mechanisms convenient to use when implementing Rete, we defined a *Rete monad* as a *State* with $s = ReteState$:

type $ReteM\ a = S.State\ ReteState\ a$

where *ReteState* actually holds the current state of Rete network. *ReteState* changes using lenses, like these three below, for graph node identifiers generator (*reteId*), α-memory cache (*reteAmems*), and the Working Memory (*reteWmes*):

$$reteId :: Lens\ ReteState\ Id$$
$$reteId\ f\ s = fmap\ (\lambda v \rightarrow s\ \{\_reteId = v\})\ (f\ (\_reteId\ s))$$

$$reteAmems :: Lens\ ReteState\ (Map.HashMap\ Wme\ Amem)$$
$$reteAmems\ f\ s = fmap\ (\lambda v \rightarrow s\ \{\_reteAmems = v\})\ (f\ (\_reteAmems\ s))$$

$$reteWmes :: Lens\ ReteState\ (Set.HashSet\ Wme)$$
$$reteWmes\ f\ s = fmap\ (\lambda v \rightarrow s\ \{\_reteWmes = v\})\ (f\ (\_reteWmes\ s))$$

The original State monad interface was replaced with the type-class specific for ReteM:

class $State\ a\ s$ **where**
  $viewS :: a \rightarrow ReteM\ s$
  $setS :: a \rightarrow s \rightarrow ReteM\ ()$

with a following variant of the basic lens-like *over* operator, named *overS*:

$$overS :: State\ a\ s \Rightarrow (s \rightarrow s) \rightarrow a \rightarrow ReteM\ ()$$
$$overS\ f\ obj = viewS\ obj \ggg setS\ obj \circ f$$

We introduced also two variants of operators for escaping the ReteM, similar to the ones in State monad, described earlier:

$$run :: ReteState \rightarrow ReteM\ a \rightarrow (a, ReteState)$$
$$run = flip\ S.runState$$

$$eval :: ReteState \rightarrow ReteM\ a \rightarrow a$$
$$eval = flip\ S.evalState$$

Every Rete node is immutable (consists solely of a unique identifier) and has a corresponding state-specific counterpart, mutable in the sense of ReteM. This separation allows creating cycles, inevitable in Rete, and unfortunately impossible to model, even in the state monadic way. Below we have an example implementation for α-memory type *Amem* with a corresponding *AmemState*:

> **instance** *State Amem AmemState* **where**
> $\quad$ *viewS amem* = *liftM* (*lookupState amem* $\circ$ *view reteAmemStates*)
> $\qquad\qquad$ (*viewS Rete*)
> $\quad$ *setS amem s* = *viewS Rete* $\ggg$ *setS Rete* $\circ$ *over reteAmemStates*
> $\qquad\qquad$ (*Map.insert amem s*)

In the case of *Amem* and *AmemState*, as well as for other node types (β-memory nodes, join nodes, etc.) the relation is implemented as a *HashMap* container:

> *lookupState* :: (*Hashable k, Eq k, Show k*) $\Rightarrow$ $k \rightarrow$ *Map.HashMap k v* $\rightarrow v$
> *lookupState k* = *Map.lookupDefault*
> $\quad$ (*error* ("`rete PANIC (1): STATE NOT FOUND FOR `" $+\!\!+$ *show k*)) k

6   The Abstraction in Action

To illustrate how the described mechanisms work, let's take a look at some example procedures. The following *activateAmem* is a procedure that passes a fact (represented by *Wme* - a Working Memory Element) to the α-memory (*Amem* instance):

> *activateAmem* :: *Amem* $\rightarrow$ *Wme* $\rightarrow$ *ReteM Agenda*
> *activateAmem amem wme*@(*Wme o a v*) = **do**
> $\quad$ *state* $\leftarrow$ *viewS amem*
> $\quad$ *setS amem* \$ (*over amemWmes* (*wme*:)
> $\quad\quad$ $\circ$ *over amemWmesByObj* $\quad$ (*wmesIndexInsert o wme*)
> $\quad\quad$ $\circ$ *over amemWmesByAttr* (*wmesIndexInsert a wme*)
> $\quad\quad$ $\circ$ *over amemWmesByVal* $\quad$ (*wmesIndexInsert v wme*))
> $\quad\quad$ *state*
> $\quad$ *agendas* $\leftarrow$ *mapM* (*rightActivateJoin wme*)
> $\quad\quad$ (*view amemSuccessors state*)
> $\quad$ *return* (*concat agendas*)

The above procedure works as follows:

1. The current state of an α-memory is read in the ReteM monad into *state* variable.

2. A series of updates on Working Memory indices called *amemWmesByObj*, *amemWmesByAttr*, and *amemWmesByObj* are made. The indices are there to speedup searching for matching Wmes for feeding newly created Amems when new productions are being added. We use *over* operator and *setS* a new state afterward.
3. Connected JoinNodes are right-activated with a Wme. Every JoinNode activation results in an updated agenda. We represent a set of all agendas created this way with a variable called *agendas*.
4. Finally all the agendas are concatenated and returned.

Similarly, activation of Join nodes also requires reading the current Join state - see *viewS join* in the beginning of the procedure below. Join nodes are stateless, so there is no need to update their state. We simply propagate matching Wmes and Tok(ens) down the network activating children of the Join node and return updated agenda.

```
leftActivateJoin :: Tok → Join → ReteM Agenda
leftActivateJoin tok join = do
    state ← viewS join
    if noJoinChildren state
      then return []
      else do
        amemState ← viewS (joinAmem join)
        let wmes = matchingAmemWmes (joinTests join) tok amemState
        agendas ← forM wmes $ λwme →
          leftActivateJoinChildren state tok wme
        return (concat agendas)
```

One thing worth mentioning in the end is the implementation of agenda. An *Agenda* is a list of *Tasks*, where the Task is a prioritized (see *taskPriority*) function that generates an updated Agenda in the ReteM monad (*taskValue*). We exploit Haskell's lazy-evaluation here:

```
data Task =
  Task
  { taskValue :: !(ReteM Agenda)
  , taskPriority :: !Int
  , taskProd   :: !(Maybe Prod)}
type Agenda = [Task]
```

The above examples only scratch the top of an iceberg with respect to the overall complexity of Rete and our realization of this algorithm. But their content is representative for the way the complexity is controlled using the elements of functional programming style and the tool-sets discussed in previous sections.

7   Final Remarks

This paper is the second in couple (together with [19]) of works dedicated to providing a high reliability and decent performance implementation of the Rete algorithm. Both the transactional implementation described in [19] and the one described here were challenging programmatically; the first was ~4300 LOC (Lines of Code) and the second ~2200 LOC. Both projects ended successfully resulting in two independent libraries for Haskell. Experiences gathered along the way when implementing them allow us to share few insights with the readers:

- Functional programming style with its expressiveness and specific means for building abstractions is a right tool for controlling and managing complexity of non-trivial algorithms like Rete. Codes are concise and the abstractions are clear and easy to use. With a fast progress in the functional languages compilation theory and practice the languages have gained production quality (see [6] for some issues in the past).
- Using the State monad is generally more tightly related to the original idea of eliminating explicit globally visible manipulations of state. Software Transactional Memory is a way do marry functional programming with global state manipulations.
- Operating in the State monad is generally a winner in terms of the performance. Unfortunately, presenting the detailed information on this exceeds the scope of this paper.

Presenting some benchmarks and real-world use cases of our functional Rete implementations is a question of future works.

References

1. Bacchus, F., Teh, Y.W.: Making forward chaining relevant. In: Proceedings of 4th International Conference AI Planning Systems (1998)
2. Ugur, K., Nau, D.: Forward-chaining planning in nondeterministic domains. In: (AAAI-04) Nineteenth National Conference on Artificial Intelligence (2004)
3. Siler, W., Buckley, J.J.: Fuzzy Expert Systems and Fuzzy Reasoning. Wiley, London (2005)
4. Sasikumar, M., Ramani, S., Muthu, R.S., Anjaneyulu, K.S.R., Chandrasekar, R.: A Practical Introduction to Rule Based Expert Systems. Narosa Publishing House, New Delhi (2007)
5. Polach, P., Valenta, J., Jirsik, V.: Knowledge coding methods for rule-based expert systems. WSEAS Trans. Inf. Sci. Appl. **8**(7), 1101–1114 (2010)
6. Clayman, S.: Developing and measuring parallel rule-based systems in a functional programming environment. Ph.D. thesis, University College London, Department of Computer Science (1993)
7. Forgy, C.: ON the efficient implementation of production systems. Carnegie-Mellon University, Department of Computer Science (1979)
8. Doorenbos, R.B.: Production matching for large learning systems. Ph.D. thesis, Computer Science Department, Carnegie Mellon University Pittsburgh, PA (1995)
9. Bird, R., Wadler, R.: Introduction to Functional Programming. Series in Computer Science. Prentice Hall International (UK) Ltd, Englewood Cliffs (1988). Editor: C.A.R. Hoare
10. O'Sullivan, B., Goerzen, J., Stewart, D.: Real World Haskell. O'Reilly Media Inc., Sebastopol (2009)

11. Lipovaca, M.: Learn You a Haskell for Great Good!: A Beginner's Guide, 1st edn. No Starch Press, San Francisco (2011)
12. Understanding monads, State: Haskell Wikibook (2015). https://en.wikibooks.org/wiki/Haskell/Understanding_monads/State
13. van Laarhoven, T.: CPS based functional references (2009). http://twanvl.nl/blog/haskell/cps-functional-references
14. O'Connor, R.: Functor is to lens as applicative is to biplate: introducing multiplate. In: ACM SIGPLAN 7th Workshop on Generic Programming, Tokyo (2011)
15. Kmett, E.: Lenses, Folds, and Travelsals - Haskell Package (2015). https://github.com/ekmett/lens
16. Arnold, J.: Lens Tutorial - Introduction. http://blog.jakubarnold.cz/2014/07/14/lens-tutorial-introduction-part-1.html
17. Grzanek, K.: A Repository of Common Haskell Utilities. https://github.com/kongra/kask-base/blob/master/Kask/Control/Lens.hs
18. Marlow, S.: Parallel and Concurrent Programming in Haskell. OReilly Media, Inc., Sebastopol (2013). ISBN: 978-1-449-33594-6. 1005 Gravenstein Highway North, CA 95472
19. Grzanek, K.: Transactional forward chaining: a functional approach. In: Rutkowski, L., Korytkowski, M., Scherer, R., Tadeusiewicz, R., Zadeh, L.A., Zurada, J.M. (eds.) Artificial Intelligence and Soft Computing. LNCS, vol. 9120, pp. 613–624. Springer, Heidelberg (2015)
20. Rete GitHub Repository. https://github.com/kongra/Rete

From SBVR to BPMN and DMN Models. Proposal of Translation from Rules to Process and Decision Models

Krzysztof Kluza[(✉)] and Krzysztof Honkisz

AGH University of Science and Technology,
al. A. Mickiewicza 30, 30-059 Krakow, Poland
kluza@agh.edu.pl, honkisz@student.agh.edu.pl

Abstract. The same business concepts can be expressed in various knowledge representations like processes or rules. This paper presents an interoperability solution for transforming a subset of the SBVR rules into the BPMN and DMN models. The translation algorithm describes how to translate the SBVR vocabulary, structural and operational rules into particular BPMN and DMN elements. The result is a combined process and decision model, which can be used for validating SBVR rules by people aware of BPMN and DMN notations.

1 Introduction

In many enterprises, there is a need to support smooth communication between business experts, software engineers and other people with technical knowledge. There are several methods of business knowledge representation, such as business rules or business process models. Both these representations can describe how the company works. However, some issues like constraints or detailed guidelines can be better represented as rules, and some other like procedures or workflows can be better represented as process models.

Although there are papers which describe how to combine processes with rules [1,2], there is no standardised solution for such integration. As SBVR (Semantics of Business Vocabulary and Business Rules) [3], BPMN (Business Process Model and Notation) [4], and DMN (Decision Model and Notation) [5] are standardised by the OMG (Object Management Group) consortium, their integration and interoperability is one of the promising solutions for this issue.

The aim of our research is to examine the possibility of combining the three standards (SBVR, BPMN and DMN) by ensuring the knowledge interoperability [6,7] between them. Especially, this paper is concerned with the translation from the SBVR representation, used to determine the business rules for people who do not have substantial technical knowledge, but have a deep knowledge how the company works, to the BPMN and DMN representations, which can be easily interpret by business analysts as well as by software engineers who can validate the knowledge.

The paper is supported by the AGH UST research grant.

L. Rutkowski et al. (Eds.): ICAISC 2016, Part II, LNAI 9693, pp. 453–462, 2016.
DOI: 10.1007/978-3-319-39384-1_39

The paper is organized as follows. In Sect. 2, we present the OMG knowledge representation standards which are used later in the paper. Section 3 provides a short overview of related approaches. In Sect. 4, we present our proposal of the translation from the SBVR rules to the BPMN and DMN models. Section 5 summarizes the paper.

2   Knowledge Representation Standards

In the following subsections, we describe the OMG standards for representing rules, processes and decisions.

2.1   Semantic of Business Vocabulary and Rules

SBVR [3] provides a metamodel for defining business vocabulary and rules by providing basic terminology and a set of keywords. Rules in SBVR are based on facts, and facts are based on terms. The vocabulary consists of noun and verb concepts. Rules, defined using terms specified in the vocabulary, can be of two kinds: structural and operational. Structural rules use such modal operators as necessary or possible/impossible. Operational rules use such modal operators as obligatory, permitted/forbidden.

A part of the SBVR standard is SBVR Structured English [8]. It defines a set of basic operators and quantifiers which can be used to define rules. It also specifies four methods of text formatting: <u>term</u> for general noun concepts, <u>name</u> for individual noun concepts, *verb* for verb concepts and keyword for keywords.

2.2   Business Process Model and Notation

BPMN [5] provides a metamodel for representing business processes. Such a process can be defined as a collection of related tasks for providing a certain service or producing a specific product for a customer [9]. Although BPMN provides several diagrams, in most solutions only process diagrams which support workflow modeling are used.

2.3   Decision Model and Notation

DMN [4] is a new standard for decision modeling. A decision in DMN is to determine the result (or select some option) based on a number of input data. The standard specifies two elements: decision requirements, which consists of the required pieces of information needed to make a decision at some point of the business process, and decision logic represented as business knowledge models. Decision requirements are specified using Decision Requirements Graphs (DRG) and business knowledge models are mostly represented as decision tables.

3 Related Works

There is a relationship between the standards described in the previous section [10]. Process and rules integration is mostly considered when concerning BPM and BRM systems integration [11]. There are also works concerning integration of particular notation like BPMN with SBVR [12]. However, in the case of interoperability between the OMG standards, Fig. 1 summarizes the existing translations for the four modeling notations: SBVR, BPMN, DMN, UML. The directed edges of the graph represent the existing translation between the two notations, and their labels refer to particular works.

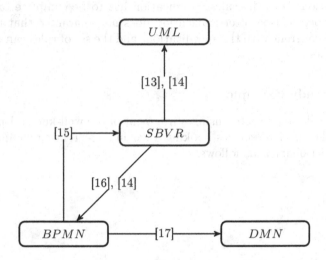

Fig. 1. The overview of the existing translations

In [13], a methodology of transforming SBVR business rules into UML diagrams is presented. The authors uses the UML activity, sequence and class diagrams. In the case of our work, the UML activity diagrams are the most similar with BPMN models. The authors developed their method in [18], by extending SBVR into SBPVR (Semantics of Business Process Vocabulary and Process Rules).

Similar solution to [13], but for the BPMN notation, was presented in [16]. In this solution binary facts are transformed into process tasks and rules are mapped into task sequences. Other method of transforming SBVR to BPMN was proposed in [14], in which the authors proposed their own metamodel – sSBVRMM (simplified SBVR metamodel) with new elements for types.

The reverse translation, i.e. SBVR rule extraction from the BPMN models was elaborated in [15]. It requires to define the set of noun concepts and verb concepts, and then the proposed algorithm can generate the SBVR business vocabulary (terms and facts).

Because the DMN standard is quite new, there are few works related to this notation. The solution for extracting DMN decision logic from BPMN diagrams was presented in [17]. In turn, the enhancing process models with decision logic was considered in [19].

4   Translation Algorithm

In this section, we present a translation algorithm which describes how to transform the SBVR rule set into a combined model of BPMN with DMN (process and decision model). For this solution, a set of the SBVR business rules has to meet certain conditions [14]: the rules specification has to be complete (adding new rules to the specification after translation does not guarantee that the process model will be coherent with the specification) and the set of rules can not contain conflicting rules.

4.1   Case Study Example

Our solution will be presented using a fragment of the well-known Eu-Rent case study example [20]. It describes booking a car in a car renting company.
The SBVR dictionary is as follows:

renter
reservation
clerk
age
income
acceptance
rejection

renter *sends* reservation
renter *receives* acceptance
renter *receives* rejection

clerk *receives* reservation
clerk *verifies* reservation
clerk *accepts* reservation
clerk *sends* acceptance
clerk *registers* reservation
clerk *rejects* reservation
clerk *sends* rejection

renter *has* age
renter *has* income

The SBVR rule set for this example is as follows:

It is obligatory that renter *sends* reservation

It is obligatory that renter *receives* acceptance or renter *receives* rejection but not both if renter *sends* reservation

It is obligatory that renter *receives* acceptance if clerk *sends* acceptance

It is obligatory that renter *receives* rejection if clerk *sends* rejection

It is obligatory that clerk *receives* reservation if renter *sends* reservation

It is obligatory that clerk *verifies* reservation if clerk *receives* reservation

It is obligatory that clerk *accepts* reservation or clerk *rejects* reservation but not both if clerk *verifies* reservation

It is obligatory that clerk *verifies* reservation requires renter information

It is obligatory that clerk *sends* acceptance if clerk *accepts* reservation

It is obligatory that clerk *registers* reservation if clerk *accepts* reservation

It is obligatory that clerk *sends* rejection if clerk *rejects* reservation

It is necessary that renter *has* age at least 18

It is necessary that renter *has* age at most 70

It is necessary that renter *has* income at least 5000

4.2 SBVR Operational Rules to BPMN Mapping

The BPMN model in our method is obtained mostly from the SBVR operational rules of the following syntax:

It is obligatory that <binary fact 1> if<binary fact 2>

The mapping of operational rules to the BPMN tasks is similar to the mapping presented in [13,16]. The specification of this mapping is presented in Table 1.

4.3 SBVR Structural Rules to DMN Mapping

In our method, the DMN model is obtained from the SBVR structural rules of the following syntax:

It is necessary that term *constraint expression*

Table 1. SBVR to BPMN mapping specification

No	SBVR Rule	Corresponding fragment of BPMN model
1	Binary facts (<u>term</u>-*verb*-<u>term</u>), e.g. <u>renter</u> *sends* <u>reservation</u>	
2	Operational rules which in both facts have the same participant, e.g. It is obligatory that <u>clerk</u> *verifies* <u>reservation</u> if <u>clerk</u> *receives* <u>reservation</u>	
3	Operational rules with facts concerning external participants, e.g. It is obligatory that <u>clerk</u> *receives* <u>reservation</u> if <u>renter</u> *sends* <u>reservation</u>	
4	Multiple rules with the same binary fact in the conditional part of rules, e.g. It is obligatory that <u>clerk</u> *sends* <u>acceptance</u> if <u>clerk</u> *accepts* <u>reservation</u> It is obligatory that <u>clerk</u> *registers* <u>reservation</u> if <u>clerk</u> *accepts* <u>reservation</u>	
5	Operational rules which contain or and but not both, and have the same participant, e.g. It is obligatory that <u>clerk</u> *accepts* <u>reservation</u> or <u>clerk</u> *rejects* <u>reservation</u> but not both if <u>clerk</u> *verifies* <u>reservation</u>	
6	Operational rules with additional requirements, e.g. It is obligatory that <u>clerk</u> *verifies* <u>reservation</u> requires <u>renter</u> information	

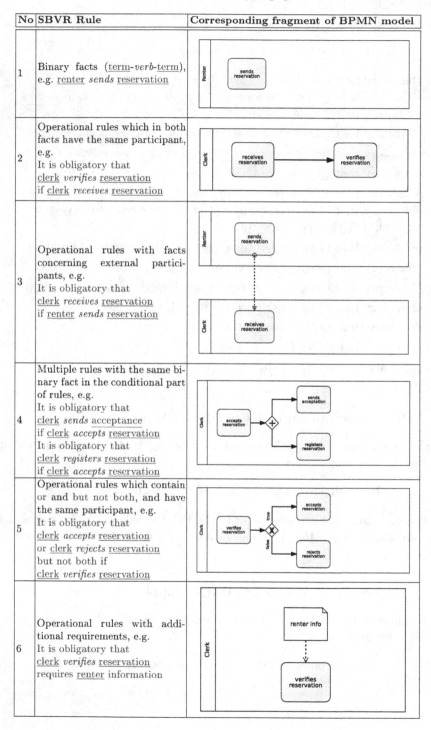

In this rule, the term is an element of the binary fact which is a business activity (business-term), and the *constraint expression* defines only the numerical constraint of the followin syntax:

$$has\ \underline{parameter}\ quantifier\ \underline{quantifier\text{-}value}$$

where quantifier is one of the following quantifiers: *at least, at most, exactly* and their combinations [3].

Such structural rules are mapped into Decision Requirements Graph (DRG) model, presenting the order of decisions, with decision tables specifying the decision logic. The mapping algorithm is specified as follows:

1. For each business-term, a corresponding a *data input* element is added to the graph. A name of the element is created based on the business-term and the word *Info*, e.g. *Renter Info.*
2. For each parameter associated with the business-term, a corresponding *business decision* is created, Its name consists of the business-term name for which a decision is made, the parameter name and the word *Decision*, e.g. *Renter Age Decision.*
3. For each decision, an associated *business knowledge model* is created. Its name is derived from the business-term and the corresponding parameter as well as the word *table*, e.g. *Renter Age Table*. For such a *business knowledge model*, a corresponding decision table is created and filled in with the decision table rules. Each SBVR structural rule specifying the constraint with the parameter of the *business knowledge model* is translated into a single decision table rule. The rule in the decision table is created as a negation of the condition in the SBVR rule with the negative decision (*DECLINE*). Then, an additional accepting rule (*ACCEPT*) is added for situations when none of the previous rules was fulfilled.
4. If the business-term has more than one parameter, the created decisions are linked into a sequence of decisions in the order the parameters appear in the SBVR rules.

Figure 2 presents the result of the translation to the DRG graph of the SBVR structural rules from our case study example:

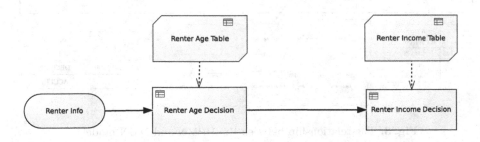

Fig. 2. The result of the translation – the DRG graph

Table 2. A decision table for the *age* parameter

LP	Age	Acceptance
		ACCEPT, DECLINE
1	<18	DECLINE
2	>70	DECLINE
3	-	ACCEPT

Table 3. A decision table for the *income* parameter

LP	Income	Acceptance
		ACCEPT, DECLINE
1	<5000	DECLINE
2	-	ACCEPT

It is necessary that <u>renter</u> *has* <u>age</u> at least <u>18</u>

It is necessary that <u>renter</u> *has* <u>age</u> at most <u>70</u>

It is necessary that <u>renter</u> *has* <u>income</u> at least <u>5000</u>

The decision tables for the *age* and *income* parameters are presented in Tables 2 and 3.

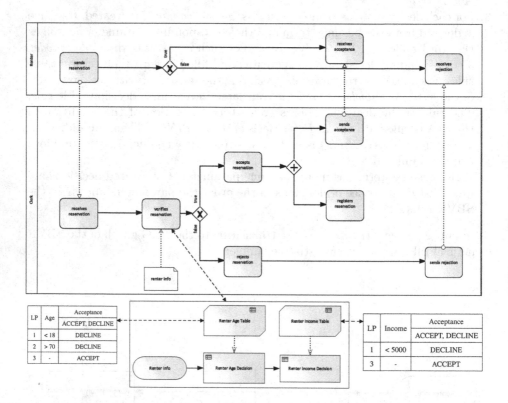

Fig. 3. The relationship between the BPMN and DMN models

4.4   The Relationship Between the BPMN and DMN Models

As the DMN specification claims that the DMN model is complementary to the BPMN model, the method proposed in this paper is consistent with this assumption. Figure 3 shows the relationship between the BPMN diagram and the DRG diagram and related decision tables of the DMN model. The dashed arrows connects the related elements between different kinds of diagrams. The model that constitutes a result of the proposed translation is a single model of business process with suitable business decisions.

5   Concluding Remarks

The goal of the research presented in this paper was to provide an interoperability solution for transforming a subset of the SBVR rules into the BPMN and DMN models. Thus, we present a translation algorithm which describes how to translate the SBVR vocabulary, structural and operational rules into particular BPMN and DMN elements. The result of the algorithm is a combined process and decision model. Our solution can be used for validating SBVR rules by people aware of BPMN and DMN notations like business analysts, software engineers, or other people familiar with the processes and decisions in the company.

As in this paper we discuss only a subset of SBVR, our future work will focus on extending the method to other subsets, implementing a useful interoperability tool for automating this method, as well as incorporating the approach into the SBVRwiki tool [21,22].

References

1. zur Muehlen, M., Indulska, M., Kamp, G.: Business process and business rule modeling languages for compliance management: a representational analysis. In: Tutorials, Posters, Panels and Industrial Contributions at the 26th International Conference on Conceptual Modeling ER 2007, Darlinghurst, Australia, vol. 83, pp. 127–132. Australian Computer Society Inc., Australian (2007)
2. Kluza, K., Maślanka, T., Nalepa, G.J., Ligęza, A.: Proposal of representing BPMN diagrams with XTT2-based business rules. In: Brazier, F.M.T., Nieuwenhuis, K., Pavlin, G., Warnier, M., Badica, C. (eds.) Intelligent Distributed Computing V. SCI, vol. 382, pp. 243–248. Springer, Heidelberg (2011)
3. OMG: Semantics of business vocabulary and business rules (SBVR). Version 1.3: formal specification. Technical report, Object Management Group (OMG) (2015)
4. OMG: Decision model and notation (DMN). Version 1.0: formal specification. Technical report, Object Management Group (OMG) (2015)
5. OMG: Business process model and notation (BPMN) Version 2.0. Technical report, Object Management Group (OMG) (2011)
6. Kaczor, K., Nalepa, G.J.: Semantically-driven rule interoperability – concept proposal. In: Rutkowski, L., Korytkowski, M., Scherer, R., Tadeusiewicz, R., Zadeh, L.A., Zurada, J.M. (eds.) ICAISC 2013, Part II. LNCS, vol. 7895, pp. 511–522. Springer, Heidelberg (2013)

7. Kaczor, K.: Practical approach to interoperability in production rule bases with SUBITO. In: Rutkowski, L., Korytkowski, M., Scherer, R., Tadeusiewicz, R., Zadeh, L.A., Zurada, J.M. (eds.) Artificial Intelligence and Soft Computing. LNCS, vol. 9120, pp. 637–648. Springer, Heidelberg (2015)
8. Lévy, F., Nazarenko, A.: Formalization of natural language regulations through SBVR structured english. In: Morgenstern, L., Stefaneas, P., Lévy, F., Wyner, A., Paschke, A. (eds.) RuleML 2013. LNCS, vol. 8035, pp. 19–33. Springer, Heidelberg (2013)
9. Lindsay, A., Dawns, D., Lunn, K.: Business processes - attempts to find a definition. Inf. Softw. Technol. 45(15), 1015–1019 (2003)
10. Linehan, M.H., de Sainte Marie, C.: The relationship of decision model and notation (DMN) to SBVR and BPMN. Bus. Rules J. 12(6) (2011). http://www.BRCommunity.com/a2011/b597.html
11. Hohwiller, J., Schlegel, D., Grieser, G., Hoekstra, Y.: Integration of BPM and BRM. In: Dijkman, R., Hofstetter, J., Koehler, J. (eds.) BPMN 2011. LNBIP, vol. 95, pp. 136–141. Springer, Heidelberg (2011)
12. Pitschke, J.: Integrating business process models and business logic: BPMN and the decision model. In: Dijkman, R., Hofstetter, J., Koehler, J. (eds.) BPMN 2011. LNBIP, vol. 95, pp. 148–153. Springer, Heidelberg (2011)
13. Raj, A., Prabhakar, T.V., Hendryx, S.: Transformation of SBVR business design to UML models. In: Proceedings of the 1st India Software Engineering Conference ISEC 2008, pp. 29–38. ACM, New York (2008)
14. Steen, B., Pires, L., Iacob, M.E.: Automatic generation of optimal business processes from business rules. In: 2010 14th IEEE International Enterprise Distributed Object Computing Conference Workshops (EDOCW), pp. 117–126, October 2010
15. Skersys, T., Kapocius, K., Butleris, R., Danikauskas, T.: Extracting business vocabularies from business process models: SBVR and BPMN standards-based approach. Comput. Sci. Inf. Syst. 11, 1515–1535 (2014)
16. Tantan, O.C., Akoka, J.: Automated transformation of business rules into business processes. In: Proceedings of the Twenty-Sixth International Conference on Software Engineering and Knowledge Engineering, pp. 684–687 (2014)
17. Batoulis, K., Meyer, A., Bazhenova, E., Decker, G., Weske, M.: Extracting decision logic from process models. In: Zdravkovic, J., Kirikova, M., Johannesson, P. (eds.) CAiSE 2015. LNCS, vol. 9097, pp. 349–366. Springer, Heidelberg (2015)
18. Raj, A., Agrawal, A., Prabhakar, T.V.: Transformation of business processes into UML models: an SBVR approach. Int. J. Sci. Eng. Res. 4(7), 647–661 (2013). ISSN: 2229-5518
19. Mertens, S., Gailly, F., Poels, G.: Enhancing declarative process models with DMN decision logic. In: Gaaloul, K., Schmidt, R., Nurcan, S., Guerreiro, S., Ma, Q. (eds.) BPMDS 2015 and EMMSAD 2015. LNBIP, vol. 214, pp. 151–165. Springer, Heidelberg (2015)
20. OMG: Semantics of business vocabulary and business rules (SBVR). Version 1.0: formal specification. Technical report, Object Management Group (OMG) (2008)
21. Nalepa, G.J., Kluza, K., Kaczor, K.: SBVRwiki a web-based tool for authoring of business rules. In: Rutkowski, L., Korytkowski, M., Scherer, R., Tadeusiewicz, R., Zadeh, L.A., Zurada, J.M. (eds.) Artificial Intelligence and Soft Computing. LNCS, vol. 9120, pp. 703–713. Springer, Heidelberg (2015)
22. Kluza, K., Kutt, K., Wozniak, M.: SBVRwiki (tool presentation). In: Nalepa, G.J., Baumeister, J. (eds.) Proceedings of 10th Workshop on Knowledge Engineering and Software Engineering (KESE10) Co-located with 21st European Conference on Artificial Intelligence (ECAI 2014), Prague, Czech Republic, 19 August 2014

On Cooperation in Multi-agent System, Based on Heterogeneous Knowledge Representation

Leszek Kotulski[1], Adam Sędziwy[1(✉)], and Barbara Strug[1,2]

[1] Department of Applied Computer Science, AGH University of Science and Technology, Al. Mickiewicza 30, 30 059 Krakow, Poland
{kotulski,sedziwy,bstrug}@agh.edu.pl
[2] Department of Physics, Astronomy and Applied Computer Science, Jagiellonian University, Lojasiewicza 11, Krakow, Poland

Abstract. Graphs are an expressive representation of projects in the domain of computer-aided design (CAD). Such a representation of a problem's structure allows for automation of a design process, what is an important property of CAD systems. It can be accomplished by using graph grammars which can represent a progress of a design process. In this paper we introduce a graph based approach to the synchronization of a design processes carried out by different and independent transformation systems supporting various aspects of a building project creation. Such a synchronization is necessary when two or more systems affect simultaneously a shared area. The proposed mechanism is illustrated by an example of successful synchronization on shared elements of an object being designed, achieved by using different representations at different layers of a design.

1 Introduction

The designing is a complex process which usually requires taking into account different aspects of an artifact being designed. Those aspects are often considered at different levels of detail or different layers. Thus a design process has to be regarded as the resultant of operations (tasks) performed on all such layers. In a large-scale design there may be a large number of layers and each a single design task can affect many of such layers. In some cases a design task may be done independently from other ones and modify/touch restricted parts or layers of the design only. In many situations a single design task may require accessing and making changes on different layers of a design. It may imply, in turn, invoking other design actions. In such cases some way of synchronization of design actions on different layers will be essential to complete successfully a design sub-process. Designing a building is such an example of a complex design task, in which a lot of different aspects have to be taken into account. The architectural design of buildings can be perceived from various perspectives: by the external design, as a structural design, as a design of the internal structure and layout, as the design of utilities and appliances or as the interior design and furnishing.

© Springer International Publishing Switzerland 2016
L. Rutkowski et al. (Eds.): ICAISC 2016, Part II, LNAI 9693, pp. 463–473, 2016.
DOI: 10.1007/978-3-319-39384-1_40

Each of these approaches can have its own separate objectives, constraints, requirements and so on. In this paper we focus mainly on differences between the external and internal aspects of building design. As the building is seen differently from the external and internal design point of view, these differences can also be reflected in various formal representations of a modeled system, what in turn can result in slightly different formal mechanisms used.

As mentioned above, each design task considered in this paper can be regarded as a superposition of a number of sub-processes carried out in different layers of the design, for example in the internal and external part of a building. While in many cases a task can be performed successfully on its own layer without interfering with other layers it is obvious that sub-processes can meet in some points. For that reason it's necessary to prepare a mechanism which ensures coherence between them in the shared areas of a project. The consistency among different aspects of a design is essential for achieving architectural goals.

The first step necessary for automation of a design process is building an appropriate knowledge representation of a designed object (building). Such a representation must be flexible enough to store different types of data, as well as structural and spatial properties of an object. Moreover, it has to support updating/modifying a knowledge in any moment. Graphs are the representation which satisfies those requirements. They allow to describe designs at different stages of their development and corresponding modifications as well. Such modifications can be modeled by notions derived from the theory of formal languages [4,5,7,18], as well as grammar systems [2,6]. Due to the potentially large graph orders in real-life tasks, there was developed the approach based on both distributed graphs (hypergraphs) and multi-agent systems. [10–15,17].

Maintaining data for building purposes has also been an object of the wide research resulting in developing BIM (Building Information Modeling) systems which became commonly used [1,3]. The data contained within hypergraph structures used in this paper can be accessed by different applications and can be exported to various formats for further processing, for example by applications which accept BIM formats, through IFC standard [1]. For the external information about a building and its position in a surrounding environment the CityGML semantic meta-model based on GML (Geography Markup Language) is a highly expressive language which allows modeling urban spaces with granularity varying from a geographical region to a building interior [8].

In this paper, hypergraphs are used as the basic representation of a building structure. For such a representation design/modification/update tasks can be represented by means of formal graph transformations (productions), applied to a structural representation of a design. These transformations can originate from independent graph grammars, which describe operations performed on different layers of a design, for example interior and exterior. Thus, it is inevitable that applying some production of one grammar (layer) impacts the elements of the other structure and thus triggers transformations carried out by that other party. We introduce in the paper a 2-phase synchronization mechanism which guaranties consistent execution of such the coupled productions, belonging to different graph grammars (layers).

The problem of synchronization was researched for a long time but in the context of an access to common resources. In this case we have to synchronize cooperation of several actions expressed in terms of graph transformations. This causes that all synchronization methods [19] based either on centralized approach (semaphores, monitors) or distributed one cannot be applied.

The work presented here is motivated by the need of a mechanism coordinating different and independent graph grammars operating on different aspects of a design, but having productions acting on shared areas of this design. The proposed approach is illustrated by the case study from the domain of architectural design, where it is used to ensure consistency of the design process performed simultaneously inside (including its internal structure) and outside (including its environment) of a building. Defining a consistent mechanism of a synchronization in shared areas is necessary for the automation of a design process covering all aspects of creation of a new building.

2   Graph-Based Design Knowledge Representation and Modification

One of the most important aspects of a design process is an appropriate knowledge representation. Such a representation should allow not only for the denotation of a static state of objects being designed but also it should constitute a formalism for the description of a design progress. One of such formalisms are graphs which can be used to both represent a state of a design at a given moment and the progress of the entire process.

In this paper a hypergraph representation and transformation model is used as a basis for creating a formal layer for the system supporting computer aided design [9]. Objects to be constructed are represented by hypergraphs, which are labeled and attributed. While simple graphs consist of nodes and edges connecting these nodes and thus each edge in such a graph connects exactly two nodes (thus, such a graph allows us to represent only binary relations between objects), a hypergraph is an extension of a simple graph, which allows for representing multi-argument relations. A hypergraph consists of hyperedges and nodes. Hyperedges are labeled, in the case of design problems, by names of the corresponding relations, and can be directed for asymmetrical relations. Hypergraph nodes represent components of a design object. To represent features of components and relations among them, attributing of hyperedges and nodes is used. Values assigned to attributes specify properties of objects represented by particular nodes and relations represented by hyperedges, allowing us to generate an instance of a hypergraph. On the basis of the standard definition of a hypergraph, two representations, being the most suitable for describing the internal and the external structure of a building, are derived and presented below.

Let Σ_E and Σ_V be fixed alphabets of hyperedge and node labels respectively. Let A_V and A_E denote sets of node and hyperedge attributes respectively.

Definition 1. *A **labeled and attributed hypergraph** over $\Sigma = \Sigma_E \cup \Sigma_V$ is a system $G = (V, E, lab, att)$, where: V is a finite set of nodes; $E \subseteq P(V)$*

is a finite set of hyperedges, such that $\forall e \in E$: *e is an ordered set of vertices;* $lb = (lb_V, lb_E)$ *is a labeling function, where:* $lb_V : V \rightarrow \Sigma_V$, $lb_E : E \rightarrow \Sigma_E$; $att = (att_V, att_E)$ *is an attributing function, where:* $att_V : \Sigma_V \rightarrow P(A_V)$, $att_E :$ $\Sigma_E \rightarrow P(A_E)$; $val = (val_V, val_E)$ *is a value assigning function, where:* $val_V :$ $A_V \times V \rightarrow D_a$, $val_E : A_E \times E \rightarrow D_a$ *assign a value to a given attribute a of a node/hyperedge in such a way that* $\forall x \in V \cup E$, $\forall a \in att(x)$: $val(a, x) \in D_a$. *A set* D_a *is referred to as a domain of a node/hyperedge attribute.*

A hypergraph in which all attributes have a value assigned (by a function *val*) is called an instance and can be interpreted by assigning geometrical components to nodes and relations to hyperedges. In Fig. 1b an example of a hypergraph representing a floor layout of a flat is depicted. The floor diagram of this layout is shown in Fig. 1a. As it can be seen, each node represents an element of the layout, nodes labeled by B represent bedroom, bathroom, K kitchen, ER eating room, H hall, LR living room, W wall and Wd window. Each section of the wall is represented by a single node labeled W. Hyperedges are drawn as rectangles with labels inside and line segments linking them to nodes belonging to a given hyperedge, the label inL represents the fact that all elements represented by nodes connected by it are positioned along straight line. To improve the readability of the figure, hyperedges which connect only two nodes are drawn as continuous line segments for those which represent adjacency and dashed-line segments for those which represent being attached to another element (for example, the hyperedge connecting a wall and a window in Fig. 1b).

While a hypergraph defined above forms a good general structure we also propose a specialization of this hypergraph which allows for better representation of building structural characteristics. It allows us to treat a building as a combination of solids.

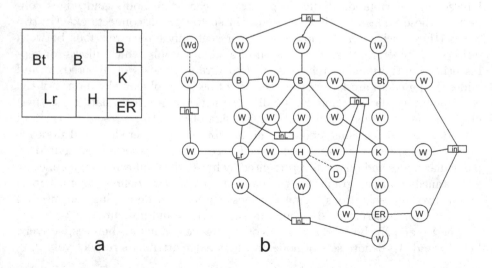

a   b

Fig. 1. (a) An example of a floor layout diagram (b) a hypergraph representing this layout

Definition 2. *External hypergraph representation of a convex polyhedron S (referred to as a simple solid) is a hypergraph $G_S = (V, A \cup H, lab, att)$ such that: V is a set of nodes representing faces of S, A set of hyperedges representing edges of S, H is a set of nodes representing vertices of S, $lab : V \cup A \cup H \rightarrow \Sigma$ is a node and hyperedge labelling function with a corresponding set of labels,Σ, $att : V \cup A \cup H \rightarrow \Gamma$ is a node and hyperedge attributing function with a corresponding set of attributes, Γ.*

A hypergraph model of a solid facilitates determining geometric relations among its faces, edges and vertices and thus is more efficient than the intuitive graph representation consisting of a graph being a polyhedral mesh of a solid.

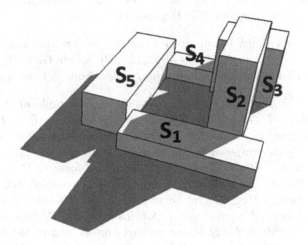

Fig. 2. Concave solid consisting of adhering buildings

The next step towards the increased expressive strength of the above formalization is modeling any solids, including the concave ones, solids with non-plane faces and solids with curved edges. The second and third case may be easily handled by means of attributing functions providing geometric data of particular entities. The first issue may be resolved when we assume that each concave solid (abbrev. CS) S is a sum of simple solids, $S_1, S_2, , S_k$, such that there exists a permutation $i(1), i(2), \ldots, i(k)$ for which solids $S_{i(j)}$ and $S_{i(j+1)}$ are adherent, for $0 < j < k$. In other words, we demand connectivity of S. Figure 2 presents the sample set of adhering buildings, $S_1, S_2, \ldots, S_5$, which form the CS satisfying the above assumption A representation of a CS is obtained by adding edges (formally hyperedges) representing adherence of solids to a set of hyperedges of G_S.

Definition 3. *Composite hypergraph representation of a connected solid S is a hypergraph $G_S = (V, A \cup H \cup R, lab, att)$ such that: V, A, H are introduced in Definition 2, $R \subset P(V)$ is a set of hyperedges such that $e = \{v_1, v_2\} \in R$ where v_1, v_2 represent adhering faces, $lab : V \cup A \cup H \cup R \rightarrow \Sigma$ is a node and hyperedge* *labeling function with a corresponding set of labels, Σ, att : $V \cup A \cup H \cup R \to \Gamma$ is a node and hyperedge attributing function with a corresponding set of attributes, Γ.*

2.1   Design Modification

Hypergraphs can represent subsequent stages of an object at different steps of a design process. They can be obtained in a design process by application of a transformation system (or so called hypergraph grammars described below). Moreover, a hypergraph transformation (also referred to as a grammar production) can be used to represent modifications of an existing hypergraph in order to introduce a required change to an object represented by this hypergraph.

The below definition introduces the notion of a hypergraph grammar being an instance of a single pushout (SPO) grammar.

Definition 4. *Hypergraph grammar G over sets of terminal and nonterminal node labels Σ_N, Σ_T is a tuple $G = (G_0, \Sigma_n, \Sigma_t, P)$, where $G_0 \in H_i$ is an initial hypergraph and P denotes a set of grammar productions defined below.*

Definition 5. *A hypergraph grammar production is a tuple of the form $P = (L, R, E, C)$, where: $L \in H_i$ is the left side of a production, $R \in H$ is the right side of a production, E stands for an embedding transformation and C is an applicability predicate, responsible for checking if P can be applied in a given context. Production P is also denoted in a simplified form as $P : L \to R$ Application of a production P to a given hypergraph G is accomplished in following steps: (1) A subgraph $H \subset G$, isomorphic with the left side of a production, i.e. with L, is taken. If a predicate C forbids applying P then the process is interrupted and terminated. (2) H is removed from G and replaced by the right side of the production, i.e. by R. All hyperedges incident with H get orphaned. (3) Finally, one has to fix all orphaned hyperedges connecting previously with H, according to the specification provided by the embedding transformation E. As a result hyperedges are (i) removed or (ii) unchanged, being reattached to R or (iii) replaced by new hyperedges.*

In order to represent a design process such a hypergraph transformation system definition needs to contain rules (productions) corresponding to all actions that can be applied in a given design task. While this approach is well defined and has been successfully used in many design problems [12–15] its main constraint is a huge number of productions in more complex, real-life design problems. In this article we show the solution of this issue, which is the usage of a system of graph transformations. Each of those graph transformations is defined and operates on a separate design layer. Thanks to this particular transformations can be executed largely independently, working on their own parts of a design.

In Fig. 3 the example of a graph transformation representing the design of an internal structure of a building is shown. This transformation is responsible for moving a window from one wall to another. When P is applied to a graph G representing an actual state of a building being designed, then a subgraph

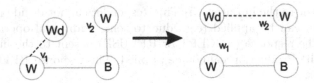

Fig. 3. The sample graph transformation (production) P

of G, isomorphic with the left hand side of production P is found and replaced by the right hand side of P in such a way that the node matched to v_1 is replaced by w_1 on the right side, v_2 by w_2 and the one labeled with B remains unchanged. When the node v_1 is replaced by w_1 all hyperedges which were attached to v_1 in the original graph are reattached to w_1 (as specified by the embedding rule E associated with this transformation). The same is done to reattach other hyperedges. The applicability predicate C for this production determines whether the wall represented by a node matched to v_2 has other objects attached to it and whether it is an external wall.

3   Synchronization Mechanism

As mentioned above the transformation systems working on separate layers of the design can operate independently, but when the operations/changes introduced by subsequent graph productions affect shared elements, a synchronization is needed. As representations of various project layers may use different types of entities and thus different labeling and attributing schemes, a set of shared elements must be agreed upon in order to facilitate communication and synchronization among processes. One of the most important attributes are common coordinate system and geometric coordinate format which have to be established. Names of attributes used by all transformation systems have to be agreed as well. Moreover, a matching between labels used in different transformation systems has to be defined. This matching enables an unambiguous mapping between elements that denote entities of the same type (obviously, it does not require the same names to be used in both systems). For example a window seen by the external transformation system can be represented by a node labeled W_{in}, by the internal layout designing system as Wd and by the interior furnishing system as W. To achieve such a matching a basic ontology supporting a communication process is built. The synchronization process proposed in this paper can be described in three steps. When one of grammars (referred to as an initiator) wants to apply a transformation affecting a shared element of a building, it has to initiate a synchronization process. Then, the second grammar (called a responder) checks data passed by an initiator and selects an appropriate transformation from its set and checks whether it can be applied. There exist three possible scenarios: (i) Production can be applied: all elements it affects are locked until the final decision from the initiator is received. The response

ACCEPT is sent to the initiator. (ii) The Responder cannot decide immediately if a production can be applied (e.g., due to some additional operations to be completed). The response (ACCEPT or REFUSE) is sent to the initiator with some delay. (iii) Production cannot be applied. The response REFUSE is sent to the initiator.

In response to the positive answer from the responder, the initiator decides whether to go on with the transformation. Even if the received response is positive, the initiator can still decide to abandon the transformation (for example, when the responder answer arrived too late and the initiator has decided to perform another action).

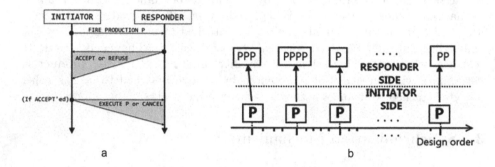

a   b

Fig. 4. Initiator-responder interactions: (a) Production synchronization scheme. Grey shaded areas denote that a message may be sent with a delay (not immediately), (b) An initiator's action P, performed in a shared environment (major ticks), require several subsequent actions on the responder's side. Minor ticks mark other actions, performed on an initiator's side only.

When the initiator decides to perform the transformation, the responder has to perform relevant operations, otherwise he releases all locked elements. Let us note that the responder action, triggered by the initiator request, may be a single production or a sequence of productions (see Fig. 4b).

4   Case Study

For a building design case study we have three types of transformations. The first one is an external design system responsible for tasks related to the project of the building solid and its external parts. The second one is responsible for the internal layout, i.e., division of the floors into spaces, flats, halls, as well as distribution of internal doors and walls. Finally, the third transformation system is used for the interior design of the spaces, that is for the furnishing of rooms.

Let us assume that the transformation system responsible for external design, working on the facade of a building, modifies it by applying subsequent productions belonging to its set of transformation rules. Suppose furthermore that one of the productions being applied, say P, contains a node representing a window being the shared element. Thus, the external transformation system (acting as the initiator in this case) cannot apply this production directly, but has to call the transformation system responsible for design and modification of the internal structure of the building, by calling an appropriate transformation, say T, of the internal system (a responder in this example). Then, as described above, there are four possible scenarios.

1. The left hand side of the production T is matched to the current graph, and the applicability predicate C returns the value TRUE, thus the internal system returns ACCEPT to the initiator.
2. The predicate C returns FALSE, meaning that there is another object attached to the wall represented by the node matched to v_2. In this case however, the responder system may trigger a sequence of productions, s, checking whether it would be possible to move the object attached to the wall to another location within the graph managed by the internal system. If the triggered productions return TRUE, the internal system blocks all elements related to all of these productions and returns ACCEPT to the initiating system.
3. The predicate C returns FALSE, as in the second case, but the responder system cannot trigger any productions to modify the internal structure (for example a place to which the window was to be moved is on the border of two walls and would be separated by the internal wall), thus the responder returns immediately REFUSE.
4. The responding system cannot apply the production directly as it shares the window with the interior design transformation system, so it has to call an appropriate production of this system, thus becoming an initiator, so the synchronization process becomes a recursive one.

When the initiating system receives REFUSE from the responder, it cannot apply the production P. If it receives ACCEPT, there are two possible scenarios:

1. Either the initiator sends EXECUTE P request to the responder which applies all required productions, or the initiator decides not to go on with applying these productions and sends the CANCEL message to the responder which unlocks all relevant elements (i.e., locked previously, in the result of the first initiator request).
2. The second scenario may occur in cases when the responding system delays its response for a very long time due to a large number of internal checks for instance. In such a situation, when a timeout has been reached, the initiator may decide to apply another transformation. Thus, when it finally receives an outdated ACCEPT message it may no longer be interested in applying P.

There are two important observations that have to be made here. Firstly, as in the case of many transformation systems operating on shared elements the recursion resulting from the scenario 4 has to stopped. Second, the synchronization process is always defined between two transformation systems, so the first initiator does not have to be aware that the second system is the initiator of another synchronization process.

5   Conclusions and Future Research

The formal mechanism of synchronization of multiple different hypergraph grammars operating on different graph representations was tested on the case study from the domain of architectural design process. The process was viewed from perspectives of interior furnishing design, internal layout design and exterior design. In the presented example, the operation of shifting a window was considered. For the external design system, it is just an object assigned to the facade of a building. From the interior perspective, a window is an entity assigned to the internal space of a building (room, hall and so on). From the interior design system point of view it is the constraint that has to be taken into account in the placing of some elements. Performing any action on objects which are shared by several environments, may potentially cause conflicts related to violation of design constraints and/or standards. It is possible, for example, that moving a window to a new location (on a building facade) may cause it to coincide with a partition wall inside a building from the internal layout perspective or be covered by a storage unit from the perspective of the furnishing system. The mechanism proposed in this paper allows two separate transformation systems to communicate when they have to perform such potentially conflicting operations and to operate independently when no cooperation is needed. At this stage, we consider a synchronization which either is carried out successfully (i.e., both transformation systems return ACCEPT) or fails altogether. In the future we plan to introduce priorities: a system having the higher priority would force, under certain conditions, changes it requires. Such situations are common in real-life design tasks. To verify the presented approach we also plan to implement it within the framework of a real-world multi-agent system.

It should also be strongly emphasized that the problem of synchronization described above (i.e., related to avoiding conflicts between different transformation systems) is not limited to this context only, and can be used in other domains. It is also worth remarking that the introduced synchronization model can be applied to (hyper-)graph representations derived from other building models (e.g., BIM-based descriptions). Such cases will be presented in our further works.

References

1. buildingSMART. IFC Specification. ISO/PAS 16739 (2005)
2. Dassow, J., Paun, G., Rozenberg, G.: Grammar systems. In: Salomaa, A., Rozenberg, G. (eds.) Handbook of Formal Languages, vol. 2, pp. 155–213. Springer, Heidelberg (1997)
3. Eastman, C., Teicholz, P., Sacks, R., Liston, K.: BIM Handbook: A guide to Building Information Modeling for Owners, Managers, Designers. Wiley, New York (2008)
4. Ehrig, H., Engels, G., Kreowski, H.-J., Rozenberg, G.: Handbook of Graph Grammars and Computing by Graph Transformation: Volume II, Applications, Languages, and Tools. Scientific Publishing, Singapore (1999)

5. Ehrig, H., Kreowski, H.-J., Montanari, U., Rozenberg, G.: Handbook of Graph Grammars and Computing by Graph Transformation: Volume III, Concurrency, Parallelism, and Distribution. Scientific Publishing, Singapore (1999)
6. Grabska, E., Strug, B.: Applying cooperating distributed graph grammars in computer aided design. In: Wyrzykowski, R., Dongarra, J., Meyer, N., Waśniewski, J. (eds.) PPAM 2005. LNCS, vol. 3911, pp. 567–574. Springer, Heidelberg (2006)
7. Grabska, E., Strug, B., Slusarczyk, G.: A graph grammar based model for distributed design. In: Artificial Intelligence and Soft Computing, EXIT (2006)
8. Groger, G., et al.: OpenGIS City Geography Markup Language (CityGML) Encoding Standard. Open Geospatial Consortium Inc., Wayland (2008). OGC 08–007r1
9. Habel, A., Kreowski, H.J.: Some structural aspects of hypergraph languages generated by hyperedge replacement. In: Brandenburg, F.J., Vidal-Naquet, G., Wirsing, M. (eds.) STACS 87. LNCS, vol. 247, pp. 207–215. Springer, Heidelberg (1987)
10. Kotulski, L.: Distributed graphs transformed by multiagent system. In: Rutkowski, L., Tadeusiewicz, R., Zadeh, L.A., Zurada, J.M. (eds.) ICAISC 2008. LNCS (LNAI), vol. 5097, pp. 1234–1242. Springer, Heidelberg (2008)
11. Kotulski, L.: GRADIS – multiagent environment supporting distributed graph transformations. In: Bubak, M., Albada, G.D., Dongarra, J., Sloot, P.M.A. (eds.) ICCS 2008, Part III. LNCS, vol. 5103, pp. 644–653. Springer, Heidelberg (2008)
12. Kotulski, L., Sędziwy, A.: Parallel graph transformations with double pushout grammars. In: Rutkowski, L., Scherer, R., Tadeusiewicz, R., Zadeh, L.A., Zurada, J.M. (eds.) ICAISC 2010, Part II. LNCS, vol. 6114, pp. 280–288. Springer, Heidelberg (2010)
13. Kotulski, L., Strug, B.: Distributed adaptive design with hierarchical autonomous graph transformation systems. In: Shi, Y., van Albada, G.D., Dongarra, J., Sloot, P.M.A. (eds.) ICCS 2007, Part II. LNCS, vol. 4488, pp. 880–887. Springer, Heidelberg (2007)
14. Kotulski, L., Strug, B.: Multi-agent system for distributed adaptive design. Key Eng. Mater. **486**, 217–220 (2011)
15. Kotulski, L., Strug, B.: Supporting communication and cooperation in distributed representation for adaptive design. Adv. Eng. Inf. **27**(2), 220–229 (2013)
16. Nikodem, P., Strug, B.: Graph transformations in evolutionary design. In: Rutkowski, L., Siekmann, J.H., Tadeusiewicz, R., Zadeh, L.A. (eds.) ICAISC 2004. LNCS (LNAI), vol. 3070, pp. 456–461. Springer, Heidelberg (2004)
17. Kotulski, L., Sedziwy, A., Strug, B.: Heterogeneous graph grammars synchronization in CAD systems supported by hypergraph representations of buildings. Expert Syst. Appl. **41**(4), 990–998 (2014)
18. Rozenberg, G.: Handbook of Graph Grammars and Computing by Graph Transformations, vol. 1. World Scientific, London (1997)
19. Tanenbaum, A.S., Van Steen, M.: Distributed Systems: Principles and Paradigms, 1st edn. Prentice Hall PTR, Upper Saddle River (2001)

Authorship Attribution of Polish Newspaper Articles

Marcin Kuta[✉], Bartłomiej Puto, and Jacek Kitowski

Department of Computer Science, Faculty of Computer Science,
Electronics and Telecommunications, AGH University of Science and Technology,
Al. Mickiewicza 30, 30-059 Krakow, Poland
{mkuta,kito}@agh.edu.pl

Abstract. This paper examines the machine learning approach to authorship attribution of articles in the Polish language. The focus is on the effect of the data volume, number of authors and thematic homogeneity on authorship attribution quality. We study the impact of feature selection under various feature selection criteria, mainly chi square and information gain measures, as well as the effect of combining features of different types. Results are reported for the *Rzeczpospolita* corpus in terms of the F_1 measure.

Keywords: Authorship attribution · Feature selection · Chi square · Information gain · Support Vector Machines · k-nearest neighbours · Decision trees · Naïve Bayes

1 Introduction

The task of assigning authorship to an anonymous document based on known writings by candidate authors is known as the authorship attribution problem. The problem of authorship attribution far predates computerization and is as old as the history of documents. One of the most well known cases of disputed attribution involves the so-called *Federalist Papers*, i.e. a set of 85 essays written in 1787–1788 by Alexander Hamilton, John Jay and James Madison. The contested portion comprised 12 articles, with Hamilton and Madison both claiming authorship. The famous solution to this problem, published by Fredrick Mosteller and David Wallace in 1964, focused on statistical methods and attributed authorship of contested articles on the basis of the frequency of function words.

Modern authorship attribution is not limited to literature but finds numerous applications in linguistic forensics (authorship of blackmail or offensive posts), terrorism prevention, suicide trials, plagiarism detection, combating copyright infringements and also (possibly undesirable) surveillance.

The aim of the paper is to improve the effectiveness of machine learning methods when applied to authorship attribution in Polish. The contribution of the paper is as follows:

© Springer International Publishing Switzerland 2016
L. Rutkowski et al. (Eds.): ICAISC 2016, Part II, LNAI 9693, pp. 474–483, 2016.
DOI: 10.1007/978-3-319-39384-1_41

- Investigating the utility of various features on different levels of the language (character, lexical, syntactic) for authorship attribution in the context of the Polish language.
- Examining the impact of feature selection and different feature selection criteria on authorship attribution accuracy.
- Examining the impact of the number of authors, data set size and thematic homogeneity of the corpus on classification accuracy.
- Finding the most suitable machine learning approach and its optimal parameters and hyperparameters for authorship attribution of news articles.
- Studying the influence of bundling features of different types.

2   Related Work

In recent year several solutions to authorship attribution have been proposed. While most of them focus on English, applications to Hebrew [1], Spanish, French, Russian, Czech and Bulgarian [2] are also presented. However, there is a lack of research in the area of the Polish language.

The unitary invariant approach takes into account only one function or marker of the text (e.g. relative frequency as a function of word length), which is believed to differ between authors and remain invariant for texts by a given author. Due to its relative simplicity it is unreliable and presently only of historical value.

Multivariate analysis aggregates many features, including style features and content features, which are used to represent documents in a multidimensional space. The author whose documents are closest (under the selected distance metric) to the document under scrutiny is attributed authorship.

Machine learning approaches are considered the state of the art in authorship attribution. However, while they yield the best results for small numbers of candidate authors, large candidate pools are more accurately processed by similarity-based techniques [3, 4].

Another important avenue of research focuses on engineering features suitable for authorship attribution, with hundreds of features representing different levels of a language (character, syntactic and semantic) proposed.

Apart from basic authorship attribution, more sophisticated problems are also considered, depending upon the number of candidate authors, $|\mathcal{C}|$:

Finding a needle-in-a-haystack $|\mathcal{C}| \to \infty$ – a variation of the authorship attribution problem, where there may be many thousands of potential candidate authors. This may happen e.g., when seeking authorship of a blog. With a large number of suspects, the machine learning approach yields poor accuracy, but acceptable results can be obtained assuming that a non-decisive'do not know' answer may be returned in certain cases.

Authorship verification $|\mathcal{C}| = 1$ – there is exactly one candidate author (a suspect). The problem is to determine whether the suspect is the author of the examined document or not. The difficulty of the problem arises from the fact that while it is straightforward to add to the corpus available texts of a suspect, it is impossible to compile a corpus representing a non-suspect class (i.e. all authors except the suspect).

Author profiling $|\mathcal{C}| = 0$ – no set of candidate authors is given and the problem is to analyze the document and determine the author's profile, including their gender, age, native language and personality dimensions.

In this paper we focus on the basic authorship attribution problem where there is a closed set of candidate authors, $0 < |\mathcal{C}| \ll \infty$, undisputed writing samples are available for each candidate and the actual author of the analyzed document belongs to $\mathcal{C}$.

3   Machine Learning Approaches

We have applied the following machine learning approaches: Support Vector Machines (SVM) [5], k-nearest neighbours (k-NN) [6], decision trees [7], naïve Bayes [8], feedforward neural networks [9] and Random Forests [10].

Support Vector Machines were used with linear kernel with optimization problem solved in primal space. In the k-NN method we used a neighborhood of size 5. To construct decision trees, an optimized version of the CART algorithm was chosen. In naïve Bayes classification multinomial distribution corresponding to the size of the vocabulary. modeled the probability of occurrence of a word in a document. Feedforward neural network (multilayer perceptron, MLP) architecture consisted of 3 layers with the number of units in the input layer equal to number of features (dimension of document vector), 200 units in the hidden layer and the number of outputs equal to the number of considered authors. The hidden layer was activated by the tanh function while the output layer used the softmax activation function [11]. Training lasted 150 epochs. Random Forest was built as an ensemble of 150 decision trees.

4   Evaluation Datasets

The authorship attribution experiments have been conducted using a subset of *Rzeczpospolita* corpus. This corpus is particularly suitable for authorship attribution experiments as its articles vary with respect to content, category and author. Each document is preannotated with its category and author. At the same time the corpus is screened for nationality/native language, author education, genre, and period during which each article was authored.

In experiments with a heterogeneous dataset, articles originated from the following 5 categories: culture, law, real estate, science and technology, and sports. Articles in single-topic datasets came from the law category. The characteristics of datasets extracted from the *Rzeczpospolita* corpus are summarized in Table 1.

The content of each article, as well as information about its category and author (for evaluation purposes), were extracted from HTML files and stored in an SQLite database. Requested feature representations of articles were created

Table 1. Characteristics of datasets used in experiments

Dataset name	Authors	Homogeneity	Training articles per author	Testing articles per author	Words per document
V1	15	Single-category	20	10	444
V2	5	Single-category	40	10	575
V3	5	Single-category	20	10	643
E1	15	Single-category	20	10	351
E2	5	Single-category	40	10	359
E3	5	Single-category	20	10	357
E3	5	Multi-category	20	10	478

on the basis of texts stored in the database. Each article corresponded to a vector in Vector Space Model space represented by features of one or many types selected from among the following: character n-grams, word n-grams (sequences of n consecutive words, where n is fixed), function words, base form and POS tags.

The character n-grams representation was straightforward to obtain. The remaining representations required text tokenization and some of them also required sentence splitting. The POS feature representation was obtained with further help from the TaKIPI POS tagger. Finally, features were subject to feature standardization so that the mean value of each feature across all documents was equal to 0 and its standard deviation was equal to 1.

Quality of authorship attribution was evaluated in terms of the F_1 measure [12], which is defined as the harmonic mean of precision, $prec$, and recall, rec:

$$F_1 = \frac{2 \cdot prec \cdot rec}{prec + rec}. \tag{1}$$

5 Experiments and Results

Seven main experiments were conducted, with a total of 1500 subexperiments performed. In six experiments we focused on classification with 3 methods: SVM, k-NN and decision trees. The seventh experiment reports results for all 6 machine learning classifiers. To reduce the dependence of results on a specific test/train dataset split, each reported measurement was computed as an arithmetic mean of 15 independent runs with random assignment to training or test article sets while maintaining the required ratio of training to test sets.

5.1 Validation

The aim of the first experiment was to find optimal values of parameters and hyperparameters: the penalty parameter, C, of the error term for SVM classifier, neighborhood size, k, of k-NN methods and number of base estimators constituting the Random Forest.

For 3 classifiers (SVM, k-NN, decision trees) the following feature type parameters were also explored: size of character n-grams, size of word n-grams, complexity of POS tags (simple vs complex tags). Values of parameters were fixed in validation data **V1–V3**, as opposed to test data. The obtained values of parameters and hyperparameters are given in Table 2.

Table 2. Optimal values of parameters and hyperparameters

Parameter	SVM	k-NN	Decision trees
Size of character n-grams	4	6	4
Size of word n-grams	2	2	2
POS tagset	Complex	Simple	Simple
Hyperparameter	SVM	k-NN	Random forest
Penalty parameter, C	1	–	–
Neighborhood size, k	–	5	–
Number of estimators	–	–	150

5.2 Effect of Data Size, Number of Authors and Thematic Homogeneity

The second experiment examined the impact of the number of candidate authors upon classification accuracy. Results are shown in Fig. 1. An intuitive dependency can be observed: the greater the number of candidate authors, the lower the accuracy. The best results are obtained with base form and character n-gram feature representations, and are much better than for all other feature representations. The drop in effectiveness along with growing number of candidate authors is much gentler than the one reported in [13].

The third experiment examined the link between the size of the available evidence (articles with known authorship) and classification accuracy. Results shown in Fig. 2 indicate that a larger body of evidence enables more accurate attribution. The plot confirms that best results are obtained with base form and character n-gram feature representations while the POS tags representation gives the worst results.

The fourth experiment investigated the effect of thematic homogeneity upon authorship attribution. Figure 3 shows the effects of thematic homogeneity for training sets consisting of 20 articles of 5 authors. Multi-category texts were easier to distinguish than single-category texts, which could be explained by the fact that, apart from implicit clues given by author style, we can exploit differences between texts imposed by thematic diversification of multi-category datasets. It is worth noting that the difference between single- and multi-category datasets is lowest for function words, compared to other feature representations. This is due to natural robustness of function words with regard to context information.

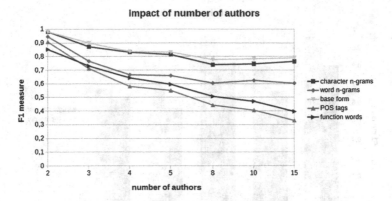

Fig. 1. Influence of the number of authors upon attribution with SVM. Evaluation performed using various feature representations of the **E1** dataset

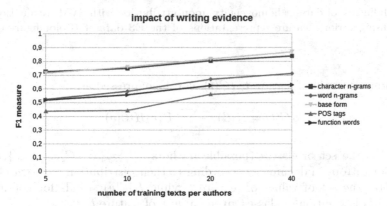

Fig. 2. Influence of the number of training texts upon attribution with SVM. Evaluation performed using various feature representations of the **E2** dataset

5.3   Feature Selection

The fifth experiment examined the effect of feature selection. As feature utility measures we used χ^2 and information gain measures, in addition to frequency criterion and random selection. The χ^2 measure of feature t is defined as follows:

$$\chi^2(t) = \sum_i \sum_j \frac{(E_{ij} - O_{ij})^2}{E_{ij}}, \tag{2}$$

where E_{ij} stands for the expected number of occurrences of feature t with value v_i in documents of the j-th class while O_{ij} stands for the observed number of occurrences of feature t with value v_i in documents of the j-th class, C_j.

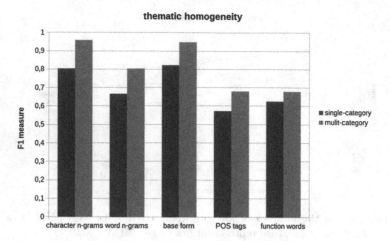

Fig. 3. Influence of dataset homogeneity upon attribution with SVM. Evaluation performed using various feature representations of the **E3** dataset (Color figure online)

Information gain of feature t, $IG(t)$, can be expressed as:

$$IG(t) = H(\mathcal{C}) - \sum_{v \in V_t} P(v)H(\mathcal{C}|v), \tag{3}$$

where $\mathcal{C}$ is the set of classes (possible authors), $\mathcal{C} = \{ C_1, C_2, \ldots C_m \}$, $H(\mathcal{C})$ stands for entropy of documents according to their distribution in target classes, V_t denotes the set of values of feature t while $H(\mathcal{C}|v)$ stands for conditional entropy of distribution of classes given value v of feature t.

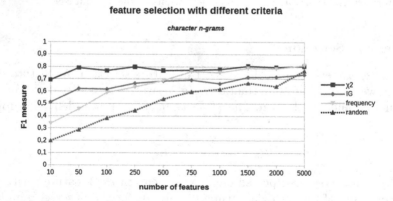

Fig. 4. Comparison of the impact of feature selection criteria upon authorship attribution with SVM. Evaluation performed on the single-topic part of the **E3** dataset represented with character n-gram features

Figure 4 presents the impact of different selection methods on authorship attribution performed using the SVM approach. In addition to χ^2 and IG criteria, the frequency criterion and a random criterion were tested. As expected the random criterion gives the worst results and is outperformed by the frequency criterion. Nevertheless, to obtain better results we have to resort to more sophisticated criteria: IG and χ^2.

The difference between χ^2 over IG is illustrated in Fig. 5, which provides more insight regarding the relation between IG and χ^2. Decreasing values of IG are not matched by similar decreases in χ^2, instead, χ^2 exhibits spikes at places of stepwise decrease of IG. The reason for this is that while IG takes into account distribution of features between authors, χ^2 depends on distribution between authors as well as between documents.

Information gain does not acknowledge per-document feature distribution differences and instead favors features which occur only for one specific author. In Fig. 5 features with greatest IG values are mostly those specific to a single author. Differences between χ^2 and IG are particularly apparent for article representations exploiting small numbers of features, which is the case for function words and POS tags representations.

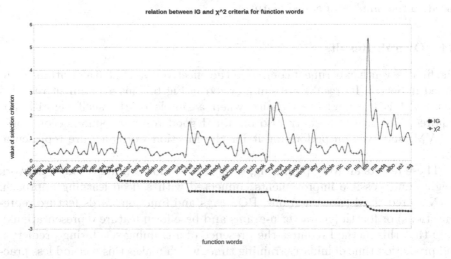

Fig. 5. Relation between IG and χ^2 feature selection measures for most frequent function words observed in the single-topic part of the E3 dataset

We conclude that the χ^2 statistic is the best feature selection criterion, yielding good attribution results with a small number of features. In contrast to other classifiers, it is hard to improve authorship attribution effectiveness with feature selection using SVM. This is in agreement with observations reported in [14].

The sixth experiment examined feature aggregation, which means combining features of different types (e.g. character n-grams, word n-grams and function words) in one article representation. In general, feature aggregation yields only

comparison of classifiers

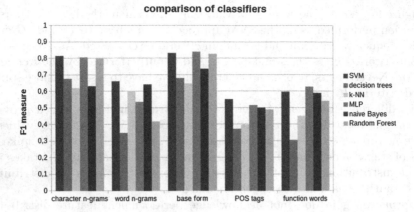

Fig. 6. Comparison of 6 machine learning approaches to authorship attribution. Evaluation performed using various feature representations of the **E3** dataset. (Color figure online)

slight improvements (according to the F_1 measure), disproportionally low compared to the number of added features.

5.4   Overall Results

The final, seventh experiment compared the effectiveness of all 6 algorithms mentioned in Sect. 3. Its results are summarized in Fig. 6. This experiment revealed that SVM is the method of choice when a simple off-the shelf algorithm is required. The neural network also obtained good results, coming second only to SVM, and even outperforming it for the function words feature representation.

These results are very promising, given the random initialization of network weights and possible improvements connected with a deep learning approach. k-NN scored third (word n-grams, POS tags and function words feature representations) or fourth (character n-grams and base form feature representations). Note that this method requires the presence of a training set during prediction and prediction time dominates training time, which makes this method less practical. The reader should be aware of these limitations as the k-NN based method was singled out for extensive analysis in [13].

Naïve Bayes usually scored last (with the exception of the word n-grams representation, where it scored second), giving better-than-expected results when employed as a baseline method.

6   Conclusions

In the paper we investigated 6 machine learning methods for authorship attribution with in-depth focus on 3 methods: SVM, k-NN and decision trees.

Datasets were represented with feature types associated with various levels of the language: character n-grams, word n-grams, base forms, function words and POS tags. Character n-gram and base form representations turned out to be the most suitable for authorship attribution in Polish. The SVM method gave the best results, however results obtained by the neural network were also very promising. Feature selection does not improve the effectiveness of SVM, but is useful for authorship attribution with other classifiers, with χ^2 being the most suitable feature selection criterion.

Acknowledgments. This research is supported by AGH - University of Science and Technology (AGH-UST) Grant no. 11.11.230.124 (statutory project).

References

1. Dershowitz, I., Koppel, M., Akiva, N., Dershowitz, N.: Computerized source criticism of biblical texts. J. Biblical Lit. **134**(2), 253–271 (2015)
2. Koppel, M., Schler, J., Argamon, S.: Computational methods in authorship attribution. J. Am. Soc. Inform. Sci. Technol. **60**(1), 9–26 (2009)
3. Koppel, M., Schler, J., Argamon, S., Messeri, E.: Authorship attribution with thousands of candidate authors. In: Proceedings of the 29th Annual International ACM SIGIR Conference on Research and Development in Information Retrieval, SIGIR 2006, pp. 659–660 (2006)
4. Luyckx, K., Daelemans, W.: Authorship attribution and verification with many authors and limited data. In: Proceedings of the Twenty-Second International Conference on Computational Linguistics (COLING 2008), Manchester, UK, pp. 513–520 (2008)
5. Cortes, C., Vapnik, V.: Support-vector networks. Mach. Learn. **20**(3), 273–297 (1995)
6. Dasarasthy, B.: Nearest Neighbor Pattern Classification Techniques. IEEE Computer Society Press, Los Alamitos (1991)
7. Quinlan, J.R.: Induction of decision trees. Mach. Learn. **1**(1), 81–106 (1986)
8. McCallum, A., Nigam, K.: A comparison of event models for Naïve Bayes text classification. In: Learning for Text Categorization: Papers from the 1998 AAAI Workshop, pp. 41–48 (1998)
9. Rumelhart, D., Hinton, G., Williams, R.: Learning representations by back-propagating errors. Nature **323**(6088), 533–536 (1986)
10. Breiman, L.: Random forests. Mach. Learn. **45**(1), 5–32 (2001)
11. Bridle, J.: Training stochastic model recognition algorithms as networks can lead to maximum mutual information estimation of parameters. In: Touretzky, D. (ed.) Advances in Neural Information Processing Systems, pp. 211–217. Morgan Kaufman (1990)
12. van Rijsbergen, C.J.: Information Retrieval. Butterworth, Newton (1979)
13. Luyckx, K., Daelemans, W.: The effect of author set size and data size in authorship attribution. Literary Linguist. Comput. **26**(1), 35–55 (2011)
14. Forman, G.: An extensive empirical study of feature selection metrics for text classification. J. Mach. Learn. Res. **3**, 1289–1305 (2003)

Use of Different Movement Mechanisms in Cockroach Swarm Optimization Algorithm for Traveling Salesman Problem

Joanna Kwiecień[(✉)]

AGH University of Science and Technology, 30 Mickiewicza Ave.,
30-059 Krakow, Poland
kwiecien@agh.edu.pl

Abstract. This paper presents a new adaptation of the cockroach swarm optimization (CSO) algorithm to effectively solve the traveling salesman problem. Proposed modifications investigate the crossover operators in *chase-swarming* procedure and directed dispersion of cockroaches. To analyze the benefits of such modifications, the performance of the considered approach is tested on well-known instances. Presented results of all experiments indicate that practical implementation of the CSO algorithm, which includes the sequential constructive crossover (SCX) and *2-opt* move is a good approach.

Keywords: Cockroach swarm optimization · Traveling salesman problem · Crossover operators · Discrete optimization

1 Introduction

Various nature-inspired metaheuristics based on existing mechanisms of a biological phenomenon have been widely studied in the literature and used in solving various optimization problems. A survey on numerous examples of these algorithms and their applications can be found in [22,23]. One of the recently proposed methods belonging to the population-based algorithms inspired by nature is the cockroach swarm optimization (CSO) algorithm, which is modeled after the habits of cockroaches looking for food [3,4]. In its structure one can find their chase-swarming, dispersing and ruthless behaviors applied to the solution search space. CSO was originally developed for continuous domains, but with some additional assumptions it can be used to solve discrete optimization problems, including flow shop scheduling problems [13,14], traveling salesman problem [5,14] and vehicle routing problem [4].

The traveling salesman problem (TSP) is one of the most intensively studied problems in discrete optimization. Various methods have been developed for solving the TSP, a comprehensive overview can be found in [7,12]. For discrete versions of known population-based algorithms, suitable parameter settings and appropriate interpretation of species movement are necessary in order for them to work effectively [6,14].

© Springer International Publishing Switzerland 2016
L. Rutkowski et al. (Eds.): ICAISC 2016, Part II, LNAI 9693, pp. 484–493, 2016.
DOI: 10.1007/978-3-319-39384-1_42

The main motivation of the paper is to improve the searching capability of the cockroach swarm optimization (CSO) algorithm through integration of crossover operators and a *2-opt* move, and to verify whether the proposed approach can be applied to the traveling salesman problem. Hence, our attention was directed to investigating the efficiency of individual movement in swarming and dispersing procedures and computational performance of the implemented algorithm.

The paper is organized as follows. In Sect. 2 we provide a short description of the traveling salesman problem and a brief overview of various methods for solving the TSP. Section 3 gives a description of the cockroach swarm optimization algorithm and its proposed modifications for solving TSP. In Sect. 4 the computational results of conducted experiments are presented. Finally, Sect. 5 contains concluding remarks.

2   Traveling Salesman Problem

For a given set of cities from 1 to N and a cost matrix $C = [c_{i,j}]$, where each value $c_{i,j}$ represents the cost of traveling between cities i and j, a solution of the traveling salesman problem can be represented as a permutation $\pi = (\pi(1), ..., \pi(N))$, $\pi(i) \in N$ represents the city visited in step i, $i = 1, ..., n$, which minimizes the following objective function [7,16]:

$$f(\pi) = \sum_{i=1}^{N-1} c_{\pi(i),\pi(i+1)} + c_{\pi(N),\pi(1)} \tag{1}$$

Therefore, the goal is to find the minimal cost of the closed tour such that all cities are visited exactly once. If all cities are described by their coordinates (x,y) and distances between cities are Euclidean, we have an Euclidean TSP. In this paper, TSP refers to the symmetric TSP: distances $c_{i,j}$ and $c_{j,i}$ between two cities i and j are equal.

The TSP arises in many applications, including logistics and transportation, where it is important to optimize routes in terms of length and duration [7]. It is also used in automated guided vehicle systems that make decisions about choosing the shortest path of robots delivering goods, in circuit board design and in X-ray crystallography [2,18]. It should be noted that the TSP is a special case of quadratic assignment problems.

There is extensive literature about the TSP and methods applied to solve this problem. A large number of varying, nature-inspired approaches have been suggested to solve the TSP [12], for example genetic algorithms [10,17], ant colony metaheuristic [8], particle swarm optimization [9,20], firefly algorithm [14, 19], cockroach swarm optimization [5,14] and cuckoo search [16].

Including local search to structure of several approximation algorithms can improve their efficiency and make the search process more complete, but does not guarantee that good solutions will be reached.

3   Cockroach Swarm Optimization and Its Adaptation to TSP

The following section will deal with the CSO for solving the TSP. In continuous optimization problems, the distance between any two cockroaches can be calculated using Euclidian distance. For combinatorial problems, one can use Hamming distance between two solutions.

3.1   Cockroach Swarm Optimization Algorithm

The cockroach swarm optimization (CSO) algorithm is inspired by observing the abilities of cockroaches to look for food. The behaviors of cockroaches such as moving in swarms and scattering or escaping from light are the basis of this method [3–5]. The initial population is randomly distributed across the entire search space. Analyzing *chase-swarming* procedure, the strongest cockroaches form small swarms and follow the global optimum. There is a possibility that in a small swarm the follower will find a better solution, because it does not move the same way as its local optimum. In the CSO algorithm, each cockroach X_i moves to local optimum P_i in the area of its visibility. The best local optimum is a global optimum at the end of the cycle, denoted as P_g. In order to assist the algorithm so as to avoid getting stuck in local minima, each cockroach is randomly dispersed. Another important concept of the CSO algorithm is the phenomenon of replacing a randomly chosen individual by the currently best individual. It imitates the natural behavior of cockroaches facing a lack of food, when the stronger cockroach eats the weaker.

The pseudo-code of the CSO algorithm can be stated as follows [3,5,22]:

Step 1. Randomly generate the initial population of n cockroaches; initialize algorithm's parameters: *step*, scope of visibility (*visual*), stopping criteria, space dimension(D); the ith individual represents a vector $X_i = (x_{i1}, x_{i2}, ..., x_{iD})$, $i = 1, 2, ..., n$.

Step 2. Search P_i (the optimal individual within the visual scope of cockroach X_i) and P_g (the global optimal individual)

Step 3. Perform chase-swarming as follows:

– If a cockroach X_i is local optimum, then it goes to P_g:

$$X_i = X_i + step * rand * (P_g - X_i) \qquad (2)$$

– Otherwise, the cockroach goes to a local optimum of P_i:

$$X_i = X_i + step * rand * (P_i - X_i) \qquad (3)$$

Update P_g

Step 4. Implement dispersing behavior: $X_i = X_i + rand(1, D)$, update P_g.

Step 5. Implement ruthless behavior by $X_k = P_g$, or $X_k = 0$; k is a random integer within $[1, n]$.

Step 6. If a termination criterion is met then output the results; otherwise go back to Step 2.

Coefficient *rand* defined in Eqs. (2) and (3) is a random number within $[0, 1]$ generated for each cockroach. It allows for a random movement towards the better individual.

3.2   CSO Adaptation for the Traveling Salesman Problem

To apply the CSO algorithm to solve the traveling salesman problem, we therefore need defining movement in the search space and to employ in the structure of the considered algorithm. Instead of redefining positions of individuals, we propose to use crossover operators known from genetic algorithms and modified dispersion that allow for the adaptation of the CSO algorithm to the considered problem. The presented adaptation incorporates three crossover operators and modifies the dispersion procedure based on the *2-opt* move. As mentioned above, each cockroach generates one solution randomly at the beginning of the process.

In *chase-swarming* procedure, a weaker cockroach tends toward the better solution, and comparing sequentially the elements in two permutations moves towards the cockroach representing a shorter route. Such a step can be defined in various ways and some movement strategies can be adapted to improve the performance of the CSO algorithm.

In the traveling salesman problem, each city may only be visited once. Therefore, traditional crossover methods may not provide a good tour. To overcome this problem, we consider various types of crossover operators such as partially-mapped, order and sequential constructive crossovers in *chase-swarming* procedure. More information on different crossover operators can be found in [15].

Partially-mapped crossover (PMX) was developed by Goldberg and Lingle [11]. While creating new solutions, the PMX operator starts with a random choice of two cut positions in permutations (the same in both parents). Cities located in such subsequence are swapped (by mapping) between two parents. Additional cities in other positions are rewritten if they are not present in the created permutations. Otherwise, if there is conflict, cities are replaced with the use of a mapping relationship.

The second well-known crossover that may be applied in the CSO algorithm is order crossover (OX) [15]. It assumes two cut points selected randomly in two parent permutations. Then, a subsequence between these points is copied into the offspring. Next, a set of nodes (not yet placed in the offspring) is created, starting from the first node after the second cut point in the second parent. After reaching the end of the parent string, to make a set complete, we continue from the beginning of this parent. Empty positions in the newly created permutation are sequentially supplemented by the nodes of the mentioned set, starting from the first node after the end of the replaced section.

As the third way of movement, the sequential constructive crossover (SCX) [1] is applied. This operator uses the evaluation procedure of the new solutions in the crossover process. A new solution is created by sequentially selecting the better of two edges of the parent solutions. In some cases, the new edges that do not exist in the parent solutions are also taken into account when creating an offspring. In this way, the chance of creating a good solution increases during such a process.

The SCX operator creates one new solution as follows [1]:

Step 1. Start from First Node (FN) of two parent solutions.

Step 2. Sequentially search both of the parent solutions and consider the first unvisited node (called *legitimate node*, LN) appearing after FN in each parent solution (let a pair of unvisited nodes be: α in the first parent solution and β in the second one). If no LN is present in any of the parent solutions, sequentially search the nodes from the set of sorted nodes and the first unvisited is considered as LN.

Step 3. If $c_{FN,\alpha} < c_{FN,\beta}$ then select node α as the next node (otherwise node β) and concatenate it to the partially constructed offspring solution. Rename the present node as FN. Stop if the offspring tour is complete; otherwise go to Step 2.

Similarly, in the dispersing procedure, there are several ways to perform a step in the search space. In the basic version of CSO presented in the literature, this is performed by the random step. In permutation problems, random movement is commonly represented by the swap operator that generates a new cockroach position by exchanging two randomly selected cities. In order to increase the efficiency of the algorithm, an alternative approach could be the use of directed dispersion based on the *2-opt* algorithm, first introduced in [14]. It relies on the idea of finding a better solution by exchanging two selected edges in the graph, such as *2-opt* algorithm. The aforementioned modification comprises reducing the set of candidate edge pairs. Edge selection for the exchange is performed at random based on the assumption that each edge in the graph is replaced with at least one randomly selected edge. If the new solution obtained by exchanging the edges is better than the current one, it becomes the current solution.

Taking into account the adaptation described above, the scheme of proposed discrete CSO algorithm for the TSP can be illustrated by Algorithm 1.

4   Experiments and Results

We developed many experiments to assess the performance of the proposed procedures. The first series of experiments aimed at determining the best crossover operator in *chase-swarming* procedure. In the second group, the performance of the proposed modification based on SCX operator and directed dispersion was tested. To compare different mechanisms of movement, many runs of the proposed approaches were executed and solution quality was taken into account. For experiments we used the benchmarks taken from the TSPLIB that is available at http://www.iwr.uni-heidelberg.de/groups/comopt/software/TSPLIB95/. In all tests the swarm size is considered to be the size of test problem, *visual* is around 40 % of population size and the maximum number of iterations is 1000.

Algorithm 1. CSO algorithm to TSP

1: Initialize:
2:   parameters of test instance from TSPLIB;
3:   parameters of CSO algorithm: k - number of cockroaches, $visual$, $MaxIT$ - maximum number of iterations
4: **for** $i = 1$ to k **do**
5:     generate randomly;
6:     evaluate quality (length of tour)
7: **end for**
8: find the best solution P_g in initial population
9: **while** iteration $< MaxIT$ **do**
10:     **for** $i = 1$ to k **do**   ▷ Start procedure: $chase - swarming$
11:       **for** $j = 1$ to k **do**
12:         **if** the tour of cockroach j is shorter than the tour of cockroach i, within its $visual$ **then**
13:           move cockroach i towards j (crossover operator)
14:         **end if**
15:         **if** the tour of cockroach i is local optimum (within its $visual$) **then**
16:           move cockroach i towards P_g (crossover operator)
17:         **end if**
18:       **end for** j
19:     **end for** i
20:     **if** new solution is better than P_g **then**
21:       update P_g (cockroach i is a current global solution)
22:     **end if**
23:     **for** $i = 1$ to k **do**   ▷ Start procedure: $random\ dispersion$
24:       move cockroach randomly (swap operator)
25:       **if** the new position is better than P_g **then**
26:         update P_g;
27:       **end if**
28:     **end for**
29:     **for** each cockroach **do**   ▷ Start procedure: $directed\ dispersion$
30:       **for** each position t_a in solution **do**
31:         select the random set of edges to remove (lk)
32:         **for** each edge $b = 1 : lk$ **do**
33:           remove edge $a = (t_a, t_{a+1})$ and b
34:           add new pair of edges according to $2\text{-}opt$
35:           calculate length of the new tour;
36:           **if** the new solution is better **then**
37:             update current solution
38:           **end if**
39:         **end for**
40:       **end for**
41:     **end for**
42:     **if** the new solution is better than Pg **then**
43:       update Pg
44:     **end if**
45:     select cockroach m randomly   ▷ Start procedure: $ruthless\ behavior$
46:     replace cockroach m by the best global cockroach
47: **end while**
48: return the best one as sub-optimal tour

It is important to note that for each instance, all experiments were done using fixed parameters during all iterations.

4.1   Crossover Operator in Chase-Swarming Procedure

Various types of crossover operators such as PMX, OX and SCX were applied to verify the impact of different movement on the results of the CSO algorithm. For experiments we used the problem *eil51* taken from the TSPLIB collection with the known value of optimal tour (426).

Detailed results of experiments are given in Table 1. The first column shows the type of crossover operator, the second column (*Best*) presents the best solutions found by the considered algorithm, the third column (*Av*) gives the average solution of 10 independent runs. The columns *Dev_best* and *Dev_av* stand for the relative deviation of the found solution from the best known value (*ref*), calculated as $Dev\_best = \frac{Best - ref}{ref} \cdot 100\,\%$ and $Dev\_av = \frac{Av - ref}{ref} \cdot 100\,\%$. We have found that the SCX operator achieves the best results in the case of *eil51*. From Table 1 one can see that the use of this operator can reduce both *Dev* results. Therefore, we recommend the choice of the SCX operator in other instances.

Table 1. Comparison of the results with different movement schemes for eil51

Operator	Best	Av	Dev_best [%]	Dev_av [%]
SCX	448,27	464,37	5,23	9,01
PMX	516,47	547,68	21,24	28,56
OX	731,51	780,66	71,72	83,26

4.2   Mechanism of Dispersion

In order to demonstrate the impact of the dispersing strategy, several benchmarks are tackled using the CSO algorithm. To achieve this goal, we conducted many experiments on 8 instances stored in TSPLIB. The dimensions of the selected problems range from 51 to 225 cities. Based on previous research, for all cases the SCX operator was used. The obtained results are summarized in Tables 2 and 3, which display the name of instances, their reference solutions from TSPLIB, the best solutions found by the implemented algorithms, the average solutions of 10 independent runs and the relative deviations of the found solutions from reference solutions (see Sect. 4.1).

Unfortunately, in none of the presented experiments were the best solutions obtained for the benchmark problems used. However, the CSO algorithm with the SCX operator and directed dispersion returned better values of goal function than one using the swap operator in dispersing procedure.

Based on the relative deviations of the found solutions from Table 3, it should be noted that for five instances (*eil51, berlin52, st70, pr76, kroA100*) the proposed approach with SCX and directed dispersion finds the best solutions near

Table 2. Results of experiments obtained by the discrete cockroach approach with SCX and swap operator

Instance	Opt	Best	Av	Dev_best [%]	Dev_av [%]
eil51	426	448,27	464,37	5,23	9,01
berlin52	7542	7732,49	7992,35	2,53	5,97
st70	675	723,93	743,74	7,25	10,18
eil76	538	576,95	584,75	7,24	8,69
pr76	108159	117351	120279,78	8,50	11,21
kroA100	21282	23271,80	23882,06	9,35	12,22
rat195	2323	2485,07	2550,23	6,98	9,78
ts225	126643	134982	137271,6	6,59	8,39

Table 3. Results of experiments obtained by the discrete cockroach approach with SCX and directed dispersion

Instance	Opt	Best	Av	Dev_best [%]	Dev_av [%]
eil51	426	428,83	432,78	0,66	1,59
berlin52	7542	7544,37	7731,22	0,03	2,51
st70	675	677,11	691,12	0,31	2,39
eil76	538	552,39	562,37	2,68	4,53
pr76	108159	109049,00	110044,67	0,82	1,74
kroA100	21282	21381,30	21596,05	0,47	1,48
rat195	2323	2436,80	2478,15	4,90	6,68
ts225	126643	128881,00	129483,75	1,77	2,24

optimal, with values of *Dev_best* less than 1 %. In all instances the results show that such directed dispersion based on *2-opt* is more efficient than random movement and for the best solution it yields *Dev_best* between 0,03 % and 4,90 %.

5   Conclusion

In this paper, we propose some modifications in a discrete version of CSO algorithm to solve the traveling salesman problem by adapting the mechanism of moving one cockroach towards another. We introduce and compare various types of movement in the discussed algorithm based on crossover operators known from genetic algorithms. Beside these, described method based on the *2-opt* move was used to assist the cockroach swarm optimization algorithm in obtaining a solution of the TSP. All tests were made to show the performance of CSO with the proposed mechanisms. It is also revealed that the proposed algorithm outperforms the results of this approach without the described modification.

Experimental results show that selecting the appropriate method in *chase-swarming* procedure and directed dispersion can improve the results of CSO. We are merely presenting a study about the quality of the obtained solutions with the considered modifications. Therefore, the results might be better in the case of using optimal settings of parameter values, higher population size or parallel version of CSO algorithm. It should be mentioned, that parallel implementation on OpenCL platform of other metaheuristics accelerates optimization tasks and provides better performance in the case of quadratic assignment problem, which models the TSP. For example in [21] parallel implementation of particle swarm optimization to solve QAP was discussed. In our approach with directed dispersion and crossover operators, the performance takes more computational time. Hence, one possibility for future research is the performance of GPU implementation for the CSO algorithm to solve combinatorial problems.

References

1. Ahmed, Z.H.: Genetic algorithm for the traveling salesman problem using sequential constructive crossover. Int. J. Biom. Bioinform. **3**, 96–105 (2010)
2. Bland, R.G., Shallcross, D.F.: Large travelling salesman problems arising from experiments in X-ray crystallography: a preliminary report on computation. Oper. Res. Lett. **8**, 125–128 (1989)
3. Chen, Z.: A modified cockroach swarm optimization. Energy Procedia **11**, 4–9 (2011)
4. Chen, Z., Tang, H.: Cockroach swarm optimization for vehicle routing problems. Energy Procedia **13**, 30–35 (2011)
5. Cheng, L., Wang, Z., Yanhong, S., Guo, A.: Cockroach swarm optimization algorithm for TSP. Adv. Eng. Forum **1**, 226–229 (2011)
6. Clerc, M.: Discrete particle swarm optimization illustrated by the traveling salesman problem. In: Onwubolu, G.C., Babu, B.V. (eds.) New Optimization Techniques in Engineering, vol. 141, pp. 219–239. Springer, Heidelberg (2004)
7. Davendra, D.: Traveling Salesman Problem, Theory and Applications. InTech Publisher, Rijeka (2010)
8. Dorigo, M., Gambardella, L.: Ant colonies for the traveling salesman problem. BioSystems **43**, 73–81 (1997)
9. Goldbarg, E., Goldbarg, M., de Souza, G.: Particle swarm optimization algorithm for the traveling salesman problem. In: Greco, F. (ed.) Travelling Salesman Problem, pp. 75–96. I-Tech Publisher, Vienna (2008)
10. Goldberg, D.E.: Genetic Algorithms in Search, Optimization, and Machine Learning. Addison-Wesley, Boston (1989)
11. Goldberg, D.E., Lingle, R.: Alleles, loci, and the traveling salesman problem. In: Proceedings of an International Conference on Genetic Algorithms and Their Applications, pp. 154–159, Pittsburgh, PA, USA (1985)
12. Gupta, D.: Solving TSP using various meta-heuristic algorithms. Int. J. Recent Contrib. Eng. Sci. IT **1**(2), 22–26 (2013)
13. Kwiecień, J., Filipowicz, B.: Comparison of firefly and cockroach algorithms in selected discrete and combinatorial problems. Bull. Pol. Acad. Sci. Tech. Sci. **62**(4), 797–804 (2014)

14. Kwiecień, J.: Swarm algorithms to solve selected problems of discrete and combinatorial optimization. AGH University of Science and Technology Press (2015). (in Polish)
15. Michalewicz, Z., Fogel, D.: How to Solve It: Modern Heuristics, 2nd edn. Springer, Heidelberg (2004)
16. Ouaarab, A., Ahiod, B., Yang, X.: Discrete cuckoo search algorithm for the travelling salesman problem. Neural Comput. Appl. **24**(7–8), 1659–1669 (2014)
17. Potvin, J.: Genetic algorithms for the traveling salesman problem. Oper. Res. **63**(3), 337–370 (1996)
18. Ravikumar, C.P.: Solving large-scale travelling salesperson problems on parallel machines. Microprocess. Microsyst. **16**(3), 149–158 (1992)
19. Sharad, N., Gopal, M.: Solving travelling salesman problem using firefly algorithm. Int. J. Res. Sci. Adv. Technol. **2**(2), 53–57 (2013)
20. Shi, X., Liang, Y., Lee, H., Lu, C., Wang, Q.: Particle swarm optimization based algorithms for TSP and generalized TSP. Inf. Process. Lett. **103**, 169–176 (2007)
21. Szwed, P., Chmiel, W., Kadłuczka, P.: OpenCL implementation of PSO algorithm for the quadratic assignment problem. In: Rutkowski, L., Korytkowski, M., Scherer, R., Tadeusiewicz, R., Zadeh, L.A., Zurada, J.M. (eds.) Artificial Intelligence and Soft Computing. LNCS, vol. 9120, pp. 223–234. Springer, Heidelberg (2015)
22. Xing, B., Gao, W.: Innovative Computational Intelligence: a Rough Guide to 134 Clever Algorithms. Springer International Publishing, Switzerland (2014)
23. Yang, X.S.: Nature-Inspired Metaheuristic Algorithms, 2nd edn. Luniver Press, Bristol (2010)

The Concept of Molecular Neurons

Łukasz Laskowski[1(✉)], Magdalena Laskowska[1], Jerzy Jelonkiewicz[1],
Henryk Piech[2], Tomasz Galkowski[1], and Arnaud Boullanger[3]

[1] Institute of Computational Intelligence, Czestochowa University of Technology,
Al. A.K. 36, 42-200 Czestochowa, Poland
lukasz.laskowski@kik.pcz.pl
[2] Institute of Computer Science, Czestochowa University of Technology,
ul. Dabrowskiego 69, 42-201 Czestochowa, Poland
[3] Chimie Moléculaire et Organisation du Solide, Institut Charles Gerhardt,
Université Montpellier II, UMR 5253 CC 1701, 2 Place E. Bataillon,
34095 Montpellier Cedex 5, France

Abstract. The paper concerns the main element of the molecular neural
network - the Molecular Neuron (MN). Molecular Neural Network idea
has been introduced in our previous articles. Here we present the structure of the Molecular Neuron element in micro and nanoscale. We have
obtained MN in hexagonal layout in the form of the thin film. In this
paper we have described self-assembly mechanism leading to the NMs
layout. Also physical properties of the MNs layer have been shown.

Keywords: Hopfield neural network · Artificial neuron · Spin-glass ·
Molecular magnet

1 Introduction

We hope that the concept of Molecular Neural Network (MNN) [24,25] will overcome all problems connected with hardware and software implementation of an
artificial neural networks [7–9,42]. This novel technology aims at the hardware
implementation of artificial neurons based on molecular techniques. The MNN
refers to a spin glass-like hardware implementation of the Hopfield neural structure. The crucial point of the idea is an array of bistable magnetic molecules
magnetically coupled through interconnection devices capable of transmitting
magnetic fields though the spinvave. In particular, this novel approach uses single magnetic molecules inside SBA-15 mesoporous silica pores. Each pore in the
SBA-15 mesostructured thin layer creates converting unit that are equivalent to
neurons in the Hopfield network with weighted interconnections between them.
Individual converting units interact with one another by means of exchange
communication and controlling of electrons coherence. It is possible to control
a magnetic field using spin-wave in dielectric [30] and to tune Fermi electron
coherency level. Having built all the necessary elements of a neural network one
can arrange them as a part of Hopfield-like network. This network works in the
same way as its physical precursor - spin glass - with all advantages: fully parallel

© Springer International Publishing Switzerland 2016
L. Rutkowski et al. (Eds.): ICAISC 2016, Part II, LNAI 9693, pp. 494–501, 2016.
DOI: 10.1007/978-3-319-39384-1_43

processing (extremely fast calculations, unavailable for any existing system) and efficiency. Importantly, no external power supply is necessary in the process of drifting to energy minimum - the system is self-polarized. Some power is needed only for setting the initial states (if necessary) or setting the interconnections. This novel technology enables fast, high density content addressable associative memory implementation. Ultimately, it is expected that the proposed approach can be scaled up to mimic memory with human-like characteristics.

The considered technology can significantly influence research and application areas, mainly artificial intelligence [1, 3–6, 10, 14, 15, 17, 18, 20, 22, 23, 29, 33–35, 39, 41, 43, 46]. For instance a straightforward application seems to be a content addressable associative memory (CAAM). This kind of memory, implemented on the molecular scale, offers both high capacity and instant access, which in turn opens up new and unprecedented possibilities for artificial intelligence. Presumably, molecular CAAM, with all kind of patterns and ease to learn new ones, can move forward the artificial intelligence research.

The technology, being a subject of the article, will also offer new opportunities for solving multi-criterion optimization problems [2, 11–13, 16, 19, 21, 26–28, 31, 36–38, 40]. Such problems, involving more than one objective function to be optimized simultaneously, what can be extremely difficult to solve. Problems of this type can be found in mathematics, engineering or economics. Vector optimization problems arise, for example, in decision making, statistics, functional analysis, approximation theory, multi-object programming or cooperative game theory. As it was proved, the Hopfield networks are very efficient in solving such problems, but also disappointingly slow. As a result, solutions can be found at the expense of computational time. When using a real parallel system, like the one described in the paper, a solution can be found instantly. Another possible application field for the molecular Hopfield network relates to a human-like expert system where fast and multi-criteria inference is needed.

The main part of MNN is a molecular neuron. In the paper we show how the molecular neurons body is created using self-assembly technology. Particularly, we described the mechanism of self-assembly of silica molecules that creates the matrix for Molecular Neurons.

2   Molecular Neuron

The Molecular Neuron is a bistable unit, capable of reacting to affecting magnetic field obtained from both electrons polarization and external magnetic field. The central part of Molecular Neuron is a molecular magnet, that can occupy only a few spin states below blocking temperature. Fixed spins configuration generates magnetic moment, that is maintained even with absence of external magnetic field. This property causes, that MN is able to generalize, as an artificial neuron.

In order to construct described above unit, it is necessary to obtain perfectly separated and fully accessible single molecule magnets. We can achieve this by using of SBA-15 thin films as a matrix. We are also capable of obtaining restricted activation of silica structure where one pore contains only one molecular magnet.

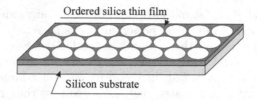

Fig. 1. 2D hexagonally arranged silica thin film with pores oriented perpendicularly to silicon wafer substrate.

The structure of silica thin films is extremely important in this case. The pores orientation in the silica layer is a vital issue. Channels orientation should be perpendicular to the substrate surface. Also their arrangement should be regular in order to allow precise localization of each neuron. The structure of considered thin silica matrix is presented in Fig. 1.

Obtaining of thin films with mesopore channels perpendicular to a substrate is still a major challenge. Nevertheless, there are a few methods to rich this goal. We consider two suitable methods for obtaining the Molecular Neurons matrix.

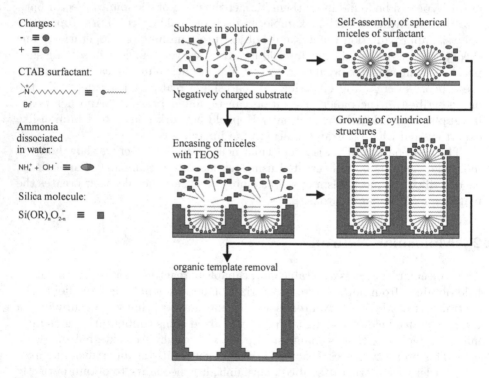

Fig. 2. Schematic representation of the formation process of ordered mesoporous silica films with perpendicular mesochannels by the Ströber solution self-assembly procedure. (Color figure online)

One of it is the electrochemically-assisted self-assembly (EASA) method [32,45]. This method applies a suitable cathodic potential to an electrode immersed in a hydrolyzed sol solution containing a surfactant template.

Second method is an ammonia-induced Ströber method. To this end we have used negatively charged substrate - in this case glass and ITO - and immersed in the sol solution containing ethanol, water, ammonia in low concentration (below 1.4 mM), tetaethylortosilicate (TEOS) and ionic surfactant - CTAB. Increasing temperature to 60°C results in formation of hexagonally arranged pores oriented perpendicularly to substrate surface.

The mechanism of such a structure creation was explained in [44]. A negative surface charge on the substrate leads to strong initial adsorption of the CTA+ surfactant molecules, forming spherical micellar structures. In a Ströber solution, the surfactant cations (CTA+) are first strongly adsorbed on a negatively charged substrate (such as glass or ITO). Next we can observe gradual transformation of silicate–CTAB composites from spherical to cylindrical micelles with

Fig. 3. Top-view TEM image of the mesoporous silica films deposited on ITO.

the assistance of ammonia hydrogen bonding and controlled silicate polymerization. This process was depicted in Fig. 2.

Using the Ströber method we obtained well-structured hexagonally arranged silica thin films, containing channels oriented perpendicularly to substrate surface. Thickness of the thin films was below 200 nm. The TEM image of obtained silica matrix can be seen in Fig. 3.

3   Conclusion

In the paper we presented the concept of a Molecular Neuron - the basic element of a Molecular Neural Network. We shown the self-assembly procedure leading to an ordered silica matrix, necessary for creating of a Molecular Neurons. We explained the self-assembly mechanism occurring in the Ströber solution during thin silica layer deposition. Also resulting thin film was shown. Considering the current status of research we are convinced that successful implementation of a molecular neuron is just a matter of time.

Aknowledgement. Financial support for this investigation has been provided by the National Centre of Science (Grant-No: 2011/03/D/ST5/05996).

References

1. Aghdam, M.H., Heidari, S.: Feature selection using particle swarm optimization in text categorization. J. Artif. Intell. Soft Comput. Res. **5**(4), 231–238 (2015)
2. Akhtar, Z., Rattani, A., Foresti, G.L.: Temporal analysis of adaptive face recognition. J. Artif. Intell. Soft Comput. Res. **4**(4), 243–255 (2014)
3. Al-askar, H., Lamb, D., Hussain, A.J., Al-Jumeily, D., Randles, M., Fergus, P.: Predicting financial time series data using artificial immune system-inspired neural networks. J. Artif. Intell. Soft Comput. Res. **5**(1), 45–68 (2015)
4. Anand, K., Raman, S., Subramanian, K.: Implementing a neuro fuzzy expert system for optimising the performance of chemical recovery boiler. J. Artif. Intell. Soft Comput. Res. **4**(2/3), 249–263 (2014)
5. Bali, S., Jha, D., Kumar, D., Pham, H.: Fuzzy multi-objective build-or-buy approach for component selection of fault tolerant software system under consensus recovery block scheme with mandatory redundancy in critical modules. J. Artif. Intell. Soft Comput. Res. **4**(2/3), 98–119 (2014)
6. Bello, O., Holzmann, J., Yaqoob, T., Teodoriu, C.: Application of artificial intelligence methods in drilling system design and operations: A review of the state of the art. J. Artif. Intell. Soft Comput. Res. **5**(2), 121–139 (2015)
7. Bilski, J., Smolag, J.: Parallel approach to learning of the recurrent jordan neural network. In: Rutkowski, L., Korytkowski, M., Scherer, R., Tadeusiewicz, R., Zadeh, L.A., Zurada, J.M. (eds.) ICAISC 2013, Part I. LNCS, vol. 7894, pp. 32–40. Springer, Heidelberg (2013)
8. Bilski, J., Smolag, J.: Parallel architectures for learning the RTRN and Elman dynamic neural networks. IEEE Trans. Parallel Distrib. Syst. **26**(9), 2561–2570 (2015)

9. Bilski, J., Smoląg, J., Galushkin, A.I.: The parallel approach to the conjugate gradient learning algorithm for the feedforward neural networks. In: Rutkowski, L., Korytkowski, M., Scherer, R., Tadeusiewicz, R., Zadeh, L.A., Zurada, J.M. (eds.) ICAISC 2014, Part I. LNCS, vol. 8467, pp. 12–21. Springer, Heidelberg (2014)

10. Chu, J.L., Krzyżak, A.: The recognition of partially occluded objects with support vector machines, convolutional neural networks and deep belief networks. J. Artif. Intell. Soft Comput. Res. 4(1), 5–19 (2014)

11. Cierniak, R.: New neural network algorithm for image reconstruction from fan-beam projections. Neurocomputing 72(13–15), 3238–3244 (2009). Hybrid Learning Machines (HAIS 2007)/Recent Developments in Natural Computation (ICNC 2007)

12. Cpalka, K.: A new method for design and reduction of neuro fuzzy classification systems. IEEE Trans. Neural Netw. 20(4), 701–714 (2009)

13. Cpalka, K., Rutkowski, L.: Flexible takagi sugeno neuro fuzzy structures for nonlinear approximation. WSEAS Trans. Syst. 5, 1450–1458 (2005)

14. Das, P., Pettersson, F., Dutta, S.: Pruned-bimodular neural networks for modelling of strength-ductility balance of HSLA steel plates. J. Artif. Intell. Soft Comput. Res. 4(4), 354–372 (2014)

15. Grycuk, R., Gabryel, M., Korytkowski, M., Scherer, R.: Content-based image indexing by data clustering and inverse document frequency. In: Kozielski, S., Mrozek, D., Kasprowski, P., Małysiak-Mrozek, B., Kostrzewa, D. (eds.) BDAS 2014. CCIS, vol. 424, pp. 374–383. Springer, Heidelberg (2014)

16. Grycuk, R., Gabryel, M., Korytkowski, M., Scherer, R., Voloshynovskiy, S.: From single image to list of objects based on edge and blob detection. In: Rutkowski, L., Korytkowski, M., Scherer, R., Tadeusiewicz, R., Zadeh, L.A., Zurada, J.M. (eds.) ICAISC 2014, Part II. LNCS, vol. 8468, pp. 605–615. Springer, Heidelberg (2014)

17. Hayashi, Y., Tanaka, Y., Takagi, T., Saito, T., Iiduka, H., Kikuchi, H., Bologna, G., Mitra, S.: Recursive-rule extraction algorithm with j48graft and applications to generating credit scores. J. Artif. Intell. Soft Comput. Res. 6(1), 35–44 (2016)

18. Katiyar, R., Pathak, V.K., Arya, K.: Human gait recognition system based on shadow free silhouettes using truncated singular value decomposition transformation model. J. Artif. Intell. Soft Comput. Res. 4(4), 283–301 (2014)

19. Korytkowski, M., Nowicki, R., Rutkowski, L., Scherer, R.: AdaBoost ensemble of DCOG rough–neuro–fuzzy systems. In: Jędrzejowicz, P., Nguyen, N.T., Hoang, K. (eds.) ICCCI 2011, Part I. LNCS, vol. 6922, pp. 62–71. Springer, Heidelberg (2011)

20. Korytkowski, M., Nowicki, R., Scherer, R.: Neuro-fuzzy rough classifier ensemble. In: Alippi, C., Polycarpou, M., Panayiotou, C., Ellinas, G. (eds.) ICANN 2009, Part I. LNCS, vol. 5768, pp. 817–823. Springer, Heidelberg (2009)

21. Korytkowski, M., Rutkowski, L., Scherer, R.: from ensemble of fuzzy classifiers to single fuzzy rule base classifier. In: Rutkowski, L., Tadeusiewicz, R., Zadeh, L.A., Zurada, J.M. (eds.) ICAISC 2008. LNCS (LNAI), vol. 5097, pp. 265–272. Springer, Heidelberg (2008)

22. Korytkowski, M., Rutkowski, L., Scherer, R.: Fast image classification by boosting fuzzy classifiers. Inf. Sci. 327, 175–182 (2016)

23. Łapa, K., Zalasiński, M., Cpałka, K.: A new method for designing and complexity reduction of neuro-fuzzy systems for nonlinear modelling. In: Rutkowski, L., Korytkowski, M., Scherer, R., Tadeusiewicz, R., Zadeh, L.A., Zurada, J.M. (eds.) ICAISC 2013, Part I. LNCS, vol. 7894, pp. 329–344. Springer, Heidelberg (2013)

24. Laskowski, Ł., Laskowska, M., Jelonkiewicz, J., Boullanger, A.: Spin-glass Implementation of a Hopfield neural structure. In: Rutkowski, L., Korytkowski, M., Scherer, R., Tadeusiewicz, R., Zadeh, L.A., Zurada, J.M. (eds.) ICAISC 2014, Part I. LNCS, vol. 8467, pp. 89–96. Springer, Heidelberg (2014)

25. Laskowski, Ł., Laskowska, M., Jelonkiewicz, J., Boullanger, A.: Molecular approach to Hopfield neural network. In: Rutkowski, L., Korytkowski, M., Scherer, R., Tadeusiewicz, R., Zadeh, L.A., Zurada, J.M. (eds.) Artificial Intelligence and Soft Computing. LNCS, vol. 9119, pp. 72–78. Springer, Heidelberg (2015)

26. Lee, P.M., Hsiao, T.C.: Applying lcs to affective image classification in spatial-frequency domain. J. Artif. Intell. Soft Comput. Res. 4(2), 99–123 (2014)

27. Nowicki, R., Pokropińska, A.: Information criterions applied to neuro-fuzzy architectures design. In: Rutkowski, L., Siekmann, J.H., Tadeusiewicz, R., Zadeh, L.A. (eds.) ICAISC 2004. LNCS (LNAI), vol. 3070, pp. 332–337. Springer, Heidelberg (2004)

28. Nowicki, R., Rutkowska, D.: Neuro-fuzzy systems based on Gödel and Sharp implication. In: Proceedings of Intern Conference Application of Fuzzy Systems and Soft Computing – ICAFS-2000, Siegen, Germany, pp. 232–237, June 2000

29. Nowicki, R., Scherer, R., Rutkowski, L.: A method for learning of hierarchical fuzzy systems. In: PS, et al. (eds.) Intelligent Technologies – Theory and Applications, pp. 124–129. IOS Press, Amsterdam (2002)

30. Oliver, T., Buettner, J., Bauer, M., Demokritov, S., Kivshar, Y., Grimalsky, V., Rapoport, Y., Slavin, A.: Linear and nonlinear diffraction of dipolar spin waves in yttrium iron garnet films observed by space- and time-resolved brillouin light scattering (1999)

31. Pabiasz, S., Starczewski, J.T.: A new approach to determine three-dimensional facial landmarks. In: Rutkowski, L., Korytkowski, M., Scherer, R., Tadeusiewicz, R., Zadeh, L.A., Zurada, J.M. (eds.) ICAISC 2013, Part II. LNCS, vol. 7895, pp. 286–296. Springer, Heidelberg (2013)

32. Robertson, C., Beanland, R., Boden, S.A., Hector, A.L., Kashtiban, R.J., Sloan, J., Smith, D.C., Walcarius, A.: Ordered mesoporous silica films with pores oriented perpendicular to a titanium nitride substrate. Phys. Chem. Chem. Phys. 17(6), 4763–4770 (2015)

33. Rutkowski, L., Jaworski, M., Pietruczuk, L., Duda, P.: Decision trees for mining data streams based on the gaussian approximation. IEEE Trans. Knowl. Data Eng. 26(1), 108–119 (2014)

34. Rutkowski, L., Jaworski, M., Pietruczuk, L., Duda, P.: A new method for data stream mining based on the misclassification error. IEEE Trans. Neural Netw. Learn. Syst. 26(5), 1048–1059 (2015)

35. Rutkowski, L., Pietruczuk, L., Duda, P., Jaworski, M.: Decision trees for mining data streams based on the mcdiarmid's bound. IEEE Trans. Knowl. Data Eng. 25(6), 1272–1279 (2013)

36. Rutkowski, L., Przybył, A., Cpałka, K., Er, M.J.: Online speed profile generation for industrial machine tool based on neuro-fuzzy approach. In: Rutkowski, L., Scherer, R., Tadeusiewicz, R., Zadeh, L.A., Zurada, J.M. (eds.) ICAISC 2010, Part II. LNCS, vol. 6114, pp. 645–650. Springer, Heidelberg (2010)

37. Scherer, R.: Neuro-fuzzy relational systems for nonlinear approximation and prediction. Nonlinear Anal. 71, e1420–e1425 (2009)

38. Scherer, R., Rutkowski, L.: A fuzzy relational system with linguistic antecedent certainty factors. In: Rutkowski, K. (ed.) Advances in Soft Computing, pp. 563–569. Springer Physica-Verlag, Heidelberg (2003)

39. Scherer, R., Rutkowski, L.: Neuro-fuzzy relational classifiers. In: Rutkowski, L., Siekmann, J.H., Tadeusiewicz, R., Zadeh, L.A. (eds.) ICAISC 2004. LNCS (LNAI), vol. 3070, pp. 376–380. Springer, Heidelberg (2004)
40. Starczewski, J.T., Scherer, R., Korytkowski, M., Nowicki, R.: Modular type-2 neuro-fuzzy systems. In: Wyrzykowski, R., Dongarra, J., Karczewski, K., Wasniewski, J. (eds.) PPAM 2007. LNCS, vol. 4967, pp. 570–578. Springer, Heidelberg (2008)
41. Starczewski, J.T.: Centroid of triangular and gaussian type-2 fuzzy sets. Inf. Sci. **280**, 289–306 (2014)
42. Szarek, A., Korytkowski, M., Rutkowski, L., Scherer, R., Szyprowski, J.: Application of neural networks in assessing changes around implant after total hip arthroplasty. In: Rutkowski, L., Korytkowski, M., Scherer, R., Tadeusiewicz, R., Zadeh, L.A., Zurada, J.M. (eds.) ICAISC 2012, Part II. LNCS, vol. 7268, pp. 335–340. Springer, Heidelberg (2012)
43. Tambouratzis, T., Souliou, D., Chalikias, M., Gregoriades, A.: Maximising accuracy and efficiency of traffic accident prediction combining information mining with computational intelligence approaches and decision trees. J. Artif. Intell. Soft Comput. Res. **4**(1), 31–42 (2014)
44. Teng, Z., Zheng, G., Dou, Y., Li, W., Mou, C.Y., Zhang, X., Asiri, A.M., Zhao, D.: Highly ordered mesoporous silica films with perpendicular mesochannels by a simple stöber-solution growth approach. Angew. Chem. Int. Ed. **51**(9), 2173–2177 (2012)
45. Urbanova, V., Walcarius, A.: Vertically-aligned mesoporous silica films. Zeitschrift für anorganische und allgemeine Chemie **640**(3–4), 537–546 (2014)
46. Zalasiński, M., Cpałka, K.: New approach for the on-line signature verification based on method of horizontal partitioning. In: Rutkowski, L., Korytkowski, M., Scherer, R., Tadeusiewicz, R., Zadeh, L.A., Zurada, J.M. (eds.) ICAISC 2013, Part II. LNCS, vol. 7895, pp. 342–350. Springer, Heidelberg (2013)

Crowd Teaches the Machine: Reducing Cost of Crowd-Based Training of Machine Classifiers

Radoslaw Nielek[✉], Filip Georgiew, and Adam Wierzbicki

Polish-Japanese Academy of Information Technology,
Koszykowa 86, 02008 Warsaw, Poland
{nielek,filip.georgiew,adamw}@pjwstk.edu.pl

Abstract. Crowdsourcing platforms are very frequently used for collecting training data. Quality assurance is the most obvious problem but not the only one. This work proposes iterative approach which helps to reduce costs of building training/testing datasets. Information about classifier confidence is used for making decision whether new labels from crowdsourcing platform are required for this particular object. Conducted experiments have confirmed that proposed method reduces costs by over 50 % in best scenarios and at the same time increases the percentage of correctly classified objects.

Keywords: Crowdsourcing · Twitter · Costs · Machine learning

1 Introduction

A heated dispute about the future of artificial intelligence (AI) and the possibility of replacing humans by it is far from decisive conclusion. AI is going to be much more capable but will it replace humans in performing some tasks? Majority (but only by small margin) of experts said in the survey conducted by PewReserachCenter[1] that technology would not displace jobs but technological progress would probably change the type of work we do. Joel Lee[2] compiled the list of six areas in which jobs are not endangered by a progress in AI (some of them are quite surprising like politicians or professional athletes). Disregard of these mostly futuristic and philosophical discussions, there is at least one place where we can observe a competition (and at the same time limitation of present AI algorithms) between AI and human workforce crowdsourcing Internet markets (e.g. mTurk[3] or Crowdflower[4]).

A significant proportion of tasks published on the mTurk platform belongs to one of two broad groups: object classification or creative content transformation (text reformulation, translation, OCR). Ten tasks with the biggest budgets from

---

[1] http://www.pewinternet.org/2014/08/06/future-of-jobs/.
[2] http://www.makeuseof.com/tag/6-human-jobs-computers-will-never-replace/.
[3] www.mturk.com.
[4] www.crowdflower.com.

© Springer International Publishing Switzerland 2016
L. Rutkowski et al. (Eds.): ICAISC 2016, Part II, LNAI 9693, pp. 502–511, 2016.
DOI: 10.1007/978-3-319-39384-1_44

the mTurk are shown on Fig. 1. These tasks, at least to some extend, may be done by computer, so why do requesters outsource it to people? There are at least couple of reasons. First, AI may not be good enough; second, human labor is often cheaper than development of a dedicated automatic algorithm[5]; and third, machine learning algorithms require labelled examples to be trained (usually the more examples the better results are obtained). Crowdsourcing platforms are a great place to collect labels very cheaply but is it possible to make it even cheaper?

A well-known method of decreasing costs of tasks outsourced to crowdsourcing platforms is the use of quality assurance mechanisms. It helps to eliminate lazy or dishonest workers and reveal correct labels for objects. These mechanisms may be very simple, like majority voting, or quite complex (e.g. expectation-maximization algorithm) but all of them require redundant tagging for single object (the more the better). On the other hand, collecting more labels for the same object generates bigger costs. Increased number of labeled training/testing examples usually improves the performance of machine learning algorithms and helps to train the classifier more efficiently (of course only if quantity goes together with quality).

To address simultaneously the issue of the costs of collecting labels and the quality of trained classifier, we proposed a heuristic composed of three steps: iterative labeling, training classifier and testing. Our approach utilizes information about classification certainty score returned by probabilistic classifiers and based on it decides whether to submit an object to microtasks platform or not. In addition, a state-of-the-art algorithm is used for detecting lazy or fraudulent workers. Results show a substantial improvement in quality of trained classifier and decrease in labeling costs. To sum up, the major contribution of this paper are:

- proposition of the algorithm for iterative labelling training data with the help of crowdsourcing platform that reduce costs,
- analysis of robustness and resistance of proposed algorithm to malicious workers and cost effectiveness.

The rest of the paper is organized as follows. The next section presents related works. Third section describes in details a proposed algorithm. Fourth section explains an conducted experiments and describes a dataset. The next section is focused on discussing and presenting obtained results and is followed by the last section that concludes the paper and sketches some ideas for future research.

2   Related Work

It may be surprising for many people but term crowdsourcing is relatively new and was coined by Jeff Jowe nad Mark Robinson, editors of Wired magazine, in 2005 and was eventually formally defined a year later in the article titled:

---

[5] While it may seem strange solving 1000 CAPTCHAs costs only a few USD.

Requester ID	Requester Name	#HIT groups	Total HITs	Rewards	Type of tasks
A3MI6MIUNWCR7F	CastingWords	48,934	73,621	$59,099	Transcription
A2IR7ETVOIULZU	Dolores Labs	1,676	320,543	$26,919	Mediator for other requesters
A2XL3J4NH6JI12	ContentGalore	1,150	23,728	$19,375	Content generation
A11970GL0WOQ3G	Smartsheet.com Clients	1,407	181,620	$17,086	Mediator for other requesters
AGW2H4I480ZX1	Paul Pullen	6,842	161,535	$11,186	Content rewriting
A1CTI3ZAWTR5AZ	Classify This	228	484,369	$9,685	Object classification
A1AQ7EJ5P7ME65	Dave	2,249	7,059	$6,448	Transcription
AD7C0BZNKYGYV	QuestionSwami	798	10,980	$2,867	Content generation and evaluation
AD14NALRDOSN9	retaildata	113	158,206	$2,118	Object classification
A2RFHBFTZHX7UN	ContentSpooling.net	555	622	$987	Content generation and evaluation

Fig. 1. Types of tasks on mTurk ordered by the amount of paid rewards

The Rise of Crowdsourcing [8]. Nowadays crowdsourcing microtasks platforms are omnipresent. Twitter use it for manual identification of trending search queries for better ads targeting, Amazon tests relevance of recommendation algorithms (among many other tasks) and countless number of researchers use it for labeling objects [2], collecting data or conducting psychological experiments [11].

Crowdsourcing has a huge impact on the labor market not only in developing countries (like India) but also in less developed areas of EU members countries (e.g. rural areas in Scotland [12]). Some researchers even focus on improving microtasks platforms usability (and profitability) for low-income workers in poor countries [9]. The in-depth study of mTurk workers demography has been conducted by Ross et al. [10].

A substantial number of workers motivated by money means that some of them may also try to maximize their income unfairly (e.g. doing tasks without proper concentration, attention or skills). Fort et al. show that obtaining the high quality annotations from crowdsourcing system is not an easy task and requires substantial amount of work [7]. A variety of approaches has been proposed to address the issue of the low quality caused by either fraudulent behavior or lack of required skills. Mechanical Turk provides the qualification mechanism that allows requester to post a test that has to be completed by worker before he or she is authorized to do hits. Downs et al. have shown that prescreening queries may be very efficient and also reveal some clues concerning demographic variables of cheaters [5]. Fraudulent behaviors are usually addressed by simple, yet powerful, approach called golden examples. This approach consists of asking workers to solve tasks and compare submitted solutions with known solutions (e.g. pictures tagged previously by requesters). If worker do not label the golden example correctly we should assume that all tasks done by this worker are poorly done (usually we ban this worker from participating in our future tasks assignments as well, what makes this heuristic more efficient in case if creating new accounts is not for free).

Golden examples work well only if an automatic comparison between solutions is possible (i.e. solutions are objective). For semi-subjective tasks without previously known solutions expectation-maximization algorithm proposed by A.

Dempster et al. [4] may be applied. The ultimate solution that combines many state-of-the-art algorithms in one system is Troia[6] developed by Panagiotis G. Ipeirotis. Troia implements ideas described in [14] and has also been used in this paper to eliminate lazy/malicious workers. Yet another approach called active learning to improve the quality of users' ratings has been proposed by Elahi et al. [6].

Crowdsourcing platforms are quite often used for preparing training data for machine learning algorithms. This coexistence has been noticed and quite extensively studied by researchers. L.C. Chen et al. tried to build an automatic classifier that would eventually outperform mTurkers [3]. Competition between mTurkers and AI is not limited to the quality of completed jobs but both parties take part in a cat-and-mouse game as well. Wang et al. checked how malicious users hired from crowdsourcing platform compete against machine learning algorithms crafted for detecting fraudulent behaviors [13]. Zhu et al. showed that in many cases increasing number of learning examples do not improve the performance of obtained classifier [16]. Surprisingly, not much research have been conducted in the area of supporting crowdsourcing workers by AI or application of AI to pre-filter examples before they are send to crowdsourcing platform. Panaiottis G Ipeirotis sketched the idea of combining AI with mturk workers in patent application [1]. The approach proposed in this paper resembles to some extent this patent application but is more focused on limiting the number of tasks that have to be assigned and improves the quality of classifier instead of detecting new features.

3   Algorithm Description

The ultimate goal of the proposed algorithm (iterative labeling/training algorithm – ILTA) is to limit the costs of collecting labels and improve the quality of obtained classifier. Let us assume that we have to assign thousands of objects (e.g. pictures, texts, songs) to one of two classes (e.g. positive or negative). Typically, we ask people to label a relatively small sample of objects and after that we train classifier with help of supervised machine learning algorithm. More labelled objects usually helps to build better classifiers but on crowdsorucing platforms we have to pay for each label and we cannot be sure of quality of them.

The proposed algorithm is composed of three steps. Firstly, we split our dataset we want to label to small chunks (e.g. 100 objects each) and collect labels for the first chunk of data from crowdsourcing platform. Next we train a classifier on labelled objects. Having classifier trained, we can proceed to the next step. Instead of submitting the whole next chunk of data to crowdsourcing platform we try to classify them with our *partially*[7] trained classifier. After that we can remove objects that are classified with enough confidence (confidence exceed a given threshold) and, thus, limit the number of objects sent to crowdsourcing

---

[6] https://github.com/ipeirotis/Troia-Server.

[7] We use word partially to stress that the initial number of cases used for training was really small and our classifier may be quite imprecise.

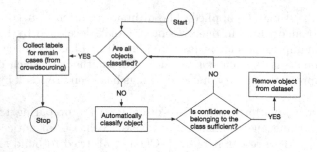

Fig. 2. Filtering out objects for which classification confidence is quite high

platform for labeling. Objects' prefiltering is shown on Fig. 2. In the next step all labeled objects (also newly collected) are used for training and validating new classifier[8].

A decreasing number of labelled objects reduces costs of preparing training dataset but may also cause a decline in the quality of obtained classifier. Objects that our classifier labels with wrong etiquette (especially those labelled with high degree of certainty) are also the most valuable in increasing performance of machine learning algorithms. On the other hand, the number of removed examples may be negligibly small and does not justify the use of proposed algorithm. The problem is even more complex when we cannot be completely sure that labels are correct (like with jobs done by poorly paid mturk workers).

4 Experiment Setup

To verify our approach we have decided to use binary classification problem, namely detection whether a tweet includes positive or negative sentiment. Motivation for selecting this particular problem is that it resembles tasks posted on the mTurk platform and, thus, may prove practical applicability of our method. Moreover, understanding of a text is one of the so-called AI complete problems and will require human assistance in foreseeable future. Semantic analysis of tweets is particularly hard because of 140 character limit, which enforce people to the extensive use of abbreviations, emoticons and references to cultural context.

4.1 Dataset

In order to ensure research reproducibility a publicly available dataset of tweets written in English has been used[9]. A random sample of 2000 tweets has been selected from the dataset. Authors have labelled all tweets and used these data as golden labels. Kappa inter-rater agreement was quite high – 0.9 – but we decided to remove examples for which raters didn't agree.

---

[8] We use a standard 10-fold cross-validation approach.

[9] http://thinknook.com/wp-content/uploads/2012/09/Sentiment-Analysis-Dataset.zip.

4.2   Data Preprocessing and Features Extraction

An important step for almost all machine learning algorithms is features' extraction[10]. Data preparation and features extraction algorithm are composed of few steps. Firstly, all common abbreviations used by people in tweets are exchanged with original words. Secondly, we replace emoticons with corresponding words. Finally, we do a part-of-speech tagging on all words in tweets. A part-of-speech tagger from NLTK toolkit[11] has been used.

4.3   Crowdsourcing Platform Simulation

Using a crowdsourcing platform as a source of labels for objects would bring the research scenario closer to the reality but has also some serious drawbacks. The most obvious is that it is impossible to control types of workers and, in particular, percentage of malicious workers among all those who accepted our task. Therefore, we decided to simulate crowdsourcing platform instead of using a real one. Based on our previous experience with a mTurk platform and literature reviews we have chosen three agents' strategies that are modelled as follows:

- honest – *has skills and put effort to solve given task correctly; it does not guarantee that he will always select right label but probability is quite high; in our simulation we use range from 0.75 to 0.95,*
- lazy – *disregard of object always submitt the same label,*
- malicious – *always submit label that is opposite to what is correct,*

Source code of a crowdsourcing platform simulator developed for this article is available on-line[12].

4.4   Machine Learning Algorithm

Proposed algorithm does not assume that any particular ML algorithm has to be used as long as selected classification algorithm returns classification certainty. In our research we decided to use simple, yet powerful, multinomial naive bayes classifier. An implementation from scikit-learn toolkit[13] has been used.

4.5   Troia

Existing crowdsourcing platforms allow quality based workers' remuneration. Requesters[14] have few days to evaluate and accept or reject submitted answers. While it might appear that this mechanism should solve problems with frauds, in reality it helps only in extreme cases. To avoid negative comments, requesters

---

[10] Deep learning algorithms are an exception.
[11] http://www.nltk.org/.
[12] http://nielek.com/crowdai/.
[13] http://scikit-learn.org/stable/.
[14] It is an official name used by Amazon for entities that outsource jobs.

usually pay to all participants but obviously cheaters are excluded from future jobs submitted by the requester. Things become even more complicated when we do not have golden examples to be compared with. Troia is a toolkit that offers the functionality of detecting low quality answers and lazy/malicious workers. It helps to reduce costs of using crowdsourcing platforms. Troia can be used as an API service or, as we run, stand-alone software. Troia implements ideas described in [15].

4.6 Tested Scenarios

We have tested four different scenarios varying in proportions of honest, lazy and malicious agents and number of tweets (balanced or unbalanced classes in the training dataset). Details are presented in Table 1. Balanced datasets are usually recommended for training classifiers but in this case, as we collect labels incrementally, we cannot assure the same number of examples in all classes. So, scenarios A and B are realistic only for data where probability of appearing both classes is roughly equal.

We limited the number of mTurk workers to 20. That may look rather small but our experience with the Amazon crowdsourcing platform indicates that for many small-to-medium tasks it is quite reasonable. For each object we collected 20 labels what is slightly more than requesters usually do but it is the number recommended by Troia developers.

Table 1. Tested scenarios and their parameters

	Scenario A	Scenario B	Scenario C	Scenario D
Honest	100 %	50 %	100 %	50 %
Lazy	0 %	25 %	0 %	25 %
Malicious	0 %	25 %	0 %	25 %
No of tweets	1000	1000	2000	2000
Positive	500	500	751	1303
Negative	500	500	1249	697

5 Results

Aggregated results are shown in Table 2. The disregard of scenarios application of proposed algorithm improves performance of classifier and reduces costs. The highest improvement is for the scenario A, which is also the easies case. Percentage of correctly classified tweets grows from 63 % to 72 % and, at the same time, costs went downy by 52 %. The decrease of costs is what was expected but the increasing of classification quality is quite surprising for this scenario, at least at

Table 2. % of correctly classified tweets and costs reduction for different scenarios

	Scenario A	Scenario B	Scenario C	Scenario D
% of corr. clas. objects (without optimization)	63 %	59 %	56 %	58 %
% of corr. clas. objects (with optimization)	72 %	66 %	61 %	62 %
Costs reduction	52 %	58 %	11,7 %	11,7 %

first glance. However, if we recall that even honest users are only partly correct in their answers, then the result becomes easier to interpret.

Adding lazy and malicious workers to the mTurk platform simulator changes the results but not as much as some may expect. For scenario B we have a fewer tweets classified correctly (more noise in the training dataset) – 66 % in comparison to 72 % in scenario A – but bigger costs reduction – 58 % (due to detection of spammers that are only partially remunerated).

Both, A and B scenarios are very special because they assume that in our dataset we have roughly the same number of examples for both classes. In real application it happens quite rarely. The problem is also that we do not know *a priori* neither the proportion nor the label, thus we cannot balance a dataset before we post it on the crowdsourcing platform. As we expected, these two scenarios are much more difficult for naive bayes classifier and for our optimization and costs reduction algorithm but proposed approach can still offer at least some improvement. For both scenarios we have been able to reduce costs by ca. 12 % and increase number of correctly classified tweets by 5 %.

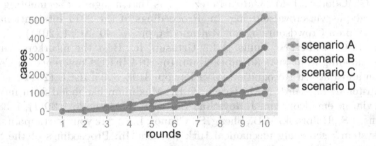

Fig. 3. Cumulative number of removed tweets for different scenarios.

The majority of costs reduction in ILTA comes from limiting number of tasks posted on the mTurk-like platform. Cumulative number of "skipped" tweets for each round of our algorithm for different scenarios is shown in Fig. 3. Figure 3 helps to understand how cost savings are connect with iterations of proposed algorithm. Exact number of skipped tweets varies for different scenarios but typically it is small for first few rounds and then increases. Stepper curve on Fig. 3 means bigger savings from applying ILTA.

It is worth mentioning that the absolute performance of tweets classifier was not the goal of this paper, so we do not invested much time in fine-tuning and data preprocessing. Using other machine learning algorithms or more carefully selected features may improve absolute performance of classifier but still can take advantage of cost reduction caused by proposed algorithm.

6   Conclusion

Presented results have confirmed that proposed approach is very promising and, in cooperation with tools like Troia, can further limit costs of gathering labels from crowdsourcing and microtasks platforms. In the future we plan to verify our results with experiments on the mTurk platform where more complex adversaries' strategies are present. Furthermore, we would like to confirm applicability of proposed algorithm beyond two class models and explore some additional ideas for costs reduction – e.g. use of uncertain labels for training classifier and increasing payments for the most important examples[15].

Acknowledgments. This project has received funding from the European Unions Horizon 2020 research and innovation programme under the Marie Sklodowska-Curie grant agreement No 690962.

References

1. Attenberg, J.M., Ipeirotis, P.G.: Task-agnostic integration of human and machine intelligence, US Patent App. 13/863,751, 16 April 2013
2. Can, G., Odobez, J.-M., Gatica-Perez, D.: Is that a jaguar?: segmenting ancient maya glyphs via crowdsourcing. In: Proceedings of the 2014 International ACM Workshop on Crowdsourcing for Multimedia, pp. 37–40. ACM (2014)
3. Chen, L.-C., Fidler, S., Yuille, A.L., Urtasun, R.: Beat the mturkers: automatic image labeling from weak 3d supervision. In: 2014 IEEE Conference on Computer Vision and Pattern Recognition (CVPR), pp. 3198–3205. IEEE (2014)
4. Dempster, A.P., Laird, N.M., Rubin, D.B.: Maximum likelihood from incomplete data via the em algorithm. J. Roy. Stat. Soc. Ser. B (Methodol.) **39**(1), 1–38 (1977)
5. Downs, J.S., Holbrook, M.B., Sheng, S., Cranor, L.F.: Are your participants gaming the system?: screening mechanical turk workers. In: Proceedings of the SIGCHI Conference on Human Factors in Computing Systems, CHI 2010, pp. 2399–2402. ACM, New York (2010)
6. Elahi, M., Ricci, F., Rubens, N.: Active learning strategies for rating elicitation in collaborative filtering: a system-wide perspective. ACM Trans. Intell. Syst. Technol. (TIST) **5**(1), 13 (2013)
7. Fort, K., Adda, G., Cohen, K.B.: Amazon mechanical turk: gold mine or coal mine? Comput. Linguist. **37**(2), 413–420 (2011)
8. Howe, J.: The rise of crowdsourcing. Wired Mag. **14**(6), 1–4 (2006)
9. Khanna, S., Ratan, A., Davis, J., Thies, W.: Evaluating and improving the usability of mechanical turk for low-income workers in India. In: Proceedings of the First ACM Symposium on Computing for Development, p. 12. ACM (2010)

---

[15] Higher vages in crowdsourcing platform increase quality and motivation of workers and can be used for collecting labels that are less noisy.

10. Ross, J., Lilly Irani, M., Silberman, A.Z., Tomlinson, B.: Who are the crowdwork-ers?: shifting demographics in mechanical turk. In: CHI 2010 Extended Abstracts on Human Factors in Computing Systems, pp. 2863–2872. ACM (2010)

11. Schneider, J.L., Weisz, J.R.: Using mechanical turk to study family processes and youth mental health: a test of feasibility. J. Child Fam. Stud. **24**(11), 3235–3246 (2015)

12. Vasantha, A., Vijayumar, G., Corney, J., AcurBakir, N., Lynn, A., Jagadeesan, A.P., Smith, M., Agarwal, A.: Social implications of crowdsourcing in rural scotland. Int. J. Soc. Sci. Hum. Behav. Study **1**(3), 47–52 (2014)

13. Wang, G., Wang, T., Zhang, H., Zhao, B.Y.: Man vs. machine: practical adversarial detection of malicious crowdsourcing workers. In: Proceedings of the 23rd USENIX Conference on Security Symposium, SEC 20114, pp. 239–254. USENIX Association, Berkeley (2014)

14. Wang, J., Ipeirotis, P.G., Provost, F.: Managing crowdsourcing workers. In: The 2011 Winter Conference on Business Intelligence, pp. 10–12 (2011)

15. Wang, J., Ipeirotis, P.G., Provost, F.: Quality-Based Pricing for Crowdsourced Workers, NYU Working Paper No. 2451/31833, June 2013. Available at SSRN: http://ssrn.com/abstract=2283000

16. Zhu, X., Vondrick, C., Ramanan, D., Fowlkes, C.: Do we need more training data or better models for object detection?. In: BMVC vol. 3, p. 5. Citeseer (2012)

Indoor Localization of a Moving Mobile Terminal by an Enhanced Particle Filter Method

Michał Okulewicz(✉), Dominika Bodzon, Marek Kozak, Michał Piwowarski, and Patryk Tenderenda

Faculty of Mathematics and Information Science,
Warsaw University of Technology, Koszykowa 75, 00-662 Warsaw, Poland
M.Okulewicz@mini.pw.edu.pl

Abstract. This article presents a method of localizing a moving mobile terminal (i.e. phone) with the usage of the Particle Filter method. The method is additionally enhanced with the predictions done by a Random Forest and the results are optimized with the usage of the Particle Swarm Optimization algorithm.

The method proposes a simple model of movement through the building, a likelihood estimation function for evaluating locations against the observed signal, and a method of generating multiple location propositions from a single point prediction statistical model on the basis of model error estimation.

The method uses a data set of the GSM and WiFi networks received signals' strengths labeled with a receiver's 3D location. The data have been gathered in a six floor building. The approach is tested on a real-world data set and compared with a single point estimation performed by a Random Forest. The Particle Filter approach has been able to improve floor recognition accuracy by around 7% and lower the median of the horizontal location error by around 15%.

Keywords: Particle Filter · Random Forest · Particle Swarm Optimization · Machine learning · Hidden Markov models · On-line mobile phone localization

1 Introduction

Localization of a mobile terminal is an important topic in the areas of public services, safety and security. While outdoor localization can be done quite precisely with the use of the satellite systems (e.g. GPS) aided with the radio based signals, creating a system localizing people inside the buildings poses more challenges. Due to the weak satellite signals such system must know either the locations of the transmitters and model the signal propagation in a given building or map the radio signals' strengths in the building [11,13,15,19–21].

In this paper we use a latter approach. Section 2 discusses the computational intelligence algorithms applied for tracking a moving mobile terminal, estimated conditional probabilities, evaluation function and the algorithm for localization

© Springer International Publishing Switzerland 2016
L. Rutkowski et al. (Eds.): ICAISC 2016, Part II, LNAI 9693, pp. 512–522, 2016.
DOI: 10.1007/978-3-319-39384-1_45

estimation built upon them. Section 3 describes the training data set and the real-world test scenarios. Subsequently, the results are presented in Sect. 4. Finally, Sect. 5 concludes the paper.

2   Indoor Localization of a Moving Terminal

In order to perform a localization of a mobile terminal in a building, given a reference data set of observed radio signals (GSM or WiFi) one may use the machine learning techniques or statistical models, such as k-NN [7], Multilayer Perceptron [9] or Random Forests [6] to learn the relation between the received signal strengths (RSS) vector and a 3D location in the building.

In this paper we take advantage of the fact that the localization could be performed in a continuous way, processing a series of RSS vectors, instead of just a single vector. A similar approach on a smaller 2D location has been presented in [20].

The structure of the remainder of this section is as follows. Section 2.1 introduces the computational intelligence methods applied in our approach. Section 2.2 defines the estimated conditional probability of the subsequent locations in the series (created either on the basis of previous location or on the basis of location provided by a single point predictor), the fitness function used interchangeably by the resampling phase and the optimization algorithm. Finally, Sect. 2.3 presents the structure of the whole algorithm.

2.1   Utilized Computational Intelligence Methods

This subsection introduces three Computational Intelligence methods used by our localization algorithm: Random Forests [2] as a single point predictor, Particle Filter [5] as a framework for the whole solution and Particle Swarm Optimization [10] as a location optimization algorithm.

Random Forest. (RF) [2] is an ensamble machine learning technique using a random subspace method [8] to create single models forming the ensemble. The concept of a Random Forest is to create a committee of a fully grown decision trees. Each tree is built on a randomly selected subset of all available features and a subset of all available data points. The final predictions are made by aggregating results from the individual models.

Particle Filter. (PF) [5] is a Hidden Markov Model [14] technique which evaluates the probabilities on the set of proposed x series (population of particles) of a hidden variable X by assuming the probability of generating the y series of an observed variable Y. In the localization problem X is a series of 3D locations and Y is a series of RSS vectors.

PF samples from the estimations of $P(X_0)$ and $P(X_i|X_{i-1})$ distributions for generating initial and subsequent propositions of locations which are then evaluated against an estimation of the likelihood $\mathcal{L}(Y_i|X_i)$ of observing a given Y_i.

Typical enhancements of the PF include resampling [1] of the set of X's generated up to a given point m on the basis of $\prod_{i=0}^{m} P(Y_i|X_i)$ and using as estimation of $P(X_i|X_{i-1}, Y_i)$ instead of $P(X_i|X_{i-1})$. In our algorithm we use the resampling interchangeably with the optimization of the last generated location by the Particle Swarm Optimization and we may look upon generating next point on the basis of a single point prediction (performed by the RF) as using an estimation of the $P(X_i|Y_i)$ distribution instead of $P(X_i|X_{i-1})$.

Particle Swarm Optimization. (PSO) (as described in [12]), is an iterative global optimization meta-heuristic method proposed in 1995 by Kennedy and Eberhart [10] and further studied and developed by many other researchers, e.g., [4,17,18]. In short, PSO utilizes the idea of swarm intelligence to solve hard optimization tasks. The underlying idea of the PSO algorithm consists of maintaining the swarm of particles moving in the search space. For each particle the set of neighboring particles which communicate their positions and function values to this particle is defined. Furthermore, each particle maintains its current position and velocity, as well as remembers its historically best (in terms of the solution quality) visited location. More precisely, in each iteration t, each particle i updates its position x_t^i and velocity v_t^i, according to the following formulas for the position and velocity update.

The position of a particle is updated according to the following equation:

$$x_{t+1}^i = x_t^i + v_t^i. \tag{1}$$

In our implementation of the PSO (based on [3,18]) the velocity v_t^i of a particle i is updated according to the following rule:

$$v_{t+1}^i = u_{U[0;g]}^{(1)}(x_{best}^{n[i]} - x_t^i) + u_{U[0;l]}^{(2)}(x_{best}^i - x_t^i) + a \cdot v_t^i \tag{2}$$

where

- g is a neighborhood attraction factor,
- $x_{best}^{n[i]}$ represents the best position (in terms of optimization) found so far by the particles belonging to the neighborhood of the ith particle,
- l is a local attraction factor,
- x_{best}^i represents the best position (in terms of optimization) found hitherto by particle i,
- a is an inertia coefficient,
- $u_{U[0;g]}^{(1)}$, $u_{U[0;l]}^{(2)}$ are random vectors with uniform distribution from the intervals $[0, g]$ and $[0, l]$, respectively.

In the case of localizing a mobile terminal the PSO is used to optimize a $3k$ dimensional function of the last k of m generated locations X_i, using a whole set as the PSO's population and $\prod_{i=m-k+1}^{m} P(Y_i|X_i)$ as a fitness function.

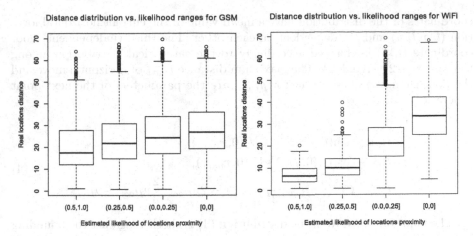

Fig. 1. The boxplots depict the relation between the ranges of estimated likelihood of locations proximity and the distribution of their real distance. The likelihood of the proximity is estimated from the radio signals observed in those locations. The left plot presents the results for GSM signals and the right one for WiFi signals.

2.2   Probability Estimations

This section describes the proposed estimated relations between the series of observed RSS vectors S and the series of estimated 3D locations L.

Location Likelihood Estimation. $\hat{\mathcal{L}}(S_i|L_i)$ relies on the reference RSS vector database for computing function $S(l)$ returning a signal observed in the location from database closest to l. Likelihood estimation consist of two factors: normalized Euclidean distance ρ between two RSS vectors (where M is a large constant grater then any ρ) and a squared number of non-zero RSS in both of the signal vectors divided by a number of non-zero RSS in each of the signal vectors.

$$\hat{\mathcal{L}}(S_i|L_i) = \frac{M - \rho(s_i, S(l_i))}{M} \frac{\left(\sum_{j=1}^{n} I(s_j * S_j(l_i) \neq 0)\right)^2}{\left(\sum_{j=1}^{n} I(s_{i,j} \neq 0)\right)\left(\sum_{j=1}^{n} I(S_j(l_i) \neq 0)\right)} \tag{3}$$

Figure 1 presents the relation between the signal distance and the location distance for the selected labeled RSS vectors from the reference database (for both the GSM and WiFi data).

Next Point. l_{i+1} for a given L series in the PF particles is created on the bases of l_i by sampling from a three dimensional probability distribution. The first two coordinates of the distribution have a mean value in the current horizontal location $(l_i.x, l_i.y)$ and are dependent on each other. The third (independent) floor coordinate $(l_i.f)$ is changed accordingly to the categorical distribution among the values $\{-2, -1, 0, 1, 2\}$. The maximum distance r_{max} of horizontal move and the floor change probability factor p_{floor} are the parameters of the next point generation.

$$l_{i+1} \sim (l_i.x + \sin(U_1(0, 2\pi)) * U_2(0, r_{max}),$$
$$l_i.y + \cos(U_1(0, 2\pi)) * U_2(0, r_{max}), \tag{4}$$
$$l_i.f + Cat(\frac{1}{3}p_{floor}, \frac{2}{3}p_{floor}, 1 - 2p_{floor}, \frac{2}{3}p_{floor}, \frac{1}{3}p_{floor})).$$

The point obtained from the distribution (4) is checked against the bounding box of the building and orthogonally projected on the exceeded boundary if necessary.

Location Prediction with the usage of the statistical model built on the reference RSS vectors database uses the estimated $(\hat{x}, \hat{y}, \hat{f})$ returned directly by the model and the error estimations $(SE_X, SE_Y, P(F|\hat{F}))$ computed on the test set extracted from the reference database (where $P(f|\hat{f})$ is estimated from the rows of the confusion matrix).

$$l_i(S_i) \sim \left(N(\hat{x}, SE_x), N(\hat{y}, SE_y), Cat(f|\hat{f}) \right) \tag{5}$$

At least one point is obtained directly from the statistical model and each of the obtained points is checked against the building's bounding box, exactly as the points generated from Eq. (4).

2.3   Localization Algorithm

The proposed localization algorithm processes a sequence of the radio signals (GSM or WiFi) measured by a mobile phone and determines a sequence of that phone locations. The flow chart of localization process is presented in Fig. 2.

The algorithm is initialized by a set of sequences of length 1, generated for the first observed signal s_0, from the Eq. (5). Subsequent points are generated either by the same way or from the Eq. (4) depending on the probability p_{RF} of using RF to generate a subsequent point. At the end of the processing of a given signal s_m the generated set of sequences (particles in PF) might be either resampled according to the weight of a given sequence L equal to $\prod_{i=0}^{m} \hat{\mathcal{L}}(S_i|L_i)$ or the last k locations might be optimized by the PSO algorithm with $\prod_{i=m-k+1}^{m} \hat{\mathcal{L}}(S_i|L_i)$ as a fitness function. The choice between the resampling and optimization depends on the p_{PSO} probability parameter. The location at

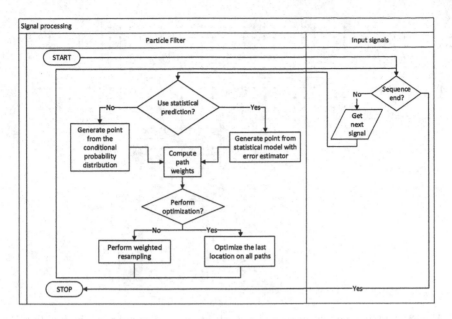

Fig. 2. A flow chart diagram of the signal processing in the localization algorithm.

the end of the series with the best value of the signal likelihood on the whole series is returned as a predicted current location.

After some initial tests the following set of common parameters have been chosen for the WiFi signals: $p_{floor} = 0.1$, $r_{max} = 3.0$, $p_{RF} = 0.5$. Within those common parameters a two different settings have been tested: $p_{PSO} = 0$ and 100 PF particles or $p_{PSO} = 1.0$, $k = 1$, 10 PSO iterations in each step and 10 PF particles.

For the GSM signals only one set of parameters has been chosen: $p_{floor} = 0.2$, $r_{max} = 10.0$, $p_{RF} = 0.0$, $p_{PSO} = 0$ and 225 PF particles. The number of PF particles in both tests has been limited by the processing time. Due to a smaller size of RSS vectors for the GSM data, larger number of particles could have been processed in a real time by a single thread of an Intel Core i5@1.9GHz machine.

3   Data Sets

As already mentioned, the data sets used to evaluate the proposed approach consisted of two parts: the reference database gathered in a stationary measurements and a real-world scenarios in which the data were gathered while a user followed a predefined path within the building while holding a mobile phone in his hand or having it in his pocket. In each of the data sets an RSS vectors of GSM and WiFi network have been gathered. Maps of all the locations where the data have been gathered and paths of the real world scenarios can be viewed on the research project's data interface website [16].

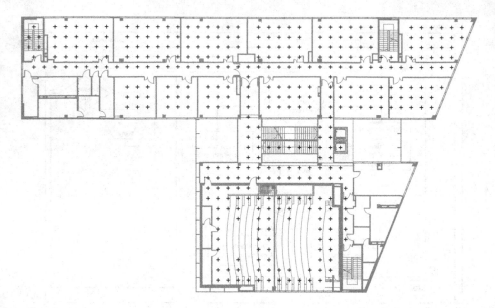

Fig. 3. The first measurments series mesh on one of the floors of the building.

Reference Database has been gathered in a similar way as described in [6,7,9] in around 3200 unique points divided into two independent measurement series. In each of the points 40 measurements have been taken in 4 different horizontal orientations (10 measurements in each direction with 500 ms periods in between). The data in each series have been gathered in a 1.5 by 1.5 meters mesh covering all of the publicly accessible areas of a six floor building. The meshes of the independent series are translated by 0.75 m in each direction. The example of a mesh on one of the floors is presented in Fig. 3. Each gathered data point consisted of an RSS vector marked with the transmitter identifier (LAC–Cell ID pair of the Base Transceiver Station for GSM data and BSSID of the Access Point for the WiFi data). Each data point has been manually labeled, when its measurements have been taken, with the x,y and $floor$ coordinates.

Test Set has been gathered while the user of the mobile phone has been moving around the building in the same areas where the reference data set has been obtained. The features of the data also contain an RSS vector marked with transmitters' identifiers. The x,y and $floor$ coordinates labeling the data points have been linearly interpolated between the way-points manually identified by the user on the reference mobile phone during the measurements.

4   Results

The algorithm has been tested on a few traversals of the three predefined paths with both GSM and WiFi data in the test set. The results from the PF and

Table 1. Floor prediction accuracy and medians of the horizontal location errors results for the GSM data divided into models, types of smoothing and scenarios

Model	Scenario	Smoothing	Accuracy	$x_{0.5}$	$y_{0.5}$
PF	1	[-15,15]	**0.45**	**4.70**	**12.02**
RF	1	[-15,15]	0.40	5.29	16.14
PF	1	0	0.40	6.28	14.18
RF	1	0	0.38	5.31	15.35
PF	1	[0,5]	0.42	5.58	13.43
RF	1	[0,5]	0.38	5.51	15.34
PF	2	[-15,15]	0.22	4.68	10.95
RF	2	[-15,15]	**0.52**	**2.23**	**4.54**
PF	2	0	0.20	6.00	12.82
RF	2	0	0.50	2.38	4.84
PF	2	[0,5]	0.21	5.30	11.56
RF	2	[0,5]	0.50	2.45	4.84
PF	3	[-15,15]	0.09	**4.17**	15.23
RF	3	[-15,15]	0.28	4.27	**4.27**
PF	3	0	0.09	6.36	17.30
RF	3	0	**0.30**	4.37	4.83
PF	3	[0,5]	0.09	4.80	16.88
RF	3	[0,5]	**0.30**	4.55	4.82

Table 2. Floor prediction accuracy and medians of the horizontal location errors results for the WiFi data divided into models and types of smoothing

Model	Smoothing	Accuracy	$x_{0.5}$	$y_{0.5}$
PF ($p_{PSO} = 1.0$)	[-15,15]	**0.74**	**2.47**	3.56
PF ($p_{PSO} = 0.0$)	[-15,15]	0.71	2.67	**3.20**
RF	[-15,15]	0.69	3.14	4.80
PF ($p_{PSO} = 1.0$)	0	**0.70**	**2.84**	3.83
PF ($p_{PSO} = 0.0$)	0	**0.70**	2.91	**3.80**
RF	0	0.67	3.14	4.86
PF ($p_{PSO} = 1.0$)	[0,5]	**0.70**	2.70	3.84
PF ($p_{PSO} = 0.0$)	[0,5]	0.69	**2.66**	**3.60**
RF	[0,5]	0.67	3.22	4.91

the RF have been additionally smoothed with a median filter for the x and y coordinates and with mode filter for the *floor*. The smoothing has been applied in 2 variants: off-line with 30 closest prediction (15 from the past and 15 from future) and on-line with 5 from the past.

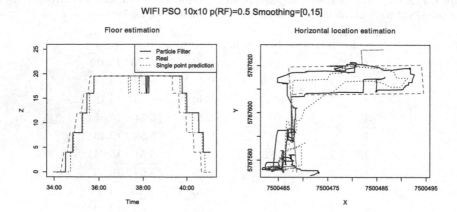

Fig. 4. Particle Filter predictions compared with a single point predictions done by a Random Forest and the real locations of the mobile terminal. Particle Filter in this example has been run with 10 particles and 10 iterations of PSO optimization for the current location. The probability of generating next location from a Random Forest predictor has been set to 0.5. Both PF and RF results are smoothed by aggregating current prediction with the previous ones (15 in the example).

The results are presented in Table 1 for the GSM data and in Table 2 for the WiFi data. Additionaly, an example of the prediction for the WiFi data is presented in Fig. 4.

As could be expected from Fig. 1 the obtained results were much worse for the GSM than for the WiFi data. On the WiFi data PF performed better or comparably well to the RF on all scenarios (resulting in significant average gain in accuracy and lowering of the median errors). On GSM data only for one of the three scenarios PF performed better, while for the other two it was much worse then RF. One of the possible explanations of that fact is that the 1st scenario spanned almost the whole building, while 2nd and 3rd scenarios concentrated more in the center (averaging trend of the RF can be observed in Fig. 4) and had many points on the floors better recognized by the RF predictor.

5   Conclusions

For the predictions based on the WiFi data the proposed approach was able to improve the results achieved by a single point Random Forest predictor, with the slight advantage of the method using PSO as the last location optimizer instead of a standard PF resampling technique. The best performance of both the PF and RF was achieved with off-line smoothing, while on-line smoothing offered very little numerical improvement over no smoothing (although the location plots were much clear even with a strong on-line smoothing).

Further research should concentrate on providing more data for the next point generation function presenting it with a more precise model of the building and possibly information extracted from the phone's accelerometer.

Acknowledgements. The research is supported by the National Centre for Research and Development, grant No PBS2/B3/24/2014, application No 208921.

References

1. Arulampalam, M., Maskell, S., Gordon, N., Clapp, T.: A tutorial on particle filters for online nonlinear/non-gaussian bayesian tracking. IEEE Trans. Signal Process. **50**(2), 174–188 (2002)
2. Breiman, L.: Random forests. Mach. Learn. **45**(1), 5–32 (2001)
3. Clerc, M.: Standard PSO 2011 (2012). http://www.particleswarm.info/
4. Cristian, I.: Trelea: the particle swarm optimization algorithm: convergence analysis and parameter selection. Inf. Process. Lett. **85**(6), 317–325 (2003)
5. Del Moral, P.: Nonlinear filtering: interacting particle solution. Markov Processes Relat. Fields **2**(4), 555–580 (1996)
6. Górak, R., Luckner, M.: Malfunction immune Wi-Fi localisation method. In: Nez, M., Nguyen, N., Camacho, D., Trawiski, B. (eds.) Computational Collective Intelligence. LNCS, vol. 9329, pp. 328–337. Springer, Heidelberg (2015). http://dx.doi.org/10.1007/978-3-319-24069-5_31
7. Grzenda, M.: On the prediction of floor identification credibility in RSS-based positioning techniques. In: Ali, M., Bosse, T., Hindriks, K.V., Hoogendoorn, M., Jonker, C.M., Treur, J. (eds.) IEA/AIE 2013. LNCS, vol. 7906, pp. 610–619. Springer, Heidelberg (2013). http://dx.doi.org/10.1007/978-3-642-38577-3_63
8. Ho, T.K.: The random subspace method for constructing decision forests. IEEE Trans. Pattern Anal. Mach. Intell. **20**(8), 832–844 (1998)
9. Karwowski, J., Okulewicz, M., Legierski, J.: Application of particle swarm optimization algorithm to neural network training process in the localization of the mobile terminal. In: Iliadis, L., Papadopoulos, H., Jayne, C. (eds.) EANN 2013. Communications in Computer and Information Science, vol. 383, pp. 122–131. Springer, Heidelberg (2013). http://dx.doi.org/10.1007/978-3-642-41013-0_13
10. Kennedy, J., Eberhart, R.: Particle swarm optimization. In: Proceedings of IEEE International Conference on Neural Networks, vol. 4, pp. 1942–1948 (1995)
11. Korbel, P., Wawrzyniak, P., Grabowski, S., Krasinska, D.: LocFusion API - programming interface for accurate multi-source mobile terminal positioning. In: 2013 Federated Conference on Computer Science and Information Systems (FedCSIS), pp. 819–823, September 2013
12. Okulewicz, M., Mańdziuk, J.: Dynamic vehicle routing problem: a Monte Carlo approach. In: Proceedings of the Selected Problems in Information Technologies, ITRIA 2015, vol. 1, pp. 119–138. ICS PAS (2015). http://phd.ipipan.waw.pl/pliki/mat_konferencyjne/12_ITRIA_2015_01.pdf#page=120
13. Papapostolou, A., Chaouchi, H.: Scene analysis indoor positioning enhancements. Ann. Télécommunications **66**, 519–533 (2011)
14. Rabiner, L., Juang, B.: An introduction to hidden Markov models. IEEE ASSP Mag. **3**(1), 4–16 (1986)

15. Roos, T., Myllymaki, P., Tirri, H., Misikangas, P., Sievanen, J.: A probabilistic approach to WLAN user location estimation. Int. J. Wireless Inf. Netw. **9**(3), 155–164 (2002)
16. Rosłan, A.: LOKKOM data viewing interface (in Polish) (2014). http://lokkom.mini.pw.edu.pl:8080/miniLocal.php
17. Shi, Y., Eberhart, R.: A modified particle swarm optimizer. In: Proceedings of IEEE International Conference on Evolutionary Computation, pp. 69–73 (1998)
18. Shi, Y., Eberhart, R.: Parameter selection in particle swarm optimization. In: Proceedings of Evolutionary Programming VII (EP98), pp. 591–600 (1998)
19. Wang, J., Hu, A., Liu, C., Li, X.: A floor-map-aided WiFi/pseudo-odometry integration algorithm for an indoor positioning system. Sensors **15**(4), 7096 (2015). http://www.mdpi.com/1424-8220/15/4/7096
20. Wawrzyniak, P., Hausman, S., Korbel, P.: Sequence detection of movement for accurate area based indoor positioning and tracking. In: 2015 9th European Conference on Antennas and Propagation (EuCAP), pp. 1–4, May 2015
21. Xiang, Z., Song, S., Chen, J., Wang, H., Huang, J., Gao, X.G.: A wireless LAN-based indoor positioning technology. IBM J. Res. Dev. **48**(5–6), 617–626 (2004)

Unsupervised Detection of Unusual Behaviors from Smart Home Energy Data

Welma Pereira[✉], Alois Ferscha, and Klemens Weigl

Institute for Pervasive Computing, Altenberger str. 69, 4040 Linz, Austria
welma.pereira@gmail.com, {pereira,ferscha,weigl}@pervasive.jku.at

Abstract. In this paper the potentials of identifying unusual user behaviors and changes of behavior from smart home energy meters are investigated. We compare the performance of the classical change detection Page-Hinkley test (PHT) with a new application of a self-adaptive stream clustering algorithm to detect novelties related to the time of use of appliances at home. With the use of annotated data, the true positive rate of the clustering-based method outperformed the PHT by at least 20 %. Moreover the method was able to identify behavior changes related to time shifts and replacement of appliances. The motivation for this study is based on the need for identifying and guiding behavior changes that can reduce energy consumption, and use this knowledge in the development of systems that can raise just-in-time warnings to save energy (e.g. avoid stand-by modes), and guide sustainable behavior changes.

Keywords: Novelty detection · Stream clustering · Behavioral change · Smart home energy saving

1 Introduction

Sustainable energy has been an important concern as energy demand continuous to rise worldwide. User behavior and lifestyle have an important impact on the energy consumption [26]. However, consumers still have a vague idea about how much their behavior influence energy consumption [24]. In order to better inform users and reduce energy consumption we need to continuously monitor energy consumption and be able to identify inefficient behaviors. While a lot of work have been done to inform users about their energy consumption using feedback displays [27–29], not much has been done to link specific changes in behavior to quantified energy uses [25].

Concerns about behavior change have also been present in other domains [21–23], and in the number of apps developed to support people to change habits related to e.g. fitness, diet, sleep, etc. [30]. Technologies for supporting health behavior change have the potential to make a meaningful impact on society [4]. This study is concerned with understanding user's behaviors over time. This is a complex task that involves the identification of routines, changes of routines

© Springer International Publishing Switzerland 2016
L. Rutkowski et al. (Eds.): ICAISC 2016, Part II, LNAI 9693, pp. 523–534, 2016.
DOI: 10.1007/978-3-319-39384-1_46

and irregular activities that might or might not be associated with changes of behavior. Since in such domains labels are rare or burdensome, unsupervised learning have been used to detect unusual events [11,28,31].

One of the challenges to improve energy efficiency is the need to design human-centric approaches to encourage people to have more sustainable behaviors. In order to do that, we turn to behavioral theory as suggested in [1], to better understand people's behaviors. We examine the value of harnessing smart energy meters data to detect unusual behaviors and changes of patterns in the use of appliances at the home environment.

As it has been shown in [2], the context (time, place and situation) in which a behavior is performed plays a crucial role in the establishment of habits. In the context of smart energy data, the locations of the appliances tend to be fixed so we assume the place to be static. The situation is hard to access, so we focus our attention on time.

Real time energy consumption data collected with the PowerIT system [5] is used to analyze how different appliances are being used at the home environment. The sensor readings include time data that is used to cluster the time-events when the appliances are turned on and off. We use a real-time clustering algorithm to continuously integrate new data into the model and characterize how appliances are being used over time. To detect changes of behavior we test and compare two novelty detection methods: the Page-Hinkley Test [3], and a measure based on deviations between the current clusters and the new sensor measurements. We show that this approach is able to detect unusual states like standby modes and unusual behaviors related to the use of common home appliances (e.g. TV, laptops, coffee machines, etc.). Furthermore the outputs during the clustering process are used to analyze how behaviors evolve in time. These outputs are used to characterize changes of behavior related to time shifts and replacement of appliances.

The approach suggested in this paper provides a way to directly and continuously access the stability of the time of use of home appliances as the sensor measurements are clustered. The stability of the time context is given by the similarity between the times at which a given behavior (e.g. to watch TV in the evening) is carried out. The method described here can identify dissimilar events such as standby modes, hence discovering energy-saving opportunities, and unusual activities that can be either punctual changes or the start point of behavior changes. We see the detection of novelties in this context as a first step towards characterizing behavior changes. The next step after a change has been identified is to determine whether this change is punctual, seasonal or long-term. In the last case we have a better ground to say that a behavior change has happened, whereas on the first and second cases the old habit is more likely to persist.

2   Related Work

The general idea for finding novelties is to build a model of the training data that has little or no examples of the novelties, and then identify deviations from this model using a threshold. The deviations are used to assign novelty scores to the novelty candidates. According to [10] novelty detections techniques can be classified as probabilistic, distance-based, reconstruction-based, domain-based, and information-theoretic. Distance-based technique assume that data are tightly clustered, and novel data occurs far away from their nearest neighbors. It includes the nearest neighbor and clustering methods. The approach for finding novelties used in this paper is based on clustering. As noted in [13] clustering is a natural choice to study broad changes in trends, since it summarizes the behavior of the data. Novelties can provide insights about the residents' activities and therefore about how their behavior change.

A monitoring system for detecting energy waste caused by malfunctioning or standby of appliances is presented in [11]. The system clusters the power consumption into states and then divides the clusters into sub-states based on the durations. The times between recurrent states are tracked and a Markov model is used to monitor state transitions. Any deviations from the models built during training are signaled as malfunctions. The approach used in this paper is also based on clustering. However, instead of clustering the power consumption, we cluster the initial time and the end time of use. Therefore the clusters that we get take into account the durations, while the clustering algorithm keeps track of the times that the appliances are used. As a result we get a picture of when and for how long the appliances are being used. This gives us more insights into the users behaviors.

A modified version of an incremental clustering algorithm (M-DBScan) is used in [12] to detect when a player changes his/her behavior in a computer game. The novelties are detected using an entropy measure based on the spatial distribution of data into clusters. Every time new data is collected and processed by the model, the entropy changes. If these variations are greater than a threshold, an alert is raised to indicate a behavior change. The paper tracks changes that happen at pre-defined moments in time related to the dynamics of a computer game (e.g. number of shots, number of deaths, mean velocity, mean distance between players, etc.). Even though the problem is similar, the data used in this work is different in nature from the one that was used in [12].

A correlation pattern mining algorithm for smart home appliances was developed in [16] to deal with the problem of mining multiple appliances instead of single ones. A study about the factors that influence energy consumption of individual devices at home was done in [17]. The results showed that the associations between the devices are often stronger than the associations based on the hour of the day or on the day of the week.

New research have been done to detect gradual changes including information about the time when they occur for the detection of forest degradation [18], and in energy-efficient mobile crowd-sensing to detect change points of contexts [19]. Also human behavior shift detection of sequences of actions that often occur together have been investigated using Markov chains in [20]. However algorithms that detect and support personalized energy-efficient changes of behavior are still missing.

3   System Architecture and Case Study

We used real data that has been collected using the PowerIT system [5,6]. The system was used to gather information about people's activities at home, in an unobtrusive way, from multiple, heterogeneous sensors that have been deployed in different households. The system's infrastructure comprises a home server, a set of energy meters and control devices. The energy meters are connected between the wall plugs and the appliances to measure their power consumption. The users can also use the system to control the ON and OFF states of the appliances. A set of approximately 20 home appliances (e.g. TV, washing machine, laptop, etc.) is connected to the energy meters and can be controlled using either a smartphone, tablet, or a smart watch.

Two households were recruited to participate in the case study that served as a test bed to evaluate the system and to acquire the data (see Table 1). The data of the first case study (H1) was recorded between June 5th and November 27th, 2014, the second case study was recorded from October 1st, 2013 to January 27th, 2014.

The data used in this paper was the recordings from the energy meters that measured the power consumption of the appliances (labeled with IDs) along with the time stamps of the records. The energy meters measured energy consumption in Watt in intervals of approximately 20s. The data was aggregated into averaged power consumption by hour.

Since we are interested in monitoring user's behaviors, we track the appliances that depend on the user interaction. We consider the appliances that belong to the categories usage dependent and fixed operation as it was proposed in [14]. Background appliances like e.g. fridges or heatings do not depend directly on the user behavior and were not used for this study.

The households used in the case study included different types of houses (e.g. family house, single flat) in order to provide different scenarios for the application of the system and energy consumption behaviors. Regarding privacy, the data was edited to hide any personal information that could be used to trace back to single case participants.

4   Methodology

4.1   Identifying Events

We define an event as the continuous time window between the start point time of use of an appliance (with a minimum power consumption of 3 W) and the end time point of use when the energy consumption reaches zero again. This event definition is the basis for the change detection algorithms in this paper.

Since there is a significant change of dynamics between weekdays, and between weekends, we separated the events in these two categories. We focused on the events during the week because they tend to be more regular, and therefore are more likely to present patterns that can be detected.

4.2   Page-Hinkley Test (PHT)

The Page-Hinkley Test [8,9] has been used to detect abrupt changes in the mean of normal behaviors in various domains. To do so, it monitors the cumulative difference between the observed values $(x_1, ..., x_t)$ and their mean $(\bar{x}_t = \frac{1}{t}\sum_{i=1}^{t} x_i)$:

$$m_t = \sum_{i=1}^{t}(x_i - \bar{x}_t - \delta) \tag{1}$$

where δ is the allowed magnitude of the changes. The test then monitors the difference:

$$PHT = m_t - min(m_t, i = 1, ..., t) \tag{2}$$

and signals a change every time this difference exceeds a threshold ϵ. We use the PHT for each individual variable: initial time, end time and power consumption. In our experiments we used: $\epsilon = 2 * mean(PHT)$.

4.3   Novelty Score Based on Stream Clustering (NSBSC)

Cluster analysis is a technique that is used to identify different groups of observations, and can be used as a baseline to identify abnormal behaviors. We apply clustering to the times of the data events to better understand the usual behaviors and to be able to identify abnormalities. Since in this application the sensor measurements are continuously gathered and are unbounded, there is a need for a stream clustering algorithm that can work online and can deal with changes. Parameters such as the number of clusters can change as time goes by therefore the algorithm should self-adapt to these changes.

To cluster the data we use ClusTree [7], a self-adaptive anytime stream clustering algorithm that performs a single pass over the data. ClusTree relies on an index structure for storing and maintaining a compact view of the current clustering. The approach is based on micro-clusters which are compact representations containing the number of objects in each cluster, their linear sum, and their squared sum. Micro-clusters are used to compute the mean and variance of the clusters incrementally. New observations are assigned to clusters according to the closest mean with respect to the Euclidean distance, and splitting is based on pairwise distances between the entries, where entries are combined into two groups such that the sum of the intra-group distances is minimal [7].

ClusTree uses a time-dependent decay function:

$$\omega(\Delta t) = 2^{-\lambda \Delta t} \tag{3}$$

that weights the significance of the data points to the clustering. The decay rate λ controls the age of the data and enables a forgetting mechanism that is used to discard old data that no longer represents the current behavior of the users. However in our experiments we keep track of the data counts in each cluster because we are also interested in tracking the evolution of behaviors.

Taking advantage of the clustering process, we can detect changes as deviations from the current clusters. So if a new event is not clustered into one of current clusters, we measure the distance between the new event and the nearest cluster. Otherwise, if the new event is clustered, we measure the distance between the new event and the cluster it entered. The novelties can then be ranked according to this distance. To shorten the list of novelties, we compare the current distance with the mean of the distances that have been calculated so far. In order to evaluate the novelty degree in a comparable scale, we normalize the distances up to the current time in a scale that goes from 0 to 1. This way we can have a more or less comparable rank of the novelties according to the degree by which they differ from the usual behavior.

The energy consumption associated with each behavior and each appliance is averaged online, as well as the event counts separated into appliances counts for each cluster. This way every behavior can be characterized with the timing and the correspondent power consumption of each appliance. Unusual values (too high or too low compared to the mean) are detected with the PHT and are target as outliers. They can be used to raise alarms but they are not averaged, because they would disturb the characterization of usual behaviors.

4.4   Exploratory Analysis of the Evolution of Behaviors

Above we presented methods to identify novelties in the data. Novelties can be unusual behaviors that never/rarely happened before or it could indicate the starting point of a new behavior. Such new behavior can be related to time shifts in the use of individual appliances or it can be related for instance to the replacement of an appliance by another. To analyze the behavior evolution of the use of appliances with relation to each other, we propose to use the Pearsons correlation between the evolution of the counts in each cluster for each appliance. To be able to compute that we would need to store at each time step the counts for each appliance. However we can calculate the correlation incrementally as in [15].

During the clustering process, clusters can appear, disappear, and merge. The disappearance of clusters can happen when a behavior is not happening anymore. Since we are interested in understanding how changes of behaviors happen, we explored the connection between the increase of one behavior related to the disappearance of other. A negative correlation in this context implies that while the event counts in one cluster increases, the other cluster dies out and restarts from zero. We monitor the correlations between cluster counts using a threshold of -0.5 to identify when a behavior might be replacing another.

The number of correlations to be computed depends on the number of appliances being monitored and the number of clusters. For example for house H1, we have 8 appliances and 6 clusters which gives a total of 2304 combinations of correlations between all clusters (with the event times) and all possible combinations of appliances used at different times. However since the correlation matrix is symmetric we only need to compute half of it (1152).

4.5 Evaluation

The evaluation of the above methods is done using the ground truth annotated data from the participants of the case study. At the end of the study the participants were presented with a list of the events of all the monitored appliances, and were asked to label the events that were consider as unusual and changes of behavior. For instance if a person is used to recharge her mobile phone only in the evenings, a recharge in the morning or afternoon is considered an unusual behavior.

The true positive rate (TPR) was used to evaluate the performances of the PHT and the NSBSC in finding novelties.

$$TPR = \frac{TP}{TP + FN} \tag{4}$$

where TP is the number of true positive instances that were labelled as unusual events by the participants and were correctly detected by the algorithm as such, and FN is the number of false negative instances that were not classified as unusual events by the algorithm but that in fact were unusual according to the participant's labels.

5 Experiments and Discussion

5.1 Results

Both methods could identify unusual events that happened during the week due to holidays of the users. For example in house H1, the TV was used for a much longer period (from 8am to 6pm) than the usual (6:30 pm to 11 pm). Standby states of laptops that were left ON during the whole night were also detected. However long periods that started or ended at usual times were not always detected by the PHT.

During the experiment a laptop that used to be recharged in the evening increasingly started to be recharged more often in the mornings. This new behavior was detected by the NSBSC method but it took longer for the PHT to stop ranking every similar event as novel.

As it can be seen in Table 1 the true positive rate is in average considerably higher for the NSBSC method. However a larger test bed would be required to better evaluate the methods, these first results indicate that the NSBSC method can identify unusual behaviors reasonably well compared to the PHT.

Using the incremental correlation between event counts of all clusters and appliances, three most significant changes were identified and can be seen in Fig. 1. The left graph shows the event counts of the three laptops used in house H1. The event counts of the Laptop 1 (Entertainment Computer) starts to increase at x = 332, while the event counts of the other two laptops go to zero and remain like that until the end of the experiment. The event counts of Laptop 2 (Accounting Computer) and Laptop 3 (Working Computer) refer to cluster 3 that before the change had on average the start time = 6.4 am, and end time

= 7.4 am. The event counts of Laptop 1 after the change refer to cluster 2 that had on average start time = 6.6 am and end time = 7.5 am. This means that from x = 332 on, the use of the Laptop 2 and Laptop 3 at about 6–7am were replaced by the use of the Laptop 1. The average energy consumption of Laptop 1 was 5.7 W per use, which is smaller than the average energy consumptions of Laptop 2 (22.2 W per use) and of Laptop 3 (8.9 W per use).

The middle graph shows the event counts of the TV in clusters 5 (t2 in the graph) and 6 (t1 in the graph). It shows that there was a time shift from t1 (average start time = 6.8 pm and end time = 9.4 pm) to t2 (average start time = 7.9 pm and end time = 9.8 pm) with a similar average power consumption (in t1 of 12.3 W per use and in t2 of 15.1 W per use).

The right graph shows the event counts of the tablet recharger in clusters 4 (t1 in the graph) and 6 (t2 in the graph). The change happened at x = 204 where cluster 4 (average start time = 5.4 pm and end time = 6.3 pm) took over cluster 6 (average start time = 6.8 pm and end time = 9.4 pm) with similar average power consumption of 6.7 W per use in t1 and 5.8 W per use in t2.

Table 1. True positive rate of the Page-Hinkley Test (PHT) and the Novelty Score based on Stream Clustering (NSBSC) for all appliances and houses.

Home	Appliance	PHT	NSBSC
H1	TV	66.7 %	66.7 %
	Entertainment Computer	12.5 %	75.0 %
	Accounting Computer	70.0 %	80.0 %
	Tablet	36.4 %	81.8 %
	Mobile Phone	100 %	100 %
	Working Computer	75.0 %	100 %
	Average	60.1 %	**84 %**
H2	TV (living room)	100 %	100 %
	Coffee Machine	0.0 %	100 %
	Rechargers	100 %	100 %
	Laptop	100 %	100 %
	TV (room)	100 %	100 %
	Average	80 %	**100 %**

5.2   Discussion

The detection of unusual behaviors is not an easy task. The labeling process is subjected to inaccuracies, because it is often hard for a person to remember if a behavior has changed, and when exactly that happened. For example, in one of the houses the exact time when the behavior of recharging a laptop in the evening

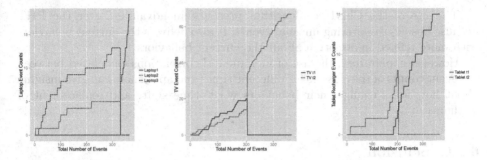

Fig. 1. Behavior evolution showing the replacement of laptops (left), time shifts of a TV (middle) and a tablet recharger(right).

shifted to the morning could not be identified. However, the user confirmed that the change has happened. Other unusual events like having an appliance ON for a long period of time could be detected if the user knew that she/he was or wasn't at home at that time. Events detected during holidays were more reliably labeled because the participants could double-check when they had holidays and could remember or judge about their most likely activities during that days. The detection of long periods of standby events can also be considered reliable because standby states are usually characterized by very low power consumption that does not depend much on the users. The replacement of laptops in house H1 was confirmed by the users with a high degree of confidence. The time shift of the TV was also confirmed, however with a lower degree of confidence, which is understandable since the change was small (the start time shifted from 6.8 pm to 7.9 pm, and the end time only changed from 9.4 pm to 9.8 pm). Similar change happened for the recharging time of a tablet. However a larger data set would be required for a more in-depth evaluation, the potentials of revealing to people their changes of behavior represent a big step towards measuring how human behavior changes and how it affects energy consumption.

Both methods demonstrated to be useful in finding unusual events in the datasets. However, repetition of the same or very similar novelty in a short time period (e.g. two following days) is still detected as novelty by the PHT. The same problem didn't happen with the NSBSC method, because once a new cluster has been created, a new observation of similar kind will be inserted into the newly created cluster, thus not yielding high novelty levels. This problem could be solved by tuning the parameters δ, and ϵ, however different appliances might require different tuned values. Both methods cannot detect novelties very well if the time events change too often.

The PHT detects better novelties that are very different from the most frequent behavior of an individual appliance, independently of the behavior of the other appliances. The NSBSC method, on the other hand detects better novelties that are different with respect to the set of appliances that tend to be used together. So if any appliance is used with an usual duration (e.g. standby) it will be detected with a higher novelty level by the NSBSC method.

The use of the ClusTree algorithm presents an advantage over the PHT because besides discovering unusual events, it also delivers the current behaviors with more refined information about the current behaviors.

However exploratory, the use of incremental correlations calculated between the event counts of the clusters for different times and appliances can give insights about how users change their behaviors w.r.t. time shifts and replacement of appliances.

6   Conclusion

This paper investigates methods to detect user behavior changes in houses equipped with smart home appliances.

The traditional change detection Page-Hinkley test (PHT) was compared with a Novelty Score based on Stream Clustering (NSBSC) method. Changes related to the times when appliances are used at home could be detected by both methods with the NSBSC performing better than the PHT (true positive rate: 84 % for house 1 and 100 % for house 2 (NSBSC), 60 % for house 1 and 80 % for house 2 (PHT)). Behavior changes related to time shifts and appliances replacement could be identified by calculating the incremental correlation between the event counts of the clusters that are increasing and the clusters that disappear.

This study presents an advance over traditional self-reported behaviors that tend to be inaccurate. It gives a basis with algorithms and technologies for assessing and analyzing the time context of behaviors connected with smart appliances at the home environment. Future research will consider a larger scale and more rigorous study to assess how the three aspects of context (location, time and situation) can influence behaviors and habits.

Acknowledgments. The project PowerIT acknowledges the financial support of FFG FIT-IT under grant number 830.605.

References

1. Hekler, E.B., Klasnja, P., Froehlich, J.E., Buman, M.P.: Mind the theoretical gap: interpreting, using, and developing behavioral theory in HCI research. In: Proceedings of the SIGCHI Conference on Human Factors in Computing Systems, pp. 3307–3316. ACM, New York (2013)
2. Danner, U.N., Aarts, H., Vries, N.K.: Habit vs. intention in the prediction of future behaviour: the role of frequency, context stability and mental accessibility of past behaviour. Br. J. Soc. Psychol. **47**, 245–265 (2008)
3. Salah, A.A., Kröse, B.J.A., Cook, D.J.: Behavior analysis for elderly. In: Salah, A.A., Kröse, B.J.A., Cook, D. (eds.) HBU 2015. LNCS, vol. 9277, pp. 1–10. Springer, Heidelberg (2015). doi:10.1007/978-3-319-24195-1_1
4. Klasnja, P., Consolvo, S., Pratt, W.: How to evaluate technologies for health behavior change in HCI research. In: Proceedings of the SIGCHI Conference on Human Factors in Computing Systems, pp. 3063–3072. ACM, New York (2011)

5. Hoelzl, G., Halbmayer, P., Rogner, H., Xue, C., Ferscha, A.: On the utilization of smart gadgets for energy aware sensitive behavior. In: The 8th International Conference on Digital Society, pp. 192–198. ACM (2014)
6. Halbmayer, P., Hoelzl, G., Ferscha, A.: A dynamic service module oriented framework for real-world situation representation. In: The 6th International Conference on Adaptive and Self-Adaptive Systems and Applications, pp. 79–84 (2014)
7. Kranen, P., Assenty, I., Baldauf, C., Seidl, T.: Self-adaptive anytime stream clustering. In: Ninth IEEE International Conference on Data Mining, pp. 249–258 (2009)
8. Page, E.S.: Continuous Inspection Schemes. Biometrika **41**, 100–115 (1954)
9. Hinkley, D.: Inference about the change-point from cumulative sum tests. Biometrika **58**, 509–523 (1971)
10. Pimentel, M.A.F., Clifton, D.A., Clifton, L., Tarassenko, L.: A review of novelty detection. Sig. Process **99**, 215–249 (2014)
11. Tanuja, G., Rahayu, D.A.P., Seetharam, D.P., Kunnath, R., Kumar, A.P., Vijay, A., Husain, S.A., Kalyanaraman, S.: SocketWatch: an autonomous appliance monitoring system. In: IEEE International Conference on Pervasive Computing and Communications, pp. 38–43. IEEE (2014)
12. Vallim, R.M.M., Andrade Filho, J.A., De Mello, R.F., De Carvalho, A.C.P.L.F.: Online behavior change detection in computer games. Expert Syst. Appl. **40**, 6258–6265 (2013)
13. Aggarwal, C.: A Survey of Change Diagnosis Algorithms in Evolving Data Streams, vol. 31, pp. 85–102. Springer, Heidelberg (2007)
14. Zaidi, A.A., Kupzog, F., Zia, T., Palensky, P.: Load recognition for automated demand response in microgrids. In: 36th Annual Conference on IEEE Industrial Electronics Society, pp. 2442–2447 (2010)
15. Wang, M., Wang, X.S.: Efficient evaluation of composite correlations for streaming time series. In: Dong, G., Tang, C., Wang, W. (eds.) WAIM 2003. LNCS, vol. 2762, pp. 369–380. Springer, Heidelberg (2003)
16. Chen, Y.C., Peng, W.C., Huang, J.L., Lee, W.C.: Significant correlation pattern mining in smart homes. ACM Trans. Intell. Syst. Technol. **6**, 35:1–35:23 (2015)
17. Rollins, S., Banerjee, N.: Using rule mining to understand appliance energy consumption patterns. In: IEEE International Conference on Pervasive Computing and Communications (PerCom), pp. 29–37 (2014)
18. Chamber, Y., Garg, A., Mithal, V., Brugere, I., Lau, M., Boriah, S., Potter, C.: A novel time series based approach to detect gradual vegetation changes in forests. In: Proceedings of the 2011 NASA Conference on Intelligent Data Understanding (CIDU) (2011)
19. Le, V.-D., Scholten, H., Havinga, P.J.M.: Online change detection for energy-efficient mobile crowdsensing. In: Awan, I., Younas, M., Franch, X., Quer, C. (eds.) MobiWIS 2014. LNCS, vol. 8640, pp. 1–16. Springer, Heidelberg (2014)
20. Aztiria, A., Farhadi, G., Aghajan, H.: User behavior shift detection in intelligent environments. In: Bravo, J., Hervás, R., Rodríguez, M. (eds.) IWAAL 2012. LNCS, vol. 7657, pp. 90–97. Springer, Heidelberg (2012)
21. Bourgeois, J., van der Linden, J., Kortuem, G., Price, B.A., Rimmer, C.: Conversations with my washing machine: an in-the-wild study of demand shifting with self-generated energy. In: Proceedings of the 2014 ACM International Joint Conference on Pervasive and Ubiquitous Computing, pp. 459–470 (2014)
22. Kawamoto, K., Tanaka, T., Kuriyama, H.: Your activity tracker knows when you quit smoking. In: Proceedings of the 2014 ACM International Symposium on Wearable Computers, pp. 107–110 (2014)

23. Doryab, A., Min, J.K., Wiese, J., Zimmerman, J., Hong, J.: Detection of behavior change in people with depression. In: AAAI Workshops (2014)
24. Darby, S.: The effectiveness of feedback on energy consumption. A review for DEFRA of the literature on metering, billing and direct displays. Technical report, Environmental Change Inst., Univ. Oxford, Oxford, U.K. (2006)
25. Tsang, F., Burge, P., Diepeveen, S., Guerin, B., Drabble, S., Bloom, E.: What works in changing energy-using behaviours in the home? A rapid evidence assessment: final report. UK Department of Energy and Climate Change. London, United Kingdom (2012)
26. Zhou, K., Yang, S.: Understanding household energy consumption behavior: the contribution of energy big data analytics. Renew. Sustain. Ener. Rev. **56**, 810–819 (2016)
27. Kjeldskov, J., Skov, M.B., Paay, J., Pathmanathan, R.: Using mobile phones to support sustainability: a field study of residential electricity consumption. In: Proceedings of the SIGCHI Conference on Human Factors in Computing Systems, pp. 2347–2356. ACM (2012)
28. Chen, Y.C., Ko, Y.L., Peng, W.C.: An intelligent system for mining usage patterns from appliance data in smart home environment. In: Technologies and Applications of Artificial Intelligence (TAAI), pp. 319–322 (2012)
29. Kjeldskov, J., Skov, M.B., Paay, J., Lund, D., Madsen, T., Nielsen, M.: Eco-forecasting for domestic electricity use. In: Proceedings of the 33rd Annual ACM Conference on Human Factors in Computing Systems, pp. 1985–1988. ACM (2015)
30. Hollis, V., Konrad, A., Whittaker, S.: Change of heart: emotion tracking to promote behavior change. In: Proceedings of the 33rd Annual ACM Conference on Human Factors in Computing Systems, pp. 2643–2652. ACM (2015)
31. Drachen, A., Thurau, C., Sifa, R., Bauckhage, C.: A comparison of methods for player clustering via behavioral telemetry. CoRR. abs/1407.3950 (2014)

Associative Memory Idea in a Nano-Environment

Henryk Piech[1], Lukasz Laskowski[2(⊠)], Jerzy Jelonkiewicz[2],
Magdalena Laskowska[2], and Arnaud Boullanger[3]

[1] Institute of Computer Science, Czestochowa University of Technology,
ul. Dabrowskiego 69, 42-201 Czestochowa, Poland
[2] Institute of Computational Intelligence, Czestochowa University of Technology,
Al. A.K. 36, 42-200 Czestochowa, Poland
`lukasz.laskowski@kik.pcz.pl`
[3] Université Montpellier II, Chimie Moléculaire et Organisation du Solide,
Institut Charles Gerhardt, UMR 5253 CC 1701, 2 Place E. Bataillon,
34095 Montpellier Cedex 5, France

Abstract. Nanotechnology is based on molecules with spin energy
[4,7,14]. These elementary particles are located outside magnetic field
[5,15,17]. Due to their chemical structure they react differently in reference to their own magnetic spin value correction [18]. The correction
refers also to the spin direction (phase θ) [20]. Technology parameters
and conditions will not be considered in the paper. We focus on idea
of finding the most correlated memory module location with given key
structure. The problem is difficult as existing solutions in traditional
computer technology with memory cells fitting comparator do not con-
form to the spin technology set of tools. Nevertheless, when we implement
operation based on probabilities of binary states after each operation we
lose measured value and phase [8]. Therefore, our proposition should be
based on different strategy of finding the closest distance among key and
context of memory blocks.

Keywords: Associative memory · Nano-technology · Magnetic spin ·
Tunneled joint · Spin transistor

1 Introduction

In associative memory given keys (attributes) locations can be found in a main
memory. This process can be parallel and iterative [1,2,8,9,16]. The keys can
have stable or dynamically extended character. The association procedure uses
comparison operations. The paper considers comparison operations implemented
for nano environment technology in a probabilistic variant. Nano-technology
imposes specific theoretical and practical constrains. The nano-environment convention brings us closer to a quantum strategy of conversion which relies on sets
of probabilistic data. There are several kinds of nano-structures. Some of them

© Springer International Publishing Switzerland 2016
L. Rutkowski et al. (Eds.): ICAISC 2016, Part II, LNAI 9693, pp. 535–545, 2016.
DOI: 10.1007/978-3-319-39384-1_47

e.g. magnetic conductor in an outside field, two layers magnetic structure and molecular spin transistor are described in Sect. 3.

The idea of such a memory entails a lot of interests in many possible application fields. It can have different meaning depending on how its role is seen in the computer system [9]:

– the material facilities, for instance, a computer memory, a physical system, or a set of elements which serve as a base for the representation of information,
– the entirety of stored representations (in life sciences, sometimes named "memories"),
– the abstract structure of knowledge that is implicit in the stored representations and their semantic relations,
– the recollections which, especially in the mental sense, may be sequences of events that are reconstructed in a process of reminiscence.

There were a few attempts to define the principles of the nano-technology information system [3, 8]. System theory leads to a challenge revealing at least the fundamentals of these principles. This approach is interesting not only because of providing physical explanations of some strategy effects but also since it brings feasible solutions to artificial systems.

2   System Models of Associative Memory

The key information is the address register. All memory is searched to find adequate (matched) key information (see: Fig. 1). There are also used tags of agreement.

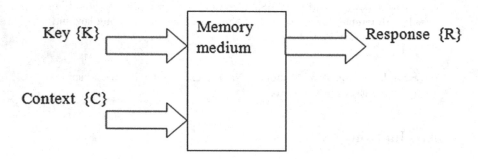

Fig. 1. Structure of memory system model with associative recall

The principle of retrieval, characteristic for biological memories, is the *associative recall* of information. When a pattern *key* (K) is applied to the input, a specific *response* pattern (R), associated with the key, is obtained at the output. Additional information, representing the *context* (C) with the stimulus, may be applied to the input [8].

When using different context options it is possible to specify an item to be recalled more closely like: selecting the pairs of input-output patterns with the most adequate content, strategy of association adaptation, structured sequences of memory events recalling procedures, knowledge representation, retrieving process recycling, patterns classification etc.

Knowledge from more complex memory structures comes from elementary observations in the process of repetitions. An information retrieving process, based on natural memorization, is represented by four channel model (Fig. 2).

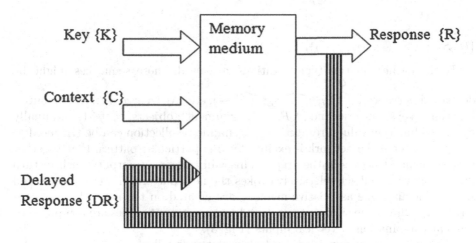

Fig. 2. Structure of associative memory model with feedback

Associative memory in this case is defined as complex procedure in which stored data set, for instance, a set of concomitant patterns, can be regarded as key excitation. One of the input patterns is the representation of an attribute, here understood as a key pattern $K(t)$ indexed by a time variable t. The second input channel carries a concomitant pattern $C(t)$ (abbreviation for context or control) which role does not differ much from that one related to an attribute. If the output pattern at time t is denoted $R(t)$ (abbreviation for response or recollection), then the third input is derived from R(t) through a delayed feedback channel $DR = R(t - \Delta)$. The adaptive physical system storage and recall may be simultaneous processes. Particularly, the system structure is such that during storage, $R(t)$ and $K(t)$ are identical. During recall, a replica of stored K must occur as an output R. An output $R = K$ is first obtained. According to the definition of associative recall, when the delayed output $R(t - \Delta)$ appears at the input, then, by virtue of the pair (C, R) used as the key, the next $R(t)$ is obtained by associative recall. The new output, again, after a delay t, acts as an input by which the third $R(t)$ is recalled, etc. It is possible to deduce that a stored sequence with context pattern C is generated.

Example. Generation of the knowledge structured graph is demonstrated when certain partial sequences of patterns, formed by $K(t) \in \{x, y, v, z, w, u, -\}$ and $C(t) \in \{Q, S, -\}$, are applied at the input of the memory type depicted in Fig. 2: the symbols $x, y, ..., Q, S$ stand for spatial patterns of signals, and $(-)$ is an empty pattern with signal values zero. (It is assumed that empty patterns do not produce responses.) It is assumed that the following timed sequences of pairs $[K(t), C(t)]$ are present at the input during storage phases:

$\{(x, Q), (y, Q), (z, Q)\};$
$\{(y, Q), (z, Q), (w, Q), (-, Q), (-, -)\};$
$\{(x, S), (v, S)\};$
$\{(v, S), (z, S)\};$
$\{(z, S), (u, S), (-, S), (-, -)\}.$

If the earlier relation-type notations are used, these sequences might be described as triples $x \overset{Q}{\frown\rightarrow} y, y \overset{R}{\frown\rightarrow} z, z \overset{S}{\frown\rightarrow} (-)$, etc. We treat $x, y, ...$ as attributes, functions, keys, patterns and $Q, R, ...$ as arguments, objects, context, and finally $y, z, ...$ as function values, respectively. Dynamic recollection can be triggered at any time later if the network is excited by one particular pattern that together with its context occurs in the graph. This will trigger an output which in turn due to delayed feedback selectively evokes the next pattern in the sequence, and so on. The analogue associative memory are created on the network base, constructed as linear physical systems. Conductance output values are computed as a linear combination of vertical inputs (Fig. 3).

Generally, the output value can be presented as follows:

$$\eta_i = \sum_{j=1}^{n} \omega_{i,j} \sigma_j, \tag{1}$$

where $\omega_{i,j}$ - crossing coefficient in order to avoid negative conductance values.

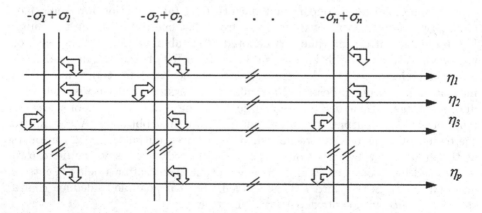

Fig. 3. Linear transformation in analogue network

An ordered set $x(t) = (\sigma_1(t),\ \sigma_2(t), ...,\ \sigma_n(t))$ is an input pattern. An output set is denoting as $y(t) = (\eta_1(t),\ \eta_2(t), ...,\ \eta_p(t))$. The $\omega_{i,j}$ are calculated as the correlation matrix of a set of pair $\{x(t),\ y(t)\}$, $t = 1, 2, ..., m$:

$$\omega_{i,j} = \sum_{t=1}^{m} \eta_i t \sigma_j t \qquad (2)$$

Considering that $x = (\sigma_1,\ \sigma_2, ...,\ \sigma_n)$, we get

$$\eta_j = \sum_{t=1}^{m}(\sum_{j=1}^{n}\sigma_j\sigma_j(t))\eta_i(t) = \sum_{t=1}^{m} w(t)\eta_i(t). \qquad (3)$$

Coefficients $w(t)$ depend on inner products of the key pattern x with the respective stored patterns $x(t)$ [8].

Another model proposed in [3] is equipped with preprocessor (Fig. 4). The stencils $x(t)$ and $y(t)$ should be selected identically. Preliminary, selectivity depends on the inner product $w(t)$ (function of the input stencil). The key patterns $x(t)$ derive from $y(t)$: the $y(t)$ is preprocessed by an operation which increased selectivity.

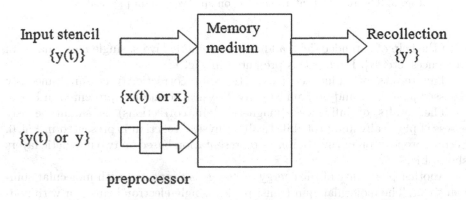

Fig. 4. System model structure of an associative memory with preprocessing

A lot of different associative memories and techniques are presented in the literature [3,8]. Only a few of them can be used in the nano-structure of the magnetic spins.

3   Nano-Enviroments for Association Strategy

The comparison procedure is the most often applied in association process. Dynamically changed attributes are merged with parts of memory medium content. In nano-technologies we have possibilities to create dynamic key parameter

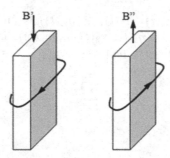

Fig. 5. Extended field as a kind of influence adequate attribute (key) parameter

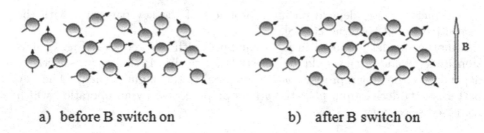

a) before B switch on   b)   after B switch on

Fig. 6. The result of influence of B on spin vectors in physical aspect

with the help of extended field, additional magnetic layers, single molecular spin influences, etc. [7]. First case is presented in Fig. 5.

The results of influences (magnetic spin corrections) is simultaneously assessed physically and probabilistically. Physical reaction is presented in Fig. 6.

The results of influences (magnetic spin corrections) is simultaneously assessed physically and probabilistically. Physical reaction is presented in Fig. 6. Second proposition of key attributes representation based on two magnetic layers shows Fig. 7.

Another possibility of the energy exchange is connected with molecular spin-transistor. The molecular spin-transistor is a single-electron transistor with non-magnetic electrodes and a single magnetic molecule as the island (Fig. 8).

The current passes through the magnetic molecule and the source and drain electrodes, while the electronic transport properties are tuned using a gate voltage Vg (Fig. 9).

According to molecular electronics [18] two experimental regimes can be distinguished, depending on the coupling between molecule and electrodes: weak-coupling limit and strong coupling limit. The presentation of molecular level changes in reference to varying the transparency of the tunnel barriers between electrodes and the molecule is depicted in Fig. 10.

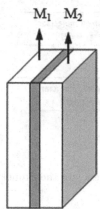

$$E_{inf} = -J\frac{M_1 M_2}{|M_1 \| M_2|}$$

One magnetic state (M_1, M_2) refers to key and second to part of analyzed memory media.

Fig. 7. Magnetic 2-layers influence representing compared arguments, E_{inf} - exchanged spin energy, $J = \{J(i,j)\}$- independent variables of mutual spin influences

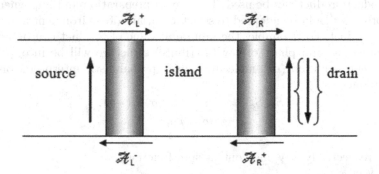

Fig. 8. The energy exchange in double tunneled joint of molecular spin-transistor, where $A_{L(R)}^{+(-)}$ - tunneling amplitudes: (+) to island, (-) from island

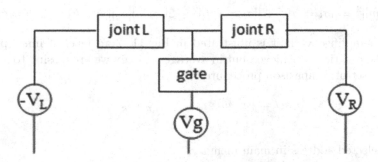

Fig. 9. Idea of molecular spin-transistor, Vg -gate voltage for tuning energy transport properties

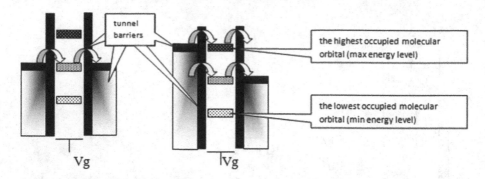

Fig. 10. Molecular level changes in reference to varying the transparency of the tunnel barriers between electrodes and the molecule

4   Comparison Procedures in Association Processes

To compare presented and other nano-environments procedure implementation inner (scalar) product can be used. The way of preparation and implementation of this process should be adapted to selected variant of environment and scheme of inner product. For example, the minimum value of product can be achieved if the spin value and phase of key (attribute) structure will be in opposite to memory representation (e.g. molecule spin in probabilistic interpretation). The scalar product:

$$(S_k, S_c) = \sum_{\sigma \in (K \cap C)} S_k(\sigma) S_c(-\sigma), \tag{4}$$

where
S_k, S_c - respectively, key and context spin functions,
σ - spin vector,
K, C - set of key and context spin configurations,
can be practically estimated in mutually compensation case by coming to spin vector values:

$$||\sigma_c om||^2 = ||\sigma_k = \sigma||^2 + ||\sigma_c = -\sigma||^2 + 2||\sigma_k|| \, ||\sigma_c|| \, cos(\theta) = 0, \, \theta = \pi. \tag{5}$$

This simplified variant is illustrated in Fig. 11. Zero level of inner product cannot be practically achieved but in average strategy we are closing to minimal level in a set of comparison procedures:

$$j\_sel = \{v : min_{j=1,...,v,...,n} (S_k, S_c)\}, \tag{6}$$

where
j_sel - selected address in main memory,
j-comparison number adequate memory location,
v- address adequate the minimal result in comparison procedure,
n-range of searching memory area.

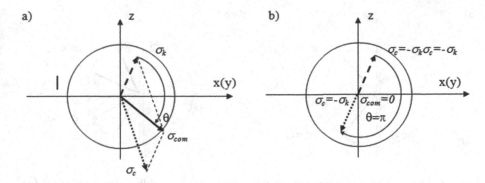

Fig. 11. The mutually compensation investigation by inner product estimation (case b)

Presented approach treated similarly as in probabilistic one may exploit Hamming distance which can be presented as follows:

$$dH = \sum_{i=1}^{m}(\widehat{\sigma}_k^{(i)}(1 - \widehat{\sigma}_c^{(i)}) + (1 - \widehat{\sigma}_k^{(i)})\widehat{\sigma}_c^{(i)}), \tag{7}$$

where
m- range of key length,
$\widehat{\sigma}_k^{(i)}, \widehat{\sigma}_c^{(i)}$ - normalized spin value on i-th key position.
Selection is achieved on the base of similar criterion:

$$j\_sel = \{v : min_{j=1,...,v,...,n}dH\}.$$

In comparison operation we can use correlation function of two spins σ_k, σ_c. The maximum correlation value will obviously meet the agreement location:

$$j\_sel = \{v : max_{j=1,...,v,...,n}Cr_{k,c}\}, \tag{8}$$

where
$Cr_{k,c} = <\sigma_k, \sigma_c> - <\sigma_k><\sigma_c>$,
$<\sigma_k>, <\sigma_c>$ - average over spin values respectively to key and memory context.

Let's turn attention to possibility of quantification degree scale adaptation referred to assess the spin values This consists in assigning the level number of spin values for discretization measuring process (Fig. 12). In these quantization procedures we can exploit both constant projection values toward the outside magnetic field direction (or assigned relative axis as in Fig. 12) and constant phase of spin vector deviations.

Random inner product has obviously probability representation in nano-environment. Therefore we use simplified criterion of selecting memory location v:
$(P_k, P_c) = \sum_{i=1}^{m} p_k(\sigma_k^{(i)})(1 - p_c(\sigma_k^{(i)}))$ which tends to minimum over $j = 1,...,v,...,n$. Formally, probability description regarding both spin value and phase refers to projection on direction of magnetic field or assigned earlier axis.

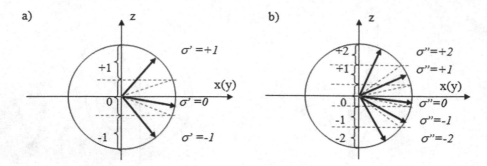

Fig. 12. The examples of quantization spin measuring procedures (three-valued (a), and five-valued (b))

5   Conclusions

The problem of associative memory idea in nano-environment has multi-dimensional aspects. Some of them we tried to name: finding applicable nano-environment, adapt criterion of association strategy, building transition information algorithm, resolve technical problems (included storage and measure processes), etc. We also suggested the approach to one operation i.e. key and context comparison implementation only. Considered strategies base on using inner product, correlation dependency and Hemming distance. Generally, they lead to probabilistic assessments and transformations. Technical aspects are currently implemented only on the experimental level using specific measurement apparatuses. The probabilistic (stochastic) approach leads to elaboration of simple form criteria that permit us to cognition memory address on the key (attribute) set base.

References

1. Bas, E.: The training of multiplicative neuron model based artificial neural networks with differential evolution algorithm for forecasting. J. Artif. Intell. Soft Comput. Res. **6**(1), 5–11 (2016)
2. Leon, M., Xiong, N.: Adapting differential evolution algorithms for continuous optimization via greedy adjustment of control parameters. J. Artif. Intell. Soft Comput. Res. **6**(2), 5103–5118 (2016)
3. Anderson, J.R., Bower, C.H.: Human Associative Memory. Winston and Sons, Washington (1973)
4. Awshalom, D.D., Flatte, M.M.: Challenges for semiconductor spintronics. Nat. Phys. **3**, 153–159 (2007)
5. Dery, H., Dalal, P., Cywinski, L., Sham, L.J.: Spin-based logic in semiconductors for reconfigurable large-scale circuits. Nature **447**, 573–576 (2007)
6. Grunberg, P., Burgler, D.E., Dassow, H., Rata, A.D., Schneider, C.M.: Spin-transfer phenomena in layered magnetic structures: physical phenomena and materials aspects. Acta Mater. **55**, 1171 (2007)

7. Kim, G.-H., Kim, T.-S.: Electronic transport in single molecule magnets on metallic surfaces. Phys. Rev. Lett. **92**, 137203 (2004)
8. Kohonen, T.: A Class of Randomly Organized Associative Memories, Acta Polytechnica Scandinavica, Electrical Engineering Series No. El 25 (1971)
9. Kohonen, T.: Introduction of the Principle of Virtual Images in Associative Memories, Acta Polytechnica Scandinavica, Electrical Engineering Series No. El f2 (1971)
10. Kouwenhoven, L.P., et al.: In: Sohn, L.L., Kouwenhoven, L.P., Schön, G. (eds.) Mesoscopic Electron Transport. Series E, vol. 345, pp. 105–214. Kluwer (1997)
11. Laskowski, L., Laskowska, M.: Functionalization of SBA-15 mesoporous silica by cu- phosphonate units: probing of synthesis route. J. Solid State Chem. **220**, 221–226 (2014)
12. Laskowski, L., Laskowska, M., Balanda, M., Fitta, M., Kwiatkowska, J., Dzilinski, K., Kaczmarska, A.: Mesoporouse silica SBA-15 functionalized by Nikel-phosphonic units: Raman and magnetic analysis. Microporous Mesoporous Mater. **200**, 253–259 (2014)
13. Lehndorff, R., Buchmeier, M., Burgler, D.E., Kakay, A., Hertel, R., Schneider, C.M.: Asymmetric spintransfer torque in single-crystalline Fe/Ag/Fe nanopillars. Phys. Rev. B **76**, 214420 (2007)
14. Misiorny, M., Barnas, J.: Magnetic switching of a single molecular magnet due to spin-polarized current. Phys. Rev. B **75**, 134425 (2007)
15. Ouyang, M., Awshalom, D.: Coherent spin-transfer between molecularly bridged quantum dots. Science **301**, 1074–1076 (2003)
16. Piech, H.: Sequence automata for researching consensus levels. In: Nguyen, N.-T. (ed.) Transactions on Computational Collective Intelligence VIII. LNCS, vol. 7430, pp. 82–101. Springer, Heidelberg (2012)
17. Ratner, M.A.: Special feature on molecular electronics. Proc. Natl. Acad. Sci. **102**, 8800–8837 (2005)
18. Romeike, C., Wegewijs, M.R., Schoeller, H.: Spin quantum tunneling in single molecule magnets: fingerprints in transport spectroscopy of current and noise. Phys. Rev. Lett. **96**, 196805 (2006)
19. Romeike, C., et al.: Charge-switchable molecular nanomagnet and spin-blockade tunneling. Phys. Rev. B **75**, 064404 (2007)
20. Sanvito, S., Rocha, A.R.: Molecular spintronics: the art of driving spin through molecules. J. Comput. Theor. Nanosci. **3**, 624–642 (2006)

A New Approach to Designing of Intelligent Emulators Working in a Distributed Environment

Andrzej Przybył[1]([⊠]) and Meng Joo Er[2]

[1] Institute of Computational Intelligence,
Częstochowa University of Technology, Częstochowa, Poland
andrzej.przybyl@iisi.pcz.pl
[2] School of Electrical and Electronic Engineering,
Nanyang Technological University, Singapore, Singapore
emjer@ntu.edu.sg

Abstract. The paper proposes a new class of the hardware emulators, namely the remote emulators. They can temporarily replace a control object to allow testing of a distributed system in a safe manner. This method is named a remote-hardware-in-the-loop (RHIL). The second issue described in the paper is a hybrid method of using the computational intelligence in the hardware emulators. This hybrid system is based on a radial-basis-function, a fuzzy-logic and a state variables theory. The proposed solutions make it possible to build a hardware emulator that can work in the RHIL systems with a good accuracy.

Keywords: Radial basis function · Nonlinear dynamics · Hardware emulator · Real-time Ethernet

1 Introduction

A hardware-in-the-loop (HIL) emulation is a popular method for testing electronic equipment. The testing process is performed in a working control system in which a control object has been temporarily replaced by an emulator. At the same time a main controller, i.e. the device to be tested, is in its normal operation mode. Such an approach is known as the closing of the feedback loop by the emulator. This HIL emulation is necessary for testing the general functions and reactions of the control system, including hardware and software. This is consistent with the conclusion presented in the work [60]. How it was indicated in the cited reference, nowadays only minor parts of the main controller software relate to the development of the feedback loop. The major parts relate to diagnostics, failure reactions, etc.

Hardware emulators are complex and quite expensive. This is due to two factors. First, they must be equipped with a number of specific analog and digital interfaces matched to the specific application. These specific interfaces are necessary in order to emulate an actual device with high fidelity. Secondly,

© Springer International Publishing Switzerland 2016
L. Rutkowski et al. (Eds.): ICAISC 2016, Part II, LNAI 9693, pp. 546–558, 2016.
DOI: 10.1007/978-3-319-39384-1_48

they must have a very high processing performance to be able to simulate a behavior of the replaced device in real-time.

Moreover, in the modern industry a real-time Ethernet-based distributed control systems are typically used instead of a centralized solution [38]. The distributed architecture enables the use of hardware emulators instead of the real control object, unnoticeably to the whole system. When emulator temporarily replaces a real control object it allows testing of a distributed system in a safe manner.

However, the emulators which are capable of operating in a distributed environment, for example by RTE, must have slightly different characteristics than the conventional emulators. Primarily, they need a high performance of the real-time communication interface to transfer a large amounts of the service data [40]. In this work we have introduced a new class of the hardware emulators, namely the remote emulators. Their specific properties are presented in the next section of the paper.

The second very important issue related to designing hardware emulators is the algorithm used for modeling of the object dynamics. Modeled objects have typically a switching nonlinear characteristics. This is due to the fact that there are many components included in the object and each of them may have an individual nonlinear characteristics. This issue is analyzed below.

Modeling of the systems is a widely developed area. In the literature many topics connected with modeling issue are considered. In the last years, besides the classic solutions, the modeling solutions based on the artificial neural networks [17,56], fuzzy logic rules [27], type-2 fuzzy systems [1,2,57–59] and neuro-fuzzy-structures [6–16,30,47,48,62–68] are presented.

It should be noted that most of the papers, which present the above-mentioned methods, relate to the fact that the system can be simply described by the "input-output" type transposition

$$y = F(u), \tag{1}$$

where y, u - are vectors of input and output signals respectively. In reality most of physical phenomena are dynamic and their state is not only depended on the input of current signals, but also on their prior states. Inclusion of historical data in the input vector u (i.e. prior values of inputs and/or outputs) enables consideration of dynamic dependences in the designed model. However, in the general case that model may be too complex and uninterpretable, which makes it not usable in the practice. This disadvantage is a characteristic for modeling by artificial neural networks and the fuzzy rules, when input vector was enlarged by the historical data.

Another and a very common way of modeling of dynamical systems [28,30] is the use of the state variables technique. State of the dynamic object model may be comprehensively described by a vector of the state variables x. In a general case the state equation has a form

$$\frac{dx}{dt} = F(x, u), \tag{2}$$

where F is a non-linear dependency in the function of state variables and input signals. However, it should be noted that many physical phenomena may be described by linear approximation (3) of non-linear dependency (2) around actual operating point and with a good accuracy. One possible way of using this technique is presented in the paper [26]. The approach to power electronics converter modeling relies on piece-wise linear passive elements. A set of discrete states is used to obtain the current values of linear state equation matrices.

The piece-wise linear model in a discrete form with time step T and first order approximation can be described as follows

$$\mathbf{x}(k+1) = \mathbf{A}_d(k)\mathbf{x}(k) + \mathbf{B}_d(k)\mathbf{u}(k), \tag{3}$$

where $\mathbf{A}_d(k)$, $\mathbf{B}_d(k)$ - are system and input matrices in a discrete form and with an appropriate size; $k = 1, 2, ...$ - is a step of simulation related with continuous time t as follows $t = k \cdot T$. Output signals of the object are defined as

$$\mathbf{y}(k) = \mathbf{C}(k)\mathbf{x}(k) + \mathbf{D}(k)\mathbf{u}(k), \tag{4}$$

where $\mathbf{C}(k)$, $\mathbf{D}(k)$ are output and transfer matrices of an appropriate size.

In the switched nonlinear dynamic systems the operating point changes over time during the process. However, in the piece-wise linear method, a local re-determination of linear approximation in any new operating point is performed. If the discretization is done with the suitable short time step T then the solution is accurate. In practice the above statement is also true in case of discontinuities in the modeled switched system. According to the paper [60] an obvious approach to handling discontinuities is to split up a sample step T into a period before and after the switching event. However, as mentioned later in the cited reference, in some cases the sample time can be very low and "close to the absolute timing resolution of the digital electronics (e.g. 100 ns). With this high-rate oversampling, switching events no long require special handling".

The second solution proposed in this paper is a new hybrid method to emulate the switched and nonlinear systems on FPGA, working with the high-rate oversampling. The method is based on an intelligent structure that switches the piece-wise linear model between discrete, pre-defined linear models. Each discrete linear model defines the object dynamics for one operating point.

This paper is organized into 3 sections. Section 2 introduces a new class of hardware emulators and presents an idea of hybrid method for modeling of switched and nonlinear systems on FPGA. Conclusions are presented in Sect. 3.

2   A New Type of Hardware-in-the-Loop Emulation

In this section we introduce a new class of hardware emulators and an intelligent hybrid method to simulate the switched and nonlinear systems in the real-time on FPGA.

2.1   New Class of Hardware Emulators - Remote-Hardware-in-the-Loop

How it was indicated in the introduction, in modern industry real-time Ethernet-based distributed control systems are typically used rather than a centralized solution. The distributed architecture enables the use of remote hardware emulators in place of the real control object in a manner transparent to the system. This remote-hardware-in-the-loop (RHIL) system is useful for the testing and development of the complex distributed control system.

Remote emulators must have slightly different characteristics than conventional emulators because they usually emulate a more complex devices. Classic emulators are typically used to simulate the combined effect of an end-driver (usually a power electronics) and a controlled object. While the emulated distributed devices can be both a simple power electronics module with controlled object as well as an integrated set of a digital controller and the end-driver (power electronics) connected to the driven object.

The examples of the last group are electric current, mechanical speed or position controllers composed of microprocessor with an integrated firmware, power electronic and driven electric motor. This types of distributed devices are controlled in a closed loop through the real-time network. In a typical case the master device manages and controls all distributed devices, for example, in a machine tool, a production line, etc.

For the reasons described above, the remote emulators must also simulate an operation algorithm, which is built-in and executed by the emulated distributed digital device. The above mentioned algorithm can be simulated by a soft-core or a hard-core processor, embedded in the FPGA project. The example of soft-core processors are MicroBlaze from Xilinx, NIOS II from Altera or TSK3000 from Altium Designer Software manufacturer. While an example of a hard-core processor is an ARM Cortex A9, included in the Xilinx Zynq7000 FPGA family.

Table 1. Comparision of two class of hardware emulators.

Feature	Classic hardware emulator	Remote hardware emulator
The method of connecting the emulator to the controller	Directly connected with a local analog and/or digital input/output interfaces Typically without a galvanic isolation	Connected through a real-time communication medium, e.g. real-time Ethernet. Provides full galvanic isolation
Response time	Starting from about of $1\,\mu s$	Starting from tens of μs
Types of applications	Modeling of an end-driver (power electronics) and the driven object	Modeling of integrated set of a digital controller, an end-driver and the driven object
The complexity and the expense	Large (i.a. because of the large number of used I/O interfaces)	Medium-large (only one I/O interface is used)

From the point of view of a master controller, the operation of the remote emulator should not significantly differ from the actual operation of the distributed device. Obviously, to achieve this the remote emulator must also be able to cooperate with the real-time network [40].

For such a defined class of emulators their most important features that distinguish it from the classic emulators are as follows:

- The required latency time (i.e. time needed to capture the input data, to process them and to deliver the results to the output) must be shorter than the cycle time of the used real-time communication solution. In modern RTE this time is the order of tens of μs or more. This is much more than in the case of classic emulators, which must prepare the response time within $1\,\mu s$ in a typical case. As a result there is no need to synchronize the time step of the remote emulator with the master controller signals.
- A physical construction of remote emulators is simpler than the classic ones. This is because the remote emulators do not need a large number of specialized analog or digital interfaces, they only require the RTE interface.
- A remote emulator works in real-life conditions, i.e. it is plugged into the communication network of the target control system. In the case of the classic emulator may exist some differences resulting from a slightly different interface connecting the master controller with the emulator and with the real object.
- In the case of the RHIL system many remote emulators may co-exist in a distributed network without any adverse mutual interaction on each other.

A summary of key features of both classes of hardware emulators are included in the Table 1. Other features that were not listed in the Table are similar for both kinds of emulators. That means they should be able to work with a very short time step of order of hundreds of nanoseconds to reproduce the switching nonlinear dynamics with high fidelity. This functionality can only provide a hardware implementation, e.g. on the FPGA. This issue is described in the next subsection.

2.2 Hybrid Method of Modeling of Nonlinear Dynamics

In the paper we propose the use of a new modeling method to simulate the switched and nonlinear systems in the real-time. The presented method was created by improving the methods previously presented in our earlier papers [3–5, 39]. The previous version of the method connects advantages of both model types: classic i.e. analytical and a fuzzy. While the modification proposed in this paper adapts the method for implementation on FPGA. This is achieved by utilizing the fact that some classes of fuzzy systems are functionally equivalent to a radial basis function (RBF) networks [24]. The RBF algorithm is well suited for implementation on FPGA.

The general idea of the proposed modeling method is shown in Fig. 1. The piece-wise linear model of the switched and nonlinear systems is used according to the Eq. 3.

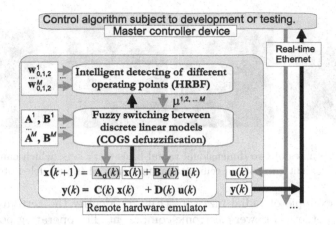

Fig. 1. The general idea of the proposed remote-hardware-in-the-loop (RHIL) system.

The proposed solution uses the hyper-radial-basis-function (HRBF) [33] to indicate the M discrete operating points of the modeled object. In the HRBF the distance of the input ($\mathbf{x}$) from the j-th ($j = 1..M$) center of the radial-basis center $\overline{\mathbf{x}}^j$ is defined as follows

$$\|\mathbf{x} - \overline{\mathbf{x}}^j\|^2 = \left(\frac{x_1 - \overline{x}_1^j}{\sigma_1^j}\right)^2 + ... + \left(\frac{x_N - \overline{x}_N^j}{\sigma_N^j}\right)^2, \tag{5}$$

where σ_i^j is the width of the HRBF for i-th input, and $\overline{x}_i^j$ is its center. The activation degree μ^j for the j-th HRBF is defined as follows

$$\mu^j = \exp\left(-\|\mathbf{x}(k) - \overline{\mathbf{x}}^j\|^2\right). \tag{6}$$

In this point of the algorithm the main computational effort is related to calculate the activation degrees for all HRBS. Therefore, the Eq. (5) can be rewritten in the following manner, which is even easier to implement on FPGA

$$\|\mathbf{x} - \overline{\mathbf{x}}^j\|^2 = w_0^j + w_{1,1}^j x_1 + w_{1,2}^j (x_1)^2 + ... + w_{N,1}^j x_N + w_{N,2}^j (x_N)^2, \tag{7}$$

where w_0^j, $w_{i,1}^j$ and $w_{i,2}^j$ are appropriately selected weight values.

It should be noted that the Eq. (7) is very versatile because it allows us to define not only the HRBF as shown in Fig. 2a,b,c but also other shapes of multi-dimensional fuzzy sets as shown in Fig. 2d. Generally speaking, this equation is well suited for identifying the operating points of the modeled object. The HRBF shown in Fig. 2a,b can be used, for example, to detect whether the module of some vector exceeds a certain limit. Such vector consists of, for example, direct and quadrature components of electrical current of a modeled electromechanical device [41]. The vector components are represented as values on the x-axis and y-axis while, the z-axis value in the Fig. 2a is the activation degree of a rule.

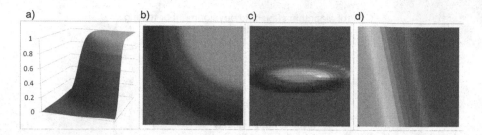

Fig. 2. Few examples of two-dimensional radial-basis-fuzzy-sets, which can be particularly useful for identifying the specific operating points of the modeled object.

The second example of radial fuzzy set (Fig. 2c) identify the certain operating point of a hypothetical power electronic component. The operating point occurs when the electric current (y-axis) is very small and at the same time the voltage (x-axis) is small. The third example (Fig. 2d) shows a radial set, which can be used to detect when the weighted sum of the two signals (for example, velocity and acceleration in motion control systems [50,51]) exceeds a certain predetermined level (threshold). The detection of such a situation (operating point) may be a signal for the start of the procedure of slowing down the motion. This approach may be useful in many other applications, for example, for tool performance prediction and degradation detection [31], etc. [18,19,22,24,25,27,32,34–37,42–46,49,52–55,61].

The proper definition of the particular RBFS is a separate issue. However, some basic guidelines are presented below. In a typical case the approximate analytical is available for a certain number M of discrete operating points [20,21]. In such a case the RBFS can be designed by an expert to obtain the intelligent piece-wise linear model of switched nonlinear system dynamics. It should be noted that in some cases the operating points of the emulated system can be determined by a suitably designed automatic identification procedure, for example, with the use of the evolutionary algorithm [20,21].

The calculated values of μ^j indicate the activation degree of j-th HRBF, which is equivalent to an indication of the activation degree of the respective discrete operating point of the modeled object. To obtain the output value of the intelligent system (i.e. the $\mathbf{A}_d$ and the $\mathbf{B}_d$ matrices) the following method is used

$$\mathbf{A}_d(k) = \frac{\sum_{j=1}^{M} \mu^j \cdot \mathbf{A}^j}{\sum_{j=1}^{M} \mu^j}, \quad \mathbf{B}_d(k) = \frac{\sum_{j=1}^{M} \mu^j \cdot \mathbf{B}^j}{\sum_{j=1}^{M} \mu^j}, \tag{8}$$

where the pairs of constant matrices $\mathbf{A}^j$ and $\mathbf{B}^j$ define the discrete linear models. Each of the j-th discrete operating point defines the equivalent linear system dynamics for different operating points of the nonlinear object. The method (8) is based on a centre of gravity for singletons (COGS) defuzzification. Thus, in this way, the radial-basis-fuzzy structure was created.

3   Conclusions

Further research is planned to prepare the details of the method of implementation on FPGA for the proposed emulators. Especially, the following two issues are considered: 1. the semi-parallel method of implementation with the use of pipelining mechanism, and 2. the use of recursive mode, in which subsequently determined operating points can use the previous results.

4   Summary

The presented paper describes a new class of the hardware emulators. It is possible to create a remote-hardware-in-the-loop (RHIL) systems using the proposed type of emulators. The study also proposes the hybrid method of modeling of the switched and nonlinear systems. This intelligent system is based on a radial-basis-function as well as on the fuzzy-logic and state variables theory. The method utilizes the fact that some classes of fuzzy systems are functionally equivalent to radial basis function networks. Therefore the algorithm is well suited for implementation on FPGA. Using the proposed solution, it is possible to build a hardware emulator that can work in the remote-hardware-in-the-loop systems with a good accuracy.

Acknowledgment. The project was financed by the National Science Centre (Poland) on the basis of the decision number DEC-2012/05/B/ST7/02138.

References

1. Bartczuk, Ł., Rutkowska, D.: Type-2 fuzzy decision trees. In: Rutkowski, L., Tadeusiewicz, R., Zadeh, L.A., Zurada, J.M. (eds.) ICAISC 2008. LNCS (LNAI), vol. 5097, pp. 197–206. Springer, Heidelberg (2008)
2. Bartczuk, Ł., Rutkowska, D.: Medical diagnosis with type-2 fuzzy decision trees. In: Kącki, E., Rudnicki, M., Stempczyńska, J. (eds.) Computers in Medical Activity. AISC, vol. 65, pp. 11–21. Springer, Heidelberg (2009)
3. Bartczuk, Ł., Przybył, A., Dziwiński, P.: Hybrid state variables - fuzzy logic modelling of nonlinear objects. In: Rutkowski, L., Korytkowski, M., Scherer, R., Tadeusiewicz, R., Zadeh, L.A., Zurada, J.M. (eds.) ICAISC 2013, Part I. LNCS, vol. 7894, pp. 227–234. Springer, Heidelberg (2013)
4. Bartczuk, Ł., Przybył, A., Koprinkova-Hristova, P.: New method for nonlinear fuzzy correction modelling of dynamic objects. In: Rutkowski, L., Korytkowski, M., Scherer, R., Tadeusiewicz, R., Zadeh, L.A., Zurada, J.M. (eds.) ICAISC 2014, Part I. LNCS, vol. 8467, pp. 169–180. Springer, Heidelberg (2014)
5. Bartczuk, Ł.: Gene expression programming in correction modelling of nonlinear dynamic objects. Adv. Intell. Syst. Comput. **429**, 125–134 (2016)
6. Cpałka, K., Rutkowski, L.: Flexible Takagi-Sugeno fuzzy systems. In: Proceedings of the 2005 IEEE International Joint Conference on IJCNN 2005, vol. 3, pp. 1764–1769 (2005)

7. Cpałka, K., Rutkowski, L.: Flexible Takagi-Sugeno neuro-fuzzy structures for non-linear approximation. WSEAS Trans. Syst. **4**(9), 1450–1458 (2005)
8. Cpałka, K.: A method for designing flexible neuro-fuzzy systems. In: Rutkowski, L., Tadeusiewicz, R., Zadeh, L.A., Żurada, J.M. (eds.) ICAISC 2006. LNCS (LNAI), vol. 4029, pp. 212–219. Springer, Heidelberg (2006)
9. Cpałka, K., Rutkowski, L.: A new method for designing and reduction of neuro-fuzzy systems. In: Proceedings of the 2006 IEEE International Conference on Fuzzy Systems (IEEE World Congress on Computational Intelligence, WCCI 2006), Vancouver, pp. 8510–8516 (2006)
10. Cpałka, K.: On evolutionary designing and learning of flexible neuro-fuzzy structures for nonlinear classification. Nonlin. Anal. Ser. A: Theor. Meth. Appl. **71**, 1659–1672 (2009). Elsevier
11. Cpałka, K., Rebrova, O., Nowicki, R., Rutkowski, L.: On design of flexible neuro-fuzzy systems for nonlinear modelling. Int. J. Gen. Syst. **42**(6), 706–720 (2013)
12. Cpałka, K., Łapa, K., Przybył, A., Zalasiński, M.: A new method for designing neuro-fuzzy systems for nonlinear modelling with interpretability aspects. Neurocomputing **135**, 203–217 (2014)
13. Cpałka, K., Zalasiński, M.: On-line signature verification using vertical signature partitioning. Expert Syst. Appl. **41**(9), 4170–4180 (2014)
14. Cpałka, K., Zalasiński, M., Rutkowski, L.: New method for the on-line signature verification based on horizontal partitioning. Pattern Recogn. **47**, 2652–2661 (2014)
15. Cpałka, K., Łapa, K., Przybył, A.: A new approach to design of control systems using genetic programming. Inf. Technol. Control **44**(4), 433–442 (2015)
16. Cpałka, K., Zalasiński, M., Rutkowski, L.: A new algorithm for identity verification based on the analysis of a handwritten dynamic signature. Applied soft computing **43**, 47–56 (2016). http://dx.doi.org/10.1016/j.asoc.2016.02.017
17. Duch, W., Korbicz, J., Rutkowski, L., Tadeusiewicz, R. (eds.): Biocybernetics and Biomedical Engineering 2000. Neural Networks, vol. 6. Akademicka Oficyna Wydawnicza, EXIT, Warsaw (2000) (in Polish)
18. Duda, P., Jaworski, M., Pietruczuk, L.: On pre-processing algorithms for data stream. In: Rutkowski, L., Korytkowski, M., Scherer, R., Tadeusiewicz, R., Zadeh, L.A., Zurada, J.M. (eds.) ICAISC 2012, Part II. LNCS, vol. 7268, pp. 56–63. Springer, Heidelberg (2012)
19. Duda, P., Hayashi, Y., Jaworski, M.: On the strong convergence of the orthogonal series-type Kernel Regression neural networks in a non-stationary environment. In: Rutkowski, L., Korytkowski, M., Scherer, R., Tadeusiewicz, R., Zadeh, L.A., Zurada, J.M. (eds.) ICAISC 2012, Part I. LNCS, vol. 7267, pp. 47–54. Springer, Heidelberg (2012)
20. Dziwiński, P., Bartczuk, Ł., Przybył, A., Avedyan, E.D.: A new algorithm for identification of significant operating points using swarm intelligence. In: Rutkowski, L., Korytkowski, M., Scherer, R., Tadeusiewicz, R., Zadeh, L.A., Zurada, J.M. (eds.) ICAISC 2014, Part II. LNCS, vol. 8468, pp. 349–362. Springer, Heidelberg (2014)
21. Dziwiński, P., Avedyan, E.D.: A new approach to nonlinear modeling based on significant operating points detection. In: Rutkowski, L., Korytkowski, M., Scherer, R., Tadeusiewicz, R., Zadeh, L.A., Zurada, J.M. (eds.) Artificial Intelligence and Soft Computing. LNCS, vol. 9120, pp. 364–378. Springer, Heidelberg (2015)
22. Er, M.J., Duda, P.: On the weak convergence of the orthogonal series-type Kernel Regresion neural networks in a non-stationary environment. In: Wyrzykowski, R., Dongarra, J., Karczewski, K., Waśniewski, J. (eds.) PPAM 2011, Part I. LNCS, vol. 7203, pp. 443–450. Springer, Heidelberg (2012)

23. Gałkowski, T., Rutkowski, L.: Nonparametric recovery of multivariate functions with applications to system identification. Proc. IEEE **73**(5), 942–943 (1985)
24. Roger Jang, J.-S., Sun, C.-T.: Functional equivalence between radial basis function networks and fuzzy inference systems. IEEE Trans. Neural Netw. **4**(1), 156–159 (1993)
25. Jaworski, M., Pietruczuk, L., Duda, P.: On resources optimization in fuzzy clustering of data streams. In: Rutkowski, L., Korytkowski, M., Scherer, R., Tadeusiewicz, R., Zadeh, L.A., Zurada, J.M. (eds.) ICAISC 2012, Part II. LNCS, vol. 7268, pp. 92–99. Springer, Heidelberg (2012)
26. Kinsy, M.A., Majstorovic, D., Haessig, P., Poon, J., Celanovic, N., Celanovic, I., Devadas, S.: High-speed real-time digital emulation for hardware-in-the-loop testing of power electronics: a new paradigm in the field of Electronic Design Automation (EDA) for power electronics systems. In: Proceedings of the International Exhibition and Conference for Power Electronics, Intelligent Motion and Power Quality 2011 (PCIM Europe 2011), 17-19 May 2011, Nuremberg, Germany, pp. 1–6 (2011). http://hdl.handle.net/1721.1/87082
27. Korytkowski, M., Rutkowski, L., Scherer, R.: Fast image classification by boosting fuzzy classifiers. Inf. Sci. **327**, 175–182 (2016)
28. Łapa, K., Przybył, A., Cpałka, K.: A new approach to designing interpretable models of dynamic systems. In: Rutkowski, L., Korytkowski, M., Scherer, R., Tadeusiewicz, R., Zadeh, L.A., Zurada, J.M. (eds.) ICAISC 2013, Part II. LNCS, vol. 7895, pp. 523–534. Springer, Heidelberg (2013)
29. Łapa, K., Zalasiński, M., Cpałka, K.: A new method for designing and complexity reduction of neuro-fuzzy systems for nonlinear modelling. In: Rutkowski, L., Korytkowski, M., Scherer, R., Tadeusiewicz, R., Zadeh, L.A., Zurada, J.M. (eds.) ICAISC 2013, Part I. LNCS, vol. 7894, pp. 329–344. Springer, Heidelberg (2013)
30. Łapa, K., Cpałka, K., Wang, L.: New method for design of fuzzy systems for nonlinear modelling using different criteria of interpretability. In: Rutkowski, L., Korytkowski, M., Scherer, R., Tadeusiewicz, R., Zadeh, L.A., Zurada, J.M. (eds.) ICAISC 2014, Part I. LNCS, vol. 8467, pp. 217–232. Springer, Heidelberg (2014)
31. Li, X., Er, M.J., Lim, B.S.: Fuzzy regression modeling for tool performance prediction and degradation detection. Int. J. Neural Syst. **20**, 405–419 (2010)
32. Murata, M., Ito, S., Tokuhisa, M., Ma, Q.: Order estimation of Japanese paragraphs by supervised machine learning and various textual features. J. Artif. Intell. Soft Comput. Res. **5**(4), 247–255 (2015)
33. Osowski, S.: Sieci neuronowe w ujęciu algorytmicznym (in Polish). WNT, Warszawa (1996). pp. 160–188
34. Pietruczuk, L., Duda, P., Jaworski, M.: A new fuzzy classifier for data streams. In: Rutkowski, L., Korytkowski, M., Scherer, R., Tadeusiewicz, R., Zadeh, L.A., Zurada, J.M. (eds.) ICAISC 2012, Part I. LNCS, vol. 7267, pp. 318–324. Springer, Heidelberg (2012)
35. Pietruczuk, L., Zurada, J.M.: Weak convergence of the recursive Parzen-Type probabilistic neural network in a non-stationary environment. In: Wyrzykowski, R., Dongarra, J., Karczewski, K., Waśniewski, J. (eds.) PPAM 2011, Part I. LNCS, vol. 7203, pp. 521–529. Springer, Heidelberg (2012)
36. Jaworski, M., Er, M.J., Pietruczuk, L.: On the application of the Parzen-Type Kernel Regression neural network and order statistics for learning in a non-stationary environment. In: Rutkowski, L., Korytkowski, M., Scherer, R., Tadeusiewicz, R., Zadeh, L.A., Zurada, J.M. (eds.) ICAISC 2012, Part I. LNCS, vol. 7267, pp. 90–98. Springer, Heidelberg (2012)

37. Pietruczuk, L., Duda, P., Jaworski, M.: Adaptation of decision trees for handling concept drift. In: Rutkowski, L., Korytkowski, M., Scherer, R., Tadeusiewicz, R., Zadeh, L.A., Zurada, J.M. (eds.) ICAISC 2013, Part I. LNCS, vol. 7894, pp. 459–473. Springer, Heidelberg (2013)

38. Przybył, A., Smolag, J., Kimla, P.: Distributed control system based on real time ethernet for computer numerical controlled machine tool (in Polish). Przegl. Elektrotechniczny **86**(2), 342–346 (2010)

39. Przybył, A., Cpałka, K.: A new method to construct of interpretable models of dynamic systems. In: Rutkowski, L., Korytkowski, M., Scherer, R., Tadeusiewicz, R., Zadeh, L.A., Zurada, J.M. (eds.) ICAISC 2012, Part II. LNCS, vol. 7268, pp. 697–705. Springer, Heidelberg (2012)

40. Przybył, A., Er, M.J.: The idea for the integration of neuro-fuzzy hardware emulators with real-time network. In: Rutkowski, L., Korytkowski, M., Scherer, R., Tadeusiewicz, R., Zadeh, L.A., Zurada, J.M. (eds.) ICAISC 2014, Part I. LNCS, vol. 8467, pp. 279–294. Springer, Heidelberg (2014)

41. Przybył, A., Szczypta, J., Wang, L.: Optimization of controller structure using evolutionary algorithm. In: Rutkowski, L., Korytkowski, M., Scherer, R., Tadeusiewicz, R., Zadeh, L.A., Zurada, J.M. (eds.) Artificial Intelligence and Soft Computing. LNCS, vol. 9120, pp. 261–271. Springer, Heidelberg (2015)

42. Rutkowski, L.: Sequential estimates of probability densities by orthogonal series and their application in pattern classification. IEEE Trans. Syst. Man Cybern. **10**(12), 918–920 (1980)

43. Rutkowski, L.: Nonparametric identification of quasi-stationary systems. Syst. Control Lett. **6**(1), 33–35 (1985)

44. Rutkowski, L.: Real-time identification of time-varying systems by non-parametric algorithms based on Parzen Kernels. Int. J. Syst. Sci. **16**(9), 1123–1130 (1985)

45. Rutkowski, L.: A general approach for nonparametric fitting of functions and their derivatives with applications to linear circuits identification. IEEE Trans. Circ. Syst. **33**(8), 812–818 (1986)

46. Rutkowski, L.: Application of multiple Fourier-series to identification of multivariable non-stationary systems. Int. J. Syst. Sci. **20**(10), 1993–2002 (1989)

47. Rutkowski, L., Cpałka, K.: Flexible structures of neuro-fuzzy systems. In: Sincak, P., Vascak, J. (eds.) Quo Vadis Computational Intelligence. Studies in Fuzziness and Soft Computing, vol. 54, pp. 479–484. Springer, Heidelberg (2000)

48. Rutkowski, L., Cpałka, K.: Compromise approach to neuro-fuzzy systems. In: Sincak, P., Vascak, J., Kvasnicka, V., Pospichal, J. (eds.) Intelligent Technologies - Theory and Applications, vol. 76, pp. 85–90. IOS Press, Amsterdam (2002)

49. Rutkowski, L.: Adaptive probabilistic neural networks for pattern classification in time-varying environment. IEEE Trans. Neural Netw. **15**(4), 811–827 (2004)

50. Rutkowski, L., Przybył, A., Cpałka, K., Er, M.J.: Online speed profile generation for industrial machine tool based on neuro-fuzzy approach. In: Rutkowski, L., Scherer, R., Tadeusiewicz, R., Zadeh, L.A., Zurada, J.M. (eds.) ICAISC 2010, Part II. LNCS, vol. 6114, pp. 645–650. Springer, Heidelberg (2010)

51. Rutkowski, L., Przybył, A., Cpałka, K.: Novel online speed profile generation for industrial machine tool based on flexible neuro-fuzzy approximation. IEEE Trans. Ind. Electron. **59**(2), 1238–1247 (2012)

52. Rutkowski, L., Pietruczuk, L., Duda, P., Jaworski, M.: Decision Trees for mining data streams based on the McDiarmid's bound. IEEE Trans. Knowl. Data Eng. **25**(6), 1272–1279 (2013)

53. Rutkowski, L., Jaworski, M., Pietruczuk, L., Duda, P.: Decision trees for mining data streams based on the Gaussian approximation. IEEE Trans. Knowl. Data Eng. **26**(1), 108–119 (2014)
54. Rutkowski, L., Jaworski, M., Pietruczuk, L., Duda, P.: The CART decision tree for mining data streams. Inf. Sci. **266**, 1–15 (2014)
55. Rutkowski, L., Jaworski, M., Pietruczuk, L., Duda, P.: A new method for data stream mining based on the misclassification error. IEEE Trans. Neural Netw. Learn. Syst. **26**(5), 1048–1059 (2015)
56. Saitoh, D., Hara, K.: Mutual learning using nonlinear perceptron. J. Artif. Intell. Soft Comput. Res. **5**(1), 71–77 (2015)
57. Starczewski, J.T., Rutkowski, L.: Connectionist structures of type 2 fuzzy inference systems. In: Wyrzykowski, R., Dongarra, J., Paprzycki, M., Waśniewski, J. (eds.) PPAM 2001. LNCS, vol. 2328, pp. 634–642. Springer, Heidelberg (2002)
58. Starczewski, J., Rutkowski, L.: Interval type 2 neuro-fuzzy systems based on interval consequents. In: Rutkowski, L., Kacprzyk, J. (eds.) Neural Networks and Soft Computing, pp. 570–577. Physica-Verlag, A Springer-Verlag Company, Heidelberg (2003)
59. Starczewski, J.T., Bartczuk, Ł., Dziwiński, P., Marvuglia, A.: Learning methods for type-2 FLS based on FCM. In: Rutkowski, L., Scherer, R., Tadeusiewicz, R., Zadeh, L.A., Zurada, J.M. (eds.) ICAISC 2010, Part I. LNCS, vol. 6113, pp. 224–231. Springer, Heidelberg (2010)
60. Schulte, T., Kiffe, A., Puschmann, F.: HIL simulation of power electronics and electric drives for automotive applications. Electronics **16**(2), 130–135 (2012)
61. Yeomans, J.S.: A parametric testing of the firefly algorithm in the determination of the optimal osmotic drying parameters of mushrooms. J. Artif. Intell. Soft Comput. Res. **4**(4), 257–266 (2014)
62. Zalasiński, M., Cpałka, K.: Novel algorithm for the on-line signature verification. In: Rutkowski, L., Korytkowski, M., Scherer, R., Tadeusiewicz, R., Zadeh, L.A., Zurada, J.M. (eds.) ICAISC 2012, Part II. LNCS, vol. 7268, pp. 362–367. Springer, Heidelberg (2012)
63. Zalasiński, M., Cpałka, K.: Novel algorithm for the on-line signature verification using selected discretization points groups. In: Rutkowski, L., Korytkowski, M., Scherer, R., Tadeusiewicz, R., Zadeh, L.A., Zurada, J.M. (eds.) ICAISC 2013, Part I. LNCS, vol. 7894, pp. 493–502. Springer, Heidelberg (2013)
64. Zalasiński, M., Łapa, K., Cpałka, K.: New algorithm for evolutionary selection of the dynamic signature global features. In: Rutkowski, L., Korytkowski, M., Scherer, R., Tadeusiewicz, R., Zadeh, L.A., Zurada, J.M. (eds.) ICAISC 2013, Part II. LNCS, vol. 7895, pp. 113–121. Springer, Heidelberg (2013)
65. Zalasiński, M., Cpałka, K., Er, M.J.: New method for dynamic signature verification using hybrid partitioning. In: Rutkowski, L., Korytkowski, M., Scherer, R., Tadeusiewicz, R., Zadeh, L.A., Zurada, J.M. (eds.) ICAISC 2014, Part II. LNCS, vol. 8468, pp. 216–230. Springer, Heidelberg (2014)
66. Zalasiński, M., Cpałka, K., Hayashi, Y.: New method for dynamic signature verification based on global features. In: Rutkowski, L., Korytkowski, M., Scherer, R., Tadeusiewicz, R., Zadeh, L.A., Zurada, J.M. (eds.) ICAISC 2014, Part II. LNCS, vol. 8468, pp. 231–245. Springer, Heidelberg (2014)
67. Zalasiński, M., Cpałka, K., Er, M.J.: A new method for the dynamic signature verification based on the stable partitions of the signature. In: Rutkowski, L., Korytkowski, M., Scherer, R., Tadeusiewicz, R., Zadeh, L.A., Zurada, J.M. (eds.) Artificial Intelligence and Soft Computing. LNCS, vol. 9120, pp. 161–174. Springer, Heidelberg (2015)

68. Zalasiński, M., Cpałka, K., Hayashi, Y.: New fast algorithm for the dynamic signature verification using global features values. In: Rutkowski, L., Korytkowski, M., Scherer, R., Tadeusiewicz, R., Zadeh, L.A., Zurada, J.M. (eds.) Artificial Intelligence and Soft Computing. LNCS, vol. 9120, pp. 175–188. Springer, Heidelberg (2015)

The Use of Rough Sets Theory to Select Supply Routes Depending on the Transport Conditions

Aleksandra Ptak[✉]

Faculty of Management, Czestochowa University of Technology,
Dabrowskiego 69, Czestochowa, Poland
olaptak@zim.pcz.pl

Abstract. Transport conditions have a direct impact on the costs of supply in the distribution network. In the wide area networks differences in transport costs depending on external conditions achieve significant meaning. The issue concerns not only the wheel transportation but also its other forms, including the transmission of different types of media (flow). However, it is felt most clearly in case of delivery with the use of the vehicle base. Among the conditions affecting the costs, one can distinguish internal (type of vehicle, the loading size) and external factors (variable capacity resulting for example from traffic, various forms of traffic disturbances). This leads to the conclusion, that costs can and should be estimated in the interval form. The consequence of such analysis will be choosing the cheapest connection configurations which will be supplemented by the system of the inference rules [11]. Such an approach is presented in the rough sets theory.

Keywords: Rough sets theory · Supply routes · Transport conditions

1 Introduction

With the above-mentioned problem we meet quite often at the stage of preliminary analysis of *"off-line"* and in real-time *"on-line"* [9] when the decision should be made during the implementation of the transportation problem. In practice, each driver, who has information about the difficulties of the journey, decides to choose another, not necessarily shorter way [15,16]. It can be seen, that the time criterion may, and sometimes has to be included in the costs of the transportation [5–7]. In the proposed approach, one chooses to use interval variables on the transportation costs. These costs can be converted with respect to the distance units, units of transported goods, or generally regarded as the weights of the tested connections, depending on the chosen optimization algorithm. Among over a dozen practically used algorithms relating to the distribution network one can mention the following (as the simplest and most commonly used): construction of the spanning tree (minimum spanning tree MST) developed by Kruskal [2,3,13] and modified by Prim and Dijkstra [14], determining the shortest path (Shortest Path SP) proposed by Dijkstra [5,14], and taking into account negative weights, developed by Moore, Belman [12] and its improved form developed

© Springer International Publishing Switzerland 2016
L. Rutkowski et al. (Eds.): ICAISC 2016, Part II, LNAI 9693, pp. 559–569, 2016.
DOI: 10.1007/978-3-319-39384-1_49

by d'Esopo and Papego [4,14], maximum flow (Max flow MF) formulated by Ford and Fulkerson [17], its improved version was submitted by Edmonds and Karp and its another form was proposed by Dinic [8]. To draw practical conclusions one proposes to use a system of rules created on the basis of the theory of rough sets [1,10] for quick decisions based on the parameters of coverage and strength. Rough set theory was introduced by Z. Pawlak. He formulated the approach to vagueness, with the use of a boundary region of a set. The set is crisp, if the boundary region of a set is empty, and by analogy, the set is rough (inexact), if the boundary region of a set is nonempty [10]. This kind of boundary region means that the knowledge of the particular set is insufficient and the set can not be defined precisely. Most of the mentioned algorithms are based on preliminary nondecreasing network connection weights and the gradual selection of the following sections as long as they meet specific conditions of the particular method (e.g. acyclicity). In the proposed solution weights connections are in the form of intervals (or fuzzy sets). Therefore problems arise from the ambiguity of choice when range of scales overlaps. Such a problem can be solved by using rough sets theory conventions, as shown in this paper.

2   Formalisms Used in Description of the Initial Stage of the Algorithm

At first, the strength of pretended objects (SPO) will be defined on the base of overlapping zones (weight intervals) OZ. The overlapping zones are created with using all object interval weights. The following definitions were created by the author with the use of the rough sets foundations. The topological sum in the Definition 1 was borrowed from Pawlak, who, in his works, was referring to the collection of physical objects.

Definition 1. Set of overlapping zone objects $(SOZO)$ is a meta-set of object groups $OG(i) = \bigcup_{k(i)\in\{1,...,N\}} O(k(i))$ $i = 1,...,lz$, lz - the number of groups, creating overlapping interval weights - overlapping zones $(OZ(i) = \bigcap_{k(i)\{1,...,N\}} WI(k(i))$ and these zones do not overlap mutually between each other: $\{OZ(i) \cap OZ(j) = \emptyset, \ i \neq j\}$, i,j-numbers of overlapping weight object groups.

$$OZ(i) = \bigcap_{k(i)\in\{1,...,N\}} WI(k(i)) \neq \emptyset \ - i\text{-th overlapping zone,}$$

$$SOZO = \{OG(1), OG(2), ..., OG(lz)\}, \tag{1}$$

$SOZ = \{OZ(1), OZ(2), ..., OZ(lz)\}$ - set of overlapping zones,

$$\{OG(1) \cup OG(2) \cup ... \cup OG(lz)\} = N, \tag{2}$$

$\min\{OG(1) \cap OG(2) \cap ... \cap OG(lz)\} = \emptyset$, at least two weight intervals are mutual separable, $\max\{OG(1) \cap OG(2) \cap ... \cap OG(lz)\} = N$ - all objects have common

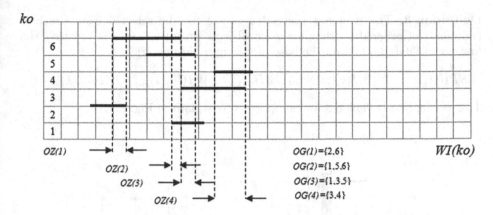

Fig. 1. Diagram of overlapping zones

part of weights $\bigcap_{i=1,2,...,N} WI(i) \neq \emptyset \Rightarrow lz = 1$. Generally, the following definition can occur useful for the implementation process:

$$\forall_{ko\in\{1,...,N\}}\exists_{max\_lz(ko)}\{\bigcap WI(i) \neq 0, \ i = l(ko,1), l(ko,2), ..., l(ko, max\_lz(ko))\}, \tag{3}$$

where:

ko - the code of the object (connection, network edge),
$max\_lz(ko)$ - the number of all objects having common weight zone,
$WI(i)$ - the interval weight of i-th object,
$l(ko,j)$ - the code of j-th component of overlapping zone for ko-th object structure.

This formalism can be interpreted as follows: for each connection we can find all objects creating with it the common zone (Fig. 1).

Definition 2. Ordered overlapping zones is a set of OZ ordered according to average of their low and up boundary regions $SOOZ = \{OOZ(1), OOZ(2), ..., OOZ(lz)\}$. In accordance with ordered overlapping zones, ordered overlapping zone objects are defined $SOOZO = \{OG(OOZ(1)), OG(OOZ(2)), ..., OG(OOZ(lz))\} = \{OOG(1), OOG(2), ..., OOG(lz)\}$.

$AOWI(v) = (OZB_{low}(v) + OZB_{up}(v))/2$ - average of v-th zone bounds,

$$AOWI(1) \leq ... \leq AOWI(v) \leq AOWI(v+1) \leq ... \leq AOWI(lz),$$

where:

$OZB_{low(v)}, OZB_{up(v)}$ - low and up boundary regions of v-th zone.
Obviously

$$OZB_{low(v)} = \max\{WI(l(v,1))_{low}, WI(l(v,2))_{low}, ..., WI(l(v, max_l z(v)))_{low}\}, \tag{4}$$

$$OZB_{up(v)} = \min\{WI(l(v,1))_{up}, WI(l(v,2))_{up}, ..., WI(l(v, max_l z(v)))_{up}\}. \tag{5}$$

Definition 3. The strongest pretended object will be selected from the first (minimal) of ordered overlapping zone objects (group of objects creating the first zone) OG(OOZ(1)) on the base of strength parameter:

$$SP(l(1,i)) = 1/(WI(l(1,i))_{low}/OZB_{up}(1) + WI(l(1,i))_{up}/OZB_{low}(1)). \quad (6)$$

This conception is depicted and supported to explain in Fig. 2.

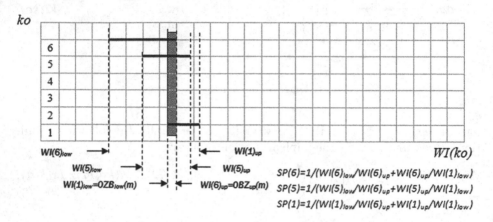

Fig. 2. The strength parameters presentation, where m-current minimal overlapping zone.

3   The Approach to an Indiscernible Relation Among Objects (Set of Pretending Connections)

Indiscernible relations generate the mathematical basis of rough sets theory. In the proposed algorithm only the first (minimal according to average of boundary regions) overlapping is considered in current algorithm stage. Indiscernible relation is base of the decision problem of choosing the current connection to optimal structure of spanning tree or shortest path. Indiscernible relation is described by codes of pretended connections and their interval weights. We cannot consider several zones simultaneously because after choosing current connection all remained pretended objects can be the new system of overlapping zones (Fig. 3). The pretended objects are presented by the set of connections creating overlapping zone or by the single connection which does not create any zone. This is an obvious conclusion inferring from following axiom:

Axiom. Excluding from pretending objects set selected connection, the overlapping zone can disappear or its rang will be extended:

$$OG(OZ(i)) \setminus O(j) \Rightarrow (OZ'(i) = \emptyset) \vee (OZB'_{up}(i) - OZB'_{low}(i))$$

$$> (OZB_{up}(i) - OZB_{low}(i)), \quad (7)$$

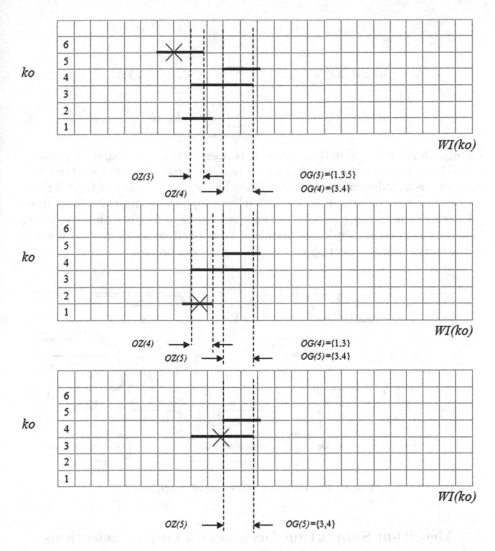

Fig. 3. Stages of pretending objects selecting; after selection object 5, objects 3 and 4 create the new overlapping zone.

where

$OZ'(i)$ - i-th overlapping zone after excluding any object,
$OZB'_{up}(i), OZB'_{low}(i)$ - boundary regions of overlapping zone after excluding any object.

It is possible to define different parameter connected with the set of interval weights connected with pretending objects set like: average of low objects boundary regions, average of up boundary regions or average of most possible value (when we dispose triangle fuzzy membership functions describing weight parameters):

$$AOZB_{low}(i) = 1/lz(i) \sum_{j=1,2,..,lz(i)} OZB_{low}(l(i,j)),$$

$$AOZB_{up}(i) = 1/lz(i) \sum_{j=1,2,..,lz(i)} OZB_{up}(l(i,j)),$$

$$AOZB_{pr}(i) = 1/lz(i) \sum_{j=1,2,..,lz(i)} OZB_{pr}(l(i,j)). \tag{8}$$

Using such prepared validation system it is possible to create rough set parameter of decision rules i.e. certainty and coverage. The procedure, exploited to select connections in indiscernibly relation (undecidable) situations, can be described by the iterative algorithm. In Fig. 4 author proposes to illustrate fundamental parts of rough sets structure i.e. universe, lower and upper approximation, boundary regions. In considered problem, mentioned structure will be fluently reconstructed during selecting and excluding objects process.

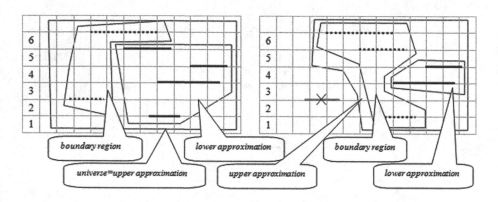

Fig. 4. The changing structure of rough sets

4 Algorithm Supporting Decision on Object Selections

The decision on object selections is the main part of most discrete optimization methods. Generally, the minimal weight object is chosen. In the considered interval weight objects ambiguous problems appear. To solve them we need special kind of analysis which is performed with the help of algorithm-example, consisting of two parts: zone selection (Fig. 5) and object selection, with the help of decision rules. The procedure presented in algorithm in Fig. 5 is realized iteratively $n-1$ times because in each iteration only one object is selected. After iteration realization the optimization method constrains (e.g. rejection of a cycling connection component) should be checked. In each iteration the new object structure defines the input date. In the iteration for each base object $(i = 1(1)n)$ full overlapping zone is found and its components (c) are created. Among zones the one with the minimum average of its boundary regions is selected min_AOZ. At first, overlapping aspects are analyzed with the help of

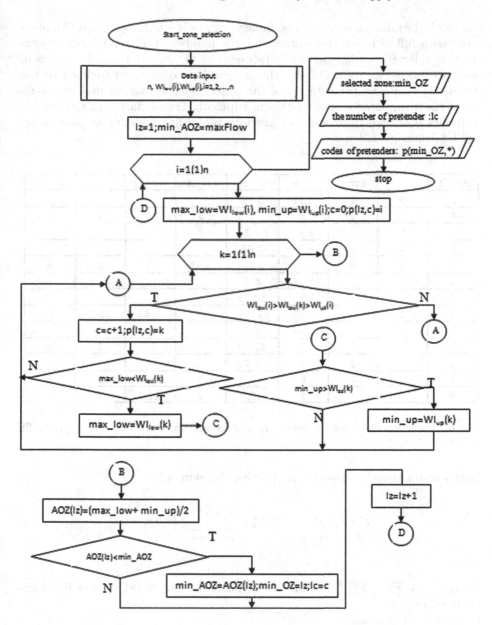

Fig. 5. Algorithm of selecting zone of pretenders.

$WI_{low}(i)$ parameter: $WI_{low}(i) > WI_{low}(ko) > WI_{up}(i)$, where ko - number of "candidate" to common zone creation object. If the mentioned condition is fulfilled the code of "candidate" is saved $p(lz, c) = ko$, where c- number of "candidate" of current zone creation. Possible corrections of current boundary regions max_low and min_up are realized. After checking all objects (label B) zone with the minimal average of boundary regions is selected (min_AOZ), obviously with full of its characteristics: lc - the number of all component objects creating selected overlapping zone, $\{p(min\_OZ, c),\ c = 0, 1, ..., lc\}$ - codes of components. Here, $p(min\_OZ, 0)$ - the code of base component (defined by the parameter i). Before presentation of the object selection algorithm one should define the main parameter of rough sets approach. Let us start with an example of results presented in iteration of previous algorithm. Rough sets parameters will be defined as follows:

iteration	c	comp	WI low	WI up	max_low	min_up	lc	sel. obj.
1	0	2	1,65	3,82				
1	1	6	3	7	3	3,82	1	2
2	0	1	6,44	8,3				
2	1	5	4,95	7,83				
2	2	6	3	7	6,44	7	2	6
3	0	1	6,44	8,3				
3	1	3	7	10,79				
3	2	5	4,95	7,83	7	7,83	2	5
4	0	1	6,44	8,3				
4	1	3	7	10,79	7	8,3	1	1
5	0	3	7	10,79				
5	1	4	9	11,2	9	10,79	1	3
6	0	4	9	11,2	9	11,2	0	4

Fig. 6. Algorithm iteration analysis - the last column contains codes of sequentially selected objects.

Normalized strength parameter supporting decision rule:

$$SPN(l(i,j)) = SP(i,j) / \sum_{p=1}^{lz} \sum_{c=0}^{lc(p)} SP(l(p,c)),\qquad(9)$$

where

$l(i,j) = j + \sum_{p=1}^{i-1} \sum_{c=0}^{lc(p)} 1$ - number of position (row in table - Fig. 6) of the analyzed object,
i - number of iteration,
j - number of component.

The coverage factor of the decision rule:

$$DC(l(i,j)) = SPN(l(i,j)) / \sum_{c=0}^{lc(p)} SP(l(p,c)),\qquad(10)$$

The certainty factor of the decision rule:

$$CC(x, l(i,j)) = SPN(l(i,j)) / \sum_{i=1}^{lz} \sum_{\{c:comp=x\}}^{lc(p)} SP(l(p,c)),$$ (11)

where

x- code of an investigated object - component (comp).

1	2	3	4	5	6	7	8	9	10	11	12
iteration	c	comp	Wl low	Wl up	max_low	min_up	strenth	str_norm	dec_cov	certainity	decision
1	0	2	1,65	3,82	3	3,82	0,59	0,091	0,646	1.00	no
1	1	6	3	7	3	3,82	0,32	0,050	0,354	0,327	yes
2	0	1	6,44	8,3	6,44	7	0,45	0,070	0,277	0,310	no
2	1	5	4,95	7,83	6,44	7	0,52	0,081	0,319	0,477	no
2	2	6	3	7	6,44	7	0,66	0,102	0,404	0,673	yes
3	0	1	6,44	8,3	7	7,83	0,50	0,077	0,337	0,341	no
3	1	3	7	10,79	7	7,83	0,41	0,064	0,277	0,299	no
3	2	5	4,95	7,83	7	7,83	0,57	0,088	0,386	0,523	yes
4	0	1	6,44	8,3	7	8,3	0,51	0,079	0,549	0,349	no
4	1	3	7	10,79	7	8,3	0,42	0,065	0,451	0,306	yes
5	0	3	7	10,79	9	10,79	0,54	0,084	0,529	0,395	no
5	1	4	9	11,2	9	10,79	0,48	0,074	0,471	0,496	yes
6	0	4	9	11,2	9	11,2	0,49	0,076	1,000	0,504	yes

Fig. 7. Rough sets parameters: strength, coverage and certainty- example.

                                                                    certainty
if iteration 1 and cover. cond. in col. 4-7 then   selection=object 2   1.00
if iteration 2 and cover. cond. in col. 4-7 then   selection=object 6   0.673
if iteration 3 and cover. cond. in col. 4-7 then   selection=object 5   0.523
if iteration 4 and cover. cond. in col. 4-7 then   selection=object 1   0.306
if iteration 5 and cover. cond. in col. 4-7 then   selection=object 3   0.496
if iteration 6 and cover. cond. in col. 4-7 then   selection=object 4   0.504

                                                                    coverage
if decision-select.=obj(2) then iter. =1 and max_low=3.0 and min_up=3.82   1.00
if decision-select.=obj(6) then iter.= 2 and max_low=6.44 and min_up=7.0   0.404
if decision-select.=obj(5) then iter.= 3 and max_low=7.0 and min_up=7.83   0.386
if decision-select.=obj(1) then iter.= 4 and max_low=7.0 and min_up=8.3   0.451
if decision-select.=obj(3) then iter.= 5 and max_low=9.0 and min_up=10.79 0.496
if decision-select.=obj(4) then iter.= 6 and max_low=9.0 and min_up=11.2   1.00

Fig. 8. The description of supporting decision rules

The results relating to the example are presented in Fig. 7.

The decision rules will be created on the base of rough set parameters in Fig. 8.

The set of rules can be extended by group of infers connected with decisions "no" (in the last column).

5   Conclusions

The rough sets approach for years has been succesfully used as a tool for the analysis in cases of no ability to define precisely a set of objects. In the paper the author have presented the algorithm referring to the distribution network depending on the transport conditions, based on the foundations of rough sets. The parameters obtained from the use of rough sets allow for more detailed assessment of the situation on the route selection in the distribution network. Well known methods of connections selection are based on their arrangement according to not decreasing weights. In the case of interval or fuzzy weights it comes to mutual coverage of weight parameters, that is the so-called similar relationships. The settlement of the decision problem, that is, to the so called selection of the route section is reduced to two steps: organizing of interval weights and the decision on the selection of the object (connection) in the first overlapping weight range. Rough sets parameters such as "certainty" and "coverage" provide the ability to assess the confidence (and risks), as well as doubts about the occurrence and selection of the same object in subsequent stages of decision-making.

References

1. Baumgarten, H.: Logistics - Management. Technische Universitaet Berlin, Berlin (2004) (in German)
2. Blackstock, T.: Keynote Speech, International Association of Food Industry Suppliers, San Francisco, CA and Gattorna J.: Supply Chains are the Business. Supply Chain Management Review, vol. 10, no. 6 (2005)
3. Chen, I.J., Paulraj, A., Lado, A.: Strategic purchasing, supply management, and firm performance. J. Oper. Manag. 22(5), 505–523 (2004)
4. Cohen, M.A., Huchzermeir, A.: Global supply chain management: a survey of research and applications. In: Tayur, S., Ganeshan, R., Magazine, M. (eds.) Quantitative Models for Supply Chain Management, pp. 669–702. Kluwer, Boston (1999)
5. Croxton, K.L., Garca-Dastugue, S.J., Lambert, D.M., Rogers, D.S.: The supply chain management processes. Int. J. Logistics Manag. 12(2), 13–36 (2001)
6. Gattorna, J.: Supply chains are the business. Supply Chain Manag. Rev. 10(6), 42–49 (2006)
7. Lambert, D.M., Cooper, M.C.: Issues in supply chain management. Ind. Mark. Manag. 29(1), 65–83 (2000)
8. Lambert, D.M., Garca-Dastugue, S.J., Croxton, K.L.: An evaluation of process-oriented supply chain management frameworks. J. Bus. Logistics 26(1), 25–51 (2005)

9. Mesjasz-Lech, A.: The use of IT systems supporting the realization of business processes in enterprises and supply chains in Poland. Pol. J. Manag. Stud. **10**, 94–103 (2014)
10. Pawlak, Z., Sugeno, M.: Decision Rules Bayes, Rule and Rough. New Decisions in Rough Sets. Springer, Berlin (1999)
11. Ptak, A., Piech, H., Zhou, N.: The setup method of the order with the help of the rough sets convention. In: Rutkowski, L., Korytkowski, M., Scherer, R., Tadeusiewicz, R., Zadeh, L.A., Zurada, J.M. (eds.) Artificial Intelligence and Soft Computing. LNCS, vol. 9120, pp. 495–503. Springer, Heidelberg (2015)
12. Sawicka, H., Zak, J.: Mathematical and simulation based modeling of the distribution system of goods. In: Proceedings of the 23-rd European Conference on Operational Research, Bonn, 5–8 July 2009
13. Straka, M., Malindzak, D.: Distribution logistics. Express Publicity, Kosice (2008)
14. Syslo, M., Deo, M., Kowalik, J.: Discrete Optimization Algorithms. Dover publications, Mineola, New York (2006)
15. Tadeusiewicz, R.: Introduction to Inteligent Systems. In: Wilamowski, B.M., Irvin, J.D. (eds.) The Industrial Electronic Handbook. CRC Press, Boca Raton (2011)
16. Tadeusiewicz, R.: Place and role of intelligence systems in computer science. Comput. Methods Mater. Sci. **10**(4), 193–206 (2010)
17. Wisner, J.D., Keong, L.G., Keah-Choon, T.: Supply Chain Management: A Balanced Approach. Thomson South-Western, Mason (2004)

Predicting Success of Bank Direct Marketing by Neuro-fuzzy Systems

Magdalena Scherer[1]([✉]), Jacek Smolag[2], and Adam Gaweda[3]

[1] Faculty of Management, Częstochowa University of Technology,
al. Armii Krajowej 19, 42-200 Częstochowa, Poland
mscherer@zim.pcz.pl
[2] Institute of Computational Intelligence, Częstochowa University of Technology,
Al. Armii Krajowej 36, 42-200 Częstochowa, Poland
jacek.smolag@iisi.pcz.pl
[3] University of Louisville, 615 South Preston, Louisville, KY 40202, USA
http://iisi.pcz.pl

Abstract. The paper concerns bank marketing selling campaign result prediction by neuro-fuzzy systems. We trained the system by the back-propagation algorithm using forty five thousand of past records. We obtained comparable prediction results with the best ones from the literature. The advantage of the proposed approach is the use of fuzzy rules, which are interpretable for humans.

Keywords: Neuro-fuzzy systems · Prediction · Bank marketing

1 Introduction

Marketing selling campaigns are established tools to improve business prosperity. Selecting the best set of customers to contact is a very hard task. Decision support systems can come to help with this task. The literature shows rare examples of banking client targeting. The bank marketing dataset used in the paper [20] was analysed earlier in the literature by multilayered neural networks [11,21] and decision trees [9]. The presented method is a novel approach to predict if the client will subscribe a bank term deposit on the basis of the client and contact data.

Neuro-fuzzy systems are artificial neural network-like structures, functionally equivalent to fuzzy inference models. They can be trained from scratch or with some initialization methods to act as we intend. Apart from realising assumed tasks they have fuzzy rules that can be used by humans to get the knowledge about a phenomena. Fuzzy rules consists of fuzzy membership functions that together are relatively easily interpretable for humans. There exists numerous variations of fuzzy systems [5–7,10,22]. Some of them use type-2 fuzzy sets [24,25]. The initial state of the system can be obtained by e.g. clustering or relational equations [23]. As neuro-fuzzy system use rules, they have better interpretability than artificial neural networks [2,4]. Several fuzzy systems can

© Springer International Publishing Switzerland 2016
L. Rutkowski et al. (Eds.): ICAISC 2016, Part II, LNAI 9693, pp. 570–576, 2016.
DOI: 10.1007/978-3-319-39384-1_50

be joined in ensembles to improve their accuracy [15–17]. In the paper we use the backpropagation algorithm to adjust the parameters of neuro-fuzzy systems. Apart from learning from scratch, machine learning systems can be initialized by evolutionary algorithms [14], data clustering [8] or particle swarm [1]. Fuzzy systems were used in various applications [3,12,13,18].

2 Mamdani-Type Neuro-fuzzy Systems

In this section we describe Mamdani neuro fuzzy systems [19]. We consider multi-input-single-output fuzzy system mapping $\mathbf{X} \to Y$, where $\mathbf{X} \subset R^n$ and $Y \subset R$. Theoretically, the system is composed of a fuzzifier, a fuzzy rule base, a fuzzy inference engine and a defuzzifier. The fuzzifier performs a mapping from the observed crisp input space $\mathbf{X} \subset R^n$ to a fuzzy set defined in X. The most commonly used fuzzifier is the singleton fuzzifier which maps $\bar{\mathbf{x}} = [\bar{x}_1, \ldots, \bar{x}_n] \in X$ into a fuzzy set $A' \subseteq X$ characterized by the membership function

$$\mu_{A'}(x) = \begin{cases} 1 \text{ if } x = \bar{x} \\ 0 \text{ if } x \neq \bar{x} \end{cases} \tag{1}$$

Equation (1) means that, in fact, we get rid of the fuzzifier. The knowledge of the system is stored in the fuzzy rule base which consists of a collection of N fuzzy IF-THEN rules in the form

$$R^{(k)} : \begin{cases} \text{IF} \quad x_1 \text{ is } A_1^k \text{ } AND \\ \qquad x_2 \text{ is } A_2^k \text{ } AND \ldots \\ \qquad x_n \text{ is } A_n^k \\ THEN \quad y \text{ is } B^k \end{cases} \tag{2}$$

or

$$R^{(k)}: \text{IF } \mathbf{x} \text{ is } A^k \text{ THEN } y \text{ is } B^k \tag{3}$$

where $\mathbf{x} = [x_1, \ldots, x_n] \in \mathbf{X}$, $y \in Y$, $A^k = A_1^k \times A_2^k \times \ldots \times A_n^k$, $A_1^k, A_2^k, \ldots, A_n^k$ are fuzzy sets characterized by membership functions $\mu_{A_i^k}(x_i)$, $i = 1, \ldots, n$, $k = 1, \ldots, N$, whereas B^k are fuzzy sets characterized by membership functions $\mu_{B^k}(y)$, $k = 1, \ldots, N$. The firing strength of the k-th rule, $k = 1, \ldots, N$, is defined by

$$\tau_k(\bar{\mathbf{x}}) = \overset{n}{\underset{i=1}{T}} \left\{ \mu_{A_i^k}(\bar{x}_i) \right\} = \mu_{A^k}(\bar{\mathbf{x}}) \tag{4}$$

The defuzzification is realized by the following formula

$$\bar{y} = \frac{\sum_{r=1}^{N} \bar{y}^r \cdot \mu_{\overline{B}^r}(\bar{y}^r)}{\sum_{r=1}^{N} \mu_{\overline{B}^r}(\bar{y}^r)}. \tag{5}$$

The membership functions of fuzzy sets $\overline{B}^r$, $r = 1, 2, \ldots, N$, are defined using the following formula:

$$\mu_{\overline{B}^r}(y) = \sup_{\mathbf{x} \in \mathbf{X}} \left\{ \mu_{A^r}(\mathbf{x}) \overset{T}{*} \mu_{A^r \to B^r}(\mathbf{x}, y) \right\}. \tag{6}$$

With singleton type fuzzification, the formula takes the form

$$\mu_{\overline{B}^r}(y) = \mu_{A^r \to B^r}(\overline{\mathbf{x}}, y) = T\left(\mu_{A^r}(\overline{\mathbf{x}}), \mu_{B^r}(y)\right). \tag{7}$$

Since

$$\mu_{A^r}(\overline{\mathbf{x}}) = \mathop{T}_{i=1}^{n}\left(\mu_{A_i^r}(\overline{x}_i)\right), \tag{8}$$

we have

$$\mu_{\overline{B}^r}(y) = \mu_{A^r \to B^r}(\overline{\mathbf{x}}, y) = T\left[\mathop{T}_{i=1}^{n}\left(\mu_{A_i^r}(\overline{x}_i)\right), \mu_{B^r}(y)\right], \tag{9}$$

where T is any t-norm. Because

$$\mu_{B^r}(\overline{y}^r) = 1 \tag{10}$$

and

$$T(a, 1) = a, \tag{11}$$

we obtain the following formula

$$\mu_{\overline{B}^r}(\overline{y}^r) = \mathop{T}_{i=1}^{n}\left(\mu_{A_i^r}(\overline{x}_i)\right). \tag{12}$$

Finally we obtain

$$\overline{y} = \frac{\sum_{r=1}^{N} \overline{y}^r \cdot T_{i=1}^{n}\left(\mu_{A_i^r}(\overline{x}_i)\right)}{\sum_{r=1}^{N} T_{i=1}^{n}\left(\mu_{A_i^r}(\overline{x}_i)\right)}. \tag{13}$$

Input linguistic variables are described by means of Gaussian membership functions, that is

$$\mu_{A_i^r}(x_i) = \exp\left[-\left(\frac{x_i - \overline{x}_i^r}{\sigma_i^r}\right)^2\right], \tag{14}$$

If we apply the Larsen (product) rule of inference, we obtain the following formula for the output of the single Mamdani neuro-fuzzy system, shown in Fig. 1

$$\overline{y} = \frac{\sum_{r=1}^{N} \overline{y}^r \left(\prod_{i=1}^{n} \exp\left[-\left(\frac{\overline{x}_i - \overline{x}_i^r}{\sigma_i^r}\right)^2\right]\right)}{\sum_{r=1}^{N} \left(\prod_{i=1}^{n} \exp\left[-\left(\frac{\overline{x}_i - \overline{x}_i^r}{\sigma_i^r}\right)^2\right]\right)}. \tag{15}$$

3 Bank Marketing Dataset and Experimental Results

In this section we describe the experiments carried out on the bank data dataset [20]. The data came from direct marketing campaigns of a Portuguese bank. The marketing campaigns were based on phone calls. Often, more than one contact to the same client was required. The goal of the experiments was to predict if a bank term deposit was subscribed or not after the contact from the bank. The dataset contains 45211 records and 20 input variables:

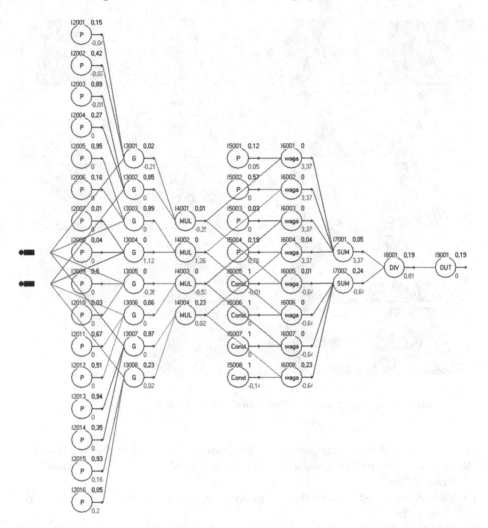

Fig. 1. An example of the Mamdani neuro-fuzzy system with two fuzzy rules.

1. age (numeric)
2. job : type of job (categorical: "admin.", "blue-collar", "entrepreneur", "housemaid", "management", "retired", "self-employed", "services", "student", "technician", "unemployed", "unknown")
3. marital : marital status (categorical: "divorced", "married", "single", "unknown"; note: "divorced" means divorced or widowed)
4. education (categorical: "basic.4y", "basic.6y", "basic.9y", "high.school", "illiterate", "professional.course", "university.degree", "unknown")
5. default: has credit in default? (categorical: "no","yes","unknown")
6. housing: has housing loan? (categorical: ' 'no", "yes", "unknown")
7. loan: has personal loan? (categorical: "no", "yes", "unknown")

Fig. 2. Fuzzy input membership functions for 19 features after learning.

8. contact: contact communication type (categorical: "cellular", "telephone")
9. month: last contact month of year (categorical: "jan", "feb", "mar", ..., "nov", "dec")
10. day_of_week: last contact day of the week (categorical: "mon", "tue", "wed", "thu", "fri")
11. duration: last contact duration, in seconds (numeric). Important note: this attribute highly affects the output target (e.g., if duration=0 then y="no"). (We discarded this feature)
12. campaign: number of contacts performed during this campaign and for this client (numeric, includes last contact)
13. pdays: number of days that passed by after the client was last contacted from a previous campaign (numeric; 999 means client was not previously contacted)
14. previous: number of contacts performed before this campaign and for this client (numeric)
15. poutcome: outcome of the previous marketing campaign (categorical: "failure", "nonexistent", "success")
16. emp.var.rate: employment variation rate - quarterly indicator (numeric)
17. cons.price.idx: consumer price index - monthly indicator (numeric)

18. cons.conf.idx: consumer confidence index - monthly indicator (numeric)
19. euribor3m: euribor 3 month rate - daily indicator (numeric)
20. nr.employed: number of employees - quarterly indicator (numeric)

and one output variable (desired target) if the client subscribed a term deposit (binary: "yes", "no"). We discarded the "duration" feature as it highly influences the output for records with unknown value of this feature.

Experiments were performed for twenty fuzzy rules in the Mamdani neuro-fuzzy system with the product t-norm. The membership functions were initially distributed evenly. The system was trained by the backpropagation algorithm for 350 epochs with the learning coefficient being equal 0.2 and the momentum term 0.4. The training set consisted of 10 % of data. We used 19 features and obtained 90,29 % classification accuracy. Input membership functions for all inputs after training are shown in Fig. 2.

4 Final Remarks

Marketing selling campaigns are established tools to improve business prosperity. The presented method is a novel approach to predict if the client will subscribe a bank term deposit on the basis of the client and contact data. We used neuro-fuzzy systems thus we can use interpretable fuzzy rules after data-driven learning by the backpropagation algorithm. Performed experiments proved the effectiveness of our method as we obtained a very high prediction rate (90, 29 %).

References

1. Aghdam, M.H., Heidari, S.: Feature selection using particle swarm optimization in text categorization. J. Artif. Intell. Soft Comput. Res. **5**(4), 231–238 (2015)
2. Bas, E.: The training of multiplicative neuron model based artificial neural networks with differential evolution algorithm for forecasting. J. Artif. Intell. Soft Comput. Res. **6**(1), 5–11 (2016)
3. Bosque, G., del Campo, I., Echanobe, J.: Fuzzy systems, neural networks and neuro-fuzzy systems: a vision on their hardware implementation and platforms over two decades. Eng. Appl. Artif. Intell. **32**, 283–331 (2014)
4. Chu, J.L., Krzyzak, A.: The recognition of partially occluded objects with support vector machines and convolutional neural networks and deep belief networks. J. Artif. Intell. Soft Comput. Res. **4**(1), 5–19 (2014)
5. Cpałka, K., Łapa, K., Przybył, A., Zalasiński, M.: A new method for designing neuro-fuzzy systems for nonlinear modelling with interpretability aspects. Neurocomputing **135**, 203–217 (2014)
6. Cpalka, K., Rebrova, O., Nowicki, R., Rutkowski, L.: On design of flexible neuro-fuzzy systems for nonlinear modelling. Int. J. Gen. Syst. **42**(6), 706–720 (2013)
7. Cpalka, K., Rutkowski, L.: A new method for designing and reduction of neuro-fuzzy systems. In: 2006 IEEE International Conference on Fuzzy Systems (2006)
8. El-Samak, A.F., Ashour, W.: Optimization of traveling salesman problem using affinity propagation clustering and genetic algorithm. J. Artif. Intell. Soft Comput. Res. **5**(4), 239–245 (2015)

9. Elsalamony, H.A.: Bank direct marketing analysis of data mining techniques. Int. J. Comput. Appl. **85**(7), 12–22 (2014)

10. Gaweda, A.E., Scherer, R.: Fuzzy number-based hierarchical fuzzy system. In: Rutkowski, L., Siekmann, J.H., Tadeusiewicz, R., Zadeh, L.A. (eds.) ICAISC 2004. LNCS (LNAI), vol. 3070, pp. 302–307. Springer, Heidelberg (2004)

11. Hany, A., Elsalamony, A.M.E.: Bank direct marketing based on neural network. Int. J. Eng. Adv. Technol. (IJEAT) **2**(6), 392–400 (2013)

12. He, Z., Wen, X., Liu, H., Du, J.: A comparative study of artificial neural network, adaptive neuro fuzzy inference system and support vector machine for forecasting river flow in the semiarid mountain region. J. Hydrol. **509**, 379–386 (2014)

13. Kar, S., Das, S., Ghosh, P.K.: Applications of neuro fuzzy systems: a brief review and future outline. Appl. Soft Comput. **15**, 243–259 (2014)

14. Kasthurirathna, D., Piraveenan, M., Uddin, S.: Evolutionary stable strategies in networked games: the influence of topology. J. Artif. Intell. Soft Comput. Res. **5**(2), 83–95 (2015)

15. Korytkowski, M., Gabryel, M., Rutkowski, L., Drozda, S.: Evolutionary methods to create interpretable modular system. In: Rutkowski, L., Tadeusiewicz, R., Zadeh, L.A., Zurada, J.M. (eds.) ICAISC 2008. LNCS (LNAI), vol. 5097, pp. 405–413. Springer, Heidelberg (2008)

16. Korytkowski, M., Nowicki, R., Scherer, R.: Neuro-fuzzy rough classifier ensemble. In: Alippi, C., Polycarpou, M., Panayiotou, C., Ellinas, G. (eds.) ICANN 2009, Part I. LNCS, vol. 5768, pp. 817–823. Springer, Heidelberg (2009)

17. Korytkowski, M., Nowicki, R., Scherer, R., Rutkowski, L.: Ensemble of rough-neuro-fuzzy systems for classification with missing features. In: IEEE International Conference on Fuzzy Systems FUZZ-IEEE 2008, (IEEE World Congress on Computational Intelligence), pp. 1745–1750. IEEE (2008)

18. Korytkowski, M., Rutkowski, L., Scherer, R.: Fast image classification by boosting fuzzy classifiers. Inf. Sci. **327**, 175–182 (2016)

19. Korytkowski, M., Scherer, R.: Negative correlation learning of neuro-fuzzy system ensembles. In: Rutkowski, L., Scherer, R., Tadeusiewicz, R., Zadeh, L.A., Zurada, J.M. (eds.) ICAISC 2010, Part I. LNCS, vol. 6113, pp. 114–119. Springer, Heidelberg (2010)

20. Moro, S., Laureano, R., Cortez, P.: Using data mining for bank direct marketing: an application of the CRISP-DM methodology. In: Novias, P., et al. (eds.) Proceedings of the European Simulation and Modelling Conference - ESM 2011, Guimaraes, Portugal, EUROSIS, pp. 117–121, October 2011

21. Moro, S., Cortez, P., Rita, P.: A data-driven approach to predict the success of bank telemarketing. Decis. Support Syst. **62**, 22–31 (2014)

22. Rutkowski, L., Cpalka, K.: Flexible neuro-fuzzy systems. Trans. Neur. Netw. **14**(3), 554–574 (2003)

23. Scherer, R., Rutkowski, L.: Relational equations initializing neuro-fuzzy system. In: Proceedings of the 10th Zittau Fuzzy Colloquium, Zittau, Germany, pp. 18–22 (2002)

24. Scherer, R., Starczewski, J.T.: Relational type-2 interval fuzzy systems. In: Dongarra, J., Karczewski, K., Wasniewski, J., Wyrzykowski, R. (eds.) PPAM 2009, Part I. LNCS, vol. 6067, pp. 360–368. Springer, Heidelberg (2010)

25. Starczewski, J.T.: Centroid of triangular and Gaussian type-2 fuzzy sets. Inf. Sci. **280**, 289–306 (2014)

The Confidence Intervals in Computer Go

Leszek Stanislaw Śliwa[(⊠)]

Faculty of Electronics and Information Technology,
The Institute of Computer Science,
Warsaw University of Technology, Warsaw, Poland
l.s.sliwa@stud.elka.pw.edu.pl
http://www.ii.pw.edu.pl

Abstract. The confidence intervals in computer Go are used in MCTS algorithm to select the potentially most promising moves that should be evaluated with Monte-Carlo simulations. Smart selection of moves for evaluation has the crucial impact on program's playing strength. This paper describes the application of confidence intervals for binomial distributed random variables in computer Go. In practice, the estimation of confidence intervals of binomial distribution is difficult and computationally exhausted. Now due to computer technology progress and functions offered by many libraries calculation of confidence intervals for discreet, binomial distribution become an easy task. This research shows that the move-selection strategy which implements calculation of the exact confidence intervals based on discreet, binomial distribution is much more effective than based on normal. The new approach shows its advantages particularly in games played on medium and large boards.

Keywords: Computer Go · AI · MCTS · UCT · Confidence intervals · Binomial distribution

1 Introduction

Go can be defined as a two-person, sequential, zero-sum, deterministic game with perfect information. The average branching factor of Go is high – 250, average game length is 150 ply and the game-tree complexity is approximately 10^{360} [1]. Computer Go game played on 9×9 or bigger boards is not solvable by brute-force methods. Classic tree-search algorithms such as $\alpha\beta$ and A^* require a strong heuristic positional evaluation function. Unfortunately, a fast and efficient evaluation function has not yet been constructed for Go.

Monte-Carlo Tree Search (MCTS) is a best-first search method guided by Monte-Carlo simulations that does not require a positional evaluation function. MCTS consists of four main steps: selection, expansion, simulation, and back-propagation. In the selection step, the tree is searched from the root node until a leaf. In the expansion step, a new node is added to the game tree. In the simulation step, random moves are played in a self-game. Finally, in the back-propagation step, the result of a simulated game is propagated from a newly

© Springer International Publishing Switzerland 2016
L. Rutkowski et al. (Eds.): ICAISC 2016, Part II, LNAI 9693, pp. 577–588, 2016.
DOI: 10.1007/978-3-319-39384-1_51

added leaf node up to the game tree root. The next part is concentrated solely on search strategy.

The goal of a selection strategy is to choose the most urgent move. The strategy attempts to balance between exploitation and exploration because on the one hand, the most promising moves should be favoured and on the other, less promising moves, because of their low scores could be a result of an unfortunate coincidence (unlucky simulations). MCTS has many variants that differ in search strategy, but most of them are based on confidence intervals and Central Limit Theorem. The Central Limit Theorem states that the probability distribution of the sum of independent and identically distributed random variables with finite variance approaches a normal distribution. The estimation of confidence intervals in the binomial distribution is difficult and computationally exhaustive. Therefore, popular remedy was to replace the binomial distribution by its normal approximation. However due to computer technology progress and functions offered by many statistical libraries, the calculation of confidence intervals for discreet, binomial distribution becomes an easy task [5,12]. The findings show that the shortest interval for a given confidence level in computer Go increases the playing strength particularly on medium 15×15 and large 19×19 boards.

The contents of the research are as follows. Section 2 is dedicated to related works and contains an overview of existing search strategies. Section 3 evaluates the effectiveness of selected search strategies. Section 4 focuses on the Central Limit Theorem and confidence intervals for binomial distribution in the context of computer Go. Section 5 presents results of experiments aimed on verification of the effectiveness of the proposed search strategy. Finally, in Sect. 6 the determinations of the research and the conclusions are drawn.

2   Related Works: Overview of the Search Strategies

The aim of the game tree search strategy is to examined and identify the most promising movements. The sequence of the game tree view is determined by finding the "best" child node (corresponding to the next movement for the current state of the game). Selection of most promising moves can be made based on various strategies: RAVE [8], MCE [4], UCT [11], UCB1-TUNED [9], OMC [6], MOSS [2], PBBM [7] and others. Most of the deterministic strategies (e.g. UCT, UCB1-TUNED, MOSS) and stochastic (e.g. OMC) are based on the Central Limit Theorem. It is worth noting that all the above strategies are universal and independent of the game.

2.1   Monte-Carlo Evaluations

In Monte-Carlo Evaluations (MCE) a value of a game state S is evaluated by performing simulations. In a simulation (payout, rollout), moves are randomly selected starting from S state in a self-game. Each simulation i gives a pay-off value P_i. The evaluation $E(S)$ of the game state S is the average of pay-off values in n simulations, i.e., $E(S) = \frac{1}{n} \sum P_i$.

2.2   Rapid Action Value Estimation

Rapid Action Value Estimation (RAVE) (Gelly and Silver 2007) heuristics allows to quickly set the initial values of nodes in the game tree. In the heuristics RAVE each node has an individual coefficient α, the value of which decreases with the number of simulation passing through the node. RAVE values are stored for both players. Weight values decrease linearly as the movements are done farther away from the current state of the game. In practice, a program must keep track of RAVE value for both players for each node in a game tree. Larger weights are applied to the nodes that are close to the root. When moves are performed the weights decrease linearly with the distance from the root.

2.3   Upper Confidence Bounds Applied to Trees

UCB1 strategy [3] is one of the most used solutions to the Multi-Armed Bandit (MAB) problem. UCB1 formula combines the estimated value of moves confidence limits. The movement having the greatest value of the formula 1 is considered to be the best:

$$k \in \underset{i \in \{1,\dots,K\}}{\arg\max} \left(v_i + C \times \sqrt{\frac{\ln n_p}{n_i}} \right), \tag{1}$$

where K is a number of child nodes, i is an index of a child node, v_i is a value of a child node i, n_i is a counter of i child node visits, n_p is a counter the parent node visits, C is an experimentally selected coefficient. A value of a child node v_i is the estimated value of the move and can be computed in several ways, e.g. it may be the average value of the results of games or be the weighted average of the results of games and the RAVE value. A variant of the algorithm MCTS, wherein the selection of the most promising of movements in the phase of viewing tree is based on UCB1 algorithm was called Upper Confidence bounds applied to Trees (UCT) [11].

2.4   UCB1-TUNNED Strategy

The choice of nodes in the tree based on a formula UCB1 works properly for those nodes that are frequently visited. However, for nodes located far from the root, which are rarely visited, the formula UCB1 excessively benefits from the accumulated knowledge. This is because it is assumed that all possible moves in a particular game state must be examined before UCB1 formula can be used. This assumption is good for a small number of options, but in the game of Go is not the case. Thus, the nodes at great depths are not significant, because not all child nodes were examined, and what's worse, some of them were selected in a strict sequence. The modified UCB1 formula was named UCB1-TUNED [9].

In the UCB1-TUNED algorithm to estimate the upper limit of confidence interval a value of an empirical standard deviation is used. The UCB1-TUNED formula is analogous to UCB1, wherein the fixed parameter C is replaced by the smaller value equal to: $1/4$ (the upper limit of the variance of the Bernoulli random variable) or V_n – the upper limit of the confidence interval calculated on the basis of observed samples. During the simulation program starts the analysis from the root of the game tree. In each node a next move k (child node) is selected according to the formula 2:

$$k \in \underset{i \in \{1,\dots,K\}}{\arg\max} \left(v_i + \sqrt{\frac{\ln n_p}{n_i}} \times \min \left(\frac{1}{4}, V_i(n_i) \right) \right),$$

(2)

where V_i function is an estimated upper limit of variance v_i and is defined by the formula 3:

$$V_i(n_i) = \left(\frac{1}{n_i} \sum_{t=1}^{n_i} R_{i,t}^2 - v_i^2 + \sqrt{\frac{2 \ln n_p}{n_i}} \right),$$

(3)

where $R_{i,t}$ is the tth payoff, obtained in node i.

In conclusion, for each child node, an upper limit value of the variance must be calculated in accordance with the formula 3. The variance, in this case, is equal to the difference of the average values of the squares of the results of games and a square value of the node (the average value of won games) – formula 4:

$$V_n(n_i) = \bar{\sigma}_i^2 + \sqrt{\frac{2 \ln n_p}{n_i}}.$$

(4)

2.5 Minimax Optimal Strategy in the Stochastic Case

Minimax Optimal Strategy in the Stochastic Case (MOSS) assumed that each arm (child node) has an index that indicates its performance (the higher the index value, the movement corresponding to this node or shoulder is more promising) [2]. In each round, in any searches of the tree, a node with the highest index value is selected. The index arm, which is selected more than n/K times is equal to the average value of empirically calculated payoffs (winnings). For other arms (moves)[1], the index value is the upper limit of the confidence interval for the mean value of payoffs.

In the "classical" UCB strategy in each node a next move k (child node) is selected in accordance with the formula 1. In the MOSS strategy in accordance with the formula 5:

$$k \in \underset{i \in \{1,\dots,K\}}{\arg\max} \left(v_i + C \times \sqrt{\frac{\max \left(\ln \left(\frac{n_p}{K n_i} \right), 0 \right)}{n_i}} \right),$$

(5)

where K is the number of arms (moves) available from the parent node.

---

[1] Search strategies (UCT, UCB1-TUNED, MOSS etc.) are often described using Multi-Armed Bandit (MAB) problem terminology.

2.6   Objective Monte-Carlo

Objective Monte-Carlo (OMC) consists of two strategies: the selection of moves during the tree search phase, and back-propagation update [6]. The idea behind the selection strategy of moves is maximum utilization of available information on the basis of Central Limit Theorem. Due to the previously stated objectives only move-selection strategy will be briefly described[2].

For the current state of the game with M possible moves, a value of objective function U is calculated for an each considered move. A value of the function for the move m can be approximated with the complementary error function, denoted $erfc$[3]:

$$U_m(O_{bj}) = erfc\left(\frac{O_{bj} - V_m}{\sigma_m\sqrt{2}}\right),\tag{6}$$

where O_{bj} is a value of the current best move, V_m is a value of move m, σ_m is a standard deviation of V_m.

The next move is randomly selected accordingly to the probability P_m:

$$P_m = \frac{U_m(O_{bj})}{\sum\limits_{i \in M} U_i(O_{bj})}.\tag{7}$$

3   Experimental Evaluation of Search Strategies

The aim of the experiments was to evaluate the effectiveness of the move-selection strategies described in the previous section. Strategies: MCE, UCT, RAVE, UCB1-TUNED, MOSS and OMC were compared in 100-game matches between the program using a strategy to be assessed, and the program using a reference strategy.

3.1   Experimental Settings

To verify the effectiveness of search strategies a self-play experiments were performed on the 9×9 board. The thinking time was limited to $3\,s$ per move. The final move was selected on the basis of the visit count (robust move). Matched strategies were implemented in the same computer program to minimize the impact of implementation details. In order to compensate an error resulting from the color of players, each program was playing 50 games with Black. RAVE heuristics was used only in a match "RAVE vs. MCE". The matches were run on 64-bit Windows based computer with dual core processor Intel(R) Core(TM) i7 2.00 GHz and 8 GB of RAM.

---

[2] Implementation of the OMC move-selection strategy does not require implementation of the back-propagation strategy. The condition, in the opposite direction, is not true.

[3] Gauss error function $erf(x) = \frac{2}{\sqrt{\pi}}\int_0^x e^{-t^2}\,dt$; $erfc(x) = 1 - erf(x) = \frac{2}{\sqrt{\pi}}\int_x^\infty e^{-t^2}\,dt$.

3.2   Results

Table 1 shows the results of competitions between programs using different search strategies. The score is presented in the form of W/L ratio (Winning/Losing games). The W/L ratio greater than 1.0 indicates that a player's strategy is more effective than the reference one played by an opponent. UCT strategy was tested with different values of C coefficient in formula (1).

Table 1. Comparison of effectiveness of search strategies.

Player's strategy	Opponent's strategy	W/L ratio
UCT	MCE	2.13
RAVE	MCE	3.17
UCT ($C = 1.4$)	MCE	1.22
UCT ($C = 1.0$)	MCE	2.33
UCT ($C = 0.85$)	MCE	2.57
UCT ($C = 0.7$)	MCE	2.13
UCB1-TUNED	UCT ($C = 0.85$)	1.70
UCB1-TUNED	MOSS	1.44
OMC	UCT ($C = 1.4$)	1.38
UCT ($C = 0.85$)	OMC	1.50

3.3   Discussion

UCT in a tournament against MCE achieved the result W/L = 2.13 and doubled the playing strength in relation to the plain Monte-Carlo Evaluation (MCE). The effectiveness of UCT strongly depends on a value of C coefficient which, in practice, must be experimentally carefully selected for a specific game and a particular implementation. **RAVE** versus MCE finished with W/L = 3.17. Simple RAVE heuristics significantly affected the playing strength of the program, more than UCT strategy. It is worth to point out that both improvements (UCT and RAVE) can be used simultaneously.

   UCB1-TUNED strategy is an improved version of UCT. The main change is the replacement of a fixed coefficient C with on-fly calculated value based on the variance of simulated games. The score of the match UCB1-TUNNED against UCT (with C = 0.85) was W/L = 1.7, what empirically proves that UCB1-TUNED strategy is more effective than UCT, but the difference is not large. Perhaps if the value of C coefficient for UCT is more closely matched the difference would be less. The great advantage of UCB1-TUNED is no need for "tuning" of C parameter as the strategy changes a value of the coefficient at run-time on the bases of results of simulated games.

In a competition **MOSS** vs. UCB1-TUNED, MOSS strategy was less effective and got the score $W/L = (1.44)^{-1} = 0.69$. The great advantage of MOSS strategy (like UCB1-TUNED) is lack of constant parameters.

OMC failed to score against UCT $(C = 0.85) - W/L = 0.67$. The result shows that OMC is clearly lagging behind UCT with a well-chosen C coefficient. But in case when OMC played against UCT $(C = 1.44)$ it obtained the result $W/L = 1.38$. The pros of OMC strategy is being self-tuned.

To summarize, Monte-Carlo evaluation is based solely on the average value of simulated games and does not benefit from any search strategy. UCB1-TUNED was the winning strategy. The playing strength of a program using UCB strategy highly depends on the empirically tuned C coefficient. Effectiveness of tested strategies is described by the following relation:

$$MCE \prec UCT(C = 1.4) \prec OMC \prec UCT(C = 0.7) \prec UCT(C = 1.0)$$
$$\prec UCT(C = 0.85) \prec MOSS \prec UCB1-TUNED,$$

where MCE is the weakest, and UCB1-TUNED is the strongest strategy. UCB1-TUNED is used as a reference strategy in further experiments.

4   Confidence Intervals in Computer Go

Confidence intervals [10] have been proposed by Jerzy Neyman in 1935 [13, 14]. The Central Limit Theorem and confidence intervals play a crucial role in search strategy in computer Go.

4.1   The Central Limit Theorem

Let R be a random variable taking the values R_i, where R_i is the end result of i game. R_i values are limited and therefore for the random variable R mean value μ and standard deviation σ can be calculated. From the Central Limit Theorem it follows that if the number of games n approaches infinity, the standard deviation of the random variable $m_n = \frac{1}{n}\sum_{i=1}^{n} R_i$ converges to $\frac{\sigma}{\sqrt{n}}$. In addition, the probability distribution of the variable m_n converges to the normal distribution $N(\mu, \frac{\sigma}{\sqrt{n}})$. For m variable, confidence intervals can be estimated. One can be 95 % confident that the mean for all games is within the interval $(m_n - \frac{2\sigma}{\sqrt{n}}, m_n + \frac{2\sigma}{\sqrt{n}})$, in other words 95 % of all confidence intervals contains the mean of all games.

In practice, nodes values are binary updated. Most algorithms approximate the value of the node using the weighted average of the values range from 0 to 1. This value can be interpreted as the probability of winning.

4.2   Confidence Intervals in MCTS

The use of uniform search of a game tree with Monte-Carlo evaluation is not effective. The main problem is to select potentially most promising moves. Let us assume that for a given node i (that corresponds to the current state of a game) n_i random playouts were simulated, within which w_i were won. Empirical expected value of a payoff based on W/L ratio can be calculated as follows:

$$\widehat{E_i} = \frac{w_i}{n_i}. \tag{8}$$

Let us assume that the evaluation of game state has a normal distribution $N(\mu, \sigma^2)$, then the confidence interval can be defined as follows:

$$P\left(x \in \left[\widehat{E_i} - C_\epsilon \times \sigma_i \, , \, \widehat{E_i} + C_\epsilon \times \sigma_i\right]\right) > 1 - \epsilon \, , \ \ \sigma_i^2 = \frac{1}{n_i}, \tag{9}$$

where C_ϵ is a constant depending on ϵ. For the node corresponding to the current game state, a child node that has the biggest value $(E_i + C_\epsilon \times \sigma_i)$ is selected.

Two additional problems must be solved. First, nodes that have not yet been evaluated should be selected as first. This can be achieved by assigning a constant (large enough) value. Second, it can always happen, for a small number of playouts, that as a result of "unlucky" coincidence the best move would have a low estimated value. In computer Go that kind of an error is corrected by multiplication of distribution value by slowly growing f function, which value depends on total number of random playouts n_p for all child nodes for e.g. $f(n_p) = \ln(n_p)$ or $f(n_p) = \sqrt{n_p}$. Constant value C_ϵ is experimentally tuned.

4.3 Confidence Intervals for Binomial Distribution

In practice, estimation of confidence intervals in Bernoulli schema (parameter of the binomial distribution) was difficult and computationally exhausted (diagrams or large tables were needed). Popular remedy was to replace the binomial distribution by its normal approximation. Now due computer technology progress and functions offered by many libraries calculation of confidence intervals for discreet, binomial distribution becomes an easy task.

If random variable X has a Bernoulli distribution with the probability of success θ:

$$P_\theta\{X = 1\} = \theta = 1 - P_\theta\{X = 0\} \, , \ 0 < \theta < 1 \tag{10}$$

then counting number of successful samples S_n is binomially distributed with parameter θ:

$$P_\theta\{S_n = k\} = \binom{n}{k}\theta^k(1-\theta)^{n-k} \, , \ k = 0, 1, \ldots, n \, , \ 0 < \theta < 1. \tag{11}$$

One can assume that $X_1, X_2, \ldots, X_n$ is a sequence of independent and identically distributed random variables with Bernoulli distribution with θ probability of success, in other words it is a sequence of n random observations[4] with distribution (11). Then $S_n = \sum_{i=1}^n X_i$ is a minimal sufficient statistic what means that its value contains all the information needed to compute any estimate of the

---

[4] In the context of Go game – payoffs, results of simulations (also called playouts or rollouts).

unknown parameter θ. Consequently all functions of observations $X_1, X_2, \ldots, X_n$ can be treated as functions of S_n statistics. The aim is to find the interval estimation of θ parameter, about which we only know that its value can be found "somewhere in the interval $(0, 1)$".

A random interval $(\underline{\theta}(S_n), \bar{\theta}(S_n))$ is called a confidence error for a proportion for a parameter θ at the confidence level $\gamma = 1 - \alpha$

$$\forall_{\theta \in (0,1)} \ P_\theta\{\underline{\theta}(S_n), \ \bar{\theta}(S_n)\} \geq 1 - \alpha. \tag{12}$$

The left end of the confidence interval is the lowest function $\theta \in (0, 1) \rightarrow d_\gamma(\theta) \in \{0, 1, \ldots, n\}$ such as

$$\forall_{\theta \in (0,1)} \ P_\theta\{S_n \leq d_\gamma(\theta)\} \geq \frac{1 + \gamma}{2}. \tag{13}$$

Calculations could be simplified with the use of the following identity:

$$\sum_{j=0}^{k} \binom{n}{j} \theta^j (1 - \theta)^{n-j} = B(n - k, \ k + 1, \ 1 - \theta), \ k = 0, 1, \ldots, n, \tag{14}$$

where $B(\alpha, \beta, t)$ denotes a cumulative distribution function (CDF) of a beta distribution with parameters (α, β), in the point $t \in [0, 1]$:

$$B(\alpha, \beta, t) = \frac{\Gamma(\alpha + \beta)}{\Gamma(\alpha)\Gamma(\beta)} \int_0^t x^{\alpha-1}(1 - x)^{\beta-1} dx. \tag{15}$$

Function $d_\gamma(\theta)$, we are looking for, is a solution of the following equation

$$B(n - S_n, \ S_n, \ 1 - \theta) = \frac{1 + \gamma}{2}. \tag{16}$$

In other words, function $d_\gamma(\theta)$ is a quantile $B^{-1}(S_n, n - S_n + 1, (1 - \gamma)/2)$ of order $(1 - \gamma)/2$ of beta distribution $B(S_n, n - S_n + 1)$. The left end of the confidence interval at the confidence level γ is equal $B^{-1}(S_n, n - S_n + 1, (1 - \gamma)/2)$.

The confidence interval at the $\gamma = 1 - \alpha$ has the form

$$\left(B^{-1}\left(S_n, \ n - S_n + 1, \ \frac{1 - \gamma}{2} \right), \ B^{-1}\left(S_n + 1, \ n - S_n, \ \frac{1 + \gamma}{2} \right) \right). \tag{17}$$

The constructed confidence interval satisfies the condition (13), for a given θ the probability is not less than assumed γ value. Due to the nature of discrete distribution, for some θ values the probability can be bigger than the postulated confidence level θ.

5 Implementation in Computer Go Program

The confidence interval for discreet binomial distribution can be calculated on the bases of (17). In a computer program *Boost* library and functions implemented in boost */math/distributions/beta* module have been used. To avoid slowing down playouts too much, the B^{-1} function values were once calculated and stored in a table before tournaments. In case the available statistical library does not have beta distribution implemented, F distribution as an alternative can be used:

$$B^{-1}(\alpha, \beta, q) = \frac{\alpha}{\alpha + \beta F^{-1}(2\beta, 2\alpha, q)} ,\qquad (18)$$

where $F^{-1}(2\beta, 2\alpha, q)$ is quantile of q order of F distribution with $(2\beta, 2\alpha)$ degrees of freedom. The game tree search strategy, using the confidence intervals based on assumption of binomial distribution and calculated with the use of the inverse cumulative beta distribution function, has been named UCT-BETA.

5.1   Experiments and Results

For the final tournament two players using compared strategies were chosen: using UCB-BETA strategy and UCB1-TUNED. To make the test more reliable three tournaments of 1000 games each with colors swapped halfway were played on boards: small 9×9 with 5.5 *komi* points[5], medium 15×15 with 5.5 *komi* points and regular 19 × 19 with 7.5 *komi* points. The thinking time was set to 3 s for a move. Number of threads was set to the maximum available. In the actual game, the move with the highest visit count was finally played. To avoid the mistake caused by a color of a player, all matchups were divided into two parts. In the first part, tested strategy was selected for Black and compared to a reference strategy set for White. In the second part, colors of players were switched. A player using strategy with confidence interval estimation based on the Central Limit Theorem and normal distribution UCB1-TUNED were compared to a player using UCB-BETA strategy with confidence interval estimation for discreet, binomial.

Table 2 presents the results of the games between players using strategies UCT-BETA and UCB1-TUNED. Data in the W/L ratio column refers for UCT-BETA player. In the tournament on 9×9 board player using UCT-BETA won 637 games and lost 363 and gained W/L ratio 1.75 and winning rate 0.64. On medium board (15×15) player using UCT-BETA won 791 games and lost 208 and finished with W/L ratio 3.78 and winning rate 0.79. On regular board (19 × 19) player using UCT-BETA won 888 games and lost 112 and finished with W/L ratio 7.93 and winning rate 0.89. UCT-BETA completely overcome its competitor.

Table 2. Comparison of effectiveness of UCT-BETA and UCB1-TUNED strategies.

Player's strategy	Opponent's strategy	W/L ratio		
		9×9	15×15	19×19
UCT-BETA	UCB1-TUNED	1.75	3.78	7.93

---

[5] Points added to the score of white stones as compensation for playing second.

6 Conclusions

The application of confidence intervals in the computer Go has been described. First part, is focused on existing search strategies used in computer Go and empirically evaluate their effectiveness in real competitions. UCB1-TUNED was the winning strategy from all implemented in a computer program and evaluated strategies, and therefore was chosen as a base-line strategy. In the second part, a calculation of the confidence intervals based on discreet, binomial distribution with the use of the inverse cumulative beta distribution function has been suggested. Three tournaments of 1000 games each played on small, medium and large board have showed that the improved move-selection strategy works particularly well in games played on medium and large boards. On a regular 19×19 board in the match against the base-line strategy achieved an outstanding result W/L ratio = 7.93.

Why does normal approximation work worse for bigger boards? Certain conditions must be met to use the normal approximation to binomial distribution. One is that a product of a number of samples and an estimate of probability of success is bigger than let's say 15. In computer Go, on a large board, with a big branching factor and limited time for thinking, this is not the case, and that is why the confidence intervals based on discreet, binomial distribution are more accurate and consequently the search strategy more effective.

References

1. Allis, V.: Searching for solutions in games and artificial intelligence. Ph.D. thesis, Rijksuniversiteit Limburg, Maastricht, The Netherlands (1994)
2. Audibert, J., Bubeck, S.: Minimax policies for adversarial and stochastic bandits. In: Proceedings of the 22nd Annual Conference on Learning Theory, Omnipress, pp. 773–818 (2004)
3. Auer, P., Cesa-Bianchi, N., Fischer, P.: Finite-time analysis of the multiarmed bandit problem. Mach. Learn. **47**, 235–256 (2002)
4. Brügmann, B.: Monte Carlo Go. Technical report, Physics Department, Syracuse University, Syracuse, NY, USA (1993)
5. Brown, L., Cai, T., DasGupta, A.: Interval estimation for a binomial proportion. Stat. Sci. **16**(2), 101–117 (2001)
6. Chaslot, G., Saito, J., Uiterwijk, J., Bouzy, B., van den Herik, H.: Monte-Carlo strategies for computer go. In: 18th BeNeLux Conference on Artificial Intelligence, pp. 83–90 (2006)
7. Coulom, R.: Efficient selectivity and backup operators in Monte-Carlo tree search. In: van den Herik, H.J., Ciancarini, P., Donkers, H.H.L.M.J. (eds.) CG 2006. LNCS, vol. 4630, pp. 72–83. Springer, Heidelberg (2007)
8. Gelly, S., Silver, D.: Combining online and offline knowledge in UCT. In: ICML 2007 Proceedings of the 24th International Conference on Machine Learning, pp. 273–280. ACM Press, New York (2007)
9. Gelly, S., Wang, Y.: Exploration exploitation in Go: UCT for Monte-Carlo Go. In: NIPS: Neural Information Processing Systems Conference On-Line Trading of Exploration and Exploitation Workshop (2006)

10. Hogg, R., McKean, J., Craig, A.: Introduction to Mathematical Statistics, 7th edn. Pearson Prentice Hall, US (2013)
11. Kocsis, L., Szepesvári, C.: Bandit based Monte-Carlo planning. In: Fürnkranz, J., Scheffer, T., Spiliopoulou, M. (eds.) ECML 2006. LNCS (LNAI), vol. 4212, pp. 282–293. Springer, Heidelberg (2006)
12. Morisette, J., Khorram, S.: Interval estimation for a binomial proportion. Photogram. Eng. Remote Sens. **64**, 281–283 (1998)
13. Neyman, J.: On the problem of confidence intervals. Ann. Math. Stat. **6**(3), 111–116 (1935)
14. Neyman, J.: Outline of a theory of statistical estimation based on the classical theory of probability. Philos. Trans. Roy. Soc. Lond. Ser. A, Math. Phys. Sci. **236**(767), 333–380 (1937)

Workshop: Visual Information Coding Meets Machine Learning

RoughCut–New Approach to Segment High-Resolution Images

Mateusz Babiuch, Bartosz Zieliński[(⊠)], and Marek Skomorowski

Faculty of Mathematics and Computer Science, The Institute of Computer Science
and Computer Mathematics, Jagiellonian University,
ul. Łojasiewicza 6, 30-348 Kraków, Poland
{mateusz.babiuch,bartosz.zielinski,marek.skomorowski}@uj.edu.pl
http://www.ii.uj.edu.pl

Abstract. We introduce a texture-based modification of the GrabCut
algorithm that significantly improves its performance for high-resolution
images but with a slight decrease in accuracy. This consists of five steps:
expansion, convolution, shrinkage, GrabCut of the shrunk image, and
enlargement. The results showed that modified algorithm is three times
faster than the original one. At the same time, there is no significant
difference between the average F1-measures obtained for both algorithms
in case of high-resolution images. Therefore, it can be successfully used
in semi-automatic segmentation of such images.

Keywords: GrabCut · Segmentation · High-resolution images · Schmid
filter bank · Texture description

1 Introduction

Maximum flow algorithms have become very popular in the fields of computer
vision because of their ability to efficiently compute a global minimum of the
given optimization problem. This algorithm was, among others, applied to segmentation (e.g., GrabCut algorithm [1]), image restoration [2], dense stereo estimation [3], and shape matching [4].

GrabCut algorithm can be used to efficiently segment low-resolution images
(with average size of 400×400 pixels) from the standard databases [5]. However,
because of its complexity, the algorithm is inefficient in case of high-resolution
images. On the other hand, the size of images increased significantly in recent
years due to high-quality commercial cameras (with up to 20 megapixels).

We introduce a texture-based modification of the GrabCut algorithm that
significantly improves its performance for high-resolution images but with a
slightly decrease in accuracy. This consists of five steps: expansion, convolution,
shrinkage, GrabCut of the shrunk image, and enlargement. Texture description
is obtained based on the Schmid filter bank [7,8] which is a "Gabor-like" filter
resistant to rotation.

© Springer International Publishing Switzerland 2016
L. Rutkowski et al. (Eds.): ICAISC 2016, Part II, LNAI 9693, pp. 591–601, 2016.
DOI: 10.1007/978-3-319-39384-1_52

As all standard databases consist of low-resolution images, we had to create our own database with high-resolution images based on existing databases of textures and shapes (see Sect. 4.1).

This paper is organized in the following manner. In Sect. 2, the original Grab-Cut algorithm is shortly described. In Sect. 3, our approach, called RoughCut, is presented in details. The obtained results and conclusions are presented in Sects. 4 and 5, respectively.

2   Original GrabCut Algorithm

GrabCut is a powerful and robust algorithm created with image segmentation in mind [1]. The successive phases of the GrabCut algorithm are as follows (see [6] for more details):

1. User generates "seed" (or trimap) to describe pixels as guaranteed foreground (FGD), guaranteed background (BGD), probably foreground (PR_FGD), or probably background (PR_BGD). FGD and BGD are considered as known pixels while PR_FGD and PR_BGD are unknown pixels.
2. Computer creates an initial image segmentation, where all FGD and PR_FGD pixels are tentatively placed in the foreground class and all BGD and PR_BGD pixels in the background class.
3. Gaussian Mixture Models (GMMs) are created for initial foreground and background classes based on the known pixels. In order to make this phase more accurate, k-means is used to generate initial components.
4. Each unknown pixel is assigned to the most likely Gaussian component in the foreground or background GMM.
5. The GMMs are thrown away and new GMMs are learned from the pixel sets created in phase 4.
6. A graph is built (using the GMMs) and Graph Cut is run to find a new tentative foreground and background classification of pixels.
7. Steps 4–6 are repeated until the classification converges.

3   Rough GrabCut Algorithm

We propose a possible improvement to the GrabCut algorithm, which we called the RoughCut algorithm. It was designed specifically with high-resolution images in mind, for which the original algorithm is inefficient. The modified algorithm supposed to approximate the general shape of the foreground object even if only limited "seed" is available. It consists of five parts: expansion, convolution, shrinkage, GrabCut of the shrunk image, and enlargement.

3.1   Expansion and Convolution

Given an image with size of $w \times h \times 3$ (in RGB color space), the algorithm first expands last dimension from 3 into 17 values in the following manner: first 3 values are left as red, green, and blue channels of the color image; 4th value is a grayscale image calculated from the color image; values 5th–17th correspond to grayscale image convoluted with filters from the Schmid filter bank [7], which contains 13 "Gabor-like" filters resistant to rotation.

3.2 Shrinkage

After expansion and convolution, the algorithm shrinks the given image using a tuned parameter s called cell size (see Sect. 4.3 for tuning description). The original image, whenever possible, is divided into squares of size $s \times s$ pixels called cells, starting from the top left corner. When w or h does not divisible by s, the algorithm picks all the pixels that would fit in the last cell (they form a rectangle, see Fig. 1a). Each cell of size $s \times s \times 17$ is reduced to a single pixel of size $1 \times 1 \times 34$, in the following manner:

```
for(i in 1:17) {
  pixel[2i - 1] = mean(cell[:, :, i])
  pixel[2i] = std(cell[:, :, i])
}
```

In result, we obtain a matrix roughly s times smaller on two first dimensions, depending on the relation between an image size and a cell size. The image has 34 values on the last dimension (17 mean values and 17 standard deviations), which describe the texture characteristic of the original image.

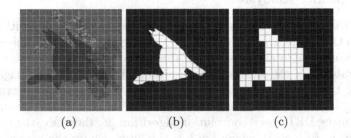

(a)   (b)   (c)

Fig. 1. Dividing image of size 500×500 pixels into cells of size 32×32 pixels (a), together with the ground truth segmentation (b) and the result obtained with Rough-Cut algorithm (c). The image in (a) is divided into cells starting from the top left corner. Therefore, right and bottom cells are not squares. Note that the cell size is visibly too large for 500×500 image size, what produces a "blocky" effect.

In order to shrink the user-defined "seed", the algorithm analyzes the pixels' flags inside the cell and determines the highest value, which is assigned to a single pixel obtained after cell reduction. The flags from the highest to the lowest value are as follows: FGD, BGD, PR_FGD, PR_BGD.

3.3   GrabCut of the Shrunk Image

In the next step, the algorithm performs the original GrabCut algorithm on the shrunk image and the shrunk "seed". In result, we a rough segmentation of the object is obtained. However, since k-means algorithm used in GrabCut requires at least k pixels, we encountered a problem with a certain combinations of the cell and image sizes. For instance, when combining 512×512 image size with 128×128 cell size, the shrunk image is of size 4×4 pixels. In result, less than six pixels corresponded to the foreground. In such a case, the algorithm randomly selects few pixels corresponding to the background and assigns them to the foreground. Although it does affect the algorithm, the results did not change much as such particular combinations fairly obviously already suffers from extreme unreliability. Such combination was chosen merely for testing purposes and while the error was certainly amplified, it can be agreed to have minimal effect on the conclusion.

3.4   Enlargement

The segmentation obtained for the shrunk image is then enlarged to the original size by expanding each pixel into the cell. The flags of the cell's pixels correspond to the value of the single pixel to which the cell was reduced, unless the original pixel was described as either guaranteed foreground or guaranteed background (FGD or BGD, see Fig. 1b, c). This produces a "blocky" effect.

3.5   Complexity Analysis

According to Sect. 2, the most complex phase of the GrabCut algorithm is running Graph Cut on the graph of size $O(w\,h)$. As the algorithm fixes the number of iteration to one, the total complexity of the original algorithm equals $O(w^3\,h^3)$.

The GrabCut of the shrunk image is iterated two times for images of size $w/s \times h/s$; therefore, its complexity equals $O(w^3 \cdot h^3/s^2)$. Complexity of the expansion, shrinkage, and enlargement equals $O(w \cdot h)$. The convolution was performed using DFT-based convolution algorithm [9]; therefore, the complexity equals $O(w \cdot h \cdot k \cdot log(k))$, where $k \times k$ is the filter size (in the case of standard Schmid filter bank $k = 49$). Therefore, the complexity of the modified algorithm equals $O(w^3 \cdot h^3/s^2 + w \cdot h \cdot k \cdot log(k))$.

While the extra steps of the RoughCut algorithm by themselves may seem costly (especially convolution), the reduction in computational complexity of GrabCut algorithm is huge and in the end beneficial. This is, however, at the cost of extra memory. The algorithm requires memory for 14 extra values of the original image's pixels and 34 extra values of the shrunk image's pixels. GMMs are also sufficiently larger because of the 34-dimensional space. Altogether, it requires $O(w \cdot h)$ extra memory, with a fairly big constant.

4   Experiment

The objective of the experiment was to compare the performance of the original GrabCut algorithm with its modification for high-resolution images. However, we encountered extreme difficulties in finding a proper testing set, as standard databases consist of low-resolution images (with average size of 400 × 400 pixels). Because of that we had to create our own database with high-resolution images. For this purpose, we used textures from Outex Texture Database [10] and shapes from Lems Brown Database [11]. Sadly, to our knowledge, the latter database is no longer available online. The sample textures and shapes are presented in Fig. 2.

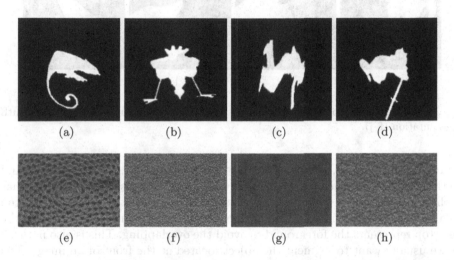

(a)   (b)   (c)   (d)

(e)   (f)   (g)   (h)

Fig. 2. Sample images from Outex Texture Database (a–e) and Lems Brown Database (f–j). The first database showcases great variety of satisfyingly natural objects, while images from the latter database have textures that can be successfully used for testing.

4.1   Generating Images with Ground Truth Segmentation

Images were generated using the following set of properties: image size (512×512, 1024×1024, 2048×2048, 4096×4096 pixels); and object number (random integer between 1 and 8). Each object added to the image has been transformed using the following phases:

1. Put a shape in the center of the generated image.
2. Enlarge the shape to 120 % of its original size to reduce the image margins.
3. Apply random scaling separately for horizontal and vertical axes, each varying from 80 % to 100 % of the original shape's size.
4. Clockwise rotation by angle randomly selected as integer between 0 and 359 degrees.
5. Translate separately for each axis by random value from −25 % to 25 % of the image size.

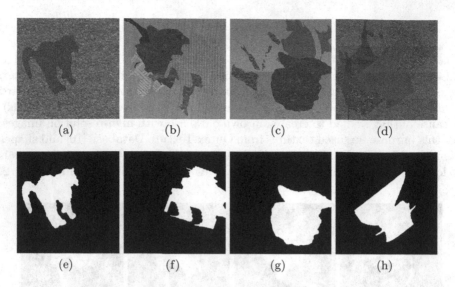

(a)   (b)   (c)   (d)

(e)   (f)   (g)   (h)

Fig. 3. The examples of randomly generated images (a–e) with their ground truth segmentation (f–j).

After transformations, random textures were assigned both to the objects and to the background. Each texture can only be chosen at most once, ensuring that each object is uniquely represented by its texture. In case of texture being too small for the object it is simply applied in a repeating manner. The object on the very top represents the foreground to avoid the overlapping. This is also natural, as we usually want to segment the object located at the front of an image. The examples of randomly generated images are presented in Fig. 3 together with their ground truth segmentation.

4.2 Experiment Setup

To get the artificial "seed" required in GrabCut algorithm, we performed erosion on the ground truth segmentation until there 10 % of the most inner pixels were left (see Fig. 4).

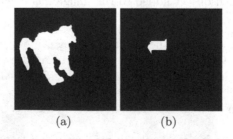

(a)   (b)

Fig. 4. Ground truth segmentation mask (a) and 10 % of the most inner pixels (b).

For each of the considered image sizes and cell sizes (8×8, 16×16, 32×32, 64×64 pixels), 100 images were generated in a way presented in Sect. 4.1. The images were segmented both with GrabCut and with RoughCut algorithm. We used one iteration for the first one and two iterations for the latter algorithm.

We used a cluster with 64 AMD Opteron(tm) Processor 6380 and 512 GB RAM. In total, we used 30 threads, each thread taking an image and testing the original and modified algorithm on that specific image. To handle multithreading, we used C++ Boost Library. The code is publicly available on GitHub: https://github.com/Babiuszek/opencv_contrib.

4.3   Results

Before comparing the original GrabCut algorithm to its modification, we decided to tune the cell size parameter. For this purpose, we compared the average F1-measures obtained for each combination of image size and cell size. The results are presented in Fig. 5. It is fairly clear that the optimal cell size is 8×8 pixels for 512×512, 1024×1024, and 4096×4096 image size and 16×16 pixels for 2048×2048 image size. It can be also observed that the accuracy suffers an extreme drop as the cell size increases, especially in case of the low-resolution images. This was expected, as in such cases, the resolution of the cells is too high to correctly reduce into a single pixel. On the other hand, in case of the high-resolution images, the objects are usually much bigger, allowing to use larger cells.

All further results presented in this section were obtained using these optimal cell sizes.

Next, we decided to check the average time for each step of the RoughCut algorithm. The results are presented in Fig. 6. The time of each step increases four times when image is four times larger (e.g., GrabCut of the shrunk image

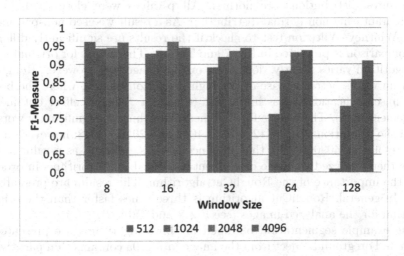

Fig. 5. The accuracy of RoughCut algorithm depending on the image size and cell size. (Color figure online)

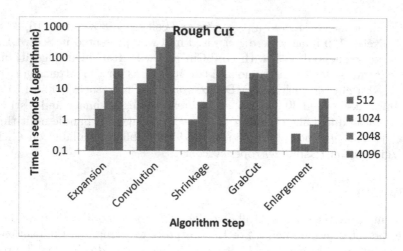

Fig. 6. The average time in seconds for each step of the RoughCut algorithm. (Color figure online)

for 512×512 images work in around $8.16\,s$, while in case of 1024×1024 images the average time is $32,81\,s$). It is worth to look closer at images that are size of 2048×2048 pixels for which the optimal cell size is 16×16 pixels. This causes the shrunk image to be of size 128×128 pixels, exactly the same as in case of the 1024×1024 images and 8×8 cells. Thus, the average time of the GrabCut of the shrunk image is nearly identical for these two combinations.

The key goal was to establish which algorithm yields the best results, the original GrabCut algorithm or its modification. In order to determine a correct statistical test, we performed Shapiro–Wilk test to establish whether the F1-measures distributions are normal. All p-values were close to 0, practically guaranteeing non-normal distribution. As a result we used non-parametric Mann–Whitney–Wilcoxon test to check if the results are significantly different. The comparison is presented in Fig. 7 and Table 1. The results for original Grab-Cut algorithm varies slightly, depending on the image size. However, RoughCut algorithm works better in case of the high-resolution images, where the border pixels misclassification is less important (due to a "blocky" effect obtained in enlargement step). The results for modified algorithm are significantly worse in case of the resolutions 512×512, 1024×1024 and 2048×2048; however, in case of the resolution 4096×4096, the difference is not significant, as p-value > 0.01.

We then analyzed the time of segmentation for both algorithms in order to prove the importance of the RoughCut algorithm. The results are presented in Fig. 8. In general, RoughCut algorithm is three times faster than the original algorithm for the analyzed images (see Fig. 8 and Table 2).

The example segmentation obtained for both algorithms are presented in Fig. 9a–h. Foreground object from the image in Fig. 9a contains thin parts which generate number of incorrectly segmented cells in case of the RoughCut algorithm (due to its "blocky" effect). On the other hand, the image in Fig. 9e is

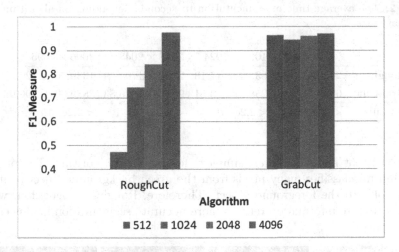

Fig. 7. The average F1-measure depending on algorithm type and image size. (Color figure online)

Table 1. The average F1-measure depending on algorithm type and image size.

	512×512	1024×1024	2048×2048	4096×4096
GrabCut	$0{,}96 \pm 0{,}07$	$0{,}94 \pm 0{,}08$	$0{,}96 \pm 0{,}09$	$0{,}97 \pm 0{,}06$
RoughCut	$0{,}47 \pm 0{,}20$	$0{,}74 \pm 0{,}17$	$0{,}84 \pm 0{,}14$	$0{,}98 \pm 0{,}04$
p-value	$< 2.2e{-}16$	$< 2.2e{-}16$	$< 2.2e{-}16$	0.01225

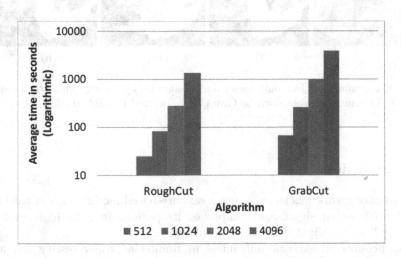

Fig. 8. The average time of segmentation in seconds depending on algorithm type and image size. (Color figure online)

Table 2. The average time of segmentation in seconds depending on algorithm type and image size.

	512 × 512	1024 × 1024	2048 × 2048	4096 × 4096
RoughCut	24,97 ± 3,14	83,04 ± 17,13	278,79 ± 93,59	1349,76 ± 129,35
GrabCut	66,71 ± 2,91	258,61 ± 5,51	981,20 ± 26,83	3889,70 ± 106,98
p-value	< 2.2e−16	< 2.2e−16	< 2.2e−16	< 2.2e−16

more consistent and, therefore, "simpler" for modified algorithm. The original algorithm misclassifies many pixels from the green background object as it has similar color to the foreground object. Therefore, RoughCut algorithm, which bases on texture information returns more accurate segmentation in this case.

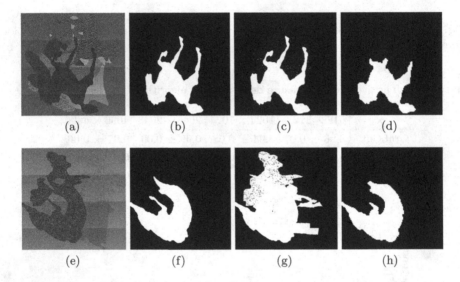

Fig. 9. The examples of randomly generated images (a, e), their ground truth segmentation (b, f), and results obtained by GrabCut (c, g) and RoughCut (d, h) algorithms.

5   Conclusion

The goal of our work was to introduce a texture-based modification of the Grab-Cut algorithm that significantly improves its performance for high-resolution images but with a slight decrease in accuracy.

We encountered extreme difficulties in finding a proper testing set, as all standard databases consist of low-resolution images (usually with average size of 400 × 400 pixels). Because of that we had to create our own database with high-resolution images.

The results showed that RoughCut is three times faster than GrabCut algorithm. Additionally, the average F1-measure obtained for modified algorithm in case of the 4096 × 4096 images is not significantly different from the one obtained for the original algorithm. Therefore, it can be successfully used in semi-automatic segmentation of the high-resolution images.

In the future, we have planed to apply other filter banks and topological methods, similar to those used by Zeppelzauer et al. [12]. Additionally, we intend to use database with more natural images. They could be supplied with shading and localized blurring of the edges. Moreover, we plan to create a database of real, high-resolution images together with their ground truth segmentation.

References

1. Rother, C., Kolmogorov, V., Blake, A.: Grabcut: interactive foreground extraction using iterated graph cuts. ACM T Graph. **23**(3), 309–314 (2004)
2. Greig, D., Porteous, B., Seheult, A.: Grabcut: exact maximum a posteriori estimation for binary images. J. Roy. Stat. Soc. Ser. B (Methodol.) **51**, 271–279 (1989)
3. Roy, S.: Grabcut: stereo without epipolar lines: a maximum-flow formulation. Int. J. Comput. Vis. **34**(2–3), 147–161 (1999)
4. Szeliski, R.: Computer Vision: Algorithms and Applications. Springer Science and Business Media, London (2010)
5. Achanta, R., Hemami, S., Estrada, F., Susstrunk, S.: Frequency-tuned salient region detection. In: IEEE Conference on Computer Vision and Pattern Recognition, pp. 1597–1604. IEEE Press (2009)
6. Talbot, J., Xu, X.: Implementing GrabCut. Brigham Young University, Citeseer, Provo (2006)
7. Schmid, C.: Constructing models for content-based image retrieval. In: IEEE Conference on Computer Vision and Pattern Recognition, pp. 11–39. IEEE Press (2001)
8. Zieliński, B., Skomorowski, M.: Schmid filter and inpainting in computer-aided erosions and osteophytes detection based on hand radiographs. In: Burduk, R., Jackowski, K., Kurzyński, M., Woźniak, M., Żołnierek, A. (eds.) CORES 2015. AISC, vol. 403, pp. 511–519. Springer, Switzerland (2015)
9. Burrus, C., Parks, T.: DFT/FFT and Convolution Algorithms: Theory and Implementation. Wiley, Inc., New York (1991)
10. Outex Texture Database. http://www.outex.oulu.fi
11. Lems Brown Database. http://www.lems.brown.edu
12. Zeppelzauer, M., Zieliński, B., Juda, M., Seidl, M.: Topological Descriptors for 3D Surface Analysis (2016). arXiv preprint arXiv:1601.06057

Vision Based Techniques of 3D Obstacle Reconfiguration for the Outdoor Drilling Mobile Robot

Andrzej Bielecki[1], Tomasz Buratowski[2(✉)], Michał Ciszewski[2],
and Piotr Śmigielski[1]

[1] Chair of Applied Computer Science, Faculty of Electrotechnics, Automation,
Computer Science and Biomedical Engineering,
AGH University of Science and Technology, Al. Mickiewicza 30,
30-059 Kraków, Poland
azbielecki@gmail.com, smigielski.piotr@gmail.com
[2] Chair of Robotics and Mechatronics,
Faculty of Mechanical Engineering and Robotics,
AGH University of Science and Technology, Al. Mickiewicza 30,
30-059 Kraków, Poland
tburatow@agh.edu.pl

Abstract. This work describes a set of techniques, based on the vision system, designed to supplement information about environment by adding three-dimensional objects representations. Described vision system plays a role of supplementary part of the SLAM technique for gathering information about surrounding environment by an autonomous robot. Algorithms are especially prepared for a mobile drilling robot. The main characteristics of the robot and its applications are defined in the first part of this paper. Then, the technical aspects and the execution steps of the algorithms utilized by the vision system are described. In the last part of this paper, the test case along with the results, presenting sample application of the vision system, is presented.

Keywords: Autonomous agent · Mobile robot · Vectorization · 3D scene representation

1 Introduction

In this paper a complex mechatronic system designed for different purposes related to drilling processes, sample extraction and its delivery to a designated area is presented. All subsystems are designed to operate in terrestrial conditions and can be adapted to space environment. The device must have possibly low mass to enable transport by an Unmanned Aerial Vehicle (UAV) to a place designated for drilling. High level of autonomy of the drilling system must be provided in order to realize drilling tasks without human supervision. In terrestrial applications, drilling performance is usually optimized due to economic

© Springer International Publishing Switzerland 2016
L. Rutkowski et al. (Eds.): ICAISC 2016, Part II, LNAI 9693, pp. 602–612, 2016.
DOI: 10.1007/978-3-319-39384-1_53

reasons. This leads to usage of high power motors and effective but heavy drilling bits to increase the rate of penetration. In space conditions the time of drilling is not an important factor, while minimization of mass and power consumptions has the highest priority. For proper operation of the system, a custom localization system has to be utilized. Its main features are base on image processing and recognition of the environment. Firstly, during transport of the drilling system to a designated place for drilling, the UAV has to scan the area of interest and select optimal starting point for the surface operation of the rover. To do this, it is required to distinguish obstacles and terrain suitable for navigation and drilling of the mobile robot. Secondly, during motion planning on the level of the surface, it is desirable to determine approximate location of obstacles based on internal camera built in the mobile robot, thus advanced image processing algorithms have to be implemented. Next, the information can be further processed and confirmed by an on-board sensing unit equipped with Laser Scanner and infrared sensors.

2   Overview of the Ultralight Mobile Drilling System

The mobile drilling system consists of three main subsystems: mobile robot MR, support module SM and drilling subsystem DR. The mobile robot is a lightweight subsystem which provides mobility in an unknown terrain. The SM is used to manipulate the drilling system and store soil and rock samples. DR subsystem consists of a core drill with complex functionality that allows drilling, latching of samples. The UMDS, as a system, weighs 22 kg and was designed to operate at the maximum distance of 100 m from the base station. Drilling and collecting samples is a very complex process, featuring multiple operations. The mission is divided into eight phases that consist in: accessing the drilling place, unfolding the SM manipulator, anchoring the system, drilling and collecting samples, undocking anchors, folding the SM manipulator and returning to the base station. The MR platform is intended for transport of SM and DR modules and has dedicated space for power supply unit, on-board computer and drive controllers. In Fig. 1 an overview of a CAD model of the mobile platform is depicted. MR has four wheels powered independently by brushless DC motors, equipped with integrated encoders and gear transmissions. A suspension system enables independent setting of extension of the left and right rocker of the rover with respect to the ground by usage of two self-locking linear drives. In addition, a passive differential system in the central part of the rover is utilized. The system provides pitch angle compensation of the mobile platform during motion on uneven terrain [1].

The mass of the MR (4.5 kg) is much lower than these of the comparable rovers. Even small rovers such as the CRAB described in [2] have over 7 times higher mass than the MR platform. The MR is equipped with a laser scanner system for precise localization in space that is based on a LIDAR mounted on a servomotor. This setting gives possibility to acquire 2D and 3D data of the environment. Additionally the robot is equipped with a camera and infrared sensors.

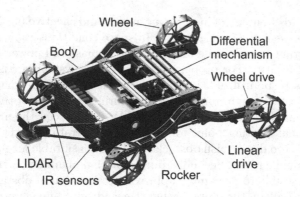

Fig. 1. Mobile robot (MR) platform with extended rockers.

2.1   Trajectory Generation

Trajectory generation of a robot in a space consists of definition of position and orientation in reference to the base coordinate system. Navigation of the robot is based on two concepts. First concept, related to Earth exploration consist of data from Inertial Measurement Unit (IMU) and Global Positioning System (GPS). Additionally, measurements from encoders mounted on wheel drives may be used as complementary information when it is possible. The second concept of navigation intended for extraterrestrial environments would be based on visual topological Simultaneous Localization and Mapping (SLAM). Such techniques are related to identification of some objects in environment to estimate robot position and orientation. Visual data of the objects can be collected by satellite imagery. There are several ways to plan robot trajectory. In our project Wavefront algorithm is utilized.

The area quantized for calculations in Wavefront algorithm must be decomposed with usage of constant cluster size grid (Constant Grid Decomposition), stretched at height corresponding to the maximum size of obstacle present in the area of exploration. The result is a projection of the grid on an uneven surface as presented in Fig. 2.

First, obstacles are marked with a 1 and the destination point is marked with 2. One can optionally surround the entire area of interest with squares numbered by 1 as well to tell the robot to avoid those squares, and/or "expand" the size of the obstacle to avoid collisions due to dead-reckoning errors. After those operations the work environment will look like the one depicted in Fig. 3.

In order to create the "wave" of values, the calculations must start at the destination, and a distance of 3 must be assigned to every square adjacent to the goal. Then a distance of 4 is assigned to every square adjacent to the squares of distance 3 (see Fig. 3). The operation should be continued until the start point is reached. When the first stage is completed, the numbers need to be followed in reverse order, and obstacles marked by 1 should be avoided. A possible path has been marked in red in Fig. 4. The goal and start point are labeled as 2 and

Fig. 2. Grid used in Wavefront algorithm adapted to exploration environment of the rover.

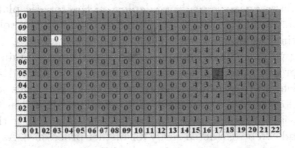

Fig. 3. First stage of trajectory generation with usage of the Wavefront algorithm. (Color figure online)

	01	02	03	04	05	06	07	08	09	10	11	12	13	14	15	16	17	18	19	20	21	22
10	1	1	1	1	1	1	1	1	1	1	1	1	1	1	1	1	1	1	1	1	1	1
09	1	17	16	15	14	13	12	11	11	11	11	1	1	6	6	6	6	6	6	6	6	1
08	1	17	16	15	14	13	12	11	10	10	10	1	6	5	5	5	5	5	5	5	6	1
07	1	17	16	15	14	13	12	1	1	9	1	1	6	5	4	4	4	4	4	5	6	1
06	1	17	16	15	14	13	12	1	10	9	8	7	6	5	4	3	3	3	4	5	6	1
05	1	17	16	15	14	13	12	11	10	9	8	1	6	5	4	3	-	3	4	5	6	1
04	1	17	16	15	14	13	12	11	10	9	8	7	6	5	4	3	3	3	4	5	6	1
03	1	1	1	15	14	13	12	11	10	9	8	1	6	5	4	4	4	4	4	5	6	1
02	1	1	1	15	14	13	12	11	10	9	9	1	6	5	5	5	5	5	5	5	6	1
01	1	1	1	1	1	1	1	1	1	1	1	1	1	1	1	1	1	1	1	1	1	1
0	01	02	03	04	05	06	07	08	09	10	11	12	13	14	15	16	17	18	19	20	21	22

Fig. 4. Generated trajectory using Wavefront algorithm. (Color figure online)

16 consecutively. This is just one of the many paths that can be used to reach the goal, and any path that follows the descending numbers correctly will be acceptable.

3   Scene Analysis for Path Planing and Obstacle Avoidance

In this section a complete scene analysis algorithm for an unmanned vehicle is described. It operates on the images taken by the sensors of the robot to reveal elements of the scene and enhance the scene model with three-dimensional models of the objects during operating in the unknown environment.

3.1   Technological Solution for the Scene Analysis Algorithm

The Python language was used for implementation of the algorithms for scene analysis. The Python is a scripting language which can be easily incorporated for autonomous, robotic systems. The Python interpreter as well as the precompiled code requires small amounts of memory. Each Python module can be easily replaced when new version is ready to deploy on the robotic platform. It only requires substitution of the with classes and methods on the robot's HDD or flash drive and the Python interpreter will automatically compile the source code modules into *.pyc precompiled module. The algorithm of obtaining the three-dimensional representation of the scene fragments is organized as a sequence of methods which are responsible for particular task. The tasks were described in [3–5] and below they are presented as a complete algorithm. The input of the method consists of a preprocessed images of the scene where the objects are clearly visible and can be extracted easily for further processing. As the method is designed to be used for various input images (different sizes, saturation, contrast and image quality), a set of parameters was incorporated in particular steps. Below is the list of parameters and their meanings. Further in this section, their specific application is described:

1. *contrast_enhance* - the numeric parameter defining the strength of the contrast enhancement function.
2. *window_size* - the range of searching for the successive points in the bordered image.
3. *outlier_threshold* - parameter used by smoothing algorithm to define which points from the object border are redundant.
4. *connect_threshold* - parameter used for connecting ends of polygonal chains which are separated but close to each other.

Below description reflects the sequence in which the complete three-dimensional model creation method is organized and executed.

Image Pre-processing

1. Contrast enhancement. If the algorithm is applied in a low visibility area, like dark interior space or during the poor weather conditions, the extraction of particular objects from the scene may cause problems. Here the contrast enhancement function, with parameter *contrast_enhance*, is applied on the input image to help reveal the shape and color of the objects in the examined scene.
2. Color extraction. In our application we assume that the image was initially preprocessed and the objects which are to be extracted are expected to be marked with majority of red color. The color extraction results in a picture with red colored objects on a white background. This is accomplished by scanning through each pixel of the input image. A new image is created by assigning the red pixel (RGB [255, 0, 0]) when red ingredient is dominating over green and blue ingredients ($R > G + B$) in the input image. Otherwise, the white pixel (RGB [255, 255, 255]) is assigned in the new picture.
3. Morphological erosion and dilatation. The methods of mathematical morphology are widely used in image processing applications [6,7]. We assume that pre-processing, even on images of well prepared scene can result in objects extraction which with high rate of errors (for example light changes on the photographed scene). In order to sharpen the edge of the extracted object and avoid separated pixels, the erosion transformation is applied. This results in shrinking of the original object. Then, to return the object to its original size, the dilatation transformation is applied.

Image Vectorization. This steps result in getting the sequence of points highlighting the border of objects in the image. The points are in the euclidean space within the domain defined by the width and height of the image. For example, having the image with size of 700 × 400 pixels will result in points (x, y) with $x \in [0, 700]$ and $y \in [0, 400]$.

1. Border extraction. That step results in obtaining two dimensional matrix of values "1" or "0". Each element contains "1" when located in place of highlighted object's border and "0" otherwise (belongs either to background or object's interior). Dimensions of the matrix are equal to image size (i.e. 700 × 400) and was implemented with Python list of lists.
2. Border points extraction. With the use of the *window*, a squared frame of size given by parameter *window_size*, is applied sequentially along the matrix elements containing "1". The result, for separate object, is a sequence (polygonal chain) of coordinates located around the original object. The points are fairly dense with distance of *window_size*/2 to maximally $\sqrt{2}window\_size/2$ between successive ones.
3. Smoothing the border. In order to remove the redundant points from the sequences the groups of points lying on a single line are identified. *outlier_threshold* parameter is used as a threshold. Those points that lays outside threshold are removed from the sequence.

Vector Post-processing

1. Connecting close ends. The vectorization method may result in obtaining opened polygonal chains, having the start and end points located close to each other. The start and end points may belong to single multiple polygonal chains. Connecting points within distance given by *connect_threshold* parameter will result in longer, well separated polygonal chains representation.

Three-Dimensional Model Building. The input for this step consists of at least two vector representation of the examined object extracted from two images taken from orthogonal directions, from the same plane (for most applications, including described in this paper, it will be horizontal plane). In some applications [5] third image, pointing from above of the examined object is used to build more detailed model.

1. Scaling of the vector representation. If the input images were taken from different distance from the object, one representation can be significantly smaller from the other. In order for the three-dimensional model building method to work properly, one of the representation has to be scaled to reflect the size of the second one. It may be noticed that, since the images were taken from single plane, scale difference can be estimated by comparing the objects height. Height is calculated by taking the lowest and the highest points from vector representation and taking absolute value of their y coordinates subtraction result.
2. Three-dimensional walls calculation. This algorithm takes one vector representation as a *reference* and calculates a set of final walls of the model by iterating through vectors from second representation. This is repeated for second representation taken as the *reference*. This step is summarized in Fig. 5 and discussed with more details in [5].

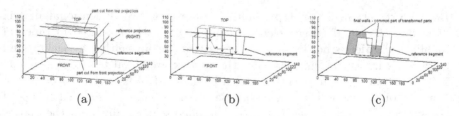

|(a)|(b)|(c)|

Fig. 5. Steps of creating walls, (a) - cutting from projections, (b) - projecting onto a plane, (c) - intersection of intermediate walls

4   Proposed Application for an Autonomous Space Rover

The method can be used by the space rover for certain applications. The model obtained with this method can enrich the scene representation built by the robot and be utilized during mission for specific tasks, including path planning. The majority of widely used methods of object's 3D model retrieving, like structure-from-motion, relays on the cloud of points which makes them computationally complex and suitable for more precise analysis of the objects [8]. The proposed three-dimensional model creation is a fast process and the resulting data structure is very memory efficient. It is based on greatly limited number of points which enables real-time analysis of the scene even with limited computational power which may be the case for ultralight autonomous rover. The algorithm can be used for building the model of the terrain obstacles which is presented below. In such scenario the mobile robot would take a pictures of the surface features, like a hill for example, to estimate if it can climb to the top in order to collect samples or take a wider picture of the surrounding area. As the area around the hill is not taken into consideration, the robot will start processing the images by extracting the feature parts which are above the level from which it observes the area.

In Figs. 6 and 7 the pre-processed test images are shown. They represent the examined obstacle - the hill.

In Fig. 8(a) the vectorization result of the first image is presented. The result of smoothing the borders of the object is shown in Fig. 8(b). Note that sequence of the points was reduced only to those that are most relevant in the suggested application. Small changes in the inclination of the hill are not relevant here.

Fig. 6. First image of the examined obstacle.

Fig. 7. Second image of the examined obstacle, taken orthogonally with respect to the first one.

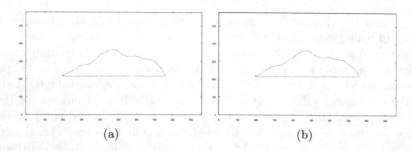

Fig. 8. Vectorization result of the first image, (a) - before smoothing of the borders, (b) - after smoothing.

Below (see Fig. 9) is the result of the vectorization of the second image of the obstacle.

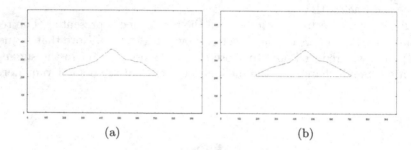

Fig. 9. Vectorization result of the second image, (a) - before smoothing of the borders, (b) - after smoothing.

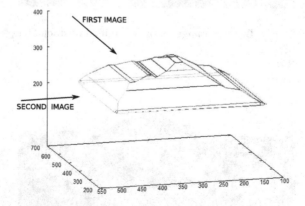

Fig. 10. Result of the three-dimensional model building (marked direction which original images were taken from).

The following figures (see Figs. 10 and 11) show the result of the execution of the three-dimensional model building method. The shape and inclination of the hill in particular levels above the ground is revealed.

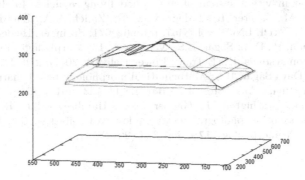

Fig. 11. Result of the three-dimensional model building.

5 Conclusions

Presented techniques related with vision system are very important in order to supplement information about robots surroundings. Idea of fusion data technique, based on LIDAR system, Infrared sensors an vision system are efficient combination of systems to gather information about the environment. For embedded systems it is very important to use less computationally complex algorithms with are able to reconstruct obstacle and recognize it. In the mobile robot's navigation, the SLAM techniques based on 2D scene recognition are used very often. Presented techniques of 3D model construction can be the a vital source of additional knowledge about the surrounding area for an autonomous robot operating in the unknown environment.

References

1. Ciszewski, M., Buratowski, T., Uhl, T., Gallina, A., Seweryn, K., Teper, W., Zwierzyski, A.J.: Design of an ultralight mobile platform for a drilling system. In: 14th World Congress in Mechanism and Machine Science, Taipei, Taiwan (2015). doi:10.6567/IFToMM.14TH.WC.OS13.027
2. Thueer, T., Lamon, P., Krebs, A., Siegwart, R.Y.: CRAB-exploration rover with advanced obstacle negotiation capabilities. In: Proceedings of the 9th ESA Workshop on Advanced Space Technologies for Robotics and Automation (ASTRA) (2006)
3. Bielecki, A., Buratowski, T., Śmigielski, P.: Syntactic algorithm of two-dimensional scene analysis for unmanned flying vehicles. In: Bolc, L., Tadeusiewicz, R., Chmielewski, L.J., Wojciechowski, K. (eds.) ICCVG 2012. LNCS, vol. 7594, pp. 304–312. Springer, Heidelberg (2012)

4. Bielecki, A., Buratowski, T., Śmigielski, P.: Recognition of two-dimensional representation of urban environment for autonomous flying agents. Expert Syst. Appl. **40**, 3623–3633 (2013)
5. Bielecki, A., Buratowski, T., Śmigielski, P.: Three-dimensional urban-type scene representation in vision system of unmanned flying vehicles. In: Rutkowski, L., Korytkowski, M., Scherer, R., Tadeusiewicz, R., Zadeh, L.A., Zurada, J.M. (eds.) ICAISC 2014, Part I. LNCS, vol. 8467, pp. 662–671. Springer, Heidelberg (2014)
6. Radhakrishnan, P., Daya Sagar, B.S., Venkatesh, B.: Morphological image analysis of transmission systems. IEEE Trans. Power Delivery **20**(1), 219–223 (2005)
7. Sharma, R., Daya Sagar, B.S.: Mathematical morphology based characterization of binary image. Image Anal. Stereology **34**(2), 111–123 (2015)
8. Westoby, M.J., Brasington, J., Glasser, N.F., Hambrey, M.J., Reynolds, J.M.: Structure-from-motion photogrammetry: a low-cost, effective tool for geoscience applications. Geomorphology **179**, 300–314 (2012)

A Clustering Based System for Automated Oil Spill Detection by Satellite Remote Sensing

Giacomo Capizzi[1(✉)], Grazia Lo Sciuto[2], Marcin Woźniak[3], and Robertas Damaševičius[4]

[1] Department of Electrical Electronics and Informatics Engineering, University of Catania, Viale Andrea Doria 6, 95125 Catania, Italy
gcapizzi@dieei.unict.it

[2] Department of Engineering, Roma Tre University, Via Vito Volterra 62, Rome, Italy
glosciuto@dii.unict.it

[3] Institute of Mathematics, Silesian University of Technology, Kaszubska 23, 44-100 Gliwice, Poland
Marcin.Wozniak@polsl.pl

[4] Software Engineering Department, Kaunas University of Technology, Studentu 50, Kaunas, Lithuania
robertas.damasevicius@ktu.lt

Abstract. In this work a new software system and environment for detecting objects with specific features within an image is presented. The developed system has been applied to a set of satellite transmitted SAR images, for the purpose of identifying objects like ships with their wake and oil slicks. The systems most interesting characteristic is its flexibility and adaptability to largely different classes of objects and images, which are of interest for several application areas. The heart of the system is represented by the clustering subsystem. This is to extract from the image objects characterized by local properties of small pixel neighborhoods. Among these objects the desired one is sought in later stages by a classifier to be plugged in, chosen from a pool including both soft-computing and conventional ones. An example of application of the system to a recognition problem is presented. The application task is to identify objects like ships with their wake and oil slicks within a set of satellite transmitted SAR images. The reported results have been obtained using a back-propagation neural network.

Keywords: Neural networks · Synthetic Aperture Radar (SAR) · Mahalanobis distance

1 Introduction

Oil spills on the sea surface are seen relatively often. The impact of not monitoring oil spills is presently unknown, but large spills of oil related petroleum products in the marine environment can have serious biological and economic impacts [1].

© Springer International Publishing Switzerland 2016
L. Rutkowski et al. (Eds.): ICAISC 2016, Part II, LNAI 9693, pp. 613–623, 2016.
DOI: 10.1007/978-3-319-39384-1_54

Active microwave sensors like Synthetic Aperture Radar (SAR) capture two-dimensional images. The image brightness is a reflection of the microwave backscattering properties of the surface. SAR deployed on satellites is today an important tool in oil spill monitoring due to its wide area coverage and day and night all-weather capabilities [2].

It is well understood that the radar image is a representation of the backscatter return and mainly proportional to the surface roughness at the scale of the radar wavelength (a phenomenon known as Bragg scattering) [3]. The radar backscatter coefficient is also a function of the viewing geometry of the SAR, and the backscatter coefficient decreases with increasing incidence angle. Oil slicks dampen the Bragg waves (wavelength of a few cm) on the ocean surface and reduce the radar backscatter coefficient. This results in dark regions or spots in a satellite SAR images.

In this work is presented a new software system and environment for detecting objects with specific features within an image [4–7]. The developed system has been applied to a set of satellite transmitted SAR images, for the purpose of identifying objects like ships with their wake and oil slicks.

The systems most interesting characteristic is its flexibility and adaptability to largely different classes of objects and images, which are of interest for several application areas, as well as the possibility to implement it within agent oriented solutions [8]. For this purpose recognition has been advantageously performed in two steps. In the first step clustering has been used in order to extract the regions of interest exhibiting the relevant properties: at this level processing involves only operations on the gray level histogram [9,10]. This step allows us to restrict the subsequent classification step to reduced portions of the entire images, thus obtaining considerable computational savings.

Developed environment allows several kinds of classifiers to be plugged into the system structure, including both soft-computing and conventional ones [11–14]. Presently a Multivariate Gaussian (MVG) classifier, a Fisher linear classifier, and a back-propagation supervised neural network (NN) have been used [15,16]. This variety of classification tools allows us to better exploit the advantageous features of any of them or a proper combination of them. Generally an NN approach is followed, but a suitable architecture for the neural network must be properly selected and then training has to be adapted according to the specific application [17–22]. Indeed representation of information to neural networks is particularly important in cases where a large amount of redundancy might be found in the input data. In such cases, the training process will inevitably detect a number of random correlations between the desired output responses and the values of some of the input components. Networks trained on such data will tend to exhibit poor generalization abilities due to these unwanted random correlations. A way of circumventing such problems is through the use of a feature transformation preprocessing which has the effect to reduce the dimensionality and hence degree of redundant information in the input information to the neural network. Such a data dimension reducing pre-processing step may be performed by using information derived from simple linear feature extractors having

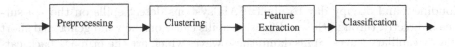

Fig. 1. Main processing steps.

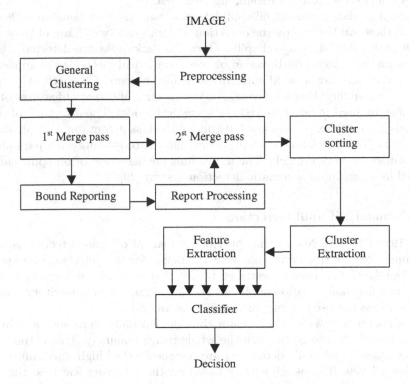

Fig. 2. Image processing system for object recognition.

only small computational demands, like Fisher's linear discriminant, where the extraction criterion used is class mean separation. The system developed has been applied to a set of satellite transmitted SAR images, for the purpose of identifying objects like ships with their wake and oil slicks. The results reported here have been obtained using an hybrid back-propagation neural network approach [23–25] as final classifier.

2   Problem Description

Oil is one of the major pollutants of the marine environment. It may be introduced in diverse ways, such as natural sources, offshore production, sea traffic, tanker accidents, atmospheric deposition, river run off and ocean dumping.

SAR systems are extensively used for the determination of oil spills in the marine environment, as they are not affected by local weather condition, cloudiness and occupy day to night. SAR systems detect spills on the sea surface indirectly, through the modification spills cause on the wind generated short gravity capillary waves. Spills damp these waves which are the primary backscatter agents of the radar signals. For this reason, an oil spill appears dark on SAR imagery in contrast to the surrounding clean sea.

Several studies aiming at oil spill detection have been implemented [26–28]. Most of these studies rely on the detection of dark areas, which are objects with a high probability of being oil spills. Once the dark areas are detected, classification methods based on Bayesian or other statistical methods are applied to characterize dark areas as oil spills or 'lookalike' objects. Characteristics (geometric, surrounding, backscattering, etc.) of spectral and spatial features of the dark area are used in order to feed the statistical model. The drawback of these methods is a complex process not fully understood, as it contains several nonlinear factors. The development of an inverse model to estimate such parameters turns out to be very difficult. The algorithms for detection of oil spills can be divided in manual and automatic detection system [29].

2.1   Manual Oil Spill Detection

Since 1994 KSAT in Norway has provided a manual oil spill detection service. Here operators are trained to analyze SAR images for the detection of oil pollution. The KSAT approach is described by [29]. External information about wind speed and direction, location of oil rigs and pipelines, national territory borders and coastlines are used as support during the analysis.

The operator uses an image viewer that can calculate some spot attributes, but he/she still has to go through the whole image manually. This is time consuming. Possible oil spills detections are assigned either high, medium or low confidence levels. The assignment is based on the following features: the contrast level to the surroundings, homogeneity of the surroundings, wind speed, nearby oil rigs and ships, natural slicks near by, and edge and shape characteristics of the spot. The determination of a confidence level is not exact science and there will always be an uncertainty connected to the results from manual inspection.

3   Automatic Algorithms for Oil Spill Detection

Automatic oil spill detection algorithms are normally divided into three steps, dark spot detection, dark spot feature extraction, and dark spot classification. Few papers are published on automatic algorithms for classification of oil spills and its look-alikes because most authors focus on the detection step.

Detection algorithms that have been proposed in the literature suffer from false alarms, and slicks classified as oil spills may be confused with look-alikes. Not all the dark areas on the SAR images of the sea surface are real oil spills and, in particular, a set of one hundred images may contain thousands of look-alikes and only hundreds of oil spills [30].

Different classifiers have been proposed in the literature, such as a statistical classifier with rule-based modification of prior probabilities proposed by Solberg et al. [30]. The probabilities assigned using Gaussian density function and derived from a signature database. The method correctly classified 94 % of oil spills and 99 % of look-alikes.

A similar statistical classification methodology was presented by Fiscella et al. [31]. They applied a Mahalanobis and a compound probability classifier. Mahalanobis classifier corresponded correctly at 71 % of the cases and a compound probability classifier at 76 % of the cases. Topouzelis et al. [32] used neural networks in both dark formation detection and oil-spill classification. During their experiment 94 % of the dark formations segmentation and 89 % accuracy of classification were obtained respectively.

Li et al., [33] used Support Vector Machine (SVM) to automatically detect oil-spill from SAR images. The average classification accuracy obtained in this study is 89.3 % for oil spills and 96.5 % for look-alikes.

Keramitsoglou et al. [34] estimated the probability of a dark formation to be oil spill using an artificial intelligence fuzzy modeling system. The method has an overall performance of 88 %.

The discrimination between oil spills and look-alikes is usually carried out with the use of a classification procedure based on the different values of certain characteristics that have been observed and reported both for oil slicks and for look-alikes. Such characteristics include the geometry, the shape, the texture and other contextual information describing the slick in relation to its surroundings.

Comparison between the different classifiers in terms of classification accuracies is very difficult. Mainly because oil spill detection approaches use different data sets, have different dark formation detection techniques, extract arbitrary number of features and in the end use different classifiers. Therefore, the reported classification accuracies can not be directly compared.

Since, almost all methods are classifying segments and not pixels, the initial step of segmentation, which leads to the extraction of possible oil spill areas, is of major importance. For this reason the main advantage of the proposed methodology with respect to the other algorithms available in the literature is the proposed two-level approach to image analysis, based first on local pixel properties, then on global features.

4 General System Description

Within the system, the target image undergoes the following steps (Fig. 1): preprocessing, clustering, feature extraction and object recognition by classification.

The preprocessing stage is intended to enhance features that are most relevant for the objects to be recognized. Preprocessing operations may include: edge extraction, smoothing, contrast enhancement, denoising, erosion, filtering, dilatation, etc.

The clustering subsystem has the task of extracting from the image objects characterized by local properties of pixels or small pixel neighborhoods. As a result, at this stage objects are viewed as subsets of pixels exhibiting relatively uniform properties. It is among these objects that the desired one will be sought in later stages. This affords greater simplicity and manageability, from a computational point of view, compared to the standard approach of scanning the image looking directly for an object with the desired features. Of course, local properties alone do not allow the intended object class to be exactly characterized. In practice, however, it has proved not too difficult to select properties which define a class that, albeit larger than the intended one, can be dealt effectively in subsequent stages.

The feature extraction module evaluates for each object a set of parameters characterizing the features that are significant for the target object class. Within the developed software environment, the parameters to be extracted may be picked from a standard set as perimeter, area, area/perimeter ratio, mean distance from center of gravity to contour, coordinates of the center of gravity, integrated optical density, gray level standard deviation etc. or suitably defined for specific applications. Each object identified by previous stages is therefore represented, and output, by this module as a parameter set. These will be examined, classified and possibly recognized by the last subsystem, i.e. the classifier.

4.1   The Recognition Process

The recognition process is structured as illustrated by the block diagram in Fig. 2, obtained from Fig. 1, by opening up the clustering block. In the following the main processing phases are described.

The general clustering block scans the image matrix horizontally, by columns (a vertical scan would work as well). Adjacent pixels are grouped in intervals depending on the local properties selected by the user. The user can also select metrics alternative to the standard Euclidean one for measuring adjacency. Each pixel interval, viewed as an elementary cluster, is represented by a quadruple: cluster number, minimum and maximum y coordinate, and column number. These quadruples are stored as entries in a cluster table.

Elementary clusters are then merged into increasingly complex ones, until a set of candidate objects is obtained. Clustering is carried out in two passes. The first pass determines, for each cluster c in a given column, the set of clusters S in the preceding column i that are adjacent according to the metrics employed. The cluster w in S that has a longer border with c is selected as a "winner", and c is renamed to w in the cluster table. Moreover, for each loser l in $S - \{w\}$, the triple (l, w, i), called a *bound*, is entered in a bound table. This information is needed because also l should be renamed to w, but doing so right now could break a previous merge between l and clusters in preceding columns. Necessary merges still pending after the first pass are performed in the second pass by processing the bound table in a suitable way. Merging is now complete, but since cluster numbers in the cluster table are neither ordered nor consecutive, a sorting procedure is employed.

By exploiting the information in the cluster table, the cluster extraction block builds the smallest bitmap containing each cluster. Such a bitmap represents a candidate object for recognition, and is further processed to extract from it the features in terms of which it will be modeled and passed to the classifier. Features can be interactively selected by the user from a user's predefined set.

In order to perform the subsequent classification step, presently three classifiers have been implemented and tested. The MVG one is based on the assumption that the feature probability density function (PDF) can be described as a multivariate normal distribution; in this case classification is performed by selecting the class with the shortest Mahalanobis distance from the test feature token. The other implemented classifiers are a simple Fisher linear classifier, and a back-propagation supervised multilayer perceptron (MLP) neural network.

5   Application

The main application on which the recognition system has been employed is the detection of ships, ship wakes and oil slicks in SAR images. The sample image shown in Fig. 3a has been acquired by the European Space Agencys ERS-2 satellite on the 18th of July 1996. The image coverage area is 40×25 km. Within it, expert human operators recognized ships, ship wakes and two oil slicks of mean sizes 12×5 km and 14×3 km. No information about misclassification error of human experts was available.

With our system, the image is first smoothed in order to decrease the high background variance (Fig. 3b), then split into 125×195 pixels blocks. Two blocks are shown in Fig. 3c, f (originals), and Fig. 3d, g (smoothed). From a gray level histogram, the minimum, maximum and most frequent luminance L_1, L_2 and L_{freq} are determined. The local properties selected as clustering conditions are that pixel luminance lies in the intervals $[\frac{L_{freq}+L_2}{2}, L_2]$ for ships, or $[L_1, \frac{L_{freq}+L_2}{2}]$ for ship wakes and oil slicks. Adjacency is evaluated with the Euclidean metrics. The effects of the clustering stage on the two blocks are shown in Fig. 3e, h. The succeeding classification step has been performed by using the three implemented classifiers i.e. MVG, Fisher and MLP; two classes have been considered for recognition: class 1 (wakes) and class 2 (oil slicks).

It is easily understandable that the classification problem is amenable to be solved by using a set of parameters correlated to the geometry of the two objects themselves: in fact wakes are thin and stretched objects, while oil slicks exhibit a round aspect. For this reason, in this case among the standard set of parameters only five have been considered for classification: i.e. area/perimeter ratio, MER, circularity, aspect ratio, maximum, minimum and mean distance from center of gravity to contour. The above parameters have been selected by virtue of their discriminating power, by examining feature spaces of increasing dimension according to the indications arisen from the Fisher procedure. The results showing the number of occurrences vs. parameter values allowed us to ascertain that superposition between the selected parameters is really negligible. The MLP architecture has been configured with 5 neurons in the input layer,

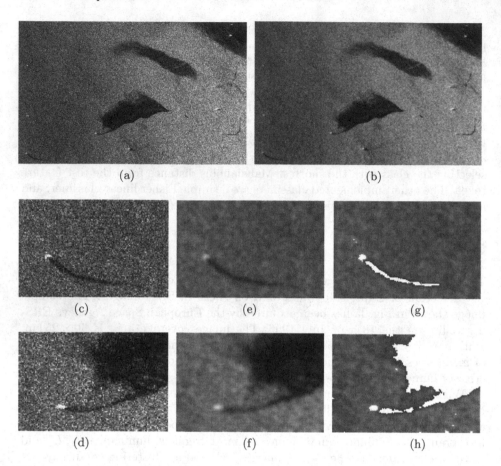

Fig. 3. (a) SAR image. (b) Smoothed image. (c, d) Image blocks analyzed. (e, f) Smoothed blocks. (g, h) Objects found by clustering (in white).

4 neurons in the hidden layer and 1 neuron in the output layer. The learning rate chosen for the experiment was 0.5 and the momentum was 0.6. The set of images which have been used for building the learning patterns consists of 31 wake images and 40 oil slick images. In the testing phase we used a test set of 400 different images suitably generated from the available ones. The observed misclassification error rate was 0.25. However all the three classifiers performed reasonably in the testing phase, for the considered applications, with the MLP neural network having a slight edge.

Some isolated pixels that can be noticed at the bottom of Fig. 3h were easily eliminated by all the classifiers.

6   Concluding Remarks

It should be noted that although the presented technique performs reasonably on the entire image, it is in practice more convenient to apply it repeatedly, after splitting rather large images (e.g. 900 × 700 pixels) into smaller blocks whose dimension is selected according to the size of the object to be detected. This strategy is more adequate for achieving better computational efficiency and for obviating to the high variability of the backgrounds statistical properties.

In the considered application, the system has proved both effective and accurate, guaranteeing a misclassification error rate lower than 1 %, while requiring limited computing time and resources. Crucial to this satisfactory performance is the proposed two-level approach to image analysis, based first on local pixel properties, then on global features.

References

1. Fan, J., Zhang, F., Zhao, D., Wang, J.: Oil spill monitoring based on SAR remote sensing imagery. Aquatic Procedia **3**, 112–118 (2015)
2. Fingas, M., Brownb, C.: Review of oil spill remote sensing. Mari. Pollut. Bull. **83**(1), 9–23 (2014)
3. Elachi, C.: Spaceborne imaging radar: geologic and oceanographic applications. Science **209**(4461), 1073–1082 (1980)
4. Woźniak, M., Napoli, C., Tramontana, E., Capizzi, G., Lo Sciuto, G., Nowicki, R.K., Starczewski, J.T.: A multiscale image compressor with RBFNN and discrete wavelet decomposition. In: Proceedings of IEEE IJCNN – IEEE International Joint Conference on Neural Networks, 12–17 July, Killarney, Ireland, pp. 1219–1225. IEEE (2015). doi:10.1109/IJCNN.2015.7280461
5. Korytkowski, M., Rutkowski, L., Scherer, R.: Fast image classification by boosting fuzzy classifiers. Inf. Sci. **327**, 175–182 (2016). http://dx.doi.org/10.1016/j.ins.2015.08.030
6. Shigeaki, S., Minoru, N.: A new approach for discovering top-k sequential patterns based on the variety of items. J. Artif. Intell. Soft Comput. Res. **5**(2), 141–153 (2015). doi:10.1515/jaiscr-2015-0025
7. Waledzik, K., Mandziuk, J.: An automatically generated evaluation function in general game playing. IEEE Trans. Comput. Intellig. AI Games **6**(3), 258–270 (2014)
8. Napoli, C., Pappalardo, G., Tramontana, E.: An agent-driven semantical identifier using radial basis neural networks and reinforcement learning. In: XV Workshop "Dagli Oggetti agli Agenti" CEUR-WS, vol. 1260 (2014)
9. Panda, D., Rosenfeld, A.: Image segmentation by pixel classification in (gray level, edge value) space. IEEE Trans. Comput. **27**(9), 875–879 (1978)
10. Sapna Varshney, S., Rajpal, N., Purwar, R.: Comparative study of image segmentation techniques and object matching using segmentation. In: Proceeding of International Conference on Methods and Models in Computer Science ICM2CS 2009, pp. 1–6, December 2009

11. Nowak, B.A., Nowicki, R.K., Woźniak, M., Napoli, C.: Multi-class nearest neighbour classifier for incomplete data handling. In: Rutkowski, L., Korytkowski, M., Scherer, R., Tadeusiewicz, R., Zadeh, L.A., Zurada, J.M. (eds.) Artificial Intelligence and Soft Computing. LNCS, vol. 9119, pp. 469–480. Springer, Heidelberg (2015)
12. Napoli, C., Pappalardo, G., Tramontana, E., Nowicki, R.K., Starczewski, J.T., Woźniak, M.: Toward work groups classification based on probabilistic neural network approach. In: Rutkowski, L., Korytkowski, M., Scherer, R., Tadeusiewicz, R., Zadeh, L.A., Zurada, J.M. (eds.) Artificial Intelligence and Soft Computing. LNCS, vol. 9119, pp. 79–89. Springer, Heidelberg (2015)
13. Dziwiński, P., Bartczuk, Ł., Przybył, A., Avedyan, E.D.: A new algorithm for identification of significant operating points using swarm intelligence. In: Rutkowski, L., Korytkowski, M., Scherer, R., Tadeusiewicz, R., Zadeh, L.A., Zurada, J.M. (eds.) ICAISC 2014, Part II. LNCS, vol. 8468, pp. 349–362. Springer, Heidelberg (2014)
14. Grycuk, R., Gabryel, M., Scherer, R., Voloshynovskiy, S.: Multi-layer architecture for storing visual data based on WCF and microsoft SQL server database. In: Proceedings of 14th International Conference on Artificial Intelligence and Soft Computing ICAISC 2015, Zakopane, Poland, 14–18 June 2015, Part I, pp. 715–726 (2015). http://dx.doi.org/10.1007/978-3-319-19324-3_64
15. Lippmann, R.: A critical overview of neural network pattern classifiers. In: Proceedings of the 1991 IEEE Workshop Neural Networks for Signal Processing, pp. 266–275, September 1991
16. Bonanno, F., Capizzi, G., Sciuto, G.L., Napoli, C., Pappalardo, G., Tramontana, E.: A cascade neural network architecture investigating surface plasmon polaritons propagation for thin metals in openMP. In: Rutkowski, L., Korytkowski, M., Scherer, R., Tadeusiewicz, R., Zadeh, L.A., Zurada, J.M. (eds.) ICAISC 2014, Part I. LNCS, vol. 8467, pp. 22–33. Springer, Heidelberg (2014)
17. Rutkowski, L., Jaworski, M., Pietruczuk, L., Duda, P.: A new method for data stream mining based on the misclassification error. IEEE Trans. Neural Netw. Learn. Syst. 26(5), 1048–1059 (2015)
18. Horzyk, A.: How does generalization and creativity come into being in neural associative systems and how does it form human-like knowledge? Neurocomputing 144, 238–257 (2014). doi:10.1016/j.neucom.2014.04.046
19. Starzyk, J., Graham, J., Raif, P., Tan, A.: Motivated learning for the development of autonomous systems. Cogn. Syst. Res. 14(1), 10–25 (2012). doi:10.1016/j.cogsys.2010.12.009
20. Graham, J., Starzyk, J., Jachyra, D.: Opportunistic behavior in motivated learning agents. IEEE Trans. Neural Netw. Learn. Syst. 26(8), 1735–1746 (2015). doi:10.1109/TNNLS.2014.2354400
21. Starczewski, J.T., Nowicki, R.K., Nowak, B.A.: Genetic fuzzy classifier with fuzzy rough sets for imprecise data. In: IEEE International Conference on Fuzzy Systems, FUZZ-IEEE 2014, Beijing, China, 6–11 July 2014, pp. 1382–1389 (2014). http://dx.doi.org/10.1109/FUZZ-IEEE.2014.6891857
22. Sou, N., Haruhiko, N., Teruya, Y., Jian-Qin, L.: Chaotic states induced by resetting process in Izhikevich neuron model. J. Artif. Intell. Soft Comput. Res. 5(2), 109–119 (2015). doi:10.1515/jaiscr-2015-0023
23. Napoli, C., Bonanno, F., Capizzi, G.: Exploiting solar wind time series correlation with magnetospheric response by using an hybrid neuro-wavelet approach. In: IAU Symposium 274, vol. 6, pp. 156–158. Cambridge University Press (2010). doi:10.1017/S1743921311006806

24. Haykin, S., Network, N.: A comprehensive foundation. In: Neural Netwoks, vol. 2 (2004)

25. Napoli, C., Bonanno, F., Capizzi, G.: An hybrid neuro-wavelet approach for long-term prediction of solar wind. In: IAU Symposium 274, pp. 247–249 (2010). doi:10.1017/S174392131100679X

26. Mart-nez, A., Moreno, V.: An oil spill monitoring system based on SAR images. Spill Sci. Technol. Bull. **3**(1–2), 65–71 (1996)

27. Galland, F., Refregier, P., Germain, O.: Synthetic aperture radar oil spill segmentation by stochastic complexity minimization. IEEE Geosci. Remote Sens. Lett. **1**(4), 295–299 (2004)

28. Caruso, M.J., Migliaccio, M., Hargrove, J.T., Garcia-Pineda, O.: Oil spills and slicks imaged by synthetic aperture radar. Oceanography **26**, 112–123 (2013)

29. Solberg, A., Storvik, G., Solberg, R., Volden, E.: Automatic detection of oil spills in ERS SAR images. IEEE Trans. Geosci. Remote Sens. **37**(4), 1916–1924 (1999)

30. Solberg, A.H.S., Brekke, C., Husoy, P.O.: Oil spill detection in Radarsat and Envisat SAR images. IEEE Trans. Geosci. Remote Sens. **45**(3), 746–755 (2007)

31. Fiscella, B., Giancaspro, A., Nirchio, F., Pavese, P., Trivero, P.: Oil spill detection using marine SAR images. Int. J. Remote Sens. **21**(18), 3561–3566 (2000)

32. Topouzelis, K., Karathanassi, V., Pavlakis, P., Rokos, D.: Detection and discrimination between oil spills and look-alike phenomena through neural networks. ISPRS J. Photogram. Remote Sens. **62**(4), 264–270 (2007)

33. Li, Y., Zhang, Y.: Synthetic aperture radar oil spills detection based on morphological characteristics. Geo-spat. Inf. Sci. **17**(1), 8–16 (2014)

34. Keramitsoglou, I., Cartalis, C., Kiranoudis, C.T.: Automatic identification of oil spills on satellite images. Environ. Model. Softw. **21**(5), 640–652 (2006)

Accelerating SVM with GPU: The State of the Art

Paweł Drozda[✉] and Krzysztof Sopyła

Department of Mathematics and Computer Sciences,
University of Warmia and Mazury, Olsztyn, Poland
pdrozda@matman.uwm.edu.pl, ksopyla@uwm.edu.pl

Abstract. This article summarizes the achievements that have been
made in the field of GPU SVM acceleration. In particular, the algorithms which allow the acceleration of SVM classification performed on
dense datasets are presented and the limitations of the dataset size are
pointed out. Moreover, the solutions which deal with large sparse collections are demonstrated. These algorithms apply different sparse dataset
formats to make possible the classification on the GPU. Finally, GPU
implementations for different SVM kernel functions are provided.

Keywords: SVM · GPGPU · CUDA · Classification · Sparse matrix

1 Introduction

Machine learning is presently one of the most important fields in computer science, which is confirmed by the development of many machine learning solutions
in various domains (for example, medicine [27,28], object detection [21], incomplete data [16] etc.). Among the algorithms implemented for machine learning,
the Support Vector Machine algorithm (SVM) is recognized as one of the most
effective solutions. This is confirmed by a large number of papers that apply
SVM classification or regression in various fields. Among these areas, we should
notice: Information Retrieval [14], Content Based Image Retrieval [7,8,12,20],
Bioinformatics [1]. In addition, a great effort has been taken to improve the SVM
algorithm in many different ways. One of the leading development directions for
the SVM is an increase of SVM classification accuracy, for example successful implementations for the linear kernel can be found in [4,23]. Another very
important goal in the SVM study is the acceleration of the algorithm execution,
which results from the fact that for large data sets the standard versions of the
SVM algorithm is very time-consuming. First attempts of accelerating the SVM
involved simplification of certain steps or approximation of calculation results.

However, one of the latest and increasingly popular trends in accelerating
the SVM algorithm is the use of graphic units (GPUs). Currently, they are
not only used as engines supporting game players, but also for time-consuming
calculations and in many cases they are specially designed for performing such
tasks. The use of the GPU allows for a distribution of small single tasks between a

© Springer International Publishing Switzerland 2016
L. Rutkowski et al. (Eds.): ICAISC 2016, Part II, LNAI 9693, pp. 624–634, 2016.
DOI: 10.1007/978-3-319-39384-1_55

great number of GPU cores, which should result in higher performance compared to CPU computation. Even the first attempts [6] demonstrated that the GPU can accelerate the SVM algorithm several times, which resulted in a growing interest in improving the SVM with the GPU.

Since a lot of research has been done in the field of GPU SVM acceleration, this paper summarizes the achievements in speeding up the SVM algorithm using the GPU. Another GPU SVM survey was proposed in [18], but since the authors did not take into account the use of sparse matrix formats of datasets that allow for processing large sets, that survey is deemed incomplete. The analysis of SVM GPU algorithms in this paper showed that there is no universal algorithm which would be appropriate for different datasets and different domains. In addition, it was found that some algorithms cope much better with dense, structured collections and others perform much better with datasets characterized by an irregular distribution of sparse elements.

The rest of the paper is organized as follows. The second section describes solutions which significantly accelerate dense collections whose size does not exceed 8 GB. The next section describes special sparse matrix formats and suggests solutions for the classification of large sparse datasets. Section 4 presents GPU implementations for various SVM kernel functions. The last section summarizes the paper and indicates directions of GPU acceleration.

2 SVM GPU Acceleration for Dense Datasets

The need for accelerating SVM algorithm derives from the fact that we deal with a still increasing amount of data in the classification process and standard solutions with the use of the CPU have become very time-consuming. This high time occupancy results mainly from the necessity of computing N scalar products, which for the SVM classification results in the matrix by vector multiplication. Therefore, attempts have been made to transfer these computations on the GPU cards in order to accelerate the calculations on multiple cores.

The first successful implementation is assigned to Catanzaro et al. [6] with the GPU SVM algorithm where part of the computation was transferred from the CPU to the GPU. In particular, the Sequential Minimal Optimization (SMO) algorithm [22] with the hybrid working set selection was implemented. The hybrid working set selection was based on the combined use of first order heuristic proposed by Keerthi et al. in [15] as well as second order heuristic [11]. The authors reported a speed up of their solution in the range of 9–35 times over the LIBSVM CPU solver for the training process. Moreover, the SVM classification time was reduced by 81–138 times. The paper also contains the authors' implementation of the CPU optimized classifier (based on the LIBSVM) for which the acceleration of the GPU SVM algorithm was 5–24 times. Results for all the methods presented in this section are summarized in Table 1.

The next GPU-based approach was proposed by Carpenter in [5], where the author proposed the CuSVM solution for SVM training. Similarly to [6], Carpenter introduced a modified version of the SMO algorithm. It involves using the second order working set selection heuristic [11] in the LIBSVM solver, which significantly reduces the number of iterations needed for solving the SVM classification problem in dual form. The author reported the acceleration in the range of 13–73 times for SVM training compared to the LIBSVM. Even higher acceleration was reached for prediction, where the CuSVM was 22–172 times faster than the LIBSVM.

Finally, in [13] Herrero et al. proposed the MultiSVM algorithm, where the potential of GPU computing was introduced for multiclass SVM classification. The training was realized by decomposition of the initial multiclass problem to many binary ones versus all classifications. Similarly to previous solutions, the modified version of the SMO algorithm was used. The main achievement of the MultiSVM was the ability to run all binary classification processes at the same time and the possibility of transferring the most time consuming tasks to the GPU unit. The main attention was focused on thread management in order to obtain the most optimized solutions. The algorithm was tested for the most popular datasets in SVM classification: firstly, in binary classification and secondly, for multiclass problems. In the first case the acceleration reached 10–32 times, while in the second 3–57 times.

One more approach, presented in [2], should be noted in this section. The authors proposed an algorithm, which transfers the calculation of dot-products on the GPU card to accelerate the SVM execution, but they did not investigate any of the state of the art machine learning datasets except the TRECVID 2007 dataset which is comprised of videos. Hence, the results provided in that paper are not comparable in any manner to the results derived in this section.

Table 1 summarizes all the presented solutions for tested datasets with the acceleration range over the LIBSVM. Unfortunately, the obtained results can not be easily compared with each other and we can not indicate which of the algorithms is the best, since each of them was carried out under different assumptions and in a different hardware and software environment making a direct comparison not possible.

The most important limitation of all the above mentioned solutions is the use of dense matrix format for storing datasets. It facilitates numerous computations in the classification process, however it greatly limits the range of datasets which can be classified with the SVM algorithm. In particular, the modern GPU units reach 8 GB of RAM memory which will not be enough for such datasets as newgroup20. Moreover, it should be noted that all algorithms presented in this section are based on RBF kernel without the possibility of changing the used kernel easily, which additionally reduces the applicability of these solutions.

3   SVM GPU Acceleration for Large Sparse Datasets

This section presents solutions, which were proposed to overcome the space limit of GPU RAM memory. In particular, all algorithms described in this section use the special sparse matrix formats for GPU SVM processing which allow for reducing the space needed for large sparse datasets.

Table 1. Training times of SVM with RBF kernel for dense matrix format

	LIBSVM [s]	GPU SVM [s]	x
Web (w8a)	2422.5	163.9	14.8x
Adult (a9a)	550.2	26.9	20.4x
Mnist	16965.8	483.1	35.1x
Forest	66523.5	2023.2	32.9x
USPS	5.1	0.58	8.8x
FACE	27.6	1.32	20.8x
	LIBSVM [s]	CuSVM [s]	x
Web (w8a)	2906.8	228.3	12.7x
Adult (a9a)	541.2	31.6	17.1x
Mnist	17267.0	498.9	34.6x
Forest	29494.3	2016.4	14.1x
	LIBSVM [s]	multiSVM [s]	x
Web (w8a)	2350	156.9	10.4x
Adult (a9a)	341.5	32.6	14.9x
Mnist	13963.4	425.9	32.7x

3.1 Sparse Matrix Formats

Due to the fact that basic SVM processing on the GPU, where the whole dataset is loaded to GPU RAM memory, meets the space limit and allows for processing datasets of up to 8 GB, SVM acceleration research has been aimed at reducing the space needed for storing the processed dataset. For this reason, three different sparse matrix formats were proposed in literature.

The first CSR holds non-zero values row-by-row and allows for good packing density. The order and the location of these values in the matrix is presented by three tables: values, columns and row pointers. The values table contains all non-zero elements from the original matrix, the columns table indicates the column for the value and the row pointers table shows the row of the considered value. In particular, the beginning and the end of ith row is determined by $rowPointer[i - 1]$ and $rowPointer[i] - 1$. An example of the CSR format is provided in Table 2.

The next sparse matrix format for GPU SVM classification under consideration is called Ellpack and its modification is called Ellpack-R [29]. This format omits the zero values and all non-zero vales are shifted to the left side. Moreover, all rows which contain fewer that the maximal number of non-zero elements are completed with zeros. For storing Ellpack format there is a need for 3 tables: values, columns and rowLength. The first table contains non-zero elements, the second table points to the numbers of columns where the non-zero values occur. To facilitate GPU processing the last table contains the number of non-zero elements for each row. The example of Ellpack-R format is shown in Table 3. The main differences between these two formats are in the level of packing density and the regularity of stored elements. On one hand, Ellpack-R is characterized by lower packing density level, but on the other, it is more regular in element storage, which greatly facilitates GPU processing.

Table 2. Example of CSR sparse matrix format

Sparse matrix	Values	Columns	Row pointers
$\begin{bmatrix} x_{00} & 0 & 0 & x_{03} & x_{04} \\ 0 & 0 & x_{12} & x_{13} & 0 \\ 0 & x_{21} & 0 & 0 & 0 \\ x_{30} & x_{31} & 0 & 0 & 0 \\ x_{40} & x_{41} & x_{42} & x_{43} & 0 \\ 0 & 0 & 0 & 0 & x_{54} \end{bmatrix}$	$\begin{bmatrix} x_{00} \; x_{03} \; x_{04} \\ x_{12} \; x_{13} \\ x_{21} \\ x_{30} \; x_{31} \\ x_{40} \; x_{41} \; x_{42} \; x_{43} \\ x_{54} \end{bmatrix}$	$\begin{bmatrix} 0 \; 3 \; 4 \\ 2 \; 3 \\ 1 \\ 0 \; 1 \\ 0 \; 1 \; 2 \; 3 \\ 4 \end{bmatrix}$	$\begin{bmatrix} 0 \\ 3 \\ 5 \\ 6 \\ 8 \\ 12 \\ 13 \end{bmatrix}$

Table 3. Example of matrix in Ellpack-R sparse format

Sparse Matrix	Values	Columns	Row length
$\begin{bmatrix} x_{00} & 0 & 0 & x_{03} & x_{04} \\ 0 & 0 & x_{12} & x_{13} & 0 \\ 0 & x_{21} & 0 & 0 & 0 \\ x_{30} & x_{31} & 0 & 0 & 0 \\ x_{40} & x_{41} & x_{42} & x_{43} & 0 \\ 0 & 0 & 0 & 0 & x_{54} \end{bmatrix}$	$\begin{bmatrix} x_{00} & x_{03} & x_{04} & 0 \\ x_{12} & x_{13} & 0 & 0 \\ x_{21} & 0 & 0 & 0 \\ x_{30} & x_{31} & 0 & 0 \\ x_{40} & x_{41} & x_{42} & x_{43} \\ x_{54} & 0 & 0 & 0 \end{bmatrix}$	$\begin{bmatrix} 0 & 3 & 4 & * \\ 2 & 3 & * & * \\ 1 & * & * & * \\ 0 & 1 & * & * \\ 0 & 1 & 2 & 3 \\ 4 & * & * & * \end{bmatrix}$	$\begin{bmatrix} 3 \\ 2 \\ 1 \\ 2 \\ 4 \\ 1 \end{bmatrix}$

The last proposed sparse matrix format in this paper is Sliced-Ellpack [10,19]. It can be considered to be a middle format between the CSR and Ellpack-R. In this format the sparse matrix is cut into slices with a predefined number of rows. Then, the created submatrices are stored in Ellpack. The presented trick allows for a reduction of the space needed for the sparse dataset storage. An example of Sliced Ellpack format is presented in Table 4.

Table 4. Example of matrix in Sliced EllR-T format with parameters: SliceSize=2 i ThreadsPerRow=2

Sparse matrix	Values	Columns	Block pointers
$\begin{bmatrix} x_{00} & 0 & 0 & x_{03} & x_{04} \\ 0 & 0 & x_{12} & x_{13} & 0 \\ 0 & x_{21} & 0 & 0 & 0 \\ x_{30} & x_{31} & 0 & 0 & 0 \\ x_{40} & x_{41} & x_{42} & x_{43} & 0 \\ 0 & 0 & 0 & 0 & x_{54} \end{bmatrix}$	$\begin{bmatrix} x_{00} \; x_{03} \; x_{04} \\ x_{12} \; x_{13} \; 0 \end{bmatrix}$ $\begin{bmatrix} x_{21} \; 0 \\ x_{30} \; x_{31} \end{bmatrix}$ $\begin{bmatrix} x_{40} \; x_{41} \; x_{42} \; x_{43} \\ x_{54} \; 0 \; 0 \; 0 \end{bmatrix}$	$\begin{bmatrix} 0 \; 3 \; 4 \\ 2 \; 3 \; * \end{bmatrix}$ $\begin{bmatrix} 1 \; * \\ 0 \; 1 \end{bmatrix}$ $\begin{bmatrix} 0 \; 1 \; 2 \; 3 \\ 4 \; * \; * \; * \end{bmatrix}$	$\begin{bmatrix} 3 \\ 2 \\ 1 \\ 2 \\ 4 \\ 1 \end{bmatrix}$

3.2   GPU SVM Sparse Matrix Solutions

This section presents available solutions which allow taking advantage of sparse data formats.

Lin and Chien [17] were the first who used the sparse matrix format for GPU SVM implementation. They chose the modification of Ellpack sparse matrix format called Ellpack-R [29]. As it was stated in the previous subsection, this format can be considered the most regular, which on the one hand greatly facilitates vector by matrix multiplication, but on the other allows a much lower dataset compression, which reduces its applicability for large sparse datasets with irregular non-zero elements. Moreover, the authors decided to store the vector used in vector by matrix multiplication in the GPU shared memory which reaches only 48 kB, hence that vector cannot have more features than 12000. This additionally reduces the spectrum of datasets, which can be processed by the SVM classifier. The authors report the reduction of the time needed for SVM training in the range of 55–134 times.

The second known algorithm was proposed in [9] and called the GPU-tailored SVM, where the authors proposed methods for training binary and multiclass SVMs on the GPU. This solution differs from the others described in this section, since instead of using any of the well-known sparse matrix formats, a special clustering algorithm is used for the reduction of the space needed for dataset storage. The vector clustering procedure groups the vectors with a similar structure of non-zero elements into the same cluster, which affects the acceleration level, but also limits its application to the datasets with only 1000 features or less. Authors present a speed-up in the range of 38–78 times, but only for small datasets such as Adult or Mnist.

The another solution dates for 2012 year is proposed in [24]. Sopyla et al. introduced another sparse matrix format called CSR [3] for SVM computation in CSR-GPU-SVM method. The main advantage of utilizing this format is the possibility of very high compression of various sparse datasets and hence, it extends the size of datasets which can be processed by SVM classifier on the GPU unit. However, CSR format is very irregular which significantly impedes part of SVM computations. For these reasons CSR-GPU-SVM algorithm allows processing larger datasets than Lin and Chien [17], for example Newsgroup20 or Real-Sim, but for the smaller datasets it achieves worse accelerations than for Ellpack-R format. It the paper authors reported speed up in order of 6–35 over the LIBSVM algorithm.

To complement the use of sparse matrix formats described in the previous subsection the SECu-SVM algorithm is proposed by Sopyla and Drozda in [26]. In that paper, the Sliced EllR-T format [10] is utilized and the solver is based on the Platt SMO algorithm [22]. Sliced EllR-T can be regarded as a middle format between the CSR and Ellpack-R formats. It takes advantage of the two previously described formats, since it preserves the regularity of stored elements, which allows the processing of datasets on the GPU unit in an uncomplicated way. Moreover, Sliced EllR-T compresses data much better than Ellpack-R format, which expands the range of possible datasets for SVM processing. In addition, the solution described in [26] introduces a solver which performs the most time consuming computations on the GPU unit, which reduces the time consumption of data copying operations between the CPU and GPU units and accelerates the whole classification process. The training time of SVM training was reduced by 4–93x against the LIBSVM methods for different datasets.

Tables 5, 6, 7 and 8 summarize all training times for all the aforementioned algorithms. It should be noted, that authors of this paper converted the solution from [17] to make it comparable with [24] and with [26] and the tests were conducted in a different environment, so the results can be slightly different from those reported in the parer.

Table 5. Training times of SVM with RBF kernel with the use of CSR sparse matrix format

Dataset	LIBSVM [s]	CSR [s]	x
Web (w8a)	907.9	70.1	12.95x
Adult (a9a)	458.5	57.2	8.06x
20 Newsgroup	3544.8	264.1	13.42x
Real-Sim	3157.7	140.0	22.56x
Rcv1.binary rev.	203917.7	6114.1	33.35x
Mnist	41173.3	494.1	83.33x
Dominionstats	642045.6	4271.9	150.30x

Table 6. Training times of SVM with RBF kernel with the use of Ellpack sparse matrix format

Dataset	LIBSVM [s]	Ellpack [s]	x
Web (w8a)	907.9	37.8	24.02x
Adult (a9a)	458.5	30.8	14.89x
20 Newsgroup	3544.8	-	-
Real-Sim	3157.7	-	-
Rcv1.binary rev.	203917.7	-	-
Mnist	41173.3	298.3	138.03x
Dominionstats	642045.6	4330.6	148.26x

4   Different Kernels for GPU SVM Acceleration

All the previous solutions described in Sects. 2 and 3 implemented the most popular RBF Gaussian kernel as the SVM kernel. This section provides the algorithms which replace the computationally expensive RBF kernel with other popular SVM kernels: Chi^2 and Exponential Chi^2 [25]. These kernels were chosen since the implementation of both functions as a scalar product is not complicated and in addition, these kernels are often used in different domains, as for example in CBIR domain. As a solver, the GPU solver was derived which performs the most time consuming operations such as working set selection and gradient updates on the GPU units. Moreover, the computation of Chi^2 and Exponential Chi^2 are made on the GPU side, which greatly reduces the cost of CPU-GPU data transfers.

Table 7. Training times of SVM with RBF kernel with the use of Slice EllR-T sparse matrix format

Dataset	LIBSVM [s]	Slice EllR-T [s]	x
Web (w8a)	907.9	36.1	25.14x
Adult (a9a)	458.5	34.1	13.45x
20 Newsgroup	3544.8	298.6	11.87x
Real-Sim	3157.7	92.5	34.14x
Rcv1.binary rev.	203917.7	3661.7	55.69x
Mnist	41173.3	260.0	158.36x
Dominionstats	642045.6	2727.9	235.36x

Table 8. Training times of SVM with RBF kernel GPU-tailored algorithm

Dataset	LIBSVM [s]	GT SVM [s]	x
Adult (a9a)	64	1.2	52x
Mnist	244	3.9	68x
TIMIT	246	3.5	78x
Cov1	16200	422	38x

Table 9. Training times of SVM for Chi^2 kernel

Dataset	LibSVM	Ellpack		Sliced EllR-T	
		T[s]	x	T[s]	x
Web (w8a)	13.3	147.7	0.09x	126.6	0.10x
Adult (a9a)	30.8	92.2	0.33x	97.4	0.31x
20 Newsgroup	338.9	-	-	404.0	0.83x
Real-Sim	218.7	-	-	355.3	0.61x
Rcv1.binary rev.	37287.4	-	-	43521.9	0.85x
Mnist*	7211.4	12763.7	0.56x	10979.6	0.65x
Dominionstats.scale	120423.1	43600.3	2.76x	41103.0	2.92x
Tweet.full	2352.8	1909.7	1.23x	1963.0	1.20x
web-spam	3409.1	596.9	5.71x	611.3	5.57x

Chi^2 and Exponential Chi^2 implementations are adapted for two sparse matrix formats: Ellpack and Sliced EllT-R and all results are provided for these formats and compared to the LIBSVM. Tables 9 and 10 summarize all the achieved results. It should be noted that an implementation of Exponential Chi^2 for both sparse formats achieved satisfactory results having a speed-up in order of 1.5–24x. On the other hand, the solution for Chi^2 proved to be completely unsuitable for GPU processing with the use of sparse matrix format. This solution achieved better results than the LIBSVM algorithm only for three datasets while for other six, it processed much more slowly.

Table 10. Training times of SVM for ExpChi^2 kernel

Dataset	LibSVM	Ellpack		Sliced EllR-T	
		T[s]	x	T[s]	x
Web (w8a)	150.2	40.8	3.7x	35.0	4.3x
Adult (a9a)	79.8	24.1	3.3x	26.9	3.0x
20 Newsgroup	755.3	-	-	498.7	1.5x
Real-Sim	1461.7	-	-	452.5	3.2x
Rcv1.binary rev.	163799.1	-	-	15882.1	10.3x
Mnist*	7486.6	571.8	13.1x	495.7	15.1x
Dominionstats.scale	98582.2	4377.0	22.5x	4120.2	23.9x
Tweet.full	6562.6	491.1	13.4x	511.8	12.8x
web-spam	3116.7	384.6	8.1x	396.6	7.9x

5 Conclusion and Future Directions

This paper summarizes the achievements made in the field of accelerating the SVM classifier with the use of GPU computing. It presents algorithms which dealt with dense datasets as well as solutions which allowed for large dataset compression. The majority of these methods reported very high acceleration over the standard LIBSVM algorithm, which could indicate the correct direction of development for the SVM classification. However, a single method can not be identified which overperforms all other for every dataset. Some solutions deal better with small and regular datasets, while the other compute the irregular large datasets faster.

One of the possible paths of future development is processing the most time consuming operations, such as working set selection, gradient updates or the computation of kernel function not only on one GPU unit but on many GPUs.

Acknowledgments. The research has been supported by grant 1309-802 from Ministry of Science and Higher Education of the Republic of Poland.

References

1. Acır, N., Güzeliş, C.: An application of support vector machine in bioinformatics: automated recognition of epileptiform patterns in EEG using SVM classifier designed by a perturbation method. In: Yakhno, T. (ed.) ADVIS 2004. LNCS, vol. 3261, pp. 462–471. Springer, Heidelberg (2004)
2. Athanasopoulos, A., Mezaris, V., Kompatsiaris, I.: GPU acceleration for support vector machines. In: 12th International Workshop on Image Analysis for Multimedia Interactive Services (2011)
3. Bell, N., Garl, M.: Efficient sparse matrix-vector multiplication on CUDA. Technical report, NVidia (2008)
4. Bottou, L.: Large-scale machine learning with stochastic gradient descent. In: Lechevallie, Y., Saporta, G. (eds.) COMPSTAT 2010, pp. 177–187. Springer, Heidelberg (2010)
5. Carpenter, A.: CUSVM: a CUDA implementation of support vector classification and regression. Technical report (2009). http://patternsonascreen.net/cuSVM.html
6. Catanzaro, B., Sundaram, N., Keutzer, K.: Fast support vector machine training and classification on graphics processors. In: Proceedings of the 25th International Conference on Machine Learning ICML 2008, pp. 104–111. ACM, New York (2008)
7. Chapelle, O., Haffner, P., Vapnik, V.N.: Support vector machines for histogram-based image classification. IEEE Trans. Neural Netw. **10**, 1055–1064 (1999)
8. Chu, J.L., Krzyzak, A.: The recognition of partially occluded objects with support vector machines, convolutional neural networks and deep belief networks. J. Artif. Intell. Soft Comput. Res. **4**, 5–19 (2014)
9. Cotter, A., Srebro, N., Keshet, J.: A GPU-tailored approach for training kernelized SVMs. In: Proceedings of the 17th ACM SIGKDD Conference KDD 2011, pp. 805–813 (2011). http://doi.acm.org/10.1145/2020408.2020548
10. Dziekonski, A., Lamecki, A., Mrozowski, M.: A memory efficient and fast sparse matrix vector product on a GPU. Prog. Electromagnet. Res. **116**, 49–63 (2011)
11. Fan, R.E., Chen, P.H., Lin, C.J.: Working set selection using the second order information for training SVM. J. Mach. Learn. Res. **6**, 1889–1918 (2005)
12. Gorecki, P., Artiemjew, P., Drozda, P., Sopyla, K.: Categorization of similar objects using bag of visual words and support vector machines. In: Filipe, J., Fred, A.L.N. (eds.) ICAART (1), pp. 231–236 (2012)
13. Herrero-Lopez, S., Williams, J.R., Sanchez, A.: Parallel multiclass classification using SVMs on GPUs. In: Proceedings of the 3rd Workshop on General-Purpose Computation on Graphics Processing Units GPGPU 2010, pp. 2–11. ACM, New York (2010)
14. Joachims, T.: Text categorization with support vector machines: learning with many relevant features. In: Nédellec, Claire, Rouveirol, Céline (eds.) ECML 1998. LNCS, vol. 1398, pp. 137–142. Springer, Heidelberg (1998)
15. Keerthi, S., Shevade, S., Bhattacharyya, C., Murthy, K.: Improvements to Platt's SMO algorithm for SVM classifier design. Neural Comput. **13**(3), 637–649 (2001)
16. Korytkowski, M., Nowicki, R., Scherer, R.: Neuro-fuzzy rough classifier ensemble. In: Alippi, C., Polycarpou, M., Panayiotou, C., Ellinas, G. (eds.) ICANN 2009, Part I. LNCS, vol. 5768, pp. 817–823. Springer, Heidelberg (2009)
17. Lin, T.K., Chien, S.Y.: Support vector machines on GPU with sparse matrix format. In: Fourth International Conference on Machine Learning and Applications, pp. 313–318 (2010)

18. Lu, Y., Zhu, Y., Han, M., He, J., Zhang, Y.: A survey of GPU accelerated SVM. In: Proceedings of the 2014 ACM Southeast Regional Conference, pp. 1–7 (2014)
19. Monakov, A., Lokhmotov, A., Avetisyan, A.: Automatically tuning sparse matrix-vector multiplication for GPU architectures. In: Patt, Y.N., Foglia, P., Duesterwald, E., Faraboschi, P., Martorell, X. (eds.) HiPEAC 2010. LNCS, vol. 5952, pp. 111–125. Springer, Heidelberg (2010)
20. Najgebauer, P., Nowak, T., Romanowski, J., Gabryel, M., Korytkowski, M., Scherer, R.: Content-based image retrieval by dictionary of local feature descriptors. In: International Joint Conference on Neural Networks, pp. 512–517 (2014)
21. Najgebauer, P., Nowak, T., Romanowski, J., Rygal, J., Korytkowski, M., Scherer, R.: Novel method for parasite detection in microscopic samples. In: 11th International Conference on Artificial Intelligence and Soft Computing, pp. 551–558 (2012)
22. Platt, J.: Fast training of support vector machines using sequential minimal optimization. In: Advances in Kernel Methods - Support Vector Learning (1998)
23. Sopyla, K., Drozda, P.: Stochastic gradient descent with Barzilai-Borwein update step for SVM. Inf. Sci. **316**(C), 218–233 (2015)
24. Sopyła, K., Drozda, P., Górecki, P.: SVM with CUDA accelerated Kernels for big sparse problems. In: Rutkowski, L., Korytkowski, M., Scherer, R., Tadeusiewicz, R., Zadeh, L.A., Zurada, J.M. (eds.) ICAISC 2012, Part I. LNCS, vol. 7267, pp. 439–447. Springer, Heidelberg (2012)
25. Sopyla, K., Drozda, P.: GPU solver with chi-square Kernels for SVM classification of big sparse problems. In: 3rd International Conference on Pattern Recognition Applications and Methods, ICPRAM, pp. 331–336 (2014)
26. Sopyla, K., Drozda, P.: GPU accelerated SVM with sparse sliced EllR-T matrix format. Int. J. Artif. Intell.Tools **24**(1), 1450012 (2015)
27. Szarek, A., Korytkowski, M., Rutkowski, L., Scherer, R., Szyprowski, J.: Application of neural networks in assessing changes around implant after total hip arthroplasty. In: Rutkowski, L., Korytkowski, M., Scherer, R., Tadeusiewicz, R., Zadeh, L.A., Zurada, J.M. (eds.) ICAISC 2012, Part II. LNCS, vol. 7268, pp. 335–340. Springer, Heidelberg (2012)
28. Szarek, A., Korytkowski, M., Rutkowski, L., Scherer, R., Szyprowski, J.: Forecasting wear of head and acetabulum in hip joint implant. In: Rutkowski, L., Korytkowski, M., Scherer, R., Tadeusiewicz, R., Zadeh, L.A., Zurada, J.M. (eds.) ICAISC 2012, Part II. LNCS, vol. 7268, pp. 341–346. Springer, Heidelberg (2012)
29. Vázquez, F., Garzón, E.M., Martinez, J.A., Fernández, J.J.: The sparse matrix vector product on GPUs. Technical report, University of Almeria, June 2009

The Bag-of-Features Algorithm for Practical Applications Using the MySQL Database

Marcin Gabryel[✉]

Institute of Computational Intelligence, Częstochowa University of Technology,
Al. Armii Krajowej 36, 42-200 Częstochowa, Poland
marcin.gabryel@iisi.pcz.pl
http://iisi.pcz.pl

Abstract. This article presents a modification of the Bag-of-Features method (also known as a Bag-of-Words or Bag-of-Visual-Words method) used for image recognition in practical applications using a relational database. Our approach utilises a modified k-means algorithm, owing to which the number of clusters is automatically selected, and also the majority votes method when making decisions in the classification process. The algorithm can be used both methods in an SQL Server database or a commonly-used MySQL one. The proposed approach minimises the necessity to use additional algorithms and/or classifiers in the image classification process. This makes it possible to significantly simplify computations and use the SQL language.

Keywords: Bag-of-features · Image classification · Image database · Modified k-means algorithm

1 Introduction

Browsing and searching image databases based on their content is required in a number of various fields of life, e.g. medicine, architecture, forensics, publishing, fashion, archives and many others. It is one of the most important challenges of computer science. The aim can be a classification of a similar image. Classification mechanisms use image recognition methods. This is a sophisticated process which requires the use of algorithms from many different areas such as computational intelligence [5,29,31,32], in particular fuzzy systems [6,15,30], rough neuro-fuzzy systems [7,23,24], evolutionary algorithms [1,9,17,18], mathematics [34], image processing [14,16,35], decision tree [33] and data mining [25–28]. One of the most widely spread algorithms used for indexation, image retrieval and classification is the bag-of-words model (BoW) [8,21], also known as a Bag-of-Features (BoF) or Bag-of-Visual-Words model. This algorithm is based on a concept of text search methods within collections of documents. Single words are stored in dictionaries with an emphasis on appearing in various documents. BoF creates dictionaries of characteristic features appearing in images in a similar way. Additionally, classification process makes it possible during a search to

© Springer International Publishing Switzerland 2016
L. Rutkowski et al. (Eds.): ICAISC 2016, Part II, LNAI 9693, pp. 635–646, 2016.
DOI: 10.1007/978-3-319-39384-1_56

determine what type of image class we are dealing with. The Bag-of-Features model comprises three main steps: (i) feature extraction, (ii) learning visual features vocabulary and (iii) image representation. In [21] we can find a detailed description of BoF and associated algorithms.

Practical aspects of the BoF algorithm implementation in image classification are rather rare in the literature. There are many modifications of this algorithm which, for example, use various image features [19,20,22] or various clustering and classification algorithms [13,36], but there are no examples of practical applications of this algorithm. Most simulations and experiments are carried out with the use of OpenCV library, Matlab environment or multi-core processors. In practice, however, applications being implemented are not supported by powerful servers or graphic cards using OpenCL or CUDA technology. Computer programs most often only have at their disposal a relational database and they operate on computers with only a few cores and limited operational memory. In this article we present an algorithm which is means to operate and work in this particular kind of environment.

The article is divided into a few sections. Section 2 outlines the algorithms of which the whole image storing system consists in the classification and database. Section 3 presents the results of the experimental research testing the efficiency of the presented algorithms as well as details connected with the database being used for the implementation of this method. The conclusions in the last Section - Sect. 4 - present ideas concerning further improvement of the system efficiency.

2   Description of the Algorithms

For the purpose of description of presented algorithms we are considering herein a set of given images $\mathbf{I}_i$, where $i = 1, ..., \mathbf{I}_L$, $\mathbf{I}_L$ is the number of all images. Each image $\mathbf{I}_i$ has a class $c(\mathbf{I}_i)$ assigned to it, where $c(\mathbf{I}_i) \in \Omega$, $\Omega = \omega_i, ..., \omega_C$ is a set of all classes and C is the number of all classes. The images $\mathbf{I}_i$ make an initial database which will be stored in the database and will be used to create a dictionary for the BoF method. The dictionary then will be created with the use of the k-means algorithm which we have modified so as to remove one of its faults, i.e. the necessity to define the number of clusters. The k-means algorithm is then started by the modified Bag-of-Features. The modification is meant to use the maximum of data storage capability in a database and performing SQL queries.

2.1   Modified k-Means

The k-means algorithm is an efficient clustering algorithm. Its basic form requires that the initial number of clusters c be defined. In our algorithm we have used the growing method used in the Growing Self-Organizing Map (GSOM) algorithm [11]. In that method a cluster is divided when the number of its data exceeds a certain threshold value Θ. Operation of the said algorithm starts with setting the threshold value Θ and defining two clusters ($c = 2$). In the subsequent steps the algorithm works as a classic k-means with the only difference being that at the end of each iteration the number of points belonging to each cluster τ_j, $j = 1, ..., c$ is checked. If the number τ_j exceeds the threshold already set Θ, then another cluster $c + 1$ is created. The algorithm is presented below in detail.

Let $\mathbf{X} = \mathbf{x}_1, ..., \mathbf{x}_n$ be a set of points in d-dimensional space, and $\mathbf{V} = \mathbf{v}_1, ..., \mathbf{v}_c$ be cluster centers, where n is the number of samples, $\mathbf{x}_i = [x_{i1}, ..., x_{id}]$, c is the number of clusters, and $\mathbf{v}_j = [v_{j1}, ..., v_{jd}]$.

1. Let the number of cluster $c = 2$. Determine Θ.
2. Randomly select c cluster centers $\mathbf{v}_j$, $j = 1, ..., c$, for example:

$$v_{ji} = rand(\min(x_{ij}), \max(x_{ij})), \tag{1}$$

   where $rand(a, b)$ is a random number generated from the interval $[a; b]$.
3. Calculate the distance d_{ij} between each data point $\mathbf{x}_i$ and cluster centers $\mathbf{v}_j$:

$$d_{ij} = \|x_i - v_j\|, \tag{2}$$

   where $\| \cdot \|$ is Euclidean distance, Cosine similarity or Manhattan distance.
4. Assign the data point $\mathbf{x}_i$ to the cluster center $\mathbf{v}_s$ whose distance from the cluster center is minimum of all the cluster centers

$$\mathbf{x}_i \in \mathbf{v}_s \rightarrow d_{is} \leq d_{im}, m = 1, ..., c \tag{3}$$

   and increase counter of winnings $\tau_s = \tau_s + 1$.
5. Recalculate the new cluster center using:

$$\mathbf{v}_i = \frac{1}{c_i} \sum_{j=1}^{c_i} \mathbf{x}_i \tag{4}$$

   where c_i represents the number of data points in i-th cluster.
6. If in the center s the number τ_s is greater than the threshold value Θ, create a new cluster, $c := c + 1$ and

$$\mathbf{v}_c = \mathbf{x}_{rand(j)} \tag{5}$$

   where $rand(j)$ generates a random index of point $\mathbf{x}$ belonging to center $\mathbf{v}_s$.
7. Remove clusters for which $\tau_s = 0$. Refresh the number of clusters c.
8. If no data point was reassigned, then stop; otherwise, repeat starting from step 3.

As a result of the algorithm operation we obtain c clusters with the centers in points $\mathbf{v}_j, j = 1, ..., c$.

2.2   The Bag-of-Features Algorithm Adjusted to a Database

For the purpose of starting the BoF algorithm operation with the use of a relational database, we have used a few modifications of the classical version of this algorithm used in image classification. Our algorithm has been divided into a few modules. The modules are operated at various times of the system operation and their task is to retrieve characteristic features and starting the modified k-means method for the purpose of creating clusters which constitute dictionary elements. The most important element of the system is the database itself as this element is responsible for storing of data and providing the result of a query about the class of a query image being tested. We do not use any classifier (e.g., the SVM algorithm which is most frequently used in the BoF method), and instead we have proposed using the majority-vote method.

The first of the BoF algorithm modules is supposed to prepare the database by creating a dictionary of characteristic features of sample images (to be used in the system learning process). This is carried out in a few steps presented below.

1. Starting operation of the algorithm generating image characteristic features. In our case we have used a well-known and fast SURF algorithm [3] which provides 64-number vectors $\mathbf{x}_i = [x_{i1}, ..., x_{1d}]$ describing the surrounding of a characteristic point, where $i = 1, ..., L$, L the total number of all characteristic points, d the dimension of the vector describing a characteristic point ($d = 64$).

2. Starting operation of the k-means clustering algorithm. We have used the algorithm version presented in Sect. 2.1. As a result we obtain c clusters with the centers in points $\mathbf{v}_j$, $j = 1, ..., c$, which are treated as words in the BoF dictionary.

3. The value of the number of classes i of cluster j is calculated and defined as k_{ji}. This value is computed by counting the points $\mathbf{x}_n$ which belong to the center j provided that $\mathbf{x}_n \in \mathbf{I}$ and $c(\mathbf{I}) = \omega_i$:

$$k_{ji} = \sum_{n=1}^{L} \delta_{nj}(i), j = 1, ..., c, i = 1, ..., C, \tag{6}$$

where:

$$\delta_{nj}(i) = \begin{cases} 1 \text{ if } d_{nj} \leq d_{nm} \text{ for } \mathbf{x}_n \in \mathbf{I} \text{ and } c(\mathbf{I}) = \omega_i, m = 1, ..., c, j \neq m \\ 0 \qquad\qquad\qquad\qquad\qquad \text{otherwise} \end{cases} \tag{7}$$

The variable $\delta_{nj}(i)$ is an indicator if a cluster $\mathbf{v}_j$ is the closest vector (a winner) for any sample $\mathbf{x}_n$ from an image $\mathbf{I}$ and $c(\mathbf{I}) = \omega_i$. Next, the values k_{ji} are normalised:

$$k_{ji} = \frac{k_{ji}}{\sum_{j=1,...,c}(k_{ji})} \tag{8}$$

4. Saving the values of centers $\mathbf{v}_j$ together with the information about the number of classes k_{ji} in the database.

Classification process, i.e. the process testing whether a given query image belongs to a particular class, requires that an additional pre-processing module be applied. This module is supposed to:

1. Use a feature extraction algorithm (the SURF algorithm) on query image $\mathbf{I}_q$ in order to obtain values of characteristic features $\mathbf{x}_i^q$, $i = 1, ..., L_q$, L_q the number of obtained features.
2. Save points $\mathbf{x}^q$ in the database.
3. Assign points $\mathbf{x}^q$ to clusters in such way so as to compute values k_i^q. Computations are carried out as follows:

$$k_i^q = \sum_{n=1}^{L_q} \alpha(i), i = 1, ..., C \qquad (9)$$

$$\alpha_n(i) = \begin{cases} k_{ji} \text{ if } \|\mathbf{v}_j - \mathbf{x}_n^q\| \le \|\mathbf{v}_m - \mathbf{x}_n^q\| \ m = 1, ..., c, j \ne m \\ 0 \qquad\qquad\qquad\qquad\qquad \text{otherwise} \end{cases} \qquad (10)$$

4. Assign to class $c(\mathbf{I}_q)$ is done by the majority vote checking the maximum value k_i^q:

$$c(\mathbf{I}_q) = \operatorname*{argmax}_{i=1,...,c} k_i^q \qquad (11)$$

The algorithm facilitates easy implementation by using only one SQL query. The algorithms details and experimental research are presented in Sect. 3.

3   Experimental Research

In this section we present the experiments which were conducted with the use of various configuration of the algorithm operation. Preprocessing algorithms were implemented in the Java language with the use of parallel computing (Concurrent library) as well as JavaCV [2] library function. JavaCV is a library which adopts functions available in OpenCV [4] for the Java language needs. The research was performed on the Caltech 101 image database (collected by L. Fei-Fei et al. [10]). Six sample categories comprising motorbikes, car sides, revolvers, airplanes, leopards and wrenches were selected. Randomly selected images are presented in the Fig. 1. Out of the remaining group of images, 20 % are randomly selected and marked as a set of testing images. They are used to test efficiency of the final classification. During the operation of the SURF algorithm over 100,000 characteristic points are identified in the database for 180 images. The main value which is used to compute classification efficiency as a percentage of correct classified images.

In the k-means algorithm distances between cluster centers and the data vector can be compared by means of different measures. All measures, however, require various kinds of computation, which in the case of a large amount of data directly affects efficiency and performance of the k-means algorithm. For our tests we chose 3 common distance measures: the Euclidean distance, the Cosine similarity and the Manhattan distance. The first of the measures requires the greatest deal of complex calculations (functions of raising to a power and extracting the root occur a number of times). The Cosine similarity requires calculating the scalar product (dot product). The last distance measure the Manhattan distance is the simplest measure, which requires only simple calculations of summation and subtraction and the calculating of absolute values.

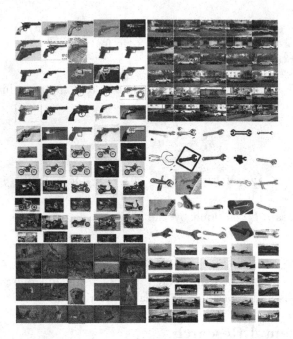

Fig. 1. Sample images from the 6 classes (revolver, car side, leopard, motorbike, wrench, airplane) selected for learning.

Table 1 shows the results of the operation of the algorithm presented in Sect. 2.2. The subsequent rows show the percentage of efficiency of both the sample (learning) and test image recognition in relation to the threshold used during the operation of the k-means algorithm and the distance measure applied. The best results for a given threshold are given in bold. The diagram picturing the classification efficiency of the test images is presented in Fig. 2. The analysis of the results brings attention to two issues. The first is the fact that the threshold value applied affects the operational accuracy of the Bag-of-features classification algorithm. A lower threshold generates a bigger number of clusters, which, in turn, translates into a lower generalization of the data mapped in the centers. In the case of the test images the optimum value is 500. The other interesting fact is that the Manhattan distance method is clearly more effective in comparison to the other two measures. It is important because this measure requires computations which are the least complicated and time-consuming for the computer processor. That is the reason why this particular measure was chosen to be implemented in the database during our research work on this algorithm.

Practical application of the presented method in image classification with the use of the database needs two modules to be used:

Table 1. Percentage results of the algorithm operation efficiency during image class recognition operations for the database of dictionary images and test images for different distance measures and different threshold values Θ

Θ	Euclidean distance		Cosine similarity		Manhattan distance	
	Train	Test	Train	Test	Train	Test
10000	**47.80**	49.65	46.03	**50.35**	45.50	46.85
5000	**52.91**	**55.24**	51.85	53.85	49.38	48.95
2000	58.02	52.45	56.61	53.15	**60.49**	**53.85**
1000	62.96	58.04	63.84	60.84	**68.61**	**63.64**
500	71.08	65.73	71.96	69.93	**76.90**	**74.13**
250	71.08	65.73	71.96	69.93	**76.90**	**74.13**
100	85.19	70.63	85.01	74.13	**90.48**	**74.83**
50	92.95	70.63	92.95	69.93	**94.71**	**74.83**
25	97.53	72.03	**97.88**	**76.22**	**97.88**	72.03
10	**99.82**	**76.22**	99.47	72.03	**99.82**	71.33

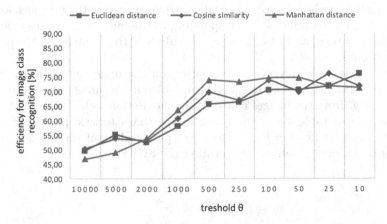

Fig. 2. Diagram of the algorithm operation efficiency for image class recognition for the test images (given in percentage) for different distance measures (different types of diagrams) and for different threshold levels (diagram horizontal axis).

- the module which is supposed to fill with the use of the Bag-of-Features algorithm the database with the cluster center values and also with the information on which class they belong to, i.e. creating the dictionary, and
- the module preparing for query image classification and saving its features in the database.

The module creating the dictionary for the database should comprise the following steps:

– preprocessing, i.e. extracting characteristic features from training images,
– starting the operation of the k-means algorithm in order to perform clustering of the data and obtaining clusters with image characteristic features,
– performing SQL queries so as to save the above data in the database.

As for the query image module, it is applied in the case of a query about an image being classified to one of the classes stored in the database. It also comprises a few steps:

– preprocesing, i.e. extracting characteristic features from a query image,
– saving data in the database,
– performing an SQL query which will produce information on the class to which a particular image belongs.

The database can be designed in different ways. However, our experimental research has shown that the simple table structure presented in the Fig. 3 has proved the most efficient. The database consists of 3 tables:

– centers - the tables subsequent rows contain the data about the cluster centers obtained from the operation of the k-means algorithm. Column `cluster_id` contains the number of cluster j obtained while operating the k-means, and k0-k5 are normalised values k_{ji} corresponding to the number of classes belonging to a given cluster, and c1-c64 being the values of the elements of the point of cluster center $\mathbf{v}_j$,
– images - this table comprises information on the query image stored in the database. `ImageId` is the image ID, and `class` the image class number, if known (e.g. from the images constituting the dictionary),
– features - this table stores the query image characteristic points. `Image_id` is the image ID (foreign key), values `pk1-pk64` values of the elements of the vector of features obtained by operating the SURF algorithm.

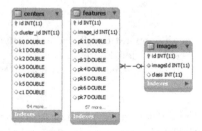

Fig. 3. Proposed structure of the tables in the database

The query about the query image class requires the pre-processing operations outlined above and their saving in the features and images tables. Next, the SQL query is performed (the version for MySQL):

```
set @rn=0, @cid=0;
SELECT sum(k0), sum(k1), sum(k2), sum(k3), sum(k4), sum(k5)
FROM
(
SELECT t.*,
@rn := if (@cid = t.fid, @rn+1, 1) as row_number,
@cid := t.fid
FROM
(
SELECT
f.id as fid,
c.id as cid,
abs(pk1-c1)+abs(pk2-c2) + + abs(pk64-c64) as mm,
c.k0, c.k1, c.k2, c.k3, c.k4, c.k5
FROM
centers c, features f
WHERE
f.image_id = ?
ORDER BY fid, mm
) t
) t2
WHERE row_number=1
```

As shown, the query is not really complex. Additional variables are used in such a way so as to make it possible to select first row per group instead of using the UNION ALL command. The most demanding factors in terms of time and computation are the Cartesian product of the centers and features tables as well as computations connected with Manhattan distance (abs(pk1-c1) + abs(pk2-c2) + ...). The answers received give the values of images belonging to a given class (numbered from 1 to 5). It is the class number with the greatest value returned which decides about the class to which a query image belongs.

4 Conclusions

Undoubtedly, the presented method cannot be said to be as efficient as the deep-learning network methods. However, it is certainly advantageous in terms of its simplicity and not having to use tools and libraries implementing complex algorithms. Moreover, its efficiency greatly depends on appropriate database configuration. The approach presented herein is sure to work efficiently enough when used in less complex applications.

Better query efficiency can be achieved by means of reducing lengths of the vectors describing particular image features. The methods which reduce the number of dimensions can be used for this purpose and these methods, for instance, include the PCA algorithm, or some other completely different feature generating algorithms. Another possible procedure reducing the number of calculations is the exclusions of those clusters which are the least likely to affect unequivocally image class determination. A similar approach was presented in [12].

References

1. Aghdam, M.H., Heidari, S.: Feature selection using particle swarm optimization in text categorization. J. Artif. Intell. Soft Comput. Res. **5**(4), 231–238 (2015)
2. Audet, S.: JavaCV (2014). http://bytedeco.org/. Accessed 1 Dec 2014
3. Bay, H., Tuytelaars, T., Van Gool, L.: SURF: speeded up robust features. In: Leonardis, A., Bischof, H., Pinz, A. (eds.) ECCV 2006, Part I. LNCS, vol. 3951, pp. 404–417. Springer, Heidelberg (2006)
4. Bradski, G.: The OpenCV library. Dr. Dobb's J. Softw. Tools **25**(11), 120–126 (2000)
5. Chen, M., Ludwig, S.A.: Particle swarm optimization based fuzzy clustering approach to identify optimal number of clusters. J. Artif. Intelli. Soft Comput. Res. **4**(1), 43–56 (2014)
6. Cpalka, K.: A new method for design and reduction of neuro-fuzzy classification systems. IEEE Trans. Neural Netw. **20**(4), 701–714 (2009)
7. Cpalka, K., Rebrova, O., Nowicki, R., Rutkowski, L.: On design of flexible neuro-fuzzy systems for nonlinear modelling. Int. J. Gen. Syst. **42**(6), 706–720 (2013)
8. Csurka, G., Dance, C.R., Fan, L., Willamowski, J., Bray, C.: Visual categorization with bags of keypoints. In: Workshop on Statistical Learning in Computer Vision, ECCV, pp. 1–22 (2004)
9. El-Samak, A.F., Ashour, W.: Optimization of traveling salesman problem using affinity propagation clustering and genetic algorithm. J. Artif. Intell. Soft Comput. Res. **5**(4), 239–245 (2015)
10. Fei-Fei, L., Fergus, R., Perona, P.: Learning generative visual models from few training examples: an incremental bayesian approach tested on 101 object categories. In: Conference on Computer Vision and Pattern Recognition Workshop, CVPRW 2004, pp. 178–178, June 2004
11. Fritzke, B.: Growing grid a self-organizing network with constant neighborhood range and adaptation strength. Neural Process. Lett. **2**(5), 9–13 (1995)
12. Gabryel, M., Grycuk, R., Korytkowski, M., Holotyak, T.: Image indexing and retrieval using GSOM algorithm. In: Rutkowski, L., Korytkowski, M., Scherer, R., Tadeusiewicz, R., Zadeh, L.A., Zurada, J.M. (eds.) ICAISC 2015. LNCS (LNAI), vol. 9119, pp. 706–714. Springer, Heidelberg (2015)
13. Gao, H., Dou, L., Chen, W., Sun, J.: Image classification with bag-of-words model based on improved sift algorithm. In: 2013 9th Asian Control Conference (ASCC), pp. 1–6, June 2013
14. Grycuk, R., Gabryel, M., Korytkowski, M., Scherer, R., Voloshynovskiy, S.: From single image to list of objects based on edge and blob detection. In: Rutkowski, L., Korytkowski, M., Scherer, R., Tadeusiewicz, R., Zadeh, L.A., Zurada, J.M. (eds.) ICAISC 2014, Part II. LNCS (LNAI), vol. 8468, pp. 605–615. Springer, Heidelberg (2014)
15. Korytkowski, M., Nowicki, R., Scherer, R.: Neuro-fuzzy rough classifier ensemble. In: Alippi, C., Polycarpou, M., Panayiotou, C., Ellinas, G. (eds.) ICANN 2009, Part I. LNCS, vol. 5768, pp. 817–823. Springer, Heidelberg (2009)
16. Korytkowski, M., Rutkowski, L., Scherer, R.: Fast image classification by boosting fuzzy classifiers. Inf. Sci. **327**, 175–182 (2016)
17. Koshiyama, A.S., Vellasco, M.M., Tanscheit, R.: Gpfis-control: a genetic fuzzy system for control tasks. J. Artif. Intell. Soft Comput. Res. **4**(3), 167–179 (2014)

18. Łapa, K., Zalasiński, M., Cpałka, K.: A new method for designing and complexity reduction of neuro-fuzzy systems for nonlinear modelling. In: Rutkowski, L., Korytkowski, M., Scherer, R., Tadeusiewicz, R., Zadeh, L.A., Zurada, J.M. (eds.) ICAISC 2013, Part I. LNCS (LNAI), vol. 7894, pp. 329–344. Springer, Heidelberg (2013)

19. Lazebnik, S., Schmid, C., Ponce, J.: Beyond bags of features: spatial pyramid matching for recognizing natural scene categories. In: 2006 IEEE Computer Society Conference on Computer Vision and Pattern Recognition, vol. 2, pp. 2169–2178 (2006)

20. Li, W., Dong, P., Xiao, B., Zhou, L.: Object recognition based on the region of interest and optimal bag of words model. Neurocomputing **172**, 271–280 (2016)

21. Liu, J.: Image retrieval based on bag-of-words model. CoRR abs/1304.5168 (2013)

22. Nanni, L., Melucci, M.: Combination of projectors, standard texture descriptors and bag of features for classifying images. Neurocomputing **173**(Part 3), 1602–1614 (2016). doi:10.1016/j.neucom.2015.09.032. http://www.sciencedirect.com/science/article/pii/S0925231215013405

23. Nowak, B.A., Nowicki, R.K., Starczewski, J.T., Marvuglia, A.: The learning of neuro-fuzzy classifier with fuzzy rough sets for imprecise datasets. In: Rutkowski, L., Korytkowski, M., Scherer, R., Tadeusiewicz, R., Zadeh, L.A., Zurada, J.M. (eds.) ICAISC 2014, Part I. LNCS (LNAI), vol. 8467, pp. 256–266. Springer, Heidelberg (2014)

24. Nowicki, R.: Rough sets in the neuro-fuzzy architectures based on monotonic fuzzy implications. In: Rutkowski, L., Siekmann, J.H., Tadeusiewicz, R., Zadeh, L.A. (eds.) ICAISC 2004. LNCS (LNAI), vol. 3070, pp. 510–517. Springer, Heidelberg (2004)

25. Rutkowski, L., Jaworski, M., Pietruczuk, L., Duda, P.: Decision trees for mining data streams based on the Gaussian approximation. IEEE Trans. Knowl. Data Eng. **26**(1), 108–119 (2014)

26. Rutkowski, L., Jaworski, M., Pietruczuk, L., Duda, P.: A new method for data stream mining based on the misclassification error. IEEE Trans. Neural Netw. Learn. Syst. **26**(5), 1048–1059 (2015)

27. Rutkowski, L., Pietruczuk, L., Duda, P., Jaworski, M.: Decision trees for mining data streams based on the mcdiarmid's bound. IEEE Trans. Knowl. Data Eng. **25**(6), 1272–1279 (2013)

28. Rutkowski, L., Jaworski, M., Pietruczuk, L., Duda, P.: The CART decision tree for mining data streams. Inf. Sci. **266**, 1–15 (2014)

29. Sakurai, S., Nishizawa, M.: A new approach for discovering top-k sequential patterns based on the variety of items. J. Artif. Intell. Soft Comput. Res. **5**(2), 141–153 (2015)

30. Starczewski, J.T.: Centroid of triangular and gaussian type-2 fuzzy sets. Inf. Sci. **280**, 289–306 (2014)

31. Szarek, A., Korytkowski, M., Rutkowski, L., Scherer, R., Szyprowski, J.: Application of neural networks in assessing changes around implant after total hip arthroplasty. In: Rutkowski, L., Korytkowski, M., Scherer, R., Tadeusiewicz, R., Zadeh, L.A., Zurada, J.M. (eds.) ICAISC 2012, Part II. LNCS, vol. 7268, pp. 335–340. Springer, Heidelberg (2012)

32. Szarek, A., Korytkowski, M., Rutkowski, L., Scherer, R., Szyprowski, J.: Forecasting wear of head and acetabulum in hip joint implant. In: Rutkowski, L., Korytkowski, M., Scherer, R., Tadeusiewicz, R., Zadeh, L.A., Zurada, J.M. (eds.) ICAISC 2012, Part II. LNCS, vol. 7268, pp. 341–346. Springer, Heidelberg (2012)

33. Tambouratzis, T., Souliou, D., Chalikias, M., Gregoriades, A.: Maximising accuracy and efficiency of traffic accident prediction combining information mining with computational intelligence approaches and decision trees. J. Artif. Intell. Soft Comput. Res. **4**(1), 31–42 (2014)
34. Woźniak, M., Kempa, W.M., Gabryel, M., Nowicki, R.K.: A finite-buffer queue with single vacation policy - analytical study with evolutionary positioning. Int. J. Appl. Math. Comput. Sci. **24**(4), 887–900 (2014)
35. Woźniak, M., Połap, D., Gabryel, M., Nowicki, R.K., Napoli, C., Tramontana, E.: Can we process 2D images using artificial bee colony? In: Rutkowski, L., Korytkowski, M., Scherer, R., Tadeusiewicz, R., Zadeh, L.A., Zurada, J.M. (eds.) ICAISC 2015. LNCS (LNAI), vol. 9119, pp. 660–671. Springer, Heidelberg (2015)
36. Zhao, C., Li, X., Cang, Y.: Bisecting k-means clustering based face recognition using block-based bag of words model. Optik - Int. J. Light Electron Opt. **126**(19), 1761–1766 (2015)

Image Descriptor Based on Edge Detection and Crawler Algorithm

Rafał Grycuk[1][(✉)], Marcin Gabryel[1], Magdalena Scherer[2],
and Sviatoslav Voloshynovskiy[3]

[1] Institute of Computational Intelligence, Częstochowa University of Technology,
Al. Armii Krajowej 36, 42-200 Częstochowa, Poland
{rafal.grycuk,marcin.gabryel}@iisi.pcz.pl
[2] Faculty of Management, Częstochowa University of Technology,
Al. Armii Krajowej 19, 42-200 Częstochowa, Poland
mscherer@zim.pcz.pl
[3] Computer Science Department, University of Geneva,
7 Route de Drize, Geneva, Switzerland
http://iisi.pcz.pl
http://sip.unige.ch

Abstract. In this paper we present a novel approach to image description. Our method is based on the Canny edge detection. After the edge detection process we apply a self-designed crawler method. The presented algorithm uses edges in order to move on pixel edges and describe the entire object. Our approach is closely related with the content-based image retrieval and it can be used as a pre-processing stage but can also be used for general purpose image description. The experiments proved the effectiveness of our method as it provides better results then the SURF descriptor.

Keywords: Content-based image retrieval · Crawler · Edge detection · Bag of Words

1 Introduction

In recent years there has been growing interest in image retrieval in the Internet and various online services as users would like to search the web for similar images. In response to this needs, many algorithms and systems were proposed [15,24]. Content-based image retrieval (CBIR, IR) is an area of expertise derived from computer vision [5,6,16,22,34] and image processing [1,3,6,13,30]. There are many approaches to this problem. A common concept is Bag of Words (BoW) [13,20,27,28]. Another type of CBIR methods is based on the user feedback (Relevance Feedback) [7]. This group of methods focuses on user responses and on which the future results are improved. The BoW approach firstly extract key features from images and creates the descriptor. There are many features on which descriptors can be created, such as color, texture, shape, local-features (keypoints). This step is crucial, because we need to extract this part of image

© Springer International Publishing Switzerland 2016
L. Rutkowski et al. (Eds.): ICAISC 2016, Part II, LNAI 9693, pp. 647–659, 2016.
DOI: 10.1007/978-3-319-39384-1_57

that contain only the object itself (this area is called ROI, Region of Interest). Descriptors must contain a mathematical description of the object. In the feature extraction stage there exist many algorithms used to extract interesting features. We can use filters, segmentation [12,37,46], keypoint detection [14,17,32], object extraction [10,21,30,35,46], and many others. After pre-processing stage (feature extraction) described above, we move to the processing stage, which is responsible for index creation. Many algorithms are used in this stage, e.g. clustering methods [19,42], neural networks [9,11,23,36,44,45], classification methods [29,39,48], deep learning [41], fuzzy systems [25,26,38,43]. The last step in CBIR, post-processing, executes the query images on previously created index (database) and retrieves the similar images. In this paper we focus on the pre-processing stage. The paper is organized as follows. Section 2 describes the Canny edge detector. Section 3 describes the proposed method for image description.

2   Canny Edge Detection

The Canny edge detector [4] is one of the most commonly used image processing methods for detecting edges [2,31,47]. The algorithm takes a gray scale image, and returns an image with the positions of tracked intensity discontinuities [8,40] and consists of four main steps [17,33]:

1. Noise reduction. The image is smoothed by applying an appropriate Gaussian filter.
2. Finding the intensity gradient of the image. During this step the edges should be marked where gradients of the image have large magnitudes.
3. Non-maxima suppression. If the gradient magnitude at a pixel is larger than those at its two neighbors in the gradient direction, mark the pixel as an edge. Otherwise, mark the pixel as the background.
4. Edge tracking by hysteresis. Final edges are determined by suppressing all edges that are not connected to genuine edges.

The result of the Canny edge detector is determined by two input parameters [17,33]:

- The width of the Gaussian filter used in the first stage directly affects the results of the Canny method,
- The thresholds used during edge tracking by hysteresis. It is difficult to give a generic threshold that works well on all images.

The algorithm basically finds the pixel intensity changes (gradients). Before this step non-important edges need to be removed. This process is performed by applying the Gaussian smooth filter [4,33] (Fig. 1)

$$K_{Gx} = \begin{bmatrix} -1 & 0 & 1 \\ -2 & 0 & 2 \\ -1 & 0 & 1 \end{bmatrix}, \tag{1}$$

Fig. 1. Canny edge detection. Left image is the input image and the right is the edge-detected image.

$$K_{Gy} = \begin{bmatrix} 1 & 2 & 1 \\ 0 & 0 & 0 \\ -1 & -2 & -1 \end{bmatrix}. \tag{2}$$

In order to determine the edge strengths we need to use the Euclidean (3) or Manhattan (4) distance measures [33]

$$|G| = \sqrt{G_x^2 + G_y^2}, \tag{3}$$

$$|G| = |G_x^2| + |G_y^2|, \tag{4}$$

where G_x is the horizontal direction gradient and G_y is the vertical direction gradient. The edge direction (angle) is determined by the following formula [4,33]

$$\Theta = \arctan\left(\frac{G_x}{G_y}\right). \tag{5}$$

3 Proposed Method for Image Description

In this section we describe our novel method for image description. It is based on the well known Canny edge detector, described in Sect. 2. The main problem in the image description is to take under consideration only the object without the surrounding area. If the non-important features are also detected, it will hinder the indexing process, thus the results also will be distorted. For example, this happens when we use local feature descriptors (e.g. SURF or SIFT). Moreover, they describe only local keypoints, which not provide comprehensive information about the entire object. Even the segmentation process will not entirely resolve the issue. Therefore we decided to develop a descriptor suitable for image retrieval. In image description, we tend to describe only the given object not the surrounding regions, e.g. background or other objects. The presented method performs edge detection on the input image and in the next step the edge linking procedure is executed. In an ideal case, the Canny edge detector should detect all edges, but the experiments shows that detected sets of pixels rarely describes a complete edge (due to noise). In order to obliterate the nuisance we used edge linking method, to complete the edges. The problem, along with the proposed solution is presented in Fig. 2. As can be seen, after the edge detection step, the edges are not complete, thus usage of edge linking method is needed. After this step the object is ready to execute the crawler on it.

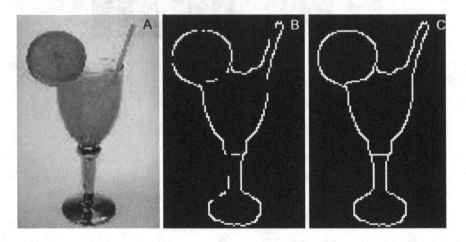

Fig. 2. The edge linking process. Figure 2A - input image, Fig. 2B - edge detection, Fig. 2C - edge linking.

3.1   Crawler Method

The main purpose of our method is to describe the entire object. The proposed algorithm allows to move between pixels and calculate angles between them. After the edge detection and edge linking, we can start crawling on the object edges. At first, we need to find the starting pixel. It is searched from up left corner of the image (position: 0,0). When the starting pixel is determined, we start crawling. In this process, finding the next pixel is crucial. The proposed method uses pixel neighbourhood for calculating the next pixel on the crawler path. Figure 3 illustrates the method of determining the pixels neighborhood. For the selected pixel (x, y) in its direct neighborhood there are pixels with common sides of the pixel. In this case, all pixels are marked in gray (0,2,4,6). As can be seen, B-neighborhood pixels are even numbers. In contrast, N-neighborhood are pixels having common corner with the selected pixels (1,3,5,7). There are two basic types of neighborhood: 4-neighborhood and 8-neighborhood.

Fig. 3. Determining pixel neighborhood

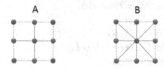

Fig. 4. A: 4-neighborhood, B: 8-neighborhood [35]

Figure 4A and B illustrate the neighborhood. Two points p and q are neighbors, if p is included the 4-neighborhood of point q $N_4(q)$ and if q is included in 4-neighborhood of the point p $N_4(p)$. Similarly, in the case of 8-neighborhood. Coherence in the sense 4 - or 8 -neighborhood can refer as well to the contours and areas [18,37]. Our method uses 8-neighborhood. In the next step we move our crawler from the current pixel to the next. If there are many neighbour pixels (branches) we choose the first pixel clockwise from the perspective of the current one (see Fig. 5). The position of the branch saved (in the form of stack, LIFO) and labeled as visited. In the next step we calculate the angle between the next pixel and the previous pixel (see Fig. 6). Angle can contain the following values: $\phi = 45, 90, 135, 180, 225, 270, 315$. Then we change the position of the crawler to the next pixel. The presented procedure is repeated until the crawler reaches the visited pixel. Then we return to the last branch and determine the next not visited pixel. If the branch stack is empty and all pixels are visited, the algorithm generates the description histogram. It is based on the previously calculated angles and determines how many pixels have a given angle (see more in Fig. 8). The descriptor size is very small and it oscillates about 64 bytes (depending on the image), however the SURF descriptor oscillates about 4 KB, which is much larger value. The described steps can be presented in the form of pseudo-code (see Algorithm 1) (Fig. 7).

45	90	135
P	C	180
315	270	225

Fig. 5. Determining the next pixel.   **Fig. 6.** Calculating the pixel angles.

INPUT: *InputImage*
OUTPUT: *Histogram*
EdgeDetectedImage := CannyEdgeDetection(InputImage);
EdgeDetectedImage := EdgeLinking(EdgeDetectedImage);
CurrentPixel := FindPositionOfNearestPixel(EdgeDetectedImage);
IsCrawlingCompleted := false;
while *IsCrawlingCompleted = true* **do**
    NextPixel = FindNextPixel();
    while *NextPixel! = NULL* **do**
        VisitedPixels.Add(CurrentPixel);
        PrevPixel := CurrentPixel;
        CurrentPixel := NextPixel;
        NextPixel := FindNextPixel();
        CurrentPixel.Angle := Angle(PrevPixel, CurrentPixel, NextPixel);
        if *VisitedPixels.Contains(NextPixel) = true* **then**
            NextPixel := NULL;
            if *Branches.Count = 0* **then**
              IsCrawlingCompleted := true;
            end
        end
    end
    if *Branches.Count > 0* **then**
        PrevPixel := NULL;
        CurrentPixel := Branches.Last();
    end
    else if *Branches.Count = 0* **then**
        IsCrawlingCompleted := true;
    end
end
Histogram := CreateAngleHistogram(VisitedPixels);

Algorithm 1. Crawler algorithm steps.

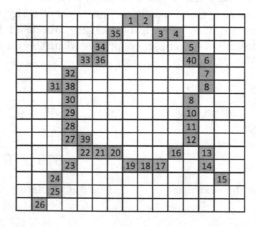

Fig. 7. Example crawler path. The numbers describe the sequence of crawler visits.

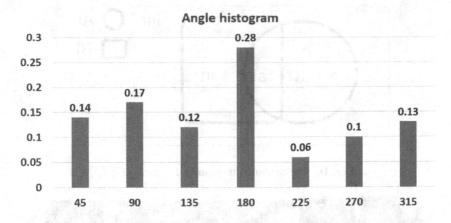

Fig. 8. Angle histogram. Each bin represents the normalized value of the given angle count.

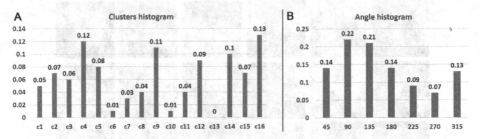

Fig. 9. Histograms comparison. Figure 9A represents histogram based on the SURF descriptor (keypoints clustering. c1, c2..., represent each cluster) and Fig. 9B shows angle histogram obtained by the proposed method. As can be seen, our method generates less data, which affects the execution time.

4 Experimental Results

In this section we described the experiments carried out using self written software presented in [15]. Test images were taken from the Corel database. We chose images with various types of objects (cars, dino, ships, mountains). In experiments we used 80 % of each class for index creating and 20 % as query images. In Table 1 we presented the retrieved factors for each query image. In this simulations we used the SURF algorithm as a descriptor. Table 2 shows simulation results for crawler descriptors. For the purposes of the performance evaluation we use two measures; *precision* and *recall* [15, 35]. Figure 10 shows the performance measures of the image retrieval. The *AI* is a set of appropriate images, that should be returned as being similar to the query image. The *RI* represents a set of returned images by the system. *Rai* is a group of properly returned images. *Iri* represents improperly returned images, *anr* proper not

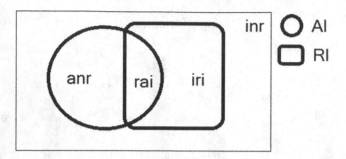

Fig. 10. Performance measures diagram. [15]

Fig. 11. Query results (Corel database). Example images from the experiment. The image with border is the query image.

returned and *inr* improper not returned images. The presented measure allows to define *precision* and *recall* by the following formulas [35]

$$precision = \frac{|rai|}{|rai + iri|}, \qquad (6)$$

$$recall = \frac{|rai|}{|rai + anr|}. \qquad (7)$$

As can be seen in Tables 1 and 2 the results are significantly improved. It is caused by better descriptor in the feature extraction phase. Our approach takes under consideration the entire object, thus the obtained histogram is more accurate and does not contain any background noise. During the simulation process we used the k-means method [17] for indexing. This algorithm is more suited for CBIR problems then the mean shift. In our experiments we used the Manhattan

Table 1. Query results for the SURF descriptor.

Image id	RI	AI	Rai	Iri	Anr	Precision	Recall
1 (1).jpg	28	30	21	7	9	0.75	0.7
1 (10).jpg	19	30	10	9	20	0.53	0.33
1 (11).jpg	26	30	19	7	11	0.73	0.63
1 (12).jpg	34	30	16	18	14	0.47	0.53
1 (13).jpg	20	30	11	9	19	0.55	0.37
1 (14).jpg	34	30	15	19	15	0.44	0.5
1 (15).jpg	18	30	9	9	21	0.5	0.3
1 (16).jpg	38	30	22	16	8	0.58	0.73
2 (1).jpg	31	30	17	14	13	0.55	0.57
2 (10).jpg	26	30	14	12	16	0.54	0.47
2 (11).jpg	40	30	24	16	6	0.6	0.8
2 (12).jpg	39	30	24	15	6	0.62	0.8
2 (13).jpg	29	30	10	19	20	0.34	0.33
2 (14).jpg	31	30	17	14	13	0.55	0.57
2 (15).jpg	31	30	14	17	16	0.45	0.47
2 (16).jpg	25	30	18	7	12	0.72	0.6
2 (17).jpg	27	30	13	14	17	0.48	0.43
2 (18).jpg	37	30	24	13	6	0.65	0.8
3 (17).jpg	35	30	24	11	6	0.69	0.8
3 (18).jpg	34	30	24	10	6	0.71	0.8
3 (19).jpg	35	30	17	18	13	0.49	0.57
3 (2).jpg	25	30	9	16	21	0.36	0.3
3 (20).jpg	34	30	18	16	12	0.53	0.6
3 (21).jpg	33	30	17	16	13	0.52	0.57
3 (22).jpg	29	30	10	19	20	0.34	0.33
3 (23).jpg	42	30	23	19	7	0.55	0.77
3 (24).jpg	30	30	18	12	12	0.6	0.6

Table 2. Query results for the proposed crawler descriptor.

Image id	RI	AI	Rai	Iri	Anr	Precision	Recall
1 (1).jpg	33	30	28	5	2	0.85	0.93
1 (10).jpg	25	30	24	1	6	0.96	0.8
1 (11).jpg	32	30	28	4	2	0.88	0.93
1 (12).jpg	30	30	26	4	4	0.87	0.87
1 (13).jpg	30	30	27	3	3	0.9	0.9
1 (14).jpg	27	30	24	3	6	0.89	0.8
1 (15).jpg	29	30	24	5	6	0.83	0.8
1 (16).jpg	22	30	21	1	9	0.95	0.7
2 (1).jpg	23	30	20	3	10	0.87	0.67
2 (10).jpg	26	30	25	1	5	0.96	0.83
2 (11).jpg	26	30	24	2	6	0.92	0.8
2 (12).jpg	33	30	27	6	3	0.82	0.9
2 (13).jpg	31	30	25	6	5	0.81	0.83
2 (14).jpg	27	30	23	4	7	0.85	0.77
2 (15).jpg	32	30	26	6	4	0.81	0.87
2 (16).jpg	31	30	26	5	4	0.84	0.87
2 (17).jpg	33	30	28	5	2	0.85	0.93
2 (18).jpg	32	30	26	6	4	0.81	0.87
3 (17).jpg	29	30	27	2	3	0.93	0.9
3 (18).jpg	25	30	22	3	8	0.88	0.73
3 (19).jpg	30	30	27	3	3	0.9	0.9
3 (2).jpg	31	30	26	5	4	0.84	0.87
3 (20).jpg	27	30	26	1	4	0.96	0.87
3 (21).jpg	32	30	26	6	4	0.81	0.87
3 (22).jpg	30	30	27	3	3	0.9	0.9
3 (23).jpg	27	30	21	6	9	0.78	0.7
3 (24).jpg	30	30	26	4	4	0.87	0.87

(see Formula 4) for comparing histograms, because it provides better results then Euclidian (see 3) or Bhattacharyya distances. The performed experiments proved the effectiveness of our method. Figure 11 shows retrieved images for a query image (the image with border).

5   Final Remarks

The presented method is a novel approach for image description. We used the Canny edge detector and edge linking for edge detection. In the further steps we applied the self designed crawler algorithm for image description. Performed experiments proved effectiveness of our method and they provide satisfying results. The presented approach can be used for content-based image retrieval tasks and image description in general. Our method allows to describe objects separately instead of the entire image thus, the resulting precision is significantly increased. As can be seen in above, our approach provides better results then the SURF descriptor.

Acknowledgments. The work presented in this paper was supported by a grant BS/MN-1-109-301/15/P "New approaches of storing and retrieving images in databases" and by the Polish National Science Centre (NCN) within project number DEC-2011/01/D/ST6/06957.

References

1. An, Y., Riaz, M., Park, J.: CBIR based on adaptive segmentation of HSV color space. In: 2010 12th International Conference on Computer Modelling and Simulation (UKSim), pp. 248–251. IEEE (2010)
2. Bao, P., Zhang, L., Wu, X.: Canny edge detection enhancement by scale multiplication. IEEE Trans. Pattern Anal. Mach. Intell. **27**(9), 1485–1490 (2005)
3. Bruździński, T., Krzyżak, A., Fevens, T., Jeleń, Ł.: Web-based framework for breast cancer classification. J. Artif. Intell. Soft Comput. Res. **4**(2), 149–162 (2014)
4. Canny, J.: A computational approach to edge detection. IEEE Trans. Pattern Anal. Mach. Intell. **6**, 679–698 (1986)
5. Chu, J.L., Krzyzak, A.: The recognition of partially occluded objects with support vector machines, convolutional neural networks and deep belief networks. J. Artif. Intell. Soft Comput. Res. **4**(1), 5–19 (2014)
6. Cierniak, R., Knop, M.: Video compression algorithm based on neural networks. In: Rutkowski, L., Korytkowski, M., Scherer, R., Tadeusiewicz, R., Zadeh, L.A., Zurada, J.M. (eds.) ICAISC 2013, Part I. LNCS (LNAI), vol. 7894, pp. 524–531. Springer, Heidelberg (2013)
7. da Silva, A.T., Xavier, A., Magalhães, L.P.: A new CBIR approach based on relevance feedback and optimum-path forest classification. J. WSCG **18**(1–3), 73–80 (2010)
8. Ding, L., Goshtasby, A.: On the Canny edge detector. Pattern Recogn. **34**(3), 721–725 (2001)
9. Gabryel, M., Grycuk, R., Korytkowski, M., Holotyak, T.: Image indexing and retrieval Using GSOM algorithm. In: Rutkowski, L., Korytkowski, M., Scherer, R., Tadeusiewicz, R., Zadeh, L.A., Zurada, J.M. (eds.) ICAISC 2015. LNCS (LNAI), vol. 9119, pp. 706–714. Springer, Heidelberg (2015)
10. Gagaudakis, G., Rosin, P.L.: Incorporating shape into histograms for CBIR. Pattern Recogn. **35**(1), 81–91 (2002)
11. Galkowski, T., Starczewski, A., Fu, X.: Improvement of the multiple-view learning based on the self-organizing maps. In: Rutkowski, L., Korytkowski, M., Scherer, R., Tadeusiewicz, R., Zadeh, L.A., Zurada, J.M. (eds.) ICAISC 2015. LNCS (LNAI), vol. 9120, pp. 3–12. Springer, Heidelberg (2015)
12. Grycuk, R., Gabryel, M., Korytkowski, M., Romanowski, J., Scherer, R.: Improved digital image segmentation based on stereo vision and mean shift algorithm. In: Wyrzykowski, R., Dongarra, J., Karczewski, K., Waśniewski, J. (eds.) PPAM 2013, Part I. LNCS, vol. 8384, pp. 433–443. Springer, Heidelberg (2014)
13. Grycuk, R., Gabryel, M., Korytkowski, M., Scherer, R.: Content-based image indexing by data clustering and inverse document frequency. In: Kozielski, S., Mrozek, D., Kasprowski, P., Małysiak-Mrozek, B. (eds.) BDAS 2014. CCIS, vol. 424, pp. 374–383. Springer, Heidelberg (2014)
14. Grycuk, R., Gabryel, M., Korytkowski, M., Scherer, R., Voloshynovskiy, S.: From single image to list of objects based on edge and blob detection. In: Rutkowski, L., Korytkowski, M., Scherer, R., Tadeusiewicz, R., Zadeh, L.A., Zurada, J.M. (eds.) ICAISC 2014, Part II. LNCS (LNAI), vol. 8468, pp. 605–615. Springer, Heidelberg (2014)

15. Grycuk, R., Gabryel, M., Scherer, R., Voloshynovskiy, S.: Multi-layer architecture for storing visual data based on WCF and Microsoft SQL server database. In: Rutkowski, L., Korytkowski, M., Scherer, R., Tadeusiewicz, R., Zadeh, L.A., Zurada, J.M. (eds.) ICAISC 2015. LNCS (LNAI), vol. 9119, pp. 715–726. Springer, Heidelberg (2015)

16. Grycuk, R., Knop, M., Mandal, S.: Video key frame detection based on SURF algorithm. In: Rutkowski, L., Korytkowski, M., Scherer, R., Tadeusiewicz, R., Zadeh, L.A., Zurada, J.M. (eds.) ICAISC 2015. LNCS (LNAI), vol. 9119, pp. 566–576. Springer, Heidelberg (2015)

17. Grycuk, R., Scherer, R., Gabryel, M.: New image descriptor from edge detector and blob extractor. J. Appl. Math. Comput. Mech. **14**(4), 31–39 (2015)

18. Haralick, R.M., Shapiro, L.G.: Image segmentation techniques. Comput. Vis. Graph. Image Process. **29**(1), 100–132 (1985)

19. Hartigan, J.A., Wong, M.A.: Algorithm as 136: a k-means clustering algorithm. Appl. Stat. **28**, 100–108 (1979)

20. Huang, J., Kumar, S., Mitra, M., Zhu, W.J., Zabih, R.: Image indexing using color correlograms. In: Proceedings of the IEEE Computer Society Conference on Computer Vision and Pattern Recognition, pp. 762–768, June 1997

21. Katto, J., Ohta, M.: Novel algorithms for object extraction using multiple camera inputs. In: Proceedings of the International Conference on Image Processing, vol. 1, pp. 863–866. IEEE (1996)

22. Knop, M., Dobosz, P.: Neural video compression algorithm. In: Choraś, R.S. (ed.) Image Processing and Communications Challenges 6. AISC, vol. 313, pp. 59–66. Springer, Heidelberg (2015)

23. Knop, M., Kapuściński, T., Mleczko, W.K.: Video key frame detection based on the restricted Boltzmann machine. J. Appl. Math. Comput. Mech. **14**(3), 49–58 (2015)

24. Korytkowski, M., Scherer, R., Staszewski, P., Woldan, P.: Bag-of-features image indexing and classification in Microsoft SQL server relational database. In: 2015 IEEE 2nd International Conference on Cybernetics (CYBCONF), pp. 478–482 (2015)

25. Korytkowski, M., Nowicki, R., Scherer, R.: Neuro-fuzzy rough classifier ensemble. In: Alippi, C., Polycarpou, M., Panayiotou, C., Ellinas, G. (eds.) ICANN 2009, Part I. LNCS, vol. 5768, pp. 817–823. Springer, Heidelberg (2009)

26. Korytkowski, M., Rutkowski, L., Scherer, R.: Fast image classification by boosting fuzzy classifiers. Inf. Sci. **327**, 175–182 (2016)

27. Korytkowski, M., Scherer, R., Staszewski, P., Woldan, P.: Bag-of-features image indexing and classification in Microsoft SQL server relational database. arXiv preprint arXiv:1506.07950 (2015)

28. Laga, H., Schreck, T., Ferreira, A., Godil, A., Pratikakis, I., Veltkamp, R.: Bag of words and local spectral descriptor for 3D partial shape retrieval. In: Eurographics Workshop on 3D Object Retrieval. Citeseer (2011)

29. Lee, P.M., Hsiao, T.C.: Applying LCS to affective image classification in spatial-frequency domain. J. Artif. Intell. Soft Comput. Res. **4**(2), 99–123 (2014)

30. Lei, Z., Fuzong, L., Bo, Z.: A CBIR method based on color-spatial feature. In: Proceedings of the IEEE Region 10 Conference, TENCON 1999, vol. 1, pp. 166–169. IEEE (1999)

31. Li, X., Jiang, J., Fan, Q.: An improved real-time hardware architecture for canny edge detection based on FPGA. In: 2012 Third International Conference on Intelligent Control and Information Processing (ICICIP), pp. 445–449. IEEE (2012)

32. Lowe, D.G.: Distinctive image features from scale-invariant keypoints. Int. J. Comput. Vis. **60**(2), 91–110 (2004)
33. Luo, Y.M., Duraiswami, R.: Canny edge detection on NVIDIA CUDA. In: IEEE Computer Society Conference on Computer Vision and Pattern Recognition Workshops, CVPRW 2008, pp. 1–8. IEEE (2008)
34. Makinana, S., Malumedzha, T., Nelwamondo, F.V.: Quality parameter assessment on iris images. J. Artif. Intell. Soft Comput. Res. **4**(1), 21–30 (2014)
35. Meskaldji, K., Boucherkha, S., Chikhi, S.: Color quantization and its impact on color histogram based image retrieval accuracy. In: First International Conference on Networked Digital Technologies, NDT 2009, pp. 515–517, July 2009
36. Mleczko, W.K., Kapuscinski, T., Nowicki, R.K.: Rough deep belief network - application to incomplete handwritten digits pattern classification. In: Dregvaite, G., Damasevicius, R. (eds.) ICIST 2015. CCIS, vol. 538, pp. 400–411. Springer, Heidelberg (2015)
37. Nakib, A., Najman, L., Talbot, H., Siarry, P.: Application of graph partitioning to image segmentation. Graph Partitioning, 249–274
38. Nowak, B.A., Nowicki, R.K., Starczewski, J.T., Marvuglia, A.: The learning of neuro-fuzzy classifier with fuzzy rough sets for imprecise datasets. In: Rutkowski, L., Korytkowski, M., Scherer, R., Tadeusiewicz, R., Zadeh, L.A., Zurada, J.M. (eds.) ICAISC 2014, Part I. LNCS (LNAI), vol. 8467, pp. 256–266. Springer, Heidelberg (2014)
39. Nowak, B.A., Nowicki, R.K., Mleczko, W.K.: A new method of improving classification accuracy of decision tree in case of incomplete samples. In: Rutkowski, L., Korytkowski, M., Scherer, R., Tadeusiewicz, R., Zadeh, L.A., Zurada, J.M. (eds.) ICAISC 2013, Part I. LNCS (LNAI), vol. 7894, pp. 448–458. Springer, Heidelberg (2013)
40. Ogawa, K., Ito, Y., Nakano, K.: Efficient Canny edge detection using a GPU. In: 2010 First International Conference on Networking and Computing (ICNC), pp. 279–280. IEEE (2010)
41. Olas, T., Mleczko, W.K., Nowicki, R.K., Wyrzykowski, R., Krzyzak, A.: Adaptation of RBM learning for intel MIC architecture. In: Rutkowski, L., Korytkowski, M., Scherer, R., Tadeusiewicz, R., Zadeh, L.A., Zurada, J.M. (eds.) ICAISC 2015. LNCS (LNAI), vol. 9119, pp. 90–101. Springer, Heidelberg (2015)
42. Serdah, A.M., Ashour, W.M.: Clustering large-scale data based on modified affinity propagation algorithm. J. Artif. Intell. Soft Comput. Res. **6**(1), 23–33 (2016)
43. Staszewski, P., Woldan, P., Ferdowsi, S.: Mobile fuzzy system for detecting loss of consciousness and epileptic seizure. In: Rutkowski, L., Korytkowski, M., Scherer, R., Tadeusiewicz, R., Zadeh, L.A., Zurada, J.M. (eds.) ICAISC 2015. LNCS (LNAI), vol. 9120, pp. 142–150. Springer, Heidelberg (2015)
44. Szarek, A., Korytkowski, M., Rutkowski, L., Scherer, R., Szyprowski, J.: Application of neural networks in assessing changes around implant after total hip arthroplasty. In: Rutkowski, L., Korytkowski, M., Scherer, R., Tadeusiewicz, R., Zadeh, L.A., Zurada, J.M. (eds.) ICAISC 2012, Part II. LNCS, vol. 7268, pp. 335–340. Springer, Heidelberg (2012)
45. Szarek, A., Korytkowski, M., Rutkowski, L., Scherer, R., Szyprowski, J.: Forecasting wear of head and acetabulum in hip joint implant. In: Rutkowski, L., Korytkowski, M., Scherer, R., Tadeusiewicz, R., Zadeh, L.A., Zurada, J.M. (eds.) ICAISC 2012, Part II. LNCS, vol. 7268, pp. 341–346. Springer, Heidelberg (2012)
46. Tamaki, T., Yamamura, T., Ohnishi, N.: Image segmentation and object extraction based on geometric features of regions. In: Electronic Imaging 1999, International Society for Optics and Photonics, pp. 937–945 (1998)

47. Wang, B., Fan, S.: An improved Canny edge detection algorithm. In: 2009 Second International Workshop on Computer Science and Engineering, pp. 497–500. IEEE (2009)
48. Wang, X., Liu, X., Japkowicz, N., Matwin, S.: Automated approach to classification of mine-like objects using multiple-aspect sonar images. J. Artif. Intelli. Soft Comput. Res. 4(2), 133–148 (2014)

Neural Video Compression Based on RBM Scene Change Detection Algorithm

Michał Knop[1]([envelope]), Tomasz Kapuściński[1], Wojciech K. Mleczko[1], and Rafał Angryk[2]

[1] Institute of Computational Intelligence, Czestochowa University of Technology, Al. Armii Krajowej 36, 42-200 Czestochowa, Poland
{michal.knop,tomasz.kapuscinski,wojciech.mleczko}@iisi.pcz.pl
[2] Department of Computer Science, Georgia State University, P.O. Box 5060, Atlanta, GA 30302-5060, USA
angryk@cs.gsu.edu
http://www.iisi.pcz.pl, http://grid.cs.gsu.edu/~rangryk/

Abstract. Video and image compression technology has evolved into a highly developed field of computer vision. It is used in a wide range of applications like HDTV, video transmission, and broadcast digital video. In this paper the new method of video compression has been proposed. Neural image compression algorithm is the key component of our method. It is based on a well know method called predictive vector quantization (PVQ). It combines two different techniques: vector quantization and differential pulse code modulation. The neural video compression method based on PVQ algorithm requires correct detection of key frames in order to improve its performance. For key frame detection our method uses techniques based on the Restricted Boltzmann Machine method (RBM).

Keywords: Restricted Boltzman Machine · Video compression · Scene change detection

1 Introduction

In recent years video and image data compression has become an increasingly important issue in all areas of computing and communications. Redundancy of the image and video data can be reduced by various data coding techniques and methods of artificial intelligence such as neural networks [2,4,5,31,34], fuzzy systems [21,22,26,32] or population algorithm [1,36]. Most algorithms and video codecs combine spatial compensation of images as well as movement compensation in time. These algorithms can be found in a wide range of applications such as video services over the satellite, cable and land based transmission channels, storage formats, and video streaming in Internet or local area network. There are many video and image compression standards. The most popular of them are MPEG, H.261 and JPEG. There is a whole family of compression standards of audiovisual data combined with the MPEG standard, which is described in more details in [10]. The well known members of MPEG family are MPEG-1, MPEG-2, and MPEG-4. H.261 is the first of entire family H.26x video

© Springer International Publishing Switzerland 2016
L. Rutkowski et al. (Eds.): ICAISC 2016, Part II, LNAI 9693, pp. 660–669, 2016.
DOI: 10.1007/978-3-319-39384-1_58

compression standards. It has been designed for handling video transmission in real time. More information about the family H.26x can be found in [3]. JPEG and JPEG2000 standards are used for image compression with an adjustable compression rate. They are also used for video compression. These methods compress each movie frames individually. In practice, these techniques prove to be inefficient because there is a lot of redundant information between frames. Therefore most compression standards analyze the video stream and divides it into scenes which can be compressed more efficiently. The first frame in the scene is called a key frame and it is the only frame in the scene for which all parameters are saved. For the remaining frames only some information needs to be stored [9,28].

In our method we used a Predictive Vector Quantization (PVQ) algorithm to compress a video sequence, which combines two techniques: Vector Quantization (VQ) and Differential Pulse Code Modulation (DPCM) [6,8]. For detection of key frames we used Restricted Boltzmann Machine (RBM) which is a recurrent probabilistic neural network [17,23]. These structures can process the probability distribution and can be applied to filtering [18], classification [19,30], image recognition [12,13,27,29], motion tracing [37], and modeling [11]. Correct detection of key frames allows to change the necessary compression parameters such as the predictor and the codebook [7,16,24].

The rest of the paper is organized as follows. Section 2 describes components of our algorithm. It includes a description of neural image compression and the key frame detection algorithm. In Sect. 3 we discuss our approach to neural video compression. Next in Sect. 4 the experimental results are presented. The final section covers conclusions and the plans for future works.

2   Related Works

2.1   Predictive Vector Quantization

PVQ is an algorithm that combines Vector Quantization method [14,15] with scalar Differential Pulse Code Modulation scheme. Vector quantization is realized by a predictor which is based on neural network. Function of DPCM is fulfilled by a codebook. Algorithm divides a frame into a grid of macroblocks $V(t)$ of the same dimentionality and processes them in horizontal lines, where t are indices of consecutive macroblocks. Each macroblock is subtracted by an output of predictor $\overline{V}(t)$. The resulting difference $E(t) = V(t) - \overline{V}(t)$ is then processed by neuro-quantizer which selects the best approximation g_j from the codebook $G = [g_0, g_1, \ldots, g_{J-1}, g_J]$. Approximation g_j is then combined with difference $\overline{V}(t)$ to obtain reconstructed input vector $\tilde{V}(t) = \overline{V}(t) + g_j$. Reconstructed vector $\tilde{V}(t)$ is later used as input to the predictor when processing macroblock $V(t+1)$ while codeword index j put into storage. For decompression, codeword indices are used to obtain corresponding codewords g_j. Codeword is combined with predictor output $\overline{V}(t)$ to obtain reconstructed macroblock $\tilde{V}(t)$. The algorithm is shown in Fig. 1.

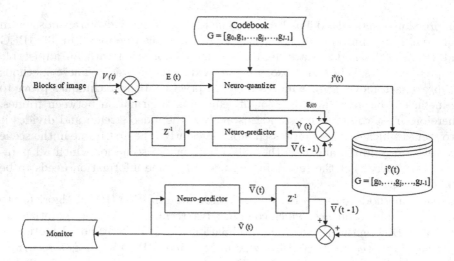

Fig. 1. PVQ compression diagram

2.2   Key Frame Detection Based on Restricted Boltzmann Machine

The key frame detection method based on Restricted Boltzmann Machine was firstly proposed by Mleczko et al. [23]. The algorithm is based on Restricted Boltzmann Machine. It is a type of two layers recurrent neural network, proposed by Smolensky [33] and further popularized by Hinton [17]. One layer, which we call visible, is connected to input values and provide output values. The second layer is called hidden and is only connected to units in visible layer. Units in visible layer are connected to all units in hidden layer and units in hidden layer are connected to all units in visible layer. There is also a bias unit to which units in visible and hidden layers are connected. The method works as follows. First, the video is divided into a stream of individual frames. The first frame is used as key frame to define input matrix for RBM network. Then we process subsequent frames using RBM and attempt to reconstruct them. We compare the error obtained from the reconstruction with assumed threshold. If the error exceeds threshold, the current frame is labeled as key frame and RBN network is trained again to recognize it. Otherwise, the network is given next frame without changing its parameters. The algorithm is shown in Fig. 2.

3   Proposed Method

In this paper we propose a video compression method which uses Predictive Vector Quantization to compress frames and Restricted Boltzmann Machine to detect key frame changes. Our approach consist of several stages. During the first steps, the algorithm divides input video into individual frames. Next it checks whether the current frame is a key frame. In this stage RBM network attempts to reconstruct the pattern of key frame based on subsequent frames delivered

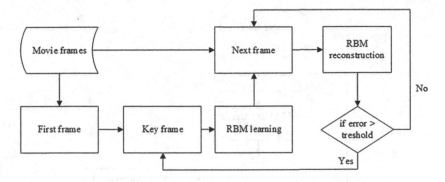

Fig. 2. RBM key frame detection diagram

to the input. This stage is crucial. As a result of the comparison of two frames (key frame and next frame) we obtain the error mapping. Next, we compare the obtained error with the assumed threshold. If the condition met is satisfied, the algorithm create a new compression parameters. These parameters are used by neural coder based on PVQ algorithm to compress all frames compatible with key frame. The diagram presented in Fig. 3 shows the proposed algorithm.

Compared to previous methods of compression also based on PVQ presented in [7,24,25], which could only compress gray-scale videos, our method has been adapted to process videos with multiple channels, including color images. Each channel is compressed independently using different compression parameters: codebooks and predictors. Before compression is performed, frame is converted to color space YC_bC_r. In this color space Y is luminance which describes brightness, C_b and C_r are chrominances which contain remaining color information. YC_bC_r is often used in image compression algorithms. Typically, luminance and chrominances don't cover full range of values from 0 to 255 like RGB values do, but in our method we used a conversion that covers full range of values. Conversion from RGB space to YC_bC_r space is presented in Eq. 1. Conversion from YC_bC_r space to RGB space is presented in Eq. 2 [20].

$$\begin{bmatrix} Y \\ C_b \\ C_r \end{bmatrix} = \begin{bmatrix} 0 \\ 128 \\ 128 \end{bmatrix} + \begin{bmatrix} 0.299 & 0.587 & 0.114 \\ -0.169 & -0.331 & 0.500 \\ 0.500 & -0.419 & -0.081 \end{bmatrix} * \begin{bmatrix} R \\ G \\ B \end{bmatrix} \tag{1}$$

$$\begin{bmatrix} R \\ G \\ B \end{bmatrix} = \begin{bmatrix} 1.000 & 0.000 & 1.400 \\ 1.000 & -0.343 & -0.711 \\ 1.000 & 1.765 & 0.000 \end{bmatrix} * \begin{bmatrix} Y \\ C_b - 128 \\ C_r - 128 \end{bmatrix} \tag{2}$$

4 Experimental Results

Algorithm stages were implemented in Java language using OpenCV library. Efficiency of our algorithm was tested using *"Akiyo"* and *"Elephants dream"*

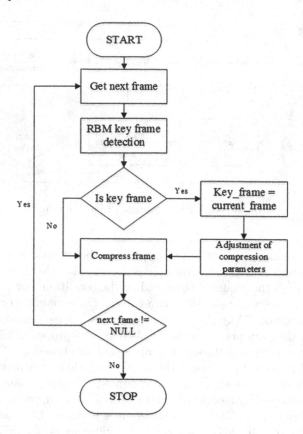

Fig. 3. Video compression diagram

sequences [35]. The first one has 300 frames of 352 × 228 resolution. The second one contains 15691 frame in full HD resolution (1920 × 1080).

We conducted a series of experiment based on two color spaces: RGB and YC_bC_r. These experiments showed that results of compression using YC_bC_r color space are of better quality than compression using standard RGB color space (Fig. 4). The average PSNR for "Akiyo" sequence after compression in RGB space is 30.82 while in YC_bC_r space PSNR is 34.70.

In our experiments we also analyzed quality of compressed images after using video filters. Figure 5 shows that median filter can decrease the amount of noticeable compression artifacts relating to macroblock processing, those making frame appear smoother. However, this does not always improve the video quality as can be seen in Fig. 6. In low resolution videos median filter can remove some details and make video appear blurry. Comparison of a video frame quality before compression, after compression, and after application of median filter is shown in Fig. 7. This figure shows that PSNR does not change significantly after using median filter in frames 19-173. This is caused by particular scene arrangement

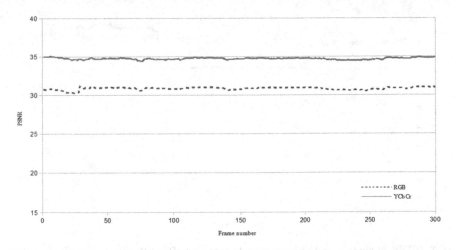

Fig. 4. PSNR after compression in RGB and YC_bC_r (Color figure online)

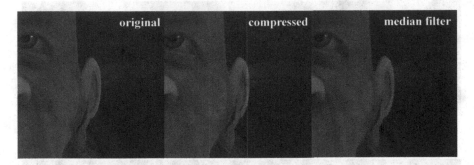

Fig. 5. Differences between images before compression, after compression and after filtering

Fig. 6. Example of frame where the median filter degrade the image quality

which contains big areas of single color and which does not change much over time (Fig. 8).

In our experiments we tested the behavior of our algorithm in two cases. In the first case we disabled key frame detection so compression

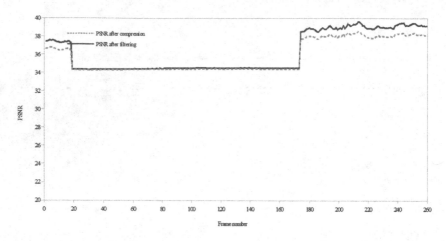

Fig. 7. PSNR of compressed video frames before and after filtering (Color figure online)

Fig. 8. First three frames of the scene with visibly lower PSNR

Fig. 9. Differences between images before compression, after compression without changing parameters, and after compression with changing parameters

parameters were determined for the first frame only and used for the rest of the video. In the second case we used our implementation of Restricted Boltzmann Machine to detect scene changes and change compression parameters accordingly. Results show that the first approach is not sufficient. Not changing compression parameters resulted in very noticeable compression artifacts which considerably degraded video quality (Fig. 9). However, changing compression parameters for each frame would increase the size of the compressed video and overall processing time. The second approach shows that changing

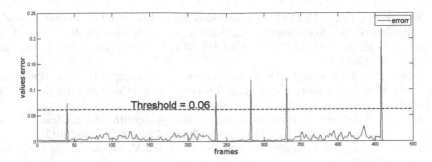

Fig. 10. RBM key frame detection diagram

parameters on frames in which scene changes were detected by RBM (Fig. 10) resulted in good video quality and, because most frames used existing parameters, smaller data storage space consumption.

5   Conclusions and Future Work

In this paper we showed that presented method can be successfully used in video compression. Key frame detection method based on Restricted Boltzmann Machine was successfully integrated with compression based on PVQ what improved its efficiency. The experimental result showed that our algorithm is a proper tool for video compression. Our future research will concentrate on further improvements to the algorithm, especially on the video quality, compression ratio and overall efficiency. We will also try to compare results of our method with that of other compression standards.

References

1. Bas, E.: The training of multiplicative neuron model based artificial neural networks with differential evolution algorithm for forecasting. J. Artif. Intell. Soft Comput. Res. **6**(1), 5–11 (2016)
2. Bilski, J., Nowicki, R., Scherer, R., Litwinski, S.: Application of signal processor TMS320C30 to neural networks realisation. In: Proceedings of the Second Conference Neural Networks and Their Applications, Czestochowa, pp. 53–59 (1996)
3. CCITT: Video codec for audio visual services at ppx 64 kbits/s (1993)
4. Chu, J.L., Krzyzak, A.: The recognition of partially occluded objects with support vector machines and convolutional neural networks and deep belief networks. J. Artif. Intell. Soft Comput. Res. **4**(1), 5–19 (2014)
5. Cierniak, R., Rutkowski, L.: Neural networks and semi-closed-loop predictive vector quantization for image compression. In: 1996 Proceedings of the International Conference on Image Processing, vol. 1, pp. 245–248, September 1996
6. Cierniak, R.: An image compression algorithm based on neural networks. In: Rutkowski, L., Siekmann, J.H., Tadeusiewicz, R., Zadeh, L.A. (eds.) ICAISC 2004. LNCS (LNAI), vol. 3070, pp. 706–711. Springer, Heidelberg (2004)

7. Cierniak, R., Knop, M.: Video compression algorithm based on neural networks. In: Rutkowski, L., Korytkowski, M., Scherer, R., Tadeusiewicz, R., Zadeh, L.A., Zurada, J.M. (eds.) ICAISC 2013, Part I. LNCS, vol. 7894, pp. 524–531. Springer, Heidelberg (2013)

8. Cierniak, R., Rutkowski, L.: On image compression by competitive neural networks and optimal linear predictors. Signal Process. Image Commun. **15**(6), 559–565 (2000)

9. Ciocca, G., Schettini, R.: Erratum to: An innovative algorithm for key frame extraction in video summarization. J. Real-Time Image Proc. **8**(2), 225 (2012)

10. Clarke, R.J.: Digital Compression of Still Images and Video. Academic Press Inc., London (1995)

11. Dourlens, S., Ramdane-Cherif, A.: Modeling & understanding environment using semantic agents. J. Artif. Intell. Soft Comput. Res. **1**(4), 301–314 (2011)

12. Duda, P., Jaworski, M., Pietruczuk, L., Scherer, R., Korytkowski, M., Gabryel, M.: On the application of fourier series density estimation for image classification based on feature description. In: Proceedings of the 8th International Conference on Knowledge, Information and Creativity Support Systems, Krakow, Poland, pp. 81–91, 7–9 November 2013

13. Galkowski, T., Pawlak, M.: Nonparametric function fitting in the presence of nonstationary noise. In: Rutkowski, L., Korytkowski, M., Scherer, R., Tadeusiewicz, R., Zadeh, L.A., Zurada, J.M. (eds.) ICAISC 2014, Part I. LNCS, vol. 8467, pp. 531–538. Springer, Heidelberg (2014)

14. Gersho, A., Gray, R.M.: Vector Quantization and Signal Compression. Kluwer Academic Publishers, Dordrecht (1991)

15. Gray, R.: Vector quantization. IEEE ASSP Mag. **1**(2), 4–29 (1984)

16. Grycuk, R., Gabryel, M., Korytkowski, M., Scherer, R., Voloshynovskiy, S.: From single image to list of objects based on edge and blob detection. In: Rutkowski, L., Korytkowski, M., Scherer, R., Tadeusiewicz, R., Zadeh, L.A., Zurada, J.M. (eds.) ICAISC 2014, Part II. LNCS, vol. 8468, pp. 605–615. Springer, Heidelberg (2014)

17. Hinton, G.: Training products of experts by minimizing contrastive divergence. Neural Comput. **14**(8), 1771–1800 (2002)

18. Hu, Y., Frank, C., Walden, J., Crawford, E., Kasturiratna, D.: Mining file repository accesses for detecting data exfiltration activities. J. Artif. Intell. Soft Comput. Res. **2**(1), 31–41 (2012)

19. Ishii, N., Torii, I., Bao, Y., Tanaka, H.: Modified reduct: nearest neighbor classification. In: Proceedings of the IEEE/ACIS 11th International Conference on Computer and Information Science (ICIS), pp. 310–315, May 2012

20. ITU-R BT.709-6: Parameter values for the HDTV standards for production and international programme exchange (2015)

21. Jaworski, M., Duda, P., Pietruczuk, L.: On fuzzy clustering of data streams with concept drift. In: Rutkowski, L., Korytkowski, M., Scherer, R., Tadeusiewicz, R., Zadeh, L.A., Zurada, J.M. (eds.) ICAISC 2012, Part II. LNCS, vol. 7268, pp. 82–91. Springer, Heidelberg (2012)

22. Jaworski, M., Pietruczuk, L., Duda, P.: On resources optimization in fuzzy clustering of data streams. In: Rutkowski, L., Korytkowski, M., Scherer, R., Tadeusiewicz, R., Zadeh, L.A., Zurada, J.M. (eds.) ICAISC 2012, Part II. LNCS, vol. 7268, pp. 92–99. Springer, Heidelberg (2012)

23. Knop, M., Kapuciski, T., Mleczko, W.K.: Video key frame detection based on the Restricted Boltzmann Machine. J. Appl. Math. Comput. Mech. **14**(3), 49–58 (2015)

24. Knop, M., Cierniak, R., Shah, N.: Video compression algorithm based on neural network structures. In: Rutkowski, L., Korytkowski, M., Scherer, R., Tadeusiewicz, R., Zadeh, L.A., Zurada, J.M. (eds.) ICAISC 2014, Part I. LNCS, vol. 8467, pp. 715–724. Springer, Heidelberg (2014)
25. Knop, M., Dobosz, P.: Neural video compression algorithm. In: Choras, R.S. (ed.) Image Processing and Communications Challenges 6. Advances in Intelligent Systems and Computing, vol. 313, pp. 59–66. Springer International Publishing, Switzerland (2015)
26. Korytkowski, M., Rutkowski, L., Scherer, R.: From ensemble of fuzzy classifiers to single fuzzy rule base classifier. In: Rutkowski, L., Tadeusiewicz, R., Zadeh, L.A., Zurada, J.M. (eds.) ICAISC 2008. LNCS (LNAI), vol. 5097, pp. 265–272. Springer, Heidelberg (2008)
27. Lee, P.M., Hsiao, T.C.: Applying LCS to affective image classification in spatial-frequency domain. J. Artif. Intell. Soft Comput. Res. 4(2), 99–123 (2014)
28. Liu, T., Kender, J.R.: Optimization algorithms for the selection of key frame sequences of variable length. In: Heyden, A., Sparr, G., Nielsen, M., Johansen, P. (eds.) ECCV 2002, Part IV. LNCS, vol. 2353, pp. 403–417. Springer, Heidelberg (2002)
29. Makinana, S., Malumedzha, T., Nelwamondo, F.V.: Quality parameter assessment on iris images. J. Artif. Intell. Soft Comput. Res. 4(1), 21–30 (2014)
30. Nowak, B.A., Nowicki, R.K., Mleczko, W.K.: A new method of improving classification accuracy of decision tree in case of incomplete samples. In: Rutkowski, L., Korytkowski, M., Scherer, R., Tadeusiewicz, R., Zadeh, L.A., Zurada, J.M. (eds.) ICAISC 2013, Part I. LNCS, vol. 7894, pp. 448–458. Springer, Heidelberg (2013)
31. Pabiasz, S., Starczewski, J.T.: Meshes vs. depth maps in face recognition systems. In: Rutkowski, L., Korytkowski, M., Scherer, R., Tadeusiewicz, R., Zadeh, L.A., Zurada, J.M. (eds.) ICAISC 2012, Part I. LNCS, vol. 7267, pp. 567–573. Springer, Heidelberg (2012)
32. Rutkowska, D., Nowicki, R.: Implication-based neuro-fuzzy architectures. Int. J. Appl. Math. Comput. Sci. 10(4), 675–701 (2000)
33. Smolensky, P.: Information processing in dynamical systems: foundations of harmony theory (1986)
34. Wozniak, M., Napoli, C., Tramontana, E., Capizzi, G., Sciuto, G., Nowicki, R., Starczewski, J.: A multiscale image compressor with RBFNN and discrete wavelet decomposition. In: 2015 International Joint Conference on Neural Networks (IJCNN), 1–7 July 2015
35. Xiph.org: Video test media. https://media.xiph.org/video/derf/. Accessed 03 Oct 2016
36. Zalasiński, M., Cpałka, K.: Novel algorithm for the on-line signature verification. In: Rutkowski, L., Korytkowski, M., Scherer, R., Tadeusiewicz, R., Zadeh, L.A., Zurada, J.M. (eds.) ICAISC 2012, Part II. LNCS, vol. 7268, pp. 362–367. Springer, Heidelberg (2012)
37. Zhao, W., Lun, R., Espy, D.D., Reinthal, M.A.: Realtime motion assessment for rehabilitation exercises: integration of kinematic modeling with fuzzy inference. J. Artif. Intell. Soft Comput. Res. 4(4), 267–285 (2014)

A Novel Convolutional Neural Network with Glial Cells

Marcin Korytkowski[✉]

Institute of Computational Intelligence, Częstochowa University of Technology,
al. Armii Krajowej 36, 42-200 Częstochowa, Poland
marcin.korytkowski@iisi.pcz.pl
http://iisi.pcz.pl

Abstract. The research presented in the paper was inspired by the work
of R. Douglas Fields. It transpired that not only neural structures in
the brain play huge role in the process of understanding but also glial
cells, which have so far been treated as passive cells with the task of
protecting neuronal cells. This was a motivation to the proposed idea
that currently extremely popular convolutional neural networks should
be equipped with some elements corresponding to glial cells. In this work
we present a modification of convolutional structures, which consist in
adding additional adjustable parameters. The parameters control convolutional filter outputs. This approach allowed us to improve the quality
of classification. In addition, the newly proposed structure is easier to
interpret by indicating which filters are specific to a particular class of
visual objects.

Keywords: Convolutional neural networks · Image classification ·
Computer vision · Glial cells

1 Introduction

Content-based image retrieval and image classification allowed to depart from
searching images by keywords and meta tags. For a long time these tasks were
realized by hand-crafted visual features and then computing similarity between
them [1,9,17–20,22,25,26]. Visual features can based on color representation
[14,21,30], textures [5,12,34], shape [16,37], edge detectors [38] or local invariant
features [3,27,29,32]. Feature descriptors have to be matched or classified. A
popular technique is bag of words [8] used in conjunction with some method
for feature detection and, in case of classification, with a classifier, e.g. support
vector machines [35].

Although artificial neural networks are a popular engineering tool [6,31],
there are still ongoing research [2] as new trends and ideas constantly emerge.
Their history dates back to 1943, when McCulloch and Pitts developed perceptron [28], i.e. the first model of a single neuron. Since then, almost continuous development takes place. It can be observed especially in recent years

© Springer International Publishing Switzerland 2016
L. Rutkowski et al. (Eds.): ICAISC 2016, Part II, LNAI 9693, pp. 670–679, 2016.
DOI: 10.1007/978-3-319-39384-1_59

with the development of convolutional neural networks (CNN) [23,33] used most often to tasks related to image and sound analysis. Now CNNs are established tool in content-based image classification, object detection and proposal and other tasks. Neural networks in terms of the architecture correspond to neuronal cells located in the human brain. Until now it was thought that precisely those cells play a major role in the mental processes, diminishing the importance of other bodies, which represent over 80 % of the brain volume — glial cells. In recent years, neuroscience research have produced an important discovery concerning the role of these cells, showing among other things that they are able to control neural cells [10,11]. Glial cells accompany neurons in processing information as they receive coded signals from synapses and produce modulatory responses. Their long-range signalling and regulated transmitter release is started to be regarded as more and more important being an inseparable part of the brain circuitry [4]. Watershed and at the same time extremely interesting fact is also an operation by a team of Polish scientists of the damaged spinal cord using glial cells. After this operation, the patient regained the ability to walk independently [36].

In the paper we propose a new convolutional neural network structure, which is inspired by glail cells. The proposed network is based on the OverFeat network [33] and we added a structure of glial cells. We trained the novel parameters on the ImageNet dataset. The main contribution and novelty of the paper is as follows:

- We present a novel CNN structure with added glial cell-like parameters.
- We achieved a significant improvement in the image classification quality.
- After learning process, the proposed glial cells allow to shed some light on knowledge regarding the interpretation of the information stored in the network.

The paper is organized as follows. Section 2 describes the proposed novel CNN architecture. Section 3 provides simulation results on the ImageNet 2012 [7] dataset.

2   Convolutional Neural Networks with Glial Cells

Convolutional Neural Networks (CNN) are derived from the multilayer perceptron to mimic a natural visual system. The visual cortex comprises elaborate structure of cells, which are sensitive to small sub-regions of the visual field, called a receptive field [15]. These cells cover the entire image and act as local filters over the image, which reflect local image variations. The CNNs structure expresses two-dimensional image space. The filters are locally connected and pooled in a consecutive layer. CNNs have smaller numbers of adjustable parameters than corresponding fully-connected neural networks. Commonly used CNNs mimic more or less cells in the visual cortex and in the paper we expand this structure by incorporating glial cells. The proposed structure is based on the OverFeat CNN [33]. This structure was chosen because its authors provided a

set of learned weights for the ImageNet. This way we can show how our modification affects positively the quality of the CNN operation. The structure with
added elements of glial cells is presented in Fig. 1. The structure contains five
convolutional layers with pooling layers between them. The convolutional layers
are the most important parts of CNNs and consist of a set of learnable filters
(kernels), which have a small receptive field. During the forward pass, each filter
is convolved with a part of the input volume, producing the dot product between
filter parameters and input pixels, computing a 2-dimensional activation map of
that filter. As a result, the network learns filters that activate when they see
some specific type of feature at some spatial position in the input. The activation maps for all filters form the full output of the convolution layer. Every
element of the output can be interpreted as an output of a neuron that looks
at a small region in the input image and shares parameters with neurons in
the same activation map. Max-pooling partitions the input image into a set of
non-overlapping rectangles and, for each such sub-region, outputs the maximum
value.

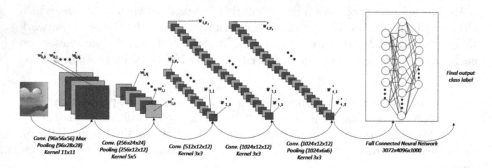

Fig. 1. The proposed convolutional network with glial cells.

Max-pooling is useful in vision for two reasons:

1. It reduces computation for upper layers by eliminating non-maximal values.
2. It provides a form of translation invariance.

The output from a CNN is a fully-connected network. In our case it is three-
layer network, which has 3071, 4096 and 1000 neurons in consecutive layers. All
neurons in convolutional and fully-connected layers use Relu activation function,
i.e. $f(x) = \max(0, x)$.

As we can observe in Fig. 1, we added parameters w^* to the standard Over-
Feat network. They should be interpreted as glial cells, which are responsible
for assessing the importance of a given feature map for a given visual class. The
glial cell is realized as a connection of an adjustable parameter (weight) and the
sigmoid function and is presented in Fig. 2. In Fig. 3 we present a very popular
in the literature schema, showing the appearance of the filters in each layer.
The filters allows interpreting the content in a successive network layers. This

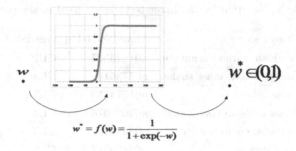

$$w^* = f(w) = \frac{1}{1 + \exp(-w)}$$

Fig. 2. Single glial cell.

structure was first used for face recognition task. The first layer is responsible for edge detection, second one stores "object parts" and the third one "knows" objects.

The use of glial cells allows us to identify these feature maps (kernel filters) which are characteristic for a class of objects. Having this knowledge we can simplify (prune) convolutional neural networks structures.

3   Experiments

The OverFeat structure was trained by Sermanet et al. [33] using images from the ImageNet 2012 [7] dataset. They used 1.2 million images from 1000 classes and each image was downsampled so that the smallest dimension is 256 pixels. They extracted then 5 random crops (and their horizontal flips) of size 221×221 pixels and presented these to the network in mini-batches of size 128. The weights in the network were initialized randomly with $(\mu, \sigma) = (0.1 \times 10^{-2})$ and then updated by stochastic gradient descent, accompanied by momentum term of 0.6 and an ℓ_2 weight decay of (0.1×10^{-5}). The learning rate was initially (5×10^{-2}) and was

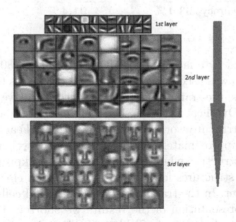

Fig. 3. Feature representation in convolutional neural network [24].

Table 1. Notation for the ImageNet classes used in the paper.

Class name	ImageNet label	Our label
Goldfish, carassius auratus	n01443537	CL1
Garter snake, grass snake	n01735189	CL2
Tarantula	n01774750	CL3
Black-and-tan coonhound	n02089078	CL4
Colobus, colobus monkey	n02488702	CL5
Digital clock	n03196217	CL6
Face powder	n03314780	CL7
Garbage truck, dustcart	n03417042	CL8
Grand piano, grand	n03452741	CL9
Jean, blue jean, denim	n03594734	CL10

Table 2. Classification results of ten ImageNet classes (CL1–CL10) for the original OverFeat and for the novel network proposed in the paper.

Class name	Original OverFeat	OverFeat with glial cells
CL1	45/50	49/50
CL2	40/50	48/50
CL3	38/50	49/50
CL4	19/50	41/50
CL5	37/50	49/50
CL6	28/50	35/50
CL7	21/50	46/50
CL8	36/50	49/50
CL9	26/50	50/50
CL10	27/50	41/50
Overall accuracy	**63.4 %**	**91.4 %**

successively decreased by a factor of 0.5 after (30,50,60,70,80) epochs. DropOut [13] with a rate of 0.5 was used on the fully connected layers (6th and 7th) in the classifier. We used the pre-trained OverFeat structure and we added glial cells to the original trained OverFeat network. The weights w were initially set to value 4, so that the new structure works as the original OverFeat as the value of the sigmoid function is approximately 1. The values of all weights in filters and in the fully-connected structure where fixed. Using the backpropagation algorithm we have trained ten structures for ten randomly chosen classes of objects from the VOC 2010 dataset. In the training process only glial cells where modified.

For more clear presentation of the results we shortened original ImageNet class names and presented them in Table 1. Table 2 shows the results of image

Table 3. Values of the five highest and the five lowest weight values for feature maps and visual classes CL1–CL10.

	Max1	Max2	Max3	Max4	Max5	Min5	Min4	Min3	Min2	Min1
CL1	**916**	694	2081	1982	1743	2631	3003	2198	1117	2119
	9.82	9.27	8.59	8.45	8.42	−33.02	−34.28	−38.46	−50.25	−51.05
CL2	**1025**	994	1192	441	2235	2805	2660	258	2344	1432
	19.32	11.97	11.09	10.73	9.85	−17.70	−18.36	−19.06	−29.09	−37.02
CL3	**1806**	417	1105	1760	1136	2918	2801	1834	2388	1960
	14.82	14.26	11.84	11.32	9.97	−31.82	−33.06	−33.54	−37.85	−38.90
CL4	**403**	2844	511	1498	1613	2346	2076	2217	2663	2776
	9.84	9.59	9.54	9.54	9.39	−22.01	−23.78	−28.85	−33.41	−33.84
CL5	**2413**	3060	2354	61	2558	1127	1140	1379	2450	1154
	19.11	10.67	10.25	10.19	9.98	−55.13	−62.19	−74.49	−80.39	−151.95
CL6	**2062**	646	2606	2043	1208	1639	1335	1236	1061	2844
	11.70	10.52	10.40	10.06	9.69	−41.71	−42.26	−44.53	−54.88	−121.56
CL7	**1872**	131	1741	65	1384	419	282	1071	2119	2670
	16.42	13.15	11.35	10.64	10.10	−37.24	−37.93	−53.97	−62.34	−73.36
CL8	**1841**	1726	1912	274	2856	2122	176	2773	1965	532
	10.34	10.05	10.03	9.98	9.93	−17.12	−22.18	−25.49	−25.63	−30.87
CL9	**1518**	2893	375	511	2782	3013	2521	1832	2381	282
	8.98	8.89	8.87	8.86	8.73	−24.27	−25.24	−26.81	−27.11	−87.14
CL10	**1670**	2528	2223	69	1068	232	484	2066	2090	1370
	12.39	10.36	10.30	9.19	9.05	−25.19	−42.94	−46.48	−51.28	−51.87

classification for 50 images for each class for the original OverFeat CNN (the second column) and for the proposed CNN modification with glial cells (the third column). Ten rows contain number of properly classified images and the last row contains overall percentage classification results. We present in Tables 3 and 4 weight values for each class to show that the use of glial cells could be interpreted as a relationship between feature maps and classes. In other words, which feature maps are characteristic for given visual classes. For this purpose, for each class we chose five feature maps in the fifth (last) network convolutional layer and presented the highest five weights and the smallest five weights. As can be seen, each of the learned class has one feature map, which is the most characteristic for this class, i.e. its value is significantly greater than the other weights. Table 5 contains feature map numbers which weights were changed the most. It should be noted that this change is significantly larger for the fifth layer. This means that the greatest influence on the decision regarding class assignment takes place precisely in this layer. Of course, we cannot remove the previous convolutional layers of the network, but there is a possibility to simplify the network structure by removing these feature maps and these neurons in the fully-connected layers for which their glial cells have values close to zero. Of course, after this process we have to re-train the whole structure.

Table 4. Values of weights for each class CL1–CL10 for multi kernels (MK).

MK	**CL**	CL1	CL2	CL3	CL4	CL5	CL6	CL7	CL8	CL9	CL10
916	CL1	**9.82**	−6.71	5.56	−6.279	3.38	−5.09	3.21	1.30	−4.73	−4.75
1025	CL2	−4.81	**19.32**	−1.81	4	2.48	−6.82	1.66	−7.05	−5.76	−1.71
1806	CL3	4	−4.47	**14.82**	−5.46	−3.27	−5.81	−5.65	−2.59	−5.32	−5.83
403	CL4	3.57	5.59	6.98	**9.84**	−4.35	4.12	−4.72	5.07	4.88	−4.58
2413	CL5	3.54	−6.18	−4.26	−6.74	**19.11**	3.18	1.50	−7.69	3.79	3.98
2062	CL6	2.57	−5.70	−4.33	−3.41	−5.94	**11.70**	−3.75	−6.89	−2.06	−0.69
1872	CL7	5.49	−5.66	−2.70	−5.72	−5.70	−5.41	**16.42**	−6.68	−3.21	−7.42
1841	CL8	−4.67	7.45	4.57	6.87	−4.21	−6.44	4.67	**10.34**	4.20	3.90
1518	CL9	5.41	8.75	−4.12	3.05	−14.97	7.09	−4.54	1.91	**8.98**	−2.97
1670	CL10	4	−4.69	5.22	−6.28	−5.82	−3.86	7.41	2.49	−0.22	**12.39**

Table 5. The largest inter-class differences between weight values for corresponding feature maps (FM) in each layer.

Layer No.	Largest difference	FM No.
1	0.0128	70
2	0.0180	230
3	0.0070	256
4	0.0108	313
5	0.2038	266

4 Conclusion

The paper presents a new convolutional neural network structure, which is inspired by the latest discoveries in neuroscience in the construction and operation of the human brain. The proposed network is based on the OverFeat network and we transformed it into a kind of a glial network. We trained the network on the ImageNet dataset. The results of the experiments showed the most important advantage of the new network concept, i.e. by learning only the added network parameters (glial cells) we achieved a significant improvement in the image classification quality. The results of the simulations showed also that the use of glial cells can provide a significant knowledge regarding the interpretation of the information stored in the network.

Acknowledgements. This work was supported by the Polish National Science Centre (NCN) within project number DEC-2011/01/D/ST6/06957.

References

1. Akusok, A., Miche, Y., Karhunen, J., Bjork, K.M., Nian, R., Lendasse, A.: Arbitrary category classification of websites based on image content. IEEE Comput. Intell. Mag. **10**(2), 30–41 (2015)
2. Bas, E.: The training of multiplicative neuron model based artificial neural networks with differential evolution algorithm for forecasting. J. Artif. Intell. Soft Comput. Res. **6**(1), 5–11 (2016)
3. Bay, H., Ess, A., Tuytelaars, T., van Gool, L.: Speeded-up robust features (surf). Comput. Vis. Image Underst. **110**(3), 346–359 (2008)
4. Bezzi, P., Volterra, A.: A neuronglia signalling network in the active brain. Curr. Opin. Neurobiol. **11**(3), 387–394 (2001)
5. Chang, T., Kuo, C.C.: Texture analysis and classification with tree-structured wavelet transform. IEEE Trans. Image Process. **2**(4), 429–441 (1993)
6. Chu, J.L., Krzyzak, A.: The recognition of partially occluded objects with support vector machines and convolutional neural networks and deep belief networks. J. Artif. Intell. Soft Comput. Res. **4**(1), 5–19 (2014)
7. Deng, J., Dong, W., Socher, R., Li, L.J., Li, K., Fei-Fei, L.: Imagenet: a large-scale hierarchical image database. In: IEEE Conference on Computer Vision and Pattern Recognition, CVPR 2009, pp. 248–255. IEEE (2009)
8. Drozda, P., Grecki, P., Sopyla, K., Artiemjew, P.: Visual words sequence alignment for image classification. In: ICCI*CC, pp. 397–402. IEEE (2013)
9. Drozda, P., Sopyła, K., Górecki, P.: Online crowdsource system supporting ground truth datasets creation. In: Rutkowski, L., Korytkowski, M., Scherer, R., Tadeusiewicz, R., Zadeh, L.A., Zurada, J.M. (eds.) ICAISC 2013, Part I. LNCS, vol. 7894, pp. 532–539. Springer, Heidelberg (2013)
10. Fields, R.D.: The Other Brain: From Dementia to Schizophrenia, How New Discoveries About the Brain are Revolutionizing Medicine and Science. Simon and Schuster, New York (2009)
11. Fields, R.D.: Neuroscience: map the other brain. Nature **501**(7465), 25–27 (2013)
12. Francos, J., Meiri, A., Porat, B.: A unified texture model based on a 2-D Wold-like decomposition. IEEE Trans. Sig. Process. **41**(8), 2665–2678 (1993)
13. Hinton, G.E., Srivastava, N., Krizhevsky, A., Sutskever, I., Salakhutdinov, R.R.: Improving neural networks by preventing co-adaptation of feature detectors (2012). arXiv preprint arXiv:1207.0580
14. Huang, J., Kumar, S., Mitra, M., Zhu, W.J., Zabih, R.: Image indexing using color correlograms. In: 1997 IEEE Computer Society Conference on Computer Vision and Pattern Recognition, pp. 762–768, June 1997
15. Hubel, D.H., Wiesel, T.N.: Receptive fields and functional architecture of monkey striate cortex. J. Physiol. **195**(1), 215–243 (1968)
16. Jagadish, H.V.: A retrieval technique for similar shapes. SIGMOD Rec. **20**(2), 208–217 (1991)
17. Jégou, H., Douze, M., Schmid, C., Pérez, P.: Aggregating local descriptors into a compact image representation. In: 2010 IEEE Conference on Computer Vision and Pattern Recognition (CVPR), pp. 3304–3311. IEEE (2010)
18. Jégou, H., Perronnin, F., Douze, M., Sanchez, J., Perez, P., Schmid, C.: Aggregating local image descriptors into compact codes. IEEE Trans. Pattern Anal. Mach. Intell. **34**(9), 1704–1716 (2012)
19. Kanimozhi, T., Latha, K.: An integrated approach to region based image retrieval using firefly algorithm and support vector machine. Neurocomputing **151**, 1099–1111 (2015). Part 3(0)

20. Karakasis, E., Amanatiadis, A., Gasteratos, A., Chatzichristofis, S.: Image moment invariants as local features for content based image retrieval using the bag-of-visual-words model. Pattern Recogn. Lett. **55**, 22–27 (2015)
21. Kiranyaz, S., Birinci, M., Gabbouj, M.: Perceptual color descriptor based on spatial distribution: a top-down approach. Image Vis. Comput. **28**(8), 1309–1326 (2010)
22. Korytkowski, M., Rutkowski, L., Scherer, R.: Fast image classification by boosting fuzzy classifiers. Inf. Sci. **327**, 175–182 (2016)
23. Le Cun, B.B., Denker, J.S., Henderson, D., Howard, R.E., Hubbard, W., Jackel, L.D.: Handwritten digit recognition with a back-propagation network. In: Advances in Neural Information Processing Systems. Morgan Kaufman (1990)
24. Lee, H., Grosse, R., Ranganath, R., Ng, A.Y.: Convolutional deep belief networks for scalable unsupervised learning of hierarchical representations. In: Proceedings of the 26th Annual International Conference on Machine Learning, pp. 609–616. ACM (2009)
25. Lin, C.H., Chen, H.Y., Wu, Y.S.: Study of image retrieval and classification based on adaptive features using genetic algorithm feature selection. Expert Syst. Appl. **41**(15), 6611–6621 (2014)
26. Liu, G.H., Yang, J.Y.: Content-based image retrieval using color difference histogram. Pattern Recogn. **46**(1), 188–198 (2013)
27. Lowe, D.G.: Distinctive image features from scale-invariant keypoints. Int. J. Comput. Vis. **60**(2), 91–110 (2004)
28. McCulloch, W.S., Pitts, W.: A logical calculus of the ideas immanent in nervous activity. Bull. Math. Biophys. **5**(4), 115–133 (1943)
29. Mikolajczyk, K., Schmid, C.: Scale and affine invariant interest point detectors. Int. J. Comput. Vis. **60**(1), 63–86 (2004)
30. Pass, G., Zabih, R.: Histogram refinement for content-based image retrieval. In: Proceedings of the 3rd IEEE Workshop on Applications of Computer Vision, WACV 1996, pp. 96–102, December 1996
31. Patgiri, C., Sarma, M., Sarma, K.K.: A class of neuro-computational methods for assamese fricative classification. J. Artif. Intell. Soft Comput. Res. **5**(1), 59–70 (2015)
32. Rublee, E., Rabaud, V., Konolige, K., Bradski, G.: ORB: an efficient alternative to sift or surf. In: 2011 IEEE International Conference on Computer Vision (ICCV), pp. 2564–2571, November 2011
33. Sermanet, P., Eigen, D., Zhang, X., Mathieu, M., Fergus, R., LeCun, Y.: Overfeat: integrated recognition, localization and detection using convolutional networks. In: International Conference on Learning Representations (ICLR 2014), p. 16. CBLS (2013)
34. Śmietański, J., Tadeusiewicz, R., Łuczyńska, E.: Texture analysis in perfusion images of prostate cancera case study. Int. J. Appl. Math. Comput. Sci. **20**(1), 149–156 (2010)
35. Sopyła, K., Drozda, P., Górecki, P.: SVM with CUDA accelerated kernels for big sparse problems. In: Rutkowski, L., Korytkowski, M., Scherer, R., Tadeusiewicz, R., Zadeh, L.A., Zurada, J.M. (eds.) ICAISC 2012, Part I. LNCS, vol. 7267, pp. 439–447. Springer, Heidelberg (2012)
36. Tabakow, P., Raisman, G., Fortuna, W., Czyz, M., Huber, J., Li, D., Szewczyk, P., Okurowski, S., Miedzybrodzki, R., Czapiga, B., et al.: Functional regeneration of supraspinal connections in a patient with transected spinal cord following transplantation of bulbar olfactory ensheathing cells with peripheral nerve bridging. Cell Transplant. **23**(12), 1631–1655 (2014)

37. Veltkamp, R.C., Hagedoorn, M.: State of the art in shape matching. In: Lew, M.S. (ed.) Principles of Visual Information Retrieval, pp. 87–119. Springer, London (2001)
38. Zitnick, C.L., Dollár, P.: Edge boxes: locating object proposals from edges. In: Fleet, D., Pajdla, T., Schiele, B., Tuytelaars, T. (eds.) ECCV 2014, Part V. LNCS, vol. 8693, pp. 391–405. Springer, Heidelberg (2014)

Examination of the Deep Neural Networks in Classification of Distorted Signals

Michał Koziarski[1](✉) and Bogusław Cyganek[2]

[1] Wrocław University of Technology, Wrocław, Poland
michalkoziarski@gmail.com
[2] AGH University of Science and Technology, Kraków, Poland

Abstract. Classification of distorted patterns poses real problem for majority of classifiers. In this paper we analyse robustness of deep neural network in classification of such patterns. Using specific convolutional network architecture, an impact of different types of noise on classification accuracy is evaluated. For highly distorted patterns to improve accuracy we propose a preprocessing method of input patterns. Finally, an influence of different types of noise on classification accuracy is also analysed.

Keywords: Noise · Image recognition · Convolutional neural networks

1 Introduction

Noise and distortions are ubiquitous in real data acquisition systems. Classification of noisy and distorted patterns still poses a real problem for majority of classifiers. The problem is especially severe if level and type of noise and distortions is unknown - such situations are frequently encountered in practice. Moreover, different types of noise and distortions may affect classification accuracy in different ways and there is no single metric of evaluation of robustness of a classifier in respect to these phenomena.

In this paper we try to evaluate the accuracy of convolutional neural network (CNN) [3] in classification task with images under different noise conditions. CNNs achieve state-of-the-art results in many image recognition [5,6,8,9] and denoising [12,13] tasks. We measure how much accuracy is lost when examined images are distorted and, in result, by how much can it be improved if successful denoising is applied. We also try to relate classifier's performance to different types of distortion metrics. Finally, a method of data preprocessing is proposed to improve CNN's classification in noisy environments.

The rest of the paper is organized as follows. Sections 2 and 3 provide a brief overview of different types of noise and metrics used to measure distortion in images. Section 4 describes conducted experiments. Section 5 presents results obtained during the experiment. Finally, Sect. 6 presents our conclusions.

© Springer International Publishing Switzerland 2016
L. Rutkowski et al. (Eds.): ICAISC 2016, Part II, LNAI 9693, pp. 680–688, 2016.
DOI: 10.1007/978-3-319-39384-1_60

2   Types of Noise

Noise is an additional, usually unwanted, component that interferes with a pure signal [2]. It occurs in images for many reasons related to various physical phenomena. In this section we provide a brief overview of types of noise encountered in image acquisition.

2.1   Gaussian Noise

Probably the most frequently occurring noise is Gaussian noise [1]. It is commonly used to model thermal distortions. Probability density $p(x)$ of Gaussian noise with mean μ and variance σ^2 is defined as

$$p(x) = \frac{1}{\sigma\sqrt{2\pi}}e^{-\frac{(x-\mu)^2}{2\sigma^2}}, \tag{1}$$

for $-\infty < x < \infty$.

2.2   Salt-and-Pepper Noise

Salt-and-pepper noise model is used when only a small amount of pixels was distorted, however, the information they carry is lost completely. Example of such situation is transmitting images over a noisy channel.

Formally, we can describe probabilities of altering particular pixel $q(x, y)$ in original image $f(x, y)$ as:

$$\Pr(q = f) = 1 - \alpha, \tag{2}$$

$$\Pr(q = max) = \frac{\alpha}{2}, \tag{3}$$

$$\Pr(q = min) = \frac{\alpha}{2}, \tag{4}$$

where max and min are maximum and minimum values pixel can obtain, respectively, and α is probability of alteration.

2.3   Quantization Noise

Quantization noise is a result of converting continuous signal into a digital representation and can be observed due to inherent inaccuracy of storing floating-point numbers in computer memory. It is usually modelled as a noise with uniform distribution, scaled to the desired range.

2.4   Photon Counting Noise

Photon counting noise, or Poisson noise, is a result of using image acquisition techniques based on counting photons. It is being modelled as a discrete random variable with Poisson distribution:

$$\Pr(X = k) = \frac{\lambda^k e^{-\lambda}}{k!}, \tag{5}$$

where X denotes the number of photons counted, k is the number of photons actually counted during the measurement, $k = 0, 1, 2, 3 \ldots$, and $\lambda > 0$ is a parameter.

3 Measures of Distortion

Having an objective measure of distortion level in images is important in assessing impact of noise on classification accuracy. In this section we present some of the most common metrics.

3.1 Mean Squared Error

Simplest and most frequently used metric is mean squared error (MSE). Let x be the original image and y distorted image. We define MSE as:

$$\mathrm{MSE}(x, y) = \frac{1}{n} \sum_{i=1}^{n} (x_i - y_i)^2, \tag{6}$$

where x_i and y_i are particular pixels, and n denotes their number.

3.2 Peak Signal-to-Noise Ratio

Another popular metric for measuring distortion level is peak signal-to-noise ratio (PSNR), measured in decibels. It takes into account the maximum value achievable by the pixels, $\mathrm{MAX}(x, y)$. PSNR is defined as:

$$\mathrm{PSNR}(x, y) = 10 \cdot \log_{10} \left(\frac{\mathrm{MAX}^2(x, y)}{\mathrm{MSE}(x, y)} \right). \tag{7}$$

3.3 Structural Similarity

Both MSE and PSNR are easy to implement and have relatively low cost of computation. Neither of them, however, matches well to perceived visual quality [14]. To take into account known characteristics of human visual system another metric was proposed: structural similarity (SSIM).

Let $c_i = (k_i \, \mathrm{MAX}(x, y))^2$ and k_i be a small constant. We can then define SSIM as:

$$\mathrm{SSIM}(x, y) = \frac{(2\mu_x \mu_y + c_1)(2\sigma_{xy} + c_2)}{(\mu_x^2 + \mu_y^2 + c_1)(\sigma_x^2 + \sigma_y^2 + c_2)}. \tag{8}$$

4   Experimental Setup

In this section we present training procedure for our CNN, specifically dataset, image preprocessing and network's architecture. Code used for conducting experiment was implemented using TensorFlow [15], software library for numerical computation.

During our experiments we used *The German Traffic Sign Recognition Benchmark* [4]. GTSRB is dataset consisting of over 50,000 images of traffic signs, each assigned to one of 43 classes. GTSRB was tested in wide range of publications [4–7], providing a good benchmark for further examination (Fig. 1).

GTSRB dataset consists of images that were extracted from camera recording and have different dimensionality, ranging from 15×15 to 250×250 pixels. Video was recorded while driving during daytime in March, October and November. As a result of data acquisition process, visual artifacts are present in images, such as low resolution, low contrast, motion blur and reflections.

Before experiment all images were reshaped to size 24×24 pixels. Additionally, their values were normalized to range from 0 to 1.

Architecture of network used during experiments was presented in Table 1. After every convolutional layer ReLU activation function was used. Additionally, dropout with probability $p = 0.5$ was applied in fully connected layer during training.

Fig. 1. Sample images from GTSRB.

CNN was trained using stochastic gradient descent with batch size of 128. Small learning rate of 0.000001 was used, together with momentum equal to 0.9. Training lasted 200 epochs and after it was over network was evaluated on test set.

5   Results

During experiments we tested performance of proposed CNN architecture, comparing it with available reported results. After that we evaluated influence of different types of artificial noise on correct classification rate (CCR). Finally, we measured correlation between different distortion metrics with classifiers performance.

Table 1. Architecture of CNN used during experiments.

Layer	Type	Size
0	Input	$24 \times 24 \times 3$
1	Convolutional	$3 \times 3 \times 32$
2	Convolutional	$3 \times 3 \times 32$
3	Max pooling	2×2
4	Convolutional	$3 \times 3 \times 64$
5	Convolutional	$3 \times 3 \times 64$
6	Max pooling	2×2
7	Convolutional	$5 \times 5 \times 128$
8	Convolutional	$5 \times 5 \times 128$
9	Max pooling	2×2
10	Fully connected	1024
11	Softmax	43

5.1 CCR for Clean Data

Experiments began with evaluating performance of CNN trained and tested on clean data. Resulting classification accuracy was presented in Table 2. Accuracy was comparable to the top methods, with only the best one, committee of CNNs, taking significant lead.

It should be noted, however, that since achieving the best accuracy possible on clean dataset was not the goal of this publication, used CNN was fairly shallow by current standards. Adding additional layers would likely further improve the classification accuracy.

Table 2. Methods that achieved best classification accuracy on GTSRB as reported in [4], with addition of CNN trained in this publication.

Accuracy (%)	Method	Publication
99.46	Committee of CNNs	[5]
99.22	Human (best individual)	[4]
98.84	Human (average)	[4]
98.31	Multi-scale CNN	[6]
98.12	**CNN**	**This publication**
96.14	Random forests	[7]

5.2   CCR for Data with Applied Distortions

After confirming that proposed CNN architecture works properly, impact of applying different types of artificial distortions on classification accuracy was tested. Evaluation was performed in two variants:

– with distortions applied only to the test, with training set unchanged,
– and with both training and test sets distorted.

In both cases four types of artificial noise were tested: Gaussian, salt-and-pepper, quantization and photon counting. Results of this stage of experiment were presented in Fig. 2.

Depending on the type of distortion applied significant drop in classification accuracy can be observed. This effect was partially mitigated in every case by training classifier using distorted data. The amount of error reduced depends on the type of noise. Significant gain in CCR was observed especially when dealing with salt-and-pepper noise.

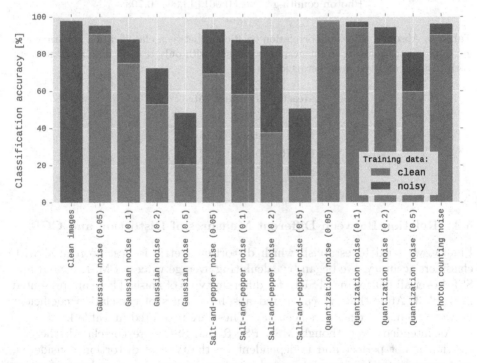

Fig. 2. Classification accuracy depending on type of artificial distortion applied, in two cases: with only test set distorted and with both training and test sets distorted. If applies, values of noise parameters where specified in parentheses, namely: standard deviation for Gaussian noise, probability of flipping pixel for salt-and-pepper noise and range of distortion for quantization noise.

Table 3. Average values of distortion metrics for different types of artificial noise.

Type of noise	MSE	PSNR	SSIM
Gaussian (0.05)	0.002	26.32	0.894
Gaussian (0.1)	0.009	20.69	0.757
Gaussian (0.2)	0.029	15.35	0.550
Gaussian (0.5)	0.119	9.25	0.248
Salt-and-pepper (0.05)	0.018	17.58	0.652
Salt-and-pepper (0.1)	0.035	14.56	0.528
Salt-and-pepper (0.2)	0.071	11.53	0.382
Salt-and-pepper (0.5)	0.177	7.54	0.166
Quantization (0.05)	0.001	31.08	0.978
Quantization (0.1)	0.003	25.10	0.928
Quantization (0.2)	0.012	19.15	0.811
Quantization (0.5)	0.074	11.44	0.524
Photon counting	0.061	13.26	0.708

Table 4. Absolute values of correlation coefficient between classification accuracy and measured distortion rate in images, in two cases: with only test set distorted and with both training and test sets distorted.

Measure	Training data	
	Clean	Distorted
MSE	0.86	0.86
PSNR	0.83	0.72
SSIM	0.98	0.87

5.3   Relation Between Different Measures of Distortion and CCR

Finally, we tried to establish which distortion metric is best correlated with classifiers accuracy. We began by calculating average values of MSE, PSNR and SSIM over all images in GTSRB, for different types of noise. These are presented in Table 3. After that we calculated absolute values of correlation coefficient between them and classifiers accuracy. These are presented in Table 4.

As intended, even though MSE/PSNR and SSIM are correlated, the correlation is not perfect and is dependent on the type of distortion considered. Furthermore, SSIM carries the most information about expected classification accuracy. We hypothesize that it might be a result of both SSIM and CNN being based on the same principles of human perception.

As a result, given the choice of specific method of denoising applied to the images during preprocessing before classification, the ones resulting in highest SSIM might yield lower classification error.

6   Conclusions

During the experiments we established that chosen CNN architecture works correctly for GTSRB data set. We later used it to test CNN's resilience to different types of synthetic noise. Depending on the type and strength of the distortion we measured significant drop in classification accuracy. We also observed that applying noise with same parameters to the training data can partially remedy this problem, with rate of improvement dependent on type of noise considered.

We also tested correlation between classifier's accuracy and distortion level measured by different metrics. Our results suggest that some metrics, especially SSIM, are more related to classification accuracy.

Overall, measured drop in classification accuracy with noise applied was significant, and applying similar noise to training data did not result in its full recovery. Because of that applying denoising to distorted images may potentially lead to noticeable performance gain. This is left for further research.

Acknowledgement. This work was supported by the Polish National Science Centre under the grant no. DEC-2014/15/B/ST6/00609.

References

1. Bovik, A.C.: Handbook of Image and Video Processing. Academic Press, Cambridge (2010)
2. Cyganek, B., Siebert, J.P.: An Introduction to 3D Computer Vision Techniques and Algorithms. Wiley, Hoboken (2011)
3. Bengio, Y., Goodfellow, I.J., Courville, A.: Deep Learning. MIT Press, Cambridge (2016)
4. Stallkamp, J., Schlipsing, M., Salmen, J., Igel, C.: Man vs. computer: benchmarking machine learning algorithms for traffic sign recognition. Neural Netw. **32**, 323–332 (2012)
5. Cireşan, D., Meier, U., Masci, J., Schmidhuber, J.: Multi-column deep neural network for traffic sign classification. Neural Netw. **32**, 333–338 (2012)
6. Sermanet, P., LeCun, Y.: Traffic sign recognition with multi-scale convolutional networks. In: The 2011 International Joint Conference on Neural Networks, pp. 2809–2813 (2011)
7. Zaklouta, F., Stanciulescu, B., Hamdoun, O.: Traffic sign classification using K-d trees and random forests. In: The 2011 International Joint Conference on Neural Networks, pp. 2151–2155 (2011)
8. Krizhevsky, A., Sutskever, I., Hinton, G.E.: Imagenet classification with deep convolutional neural networks. In: Advances in Neural Information Processing Systems, pp. 1097–1105 (2012)
9. Simonyan, K., Zisserman, A.: Very deep convolutional networks for large-scale image recognition. arXiv preprint arXiv:1409.1556 (2014)
10. Nair, V., Hinton, G.E.: Rectified linear units improve restricted boltzmann machines. In: Proceedings of the 27th International Conference on Machine Learning, pp. 807–814 (2010)

11. Srivastava, N., Hinton, G., Krizhevsky, A., Sutskever, I., Salakhutdinov, R.: Dropout: a simple way to prevent neural networks from overfitting. J. Mach. Learn. Res. **15**(1), 1929–1958 (2014)
12. Eigen, D., Krishnan, D., Fergus, R.: Restoring an image taken through a window covered with dirt or rain. In: 2013 IEEE International Conference on Computer Vision, pp. 633–640 (2013)
13. Jain, V., Seung, S.: Natural image denoising with convolutional networks. In: Advances in Neural Information Processing Systems, pp. 769–776 (2009)
14. Wang, Z., Bovik, A.C., Sheikh, H.R., Simoncelli, E.P.: Image quality assessment: from error visibility to structural similarity. IEEE Trans. Image Process. **13**(4), 600–612 (2004)
15. Abadi, M., Agarwal, A., Barham, P., Brevdo, E., Chen, Z., Citro, C., Corrado, G.S., Davis, A., Dean, J., Devin, M., Ghemawat, S.: TensorFlow: large-scale machine learning on heterogeneous systems (2015). tensorflow.org

Color-Based Large-Scale Image Retrieval with Limited Hardware Resources

Michał Lągiewka[1], Rafał Scherer[1(✉)], and Rafal Angryk[2]

[1] Institute of Computational Intelligence, Częstochowa University of Technology,
Al. Armii Krajowej 36, 42-200 Częstochowa, Poland
{michal.lagiewka,rafal.scherer}@iisi.pcz.pl
[2] Department of Computer Science, Georgia State University,
Atlanta, GA 30302-5060, USA
angryk@cs.gsu.edu
http://iisi.pcz.pl
http://grid.cs.gsu.edu/rangryk/

Abstract. This paper is an attempt to design a fast image retrieval system with limited hardware resources. To this end, we use two-stage color-based features, Hadoop with HDFS to ensure file system flexibility, even in the case of sprawling into cloud projects and JAVA environment to run on every operating system. Namely, we retrieve images by color histogram and then by the color coherence vector to pick the best match from the results found by the previous algorithm. We tested the system on a large set of Microsoft COCO images.

Keywords: Hadoop · HDFS · Content-based image retrieval · Map/reduce · Image color representation

1 Introduction

Image retrieval and classification [5,6] are one of the most important applications of computer vision. Content-based image retrieval methods are usually targeted for precision. Our goal is to build an image retrieval system, which has a relatively high precision of results and high-speed of data manipulation for low-end, limited hardware. Users of such systems would not like to wait and most probably do not need all of the possible results, just the most relevant to their expectations. Moreover, it is sometimes impossible to browse all the results by a man. This is the main reason we decided to focus on the way of searching instead of improving compare algorithm or creating a new one. We made also an assumption that there is no limit for dataset to keep growing, but we are still limited by hardware. It is very probable that the end-user will not dispose a powerful server or even close to such a hardware. We searched for an easily-adjustable solution for small, medium and large data processing. Analysing very large datasets for some pattern requires huge computing power. To make our system as computationally efficient as possible, we picked color information as

© Springer International Publishing Switzerland 2016
L. Rutkowski et al. (Eds.): ICAISC 2016, Part II, LNAI 9693, pp. 689–699, 2016.
DOI: 10.1007/978-3-319-39384-1_61

the visual feature to retrieve images. Moreover, we store processed images as well as the original ones, because storage is cheaper than adding or upgrading processors or memory, hard disks are widely available with higher and higher capacities. This leads us to conclusion, that splitting retrieval into several steps can reduce computing power needed to execute exactly the same tasks, unless data is corrupted. That prompted an important problem how to avoid data loss? The answer came with the Hadoop and Hadoop Distributed File System (HDFS). Because Hadoop replicates blocks of incoming data, it is not likely to lose all copies of the corrupted fragment [1]. Hadoop can be accessed in two ways: locally via file system (e.g. /home/hduser/hadoop/) or globally via a domain (e.g. hdfs://example.com/). Thanks to the HDFS file system, we were able to split our system in two parts - user-device and mass-storage device, which may be useful if available, but is not necessary. We planned our system to be the most effective for low efficient hardware, so we acknowledge, that distributed file system as is HDFS is a solution for this worries, because it can be set up for multiple data nodes on multiple hard drives (if available). Bearing in mind that Hadoop replicate blocks of data through data nodes, we can assume, the worst scenario is when all blocks of data are contained by a single node.

Image retrieval can be based on various features [3,11]. Although, color histogram-based algorithms [4,11] are good for analyzing color distribution in blurred images, they do not really provide detailed content analysis. We decided to use histograms to reduce initial set of images, as a preparation for more a complicated algorithm. The narrowed pool consists of images that have enough of common colors with the query image (above 5% of dominating colors). We used the color coherence vector algorithm (CCV) [8,9] to build a color map for each picture which met our conditions. This process was placed at Hadoop Job to utilize map/reduce methods in the most optimal way. Then we were able to order images by most relevance of color map to the query image color map created with this algorithm.

The paper is organized as follows. Section 2 describes a general framework of the proposed system and Sect. 3 provides a detailed description of every stage of the image retrieval. Experiments on Microsoft COCO images are presented in Sect. 4. Section 5 concludes the paper and provides future directions.

2   System Model

The proposed system is presented in Fig. 1 with image storage based on a database. The most computational demanding are three core steps: the color histogram algorithm (CHA) of a blurred input image (i.e. its copy), comparison in database to reduce possible outcomes to the next step and, finally the color coherence vector algorithm on specified images. As the most complicated method, we decided to implement CCV in Hadoop Map/Reduce component. CHA and CCV in combination allowed us to obtain results, which are most relevant and with moderate demand for computing power.

We decided to test it empirically in conditions of variety CPU's and RAM. We assumed to test the whole system on given terms:

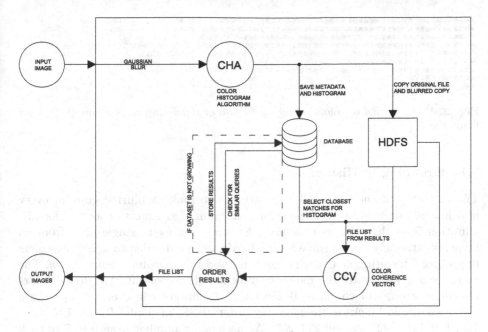

Fig. 1. Model of the proposed system for image retrieval based on color.

1. 1 CPU (single core), 1024 MB RAM,
2. 1 CPU (single core), 2048 MB RAM,
3. 1 CPU (single core), 4096 MB RAM,
4. 1 CPU (two cores), 1024 MB RAM,
5. 1 CPU (two cores), 2048 MB RAM,
6. 1 CPU (two cores), 4096 MB RAM.
7. 1 CPU (four cores), 1024 MB RAM,
8. 1 CPU (four cores), 2048 MB RAM,
9. 1 CPU (four cores), 4096 MB RAM.

The operating system (i.e. Linux Server with graphical interface Ubuntu, ver. 15.10) was installed on a virtual machine with a standard magnetic hard drive (not a solid state drive). This solution was designed to work with Hadoop 2.7.2 and Java 8 platform. Additionally we used MySQL, later migrated to Spark SQL database for better big data managing.

3   Image Retrieval

Digital images have four channels of ARGB or RGBA. We can treat the alpha channel like a separated channel or we can ignore it and use only the RGB color set only on RGB. We used the first, more detailed representation in the experiments.

Fig. 2. Eight groups of colors combined from 3 channels (alpha is ignored). (Colour figure online)

3.1   Grouping in Histogram

The first step of the proposed framework is to make a blurred copy of every new image. Later on, we use the color histogram algorithm to collect color distribution from these blurred pictures. As analyzing every single pixel from an image is extremely burdensome for the hardware, we decided to aggregate colors in groups. Clustering is a very popular method in computer science [2,10]. The more groups we create, the more accurate results we obtain. We divide colors into eight groups (4 channels, 0–255 each, 32 numbers in every group). As a result we obtain blocks in the following order: 0–31, 32–63, 64–95, 96–127, 128–159, 160–191, 192–223 and 224–255. We assigned a number from 0 to 7 to each group. The eight groups are presented in Fig. 2 Decision about splitting each channel into eight groups was made empirically, because it brings good trade-off between performance on a limited hardware and the retrieval accuracy. As a result we obtain the possibility to create a 4-dimensional array to store the sum of pixels which belong to every combination of four groups. Below we present the histogram function implemented in Java:

```
public static int[][][][] histogram(BufferedImage image)
    throws Exception {
  int m = 8;
  int n = 256 / m;
  int[][][][] ch = new int[m][m][m][m];
  for (int x = 0; x < image.getWidth(); x++) {
    for (int y = 0; y < image.getHeight(); y++) {
      int color = image.getRGB(x, y);
      int alpha = (color & 0xff000000) >> 24;
      int red = (color & 0x00ff0000) >> 16;
      int green = (color & 0x0000ff00) >> 8;
      int blue = color & 0x000000ff;
      ch[alpha / n][red / n][green / n][blue / n]++;
    }
  }
  int pixels = image.getHeight() * image.getWidth();
  for (int a = 0; a < ch.length; a++) {
    for (int r = 0; r < ch[a].length; r++) {
      for (int g = 0; g < ch[a][r].length; g++) {
        for (int b = 0; b < ch[a][r][g].length; b++) {
```

```
            ch[a][r][g][b] = (int) (ch[a][r][g][b] * 100 /
              pixels);
          if (ch[a][r][g][b] < 5) {
            ch[a][r][g][b] = 0;
          }
        }
      }
    }
  }
  return ch;
}
```

The code above counts every color from each pixel as its group from $\{0,0,0,0\}$ to $\{7,7,7,7\}$ and skips groups being under 5 % of total pixels. The function takes BufferedImage object as argument. We decided to use full images instead of relative or absolute path to retain possibility to move this function to Hadoop Job if needed. The integer m represents number of groups we split 4 channels into. The next integer is n, which is the value of range in each group (in this case 32 elements). After that, we declare 4-dimensional array to store number of pixels that belongs to each combined group. We traverse through the image width and height and get values for each channel (RGBA) in for loops. We divide channel value by group amount, thus as a result we increase value in a certain group by its number.

In the second part of the presented function we change the obtained pixel numbers into percentage of all image pixels. We decided to ignore smaller values (under 5 %), thus we replaced those with zeros. The most common matching function for this method is the Euclidean distance. To be able to store results of the above method we had to prepare an SQL table:

Field	Type	Null	Key	Default	Extra
id	char(36)	NO		NULL	
realname	varchar(255)	NO		NULL	
type	char(3)	NO		jpg	
a	int(11)	NO		NULL	
r	int(11)	NO		NULL	
g	int(11)	NO		NULL	
b	int(11)	NO		NULL	
v	int(11)	NO		NULL	

The table stores HDFS file name (id), HDFS file extension (type), uploaded file name with extension (realname), ARGB group numbers (a,r,g,b) and the percentage of color in image (above 5 %). In columns a, r, g and b we stored group number from the current comparison, e.g. if we had a group represented by $ch(\{0,0,0,0\}) = 70$ it means there are 70 percent of all pixels, which belong to the combined group 0 (each A, R, G and B are between 0 and 31). We only store values higher than 5 % of the image size. The example SQL insert would look

```
INSERT INTO images (id, realname, a, r, g, b, v) VALUES
(UUID, 'image.jpg', 'jpg', 0, 0, 0, 0, 53),
(UUID, 'image.jpg', 'jpg',  0, 0, 1, 0, 17),
(UUID, 'image.jpg', 'jpg', 0, 3, 3, 1, 8);
```

where we assume that UUID is a parameter for the universally unique identifier UUID() function. If we consider selecting histogram by the top three colors from recently created, the query should look like this:

```
SELECT DISTINCT id, realname, type FROM images WHERE
(a=0 AND r=0 AND g=0 AND b=0 AND v BETWEEN 53-5 AND 53+5)
AND
(a=0 AND r=0 AND g=1 AND b=0 AND v BETWEEN 17-5 AND 17+5)
AND
(a=0 AND r=3 AND g=1 AND b=1 AND v BETWEEN 8-5 AND 8+5)
ORDER BY v;
```

This will return all rows which contain ARGB from given groups in a certain bin. The other method we can use besides using the range 'from – to' round to tens while inserting to get smoother dataset. If there was not more color groups assigned we can assume, that not inserted ones were groups which had less than 5 % impact on the image (separated). This is where we already know that we need to find similar images in which has similar proportions – it could have more colors considered as less than the lowest picked color in query image. This means we could look for an image which has been scaled or its content has been transformed. Additionally we loop our searching in the case of no results found with increasing range of the v parameter. If have not found any result within the first step $(+/-5)$ we increase it by another $5(+/-10)$ and so on.

3.2   Color Coherence Vector

After we have obtained the reduced list of file names we order them by the best match. The simplest way was to use the color coherence vector algorithm to create color map for every image. To optimize this algorithm we had to divide images into percentage areas (5 % of image width and 5 % of image height each). The more fragments we create (smaller ones) the more exacts results will be, but at the price of computing speed trade-off. Using such method as combining two algorithms is an efficient way of obtaining results with reduced computing unit activity to minimum. In this way we created a vector sized as 400 (number of percentage areas). At first, we assigned to every cell the value of the most dominant color at a particular area. Next, if the assigned color matched with the same area we increased match counter for this cell by 3. But what if the image was transformed? To consider the image color vector in a transformed

Table 1. Example of color assignment in color vector – 25 % × 25 % fragment of query image.

[1][3][2][1]	[8][5][4][2]	[1][3][2][1]	[8][5][4][2]	[1][3][2][1]
[8][5][4][2]	[0][0][0][0]	[0][0][0][0]	[0][0][0][0]	[8][5][4][2]
[1][3][2][1]	[0][0][0][0]	[0][0][0][0]	[0][0][0][0]	[1][3][2][1]
[8][5][4][2]	[0][0][0][0]	[0][0][0][0]	[0][0][0][0]	[8][5][4][2]
[1][3][2][1]	[8][5][4][2]	[1][3][2][1]	[8][5][4][2]	[1][3][2][1]

Table 2. Example of color assignment in color vector – fragment of image from dataset matching position of picture from Table 1.

[1][3][2][1]	[2][1][5][7]	[2][1][5][7]	[2][1][5][7]	[1][3][2][1]
[2][1][5][7]	[0][0][0][0]	[0][0][0][0]	[0][0][0][0]	[2][1][5][7]
[1][3][2][1]	[0][0][0][0]	[0][0][0][0]	[0][0][0][0]	[1][3][2][1]
[2][1][5][7]	[0][0][0][0]	[0][0][0][0]	[0][0][0][0]	[2][1][5][7]
[1][3][2][1]	[2][1][5][7]	[1][3][2][1]	[2][1][5][7]	[1][3][2][1]

Table 3. Example of value assignment in counter vector based on Table 2.

3	0	3	0	3
0	6	6	6	0
3	6	11	6	3
0	6	6	6	0
3	0	3	0	3

image we increased by 1 counters for surrounding cells if their color matched with the current cell. For example, if current cell belongs to group $\{1, 3, 7, 2\}$, its counter is increased by 3, but if the cell next to it has the same color, the counter for next cell is increased by 1. Additionally, if the next cell from our example match with query image cell at the same position it is increased by 3 again. Thus, if we got a square of cells with the same group of color, the middle one will have a value of $11 - 3$ for itself and 1 for each surrounding cell with the same color. When the color does not match the query image, we assign 0 to this cell.

Why do we point the matched color and the next one only if they are the same? We made this choice because of the blur operation in the first step. Working with blurred images brings a risk of losing sharp shapes and we were aware of this fact. Not pointing neighbour areas for matching color in the current cell if they are different helped us with bounds of color changing shapes. After building a vector (an array) of counters we sum values included and sort the returned images in order to received score of image from the highest to the lowest. The most optimistic situation is, when the query image and picture from dataset are exactly the same (or resized) – sum value is 4400. The worst scenario is, when both images does not match – sum is 0 – but the image from the dataset contains large amount of dominant colors we searched for. When the result of CCV sum is 0, we have a choice of showing that image as last or skip it. Just because our point was to search through the color attribute we decided to display those results as last – those images still contain dominant colors. At this point we are able to return ordered names of images from the retrieval process. In our system we decided to return them as a list of URLs. We could also consider returning a JSON object with final values, realname value from the database for each image, but we found this not necessary since those results will be displayed as images, not text.

3.3   Returning Images

To return images retrieved in our system we can use hdfs:// protocol to import images via local network defined in Hadoop configuration or by using the following Hadoop command:

```
hadoop fs -copyToLocal /path/a.jpg /home/user/images/
```

But what if we want to return our results through the Internet? Hadoop offers additional service for sharing resources via HTTP protocol – HttpFS which is a part of NameNode and below we present an example of the access

```
HTTP://<DOMAIN>:<PORT>/WEBHDFS/V1/<HADOOP
DIRECTORY>/<FILENAME>
```

or via regular Hadoop service browsing:

```
http://example.com:50070/explorer.html
```

which leads to: http://example.com:50070/webhdfs/v1/images/example.jpg. As we designed our solution, we assumed it will mostly work in a local network. The most important thing in using external URI to access to HDFS is to use correct configuration and URL parameters.

```
http://example.com:50070/webhdfs/v1/images/
00039cd4-e14b-11e5-925d-08002760e809.jpg?op=OPEN
```

The parameter op=open means, that request is meant to open requested file with read-only permission. This method can provide supplying results through the network e.g. to mobile devices. If requested resource was found, its returned as a downloadable file, otherwise Java IOException is returned in the JSON format.

4   Numerical Experiments

To make sure this solution is applicable for not-powerful devices we decided to compare results received on virtual machines with one, two and four cores (64-bit only) mentioned in Sect. 2. The operating system we chosen was Linux, to reduce background tasks and visual effects, which could disturb our tests. Due to using cross-platform solutions like Java, it is not a problem to run the system in other environments – even mobile. The configuration was tested on two Microsoft COCO datasets: small – 2 GB and large – 13 GB [7]. As we can see in Table 4 hardware resources such as cores in processors influence the results as well as the amount of RAM. Computing power required to proceed retrieval is the primary reason we had to reduce the amount of images to search by combining two algorithms. However, we still do not have to consider every single pixel of a picture as a factor, we can determine a proportion of groups extracted from blurred images. This operation saves computing power, but still requires RAM to store temporary data and calculations. We tested the most popular amounts of RAM installed in common personal computers – 1 GB, 2 GB and 4 GB.

Table 4. Results (in milliseconds) of testing the system with the same input image in ten attempts in system various conditions.

TYPE	RAM (MB)	2 GB (18 000 items) retrieval time [ms]		13 GB (80 000 items) retrieval time [ms]	
		min	max	min	max
Single core	1024	2538	11854	8456	18953
	2048	2422	11203	8023	17984
	4096	2418	10897	7998	17985
Dual core	1024	2036	8518	7231	16057
	2048	1931	8165	6986	16102
	4096	1850	8103	6850	15968
Quad core	1024	1826	6304	4825	14846
	2048	1695	6158	4171	14145
	4096	1612	5984	4093	14121

By testing certain image on the system input we observed several patterns within many attempts of repeating retrieval. We determined the minimum attempts of searching to obtain reliable results – 10 was enough to compare the lowest and the greatest times of searching through the dataset. The minimum time reached was decreasing along with additional cores and RAM. This occurrence is strictly related to operating system memory managing and background tasks related to our solution (e.g. uploading to HDFS).

We observed a very satisfactory correlation between the highest times of searching between small and large dataset. We expected those times to grow proportionally, instead we obtained much shorter times for larger dataset than we expected. Those results assured us, that we picked the correct components to build such retrieval system.

5 Conclusion

Combining two algorithms along with the distributed filesystem to reduce potential failure results and to improve access speed transpired to be a good solution for every limited resource computer system. The components used to create the system made it adjustable to a much larger infrastructure.

We would not be able to achieve such efficient results without sacrificing some precision in consequence of grouping colors in larger groups at the histogram phase and using color dominance at certain areas in building color coherence vector.

The results could be improved if we drop the precision even more, but we consider this exertions not obligatory as we want our final results to have the most probability of what user expected to be returned. Colour is a very flexible image attribute and can be very helpful in fast content-based retrieval systems. To be more precise, when we already reduce our dataset to images, which have all necessary colors required to consider the images similar to the query image, we can use other algorithms to classify objects in these images. This means that our system can be used for further research for optimizing and improving image retrieval.

An another aspect we can take into consideration is reducing ARGB channels into RGB to provide less comparison as of one channel less. Channel Alpha informs us about the opacity/transparency of a pixel. In our experiment we considered it as a factor influencing the color for better adjusting to images with transparent areas.

Our system is easy to extend to a larger infrastructure by adding a new functionality to image retrieval not just retrieval by color, but many other features, attributes and content. The easiest to provide are limitations, e.g. limit results to certain parameters such as width and height or brightness. Another option is to add a possibility to pick up a single color and search for images with the picked color as dominant combined with the query image. The system is independent from third party providers and was meant for limited resources. In a consequence, it can be installed for home users to search through image libraries (even on home cloud services) or in companies storing large amount of images e.g. advertising agencies, photo agencies etc.

Acknowledgements. This work was supported by the Polish National Science Centre (NCN) within project number DEC-2011/01/D/ST6/06957.

References

1. Borthakur, D.: HDFS architecture guide. HADOOP APACHE PROJECT (2008). http://hadoop.apache.org/common/docs/current/hdfsdesign.pdf
2. El-Samak, A.F., Ashour, W.: Optimization of traveling salesman problem using affinity propagation clustering and genetic algorithm. J. Artif. Intell. Soft Comput. Res. **5**(4), 239–245 (2015)
3. Gabryel, M., Grycuk, R., Korytkowski, M., Holotyak, T.: Image indexing and retrieval using GSOM algorithm. In: Rutkowski, L., Korytkowski, M., Scherer, R., Tadeusiewicz, R., Zadeh, L.A., Zurada, J.M. (eds.) Artificial Intelligence and Soft Computing. LNCS, vol. 9119, pp. 706–714. Springer, Heidelberg (2015)
4. Hafner, J., Sawhney, H.S., Equitz, W., Flickner, M., Niblack, W.: Efficient color histogram indexing for quadratic form distance functions. IEEE Trans. Pattern Anal. Mach. Intell. **17**(7), 729–736 (1995)
5. Korytkowski, M., Rutkowski, L., Scherer, R.: Fast image classification by boosting fuzzy classifiers. Inf. Sci. **327**, 175–182 (2016)
6. Lee, P.M., Hsiao, T.C.: Applying LCS to affective image classification in spatial-frequency domain. J. Artif. Intell. Soft Comput. Res. **4**(2), 99–123 (2014)
7. Lin, T.-Y., Maire, M., Belongie, S., Hays, J., Perona, P., Ramanan, D., Dollár, P., Zitnick, C.L.: Microsoft COCO: common objects in context. In: Fleet, D., Pajdla, T., Schiele, B., Tuytelaars, T. (eds.) ECCV 2014, Part V. LNCS, vol. 8693, pp. 740–755. Springer, Heidelberg (2014)
8. Pass, G., Zabih, R.: Histogram refinement for content-based image retrieval. In: Proceedings 3rd IEEE Workshop on Applications of Computer Vision, WACV 1996, pp. 96–102. IEEE (1996)
9. Pass, G., Zabih, R., Miller, J.: Comparing images using color coherence vectors. In: Proceedings of the Fourth ACM International Conference on Multimedia, pp. 65–73. ACM (1997)
10. Serdah, A.M., Ashour, W.M.: Clustering large-scale data based on modified affinity propagation algorithm. J. Artif. Intell. Soft Comput. Res. **6**(1), 23–33 (2016)
11. Sural, S., Qian, G., Pramanik, S.: Segmentation and histogram generation using the hsv color space for image retrieval. In: 2002 International Conference on Image Processing, Proceedings, vol. 2, p. II-589. IEEE (2002)

Intelligent Driving Assistant System

Jacek Mazurkiewicz[1(✉)], Tomasz Serafin[1], and Michal Jankowski[2]

[1] Faculty of Electronics, Department of Computer Engineering,
Wroclaw University of Science and Technology, Ul. Wybrzeze Wyspianskiego 27,
50-370 Wroclaw, Poland
{Jacek.Mazurkiewicz,Tomasz.Serafin}@pwr.edu.pl
[2] Dollar Financial, Castlebridge Office Village,
Kirtley Dr, Nottingham NG7 1LD, UK
mikimicha@gmail.com

Abstract. The paper presents the intelligent driving assistant system as a device to increase a car active safety without any interference with a driving process. The system - based on the softcomputing methodology working "on-line" - is able to overtake the driver's reaction. The system analyses pictures in front of the vehicle and recognises road events and the grip of the road. The driver is informed about the each kind of recognised event. To resolve the problem of the road event recognition entirely new picture preprocessing approach has been used. The learning for multilayer perceptron realised by such data gives very good results. The new way of extracting data from pictures is a promising solution. The algorithm was implemented as part of a real system to support the on-line driver decision. The system was tested in the real car in real traffic with very promising results.

1 Introduction

The intelligent driving assistant system is an effort to use the intelligent processing methods in vehicles to increase an active safety without any interference with a driving process. The main goal of this system is overtaking driver's reactions. The driver analyses pictures in front of the vehicle and tries to decide which kind of reaction is suitable for a specific road event. The situation when driver's reaction is too slow happens very often [1]. It is connected with many factors. The explanation why people are not able to pay 100 % attention and react always fast and correct is not easy. The human's nature and mind is really difficult to analyse. That is the reason why the better way to increase driving safety is creating systems like described is the paper. The system must be faster than human being in analysing pictures in front of the vehicle and recognising road events [7,8]. This system should inform driver about each kind of recognised event. The information about recognition should be transmitted as a voice or as a picture message [9,13]. The type of message is connected with the specific conditions. To get results in creating the approach, there is necessity to use advanced computing methods connected with pictures analysis and shapes recognition. The system is going to be an autonomic solution without any connection to any kind

© Springer International Publishing Switzerland 2016
L. Rutkowski et al. (Eds.): ICAISC 2016, Part II, LNAI 9693, pp. 700–711, 2016.
DOI: 10.1007/978-3-319-39384-1_62

of database or other remote resource. This system should be able to learn in its whole life cycle. Each "turning on" should start learning procedure from patterns collected previously.

2 System Description

The system is divided into two subparts. The first one is responsible for various types of road events e.g. recognises speed limits, traffic jams, obstacles. It consists of the three main elements: computing unit, CCD camera and sound system. The computing unit is the PC computer powered by the car's electrical installation and connected by wires with the camera and speakers. The second part recognises the surface of the road. It has been build up from several components: speed sensor, brake pedal position sensor, microcontroller (MCU), camera and PC computer. The MCU constantly reads signals and stores them for later sending. The computer requests data from microcontroller device every 20 milliseconds. Also special application running on PC is controlling camera and takes photo every second. Information about the speed and about the surface type is enough to predict stopping distance. The data describing the speed are ready to use just after the end of the reading procedure. The surface recognition is more time consuming process and needs next "solid steps" for implementation. Firstly already taken photo is normalized then preprocessed and neural network is used as classifier of the presented surface [2,6]. Lastly - based on obtained data and knowledge acquired from learning data - the stopping distance is computed.

3 Road Events Recognition System

The application for the system is built from modules. Each module is the part of the application which is responsible for the special task. Modules are grouped into functional blocks (Frames block - Extraction block - Classifier block) (Fig. 1). The functional blocks and modules communicate with themselves with some specified data and parameters transfers. ADC is a device which converts a camera signal to the digital frames in the specified format readable for the system application. Extraction block is the set of modules which processes the frames. The contours selector is responsible for finding and selecting contours in the frame which is processed at the moment. The number and the type of contours is controlled by the external parameters. The segments manipulation module starts working when the contours selector gives its output. The manipulation on the segment is understood as the scaling process (scaling is in this case is the equivalent of the normalization process). After this process, selected and normalised segments are the input for the classifier block and if the classification process matches some segments to some classes, they will be sent to the files output module (it is the part of the self-learning process) (Fig. 2). Classifier block is the set of modules which consists of two subsystems - classifier [12] and the learning subsystem [10]. The first one works in "the real time", when the system is running. The learning subsystem starts working after the turning on and

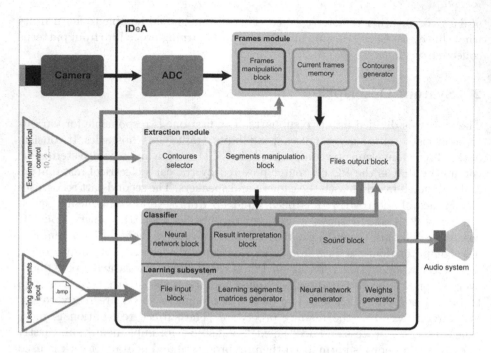

Fig. 1. Road events recognition system architecture

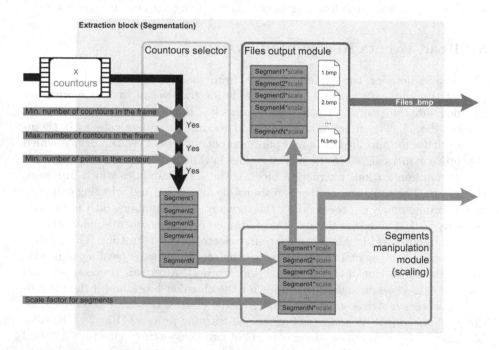

Fig. 2. Road events recognition system - extraction block

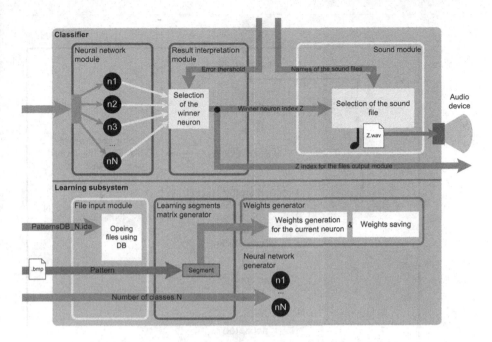

Fig. 3. Road events recognition system - classifier block

is responsible for the system initial learning from the patterns collected in the bitmaps (bmp files) stored on the hard disk (the file input module). The result interpretation module is connected with the voice module and file input module. After matching segment to the specified class it sends information about segment to store on the hard disk (in the specified class folder) - it will be used to the next learning procedure. Simultaneously it gives the specified class name to the voice module and then the sound with alert is played (Fig. 3). The application for the system works in the three main cycles. The first one is the pre-initialization in which the application checks if it can start correctly. This cycle examines the input parameters and files if they are correct. If this process finishes correctly, starts the second cycle called initialization. In this process are created all data structures needed by the system third cycle called work. The learning process is connected with generating learning structures which data comes from the stored bitmap files and folder structure (the folder structure is the mirror of classes which can be used in the work cycle). The work cycle is described below (Fig. 4). It starts only if the first and the second cycle finish with success. It works in the infinite loop. It stops when the user turns off the system or the car engine will be turned off.

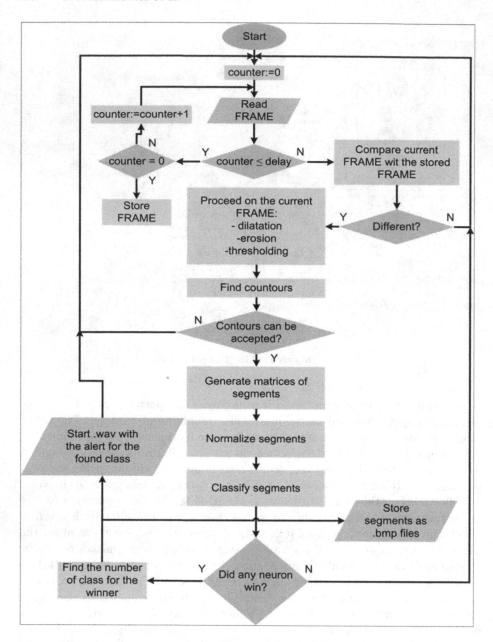

Fig. 4. Road events recognition system - main algorithm

4   Learning Data for Road Surface Recognition

We can point two special areas for collected data. The stopping distance prediction is the main goal of the system the data about retardation on each surface was needful. Using this information square function was discovered for each surface that system is recognising. The functions describe the relation between the speed and the stooping distance. The main topic is to learn the neural network to recognize road surfaces based on the photos of the road. So the pictures for each type of the road surface for different types of weather conditions have been collected. As a result the data describing: asphalt, sett, snow, and off-road in 22 different variations like: day, night wet, dry, good quality, bad quality. The road surface is recognised not based on the entire view but using only the piece of the photo, patterns are populated by copying the different areas of the same picture. The neural network is trained using around 150 patterns for the each type of the road [2,11].

5 Image Recognition

The system can recognize three types of surfaces: snow, asphalt and sett. The discovered preprocessing approach can be easily extended for more types of the road. The camera takes the photos of the road. The photos are processed to detect the surface type. Firstly the square is cut out from the photo in a place where the right car wheel is going to contact the road surface. It cannot be taken from the area between wheels as there could be different type of the surface. For example in winter time we can find a snow is in a middle of a road but the car wheels go on the clean asphalt surface. Before the image cropping the thresholds for image normalization are calculated. After the cropping the small square is normalized using previously found thresholds. Next the histogram equalisation is used. This way the picture seems to be more clear and unequivocal [6]. At the end the prepared square is ready for subsequent processing.

5.1 Snow Recognition

The average colour of the picture square creates the basis of the solution. It is little bit surprising that snow surface is not always the brightest surface. Sometimes the sett can be brighter and it depends only on auto exposition of a camera. Therefore lightens is not something that the algorithm can rely on. The key observation is that snow has one dominating colour component. This is usual situation, many times something what we recognize as white it is a bit blue e.g. white paper for printer is also blue [6]. Lastly as a result of dominating component also saturation of the colour is noticeable. Putting all of the mentioned steps together we create the snow recognition algorithm. The average colour in picture square is calculated for all R, G and B channels separately. For the RGB colour the HSL representation is also computed. If the B (blue) is dominating component and H (hue) is greater than 6 % the picture is recognized as a snow.

5.2 Asphalt and Sett Recognition

If the picture is not pointed as snow the next step is made and the neural network gives and answer if the presented photo includes the sett or the asphalt probe.

Apparently the distinguish between the asphalt and the sett is unexpectedly difficult. It seems that pattern of relatively smooth and uniform asphalt differs from sett significantly and therefore it is trivial to make the classifier for it. However simple preprocessing gives no valuable results. The neural network is trained with the following types of images: grayscale, B&W, B&W using the median algorithm to remove the ragged edges. We tried to build the input based on the already detected corners or based on the B&W image with detected corners. The approaches are the completely blind ways - the neural network is not able to learn. It is clear that the completely new way of data extracting is necessary.

6   Growing Bubbles Algorithm

The "Growing Bubbles Algorithm" is developed especially to find an answer: is presented image the probe of the asphalt or the probe of the sett. Apparently differences between patterns for the same type of the road are so significant that the neural networks are not able to recognize it properly [2]. The following observation can be converted to a solution. The proportion of black and white areas analysis and the frequency of appearance can potentially point to correct answers. In this case place and rotation of pattern are ignored and it is the issue with the previous preprocessing types. As a consequence, a unique algorithm is developed. The photos of a sett contains quite significant white areas divided by the dark lines. In general it is difficult to find these lines as a result of bad image quality. For the asphalt probe the only common pattern are the little black spots. The mentioned observations create a base of the "Growing Bubbles Algorithm". Therefore a task for the algorithm is to extract only the information about the sizes and the frequency of the appearance for solid colour areas. The idea is to fill the white and black areas, to count them and to measure its sizes. It could be the key information for detecting the sett. However usually the stones presented in the photos stick together in such a way that there is no gap between them and simple filling will fail in a such situation. We have to limit an expansion of the filling areas and this is exactly what bubbles do. The areas are filled by the bubbles instead of the simple colour. The bubbles cannot grow bigger than the sett stones and consequently are able to preserve its sizes. The bubbles size for black and white areas analysis can be the device to distinguish between the sett probe and the asphalt probe [5].

Figure 5 shows the example for the sett and the asphalt probe preprocessing. It can be easily noticed that sizes of bubbles are more systematic for the sett pattern than for the asphalt pattern. The information about bubbles sizes and numbers allows to remove the noise recorded in the plane images: the angle of sett, the shape of sett, etc.

6.1   Implementation

The algorithm goes true all pixels in the image. If the white pixels area of radius equal to four is available it draws circle there. Next it tries to enlarge and move

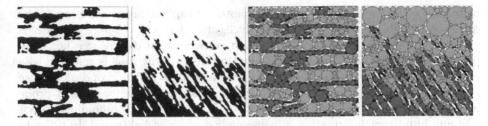

Fig. 5. Comparison of simple B&W with median algorithm to bubbles preprocessing. Counting from left: (1) B&W with median sett, (2) B&W with median asphalt, (3) bubbles sett, (4) bubbles asphalt (Colour figure online)

the circle around the white area to possibly best fit in the solid colour space. It stops enlarging when the circle is going to overlay the black zone or the already drown circle. The process is repeated until all white regions are touched. Meanwhile in analogical way the black areas are processed where the second set of bubbles is created. In fact the process of enlarging is not stopped immediately if the circle overlaps the single pixel. A little bit of overlapping is allowed and thanks to that the circles can fit better ragged edges. As the consequence - the circles are filled with colour. Later when new circle is looking for a place it calculates how many pixels overlaps already.

1. Set R to 4.
2. Iterate through all of the pixels.
3. If actual pixel is white then take red colour, If it is black then take the blue colour, otherwise go to Point 2.
4. Set error variable to zero.
5. In place pointed by the actual pixel draw the circle of radius R pixels with a chosen colour.
6. For each pixel out of the picture or overlapping different colour increment error variable and save average error place.
7. If error variable not larger then increment R and go back to Point 4.
8. If error is to big then move circle in an opposite side to the average error place and draw again.
9. If error variable is less than before then increment R and go to Point 4.
10. If error variable is bigger than draw the previous circle and fill it with chosen colour.
11. If it was not the last pixel in the picture go to Point 2.
12. Calculate pattern - count bubbles grouped by sizes and colours.

6.2   Retrieving Pattern

When all bubbles are drawn it is a time for the actual data retrieving. All circles are grouped by intervals of sizes and colours. The members of each group are counted and the cardinalities of groups are the classifier input. There is one more factor to extract from the picture. The photos of asphalt probe can provide the direction of light as one corner is usually lighter than the other. This effect is as strong as strong the light is and is not noticeable in cloudy weather. In a process of thresholding almost all information in the light zone is removed as a result of low dynamic range. It is because the asphalt is the kind of dark texture that is close to solid colour. At the same time dynamic range for the sett probe is high as stone is light and gaps are usually dark. The thresholding do not lose any important information in consequence of scene lightening. In order to preserve information about the asphalt light direction the picture is splitted by four squares [5]. The counting bubbles algorithm is done for each of the square separately. In (Fig. 6) there is print out for the obtained data calculated by the bubbles preprocessing. It is found for top left square and white areas: 37 circles of size 4–5, 31 circles of size 6–7 ... 5 circles of size greater than 26.

```
Black Top Left:        8   5   2   0   0   0   0   0   0   0   0   0
White Top Left:       37  31  13   6   2   2   4   0   0   1   2   5
Black Top Right:      43  26  12   3   2   0   2   2   0   1   0   2
White Top Right:      45  34  15   3   2   2   0   1   1   1   2   1
Black Bottom Left:    38  31   8   6   4   2   1   0   0   1   3   5
White Bottom Left:    24  22   6   2   0   0   1   0   0   1   0   0
Black Bottom Right:    8  12   5   2   2   3   0   0   0   1   1   1
White Bottom Right:   30  22   9   5   1   1   2   1   0   0   0   5
```

Fig. 6. Example of classifier data input

7   Results

7.1   Road Events Recognition Results

The (Fig. 7) shows the results of the tests which were made for two road signs: no overtaking and give a way. Besides those two signs, there were made other stimulations considered as the noise. If the number of correct classifications for the noises is the same as the number of simulations for that noise, it means that system is resistant to that kind of noise. The base of learning patterns consisted of 200 patterns for the "no overtaking" sign and from 100 patterns for the "give way" sign. The results are satisfactory. The road sign "no overtaking" had the bigger patterns database and its results are better in the classification process. The resistance to classifying other signs as the signs for two classes is also on the accepted level. However those results should be improved. Probably the patterns database is too small. There were made the real environment tests for the system (Fig. 8). Their task was to check the segmentation methods used in the propsed approach. It was necessary to start developing the classifier. The classifier with the wrong segments cannot work. The results were very satisfactory. The base of patterns contained the segments with 100 % of the road signs from the tested road fragment.

Stimulation	Number of stimulations	CORRECT classifications	WRONG classifications
 (two cars sign)	50	40	10
 (triangle sign)	50	34	6
Hand move	20	20	0
Other signs	40	31	9
Washing cat	10	10	0
Human being on the move	10	10	0

Fig. 7. The laboratory tests results

7.2 Snow Recognition Results

The snow recognition algorithm works with very promising accuracy of 100 % correctly recognized patterns of the collected data. There is only one condition for the proper recognition of the snow. The white balance ought to be correct. The cameras set it in automatic way but it gives appropriate results rarely. The way to solve it is to put some neutral colour object in a view of a camera. It would be possible then to correct the white balance based on registered colour of the neutral object.

7.3 Asphalt and Sett Recognition Results

The patterns for the asphalt and the sett differ significantly although the neural network training based on the traditional preprocessing methods gives no sensible results. The three-layer MLP is used as a device for recognition process. The output layer includes two neurons, the number of neurons in the input layer is fixed to the actual size of the input signal. The number of neurons in the hidden layer is tuned by the experimental way. The backpropagation algorithm with momentum parameter is used for the training procedure. The momentum parameter and the speed of the training is fixed by the set of experiments: momentum equals to 0.8, step - 0.001. The results are grouped in the table (Fig. 9) - where: *input* - number of input neurons, *hidden* - number of hidden neurons, *step* - speed of the space exploring the of solutions, *mom* - momentum parameter, *epochs* - number of training iterations, *train* - training set accuracy, *gener.* - generalization set accuracy, *valid.* - validation set accuracy. "Growing Bubbles Algorithm" with best result of **96,15 %** of recognized photos has clear advantage over other solutions in recognition between the asphalt and the sett - when we use traditional preprocessing with 400 or even 1600 input pixels of the picture.

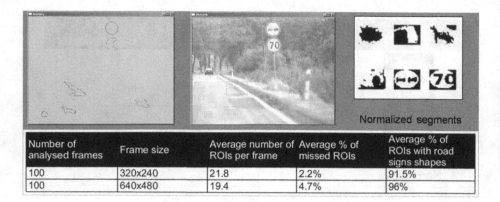

Number of analysed frames	Frame size	Average number of ROIs per frame	Average % of missed ROIs	Average % of ROIs with road signs shapes
100	320x240	21.8	2.2%	91.5%
100	640x480	19.4	4.7%	96%

Fig. 8. The real environment tests results

					accuracy			MSE		
input	hidden	step	mom.	epochs	train	gener.	valid.	train	gener.	valid.
96	20	0,001	0,8	150000	98,08	90,38	82,69	0,00065	0,0501	0,0782
96	20	0,001	0,8	150000	100	90,38	88,46	0,000153	0,0477	0,0574
96	20	0,001	0,8	150000	94,44	90,38	76,92	0,025761	0,0517	0,1281
96	19	0,001	0,8	150000	99,36	90,38	86,54	0,001198	0,0451	0,0277
96	19	0,001	0,8	150000	99,36	90,38	84,62	0,006379	0,0679	0,0842
96	19	0,001	0,8	150000	100	88,46	86,54	0,000006	0,0546	0,1032
96	18	0,001	0,8	150000	95,51	90,38	92,31	0,036066	0,0843	0,0500
96	18	0,001	0,8	150000	98,72	90,38	94,23	0,000491	0,0427	0,0339
96	18	0,001	0,8	150000	100	88,46	84,62	0,000005	0,1025	0,0958
96	17	0,001	0,8	150000	100	86,54	88,46	0,000005	0,0539	0,1009
96	17	0,001	0,8	150000	100	90,38	92,31	0,000301	0,0557	0,0247

Fig. 9. Training for Growing Bubbles Algorithm

8 Conclusion

Although a bit more types of the road surfaces could be recognized it is possible
to make surface recognition with good results based on the photo taken "on-line"
during the car movement. The recognition between the good quality asphalt and
the bad quality asphalt could be also done with use of bubbles algorithm. When
thinking about a final product ready for customers, there will be need for a way
of calibrating the system. While the road recognition will be the same for each
vehicle and speed reading can be customized for different cars, the retardation
quadratic functions will have to be discovered automatically by each user. There
are too many variables to customize this product for each car, tires and brakes
[3,4]. Each part of the system hardware was collected, algorithms were created
and developed, laboratory tests are finished. Road tests were carried out too.
The results are very promising and they enhanced the end-users features of the

commercial solutions available in some makes of cars at the market. The learning patterns base is still not sufficient for the real environment. We try to improve it and to tune the system in more detailed way to real traffic requirements. The system of braking distance prediction is satisfactory and could be developed up to customer ready product. The algorithm was implemented as part of a real system to support the on-line driver decision.

References

1. Barcelo, J., Codina, E., Casas, J., Ferrer, J.L., Garcia, D.: Microscopic traffic simulation: a tool for the design, analysis and evaluation of intelligent transport systems. J. Intell. Robot. Syst. Theory Appl. **41**, 173–203 (2005)
2. Du, K.L., Swamy, M.N.S.: Neural Networks in a Softcomputing Framework. Springer, London (2010)
3. Han, J., Kamber, M., Pei, J.: Data Mining. Morgen Kaufmann, Waltham (2012)
4. Anti-lock Braking System (ABS). Traction Control (2012). http://www.samarins. com/glossary/abs.html#.T-2dSLV1Dj8
5. Circle-Drawing Algorithms (2012). http://groups.csail.mit.edu/graphics/classes/ 6.837/F98/Lecture6/circle.html
6. Levine, M.D., Gandhi, M.R., Bhattacharyya J.: Image Normalization for Illumination Compensation in Facial Images (2012). http://wwwhomes.uni-bielefeld.de/ ggoetze/B/IlluminationReport.pdf
7. Li, H., Nashashibi, F.: Multi-vehicle cooperative perception and augmented reality for driver assistance: a possibility to "see" through front vehicle. In: 14th International IEEE Conference on Inteligent Transportation Systems, Washington DC (2011)
8. Lindner, F., Kressel, U., Kaelberer, S.: Robust recognition of traffic signals. In: IEEE Intelligent Vehicles Symposium. University of Parma (2004)
9. Narzt, W., Pomberger, G., Ferscha, A., Kold, D., Muller, R., Wieghardt, J., Hortner, H., Lindinger, C.: Augmented Reality Navigation Systems. Springer, Berlin (2005). Published online
10. Rutkowski, L.: Methods and Techniques of Artificial Intelligence (in Polish). PWN, Warszawa (2009)
11. Serafin, T.P., Mazurkiewicz, J.: IDEA - intelligent driving E-assistant system. In: Problems of Dependability and Modelling. Oficyna Wydawnicza Politechniki Wroclawskiej, Wroclaw (2011)
12. Tadeusiewicz, R.: Neural Networks (in Polish). Akademicka Oficyna Wydawnicza RM, Warszawa (1993)
13. World First: Automated Driving in Real Urban Traffic. http://www.dlr.de/en/ desktopdefault.aspx/tabid-6216/10226_read-26991/

Novel Image Descriptor Based on Color Spatial Distribution

Patryk Najgebauer[1], Marcin Korytkowski[1], Carlos D. Barranco[2], and Rafal Scherer[1(✉)]

[1] Institute of Computational Intelligence, Częstochowa University of Technology, al. Armii Krajowej 36, 42-200 Częstochowa, Poland
{patryk.najgebauer,marcin.korytkowski,rafal.scherer}@iisi.pcz.pl
[2] Intelligent Data Analysis (DATAi), Division of Computer Science, Universidad Pablo de Olavide, 41013 Seville, Spain
cbarranco@upo.es
http://iisi.pcz.pl

Abstract. This paper proposes a new image descriptor based on color spatial distribution for image similarity comparison. It is similar to methods based on HOG and spatial pyramid but in contrast to them operates on colors and color directions instead of oriented gradients. The presented method assumes using two types of descriptors. The first one is used to describe segments of similar color and the second sub-descriptor describes connections between different adjacent segments. By this means we gain the ability to describe image parts in a more complex way as is in the case of the histogram of oriented gradients (HOG) algorithm but more general as is in the case of keypoint-based methods such as SURF or SIFT. Moreover, in comparison to the keypoint-based methods, the proposed descriptor is less memory demanding and needs only a single step of image data processing. Descriptor comparing is more complicated but allows for descriptor ordering and for avoiding some unnecessary comparison operations.

Keywords: Content-based image retrieval · Color-based image matching

1 Introduction

Developing content-based image comparison methods that simulate human visual perception is a very hard and complicated process. Image recognition is natural and very simple for human but when we try to mimic the process we face many problems as it is very complicated, uses multiple hidden techniques developed during the evolution and we only have a rough sense of how the brain works. Most of them, e.g. human imagination, are currently unavailable for computer systems. Also huge knowledge, which humans acquire though the entire life is hard to store for machine learning systems and we excel in visual identification. Thus, image comparison algorithms try to extract and simplify this large

© Springer International Publishing Switzerland 2016
L. Rutkowski et al. (Eds.): ICAISC 2016, Part II, LNAI 9693, pp. 712–722, 2016.
DOI: 10.1007/978-3-319-39384-1_63

amount of data from images to form a structurized description that is easy to compare for computers, such as human text writing [1,11]. But image description is extracted only from the image pixel spatial distribution and is not supported by human imagination or knowledge. That caused that image description in most cases is not fully satisfactory for human users. Image features can be generally divided into global and local methods.

Global methods extract features from the entire image without dividing into more and less significant areas. To this group we can include histogram based algorithms such as histogram of oriented gradients (HOG) or color coherence vector (CCV) [6,14]. In most cases they generate constant amount of description data which is easier to compare and store, on the other hand, image comparison by histogram based algorithms gives only a vague similarity for a user.

Local feature-based methods try at first to find significant characteristic areas of an image based on Laplacian of Gaussian (LoG) or Difference of Gaussian (DoG) algorithms [8,20]. And then they generate a description of their neighbourhood. These methods are more accurate, on the other hand can generate far more description data and that amount varies per image. Local feature methods based on keypoints are efficient in similarity detection between images but less in content recognition. Commonly used methods of this kind are SIFT, SURF, ORB, BRIEF, FAST [3,5,12,16,17].

The aforementioned methods are often used to simple similarity comparison between images. There are many ways to compare features, from vector distance measures to fuzzy set-related [9]. In some cases it is required to classify images by their content. To this end, many methods were developed that could learn a combination of image features specific for a visual class. In the case of image classification, usually visual feature extraction methods are combined with machine learning, e.g. with support vector machines [18] or artificial neural networks [2]. Classifiers in most cases at first need to be trained by a set of prepared data of known classes [15]. Sometimes images are divided into regular sectors and within them descriptors are generated and classifiers are trained. Local feature-based algorithms can be also used with a spatial localization of keypoints [13]. Classifiers are often joined with the bag-of-features algorithm [7]. Global feature algorithms are far easier applicable to classification because of the constant number of feature data per image.

The paper is organized as follows. Section 2 describes the motivation behind the proposed research and Sect. 3 describes the novel method for image description. Experiments with various types of images are presented in Sect. 4.

2   Problem Description

In most global feature methods, image description is too simple and cannot provide satisfactory results for reliable image comparison or classification. Results of color histogram-based methods in most cases bring only vague similarity. On the other hand, they are efficient in comparing large sets of images. In the case of local feature-based algorithms, we face different problems: difficult comparison and classification due to an irregular keypoints distribution over the image and descriptors that describe only a small scrap of space around the keypoint. Local keypoint descriptors represent blobs and corners of the image which not fully represent the real, abstract image content.

To address the aforementioned problems, the research presented in the paper focuses on several goals:

- Describing image in a more precise way as is in global, histogram-based features. We want to describe image in a more readable way for human. Color histogram-based methods describe only colors that not allow to guess the image content for a human. Similarly, local features are hard to recognize by humans as they describe many single elements of image. This problem was shown in Fig. 1.
- Obtaining a small number of generated descriptors per image. Local feature-based methods generate hundreds of keypoints (vectors) per image. In many cases, keypoints are localized on the same structure. In our method we want to create a single descriptor for the entire structure that would replace multiple keypoints. For example, in the case of a triangle, we obtain three SURF keypoints (Fig. 1), whereas in our method we try to represent the entire triangle by a single descriptor.
- Creating a descriptor that will be able to be sorted for comparison speed-up. Most local and global feature descriptors do not distinguish more or less important values. Each descriptor parameter corresponds to equivalent element of space around keypoints or for single color in the case of histograms. They need to be compared directly each to each. In our work, we aim at creating a descriptor that could omit some comparison operations.
- Creating a descriptor that will be small and normalized. In the SURF algorithm, descriptors that describe surrounding neighbourhood of keypoints contain 64 floating points values, whereas in the proposed method we reduce this amount of data to speed up comparison and to reduce memory usage.

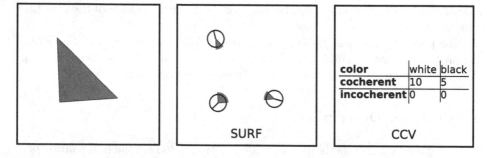

Fig. 1. Example results of SURF and CCV algorithm

3 Method Description

In this paper we propose a method that is a combination of local and global features and is focused on color images to describe image patterns. It can also work with gray scale images as is with HOG and most of keypoint-based methods but with worse results as we loose the color information. The proposed descriptors refers slightly to the HOG and CCV algorithms but work in a different way.

3.1 Image Processing

In the proposed method image features are extracted during color segmentation process which, in our case, is not preceded by any additional processing such as smoothing. Thus, the entire feature extraction is performed in a single pass, contrary to local keypoint-based methods that use multiple passes for size detection. An image is divided into regular fragments as is in spatial pyramid-based algorithms [4,10,19]. The method performs segmentation and extraction of descriptors, which were collected from each area, into a single set.

During segmentation stage, the method counts for each color group the number of segments and the number of segment's pixels. To reduce the combination of segments and memory usage, the colors of each segments are reduced to 64 color space. In this process borders between segments are also counted as histograms where position in the histogram corresponds to the direction of the edge created by the border (Fig. 2). Histograms of borders are counted for each colors combination, thus, they not exactly represent segments' shape but the distribution of relationship between colors.

Thanks to color space reduction to 64, the method during any image processing needs an array of 64×2 variables for image color counting (number of segments, numbers of pixels) and also an array of $64 \times 64 \times 4$ variables for border histograms counting (half of eight-value histogram).

After image fragment processing, the method selects up to 10 most significant colors. For each of the selected colors, the method generates the main color descriptor. After that, for each color we create sub-descriptors of color relationships.

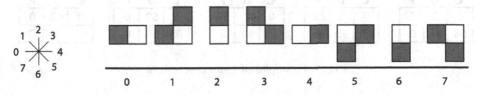

Fig. 2. Histogram of border directions.

3.2   Color Descriptor

The first and main descriptor represents color that occurs in an image fragment by describing color domination and fragmentation. By this, it is possible to distinguish solid or sprayed color patterns and their participation in the image. The descriptor contains three base values (Fig. 3). Some of them are normalized into the range between 0–255 for efficient comparison and memory usage. The first is the color number (C) for descriptors sorting or identification. Only descriptors of similar color are compared. The second block consists of normalized values describing color domination (D) and fragmentation (F). The domination is the ratio of the number of pixels of the same color with respect to the number of all pixels in the sector. The fragmentation is a number of segments scaled compared to the number of color pixels. Additional three values represent descriptor relation between sectors. Values of min and max y describe range of vertical descriptor distribution over sectors. And the last value (sector count) describes a number of sectors where this descriptor occurred. Thus, our main descriptor requires only 6 bytes of memory. Figure 4 presents descriptors for a set of simple example images. Each image contains only two colors, thus, we have only two descriptors. Color 0 is black and 63 is white. As wee can see, it is possible to distinguish images which are more fragmented and which color is dominant.

color 0-63	domination 0-255	fragmentation 0-255	min y 0-255	max y 0-255	sector count 0-255

Fig. 3. Structure of the main descriptor.

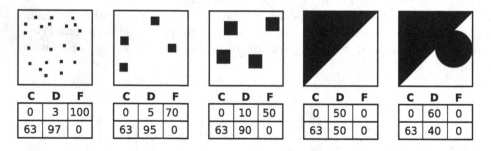

Fig. 4. Examples of main descriptors.

3.3   Color Relationship Sub-descriptor

Using the main descriptor we are not able to compare and distinguish squared or rounded segments. To resolve this, we designed a second sub-descriptor to describe a structure of color relationships to other colors. The proposed sub-descriptor is closely related to the single main descriptor and indicates border related color. Figure 5 presents the descriptor structure. The first value of descriptor is the aforementioned color, the second is a normalized value of domination of this color compared to other sub-descriptors. The last eight values constitute a normalized histogram of border edge directions.

Figure 6 presents examples of sub-descriptors. Tables under images contain related main descriptor color values (MC), sub-descriptor colors (C), relation dominations (D), histograms of relationship directions (H). As we see in this example, by using this additional descriptions it is possible to distinguish between structure of patterns, such as e.g. circles, squares or lines. Also gradient pattern can be described as a relation in a single similar direction between different segments.

color 0-63	domination 0-255	←	↖	↑	↗	→	↘	↓	↙
		0-255	0-255	0-255	0-255	0-255	0-255	0-255	0-255

Fig. 5. Structure of sub-descriptor.

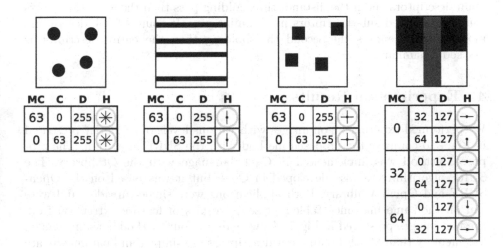

Fig. 6. Example of sub-descriptors.

3.4 Descriptors Comparison

Image comparing based on the proposed descriptors is more complex than in the case of the mentioned earlier local and global methods. Local feature-based methods describe image fragments very precisely, thus, when some descriptors will be equal between images we could say that the image contains exactly similar content. Global methods such as CCV, generate a single descriptor per image, which describes the entire color space, thus, it can be compared in a simple way based on the distance between vectors. In our method we divide it into smaller descriptors that describe only present colors. In this approach we lose information of colors which are not present on the image. This could be problematic because our method compares descriptors of similar color and a lot of images could be matched by a single common descriptor, even if other not common descriptors dominated the image. Because of this, our method checks the level of dissimilarity that is similar to a relative error. Comparison algorithm use two counters of weighed descriptors number. The first one counts all descriptors. The weight of descriptor is ranked by his strength and it is calculated by formula (1) where D is domination and SC is sector count.

$$C = D * SC \qquad (1)$$

Descriptors' similarity is checked by modulo distance matching with value thresholding, similarly to other feature descriptors. At first, the method checks main descriptors and if the distance thresholding pass then the algorithm starts comparing linked sub-descriptors in a similar way. If count of sub-descriptors modulo distance pass the second thresholding then the entire descriptor is marked as similar.

4 Experimental Results

We performed experiments on images with various levels of similarity presented in Fig. 7 to compare the proposed method with the SURF algorithm. The proposed method was implemented in C++ language with the Qt library. The SURF algorithm was also developed in C++ but it was based on the Open-SURF and OpenCV library. Both applications were single-threaded and were run on the same machine. Table 1 presents results of feature extraction from the test images presented in Fig. 7. As we can see, our method consumes much less memory than SURF because our descriptors are simpler and parameters are scaled to a single byte value versus the SURF descriptors of 64 float numbers.

In our method the number of extracted descriptors increases with increasing number of colors and their combination but not with the image size. In the SURF algorithm the number of descriptors increases rapidly with the image size and complexity. In this experiment the number of main descriptors and sub-descriptors sum was about 46 % of the SURF descriptors. Moreover, our method consumes about 1.6 % memory when compared to SURF.

Fig. 7. Set of images used in experiments.

The SURF algorithm perfectly locates and describes single characteristic points of images but achieves worse results on complicated patterns. Our method inversely, reaches better results with complicated patterns and single elements even can be omitted. It is due to the fact that the method extracts descriptors from a determined sector in contrast to SURF that at first performs keypoint localization.

Table 1. Results of image descriptors extraction from Fig. 7

The proposed method			SURF	
Descriptors	Sub-descriptors	Memory [KB]	Descriptors	Memory [KB]
31	87	1.031	134	33.500
39	102	1.225	153	38.250
33	79	0.965	69	17.250
70	299	3.330	156	39.000
37	117	1.359	150	37.500
26	41	0.553	42	10.500
45	81	1.055	72	18.000
23	38	0.506	29	7.250
8	6	0.105	0	0.000
3	2	0.037	0	0.000
18	28	0.379	0	0.000
7	6	0.100	11	2.750
142	794	8.586	9910	2477.500
153	707	7.801	4893	1223.250
147	618	6.896	3648	912.000
155	737	8.105	5806	1451.500
154	913	9.818	1077	269.250
156	875	9.459	760	190.000
155	961	10.293	1125	281.250
160	963	10.342	1008	252.000
158	1029	10.975	1276	319.000
159	1024	10.932	1255	313.750
151	975	10.406	1324	331.000
158	876	9.480	1011	252.750
160	858	9.316	1010	252.500
160	828	9.023	940	235.000
153	960	10.271	1334	333.500
96	353	4.010	39	9.750
156	1011	10.787	1760	440.000
152	897	9.650	2153	538.250
145	957	10.195	1945	486.250
152	957	10.236	1866	466.500
142	879	9.416	3819	954.750

5 Conclusion

After analysing results of our experiments, we can claim that our new image descriptor is efficient in terms of memory usage and feature extraction and comparison speed versus e.g. SURF. The new method describes images in a more detailed way than CCV but less than SURF, whereby it could be used to fast search for similar images without necessity to contain exactly the same content. It could compare images by pattern content in an initial prefiltering process to speed up a more complex method. It could by used in a similar way to the HOG algorithm in spatial pyramid-based methods in content classification applications because of similar advantages such as merging descriptors from sectors to describe a larger area.

Acknowledgements. This work was supported by the Polish National Science Centre (NCN) within project number DEC-2011/01/D/ST6/06957.

References

1. Aghdam, M.H., Heidari, S.: Feature selection using particle swarm optimization in text categorization. J. Artif. Intell. Soft Comput. Res. **5**(4), 231–238 (2015)
2. Bas, E.: The training of multiplicative neuron model based artificial neural networks with differential evolution algorithm for forecasting. J. Artif. Intell. Soft Comput. Res. **6**(1), 5–11 (2016)
3. Bay, H., Tuytelaars, T., Van Gool, L.: SURF: speeded up robust features. In: Leonardis, A., Bischof, H., Pinz, A. (eds.) ECCV 2006, Part I. LNCS, vol. 3951, pp. 404–417. Springer, Heidelberg (2006)
4. Bosch, A., Zisserman, A., Munoz, X.: Representing shape with a spatial pyramid kernel. In: Proceedings of the 6th ACM International Conference on Image and Video Retrieval, pp. 401–408. ACM (2007)
5. Calonder, M., Lepetit, V., Strecha, C., Fua, P.: BRIEF: binary robust independent elementary features. In: Daniilidis, K., Maragos, P., Paragios, N. (eds.) ECCV 2010, Part IV. LNCS, vol. 6314, pp. 778–792. Springer, Heidelberg (2010)
6. Dalal, N., Triggs, B.: Histograms of oriented gradients for human detection. In: IEEE Computer Society Conference on Computer Vision and Pattern Recognition, CVPR 2005, vol. 1, pp. 886–893. IEEE (2005)
7. Drozda, P., Grecki, P., Sopyla, K., Artiemjew, P.: Visual words sequence alignment for image classification. In: ICCI*CC, pp. 397–402. IEEE (2013)
8. Gunn, S.R.: On the discrete representation of the Laplacian of Gaussian. Pattern Recogn. **32**(8), 1463–1472 (1999)
9. Korytkowski, M., Rutkowski, L., Scherer, R.: Fast image classification by boosting fuzzy classifiers. Inf. Sci. **327**, 175–182 (2016)
10. Lazebnik, S., Schmid, C., Ponce, J.: Beyond bags of features: spatial pyramid matching for recognizing natural scene categories. In: 2006 IEEE Computer Society Conference on Computer Vision and Pattern Recognition, vol. 2, pp. 2169–2178. IEEE (2006)
11. Murata, M., Ito, S., Tokuhisa, M., Ma, Q.: Order estimation of Japanese paragraphs by supervised machine learning and various textual features. J. Artif. Intell. Soft Comput. Res. **5**(4), 247–255 (2015)

12. Ng, P.C., Henikoff, S.: SIFT: predicting amino acid changes that affect protein function. Nucleic Acids Res. **31**(13), 3812–3814 (2003)
13. Nowak, T., Najgebauer, P., Romanowski, J., Gabryel, M., Korytkowski, M., Scherer, R., Kostadinov, D.: Spatial keypoint representation for visual object retrieval. In: Rutkowski, L., Korytkowski, M., Scherer, R., Tadeusiewicz, R., Zadeh, L.A., Zurada, J.M. (eds.) ICAISC 2014, Part II. LNCS, vol. 8468, pp. 639–650. Springer, Heidelberg (2014)
14. Pass, G., Zabih, R., Miller, J.: Comparing images using color coherence vectors. In: Proceedings of the Fourth ACM International Conference on Multimedia, pp. 65–73. ACM (1997)
15. Patgiri, C., Sarma, M., Sarma, K.K.: A class of neuro-computational methods for assamese fricative classification. J. Artif. Intell. Soft Comput. Res. **5**(1), 59–70 (2015)
16. Rosten, E., Drummond, T.W.: Machine learning for high-speed corner detection. In: Leonardis, A., Bischof, H., Pinz, A. (eds.) ECCV 2006, Part I. LNCS, vol. 3951, pp. 430–443. Springer, Heidelberg (2006)
17. Rublee, E., Rabaud, V., Konolige, K., Bradski, G.: ORB: an efficient alternative to SIFT or SURF. In: 2011 IEEE International Conference on Computer Vision (ICCV), pp. 2564–2571. IEEE (2011)
18. Sopyła, K., Drozda, P., Górecki, P.: SVM with CUDA accelerated kernels for big sparse problems. In: Rutkowski, L., Korytkowski, M., Scherer, R., Tadeusiewicz, R., Zadeh, L.A., Zurada, J.M. (eds.) ICAISC 2012, Part I. LNCS, vol. 7267, pp. 439–447. Springer, Heidelberg (2012)
19. Yang, J., Yu, K., Gong, Y., Huang, T.: Linear spatial pyramid matching using sparse coding for image classification. In: IEEE Conference on Computer Vision and Pattern Recognition, CVPR 2009, pp. 1794–1801. IEEE (2009)
20. Young, R.A.: The gaussian derivative model for spatial vision: I. Retinal mechanisms. Spat. Vis. **2**(4), 273–293 (1987)

Stereo Matching by Using Self-distributed Segmentation and Massively Parallel GPU Computing

Wenbao Qiao(✉) and Jean-Charles Créput

IRTES-SET, University of Technology of Belfort-Montbéliard, Belfort, France
rapidbao@gmail.com

Abstract. As an extension of using image segmentation to do stereo matching, firstly, by using self-organizing map (som) and K-means algorithms, this paper provides a self-distributed segmentation method that allocates segments according to image's texture changement where in most cases depth discontinuities appear. Then, for stereo, under the fact that the segmentation of left image is not exactly same with the segmentation of right image, we provide a matching strategy that matches segments of left image to pixels of right image as well as taking advantage of border information from these segments. Also, to help detect occluded regions, an improved aggregation cost that considers neighbor valid segments and their matching characteristics is provided. For post processing, a gradient border based median filter that considers the closest adjacent valid disparity values instead of all pixels' disparity values within a rectangle window is provided. As we focus on real-time execution, these time-consumming works for segmentation and stereo matching are executed on a massively parallel cellular matrix GPU computing model. Finaly, we provide our visual dense disparity maps before post processing and final evaluation of sparse results after post-processing to allow comparison with several ranking methods top listed on Middlebury.

Keywords: Stereo · Image segmentation · SOM · Self-distributed segments

1 Introduction

Stereo matching from two 2D images is a process to estimate 3D scene but with acceptable error under the fact that we can not get really true disparity values for every pixel. Many solutions have been proposed for stereo to meet different requirements in various artificial intelligence research. These solutions can be categorized into four basic optimization approaches: local, global, cooperative and semi-global [1], among which the local methods are usually applied to real-time applications. Generally, local stereo methods work base on four steps: matching cost computation, cost aggregation, disparity computation and disparity refinement [2]. The cost aggregation step plays a more important influence on obtaining good results. For example, classical fixed window aggregation method using

© Springer International Publishing Switzerland 2016
L. Rutkowski et al. (Eds.): ICAISC 2016, Part II, LNAI 9693, pp. 723–733, 2016.
DOI: 10.1007/978-3-319-39384-1_64

matching cost such as color/grey absolute difference (AD) or mutual information [3] all suffers poor performance at depth discontinuities and in texture-less areas [4], leading to consequences like foreground fattening effect.

Researchers believe image segments can contribute border information to help distinguish background from foreground. Normally, these segments are small over-segments [5,6] under the assumption that disparity values of pixels within the same segment are same or vary smoothly. Considering the same matching strategy, even though there are few side-effects at curved surface regions compared with pixel-based dense matching method, the adavantages of segment-based techniques are well known: lessening computational complexity, enhancing noise tolerance [5] and border distinguishment.

Aiming at real-time execution, this paper proposes to use self-distributed image segmentation as main contribution to a newly proposed cost aggregation method. And because we train initial segment centers according to texture changement, our self-distributed segmentation method maybe an interesting solution to the difficulty cited by Yoon and Kweon [7]: the segmentation-based stereo methods require precise color segmentation that is difficult when dealing with highly textured images [7]. Our stereo's cost aggregation strategies are inspired by another real-time algorithm listed in top 20 methods on Middlebury [8], wrote by Hirschmüller et al. [9]. Hirschmüller uses selected multiple rectangular windows to compute Sum of Absolute Differences (SAD) for each pixel and applies only two optimization steps (error disparity filter and border correction) to get state-of-art results. As far as we can see, the multiple small windows which Hirschmüller used can be substituted by the segments produced by our algorithm, because his small windows may across depth discontinuity areas and introduce errors [9], but most of our segments will not. And through using segments, we lessen the most heavy computation part of [9] to get acceptable stereo matching quality for a local stereo method with little complexity.

In most cases, stereo matching processes for each matching unit is same, that is why people can use CUDA programming [10] to do parallel computing instead of calculating one unit after another sequentially by CPU. However, that is not new for stereo, here we not only decompose the input data into parts as usual but also use a massive cellular matrix model to execute neural networks with jobs like: training data, spiral search [11], zooming in/out at different levels of an original image, stereo matching, in a parallel and non-conflict way.

The rest of this paper is organized as follows. Section 2 presents previous work about different strategies using various image segmentation methods for stereo. Section 3 provides our proposed approaches including brief introduction of our cellular matrix model, how we get self-distributed segmentation and the way we use these segments to do stereo matching. Section 4 includes results visualization and discussion.

2   Previous Work

Various image segmentation methods have been proposed for stereo matching and researchers use different strategies to contribute segments to stereo.

Probabilistic-based methods such as Zitnick and Kang [5] use iterative K-means algorthm to produce color-based segmentation, which evolve to be SLIC [12] later. Then a Markov Random Field(MRF) is constructed by using segments as probability events. Through computing all pixels' Sum of Squared Differences(SSD) within one segment, Zitnick constructs that segment's matching probability for the MRF.

Global optimization methods such as Klaus et al. [6] applies Mean shift color segmentation, but the preliminary disparity values before post processing are calculated by computing color and gradient SAD of all pixels within a fixed pixel-level window. Segments are mainly used in post processing steps to refine each pixel's disparity value.

Another bottom-up segmentation method proposed by Bruzzone and Carlin [13] is also used in Xiao et al. [14]. However, Xiao et al. [14] only computes disparity values of segment's edge line points, counts their disparities and selects the most frequently appeared value as disparity for the segment region [14]. In fact, the edge line points used in [14] may turn out to belong to a slanting surface or curved surface whose disparity values vary hugely from center pixels to edge line pixels.

State-of-art local stereo methods such as Gerrits and Bekaert [15] additionally considers image segmentation information within rectanglar fixed window support region. The author segments the reference image and considers all window pixels outside the image segment that contains the pixel under consideration as outliers and greatly reduces their weight [15]. Tombari et al. [16] does similarly with Gerrits, the differences are that Tombari segments both reference and target images and introduces a modified weight function similar to adaptive weight method presented by Yoon and Kweon [7].

3   Proposed Approach

3.1   Overview

Under the fact that left and right images' segmentation maps are not exactly same and problems such as big segments may represent slanting or curved surfaces, it can bring matching errors when we only consider the border information extracted from segments. To tackle these problems when using segmentation to do stereo matching, we propose following two parts base on the assumption that objects' surfaces are piece-wise smooth like people treat a circle as a polygon with n sides:

- An image self-distributed over-segmentation method that allocates segments according to texture density or color changement where depth discontinuities usually appear.
- A stereo cost aggregation strategy that not only uses segments as matching units but also involves neighboring segments' matching characteristic to help detect some occluded regions.

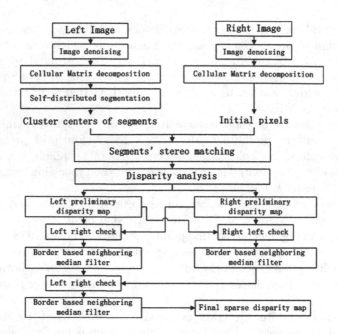

Fig. 1. Overall algorithm flow of our self-distributed segmentation-based stereo algorithm.

Futher more, we provide an improved gradient border-based median filter that considers the closest valid disparity values instead of involving all neighboring disparity values within a fixed window. And also, a cellular matrix parallel GPU computing model is provided to execute time-consumming jobs during processes of segmentation and stereo matching. We provide our algorithm's overall flow chart in Fig. 1.

3.2   Self-distributed Segmentation

We provide a cellular matrix model to execute neural networks and do parallel CUDA computation, this model contains following basic concepts:

– A concept of low level topological grid (neural network) with the same size as input image and its node (neuron) contains all attributes of its corresponding original pixel, as shown in Fig. 2 upper (a), here, too small to show details;
– Extracting nodes with a topological radius r on the low level grid, these nodes compose a higher level grids named base level shown in Fig. 2 upper (b, c). Here, each hexagon delimits one cell containing the decomposed low level nodes for GPU to do parallel jobs;
– Neighborhood search operators that can do local spiral search centered by each node within different topology radius of different levels' grid.

To produce self-distributed segments, firstly, we initialize K cluster centers for each final segment. Actually, these cluster centers are same with hexagonal

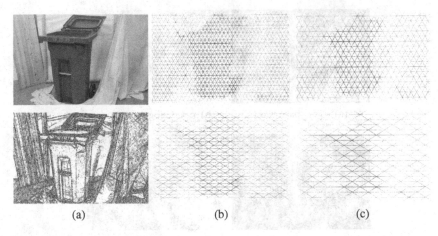

(a)   (b)   (c)

Fig. 2. Cellular matrix model for GPU parallel computation. Up (a) input left image of Recycle dataset from Middlebury [8], each pixel corresponds to one node belonging to the low level hexagonal grid; Up (b) base level with topological radius $r = 20$; Up (c) base level with topological radius $r = 30$; Down (a) gradient information of the input image; Down (b, c) second higher level grid extracted from Up (b, c) separately, namely geometric dual level.

nodes on base level shown in Fig. 2 upper (b, c). And the topological radius r decides the number of nodes, which finally influences stereo matching quality. Then, we use online-SOM [17] to train these initial cluster centers (neurons), aiming at allocating more neurons to areas where exists more color changement. Because the cluster centers are on the base level topological grid, the decomposition of these nodes for parallel computation should be on geometric dual level shown in Fig. 2 lower (b, c), in which each dual hexagon can be considered as a cell S_i containing equal number of cluster centers at beginning. And the learning direction of these cluster centers is controled by randomly determining which cell can do the training step of SOM by using an activity possibility stated in Eq. (1).

$$p_i = \frac{S_i}{\max\{S_1, S_2, \ldots, S_{num}\}} \tag{1}$$

Here, p_i is the activity probability of cell i; S_i is sum of initial gradient values of all the input pixels in cell i; and num is the quantity of cells.

After that, we slightly "exchange" these cluster centers to mean color position of all its similar color neighbor pixels as K-means does and get cluster center pixels. Here we only concern color difference when choosing the closest neighbor pixels for K-means because of the assumption that depth discontinuities always appear with color changement. Then these neighboring pixels are marked belong to that cluster center pixel and we get final self-distributed segmentation shown in Fig. 3(b, d). And the cluster center pixel's color information can represent all its subordinate pixels' color information. Comparing Fig. 3(b, d) with Fig. 2 upper (a), we can figure out that the allocation of self-distributed segments

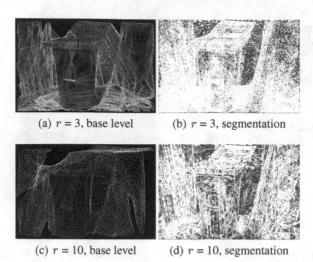

(a) $r = 3$, base level   (b) $r = 3$, segmentation

(c) $r = 10$, base level   (d) $r = 10$, segmentation

Fig. 3. Self-distributed cluster centers and the final segmentation for stereo matching. (a, c) Online-som results with topological radius $r = 3$ and $r = 10$ separately; (b, d) final self-distributed segmentation, the white lines indicate borders of these segments.

reflects texture changement of the input image, where higher color changement regions have more and smaller segments while segments in texture-less regions can also support our assumptions.

3.3 Stereo Matching by Using Segments

As we use the cluster center pixles as representatives of the self-distributed segments, the basic strategy that we contribute segments to stereo matching is to match these cluster center pixels of left image to pixels of right image. Of course, image denoising step is indispensable to reduce influence of noise pixels. This strategy works base on the fact that cluster centers pixel has mean color value of its segment and the segment are very small, just like people treat a circle as a polygon with n sides.

Then, only considering left image's segmentation, for each current cluster center pixel p_{iL} which we are dealing with, we spiral search all its neighbor cluster center pixels p_{jL} within another topological radiu r_S. Under the assumption that depth discontinuity appears with color discontinuity, here we set an empirical threshold (β) of color AD between p_{iL} and its neighbor cluster center pixel p_{jL} using Eq. (2), to decide n_{jL} valid neighbor segments that can contribute to p_{iL}'s aggregation cost in Eq. (4). We also count the number (n_{jR}) of valid projection pixels P'_{jR} whose color AD with p_{iL} less than the same threshold (β) in the right image, the bigger the difference between n_{jL} and n_{jR}, the smaller chance this candidate disparity value is correct.

$$AD(p_{iL}, p_{jL}) = \left[\left| \begin{matrix} R_{p_{iL}} - R_{p_{jL}} \\ G_{p_{iL}} - G_{p_{jL}} \\ B_{p_{iL}} - B_{p_{jL}} \end{matrix} \right| \right] \tag{2}$$

Here p_{jL} is the closest neighbor cluster center pixles surrounding p_{iL} in the left image.

$$SAD(p_{iL}, s) = \sum_{p_0}^{p_{n_{jL}}} \left(\left[\left| \begin{matrix} R_{P_{jL}}(p_{jx}, p_{jy}) - R_{P'_{jR}}(p_{jx} - s, p_{jy}) \\ G_{P_{jL}}(p_{jx}, p_{jy}) - G_{P'_{jR}}(p_{jx} - s, p_{jy}) \\ B_{P_{jL}}(p_{jx}, p_{jy}) - B_{P'_{jR}}(p_{jx} - s, p_{jy}) \end{matrix} \right| \right] \right) \tag{3}$$

Here $P_{jL} = (p_0, p_1 ... p_{n_{jL}})$ are neighbor valid cluster center pixels of p_{iL}, n_{jL} represents the quantity; s is candidate disparity value within the disparity range given by Middlebury; P'_{jR} are the projection pixels of P_{jL} on the right image with s.

$$C(p_{iL}, s) = \beta * SAD(p_{iL}, s) + (1 - \beta) \left| n_{jL} - n_{j'R} \right| \tag{4}$$

Here, n_{jR} is the quantity of valid neighbor projection pixels P'_{jR} in the right image.

Then, the candidate disparity value that minimize the aggregation cost $C(p_{iL}, s)$ is considered as the preliminary disparity result of p_{iL}. We adapt this disparity value to all the subordinate pixels belong to p_{iL} and get disparity map shown in Fig. 4(c) without post processing steps.

However, only selecting the minimum aggregation cost by Eqs. (2)–(4) can not solve the occluded region marked in Fig. 4(a), because this region corresponds to nothing correctly in the right image. To detect this kind of occluded region, at process of computing Eq. (3), we set another threshold (θ) of color AD between the valid left neighbor cluster center pixels and its candidate projection pixels on the right image, shown in Eq. (5). This means we check the neighbor segments' matching characteristics when we compute the aggregation cost for p_{iL}. Then, our segmentation-based aggregation cost can detect that occluded region as shown in Fig. 4(d).

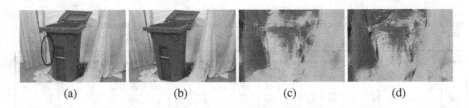

(a)	(b)	(c)	(d)

Fig. 4. Preliminary disparity maps with radius parameters $r = 5$ and $r_S = 3$ before post-processing. (a) input left image with one kind of occluded region being marked with black ellipse; (b) input right image; (c) disparity map got by using Eqs. (2)–(4) for the left image; (d) improved disparity map got by adding Eqs. (5) to Eq. (3), the occluded region marked in (a) has been detected.

$$AD(P_{jL}, P'_{jR}) = \left[\begin{array}{l} |R_{P_{jL}}(p_{jx}, p_{jy}) - R_{P'_{jR}}(p_{jx} - s, p_{jy})| \\ |G_{P_{jL}}(p_{jx}, p_{jy}) - G_{P'_{jR}}(p_{jx} - s, p_{jy})| \\ |B_{P_{jL}}(p_{jx}, p_{jy}) - B_{P'_{jR}}(p_{jx} - s, p_{jy})| \end{array} \right] \tag{5}$$

Here, P_{jL} are the neighbor valid cluster center pixels surrounding p_{iL}; P'_{jR} are the candidate correspondences of P_{jL} in the right image with candidate disparity value s.

4 Post Processing and Result Evaluation

As we put emphasis on the quality of preliminary disparity map before post-processing, we make a comparison of our preliminary dense results with three top ranking results after post-processing, shown in Fig. 6. We can discern the smoothness of our results compared with BSM in some regions where disparity values seem correct and the clear distinguishment of foreground with background compared with R-NCC. Though our preliminary results before post processing can not compete with these two methods on Middlebury, our results can be improved by adding many other optimization steps that have been proved by many other researchers.

For example, before post-processing, we borrow idea from Hirschmüller et al. [9] and use his disparity analysis strategy. After left-right cross check (LRC), we use a gradient border-based median filter as post-processing step, which can avoid fuzzy borders that usually happen with normal window-based median filter: we firstly exclude small gradient values from initial gradient image and get the gradient boundaries similar as Fig. 2 down (a); then we spiral search neighboring valid disparities surrounding the bad pixel detected by LRC instead of using fixed rectangle window surrounding that bad pixel; if the searcher touches the gradient boundaries or bigger than a certain searching radius, it stops; also we do not fix these bad pixels locating on gradient boundaries. The final evaluation of our sparse disparity maps (SDSWTA) on Middlebury shows

Set: training dense training sparse
Metric: bad 0.5 bad 1.0 bad 2.0 bad 4.0 avgerr rms A50 A90 A95 A99 time time/MP time/GD
Mask: nonocc all
plot selected show invalid Reset sort

Date	Name (bad 0.5 (%))	Res	Avg (Weight)	Adiron MP: 5.7 nd: 290 im0 im1 GT nonocc	ArtL MP: 1.5 nd: 256 im0 im1 GT nonocc	Jadepl MP: 5.2 nd: 640 im0 im1 GT nonocc	Motor MP: 5.9 nd: 280 im0 im1 GT nonocc	MotorE MP: 5.9 nd: 280 im0 im1 GT nonocc	Piano MP: 5.4 nd: 260 im0 im1 GT nonocc	PianoL MP: 5.4 nd: 260 im0 im1 GT nonocc	Pipes MP: 5.7 nd: 300 im0 im1 GT nonocc	Playrm MP: 5.3 nd: 330 im0 im1 GT nonocc	Playt MP: 5 nd: 290 im0 im1 GT nonocc	PlaytP MP: 5 nd: 290 im0 im1 GT nonocc	Recyc MP: 5.6 nd: 260 im0 im1 GT nonocc	Shelvs MP: 5.9 nd: 240 im0 im1 GT nonocc	Teddy MP: 2.7 nd: 256 im0 im1 GT nonocc	Vintge MP: 5.5 nd: 760 im0 im1 GT nonocc
04/08/15	REAF	H	66.6 31	66.7 31	63.8 30	64.6 31	63.5 30	62.3 27	66.1 31	72.3 30	61.1 31	71.7 32	79.3 32	64.9 31	66.1 31	80.3 32	62.3 30	79.8 32
03/03/16	SDSWTA	Q	71.4 32	71.0 32	82.0 34	58.4 29	72.1 32	71.7 30	70.9 32	77.8 32	69.7 32	68.7 31	66.2 23	68.3 32	74.8 32	73.8 20	73.7 32	73.6 30
01/21/15	TSGO	F	78.1 33	76.8 33	69.2 32	86.2 34	74.7 33	76.2 31	80.6 33	86.9 33	74.2 33	85.7 34	81.9 33	73.6 33	75.6 33	85.0 33	76.1 33	87.9 34
08/31/14	BSM	Q	82.2 34	80.6 34	79.8 33	82.9 33	79.4 34	79.1 32	82.3 34	88.6 34	80.4 34	84.5 33	87.5 34	81.9 34	81.5 34	88.0 34	81.0 34	87.6 33

Fig. 5. Evaluation of our sparse disparity results after post processing (SDSWTA). This evaluation only concerns the percentage of bad pixel 0.5 without occluded parts of the left image.

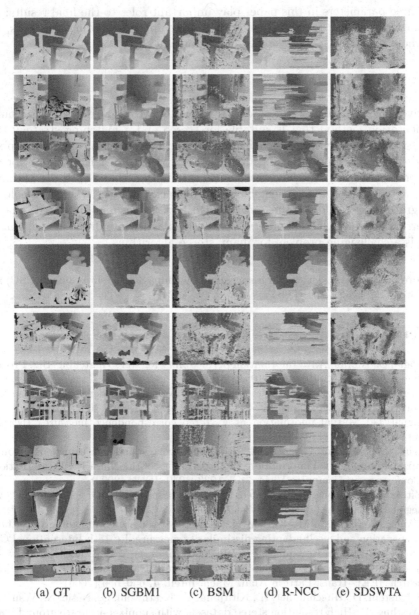

(a) GT   (b) SGBM1   (c) BSM   (d) R-NCC   (e) SDSWTA

Fig. 6. Comparison of our preliminary dense results before post processing with three top ranking methods listed on Middlebury. (a) Ground Truth; (b) SGBM1; (c) BSM; (d) R-NCC; (e) Our method, SDSWTA.

that our method can reach an interesting accuracy. One of the best evaluations is shown in Fig. 5.

Three parameters in this paper play important roles to the final results: the topological radius r for SOM and r_S for searching neighboring segments, the threshold θ to select valid neighbor correspondences.

5   Conclusion

To give an objective assessment of our methods, we provide a self distributed segmentation method that is suitable for stereo and a matching strategy that adapts to this segmentation. The aggregation cost may not be suitable for pixel-based dense matching method, but we have proved that it is adequate for our segments-based strategy. The reasonable assumption that depth discontinuity happens with color changement has its drawbacks at cases where the color of background is very close to the foreground's. Just as shown in Fig. 4(c, d), matching errors appear near the borders of white wall and white drape in Fig. 4(a, b). This is a challenging problem for many stereo algorithms.

Acknowledgments. This paper is sponsored by China Scholarship Council(CSC) and laboratory IRTES-SET of UTBM.

References

1. Cigla, C., Alatan, A.A.: Information permeability for stereo matching. Sig. Process. Image Commun. **28**(9), 1072–1088 (2013)
2. Scharstein, D., Szeliski, R.: A taxonomy and evaluation of dense two-frame stereo correspondence algorithms. Int. J. Comput. Vis. **47**(1–3), 7–42 (2002)
3. Egnal, G.: Mutual information as a stereo correspondence measure. Technical reports (CIS), p. 113 (2000)
4. Kim, J., Kolmogorov, V., Zabih, R.: Visual correspondence using energy minimization and mutual information. In: Proceedings of the Ninth IEEE International Conference on Computer Vision, pp. 1033–1040. IEEE (2003)
5. Zitnick, C.L., Kang, S.B.: Stereo for image-based rendering using image over-segmentation. Int. J. Comput. Vis. **75**(1), 49–65 (2007)
6. Klaus, A., Sormann, M., Karner, K.: Segment-based stereo matching using belief propagation and a self-adapting dissimilarity measure. In: 18th International Conference on Pattern Recognition, ICPR 2006, vol. 3, pp. 15–18. IEEE (2006)
7. Yoon, K.-J., Kweon, I.S.: Adaptive support-weight approach for correspondence search. IEEE Trans. Pattern Anal. Mach. Intell. **4**, 650–656 (2006)
8. Scharstein, D., Hirschmüller, H., Kitajima, Y., Krathwohl, G., Nešić, N., Wang, X., Westling, P.: High-resolution stereo datasets with subpixel-accurate ground truth. In: Jiang, X., Hornegger, J., Koch, R. (eds.) GCPR 2014. LNCS, vol. 8753, pp. 31–42. Springer, Heidelberg (2014)
9. Hirschmüller, H., Innocent, P.R., Garibaldi, J.: Real-time correlation-based stereo vision with reduced border errors. Int. J. Comput. Vis. **47**(1–3), 229–246 (2002)
10. NVIDIA: CUDA C Programming Guide 4.2, CURAND Library, Profiler User's Guide (2012). http://docs.nvidia.com/cuda

11. Bentley, J.L., Weide, B.W., Yao, A.C.: Optimal expected-time algorithms for clos-
    est point problems. ACM Trans. Math. Softw. (TOMS) **6**(4), 563–580 (1980)
12. Achanta, R., Shaji, A., Smith, K., Lucchi, A., Fua, P., Susstrunk, S.: Slic superpix-
    els compared to state-of-the-art superpixel methods. IEEE Trans. Pattern Anal.
    Mach. Intell. **34**(11), 2274–2282 (2012)
13. Bruzzone, L., Carlin, L.: A multilevel context-based system for classification of very
    high spatial resolution images. IEEE Trans. Geosci. Remote Sens. **44**(9), 2587–2600
    (2006)
14. Xiao, J., Xia, L., Lin, L.: Segment-based stereo matching using edge dynamic
    programming. In: 2010 3rd International Congress on Image and Signal Processing
    (CISP), vol. 4, pp. 1676–1679. IEEE (2010)
15. Gerrits, M., Bekaert, P.: Local stereo matching with segmentation-based outlier
    rejection. In: The 3rd Canadian Conference on Computer and Robot Vision, 2006,
    p. 66. IEEE (2006)
16. Tombari, F., Mattoccia, S., Di Stefano, L.: Segmentation-based adaptive support
    for accurate stereo correspondence. In: Mery, D., Rueda, L. (eds.) PSIVT 2007.
    LNCS, vol. 4872, pp. 427–438. Springer, Heidelberg (2007)
17. Kohonen, T.: The self-organizing map. Proc. IEEE **78**(9), 1464–1480 (1990)

Diabetic Retinopathy Related Lesions Detection and Classification Using Machine Learning Technology

Rituparna Saha, Amrita Roy Chowdhury, and Sreeparna Banerjee[✉]

Department of Computer Science and Engineering,
West Bengal University of Technology, Kolkata, India
sreeparna.banerjee@wbut.ac.in

Abstract. A novel Computer Aided Diagnosis System for early diagnosis of Diabetic Retinopathy is proposed for the detection and classification of Bright lesion classes and Dark lesion classes of Fundus Retina images using machine learning mechanisms. In the proposed methodology, the detection procedure is based on Fuzzy C Means (FCM) clustering technique to segment the candidate region areas. In the Dark lesion category, attempts are being made to modify the Micro aneurysms detection and Blood vessel elimination with the help of improvised algorithms. For the classification of each Bright and Dark lesion classes a classification system is built using machine learning algorithms namely Naive Bayes and Support Vector Machine. A comparative study between the two machine learning algorithms yield accuracy of 97.0588 % for Bright lesion classification using Naive Bayes classifier and accuracy of 88.8889 % for Dark lesion classification using Support Vector Machine classifier.

Keywords: Diabetic retinopathy · Fuzzy C means · Nave Bayes classifier · Support Vector Machine classifier

1 Introduction

Diabetic retinopathy (DR) a leading cause of vision loss in Diabetic patients, can occur in two stages namely Non-Proliferative Diabetic Retinopathy (NPDR) and Proliferative Diabetic Retinopathy (PDR). Manifestations of DR groups of lesions are found in the retina of individuals suffering from diabetes. The visible signs of DR are mainly Dark lesions like Micro Aneurysms (MA) and Hemorrhages (HEM) and Bright lesions mainly denotes the exudates like Hard Exudates (HE) and Cotton Wool Spots (CWS). On opthalomoscopic examination, Micro Aneurysms (MA), Hemorrhages (HEM) and Hard Exudates (HE) are visible in Non-Proliferative Diabetic Retinopathy (NPDR) which is the early stage of DR and Cotton Wool Spots (CWS) are observed during the later stages of NPDR. Dark lesions are red in color due to presence of blood. The first clinically observable lesions indicating DR are Micro aneurysms appeared as small red dots located within the deep retinal capillary network. Hemorrhages caused

© Springer International Publishing Switzerland 2016
L. Rutkowski et al. (Eds.): ICAISC 2016, Part II, LNAI 9693, pp. 734–745, 2016.
DOI: 10.1007/978-3-319-39384-1_65

by bleeding are also one of the most notable symptoms of DR occurring during later stages of NPDR and extending into Proliferative Diabetic Retinopathy (PDR). Hard Exudates (HE) are one type of Bright lesions visible as bright yellowish color occurring due to leakage of lipoproteins. The presence of HE are manifested as discrete bright yellow lesions, varying in size and most frequently seen in the posterior pole. Cotton Wool Spots (CWS) or Soft Exudates (SE) are superficial retinal infarcts. They have white fluffy appearance and ill-defined edges. In the present time through Computer Aided Diagnosis (CAD) system attempts are being made to modify the diagnosis of DR. Monitoring and checking of the progress of this disease from the fundus retina images using CAD system is more efficient than normal screening technique.

This paper aims at integrating image processing and machine learning approaches in order to remove regular structures like Blood vessels and Optic Disk from the retina images and extract the Region of Interest (ROI) areas of the lesions occurring during various stages of NPDR and then perform comparative study between two machine learning based classification techniques to identify the particular lesion type. The classification system bears the advantage of using metadata as well as the ability to perform satisfactorily even with incomplete data. This paper gives a suitable approach for diagnosis the early stage of DR i.e. the NPDR stage.

The next section, Sect. 2 discusses the related works on this field that is followed by a description of the various stages of the proposed methodology in Sect. 3. In Sect. 4, experimental results are presented. Conclusion and Future Work are given in Sects. 5 and 6, respectively.

2   Related Works

Several attempts have been made to detect and classify DR through various methodologies. A comparative analysis of Support Vector Machine and Neural Network is performed for exudate classification in [1]. Another comparative analysis of exudate classification was done using Fuzzy logic and K-means in [2]. Zhang and Opas proposed local contrast enhancement processing and improved Fuzzy C means in LUV color space to segment Bright lesion areas and also used hierarchical Support Vector Machine for classification in [3]. In [4] series of experiments on feature selection and exudate classification using Support Vector Machine classifier is presented. In [5] Gaussian Scale space is used for exudate detection, Support Vector Machine is used for classification and beside that also proposed severity detection method. Niemeijer et al. [6] proposed a unique technique for detection and classification of Bright lesion areas consisting Drusens, Hard Exudates and Cotton Wool Spots using machine learning mechanisms. Rocha et al. [7] proposed a novel method using SURF features and using a machine learning method for detecting Bright lesions. In [8] the LibSVM package is used for classification of Soft and Hard Exudates. Zhang et al. [9] used random forest based classification method for exudate detection.

Influenced by many ideas this paper attempts to propose a suitable approach for DR related Bright lesions mainly denoting the exudates and Dark lesions denoting MA, HEM. At the same time a suitable algorithm is also proposed for Micro Aneurysm detection based on edge detection and some statistical feature values. The Bright lesions and Dark lesions of diabetic retinopathy images are extracted using Fuzzy C Means segmentation method and subsequently the classes of Bright lesion regions and Dark lesion regions are classified using machine learning methods, namely Naive Bayes Classifier and Support Vector Machine Classifier, after removal of regular objects like Blood Vessel tree and Optic Disk (OD) area.

3   Proposed Methodology

The proposed methodology is divided into 4 parts, I. Preprocessing part, II. Dark lesions and Bright lesions extraction part & Removal of Optic Disk and Blood Vessel areas, III. Feature extraction part and IV. Classification part. The overview of the method is shown in Fig. 1.

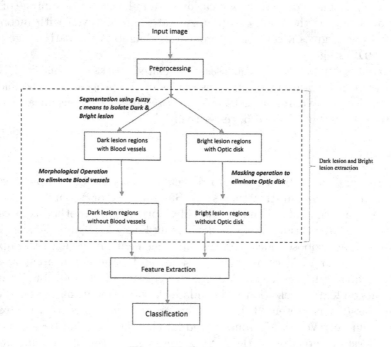

Fig. 1. Method overview

Database: Database consists of 40 fundus retina images of DR patients collected from ophthalmologist of city hospital and 100 images from publicly available DIARETDB0 database are used for the experiment. The MATLAB and Weka 3.7 [10] software tools are used for algorithm development and classification purpose respectively.

3.1   Preprocessing Phase

Preprocessing steps help in accurate feature extraction and also used to remove noise parts in fundus retina images. In order to improve the quality of the input fundus retina image Histogram Specification is done. This technique modifies the shape of the histogram of the input image according to the specified shape of the histogram of the referenced image. Further, the image has been Cropped to eliminate the black corners of the fundus image. In the following Green channel (G) is extracted from the RGB processed image as it contains the most useful information of lesions. The Green channel is mainly highly sensitive to the Blood vessels and the Dark lesions than the Red channel (R) and Blue channel (B). The extracted channel has been filtered using Median filtering to remove noise and smooth images. Contrast Limited Adaptive Histogram Equalization (CLAHE) is used to improve the local contrast of filtered image. Another contrast enhancement approach for the low contrast gray scale image is also used through specifying the range of intensity value.

3.2   Extraction of Dark and Bright Lesion Phase

The preprocessed image is segmented using Fuzzy C Means (FCM) clustering method based on the intensity level of pixels. Generally the number of clusters is specified as three because of a retinal image contains mainly three types of color [11], dark red color for Blood Vessel tree, Hemorrhages and Micro aneurysms; bright yellow color for Optic Disk, Hard Exudates and Cotton Wool Spots and reddish yellow color for retinal membrane and fluid. But, after thoroughly observing many experimental results of the segmentation, number of clusters specified as three does not always give good results for Dark and Bright lesion detection. It is mainly due to wide variation of color into the retina surface area. In this proposed methodology the number of clusters is selected as four for Bright lesion detection and seven for Dark lesion detection after observing the results of several trials. After segmentation the resultant extracted Bright lesion region contains the Optic Disk (OD) region. To eliminate the OD region a mask image is formed depending on the position and size of OD, then logical operation (OR operation) and subtraction operation are applied between the mask image and image of extracted Bright lesion region with OD. Similarly the resultant extracted Dark lesion region after segmentation contains the blood vessel trees. To eliminate the unnecessary blood vessel regions, they need to be detected separately. The steps to detect blood vessel tree are depicted below.

Algorithm: Blood Vessel Detection
Input Image: Color fundus image
Output: Image containing only Blood Vessel
Step 1: The input image is passed through the proposed preprocessing steps.
Step 2: Closing (morphology) operation is applied on the resultant preprocessed image.The closing operator is a dilation followed by erosion defined in equation (1) where morphological dilation operation adds pixels to the boundaries of objects in an image and morphological erosion operation removes pixels on

object boundaries.

$$(A \bullet B) = (A \oplus B) \odot B \tag{1}$$

Step 3: The closing image is subtracted from the preprocessed image.
Step 4: The contrast of the subtracted image is enhanced.
Step 5: The resultant image is converted to binary image.
Step 6: Blood vessels are selected from the resultant image using concept of compactness. Compactness is calculated using equation (2) defined by

$$C = \left(\frac{A_R}{P_R^2}\right) \tag{2}$$

where A_R and P^2_R are area and perimeter of the region R respectively. It has been checked that perfect circular regions have compactness 0.08 and those regions which are nearly circular have compactness less than 1.5. For this reasons, region having compactness range between 1.6 to 2 are selected as vessels. Figure 2 shows the images obtained after different steps of Blood Vessel Extraction.

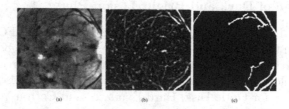

Fig. 2. Blood vessel extraction, (a) Preprocessed image (b) Contrast enhanced image after closing operation and subtraction operation (c) Final blood vessel extracted image

To eliminate the blood vessel tree from the segmented Dark lesion region, logical operation (OR operation) and subtraction operation are applied between the image containing only blood vessel tree and image containing all Dark lesions with blood vessel tree. Figures 3 and 4 represents the images obtained after different steps of Dark Lesion and Bright lesion Extraction respectively.

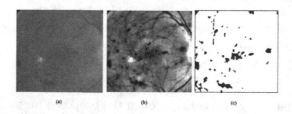

Fig. 3. Dark lesion extraction (a) Original image (b) Preprocessed image (c) Dark lesion extraction

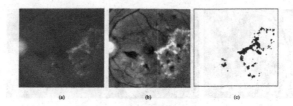

Fig. 4. Bright lesion extraction (a) Original image (b) Preprocessed image (c) Bright lesion extracted image

Micro aneurysms (MA) are the first clinical observable sign of DR, but are very hard to detect due to their low contrast and small size. It is also difficult to distinguish MA from noise or pigmentation. Therefore segmentation using FCM clustering cannot select all Micro aneurysm areas properly. In this proposed methodology, to select Micro aneurysms accurately a unique method is applied. The algorithm for detecting Micro aneurysms is discussed below.

Algorithm: Micro Aneurysm detection
Input Image: Color fundus image.
Output: Image containing only Micro Aneurysms.
Step 1: The input image is passed through the proposed preprocessing steps.
Step 2: Edge detection method is performed on the preprocessed image using Canny edge detection method.
Step 3: The enclosed areas of the edge detected image are filled up.
Step 4: The output image containing detected edges obtained in step 2 is subtracted from the area filled image obtained in step 3. Through this procedure along with these Micro aneurysm, some regions not containing Micro aneurysms are also selected. To remove unwanted areas steps 5, 6 and 7 are followed.
Step 5: As Micro aneurysms are very small in size, the larger areas are removed using Matlab function.
Step 6: Micro aneurysms are considered here with less than 12 pixels. The regions having low intensity value, pixels with intensity less than 60 are selected.
Step 7: The Solidity and Circularity of the selected regions are calculated using equation (3) and (4) respectively. Regions having Solidity greater than and equal to 0.8 or Circularity greater than or equal to 0.45 are ultimately considered as Micro aneurysms. Figure 5 represents the images obtained after different steps of Micro Aneurysm Detection.

$$Solidity = (Area/ConvexArea) \qquad (3)$$

$$Circularity = \left(Perimeter^2\right) \times (4 \times \pi \times Area) \qquad (4)$$

3.3   Feature Extraction Phase

After extracting the Regions of Interest (ROI) areas of retina i.e. the Bright lesion parts and Dark lesion parts, the next important step is the feature extraction. Based on the distinguishable characteristics of retinal abnormalities a total number of 9 statistical features are selected of which 6 are Shape based and 3 are Texture based features. Table 1 lists all the features that are extracted.

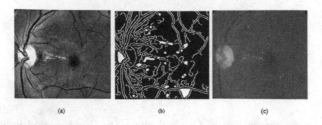

Fig. 5. Micro aneurysm detection (a) Original image (b) Preprocessed image (c) Detected micro aneurysm

Table 1. List of extracted features

Feature Type	Feature names	Explanation
Shape based Features	1. Area of Connected region	Number of Pixels in the region
	2. Perimeter of Region	Distance between each adjoining pair of pixels around the boarder of the region.
	3. Convex Area of Region	Specifies number of pixels in Convex image.
	4. Solidity of Region	Solidity= Area / Convex Area
	5. Circularity of Region	Circularity= (Perimeter ^2)*(4*pi*Area)
	6. Compactness of Region	Compactness= Area / (Perimeter^2)
Texture based Features	7. Mean (M) of Region	$$M = \sum_{i=0}^{L-1} z_i\, p(z_i)$$ Where z_i is a variable indicating intensity at location i, $p(z_i)$ is the histogram of the intensity levels in a region
	8. Standard Deviation (σ) of Region	$$\sigma = \sqrt{\frac{1}{L-1}\sum_{i=0}^{L-1}(z_i - \mu)^2}$$ Where z_i is a variable indicating intensity at location i, μ denotes simple mean intensity value of region
	9. Smoothness (R) of Region	$R = 1 - 1/(1+\sigma^2)$ Where σ denotes the Standard deviation

3.4   Classification Phase

In our proposed methodology, a classification system is developed using machine learning mechanisms that follows the feature extraction part. The classification system using supervised learning techniques is used to classify the candidate region areas based on their feature values. The system is trained individually using 2 datasets of the above mentioned feature vectors for perfectly classification of Bright lesion and Dark lesion regions. The detail information of training datasets and testing datasets for Dark lesion classification and Bright lesion classification is shown in Table 2. A comparative study between two well-known machine learning algorithms namely Naive Bayes Classifier and Support Vector Machine (SVM) Classifier is done to classify Bright lesions into Micro aneurysms

(MA), Hemorrhages (HEM) and Dark lesions into Hard Exudates (HE), Cotton Wool Spots (CWS). SVM is used to find best hyper plane that define decision boundaries between two classes of data. The books (Vapnik, 1995; Vapnik, 1998) contains the explanation of SVM. Naive Bayes classifier is probabilistic approach based on Bayes theorem with independence assumptions between predictors [12]. The proposed experiment is evaluated on SVM using Polynomial Kernel and the same experiment is also evaluated on Naive Bayes classifier. A detailed analysis of the performance of the two classifier is discussed in the following part.

Table 2. Training and testing set of classification system

DR lesion type	Training Set	Testing Set
Dark lesion	HEM lesions = 71 MA lesions =39	HEM lesions = 35 MA lesions= 28
Bright lesion	HE lesions = 65 CWS lesions=15	HE lesions = 27 CWS lesions = 7

4   Experimental Results and Discussions

Performance of the classification system using the Naive Bayes (NB) classifier and Support vector machine (SVM) classifier is evaluated from the data of confusion matrices. A confusion matrix contains information about actual and predicted classification done by a classification system [13]. The comparative analysis of confusion matrix result of the testing sets are depicted in Fig. 6.

The results for Bright lesion classification in Fig. 6(a) using NB classifier shows better results than in Fig. 6(b) using SVM classifier. For Bright lesion using NB classifier among 7 CWS, 7 are correctly classified and among 27 HE, 26 are correctly classified whereas for SVM classifier among 7 CWS 6 are correctly classified and among 27 HE 26 are correctly classified.

In case of Dark lesion classification the Fig. 6(d) using SVM classifier shows better results than the Fig. 6(c) using NB classifier. For Dark lesion using NB classifier among 35 HEM 26 are correctly classified and among 28 MA 26 are correctly classified whereas for SVM classifier among 35 HEM 34 are correctly classified and among 28 MA 22 are correctly classified.

Figure 6(a) shows Confusion matrix of the Bright lesion classification using Naive Bayes classifier, Fig. 6(b) shows Confusion matrix of the Bright lesion classification using Support Vector Machine classifier, Fig. 6(c) shows Confusion matrix of the Dark lesion classification using Naive Bayes classifier, Fig. 6(d) shows Confusion matrix of the Dark lesion classification using Support Vector Machine classifier.

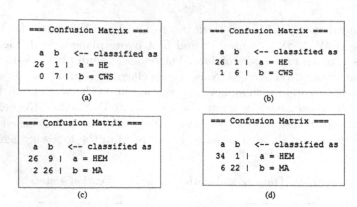

Fig. 6. Confusion matrix result of testing sets of dark lesions and bright lesions

For performance comparison sensitivity and specificity values are measured. Sensitivity specifies percentage of true positivity, Specificity specifies percentage of false positivity and Accuracy is overall success rate. All these measures are calculated based on 4 values True Positive rate (TP), False Positive rate (FP), False Negative rate (FN), True Negative rate (TN). These measures are defined in the following equations.

$$Sensitivity = \left(\frac{TP}{TP + FN} \right) \tag{5}$$

$$Specificity = \left(\frac{TN}{TN + FP} \right) \tag{6}$$

$$Accuracy = \left(\frac{TP + TN}{TN + FP + TP + FN} \right) \tag{7}$$

For a particular class, True Positive Rate (TP) denotes number of lesions correctly classified in that class. False Negative (FN) denotes number of lesions of the particular class that are incorrectly classified. False Positive (FP) denotes number of lesions of other classes incorrectly classified. True Negative (TN) denotes number of lesions of other classes correctly classified.

Performance comparison of Dark lesion and Bright lesion regions are shown in Tables 3 and 4, respectively. It is clearly visible that from the comparative results shown in Table 3, SVM gives better result than Naive Bayes for classifying Dark

Table 3. Performance comparison result of dark lesion classification

Machine Learning Algorithm	Sensitivity	Specificity	Accuracy
Naive Bayes Classifier	96.29%	100%	82.5397%
SVM	96.29%	85.71%	88.8889%

Table 4. Performance comparison result of bright lesion classification

Machine Learning Algorithm	Sensitivity	Specificity	Accuracy
Naive Bayes Classifier	74.28%	92.85%	97.0588%
SVM	97.14%	78.57%	94.116%

lesions and from the comparative results shown in Table 4, Naive Bayes is slightly superior to SVM for classifying Bright lesions.

5 Conclusion

Our classification is totally feature based. In this proposed method, a total number of 9 features have been used. These are effective in the classification of the Bright lesion classes and Dark lesion classes. The 9 features includes 6 shape based features and 3 texture based features. Among these 9 features, those feature results are very useful for classification, are labeled as Grade I and those features that are partly useful are labeled as Grade II. In case of Dark lesions of DR, Feature 1, 2, 3, 4, 6 and 9 i.e. Area, Perimeter, Solidity, Convex area, Compactness and Smoothness respectively yield good results for isolating Micro aneurysms from Hemorrhages. Mean intensity feature is useful for differentiating the Dark and Bright lesions. In case of Bright lesions, Feature 6, 8 and 9 i.e. Compactness, Standard deviation and Smoothness features show better result for differentiating Hard exudates from Cotton wool spots. Therefore, based on experimental results using this proposed method, for Dark lesion classification Feature 1, 2, 3, 4, 6, 7, 9 are labeled as Grade I features and Feature 5, 8 are labeled as Grade II features. Similarly for Bright lesion classification Feature 6, 7, 8 and 9 are labeled as Grade I and Feature 1, 2, 3, 4 and 5 are labeled as Grade II feature. In Table 5 the grading of features are shown.

Table 5. Feature grade table

	Grade I Features	Grade II Features
For Dark Lesions	Feature 1. Area of connected region Feature 2. Perimeter of region Feature 3. Solidity of region Feature 4. Convex area of region Feature 6. Compactness of region Feature 7. Mean intensity value of region Feature 9. Smoothness of region	Feature 5. Circularity of region Feature 8. Standard deviation of region intensity value
For Bright Lesions	Feature 6. Compactness of region Feature 7. Mean intensity value of region Feature 8. Standard deviation of region intensity value Feature 9. Smoothness of region	Feature 1. Area of connected region Feature 2. Perimeter of region Feature 3. Solidity of region Feature 4. Convex area of region Feature 5. Circularity of region

Table 6. Comparison table of accuracy for dark lesion and bright lesion classification

Dark Lesion		Bright Lesion	
Method	Accuracy	Method	Accuracy
Nayak et al. [14]	82.6%	Nayak et al. [14]	88.3%
Niemeijer et al. [15]	92.9%	Walter et al. [16]	92.7%
Akram et al. [17]	93.71%	Akram et al. [17]	94.73%
Proposed method	97.0588%	Proposed method	88.8889%

In this work we have used total 140 Diabetic Retinopathy images. The novelty of the method lies in proposing a computer based system that can select Bright lesions and Dark lesions separately using Fuzzy C means clustering, at the same time shows a better approach to detect the Micro aneurysms and blood vessel tree and classify the each classes of Bright lesions using Naive Bayes classifier with 97.0588 % accuracy and the each classes of Dark lesions using Support Vector Machine Classifier with 88.8889 % accuracy, which appears to be promising in the diagnosis of DR. The comparison of accuracy for both Dark lesions and Bright lesions of the proposed method with other research works [14–17] is shown in Table 6.

6   Future Work

This proposed methodology involves heterogeneous information such as images and contextual information. The aggregation of the variables and consideration of missing information might hamper the process flow of the methodology. Machine learning mechanisms are more suited for retrieving and processing of these heterogeneous as well as incomplete information. With large data sets, the classifier to be used can be standardized. The clinical efficiency of our system can be improved by taking more retinal image under uniform lighting. In future, more images, including those obtained from hospitals, will be used for experiment purpose. This will be helpful for standardization of the type of classifier to be used.

Acknowledgment. The authors would like to acknowledge a grant from TEQIP and Department of Biotechnology, Government of India (No. BT/PR4256/BID/7/393/2012 dated 02.08.2012) for supporting this research.

References

1. Osareh, A., Mirmehdi, M., Thomas, B., Markham, R.: Comparative exudate classification using support vector machines and neural networks. In: Dohi, T., Kikinis, R. (eds.) MICCAI 2002, Part II. LNCS, vol. 2489, pp. 413–420. Springer, Heidelberg (2002)
2. Vandarkuzhali, T., Ravichandran, C.S., Preethi, D.: Detection of exudates caused by diabetic retinopathy in fundus retinal image using fuzzy k means and neural network. IOSR J. Electr. Electron. Eng. (IOSR-JEEE) **6**(1), 22–27 (2013)

3. Xiaohui, Z., Chutatape, O.: Top-down and bottom-up strategies in lesion detection of background diabetic retinopathy. In: IEEE Computer Society Conference on Computer Vision and Pattern Recognition (CVPR), pp. 422–428 (2005)

4. Wisaeng, K., Hiransakolwong, N., Pothiruk, E.: Automatic detection of retinal exudates using a support vector machine. Appl. Med. Inform. **32**(1), 33–42 (2013)

5. Haloi, M., Dandapat, S., Sinha, R.: A Gaussian scale space approach for exudates detection, classification and severity prediction. arXiv:1505.00737v1 [cs.CV] (2015)

6. Niemeijer, M., Ginneken, B.V., Russell, S.R., Suttorp-Schulten, M.S.A., Abramoff, M.D.: Automated detection and differentiation of drusen, exudates, and cotton-wool spots in digital color fundus photographs for diabetic retinopathy diagnosis. Invest. Ophthalmol. Vis. Sci. **48**, 2260–2267 (2007)

7. Rocha, A., Carvalho, T., Jelinek, H.F., Goldenstein, S., Wainer, J.: Points of interest and visual dictionaries for automatic retinal lesion detection. IEEE Trans. Biomed. Eng. **59**(8), 2244–2253 (2012)

8. Chang, C.-C., Lin, C.-J.: LIBSVM: a library for support vector machines. ACM Trans. Intell. Syst. Technol. **2**, 27 (2011)

9. Zhang, X., et al.: Exudate detection in color retinal images for mass screening of diabetic retinopathy. Med. Image Anal. **18**(7), 1026–1043 (2014)

10. http://www.cs.waikato.ac.nz/ml/weka/documentation.html

11. Banerjee, S., Chowdhury, R.A.: Case based reasoning in the detection of retinal abnormalities using decision trees. In: International Conference on Information and Communication Technologies (ICICT 2014). Procedia Comput. Sci. **46**, 402–408 (2015)

12. Huang, G.M., Huang, K.Y., Lee, T.Y., Weng, J.T.Y.: An interpretable rule-based diagnostic classification of diabetic nephropathy among type 2 diabetes patients. BMC Bioinform. **16**(1), 1–10 (2015)

13. http://www2.cs.uregina.ca/dbd/cs831/notes/confusion_matrix/confusion_matrix. html

14. Nayak, J., Subbanna Bhat, P., Rajendra Acharya, U., Lim, C.M., Kagathi, M.: Automated identification of diabetic retinopathy stages using digital fundus images. J. Med. Syst. **32**, 107–115 (2008)

15. Niemeijer, M., Abramoff, M.D., Ginneken, B.V.: Infor-mation fusion for diabetic retinopathy CAD in digital color fundus photographs. IEEE Trans. Med. Imaging **28**(5), 775–785 (2009)

16. Walter, T., Klein, J.C., Massin, P., Erginay, A.: A con-tribution of image processing to the diagnosis of diabetic retinopathy-detection of exudates in color fundus images of the human retina. IEEE Trans. Med. Imaging **21**(10), 1236–1243 (2002)

17. Akram, U.M., Khan, S.A.: Automated detection of dark and bright lesions in retinal images for early detection of diabetic retinopathy. J. Med. Syst. **36**(5), 3151–3162 (2012)

Query-by-Example Image Retrieval
in Microsoft SQL Server

Paweł Staszewski[1], Piotr Woldan[1], Marcin Korytkowski[1],
Rafał Scherer[1(✉)], and Lipo Wang[2]

[1] Institute of Computational Intelligence, Częstochowa University of Technology,
Al. Armii Krajowej 36, 42-200 Częstochowa, Poland
`rafal.scherer@iisi.pcz.pl`
[2] School of Electrical and Electronic Engineering,
Nanyang Technological University, Block S1,
Nanyang Avenue, Singapore 639798, Singapore
`http://iisi.pcz.pl`

Abstract. In this paper we present a system intended for content-based
image retrieval tightly integrated with a relational database management
system. Users can send query images over the appropriate web service
channel or construct database queries locally. The presented framework
analyses the query image based on descriptors which are generated by the
bag-of-features algorithm and local interest points. The system returns
the sequence of similar images with a similarity level to the query image.
The software was implemented in .NET technology and Microsoft SQL
Server 2012. The modular construction allows to customize the system
functionality to client needs but it is especially dedicated to business
applications. Important advantage of the presented approach is the support by SOA (Service-Oriented Architecture), which allows to use the
system in a remote way. It is possible to build software which uses functions of the presented system by communicating over the web service
API with the WCF technology.

Keywords: Content-based image retrieval · Relational databases ·
Bag-of-features · Query by image · WCF · Microsoft SQL Server

1 Introduction

Content-based image retrieval (CBIR) is part of a broader computer vision area.
Thanks to CBIR-related methods [1,5,6,13,14,20,21,23,27,33] we are able to
search for similar images and classify them [35,41]. To compare images we have
to extract some form of visual features, e.g. color [10,16,30], textures [3,8,12,37],
shape [11,15,39] or edges [43]. Other choice can be local invariant features [24–
26,28,36] with the most popular detectors and descriptors SURF [2], SIFT [24]
and ORB [34]. To find similar images to a query image, we need to compare all
feature descriptors of all images usually by some distance measures. Such comparison is enormously time consuming and there is ongoing worldwide research

© Springer International Publishing Switzerland 2016
L. Rutkowski et al. (Eds.): ICAISC 2016, Part II, LNAI 9693, pp. 746–754, 2016.
DOI: 10.1007/978-3-319-39384-1_66

to speed up the process. Yet, the current state of the art in the case of high-dimensional computer vision applications is not fully satisfactory. The literature presents countless methods, e.g. [32] and they are mostly based on some form of approximate search. Generally, when the amount of data is increasing, in a consequence the compunctions are more complex. Moreover, the process of loading images from storage requires more time.

Recently, the bag-of-features (BoF) approach [9,22,29,31,36,40,42] has gained in popularity. In the BoF method, clustered vectors of image features are collected and sorted by the count of occurrence (histograms). All individual descriptors or approximations of sets of descriptors presented in the histogram form must be compared. The information contained in descriptors allows for finding a similar image to the query image. Such calculations are computationally expensive. Moreover, the BoF approach requires to redesign the classifiers when new visual classes are added to the system.

All these aforementioned methods require a large amount of data and computing power to provide an appropriate efficiency. Despite applying some optimization methods to these algorithms, the data loading process is time-consuming. In the case of storing the data in the database, when a table contains n records, the similarity search requires $O(log_2 n)$ comparisons. Image comparison procedure can take less time when some sorting mechanisms are applied in a database management system. Noteworthy solutions are proposed by different database products [4,19,38]. A system designed for the image classification task based on fuzzy logic was presented in [18] and on BoF with a MS SQL Server database was presented in [17]. The system structure allowed to modify crucial components without resulting in interferences with the other modules. Thus, authors of the current paper modify the system to adapt it to image retrieval task, i.e. to detect similar images to the query image which was presented on the system input.

MS SQL Server offers the FileTable mechanisms thanks to the SQL Server FILESTREAM technology to store large files a filesystem. Modifying the content of objects stored in a FileTable can be performed by adding, or removing data from directories linked to this table and the changes are visible in the table automatically.

The paper is organizes as follows. In Sect. 2 the proposed approach for system architecture and functionality was presented. Section 3 contains examples of the system response to query images.

2   Description of the Proposed System

The system described in this paper allows to search similar images to the query image which was provided by a user or a client program. Users are able to interact with our system by executing a stored procedure. There is also a possibility of calling the methods from a WCF service in a remote way. This operation can be performed in a client software. When the user interacts with the system locally, the query images can by copied to a special directory called Test, which is the integral part of the database FileTable structure. As a consequence, the appropriate trigger is executed and adequate testing stored procedure is called. When client software connects to our system remotely, it is necessary to transfer the query image as stream over the network. The authors provided API mechanisms to perform this kind of interaction.

2.1   Architecture of the System

The main target of the system are business applications that need a fast CBIR functionality. It encapsulates computer vision algorithms and other mechanisms, thus the user do not have to know how to implement them. MS SQL Server 2012 provides the UDT mechanism (User Defined Types) which was used for crucial elements such as image keypoints, dictionaries, or descriptors. All UDT types were programmed with custom serialization mechanisms. These types are stored in assemblies included in the database which is linked to our system. The software was based on .NET platform. Moreover, the additional advantage is the use of the Filestream technology which is included in MS SQL Server. As a consequence, reading high resolution images is much faster than with using classical methods. The aforementioned technology provides the interaction with image database, based on the content of appropriate folders (linked to FileTable objects), designed to storing images. Placing new images in these folders fires the adequate trigger. It gives the advantage of automatic initialization of the corresponding database objects without additional operations. Users have to indicate a query image to compare. As a result, the system returns the sequence of images similar to the content of the query image. The process of extending the set of indexed images in the database boils down to copying images to FileTable directories. Then, the dictionary and descriptors are be generated automatically after inserting the number of words for dictionary in an appropriate stored procedure. Figure 1 presents the architecture which was divided into four layers. In the first layer, the user selects a query image for transferring to the system over the remote WCF channel or by copying to the Test folder locally. After processing the query image, user obtains the response as the sequence of similar images (sorted in descending order from the most similar image). The second layer is an interface which allows to perform queries to the system database. The list of similar images consists of file paths from a database and similarity levels assigned to appropriate files. The third layer acts as the physical MS SQL Server database. This is the place of storing the information about the images and their descriptors. The table with descriptors is indexed to speed up generating response. At this level it is also possible to execute a stored procedure which contributes to running the bag-of-features algorithm and indicating similar images over the WCF endpoint. The last layer contains the WCF service functionality. Methods shared by the web service module run the main algorithms, generate keypoints and descriptors basing on the dictionary. Having the dictionary, it is possible to perform the similarity calculation procedure. The response collected from the system contains a sorted list which is transferred to the second layer. The list stores top_n most similar images, which can be accessed from the first layer.

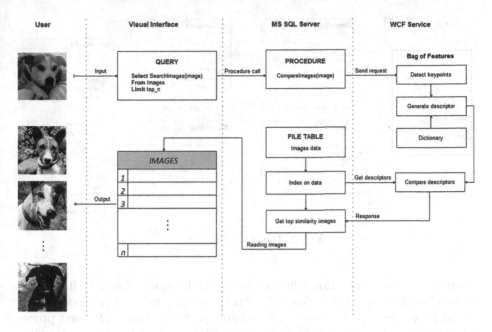

Fig. 1. System architecture.

2.2   System Functionality

The system was divided into modules, which are dedicated for specific functions. These modules include communication interfaces with other modules. The layered software implementation allows to modify some modules, without interfering with the other architecture parts of the system.

The domain model layer is a fundamental module for business logic of the system and was created with the Database First approach. Figure 2 presents the database diagram. Considering the integration of the applied mechanisms from .NET platform, Microsoft SQL Server 2012 was chosen. The database structure was designed based on the bag-of-features algorithm. Keypoints, dictionaries and descriptors were stored in the database as UDT (User Defined Types), for which serialization mechanisms were implemented. System functionality is mainly based on the bag-of-features algorithm [29]. This algorithm was chosen by the authors of this paper because of the relatively high effectiveness and fast operation. Keypoints are calculated using the SIFT method, nevertheless the system can use other visual feature generation techniques. The local features calculated for images are stored in the database along with the dictionary structures and descriptors generated basing on these dictionaries. This approach entails the requirement of only one generation of crucial data structures for the system. The Images_FT table was designed with the FileTable technology and contains images which are necessary for the training process. As a consequence, the entire content of this table influences cluster calculation and effectiveness of similarity detection.

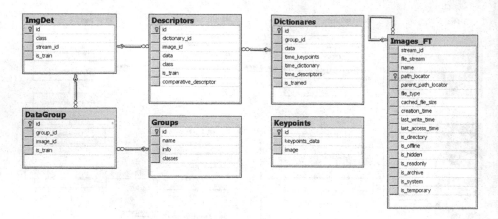

Fig. 2. Database diagram.

Query by image operation relies on the initial dictionary loading with appropriate identification number from the `Dictionaries` table. This operation is crucial for calculating descriptors for the adequate dictionary. The next procedure compares the query image descriptor with the other descriptors stored in the database. Vectors $x = \{x_1, x_2, \cdots, x_n\}$ are generated for images from the database, and $y = \{y_1, y_2, \cdots, y_n\}$ is calculated for the query image. The next procedure is responsible for comparing descriptors by the Euclidean distance. As a result, we determine the similarity factors for all comparisons sorted in descending order.

Our software has the functionality of classifying the query image, basing on the support vector machine (SVM) classifiers trained on descriptor collection. Information about the class membership can be used with the similarity results. The SVM classifiers are stored in the database after the process of training with the collection of descriptors from `Images_FT` table.

In an attempt to provide remote interaction with the system, we implemented SOA layer (Service Oriented Architectures) in .NET technology. To achieve this essential aim, WCF (Windows Communication Foundation) web service was programmed. In this case client software can execute procedures remotely. The system architecture also provides the distributed processing system, when a database server is situated in a different physical location. Hence, we implemented remotely executed WCF methods from stored procedures.

3   Numerical Experiments

In this section we present the results of example experiments performed to validate the correctness of the system. We used images taken from the PASCAL Visual Object Classes (VOC) dataset [7]. We queried the database with images and the returned images are shown with the distances to the query descriptor.

The first part of the tests was performed for query images which were not included in the database. When an image is presented on the system input, the response vector $R = S(x, y1), S(x, y2), ..., S(x, yN)$ obviously did not include similarity values being equal zero. It contained k similar images from an appropriate class of the query image. Figure 3 presents the example with several returned images. The next experiments consisted in showing images which had the exact representation in the database (in Images_FT table), i.e. they were included in the dictionary building process. In this case, the response vector obviously included the output with m values equal zero, when m indicates the amount of identical images contained in the database. If the request was configured for including the k similar images, when $k > m$, then response vector should comprise $k > m$ values greater than zero. Figure 4 shows an example of querying the database with an image that existed in the database.

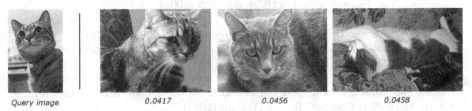

Query image   0.0417   0.0456   0.0458

Fig. 3. Querying test performed for an image which is not included in the database. The distance to the query image is given for each returned image.

Query image   0.0   0.0877   0.0903

Fig. 4. Querying test performed for an image which was included in the database. The distance to the query image is given for each returned image.

4 Conclusions

We developed a system dedicated to image retrieval by providing an integrated environment for image analysis in a relational database management system environment. Nowadays RDBMS are used for collecting very large amount of data, thus it is crucial to integrate them with content-based visual querying methods. In the proposed system computations concerning visual similarity are encapsulated in the business logic of our system, users are only required to have knowledge about communication interfaces included in the proposed software. Applying database indexing methods affects positively speeding up the image retrieval.

Moreover, our system is integrated with .NET platform. The authors chose the WCF technology for providing the remote interaction with the system. MS SQL Sever allows to attach assemblies implemented in .NET to the database dedicated for image analysis. As a consequence, users can interact with the system locally by SQL commands, which execute remote procedures. It is an important advantage of the system. The system retrieves images in near real-time.

References

1. Akhtar, Z., Rattani, A., Foresti, G.L.: Temporal analysis of adaptive face recognition. J. Artif. Intell. Soft Comput. Res. **4**(4), 243–255 (2014)
2. Bay, H., Ess, A., Tuytelaars, T., Van Gool, L.: Speeded-up robust features (SURF). Comput. Vis. Image Underst. **110**(3), 346–359 (2008)
3. Chang, T., Kuo, C.C.: Texture analysis and classification with tree-structured wavelet transform. IEEE Trans. Image Process. **2**(4), 429–441 (1993)
4. Chaudhuri, S., Narasayya, V.R.: An efficient, cost-driven index selection tool for Microsoft SQL server. VLDB **97**, 146–155 (1997)
5. Chu, J.L., Krzyzak, A.: The recognition of partially occluded objects with support vector machines and convolutional neural networks and deep belief networks. J. Artif. Intell. Soft Comput. Res. **4**(1), 5–19 (2014)
6. Drozda, P., Sopyła, K., Górecki, P.: Online crowdsource system supporting ground truth datasets creation. In: Rutkowski, L., Korytkowski, M., Scherer, R., Tadeusiewicz, R., Zadeh, L.A., Zurada, J.M. (eds.) ICAISC 2013, Part I. LNCS, vol. 7894, pp. 532–539. Springer, Heidelberg (2013)
7. Everingham, M., Van Gool, L., Williams, C.K.I., Winn, J., Zisserman, A.: The pascal visual object classes (VOC) challenge. Int. J. Comput. Vis. **88**(2), 303–338 (2010)
8. Francos, J., Meiri, A., Porat, B.: A unified texture model based on a 2-D Wold-like decomposition. IEEE Trans. Signal Process. **41**(8), 2665–2678 (1993)
9. Grauman, K., Darrell, T.: Efficient image matching with distributions of local invariant features. In: 2005 IEEE Computer Society Conference on Computer Vision and Pattern Recognition, CVPR 2005, vol. 2, pp. 627–634, June 2005
10. Huang, J., Kumar, S., Mitra, M., Zhu, W.J., Zabih, R.: Image indexing using color correlograms. In: 1997 IEEE Computer Society Conference on Computer Vision and Pattern Recognition, Proceedings, pp. 762–768, June 1997
11. Jagadish, H.V.: A retrieval technique for similar shapes. SIGMOD Rec. **20**(2), 208–217 (1991)
12. Jain, A.K., Farrokhnia, F.: Unsupervised texture segmentation using gabor filters. Pattern Recogn. **24**(12), 1167–1186 (1991)
13. Kanimozhi, T., Latha, K.: An integrated approach to region based image retrieval using firefly algorithm and support vector machine. Neurocomputing **151**, 1099–1111 (2015)
14. Karakasis, E., Amanatiadis, A., Gasteratos, A., Chatzichristofis, S.: Image moment invariants as local features for content based image retrieval using the bag-of-visual-words model. Pattern Recogn. Lett. **55**, 22–27 (2015)
15. Kauppinen, H., Seppanen, T., Pietikainen, M.: An experimental comparison of autoregressive and Fourier-based descriptors in 2D shape classification. IEEE Trans. Pattern Anal. Mach. Intell. **17**(2), 201–207 (1995)

16. Kiranyaz, S., Birinci, M., Gabbouj, M.: Perceptual color descriptor based on spatial distribution: a top-down approach. Image Vis. Comput. **28**(8), 1309–1326 (2010)
17. Korytkowski, M., Scherer, R., Staszewski, P., Woldan, P.: Bag-of-features image indexing and classification in Microsoft SQL server relational database. In: 2015 IEEE 2nd International Conference on Cybernetics (CYBCONF), pp. 478–482 (2015)
18. Korytkowski, M., Rutkowski, L., Scherer, R.: Fast image classification by boosting fuzzy classifiers. Inf. Sci. **327**, 175–182 (2016)
19. Larson, P., Clinciu, C., Hanson, E.N., Oks, A., Price, S.L., Rangarajan, S., Surna, A., Zhou, Q.: SQL server column store indexes. In: Proceedings of the 2011 ACM SIGMOD International Conference on Management of Data, pp. 1177–1184. ACM (2011)
20. Lin, C.H., Chen, H.Y., Wu, Y.S.: Study of image retrieval and classification based on adaptive features using genetic algorithm feature selection. Expert Syst. Appl. **41**(15), 6611–6621 (2014)
21. Liu, G.H., Yang, J.Y.: Content-based image retrieval using color difference histogram. Pattern Recogn. **46**(1), 188–198 (2013)
22. Liu, J.: Image retrieval based on bag-of-words model (2013). arXiv preprint arXiv:1304.5168
23. Liu, S., Bai, X.: Discriminative features for image classification and retrieval. Pattern Recogn. Lett. **33**(6), 744–751 (2012)
24. Lowe, D.G.: Distinctive image features from scale-invariant keypoints. Int. J. Comput. Vis. **60**(2), 91–110 (2004)
25. Matas, J., Chum, O., Urban, M., Pajdla, T.: Robust wide-baseline stereo from maximally stable extremal regions. Image Vis. Comput. **22**(10), 761–767 (2004). British Machine Vision Computing 2002
26. Mikolajczyk, K., Schmid, C.: Scale and affine invariant interest point detectors. Int. J. Comput. Vis. **60**(1), 63–86 (2004)
27. Murata, M., Ito, S., Tokuhisa, M., Ma, Q.: Order estimation of Japanese paragraphs by supervised machine learning and various textual features. J. Artif. Intell. Soft Comput. Res. **5**(4), 247–255 (2015)
28. Nister, D., Stewenius, H.: Scalable recognition with a vocabulary tree. In: Proceedings of the 2006 IEEE Computer Society Conference on Computer Vision and Pattern Recognition, CVPR 2006, vol. 2, pp. 2161–2168. IEEE, Computer Society, Washington, DC (2006)
29. O'Hara, S., Draper, B.A.: Introduction to the bag of features paradigm for image classification and retrieval (2011). arXiv preprint arXiv:1101.3354
30. Pass, G., Zabih, R.: Histogram refinement for content-based image retrieval. In: Proceedings of the 3rd IEEE Workshop on Applications of Computer Vision, WACV 1996, pp. 96–102, December 1996
31. Philbin, J., Chum, O., Isard, M., Sivic, J., Zisserman, A.: Object retrieval with large vocabularies and fast spatial matching. In: 2007 IEEE Conference on Computer Vision and Pattern Recognition, CVPR 2007, pp. 1–8, June 2007
32. Rafiei, D., Mendelzon, A.O.: Efficient retrieval of similar shapes. VLDB J. **11**(1), 17–27 (2002)
33. Rashedi, E., Nezamabadi-pour, H., Saryazdi, S.: A simultaneous feature adaptation and feature selection method for content-based image retrieval systems. Knowl. Based Syst. **39**, 85–94 (2013)
34. Rublee, E., Rabaud, V., Konolige, K., Bradski, G.: Orb: An efficient alternative to sift or surf. In: 2011 IEEE International Conference on Computer Vision (ICCV), pp. 2564–2571, November 2011

35. Shrivastava, N., Tyagi, V.: Content based image retrieval based on relative loca-
    tions of multiple regions of interest using selective regions matching. Inf. Sci. **259**,
    212–224 (2014)
36. Sivic, J., Zisserman, A.: Video google: a text retrieval approach to object matching
    in videos. In: Proceedings of the 2003 Ninth IEEE International Conference on
    Computer Vision, vol. 2, pp. 1470–1477, October 2003
37. Śmietański, J., Tadeusiewicz, R., Łuczyńska, E.: Texture analysis in perfusion
    images of prostate cancer–a case study. Int. J. Appl. Math. Comput. Sci. **20**(1),
    149–156 (2010)
38. Srinivasan, J., De Fazio, S., Nori, A., Das, S., Freiwald, C., Banerjee, J.: Index with
    entries that store the key of a row and all non-key values of the row. US Patent
    6,128,610, 3 October 2000
39. Veltkamp, R.C., Hagedoorn, M.: State of the art in shape matching. In: Lew,
    M.S. (ed.) Principles of Visual Information Retrieval, pp. 87–119. Springer, London
    (2001)
40. Voloshynovskiy, S., Diephuis, M., Kostadinov, D., Farhadzadeh, F., Holotyak,
    T.: On accuracy, robustness, and security of bag-of-word search systems. In:
    IS&T/SPIE Electronic Imaging, International Society for Optics and Photonics,
    p. 902807 (2014)
41. Yang, J., Yu, K., Gong, Y., Huang, T.: Linear spatial pyramid matching using
    sparse coding for image classification. In: 2009 IEEE Conference on Computer
    Vision and Pattern Recognition, CVPR 2009, pp. 1794–1801, June 2009
42. Zhang, J., Marszalek, M., Lazebnik, S., Schmid, C.: Local features and kernels
    for classification of texture and object categories: a comprehensive study. In: 2006
    Conference on Computer Vision and Pattern Recognition Workshopp, CVPRW
    2006, p. 13, June 2006
43. Zitnick, C.L., Dollár, P.: Edge boxes: locating object proposals from edges. In:
    Fleet, D., Pajdla, T., Schiele, B., Tuytelaars, T. (eds.) ECCV 2014, Part V. LNCS,
    vol. 8693, pp. 391–405. Springer, Heidelberg (2014)

New Algorithms for a Granular Image Recognition System

Krzysztof Wiaderek[1(✉)], Danuta Rutkowska[1,2],
and Elisabeth Rakus-Andersson[3]

[1] Institute of Computer and Information Sciences,
Czestochowa University of Technology, 42-201 Czestochowa, Poland
{krzysztof.wiaderek,danuta.rutkowska}@icis.pcz.pl
[2] Information Technology Institute,
University of Social Sciences, 90-113 Lodz, Poland
[3] Department of Mathematics and Natural Sciences,
Blekinge Institute of Technology, 37179 Karlskrona, Sweden
elisabeth.andersson@bth.se

Abstract. The paper describes new algorithms proposed for the granular pattern recognition system that retrieves an image from a collection of color digital pictures based on the knowledge contained in the object information granule (OIG). The algorithms use the granulation approach that employs fuzzy and rough granules. The information granules present knowledge concerning attributes of the object to be recognized. Different problems are considered depending on the full or partial knowledge where attributes are "color", "location", "size", "shape".

Keywords: Image recognition · Information granulation · Fuzzy sets · Rough sets · Knowledge-based system

1 Introduction

This paper refers to our previous articles where the granulation approach to color digital picture (image) recognition is presented. In [24] the granular pattern recognition system (GPRS) and object information granules are introduced. In addition, examples of image recognition problems to be solved by the GPRS are proposed and described.

Different information granules (e.g. color granule, location granule) are considered in [22–24]. With regard to the object attributes such as color, location, size and shape, fuzzy and rough granules based on the fuzzy set [25] and rough set theory [9], respectively, are employed.

In this paper, we propose new algorithms for particular cases of the knowledge concerning the attributes of the granules describing the object to be recognized.

2 Granular Image Recognition System

In our previous article [24] we introduced the concept of the OIG (Object Information Granule) and the GPRS (Granular Pattern Recognition System). The

L. Rutkowski et al. (Eds.): ICAISC 2016, Part II, LNAI 9693, pp. 755–766, 2016.
DOI: 10.1007/978-3-319-39384-1_67

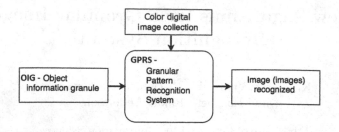

Fig. 1. Diagram of the granular image recognition system

OIG includes some knowledge describing the object that must be recognized within the image collection. Figure 1 portrays the OIG at the input of the GPRS, as well as the collection of photos (images). The output of the GPRS presents the color digital picture (or pictures) retrieved from the image collection.

The algorithm employed by the GPRS, proposed in this paper, is illustrated in Fig. 2. As we see, different cases of particular algorithms are applied according to the knowledge contained in the OIG. Details of these algorithms are described in Sect. 4.

The algorithm presented in Fig. 2 allows to solve the problem of image recognition introduced in [21–23]. Different tasks are distinguished within this problem, depending on the knowledge containing in the OIG. These particular tasks – corresponding to the algorithms shown in Fig. 2 and described in Sect. 4 – are explained in Sect. 3 (see Fig. 3), as well as in Sect. 5.

In this general algorithm there are eight special algorithms used depending on the available knowledge, i.e. attribute values in the OIG. Names of these algorithms, shown in Fig. 2, indicate the number and type of the attributes. For example, A1 – is the algorithm for the granule of one known attribute – color, A4 – algorithm for the OIG with all four attributes known, A2 and A3 – algorithms for, respectively, two and three known attributes in the OIG. Because the color attribute is always present (in all input granules) it is omitted in the names of the algorithms, so only the remaining known attributes are given in the index names of the algorithms. For example, $A3_{Loc-Siz}$ – means the algorithm for the OIG with three known attributes: color, location, and size. More information about the original input granules is included in Sect. 3.

3   Different Object Information Granules and the Corresponding Algorithms for the GPRS

To select from a collection of photos, the image (images) containing the object described by the given attributes such as color, location, size and shape, the OIG is created and applied to the input of the GPRS, as shown in Fig. 1 (Sect. 2). The image recognition system uses the proper algorithm that corresponds to the knowledge included in the OIG, in order to accomplish this task.

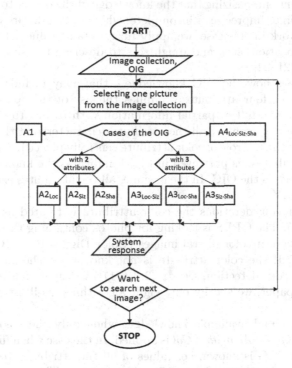

Fig. 2. General algorithm for the GPRS

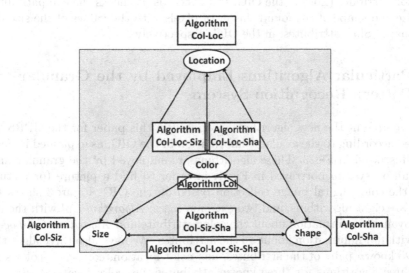

Fig. 3. Eight algorithms for the granular image recognition system

It is important emphasizing that the knowledge of the object to be recognized may be uncertain or imprecise or incomplete, which in fact occurs very often. For the system to work in this case, we apply fuzzy sets as values of the attributes such as color, location, size, and rough sets to describe the shape attribute of the object; see [21–24].

Figure 3 shows how the OIG knowledge - that may include values of one or two or three or four attributes - implies the use of the special algorithms corresponding to the full or partial information with regard to the object. We see that its base is presenting all the attributes characterizing the object to be recognized (with the key role of color attribute centrally placed). The relationship between the attributes, as portrayed in Fig. 3, indicates the knowledge that can describe an object as the OIG. In the granule, all the attributes except color can be known or not.

Thus, in our considerations the color attribute is treated as primary (the most important). The GPRS is looking for photos containing the object (OIG), from the collection of color digital images (Color Digital Image Collection), as shown in Fig. 1. If the color attribute is not known, we should employ other algorithms (e.g. edge detection, see e.g. [2,3,6,17]) which are not included in the GPRS. In this paper, we specify only eight algorithms, as illustrated in Figs. 2 and 3.

With the minimal availaible knowledge, when only the color attribute is known in the OIG, the *Algorithm Col* is applied. In the case when full information contained in the OIG is known, i.e. values of all the attributes (color, location, size, shape), the *Algorithm Col-Loc-Size-Sha* is used. The latter algorithm is looking for the clusters of pixels of a color corresponding to the color attribute (Col) in the location (in the analyzed image) described by the value of the location attribute (Loc) in the OIG. If it succeeds, it checks the compatibility of the size and shape of the found cluster of pixels with the values of the size (Siz) and shape (Sha) attributes, in the OIG, respectively.

4   Particular Algorithms Employed by the Granular Pattern Recognition System

Now we present the new algorithms, proposed in this paper for the GPRS, and applied according to the available information in the OIG, as explained in Sect. 3 and illustrated in Fig. 3. These algorithms are employed by the granular image recognition system portrayed in Fig. 1, in order to find a picture (or pictures) from the color digital image collection based on the OIG. Figure 3 shows that there are eight algorithms, and two extreme cases: *Algorithm Col* with the minimal available information about the color attribute and *Algorithm Col-Loc-Siz-Sha* with full information about all the attributes. We have also three algorithms for two known pairs of the attributes, i.e.: color-location, color-size, color-shape and three algorithms for three known attributes, i.e. color-location-size; color-location-shape; color-size-shape. As a result, we have in total eight different algorithms depending on the available information.

4.1   Algorithm Col (With Color Attribute Only)

We use this algorithm when we have only one attribute – the color attribute. It is an extreme case – with the minimal available information about the image to be recognized, so the GPRS would be able to search the answer in an image collection, where "answer" means an image containing an object whose only known feature is the color (no other information is available). Then the algorithm begins with the selection of a pixel (more precisely – the position in the analysed image) from which we start the analysis; that means comparing the color of the selected pixel with a given color. The easiest way is randomly selecting a pixel, and we present an algorithm for this method:

1. Randomly select a pixel from the analyzed image
2. Check if the color of the selected pixel corresponds to the value of the color attribute (Col), in the OIG;
   - (a) if not
     - randomly select the next pixel of the remaining pixels and check its color (if it corresponds to the value of the color attribute (Col)) until they are available in the image; if not found then the analysed image is rejected,
   - (b) if yes
     - examine the color of neighbouring pixels and those which have a given color are attached to the group until the availability of all the neighbouring pixels of a given color. At the same time, add the next pixels to the cluster of the pixels, and count them (it will be useful later). In other words, we are looking for clusters of pixels "of the same color". Of course, the color is treated in the fuzzy sense (equality or similarity of fuzzy sets in the CIE color space [21]). The resulting cluster of pixels is the granule of color of the object to be retrieved.
3. The image containing a group (cluster) of pixels of a given color is the answer.
   - (a) if it is enough for a user, it is over
   - (b) if not, the system can also look for the next groups of pixels with a given color in this analyzed image, repeating from point 1 until a satisfactory end result (from the user's perspective).

4.2   Algorithm Col-Loc-Siz-Sha (With All Attributes)

We use this algorithm when we know all the attributes, that means: color, location, size, shape. This is the second extreme case – with full information about the object to be recognized. This algorithm applies the idea of macropixels, introduced in [22]:

1. Using the size attribute (Siz) of the object, determine the size of the macropixel as a rectangle with a size corresponding to the size of the object.
2. On the basis of the location attribute (Loc) of the object, define the proper macropixel within the analyzed image. That means: select the macropixel which has the same location as the object to be retrieved, and the rest of the macropixels of the analyzed image are skipped;

3. In the selected macropixel, search groups (clusters) of pixels with a color corresponding to the value of the known color attribute (Col) of the object, as described in Subsect. 4.1, point 1;
   - (a) if such clusters of pixels are not found, the analyzed image is rejected,
   - (b) if found, then go to point 4.
4. Check if the found cluster of pixels has a shape similar to the shape attribute (Sha) of the object to be retrieved;
   - (a) if not, then look for the next cluster similar to that indicated by the shape attribute (Sha) of the object until it is available; if such a cluster has not been found then the analyzed image is rejected,
   - (b) if yes, the analyzed image is the system answer.

4.3   Algorithm Col-Loc-Siz

We use this algorithm when we know the three attributes, that means: color, location, size. It is a case of incomplete information about the object to be retrieved; a shape attribute (Sha) is unknown. This algorithm uses some steps of the *Algorithm Col-Loc-Siz-Sha:*

1. Repeat the actions from Subsect. 4.2, points 1–3a.
2. If a cluster of pixels with a color corresponding to the value of the color attribute (Col) of the object to be retrieved has been found, the analyzed image is a system answer. In this case, the macropixel is a "window" (frame), which contains the object to be recognized, that can be represented by rough sets (top, bottom approximation).

4.4   Algorithm Col-Loc-Sha

We use this algorithm when we know the three attributes, that means: color, location, shape. It is a case of incomplete information about the object to be recognized; a size attribute (Siz) is unknown. This algorithm uses a procedure similar to that in *Algorithm Col:*

1. For all the pixels lying in a given location, corresponding to the value of the location attribute (Loc) of the object to be retrieved, check the compatibility of the color of the pixel, with the given value of the color attribute (Col) of the object, and look for clusters of pixels with the same color, analogously to Subsect. 4.1;
   - (a) if such clusters of pixels are not found, the analyzed image is rejected,
   - (b) if found, then go to point 2.
2. Check if the found cluster of pixels has a shape similar to the value of the shape attribute (Sha) of the object to be retrieved;
   - (a) if not, then the analysed image is rejected,
   - (b) if yes, then the analysed image is a system answer.

4.5 Algorithm Col-Siz-Sha

We use this algorithm when we know the three attributes, that means: color, size, shape. This is a case of incomplete information about the object to be recognized; a value of the location attribute (Loc) is unknown. This algorithm uses a procedure similar to that in *Algorithm Col:*

1. Set the size of the macropixel corresponding to the value of the indicated size attribute (Siz) of the object to be retrieved.
2. Randomly select the macropixels and look for clusters of pixels of a color corresponding to the value of the color attribute (Col) of the object to be retrieved, similarly as in Sect. 4.1;
   - (a) if such clusters of pixels are not found, reject the analyzed image,
   - (b) if found, go to point 3.
3. Verify if a found cluster of pixels has a shape corresponding to the value of the shape attribute (Sha) of the object to be retrieved;
   - (a) if not, reject the analyzed image,
   - (b) if yes, go to point 4.
4. Check if the number of pixels included in point 2 corresponds to the value of the size attribute (Siz) of the object to be retrieved;
   - (a) if not, reject the analyzed image,
   - (b) if yes, the analyzed image is the system answer.

4.6 Algorithm Col-Loc

We use this algorithm when we know two attributes, i.e.: color (Col) and location (Loc). This is a case with incomplete information about the object to be recognized; the size (Siz) and shape (Sha) attributes are unknown. This algorithm uses a procedure similar to that in *Algorithm Col:*

1. For all the pixels lying in a location corresponding to the value of a given attribute location (Loc) of the item, check the compatibility of the color of a pixel with a given value of the color attribute (Col) of the object to be retrieved, and look for the cluster of pixels of the same color, as described in Subsect. 4.1;
   - (a) if any cluster of pixels has not been found then the analyzed image is rejected,
   - (b) if found, then this image is the system answer.

4.7 Algorithm Col-Siz

We use this algorithm when we know two attributes, i.e.: color (Col) and size (Siz). This is the case with incomplete information about the object to be recognized; the location (Loc) and shape (Sha) attributes are unknown. In this case, use the additional information about the number of pixels in the cluster obtained during clustering pixels of the same color – see Subsect. 4.1, point 2b. Thus, some procedures employed by *Algorithm Col* are used:

1. Proceed the same way as Subsect. 4.1, points 1–2b, i.e. looking for the clusters of pixels corresponding to the value of the color attribute (Col) of the object to be retrieved, and for each found cluster of pixels check whether the number of pixels corresponds to the size attribute (Siz) of the object;
   - (a) if any clusters in the analyzed image, whose number of pixels corresponds to the value of the size attribute (Siz) of the object to be retrieved, has not been found then the image is rejected,
   - (b) if found, then the image is the system answer.

4.8   Algorithm Col-Sha

We use this algorithm when we know two attributes, i.e.: color (Col) and shape (Sha). This is a case with incomplete information about the object to be recognized; the location (Loc) and size (Siz) attributes are unknown. This algorithm is similar to the previous one (see Subsect. 4.7) but instead of the size we are given the shape of the object to be recognized:

1. Proceed the same way as Subsect. 4.1, points 1–2b, i.e. looking for the clusters of pixels corresponding to the value of the color attribute (Col) of the object and for each found cluster of pixels check whether the shape corresponds to the value of the shape attribute (Sha) of the object to be retrieved;
   - (a) if any clusters in the analyzed image whose shape corresponds to the value of the shape attribute (Sha) of the object to be retrieved has not been found, then the image is rejected,
   - (b) if found, then the image is the system answer.

5   Particular Problems Solved by the Granular Image Recognition System

The particular algorithms portrayed in Fig. 2, and described in Sect. 4, concern special cases of the OIG knowledge (see Sect. 3 and Fig. 3). Each of them corresponds to the specific problem of the image recognition, from the color digital image collection, solved by the GPRS (see Fig. 1).

Different problems can be formulated depending on the OIG knowledge presented at the input of the system. Every OIG contain values of the attributes such as color, location, size, and shape – that describe the object at the picture to be retrieved from the image collection. It is important to emphasizing that some values of these attributes may be unknown. Therefore, we consider eight cases of the OIG knowledge as shown in Fig. 3. Thus, we may know values of only one attribute (color) or two attributes (color-location, color-size, color-shape) or three attributes (color-location-size, color-location-shape, color-size-shape) or four attributes (color-location-size-shape). The last case that employs the *Algorithm Col-Loc-Siz-Sha* represents full knowledge of the OIG while the *Algorithm Col* concerns the case where only color attribute is known. It seems obvious that it is much easier to find the object with full OIG knowledge that in other cases.

The particular problems that can be solved by the GPRS are introduced in [22–24]. Some examples, associated with the proper algorithm for that problem, are following:

- "an object of a color close to red" – *Algorithm Col* ($A1$)
- "an object of a color close to red, located in the center" – *Algorithm Col-Loc* ($A2_{Loc}$)
- "a big object of a color close to red" – *Algorithm Col-Siz* ($A2_{Siz}$)
- "an object of a color close to red, and round shape" – *Algorithm Col-Sha* ($A2_{Sha}$)
- "a big object of a color close to red, located in the center" – *Algorithm Col-Loc-Siz* ($A3_{Loc-Siz}$)
- "an object of a color close to red, round shape, and located in the center" – *Algorithm Col-Loc-Sha* ($A3_{Loc-Sha}$)
- "a big object of a color close to red, and round shape" – *Algorithm Col-Siz-Sha* ($A3_{Siz-Sha}$)
- "a big object of a color close to red, a shape close to hat, and located in the center" – *Algorithm Col-Loc-Siz-Sha* ($A4_{Loc-Siz-Sha}$)

As we see, to solve a problem when we know values of the all attributes, i.e. color, location, size and shape, e.g. for the input like to "a big object of a color close to red, located in the right–upper corner and round shape" we employ the *Algorithm Col-Loc-Siz-Sha* ($A4_{Loc-Siz-Sha}$), but for the input "an object of a color close to red, located in the center" we should apply the *Algorithm Col-Loc* ($A2_{Loc}$).

6 Conclusions and Final Remarks

In our granulation approach, we assume that the color granule is treated as primary in the OIG, as presented in Sect. 3 (see Fig. 3). The OIG is the information granule composed of the particular granules such as the color granule, location granule, size granule, and shape granule [26]. Thus, in the problems, listed in Sect. 5, the color attribute of the object to be recognized is always most important even in the case when the size attribute is first in the object description. This means that the GPRS, employing the algorithms proposed in this paper, retrieves pictures from the color digital image collection, with an object characterized first of all by a specific color. More precisely, the system is looking for the color granule, in the pictures, that matches to the OIG. In addition, other granules (location, size, shape) are used in the particular algorithms, shown in Fig. 3 and described in Sect. 4.

The color granule refers to the color space granulation, based on the CIE chromaticity triangle (see [5,21,22]), considered in [23]. The location granules, as well as the size and shape granules, concern the pixel space granulation [23] and apply the idea of macropixels introduced in [22]. The granulation employs fuzzy and rough sets to represent the granules [10,27]. Other papers presenting fuzzy and rough granulation and their applications are e.g. [8,11–13,18].

With regard to the GPRS, it is worth mentioning that e.g. the FaceNet system produced by Google performs recognition, verification, and clustering of human faces, applying an artificial intelligence method called deep learning [20]. In contrary, our system, introduced in [24] and illustrated in Fig. 1 does not require this kind of techniques because instead of recognizing details, the aim of the GPRS is to detect a color picture (or pictures) including an object described roughly or in a fuzzy way.

The GPRS is a knowledge-based system that realizes an inference algorithm by means of appropriate fuzzy rules and the rules formulated by use of the rough set theory. The IF-THEN rules employ the information granules represented by fuzzy and rough sets, respectively [24]. The new algorithms, proposed in this paper (Sect. 4), support the inference of the GPRS. Other computational intelligence methods applied in order to enrich performance of the GPRS are studied in [14–16].

Further research may concern an interesting problem of image understanding (see e.g. [19]) based on the fuzzy and rough granulation [23]. It is worth mentioning that in our approach to the image recognition the most important is the description of an object (to be found) by linguistic terms, as presented in the examples listed in Sect. 5. This may be the first step to study the problem of understanding an image, described by words and sentences of a natural language, by means of computing with words introduced by Zadeh [26].

The GPRS will be developed with regard to theoretical and practical aspects of this pattern (image) recognition tasks, so it is not constrained only to the problems and algorithms presented in this paper. To realize the further research of development of the system [1, 4, 7], among many others, may be helpful.

References

1. Akimoto, T., Ogata, T.: Experimental development of focalization mechanism in an integrated narrative generation system. J. Artif. Intell. Soft Comput. Res. **5**(3), 177–188 (2015)
2. Biniaz, A., Abbasi, A.: Segmentation and edge detection based on modified ant colony optimization for IRIS image processing. J. Artif. Intell. Soft Comput. Res. **3**(2), 133–141 (2013)
3. Bruzdzinski, T., Krzyzak, A., Fevens, T., Jelen, L.: Web-based framework or breast cancer classification. J. Artif. Intell. Soft Comput. Res. **4**(2), 149–162 (2014)
4. Chu, J.L., Krzyzak, A.: The recognition of partially occluded objects with support vector machines, convolutional neural networks and deep belief networks. J. Artif. Intell. Soft Comput. Res. **4**(1), 5–19 (2014)
5. Fortner, B., Meyer, T.E.: Number by Color. A Guide to Using Color to Understand Technical Data. Springer, Heidelberg (1997)
6. Karimi, B., Krzyzak, A.: A novel approach for automatic detection and classification of suspicious lesions in breast ultrasound images. J. Artif. Intell. Soft Comput. Res. **3**(3), 265–276 (2013)
7. Murata, M., Ito, S., Tokuhisa, M., Ma, Q.: Order estimation of Japanese paragraphs by supervised machine learning and various textual features. J. Artif. Intell. Soft Comput. Res. **5**(4), 247–255 (2015)

8. Pal, S.K., Meher, S.K., Dutta, S.: Class-dependent rough-fuzzy granular space, dispersion index and classification. Pattern Recogn. **45**, 2690–2707 (2012)
9. Pawlak, Z.: Rough Sets. Theoretical Aspects of Reasoning About Data. Kluwer Academic Publishers, Dordrecht (1991)
10. Pawlak, Z.: Granularity of knowledge, indiscernibility and rough sets. In: Fuzzy Systems Proceedings. IEEE World Congress on Computational Intelligence, vol. 1, pp. 106–110 (1998)
11. Pedrycz, W., Vukovich, G.: Granular computing in pattern recognition. In: Bunke, H., Kandel, A. (eds.) Neuro-Fuzzy Pattern Recognition, pp. 125–143. World Scientific, Singapore (2000)
12. Pedrycz, W., Park, B.J., Oh, S.K.: The design of granular classifiers: a study in the synergy of interval calculus and fuzzy sets in pattern recognition. Pattern Recogn. **41**, 3720–3735 (2008)
13. Peters, J.F., Skowron, A., Synak, P., Ramanna, S.: Rough sets and information granulation. In: Bilgic, T., De Baets, B., Kaynak, O. (eds.) IFSA 2003. LNCS (LNAI), vol. 2715, pp. 370–377. Springer, Heidelberg (2003)
14. Rakus-Andersson, E.: Fuzzy and Rough Techniques in Medical Diagnosis and Medication. Springer, Heidelberg (2007)
15. Rakus-Andersson, E.: Approximation and rough classification of letter-like polygon shapes. In: Skowron, A., Suraj, Z. (eds.) Rough Sets and Intelligent Systems, pp. 455–474. Springer, Heidelberg (2013)
16. Rutkowska, D.: Neuro-Fuzzy Architectures and Hybrid Learning. Springer, Heidelberg (2002)
17. Salazar-Gonzales, A., Li, Y., Liu, X.: Automatic graph cut based segmentation of retinal optic disc by incorporating blood vessel compensation. J. Artif. Intell. Soft Comput. Res. **2**(3), 235–245 (2012)
18. Skowron, A., Stepaniuk, J.: Information granules: towards foundations of granular computing. Int. J. Intell. Syst. **16**(1), 57–85 (2001)
19. Tadeusiewicz, R., Ogiela, M.R.: Why automatic understanding? In: Beliczynski, B., Dzielinski, A., Iwanowski, M., Ribeiro, B. (eds.) ICANNGA 2007. LNCS, vol. 4432, pp. 477–491. Springer, Heidelberg (2007)
20. Taigman, Y., Yang, M., Ranzato, M.A., Wolf, L.: Deepface: closing the gap to human-level performance in face verification. In: Proceedings of IEEE Conference on Computer Vision and Pattern Recognition (CVPR), pp. 1701–1708 (2014)
21. Wiaderek, K.: Fuzzy sets in colour image processing based on the CIE chromaticity triangle. In: Rutkowska, D., Cader, A., Przybyszewski, K. (eds.) Selected Topics in Computer Science Applications, pp. 3–26. Academic Publishing House EXIT, Warsaw (2011)
22. Wiaderek, K., Rutkowska, D.: Fuzzy granulation approach to color digital picture recognition. In: Rutkowski, L., Korytkowski, M., Scherer, R., Tadeusiewicz, R., Zadeh, L.A., Zurada, J.M. (eds.) ICAISC 2013, Part I. LNCS, vol. 7894, pp. 412–425. Springer, Heidelberg (2013)
23. Wiaderek, K., Rutkowska, D., Rakus-Andersson, E.: Color digital picture recognition based on fuzzy granulation approach. In: Rutkowski, L., Korytkowski, M., Scherer, R., Tadeusiewicz, R., Zadeh, L.A., Zurada, J.M. (eds.) ICAISC 2014, Part I. LNCS, vol. 8467, pp. 319–332. Springer, Heidelberg (2014)
24. Wiaderek, K., Rutkowska, D., Rakus-Andersson, E.: Information granules in application to image recognition. In: Rutkowski, L., Korytkowski, M., Scherer, R., Tadeusiewicz, R., Zadeh, L.A., Zurada, J.M. (eds.) ICAISC 2015, Part I. LNCS (LNAI), vol. 9119, pp. 649–659. Springer, Heidelberg (2015)

25. Zadeh, L.A.: Fuzzy sets. Inf. Control **8**, 338–353 (1965)
26. Zadeh, L.A.: Fuzzy logic = computing with words. IEEE Trans. Fuzzy Syst. **4**, 103–111 (1996)
27. Zadeh, L.A.: Toward a theory of fuzzy information granulation and its centrality in human reasoning and fuzzy logic. Fuzzy Sets Syst. **90**, 111–127 (1997)

Author Index

Printed in the United States
By Bookmasters

Printed in the United States
By Bookmasters